C000075607

ISBN 978-1-5279-1093-5
PIBN 10940175

FB &c Ltd, Dalton House, 60 Windsor Avenue, London, SW19 2RR.
Company number 08720141. Registered in England and Wales.

For support please visit www.forgottenbooks.com

POETRY.

TALES.

THE LIVING AGE.

No. 879.—6 April, 1861.

CONTENTS.

NEW BOOKS.

SECOND ADDRESS TO THE PEOPLE OF MARYLAND. By William H. Collins, of Baltimore. [This is worthy of the former Address, and has no doubt done good service.]

PUBLISHED EVERY SATURDAY BY

LITTELL, SON, & CO., BOSTON.

For Six Dollars a year, in advance, *remitted directly to the Publishers,* the LIVING AGE will be punctually forwarded *free of postage.*

Complete sets of the First Series, in thirty-six volumes, and of the Second Series, in twenty volumes, handsomely bound, packed in neat boxes, and delivered in all the principal cities, free of expense of freight, are for sale at two dollars a volume.

ANY VOLUME may be had separately, at two dollars, bound, or a dollar and a half in numbers.

ANY NUMBER may be had for 13 cents; and it is well worth while for subscribers or purchasers to complete any broken volumes they may have, and thus greatly enhance their value.

"DIOGENES" is just as rude as he used to be. He thinks we have had "enough Secession poetry," and implies that we print it to please Secession subscribers. We are sorry to inform him that we have very few subscribers among this class, having lost them some years ago, when, deprecating the everlasting discussion upon slavery, we asserted, from our own recollection, that the excitement was created by Mr. Calhoun for the purpose of uniting the South against the North. Little did we dream that his doctrines had taken such root as to destroy the patriotism of so many!

Another correspondent is "wonderstruck at our copying those wretched doggerels." We have done so, as a part of the living age, not considering them as poetry, but as curiosities, we may say monstrosities, of literature. They show how much the affections, as well as the reason, may be distorted, when people so give themselves up to one idea that they will permit no other to be spoken.

We have no sympathy for such literature. And for the leading spirits, who have weakened and degraded the country in the sight of Europe, we have the same feeling as we should have for the man who would knock down our mother. For all that "has come and gone yet," we do not despair of the love of country in the mass of voters in any State; though we could not have dreamed that insults to the national flag would have been anywhere permitted.

Thank God that our new President enters upon the difficult task of sustaining the government, with an earnest desire to avoid bloodshed. It will be the more difficult for him to do so, because the conspirators are anxious to hurry their dupes into violence, in order to make them desperate.

Some people say, "Let them go! let the separation be peaceful!" This is not so easy to carry out practically. In every one of the Seceding States, there are many true patriots who have been for the moment carried away by falsehood, or terrified into silence by the sudden outbreak of a well-concocted conspiracy which has been drilled for thirty years. We believe that in every one of them, except perhaps South Carolina, a majority would, if they dared, give their votes against Secession. And that this is the opinion of the usurpers is evident, from their refusal to submit their doings to the ratification of the people. Were it otherwise, could we have any reliable evidence that the leading politicians are sustained by the great body of the people of their States, we should feel that the nation would be happier and stronger for cutting them off;—and should be willing to vote for such an amendment to the Constitution as would give to the President and Congress the power to agree to terms of separation.

A physician in Columbus, Ga., a friend of the Union, has written the following poem:—

"SECESSION CONSUMMATED.

"Yankee Doodle took a saw,
With patriot devotion,
To trim the Tree of Liberty,
According to his 'notion'!

"Yankee Doodle on a limb,
Like another noodle,
Cut *between* the *tree* and *him*,
And down came Yankee Doodle.

"Yankee Doodle broke his neck,
Every bone about him,
And then the Tree of Liberty
Did very well without him!"

Let our statesmen keep prominently the true and simple issue before the people: this attempt at revolution is not caused by any wrong done or threatened, but because people who have ruled the country almost ever since the Union was consecrated, have been defeated in an election. The pretended plea of the right of Secession is one that would make all government impossible. If the Supreme Law which is above all state laws or constitutions, can be set aside at pleasure, much more may a part of a state separate itself from another part;—and this is already talked of in Alabama and Georgia.

Much of this misery is the fruit of the doctrine of State Sovereignty, in which so many Southern people have been educated by leaders who invented it for a weapon against the national government, at a time when they were in opposition to John Adams. We were born in New Jersey, lived long in Pennsylvania, and have now been nearly a score of years a citizen of Massachusetts, to whose people we are greatly indebted, and in whose soil we shall soon be buried. For each of these states we have an especial love; but wider, deeper, high over all, is the love of OUR COUNTRY. Surely, this is an *instinctive* feeling, not absent in any men except in the "dangerous classes."

The *Times* says that we can never again be so great a nation as we have been. We are indeed greatly humbled, but may take heart by remembering that Great Britain is now far stronger than she was before that *Mutiny at the Nore* which threatened to undermine her naval power, and bring her very existence into peril.

"God is our refuge in distress;
A present help when dangers press.
In him undaunted we'll confide."

From The National Review.

EUGENIE DE GUERIN.

Eugénie de Guérin. Reliquiæ. Publié par Jules Barbey d'Aurevilly et G. S. Trebutien. Caen. Ce volume ne se vend pas.

THE "Remains of Eugénie de Guérin" consist of a short Memoir written by a friend, her own Journal, and some of her Letters. The book has not been published, and the papers were never intended to see the light. Mdlle. de Guérin herself was in noways remarkable by her position; she was merely a lady of good family, who lived and died in almost total seclusion from the world. That she numbered one or two men of letters among her friends was due to their connection with her brother, a poet, with some resemblance to Keats in the style of his talent and in his early death. Eugénie de Guérin appears to have shared her brother's artistic temperament; her perceptions of nature were keen, her literary taste good, and her style, commonly of an intense simplicity, is at times relieved by a playful conversational grace. But in all mere intellectual qualities she has been excelled by a dozen women whose names are in every mouth. The matchless charm of her writings lies in the fact that they are the record of a life, written without affectation but also without disguise, intended only for the eyes of a brother and of a friend from whom no thought was a secret; even the father whom she loved passionately was not suffered to see them, lest their melancholy should distress him. Complete up to a certain point, they are also guarded by a feminine reserve from all sentimentalism; they contain much that could never have been said in public, but nothing that might not have been said aloud. The need of a southern and artistic nature to express a portion of what it feels in words has never been suffered to degenerate into chronic garrulity; it was only from time to time that half a dozen sentences, the expression of many days' experiences, were written down; and the few pages that were thus filled are rather the index of a life than an autobiography.

Eugénie was the eldest daughter of a gentleman whose estate had been reduced by the Revolution to the single chateau of Cayla in Languedoc. The little country-house, with its terrace and garden, in the style of Louis Quinze, lay hidden among mountains and woods; the neighbors consisted of a few cousins and the clergy. When only fourteen, Eugénie, who slept in the same room with her mother, woke up to find her dying. Placed by this bereavement virtually at the head of the family, the young girl, who had been lively and fond of laughter, became thoughtful and collected; her life changed all at once; "it was like a flower thrown upon a coffin." To deep religious impressions she now joined an unusual solidity of character. Partly, perhaps, from a wish to share the studies of her brother Maurice, whom she loved passionately, partly that she might better understand the services of her Church, she insisted on learning Latin. Shut out as she was from books and society, she seems to have felt, what Luther so powerfully expressed, that the human heart is like mill-stones, which, in default of other grist, will grind themselves. As her brother grew up, he of course left home to go into the world. His sisters were too well-born to marry into the *bourgeoisie*, and too poor to be sought in marriage by men of their own rank. Except for the occasion of her brother's wedding, and once after his death, Eugénie never seems to have stayed in Paris; and in her father's house, where a stranger was an event to be recorded and talked over, she was thrown completely upon her own resources. Fortunately, the routine of her days has been described by her sister.

"She rose, except when she was unwell, at six o'clock. After dressing she prayed aloud or in thought; and when she was in a town, she never missed going to hear Mass at the nearest altar. At Cayla, after her prayers, she went into her father's room, either to attend to him or to give him his breakfast, during which she read to him. At nine o'clock she came back into her own room, and repeated the prayers of the Mass. If her father was well and did not want her attendance, she employed herself in writing or reading, or in working, of which she was very fond, having the same fairy-like quickness of finger as of mind; or perhaps she looked over household matters, which she managed with great taste and good sense. At noon she went back to her room, and repeated the *Angelus*; then came dinner-time. After dinner, if the weather allowed, she took a walk to amuse her father, or sometimes that she might visit the neighboring village, if there was a sick person to see or any one in sorrow to comfort. If, on coming back, about two o'clock, she resumed her reading, she always took her work, and knitted as she read, not liking even the shadow of an idle hour. At three o'clock she went back to her room, where she commonly read the 'Visit to the Holy Sacrament,' by St. Alphonso Liguori, or perhaps the life of the saint of the day. After that she wrote till five o'clock, if her father did not send for her. At five she recited the Rosary, and meditated till supper-time. At seven she joined the family circle, but never stopped working. After supper she went to the kitchen, to pray with the servants, or often, during the vintage, to teach some little ignorant boy his catechism. The rest of the evening was spent in needlework; and at ten o'clock she was in bed, having first read over the subject on which she meant to meditate next day, in order that she might fall asleep with this good thought. Lastly, it is right to add, that every month she prepared herself for death, and chose one of the saints whom she was most drawn to as a model for imitation."

A few details as to the books she read may be gleaned from her Journal. Her favorites are mostly such as a devout woman of strong sense might be expected to choose —"the marvellous thinker, Pascal, Bossuet, and St. Theresa, whose passionate mysticism was so wonderfully tempered by shrewd common sense and by the habit of government." Among more profane authors, Molière and Xavier de Maistre seems to have been the best approved; the latter, a friend of her brother, has evidently influenced her style. Modern literature, perhaps fortunately, was a little rare at Cayla; the *Mémoires d'Andryane*, after some censures, are dismissed with high praise; and De Custine receives more qualified commendation as amusing. Once Victor Hugo's *Notre Dame* was sent for from a neighboring town. It had been a question whether she ought to read it; but she was now in mature life, and decided that she might "meet the Devil without making him a friend." The book was never procured: but we find her soon afterwards sending back *Delphine* unfinished and in disgust. "Mme. de Staël," she observes, "is always preaching right and acting wrong. I detest those women who mount the pulpit and lay their passions bare." Scott, and up to a certain point Lamartine, were the only novelists whom she cordially admired. Her reading was evidently intensive rather than wide. But the passages which she quotes are without exception of high merit. The few lines of poetry that occur make us regret that the editor has not indicated the sources. Once she quotes from Shakspeare with a characteristic comment: "'There are beings who are taken from the world for little faults; it is in love and to save them from fresh falls. If one did not know that this thought was Shakspeare's, one would think it Fénelon's. Oh, I know to whom I apply it."

The application in her own mind was no doubt to her brother Maurice. What the little frailties were which his sister felt so deeply we need scarcely ask. Shortly after his marriage he sickened, and in a few months died. "The affection which covered all others, the heart of her heart," was taken from her. The death was not unexpected, for his health had always been weak; even when she danced at his wedding, Eugénie's presaging affection had tormented her with a second-sight of coffins placed round the room; but the blow was not the less terrible; "If the heavens were to fall," she said, "it would add nothing to my distress." Henceforward only two wishes kept her alive,—the desire to cherish her father's old age, and the hope of publishing her brother's works. Slight as this last wish may appear, it, for some unknown reason, has never yet been accomplished; and Maurice de Guérin is only remembered by the single fragment which George Sand edited, the "Centaur." Mdlle. de Guérin lived on through ten years of monotonous suffering, only consoled by the devoted friendship of her own and her brother's friends. For one of these last the latter part of her Journal was kept; to another the few letters that have been printed were addressed. It is curious to find the same gentleman the correspondent of George Sand and of Mdlle. de Guérin. Probably, to quote an expression of her own, she had placed the cross between her friend and herself to sustain both. At last, in 1848, the end arrived. "I believe," says her sister, "she saw the approach of death, but she never spoke of it; she would have feared to pain us." One of her last directions was, that her papers should be burned.

The private journals and letters from which our extracts have been made were saved from destruction, probably, because they were not in the hands of the family. They have been printed for circulation among a few friends. As time removes the reasons for privacy, it is to be hoped that they will be given to the world. Generally, there is a certain indecorum in publishing private experiences or feelings of any kind. But the life of a woman like Mdlle. de Guérin is at once so transparent and so deep, that it may bear any scrutiny, and will never be penetrated except by the subtle insight of sympathy. Memoirs of this kind are so scarce that, to the few who value them at all, they are inestimable. But on other and higher grounds their publication is desirable. The large public of honest men and pure women in France are little aware how much their national character is depreciated by the nameless baseness and badness of their novel-literature. It is no inveterate prejudice that leads Englishmen to ascribe the morals of stock-jobbers and of lorettes to a great people whom we sincerely wish to respect; most of us are constrained to take our information second-hand, and to trust to the pictures of French society which native novelists draw; and France suffers for the faults of a class who base their ideal of life on the breach of every commandment except the fifth; just as English society on the Continent is too often judged from the noisy and underbred among our countrymen. Nothing is more likely to remove such misconceptions than the knowledge of such a family interior as the memoirs of Mdlle. de Guérin show us, in which delicacy, purity, and the practice of little household charities seem as native to the daily life as they could be in the most blameless English home. With a little change of names and local coloring, the Journal might have been kept, and the life lived, by hundreds of English ladies. It is wonderful to see how slightly even the chief difference, that of faith, affects the writer's character. Probably many English Protestants will be startled to hear of a Catholic lady who was eminently devout, and who yet felt no attractions to conventual life, and disliked confessing to a priest who was not a friend. Only perhaps in one point is there a marked difference. A sensible Englishwoman would regard cheerfulness as a duty in itself, and would shrink from expressing any disgust with life. The ascetic element in Catholicism inspires a different tone; and Mdlle. de Guérin never hesitates to confess that life has no attractions, and that she will be glad to lay it down. "At the bottom of all we find emptiness and nothing," the phrase she quotes from Bossuet, is the key-note to her confessions.

We proceed to quote at some length one or two passages from the Journal. The first that occurs opens cheerfully; it was written before her great loss.

"En lisant un livre de géologie, j'ai rencontré un éléphant fossile découvert dans la Laponie, et une pirogue déterrée dans l'Ile des Cygnes en creusant les fondations du Pont des Invalides. Me voilà sur l'éléphant, me voilà dans la pirogue faisant le tour des mers du Nord et de l'Ile des Cygnes. Voyant ces lieux du temps de ces choses: la Laponie chaude, verdoyante et peuplée, non de nains, mais d'hommes beaux et grands, de femmes s'en allant en promenade sur un éléphant dans ces forêts, sous ces monts pétrifiés aujourd'hui, et l'Ile des Cygnes, blanche de fleurs et de leur duvet. Oh, que je la trouve belle! Et ses habitants qui sont-ils, que font-ils dans ce coin du globe? Descendants comme nous de l'exile d'Eden, connaissent-ils sa naissance, sa vie, sa chute, sa lamentable et merveilleuse histoire; cette Eve pour laquelle il a perdu le ciel, tant de malheur et de bonheur ensemble, tant d'espérances dans la foi, tant de larmes sur leurs enfants, tant et tant de choses que nous savons, que savait peut-être avant nuos ce peuple, dont il ne reste qu'une planche? Naufrages de l'humanité que Dieu seul connait dont il a laché dans les profondeurs de la terre, comme pour les dérober à notre curiosité. S'il en laisse voir quelque chose, c'est pour nous apprendre que ce globe est un abime de malheurs, que ce qu'on gagne à remuer ses entrailles c'est de découvrir des inscriptions funéraires, des cimetières. La mort est au fond de tout, et on creuse toujours comme qui cherche l'immortalité."

["In reading a book on geology, I met with a fossil elephant discovered in Lapland; and with a canoe, found in the Ile des Cygnes in digging the foundation of the Pont des Invalides. Behold me on the elephant; behold me in the canoe, gliding over the seas of the north and of the Ile des Cygnes. Looking at these places in the times of these things: Lapland, warm, verdant, and peopled not with dwarfs, but with tall and handsome men; women riding on an elephant in these forests, under these now frozen mountains, and the Ile des Cygnes, white with flowers and swan's down. Oh, how beautiful it is! And the inhabitants, who are they? What are they doing in that corner of the world? Descendants like ourselves, of the exile of Eden, do they know the story of his birth, his fall, his lamentable and marvellous history: this Eve for whom he lost heaven, so much sorrow and joy together, so many hopes in faith, so many tears shed over their children, so many, many things which we know, how many of them were known before us to this people of whose existence only a single plank remains to testify? Shipwrecks of humanity known only to God; concealed by him in the depths of the earth as if to hide them from our curiosity. If he has suffered us to see something of them, it is to teach us that this globe is an abyss of sorrow; that all that is gained by stirring its depths, is the discovery of cemeteries, of funeral inscriptions. Death is at the bottom of all things,—yet we continue to search, as one who seeks there for immortality."]

The transition from a string of playful fancies to religion in its most sombre sentiments is highly characteristic of the writer. A strong feeling of any kind, even despair, seems to be a relief from the *ennui* of ordinary life. We in England know something of the craving for occupation in any shape that possesses unmarried women of strong character; but among us it finds vent in a hundred useful or harmless forms,—in district societies, in the study of new sciences, or in writing religious novels. There is comparatively little of this in France. Sisterhoods of Martha and Mary, and such-like kindred forms of ladies' committees, no doubt exist; but they find the poor more jealous of interference than our own are, and the ground is already occupied by the priests, and by those regular fraternities. The prejudice against educated women, which is still far from extinct in England, is infinitely stronger in France, except in a few of the higher circles of the capital. This is no doubt chiefly the result of habit; the ideal of women has been formed from those who are trained in convents and under the priests; and the worthy directresses of schools shrink very naturally from any approach to *la femme émancipée*, and view secular studies beyond the common bent with extreme suspicion. It is something of the same feeling which regards the cultivation of the physique as indelicate, and shrinks from "the rude unfeeling health" which English ladies derive from riding and long country walks. The native quickness and unrivalled conversational talent of French women enables them to talk, and even to think, well on less knowledge than would sustain any other race. If they marry early, they scarcely feel the want of high intellectual training; or if they come in contact with superior men, they easily seize the ideas that circulate around them. But the want of thought tells none the less, and avenges itself naturally; it leads to a brilliant hollowness in the intercourse of the *salons*, where trifles, scandals, and little narrow views of faith or politics take the place of serious ideas: it is the source of vice, or at least of indiscretion, among the more impulsive and worse trained, who take refuge from vacuity in passion; and in nobler natures, like that of Mdlle. de Guérin, it wears away life itself, by the ceaseless tension of the soul. Her position did not often bring her into mixed society. When she saw the world in her visits to Paris, she was able to remain outside it, enjoying it but self-sphered. The relief from solitude and the glitter of new ideas did not attract her so much as the insincerity disgusted her. The judgment she passes is the more remarkable in one who, we are told, made a great success by her character and originality, in spite of her provincial training.

"Tant d'habileté, de finesse, de *chatterie*, de souplesse ne s'obtiennent pas sans préjudice, sans leur sacrifier point de grâces. Et néanmoins je les aime, j'aime tout ce qui est élégance, bon goût, belles et nobles manières. Je m'enchante aux conversations distinguées et sérieuses des hommes, comme aux causeries perles fines des femmes, à ce jeu si joli, si délicat de leurs lèvres dont je n'avais pas idée. C'est charmant, *oui, c'est charmant en vérité* (chanson), pour qui se prend aux apparences, mais je ne m'en contente pas. Le moyen de s'en contenter, quand on tient à la valeur morale des choses? Ceci dit dans le sens de faire vie dans le monde, d'en tirer du bonheur, d'y fonder des espérances sérieuses, d'y croire à quelque chose. Mmes. de . . . sont venues, je les ai crues longtemps amies, à entendre leurs paroles expansives, leur mutuel témoignage d'interêt, et ce délicieux *ma chère* de Paris: oui, c'est à les croire amies, et c'est vrai tant qu'elles sont en présence, mais au départ on dirait que chacune a laissé sa caricature à l'autre. Plaisantes liaisons! mais il en existe d'autres heureusement pour moi."

["So much cleverness, acuteness, kitten-like playfulness, and pliantness, cannot be obtained without injury, without sacrificing to them some graces. And nevertheless I like them; I like all that is elegant, in good taste, of noble and beautiful manners. I am delighted with the dignified and serious conversations of the men, as well as with the lighter talk, pearl-fine, of the women; this play of their lips, pretty and delicate to a degree of which I had not an idea. It is charming, 'Yes, it is charming in truth,' for whoever will be satisfied with appearances, but I am not content with them. How can they content any one who has regard to the moral value of things. Who looks at the world with a view of true life in it, of drawing happiness from it, of founding serious hopes upon it, of believing in something in it. Mmes. de —— meet: to hear their candid greetings, their mutual protestations of interest and the delicious 'ma chere' of Paris, I should take them for old friends. Yes, one would think them friends, and so long as they are together it is true; but when they part one would say that each had left her caricature with the other. Pleasant connections! but happily for me there are other kinds in the world."]

How exalted her notion of friendship was, we learn from another passage, which is in itself sufficiently remarkable. It will serve to complete the hasty sketch, to which our space limits us, of a life that deserves to be studied in its entirety.

"J'ai toujours cherché une amitié forte et telle que la mort seule la pût renverser, bonheur et malheur que j'ai eu, hélas! dans Maurice. Nulle femme n'a pu ni ne le pourra remplacer; nulle même la plus distinguée n'a pu m'offrir cette liaison d'intelligence et de goûts, cette relation large, unie et de tenue. Rien de fixe, de durée, de vital dans les sentiments des femmes; leurs attachements entr'elles ne sont que de jolis nœuds de rubans. Je les remarque ces légères tendresses dans toutes les amies. Ne pouvons-nous donc pas nous aimer autrement? Je ne sais ni n'en connais d'exemple au présent, pas même dans l'histoire. Oreste et Pylade n'ont pas de sœurs. Cela m'impatiente quand j'y pense, et que vous autres ayez au cœur une chose qui nous y manque. En revanche, nous avons le dévouement."

["I have always sought a strong friendship —such an one as death alone could destroy, a happiness and a sorrow which I have had, alas! in Maurice. No woman could nor can take his place; none, even the most distinguished, could offer me that fellowship of intelligence and of tastes; that intimate relationship so large, strong, and tender. There is nothing fixed, durable, vital in the sentiments of women; their attachments among themselves are only pretty knots of ribbon. I remark these light tendernesses in all female friends. Can we not then, love each other in any other fashion? I know no such example at present, and I know of none even in history. Orestes and Pylades have no sisters. It vexes me to think of it, and that you men have in your hearts one thing which is wanting in ours. Instead of it, we have devotedness."]

Marine and Land Compasses.—The variation of the compass in different parts of the world is a fact to which scientific men have directed much attention. At present, a balanced magnetic needle points to twenty-two and a half degrees west of the true north. There is also a diurnal change, but the variations are very small, and doubtless occasioned by the temperature. The proper making of magnets involves great skill and care. When made, they may be preserved a long while if placed parallel with the north-pointing end of one against the south-pointing end of another. They will thus strengthen each other. After taking a needle off its bearing it should be placed in the position it seemed to prefer, and then it will not be injured. Rough usage, shaking, cleaning with sand paper, etc., injure them. Different from the mariner's, the land compass has no cord, and the needle alone is used. The needle ought not to be too heavy, and should have its magnetism equally distributed. The two ends of the magnet ought to have the same amount of detective force, otherwise it will not point exactly in its proper direction, while its axis of figure must correspond with its magnetic axis. There seems to be a great objection to having needles too long or too short; the best length is thought to be about five inches.

From The Examiner.

*Works and Correspondence of Alexis de Tocqueville.** Edited by Gustave de Beaumont, Membre de l'Institut.

To M. Gustave de Beaumont, one of the earliest and most attached of the numerous friends of Alexis de Tocqueville, whose death two years since deprived France of a great and good man, has fallen the duty of editing his correspondence, which has been performed in a manner to prove that the labor was one of love. It is satisfactory to know that the extremely interesting collection of letters before us is by no means exhausted by the present publication, many being withheld for reasons which scarcely require explanation, the writer's opinions considered, and the existing state of the press in France.

M. de Tocqueville's high reputation as a statesman is well known, but these letters make us acquainted with a great man in private life, and show "the very life of the machine." Always correct in judgment and clear in appreciation, his expressed opinions in familiar writing have a prophetic character in their political and moral justness, which events have proved in a remarkable manner, and not only is his foresight displayed and his wisdom confirmed, but every sentiment he utters is full of noble feeling, and chivalrous, almost romantic, generosity of thought. Truth was his goal, and its light shines out in all his words as it did in all his acts. Whatever subject he took in hand he studied minutely, in order to make himself master of it, and allow no room for prejudice or self-deception. It was thus he judged the English nation, and on this account his opinions are of more weight than those of almost all the rest of his countrymen, who generally persist in seeing our institutions from a point of view peculiar to their own habits and customs. The letters he addresses to numerous Englishmen of note on this subject are most valuable, and will be eagerly read. Those of a more domestic character possess a singular charm in the warmth of their friendliness and the kindness of heart they exhibit; not the least charming are those in which the amiable lady who has the misfortune to be his widow is named. All received notions of the imperfections of a French *ménage* are refuted by the pleasant glimpses he affords of his interior. He chose his English wife for her virtues alone, and during their union of five-and-twenty years their happiness evidently knew no diminution; he dwells on her merits with fondness, associates her with all his studies and all his pleasures, and fails not to excite in the reader more than a stranger's interest for one so accomplished and so devoted.

He visited England several times, but regrets the shortness of his stay, though, however brief it may have been, the observations he made on our laws, our people, and our constitution could hardly have been more lucid and correct from longer acquaintance. His modesty as to his own acquirements and his earnest striving after truth make him difficult in satisfying himself, and, in this, his example is worth following by many less gifted and less conscientious writers. There is a certain resemblance in this respect in some of his letters to those of Schiller, to Körner, and, to judge by his early writings, one might be induced to think nature hesitated as to whether her child should be a great poet or an eminent statesman. A calm severity of thought and serious view of human affairs subdued the poet within him, and gave to reality what would have been precious to fancy under other circumstances.

M. de Beaumont's memoir of his admirable and illustrious friend is pleasing, though rather labored, and he is sometimes wanting in that simplicity which was a characteristic of De Tocqueville; no doubt he has had to struggle with difficulties to which a French writer of the biography of an honest and liberal lover of his country is subject at this moment. The notice is, however, of much value as to facts, and presents the man from youth to premature decay in a clear and satisfactory view, while it breathes a spirit of love and admiration entirely deserved by its object, as the letters which follow most fully demonstrate.

"Besides," remarks the biographer, "the writer, whose merits are universally known, there is in Alexis de Tocqueville, to be considered the man himself, less understood, of whom an intimacy of thirty years has allowed me to judge better than another. It

* "Œuvres et Correspondance inedites d'Alexis de Tocqueville," Pudlicés et Precedées d'une notice par Gustave de Beaumont, Membre de l'Institut. Paris: Michel Lévy Frères. 1861.

is therefore the man whom I have been desirous to paint in the notice to this publication; and," he adds, "the best means of causing him to be both admired and loved is to represent him impartially as he really was, without panegyric or other ornament than sincerity."

He was born in Paris, in 1805, of a noble Norman family, and, by his mother's side, was descended from Malesherbes. His father, the Count de Tocqueville, a peer of France, was, under the Restoration, successively Prefêt of Metz, Amiens, and Versailles. "Except good manners and good sentiments," the clever boy learned little at home; but, weak in Latin and Greek, he contrived at the end of his first year at the Academy of Metz to carry off the first prize for French composition. A passion for travel, with a view to examine questions which already sprung in his mind, caused him to abandon his studies too soon, according to his after-view of the case, though the world has little reason to agree with him. He has left a manuscript account of his wanderings in Italy and Sicily with his brother, which is curious as proving the earnestness with which he observed and his desire to gain real information. Dazzled by the glories of ancient architecture, his first wish was to study it in its fundamental principles, in order to the guidance of his taste and the perfection of his judgment. While contemplating the ruins of Rome, his characteristic remark is that "her fall dated from the day her liberties were lost." The beauties of Sicilian scenery, in admiration of which he is enthusiastic, absorb him less than regret for the debasement of her people and anxiety to discover a remedy for their suffering. His forensic career began in 1827, when he was just twenty-one, and immediately the superiority of his mind became conspicuous; he soon felt that a wider field of usefulness lay before him than his mere profession, and the stirring spirit of the time acted upon and urged him to action. "It is difficult," says M. de Beaumont, "for those who did not witness the state of affairs in 1827–8 to understand the ardor of feeling then existing. The empire had fallen twelve years before; for the first time France had known liberty and loved it. Liberty, a consolation to some, a sovereign good to others, had created for all a new country. Institutions in place of a single man, new manners, and, in the midst of profound peace, the development of new instincts, sentiments, and wants. All contributed to spread fresh life and to regenerate the nation. France was then sincerely liberal, and the great problem of constitutional liberty was seriously considered for the first time."

De Tocqueville, to whom arbitrary power was equally distasteful with revolution, threw himself with avidity into the great struggle to maintain liberty so lately and so dearly gained. His fixed opinion was that a people, worthy to be so called, had a right to participate in the government of its own affairs, and that neither true greatness nor true dignity could exist in a nation without free institutions; consequently, a constitutional monarchy was what he desired for France, and he supported the government of the elder branch of the Bourbons because he thought the end more likely to be attained by that means than by one springing from a revolutionary origin. The difficulties and dangers attending equality were present to his mind, and caused him to meditate profoundly on the possibility of preventing the power, issuing from democracy, from becoming tyrannical. This was the great question which occupied his life from first to last. He was a thinker, untired by obstacles and unwedded to opinion, resolute to examine and never satisfied with striving for truth. Like all great minds he began with doubt, as some early notes of his prove. Thus he wrote:—

"There is no absolute truth;" adding, "If I were charged to classify human misery, I should place it in this order, 1, Sickness; 2, Death; 3, Doubt."

It was the rule he doubted, not the duty, and, the rule once admitted, he never swerved: being as resolute in action as he had been timid in deciding on a course. He saw far and rapidly, and these qualities of mind he brought to the study of modern history.

He gave in his adherence to the new reign after the revolution of 1830, unsatisfied but hopeful, and it was at that period that he visited the United States in order to study the great principles he believed in on the spot. The ostensible reason for this journey was the utility, in his quality of magistrate, of examining the penitentiary system pursued in America, and with this mission he departed. One of the results was his first work, "Enquête sur le Pénitencier de Philadelphie," but the earliest ideas of his great work on democracy hence took their rise. The romance of the affair was his desire, accomplished with great perseverance, to advance in the untrodden forests of that vast world to the very limit of civilization. A pamphlet, now first edited, which he called "A Fortnight in the Desert," is a record of his impressions, and in this the poetical element within him is developed. His imagination was so much charmed by all he saw in his mysterious travels, that the chances seemed great as to whether another Chateaubriand or Lamartine would not extinguish the magistrate and statesman De Tocqueville. M. de Beaumont gives part of his own diary at this time, he being his companion in adventure, and extremely interesting and exciting it is; the pleasure, however, it affords is dashed with the fear that the hardships De Tocqueville underwent in his rambles in this ungenial clime, ripened the seeds of that insidious disease which afterwards destroyed him.

The first two volumes of "Democracy in America" appeared in January, 1835; of that remarkable work it is enough to say, with M. Royer-Collard, "Since Montesquieu nothing has appeared like it." A judgment repeated after twenty years, as M. de Barente has observed, in 1859.

A curious instance of the encouragement given by publishers to an author hitherto without renown occurred on the occasion of the first appearance of a work which soon reached a fourteenth edition. The bookseller had agreed to bring out the offered book, which had already been rejected by others, but would only agree to print five hundred copies, being excessively afraid of its failure. After the rapid success it met with the publisher received M. de Tocqueville with the remark, "It seems you have written something extraordinary," and therefore proposed terms in his own favor which the un-business-like author agreed to, believing that he was as well treated as he deserved to be.

The sensation that De Tocqueville's work created in Europe was even more vividly felt in America, when it was at once acknowledged that he had explained their institutions and their manners with a sagacity and logical clearness which showed them at a glance all that they had hitherto seen confusedly. Every eminent man in the United States thanked him for teaching them the "spirit of the laws" of America.

From this moment De Tocqueville became a famous man, sought and esteemed by all the great personages of his time, both at home and abroad. His visits to England appear to have gratified him extremely; the warmth of his reception by members of all parties, and the just appreciation of his genius and his motives, seems to have dwelt very pleasantly on his memory. About this time he married, and as a contrast to grave letters written to Mr. Grote, Sir George Cornewall Lewis, John Stuart Mill, Henry Reeve, Lord Radnor, etc., we extract a charming one of the husband of a year to his oldest friend, Louis de Kergolay.

"Nacqueville [near Cherbourg, his brother's chateau], 10 Oct., 1836.

". . . I cannot tell you the inexpressible charm that I find in living thus incessantly with Mary, nor the fresh resources that I discover every moment in her heart. You know that in travelling I am even more than commonly unequal, irritable, and impatient. I scolded often, and was almost always in the wrong, and under every circumstance I see in her inexhaustible springs of tenderness and indulgence; and how shall I explain to you the happiness one feels in the habitual society of a woman in whom all that is good in your own soul is reflected naturally and appears enhanced. When I do or say any thing with which I am perfectly content, I read immediately in the features of Mary a sentiment of joy and pride which raises me in my own esteem. In the same manner, if my conscience reproaches me with any thing, I see at once a cloud passing over her eyes. Although master of her affections in a remarkable degree, I observe with pleasure that I can be intimidated by her influence; and while I continue to love her as I do, I feel certain of never being induced to act otherwise than well. Not a day passes that I do not thank Heaven for placing Mary in my path, nor in which I do not think that if happiness is to be gained on earth it is with such a companion."

Five-and-twenty years from the date of this lover's letter he wrote and felt with the same warmth and devotion of his estimable wife, dearer to him than all the fame he had acquired.

Traits of humor are not rare in the letters, and a natural gayety of character frequently shines out amidst his grave pursuits. He had written a great work, as if by inspiration, but he resolved that in future he would not remain ignorant of much which he imagined would improve his style of composition, as well as confirm his opinions. Thus he read with avidity and enthusiasm Plato, Plutarch, Machiavel, Montaigne, Rousseau, and others. "I feel," he remarks, "when reading these books, which it is degrading not to know, and which but yesterday I was scarcely acquainted with, the same pleasure as Marshal Soult felt in learning geography when he was made minister for foreign affairs."

Political life now opened to De Tocqueville, and often drew him from his retreat in Normandy, to which he returned from time to time with extreme delight, only to go back to public life with more vigor and power. His aristocratic birth stood in his way at first in his own province, but at length by an immense majority he was elected for the arrondissement of Valognes (Manche) in 1839. For two years he continued to represent the same interests, and to combat all the false policy which grew around the throne of Louis Philippe; but he was not an orator, owing to the weakness of his lungs, and it was not before the public in that character that he most distinguished himself. "He had an unextinguishable dislike," drily remarks M. de Beaumont, "to *commonplace*, an excellent quality in writing a book, but the most damaging imaginable to an orator addressing great assemblies, amongst whom commonplace is in high favor."

In a speech, however, that he made in the Chamber of Deputies on the 27th January, 1848, he almost prophetically announced the revolution which was about to burst forth:—

"It is asserted," he exclaimed, "that no danger exists because there is no outbreak: it is said that since there is no material disorder on the surface of society, revolution is distant. I think this a mistake. Doubtless disorder is not perceived in actions, but it has taken deep hold on the general mind. Observe the working classes, who are at present, I acknowledge, quiet. It is true that they are not disturbed by political passions, properly so called, in the same degree as formerly, but do you not see that, from being political, they are becoming socialistic? Do you not see that by little and little ideas and opinions are growing in their minds which tend not merely to overthrow such and such laws, ministers, or government, but society itself, and to shake it to the foundation on which it rests at this moment? Do you not hear what they are continually repeating amongst themselves? that all above them are incapable and unworthy to be their governors; that the distribution of property hitherto existing in the world is unjust. And do you not think that, when such opinions have taken root, when they are spread in a manner almost universal, when they have taken profound possession of the masses, it must bring about, sooner or later—I know not when—I know not how—but that it must bring, soon or late, the most tremendous revolutions. This is my conviction. I think that we are sleeping at this moment over a volcano—of that I am profoundly convinced."

The revolution of February 24th, 1848, did not, therefore, take De Tocqueville by surprise, bitterly as he regretted it; but he considered that the republic which it was sought to establish afterwards was the only chance left for the liberties of France; and although he differed with the ruling men of the day on vital points, he decided to support General Cavaignac. His correspondence with M. de Beaumont during this period would explain the views he took on the state of affairs, and exhibit him in all the power of his judgment, were it possible that it could be added to this collection under the present régime, but that being impossible, a dead silence must fall upon that part of his political opinions. How he became plenipotentiary for France at Brussels, and Minister of Foreign Affairs under Barrot's Ministry, finishing his career at Vincennes, is a matter of history, only to be alluded to by his biographer, whose remark, "Here ceased the political life of De Tocqueville: it ended with the liberty of France," has peculiar meaning.

From The Saturday Review.

A STORY OF ETIQUETTE.

THE refinements of diplomatic etiquette in Europe were once upon a time carried to almost as extravagant a pitch as Chinese punctilio itself. Long after the days of Sir John Finett courtesy was meted out to the various members of diplomatic circles according to the power and influence of the nation which each respectively represented. The ambassadors of Savoy, as in duty bound, used to quarrel with the envoys of Florence for precedence. Cardinal Richelieu, to solve difficult problems of relative dignity, took to his bed, and received the English negotiators in an attitude which compromised nobody. French ambassadors found themselves prevented by a sudden fit of ague from attending masks where the Spanish representative was to have the first place. In our own country, disputes between Venetian, Spaniard, Dutch, and French legations fully occupied the time of one rather bewildered master of the ceremonies. Only the Muscovite ambassador was left out of the pale of social consideration. That functionary did not then hold in Europe the position he now fills. He was regarded as a person who knew little about the great science of etiquette, and who might safely be imposed upon. Even the courtly Sir John Finett seems to have treated him at the English court with that good-humored contempt which beams in the eye of a bishop's footman as he surveys a host of banqueting curates. On one occasion the Russian, exhibiting more susceptibility than could have been expected, complained that, at his reception, only one lord was in waiting to receive him at the stair's-head. Sir John's answer, for an impromptu, was amusing enough. He gravely assured his excellency that in England it was considered a greater honor to be received by one lord in waiting than by two.

Diplomatic etiquette is not, of course, now what it was then; but it is still a science, and naturally a science of some nicety. Countries which are governed constitutionally, and whose sovereign is not personally mixed up in political disputes, stand less in need of the science, it is true; although, so long as the sovereign is the personage in whose name business is transacted, it may still be conventional to mark coolness in international relations by a temporary withdrawal of the personal favor of the court. But on the Continent, where the monarch in person directs the policy of his Cabinet, the case is different. Minute shades of policy are properly indicated by minute distinctions of manner and cordiality at court balls, at state receptions, and at royal or imperial banquets. If Napoleon III. frowns on the Austrian ambassador on January 1, he means to let the world know that France and Austria may possibly be at war before the spring. If Francis Joseph and the emperor of Russia talk much and warmly over a friendly dinner, we infer that the fate of Hungary is in the balance. There are some countries whose foreign policy is often notoriously the result of the personal feelings and predilections of the reigning monarch. Where that is the case, the tones of his voice, or the play of the muscles of his face upon great occasions become matters of real consequence, as they are the index of the temper of a man whose temper is a subject of as much interest in the political as the weather is in the domestic world. There is one nation pre-eminently whose policy previously to the Crimean war for many years was decided by the private piques, inclinations, and prejudices of her ruler. That nation is Russia. On the other hand, it happens that French politics, during a similar period, have turned mainly upon questions of dynasty. It is accordingly in the history of the relations between the courts of St. Petersburg and Paris during the last forty years that we should expect to find, if anywhere, battles of diplomatic etiquette. In a contemporary French review, M. Guizot last week published a diplomatic correspondence which contains the account of a curious quarrel between France and Russia in 1842. The story is amusing, and well deserves the perusal of all who wish to know how an international coolness may be brought about by means of a diplomatic cold. If Sir John Finett had lived till now he would have been pleased to see the Muscovite, whom he considered a mere novice in etiquette, hold his own so ably against the envoys of that polite nation from whom Sir John borrowed the principles of his ingenious code.

Dissatisfied at the changes that had taken place in France in 1830, the Emperor Nicholas for eleven years had treated Louis Philippe with offensive coolness and *hauteur*. In his letters he consistently abstained from addressing the French king by the conventional title of *Monsieur mon frère*, which it was his custom to employ in similar communications. Finally, at the close of 1841, the Russian ambassador, whose business it would otherwise become through the indisposition of Count Appony, the Austrian representative, to address the king on the first day of the new year as the spokesman of the Corps Diplomatique, received a significant recall. The patience of the French Cabinet was exhausted by this unmistakable slight, and M. Guizot addressed a letter to M. Casimir Périer, *chargè d'affaires* at St. Petersburg, from which we reprint the following extract:—

"Monsieur le Comte de Pahlen a reçu l'ordre fort inattendu de se rendre à St. Petersbourg. . . . La cause réelle, qui n'est un mystére pour personne, c'est que par suite de l'absence de M. le Comte Appony, l'ambassadeur de Russie se trouvait appelé à complimenter le roi, le premier jour de l'an au nom du corps diplomatique. . . . Une seule réponse nous convient. Le jour de la Saint-Nicholas, la légation française à St. Petersbourg restera renfermée dans son hôtel. Vous n'aurez à donner aucun motif sérieux pour expliquer cette retraite inaccoutumée. Vous vous bornerez en répondant à l'invitation que vous recevrez sans doute de M. de Nesselrode à alléguer une indisposition. . . . Jusqu'au 18 Décembre, vous garderez sur l'ordre que je vous donne, le silence le plus absolu. Et d'ici là vous eviterez avec le plus grand soin la moindre altération dans vos rapports avec le cabinet de St. Petersbourg."

["M. le Comte de Pahlen has received a very unlooked-for order, to return to St. Petersburg. . . . The real cause, which is a mystery to no one, is that in consequence of the absence of M. le Comte Appony, the Russian ambassador found himself called upon to make the complimentary address on New Year's day to the king in the name of the diplomatic corps. . . . One answer alone becomes us. On St. Nicholas day, the French Legation at St. Petersburg will remain shut up in their hotel. You will not have to assign any serious reason for this unusual seclusion. You will merely, in replying to the invitation which you will without doubt receive from M. de Nesselrode, allege indisposition. . . . Until the 18th December, you will maintain the most profound silence as to this order. And till that time you will avoid with the greatest care, the least alteration in your intercourse with the Cabinet of St. Petersburg."]

In due time M. Casimir Périer received the order by the courier's hands to whom it had been entrusted, and preserved it a profound secret till the 18th of December, the day of the fête of St. Nicholas. He then faithfully carried it into execution. For forty-eight hours the entire French Legation, without a single exception, were confined to their hotel by indisposition. Not a man appeared out of doors even for the emperor's ball on the day after. The consternation produced in the capital was considerable. The emperor himself was furious, and in a burst of passion resolved, so ran the story, to suppress the Russian embassy at Paris. Finally, he determined to revenge himself in a more indirect but equally telling way. The cue was given to the leaders of the fashionable world, and from the 18th of December, the French Legation found itself put under ban. Nobody came to call. Nobody invited Madame Périer to dinner. Lastly, all who had already issued invitations sent at the last moment to say their parties were suddenly, unavoidably, and indefinitely postponed. The war being nominally one of social etiquette, business was as usual transacted between the embassy and the Russian government. But for all festive purposes M. Périer and his suite found themselves under an interdict. Even a young Russian who paid his compliments to Madame Périer at the theatre received an official intimation that loyalty was not to be sacrificed to politeness. At an official ball, at which M. Périer thought it his duty to appear in virtue of his uniform, he found himself the centre of cold looks. Lastly, at Paris, on the first of January, indisposition attacked a fresh victim in the person of M. de Kisselef, who, during the absence of Count Pahlen, was left in charge of the Russian embassy. He was quite unable to appear at the king's reception, and remained at home all day.

Meantime, at St. Petersburg the situation of affairs was very gloomy. At all court balls the embassy of course were present, and the emperor and empress showed no lack of personal courtesy towards them. "Comment ca va-t-il depuis que nous ne nous sommes vus?" he says on one occasion, good-humoredly, to M. Périer; "ça va mieux n'est-ce pas?" But a general suspension of hospitalities was still the order of the day. Previously to the rupture, M. Périer and his lady had been popular enough. Suddenly they were excluded from all society. During eight months of solitude, the sense of his abandoned position preyed upon the soul of the deserted son of France. He endeavored to bear the misfortune of the general stoppage of entertainments like a man, and to prevent Madame Périer from bearing it like a woman. During this part of the crisis, his letters to M. Guizot are tinged with delicate pathos. They are the letters of a man who suffers, but who suffers for his country. To be deprived of balls is sad, but to maintain dignity intact is sweet. What became of the junior members of the embassy since the day when they had with cheerfulness partaken of the indisposition of their chief, is not recorded. Doubtless they became gloomy and misanthropical, and neglected their personal appearance in a way sufficient to alarm their friends. Even M. Guizot, in his epistles from Paris, shares the general melancholy. He consoles his bereaved countryman in the tone of a man who has a heart, and can sympathize with the persecuted. The end of M. Périer's expatriation was, however, at hand. Indisposition finally attacked one more victim—that victim was Madame Périer. The sad state of her health imperatively demanded a journey to Paris, and M. Périer solicited his recall. He obtained it, together with the cross of the Legion of Honor, and in course of time resigned his functions into the hands of M. d'André, second secretary of Legation.

The ambassadors of France and of Russia meanwhile were both enjoying prolonged leave of absence from their respective posts. Neither would go back, until the other had gone back first. The emperor would not send M. de Pahlen to Paris, before M. de Barante had returned to St. Petersburg. Matters were in this situation at the moment of the unhappy death of the Duke of Orleans, which cast so deep a gloom over Europe. The emperor of Russia exhibited, on the arrival of the sad news, all the feeling of a high-bred gentlemen. A ball which was to have been given the same night by the Grand Duchess Olga, was countermanded; and though he refused to write any autograph letter of condolence to Louis Philippe, he sent a very friendly message by a special courier to be transmitted through the embassy at Paris. A personal congratulation to M. Guizot upon the oratorical successes he had achieved in the French Chambers, combined with a rather bitter allusion to his supposed private hostility to Russia, soon after entailed a correspondence between the two Cabinets, full of explanation and recrimination. Not much alteration took place in consequence. Neither ambassador returned to his post; and business was managed in each case by a *chargé d'affaires*. For the relief of the fairer portion of our readers, it is humane to mention that by the end of 1842, the French Legation, under the social banner of M. d'André, was once more admitted to the enjoyments of festive life. The political coolness lasted; but the social inconveniences, so terrible and so heart-rending, to which it gave rise, passed away. A letter from M. de Guizot to the Count de Flahault, the French representative at Vienna, sums up the moral of the whole:—

"Nous avons atteint notre but, et nous sommes parfaitement en règle. *Officiellement*, le Comte de Pahlen a été rappelé à Pétersbourg pour causer avec l'empereur: M. Casimer Périer a été malade le 18 Décembre, et M. de Kisselef le 1er Janvier. En réalité, l'empereur n'a pas voulu que M. de Pahlen complimentât le roi, et nous n'avons pas voulu que ce mauvais procédé passât inaperçu. De part et d'autre, tout est correct, et tout est compris. Les convenances extérieures ont été observées, et les intentions rèelles senties. Cela nous suffit, et nous nous tenons pour quittes."

["We have accomplished our object and are perfectly *en règle*. *Officially* the Comte de Pahlen has been recalled to St. Petersburg to speak with the emperor; M. Casimir Périer was ill on the 18th December, and M. de Kisselef on the 1st. January. In reality the emperor would not allow M. de Pahlen to compliment the king, and we would not allow this misbehavior to pass unnoticed. On both sides, all is correct, and all is understood. Outside convenances have been observed, and real intentions felt. That is enough for us, and we are quits."]

From The Cornhill Magazine.

HORACE SALTOUN.

PART I.—EARLY DAYS WITH GRIND AND GRINDERS.

It is now many a long year since I and Horace Saltoun found ourselves extended one fine summer's day on a luxuriously mossy bank that overlooked one of the loveliest dales of the north-west of England. We had achieved our small triumph, which, however, appeared magnificent in our eyes; namely, we had successfully passed the hall and the college; and having worked like men, we were ready to play like boys. So while we smoked our short pipes we philosophized after our crude fashion, pitied the fellows who had been "spun," as the phrase goes, and pronounced dogmatically enough on the merits of the case.

We were new at our work then, and regarded the examiners as our natural enemies, to be outwitted, dogged, discomfited, or at any rate to be circumvented somehow; forgetting that the balance of power adjusts itself even in the dreaded chamber of ordeal, and that the instinct of fair play common to all Englishmen is assisted by artificial means. For instance, an examiner does not propose questions to a pupil from his own hospital, but he sits by to hear those whom he instructed undergo their trial, and if they fail from nervousness, not inability, he is permitted to explain the query fairly to them, and ascertain that they completely understand its meaning; while, if they are unduly pressed, though he may be—and, as man is but man, he probably often *is*—in a rage, it is always in his power to torment his rival by a little extra severity on the other men; so that even appealing to the selfish part of human nature—and that is perhaps the safest, inasmuch as it is never wanting, but is always there to be appealed to—the examinations cannot be otherwise than conducted with ordinary justice. All this, however, as I have said, we did not reflect on, but blamed and critcised pretty freely. One gentleman was a sneak, another "a pagan," and a third "a good fellow, and no mistake."

As for me, I was the only son of a widowed mother, and I need not say how disastrous to our hopes, and crushing to the slender means (already largely drawn on for my necessary expenses), a failure would have been. I recounted to Horace for the twentieth time, almost with tears in my eyes, how I could have wrung off the hand of old —— in sheer gratitude when he interposed, "Take courage, young gentleman; don't hurry. Do you quite understand what Mr. —— means? It is," etc. And in a few words a question that had been put in a most involved and ambiguous form, was made so clear that it was satisfactorily answered. My spirits and hopes rose, and I felt an internal conviction that I should get through. Well—well! all that is past and gone; and boys with faces as white as their own shirts have stood before *me* since then. But you may be sure I do not forget the hour when I occupied their place, sick with anxiety, and my heart thumping against my side as though it would break my ribs. And if I see the honest face of a painstaking lad hopelessly troubled, for the sake of that memory I give him a helping hand, or a word of encouragement. And if, as will happen, young fellows present themselves who have been idle three-fourths of their time, and have frantically ground and crammed into them in six months that which ought to have been carefully acquired in five years (and though they may shave off their moustaches, and turn up their shirt-collars, we *do* happen to know these young gentlemen by sight), I try that their rejection, which really the slightest regard for the good of mankind renders imperative, shall be accomplished by such words and recommendations as shall not dispirit them from making another, and often a more successful, endeavor.

But I am digressing. I must try to convey some idea of the tall, loose-limbed, bulky young fellow who was lounging by my side. He possessed a massive and exceeding well-developed forehead, a full, light-gray eye the iris of which was curiously flecked with dark patches, somewhat irregular features, rather thin, twitching lips, a complexion that was habitually of a muddy pallor, and a quantity of disorderly hair of no very obvious color.

At fifteen, Horace Saltoun was a dull, heavy lad, whose brain seemed overweighted. He was as stupid in his intellectual efforts as he was slow and clumsy in the active sports of his schoolfellows. He was the despair of his tutors, though to do him justice, he received their reproaches with the most phlegmatic stolidity, and the butt of his fellows, as far as they dared, for his fists were known to be like sledge-hammers, and his blows to rarely miss their aim. It was, indeed, said of him, that as he never knew when to begin fighting, he never knew when to leave off; and that slow as he was to be roused, he was slower still to be appeased. The head-master, however, differed from the others in his estimation of the character of young Horace, and was wont to say, "There is no need to hurry; he will get the use of his faculties all in good time, and, God sparing his health, he will some day be an extraordinary man: he is inert, but there is great dormant power. With such a head as that I never despair."

The doctor's prediction seemed likely to realize itself, though not till after Saltoun quitted his care. At nineteen his ponderous powers came into play, and at twenty-two he was one of our most rising and analytical chemists, and had distinguished himself in microscopic investigations; he had likewise effected one or two small but important improvements in certain philosophical apparatus, the result of which had been to bring him under the favorable notice of some of the leading scientific men of the day, while his prodigious ability in mental arithmetic and quantitative analysis had already caused him to be looked on as no mean authority. I can see him now as he used to sit in his student days in the front rank at the lecture, apparently utterly dead to all that was going on around him, with his huge shoulders up to his ears, his eyes half closed, and his head resting on his hand, until he resembled a great contemplative sloth. But if a knotty point or a contested theory were started, he would show signs of life, move incessantly on his seat, run his fingers through his long, untidy locks, wake up, and in a wonderfully short space of time he had sifted and digested the information, added one or two odd-looking hieroglyphics to those that already adorned his note-book, and would then relapse into his former sluggish attitude.

As the intellectual dulness which characterized his boyhood utterly disappeared, so did his moral disposition undergo a marked change. The phlegmatic tone vanished; he became more delusive in kindness and more sensitive to rebuke, more ready to love or hate, to rejoice or to mourn, and, as a consequence, proportionably more popular. As a student he was a reckless liver, drawing unsparingly on his health and his brains. Whether it were boating or reading, fighting or gambling, a daring experiment in surgery or a night expedition to procure anatomical subjects, a war among the dons or a row with the Thames watermen (at all times rough customers), no man threw himself into the ring with such haste and zeal as Saltoun. His rough, natural eloquence, and his iron power of endurance, made him an invariable boon companion; for he seemed to be indifferent to heated rooms and abominable smells; and the longest orgie failed to exhaust him, for he apparently postponed sleep at will, and summoned it at his own pleasure.

I ought, perhaps, to have said before that the lower part of his head and face was inferior to the upper, and even somewhat animal in the expression; and from this there ran a certain tendency to coarseness which marred the harmony of the impression given by his whole appearance. He, nevertheless, had his impulses under strict control: he never touched any spirituous liquor, and none of us ever saw him deviate from what seemed to be a fixed resolution on this point; he was, however, a votary of tobacco, and a passionate lover of all games of chance; so that he had weaknesses enough to compensate for his temperance in other respects. Gambling, however, he renounced in a great measure; and after he commenced his professional career, he did so entirely, alleging he had not time for it. In one department of medical student-life he won laurels. His invariable and unselfish kindness to the poor; his persevering attention; his constant readiness to give up his time and pleasure for their benefit, made him regarded almost as a deity among them; and "young Dr. Saltoun" had been reported to many of his superiors long before he had acquired the legal license to cure or kill. He thus laid the foundation of a large, though, perhaps, not lucrative practice.

He did not, as has been said, neglect his books; but he profited more by direct experience than any man I ever saw. In these matters he passed his fellows, as one wave will occasionally head all the rest, and roll far beyond that thin line of froth which marks on the sand the spent force of the others. What he found to do he did with all his might; but it was generally tinted by a certain pervading recklessness; and from the time when his intellect first seemed to respond to the calls which were made on it, in all his ways there was a something which betrayed the craving instinct for excitement which seemed to be a component of his changed character. Like most temperaments of this order, his spirits were subject to great alternations: he had fits of gloom, of ill-will to particular individuals, and great irresolution in adopting any plan. Whether it was that his mind was too divided to fix on any line of action, and that he anticipated a failure; or that his too highly taxed physical strength encouraged a regretful state of mind; or that the voluntary power was too much enfeebled to be exerted with effect, cannot be safely pronounced on; but at these seasons he was unlike himself, moody and taciturn in society, and in gesture irritable and petulant. But, with all his faults, he was pre-eminently generous, humble-minded, and truthful, ever ready to see merit, and slow to believe evil; and our intimacy as schoolboys and fellow-students laid the foundation of a friendship which after years cemented into an abiding affection.

So much for my companion: and if I have appeared to sketch his character at a greater length than requisite, it must be borne in mind that it is necessary to bring his peculiarities prominently before the reader, in order to appreciate the after troubles of his career.

Below the mossy bank on which Horace and I reclined, was a cascade, rather celebrated in those parts. The water came pouring over the fall in foaming torrents; and, once in that deep, turbid hollow, they revolved round and round, as life does in large towns, like thick, boiling scum; then the spots of discolored foam congregated sullenly, those that escaped fell over a few stones into a rapid, clear brook, and were carried swiftly out of hearing of the din and tumult above. Opposite to us rose a hill, clothed to its very summit with birch, alder, holly, furze, and fern; beyond it, to the right, lay a plain, dotted over with isolated rocks, of that peculiar coffin-like shape which so often indicates the limestone formation; and stretching away from this, lay range after range of those broad, lofty mountains which guard our native dales: indented, scored steppes of stone formed frequent distinct lines of terraces, some of which must have been upwards of sixty feet in depth. A dark strip of pine formed an angle on the summit of the hill, and the small expanse of sky which was visible through this angle marked the pass of the "Grip Hag."

After smoking for a considerable time in silence, I slipped from my seat, and, making my way among the tangled branches of the stunted trees and over the rough blocks of stone, I reached the river, and, filling my horn with the sparkling water, mixed it with some whiskey, supposed to be of peculiar excellence, which I had procured on my road. I tossed it off, half filled it again, and, scrambling up, rejoined Horace, and, with the foolish idea of vanquishing his determined practice of drinking nothing but water, I proceeded to mix for him. At first he refused; but when the odor from the flask was wafted into his nostrils, he wavered, and at last acquiesced, with an odd grimace. "If I must take it, Paul, give me it neat." I complied, and poured the yellow, fragrant liquid out alone. As I placed the horn in his hand, I was struck by the greedy, anxious expression of his eyes. He held it for an instant to his lips, and then, without touching the liquor, jerked the horn and its contents into the little river, where, after a few bobbings about, it proceeded on its brief and uneven voyage. "What an ass you are, Horace!" I said, heatedly.

"I dare say I am," he replied, twisting his face into a horrible contortion. "But I should have been a greater ass if I had tasted that stuff. Stay, old fellow, don't be waxy, when I tell you why, by a safe inspiration, I threw it out of my reach. I shall tell you what I never trusted to any human being before, and you will change your mind about me, or I am far wrong. They say every house has its skeleton. Now, intoxicating liquors have been the bane of my family. We have, most of us, a morbid propensity to drink any thing, no matter what, provided it intoxicates us. I don't say we all have it; but we never know in which of us it is to break out. We don't drink for *drinkee*, as the black man says, but for *drunkee*. It's no outbreak of convivial cheer, but a mad, animal instinct for solitary excess. My grandfather was hardly ever seen drunk:

amid the excesses so common in those days, when three-bottle men abounded, he was singular by his abstemiousness; but at isolated periods, when quite alone, he took the most awful doses of raw spirits: he craved the poison with a fatal obstinacy, and obtained it by a marvellous cunning; and his very sobriety in public made it an easier matter for him to slaughter himself unprevented in private. He died in a madhouse. My uncle exhibited the same tendency: he cut his own throat. My father was all his life, a rigid water-drinker; he was not a long-lived man, but when he was made aware that his end was approaching, he called me to his bedside, detailed these terrible particulars, and warned me, in words that made a deep impression on my mind. Since then I have never tasted wine or spirits: in fact, *you* know how strictly I have abstained. But sometimes, in the dead of night, when I have been previously overworked, or worried and anxious, I have felt the most awful craving for a stimulant; and I have broken out into a cold sweat with terror, lest the fiend was come to take possession, and the family degradation about to break out in my person. At those times I could fancy that the very scent of spirits would be enough to make my resolution vanish into thin air. It seems to me as if the most infernal compounds—British gin, or spirits of wine—any thing, in short, that would excite me, would be drunk to the dregs, as if it were nectar. With such a history to my back, Paul, you, for one, will never blame me for avoiding that which is to me the accursed thing."

"Nay, old fellow," was my answer; "if I had known this, you may trust me, I'd sooner have cut off my right hand than have pressed it on you."

There is more generosity and frank sympathy in youth than in after years; had we both come to ripe manhood, perhaps Horace would have hesitated to make this confession. As it was, the mutual knowledge of it only cemented more firmly our friendship; and his very distrust of himself lent him, in my eyes, a deeper interest.

Shortly after this period, fortune separated us; Saltoun remained in England, while I was appointed surgeon to an East Indiaman. We kept up a correspondence, though of course at intervals.

Meanwhile, circumstances occurred that made me anxious to quit the naval service. It did not suit me for many reasons: the facilities afforded to young medical officers were limited in extent, and very rarely vouchsafed at all; moreover, the life was to me an intolerably idle one: often for days becalmed in the blue Indian seas, beneath a tropical sun, and with a thermometer 98° in the shade, our sole endeavors seemed directed to invent what might, if possible, keep us cool. My business was in general of the lightest description, and there was much to see and observe in the fashions and manners of the passengers, some of which were amusing enough. Still there was a monotony about it all.

I speak, be it remembered, of things as they were twenty-five years ago, at which time there was a much greater approximation to similarity in the character and appearance of those who went out. They were all people who were descended from those connected with India by ties of different kinds; they had been bred to look forward to it, if not as their home, at least as their appointed sphere, wherein to earn a fortune or win a husband: and there was by no means that bitter and contemptuous mode of speaking of the natives which has of late years become the fashion. About four years after I entered I was invalided, with leave of absence for some months. I resolved not to sail again if I could avoid it, but endeavor, instead, to obtain, the superintendence of some establishment for the insane, and devote myself entirely to the psychological branch of my profession, for which I had always felt a strong preference.

While I was recruiting my health in one of the watering-places in the south-west of England, busied in plans and correspondence, I got a letter from Horace, and found that his mother and sister were residing temporarily in the same neighborhood; furthermore he required me to call on them. He gave me a flourishing account of his own affairs: his practice was already large, his private pupils were rapidly increasing, and he had received a hint that the professorship of anatomy at —— Hospital was open to his acceptance. Moreover, he thought he had heard of something which would exactly meet my requirements. Many more warm and kind-hearted things he said, which showed to me that his disposition was unaltered, and he concluded by enclosing the address of a well-known physician who proposed to resign the active duties of his establishment in favor of a younger man. The idea pleased me much, chiming in as it did with my secret wishes, and I wrote respecting it without an hour's delay.

That evening, after a hard day's work, I had just seated myself with a new number of the "Blue and Yellow" quarterly, then in the zenith of its fame, and was deep in one of its brilliant and slashing articles, when a note, the handwriting of which was not familiar to me, was placed in my hand. It was marked *urgent*. I could hardly guess what should procure such a summons for a poor invalid medical officer, and I hastily mastered its contents. It was from Mrs. Saltoun, and contained a hurried request to me, as the friend of her son, to lose no time in repairing to her house, as her daughter, suffering under a feverish attack, had become rapidly worse, and was now delirious: would I follow the messenger forthwith? Of course I hastened to dismiss the *Edinburgh*, and set out immediately, wondering meanwhile how it had happened that a medical man had not been called in before, and whether they had sent for Horace. No doubt he had named me to his mother, and hence the application.

The stars looked down steadily, the air was of an oppressive sultriness, and the sky of that deep blue which almost reminds one of southern climes, as I listened to the echo of our steps while the boy and I paced along the solitary road. I could not help calling to mind the many nights when, almost smothered, I had leaned out of my little cabin window, trying vainly to get a breath of air, or at last, totally unable to sleep, quitted the berth and spent the night on deck in company with the officer of the watch, enjoying the strange calm beauty of night in the southern hemisphere. Amid thoughts like these I was called back to business by the servant stopping at the iron gates of a low white house which stood in some pleasure-grounds: these, though only of limited extent, were laid out with much taste. As we proceeded up the short avenue, I observed that the two upper windows were open from the top only, and that the room was apparently lighted up; the blinds, however, were drawn down, and were flapping idly to and fro, and I could perceive the shadow of a woman's figure passing hastily backwards and forwards. In a minute after I stood in the presence of Mrs. Saltoun. She was a good deal altered since the days when she had welcomed me, then a mere boy, to her house. She was still a fine-looking woman, with a pair of gentle eyes, and a natural graciousness of manner which was very winning. She professed to recall my face at once, and welcomed me with much kindness.

"I am rejoiced to see you, my dear Paul —I must call you doctor, now. You will perhaps feel surprised at this hurried message, but we have only recently settled in this neighborhood, and hearing from Horace that you were here also, he begged we would find you out; and I am glad to do so, though this is a melancholy occasion."

I mentioned the substance of his letter, and added my regrets as to her daughter's illness.

"Yes, Emily's illness seems more serious than I anticipated, so I decided on sending for you in your medical capacity." I expressed suitable acknowledgments. "Nay, it is very pleasant when a physician is also a friend. I have sent express for Horace."

"And when may we look for him?"

"Not before to-morrow, I fear."

The poor lady seemed a good deal flurried; and I noticed, or fancied I did, a slight hesitation of speech and a hardly perceptible expression of the face which induced me to suppose she had recently experienced a threatening of paralysis. I inquired whether it would not be advisable for me at once to see Miss Saltoun. She rang the bell, sent for Miss Emily's maid, and then pursued the conversation.

"Mdlle. Justine is an invaluable person; I hardly know what we should have done without her: unfortunately she does not speak English, but even with that drawback she is quite a treasure."

I made no comment on this, as I have a secret aversion to treasures of this description.

"And how have you kept your own health, Mrs. Saltoun?"

"Oh, I have not been very strong; Emily has been for some time very far from well, and in strangely uneven spirits."

I did not like to hazard the direct inquiry,

which is nevertheless the first real thought of every experienced medical man: "Has she any known cause for mental disquiet?" but substituted, "Have her spirits always been so variable?"

"No: yesterday she really alarmed me; but she was exceedingly opposed to having advice. Justine, too, thought it unnecessary, so that I am now too sensible that I have delayed it longer than I ought to have done," continued the poor lady. "To-night she is quite delirious, and frightened me sadly. I am not often able to go up-stairs," she added, with a calm, pleasant smile, "and my old limbs remind me that the days are gone by, never to return, when three or four flights of steps were as nothing to me."

At this instant the door opened, and Mdlle. Justine entered. She was a middle-aged, firmly built, olive-complexioned woman, with a pair of fine dark eyes beneath strongly defiant black brows, a thin-lipped and rather wide mouth, with that square iron-looking jaw so often seen in Frenchwomen of the lower class. Not one moment elapsed before I felt positive I had seen that face before in other scenes, and taxed my memory to recollect where.

"Had madame called her?" she inquired in French. "Yes, Justine," Mrs. Saltoun replied in the same language; "is my daughter prepared to see the doctor?"

"Assuredly, madame."

"Is Mdlle. Louise the sole attendant on Miss Saltoun?" I asked, remembering what I had been told, that the waiting-maid did not understand English.

"Oh, yes; she hardly leaves her for an instant."

Justine's eyes flickered, and then turned with a steady, and I thought, rather insolent, glance on me. I was not duped; she understood English as well as I did, of that I was clear.

"Her name is Justine, not Louise," replied Mrs. Saltoun, innocently; "but it's no matter."

Justine vanished instanter, and darted up-stairs, with a singular alacrity. The old lady leaned on my arm, and we proceeded slowly to ascend the staircase. As we approached the chamber door, I heard a hasty exclamation in French, then a low muttering, and a groan.

I had left Miss Saltoun a little girl of ten years old, and should certainly hardly have recognized her at first sight. She was in bed. I could trace considerable resemblance to Horace in her expressive and irregular features; there was a good deal, too, of the same promise of mental power about the head, but it was so far refined down as to make her a woman almost handsome, and certainly attractive in no ordinary degree. Her long hair lay loose and in disorder about the pillow; her arms were outside the sheets, which I observed by the way were firmly swathed and banded down to the bed. Her eyes were glistening, and their expression was full of a sort of expectant fear. She made several attempts to spring up, but Justine held her forcibly but quietly down. There was something about it all I thought very peculiar. I proceeded to feel her pulse. Oh, that valuable minute which is allowed to us, when with watch in hand we have time to think, if we only preserve that absorbed expression which is necessary! I quickly ran over the symptoms in my mind, especially the tremulous motion of the head, and the twitching of the eyelids. As I sat perfectly still, holding my fingers on the wrist, I was aware that I had long exceeded the single minute, and I could feel that Mdlle. Justine was watching me with ill-dissembled anxiety. I quickly made up my mind how to act.

"What food has Miss Saltoun taken?" I asked in English, of Justine.

She referred to Mrs. Saltoun, who repeated the question in French, when the maid condescended to reply in the same language,—

"Oh, very little: for the last six weeks, less and less."

"Yes; and what liquids?" (Again her eye flickered.)

Mrs. Saltoun replied for her, "Chiefly soda-water, sometimes lemonade." The look of uneasiness wore off Justine's countenance, as Mrs. Saltoun said this.

Now of two things I had gradually become convinced during these few minutes: one was, that the name of Justine was assumed for some reason or other, and that I had known the attendant in very different circumstances as "Louise;" the other was, that this being the case, she understood

English as well as I did. Granting this, and that she was aware of my discoveries, I should have a pretty strong hold on her.

I walked to the window and tried to open the lower part, but found it was nailed fast down. Good. Evidently Justine, who knew more about it than any of us, had taken the same view of the case that presented itself to me. She came forward with some explanation. "Do not apologize, mademoiselle," I said; "you have done quite right: I am aware of your reason." I drew a little writing-table to me, and began a prescription, and wrote also a note to a medical friend on whom I could depend, requesting him to send me instantly a trustworthy nurse. As I was thus engaged, Miss Saltoun raised herself gently up and peered over the side of the bed. A nervous tremor ran through her whole body, and her face wore an expression of abject terror.

"There is something black," she said to me. "A horrid, crawling, twisting black thing under my bed. I wish you could take it away; it comes up to me constantly: can't it be removed? it ought not to be permitted to stay," she added, cowering back into her bed.

"Be comforted," I said; "I'll have it removed, and the whole room cleared out. I'll see that it does not annoy you. Mrs. Saltoun, will you be so good as to send off these two notes immediately; I will wait here until the messenger returns. How long did you say it would be before Horace will be here?"

"He cannot come before morning," she answered. "But surely, my poor child wanders strangely. Do you suppose the fever is infectious? Is not delirium a sign of danger?"

"Not necessarily so, my dear madam. As to its being infectious, I cannot pronounce definitely at this stage; but, decidedly, no one who has not been previously in attendance should be much in the room." I did this to prevent Miss Saltoun being seen by more eyes than needful. "Mdlle. Justine looks a little knocked up. I have sent for assistance, which I doubt not will be very acceptable to her; she must require relief." I gave her a keen glance, which she returned with a stare of considerably less perfect effrontery than before. "With your permission, Mrs. Saltoun, I'll speak to her for a moment. Step this way, mademoiselle," I said to her in French. She followed me, rather unwillingly, into the next room. I turned sharply round on her as soon as we were out of hearing, and said abruptly in English: "Now, your young mistress has not got a fever, you know; what has she been in the habit of drinking?"

"*Je ne comprends pas, monsieur,*" she replied.

I repeated the question, with the same result. "If *you* don't understand," I said, very slowly, "I do. Mademoiselle, *I* understand that your name is not Justine, but Louise; and that you speak and comprehend English perfectly. *Now*, what has your mistress been drinking?"

"It is as I had the honor of telling monsieur," she said in English, perfectly unabashed; "tea and soda-water or lemonade."

Now on earth there is no race of people who lie more audaciously than the French: they attach so little regard to truth that detection causes them no shame; and of all liars, perhaps a French Abigail is most at home in this art; but then stupidity is not among her faults—and if she can clearly perceive it is to her own interest to retrace her steps, she has neither shame nor dignity to prevent her doing so.

"Now, Louise," I said, "this wont do. I will not inform Mrs. Saltoun, if you will tell the truth for once; and if you can't, or wont, I'll get you discharged before I leave this house. What is it your mistress has been drinking?"

"*Mon Dieu! que sais-je?*" she was commencing.

"Speak English, if you please," I said.

"Ether, eau-de-Cologne, spirits of lavender."

"Yes, yes, I know that; but that is not all. What is it she has had that you buy and bring in quietly?" I said this on supposition, but I saw I had hit on the truth.

"Gin, since you will have it, monsieur. She has been a little ill before, but never so bad as this." Here she relapsed into mendacity, and declared how unwillingly she had consented to procure the liquor; how much pain it had cost her do so, with other items exculpatory, which I interrupted.

"How long have these fits of drinking lasted?"

"About three weeks."

"Good; now, that will do. I need not advise you to keep your own counsel. You must stay with your young mistress until the nurse arrives. You have nailed down the window, I perceived; that was a very happy precaution, and proves that you knew what it was all about. Keep her from jumping out of bed, if possible; and don't leave her for an instant, under any pretence whatsoever. It is as much as her life and your place are worth put together."

I administered the proper medicines, and by the time that the nurse (a vigilant, reserved-looking individual) made her appearance, I had the satisfaction of finding that my patient appeared inclined to sleep, and that the frightfully irritable state of the nervous system showed symptoms of submitting to the remedies.

Horace arrived early the next morning, and I found him in the room with his mother when I paid my visit. I shook hands with him, and, of course, my first inquiry was whether Miss Saltoun had slept. It was a real relief to me when I received an answer in the affirmative; under the circumstances I naturally attributed the utmost importance to the fact.

"Excuse me, Paul," Horace broke in, "but I think you must be mad, if, as I am told, Emily has a fever, and you are prescribing morphia, brandy, and ammonia."

I tried to laugh, but it was a very poor attempt, for Mrs. Saltoun was looking anxiously and nervously from one to the other.

"I am open to correction, Horace. However, she appears to be better; and we will have a consultation." I took his arm, and we went out together. "You have not awakened her, have you?"

"No, not I," he replied; "I only just saw her, without disturbing her in the slightest degree. I tasted the medicines, which struck me as very oddly chosen for this particular case;" and he fixed on me an angry and suspicious eye.

How was I to break the painful truth to the poor fellow? I durst not dissemble: indeed, it could have answered no good purpose, so I said at once, "Horace, it is better that you should know the fact. It is not a fever under which your sister is suffering, it is a slight attack of *delirium tremens;*" and I proceeded to give him the substance of what I had extracted from Justine. He whitened visibly, as I spoke, and his knitted brows and twitching lips testified how terribly he was shaken.

"That fatal madness!" he gasped, and the drops of perspiration stood on his forehead. "Of course, the first thing is to discharge Justine. But I dare not tell my mother; it would kill her. And yet how to account for it? Do you think I can conceal the worst part of the affair?"

"I'll tell you my plan," I said; "and after you have heard it, take it or not, as you think advisable. Justine is not a conscientious individual; but she has plenty both of pluck and firmness, with a keen eye to her own interest, and is very difficult to deceive. She alone knows of this sad weakness, except the nurse—and her silence I'll undertake to secure. Of course the fewer that are aware of it the better. Make it to her advantage to serve you faithfully and discreetly; double, or, if needs be, treble her wages, and tell her that you will pay her at that rate so long as she keeps silence, and your sister keeps her health. Impress upon her that if another attack of the same kind even threatens to appear, she will be turned off forthwith, and without any recommendation."

Horace fell in at once with my proposal; requesting me, however, to make the necessary treaty with Justine, since, from my being not quite unacquainted with her former history, I had the greater chance of influence. She agreed, without making any objection or testifying any surprise.

"You understand, Louise, that you, and you only, are responsible. I'm quite sure that, with your quickness and penetration, Miss Saltoun will never be able to obtain spirits without your knowing of it, and I am confident that your good feeling as a woman will induce you to assist with all your might Mr. Saltoun's efforts to rescue his sister from such a melancholy fate: for that she will be liable to seek to indulge the craving from time to time I do not doubt. Besides, Louise, letting alone your affection for your mistress," Louise put on a sentimental air at this point, "it is obviously to your advantage to do so."

She assumed her natural manner again, and even exchanged glances which announced that we understood each other.

"No, she had no objection. As to *bonté de cœur*—she did not know; Miss Saltoun had always been very kind, and a benefactress to her. Yes, she would undertake the task. Three times her old salary, that was 1,500 francs. Yes, she would certainly undertake it, and if danger appeared she would instantly communicate with me or Mr. Horace."

I hastened back, made known my success, and counselled him earnestly to stay with his sister until she recovered.

"And then tell her, Horace, that you know what the nature of her malady was, and what has occasioned it. Tell her what you have told me about other members of your family, so that she may feel that you are not without sympathy for her—that she does not stand alone—and that, above all, you understand the struggles that are before her, and that you are prepared to stand by her to assist her in them. Don't say a word about my having seen her in that state: enlist her pride, as well as her fears, on her own behalf; and if you can procure her some female friendship, and society of her own sex, it would be very advisable."

"You are right; solitude does engender the craving; whether it be due to counter-excitement or to the dread of shame, mixing in society tends to check it."

I hardly like to think of that interview between the brother and sister! How must it come from a man and a gentleman to a woman—and that woman his sister! Yet they were both to some extent fellow-sufferers; though he, forewarned by his father, had also been forearmed. But look at it how one will, it must have been a saddening and humbling interview. He had such a natural generosity and tact, that I felt sure he would seek to break the intelligence to her with all tenderness, and to save her from her own reflections under that terrible reaction which invariably follows those attacks.

I believe in all this he perfectly succeeded; and, as one consequence, Emily recovered rapidly. A week after, Horace put into my hand a letter containing a proposal which so exactly coincided with my own earnest desires that I at once resigned my naval appointment.

I warmly thanked Horace, and very naturally asked him about his prospects. He gave vent to a most uproarious laugh, and then subsided into total silence. I regarded him attentively.

"You have something to tell, I suppose, Horace, when you have done your internal reflections."

"Well, Paul, don't you feel that I should think of settling?"

"Taking a wife, you mean, I suppose: why, it is what we all hope for, Horace; and I suppose to no man is a wife more necessary than to a doctor."

I was rather surprised; though perhaps I had no right to be. He lay down on the sofa, lit his cigar with great deliberation, emitted some mouthfuls of smoke, and then the secret came out.

"Well, I'm engaged to be married, old boy, congratulate me."

I burst out laughing and said, "Not till I know who to."

"To Cecile Otway. It is not a bad match in a worldly point of view: though, you know, that need not be a desideratum with me; and it's all I could wish in every other way."

"Do you mean the daughter of Mr. Otway of the firm 'Otway and Kennedy,' East India people?"

"The very one. Do you know her?"

"Know her!—I think I do know her."

"Then," hastily interrupted Horace, "if you know her, of course you admire her: at least, if you don't you need not say it; though I should like to hear your opinion," he continued, with a lover's usual logic.

"I remember admiring her," I said, cautiously.

"I met her some time ago, you must know, Paul, before you were in England, and was struck immediately. I know you wont suspect me of coxcombry; indeed, such an uncouth fellow as I am has no right to entertain delusive notions of the sort; but she showed me a certain preference. Mr. Otway appeared so well inclined towards me that a few days ago—before I came down here, mark you—I proposed, and was accepted. Now, I want to consult you on one point. Do you think this unhappy secret about my sister's illness will ooze out?"

"No," I replied. "It has not, and need not do so. Your mother has not the faintest suspicion. Justine will, for her own sake, hold her tongue. There only remain you and I."

"Well, now, we will suppose that safe. Now I want your candid opinion, as an honorable man. *Ought* I—is it my duty—to acquaint Miss Otway with it?"

"I don't see the slightest reason why you should. It concerns your sister, not yourself; it would be an unkind step as regards her, and an unnecessary one as respects yourself."

"You really think so, Paul?"

"I do, indeed, Horace."

"Good! then henceforth let it be not named between us. You don't know what a load you have taken from my mind by giving me this assurance." A pause followed.

"When are you to be married?" I demanded with a countenance, I fear, not so congratulatory as he expected. He looked a little cast down.

"I have no right to hurry the thing on, you see; and she is very reserved. Some people might fancy she was cold, but to me she is the very incarnation of feminine purity!"

A good deal more he added in the same strain, before we parted for the night. The upshot of the business appeared to be, that, after a rather short acquaintance, Horace was an engaged man. I was not astonished at his success, with the daughter even of so wealthy a man as Mr. Otway was reputed to be, for already he was named as a most rising man, with every chance of a brilliant future in his profession; and his remarkable powers of wit and illustration distinguished him, even in general society, from his fellows. My acquaintance with both father and daughter chanced thus. Mr. Otway had a connection with some of the foreign mercantile houses, and frequently made voyages in person. On one of these occasions he and his daughter were passengers on board the ship to which I had the honor of being junior surgeon, and I had watched that young lady's proceedings with a good deal of amusement. I remembered her as a very elegant young woman, with a pair of steely-blue eyes, fair hair, a singular purity of complexion—which, I suspected, had to do duty for purity of purpose, and a catlike grace and stealthiness of movement. One drawback I must add—she possessed a certain thinness and sharpness in the quality of her voice, which could be unpleasant occasionally, when she spoke and was ill-pleased, and which certainly forbade her ever to attempt to increase the number of her charms by the aid of song. These were the most noticeable features of her *personnel;* as to the rest—I am not often uncharitable—but I knew that she had been engaged once or twice, and that a good many young men considered themselves exceedingly ill-treated by her. If Horace were to marry, I wished heartily that he had selected some one of whom I had formed a less unfavorable opinion. But advice is rarely taken, even when asked for, in such affairs.

A few months glided rapidly away, and witnessed our taking possession of our respective positions. I obtained my diploma, and was established as resident physician at —— Grange, while Horace stood before the world as the accepted lover of the wealthy Miss Otway. She used her power a little mercilessly: he was literally harnessed to the wheels of her chariot, and everywhere graced her triumph. Thus Horace had to appear in a triple character—a devoted lover, an active surgeon, a popular lecturer; not to count that she also expected him to shine in society. He rose early, and arranged for his morning lecture to his private pupils; then he saw a large number of out-patients, made his rounds—where, as his fame extended, he had frequently to perform difficult and delicate surgical operations—then to his evening lecture again. After a hasty dinner he would repair to some scientific or medical meeting, and read a brilliant and effective paper prepared Heaven knows when; from which he proceeded to attend Miss Otway to a ball, or the opera, or wherever that young lady chose to be seen with him; and once there—owing, perhaps, to the presence of the object of his affections, the excitement of company, and his variable spirits—he was unsparing of his apparently never-flagging powers, was applauded, admired, and quoted. This gratified his impulsive nature, as it exhausted his energies; and at two or three A.M., more or less jaded, he would snatch a few hours' sleep, until his multifarious duties again summoned him. But that he could, as I said before, sleep almost at will, he must have given way under it.

I may be accused of judging Miss Otway a little harshly, but the result will bear me guiltless. I heard *of* Horace frequently, and directly from him occasionally. More than once I met them both at different houses, and had full opportunity to verify my opinion. Miss Otway's manner towards him was, to my mind, very cold; and if her smile was bright, it had also that heartless, set expression, which bears about as much relation to a warm heart as the flame of a spirit-lamp does to a coal fire. However, he always spoke of her with the utmost generosity, lamenting only that he could not prevail on her to fix the marriage for a definite day; but added that he should be unreasonable indeed to complain, for that their house and table were always open to him; that he never went without receiving a hearty welcome from Mr. Otway, and that Cecile's manner was in private all a lover could wish for. Indeed, even if a day passed without their seeing each other, the next was sure to bring him a summons; and I knew quite well what a pile of tiny three-cornered pink-tinted notes he had treasured up.

When I encountered Miss Otway in society—which, however, from my onerous avocations, I was rarely enabled to do—she received me from the first with a marked cordiality, hardly warranted by our previous very slight acquaintance. Was this, as she took care to inform me, because I was the friend of Horace? or was it rather to enlist my sympathy and secure my silence as to what I might have formerly seen and heard of her character? I was uncharitable enough to believe the latter; and if I considered her a thorough coquette, I had the satisfaction of knowing that a good many men, and a large majority of women, were of my way of thinking. However, it was obviously not my place to interfere. I tried to give her credit for future good intentions, and to believe in her affection for Horace, against my own conviction. And I am not the first man, nor shall I be the last, who has lent credit to a fair face.

"Yes, I am proud of Horace," she said to me one evening, when the fancy took her to lean confidingly on my arm. We both watched his powerful, and, if the truth be said, somewhat clumsy, person, shouldering a path in the crowd, easily visible from his great height. "Every thing he does is so masculine and characteristic."

"He has a very warm and affectionate disposition, and a most unselfish heart, Miss Otway; and that, let me tell you, is a very rare qualification among our sex." No reply. "And it generally fails to meet with its deserts," I added, a little sadly.

"You know Horace can do no wrong in my eyes, doctor," returned Cecile, "and that ought to content even *your* friendship, exigeant as it is." And again the old honeyed smile.

"We will hope it may always continue to be the case," I replied, in a rather churlish manner.

A few weeks after this Horace came to me, looking terribly out of sorts. He lit a large cigar, and puffed away at it furiously, as if he wished to get rid of some secret irritation. I continued writing, without boring him by inquiries. At last out came his grievance.

"I say, Paul, old Otway is going abroad for a twelvemonth, and Cecile is going with him."

"How does she like that?" I asked.

"That is the point. I can't understand it," he said, dashing down his cigar in uncontrolled impatience. "She likes it very well indeed, and takes to it as a child does to new milk. She says she is very much grieved, and all that: indeed, she shed tears" (this with a little softening in his tone), "and I may have pressed her too hard; but still she does not really care—she hardly pretends."

"Why not marry at once, and save her the trouble and expense of the voyage; or, at least, let her make the tour in your company, instead of her father's?"

"Exactly what I urged: you know there is no earthly reason why we should not. I am making more than £900 per annum now, besides £200 a year of my own, and the absolute certainty of more at my mother's death; and, as to a house, one can procure any thing for money in London, from a castle down to a wigwam. I did implore and beg. Was ever any woman yet so cold and so gentle? She wept, and caressed, and talked about her duty to her father, until I was bewildered."

I said nothing: but I thought she owed a

duty to her intended husband no less than to her father, who was in perfect health, and by no means a gentleman who laid solitude much to heart. Indeed, if she shed tears, she should have let her father see them, as I had ample reason to know that he never denied her any request.

"She says she cannot bear the idea of her father being quite alone," he continued.

"She knows he would most likely marry again if he were," I said, coolly.

Horace looked disgusted. "What a brute you are! I almost hate you, Paul." Then the poor fellow began to reproach himself for ever having blamed her even for an instant. "It's not that I doubt her truth and constancy, however little I am worthy of her," he said, humbly. "I believe in her," continued the good, trusting heart, "as I do in Heaven! But my lonely home —my solitary hearth—that is what cows me. Oh! the horror of going every night into the house which contains no face to gladden at your presence, no ear to listen for your footstep, no eye to brighten at your approach. I tell you it is the knowledge that as I pace these weary, crowded, seething streets, if I were to fall down dead I should be carried to the nearest hospital, and no moan would be made—none would own me, unless one of my own lads got hold of me—"

"Nay—this is morbid, Horace. It is not true that no one cares for you, and you know it. Cecile Otway is not the only woman in the world."

"She is all that this world has of woman for me," he returned, with a dogged dismalness that almost tempted me to smile, provoked as I was at the whole affair. "She complains of my impetuosity, Paul, though her words are gentle enough. If I am impetuous, it is not without reason. Women hardly understand how far they try a man when they make regulations simply by the light of their own experience. However, I must submit. I know her truth. I am well assured of her real love; and I'll do my duty, never doubting, and 'take the first *best* that offers,' as the German sage says."

In due time the vessel sailed, the Otways left England, and Horace was no longer fevered by the presence of Cecile. He was rather gloomy and moping at first, but soon threw himself with ardor into hard work; which is, after all, the best specific in love. *Cedit amor rebus: res age, tutus eris.* He was soon after formally offered the professorship of —— at ——Hospital. At first I urged him to accept it, in spite of his exhibiting a most unaccountable disinclination to do so.

"I'm more independent as I am, Paul," he argued. "I lecture my own men: I can say what I please, as I please, when and where I please; the number of my pupils increases every term, so that I make a fair income independent of my practice. You know I'm an odd fellow: I don't like binding myself down to any particular views, or to be pledged to any unchangeable round of duty. Come and see my fellows some day, and judge for yourself."

I took him at his word, and some little time after this conversation I repaired in good time in the morning to the large, dingy room in a certain quiet street, where he held his classes. There were, I suppose, upwards of a hundred students assembled, every description of man being there represented. One or two I recognized as old acquaintances, and others I knew owing to my connection with —— Hospital. Take them altogether, they were a rough-looking lot, though several were dressed in the extreme of fashion; but these were exceptions. I saw a face I knew; it was that of a sallow, sodden-visaged fellow, the son of a hard-working incumbent in the south. He had long been the plague of his father's heart, and for the last three years he had been cut down to a pound a week, paid every Monday morning. Here was an earnest, slow-witted, pale-faced lad, who looked as if he wished to study, but couldn't. And here was another, of unmistakably Hebrew descent, all rings, and chains, and oaths. Beards were not as common then as they are now; but there was a large sprinkling of moustaches, a great dearth of clean shirts, and an all-pervading smell of tobacco.

Very soon Saltoun strode in, dashed down his hat, and without notes or papers—without, apparently, preparation of any kind—he at once plunged into his subject. It comprehended some of the more intricate anatomy of part of the knee-joint; and I was amazed at the striking and lucid manner in which he handled so dry a subject. He did it in a thoroughly masterly style, illustrating it with imagery, sometimes forcible, sometimes grotesque, and clenching the point with some humorous remark, or some anecdote strictly suitable to an audience whose fault was not that of being too fastidious. He was a swift and skilful draughtsman, and the sketches he made as he proceeded were such that the veriest dolt must needs have learned somewhat. A few on the front benches were the constant object of his lecture, half conversational as it was; and from time to time he declared that he read that in their countenances which induced him to believe they wished and felt competent themselves to elucidate the point in hand. The unfortunate men who thus found themselves the object of attention to the whole class, could not shirk this public appeal; and accordingly, as they acquitted themselves, they were rewarded by the applause or the jeers of their fellows. There was about Saltoun an energy which seemed to diffuse itself irresistibly among the men; a kind of concentrated vitality, which, by the power of his strong individual will, inspired those near him, and carried them with him.

After nearly two hours of brilliant demonstration, Horace suddenly caught my eye, and concluded by saying,—

"And now, gentlemen, I wish you a very good-morning."

In a moment every man was on his legs. Horace pushed through the crowd, slipped his arm through mine, and we passed into the hall, where a few men were exchanging students' chaff with the untidy maid who acted as gyp for the whole establishment; and to do her justice, she appeared on the best of terms with the young fellows, and in the encounter of wits it was not *she* who had the worst of it.

"How do you like my crew, Paul?—a rough lot, eh? But some of them are very good fellows, in their way. You see it is not the most elegant, nor yet the most promising of the students, who resort to me; but the black sheep, and the lost, the lazy, the hopelessly stupid, prodigal sons generally, and the often-plucked ones particularly: they all come to me." And he gave his old boisterous, genial laugh.

"Surely, Horace, I saw one or two men who were mates of mine?"

"I dare say you did. They have stuck in the mud, and it is Hercules' own work to hoist them out again. Did you notice that scampish, quick-eyed, dissipated fellow to the right front? He was plucked years ago; since then he has been dresser and assistant abroad with one of the contingents. He is up to his work—indeed, a good many of them are; but they either cannot or will not read. When the bigwigs say, 'Now, Mr. ——, in such a case, what would you do?' they mostly answer right enough; but when they demand, further, 'Why would you pursue that course of treatment?' they are altogether at sea. One of my men answered, boldly, 'Because it's the best plan to cure your patient;' and I defy the college to improve on it. It got him through; but he told it about, and some of the hopeless ones looked on it as a charm, tried the same dodge, and were sent to the right about: 'recommended to pursue their studies for six months longer'—I think that is the euphemistic phrase employed."

"Who was that dull, grave, dispirited-looking man in a corner?"

"Oh, the men call him, rather profanely, the 'God-forgotten man.' He has been grinding away under different tutors for five years, and he has not passed yet. Poor fellow, I hope he will: he is dresser at one place and dispenser at another, and is a hard plodder; but somehow his brain wants quality. His wife came to me the other day: 'Now, Mr. Saltoun, Alfred knows the cavity of the chest, and the muscles of the face and neck, and the thoraic regions, but he is not up in the knee-joint, the wrist, and carpal articulations.' Fancy that! he is a married man: so I gave him the knee to-day. Those eight in the front rank go up to-night: two of them will be spun; two more *may* pass; the other four *must*, if they are ordinarily easy examinations."

"And you like this better than a professor's chair?"

"Yes, I do; I enjoy it. I get quite fond of my *enfans terribles*, and I am as keenly interested in their success as it is possible to be. I live my student life over again in them: yet some of them are the most awful scamps, too," he added, laughing.

"I think you infuse energy into them."

"It is, depend on it, a reciprocal action, then; for they infect me with their youth."

I may mention here, that, owing to unforeseen circumstances, the opportunity for purchasing the entire of the practice on which I had entered presented itself much sooner than I anticipated; and as I have already explained that I was entirely dependent on my own exertions, it found me unprepared—in truth I had not had time to save, and I was reluctantly about to relinquish the idea of succeeding to it. This reached Saltoun's ears, and quite unsolicited, he advanced the money in the most delicate manner, without my knowledge; refusing to accept any formal acknowledgment. I was able in a short time to repay him; but I was deeply touched by his kindness. This is only one of his many generous actions to old friends, always performed with the same absence of ostentation. When I endeavored to thank him, and to insist on his taking some security, he made the most frightful grimaces, and begged me, as I valued his peace, to let the subject drop.

About six or eight months after this he surprised me with a visit; as I knew it was not his disengaged time, it was the more unexpected when he announced that he meant to stay some days; and I observed with real anxiety, that he was very thin—for him almost emaciated—and seemed wretchedly out of spirits. The dinner-bell rang, but he did not appear, so I went up to his room with an exordium on punctuality, ready to deliver; I found him with his razors out, coolly preparing to shave.

"My good fellow, leave your stubble till after dinner."

"I've sharpened my razors," he said, obstinately, "and I may as well use them."

"But the dinner?"

"Stay until I've finished," he replied; "if you do, I promise you you will see me down a good deal earlier than you otherwise would."

I concluded he was in one of his queer humors, and, unwilling to cross him, I sat down until the operation was concluded. We then went down-stairs. Now I can hardly account for it except by some sort of instinct; but I gave previous orders that no wine should appear at dinner, and when the deficiency became manifest, I contented myself with remarking, "I know you are a water-drinker, and I find it too heating this warm weather."

He acquiesced, and so it passed; but that night, after our evening cigar, just before we turned in, he grasped my shoulder, or rather clutched it, and said,—

"Tell me the truth, Paul; what made you order that there should be no wine? Did I look as if I wanted drink? Do you think other people can detect the demon that possesses me?"

This confirmed my secret idea.

I merely replied, "It is better never to enter into temptation; but I'm quite certain, Horace, no one imagines that such an occasional impulse exists with you."

He compressed his lips. "Well, Paul, put me under treatment; for when I came down to you it was because I knew it was my safety. I felt the most awful, infernal craving that any one out of hell can imagine. I don't want to drink. It is—O God!—it is that I want to feel *drunk*. I don't often undergo it, and I know when it is coming on. I begin to feel miserable and gloomy without knowing why—only that every thing seems going wrong, and that something dreadful is about to happen; or else I feel so irritated and quarrelsome at the slightest contradiction from others that I turn away and actually shed tears because I must not strike them; when that wears off, this terrible desire to get madly intoxicated follows. I think of it with rapture: it seems to promise me heaven—oblivion from all present misery; and at the bare thought of it excessive joy comes to me. I felt gloomy enough to hang myself this morning as I came down here."

"Or cut your throat?" I said.

"Or cut my throat," he repeated with emphasis.

The only thing to be done was to nip it in the bud, if possible. I put him under a course of sedatives, combined with tonics; insisted on regular hours, cheerful society, bathing, etc.; and I had the satisfaction of seeing my prescription do its work. The tears came into his eyes as he wrung my hand in parting.

"You will always find me here, Horace, and a welcome for you."

"All right, old fellow," he replied, with the most perfect composure. "I hope the next visit will not be for aye and forever."

So we parted.

From The Examiner.

The Autobiography and Correspondence of Mary Granville, Mrs. Delany; with interesting Reminiscences of King George the Third and Queen Charlotte. Edited by the Right Hon. Lady Llanover. 3 Vols. Bentley.

This book gives us a real old picture without any of the touching and varnishing employed too often by editors of memoirs, who consider themselves as artists bound to present a glossy portrait of the person whose living features they propose to represent. Lady Llanover has represented the life of her kinswoman, Mrs. Delany, as detailed by herself in her correspondence with her sister and most intimate friends. Here we have "the familiar matter, joy and pain," which makes up daily life in every century, and which can be written and spoken of only in the innocent unreserve of domestic intercourse. We are admitted to the privilege of intimacy and relationship with one who is almost an ideal Englishwoman. Mrs. Delany's letters were not meant for any eyes except those of the dear sister to whom chiefly they are addressed. They have the charm of a perfect unconsciousness, the modest unreserve which had no secrets except those which come of innate good sense and reverence for all that is pure. There is a dignified reticence upon subjects about which mere talk is undesirable, affording healthy contrast to the morbid self-analysis of which examples are not few. These letters contain simple, natural, and living words; the reader is taken by them into the heart of life and manners as they were a hundred and sixty years ago, and finds in it nothing stiff or old-fashioned. We may look at old portraits of great-grandmothers, and wonder where their human nature was, when we see only the cumbrous embroidery and the uncomfortable fashions of their clothes. In these volumes women, whom we know only as great-grandmothers, live in the freshness of their youth and beauty, coming out in new fashions, stirring, gossiping, and amusing themselves. The work illustrates that English life of the last century which is best known to us through Tom Jones, and Sir Charles Grandison.

There may be complaint that the editor has given every thing without selection, and has troubled us with much that is minute in detail and of merely private interest. The book in fact carries to defect the merit of not being "made up," and we bear with its bulk for the sake of the scrupulous reverence with which Lady Llanover has given us the letters untouched and uncurtailed. The industry, indeed, of a loving zeal on the editor's part is a pleasant feature in the volumes, apart from the value of her notes, illustrative and biographical. It is a grave fault that there is no index, but the memoirs are not yet complete. An ample index doubtless is reserved for their last volume. The three volumes now before us only reach halfway through Mrs. Delany's life—to the first break in the chain of her domestic ties, the death of her dear and only sister, Mrs. d'Ewes, to whom most of her letters are addressed. Illustrations of her life with the Court of George the Third and Queen Charlotte, are yet to come. One fitness there is in the prolixity of detail illustrative of a private lady's life in the last century. The life itself of those days was very much slower than it is at present, and it would have been difficult, without thus covering time and space, to convey an idea of the stately coach-and-six movement with which all business was in those days transacted. The whole interest, too, is so minute, so entirely personal, that it would have been difficult to select matter for omission. The conservative genius of the editor, leaving the old life story just as it was, suits well with the humor of the past presented by it. Some of the notes are too long, and there are unnecessary extracts from familiar books. But for Mrs. Delany's own letters, they become almost as welcome to us as they once were to her sister.

The three volumes are daintily illustrated with portraits of the chief persons mentioned in their text. There is Ann Granville, afterwards Mrs. D'Ewes, with a beautiful face expressive of all womanly good sense. There is the Duchess of Portland, most bewitching of fine ladies; Mrs. Elizabeth Carter, pleasantly strong-minded; Lady Mary Wortley Montague, as she was before she had begun to despise fine clothes and cleanliness; the Duchess of Queensbury, brilliant in a nunlike costume; what must she have been in her court-suit and jewels? Of course, too, there is Mrs. Delany herself—who, both as young Mary Granville and in her old and honored age, looked like a worthy woman, gentle, sagacious, kind, and strong. There are other portraits of women who in their day and generation counted broken-hearted lovers by the score. But there are only two male portraits, one that of George Granville Lord Lansdowne, the courtly wit and poet, and another a delightful miniature of a little boy who we are told in a note was—grandfather to the present Duke of Portland.

Mary Granville, Mrs. Delany, was the daughter of Bernard Granville, brother to George Granville, created Lord Lansdowne by Queen Anne. She was born May 14, 1700, at Coulston, in Wiltshire. Her father and uncle were grandsons of Sir Bevil Granville, who was killed at Lansdowne whilst fighting on the Royalist side in the parliamentary wars. One of Mrs. Delany's earliest recollections is a visit which Handel paid them in 1710; she says,—

"We had no better instrument in the house than a little spinnet of mine, on which that great musician performed wonders. I was much struck with his playing, but struck as a child, not as a judge; for the moment he was gone I seated myself to my instrument, and played the best lesson I had then learnt. My uncle actually asked me whether I thought I should ever play as well as Mr. Handel. 'If I did not think I should,' cried I, 'I would burn my instrument.'"

One of the most curious and entertaining portions of the Memoirs is the autobiography addressed in letters to Mrs. Delany's early and life-long friend, the celebrated Duchess of Portland. It is written with fictitious names, to which, however, we have the key given us. The style is singularly simple and flowing. There is no attempt at fine writing or effect, and the result is an excitement of the strongest interest. One of the first remarkable events that befell her was finding, when she awoke one morning, two soldiers with guns in their hands standing beside her bed! They had come to arrest the whole family on a Secretary of State's warrant, granted on suspicion that her father was about to leave England on the Pretender's business. All the Granvilles had hereditary affection for the House of Stuart.

Mrs. Delany had been brought up in the expectation of being maid of honor to Queen Anne, but the death of the queen and the imprisonment of Lord Lansdowne made a great change in her destiny. Her father retired to a small estate in Gloucestershire called Buckland, given to him by his brother, and thither at the age of fifteen Mary Granville was taken when she had barely looked at the delights of a town life. It was five days' journey from London into Gloucestershire, the travel was in November, and the house at which they arrived was found to be blocked up by a fall of snow. The girl was young enough to regret keenly the loss of plays and operas, but she bore the girlish trouble sensibly, and exerted herself to be cheerful for the comfort of her father and mother. She had no resources outside her own home. The account of her life shows that "les plaisirs innocens" have interest of their own, even in innocent detail. For us, too, the description is a welcome picture of old English life in the depths of the country. Mary Granville's great friend was a Miss Kirkham, who afterwards became Mrs. Chapone, and whose son married the famous mistress of all young women who would be taught by her letters. Lord Lansdowne was the grand relative of the family. Mrs. Delany's father was dependent on him for his income. When, after two years of imprisonment, my lord and the countess were released from the Tower, Mary Granville was invited to stay with them at their house near Bath. He was a fascinating man, very fond also of his niece, but he was selfish and unscrupulous. One of his old friends was Mr. Pendarves, a man of large possessions, sixty years of age. Mr. Pendarves, who was of a repulsive person and habits, bad tempered and generally ill-conditioned, fell in love with the beautiful Mary Granville, then just seventeen. Lord Lansdowne insisted that his niece should accept the old suitor's proposals, and in spite of tears and entreaties he compelled her to marry him. She was married, as she says, "in great pomp, and never was woe dressed out in gayer colors." A young man who had been tenderly attached to her was struck with paralysis on hearing of her marriage, and he died in less than a year. Under the pillow of his death-bed there was found a piece of cut paper which he had stolen from Mary's closet at home. Mr. Pendarves carried his young wife to a dreary old family seat, Roscrow, in Cornwall.

The house had not been inhabited for thirty years. Yet here, shut up with a surly husband, the woman's fine and courageous nature could assert itself. She exerted herself to be good and pleasant to her husband, and to make the best of her position. Young, beautiful, courted by all the men who came near her, linked with an old, unloved husband, who, though stupidly jealous, would have been easily blinded, young Mrs. Pendarves looked neither to the right hand nor the left. She wasted no time on commiseration of herself, and she sought no sympathy from others; would accept no homage to her vanity or sensibility, but quietly and cheerfully endured her lot, and did her duty in the state she had accepted. Always noble and tender, a true heroine, English Mrs. Delany was; as unlike the heroine of a French novel or drama as if she had belonged to another race of beings. We commend her history to the attentive study of all fidgety *femmes incomprises*.

After seven years of this marriage, Mr. Pendarves died, but he did not leave the patient wife a well-dowered widow, for his will was not signed, and her jointure was a slender one. Yet she made no complaint. When, after awhile, established in London, she could gather a bright circle of friends about her, and see the great world, she gave lively and happy pictures of it in letters to her sister, with whom she kept up a constant correspondence. Here we have very minute details of her life and occupations. The letters are not less lively than those of Lady Mary Wortley Montague, but the good nature that warms them makes them pleasanter to read. "That morning I was entertained with Cuzzoni. Oh, how charming! How did I wish for all I love and like to be with me; my senses were ravished with harmony!" Again she mentions "hearing Mr. Handel's opera performed by Faustina, Cuzzoni, and Sennesino." She gives an account of the coronation of George II., and of a subsequent entertainment at the Mansion House when king and queen were present. When she goes to Queen Caroline's birthday the queen thanks Lady Carteret for bringing her, and is obliged to Mrs. Pendarves for her pretty clothes. The fashions are superb—the king in blue velvet, with diamond buttons; the Prince of Wales in mouse-colored velvet, turned up with scarlet. There is mention, too, of the famous Countess of Huntingdon's appearance at a birthday, in velvet embroidered with an immense flower-pot, the flowers growing out of it and covering the whole dress.

It is charming to see the true natural woman thus enjoying gayety of life for the first time. But she had another trial. Lord Baltimore, a young and fascinating man, took pains to win her heart, succeeded, coquetted, was met with a womanly dignity, and jilted her, marrying for money. Mrs. Pendarves never pities herself, or speaks of her disappointment, but does her best to get over it. She speaks of Lord Baltimore without any bitterness, and makes no ill-natured comment on his marriage.

It was after the serious illness caused by this affair that she went to Ireland, and first saw her future husband, Dr. Delany. She was admired by Swift, who wrote her charming letters. The account of country life in Ireland at that period is full of a decorous jollity. Mrs. Delany's second residence in Ireland is not in the description so amusing as her first visit, but there is much good matter nevertheless, and the maturing of her character is very marked.

Decay of Idolatry in India.—A traveller from Madras to Jaffna states that but few of the heathen temples he passed were in good order; those regularly repaired and used are comparatively few. Many of the temples are gradually going to ruin—towers, walls, and rooms where the idols sit are broken; many of the idols that were carried with great parade are now resting in their places, with no one to wipe or clean them. Many idol cars, once drawn with great pomp and parade, are so neglected that they can only be used for fuel. The impression is steadily gaining ground among the people that their idol system has had its day, and that the religion of the gospel will eventually fill the whole land.

From The Athenæum.

Correspondence between the Bishop of Exeter and Right Hon. T. B. Macaulay, in January, 1849, on certain Statements respecting the Church of England, in the First Chapter of his History of England. Murray.

A FAIR fight between two such doughty and adroit champions as the present Lord Bishop of Exeter and the late Lord Macaulay is good to see. A generation which delights in personal prowess and in personal encounters,—which has raised John Heenan and Tom Sayers into the rank of immortals, and made the meadow at Farnborough classical ground, will rejoice to see the prelate tuck up his lawn, and mark the historian bound into the ring. The challenge came from Bishopstowe, the response from the Albany. At first, the note of offence is mild and honeyed; perhaps the episcopal Heenan is afraid of his man; perhaps it is only his natural modesty or a desire to excite the sympathy of spectators. The historical Tom Sayers, confident with many victories, politely contemptuous in reply, accepts the battle, if his adversary should be really indiscreet enough to force him into an attitude of self-defence. So they shake hands, square, and strike out. Tom, we are sorry to say, gets many a knock-down blow; it is wonderful to see him rally to the call, laugh in his powerful adversary's face, lunge out right and left, and now and then, by an unexpected hit, send the big man staggering, stunned, and blinded, into his corner of the ring. At last they close, and Tom goes down. The fight ends in a hubbub; and if the historical and rhetorical Tom's friends claim a drawn battle, the prelatical Heenan enjoys at least the last shout of victory, and, in his own opinion, establishes his claims to the belt.

How courteous is the first challenge from Bishopstowe to the Albany! The bishop writes to Macaulay on his "History:"—

"All must admire it for its unequalled ability, eloquence, force of expression, power of condensation, where condensation is necessary, power of expansion and graphic detail, where your subject admits of expansion and detail. In truth, never in a single instance did I wish your narrative or your comment abridged. But your highest merit is your unequalled *truthfulness*."

There is a hint—no more than a hint—unless the prelate is ironical—that Lord Macaulay may, in spite of his marvellous "truthfulness," be a little of a partisan:—

"Biassed as you must be by your political creed, your party, and connections, it is quite clear that you will never sacrifice the smallest particle of truth to those considerations. If I think that you are not sufficiently on your guard against those partialities in any instance, it is in your estimate of William the Third. The deep stain of vice in his private morals is not I think, stated as it ought to have been, especially of the brutal manner in which he prosecuted his scandalous adulteries with the ladies of his queen's own household under her very eye."

This gentle flattery introduces the real subject of the communication,—the point on which controversy is challenged:—

My object is not to criticise your History, but to state to you, as briefly as I may, one or two particulars, on which you are already aware that I think you are somewhat in error. I especially refer to some things said by you respecting *Cranmer* and the history of *the Church of England in his time*."

Then follows a most subtle and searching inquiry into the authorities on which Macaulay relies for his portrait of Cranmer. Macaulay's picture of the great Protestant archbishop is well known. In his "Essays" and in his "History" he has painted the figure of a loose, worldly, and uncourageous priest, more zealous for his order than for the truth, a persecutor in power, a whining sycophant in adversity. Cranmer's conduct cannot be wholly defended, nor does the bishop seek to excuse it in every part. But he produces plenty of evidence to show that Macaulay was mistaken as to many of his facts and unjust in most of his inferences. Into this debate we do not ourselves mean to go; it is a question of those small details, of those microscopic comparisons and verbal constructions, which are wearying to the general mind, unless stated in full and surrounded by the accessory facts. Those who care for Cranmer's reputation will read for themselves all that the defender of his honor has to say in his behalf. Suffice it, that the bishop defends Cranmer from the imputation of baseness and worldliness:—

"There never was a person in any thing like the eminent station occupied by *Cran-*

mer, so long conversant with kings and courts, who was so free as he, not only from statecraft, but from every thing like the habits, views, and policy of a statesman. From disposition, and probably from prudence, he avoided further than could have been thought possible all mixture in the statesmanship of the times. *Gardyner* was the episcopal statesman; and *Cranmer* probably owed much of his influence over Henry to his entire abstinence from all dealing with matters of state. His whole conduct was, I think, dictated by a cautious and wary vigilance to observe every occasion on which the Reformation of our Church from the corruptions of Rome could be advanced, and to interpose every check to Henry's frequent desire to bring back every *doctrinal* error, which he, with the aid of *Gardyner*, could again fasten on our system. *Cranmer's* success in this endeavor was wonderful. But I spare you details."

But the bishop's gage of battle is not the character of Cranmer, singularly important to the Church of England as that character must ever be: it is the whole scheme of Macaulay's presentation of the Church, in its early, organizing days, to which the Lord of Exeter objects. His objections to the tone, statement, and presentation of the subject in the "History" are expressed at length, and with very great force of statement and citation.

Mr. Macaulay answers these criticisms in a manner quite his own:—

"I beg you to accept my thanks for your highly interesting letter. I have seldom been more gratified than by your approbation; and I can with truth assure you that I am not solicitous to defend my book against any criticisms to which it may be justly open. I have undertaken a task which makes it necessary for me to treat of many subjects with which it is impossible that one man should be more than superficially acquainted—law, divinity, military affairs, maritime affairs, trade, finance, manufactures, letters, arts, sciences. It would therefore be the height of folly and arrogance in me to receive ungraciously suggestions offered in a friendly spirit, by persons who have studied profoundly branches of knowledge to which I have been able to give only a passing attention. I should not, I assure you, feel at all mortified or humbled at being compelled to own that I had been set right by an able and learned prelate on a question of ecclesiastical history. I really think, however, that it is in my power to vindicate myself from the charge of having misrepresented the sentiments of the English Reformers concerning Church Government."

How vindicate himself? By asserting that his correspondence has wholly missed his meaning in the most material points. "The truth is, that you altogether misapprehend the use which I make of Cranmer's answer." After a long defence, which is always dexterous and sometimes successful, Macaulay ends in a less confident tone than he began: "The difference between us is a difference of degree, and differences of degree are not easily expressed with precision in words. I do not, I must own, feel satisfied that the language which I have used requires any modification. But if reading and reflection should lead me to a different opinion, false shame shall not prevent me from making a public retraction."

The bishop now feels his advantage, and he presses home on his antagonist. The elaborate courtesy—or irony—of the first communication disappears; and, at the very beginning of the reply, there is a *brusque* intimation that verbal civilities are at an end. After quoting a few lines from the "History," the bishop says, with the utmost plainness:—

"When I say that *this I emphatically deny*, you will, I am sure, understand me as only intending to express my meaning plainly, not offensively, and as disencumbering both of us from the necessity of making apologies at every step of our discussion."

This is stripping for the fight; and into it the bishop goes, feeling his strength increase as he pounds away at his adversary, and sometimes showing very plainly that he strikes in mere contempt. Such a passage as this following must have been gall and wormwood to the historian:—

"In respect to *Cranmer*, I spare you and myself a detailed argument. I am content with saying, that after a rigid search, I can find not a particle of evidence in favor of your statement of his doctrine on this subject, except the one answer to the 9th question proposed in the Commission of 1540, in which answer not one of the bishops and divines joined with him in the Commission concurred. They all decided contrary to him, and that decision of theirs he reported to Henry as the decision of the Commission, *not saying one word of his own*."

And this:—

"I shall not hesitate to say (though I hope you will not ascribe my saying it to a want of high respect to both yourself and Lord Clarendon) that you have grievously misapprehended the case. Such never was the law of the Church of England."

And this one, also:—

"'As the government,' you say, 'needed the support of the Protestants, so the Protestants needed the protection of the government. Much was therefore given up on both sides; an union was effected, and the fruit of that union was the Church of England.'—51. It is a pity to disturb so exquisitely antithetic a system. But, undoubtedly, it is so totally opposed to the most glaring and notorious facts, that it is better it should be disturbed by a friend (forgive me for presuming so to call myself) than by a foe."

The bishop concludes his first set of charges against the version of Church history put forth by Macaulay in these words:—

"I will not trespass longer upon you. I think that you will require no apology for what I have written. You will do yourself and me the justice of seeing that it could not have proceeded from any other than the most respectful feeling towards you and your immortal work. I grieve to think that in that work should be embalmed errors so grievously injurious to the Church, as those on which I have presumed to address you. Would that what I have written may induce you to look more closely into the various matters which I have brought to your attention."

To the vast body of historical reference, on Church history, contained in the bishop's Letters, Macaulay briefly replied. He began, in a far less confident tone than before, though still clinging to his expressed opinion:—

"I should be most ungrateful if I did not thankfully acknowledge my obligations to your lordship for the highly interesting and very friendly letters with which you have honored me. Before another edition of my book appears I shall have time to weigh your observations carefully, and to examine the works to which you have called my attention. You have convinced me of the propriety of making some alterations. But I hope that you will not accuse me of pertinacity if I add that, as far as I can at present judge, those alterations will be slight, and that, on the great points in issue, my opinion is unchanged."

Macaulay goes, at some length, into a defence of various controverted statements in his "History." But he does not mollify his adroit antagonist, even when, in repetitions of respect for these criticisms, and his desire to improve by them, he says: "I again assure your lordship that I will carefully reconsider the opinion which I have formed on these important matters, and will weigh with attention the many valuable observations contained in your letters." Exeter answers, in a last word, full of confidence: "I am not going to inflict another long letter upon you; but I am confident that you would rather know what I think of the new matter stated in your letter."

The last words of all in this Correspondence, touching the value of a paper to which Macaulay had assigned an unwarranted value, are the most trenchant; and the facts which they contain are, perhaps, the most damaging to the historian:—

"The stress laid by you on the paper cited in *Strype*, Mem. i., ch. 17, *astonishes* me. No lighter word would do justice to my feeling. 'A Paper,' found in a public library, '*without name* and *without date*,' '*seems*' to *Strype* (a most inaccurate and ill-judging, though very honest writer), 'to be in the hand of *Stephen Gardiner*,' who had been dead nearly a century and a half when this judgment is pronounced upon his handwriting, and the same *Strype* '*thinks* it *may* belong to 1532.' Upon this, you gravely state in your History, that it is 'a very curious paper which *Strype believed* to be in *Gardiner's* handwriting,' and, though the paper does no more than ask some unnamed lord, temporal or spiritual, 'whether your lordship think convenient that *we*' (whosoever *we* might have been) 'should endeavor ourselves to prove these Articles following'—stating, amongst others, two outrageous propositions, of which there is not a particle of proof (nor, I must insist, of likelihood) that they were *ever* brought forwards—you say of it, also, in your HISTORY that '*when it was objected etc., it was answered*,' etc., and, in your letter, that 'this paper was *evidently* meant as a kind of *brief* for the Courtly Party *in the Convocation*.' Do not think me very saucy, when I say, that a person *willing* to come to such a conclusion on such evidence would make an invaluable foreman of a jury to convict another *Algernon Sydney*. Seriously, I never met with so monstrous an attempt to support a foregone conclusion."

Macaulay does not appear to have answered this last denunciation!

From The Examiner.

Port Royal: a Contribution to the History of Religion and Literature in France. By Charles Beard, B.A. Two Volumes. Longmans.

In minute and exhaustive research Mr. Beard's volumes are not equal to the elaborate work on Port Royal which M. Sainte-Beuve commenced more than twenty years ago, and finished only a few months back. They contain, however, as much information, honestly collected and skilfully put together, as the majority of English readers will care for, and are far in advance of the somewhat crude memoirs through which Mrs. Schimmel-Penninck had the merit of calling attention to a very valuable subject. It is a chapter out of history well worthy of careful study. It includes the story of more than half of all that is noteworthy in French literature, and it presents in clear perspective one of the most eventful battles that the world has ever seen between the best and the worst developments of Romanism. He who would trace the working by which some of the noblest human intellects strove to bring good out of the papal system, and the opposition which they received from the inherent evils of that system, can find no better subject for his study than the history of Port Royal; and the history has nowhere been told in a better spirit than in Mr. Beard's eloquent and impartial narrative.

It is by a strange gathering of circumstances that an obscure nunnery should, through nearly a century, have been the centre of the noblest intellectual life of which France can boast. The name Port Royal is apparently a corruption from Porrois—in Latin, Portus Regius—a valley near Chevreuse, six leagues west of Paris. There, in the thirteenth century, a religious house was founded, in accordance with the Cistercian rule, Simon de Montfort being one of its earliest patrons. The community was small and poor, and its progress finds scanty record in history until the year 1602, when Jacqueline Arnauld, best known as La Mère Angélique, was appointed abbess. There have been few saintlier women than Angélique, and very few who, desiring to live meekly and unostentatiously, have held stations of greater influence. She was not eleven years old when she was made abbess, and during her youth she had no leaning to monastic life. When she was fifteen, only illness hindered her from renouncing the office in which she had been placed and fleeing to some Huguenot kindred. But when she found that her position was unalterable, she set herself honestly to fulfil its duties. As soon as she was old enough, she commenced reforming the establishment, which had fallen into listless and worldly habits. Many patient years were spent in restoring the forgotten rules of the foundation, and in winning over by love a body of sisters who, all older than their abbess, were yet young enough to have their hearts set on worldly things. Insisting upon little, she won, by the example of her own austere virtue which she knew how to couple with proper cheerfulness and gayety, more hearty obedience than any laws could have enforced. Under her guidance the community grew partly in numbers, but much more in influence. In 1625 it was found necessary to transfer it to a larger house in Paris, and in 1648 both establishments were put in use; so that henceforth there was a Port Royal de Paris and a Port Royal des Champs.

In Paris Angélique found in M. de Saint-Cyran a confessor whose honest frankness won her reverence. Saint-Cyran was the friend of Jansen, and the first great champion of Jansenist doctrine in France. His learning and genius might have secured for him high place in the Church, and Richelieu tried repeatedly to prefer him. Five bishoprics were offered to him in succession; but he was resolute in his determination to be nothing but a simple priest, uninterrupted by worldly honor, and with best opportunity for doing the work which he had at heart. He desired above every thing to enforce the purer doctrine which Augustine had set forth and which Jansen had revived, and in doing this he was brought into fierce conflict with the Jesuits. To them his wholesome views of Christian duty, and of the responsibility of the soul to Heaven alone, were hateful in the extreme. No sooner had Angélique and the nuns of Port Royal found in him a wise spiritual guide, than the Jesuit suspicions, which had been aroused by the recent reforms, began to shape themselves into plans for persecution. In this way the name Port Royal was gradually becoming the watchword for a new religious activity.

Round Saint-Cyran was growing a little company of earnest thinkers who knew his worth and could understand his teaching. Among them were Singlin and Lancelot. Two others, Le Maitre and De Sericourt, were nephews of the abbess of Port Royal. Taking them for his nucleus, Saint-Cyran designed forming a little hermit community, in connection with the sisterhood. He was soon taken, on charge of heresy, to be imprisoned in the Bastille, and only to be released in time to die outside its gates; but the society was strengthened by his sufferings, and made more anxious to protest against the enemy which sought to crush him. Its members, growing numerous, began to be known as the Messieurs de Port Royal. They pledged obedience to no common rule, and wore no special dress; but the same mental likeness which parted them off from the world induced in them similarity of conduct. They met often each day for social prayer and once for a scanty dinner; but at other times they sought to be alone, holding company to be burdensome, and useless speech to be wicked.

While this unhealthy tendency was gaining ground, worthier successors to Saint-Cyran were rising up among men who did not choose so entirely to cut themselves off from the world. Foremost of these, in point of time, was Antoine Arnauld, the youngest brother of Angélique; raised by his learning to be a doctor of the Sorbonne, he soon suffered scandal for his writings in support of Jansenism. In December, 1655, and in the following January he was condemned, for asserting that certain heretical propositions had not been taught by Jansen, and for enouncing one heresy of his own. The seventy-one doctors who voted in his favor shared his expulsion. This trial is noteworthy as a grand beginning of the persecutions of the Port-Royalists: but it has a still greater interest in literary history. During the course of the investigation, Arnauld's friends were accustomed to meet with him and talk over its progress. One day they urged him to prepare a pamphlet in defence of his views. This he did, but the friends were not able to praise it. "I see," he said, "that you do not like my paper, and I think you are right. But you," he added, turning to the most youthful of the company, "you are young, and ought to do something." The challenge was accepted, and next day they met to hear, and be charmed by, "A Letter written to a Provincial by one of his Friends." The tract was published at once, and seventeen others followed it at intervals. They took the public altogether by surprise. Wits and scholars found in them keener satire and more eloquent argument than had ever yet been uttered in French. The Jesuits were goaded to madness by their vigorous statements of the truth. Thousands read them with delight, and took in all the lessons of religious liberty which they were intended to convey. All men asked eagerly who was writing these wonderful Provincial Letters, but it was only known to a chosen few, that their author was Blaise Pascal.

Pascal was at this time in his thirty-third year. In his youth he had made himself famous as a student of science. All the world knows the story of his having in boyhood, before he was taught any thing of geometry, invented a First Book of Euclid for himself; and there was some excuse for the fable. He detected many important natural truths, and might, had he chosen to prosecute his researches, have rivalled the success of Galileo and Descartes. But circumstances brought him into close contact with all that was worthiest among the Port-Royalists. Jacqueline, the sister whom he most loved, was a member of the convent. He was gradually led to give up his science and apply himself to theology, bringing to it all the caustic wit and shrewd common sense which he had formerly employed on other things. Of this the "Provincial Letters" are the best possible illustration. With special reference to the ground of Arnauld's trial, he begins by playfully describing how he went among Jansenists and Molinists to gain instruction upon the points at issue. We need not attempt to follow his argument or to enter upon the theological details. Every word has force, and every sentence contains polished satire. Gradually his language grows sterner. He boldly denounces the casuistry of the Jesuits, and shows how it is equally ruinous to those who use it and to those against whom it is employed. "The best comedies of Molière," wrote Voltaire, "have not more wit than the first 'Provincial Letters:' Bossuet has nothing more sublime than the later ones."

Pascal's eloquence, if it won for his party everlasting fame, chiefly served in his own day to add fury to the spirit of persecution. The years which followed were years of deadly combat between the Port-Royalists and the Jesuits. Fierce abuse and cruel calumny were hurled by the self-appointed champions of the Church. Lacking real objects worthy of attack, they invented heresies and immoralities with which to charge their enemies. They, on the other hand, were not slow in self-defence and counter-attack. There is small interest now in the heap of theological pamphlets which attest the zeal of the combatants: but there is very living value in the spectacle of a small community of men and women bravely holding ground against enemies armed with all the wealth and power, if with not much of the genius, of Catholic Christendom. Death struck heavier blows than any which the Jesuits could level. Pascal died in August, 1662, having only just completed his thirty-ninth year. Angélique ended her life twelve months before, at the age of seventy.

From the turmoil outside it is pleasant to turn to the cloister of this noble woman. Having begun life by commanding, she chose in later years to become subordinate to others, saying that she needed thus to learn humility. When her nuns boasted of the antiquity of Port Royal, and the splendor of the Cistercian Order, she reproved them, exclaiming, "As for me, I am of the Order of all the saints, and all the saints are of my Order." Once she thanked her physician for the services he had rendered her, and he replied that all he could do for her was as nothing. "Say not so," she answered, "nothing is little that is done for God." Upon her death-bed, when the troubles were too great for De Saci, her nephew and confessor, to visit her as she wished, she remarked, "It is God's will; it troubles me not. My nephew, without God, could do nothing for me; and God, without my nephew, will be all in all."

Hardly was the first requiem chanted over her grave before new troubles fell upon the convent. A formulary was prepared, condemning the doctrines of Jansen, and every sister was commanded to sign it. Many held that, with slight reservation, this might be done. Jacqueline Pascal, who survived the abbess only two months, was foremost among those who protested nobly against the least semblance of casuistry. "I know well," she wrote, "that men say that it is not for women to defend the truth; although they might say—since, by a sad accident and confusion of the times in which we live, bishops have no more than women's courage—that women ought to have the courage of bishops. But if it is not our part to defend the truth, it is ours at least to die for it." The mental strain of her brave bearing brought on illness and death at the age of thirty-six; but there were others to remember and act upon her words. The sisterhood refused all treacherous compromise. After four years of threats and remonstrances, the Archbishop of Paris could brook their defiance no longer. He declared them "pure as angels, but proud as devils," and went down in state to take twelve of the most incorrigible and lodge them in prison, putting in their place some women commissioned to break the spirit of the rest. "The archbishop has dealt too gently with the nuns of Port-Royal," said one; "if it had been in Spain, they would have been dressed like devils and burned alive." The harsh treatment which they did receive, however, made no change in their resolution. Not till 1669, after the peace of the Church had been effected, and when a modified formulary was presented to them, did they consent to sign.

Ten years of moderate prosperity followed the peace of the Church, and then came twenty years of final persecution. A new generation had started up, but the old independence of thought was perpetuated, and the old purity of life found loving imitation. Therefore in October, 1709, the order was sent down for the breaking-up of the community. The sisters were summoned and sent off singly to be imprisoned in distant convents. When in later years the archbishop of Paris found himself in trouble, Madlle de Jouenix exclaimed, "What would you have? God is just, my lord; and these are the stones of Port-Royal falling back upon your head."

On the literary history of Port Royal—with which Mr. Beard fills pleasantly the chief part of his second volume—we have no space to dwell. In Pascal's work alone there is boundless theme for story and for criticism. The "Provincial Letters" occupy middle ground between his earlier scientific tracts and the stern, unwise asceticism often exhibited in the "Thoughts" of his later years. But Pascal was only captain of a whole army of noble writers. Saint-Cyran and Singlin were eloquent pleaders in theology. Nicoll and Arnauld left broad marks of their honesty and learning upon many branches of knowledge—their most important work, outside the circle of technical theology, perhaps being the "Port Royal Logic," even now the best school-book on the science. The modern method of teaching the classics was almost started by Lancelot and his coadjutors in the Port Royal schools. Racine was a Port-Royalist, though he wandered in paths which his school denounced; his plays retain to the last the marked influence of its teaching. On his death-bed he implored the honor of burial within the walls of Port Royal, "although," he said, "I acknowledge myself very unworthy of it, both by the scandals of my past life and by the little use that I have made of the excellent education which I formerly received in that house."

GERMAN BOOKS.—We have spoken of some characteristic French books. To-day we may name one or two that are characteristically German. All are upon practical subjects. Dr. Wilhelm Koch has published at Marburg, after a pause of some years, the concluding part of his laborious work upon the German Railways (Deutschland's Eisenbahnen). It is a book of substantial value to all Englishmen concerned in foreign railway lines; being especially an exposition of the German Railway Law as between directors, customers, and the States through which a line may pass. But with what subtleties of argument the plain statement of actual law is mixed! In our own island the lines all run over ground subject to a single government, but on the Continent, especially in Germany, the rights of many great and little States have to be properly considered. The profound question of a railway's local responsibility—whether a line be answerable along its length, or only at the point to which, let us say, a parcel is addressed, or at the point from which it is sent for any default causing litigation—the jurisdiction being in each case different, is discussed with an acute relish that revives the day when lawyers argued together over such questions as Who is the owner of an egg laid in a nest frequented by the fowls of many households?

Another new German book, and one of great mark, too, is a laborious work on Political Economy by an entirely German Adam Smith, Herr Adolf Trendelenburg. Its title is "Natural Law based upon Ethics," ("Naturrecht auf dem Grunde der Ethik," [Leipzig, S. Hirzel]), and there can be no doubt that it is the best German work of the kind that has for some time been published. But the sublime ethical view founded on an ideal of society and disdaining reference to your mere practical politics is edification for the English reader. Edification of edifications, however, in this way is a book of Writing Lessons,—elementary writing-lessons setting out with lines and pothooks, called "Der Schreibunterricht, etc.," "(Instruction in Writing), an Attempt to base the Method of this Object of Instruction on Psychology." From a long prelude upon Herbert's Psychology we pass to the first psychological view of an empty copy-book. The work is not a large or costly treatise but a tractate of about a hundred pages, published at Schweidnitz; as a national psychological curiosity it is worth getting.

JOHN BRIGHT! JOHN BRIGHT!

IN Birmingham town, when Scholefield sat down,
Arose on his legs a vociferous wight,
With vehement words to pitch into the lords,
And abolish the army, John Bright, John Bright.

Our expenses, quoth he, seventy millions will be,
And all through those Tories who want us to fight,
And the captains and colonels who write in the journals,
Creating a panic, quoth Bright, John Bright.

But really friend Nap is a peaceable chap;
Besides, he's our partner, and means to do right—
It's gazetted, you know, "France, England, and Co.,"
And Dick Cobden's their bagman, says Bright, John Bright.

These boys pleased with trifles are your Volunteer Rifles;
If they stuck to their shops 'twere a much better sight.
To use a yard measure should give them more pleasure
Than a dangerous gun, says John Bright, John Bright.

We peaceful civilians have to pay seventy millions
For the red-coated people whose trade is to fight,
And to keep up the Crown, which some day must go down—
Not while there's a rifle in England, John Bright!

—*The Press.*

From The Spectator.

THE DECADENCE OF ASIA.

It is just now the fashion to reckon the philosophy of history among the exact sciences. Scores of writers of all grades of intellect, from Mr. Hallam to Sir Archibald Alison, are ready to explain to us all the causes of events. Every thing has occurred because of some law which the victorious analysis of the nineteenth century has, for the first time, revealed. There are some large problems, nevertheless, which are not, perhaps, quite satisfactorily resolved. Can anybody tell us, for example, why one conquering race should suddenly cease to multiply, while another conquering race grows till it seems ready to populate the world? Yet French and British history will one day be slightly affected by the relative rate of increase. Or can any man explain why Europe in its internecine conflict with Asia, should always have won the game? Every cause assigned by the philosophy of history seems somehow or other to break down. Climate is no explanation, for the climate of Greece is the climate of Asia Minor, and the Greek was the victor there. Besides, the climate of Scotland produces in Tasmania an Australian aborigine, who is, except the Bornese, the nearest known approach to a chimpanzee. To talk of comparative courage, merely evades the question, which is *why* the European in the same climate should be braver than the Asiatic. The "circumstances of locality" sound like a reason, but what advantage in that respect had Greece which Egypt did not possess? Superior morality may be suggested; but the difference between the morals of Lucullus and the morals of Mithridates is not very appreciable. Is it number? Number has been on the Asiatic side. Intellect? All modern philosophy finds its root in the Sanscrit; all religion its key in Hebrew; all physical science its germ in Arabic. Discipline? Darius was the head of an army organized for centuries: the sepoys in yesterday's contest were trained veterans. Physical resources? What resource had the little province of Macedonia which the empires it subdued did not possess tenfold?

Yet there the fact remains. Asia for three thousand years has precipitated itself spasmodically on Europe, and, save in one instance, has invariably been beaten back. A king of Persia, after conquering half Asia, wanted to punish Attica, a country which would have been lost in one of his own parks. He invaded it with an army, allowing for all exaggerations, greater than the whole population, and was not only defeated, but, as an imperial power destroyed. The king of a province equal to one Persian satrapy, and an army about as large as the personal guard of his rival, resolved to conquer Western Asia. Not only did he conquer it, but when he died, each of his generals, dividing that army, founded an historic dynasty, one of which, at least, endured for centuries. Rome before Tiberius can never have drawn recruits from ten millions of freemen, yet she not only conquered Western Asia, but so moulded it, that only one province ever rebelled, and her stamp remained impressed throughout her Asiatic dominion till the Arab invasion. Once, as we have said, the Asiatic remained master, but the races who swallowed Rome failed till centuries of forest life had made them European, and when they won they adopted creed and civilization from the conquered. Western Asia never recovered its conquest by Rome, till in 550 a new race once more risked her strength against Europe with the usual result. The Arabs, after conquering Asia, stopped the day they met a European army, and after centuries of conflict failed to keep a corner of Europe in which they had reared a successful organization. Once, and once only, did the European succumb. The whole strength of the continent proved insufficient to wrest Syria from the Saracens, but even there they were beaten rather by the climate than by man. Then followed an extraordinary interval, during which the very existence of Asia seemed blotted out of the European mind. Even its geography was forgotten. Countries as familiar to Rome as Sicily or Gaul, were described by Italians as if they had been portions of another planet. The great Asiatic invasion of Timour passed away without a permanent trace, and the Othmans were dreaded only as a European power. While Western Europe trembled at the name of Solyman, there was, probably, not a statesman alive who could run off with accuracy a list of Solyman's Asiatic provinces. That wave, the last from Asia, and only formidable because swelled by the renegade tribes of Southern

Europe, and an army filled almost exclusively with European slaves, as usual receded, having swallowed up but a single European state.

Then ensued a period during which the feeblest of European powers made itself feared in Asia, and at last, a century ago, the process, as old as history, began to recommence. Europe once more attended to Asiatic affairs, and once more the independence of the Asiatic empires faded away. An English trading company, with a regiment at its disposal, quarrelled with a satrap of the Great Mogul, and in twenty years England, against her own will, was sovereign over one-third of the Asiatic world. For a hundred years the restless aggression has never ceased, until at last Europe is admittedly supreme. No European State has ever fairly set before it the conquest of Asia. No European State, till 1857, ever despatched to Asia an army large enough to be appreciable in European politics. Yet from Scutari to Kamschatka, there is but one State in Asia in which the authoritative influence of Europe is not felt. Russia is sovereign of the entire north, from the Ural to the Sea of Okhotsk, from Bokhara to the Pole. Turkey exists because Europe is puzzled how to divide the Turkish inheritance. An English remonstrance sends the Shereef of Mecca into exile, and an English ship of war brings the only Arabian port into submission. The action of Persia is regulated from St. Petersburg. India belongs, even in theory, to a European state. The Birman empire is only maintained, because its profitable provinces are in our own hands. The king of Siam talks English, and releases Europeans from the operation of his laws. The ruler of Cochin-China cannot descend his own river for fear of capture by a French fleet. Malaya is a tributary province of a British bonding warehouse. The islands of the Archipelago are claimed by the Dutch, and ruled by princes whose idea of success or failure is confined to Dutch approval or remonstrance. Japan has given up an island to Russia, and all her principles of action to Great Britain. Finally, as if to indicate to the world that the term of the Asiatic empires had arrived, an army, just half as large as the emperor's guard, has invaded China, entered the capital, reduced the governing class to reason, and extorted terms from a sovereign still absolute over a third of the human race. There is at this moment no country in Asia, save Thibet, where the European is not regarded as a superior; none, save Cochin-China, in which the officials do not hold their posts on the tenure of exempting him from insult. The political force of these monarchs had previously disappeared. Less than a century and a half ago, no European entered Asia save by permission of an Asiatic. Now, the order of the Sultan would not stop an English boat in the Red Sea, or a decree of the emperor of China impede a steamer on the Yang-tse-kiang. Less than a century since every Christian in Asia paid tribute for liberty to exist. There are now but three countries on the continent in which Christians have not a legal and independent status.

The change we have described is sufficiently vast, but it is only a portion of a mightier revolution. These vast Asiatic monarchies do not merely yield to an external pressure, they are all simultaneously rotting down. Only a century since they were to external appearance powerful states, possessed of an apparently firm organization, so far well governed as to permit the increase of an already vast population. To-day the sultan with difficulty holds together the shattered fragments of his empire. His army is destroyed, his finances dependent upon loans from Paris, his cities universally decaying. The only vitality left in India is that of Europeans; throughout that immense section of Asia no Asiatic can rise to a post higher than the judge of a county court. The king of Burmah lives on small monopolies of produce. The empire of Cochin China is too weak to drive 1,500 sickly Frenchmen from the gates of its capital. Russia takes slices from Tartary at her own convenience. The Chinese empire is one vast scene of anarchy and confusion, with cities as rich as European capitals sinking fast into decay. The British found Pekin a mass of ruinous hovels, surrounding one huge palace the emperor was too powerless to defend. Japan is still apparently intact, but throughout the remainder of Asia there is but one scene of decline, and feebleness, and despair. Religious men may well doubt whether the progress of mankind exactly agrees with the theory of philosophers. Europe may be advancing, though the Roman slave worked six hours a day, and the English freeman works twelve; but the European race is but a section of mankind. His Asiatic brethren, at least twice as numerous, will scarcely join in his pæans over the approaching reign of a Parisian Paradise on earth.

What is to be the end of this growth of European control? Hitherto Europe has only settled in Asia to be Asiaticized. The man of the South, who was the old instrument of conquest, and could live in the tropics, rather approved, on the whole, the Oriental tone of life. The Northern, who has taken his place, will neither assimilate nor reside. Still less will he depart. Civilization is armed at last, and all the resources of numbers, climate, and position do not avail to counterpoise the destructive power of science. Even were a new Atilla possible, what could he do against the Armstrong shell? Mr. Prinsep, in one of his able monographs, talks of some vast horde which has been organizing cavalry for years for an invasion of Hindostan. Suppose it all true, what is the force of any number of undisciplined cavalry against a couple of rocket batteries? The European conquest, so far as the human eye can see, is this time complete and final. No force we can imagine developed in Asia can be efficient for more than massacre. No movement, however general, even if led by a new prophet and accompanied by a new creed, could avail to shake the European grasp. What could fanaticism do for the capture of a steamer? Yet nothing can be more certain than that the Asiatic, however capable of development, does not develop under European tutelage. The educated Hindoo, whatever his merits, has lost all his originality. Indeed, if our experience in Hindostan is to be the guide, the vital force of the Asiatic is extinct. For two entire years the people of Upper India were practically free. Every career was open, every dream was a possibility, every man enjoyed his full capability of development. All India, thus fairly brought to the test, did not produce one statesman, one organizer, one leader with more than the capacity of a bandit. The race which built the Taj placed its rulers in European huts; the race who organized the system of castes, placidly mimicked their conquerors' notions of civil order. The human race cannot, it is believed, lose its vitality, but of all the problems now presented to the thought of Europe, the future of Asia is the most disheartening.

Application of Soluble Glass.—It is found that the richer soluble glass is in silica, the less fusible it is; and to attain the maximum of fusibility, it must contain both soda and potash. By pouring a concentrated solution of silicate of soda into alcohol, there is formed, by degrees, a mucous deposit insoluble in alcohol, which hardens after some days. This deposit is soluble in water. By triturating soluble glass with quick lime, the silicate rapidly hardens, forming silicate of lime and caustic soda. With oxide of zinc, soluble glass forms a viscous liquid, containing some silicate of zinc, which has already led to the idea of using soluble glass with oxide of zinc in painting. Combined with hydraulic lime, the silicate forms a good cement for fastening stones; united with fluor spar and pounded glass, it becomes like porcelain or marble. Two parts of fluoride of calcium and one part of glass in impalpable powder, are made into a semi-fluid mass, with a solution of soluble glass; this is applied to the parts which are to be joined, and the pieces are then pressed together until the cement is dry.

Steam Navigation on English Canals.—It is rather singular that steam navigation on American canals should have been unsuccessful, as described on page thirty-nine of the present volume of the Scientific American, while in England it has become so successful as to reduce the cost of conveying freight no less than twenty-five per cent. The Grand Junction Canal Company, which formerly used to tow their boats with horses, have dispensed with animal power, and now use steam alone.

There are five thousand miles of canal in Great Britain, representing a capital of about $200,000,000, and since the adoption of steam as the propelling agent, the traffic increased last year twenty-five thousand tons. The most peculiar feature in the steamboats which are now employed by the Grand Junction Company, plying between London and Birmingham or Manchester, is an improved form of screw propeller, called the "waggle tail," which has the advantage of keeping all the disturbance of the water immediately behind the stern of the boat, instead of spreading it right and left. The effect of this improvement is at once to secure the canal banks from being damaged by the wash, and to economize the motive power.

From The Spectator, 23 Feb.

THE NEW KINGDOM.

The present generation scarcely need Mr. Kingsley's poetry to tell them that "the world is young." If boiling life and activity, incessant change and portentous incident, be the signs of youth; then was the world never younger than it is this day. All around us the fabric of the old world, the edifice we have come to regard as durable as nature, is visibly breaking up. The air is choked with the dust of the crumbling of rotten thrones, vivid with the light which heralds the birth of new nationalities. The electric telegraph can scarcely keep pace with the speed of accomplished facts. Events, each of which would once have illustrated a century, are crammed into a week. The existence of the Austrian empire probably depends on the resolves of the next few days. On the 4th of March Mr. Lincoln will be installed at Washington, and the great republic, to which men pointed as the ultimate hope of mankind, and which in a century has risen from a colony into a first-class power, will be finally rent asunder. On the 3d of March, a nation of serfs, more numerous than the population of any European state, will be solemnly pronounced free. And now, already on the 18th instant, a nation, for eight hundred years parcelled out among citizens and strangers, has resumed her place in the European family, and once more recommenced her national life.

It is scarcely possible to write of an event such as this, without falling unconsciously into a tone of exaggeration. Men who, like Mr. Bright, consider the new birth of Italy a small event, overlook in their shallow philosophy all that human freedom may produce. The freedom of Italy means, among other things, the addition of twenty millions of brains to the intellectual reservoir of the world, and those brains Italian. It has been the function of the "party of order" all over Europe to decry the Italians, to assert that the only race among whom genius is endemic, is exhausted and effete. So long and continuous has been the cry, that it has imposed even on men who do not, like Mr. Cobden, hold the *Times* more valuable than Thucydides. Yet it would not be difficult to prove that Italy under all its degradation, has always asserted its right to a front rank in the war of thought. We need not speak of literature, of the poets whose words have become a European treasure, or even of the artists, for whose works states still jealously compete. The English middle class scarcely feel the value of Dante, and would probably pronounce Michael Angelo improper. But cotton-spinners may surely allow that the Genoese whom Englishmen call Columbus was of some slight service to the world. Science alone may recognize the rank of Galileo, but a thought of Galvani is to-day paying dividends in the city. Is there a name in physics more honorable than that of Volta, in economy than Beccaria, or in learning than the last of the Della Scalas? Or is it that practical intellect has worn out, that, like the intellect of Greece, its absence only proves the utter degradation of the Greeks? Modern Europe honors many generals, and Lord Clyde and Marshal Pelissier, General Benedek and Col. Todtleben are doubtless practical soldiers. But the one Italian of pure blood who in these days has commanded a great army, mastered Europe in ten years. Soldiership is a practical faculty, but an abler than Napoleon, son of a pure Romagnese family, would be hard to seek. Revolution is practical work but the solitary successful leader of revolution has been an Italian. What argument is it by which we are to place Lamartine, or Kossuth, or Proudhon above Garibaldi? Statesmanship is practical, but where is the statesman in Europe who believes himself the superior of Cavour? When England is in despair for a statue, she commissions Baron Marochetti. When a French emperor would regenerate Paris, he calls on Visconti for a plan. Genius, we may be told, is universal and unfettered by race, and it is in the people alone that real strength is to be found. So be it. Which is the nobler, the French revolution or the Italian? Or, if we must introduce the question of race, which is the greater, the people who, unable to produce a statesman, are suffering a successful republic to shatter down, or the people who, in the face of hostile Europe, and in spite of every inducement to disunion, are welding the states of Italy into one harmonious whole? Compare Congress with the Parliament of Italy, Buchanan with Cavour, Governor Pickens with Ricasoli, General Floyd with La Marmora, and it is not the Anglo-Saxon which has reason to be proud of its "practical" capabilities. It is useless, however, to run over a bead-roll of names. With men who can forget that one and the same race built the Roman empire, the Catholic Church, and the kingdom of Italy, argument on national capabilities is but a waste of time.

The Italian Parliament met in a building strangely typical of the new kingdom. Hastily constructed, and altogether of wood, it still extorts the admiration of the spectator by its beauty and completeness of design. The scene must have presented to Italians a strange jumble of things old and new. The ..an-new Parliament thronged into the bran-new building as representatives of provinces which bore the same names under the Roman empire, and cities whose history extends to the limit of human record. They assembled to organize a new monarchy under a king whose race was ruling during the brief revival of the empire of the West, and from that day to this has struggled for the position Victor Emmanuel has attained. The king's first speech, like all his public acts, was dignified and reserved. In a few words he indicated to Parliament its most pressing duties, to organize municipal government without impairing the unity of the State, and to aid the sovereign in strengthening the national armament. The absence of the French representative was deplored; but "France and Italy have riveted at Magenta and Solferino ties of amity which will be indissoluble." The good offices of England will be preserved "in imperishable remembrance;" and for the rest of the hostile world, for the princes intriguing for their thrones, for Austria still menacing Italian rebels, and Russia still refusing to acknowledge Italy, there is only a proud silence. The solitary allusion to Germany is a note of welcome to the new sovereign of Prussia. The king concludes by a simple appeal to the courage with which he has risked his crown, as the best argument for his honesty, when he urges patience and moderation. In the whole speech there is not a word of undue exultation, not a sentence implying vindictiveness against the clouds of enemies with whom the new monarchy has still to contend. No allusion is made to annexation, not even to the accession of the Two Sicilies. The king accepts Italy, "almost united," as a fact, and urges Parliament to advance, in words which an English sovereign might have employed. It is on this determined reticence, this grave, deliberate preference of strong action to high phrase, that Englishmen found their confidence in the political future of the State. When the people of the South are content with measures such as Victor Emmanuel recommends, and a Parliament such as that now assembled at Turin, there is little fear that their future will be sacrificed to a turbulent impatience of delay.

The first duty of the new Parliament will be the organization of a force adequate to the necessities of the time. The extent, and in some degree the character, of this force must be dependent on the weight of taxation to which the people are willing to submit. Fortunately, they have not been accustomed to cheap government. Italian statistics form the most complex of arithmetical puzzles, but the population ought to be able to contribute at half the French rate, or £35,000,000 a year. With that revenue the king may keep on foot a standing army of 400,000 men, backed by a national rifle organization, and the largest park of artillery in Europe. With such a force Italy might treat for Venice on terms of equality, and reply to a French demand of more territory by the calm assertion that Italy is prepared to defend the unity she has secured. It is this which will be the testing-point of the capacity of Italians for self-government. They have demonstrated the possession of high military qualities, of the self-restraint which is the first essential of civil freedom. They have yet to prove that they will submit voluntarily to the searching taxation modern armaments so imperatively demand.

From The Saturday Review, 23 Feb.

FRANCE, ENGLAND, AND ITALY.

Of the power of the French emperor for good or evil there can, unfortunately, be no doubt; and there is probably now little conflict of opinion as to the general objects for which his power is wielded. But as to his intellect, there are two theories—the natural and the supernatural. It is agreed on all hands that his wisdom is not visible on the surface; the question is, whether it lies hid in the depths below, or whether things really are pretty much as they seem. We cannot imagine a more decisive argument in favor of the natural view than his conduct towards Italy, as it has been from the outset, and as it is now. Impulse succeeding to impulse, scheme supplanting scheme, intrigue crossing intrigue, reveal the habits of the adventurer and conspirator; but proof of far-sighted sagacity or resolute purpose there is none. Clear away the cloud of dark and mysterious grandeur with which the imaginations of men invest every thing that has power to do them harm, and you see nothing but a small, tortuous intellect, called upon to grapple with great events, and not guided through their perplexities by the inspiration of an honest and generous heart. Mysterious reticences and oracular utterances keep the world in an awful suspense; but the laboring mountain on which all eyes are fixed at length brings forth a pamphlet by M. de la Guerronière.

A fear and a necessity drove the French emperor to interfere in Italy. He feared the daggers of the revolutionary fraternity who, by a strange freak of fortune, found one of their members on a throne. He felt, as the chief of a military despotism will always feel, the devouring necessity of war.

He knew that, from the superiority of his troops, the chances of the game were in his favor, and he is a gambler who, to do him justice, does not throw the dice with a trembling hand. He had also moved armies on paper, and formed plans of battle, as of politics, diplomacy, and legislation, which were imitations of those of his uncle. The miraculous escape of Magenta, the bloody chaos of which he was a helpless spectator at Solferino, dispelled his delusion, and his mind turned wildly from the difficulties which surrounded him to a different scheme. He made overtures for peace to the emperor of Austria, and offered the restoration of Lombardy as the price of connivance on the Rhine. Safe out of his scrape and in the Tuileries again, he recovered heart, thought once more of the Orsinis and of his fame as a liberator, and passed the word to the Tuscans to break the Treaty of Villafranca. Then followed the natural consequences—the rising of Italy and the Dictatorship of Sardinia. Yet for these consequences, natural as they were, the sagacity of the emperor was not prepared. He saw, against all the traditions of French diplomacy, a powerful kingdom rising on the borders of France, and he knew neither how to suffer this result nor how to prevent it. He propounded a scheme for a federal Italy, with the pope at its head, which proved so immediately abortive that the world has forgotten that it was ever propounded. Since that time he has assumed an undecisive, ungenerous, half hostile attitude, condemning, thwarting, threatening, irritating, yet fearing to interpose; covering himself with odium and contempt by delaying the fall of Gaeta, yet allowing it to fall at last; countenancing the reactionary movement only to prolong confusion and waste blood, alienating the Italians by withdrawing his envoy from Turin, but not speaking the word that would have restrained Cavour. Is this policy inscrutably sagacious, or is it inscrutable alone? What should we, who think our diplomacy so blundering and inconsistent, have said to an English ministry which had thus converted into hatred the gratitude earned by a Magenta and Solferino?

What is the key to Louis Napoleon's present conduct in the matter of Rome? We are persuaded that it is mere perplexity—the perplexity of short-sighted selfishness, unable to make out which way its interest lies. On the one hand, he finds his position growing hourly more untenable. On the other hand, he cannot bear to withdraw the forces by which he still prevents the complete union of Italy, keeps the game open, and retains his hold on Italian affairs. He is pressed by the Liberal party and the English government on one side; he is pressed by the Ultramontanists on the other; and the relative force of these influences varies from hour to hour. Now he bullies the pope, and now he cajoles him—sends fresh troops to the support of his temporal power, and dictates pamphlets against its continuance. "The spiritual authority of the pope," said Voltaire, "always a little mingled with temporal authority, is destroyed and detested in half Christendom; and if in the other half he is regarded as a father, he has children who sometimes resist him with reason and success. The maxim of France is to regard him as a sacred but enterprising personage, whose feet must be kissed, but whose hands must be sometimes tied." Such, no doubt, is the view which the eldest son of the Church at this moment takes of his duty towards his holy father. He does his best to observe the rule of diplomatic etiquette in both its parts. Whatever injury or humiliation he inflicts on the chief of Christendom is always preceded by the regulation kiss. The Byzantine rhetoric and the Byzantine adulation of M. de la Guerronière's pamphlet have been sufficiently noticed. Its "modest churches," its "fertile plains watered by the Po," its reverent exposition of the providential dispensations of imperial goodness and wisdom, have received the due meed of literary and moral approbation. The unctuous hypocrisy which is its distinguishing feature has not been so clearly pointed out. The writer, while producing the handcuffs, kisses "with ardor" the consecrated feet. It is not quite so easy, however, to kiss the feet and tie the hands at the same time. Hypocrisy denotes fear and weakness; and this the eye of an Antonelli is quick to discern. While Louis Napoleon is pious, it is a sign that the priest party in France has power. While the priest party in France has power, the French troops will not be withdrawn. And till the French troops are withdrawn, Antonelli, like Francis II., will play his own game. When the support of France is gone, it will be time to give in an adhesion to the Italian nation. Nothing worse can come at last than a "spiritual" dominion in place of the patrimony, and a great ingathering of "souls" to Peter instead of pence.

England has certainly no reason to boast of any direct aid given to Italy. As a nation, she has spent no treasure and no blood. But we have the satisfaction of being assured by the chief of the Italian cause that the sympathy of a free people has not failed to afford support to those who were struggling to be free. That sympathy has been given in unbounded measure, and without misgiving or hesitation, so far as the cause of Italy was concerned. If England looked on with divided feelings at Magenta and Solferino, it was because, not the cause of Italy alone, but that of the world also, was at issue in those fields, and if the interest of Italy was clear, that of the world was by no means so. There might be a doubt which of the two contending despotisms—that of France or that of Austria—was the worst in itself; there could be no doubt which was the most formidable, the most actively retrograde, the most aggressive, the most menacing to the liberties of the world. Whether Italy herself will have gained in the long run by the intervention of France, is even now a question, the solution of which must depend upon the further question whether the Austrian tyranny would or would not have been broken up, without the appliance of external force, by bankruptcy and other internal causes of dissolution. But it is only too clear that the interests of the world have suffered by the exaltation of the French military power, the elation of the French soldiery, the strength which victory has added to the military despotism, and the decisive preponderance given to the warlike over the pacific and commercial element in the French nation. The time is probably not remote when all free nations will have reason to rejoice that England has husbanded her resources for the supreme exigencies of European freedom.

From The Saturday Review, 23 Feb.

POINTS OF CONTRAST BETWEEN ENGLISH AND AMERICAN POLITICS.

The suddenness, the unexpectedness, and the overwhelming importance of the events which are occurring in America have naturally tempted Englishmen to speculate on their course and probable issue, rather than on the effects which in their ultimate result they will assuredly produce on English society. The only point on which we have hitherto had time to concentrate our interest has been what will be the next stage in this amazing history. We have asked ourselves, in turn, whether South Carolina would really secede?—whether her example would be followed by any other Cotton State?—whether the Republican party would be cowed into offering any compromise?—whether any compromise could be invented which would preserve the border States to the Union? All these questions, except the last, have successively received the answer which, at first sight, seemed the least probable and was certainly the most unfortunate; and, even on the point which remains to be solved,—the possibility of keeping Virginia, Kentucky, and Tennessee from withdrawing,—the latest news seems to show that the evil genius of the Federation is likely to have his way. Unless Mr. Lincoln, continuing the incredible policy of Mr. Buchanan, should allow a second nation to form itself peaceably in North America, we seem sufficiently near a great and bloody struggle to be excused for reflecting how far it involves consequences important to ourselves.

If we turn our attention to the influence of the American rupture on England, the first thought which suggests itself is, that the quarrel has a material bearing on the question of parliamentary reform. That there is so close a connection between the two topics is not the fault of reflecting politicians in this country. They, at all events, have always denied that, except within certain limits, American experience had any value for English legislators. The shallow demagogues of the Birmingham and other kindred platforms must bear the blame of the inference, drawn nearly universally at the present moment, that, if the United States become involved in hopeless difficulties, it would be madness to lower the qualification for the suffrage in England. The conclusion may not be warrantable, but whose fault is that? It is equally warrantable with the positions of the only advocates of a Reform Bill who have forced the English public to give them a hearing. If it be of importance to point out that the United States can do without an army, it is an equally cogent observation that the want of an army is exposing what was but yesterday one of the greatest governments on earth to contempt, contumely, and ruin. If the comparison of English with American taxation has the slightest bearing on English politics, so has the obvious truth that, for want of an adequate establishment, the Americans of the Northern States are likely to have to make more sacrifices, personal and fiscal, than Englishmen have submitted to since the two countries separated. If it be argued that something like universal suffrage ought to be adopted in England because law, order, and property are respected in America, it is answer enough that the very quarrel which distracts the Union takes the form of a complaint, on one side, that the rights of property have been lawlessly violated, and on the other, that a minority is outraging the first principle of constitutional government by refusing to give way to a majority. The replies are not ours, but they are conclusive as to the emptiness of the arguments, which are not ours either. *We* can separate the cause of England from that of America. We can show that the shipwreck of one set of institutions, even were it more complete than it is, would prove nothing as to the fate of the other. We could, perhaps, even establish that the miscarriage of an extended franchise in the United States has but a restricted bearing on the extension of the franchise in England. But were we to make the attempt, we should probably convince nobody, for the simple reason that Mr. Bright has succeeded in persuading a great number of influential persons that the admission of working men into the constituencies is chiefly, if not solely, desirable on the ground that it has succeeded so admirably in America, and has proved a sovereign panacea against the war, taxation, and confusion which are the curses of old governments in Europe.

Even if the Americans should succeed in adjusting their differences, the rebuke to English agitators would be equally severe. Even if the gulf close, the fact remains that it once opened, and there is no more security for those who have seen an abyss at their feet. But should this unhappy quarrel come to bloodshed, its influence on England will be not simply moral or speculative, but direct, practical, and material. We cannot share in the confidence so freely expressed that the staple of English industry will remain long undisturbed by American convulsions. Knowing of what stock the Northern Americans come, it is hard to believe that they will resign half an empire without a struggle. What was India, for which three years since we made so mighty an effort, compared with those securities for national and material greatness which the men of the Northern States are threatened with losing? But, even if a Confederation of the Southern States succeed momentarily in forming itself (as it seems likely to do) through the utter bewilderment and perplexity of the North, nothing more would be gained, we are convinced, than a mere respite from battle. How can a Southern Union remain in peace with a country which will be one great receptacle of fugitive slaves? How can the North look on with indifference while the slave trade is revived and Mexico absorbed? In every event, the cotton on which so many of our millions depend for sustenance will be produced in smaller quantities or exported under greater difficulties. A short supply of cotton at Liverpool must be the consequence; and a scarcity of cotton is in this country not merely a commercial, but a political event. It implies low wages and slack work; and doubtless, with low wages and slack work will recommence the era of Mr. Bright's maleficent activity. It is a curious circumstance that the very occurrences on the other side of the Atlantic which have led almost all Englishmen who can think at all to review their hasty acquiescence in the demand for an organic change, are likely to produce a clamor for organic change from those Englishmen who unhappily think but little. We presume that as soon as want begins to pinch the manufacturing operatives, Mr. Bright will make their sufferings the pretext for instructing them as to their wrongs. That the British aristocracy will be shown to have caused or aggravated the scarcity may be taken for granted. That the institutions of the United States will be proved to have had no share in producing it may be equally assumed. The exact turn which the arguments will take is matter of interesting speculation.

It is but too probable that we must be prepared for a period of considerable, perhaps of severe distress. When the causes of such a calamity are perfectly plain, and apparently beyond help, there is always a yearning among the suffering class for the remedies which lie furthest away from ordinary experience. The factory hands who cannot get work because the negroes in America do not hoe sufficient cotton will long for admission to the franchise, just as the victim of a cancer flies to a quack medicine. It is imperative, with such a prospect before us, that we should all review our reasons for advocating or opposing a Reform Bill. It is possible that the silence of the country which has disheartened Lord John Russell may not always continue, and that there may one day be reason enough for altering the Constitution, if clamor be a reason. It is time that politicians even of the most moderate patriotism left off the affectation of talking of themselves as mere straws in the popular wind, and making up their minds in good earnest whether the reconstruction of Parliament be a measure in itself and on its own grounds desirable.

From The Spectator, 23 Feb.

THE RUSSIAN REVOLUTION.

On the 3d March, says the *Indépendence Belge*, the Emperor Alexander will decree the final emancipation of the serfs. The statement reads simple enough, but for ages no event has occurred so huge at once in its proportions and its consequences. The slavery of Russia differs materially from any form of that great curse hitherto known among men, from the slavery which dried up the vitality of the Roman world as much as from the slavery which is the disgrace of North America. It was a purely Asiatic institution, the logical complement of an Asiatic theory of society, and Russia, in renouncing it, renounces Asia, and enters Europe not merely as a power—the Sultanut was once a power—but as a nation, with European objects, and a European capacity for limitless development.

The modern system of serfage commenced in 1599 with a decree of the usurper Boris Godunoff. As he was a usurper, philosophical historians suppose he intended to conciliate the noblesse, but there is not the slightest evidence of any such intention. At that time the agricultural classes were marked by a spirit of restlessness which seemed to Russian statesmen dangerous and unreasonable. Villages were always on the move. Every fifth or sixth year the commune, which is, so to speak, the integer of Russian society, would migrate to some new locality, disappear perhaps in a night, without warning or signal, to be heard of only after a march of a hundred miles. They retained, in fact, say Western philosophers, the nomadic instincts of their ancestry. Nothing of the sort. They disliked unnecessary work just as Western philosophers dislike it, and in a country where land is valueless it is easier to break up a virgin soil than to re-invigorate an old one. Exactly the same tendency at this moment puzzles British administrators in Burmah, and American politicians in the far South. The system, of course, is exceedingly unpleasant to any government advanced beyond the stage of Tartar Khans. It very nearly destroys the possibility of conscription, and completely paralyzes the fiscal authorities. It is, moreover, injurious to civilization. A race which contemplates migration as an ordinary incident of life will neither fence, nor drain, nor build, and has a trick of preferring stock breeding to cultivation. Influenced by all these motives, the councillors of Boris Godunoff resolved to prevent locomotion, and in a rough arbitrary way alone intelligible to Asiatics, they passed a Law of Settlement. In less civilised phrase, they bound the peasant to the soil, thus changing at once freemen into "ryots." As the soil, in *their* theory, belonged to the boyars, they ordered the peasant to pay three days' labor in the week for the privilege of working on the other three; and it is in the continued effort to realise this rental that the root of modern serfage must be sought. Gradually the class who held, though they did not own, the land, and who could directly influence the throne, drew all privileges to themselves. The right of selecting conscripts gave them one weapon, the right of enforcing obedience to orders necessary for cultivation, another; but to this hour the power of the Russian slaveholder is based rather on encroachment hardened into right than on any positive law. The throne neither felt nor pretended any interest in oppressing the peasant for the sake of the proprietor. It was the strain to protect the land rental which vested the landowner in Russia, as in Bengal it vests the Zemindar, with such tremendous power. The law, for example, intends that every man who shares the produce of certain land shall pay his share of rent in service and obedience. But there is no law enabling the proprietor who permits his serf to emigrate to follow him with a personal tax. All he can legally do, is to summon him back to the estate, though, as the summons implies to the serf of the cities utter ruin, it is amply sufficient to ensure obedience. In practice, partly through the operation of the law, partly through long-continued custom, and chiefly through the steady bias of all officials towards the proprietor and against the serf, the landowner has become absolute over individuals. He can order any man to be beaten, without limit as to the number of blows; he can, when hard pressed, evade the law prohibiting sale by letting the serf for ninety years; he can make life unendurable by petty exactions and incessant work, by insults it is impossible to resent, and demands it is difficult to evade. The actual conduct of the class is differently represented by different observers, but the evidence is heavy against the landowners. Most, if not all, of the favorable accounts have been written by foreigners. Russian writers usually admit that the system is oppressive, and the literature of the populace teems with stories of the grotesque and usually filthy tyranny of the noblesse. *Uncle Tom's Cabin* was circulated in Russia with a speed which in such a country could be produced only by the sympathy arising from similarity of condition. Above all, it is a certainty that the Russian peasant detested his position, that local insurrections were incessant, and that only hope—the hope now justified by the emperor—prevented them from becoming universal. Russian slavery in its best form destroys individual interest, and therefore general progress, renders a true middle class impossible, and poisons the national mind with discontent. In its worst forms it is better than negro slavery only in the absence of race hatred, and in the peculiarity we may now describe.

While the master is thus absolute over the individual, he is powerless as against the community, or against a general right. No proprietor in Russia claims a *right* to sell children, or separate husband and wife, or breed slaves for sale. He may perform isolated acts of tyranny, tending to those results, but he performs them in the face of the law and public opinion, and not with their support. As to communities, he is powerless both in theory and practice. The Russian, like every other Asiatic, considers that the land belongs to him and his commune. He may be compelled to pay rent, or give service, but his right is wholly unimpaired. Like other Asiatics, too, he will fight for this single right with the most utter indifference to consequences. The same man who will bear insult and blows and taxation without a murmur, is a freeman the instant his land is menaced. A real assault on his village rights produces an insurrection as certainly as a cloud produces rain. His land has, therefore, been respected, and it is this remnant of citizenship, this last relic of property right, which has saved him from degradation, and which now forms the difficulty of emancipation.

The House of Romanoff, though the largest serf-holder in the empire, has almost from its accession been hostile to Russian serfage. There is no need to account for the fact by supposing the czars either enlightened beyond all other Russians, or moved by any very recondite policy. Absolute monarchs usually dislike the classes which can resist them, and the nobles have been the resisting force of Russia. Absolute monarchs, on the other hand, are apt to regard all their subjects as equal, to care as much for the peasantry as the middle class. The Cæsar alone among Romans tried to alleviate slavery. Oriental kings in their fits of good government always hang a few satraps, and secure a decent tenure for the cultivators. The Russian house, moreover, has thirsted for generations for a high place in Europe, has keenly felt the loss of position involved in ruling over serfs. Indeed, this latter feeling may have been the strongest of all, for Nicholas, the only czar who ever attained a commanding position in Europe, was also the only one who never attempted any thing for the serfs. Other emperors have not done much, but they have done enough to indicate their tendencies, and make themselves recognized as the sole protectors of the peasantry. This feeling has been their strength, and when on his accession to the throne the emperor distinctly pledged himself to emancipation, it was his security. Within a fortnight of the issue of the first decree, ordering inquiry, it was known throughout the remotest villages of Russia. A glad and overpowering emotion ran through the land, and in an instant the power of the nobles as a corporation was destroyed. They might remonstrate, or even delay, but their power of resistance had disappeared. One wave of the emperor's finger, and the class would have been swept away. The old "constitutional check" in Russia, the right of assassination, was at an end. The ablest nobles admitted that the death of the czar, even from natural causes, would be the signal for the universal massacre of the Order. They protested and implored, and suggested impossible compromises, but even in Moscow no dream of resistance was ever entertained. The peasantry, with that strange self-control which is the first characteristic of Asiatics, waited in patience for the emperor's will. It has been uttered at last, and from the 3d March every Russian in the empire will be free. He may have rent to pay, though we doubt it; he may have a compensation fund to make up, though we disbelieve it; but he will be free of the stick, free of labor for another's advantage, free above all to remove himself to the cities, and there reap the advantage of his almost Parisian shiftiness and address.

It is not, perhaps, necessary to examine very carefully the consequences of this great deed. There are occasions in the history of nations, as in the lives of individuals, when the act to be done is too vast for human foresight, when the single advice worth hearing is to do right, and leave the consequences to the God you have obeyed. But there are one or two results which, unless all history is valueless, may safely be predicted from the revolution.

The first is an increase in the political strength of Russia. The House of Romanoff, with all its despotic principles, has been for ages in fair accord with its people. The masses, while distrusting the "Tchin," and detesting the aristocracy, have been steadfastly loyal to the throne. A mob obeys the direct order of the czar as submissively as his soldiery. "God and the czar" is the cry of the Russian peasant, and he does not always distinguish accurately between the two Beneficences. If this has been his habitual feeling, what will it be when the emperor has conceded the freedom his nobles would have withheld? Henceforward, the man who menaces the dynasty will be regarded in Russia as he would be in England —as a dangerous, but still contemptible fool. That result alone strengthens the czars almost inconceivably. Add to this that serfage is the first cause of the poverty of the Russian fisc, that its abolition renders direct taxation on the masses possible, and must increase the customs receipts indefinitely, that half the abuses of the army have their root in serfage, and, finally, that the moral weight of Russia is crippled by her adherence to slavery, and we may gain some idea of the advantages which will repay the reigning house for the enormous sacrifice they have made.

The second result is, we imagine, the temporary extinction of the Russian aristocracy.

That body numbers some 100,000 slaveholders, whose properties are thus distributed:—

1,424	possess	more than	1,000	peasants
2,273	"	"	500	"
16,740	"	"	100	"
30,417	"	"	20	"
58,457	"	less than	20	"

There is talk of pecuniary compensation, and the emancipation will, doubtless, be accompanied by a decree authorizing the collection of rent: but both palliatives must, we conceive, break down. The fee-simple of an empire is not purchasable with money, and the loan Russia has raised will not fairly compensate for the *obrok* alone. As to the right to rent it would be invaluable if it could be enforced; but the means of enforcing it are not clear. The Russian peasant will certainly not become a tenant at will. The attempt to consider him such would end in a catastrophe to which the Indian Mutiny would be a trifle. Yet, if not a tenant at will, how is the peasant to be made to pay? He has no idea of doing it voluntarily. The land is *his*, and popular landlords have been promised by their serfs that their homesteads should be left them, as a friendly concession. The idea of employing force has no just place here. The army is composed of peasants, and if it were not, the army is powerless against united Russia—united, too, on the one point the people hold dearer than their lives. The wild lands the nobles may retain, but there will be no laborers to cultivate them. Some families, like the Demidoffs and Sheremetioffs, who own provinces and cities, whose factories will pay under free labor, and whose mines will be productive under any system of working, may survive the shock, and hereafter grow wealthier than before. But the mass of the aristocracy, the men with less than a thousand peasants, must go down, and be replaced by the moneyed class already rising in the scale. They can be spared. They have added nothing to European society beyond a somewhat bizarre magnificence, and in Russia their absence will be felt only in a sense of relief from a dead weight on human energy. On the whole, we believe the decree of emancipation will add, at once, forty millions to the list of European freemen, without a single serious disadvantage. What it may effect in the future, is a theme rather for the poet than the journalist. In Russia alone, of European countries, is there room for the development of new forms of life and social habit. The Russian is the only race in Europe which carries communist ideas into effect, the only one in which thorough and startling originality has been found compatible with an adamantine social order.

From The Spectator, 23 Feb.

BRENNUS DE ROMA.

The daily press has, we think, erred in attributing so slight an importance to the last imperial brochure. M. de la Guerronnière, it is true, tells us less than in the pamphlet which preceded the Italian war, and has lost the interest which must always attach to the words of a French ruler when threatening war. But the publication of *La France, Rome, et l'Italie* is none the less an event. Carefully studied, it breathes in every line that independence of the Church which the Revolution has always asserted, and the Empire seems hitherto to have forgotten. But one spirit pervades its remarks, whether upon the pope, or upon the "parti prêtre," and that is one of utter, irrepressible scorn. A Protestant would scarcely venture to ridicule the pope in the style employed by M. de la Guerronnière, when describing the advent of Lamoricière at Rome. "And when one thinks," he says, "that these ridiculous scenes" (the receptions granted by the pope to French provincial deputations to protest against the court) "occurred in some sort under the protection of the French army, one may estimate the moderation of the emperor. This parody of Coblentz, these puerile imitations of the times of Gregory the Seventh, this strange distinction between Frenchman and Bretons, this homage offered to the pope, not as the chief of the Church, but as a sovereign, did not deserve that the emperor should lose that calm which he found in his strength and in his right; but if he saw in it no danger, he found in it none the less an irrefragable proof of the feelings which impelled Rome against France and the sovereign of her choice." And M. About might be proud of the subtle scorn alike of priests and legitimists which underlies this masterly paragraph. "The emperor has always recommended to the pope the creation of a national army as the proof of re-established order and the pledge of future security. The Roman government, which had remained deaf to that advice, tried to form an army without either nationality or unity. The attempt was made with an éclat which sought to recall the great religious manifestations of another epoch, and that nothing might be wanting to the *mise en scène*, they placed at the head of this crusade a general whom France had *not* seen under her eagles in the heroic struggles of Italy and the Crimea. Let us say it freely: when a Roman prelate, notorious for his personal antipathy to the French policy, sought the recesses of Anjou, to appeal to the courage and devotion of M. de Lamoricière, he selected less the hero of Constantine than the politician at variance with the government of his country. The emperor, occupied with higher thoughts, did not oppose the choice, although an indiscreet speech had already betrayed the hopes attached to the name of the papal commander-in-chief. . . . The general himself, on his return to France after that campaign of a day, marked its true character by declining the offer of a sword of honor." The emperor of the French, roundly condemning the papacy, actually quizzes the *parti prêtre*. Able rulers do not satirize those whom they fear, and the fact that Louis Napoleon can laugh at priestly antics, indicates a total change in the position of his dynasty. It rests no longer on the support of the clergy, who, he says, "marched at the head of their flocks to vote for his election," and in that change, far better than in any solemn assurance, men may perceive the future of the papacy. When the *parti prêtre* is called by the emperor himself, the party which "desires to make God the accomplice of its designs," when the curés are warned to beware of "men who, without titles or rights, arrogate to themselves a dictatorial control," and the pope himself is told to "submit in his temporal capacity to the ordinary conditions of human power," the policy of Louis Napoleon is not difficult to divine.

And it must be remembered his policy alone controls the situation, and arrests the extension of Italian unity to Rome. This pamphlet reveals, for the first time, that the Catholic powers have formally abandoned the papal cause. The Count de Rechberg assented to proposals which left to the papacy only the patrimony of St. Peter. The minister of Naples concurred in the same arrangement. The Spanish secretary for foreign affairs "declined to deny the obstinacy of the holy father," and thought the proposal the only one calculated to arrest the destruction of the temporal power. And the Portuguese minister of foreign affairs coolly remarked that, as the pope refused all concession, "there was nothing to be done but leave him to his fate." The remaining powers are Protestant or Greek; one of them ardently contending for the unity of Italy, another "not indisposed to see Italy a power." With France contemptuous, Italy hostile, and the ultramontane world quiescent, the temporal power is, at least, trembling to its fall. In what way the last stroke is to be given, whether the French army will be suddenly withdrawn from Rome, or whether, as the *Allgemeine Zeitung* affirms, it will be simply replaced by Sardinian troops, and the papal dominion terminated by the mere absence of force to execute its decrees, may be hard to predict. But the following sentence of the pamphlet is too precisely identical with that by which M. de Manteucci recently defined the policy of Cavour for the coincidence to be accidental.

"But if Italy is free she is not organized, and the obstacle to her organization is Rome. It is as difficult to conceive of Italy without the pope, as of the pope without Italy. They are bound together by history, by tradition, by the universal respect of all Catholic nations towards the chief of the Church. When the emperor entered on his contest with Austria, he designed to re-establish that precious bond. On the day on which that grand thought shall be accomplished, we shall see the papacy regain in modern society an authority as high as its origin and its mission. We shall see Italy add to the weight of its independence the moral strength of a position altogether unique, as the home of the spiritual sovereignty whose empire extends to the confines of the world."

The Roman question, we submit, draws near to its solution.

From The Economist, 23 Feb.

ASPECT OF FOREIGN AFFAIRS.

It cannot be a pleasant thing to be foreign minister of a nation on whose dominion the sun never sets, whose ships swarm on every sea, and whose merchants have factories on every shore. Day by day he is called upon to consider not only the great and stirring questions of European policy, such as Italian Unity, or Syrian Massacres, which interest every heart, but plaguing bagatelles about Mexican Bondholders or Mozambique Consuls, which interest no one but the parties personally concerned. And he must consider even the smallest and dullest of these matters cautiously and fully, since future wars and catastrophes, which will agitate the world and cost us millions, may easily grow out of disputes which now seem trivial even below contempt; and a cloud no bigger than a man's hand, if neglected or mismanaged, may in a few years swell into the cause of tempests and of earthquakes. At a moment when he would fain devote his continuous and undivided attention to the perplexing complications which America, Hungary, and Venetia are preparing for us, he is bothered out of his life by being suddenly called off, to watch the French in Cochin China, or the Russians in Servia, or the Germans in Schleswig-Holstein; or Juarez at Vera Cruz, or M. de Lesseps at the Suez Canal. All this must be exceedingly annoying, even to so highly placed and highly paid a functionary: if the same obligations in their fullest extent were entailed upon unhappy journalists, life would become an unendurable burden. Fortunately, however, less is required of us; and the public is satisfied and considers itself honestly served, if we take cognizance only of those more prominent and important foreign questions, which the people as a whole wish to follow and to understand.

In Europe, since we last called attention to the subject, affairs have been advancing towards an inevitable issue, but so slowly and so obscurely that we can only just register the progress without being able in the least to predict when or by what precise road that issue will be reached. In reference to the Italian question three events have to be noted. The first Italian Parliament has met at Turin, and has been opened by Victor Emmanuel in a temperate, but not very explicit or informing, speech. The essential point, however, is that Count Cavour has secured a large majority at the elections: it is obvious that the great mass of the Italian people are well inclined to place confidence and power in the hands of the statesman to whose ability, judgment, and patriotism they mainly owe their present proud position, and to trust him with the completion of the work he has so splendidly conducted hitherto. Gaeta, too, has at length fallen; King Bomba is an exile, dethroned, wealthy, unpitied, but scarcely yet quite innocuous; for he has gone to Rome, a most convenient place from which to direct reactionary plots; and though we do not know the conditions of his surrender, we know enough of the man to be certain that, if they are stringent and disadvantageous, he will not observe them an hour longer than he must. We do not learn that the surrender of Messina was included in the capitulation, but there can be now no excuse for prolonging its anomalous position. The dethroned monarch can scarcely intend to put Victor Emmanuel to the cost and trouble of another lengthened siege; and even were he disposed to do so, the garrison would scarcely deem it worth their while to encounter suffering and death to no purpose, on behalf of a monarch who has no longer any right to command them or any power to reward them. The third event is the issue of another pamphlet-oracle from the Delphi of the Tuileries, propounding, or professing to propound, the emperor's policy with reference to Rome. The utterance is, as usual, perplexing and obscure: its meaning, however, appears to be that the pope must remain at Rome, but that he must remain on terms which will prevent him from being a permanent obstacle to the completion of Italian unity. The emperor will not suffer him to be forcibly driven away, nor yet to be a hinderance to the developments rendered necessary by "the inexorable logic of facts." As to *how* this combination of objects is to be achieved, the oracle is silent. Perhaps Louis Napoleon has adopted the suggestion of the *Edinburgh Review*—that Florence shall be the capital of Italy and the seat of the temporal government; and that Rome shall be simply the Holy City, graced by the residence of the spiritual potentate. Or, perhaps, he does not see his way to a feasible solution more clearly than the rest of us, but is determined to protect the person of the pope from outrage, and trusts to time and accident for offering some way out of the dilemma. Certainly the whole tone of the document is as unfavorable to the pope's temporal sovereignty as it is friendly to the pope himself.

The dispute between Austria and Hungary has reached another phase. The Hungarians, whatever may be the differences of opinion among themselves, maintain one resolute and unchanging attitude towards Vienna. They stand upon their old Constitution, because it was legal and ancient, though admittedly imperfect. They will pay no taxes but such as are voted by the Diet; and they will elect their Diet by no forms except those prescribed by the electoral law of 1848. The emperor is willing to concede every thing which will leave him master of the financial and military resources of Hungary, for without these he cannot face Italy or coerce Venice; but he will not go a step further, since to do so would be to sacrifice the ends to the means. The Hungarians, knowing his object as plainly as he knows it himself, are resolved that neither their revenue nor their soldiers shall be employed against Italy, and are convinced also that, unless they retain the constitutional command of these essentials, all other concessions will be evaded or revoked. The consequence is that the attitude of the emperor towards Hungary has within the last three weeks become decidedly more obstinate and hostile. Finding that he cannot gain by conciliation the point for which alone he was willing to conciliate, he seems preparing again to be stiff and reactionary. Meanwhile there appears to be great restlessness, to say the least, in Servia, Montenegro, and the Principalities; and Russia, on the very eve of a vast internal change, the emancipation of twenty millions of serfs, is said to be moving troops with a view to intervention, unless France and England shall forbid the step. Prussia and Denmark also are at issue about the duchies; and altogether there are several causes of war extant and in operation which it would be very easy to fan into a flame, and which it will be very difficult, we fear, to reduce to perfect harmlessness.

The position of affairs in America is alluded to in another part of our paper. Certain difficulties have arisen with reference to the want of customs officers qualified to give clearances to ships which shall be recognized as valid by both the contending parties; and the attorney-general of the Union, when applied to by the foreign ministers at Washington, has been most feeble and unsatisfactory in his reply. Shippers and merchants, however, are ingenious and usually successful in surmounting embarrassments of this sort. A more serious impediment to a large and lucrative commerce with America this year seems likely to arise from the confused state of the interior. Commerce hates disturbances and shrinks from *prospective* engagements with chaotic countries; and till *some* settlement is effected, we must expect that dealers will exhaust their stocks rather than send out fresh orders. Cotton, however, will continue to come forward for the two simple and omnipotent reasons, that Europe *must* have it, and that America *must* have the money which it brings. The tone of commercial advices, however, is decidedly uncomfortable.

From The Economist, 23 Feb.

"MANIFEST DESTINY" OF CANADA.

THE discussions in the Northern States of the American Union, while they seem to show every day more clearly the hopelessness of any reconciliation between North and South, have brought prominently forward one political issue on which it seems not unlikely that the Democratic and Republican parties will combine. "Manifest Destiny," who has hitherto turned her eyes southward, now wheels round and gazes in the opposite direction; and as she looks the boundary line of the Ashburton Treaty disappears from the map. The annexation of Canada is spoken of in the Democratic organs of the North as the only proper equivalent for the loss of political importance caused by the Southern secession. "The territory which the Canadians hold," says the *New York Herald*, "is about three hundred and fifty thousand square miles. It would, therefore, make thirteen Sovereign States, averaging in area thirteen States of the Northern Confederacy. Such a prize is not to be lost. . . . Now that the Confederacy is to be shorn of more than half its strength in territory, and more than a third of its population, it is necessary to repair the loss, else we would sink to a third or fourth-rate power. *By peaceable means or force, therefore, Canada must be annexed.*" Now the policy of swelling the free States by the accession of the Canadas and British Columbia was expressly foreshadowed by Mr. Seward last autumn in his great presidential canvass, and now that the Republicans are on the look-out for some means of healing the breach with their Democratic opponents, it is not probable that the Republican leaders will in any way discountenance the agitation for "redressing the disturbed balance of power" in this way. Even the Democratic organs admit that the Southern Confederacy "aspires to the early absorption of Mexico, Central America, and the island of Cuba." The more clearly they see in the secession movement a premeditated scheme for carrying Southern empire down to the Isthmus and for absorbing the West India Islands, the more anxiously do the States of the Northern Confederation scan the area within which alone they can hope to expand. The annexation of the Canadas will be a question of daily increasing interest in the Northern States, as the power of the South is consolidated. The Democrats, with that passion for dominion which has never in any era of the world's history taken so unscrupulous or impudent a form, will identify themselves with the step. The Republicans, though far more scrupulous and modest in their party-aims, yet as in some sense the authors of the disruption which has so clipped the power of the Union, and as having themselves first pointed to this equivalent for the growing power of the South, can scarcely help lending their influence, more or less, to this movement. The sooner, therefore we consider the attitude that England ought deliberately to assume, the more consistent and dignified our policy will be.

It seems to us clear that we should take our stand on the policy indicated long ago by Lord Derby (then Lord Stanley) and Sir Robert Peel, that if the people of the Canadas universally wish to throw off the yoke of England and annex themselves to the United States, no obstacle will be interposed on the part of Great Britain. To us Canada is, from a military point of view, expensive; and to defend for her so long a frontier line is no little responsibility in case of war with the United States. And even if this were not so, to keep down a vast and populous dependency, anxious to revolt, on the other side of the Atlantic, is a policy, on which we are not likely to embark twice. Moreover, we sincerely believe that this is the policy which is most likely to retain for England the affection of the Canadas. The political jealousy of any thing like interference in all independent dependencies, if we may be excused the expression, is naturally very great. And the least symptom of any wish on the part of England to coerce the political movements of Canada would immediately engender a feeling of disloyalty, however loyal the previous temper of the population.

And if we refrain from any thing like menace or coercion in the matter, contenting ourselves with simply defending Canada against any aggressive movement of the American States, we do not think the people of that country will be disposed to listen to the voice of the Democratic charmers, "charm they ever so wisely." It is true that with the obliteration of slavery from the institutions of the Northern Confederation, by far the greatest obstacle to the Union will have been removed. But though the institution of slavery would have kept an impassable barrier between the people of the American Union and of the British dependency,—there are other, not indeed so great, but very serious objections to an amalgamation, which we do not think the Canadians will be disposed to surmount if they feel absolutely free to act exactly as they please. If, as our New York contemporary tells us, the Canadians have long been "panting for more freedom than they can enjoy under British rule," we do not think it very likely that they will look to find it in the American Union. The protectionist policy which the Northern States are now so madly adopting is unfortunately not likely to deter Canada, as her own Legislature has embarked in the same course. But the result of the union with the United States would be the partition of Canada into a number of "Sovereign" States, as they are called, each with the complete direction of its own policy in all matters except those of which the Federal authority in Washington takes account. Lower Canada would be permitted to be as intolerantly Roman Catholic as it chose, Upper Canada as intolerantly Orange. The result of this removal of the tempering influence of a central government empowered to deal with all subjects of public importance would soon be felt in a fatal localization of petty tyrannies. The truth is, that the partition of powers between Federal and State authorities does not work well for the interests of true freedom. The State appears to be much too *small* a unit for the good use of sovereign power. The petty tendencies of place and prejudice exercise too large an influence. The Federal Union ought to exercise many of the powers which the State really possesses. And this the Canadians can scarcely help seeing. They will not envy the States of America that so-called liberty which consists in enthroning the popular opinion of a very confined district, and investing it with sovereign power over all the most important departments of human life.

THE STATES OF THE BORDER.

Air.—"All the Blue Bonnets are over the Border."

HASTE, haste! Men of the Union, all,
Willing to save us from wrath and disorder!
Haste, haste! Fail not to meet the call
Made on the true by the States of the Border.
Broadly, still, overhead,
Star-spangled banners spread,
Dimmed in their radiance, but not in their story!
Hasten, oh! hasten then,
Called by the Border men,
Sons of the free, to restore them their glory.

Come from the hills of the swift Susquehanna,
Come from the cities that stand by the sea;
Come from each mountain and glen and savannah,
Hallowed of old, by the flag of the free.
Turmoil is round us—
Evils confound us—
True men alone can restore us to order;
Come, then, oh, come, then,
Fearless and gallant men,
Come when convened by the States of the Border.

Come, Indiana, Missouri, Rhode Island,
Come, Tennessee, Arkansas, Illinois,
Come, Jersey, Ohio, come lowland and highland,
New York, and Kentucky, let none remain coy.
Leave party behind us,
Its instincts but blind us,
Platforms must yield, if it's needed, to save us.
Are we not brothers?
Then, by our mothers,
Swear to preserve what our forefathers gave us.

Come, with no purpose of force or coercion;
Come, but as freemen should come to the free;
Come with affection, and not with aversion,
Come, not for contest, but come to agree.
Then, as the sunbeams
Chase from the summer streams
Fogs of the morning, with sickness their story,
So shall be lightened,
Made broader and brightened,
The star-spangled banner, in all its old glory.

Hasten then, hasten then—men of the Union all.
Palm tree, or pine tree, what matters the sign?
Thousands on thousands will tearfully greet you all,
Praying, for each, inspiration divine,
You but agreeing—
Anarchy fleeing,
End shall be put unto wrath and disorder;
And, to the latest days,
Loudly shall millions praise
Those who convened at the call of the Border.

—*Baltimore American.*

From Chambers's Journal.

SCIENCE AND ARTS FOR JANUARY.

The year opens with renewed conviction to many minds, that the accomplishment of many good works, though long desired, still remains to be striven after by philosophers and savants. The lamentable loss of life by the fearful colliery explosion at Risca, and at Hetton, indicates very emphatically what one of the first of these much-desired good works should be—the discovery or application of a method by which mining operations may be carried on free from the terrible risk to which miners are now subject. We cannot believe that Science has come to the end of her skill in this matter: Mr. Gassiot's experiments, shown before the Royal Society, demonstrate that a brilliant electric light is producible within a glass globe or cylinder from which the surrounding atmosphere is perfectly excluded. May not this fact be accepted as proof that some safe application of the electric light is possible, even in the most dangerous workings? Moreover, something was said a few years ago about a means for burning the choke-damp as fast as it accumulated, whereby explosions would become impossible. Has this notion ever been put into practice? Let us hope that 1861 will not pass away without the removal of what may be regarded as a reproach on our national character: the oft-recurring sacrifice of human life in the pursuits of industry.

We want pure gas to burn in our houses; we want the purest of drinking water; we want a way to save the thousands of tons of good fuel which are now smoked off to waste in the air; we want a simple and effectual method of ventilation applicable to all sorts of buildings; we want a sure way of passing signals to the guard of a railway-train while in motion, whereby passengers may give timely warning of fire, breakage of wheels, and the like; we want improved means of vehicular locomotion in streets which shall entirely prevent the numerous fatal accidents which now occur every year in London and other large towns of busy traffic. Is it not an opprobrium to our civilization to be able to cross a street only with risk of life? We want wider applications of the electric telegraph in large towns, as well as to all parts of the realm, for social as well as commercial purposes. The District Telegraph, wherever available in London, is found to be singularly useful. A friend of ours who left his home in Islington one morning with anticipation of a supper-party in the evening, discovering at 4 P.M. that his expected guests would not be able to appear, immediately flashed the information to his wife, and thus, by a payment of fourpence, saved materfamilias from useless trouble. We could fill a column with desiderata; but if 1861 should accomplish those we have pointed out in addition to its promised Great Exhibition, and the realization of the superb scheme of what is now the Royal Horticultural Society, it will be a year exceedingly memorable.

So far as gas is concerned, there is prospect of relief from those impurities which at present render the brilliant light so prejudicial in a dwelling-house. A paper by the Rev. W. R. Bowditch, read before the Royal Society, describes a series of experiments undertaken for the discovery of a method of purification, and the results. Heated clay appears to be a valuable purifier, as it removes many injurious products from the gas; but the greatest success is obtained by lime at about a temperature of 108 degrees, as it completely neutralizes the bisulphide of carbon which, with another sulphurous product, are felt so oppressively in the atmosphere of a room where gas has been burning a few hours. Seeing that, generally speaking, two hundred grains of sulphur are given off by every thousand feet of gas consumed, the oppressiveness complained of is not to be wondered at, nor that gilding and the binding of books are spoiled. No means were known by which this sulphur could be got rid of, and even the ablest chemists regarded it as an inevitable evil. But Mr. Bowditch, to whom gas-makers are indebted for the introduction of clay as a purifier, animated by his success, made further experiments, and found, as above stated, the desired means of purification in lime, and without any loss of light-giving constituents from the gas. When once his process shall have come into general use, some of the objections now made to the lighting of picture-galleries, museums, and libraries by gas will no longer apply. We assist the more willing in making this subject known, as it is one of much importance from the domestic as well as the commercial point of view. Some readers will perhaps take interest in the fact, that the clay used in the purifying is afterwards valuable as a fertilizer.

A happy result of the attempt made to familiarize sea-side folk with a scientific instrument deserves notice. The fishermen of Cullercoats, one of the villages where a barometer was set up at the cost of the Duke of Northumberland, observing a fall of the mercury during their preparations for sea, put off their departure, and thus saved themselves from a gale, which came on a few hours later.—An apparatus has been invented for pumping a leaky ship: a two-bladed screw, placed in the water behind the stern, turns a rod and crank shaft, which keep the pump working; and the faster the vessel sails, the more water will be pumped out, and without fatigue to the crew.—An American inventor now builds boats by machinery, and turns out a cutter thirty-six feet long, in ten hours; a task that, by the usual method, takes eight days.—And now the much-talked-of iron frigate *Warrior* is fairly launched, the largest ship in the world except the *Great Eastern*; and by and by we shall know whether a vessel cased in ponderous armor is, like the iron-clad knights of the olden time, too heavy to be useful.

Mr. David Forbes, brother of the late Professor Edward Forbes, has read a paper before the Geological Society, giving the results of his geological explorations of Bolivia and Southern Peru, where he has spent some years, and met with much adventure. Examination of the Peruvian coast leads him to the conclusion, that it has undergone no elevation since the Spanish Conquest, although along the neighboring coast of Chili a remarkable upheaval has taken place. The saline formations extend over five hundred and fifty miles of the rainless region, and contain prodigious quantities of nitrate of soda—a valuable article in commerce, besides considerable deposits of borate of lime. Among the fossils brought home by Mr. Forbes are certain Silurian species, which were collected on the mountains at great heights above the sea; and geologists are much interested in the fact, that perhaps a hundred thousand square miles of the great chain of the Cordilleras are now known to comprise Silurian rocks, which yield fossils even at a height of 20,000 feet. Notwithstanding the risks and wounds received during revolutionary contests, Mr. Forbes intends returning to Bolivia to resume his explorations, and to climb, if possible, to the highest of the mountain summits.—The iron-sand, which covers many miles of country in New Zealand, to the great annoyance of settlers in windy weather, is likely to become a considerable source of profit; for analysis of samples brought to England shows it to be composed of a peroxide of iron, with twelve per cent of titanium—a rare combination. It is, moreover, readily convertible into steel of singularly good quality; and sundry manufactured specimens which have been put to the test as razor-blades, and other cutting instruments, show proof of a keen edge, a surface less easily tarnished than that of ordinary steel, and unusual hardness. Hence, in their so-called sand, which is attracted as readily as steel-filings by the magnet, we may believe that the New Zealand colonists have a metalliferous resource valuable to them as gold-fields; that is, should "Taranaki steel" maintain its present reputation among manufacturers.—In a communication to the Geological Society of Dublin, Mr. Alphonse Gages announces his discovery of the structure of certain mineral substances; he immersed a small piece of fibrous dolomite in dilute sulphuric acid, and found, at the end of some days, that certain parts were dissolved out, leaving only a skeleton form. In other instances, he finds one skeleton superposed on another; and he is now trying to discover the origin of serpentine, which is composed, perhaps, of three skeletons, whose interstices are filled up by another substance.

The Geographical Society, desirous to promote African discovery, are raising a subscription of £2,000 wherewith to equip Mr. Petherick for another exploration towards the head waters of the Nile.—From Australia the news of Mr. Stuart's expedition to explore the interior has surprised alike colonists and geographers; for instead of the vast traditionary desert, the scorching wilderness, and source of the suffocating "brickfielders," he found a fertile and well-watered country, suited for pastoral purposes. At the last accounts, he had returned to the settlements to report progress and replenish his supplies, but intended to repeat his endeavor to solve the mystery of the unknown interior. The happiest discovery he could make would be a chain of mountains, but failing that, it is gratifying to know that grassy plains and woods exist where, according to theory, nothing was to be met with but barren sand.

Not fewer than five hundred pages of the last published volume of the *Mémoires* of the Academy of Sciences at Paris are filled with a dissertation on the silkworm disease, comprising facts observed up to the latest available period in 1859. The history and phenomena of the disease are set forth, the causes and means of cure are sought out and explained; and the prime conclusion is, that the best remedy consists in hygienic means, and that the visitation is temporary in its nature. The importance of this question to our neighbors may be inferred from the fact, that in 1853 France raised 26,000,000 kilogrammes of cocoons, worth 130,000,000 francs; and that, owing to the progress of the disease year by year, the quantity was less in 1856 by 7,500,000 kilogrammes. As we mentioned some time since, attempts have been made to introduce new species of silkworms, among which the most successful is the *Bombyx arrindia*, the silkworm which feeds on the *Palma Christi*, or castor-oil plant. It was brought first from China about four years ago; was reared and propagated at Turin; has been found to thrive in Algeria, and to survive the winter of the south of France; and is, besides, remarkably productive, for, to quote Professor Milne-Edwards, it yields six or seven broods within a year. It is of the silk of this worm that India handkerchiefs are made.

Great surprise was manifested a short time since at a statement laid before the Société d'Encouragement, concerning the enormous quantity of albumen consumed by the dyers of cotton-prints in the manufacturing districts of France; for it was shown that 33,000,000 of eggs were required every year to supply the demand; the quantity produced being 125,000 kilogrammes, and each kilogramme worth twelve francs. The yolks of all these eggs were for the most part wasted, until it was found that they were convertible into soap; but even then, it was felt that to consume the eggs as food would be better than employing them in the preparation of mordants. There is no fear of lack of customers while English ports are open for all that France can send. The question would be solved if an artificial albumen could be produced from some substance not of prime importance as an aliment; and for some time past the Société Industrielle of Mulhausen has offered a prize of 17,500 francs for the discovery of a material which will not require the use of eggs. The same problem has been seriously studied at Manchester, and not fruitlessly; and we now see that the Abbé Moigno announces in his weekly journal, a discovery made by M. Hannon, a miller and baker, that the waste gluten of starch-factories yields the substitute for albumen which has been so long desired. By a process of fermentation, and subsequent drying in moulds, and in a stove, with certain precautions, cakes are produced of what the inventor calls "albumoid glue," which is applicable to other uses as well as those of the dyer: it answers as a glue for carpenters and cabinet-makers, for workers in leather, paper, and pasteboard, for menders of glass, porcelain crystals, shells, and so forth, for clarifiers of beer, for the finishers of silk and woollen goods, and in the fabrication of gums; and with all this utility its price is but one-fourth that of the albumen of eggs.

A pamphlet lately published under the title, *Why the Shoe Pinches*, deserves a word of notice here, and claims the attention of all who wear shoes, because of the importance of its subject. It is a translation of Dr. Hermann Meyer's short treatise on the best form of shoe for the human foot, regarded from the anatomical point of view; the which point, we take leave to say, is the primary one in the question. Let those who fear to wear a comfortable shoe lest their feet should be thought "big," read Dr. Meyer's explanations and examine his engravings, and they will see the evil and sometimes fatal consequences of denying fair play to the six-and-twenty bones of the foot. They will see such deformities wrought by fashion, that leave us but little to boast of in the treatment of our feet over the much-wondered-at ladies of China. They will learn what are the true principles on which the foot-covering should be shaped, and many a mother will perhaps rejoice that they have been saved from the cruelty of distorting their infants' feet. It is scarcely possible to convey the description without the aid of engravings; but the essential particulars are that, in forming the sole, a straight line drawn from the ball of the great toe—the toe being in its natural position—shall pass exactly through the centre of the heel; that the edge of the sole shall be straight along its inner side from its foremost extremity to the base of the great toe; and that none but what are called "rights and lefts" should be worn. We recommend perusal of the pamphlet to all concerned—and they are not few; and especially to shoemakers, who are commonly so apt to be dogmatic, and fancy they have nothing to learn, and who torture their customers without remorse.

Of the gorgeous Christmas books, the perfection of whose type, illustrations, and binding seems to merit a notice in this our record of the Arts as well as the Sciences, these two are especially commendable—the new edition of the *Lyra Germanica* (Longmans) and the *Ore-seeker* (Macmillan). The hymns contained in the former were perhaps some of the first compositions produced in types at the dawn of printing, and the book before us is probably the best specimen of modern art. The means employed are nearly the same, both being the production of the hand-press; but how wide the difference between the black-letter folio and the result which is now attained, itself a record of the progress of civilization! The illustrations, which are engraved under the superintendence of John Leighton, F.R.S., are as excellent and appropriate to their subjects as can be conceived. The *Ore-seeker* is also an admirably executed volume, concerning whose charming story and beautiful illustrations the only thing to be regretted is, that the author and artist are both anonymous.

Shakspeare, Derivation of.—The name, Shakspeare, no doubt originated in the Norman or French edition of the double beloved-disciple name (Jacques-pierre, James-peter, Jakespear), of which it is composed; the initial *J* being pronounced *sh*, as in many other instances; viz., in

Shenkins for Jenkins.
Sherard " Gerard.
Shiles " Giles.
Sherry " Jerry.
Sheridan " Jeridan (old Jerry).
Shenstone " Johnstone (Johnson).
She " Je, in Switzerland and elsewhere, where the French language is provincialized, etc.

With such a self-evident derivation before us, we may therefore dispense with the unlikely refference to the shaking of a spear, which most probably had nothing to do with the origin of the name, when first invented; being only a suggestion from its accidental English form; though the idea once started, the name may with some have seemed to be recommended by it.

Those who consider that Shakspeare originated in spear-shaking rely on "Breakspear," "Winspear," etc., as analogous, these names having a like termination in, and apparent reference to, action with a spear; but this illustration is of the kind "ignotum per ignotius." We do not know enough of Brakespeare, etc., to justify us in saying that their origin was connected with spears; nor applying any inferences from them to other names. Probably Breakspear (a priest) was in part named after St. Peter, the chief of the apostles, and not after spears. Winspear almost looks like "Owen" (or John?) "Peter."—*Notes and Queries.*

Church: Number to form a Congregation.—A provincial paper states, that on one of these last cold Sundays, the curate of a rural parish dismissed a very small assemblage of parishioners to their homes without performing the service. A London weekly journal of about the same date, in answer to a correspondent, states, "Nine persons form a congregation, and cannot be legally dismissed without the usual services being performed. 'Two or three gathered together' are generally understood to form a congregation." Is there any law by which the number is defined to be larger than that which is required to ensure the Divine presence, Matthew xviii. 20?—*Notes and Queries.*

"Begone, dull Care."—It appears to me that the following verse, which I have frequently heard sung by a lady, who learned it in childhood from the singing of others in this neighborhood, is a powerful addition to the well-known song, "Begone, dull Care." In any company in which I have heard it sung it produced a great effect. Is it known as originally forming the concluding part of the lyric? I should say it has seldom been surpassed in that class of composition:—

"This world, they say, was made of naught,
And all that is therein—
And at the end of time it will
To naught return again.
Since this world at best
Then's [Is?] but a jest,
And life will soon decay;
Then while we're here,
My friends most dear,
Let's drive dull Care away.
Begone, dull Care," etc., etc.
—*Notes and Queries.*

The following article is copied from *The New York World*, 11 March, and shows that Mr. Douglas might have made for himself a reputation as a statesman.

The *material* benefits of our national Union are, 1. Peace with one another. 2. Free trade with one another. 3. Strength against "outside pressure." If this "Zoll-verein" could be accomplished so as to give us the second of these advantages with British America and Mexico, the first would be very likely to follow it.

The hope of accomplishing so great an advancement as is held forth in this suggestion, is an additional argument in favor of such caution and moderation in the adjustment of our own tariff, as may make it an acceptable basis for British America, Mexico, and any *other power* which may arise in our neighborhood—if such calamity should befall us.

A NORTH AMERICAN ZOLL-VEREIN.

DURING the recent discussions on the new tariff bill, in the United States Senate, some ideas were thrown out by Senator Douglas, which seem to us to deserve a greater share of the pu lic attention than they have yet attracted. bSo important, indeed, is the subject to which they relate, embodying, as it does, the germs of a great continental policy—a policy worthy of consideration if the Union is preserved, and doubly worthy of consideration if it should be broken—that the American people can hardly devote attention to a question better deserving profound study. It is a subject which has already engaged the earnest thoughts of some of the most sagacious minds among us, but the views toward which they tend have never been so distinctly expressed by any leading statesman as they were by Senator Douglas in the remarks to which we have alluded. "I had hoped," said Mr. Douglas, "that the time had arrived when we could mature and adopt a continental system that would embrace, in one commercial union, all the States of the North American continent, with a uniform system of duties. Such a commercial union could be adopted, in my opinion, that would be beneficial to all the states and countries who should become parties to it. I would like to see it embrace not only the United States but the Canadas upon the north, the British possessions upon the east and the north-west, and Mexico, Cuba, and the Central American States upon the south. I would like to see them all brought within the circle of one commercial union and a uniform system of duties, so far as all these states were concerned. I desire to see all custom-houses in the interior abolished, all restrictions upon internal commerce done away with, so that there should be entire free trade unrestricted between every state, province, or country upon the American continent and the adjacent islands."

This, it will be seen, proposes, for the adoption of all North America, a system nearly identical in its essential features with the well-known *Zoll-verein*, or customs-union, of the German States. There can be little doubt that, if practicable, it would promote the interests of trade, open extensive markets for our productions and new theatres for our enterprise, and would give a fresh and powerful impetus to the growth and development of the great regions on this continent to the north and south of us. The time approaches when the commercial relations of this country with Canada, Mexico, and Cuba will demand the attention of the government. The Canadian reciprocity treaty fails to meet the expectations of its friends on this side of the frontier, in consequence of recent legislation by the Canadian Parliament violative of its spirit. From the geographical configuration of the country, commercial intercourse with us is indispensable to the Canadians, and our government owes it to its citizens that this intercourse should be put on such a basis that its advantages shall not be all on the other side. Our commercial relations with Mexico have long been in an unsatisfactory state, and the recent accession to power of the liberal party in that country is favorable to their early revision. Our trade with Cuba, also, needs to be put on a better footing; the unsuccessful negotiations of many years have failed to procure for us the advantages we desire. It is not to be expected that all the countries on the northern part of the continent can be simultaneously brought into the Zoll-verein arrangement; but if our government would now begin to look at our commercial relations from this point of view, and direct its diplomacy to the building up of a great continental policy, the project is so conducive to the interests of every part of North America there can be little doubt of its ultimate success. Canada is already ripe for it, and the other parts of the continent are rapidly ripening.

The proposed union does not contemplate any change in the *political* condition of the countries that would be parties to it. That is to say, we should get all the *commercial* advantages which would result from the annexation of Canada, Mexico and Cuba to this country without incorporating incongruous populations under one government, or incurring the expenses of maintaining civil order in communities that would not readily assimilate with our own. A wide field would be opened to Anglo-American enterprise; capital would be attracted to Mexico and Central America, and, by furnishing employment to labor, not only would the wealth of these countries and their ability to purchase of us be increased, but the spirit of restless insubordination which has been the bane of Mexico, and which has resulted, in part, from lack of encouragement to steady industry, would be greatly diminished. The great numbers of our citizens who would emigrate to those regions so favored by nature would naturally touch the nerves of industry and develop trade, but would tend to the diffusion of Anglo-American ideas and habits of thought. The benefits to our industry would be double. By cheapening the cost of tropical commodities, the expense of living, and consequently the cost of production, would be diminished, and industry would be further encouraged by the extension of our markets.

If, unfortunately, the upshot of our present troubles should be the permanent severance of the self-styled Confederate States from the Union, such a system would partially retrieve the loss, by retaining the mutually profitable commercial intercourse between the sections. Our national Constitution had its inception in the exigencies of trade; it was framed mainly because of the conflicting commercial regulations by which trade was prostrated and paralyzed under the old confederation. But whether the Union be dissolved or preserved, this idea of a North American Zoll-verein contains the germ of a great continental policy which deserves the profoundest study of our statesmen and our people.

From The Saturday Review, 23 Feb.

THE EMANCIPATION OF SERFS IN RUSSIA.

The anniversary of the emperor's accession, the 3d of March, has been selected as the day on which a proclamation is to terminate Russian serfdom. For three centuries the nomadic instinct of a half-barbarous and Asiatic people has been restrained, and their indolence overpowered, by a system which has made them stationary, and as industrious as men ever are who work against their will. Whether serfdom has been a necessity or a mistake, can never be proved; but it has unquestionably kept together a supply of labor which would have been lost if dissipated over the vast steppes of Russia; while, on the other hand, it has been fruitful of cruelty, injustice, and of the hatred of class against class. During half the term of its existence the czars have striven to abolish, and the nobles to maintain it. The interests as well as the prejudices of the serf-owners have inspired them with a strong resolution to preserve a privilege which relieves them from the anxieties of an uncertain income, permitted them to indulge in the delights of absenteeism, and imparted to them the supreme distinction of owning not only lands, but souls. The serfs have not, until recent years, cared much to change their lot. Men of exceptional ability and industry may have resented the narrow limits in which their powers were confined, and gross outrages may have stirred the breasts of injured husbands and fathers; but the mass cherished a system which saved them the trouble of thinking, and sheltered them from want and a neglected old age. The czars, however, have long perceived the political difficulties which serfdom threw in the way of imperial supremacy. As a rule, the emperor and his immediate advisers have been much in advance of the leading territorial aristocracy; and the beneficial changes they have sought to introduce have been thwarted by the immovable conservatism of the magnates. To preserve the serf system was the cardinal tenet of this conservatism. Freedom of the souls on their lands was not a political change affecting the government, and felt principally at the capital; it was an alteration in all the habits of daily life—it was an abolition of the oldest family usages—it was a confusion of the differences which made the great men great. For many years the nobles withstood the czars successfully. It is much easier to say that serfs shall be free than to say what is the exact way in which their freedom shall be worked out. The czar might order, as in Esthonia, that serfdom should cease, but the failure of the experiment might have been easily anticipated when it was determined that the nobles should be entrusted with the fulfilment of the emperor's commands. It is only by the operation of that great silent change which passes over all classes in a nation which is beginning to get rich, to read and think, and to mix with more advanced nations, that the extinction of serfdom has become possible. Villeinage passed away in England when all ranks began to grow rich, and to be transfused with the same religious and political ideas. This is the stage at which Russia has now arrived. There is no inherent distinction between the master and his serf. There is no barrier like that which race builds up between the white man and the negro. Serf and master are both Russians, and when agriculture has become possible without compulsory labor, and the serf has learned that his soul is his own, a distinction that has been rendered superfluous ceases to be possible.

The nobles, however, have resisted the change to the last, and emancipation has been forced on them by the strong hand of a resolute government, backed by the newly formed desire of the serfs for freedom. The serf-owners have loudly protested that they will suffer greatly by the change, and that the money they may receive as compensation for the lands assigned to the emancipated serfs cannot possibly make up for the loss. They may very probably be right in this. The twenty millions sterling paid to our own slave-owners did not, as we know, prevent the West Indies from falling into the most lamentable state of pauperism and decay. The landowner is by no means sure of finding free labor at his door ready and willing to be employed. The freed men will have to attend to the cultivation of their own lands; and although the increase of population and the certainty that many small proprietors will sell their holdings might in time be depended on to provide a sufficiency of laborers glad to earn wages, the landowner feels a natural anxiety to know how he is to get on meanwhile. There is also a further cause for alarm. An enormous portion of the area of Russia is practically unoccupied, and it so happens that of this portion a considerable fraction is situated in the more recently acquired provinces of the south. The climate and the soil are much more favorable to cultivation in the south, and it is highly probable that when the serfs find themselves free to wander and capable of owning land, they will migrate to those boundless plains of virgin soil which, if properly tilled, would soon become the granary of Europe.

The northern proprietor may therefore find himself in a position painfully resembling that of a Jamaica planter. And if the larger landowner suffers anxiety and temporary distress, the smaller men may easily be swept away altogether. Many of them are deeply embarrassed already, and possess a number of serfs disproportionately great in comparison with their property. They have kept themselves afloat by the credit which the possession of serfs carries with it, and by the certainty that, if they wished to get rid of these ornamental dependants, some one else who longed to possess the coveted distinction would buy the souls they had to sell. These men will have no place in society when serfdom is gone. It is true that they will be no loss, and it is also true that the national advantages of freeing the serfs largely outweigh all the inconveniences to which the nobles can be exposed. But this does not diminish the probability that the period of transition through which Russia is now to pass will be one of great suffering and great discontent.

The attitude which the serfs have preserved since their coming emancipation was first decreed, shows how inevitable it was that a gift so keenly desired and so patiently expected should be accorded. The serf is free because it is impossible he should not be free. With the crown serfs already enfranchised—with the government, for social and political reasons, bent on a general emancipation—and with the serfs of private owners sufficiently advanced to conceive a wish, not spasmodic but permanent, for freedom—the choice really lay between an extinction of serfdom and a revolution that would have rudely shaken the fabric of society. But it must not be expected that the serf will at once and universally assume the position of a free laborer. It is probable that some imitation of the communal system obtaining in the crown lands will be largely called into play, in order to protect those long accustomed to being guided and cared for from the effects of an absolute independence. It is only the exceptional men who will feel all the gain of freedom in the first instance. The native merchant who has hitherto paid a rent to his lord for his personal liberty, and has lived in dread of arbitrary exactions, will now enjoy the luxury of security and self-respect. He will rise in the scale of society, and thus the greatest want of Russia will be supplied, and a middle-class created. The industrious, capable, thrifty cultivator will increase his holding little by little, until he makes it possible for his descendants to pass into the rank of the territorial gentry. For some years, in all likelihood, this is all the change that will be perceptible. Here and there an individual will be seen laying the foundation of a new order of things, while the mass are still too inert, too timid and improvident to depend on themselves. But in time one change will produce another, and the circles of growth will widen. We may be sure that this emancipation of the Russian serfs is the first step to innovations which will profoundly affect Eastern Europe. More especially the Greek Church, the most stagnant form exhibited by Christianity, is certain to be roused into life or to pass into a new phase, when increasing wealth and habitual activity have given new energies to the peasant and the nobles. Nor is it easy to conceive that the scandalous extortions and caprices of the bureaucracy will be endured when free critics are at hand to watch and report their proceedings. The religion, the politics, the habits, and the morals of Russia must all undergo a gradual transformation now that serfdom is extinguished, and how powerfully and widely that transformation will affect the rest of the world no man living can even conceive.

From The Saturday Review.

MARRIAGE ENGAGEMENTS.

THERE are two things which almost every one finds it difficult to do easily and with grace. One is for a man to announce orally that he is going to be married, and the other is to congratulate him. Why the announcement should cause embarrassment is obvious. However proud the happy lover may feel in his heart, he knows that by saying he is going to be married he at least exposes himself to the criticism of friendly curiosity. The friend to whom the announcement is made has also many reasons for feeling a little nervous. Not being a foreigner, he cannot throw himself on his friend's neck and have a good blubber, and he must confine his congratulations within the limits of English reserve. The surprise and the oddity of the thing, again, often, overpower every deeper feeling for the moment, and even the sincerest and warmest friend has been known to receive the affecting intelligence with no other answer than one long peal of laughter. And there is also a deeper cause of embarrassment. It is for the person to whom the news is imparted to continue the conversation. He must ask something, and what is he to ask? So far as the lady's name goes, and the place of her residence, all is straightforward. But what is to come next? It is absurd to ask whether she is pretty, for it is painful to the lover, if he is honest, to have to say she is not; and if he says she is, every one sets it down as a natural delusion. Delicacy equally forbids any inquiries as to her money. It is taking so very marketing a view to look at the affair of a friend's heart as a mere bargain. The only obvious and unexceptionable question is to ask whether it is to be soon, and to hear whether there is to be an engagement or an immediate marriage. If there is to be no engagement, the hero is thought more fortunate than ever. Not to wait at all, but to go in at once to connubial happiness and the smoothest of all possible loves, is considered a great triumph. The best imaginable lot is when a man has nothing to do but to hang up his hat in his wife's house. Any thing like an engagement is a diminution of the glory of matrimony. Engagements are romantic, but they are not business-like, and friends always take a remarkably business-like view of each other's marriages; or, if they do not do so really, at any rate, they pretend to do so, in order that their reputation as smart wordly people may not accidentally suffer.

Engagements, however, are really the natural corollaries of the modern theory of marriage which supposes that unions spring from affection based on compatibility of temper, tastes, and principles. On the contrary theory, engagements are unreasonable. If married happiness, depends, as many hold, not on this preliminary romance, or any antecedent harmony, but merely on that power of adaptation which enables any two human being who are forced to live together to get on pretty well, and fall in with each other's ways, there is no object in forming an engagement. If A is not ready to marry, B is; and, according to the hypothesis, B will do just as well. The great advantage possessed by those who hold this view of marriage is that they can appeal to facts. They say that, however marriages are commenced, they all end in about the same average of happiness. Great trials arising from worldly inconveniences being avoided, as many married people will get on well if they meet for the first time at the altar as if they have spent a couple of years in eager flirtation. Their adversaries are obliged to shirk this appeal to facts, and rest their case on the human heart. If nature has given a taste for poetry, a belief in constancy, a passion for romantic excitement, a possibility of a partial or total absorption in another person, it seems a pity to throw all this away because in course of time housekeeping will go on moderately well whether it has been thrown away or cultivated. If love is to have any thing like the place in life which it holds in poetry, room ought to be given it to expand. Long engagements are, in their way, bad things, but they are justifiable bad things. If two persons love each other, and love is the one great thing in their lives that makes their lives valuable, it is very difficult to show that they do not gain by a long engagement. It is said that the girl loses the best years of her life, and wastes away without the happiness and respectability of being married. Observations like this clearly proceed from the secret belief that one man would really do as well for her as another. If only one man would do, a crumb that falls from his table must be better than the richest banquet of any one else. Long engagements are, at any rate, better than nothing; and if life is a blank without this particular love, a faint existence is preferable to annihilation. Both parties would have a more equable and peaceful life if they agreed to forget and keep their resolution. But the people who prefer equanimity to love ought scarcely to judge of others who have a contrary taste. The real reason why long engagements are objected to is, that as a matter of fact all the love that most people are capable of may be satisfactorily excited not only by any one of a considerable number of persons, but by more than one person in succession. If an engagement is forbidden, the common run of lovers are quite happy in a few months, and are on the look-out for a serener courtship. But the exceptions—those who really love when they are about it, who cannot repeat or transfer their feelings—unquestionably gain by not having to undergo a total separation. No man or woman of a really tender and constant nature, and once absorbed in a great passion, either refuse to enter on a long engagement or regretted having formed one. The only thing is, that engagements affect not only the parties themselves but their friends, and why should friends go through all the anxiety and trouble of a long engagement when exceptional lovers are so rare? It is in the interest of society that these engagements are discountenanced.

The lovers themselves—if the modern English theory of marriage is true—certainly profit by an engagement of some moderate length preceding marriage. It is not only that they learn to know each other, and have opportunities of seeing whether the desired harmony really exists, but many fine feelings never blossom at all if marriage immediately follows on a chance acquaintanceship. The niceties of courtship are superseded by this levelling rapidity. In the first place, there are no letters, or at any rate none worth speaking of. There is a smack of furniture and dress about the correspondence of a couple that will not condescend to wait. Now, on all the principles of romance and poetry, letters are among the choicest flowers of love. They express feelings which would be nipped in the bud if they were not put on paper. Receiving a love-letter is undoubtedly a sensation, and a very pleasant sensation, and why should it not be experienced? Probably many engagements are shortened purposely, because one, or both, of the parties are conscious that they have nothing to say. But real lovers can go on for pages, and, what is more, can bear to read the pages they receive. A lover—a truly happy, ardent, passionate lover—can stand crossing and scented note-paper, and both are trials to the male heart in its natural state. Poetry, too, ought to be written, or at least there ought to be songs without words, passing to and fro. Young people cannot be much in love if they do not have "imaginings." But if they are to be married immediately, poetry is quite out of place. If a wife is a bargain, no one who has just paid earnest for her is likely to sing hymns to her. The Arab wrote his pretty verses to the horse he supposed he was going to lose, and not to one that was just being trotted to his tent. There appears to us to be no answer to this apology for engagements. The pleasure they offer is one which marriage does not offer; therefore, to forego it is to lose something, and the something that is lost is the very thing which is supposed to be the leading characteristic of English matches. If every one went through the love vicissitudes of a novel there would be no necessity for an engagement. If there was always a stern father who interfered exactly when a passion had been formed, if the parted couple were being continually thrown together by the most astonishing coincidences, and if the sudden wealth and dignity of the hero ultimately brought every one round, there would have been plenty of love-making, and the sooner the parson was applied to the better. But in real life things are tamer. If an immediate marriage is impossible, it is generally a choice between total separation and an engagement; and if the lovers adopt the latter course they gain more by it than they would have gained by being married immediately—that is, if they have any taste for the poetical and any feelings to express. If not, the sooner they get to paying taxes and ordering dinner the less will their course in life be ruffled.

The person who really suffers from engagements is the intended mother-in-law. It is she who is constantly on the watch and in constant anxiety, without any romance to keep her up. What are the notes and verses in a fine manly hand to her? She has trouble on trouble to bear up against. She has to care for the respectabilties, to decide what her daughter may be seen doing, and what not; when she ought to appear, and when not; who is to be kept informed of all that goes on, and how. She has to endure the condoling congratulations of dear friends who intimate a conviction that the marriage will never take place. She has to repeat a thousand times the version of facts which she has settled on as calculated to put the best front on things. She has to guard the interests of all those members of her family who are not engaged, and to keep their chances in life still open. If her daughter is unhappy, she has to receive her confidences, to cheer, console, and reason. If the lover is too intrusive or too negligent, she has to admonish him without making him enter on marriage with a settled hatred of her. Mothers who love their daughters, and who are capable of undergoing anxiety in patience, will endure all this, and smile under it. But those who are nervous, or who have only that limp feeling of intermittent regard which is often the only emotion daughters awaken in a mother's breast, either cannot or will not bear this burden. They begin to tease, discomfort, and worry their daughter, as the tedium of the affair tells upon them. They cannot forgive her for bringing them into a less pleasant position than they can fancy. If only the girl had married some one who would have taken her away directly he had fallen in love with her! It is impossible to say that an engagement which throws the mamma into such a state is a good thing. There may be penalties too heavy to pay for the development of poetical feeling and the delights of loving without thoughts of cooks and nurses; and one of these penalties is the unhappiness or the unkindness of a mother.

Even where the mother bears her lot sweetly, and where an engagement protracted in hope offers every opportunity for the blossoms of romance to spring up, the young people should always remember that they unavoidably give a great deal of trouble. The lover, especially, should move continually with the meekness proper to a man who is convinced he is a nuisance. The love-making of engaged people is very inconvenient. They want a clear room to themselves; they believe that no one notices their most patent overtures; they think that any thing like regularity of hours would be ludicrous in them. The lady has, indeed, a suspicion of the feelings with which her relatives regard the process that is so interesting to her, but it is very hard for the lover to realize he is a bore. Young men never see any household difficulties. Dinner grows for them; it is not cooked by a fiend who adds insolence to a love of perquisites and flirtation. Bedrooms clean themselves, furniture repairs itself. If the thought occurs that things must be done by somebody, they content themselves with a general persuasion that every thing can be achieved by the simple means of giving a cad half a crown. The ease with which they confront household difficulties is immeasurably increased when they come into the house as triumphant lovers. They are happy, and why should any one else be unhappy? The people who are in love are born to rule, and the people who are not, are destined to be slaves while the love-making is going on. Nothing but the most assiduous reflection could fix in their minds that, however little they may care for it, they are disarranging the whole course of family life, causing daily and hourly anxiety, and sowing a prolific crop of tiny difficulties. There is no moral in this. It does not show that engagements are, on the whole, bad things. The nuisance may be amply compensated by a deep and substantial happiness diffused through the family. Only, if he could but see the whole truth, the new-comer would be inclined to feel grateful for the patience that is exercised towards him. The best of all arrangements is an engagement long enough to give the poetry of love its full swing, and not so long as to tire out the long-suffering of the lady's relations.

DRINK AND AWAY.

"There is a beautiful rill in Barbary, received into a large basin, which bears a name signifying 'Drink, *and away!*' from the great danger of meeting with rogues and assassins."—*Dr. Shaw.*

UP, pilgrim and rover!
Redouble thy haste,
Nor rest thee till over
Life's wearisome waste:
Ere the wild forest ranger
Thy footsteps betray
To trouble and danger,
Oh, drink, and away!

Here lurks the dark savage
By night and by day,
To rob and to ravage,
Nor scruples to slay!
He waits for the slaughter;
The blood of his prey
Shall stain the still waters;
Then drink, and away!

With toil though thou languish,
The mandate obey:
Spur on, though in anguish:
There's death in delay.
No blood-hound, want-wasted,
Is fiercer than they;
Pass by it untasted,
Or drink, and away!

Though sore be the trial,
Thy God is thy stay:
Though deep the denial,
Yield not in dismay;
But, rapt in high vision,
Look on to the day
When fountains Elysian
Thy thirst shall allay.

Then shalt thou forever
Enjoy thy repose,
Where life's gentle river
Eternally flows.
Yea, there shalt thou rest thee
Forever and aye
With none to molest thee:
Then drink, and away!

—*Dr. Croswell.*

TO A DEAD HOPE.

LIE still, lie deep and still,
O my dead hope! my withered flower!
Bright nursling of a short spring hour!
Thus thy untimely grave I fill,
And treading in the sullen clay,
Prison thee down with a roof of stone,
And leave thee in thy shroud alone,
Turning, with foot resolved, away,
To the sound of thy funeral knell—
"Farewell! utterly farewell!"

Now sleep, forever sleep;
For should thy ghost arise, and glide
With its smile and its whisper to my side,
My rebel soul must fail to keep,
Against the magic of thy beauty,
Its faith with self, its league with duty;
But, in thy burial garments clad,
Would force thee back to life and me;
Or, if too strong a fate forbade,
Would choose a living death with thee;
Would madly follow to share thy doom
In the dust and the shame of the hopeless tomb;
Therefore I ring so stern a knell,—
"Utterly, utterly farewell."

Lie still till I am still.
When to thine image I am cold,
When the bosom which fostered thee is old,
When my heart has forgotten its restless thrill,
If this, which seems so strange, may be,—
Then will I dare, in leisure hours,
Beside this grave, to muse on thee;
And I will strew it with late flowers;
And thy dim spirit shall be free
From its long prison to arise
And flit before my tearless eyes.
But until then obey thy knell,—
"Buried hope, farewell, farewell."

In thy young beauty sleep!
What Time, the prover, might have shown
I cannot tell. Thou mightst have sown
What it were bitterness to reap.
Thine infant smiles might have grown
Into a cunning, baleful guest,—
Into a giant fierce and strong,
A power of tyranny and wrong
To crush the life from its nurse's breast.
But now in love and honor rest,
Only, while I ring thy knell.
I will believe 'tis wise, 'tis well
To say thus utterly—Farewell!

—*Frasers's Magazine.* E. HINXMAN.

THE STUDENT.

Air.—"Oh! may I marry thee?"

THE live-long day, and many a night,
Upon my books I pore,
And is it all for fame's delight,
Or all for golden store?
It is not for the golden pay,
Or fame's bright face to see,
But oh! to hurry on the day
When I may marry thee,
My love,
When I may marry thee.

The breezy morn, the sunset bright,
To me no gladness bring,
Nor summer with its bloom and light,
Nor freshness of the spring;—
Yet I have glimpses of a ray
As bright as they can be—
Thy fond look on that happy day
When I may marry thee,
My love,
When I may marry thee.

I thought to seek a soldier's lot,—
Bright fame, or narrow bed,—
Yet I am chained to one lone spot,
By love-hopes only led;
But heart and brain shall win their way
To some good destiny,
And hurry on the blissful day
When I may marry thee,
My love,
When I may marry thee.

ROBERT DWYER JOYCE.

THE LIVING AGE.

No. 880.—13 April, 1861.

CONTENTS.

NEW BOOKS.

Twelve Sermons: Delivered at Antioch College, by Horace Mann. Boston: Ticknor and Fields.

PUBLISHED EVERY SATURDAY BY

LITTELL, SON, & CO., BOSTON.

For Six Dollars a year, in advance, *remitted directly to the Publishers*, the Living Age will be punctually forwarded *free of postage*.

Complete sets of the First Series, in thirty-six volumes, and of the Second Series, in twenty volumes, handsomely bound, packed in neat boxes, and delivered in all the principal cities, free of expense of freight, are for sale at two dollars a volume.

Any volume may be had separately, at two dollars, bound, or a dollar and a half in numbers.

Any number may be had for 13 cents; and it is well worth while for subscribers or purchasers to complete any broken volumes they may have, and thus greatly enhance their value.

predecessors to their proper duties, which, we beg leave to observe, are not those of an oracle, but those of an educator. As, by the reviewer's own showing, his latent atheists are "silent," neither he nor we can divine their miserable state except from their actions. And their actions are those of men with a sufficient religious and moral faith to support them in a course of active and cheerful duty. There can be no surer outward proof of tolerable peace of mind, as those who have seen in Oxford itself the effects of deep religious perplexity on a man's practical life, are well aware. The dismal announcements of the *Westminster* as to the state of the Oxford mind are worth just as much as its assertion that "the school-book, the text-book, the manuals for study of youth and manhood, *the whole mental food* of the day," is "written almost exclusively by men who have long ceased to believe." Certainly this writer has a good right to deal out charges of "recklessness" against his opponents.

The fact is, that amidst all the critical disquisitions that are going on, and the importance of which to those within whose sphere of duty they fall we would by no means depreciate, the mass of men are guided in their choice or retention of a religious creed by an instinct which is called practical, but which really coincides with the deepest philosophy. They know that the one sure proof of an advance in religious and moral truth is (and till Providence belies itself must be) a corresponding advance in religious and moral character; and they look in vain for any thing practically higher than Christianity. Is any thing higher than Christianity presented by the apostles of "Positivism," or "Development," or "Humanitarianism," or whatever they choose their creed to be called? Have they made an improvement on the moral type of the founders of Christianity corresponding to that which the founders of Christianity made on those who went before them, and by which, not by intellectual arguments, they won the allegiance of the world? In their own opinion, they unquestionably have made such an improvement. We, of course, possess no criterion but the character exhibited in their books. Turn to the works of M. Comte—they are the most portentous exhibition of egotism in literature, not excepting the *Confessions* of Rousseau. The famous passage in which the founder of positivism informs the world that at first he was only an Aristotle, but that subsequently love made him a St. Paul, is the climax of the whole; but it by no means stands by itself. Not only so; but this teacher, for whom "Love thy neighbor as thyself" was not enough, but he must turn it into "Live wholly for thy neighbor," is perpetually betraying his intense hatred against the most eminent intellectual men of his time and country because they had failed to appreciate his superior merits. This sect, indeed, has at least so much of ordinary humanity that it hates those who (according to its own theory of progressive development) are nearest to it, but who are not of it, with a peculiar intensity. Turn now to the writings of Mr. Buckle. Ask yourself whether in them there shines forth a nobler character, a more entire forgetfulness of self, than Christianity can produce. Read his attack on Sir John Coleridge in *Fraser*, and say, granting the assailant to be in the right, what sort of temper he displays, and whether you would find it very easy, morally speaking, to sell all you have and follow Mr. Buckle. The *Westminster Review* fixes on "charity" as a virtue of which there has been a great development since the time of the apostles—though he would probably allow that its germ is to be found in St. Paul. To show his own exceeding "charity," he addresses a person of Dr. Temple's character and intellect in this style:—

"The fact is that the whole Essay is a mere mystification. Dr. Temple does not adopt, and scarcely, perhaps, comprehends, the notion of the life of the human race, or its growth by invariable laws. This view of the colossal man is a mere rhetorical phrase, *recklessly borrowed*, and loosely adapted. We spend (*sic*) so long upon it for two reasons. In the first place, it is *a flagrant instance* of the habit now prevalent among Churchmen (though rare in this book) of snatching up the language or the ideas of really free thinking (*sic*), and using them for their purposes *in a way which is utterly thoughtless or shamefully dishonest*. . . . We are far from attributing to the other writers *the same audacious inconsequence and the same spirit of glib adaptation*, but we find in each of them the same leading principles."

In the same passage, "shuffling morality" is sweepingly predicated of both Universities, though the one particularly alluded to has during the last five-and-twenty years absolutely teemed with sacrifices of worldly prospects for conscience' sake. Those who happen to know the Universities may also perceive here and there insolent personal allusions thrown in, not for the sake of the argument, but simply to indulge a petulant temper. No doubt this proves that by an "invariable law" "charity" is being rapidly "developed." In its mode of treating the unconverted, the *Westminster* is eighteen centuries at least in advance of "I would to God that not only thou, but also all that hear me this day, were both almost and altogether such as I am, except these bonds." "Pride," too, it seems, is a vice inadequately condemned by the religion whose Founder washed His disciples' feet. Christians do not sufficiently apply the gentle name of "pedants" to people whose education has been the same as their own, and whose moral experience is perhaps more extensive. On the whole, the evidence leads us to doubt whether a better thing than Christianity has yet been born into the world.

For the rest, we perceive even in this article some symptoms of a disposition on the part of "Positive Sociology" to draw in its horns. "No rational thinker hopes to discover more than some few primary axioms of law, and some approximating theory of growth." If this is the case, is so limited a science likely to do more towards "healing the wounds of society" than the primary axiom, "Thou shalt love thy neighbor as thyself"? We perceive, also, that the Comtian and Buckleian hypotheses of humanity are beginning to rest their claims to public approbation on grounds distinct from their correctness. But the most significant symptom of all is the decided tendency here manifested to relapse into the "theological" stage of science after the "positive" stage had been reached. This writer talks of "God" and of the "Creation," deplores the prevailing "irreligion," and is fond of using the term "spiritual" instead of "moral." Not only so, but he speaks of the "masses" as "lying in brutal *heathenism*." Does he use these phrases—the last especially—in the same spirit of "glib" and "reckless" adaptation and of "dishonest appropriation with which he reproaches the authors of *Essays and Reviews*? Or does he believe that men cannot live without religion? If such is his belief, he shows a strong sense of responsibility by thus cutting, in a slashing, anonymous article, at the roots of the only religion the world knows, without being prepared to offer any thing whatever in its place, except a sort of Church of Humanity, which he might be compelled, by any one who wished to push him over a precipice, to exchange for a Church of Animality, including not only the "fetichist populations" of Africa, but the African apes.

We have one thing more to say. The article concludes with a high-wrought appeal, in the style of the most impassioned "Union" peroration, evidently pointed to the young hearts which the writer believes to be in a state of religious unsettlement, stimulating them to have done with "hypocrisy" and "hollow peace" and "conformity," and, regardless of their own ties and the peace of their families, to leave all they have and follow—the Darwinian monad. Now, let us ask the reviewer whether he considers that a man of his opinions is guilty of "conformity" by holding a Church-of-England fellowship under an obligation to attend the daily service of that Church? If not, we do not in the slightest degree impeach his view of conscientious obligation, but there seems to be no reason why he should require any one else to do any thing very Quixotic or precipitate.

From The Examiner.

Henry Hudson the Navigator: the original Documents in which his Career is recorded. Collected, partly Translated, Annotated, with an Introduction, by G. M. Asher, LL.D. Printed for the Hakluyt Society.

The name of Hudson is inscribed upon such mighty monuments as Hudson's River, Hudson's Strait, and Hudson's Bay. He was one of a crowd of Englishmen who spent their strength in bold adventure and heroic suffering, of which the least valuable result has been increase of geographical knowledge. The story of their deeds, from the earliest day down to Franklin, has been one of unstained triumph, and often the real conquest has been greatest when there has been most show of failure.

Ohthere, a Scandinavian, was, as far as we know, Hudson's first forerunner in Arctic research. Living a thousand years ago, he journeyed to the North Cape, and thence round through Finnish districts, observing the features of a region and the manners of a people before unknown to the civilized world. He brought back strange, but for the most part truthful, accounts, which he related to Alfred the Great, and for which the wise king found place in his translation of Orosius. Through the following centuries Ohthere's countrymen strayed often in the icy seas, carrying settlements to Greenland, and even, it is supposed, to the coasts of America. It was the tradition of their doings, perhaps, that first filled Columbus and the Cabots with zeal, and set them upon their different tracks to the New World. Only an accident, which we may turn aside for a moment to recount, shut out from England the glory of having provided Columbus with men and material for his discovery. Having in vain sought aid from Portugal, he sent his brother Bartholomew to make petition to the English king. Bartholomew proceeded on his journey, but was seized and plundered by corsairs, and brought thereby to such poverty, that for some years he could do nothing but keep himself alive by chart-making. But when at length he was able to give his message, he met with far more generous treatment from Henry the Seventh than Christopher had found elsewhere. The king declared himself willing to undertake the work, and Bartholomew returned in high spirits to inform his brother, but learned on his road that the discovery had already been made under the auspices of Isabella of Spain, and that Columbus had even set forth on a second voyage.

There were other voyagers, however, whom Henry the Seventh had the merit of aiding. In 1496 John Cabot, a Venetian residing at Bristol, received from him letters patent for finding new lands, and next year he discovered what is now known as Newfoundland, but what he and others thought was "the territory of the Great Chan." Another Venetian, at that time in London, writing pleasantly about the greatest subject of the day, indicates the spirit which has always marked us as a people. "Vast honor," he says, "is paid to him, and he dresses in silk; and these English ran after him like mad people, so that he can enlist as many of them as he pleases, and a number of our own rogues besides."

John Cabot was the first whom we know to have set foot on America, Columbus having gone no further than the West Indies. The continent, however, he regarded as only a stumbling-block in the way towards Asia. He died in the year of his success, but his son Sebastian carried on the plan of discovery. By him the earliest voyage in quest of a strictly north-west passage was made. In 1498 he set off at the head of a little squadron, still largely helped by King Henry. Of his voyage scanty particulars are known. It seems that having failed, as his successors were to fail through three centuries and a half in detecting the coveted route, he wisely turned round and explored and defined a portion of the North American coast. Other voyages followed in quick succession. For a time England, France, Spain, and Portugal vied with one another, although our own country alone steadily persevered in the undertaking. The first great Englishman was Willoughby, who taking a new beat in 1553, essayed a north-east passage. He, however, after some months of fortunate sailing, perished miserably, along with a crew of seventy men. His companion, Chancellor, fared better. "He held on his course," we learn, "towards that unknown part of the world, and sailed so far that he came at last to the place where he found no night at all, but a continual light and brightness of the sun, shining clearly upon the great and mighty sea." This was in the region of the White Sea and Nova Zembla.

After a short pause we meet with a fresh cluster of great names. Frobisher, petted almost overmuch by Queen Elizabeth and her courtiers, made three important voyages in 1576 and the two following years. Finding little new, he did much towards showing the landmarks of what was already known. After him was John Davis, whose first expedition was in 1585, when he struck upon an unexplored part of Greenland, so rocky, ice-bound, and foggy, that he called it the Land of Desolation. Next year he sailed again, and in 1588 he thought himself sure of success. He reached the entrance of the bay afterwards marked out by Baffin, which he described as "no ice, but a great sea, free, large, very salt, and very blue." But contrary winds drove him home, and the people who had shouted with hope on his departure began to exclaim, "This Davis hath been three times employed; why hath he not found the passage?" Two great Dutchmen, Willem Barents and Jacob van Heemskerk, carried on the search; but Davis' first notable English successor was Henry Hudson, whose movements Dr. Asher's volume helps us to watch in detail.

Every thing known of Hudson is the story of four voyages occupying his four last years of life. The only family fact on record is that he had a son named John, who shared his journeys and his death. We first meet with him on the 19th of April, 1607. On that day, along with his son and ten others, he took the sacrament, "purposing to goe to sea foure dayes after, for to discover a passage by the North Pole to Japan and China."

Of the three attempted routes, all of which Hudson tried in turn, this, started in idea by Robert Thorne in 1527, was the wildest. To sail in an almost direct line towards the North Pole would be accounted a mad freak even in our own day, with the stoutest ships and the amplest supplies. Our voyager, however, with his little band of eleven seamen, boldly undertook it. He received the command of a small ship belonging to the Muscovy Company, an association formed for commercial purposes, but at that time solely devoted to the search for a northern route to the Indies. The party quitted Gravesend on the 1st of May. Harassed by adverse winds, they were nearly a month in reaching the Shetland Islands, but in another fortnight they came within sight of Greenland, to visit which they had turned somewhat out of their course. There they began to feel the hardships of their work. Thick fogs coming from the land wrapped up their ship and froze their sails and shrouds. Stiff winds set in, which hindered them from spreading any cloth. Great blocks of ice floated towards them. They worked their way on, however, and by the middle of July they arrived at Spitzbergen, which had shortly before been discovered by Barents, and by him named Newland. Hudson explored parts of it, and then favored often by clear weather and fit breezes, he proceeded on his voyage. But one day a dense fog closed round; through the darkness the men heard a great rumbling of sea and ice, and they found themselves drifting nearer and nearer to the frozen mass. There is eloquence in the simplicity with which this danger and the escape from it are spoken of, very indicative of the mind of such men as Hudson and his crew, anxious to do Heaven honor, but careless of saying one word about themselves.

"Wee heaved out our boat, and rowed to towe out our ship farther from the danger; which would have beene to small purpose, by meanes the sea went so high; but in this extremitie it pleased God to give us a small gale at north-west and by west. We steered away south-east, four leagues, till noone. Here we had finished our discoverie, if the wind had continued that brought us hither, or if it had continued calme; but it pleased God to make this north-west and by west wind the meanes of our deliverance: which wind wee had not found common in this voyage. God give us thankfull hearts for so great deliverance."

The year was too far gone for them to journey further with safety or hope of success, and they therefore soon retraced their course, reaching England in the middle of September.

This was Hudson's only attempt at sailing due north. The route was too barren and icy to offer encouragement to any but the most sanguine explorers. The north-eastern search, which was next undertaken, had more ground for reasonable hope, notwithstanding the gloom thrown over it by Willoughby's fate. Hudson started in April,

1608, at the expense of the London merchants, and accompanied by fourteen seamen. His plan was to find a way between Spitzbergen and Nova Zembla. After one narrow escape, in which the ship broke through a prison of ice, with only "a few rubbes," his party had opportunity for gossip and speculation.

"This morning [the fifteenth of June], one of our companie, looking overboard, saw a mermaid, and calling up some of the companie to see her, one more came up, and by that time shee was come close to the ship's side, looking earnestly on the men. A littil after, a sea came and overturned her: from the navill upward, her backe and breasts were like a woman's, as they say that saw her; her body as big as one of us; her skin very white; and long haire downe behinde, of colour blacke; in her going downe they saw her tayle, which was like the tayle of a porposse and speckled like a macrell."

Hudson's sailors must have been thrifty men if only two could spare the time for seeing a seal, thus beautified into a mermaid. A year ago there were thousands of Londoners ready to look at a less fortunate seal, degraded into a talking fish. Other animals were observed and captured by Hudson. He pursued his journey, visiting many parts of Nova Zembla and the regions within reach, and storing up much useful information. He would have gone further had not the ice begun to gather and beat past him, "very fearfull to look on." He then became convinced, not only of the wisdom of hastening home for that season, but of the impracticability of finding any North-eastern Passage.

By this time his fame was spread abroad. Soon after his return he was invited to Amsterdam, with the view of laying before the Dutch East India Company his schemes for seeking a North-west Passage, that being the direction in which his thoughts were now turned. So great was the stir that, had the company not engaged his services, the Belgians were in readiness to form an association, of which Henry the Fourth of France would have been patron and Hudson the first captain. Concerning these arrangements pleasant matter is on record in the form of a letter, written by the President Jeannin to the French king, and printed both in the original and in translation by Dr. Asher. Hudson's project in which he was supported especially by Plaucius, a great mathematician and geographer of the day—was to go further north than the other voyagers had done. For in mid-ocean, he said, there could be neither ice nor currents, it being warmer near the Pole than in the parts mostly frequented; and in this way, moreover, the circumference to be traversed would be lessened. The whole voyage to the Indies and back again could be effected in six months, whereas the journey round the Cape of Good Hope occupied three years. Jeannin liked the thought, and urged its execution. When Columbus started for the West Indies, he argued, the project was really hazardous and men might well believe it impossible; but here was a plan almost without risk, and full of hope. In the northern parts were doubtless many countries yet to be discovered, and which, it might be, God was keeping for the glory and profit of other States, unwilling to give every thing to Spain alone. Even if nothing came of the search, it would be always honorable to have undertaken it.

Before these arguments could prevail, however, Hudson was engaged by the Dutch Company. He quitted Amsterdam on the 6th of April, 1609, having a mixed band of Dutch and English seamen. This crew, ill-assorted, brought him serious trouble, and, as far as the North-west Passage was concerned, made his voyage useless. Yet it can hardly be regretted, as he was forced into the exploration of more important regions. In prosecution of his design he had sailed as far as Nova Zembla, when a threatened mutiny compelled him to turn round and make his way across the Atlantic to Nova Scotia. Ranging the coast and noticing its peculiarities, he visited many important places; chief of which were Chesapeake Bay, Delaware Bay, and the river which bears his own name. This river had been discovered eighty-five years before by Verragano, whose amusing account of his observations is properly given as an appendix to the volume before us. Yet the water is rightly called Hudson's River, for it was Hudson who first marked out its locality and brought it into notice.

In September he landed and made acquaintance with the Indians. A native tradition about him is well worth repeating in brief. Before white skins were known, say the people, when some red men had one day gone out fishing, they were surprised to see afar off a great strange thing swimming or floating towards them. In wonderment they hurried home to tell their kinsmen, and all flocked out to watch what some thought a huge fish, others a large house. As it drew near, they felt assured that Manitto, the Great Spirit, was coming to them, and all made ready for a great sacrifice and a great feast. In due time the marvel reached the shore, and it was seen to be a sort of house, full of unheard-of furniture, and with white-skinned men running about in it. The stateliest of the white men was clothed in red, their own color, but brighter and more beautiful; and by that token they were assured that he was the Great Being. Many were for running away, but the dread of rousing his anger held them back. The chiefs and wise men drew up in a circle as Manitto and two of his followers came up to them. He greeted them with friendly countenance, and they replied after their manner. Presently one of his servants brought him a sort of gourd, and out of it he poured something into a cup, and drank from it. Then he filled the cup again, and gave it to the nearest red man. The red man smelt but would not drink, and handed it to his neighbor, and so the cup passed round, and was about to be given back to Manitto, when one, a brave warrior, rose up and spoke. He said that Manitto, having drunk himself, had clearly meant that they should also drink, and if they did not he would be very angry; it was better for one man to die than for the whole tribe to be destroyed. Then he took the glass and bade them all farewell, and drank what was in it. All watched to see what should follow, and soon they saw him stagger, and soon after that he fell down as dead. Yet he was not dead: presently he rose up and began to dance, and tell them there was more joy in his heart than he had ever known before. He asked for more drink, and it was given him; and one by one they all drank, and did as the first man had done. Next day the Red-clothed One came again, and they were glad to see him; and he brought beads and axes, and hoes and stockings, and such like things, and gave one to one, and another to another, and they were all glad, and by signs they understood him. Often he came to them, and at last he said he must go now, but he would return next year. Next year the white strangers did come back; and they laughed at the red men because they hung their axes and hoes from their necks as ornaments, and made tobacco pouches of the stockings. They taught them how to use them, and then the red men were lost in wonder when they saw great trees cut down and shaped into houses. Every white man they thought was a Manitto, but the supreme Manitto was he who wore red clothes. After awhile the strangers asked for land—a little bit, just so much as a bullock's hide would encompass, and they gladly promised it. But they marvelled greatly at the white man's shrewdness when they saw them take the hide and cut it into strips no bigger than a child's finger, and so fashion a long rope with which they enclosed a great heap of land. That was the beginning of Mannahattanink, which the white men call New York.

Dr. Asher has no doubt that this story refers to Hudson, who had much friendly intercourse with the Indians. This was a cause of frequent quarrelling with his crew. To the cruelty which they were fond of showing he steadily and manfully objected. On his way back to Amsterdam he put in at Dartmouth, and there the English kept him. Seeing the importance of his discoveries they would not let him make report to his Dutch masters, and resolved, in summary way, to use him for themselves.

Next spring, therefore, he set off on his last voyage, in the employ of a company of London merchants. This voyage was by far the most important of the four, and the one in which Hudson prosecuted his long-cherished search for the North-west Passage; but the accounts of it are not altogether trustworthy, for the voyager never returned to see justice done to his work. He discovered and examined several important coasts and seas, the chief of which were the strait and bay known by his name. When winter came, rather than go home and give up his advantages, he adopted the then rare expedient of wintering in the icy regions. Having put up in James Bay, he resumed his voyage in June, 1611, but then a long-smouldering mutiny broke out. He had unwisely admitted into his crew some of his former rebellious party, and often before the crisis came they had shown spirit of opposition, whereby his progress had been retarded. One of the crew was a young man named Henry Green, whom Hudson had taken up out of compassion. This man soon quarrelled with some of his comrades, and afterwards with his master. On the 21st of June he gathered some of his companions, told them that there was not fourteen days' food left in the ship, that the master was the cause of all, and that unless they were rid of him and all the sick men, and so were able to sail back unencumbered, they must surely be starved. Such language found ready hearing with "those monsters of treacherie and bloodie crueltie," as Purchas calls them. A plan was promptly arranged and executed, by which Hudson and eight others were bound and placed in an open shallop and left to their fate. Thus perished one of the bravest and worthiest of the arctic explorers. A proper retribution fell upon the leaders of the mutiny. Sailing homeward past Diggs' Island, Green and his chief companions visited the coast, and there fell in with some natives. "The savages," we are told by Purchas, "entertained him with a cunning ambush, and at the first ambush shot this mutinous ringleader into the heart, and Wilson, his brother in evil, had the like bloody inheritance, dying swearing and cursing; Perse, Thomas, and Moter, dyed a few dayes after of their wounds. Everywhere can Divine justice find executioners." The rest on reaching home were thrown into prison, with what punishment we know not. An expedition was at once sent out in fruitless quest of the lost captain, and other expeditions followed. In this way the arctic search was kept alive. Hudson was never found; but Hudson's work, was continued, his discoveries were more cleary marked, and his guesses were many of them realized.

We have left ourselves little space to express the praise which is due to the Hakluyt Society and its able editor for the preparation of the volume before us. Dr. Asher, with real love for his subject, has collected every fragment of original and contemporary information respecting his hero, and explained all that was needful in a very pleasant introduction, which, though filling nearly half the volume, is not a page too long. The whole work, though of highest value to the student of geographical history, has interest enough for the general reader to find fitting place among the best popular reading. In time of frost and nipping wind there is special attraction in the story of a noble man who spent his life, and lost it, in service among icebergs and frozen seas.

IMPERIAL ASSURANCE.

In politics—to say it much I grieve—
The world, albeit in the face of facts,
Inexorable logic, wont believe
In totally disinterested acts.
All I can say is, that Savoy and Nice
Irrevocably are rejoined to France;
So now let commerce calculate on peace,
Take a new start, assured no war will chance.

To aid a just cause, France may draw the sword,
Quite without thought—save afterthought—of gain,
Whereof events occasion may afford;
New provinces, for instance, to obtain.
To vindicate her honor, if 'tis hurt,
France, too, may fight, but not with further aim,
Except her will and pleasure to assert,
And generous ideas to proclaim.

With forty millions, France can threats despise,
Armed to the teeth by sea as well as land,
Yet she inspires mistrust, to my surprise,
Suspicion, which I cannot understand!
Her army is invincible, all know,
Invulnerable is her iron fleet.
Then who to war with her will idly go,
With the dead certainty of being beat?

Come, therefore, drooping Confidence, revive.
Cheer up, dull Business; clear thy cloudy brow.
Now, languid Speculation, look alive.
Take courage, Capital, and fear no row.
Secure in strength, France feels herself at ease,
For none her enmity will dare provoke;
Europe must let her do what she may please:
Then European concord wont be broke.

—*Punch.*

From The Athenæum.

SURVEY OF THE NORTH ATLANTIC.

It has been the privilege of commercial and scientific enterprise to be pleasantly and profitably associated. The merchant, eager to push his ventures to the ends of the earth, by discovering new markets for his goods, makes the scientific man acquainted with fresh fields for his researches; and, on the other hand, the man of science in the course of his investigations not unfrequently reveals paths which the merchant gladly takes advantage of. It was the keen desire to reach Cathay by a shorter and less perilous route than that round the Cape of Storms that made us acquainted with the wonderful phenomena of the Arctic Regions; and we are now indebted to the great but very natural wish to connect the Old and New Worlds by the electric chain for much interesting information respecting Greenland and the North Atlantic.

The promoters of the North Atlantic Telegraph purchased, as will be remembered, the steam-yacht Fox, and giving the command to Capt. Allen Young, she was sent to co-operate with the Bull Dog in the survey of the contemplated route for the telegraph to North America. Capt. Allen Young has drawn up a report of his Expedition, from which we purpose making a few extracts. The Fox reached the Faroe Islands on the 2nd of August last. The scenery on the Fiords in these islands is magnificent; the land on either side rising to the height of from 1,500 to to 2,000 feet, pierced by vast basaltic caverns and faced by huge columns, but having many fine harbors where ships can lie in safety, and into which an electric cable can be carried. The violent currents supposed to exist among these islands are found to have been exaggerated with respect to their violence, and it has been ascertained that a cable can be laid down easily across the country. On the 12th of August, Capt. Young anchored off East Iceland, having taken occasional soundings from the Faroe Islands, the deepest being 624 fathoms. A travelling party, consisting of Dr. Rae, Col. Shaffner and Lieut. von Zeilau, crossed Iceland for the purpose of selecting a route for the telegraph, while the Fox explored the coasts. From observation and information gained from trustworthy authorities, it appears that no icebergs ever reach Iceland. Drift-ice is occasionally seen off the north and east coasts; it is called in Iceland "Greenland ice," and is the ordinary washed and decayed floe-ice. An extensive trade is carried on at Bernfiord in oil, expressed from the livers of sharks which are caught by Icelanders, and in cod-fishing, which is carried on by the French, who have generally from 100 to 150 fishing vessels on the coast.

The results of the examination of Iceland were, that Capt. Young determined on reporting Bernfiord, on the east coast, and Kral Fiord, on the west coast, as the most suitable places for the termini of the Icelandic sections of the cable,—and he recommends the south coast to be avoided, on account of recent very extensive submarine action having occurred there.

On the 12th of September, the Fox arrived off the east coast of Greenland, and on the 14th she was in lat. 60° N., long. 40° 10′ W., where soundings were obtained in 1,230 fathoms. This is a great depth; but not far from this locality, and nearly midway between the north of Ireland and Cape Farewell, soundings were obtained by the officers of the Bull Dog of 1,260 fathoms, and it was here that the ocean depths gave up a marvellous secret. The sounding apparatus, which was of a very perfect description, brought to the surface a large mass of coarse muddy matter, no less than ninety-five per cent of which consisted of the shelly remains of Globigerina, a genus of Foraminifera,—thus testifying that the ocean floor at that locality must be paved by countless millions of these animals, some of which were alive. But, more marvellous still, from this great depth, the sounding line brought up starfish in full activity, radiant with beauty, which probably enjoyed life, though subjected to the enormous pressure of a ton and a half on the square inch. This most interesting discovery, to which the scientific world is more immediately indebted to Dr. Wallich, who accompanied the Bull Dog in the capacity of naturalist, shows that no limit of life can be drawn in the sea. It has been found that the air on the summit of Etna, 12,000 feet above the sea level, abounds with Diatomaceæ,—and now, the ocean, at a depth of upwards of 7,000 feet, and about 500 miles from Greenland, is found to teem with animals which have hitherto been supposed capable of living only in much shallower water. "Here, truly," says Dr. Wallich, "is a fresh starting-point in the natural history of the sea." The presence of this deep-sea life is very important with reference to the question of the telegraph. Great pains should be taken to ascertain precisely the various species of animals inhabiting the ocean where it is proposed to lay the cable, for should this precaution be neglected it may be discovered, when too late, that some animal with boring habits exists at unsearched depths which would be fatal to a telegraphic cable covered in the ordinary manner.

We may also notice incidentally, as affecting ourselves, that while the great deep proved thus prolific in life, Dr. Wallich found the surface of the ocean barren in the species of animals which are usually found in its upper waters. This circumstance and the remarkable absence of drift timber are accounted for by the usual course of the Gulf-stream having been deflected by the Arctic-stream which, during the past summer and autumn, flowed from the north with extraordinary force, and thus probably lowered the temperature in Europe.

On striking the coast of East Greenland, Capt. Young commenced a series of explorations for the purpose of ascertaining where the electric cable could be safely landed from the Faroe Islands, and he came to the conclusion that Julianshaab Fiord is an eligible locality. This was carefully surveyed, and it was found that a depth of not less than 150 to 160 fathoms can be carried from the middle of the fiord abreast the settlement out to sea, with a general muddy bottom. This depth of water, it is believed, will effectually preclude injury to the cable from the largest icebergs ever seen upon the coast, as it is only by icebergs that a cable, if properly laid at the bottom of the ocean, is at all likely to be injured. It is interesting to hear Capt. Young's opinion respecting the nature of the ice around the Greenland coast. He is particularly entitled to be heard on this point because he has navigated the entire west coast of Greenland, visited the principal settlements, and passed through the instructive, though unpleasant, ordeal of spending a winter in the drift-ice.

He is of opinion that around the coast of Greenland, westward of Cape Farewell, there are two distinct descriptions of drift-ice, ever approaching but never meeting. One is found in the vast area of Baffin's Sea and the channels leading into it west of Greenland. This is called by the Greenlanders the West Ice, and, though it often blocks up the upper part of Melville Bay, there is always open water between it and Greenland, as far up as Holsteinberg. The second description of ice is the Spitzbergen, or store-ice, which comes down the east coast of Greenland, drifts round Cape Farewell, and is carried by the current up the west coast, occasionally even to the arctic circle,—but before reaching this zone it is usually broken up, and finally disappears in the current passing through Davis' Straits into the Atlantic. So near do these two great ice streams approximate, that ships bound to the colonies have in early spring passed up Davis' Straits between the West Ice and the Spitzbergen Ice.

But as there are two kinds of oceanic ice, so also are there two distinct classes of icebergs; viz., those from the stupendous glaciers far up the west coast of Greenland, and those launched from the glaciers high up the east coast of Greenland and from those on Spitzbergen. The West Greenland icebergs accompany and sometimes proceed faster than the west ice, and it is only in very exceptional cases that they are blown by gales on the Greenland coast, below the parallel of the arctic circle. The East Greenland and Spitzbergen icebergs frequenting the south coast of Greenland are very much smaller than those generated on the west coast; and on being exposed during their long passage southward to the warmer Atlantic wind and heavy swell, they are considerably reduced in dimensions before they reach Cape Farewell.

With regard to the "floatation" of ice, Capt. Young believes that the usual calculation, that seven-eighths of a cubical mass of ice is immersed, does not apply to icebergs, which he conceives are immersed in the proportion of six feet below to one foot perpendicular height above water. Therefore, in 150 fathoms of water, the smallest soundings at Julianshaab Fiord,—where it is recommended to land the cable,—no iceberg of the dimensions common to the east and south coast of Greenland could be grounded.

Capt. Young does not, therefore, as will be seen, apprehend any difficulties which may not be overcome in laying an electric cable in these stormy northern waters. But, after the failures which have occurred, we sincerely trust that the promoters of the great and laudable scheme of linking the Old and New Worlds together will deliberate long and wisely before they commence operations.

PART II.—DE PROFUNDIS.

SOUTHAMPTON WATERS lay, as usual, placid as a lake: the sultry heat of the passing day still hung heavily on the atmosphere: though somewhat of a breeze got up towards the evening, it was hot wind, as though it were blown from a furnace or across a desert. Lights had begun to twinkle in the windows of Hythe and Southampton. The moon was beginning to show part of her pale crescent to the south, a few angry clouds were gathering, and to this sign from the heavens the sea responded in heavy rolls and swells, and the breaking of the surf on the distant shore began to have a hollow and threatening sound.

Far out on the point beyond Netley and its fair abbey a tall, large-limbed man was pacing hurriedly up and down. He examined the sky, strained his eyes over the waves towards the horizon, and then began to walk again. This man was Horace Saltoun. True to his promise, he was on the look-out for the ship which bore homeward his lady-love. Some accident to the machinery had delayed it two days beyond the date of being due; and what with expectant relatives and anxious friends, the clerk who ought first to receive intelligence was pretty nearly driven wild with their importunity. Horace had repaired, like the rest, to hear the eternal reply, "No news of the ship." He was chafing with impatience and the idea of two days being lost to him, well aware that he was wanted in town. He thought he ought not to stay a day longer, and yet he could not bring himself to leave; he went down that night with an irresistible conviction that the ship would come, and yet, as he afterwards told me, with an impression not to be shaken off that it would bring him no good news.

Heavy drops, precursors of a summer storm, began to fall; which, however, in his excited state, he hardly noticed. Again he swept the horizon with his glass. Did his eyes deceive him, or was that really the smoke of the East Indiaman? Yes, he felt sure of it. Then he saw a signal; but the light danced about before his eyes like a treacherous will-o'-the-wisp, and he felt as if his senses were not to be depended on. Just then a broad sheet of lightning flashed over the waters, displaying the ship in its full dimensions, huge and black, so close to him he could have touched it with his hand. He saw a swarm of black faces on board, but not the one that his heart sickened for. He answered the hail of the sailors, careless that his voice was drowned in the crash of Heaven's artillery. The next flash showed him that his phantom ship had vanished utterly, and he was alone. He bared his head and let the cool rain beat on it, and then set off and ran into the town as if a demon were at his heels. As he neared it, he heard the cannon boom, and felt quite sure that the greeting would be, as indeed it actually was, "The ship is signalled, sir."

"I know that," was his brief reply.

"But it will not be in till morning, sir," pursued the disappointed "boots."

Horace did not go to bed or even close an eye that night, and by the break of dawn he was one of the first on board. There was no bad news for him, so far, at least. There was the usual number of helpless native servants, being frightfully bullied in their own language by their respective owners, who woke out of their ordinary languor for this laudable purpose. Bags of specie were in course of transport, sailors passed to and fro, and commission agents were trying to discover those who sent for them. When Horace could make his way among the distracted friends, unhappy guardians, overjoyed mothers and children, and all the rest of the motley crew who were calling, fussing, crying, weeping, and kissing, he discovered the person whom he sought—Miss Otway.

She welcomed him with a sprightly coldness, which rather staggered him; and whereas his spirits had been high they now sank to zero, and the man generally so eloquent had hardly a word to say: at least not any thing but exclamations not the most fitting to welcome home his *fiancée*. We all have, some time or other, seen the yearning expression of disappointed affection; we have most of us, at least once in our lives, had a dim insight into what that sort of feeling is, when

"We know the change, and feel it,
When there is none to heal it,
Nor numbèd sense to steal it."

On these occasions memory sometimes for a brief space does duty for hope; yet assuredly there are times other than when man "goeth to his long home," that "fears shall be in the way, and desire shall fail."

Exactly a fortnight after this I was in Saltoun's rooms, towards evening. His servant said he expected him in every instant, and I had fallen into a half doze in the depths of one of those comfortable, untidy arm-chairs which a bachelor who knows what ease is generally supplies his rooms, when the door opened, and Saltoun walked—or rather staggered—in, and threw himself down on the sofa. On perceiving me he gave me a half glance, and then covered his face with his hands.

"What's wrong, Horace?"

"Every thing, Paul. Cecile Otway has sent me about my business; whatever that may be now, for I don't feel as if I had any on earth."

"Do you mean that you have quarrelled?"

"No, I don't. Do you think I would have ever quarrelled with what I love better than my own life? I mean," he said, raising his voice, and speaking with extreme bitterness, "that she has this day, of her own accord, without compulsion upon her, without reason offered, sent me to the Devil. O Paul!" he continued more gently, "for more than two years I have been faithful to her—you know how faithful; for her sake I have defied temptation, as few men think it necessary even to pretend to do. Her very coldness was to me the idea of purity. That was a mistake, Paul; but no matter; I'll go on. I could not let a woman be ashamed of me. I did not want to have to blush under her eyes—so innocent and truthful and good as I thought them to be. Why did I ever agree to wait? What infernal infatuation! 'But it was her duty,' she said; and it sounded so well, too. And something else she said, of the joy of meeting when I had proved to her my patience and constancy. Good. Well, then, at her express desire, I went down to Southampton, and watched hour after hour for that hateful ship, until, but for the hope in my heart and the love I bore her, I should have gone mad with that darkening, dreary sea forever chiming out its monotonous song to me. Then one morning, you know, old fellow, before sunrise, one sees white sails puffed out, and the great ship, that looks but like a toy of the ocean, and bears my heart's treasure, comes on, smiling and bending in the wind, as a girl does in the dance." He stopped here.

"Well, Horace, what did she say to you?"

"She said, 'O Horace, is that you?—do get out of my way.' I can hardly help laughing now, to think how a child might have knocked me down the instant after she made that speech. I don't remember any thing more then: no, not even how I left the ship. She said afterwards that she was very glad to see me; but for the first time—no, not quite the first time—her smile struck me as being not changed, but cold: very, very cold: it was like lightning on the snow, a sort of refrigerating blaze; and she laughed her peculiar silvery laugh,"—he tried to imitate it.

Now, lovers are of different opinions to every one else. He admired her laugh; I always thought it a singularly heartless one. But to hear his deep, rough voice essaying to reproduce it was something too absurd. I laughed outright. He filled his short, black clay, lit it, and puffed away vengefully for a few minutes, then proceeded:—

"Well, Paul, when I saw her at her own house, I fancied, somehow, there was a difference; though I cannot say she refused me one favor that she ever granted me, yet in some fashion her favors did not taste the same—the flavor had gone; and they were always from the very first dealt scantily out. When I spoke of our speedy union—which surely I had a right to do—she said there was much to be done first; that she had friends whom she must first visit, plans which she must arrange, business, etc.: in short, on one pretence or another, she sent me from her presence for ten days; which time she allowed me to infer I might employ in sweeping aside my work, and procuring a substitute for cases of emergency, with a view to the speedy termination of our engagement.

"'Surely,' I said to myself, 'at last she will be mine—mine only.' I began to count the days and hours. Very well, then,"—here he moved uneasily about the room, as if he flinched at detailing the rest, and laid down his pipe, out of which he had been puffing volumes of smoke—"I went the earliest day I had permission to do so. She played deliciously to me; her music is something to wile one's senses away. I insisted on a private interview, which she accorded apparently quite willingly; then she said to me very singular things," he spoke slowly, and his complexion, never very clear, grew of a muddy whiteness; "she spoke of her duty to her God, and to herself; she affirmed that our tempers did not suit; that I was too impetuous, that she was afraid of me, and did not respect me; that she should, in fact, think it wrong, with these sentiments, to marry me; that she had long regretted our engagement, but had lacked courage to break it off. But that now she wished us to be friends—and friends only: to part! without bitterness, if that might be; but at any rate to part. It was best so, she said. I was astounded, Paul. What wickedness was this? 'Tell me, Cecile,' I said, 'I insist on your replying; did you contemplate this? Had you that design in your heart when you bade me farewell and renewed your troth to me, now a year ago?' She replied distinctly and calmly in the affirmative; so that her treachery was not a thought of yesterday's growth. I wondered that she could stand so quietly, and speak such words to me: I wondered she did not fear I should kill her. But she bore my long, wistful gaze without any sign of repentance or misgiving; though her eye flickered a little. Part without bitterness! Why add to the farce? It can never be without bitterness that men part from women who have dealt thus by them: for, Paul, it was not that she had lost to me three years of my life; for life is naught—now less than ever is it of value to me; but she has wasted my love, deceived me treacherously, stolen my faith, shattered my long-nursed dream and hope. 'I love you no less,' she said, 'but I wish, and have long wished, to break off all connection between us, beyond that sincere friendship which I shall ever feel.' She was proceeding with this odious hypocrisy: 'Now God forgive you, Cecile,' I said: I don't know why; perhaps because when one has ever deeply loved, that cry is the first which rises to the lips of those who are stricken to the quick. For if God does take cognisance of such things, he can hardly forgive her on her own defence. How could she be forgiven as she stood there, heartless and impenitent, looking with a certain cruel complacency at her work? If she had but shown one gleam of compunction—had she but affected to grieve over the agony she saw and knew she was inflicting—I had never told you this, Paul." Here he burst into a succession of quivering sobs, which shook him from head to foot. Ah me, that tearless sobbing in a man is a terrible sight! He went on again, after a little:—

"You cannot guess how the blood curdled round my heart and then coursed back into my veins until my fingers tingled and my brain felt as if it were on fire."

I began to question; but he anticipated me.

"Angry, no; not she: as cool and pleasant as iced porter," he added, with a dismal pleasantry. "Well, hot iron sears, but it is cold steel that cuts; and while she was smiling I felt as if she had severed an artery and I was bleeding to death inwardly. I forget what I said; I hardly knew what I did; but I knelt to her and implored her, not to take me back, but to tell me that it was not a premeditated deed; that she had not continued up to the very last to appear to smile and love, while waiting only for a fair chance to strike me thus. I prayed her for mercy to say that it was but lately conceived, that she grieved over the blow; that she had not kept it for two years in her heart to enjoy my suffering, as she enjoys it now!" he exclaimed, fiercely. "In short, I besought her, for dear life, to feel, or to feign to feel. Ah, my defeated supplications! how you stare me in the face! As well expect water to feel when you divide it. I was addressing prayers to the heart, and she has no such incumbrance; I was appealing to that which was profitless, *les souvenirs d'une femme qui a perdu sa mémoire*."

There was a long pause, and he began to smoke again.

"So do the hopes of our early years become the regrets of our after lives, Paul; and so the game goes on. '*Rouge et noir*, gentlemen; make your game:' we begin *rouge*, and we lose,—we end *noir*, and we lose still."

He made this sad attempt at appearing careless; but it was to me all the more unnatural and painful. Medical men ought to keep their heads and hearts as cool as they can, but I confess I left poor Saltoun with much uneasiness, and in a most unprofessional state of wrath at the conduct of Miss Otway. I was by that time on tolerably intimate terms with her family, and having an opportunity the following day of meeting the lady, I determined to have my say, and deliver my opinion to her in plain terms; if

I could not first influence her to alter her decision respecting Horace. Had I been as old then as I am now, I should have been wiser, and remembered the French proverb, *Entre l'arbre et l'écorce ne mettez pas le doigt;* but I conceived that Saltoun might have misunderstood her character, and in my conceit I thought I could mend matters. Under cover, then, of a chorus at the opera, I found my occasion.

"Forgive me, Miss Otway; but will you let me say how sincerely grieved I am that you have broken with Horace? Can nothing be done in the matter in his behalf? It is now three years since he placed his future in your hands; and his whole heart is bound up in you. You were never surely designed to be the quicksand which should wreck so noble a vessel."

She was amazingly self-possessed, and turning her blue eyes full on me, demanded point-blank,—

"Has Mr. Saltoun been complaining to you?"

"He told me how the matter rests," I replied; "you best know whether a true account thereof hath in it the nature of complaint."

She raised her eyebrows, and prepared to assume the terrible, because unassailable, attitude of a victim.

"I was very wrong ever to have accepted him—very wrong, and for that I do blame myself most severely; but I have long felt that this could not go on forever."

"No one expects that an engagement should last forever, Miss Otway; in the natural order of things, it usually terminates in a marriage."

She proceeded without taking any notice of this. "I made up my mind to put an end entirely to existing relations, which have indeed burdened my conscience most terribly."

I hardly knew how to meet this very singular line of defence, which seemed to assume that no wrong had been committed, and I asked her in what he had failed, that solemn promises made to him were to be broken at will. I descanted on his laborious life, his blameless moral character, and his deep and absorbing affection for her: I alluded to the pride he had in her, and hinted how deep would be the responsibility of those who on frivolous grounds dealt so terrible a blow to a man so affectionate and sensitive in disposition. Vainly; I might as well have talked to the winds.

"Did you ever love him, Miss Otway?"

She might justifiably have refused to answer this question; but she replied, with a provoking calm and an apparent sadness,—

"No, I never did; though I hoped I should do: and now, doctor, may I in my turn inquire if he commissioned you to put that question?"

"No, he did not: he uttered no complaint, still less desired any mediation. For this transgression I am alone responsible."

She paused a little, and played with her bouquet. "I assure you I have a sincere regard for him."

I made an impatient gesture of dissent. She went on, unheeding, "It is quite natural he should think hardly of me. I am prepared for that; but my conscience acquits me; with a temper so impetuous, rash; and masterful, we never could have been happy together. It was foolish cowardice of me to hesitate to tell him so before, and so spare all these painful scenes."

"Scenes which never would have occurred had you not thought fit to play your part in the farce a little too long. I don't envy you the ease of conscience you profess to have, Miss Otway; you should have consulted these scruples before you entered into a contract by which you secured your right to his love and devotion, his time and talents: you have used them, without sparing them, for three years. Well, you have thrown away a true and loyal heart, and a distinguished position; for there is that in him which must raise him to the head of his profession."

Her eye flickered again, and her attention was at once secured. A silence followed, which she appeared determined not to break. Perhaps silence is the most aggravating form of opposition which women adopt, especially when it is accompanied by a smile; and she smiled when she saw that I noticed her slight *empressement* as I spoke of the worldly position of Saltoun. I pursued with some heat: "You have acted very wickedly, if, as you say, you never loved him."

"It would be doing worse to marry him, now that I am more and more convinced I don't," with a smile of the most perfect heartlessness, "and you may be sure I will not continue in wrong-doing, and unnecessarily burden my conscience." She paused a little for a parting blow: "And you may tell him, from me, that he has not improved matters by allowing you to try to assist him."

I essayed to convince her that I was wholly unauthorised—that I had exceeded my own intentions. I might as well have remonstrated with a marble statue. The young lady left me, angry with her, indignant for Horace, and most heartily repenting my own meddling. The sage has well said, "*Give me any plague but the plague of the heart, and any wickedness but the wickedness of a woman.*"

It is perhaps according to human nature that Horace should have received my account very ill: he flew into a passion with me; blamed his clumsiness, my officiousness, his own petulance, and what he was pleased to call my want of temper and judgment, every thing, in short, but her heartless hypocrisy. Indeed, I felt pretty sharply that I had done no good, and I made an inward vow never again, on any inducement, to meddle in love matters. It did not add to the comfort of my reflections to hear Horace announce that he intended to meet her at a ball that night, and declare that nothing on earth should dissuade him. Knowing how violent his feelings were, and the serene bloodlessness of Miss Otway's, I imagined there would be a scene, in which Horace would only come off second best: however, he swore a mighty oath that go he would, and he kept his word—most unfortunately.

Late in the evening of the second day after the ball, a young man, who had for some years acted as his assistant, came to me in great distress. All those who were in daily intercourse with Horace became warmly attached to him; and the manner of this poor fellow plainly testified to the affection with which his master had inspired him.

Mr. Saltoun had, contrary to his usual custom, desired him to sit up until his return from the ball. Horace came back between one and two in the morning, unlocked his desk, took out a considerable quantity of gold, and then went out, without changing his dress or saying where he was going. He was a good deal agitated, as it would appear; and from that time nothing had been heard of him. This intelligence disturbed me very much: it was so unlike his usual habits; and from the fact of his not having changed his dress-coat and merely taking money, I feared that his interview with Miss Otway had urged him to some recklessness. I caused inquiries to be set on foot; but without success: altogether, there was so much mystery about the affair, that I placed it in the hands of the detective police.

Three days more passed in suspense, and nothing was ascertained, further than that he had been seen, within two hours of his leaving his own residence, with some characters of a worse than suspicious order, and that he then appeared to be much intoxicated. The night following, as I was entering the small house which I occupied when called to town, I was touched on the shoulder by a shabbily dressed man. "You are on the look-out, I take it, sir, for Dr. Saltoun" (the poor always call surgeons doctor, and address physicians merely as Mr. So-and-so). I replied eagerly in the affirmative. He said he knew where he was, and that he was safe and cared for; that it would be difficult, but not impossible, to get at him; but that he would, if I liked, manage it; and then I might, if I had pluck, get him away.

I knew my informant well; the name by which he was generally known was "Round-the-corner-Bob;" he gained his living by "looking after lost articles," to use his own words, and had been more than once "in trouble," as the phrase goes: his low brow, short-cropped head, and that indefinably suspicious look which constant apprehension of justice gives, stamped him in legible type as one of "the dangerous classes." But I had had opportunities of showing him kindness, and felt certain that he would do his best to assist me.

I made further inquiries, and ascertained sufficient to decide me at once to accompany him that night. It would be uninteresting to detail our conversation to the reader, for it was so completely interlarded with thieves' slang as to be utterly unintelligible to the uninitiated. If my starting on this expedition with a well-known bad character be considered foolhardy, I would remark that, with the exception, perhaps, of city missionaries, there is no class of men who so readily gain free access into disreputable houses and dens of infamy in London as medical students. Whether it be that we are a recognized necessity of humanity, or that we are accustomed to give without charge the benefit of our professional skill, or that we are distinguished, especially when young and on the up-hill side of life, by a breadth, bordering on latitudinarianism, in our views of the failings of humanity, I can hardly say: certain it is, that hardly any door is closed to the medical student, and the words, "It's only the doctor," give us the *entrée* into places where policemen are rarely seen, and even then, never alone. I must own, that the wilder the student the greater his chance of a welcome; while the freedom of admission decreases in inverse proportion with the respectability of the physician.

Within the hour I was following Bob; and we traversed above a mile on foot, through regions of misery, poverty, and crime. At that time "Seven Dials" was in the full swing of lawlessness and disorder. As we passed through, each of the numerous lanes were literally choked with people, moving to and fro with the sort of restless, aimless motion of maggots in a cheese. Women without caps, with disordered hair and ragged gowns, shouted in that peculiar, husky, cracked voice which certifies to a hard life and dissolute habits; gas flared, and children swarmed; "city arabs," ragged, stunted, unwashed, unwholesome, but of a precocious vice. There was a street chanter, singing some doggerel rhymes of the gallows literature class, to which he obtained an audience tolerably attentive. At one gin-palace there was some uproar going on within, and the glare threw out in shadow against the decorated windows figures engaged in active combat; the women had crowded round, and were actually kneeling on each other's shoulders, or holding their children up in their arms, to have a better view of the fray; the unfortunate little creatures screaming with delight, and reporting progress in language of astonishing vileness, interspersed with a variety of oaths. We passed on, and soon gained some more retired streets, which are, towards midnight, though in the heart of all this seething movement, generally very still. The houses seemed without life; the inhabitants dead or asleep. Two or three roystering fellows broke into a song, but we turned the corner and it died away; a couple of cabs and wretched-looking horses were standing, vainly hoping for a fare; they looked fit for the knackers, and the men were asleep on their boxes, having the look of fixtures in that deserted thoroughfare. We emerged presently from this to a district nearer to the fashionable part of London, but not a whit more respectable.*

In a forlorn quarter, branching from one of the many deserted and disreputable narrow streets, was a little court, swarming with people. The entrance was almost blocked up by men of a low-lived, sinister aspect, unshorn, unwashed; the small black clay pipe ever between their lips. Not without difficulty, we made our way through them, and then plunged into an interior darkness. We had no light, as, of course, we avoided every thing which could attract observation, so I nearly fell over what I imagined to be a bundle of rags, but which was, in reality, a human being stretched in a doorway: an oath, and some filthy language, was the return for my awkwardness. We entered a large, low room, which I knew at once to be one of those places that, under the pretence of lodging-houses, are, in reality, haunts of thieves, and are chiefly frequented by receivers of stolen goods, and abandoned women,† under the nominal superintendence of an old Israelite of the worst description.

At a table were seated, in close confabulation, two sinister-visaged men—their closely cropped heads betrayed their recent place of residence; a couple of bareheaded, coarse-featured women, their ears adorned with enormous ear-rings, were plying them with liquor, and the men were already more than three parts intoxicated. A well-to-do seafaring man, very probably the master of a merchant-vessel, was standing in parley with a brazen-faced Jewess, who was endeavoring to inveigle him into some wickedness, to judge by her abominable leer. A surly spoken female rose on our entrance, and

* Marylebone, which had, about the time I write of, 145,000 inhabitants to every 1,500 statute acres, and was densely populated by the lower orders, though nothing in comparison to what it is at present.

† In such houses, often the real owner of the property has no control over those who inhabit them. A house is let to one man, who sublets it; and these tenants often repeat the operation, so as to produce an indefinite number of vagrants in possession, who defy any ordinary means of turning them out.

seemed about to bar our further progress; but a few words, unintelligible to me—cant pass-words, no doubt—satisfied her. Another dark, ruffianly looking fellow sprang up, and put some questions in the same slang; it was replied to in a similar strain, and he also seemed content.

We passed through an inner passage and commenced climbing a narrow staircase. The air below reeked with the smell of spirits and tobacco; but as we ascended, the atmosphere had a peculiar miasma about it which my practised organs recognized instantly. "Yes, it's very bad," returned the man, in answer to an observation from me. "You see we've been down in the fever, near all of us, and that makes it not anyways sweet. Oh, yes, there's a many dead; and sometimes we hardly know what to do with their bodies till they are put under."

"How did you get the fever?"

"Well, I do believe it were some furniture which old Zacchy bought cheap; they said it came from a fever house: it were cheap, tho'."

We crossed a room devoid of any furniture except a bed, and beneath the counterpane my eye could trace the sharpened outline of a human figure; the death-odor proclaimed the rest. Up another round of steep and rotten steps, and a poor girl, one of those known as the unfortunate class, came forward. She was no stranger to me, having been for some months an out-patient in —— Hospital. She made no difficulty, asked no question, but, placing her hand on my shoulder, urged me forward, and pointed silently to a mattress on the floor in a corner of the room, with a couple of blankets tossed on to it; there, unclothed, senseless, and hopelessly intoxicated, lay, or rather crouched, Horace Saltoun. But oh! how changed and fallen from his high estate! "*Yea, many there be that have run out of their wits for women; many also have perished, have erred, and sinned for women.*"

I quickly learned all that was needful to know. For five days he had been in this wretched condition; and when robbed, stripped, plundered, and utterly helpless, he fell into this poor girl's hands, who, finding him abandoned, as being good for nothing more, took charge of him and sent to warn his friends.

"Yes, sir, it's a terrible thing: but I knew him well when I was at —— Hospital; he was always very kind to me. It was of no manner of use trying to get hold of him while he had any money left; they kept him too close for that. But here is his watch, sir,"—she drew it from some folds of her poor, shabby dress,—"a friend of mine took it from him early on, and gave it to me, because she knew he had been good to some of us poor girls. He was tearing drunk now most of six days; but he's quite stupid now: he hasn't eaten any thing that I know of."

She gave a sharp, hard cough.

"I'm afraid you are badly, Ellen."

She pointed to the unglazed hole in the roof that did duty for a window. "How should I not be, sir? I can see the stars through the roof as I lie in bed of a night, and most nights in winter I'm soaked through. I often think I'd be glad if I was took before the snow were come. You'll please to keep it quiet about the watch, sir," indicating with her finger the man outside.

Poor Ellen! her troubles on this earth were over before the old year faded into the new. With her assistance I contrived, not without difficulty, to get Horace conveyed away into his own residence with as much privacy as possible, where I established him under suitable care. Of course he had to be recovered very gradually, and it was some time before he could be pronounced sober. Alas! those were days of darkness, and humiliation, and desolating thoughts—seed, the fruit of which was bitterness and remorse. For six days this highly gifted man had herded with the scum of society—degraded far below the level of the beasts that perish—without, as far as I could ascertain, one sensible interval.

It is well for us all, perhaps, that women see us rather as we appear to be than as we are, or have been. Which of us has attained to manhood whose conscience is free from reproach? And when the day comes,—for which we all hope in our heart,—and we wring the hand of the father who wishes us God-speed, and of the poor mother who tries to smile that she may not weep, and amid the plaudits of friends we take our place by the side of the woman we have just sworn to love, honor, and cherish till death, which of us, I say, even the best among us, could not repent in sackcloth and ashes of scenes of wretched license where we have desecrated our better selves? Do none of us feel inclined to lay our hand on our lips, and wish that these saddened memories of shameful things could be forever sunk in the Lethean waters, and that we could, in ever so faint a degree, match ourselves with the innocence and purity of the wife whose future happiness lies in our hands?

How Horace escaped a fit of delirium tremens I cannot tell. This was his first outbreak, and a most awful one it was. Surely, the curse of his family had broken loose. I, perhaps, was the only human being who knew of his long-kept resolution, of his secret temptations, his victorious struggles. I remembered the particulars of his family history, the unfortunate episode of his sister's life, and, in spite of myself, I trembled for the future. It testified to the wonderful strength of his constitution that he recovered as he did. I kept him for some time under the influence of sedatives, and he did little but sleep for some days. At first, it was more than half a lethargic stupor, and much disturbed by dreams, but it gradually acquired a better tone. I used to marvel sometimes as I watched him in a sleep so profound that hardly any thing disturbed him. Then followed some weeks of very variable spirits, and he complained much of distraction and inability to fix his thoughts.

His recovery at length seemed complete, and he applied himself with his accustomed ardor to his old pursuits. His escapade had not oozed out, and not long after, a public appointment being vacant as lecturer at —— Hospital, it was signified to him on the part of the authorities, who were not unnaturally anxious to place on their staff a man of such recognized ability, that if he should stand he would have every chance of success. To the surprise of every one, he declined; alleging his love of independence and his attachment to his present employment. When in private I made allusion to it, he exclaimed, with much bitterness, "What right has such a devil-tempted man as you know me to be, to place himself wilfully on a pedestal, only to be inevitably hurled thence at some future day with the greater ignominy! No, no; the young vagabonds who form my audience are the most fit for me: if I have black sheep, so much the better; they cannot find fault with a shepherd of the same hue." Against this I had nothing to urge in reality, though I made some slight pretence of doing so in appearance; the insincerity of which he instantly detected and pshawed down.

An interval of fifteen months elapsed, during which, owing to engagements, I saw but little of him; though, as may be supposed, I was not without anxious thoughts. Towards the close of that period, a young surgeon told me of a disagreeable occurrence. On my asking after Saltoun, he shook his head.

"I don't know, but I think there is something wrong there. The attendance at his classes is enormous, and he does manage to pass the most prodigious dolts that ever were born. Any man that he pronounces fit, may be safely backed to pass: it's almost impossible for the college to pluck him; and he vexes the hearts of the authorities terribly by his unvarying success, of which he, perhaps, makes too much boast. He is confessedly the most original and able grinder that ever appeared, and a perfect godsend to all the idle scapegraces, as they know full well: moreover, he inspires most of them, and, indeed, all who know him, with a really personal affection. But this is not what I had to tell you. Last week I called him in to a patient, to consult on the advisability of an operation. He pronounced it necessary; and it was agreed that at a certain hour next day he should perform it, with my assistance. I was detained a few minutes by my cab breaking down, and was a little after time. To my surprise I found that he had commenced without me. I entered the house; there was no one to bar my progress, so I went straight into the patient's room, and he had then nearly completed the operation." Here he gave me the details, which, however, could not interest general readers: it will suffice to add, that, though not a complicated operation, it was one in which the slightest mistake would be dangerous, if not fatal. "I glided in noiselessly, and stood behind the patient, and then I was immediately struck by the deathly pallor of Saltoun's face. He looked up for an instant, but cut away with a steady and dexterous hand. But that single glance told me his state—that staring, vacant eye, and stolid, expressionless face. He was at that moment completely intoxicated. My blood ran cold, and my face grew as white as his when the awful consequences flashed on my mind of the smallest tremor or failure of nerve. I dare say the whole thing did not occupy three-quarters of a minute; but it seemed an hour to me. He completed it with perfect skill, and sat down without a word, staring stolidly at the knife, and the blood on his hands. I stepped forward, and in silence arranged the bandages, as though I had only been waiting in order to do so; and as soon as decency permitted, I passed my arm through his, and we left the house together. I quickly found my suspicions were correct: he was stolidly drunk, and when he had gained his own rooms, he burst into a torrent of abuse on me for what he was pleased to call my cursed officious meddling. Then he shed some maudlin tears. But bah! it's horrid to see this, or to have to speak of it in such a fine gifted fellow as he is. I gave strict charge to his servant, and to Mr. ——, his assistant, and I hope it will be a warning to him; for had any one beside myself perceived his state, or had his knife slipped, nothing could have saved the life of that unlucky man he was operating on, or of his own character: for he was too stupefied to have corrected any mistake. How he did it at all is a marvel: only the mechanical dexterity of long practice got him through." I received this news very gloomily. "Nay," he said, "it is a bad habit, but not a deadly one. There are many more old drunkards, you know, than old physicians." And with this scrap of Rabelaisian philosophy, he left me.

After this no one will be surprised to learn that I was quickly summoned to attend Saltoun in a severe attack of delirium tremens. There lay the strong man, raving of devils and snakes, and, as he expressed it, creeping things innumerable, both small and great; his face flushed, his eyes bloodshot and glistening, his tongue bitten through, and his black lips streaked with foam. He was struggling with all his strength against imaginary demons, and shouting at the top of his voice that he was devil-possessed, and that his time was come to go to outer darkness. "Oh, devils of the air, how they glare on me! Messengers of Satan, sent to buffet me, I'll have it out with you yet. Off, off! I say, crawl, crawl, creep, creep." Then would ensue a fearful paroxysm, and he would make snatches at the bedclothes, or cower beneath them, or peer over the edge of the bed, with an expression of horror and fright difficult to forget—murderous in its terror. The delirium was not, perhaps, of a more than usually violent kind, but it appeared so from the great bulk and the enormous personal strength of the patient. It required the utmost efforts of four able men to keep him down in bed. Now, unless physical force be applied so as not only to be perfectly adequate but also to *appear* overwhelming, I have always found it productive of more harm than good: so, after repeated trials, I adopted the plan of keeping him in a recumbent position by means of a strong webbing across his chest, which was fastened down to the two sides of the bed. He made several attempts, when he broke loose by accident, to throw himself out of the window. He told me afterwards that he perfectly remembered this, and that he did it, not from the desire of suicide which he afterwards experienced, but that he felt the conviction of being able to float painlessly on the air.

His screams and yells were awful, and when they ceased he gabbled incessantly—it seemed a veritable diarrhœa of words, sometimes in senseless soliloquy, sometimes in ejaculations addressed to the imaginary beings who crowded his chamber; imploring their pity, or deprecating their insults. Throughout, consciousness was, as it were, broken up into fragments, exhibiting an utter absence of that alternate continuity which I have had occasion to remark as present in genuine insanity. In brain fever the same incoherency is generally noticeable. When he became a little more quiet, he was a prey to a sort of universal dread, in which every form—every sound—all the relations of existence seemed to inspire him with a nameless fear. For this he did not attempt to assign any reasonable cause; and it was pitiable to see how he would start and tremble even at the shutting of a door or the entrance of his servant into the room.

The delirium ran its course, leaving him in a state of settled dejection: for days he would, if allowed, sit dumb and motionless, apparently without desire or will; his arms folded, his head sunk on his chest, and his eyes fixed on the ground with an expression of the deepest gloom; the utmost that could be extracted from him in reply to any question was, "yes," or "no." Here was the depression of the mind without fever so well delineated by an ancient writer,* who expressly distinguishes it from delirium or insanity, and directs attention to its periodic nature. At length he began to lament his fate in words: this was an improvement. "Every thing reproaches me," he would exclaim. "I have failed miserably, shamefully; and what is worse, I have no power to reform. Would to God that such a devil-possessed man as I am were no longer here to trouble the earth! The same thing, always the same—how am I to escape? Oh, wretched man that I am! for what I would, that I do not; but what I hate, that I do!"

The society of others, fine scenery, a bright sky, only seemed to aggravate his melancholy.

"Light!" he said, "I wish to God I were in darkness that should be eternal: the sunshine bursts on me charged with the memories of other days—of joys that I shall never know again!"†

"I admit, Horace, that you regard life thus at present; but you know as well as I do that it is because you have by your excess lamentably deranged your health. You have congestion of the liver at this moment."

He quoted the heathen maxim, "*Mori licet cui vivere non placet.*"

"If God had not intended you for some purpose he would not have saved your life. You have life, therefore you have work."

To all he would only gloomily shake his head. He brought forward the famous argument of antiquity: "*A malis igitur mors abducit, non a bonis.*"

"Look at yourself from out of yourself," I urged, "if that be possible: resist this foul fiend; prescribe for yourself as you would for another man."

I insisted on reading him the description given of the insanity of melancholy by various writers of the middle ages; also the treatises of St. Chrysostom and Castianus, who term it Athumia, or Acedia, and describe admirably that nervous despondent state which so frequently terminated in suicide among the monks.* By this he was entrapped into taking a professional view of the disease; but he relapsed when he perceived his inconsistency, and quoted, finally, Cicero,—

"Cause why I should commit suicide, there was *none*; why I should wish it, *much*!"

"That," I said, "was the Roman's reason for living, and not dying, and goes against you.

This he denied strenuously at first, but more faintly afterwards. However, I was too well pleased that I could move him to the exertion of argument to care much which of us got the best of it; the point was not to let the matter drop, and the discussion continued for several days on both sides with great earnestness. I on my part promised that if he convinced me, I would not only not interfere to prevent his suicide, but would advise him as to the easiest means of carrying out his purpose. After some little time it was evident to me that though he still argued, he did it as it were out of himself, and against his own inclinations. I felt his pulse.

"Confess," I said, "that you are cured: no man whose pulsations are as firm and regular as yours seriously contemplates self-destruction—the most cowardly crime, and also the greatest mistake, a man can commit."

He gave a genuine hearty laugh, the first I had heard since his illness, and owned that I spoke truth. From that day his spirits rose; he began to take open-air exercise, to notice children and dogs, and, in fact, to approach in some degree to his old condition.

"Horace," I said, the night before he left me, "I wish much that you would, if you can, give me an account, as far as it is possible, of your sensations previous to these two attacks."

He acquiesced at once.

"I hardly know how to commence, Paul. Do you mean when it was that I first felt a desire for spirits?"

* Aretæus of Cappadocia, in his book on the causes and symptoms of chronic diseases.

† I may remark that if Miss Otway jilted Horace it was not because she loved any one else, but from innate heartlessness. She pursued the same system until the bloom of youth had faded, and at last married a notorious profligate. Saltoun hardly ever alluded to her after his recovery. When love is extinguished by an illness it may be fairly supposed it was rather a passion of the physical nature than a true affection of the soul.

* Castianus, lib. ix.

"I mean when and how you first became sensible of it."

"Well, I am not sure, but I think ever since I was about fourteen. I liked the smell sometimes more than at others: there are days when I have smelt at a bottle of spirits of wine or whiskey with the strangest pleasure; but occasionally it has, on the contrary, caused me to shudder."

"Did you never taste?"

"No; not since my father's death. I was about seventeen then, and I made a solemn resolution not to do so: neither did the effort to keep it cost me as much as might be thought, for I had an inward conviction that the first failure would be a costly one. As months went on I became aware that these sensations of craving were much stronger at certain times; that they were preceded by dejection of spirits, extreme unrest, and irritability, and an odd feeling of sinking and faintness."

"Well, but when was the first occasion?"

"Let me alone, will you, Paul? I'm coming to that. The time when the fiend first grasped me so as to be felt, was immediately after my sister's attack: for five days I kept my own room, a prey to the most unaccountable and unreasonable mental anguish. At the expiration of that time it passed away, and I resumed my usual employment. Once again it made its presence known, and this time more severely. I used to awake at night and lie for hours full of terror and misery; the cold sweat breaking out on me at every pore: it was prolonged also, and it was the secret reason of my hasty visit to you; indeed, it so far worked on me that if, on the occasion of your coming up to hurry me down to dinner, you had entered the room five minutes later, you would have found only my lifeless body."

"Now, Horace! People usually have a motive, rational or irrational, which they assign to themselves when they purpose suicide; what would yours have been?"

"I can hardly say: not actually unhappiness, for, though at the moment I was gloomy at the separation that had just taken place, I was not hopeless; not *tædium vitæ*, for I loved life, and enjoyed it after my fashion; but the conviction came to me that sooner or later this accursed propensity would get the better of me—and if it does, Paul, surely, it were better for me to die than to live. Again it passed off, and for eighteen months I was free. Of the miserable night when I actually fell, I can give little or no account. I remember feeling stunned, choking, and miserable: wherever I turned one peculiar laugh haunted me; then I grew sick and faint, almost senseless; then I went home for money. I recollect gulping down glass after glass of raw spirits without one minute's interval: I did it quickly and greedily; beyond that all is blank. Since then I have not been my own master. The demon is occasionally still, but it is in possession. I have a distinct remembrance of the premonitory stages of the last attack: how the first instant that the mad craving for intoxication came I groaned aloud. I knew it, and burst into a cold sweat in anticipation of the horrors to come. I sought to hide myself from view: I loathed and hated myself, and every thing else. I passed the night in dreams; alternately enjoying the ecstasy of intoxication, and beholding myself as it were out of myself, wallowing in every sort of degradation."

"Why not have come to me?"

"I meant it, Paul. I had packed my carpet-bag; but I threw myself on the ground in a paroxysm of wretchedness, to which I never experienced any parallel. I fainted away twice; and when I recovered my senses, I felt that nothing but spirits could satisfy me. I could not eat or sleep for thinking of it. At last I took a bottle of spirits of wine in my hand and smelt at it. It made me shiver all over with a strange joy: it seemed to promise relief—happiness. In another instant I swallowed half of it ravenously; then more and more succeeded as quickly as possible. I never felt it burn my mouth; I only thought how happy I should soon be."

"Do you remember performing the operation on ——?"

"Not in the slightest degree. My first awakening to consciousness was to find myself fastened down in my bed, forcibly held, a prey to horrors unutterable. Hideous things glared at me from the walls; the most disgusting reptiles crawled over me in swarms; there seemed to my imagination millions of them—on the floor, on the ceiling, under the door: in vain I attempted to throw them off me."

"Do you recollect struggling to leave your bed?"

"No; and, Paul, I'm quite certain that I did not, for I conceived that the fiends were under the bed, and floating in the air, and that bed was the safest place for me. They frequently touched me, and I was surprised to find they did not burn; but, on the contrary, they felt cold and moist. I thought they repeatedly stretched out long glistening arms to drag me out. Then the tomb in Westminster Abbey recurred to me—you have seen it—where Death is starting from out of the tomb to strike his prey."

I argued the matter with him for a minute or two, stating that he had uniformly attempted to leave his bed and the room; but he maintained with singular pertinacity, that the reverse had been the case.

"There is one thing I observe, Horace—you always speak of being devil-possessed. Now, metaphorically speaking, of course the propensity to drink is a demon; but you don't attach more meaning than that to the phrase?"

"Yes, I do," he returned, quite stubbornly. "I firmly believe that a demon, bequeathed to me by direct descent, possesses me—"

"Collateral descent, I should say; for you told me your father was not so plagued."

He proceeded without noticing my interruption: "That this is entailed on me, and that it is an active and malignant spirit. I knew this perfectly well when I was tied down in bed; and I remember accounting for it on the supposition that it was one of the aërial devils named by certain ancient writers, which are slender and spiral-shaped, and thus enter into men's bodies."

"Spiral-shaped devils?" I said, laughing, in spite of myself, at this crowning absurdity. "You don't mean you believe *that*, Horace?"

"No; I believe the fact, but not the solution. Indeed," he added, quite seriously, "It's no matter how one of them obtains possession, provided it effects a lodgement."

His settled conviction of these impressions being facts—namely, his dreadful efforts to remain in bed, and his reception of the spiral devil—was quite too strong to be vanquished. What had entered the herd of swine might surely possess him, he affirmed: so at last I yielded the point, but under protest. This filled my mind with sad apprehensions for the future: was this a taint of insanity, or the effects of hypochondria? That when his health was quite restored, he should obstinately continue to maintain these delusions or hallucinations, was extraordinary. Was it the harbinger of cerebral disease—the first sentinel cry of the brain, to warn that the judgment was becoming impaired?

From many particulars conveyed in his curious description of his sufferings, I could no longer doubt that my unfortunate friend was a dipsomaniac: at least, that he was periodically attacked by that particular form of insanity popularly so called. In all he said the account was strictly consistent with the laws (so far as we know them) which regulate mental disease. The feelings first change; then—and not till then—the intellect suffers. The premonitory stage may be short, or long—years, months, or days; but before any real delusion is entertained, the feelings towards those around undergo a sensible alteration. This is what is termed the incubation of insanity, against which the patient is too often left to struggle unaided.

Simple intoxication is impeded spontaneity of the organs of sense and motion, but yet with increased vitality; in which latter respect it differs from sleep: into this, however, it ultimately passes, in obedience to the laws of oscillation, whereby tension is succeeded by relaxation. Delirium tremens so called from the nervous tremors which characterize it—is simply exhausted vitality of the nervous system. It is accompanied by sensations of terror, crawling, and so forth. After repeated attacks, the brain generally softens, the mind gives way, and the patient becomes demented.

Polydipsia ebriosa, or drinking to drunkenness, is not insanity, though it often causes it. A man may get drunk at a dinner party, or on a holiday, or some favorable occasion; others, especially among the lower orders, will have what they call a "spree," but return to their work in a day or two: some get drunk habitually every Saturday night, and continue so till the Monday; others get drunk systematically every night of their lives, but by following their usual avocations all day in the open air, they escape serious consequences for a wonderfully long time; but the insanity which is known as Dipsomania differs from all these. The patient has no pleasure in mirth, company, Anacreontic songs, and so forth. He rarely drinks in society, and is often abstinent between the fits, and even shudders at wine or alcohol after a severe attack. It is preceded by great mental misery, causeless dread, sensations of sinking. It is not with boon companions that he drinks, nor for the pleasure of drinking, but it is in order to become intoxicated; and it is in haste, in solitude and gloom, that he gulps down glass after glass of any thing that will gratify this morbid craving.

Bearing these distinctions in mind, the apparent inconsistency, the mixture of strength and feebleness, in Saltoun's conduct, will be understood, and the better traced to its true source. He recovered, to all appearance, completely, and for upwards of three years enjoyed perfect health. His conduct was remarkable for its regularity; his upward course in his professional career was rapid; his fame increased, and of course his income in the same proportion. He obtained the reputation of being the most successful private tutor ("coach" or "grinder" is the term) that ever defied the College of Surgeons.

"Grinding is a bad system," he often said to me. "A yearly examination of each pupil, by properly constituted authorities, as to the progress made would almost destroy my business, and would choke off all the blockheads and idle scamps that crowd into every profession."

"It's a monotonous employment."

"It would be if I always taught the same men, but I don't. My grand secret lies in this: I teach them only what is essential to pass them, and cut away any superfluous burden on the memory without mercy; I sift the lectures and books for the men, and give them the essence."

He seemed so well, that I was quite satisfied; in fact, I was too glad to condemn my own theory, and believe him a cured man.

THOSE DOGS OF ITALIANS!

"No doubt all the people in Italy might be called Italians,—

"As hounds and greyhounds, mongrels, spaniels, curs,
Shoughs, water-rugs, and demi-wolves, are 'cleped
All by the name of dogs."—*Lord Derby's Speech on the Address.*

Thanks, courteous Rupert, for the gentle gird;
We thank thee, peer, for teaching us the word.
As dogs are dogs, whate'er their build or breed,
Italians *are* Italians, be their seed
From Alp or Apennine, reared north or south,
In Milan's moisture or Apulia's drouth.
And why should Italy the image spurn,
And from such parallel in anger turn?
If "every dog," we're told, "will have his day,"
Sure Italy for *hers* may hope and pray.
Then dogs have such true hearts, such faithful natures,
Poets have ranked them o'er their fellow-creatures:
And dogs are blest with scent, to smell out vermin,
Shroud they in sackcloth, crouch they under ermine;
And dogs are swift their quarry to pursue;
And dogs are sharp of teeth to rend it, too,—
And most in this, dogs' wit our own transcends—
The precious art of knowing foes from friends;
And Dante doggedly through hell did jog;
And Michael Angelo's a grand old dog;
From all "sly dogs," who claims to bear the bell?
The subtle, supple, smooth Machiavel;
Columbus kept his dog-watch not in vain;
And Galileo's tube dogged Dian's train.
What was the *soubriquet* that came most handy,
To great Verona's greatest lord?—*Can Grande*—
Which means "Big Dog," and this was he whose power
Found Dante shelter in his exiled hour.
Nay, turning to the present from the past,
Upon what jollier dog was crown e'er cast,
Than Victor, at Turin? Does land or sea know
A sadder dog than wretched Bombalino?
Yet, ringed with fire at ever lessening distance,
He offers still a doggèd, *dour* resistance.
Venetia writhing Austria's hoof beneath,
Aye shows—and soon may use—her canine teeth.
And soon the parallel may hold more far,
Should Italy reslip her dogs of war.
Those dogs, who stoutly swam the Tyrrhene sea,
With Garibaldi—grand old sea-dog he!
Who—units braving hundreds—sprang to shore,
And swept—heroic pack—Trinacria o'er.
Let stormed Palermo, let Melazzo say,
When British bull-dogs showed more pluck than they?
Laughing to scorn e'en Scylla's rival bark,
And dodging fierce Charybdis in the dark,
To run, close-mouthed, their Royal Reynard down,
Till he took earth in Gaëta's walled town.
Stanch, steady, dogs, how quick you worked and quiet,
Scarce, here and there, one young hound running riot,
Till in Caserta's parks and paddocks tame
Hunting once more showed out—a royal game.
Yes, courteous Rupert—well the image holds—
Italy's dogs are up! Wolves—ware the folds!

—*Punch.*

From The Spectator.

THE CONSTITUTIONAL HISTORY OF ENGLAND.* THE POWER OF THE CROWN.

PUBLIC opinion for the moment has agreed to consider democracy the one danger of the British Constitution. Less than a hundred years ago, however, our fathers looked to the royal authority as *the* influence it was the duty of Englishmen steadily to resist. The distrust of the crown, it is said, though it has died out among a middle class, conciliated by the virtues of the present reign, still endures in the higher ranks, growing keener and keener as we approach the throne. Lord Brougham, who understood the position of at least one king, pronounces the Constitution safe until the royal line produces a man of genius. Lord George Bentinck, Whig by instinct and tradition, though not by party connection, always avowed his dread of the influence of the throne. The Peers have once or twice muttered at what they deemed stretches of the prerogative, passed over lightly by the Commons, and have once within the present reign compelled the sovereign to recede. Lord Macaulay, shortly before his death, declared the crown was regaining power, that the throne "was a more active estate than it had been since George III." It is certain that the authority of the sovereign, though usually concealed with care, makes itself every now and then distinctly felt, more especially in foreign politics, and that twice at least in the present reign the crown has beaten strong ministers on very essential points. There are not wanting observers who believe that in any great conflict of parties the crown might assert practically, though not openly, its old supremacy. Those who entertain these ideas may well read with interest Mr. May's sketch of the last open struggle of a British sovereign for personal ascendency. His first volume, though nominally covering the whole field of constitutional practice, is really directed to the elucidation of this great struggle, and is in that sense a most valuable contribution to English history. The story has been related in every point of view, from that of Mr. Disraeli, who holds that the king had determined not to be a Doge, to that of Mr. Thackeray, who thinks the king apparently a blundering maniac. But they all fail to explain the one point interesting to the politician, the *means* by which the king attained the measure of power he is admitted by all to have acquired. All rely too much on what they call the "influence" of royalty, forgetting that in the best days of George III. he never possessed a tithe of the "influence" of our present sovereign. We are indebted to Mr. May for making this point clear, for displaying with the minuteness of a statist rather than an historian, the material resources then wielded by the king, and available in his struggle for independent power.

George III. ascended the throne at a singular crisis in the party history of England. The great Whig houses who had stood in the van of the nation during its second and successful struggle with the Stuarts, had outlived their popularity. For nearly a hundred years their sway, though temperate and on the whole wise, had been characterized by that singular infecundity which is the bane of aristocratic administrations. The party had ceased to advance, more especially in the direction of social politics. They had become too exclusive, too much inclined to believe the Revolution the end of human progress, above all, too apt to consider power as a right purchased by their courage and their sacrifices. The nation was very weary, and had the new dynasty shown high qualities of any one kind, it might have restored a form of government more nearly approaching to the Stuart regime. Fortunately for England, the first two Georges, though not the brutes Mr. Thackeray chooses to believe them, were men singularly unpalatable to the English people. The nation, it is true, did not care a jot about the personal vices satirists so eagerly attacked. A popular king might have had a dozen mistresses as ugly as the Duchess of Kendal, or as fat as Madame Walmoden, without exciting wrath among a people always careless about royal amours. But the nation detested the German ways, tongue, and brusquerie of the new House, and was painfully alive to the loss of the imperial position Marlborough's victories had secured. Failing the kings, they endured the Whig magnates, though with an indifference, "a universal deadness" of spirit, which twice placed Whigs and dynasty in jeopardy together. The accession of a king

* *The Constitutional History of England, since the Accession of George III.* By Thomas Erskine May, C. B. Longmans.

young, frank, and English, re-created loyalty, and from that moment the power of the Whig houses began to decline.

The occasion was favorable for the development of monarchical power, and the new monarch ascended the throne with the steady resolve to rule. He would be a king after the ancient type, the real leader of the people, the active as well as nominal source of honor and advancement. The work he perceived was a difficult one, but he brought to the task some personal and many extraneous advantages. It is the fashion, now-a-days, to deny him all credit for capacity, and, doubtless, he was by no means the sort of monarch likely to succeed in a competitive examination. He could hardly spell better than Frederick the Great, disliked litterateurs as much as Napoleon, and had no more feeling for art than Peter the Great. It is nevertheless quite certain that he did, single-handed, change the position of the English monarch, that if he failed to attain his own end he did crush the dominant aristocracy, and that he did for sixty years secure to himself the largest share in the executive of Great Britain. Those achievements are not very consistent with mental weakness, and in truth his intellect was not weak. It was only narrow, as strong minds without culture are apt to be, and this narrowness added force to a will marked from the first by the vehement intensity, which so often precedes or produces incipient insanity. His capacity was, perhaps, never more clearly demonstrated than in the means he adopted to secure his end. In his pursuit of power George III. never committed a mistake. He never once gave his opponents a fair ground to attack his prerogative, never once induced his people to transfer their dislike from him to the kingly office. No monarch has been subjected to a more searching criticism, yet, under that microscopic examination, no trace of a plan to evade or dispense with the action of the legislature has been found. The king set himself to rule, not in spite of Parliament, but through it, and to this end sought from the beginning to secure three objects: first, a following in both Houses sufficient to secure him a free choice between the two parties; secondly, a commanding influence in the election of that following; and, thirdly, a ministry willing to obey his behests.

He attained them all, only to find that all were insufficient to secure to one man the personal sovereignty of the British people, and the process by which he worked out his design is the most instructive episode in constitutional history.

The king, it will be remembered, wanted power for himself, not for his ministers. He could not, therefore, avail himself, except when supported by his premier, of all the ministerial boroughs. He managed, it is true, to filch a few seats, but, as a rule, he was compelled to find seats pretty much like any other great borough dealer. The power of creating peerages was his only special resource, but, considered as an ordinary dealer, his resources were still large. He had, for example, certainly ten times the pecuniary means of any private noble. The civil list alone was £800,000 a year, and though this income was heavily burdened, more than half remained at the disposal of the king. He was also possessed of the hereditary revenue of Scotland, an Irish civil list, certain duties, the droits of the crown, and the revenues of Lancaster and Cornwall, amounting in all to at least a million more. These resources were husbanded with a frugality which made him the butt of the satirists, yet, in the first seventeen years of his reign, he ran in debt to the extent of eleven hundred thousand pounds, which sums were voted by the Parliament they had helped to buy. The people, unable to comprehend such expenditure and such frugality,—a king who dined on mutton, and ran in debt for a million,—affirmed that the money was squandered on Germany. Members favored an idea which screened themselves, and the king, while living on the revenue of Osnabruck, was supposed to be exhausting England for the benefit of Hanover. The money was really spent in purchasing a faction in the House of Commons, and all the patronage the king could seize was devoted to the same end. The sleepless jealousy of the country party had reduced the placemen in the House from two hundred and seventy-one to sixty-nine, but there were other influences besides votes to be purchased. Offices were showered on borough owners, on powerful constituents, on the relatives of members. The secret service money was used to purchase special votes on important occasions, one treaty, for instance, costing

£25,000 in one day. Lottery tickets were assigned to members, and the preference given them on loans. One loan in particular, for £12,000,000, was issued on terms so favorable that the nation lost a million sterling, and half the loan was assigned to members of the House. Meanwhile the Peers were controlled by less dishonorable, but more despotic means. When George III. ascended the throne, there were but one hundred and seventy-eight Peers of Parliament. Before he died he had added three hundred and eighty-eight, two entire thirds of the House being his own creation.

With absolute sway in one House, and some eighty votes in the other, enough to ensure him the casting voice in all disputes, what degree of political authority did the king acquire? Simply none. The power thus purchased from day to day secured him, indeed, vast influence as the dispenser of patronage, but it was an influence sacrificed day by day to preserve itself. The king never once succeeded either in arresting or defying the national will. He scarcely succeeded in defeating the aristocracy. Three times he was compelled to accept ministers he detested. Twice he was compelled to give up ministers he loved. He was beaten by a London demagogue, beaten by the printers, beaten by Parliament, over and over again. Twice, it is true, he enjoyed a full measure of power, but how? Because he had selected as ministers, men (the two Pitts) who were the idols of the nation and the aristocracy, and whose minds completely dominated his own. After sixty years of devotion to one end, pursued with unswerving purpose, with marvellous skill, and means such as no British sovereign ever possessed, George III. left the royal power weaker than when it came into his hands. His predecessor could veto an Act, his successor could not stop the one measure on which even his hardened conscience felt a qualm.

A FEW SIMPLE REASONS AGAINST SMOKING.

(Principally addressed to Sir Benjamin Brodie, in answer to his letter on that abominable practice.)

BY THE MOTHER OF A LARGE FAMILY, AND THE WIDOW OF THREE HUSBANDS, WHO ALL SMOKED.

1. Because it injures the curtains.

2. Because it is injurious to the furniture generally.

3. Because it is not agreeable to breakfast in the room when the gentlemen have been smoking overnight.

4. Because no man's temper is the better for it the next morning.

5. Because it keeps persons up to late hours, when every respectable person ought to be in bed.

6. Because the smell haunts a man's clothes, and his beard, and his hair, and his whiskers, and his whole body, for days afterwards—so much so that it is positively uncomfortable sometimes to go near him.

7. Because it is a selfish gratification that not only injures those who partake of it, but has the further effect of driving the ladies out of the room.

8. Because it is, also, an expensive habit which the ladies, not participating in its so-called enjoyments, cannot possibly have the smallest sympathy with or appreciation for.

9. Because it has the further effect of making gentlemen drink a great deal more than they otherwise would, and so weaken their purses besides ruining their constitutions, to say nothing of the many comforts and new dresses that their dear wives and children may have been unjustly deprived of, supposing the same amount of money had only been judiciously laid out at home.

10. Because it gives extra trouble to the servants who have to clean and to ventilate the room the next morning.

11. Because how are one's daughters to get married, if the gentlemen are always locked up in a separate room paying court to their filthy pipes and cigars?

12. Because it unfits a young man, who is wedded to it, for the refining influences of female society.

13. Because it puts a stop to music, singing, flirting, and all rational enjoyments.

14. Because it is a custom originally imported from the savages.

15. Because we see the nations that smoke the most are mostly the stupidest, heaviest, laziest, dreariest, dreamiest, most senseless, and worthless beings that encumber—like so many weeds, only capable of emitting so much smoke—the face of the earth.

16. Because when a man says he is going out to smoke a cigar, there's no knowing what mischief he is bent upon, or the harm the monster may be likely to get into.

17. Because it is not allowed in the Palace, or Windsor Castle, or in any respectable establishment.

18. Because the majority of husbands only do it because they know it is offensive to their wives.

And a thousand other good reasons, if one only had the patience to enumerate them all. Pray did Adam smoke?—Punch.

From The New Monthly Magazine.

MARY TUDOR.

NOTWITHSTANDING the sanguine stigma indelibly branded on her name—the predominant *gules* of her escutcheon, *rouge et noir* (as it were) in one—we have always felt a sneaking kindness at the least, a sort of vexed and mortified good-will, a something of chagrined but compassionate interest, in the character of Mary Tudor.

Unamiable and unattractive as she so pre-eminently was, there was an underlying nobility in her moral nature, such as we fail to discover (or are wilfully or judicially blind else) in her all-popular sister, Elizabeth. Mary was, at any rate, sternly sincere; and she was memorably capable of two passionate attachments, which, otherwise directed and controlled, might have won the world's love and admiration, instead of involving her in scorn and reproach,—she was even servile in her hearty devotion to the cause of her Church, and she was not only profuse but constant in her affection to a very cold, neglectful, and thankless husband.

If it be true, as alleged, that a blunder is worse than a crime, then was Mary's reign worse than criminal, for it was a blunder throughout. She was not strong enough for the place. For her the post of honor would have been a private station,—the more private the better. Haply she might not, in that case, and on that condition, have belied the promise of her youth,—

> "She is young, and of a noble, modest nature;
> I hope she will deserve well," *

as Shakspeare (albeit a true Elizabethan), unstinted in sympathy with them both, makes dying Katherine say of her "young daughter," when praying that the dews of heaven may fall thick in blessings on her, and, as a last request, beseeching the king not to neglect this "model of their chaste loves," but to "give her virtuous breeding," and preserve his motherless girl from the pangs of absolute orphanage.

Mary had been educated according to the austere directions of that second Quintilian, as his contemporaries called him, the learned Spaniard, Ludovicus Vives, whom Katherine had desired to draw up a code of instructions for the observance of her daughter. Rigid were the rules enforced by Vives, in compliance with royal request. Mary was to read no idle books of chivalry or romance. All such productions as Amadis of Gaul, or Margalone and the Fairy Melusina, he would consign to the flames, as unrelentingly as the curate in "Don Quixote." Pyramus and Thisbe (in the Flemish) and Tirante the White (in the Spanish) are entered in his Index Prohibitorum. Lancelot de Lac, and Florice and Blanche, and ever so many more, he denounces as *libri pestiferi*, to be abjured by all young Christian souls. He prescribes in their room and stead (in addition to selected portions of the Old and New Testaments) the works of Cyprian, Jerome, Augustine, and Ambrose; Plato, Cicero, Seneca's Maxims, the Paraphrase of Erasmus, and the Utopia of Sir Thomas More. From his allowance of classical poets he does not exclude the Pharsalia of Lucan, the tragedies of Seneca, and elegant extracts from Horace. Cards, dice, and showy attire, he thinks only not worse than the pestiferous romances aforesaid. Mary is to work hard at Greek and Latin, learning the rules and exercises by heart, daily, and reading them two or three times over before going to bed. She is to converse with her tutor in Latin, and to be frequently translating English into that language. If stories or story-books or some kind she must have, they are to be exclusively historical, sacred, or classical—his only exception being the story of Griselda, which is recognized as a permissible fiction for the delectation of young folks. Griselda, by the way, came afterwards to be considered in England, by one (the Spanish) party at least, as the prototype of poor, patient, sorely tried, and cruelly provoked Queen Katherine.

The system authorized by Vives was faithfully carried out, to Mary's life-long prejudice. Miss Strickland holds her forth as an historical example of "the noxious effect that over-education has at a very tender age," * and is convinced that these precocious studies laid the foundation for her melancholy temperament and delicate health.

At the same time it is observable that the young lady did not absolutely debar herself of recreation, and that of a questionable kind. She seems to have been fond of betting, and to have lost a tidy sum now and then in certain gambling transactions. But no shadow of a stain rests on her perfect

* King Henry VIII., Act IV. Sc. 2.

* Lives of the Queens of England, vol. v.

propriety in other respects. Vainly have the disaffected endeavored to hunt up charges against her, or searched diaries and documents through and through for matter for an indictment. "The search has been vain: these records speak only of charity, affection to her little sister, kindness to her dependants, feminine accomplishments, delicate health, generosity to her god-children, many of whom were orphans dependent on her alms, fondness for birds—very little hunting and hawking is mentioned, and no bear-baiting. Her time, indeed, passed most blamelessly, if the gaming propensities above mentioned may be considered rather faults of the court when she visited it, than faults of hers." *

In this gambling propensity she was her father's daughter. In few other respects did she take after that side of the house. She was in the main her mother's child, born and bred. And in that mother's misfortunes she shared only too deeply, and too soon. Keenly she resented Katherine's wrongs, and warmly asserted her indefeasible rights. She wrote strongly-worded letters † to her father, in defence of her own legitimacy and righteous title to the throne, which Henry was pleased to treat as the outburst of a petulant child. A tight curb must be kept on this fractious girl; but though her spirit might be, and was considerably, depressed and cowed, it had too much of the Tudor in it to be broken. Sharply tried must it have been, to the utmost tension, when baby Elizabeth, giddy Anne Boleyn's child,—the child of that adventuress commoner by whom Mary's mother had been supplanted,—was declared heiress of the realm; while Mary herself was denied the title of princess, and kept as a kind of state prisoner, apart from the divorced queen her mother. No wonder the iron entered into her soul.

The lessons of adversity, as Sir Bulwer Lytton has remarked, are not always salutary—sometimes they soften and amend, but as often they indurate and pervert. "If we consider ourselves more harshly treated by fate than those around us, and do not acknowledge in our own deeds the justice of the severity, we become too apt to deem the world our enemy, to case ourselves in defiance, to wrestle against our softer self, and to indulge the darker passions which are so easily fermented by the sense of injustice." * Through some such process as this had Mary's inner being to pass; and the result was bitterness to herself and others.

How happy had it been for Mary, exclaims Hartley Coleridge, had she died a nun, or sunk uncrowned beneath the weight of royal sorrow! The comfort of a worse than widowed mother—the duteous daughter of a father who disowned and bastardized her, the devoted confessor of an oppressed and plundered Church, she had been a saint to a generous Protestant no less than to the sympathizing Catholic, had her rival's success consigned her to the cloister, or the overthrow of her religion to a grave. "The Princess Mary had been consecrated to memory had the Queen Mary never reigned." †

Hartley speaks in the tolerant spirit of a generation which can allude to Mary without the invariable prefix of that damning epithet, which our Protestant forefathers were apt to account (at least in practice) an indispensable adjunct. Nay, we find the elder Coleridge, at one time, protesting against the growing disinclination to so orthodox a traditional title as that of Bloody Mary. It was a squeamish-looking sign of the times, he augured, and boded no good to Church or State. His satire is pointed blank against the spurious sentimentalism which

"Lamonts the advice that soured a milky queen
(For "bloody" all enlightened men confess
An antiquated error of the press);
Who, rapt by zeal beyond her sex's bounds,
With actual cautery stanched the Church's wounds." ‡

Certainly no one will suppose Queen Mary to be the subject of Prior's stanza, in a feeble copy of verses that glorify one of our sovereign ladies—

"She held the sword and balance right,
And sought her people's good;
In clemency she did delight,
Her reign not stained with blood;" §

the two last lines being so exquisitely inappropriate to *la sanglante*. But the good taste of the times has ratified the disuse, by degrees, of an adjective which now appears to be the hideous word-of-all-work in the

* Lives of the Queens of England, vol. v.

† See Froude's History of England, vol. ii. ch. vii.

* The Last Days of Pompeii, book iii. ch. xi.

† Ignoramus on the Fine Arts, Essay ii.

‡ Poems by S. T. Coleridge: *Sancti Dominici Pallium.*

§ Prior, The Viceroy.

working man's table of execrations. A word so emphatically monopolized by cads and cadgers, cabbies and costermongers, tinkers and dustmen, coalheavers and bargees, as their favorite expletive, when swelling out a period with something that shall sound spicily profane,—and, to do them justice, they are as lavish of this expletive, throughout the members of a sentence, as ever were the Greeks with their innocent *δε*,—now that the adjective aforesaid is thus appropriated by street blackguards, and by them made to form the backbone (and ribs) of their mother-tongue, one cannot but think it time, for this if for no other reason, to drop the "bloody" when speaking of Queen Mary—at any rate out of Exeter Hall, in the month of May.

Let us take a hasty survey of some of the sentences passed upon Mary's memory, by historical judges of different schools and opposite tempers. David Hume—whose prestige it still is, deservedly or otherwise, to have written The History of England—pronounces her to have possessed few qualities either estimable or amiable, and her person to have been as little engaging as her behavior and address. Her characteristics are tabulated in a category unpleasantly composed of obstinacy, bigotry, violence, cruelty, malignity, revenge, and tyranny; all of which are said to have taken a tincture from her bad temper and narrow understanding. And amidst that complication of vices which entered into her composition, Mr. Hume can "scarcely find any virtue but sincerity," a quality which he owns her to have (seemingly) maintained through her whole life, except in the beginning of her reign, "when the necessity of her affairs obliged her to make some promises to the Protestants, which she certainly never intended to perform. But in these cases a weak, bigoted woman, under the government of priests, easily finds casuistry sufficient to justify to herself the violation of a promise." The historian allows,* too, that Mary appears, as well as her father, to have been "susceptible of some attachments of friendship" —and this, in her case, without the caprice and inconsistency which were so remarkable in Henry. Nor does he blink the fact, that in many circumstances of her life she gave indications of resolution and vigor of mind —a quality, he remarks, which seems to have been inherent in her family.

* Hume, History of England, ch. xxxvii.

No one of our historians, as Mr. Hallam observes, has been so severe on Mary's reign, except on a religious account, as Carte, on the authority of the letters of Noailles; while Dr. Lingard, though with these letters before him, has softened and suppressed, till she appears honest and even amiable. To Mr. Hallam himself,—admitting that the French ambassador had a temptation to exaggerate the faults of a government wholly devoted to Spain,—it is quite manifest, that Mary's reign was inglorious, her capacity narrow, and her temper sanguinary; that, although conscientious in some respects, she was as capable of dissimulation as her sister, and of breach of faith as her husband; that she obstinately and wilfully sacrificed her subjects' affections and interests to a misplaced and discreditable attachment; and that the words with which Carte has concluded the character of this unlamented sovereign, though little pleasing to men of Dr. Lingard's profession, are perfectly just.

The words are simply and severely these: "Having reduced the nation to the brink of ruin, she left it, by her seasonable disease, to be restored by her admirable successor to its ancient prosperity and glory." *

Professor Blunt's is but a pungent paraphrase of Carte's summing-up, when he says, in reference to the fires of Smithfield and elsewhere, "How many more might have been added to the number of victims, had Mary's life been spared, it is impossible to conjecture, but happily those days were shortened; and on the 17th of November she herself ended a reign of continued disaster: Calais, which had been in possession of the English since the battle of Crecy, and then reckoned the jewel of the crown, lost; and lost apparently because the government dared not call a parliament to provide means of defence, such was its unpopularity; . . . an exchequer too much exhausted to right itself; the learned men in exile; . . . capital offences greatly multiplied, fifty-two persons being executed at Oxford at one sessions; a pestilence depopulating the country

* At the same time, Mr. Hallam fully admits that Lingard has proved Elizabeth to have been as dangerous a prisoner, as she afterwards found the Queen of Scotts.—*Constitutional History of England, vol. i. ch. ii.*

to such a degree as to excite fears of a French invasion by reason of the nation's weakness; for the inhabitants of the village ceased, might Elizabeth say on her accession; they ceased in Israel, until that I arose, that I arose a mother in Israel." *

We are as far removed as possible—*quàm longissimè*—from those who would "diminish the aversion" (in Burnet's phrase) felt towards the Marian persecutions—and whom Mr. Hallam somewhat sternly counsels to "avoid for the future either such panegyrics on Mary and her advisers, or such insidious extenuations of her persecutions as we have lately read," † and which he not unreasonably says, do not excite a favorable impression of the sincerity of these writers in the principles of toleration to which they profess to have been converted. With or for polemics of this order we have not a word to say.

A more tolerant feeling towards the unhappy queen need not, however, be at all symptomatic of a less distaste for Smithfield fires and fagots. Partisan apologists apart, Protestantism is learning to make allowances for individual infirmities, and to recognize the possible conjunction of a bigoted will with hysterical sincerity of creed. Mary might shed much blood, and yet not be bloodthirsty, after the tigress type. She might sign the death-warrants of four or five hundred men, women, and children, gentle and simple, learned and untaught, and yet have a certain "piety" of her own, to the morbid excess of which, in fact, these poor people owed their death. Hear, on this point, the unimpeachable testimony of a Lady Margaret Professor of Divinity, already our creditor for one citation. "Her sincere and disinterested devotion to the Roman Catholic persuasion was the virtue, the passion it might rather be said, of her life; the piety of her mother had imparted to her in her cradle a faith, which the subsequent sufferings of that mother must have hallowed in her sight." * A more recent contributor to the *Quarterly Review*, who, while admitting Elizabeth to have been a born ruler, pronounces her inferior to Mary in every moral quality, says of the latter, that "her somewhat austere virtues, her unbending rectitude, her sincere, though mistaken piety, would have rendered her respected in private life," * though on the throne they proved so injurious to both ruler and realm. Mr. Leigh Hunt, again, confessed long since that he pitied "'Bloody Mary,' as she has been called," almost as much as any unfortunate sovereign on record. She caused horrible and odious suffering, he admits; but she also suffered horribly herself, and became odious where she would fain have been loved. "She had a bigoted education and a complexional melancholy; was stunted in person, plain in face, with impressive but gloomy eyes; a wife with affections unrequited; and a persecuting, unpopular, but conscientious sovereign. She derived little pleasure apparently from having her way, even in religious matters; but acted as she did out of a narrow sense of duty; and she proved her honesty, however perverted, by a perpetual anxiety and uneasiness." † In another work the same kindly writer expresses his deep commiseration for one who ended with having nobody to love her, not even the bigots in whose cause she lost the love of her people. And he would have us remember whose daughter she was, and under what circumstances born and bred: that she inherited the tyrannical tendencies of her father, and the melancholy and stubbornness of her Spanish mother; and that she "had the misfortune, say rather the unspeakable misery, of being taught to think it just to commit her fellow-creatures to the flames, for doing no more than she stubbornly did herself, namely, vindicate the right of having their own opinion." Above all, he would have us remember, that she was not happy; that it was not in gayety or sheer unfeelingness that she did what she thus frightfully thought to be her duty.

"She suffered bitterly herself; and suffered too, not merely for herself and her own personal sorrows, but sharply for her sense of the public welfare, and that of men's very souls. In sending people to the stake, she fancied (with the dreadful involuntary blasphemy taught her by her creed) that the measure was necessary, in order to save millions from eternal wretchedness; and if in this perverted sense of duty there was a willing participation of the harsher parts of her

* Blunt, Reformation in England, ch. xii.

† Const. Hist., i. 106. Fifth edit.

‡ Prof. Blunt, the Reformation in England, ch. xii.

* *Quarterly Review*, July, 1854, p. 224.

† The Town: its Memorable Characters and Events, vol. ii. ch. xi.

character, she had sensibility enough to die of a broken heart. Peace and pardon to her memory. Which of us might not have done the same, had we been as unhappily situated?" *

Mr. Froude says that "Queen Mary, cruelly as she was wronged in her young days, is not one of those persons whom it is possible to hate, and we pity her even in her crimes." From her childhood, as he reminds us, she had been the plaything of a fortune which had bound her heart in ice, and her woman's feelings, as she brooded over her own and her mother's wrongs, had curdled into bitterness. With a more powerful nature, injuries such as hers would have brought about some tragical catastrophe; but such a result was prevented by the poverty of her disposition, and she was transformed instead into a wretched being who could neither love nor be loved.

"If her husband," this historian affirms, "had treated her even with ordinary kindness,—inexperienced as she, who had never known kindness at all, must have been in distinguishing between the degrees of it—it might have satisfied her self-flattery; and if those other hopes had not deceived her, and if in becoming a mother fresh springs of affection had been allowed to open for her, it is not impossible that the hard, frost-bound soil might have thawed, and the latent humanity shot up again." †

So it might have been, this historian is fain to believe; and those dark blots which will now lie on her name forever, might either never have been, or have been washed away by repentance. But so it was not to be; and, as Mr. Carlyle observes of the wide world's history, these same "might-have-beens" are mostly a vanity.

A sorry spouse she found in the King of Spain. Like the complaining dame in Beaumont and Fletcher she might soothly swear,

"I have been gulled in a shining carbuncle,
A very glowworm, that I thought had fire in't,
And 'tis as cold as ice." ‡

It was not unlike a new version of the story of her poor mad aunt, Joanna, who also had a Philip for her husband, and one whose indifference to her so mortified her parents, Ferdinand and Isabella, and went far to derange her own wits. Joanna, too, like Mary, had few personal attractions, and, as Prescott says,* cooled the affections of *her* Philip by alternations of excessive fondness and irritable jealousy, for which last the levity of his conduct gave her too much occasion.

Describing Mary at her nuptial period, M. Michelet styles her "vieille fille, âcre de passions retardées," "petite femme, maigre et rouge." † Of the portrait of her by Sir Antonio More—who received for it, from Philip, not only a chain of gold, but the more substantial honorarium of £400 a year as painter to the king ‡—of this portrait Hartley Coleridge remarks, that if Sir Antonio painted the traditional likeness of Mary, he was no flatterer—she being old and ugly enough for a frontispiece to the Book of Martyrs. One would scarce have suspected Philip of loving his wife well enough to give away chains for her vinegar features; and if Sir Antonio received a salary of £400, he was better paid than he could possibly deserve. Holbein's pension was only two hundred florins. §

Leigh Hunt describes her as "plain, petty of stature, ill-colored, and fierce-eyed, with a voice almost as deep as a man's." True, that Michele, the Venetian ambassador, in the account which he wrote of her, pronounces her "moderately pretty;" ‖ but if Giovanni the diplomatist was not, *ex officio*, "lying abroad" (to adopt Wotton's now proverbial pun)—if he did not "use the words as good-naturedly implying something different," then, as Leigh Hunt too truly says, ¶ he goes counter to all which is understood of Mary's face in history, and certainly to the prints of it, which are representative of a melancholy and homely vixen.

Not, at any rate, the sort of face and expression to captivate Philip, who was a coarse and eager sensualist—as unrefined in his amours as in his palate; and as re-

* Leigh Hunt, Female Sovereigns of England.

† See the historical essay on Mary Tudor in the *Westminster Review*, No. V., New Series;—an essay equal in its better parts to the best parts of the author's History of England under the Tudors, and which may be said indeed to contain the pith or marrow of the sixth volume of that very able work. (*Living Age*, *Vol.* 36. p. 347.)

‡ Wit at Several Weapons, Act II. Sc. 1.

* History of Ferdinand and Isabella, part ii. ch. iii.

† Guerres de Religion, ch. viii.

‡ Allan Cunningham, Lives of the Painters.

§ Essays and Marginalia. by Hartley Coleridge.

‖ Ellis' Original Letters, illustrative of English History, etc. Second Series, vol. ii.

¶ Men, Women, and Books, I. 307.

gards the latter we know that of all dainty dishes you could set before the king, he preferred huge masses of bacon fat—if from a pig of some forty score weight, so much the better.

Mary had the misfortune, as the latest and best of her husband's historians describes it, to labor under a chronic infirmity, which confined her for weeks, and indeed months, of every year to her chamber, and which, with her domestic troubles, gave her an air of melancholy, that in later years settled into a repulsive austerity.* Mr. Lothrop Motley avows his almost compassion for Mary Tudor, when her passionate efforts to inspire Philip with affection are contrasted with his impassiveness. "Tyrant, bigot, murderess though she was, she was still woman, and she lavished on her husband all that was not ferocious in her nature. Forbidding prayers to be said for the soul of her father, hating her sister and her people, burning bishops, bathing herself in the blood of heretics, to Philip she was all submissiveness and feminine devotion.

"It was a most singular contrast, Mary the queen of England, and Mary the wife of Philip. Small, lean, and sickly, painfully near-sighted, yet with an eye of fierceness and fire, her face wrinkled by care and evil passions still more than by time, with a big man's voice, whose harshness made those in the next room tremble, yet feminine in her tastes, skilful with her needle, fond of embroidery, striking the lute with a touch remarkable for its science and feeling, speaking many languages, including Latin, with fluency and grace; most feminine, too, in her constitutional sufferings, hysterical of habit, shedding floods of tears daily at Philip's coldness, undisguised infidelity, and frequent absences from England—she almost awakens compassion, and causes a momentary oblivion of her identity."†

Philip's frequent absences from England might more properly be rendered his very rare presence there, for he gave our island and its queen very little of his company. England did not care how little; but the queen did. Philip made himself scarce; and the English liked him none the worse for that. But it was pain and grief to Mary, and the fire was hot within her, and she spoke upbraidingly with her mouth, and wrote reproachfully with her pen. But hardly could the gentle lady married to the Moor be more devoted in her attachment, or say more sincerely,—

> "Unkindness may do much;
> And his unkindness may defeat my life,
> But never taint my love."*

When Philip bade his dejected wife a final adieu, nothing, as Prescott says, could be more forlorn than her condition. Her health wasting under a disease that "cheated her with illusory hopes" of an heir, and so made her ridiculous in the eyes of the world; her throne, her very life, continually menaced by conspiracies, to some of which even her own sister was supposed to be privy; her spirits affected by the consciousness of the decline of her popularity under the gloomy system of persecution into which she had been led by her ghostly advisers; without friends, without children, almost it might be said without a husband,—she was alone in the world, more to be commiserated than the meanest subject in her dominions. She has had little commiseration, however, Mr. Prescott continues, "from Protestant writers, who paint her in the odious colors of a fanatic. This has been compensated, it may be thought, by the Roman Catholic historians, who have invested the English queen with all the glories of the saint and the martyr." Experience may convince us, he adds, that public acts do not always furnish a safe criterion of private character,—particularly when these acts are connected with religion. "A larger examination of contemporary documents, especially of the queen's own correspondence, justifies the inference, that, with all the infirmities of a temper soured by disease, and by the difficulties of her position, she possessed many of the good qualities of her illustrious progenitors, Katherine of Aragon and Isabella of Castile; the same conjugal tenderness and devotion, the same courage in times of danger, the same earnest desire, misguided as she was, to do her duty,—and, unfortunately, the same bigotry. It was, indeed, most unfortunate, in Mary's case, as in that of the Catholic queen, that this bigotry, from their position as independent sovereigns, should have been attended with such fatal

* Prescott, History of Philip II.

† J. L. Motley, Rise of the Dutch Republic, vol. i. ch. i.

* Othello, IV. 2.

consequences as have left an indelible blot on the history of their reigns." *

Michelet declares that nothing can be more curious than to watch the phantasmagoria of the Marian policy, as displayed in the despatches of Renard, the Spanish envoy, who acted as Mary's right-hand counsellor, urged her on, and supported her with adroit zeal. "Marie, ignorante, intrépide de son ignorance, qui ne sait rien, ne comprend rien, croit toute l'Angleterre catholique." She blunders on, blind in the belief of that one blunder, and acting upon it as an axiom in her laws of government, a postulate in her system of politics. She steers her way right onward—*va droit, sans avoir peur de rien.* She has no fear of losing her kingdom; but even were such a contingency probable, she might think a kingdom not ill lost for a mass. And yet, *péril énorme! La première messe fait une sanglante émeute à Londres.* † What matter, in comparison with the weal of Mother Church? Mary may be vexed and soured by refractory Protestantism, but she will not desist or be turned aside—for she, too, in her crabbed way, has full purpose of heart to cleave steadfastly to the faith she regards as pure and undefiled—she, too, is wholly resolved to contend earnestly for what she accounts the faith once delivered to the saints.

And thus arose, in its baleful horror, what Shenstone calls

> "The pest gigantic, whose revengeful stroke
> Tinged the red annals of Maria's reign." ‡

Upon the *class* character of the persecution, Mr. Froude forcibly remarks, that although Pole and Mary could have laid their hands on earl and baron, knight and gentleman, whose heresy was notorious, although, in the queen's own guard, there were many who never listened to a mass, § they durst not strike where there was danger that they would be struck in return. They went out, as he describes it, into the highways and hedges; they gathered up the lame, the halt, and the blind; they took the weaver from his loom, the carpenter from his workshop, the husbandman from his plough; they laid hands on maidens and boys "who had never heard of any other religion than that they were called on to abjure," * old men tottering into the grave, and children whose lips could but just lisp the articles of their creed; and of these they made their burnt-offerings; of these they crowded their prisons, and when filth and famine killed them, they flung them out to rot. How long England would have endured the repetition of the horrid spectacles is hard to say. The persecution lasted three years, and in that time something less than three hundred persons were burnt at the stake. † "By imprisonment," said Lord Burleigh, "by torment, by famine, by fire, almost the number of four hundred were," in their various ways, "lamentably destroyed." ‡

It is only your stage Jesuit, ironically personified, who will be found to maintain that

> "Too sparing was the time, too mild the day,
> When our great Mary bore the English sway!
> Unqueenlike pity marred her royal power,
> Nor was her purple dyed enough in gore.
> Four or five hundred, such like petty sum,
> Might fall perhaps a sacrifice to Rome,
> Scarce worth the naming: had *I* had the power,
> Or been thought fit to have been her counsellor,
> She should have raised it to a nobler score,
> Big bonfires should have blazed, and shone each day,
> To tell our triumphs, and make bright our way;
> And when 'twas dark in every lane and street,
> Thick flaming heretics should serve to light,
> And save the needless charge of links by night;
> Smithfield should still have kept a constant fire,
> Which never should be quenched, never expire,
> But with the lives of all the miscreant rout,
> Till the last gasping breath had blown it out." §

The late Lord Nugent had some reason for complaining that, although our histories, up to the time of his writing (1826), had not, he believed, stated what is untrue of Queen Mary, nor, perhaps, had very much exaggerated what is true of her; yet, "our arguers, whose only talk is of Smithfield, are generally very uncandid in what they con-

* See Tytler's valuable work, Reigns of Edward VI. and Mary. The compilation of this work led its candid author to conclusions eminently favorable to the personal character of Queen Mary.—*Prescott, History of Philip II., book i. ch. vii.*
† Histoire de France, t. ix. p. 135.
‡ Shenstone, The Ruined Abbey.
§ Underhill's Narrative.

* Burleigh's Execution of Justice.
† The number is variously computed at 270, 280, and 290.
‡ Froude, VI. 532-3.
§ Oldham, Satires upon the Jesuits.

zeal." It seemed to be commonly ignored, that the statutes which enabled Mary to burn those who had conformed to the Church of her father and brother, were Protestant statutes, declaring the common law against heresy, and framed by her father, Henry the Eighth, and confirmed and acted upon by Order of Council of her brother, Edward the Sixth, enabling that mild and temperate young sovereign to burn divers misbelievers, by sentence of commissioners. "It would appear to be seldom considered, that her zeal might very possibly have been warmed by the circumstance of both her chaplains having been imprisoned for their religion, and herself arbitrarily detained, and her safety threatened during the short but persecuting reign of her brother." * His lordship further reminds all whom it concerns, that the sad evidences of the violence of those days are by no means confined to her acts alone; that the fagots of persecution were not kindled by papists only, nor did they cease to blaze when the power of using them as instruments of conversion ceased to be in popish hands.

Hartley Coleridge, on this topic, adopts the tactics of those who apologize for the Elizabethan persecution. He asserts that the real grounds of the Marian persecution were political, not religious. Religion, he contends, was only called in to smother the consciences of the persecutors, some of whom would have shrunk from the deadly acts of vengeance which they perpetrated, if they could not have contrived to believe that they were vindicating the true Church against soul-killing heresy. Not that he denies the appearance, here and there, of a Bonner or a Jeffreys, in whom the lust of blood is not a mere metaphor, but a physical appetite—though he believes such to be as rare a phenomenon as the Siamese twins. But he doubts whether Christianity, however corrupted with error, ever urged one human being to oppress or destroy another. "An erring piety may *consent* to persecution; but the promoters of persecutions are revenge, ambition, avarice, and the other bastards of the world, which the Church adopted when she married the world. It may be said that among the victims in Mary's reign, there were many poor insignificant individuals, that could be formidable to no government; but if it were possible, at this distance of time, to investigate the history of such cases, we should find that there was some old quarrel, some malicious neighbor, some *Tony-fire-the-fagot* at the bottom of it." * Elsewhere Hartley affirms, that, in the black list of persecutors, depend upon it, there have been three atheists to one sincere bigot.

Be that as it may, we have, at any rate, one most sincere bigot in the person of Mary Tudor. It is just this quality that makes Macaulay exalt her, in this one respect, to the prejudice of her right royal sister. He calls it the great stain on the character of Elizabeth, that being herself an Adiaphorist, having no scruple about conforming to the Romish Church when conformity was necessary to her own safety, retaining to the last moment of her life a fondness for much of the doctrine and much of the ceremonial of that Church, she yet subjected that Church to a persecution even more odious than the persecution with which her sister had harassed the Protestants. "We say more odious. For Mary had at least the plea of fanaticism. She did nothing for her religion which she was not prepared to suffer for it. She had held it firmly under persecution. She fully believed it to be essential to salvation. If she burned the bodies of her subjects, it was in order to rescue their souls." † Whereas Elizabeth, as he insists, had no such pretext—being a half Protestant, or wholly a Catholic, as opportunity might offer, or exigency require.

In Queen Mary, as the historian of the Tudors not only says but clearly shows, early ill-usage had trampled out the natural woman, and delivered her up to Catholicism, to be moulded by it exclusively and completely. He finely and feelingly pictures her as one who, with a resolute wish to do the will of God, without one bad passion, careless of herself, and only caring for what she believed to be her duty, had no idea of what duty meant, except what she gathered from her creed; and all whose loves, all whose hatreds, submitted to the literal control of the propositions of it, uncounteracted and uninfluenced by a single human emotion. Her life on earth, as he says, was one long mistake, and but for the

* Lord Nugent's Plain Statement on the Catholic Question, 1826.

* Hartley Coleridge Life of Roger Ascham.

† Essay on Burleigh and his times. (1832).

brief delusive interval, which only served to make her cup more bitter, it was one long misery. "The symptoms which she had mistaken for pregnancy were the approaches of a hideous disease. Her husband, for whom she had sacrificed the hearts of her people, detested her, and, brute as he was, took no pains to conceal his aversion. He insulted her by infamous solicitations of the ladies of her court; when they turned with disdain from him, he consoled himself with vulgar debauchery; and making no secret of the motives which had induced him to accept her hand, when the policy burst like an air-bubble, he hastened to leave a country which was always execrable to him, and a wife whose presence was a reproach."*

And would he not come again? never again? Give him up, she could not, contemptuous ingrate though he was. One might almost transfer to Mary, in his regard, the language of Lady Frampul in Jonson's play:—

"Thou dost not know my sufferings, what I feel,
My fires and fears are met; I burn and freeze,
My liver's one great coal, my heart shrunk up
With all the fibres, and the mass of blood
Within me, is a standing lake of fire,
Curled with the cold wind of my gelid sighs,
That drive a drift of sleet through all my body,
And shoot a February through my veins.
Until I see him, I am drunk with thirst,
And surfeited with hunger of his presence."†

But the separation was final; and thus bitterly was Mary's heart "flung back upon itself; and with seared feelings and breaking health, she threw herself with undivided heart upon her religion to fulfil the mission on which she believed that she had been sent by God." In proof, were proof wanting, that Mary, and not Philip, was the author of the persecution, Mr. Froude refers to the fact, that the most severe edict which was issued, went out after her husband had left her. Victims were multiplied exceedingly, and curses loud as well as deep began to penetrate within palace walls, needing no bird of the air to carry the matter, even within the queen's chamber.

She saw that she was hated by her people, widely and intensely hated. But she clung to her disastrous mission only the more. She felt that she was dying by inches, but this only quickened her zeal to work while it was called to-day, the night being so near in which she could work no more.

They tell us it was the loss of Calais that broke Mary's heart. It came upon her with the shock of an unforeseen disaster. Calamities had taken such hold upon her that she was not able to look up; and this was the finishing stroke.

Here is Michelet's vigorous outline of the closing scene. "Marie, avec son légat Pole, dans ses quatre ans de supplice, avait usé la Terreur catholique. Vaincue par les martyrs, elle se sentait impuissante et comme submergée dans la grande marée montante du protestantisme vainqueur. Négligée de son cher époux le *roi velu*, et furieuse de ses nuits veuves, blessée par Rome qu'elle servait si bien, excommuniée par un pape imbécile, elle reçut encore cet horrible coup de Calais, honte nationale que l'Angleterre lui mit comme une pierre sur le cœur. Elle n'y survécut guère, et mournut conspuée du peuple, laissant le trône à celle qu'elle baissait à mort, la protestante Elisabeth (novembre, 1558)."*

The Calais *coup* is assumed to have been her death-blow. Where there were so few to speak comfort to her, Mary can hardly be said to have refused comfort: else might one picture her rejecting the ordinary

Console-toi pourtant de ton malheur,

in the spirit of Molière's Alcippe—

Qui, moi? J'aurai toujours *ce coup-là sur le cœur*.†

In the spirit, and to the letter too; for we all know what the moribund woman said about Calais and her heart.

Measured by substantial value, Mr. Froude computes the loss of Calais to have been a gain; English princes were never again to lay claim to the crown of France, and the possession of a fortress on French soil was a perpetual irritation. But Calais was called the "brightest jewel in the English crown." A jewel it was, useless, costly but dearly prized. Over the gate of Calais had once stood the insolent inscription:—

"Then shall the Frenchmen Calais win,
When iron and lead like cork shall swim;"

and the Frenchmen had won it, won it in fair and gallant fight.

"If Spain should rise suddenly into her ancient strength and tear Gibraltar from us, our mortification would be faint, compared to the anguish of humiliated pride with which the loss of Calais distracted the subjects of Queen Mary,"‡

* Essay on Mary Tudor, in *Westminster Review*, V. 32.

† Ben Jonson. The New Inn, Act V. Sc. 1.

* Guerres de Religion, p. 148.

† Les Fâcheux, II. 8.

‡ Froude, vol. vi. p. 506.

Hear how a jolly Briton, nearly three centuries after the event, expresses his feelings upon it, on a return from perambulating the fortifications of Calais. We quote from Sir Walter Scott's diary, as kept in France, in the autumn of 1826. The extract may serve by way of relief by contrast to the tone and accent of what precedes and follows it. "Lost, as all know, by the bloody papist bitch (one must be vernacular when on French ground) Queen Mary, of red-hot memory. I would rather she had burned a score more of bishops. If she had kept it, her sister Bess would sooner have parted with her virginity." And then the hearty old baronet speculates on the chances of keeping it under the Stuarts. Charles I., he says, had no temptation to part with it—and though it might, indeed, have shuffled out of our hands during the Civil Wars, he is clear that Noll would have as soon let Monsieur draw one of his grinders—then Charles II., he assumes, would hardly have dared to sell such an old possession, as he did Dunkirk; and after that the French had little chance till the revolution. "Even then, I think, we could have held a place that could be supplied from our own element, the sea. *Cui bono?* None, I think, but to plague the rogues."* The very reason why so many latter-day politicians think it a good riddance, in the cause and interests of peace. But let that pass.

Memorable is the saying attributed to Mary, that the name of Calais would be found imprinted on her heart when dead. She could not get the better of this scathing blow. Of the surrendered town she might have said, as Milton's Adam of a merely imagined bereavement,—

"Loss of thee
Will never from my heart."

We have seen Michelet's description of her, as "furieuse de ses nuits veuves." More tumultuous agitation now afflicted her in the night season. George Buchanan's Latin ode on the taking of Calais, includes a dark sketch of Mary's remorse and shame,—with this among the other woes of her unrest:—

"Umbræque nocturnæ, quietem
Terrificis agitant figuris." †

Mary's death was now openly prayed for in the churches; and reverend refugees in Germany were not backward to send over pamphlets to the tune of Killing No Murder, in a case like hers. But she saved their disciples the trouble of summary slaughter, by dying, almost as soon, and quite as miserably, as they could wish. Unwept, unsolaced, she died,—with a last prayer that she might be buried in the garb of a poor *religieuse*—in which alone, a kindly critic affirms, it would have been well for her if she had lived.

No English sovereign, says Mr. Froude, ever ascended the throne with larger popularity than Mary Tudor. The country was eager to atone to her for her mother's injuries; and the instinctive loyalty of the English towards their natural sovereign was enhanced by the abortive efforts of Northumberland to rob her of her inheritance. She had reigned little more than five years, and she descended into the grave amidst curses deeper than the acclamations which had welcomed her accession. In that brief time she had swathed her name in the horrid epithet which will cling to it forever; and yet from the passions which in general tempt sovereigns into crime, she was entirely free; to the time of her accession she had lived a blameless, and, in many respects, a noble life; and few men or women have lived less capable of doing knowingly a wrong thing.

"Philip's conduct, which could not extinguish her passion for him, and the collapse of the inflated imaginations which had surrounded her supposed pregnancy, it can hardly be doubted, affected her sanity. Those forlorn hours when she would sit on the ground with her knees drawn to her face; those restless days and nights when, like a ghost, she would wander about the palace galleries, rousing herself only to write tear-blotted letters to her husband; those bursts of fury over the libels dropped in her way; or the marching in procession behind the Host in the London streets—these are all symptoms of hysterical derangement, and leave little room, as we think of her, for other feelings than pity. But if Mary was insane, the madness was of a kind which placed her absolutely under her spiritual directors; and the responsibility for her cruelties, if responsibility be any thing but a name, rests first with Gardiner, who commenced them, and, secondly, and in a higher degree, with Reginald Pole."*

All these have gone, long since, every man to his own place; and to their own Master they stand or fall. But let us, who judge none of them, compassionate her who stood forth the most prominently of them all, and who more than either of them bore the burden and heat of the day, the glooms of its wintry morning, and the darkness that might be felt when its even-tide saddened into night.

* Lockhart's Life of Scott, ch. lxxxii.

† Ad Franciæ Regem, Henricum II., post ictos Caletes, Georgius Buchanan.

* Froude, History of England, vol. vi. p. 528.

From The Economist, 2 March.

PROGRESS OF AMERICAN DISUNION.

The great drama of disruption is surely and not very slowly evolving in the United States. There are still some features in the case which foreigners cannot well understand, and which seem not perfectly clear even to Americans themselves. But two or three points are becoming plainer day by day. It now appears that Secession has not been an act hastily forced upon the seceding States by Mr. Lincoln's election, or by any *bonâ fide* fears brought home to them by that event, of fresh aggressions upon their "peculiar institution;" but that it is an occurrence which has not only been long foreseen and prepared for, but resolutely determined upon. It is obvious that the South were ready to remain in the Union, so long as they could unreservedly dictate its policy and nominate to all places of power and trust, but not one hour longer;—that they had for some time perceived symptoms that this supremacy was about to be wrested from them;—and that Mr. Lincoln's election merely indicated to them that it was gone, and that the expected moment for action had, therefore, arrived. From that date there has been neither hesitation nor delay; they never attempted to make terms; they never proposed any real scheme of arrangement; they never showed the slightest desire or intention of remaining in the Union; but, on the contrary, pushed forward their proceedings with a reckless and indecent haste, as if they dreaded nothing so much as a compromise which would stop the Secession movement at the outset. While the Border States have been concocting schemes of adjustment, while the Northern politicians have been bringing forward project after project for what is called "conciliation," but which in fact is nothing less than ignominious capitulation, the seceding States have not given one moment's attention to any of these countless propositions, but have rushed at once upon action, in a manner which betrays three things as clearly as the sun at noonday. *First*, a violence and intemperate haste which augur ill for the future wisdom and decency of their government, *secondly*, a resolution that *nothing* now shall balk them of their purpose; and *thirdly*, the absolute certainty that their plans have been laid for months if not for years, and at least the *first* steps consequent upon separation carefully determined on beforehand. They at once seized, where they could, upon the Federal fortresses and stores; they fired on Federal ships; they obstructed the entrances to their harbors; they summoned conventions to meet without an hour's delay; and—while Virginia is still offering her mediation, while senators at Washington are still discussing terms of accommodation, while the obnoxious Lincoln is still uninstalled and powerless—they have already chosen the style and title of their new Republic, and nominated Mr. Jefferson Davis President of the Southern Confederation. Nay, more, it seems highly *probable*—for without further proof we are unwilling to speak with any thing like positive conviction—that at least three members of Mr. Buchanan's Cabinet, in fact all his chief ministers have been for some time traitorously and fraudulently using their positions to facilitate separation, and to make the North comparatively powerless to resist it when it came. There is reason to believe—indeed, there is something amounting to official proof—that the late Secretary at War, the Secretary of the Treasury, and the Secretary of the Interior have combined with each other to manipulate the army appointments and the public chest, with the purpose of impoverishing and disarming the North, and enriching and organizing the South in the immediate view of the Secession crisis. It is not easy either, as far as appearances at present go, to acquit Mr. Buchanan himself of a guilty knowledge and tolerance of their proceedings—at all events to some extent.

With such promptitude, too, have the Secessionists acted, and so resolute do they seem not to lose a single hour, that they have framed their new constitution without a single attempt to improve it in any one of the particulars in which experience had shown it to be defective. They have, in fact, merely re-enacted the old Federal institutions and the old Federal laws. The truth is—and we do not wonder at it—their imaginations have been so fired and their cupidity so excited at the prospect of a vast Slave Empire, with uncontrolled dominion and almost illimitable territory, stretching over all the magnificent lands which lie between Virginia on the North and the Isthmus of Panama on the South, that they are actually intoxicated by the dream; and are resolved, cost what it may, to shake off the incubus of the Northern States, whose citizens they both despise and detest as pedantic and shopkeeping quill-drivers, and envy as being at once more numerous, more wealthy, and more clever than themselves. There is perhaps scarcely a Southerner now who does not fancy himself a member of the ruling class in a Republic exercising absolute sway over Central America, Cuba, the Antilles, and the whole of the Gulf of Mexico, as well as over the largest portion of the old Union itself. The Southerners are a very excitable race, and usually very ignorant of their relative power and position in the world: they see no difficulties, and make light of all dangers; they seem actually to have no scruples, and their morality on all points seems to have been strangely warped by slavery.

There are already indications, however, that in their reckless violence and haste they have somewhat overshot their mark. The Border States, whose cause is not identical, whose real interests in the strife are far from clear or simple, and who would have protected the seceders against Northern coercion, are by no means all inclined to join or encourage them, now that their policy is so obviously one of aggression. Though the Southerners have introduced into the laws of their new Confederation an absolute prohibition of the African slave trade—with a view to *bribe* the Border States, and a contingent prohibition of the internal slave-trade from non-seceding States—with a view to *alarm* them,—neither Kentucky, Tennessee, Virginia, nor Maryland, has given in its adhesion to the separation: on the contrary, they are all pronouncing more and more distinctly in favor of the maintenance of the old Union. We do not for a moment fancy that any line of action adopted by these States can now prevent the consummation of the severance, but their adherence to the North will materially affect both the terms of separation, and the relative prospects of the two Republics.

Meanwhile the intentions of the Northern politicians seem to be undetermined, or far from unanimous. They are by no means either as clear or as resolute as their antagonists. They still talk hopefully of the maintenance of the Union. They still go on discussing proposals of compromise and adjustment. They say, with perfect truth, as Mr. Lincoln has well put it in one of his recent speeches, that the crisis is "artificial;" that there are no new grounds for disunion, and that, if time be given for angry passions and unreasoning panic to die away, the danger will blow over, and the South will return to its allegiance. It is difficult to know how far they believe this in their hearts. Some are for coercion, some are for conciliation, some are for a policy of "masterly inaction." The President-elect seems to be of the number of these last. To our thinking, though, of course, we speak with diffidence, they are all wrong. Coercion we hold to be nearly if not wholly impossible; but whether possible or not, we are sure it would be very foolish. What would they gain by *compelling* eight millions of men to remain members of the Union against their will? How could such compulsion be permanently continued in a Republican nation? How could the government at Washington be carried on in the face of such a virulent and hostile minority of representatives as the coerced States would send up? No—depend upon it, it is not for Americans to take a leaf out of the book of Austria. Mr. Lincoln says that retaking by force the Federal fortresses and property from the States which have so lawlessly seized them, would not be coercion or invasion. This may be very true; but where would be the use of retaking them? The moment the separation is effected and acknowledged, the fortresses would necessarily be surrendered, or sold to the Southern Confederation, or to the separate States composing it. *Half* the property in them belongs to the South, if a peaceable and equitable division of territory and property is effected; and it would be simply idle to make South Carolina purchase Fort Sumter, and then return her half the purchase money, and then perform a counterbalancing operation on one of the Northern forts, and pay half the price of that to the Southern Confederation. If the Secession be consummated by agreement, of course all the strong places in the seceding States will be given up to them; if consummated by connivance and reluctant acquiescence (which it will be, if no coercion is to be used), then why be at all the pains of retaking what no one would dream of *permanently* holding as a menace and an irritating sore?

Again, why endeavor to retain the reluctant Southerners by compromise which *must* be humiliating and an admission of defeat, and yet could only for a short period postpone the evil day? Does any one in his heart believe that the fiery and ambitious citizens of the Slave States will submit to remain in the Union—the power of which, by the inevitable operation of the existing constitution, must yearly be handed over more and more completely to the increasing population of the North—unless they can do so on their own terms? or that these terms will or can be any thing short of virtual and secure supremacy? If they remain in the Union, they see clearly enough, they must do so *as a minority*—and a minority which every year becomes more decided;—and how can a minority hope permanently to govern under democratic institutions? Let them go then, since they can only be retained at the price of servility and dishonor.

The policy of "inaction" might have much to say for it, if the South were really in a panic or merely in a passion, and were likely to come round if time were allowed it. But, as we have said, there is ample evidence that this is not the case. The seceding States have long since determined to be free.

Moreover, the position of affairs is growing too serious in the commercial world to permit the continuance of uncertainty. Politicians might live for awhile in a provisional condition and wait for the natural development of the crisis; but merchants cannot do so. Already great difficulty and uneasiness is felt, and this must increase day by day till a final settlement is effected. Property is decreasing rapidly in salable value; cautious men are curtailing their transactions; loans can scarcely be negotiated, because no one knows what positive security can be offered; and, what is still more embarrassing, debtors in the South are withholding payment from their Northern creditors (even where they are not infamous enough openly to speak of repudiation); and merchants, at New York deprived of their remittances on account of the planters of Alabama, Carolina, and Mississippi, are beginning to feel anxious about their power of meeting their own engagements. A continuance of this uncertainty for three months longer, would in all likelihood bring about a more wide-spread commercial ruin than has been seen for many years. On any account, therefore, an immediate termination of the crisis has become imperatively needed; and we confess we cannot see any termination that would be at once desirable, possible, and permanent, except *a separation by acquiescence and negotiation.* We are sure that a peaceable severance on such terms as would induce the Border States to adhere to the Northern Confederation (which sooner or later they must ultimately join), every friend of humanity ought to hail with joy.

From The Saturday Review, 2 March.

THE AMERICAN BORDER STATES.

The affairs of the North American States are rather a trial to the English journalist. Their overwhelming importance renders it impossible to pass them over in silence, but it is wearisome to have to chronicle events of which the commonest caution teaches us neither to draw the moral nor to predict the issue. The absurdity of taking a confident view of them is especially great at the present moment. In two days after the time at which these lines come under the eye of the reader, the most critical passage in this revolution will have been reached without its being possible for us to know whether it has been fatal to what remains of the American Union or whether it has been successfully surmounted. Mr. Lincoln ought to assume office on March 4th, but the best-informed Americans on this side of the Atlantic are still uncertain whether he will be allowed to do so in constitutional form. The mob of Washington and of the neighboring slave-country has unquestionably been tampered with by conspirators who wish to place the Secessionists beyond the reach of interference by disorganizing the heart of the government; and it is by no means improbable that, if Mr. Buchanan had retained the Cabinet which surrounded him at the commencement of these troubles, Mr. Lincoln would have been actually prevented from installing himself in the chief magistracy. The now proved treason of the person, Mr. Floyd, who was then Secretary at War—proved by his own direct avowals that he did his best to place the government of the United States in the worst possible position for resisting a disruption—leaves little room for doubt that the military forces of the Union would have been carefully disposed in such a manner as to give free play to the ruffianism of the Washington rioters on the day of installation. But Mr. Buchanan is now served by ministers who, while they appear to share his hesitations, are still faithful to the trust reposed in them. It is understood that the first soldier in the Republic, General Scott, has been directed to make his own arrangements for the prevention and repression of violent disturbance. Though the troops at his command are reported as far from numerous enough to furnish absolute security, the belief, on the whole, seems to be, that the change of government is more likely than not to be peaceably effected.

The only point cleared up by the latest advices is the state of opinion in the Southern Border States. Delaware, Maryland, and even Tennessee, which is further off, have pronounced for remaining in the Union. Kentucky has been safe for some time past, and it seems to be taken for granted that the decision of Virginia will be the same with that of the States similarly circumstanced. This result is not, we think, attributable to any dissatisfaction with slavery in these more northerly Slave States; for though we have much evidence that in all of them there is a minority, and perhaps an increasing one, which prefers free labor to the empty right of purchasing negroes, it is not large enough to make itself heard even under more favorable circumstances than can be supposed to exist in the present excitement and confusion. The real truth seems to be, that the citizens of these Border States are strange to the fanatical hatred, suspicion, and terror of the North which possess the cotton planters. Intercourse and commercial interchange have produced the effects which they never fail to carry with them; and, as the Americans on the two sides of the Border line understand each other better, they hate each other less than those residents in the extreme North and in the extreme South, who may almost be said to belong to two different races. It has often been noticed that the heartiest and most enthusiastic of Northern movements could never hurry away the dwellers on the Southern boundary. In the struggle of 1856, every thing turned on the vote of Pennsylvania; but Pennsylvania was lost to Colonel Fremont because the counties immediately adjacent to slave soil could not be got to sympathize even with the wrongs of Kansas. The present is an analogous phenomenon. In spite of the widely diffused conviction that Mr. Lincoln's presidency is likely to be injurious to slavery, the Kentuckians, Virginians, Marylanders, and Tennesseeans cannot be persuaded that their white brethren intend them all the mischief which the more distant traffickers in cotton believe to be brooding, and show themselves disinclined to throw aside the historical grandeur and material greatness of the Federation on the score of apprehensions which they instinctively feel to be groundless or half founded The reluctance to break with the North is the more significant, because these States have no less important interests staked on slavery than Louisiana or South Carolina. A community which depends to any considerable extent on breeding slaves would be more immediately and seriously affected by the discouragement of slavery than one which employs them in the cultivation of the soil. It is, indeed, probably true that all the Border States would be better in the long run for abandoning slavery altogether. But it is extremely improbable that such an eventuality enters at all into their calculations. Men in large masses can rarely be got to welcome changes which will require time to bear fruit, and will probably benefit future generations at the expense of the present.

All that these votes of the Border States prove, is their inclination to remain in the Federation. They by no means establish the certainty that this wish, though undoubted, will be realized. Unfortunately, the Cotton States are able to apply to them at one point the most galling pressure; and the newly formed Southern Confederation has plainly declared that it will not spare the means of annoyance which it possesses. The Constitution of the newly Confederate States differs from the old Constitution of the United States in two particulars principally. It substitutes the plain word "slave" for the gingerly circumlocutions of the older instrument, and it prohibits the importation of slaves from any State not included in the new association. The clause last mentioned may possibly be intended to conciliate our own country by an ambiguous prohibition of the slave-trade, but its principal object is, of course, to intimidate the Border States. Their prosperity is intimately bound up with their artificial relation as slave-breeders to the Planting States, and it seems easy to bring them to terms by depriving them of a privilege to which they can put in no tangible claim. At the same time, it must be recollected that the seceders must always have been suspected of intending to use this instrument against Virginia, Maryland, and Kentucky, and this very circumstance invests with still greater importance the manifested desire of those States to remain in the Union. For they cannot have come to this decision without convincing themselves that the North will have the best of it in the coming struggle. By their own adhesion they still further strengthen the hands of the North. If the number of seceders does not increase, it is scarcely possible for the Southern Confederacy to stand. Great as are some of its natural advantages, the benefits it may calculate on deriving from them are not of such a kind that it can enter immediately on their enjoyment. The first drawback in its prospects is obviously its lack of money and credit. All the States which have joined it are extremely poor in available capital, almost all their wealth taking the form of negroes, which, of course, diminish in exchangeable value according as public confidence is shaken, and according as the area over which they will pass as an article of commerce is restricted in extent. It is almost needless to add that they have even less credit than money. By an odd chance, they include all the governments which have most astonished the world by their shameless dishonesty. The Southern Confederation is, in fact, a very Adullam of insolvency, and it will be curious to observe the market price of the bonds which it is said to have assurance enough to think of negotiating. This want of funds is its real difficulty, and the North is likely to find in it an advantage equivalent to that which the seceders are making the most of against the Border States. The incoming President has evidently his eye on the weak point. The one announcement he has made concerning his policy is that he intends to collect the customs duties as if no secession had occurred. If he does this, he will dry up the only source from which the Southern Confederacy can hope to draw a sufficient revenue. The crushing direct taxation which it now imposes cannot long be continued.

From The Saturday Review, 2 March.

THE MOTIVES TO SECESSION.

MUCH as the disruption of the United States has been discussed, it still seems to be little understood. If any ten English gentlemen were asked what motives had led the Southern States to propose secession, it would be a great chance if two of them could tell. At first sight, it looks unaccountable that a third of the people of that country should break off from their allegiance simply because a President has been elected whose principles differ from their own. This seems still more strange when we remember that he has neither the will nor the power to lay the lightest finger upon any part of their institutions. Neither Mr. Lincoln nor the Republican party, of which he is the head, dream of the abolition of slavery. They are opposed to the extension of slavery beyond its present limits; nor will they consent to lay down the principle that slavery is to be assumed to exist until it has been abolished by law. But apparently there is nothing in this to terrify or exasperate those States in which slavery is already rooted. And as the Democratic party had a majority both in the Senate and in Congress, there was no reason to fear any change of policy even in these respects. At first sight, therefore, there was nothing in the election of Mr. Lincoln to justify the Southern States in breaking up the Union. But, in fact, although it was the election of a President whom they abhorred that made their wrath boil over, they had long been inflamed against their Northern brethren with a most intense hostility. Our gentle jars between Whigs and Tories can but give us a faint idea of the vehemence of party feeling between the South and the North. The Democrats hate the Republicans with a perfect hatred. It is only natural for them to do so. They are told every day that their social system is detestable; that they are living in defiance of the law of God; that their much-loved institution is the scandal of the world; and they are not likely to show that Christian feeling which they are denied to possess by a meek submission to these insults. Their rage, too, has the powerful stimulus of fear. They dread that the principles laid down by the North should catch the ear of their slaves, and lead to that most terrible of all calamities—a servile insurrection. Every thing, in short, has helped to lash into excitement the antipathies of the Southern against the Northern States. So long as the President was of their own choosing, and the whole policy of the United States was in their hands, this feeling, however deep, could remain quiescent. But at the least check the tide was sure to overflow. The election of a Republican President could not but make the slave-owners feel that the sceptre was passing from their hands. They were no longer to control the destinies of the United States. Their power and prestige were gone. Even patient men might have felt some exasperation at such a change; and patience is not the virtue by which the Southern planters are marked. Probably no men in the world are less accustomed to self-control. No wonder that a burst of rage ensued that shook the Union to its base. It would, however, be a mistake to imagine that the disruption of the United States has been simply owing to an uncalculating access of fury. In fact, that gust of rage is dying away, and yet these long-headed Southerners are not the less keen for secession. It is from the North, not from the South, that the desire for a compromise has arisen. Generally, the Southern States have made up their minds that true policy requires them to secede. They look forward to their future with confidence, and their conduct is that of men who see good reasons for what they are about to do.

In the first place, their politicians are profoundly imbued with the idea that, as regards their "domestic institution," attack is the true method of defence. To stand still is to be lost. Their wise policy is, not to let the North outweigh them, but to extend slavery over a boundless extent of new territory, and thus to build up a confederacy of Slave States whose importance should command the respect, not only of their Northern brethren, but of the whole world. We are by no means prepared to say that, given slavery as a postulate, this view is short-sighted or unstatesman-like. And then, again, many thoughtful men in the Southern States feel this—they find themselves radically at variance with their Northern brethren with respect to the most essential principles that can bear on their daily life as private men, and on their policy as a State. Every year deepens the Northerner's abhorrence of slavery. Every year deepens the Southerner's conviction that slavery is right; that the negro is born to be a bondsman; that slavery is the true gospel of wealth, civilization, and Christianity. And who shall blame them for deeming that, with principles so utterly at war, it is not possible for two great countries, such as the Northern and the Southern States, to be really and in truth bound together as one people? This fictitious outward union does but cause grievous heart-burnings; and it would, in fact, tend to peace and neighborly feeling to make an outward division, where all views and interests are so utterly sundered. Let us, they say, form one mighty Confederation, imbued with the same principles, aiming at the same ends, setting before the world the example of the beneficence of our noble institution. Let us no longer be dragged back in the course which Providence has prepared for us, by tying ourselves to those who abhor our social system, and whose passionate desire is to thwart our undertakings. Coming down from this lofty ground, they know well that a free-trade tariff would enormously enhance the prosperity of their country. Having no manufactures to protect, to them the relaxation of custom-house restrictions on trade would be an unmixed boon. And yet, so long as they are bound to the Union, they cannot withstand the superior influence of the North, strenuously exerted as it is, and will be in favor of a protectionist tariff. These we believe to be the main inducements that have led the upper class in the Southern States to desire secession.

In fact, however, if the upper class had not joined in the cry, they would have been powerless to resist; for they number but a few hundred thousands, while the mass of whites amounts to more than seven millions. And since every white man has a vote, of course mere numbers carry all before them. The inducement to the lower ranks of whites to demand secession is mainly their desire to re-open the African slave-trade. In the Southern States, social position almost entirely rests, not on birth, not even upon general wealth, but upon the possession of slaves. The man who has not a nigger at his command is looked upon with as much contempt as the poor wretch spoken of by Juvenal, who could not call himself the owner even "*unius lacertæ*." But, despised as the mean whites are, they will not put themselves on the level of the slaves by engaging in manual labor. They would rather live in penury than work for their bread. Their golden day-dream is to have niggers of their own to wallop. Now hitherto, the Northern States, in conjunction with the breeding States, have been able to keep in check this longing for an influx of cheap slaves. In the last two or three years, however, the whites of the Southern States have grown restless under this yoke, and now their resolute determination is to open up a trade in slaves with Africa, and thus reduce the price of negroes. Nor is this only with the view of increasing their private wealth and importance. Their idea is, that by covering new territories with negroes they shall build up a great confederacy of Slave States occupying the whole southern portion of North America. This thirst for an African slave-trade has been the chief motive that has influenced the secessionists, and which makes a compromise almost impossible. The Northern States would be too glad to make any reasonable, and perhaps some unreasonable, concessions; but nothing, we believe, would induce them to acquiesce in legalizing that atrocious traffic.

And yet one might have thought that even the strong appetite for gain would hardly have blinded the white men of the Southern States to the great loss and the great risk which they are about to incur. To our minds the loss would seem to be so enormous as far to outweigh any pecuniary gain. They would at once cease to belong to one of the greatest nations of the world, and sink into members of a comparatively small State with no history, no renown, no prestige. All the traditions that gather round the great North American people, and of which that people has been so proud, would cease to be theirs. But if patriotic pride does not sway them, still we cannot help wondering at their readiness to incur the heavy taxation which a separate Confederacy must entail. It will be necessary for them to maintain a fleet and an army, unless they choose to be exposed to insults from their Northern neighbor. The whole cost of the civil administration, hitherto divided between the North and the South, will fall upon them. But more than all this, there is the risk that, should civil war break out, the negroes might take part in it against their masters; and that in any case the neighborhood of a Free State, whose enmity to slavery has been inflamed by these dissensions, will render insubordination and desertions far more frequent among the slaves.

No event of our own day has been half so wonderful as the one before us. Who, *à priori*, could have believed that in the nineteenth century a new State should be organized, by the grandsons of Englishmen, solely on the principle of preserving and extending a system of slavery! A more ignoble basis for a great Confederacy it is impossible to conceive, nor one in the long run more precarious. The permanent renunciation of sound principles and natural laws must in due time bring ruin. No great career can lie before the Southern States, bound together solely by the tie of having a working-class of negro bondsmen. Assuredly it will be the Northern Confederacy, based on the principle of freedom, with a policy untainted by crime, with a free working-class of white men, that will be the one to go on and prosper, and become the leader of the New World.

From The Saturday Review.

ROYAL MARRIAGES.

THERE is an institution in London called the Marriage Law Defence Association. We are not aware whether the functions of this body are œcumenical, or whether they profess to redress the present wrongs to which the Marriage Law is subjected as well as to resist future encroachments on its limits. If so, a fine field has just been opened for its exertions. England and France—and that, too, in the reigning families of either kingdom—have cases before their respective law courts which, as it seems, are almost ludicrously similar. So curious and complete is the parallel between the claims of the descendants of M. Jerome Bonaparte and of the so-called Princess Olive of Cumberland to be admitted to the doubtful honors of royal descent, that had these two cases occurred in history a couple of thousand years old, critical historians would have said that they were versions of the same fact. M. Jerome Bonaparte, at the age of eighteen or twenty-two,—and the fact of his having or not having attained his majority in the year 1803 is the pivot upon which the French case turns,—married a pretty American girl, named Paterson, and subsequently becoming a great man and a king of a certain sort, repudiated the wife of his love and youth, and contracted a second marriage with a princess of Wurtemberg. Of both marriages there was issue, and upon the recent death of the royal and imperial bigamist the descendants of the first marriage claim to inherit; and the French courts will have to decide whether the issue of the first or second marriage is legitimate. The English case is this: Henry Frederick, Duke of Cumberland, younger brother of George III., and one of the nine children of Frederick Prince of Wales, is said to have married Olive, the daughter of a certain clergyman named Wilmot, in the year 1767. This Dr. Wilmot was himself an adventurer in marriage, and his wife, with whom he had contracted a private marriage, was a king's daughter, though a king of Poland. That there are unquestionably suspicious circumstances connected with Miss Wilmot's marriage is indisputable. The duke and Olive Wilmot were, it is alleged, married by the bride's father, at the house of Lord Archer, in St. James' Square, in the presence—of all people in the world—of George III. himself, the great Lord Chatham, and Lords Warwick and Archer. It is quite true that the date of the marriage is 1767, and the Royal Marriage Act was not passed till 1772, and it is within belief that George III. might have objections to clandestine unions of his own children, while he had none to assist as paranymph at his brother's private wedding. Of this marriage a daughter was the fruit—a lady notorious some forty years ago as the Princess Olive of Cumberland by birth, and Mrs. Olive Serres by marriage. Four years afterwards the royal Cumberland contracted a second marriage with the widow of Lord Carhampton, and became in the eyes of his brother a bigamist. This marriage did not please George III., as some people say, because his majesty disliked the lady, or, as the Serres family say, because the king was privy to his brother's previous marriage. Hence it is said the Royal Marriage Act of 1772, which required the king's assent to every marriage in the royal family. The Princess Olive married a marine painter named Serres, from whom, by the way, she was separated, and of this marriage one Lavinia Juvanella Horton appears as the eldest survivor. This lady married a Mr. Ryves, from whom, however, she has been divorced; and it is a curious feature that all these marriages seem to have been particularly unhappy. Mrs. Ryves now claims that her mother's legitimacy should be established; in other words, she comes into the Court of Probate and Divorce to procure a decree for the validity of the marriage between the Duke of Cumberland and Olive Wilmot. Here the parallel between the French and English cases ends. We have not heard that the ex-king of Westphalia left much money behind him. All that the Paterson-Bonapartes claim is to vindicate the fair fame of the first wife of Jerome; but Mrs. Ryves reminds the courts that the Duke of Cumberland was also Duke of Lancaster, and if the facts are as she states them, her claim on the royal property is a little more than a million of money. Without anticipating the legal points of the two cases, we may just remark, that in the French case the only point worth contesting is the age of Jerome at the first marriage; while in the Cumberland case, both document and alleged fact come before the court with some improbability on their face. Not only has the very curious marriage of the Duke of Cumberland to be proved, but even if Mrs. Ryves is the daughter of the Duke of Cumberland's daughter, her claim upon the royal estates is not concluded by what has taken place before Sir Cresswell Cresswell.

The social aspect of royal marriages, however, may be looked at without any reference to these two curious cases. We have been informed on recent authority, that, as regards marriage, there ought to be, as perhaps in fact there is, one law for the Porphyrogeniti and one law for common folk; that kings and princes may take wives and get rid of them as reasons of state require, but that Jack and Jill must be tied together for life. There is nothing very new in the fact, but there is something very new in its justification upon principle. As to the fact, we all remember that Luther, in the case of Elector of Saxony, allowed that bigamy or polygamy was, for reasons of state, permissible. Henry VIII. certainly was not slow to avail himself of the royal privilegium to dispense with the laws of Christian matrimony. A license has been assumed by princes which is not accorded to the general. Protestantism, in the cases just mentioned, was only not behind the easy dispensations of the court of Rome, which was ready to dispense not only with the laws of the Church but the laws of nature—for a consideration; and Morganatic marriages have been invented to justify a distinction which, were it permitted to the mass of mankind, would certainly destroy the bonds of society. Among our own sovereigns it will be remembered that marriages exactly similar to those of the Duke of Cumberland and Jerome Bonaparte have been matters of suspicion or fact in almost a regular succession. It was given out and believed by the partisans of Monmouth that Charles II. had married Lucy Waters. George III. was often charged with being the husband of the fair Quakeress. The Duke of Clarence was thought to have lawfully loved Mrs. Jordan; and it is an incontestable fact that Mrs. Fitzherbert was the wife of George IV. Had there been any issue by the last-named union, we should have been assured that such child was the legitimate offspring of Mr. George Guelph,—if Guelph were the family name of the House of Hanover,—and the Princess Charlotte the equally legitimate daughter of George Prince of Wales. This is the doctrine, at once a distinction and a solvent, which has been applied to the family of M. Jerome Bonaparte. "M. Jerome Bonaparte is the lawful son of Lieutenant Bonaparte, and Prince Napoleon is the lawful son of the king of Westphalia." This decision—happily as yet it is not the decision of the courts—opens out some curious results. At what point of temporal success does repudiation of one's wife come in? May a curate, when he becomes a bishop, have two lawful wives and two lawful families—the one begotten in Bethnal-green lodgings, the other the children of the palace? Is it seriously meant that a judge may take the daughter of a Scotch earl in his successful senescence, though the wife of his youth, won and wed in his briefless days, still survives? If a considerable rise in the world, such as that from a lieutenant in the navy to the throne of Westphalia, justifies bigamy, how low in the social scale may this privilege be extended; or again, how high is it to reach? A squire promoted to a baronetcy may, we suppose, keep a mistress; when promoted to the Upper House he may establish two wives. And then in an arithmetical ratio, if the king of Westphalia might have two living wives, an emperor might indulge in a harem. At any rate, this view accounts for that profusion in matrimonial engagements which characterized Solomon in all his glory. We must say that this rationale of the Marriage Law, as applied to sovereign princes, strikes us as somewhat akin to barbarism. It is carried out with entire consistency among the potentates of Africa; and the king of Dahomey is, like Napoleon and his brothers, to be "justified from dynastic exigencies." These exigencies are now formally pleaded; we are invited "to construe the laws of matrimony with latitude when crowns and kingdoms are at stake." If crowns and kingdoms, why not estates—why not social position? The simplest expression of the new theory of the obligation of marriage would be in all cases to allow a marriage of affection and a *mariage de convenance.* If we were all permitted our Rebekah and our Leah, it would avoid the present anomaly and conflict between the Royal Marriage Law and that law which alone holds Christian society together.

ORDER FOR MOURNING.

Lord Chamberlain's Office, February 21, 1861.

The lord chamberlain and dramatic censor has just been apprised of the removal of M. Eugène Scribe from the sublunary scene. The lord chamberlain therefore suggests that British dramatic authors do forthwith put their Boyer's Dictionaries into decent mourning. Gentlemen who have annexed the entire plot and dialogue of any of M. Scribe's pieces will have their dictionaries re-bound in black, while for authors who have simply "adapted," a temporary cover of black calico will suffice. Appropriators of fragments and epigrams from the same source will insert black bookmarks or strips of black ribbon. Half mourning to commence on Easter Monday with the holiday spectacles, and on Shakspeare's birthday the authors will go out of mourning.—*Punch.*

From The National Magazine.

THE WIDOW MINARDS' FIRST LOVE.

The fire cracked cheerfully on the broad hearth of an old-fashioned fireplace in an old-fashioned public house, in an old-fashioned village, down in Cornwall. A cat and three kittens basked in the warmth, and a decrepit yellow dog, lying full in the reflection of the blaze, wrinkled his black nose approvingly, as he turned his hind feet where his fore feet had been. Over the chimney hung several fine hams and pieces of dried beef. Apples were festooned along the ceiling, and other signs of plenty and good cheer were scattered profusely about. There were plants, too, on the window ledges, horse-shoe geraniums, and dew-plants, and a monthly rose just budding, to say nothing of pots of violets that perfumed the whole place whenever they took it into their purple heads to bloom. The floor was carefully swept, the chairs had not a speck of dust upon leg or round, the long settle near the fireplace shone as if it had been just varnished, and the eight-day clock in the corner had had its white face newly washed, and seemed determined to tick the louder for it. Two arm-chairs were drawn up at a cosy distance from the hearth and each other, a candle, a newspaper, a pair of spectacles, a dish of red-cheeked apples, and a pitcher of cider, filled a little table between them. In one of these chairs sat a comfortable-looking woman about forty-five, with cheeks as red as the apples, and eyes as dark and bright as they had ever been, resting her elbow on the table, and her head upon her hand, and looking thoughtfully into the fire. This was the Widow Minards, "relict" of Mr. Levi Minards, who had been mouldering into dust in the neighboring churchyard for more than seven years. She was thinking of her dead husband, possibly because all her work being done, and the servant gone to bed, the sight of his empty chair at the other side of the table, and the silence of the room, made her a little lonely.

"Seven years," so the widow's reverie ran; "it seems as if it were more than fifty, and yet I don't look so very old neither. Perhaps it's not having any children to bother my life out, as other people have. They may say what they like—children are more plague than profit, that's my opinion. Look at my sister Jerusha, with her six boys. She's worn to a shadow, and I'm sure they have done it, though she never will own it."

The widow took an apple from the dish and began to peel it.

"How fond Mr. Minards used to be of these apples. He never will eat any more of them, poor fellow, for I don't suppose they have apples where he has gone to. Heigho! I remember very well how I used to throw apple peel over my head when I was a girl to see who I was going to marry."

Mrs. Minards stopped short and blushed, for in those days she did not know Mr. M., and was always looking eagerly to see if the peel had formed a capital "S." Her meditations took a new turn.

"How handsome Sam Payson was, and how much I used to care about him. I wonder what has become of him! Jerusha says he went away from our village just after I did, and no one has ever heard of him since. And what a silly thing that quarrel was! If it had not been for that—"

Here came a long pause, during which the widow looked very steadfastly at the empty arm-chair of Levi Minards, deceased. Her fingers played carelessly with the apple-peel, she drew it safely towards her, and looked around the room.

"Upon my word it is very ridiculous, and I don't know what the neighbors would say if the saw me."

Still the plump fingers drew the red peel nearer.

"But then they can't see me, that's a comfort, and the cat and old Bowse never will know what it means. Of course I don't believe any thing about it."

The peel hung gracefully from her hand.

"But still, I should like to try; it would seem like old times, and—"

Over her head it went, and curled up quietly on the floor at a little distance. Old Bowse, who always slept with one eye open, saw it fall, and marched deliberately up to smell it.

"Bowse—Bowse—don't touch!" cried his mistress, and bending over it with a beating heart, she turned as red as fire. There was as handsome a capital "S" as any one could wish to see.

A great knock came suddenly at the door. Bowse growled, and the widow screamed, and snatched up the apple-peel.

"It's Mr. M.—it's his spirit come back again, because I tried that silly trick," she thought fearfully to herself.

Another knock—louder than the first, and a man's voice exclaimed,—

"Hillo—the house!"

"Who is it?" asked the widow, somewhat relieved to find that the departed Levi was still safe in his grave upon the hill-side.

"A stranger," said the voice.

"What do you want?"

"To get a lodging here for the night."

The widow deliberated.

"Can't you go on? There's a house half a mile further, if you keep to the right-hand side of the road, and turn to the left after you get by—"

"It's raining cats and dogs, and I'm very delicate," said the stranger, coughing. "I'm wet to the skin; don't you think you can accommodate me?—I don't mind sleeping on the floor."

"Raining, is it? I didn't know that," and the kind-hearted little woman unbarred the door very quickly. "Come in, whoever you may be; I only asked you to go on because I am a lone woman, with only one servant in the house."

The stranger entered, shaking himself like a Newfoundland dog upon the step, and scattering a little shower of drops over his hostess and her nicely swept floor.

"Ah, that looks comfortable after a man has been out for hours in a storm," he said as he caught sight of the fire, and striding along towards the hearth, followed by Bowse, who sniffed suspiciously at his heels, he stationed himself in the arm-chair—*Mr. Minards' arm-chair!* which had been kept "sacred to his memory" for seven years. The widow was horrified, but her guest looked so weary and worn out that she could not ask him to move, but busied herself in stirring up the blaze that he might the sooner dry his dripping clothes. A new thought struck her; Mr. M. had worn a comfortable dressing-gown during his illness, which still hung in the closet at her right. She could not let this poor man catch his death, by sitting in that wet coat; if he was in Mr. Minards' chair, why should he not be in Mr. Minards' wrapper? She went nimbly to the closet, took it down, fished out a pair of slippers from a boot-rack below, and brought them to him.

"I think you had better take off your coat and boots—you will have the rheumatic fever, or something like it, if you don't. Here are some things for you to wear while they are drying. And you must be hungry too; I will go into the pantry and get you something to eat."

She bustled away, "on hospitable thoughts intent," and the stranger made the exchange with a quizzical smile playing around his lips. He was a tall, well-formed man, with a bold but handsome face, sun-burned and heavily bearded, and looking any thing but "delicate," though his blue eyes glanced out from under a forehead as white as snow. He looked around the kitchen with a mischievous air, and stretched out his feet before him, decorated with the defunct Boniface's slippers.

"Upon my word, this is stepping into the old man's shoes with a vengeance! And what a hearty, good-humored looking woman she is! Kind as a kitten," and he leaned forward and stroked the cat and her brood, and then patted old Bowse upon the head. The widow bringing in sundry good things, looked pleased at his attention to her dumb friends.

"It's a wonder Bowse does not growl; he generally does if strangers touch him. Dear me, how stupid!"

The last remark was neither addressed to the stranger, nor to the dog, but to herself. She had forgotten that the little stand was not empty, and there was no room on it for the things she held.

"Oh, I'll manage it," said her guest, gathering up paper, candle, apples, and spectacles (it was not without a little pang that she saw them in his hand, for they had been the landlord's, and were placed each night, like the arm-chair, beside her), and depositing them on the settle.

"Give me the tablecloth, ma'am, I can spread it as well as any woman; I've learned that, along with scores of other things, in my wanderings. Now let me relieve you of those dishes, they are far too heavy for those hands," the widow blushed; "and now please to sit down with me, or I cannot eat a morsel."

"I had supper long ago, but really I think I can take something more," said Mrs. Minards, drawing her chair nearer to the table.

"Of course you can, my dear lady; in

this cold autumn weather people ought to eat twice as much as they do in warm. Let me give you a piece of this ham, your own curing, I dare say."

"Yes; my poor husband was very fond of it. He used to say that no one understood curing ham and drying beef better than I."

"He was a most sensible man, I am sure. I drink your health, ma'am, in this cider."

He took a long draught, and set down his glass.

"It is like nectar."

The widow was feeding Bowse and the cat (who thought they were entitled to a share of every meal eaten in the house), and did not quite hear what he said. I fancy she would hardly have known what "nectar" was—so it was quite as well.

"Fine dog, ma'am, and a very pretty cat."

"They were my husband's favorites," and a sigh followed the answer.

"Ah, your husband must have been a very happy man."

The blue eyes looked at her so long, that she grew flurried.

"Is there any thing more I can get for you, sir?" she asked, at last.

"Nothing, thank you, I have finished."

She rose to clear the things away. He assisted her, and somehow their hands had a queer knack of touching as they carried the dishes to the pantry shelves. Coming back to the kitchen, she put the apples and cider in their old places, and brought out a clean pipe and a box of tobacco from an arched recess near the chimney.

"My husband always said he could not sleep after eating supper late unless he smoked," she said. "Perhaps you would like to try it."

"Not if it is to drive you away," he answered, for she had her candle in her hand.

"Oh, no; I do not object to smoke at all." She put the candle down, some faint suggestion about "propriety" troubled her, but she glanced at the old clock, and felt re-assured. It was only half-past nine.

The stranger pushed the stand back after the pipe was lit, and drew her easy-chair a little nearer the fire, and his own.

"Come, sit down," he said pleadingly; "it's not late, and when a man has been knocking about in California and all sorts of places, for a score of years, he is glad enough to get into a berth like this, and to have a pretty woman to speak to once again."

"California! Have you been in California?" she exclaimed, dropping into the chair at once. Unconsciously, she had long cherished the idea that Sam Payson, the lover of her youth, with whom she had so foolishly quarrelled, had pitched his tent, after many wanderings in that far-off land. Her heart warmed to one who, with something of Sam's looks and ways about him, had also been sojourning in that country, and who very possibly had met him—perhaps had known him intimately! At that thought her heart beat quick, and she looked very graciously at the bearded stranger, who, wrapped in Mr. Minards' dressing-gown, wearing Mr. Minards' slippers, and sitting in Mr. Minards' chair, beside Mr. Minards' wife, smoked Mr. Minards' pipe with such an air of feeling most thoroughly and comfortably at home!

"Yes, ma'am, I've been in California for the last six years. And before that I went quite round the world in a whaling ship!"

"Good gracious!"

The stranger sent a puff of smoke curling gracefully over his head.

"It's very strange, my dear lady, how often you see one thing as you go wandering about the world after that fashion."

"And what is that?"

"Men, without house or home above their heads, roving here and there, and turning up in all sorts of odd places; caring very little for life as a general thing, and making fortunes just to fling them away again, and all for one reason. You don't ask me what *that* is? No doubt you know already very well."

"I think not, sir."

"Because a woman has jilted them!"

Here was a long pause, and Mr. Minards' pipe emitted short puffs with surprising rapidity. A guilty conscience needs no accuser, and the widow's cheek was dyed with blushes as she thought of the absent Sam.

"I wonder how women manage when *they* get served in the same way," said the stranger, musingly; "you never meet *them* roaming up and down in that style."

"No," said Mrs. Minards, with some spirit, "if a woman is in trouble she must stay at home and bear it, the best way she can. And there's more women bearing such things than we know of, I dare say."

From The Spectator.

THE RECREATIONS OF A COUNTRY PARSON.*

Those who cultivate the lighter literature of the day will not require to be told that this volume is the second series of a collection of essays by a writer signing himself "A. K. H. B.," published at various times during the last three years in *Fraser's Magazine*. To a reader unacquainted with them a tolerably adequate idea of their character will be conveyed by saying that they belong to the class of composition of which "Friends in Council" is one of the best known types, and that they claim a more distant affinity with the "Essays of Elia" and those of Hartley Coleridge. The present volume deals with the subjects of "Disappointment and Success"—of "Giving up and Coming Down"—of the "Worries of Life"—of the "Dignity of Dulness"—of "Growing Old"—of "Scylla and Charybdis"—of "Churchyards"—and of "Summer Days." On all these topics the country parson discourses with a meditative and generally pleasant pen, touching on matters which interest most of us, and making observations which are just sufficiently below the surface not to have occurred to us on the bare announcement of the title, and not too far-fetched to be beyond the verification of ordinary experience. His style is, for the most part, good; he always writes like a gentleman, and though there is little evidence of wide reading or deep culture in his pages, the want is partly supplied by some practical acquaintance with human nature, and a kindly sympathy with a certain though not a very large portion of it.

Those who like these essays will probably like them very much; but if they are persons of tact they will not recommend them so indiscriminately as they would do the last new novel. For nothing is more curious, in a small way, than to observe what very different judgments are pronounced upon books of this sort by persons of different ages and temperaments, and how you may pass from one circle where the writer is thought a guide, philosopher, and friend, to another where he is nothing but an insufferable twaddler or a pedantic coxcomb. A. K. H. B.'s former volume was a success, and we should not be surprised to hear that some of his more enthusiastic admirers had gone the length of writing to tell him how eagerly they looked forward to the next number of *Fraser*, and how much they wished they had such a parson in their church. The worst he appears to have heard of himself is that he is light, or frivolous, because an amusing writer, and that his essays are "sermons played in polka time." He would, perhaps, be astonished, and would certainly gain some illustrations for the next edition of his paper "On the Art of putting Things," if he could hear the unvarnished manner in which he is sometimes spoken of by persons whose sincerity he would not deny and whose capacity he could not despise. But it has always seemed to us that both the excessive admiration and violent dispraise of which he is occasionally the object rest upon a mistaken footing, and cannot be adjudged in any case of this sort upon grounds which are to be considered absolute for all the world. Some people, perhaps, prefer him, for their own consumption, to Charles Lamb; while some think him little better than Mr. Martin Tupper. Both are right in their way, for the case is one in which there is no appeal from the verdict of the individual.

The truth appears to be that every book of the moral essay class, addressed itself to a certain moral temper and to a certain degree of intellectual development, and not to any other. Some moralizers are of a very elementary sort; and though it may be true that they have made their discoveries themselves, the world made the same discoveries long ago, and people are ignorant of them only when very young. But at that time they come in usefully, as a part of education, to those who are disposed to think at all. We should be sorry to have to go through a course of the "Proverbial Philosophy," but we do not question that there is a time of life at which it may be beneficial. All that is required is to stimulate thought, and a book which effects this is good, however much we may be led to look down upon it afterwards. Some books are intellectual baby-jumpers; and the successive stages of perambulators, Shetland ponies, and hacks and hunters, have also their counterparts in the world of mental development. If we take up a book of this class at its proper time, it hits us, like a gun that has been trained to the proper range of the bit of road where

* *The Recreations of a Country Parson.* Second Series. Parker and Bourn.

sisted, but it was a magnetic touch, the rosy palm lay quietly in his, and the dark beard bent so low that it nearly touched her shoulder. It did not matter much. Was he not Samuel's dear friend? If he was not the rose, had he not dwelt very near it, for a long, long time?"

"It was a foolish quarrel that parted them," said the stranger, softly.

"Did he tell you about it?"

"Yes, on board the whaler."

"Did he blame her much?"

"Not so much as himself. He said that his jealousy and ill-temper drove her to break off the match; but he thought sometimes if he had only gone back and spoken kindly to her, she would have married him after all."

"I am sure she would," said the widow piteously. "She has owned it to me more than a thousand times."

"She was not happy, then, with another."

"Mr.—that is to say, her husband—was very good and kind," said the little woman, thinking of the lonely grave out on the hillside rather penitently, "and they lived very pleasantly together. There never was a harsh word between them."

"Still—might she not have been happier with Sam? Be honest, now, and say just what you think."

"Yes."

"Bravo! that is what I wanted to come at. And now I have a secret to tell you, and you must break it to her."

Mrs. Minards looked rather scared.

"What is it?"

"I want you to go and see her, wherever she may be, and say to her, 'Maria,'—what makes you start so?"

"Nothing; only you speak so like some one I used to know, once in awhile."

"Do I? Well, take the rest of the message. Tell her that Sam loved her through the whole; that, when he heard she was free, he began to work hard at making a fortune. He has got it; and he is coming to share it with her, if she will let him. Will you tell her this?"

The widow did not answer. She had freed her hand from his, and covered her face with it. By and by she looked up again—he was waiting patiently.

"Well?"

"I will tell her."

He rose from his seat, and walked up and down the room. Then he came back, and, leaning on the mantel-piece, stroked the yellow hide of Bowse with his slipper.

"Make her quite understand that he wants her for his wife. She may live where she likes, and how she likes, only it must be with him."

"I will tell her."

"Say he has grown old, but not cold; that he loves her now perhaps better than he did twenty years ago; that he has been faithful to her all through his life, and that he will be faithful till he dies—"

The Californian broke off suddenly. The widow answered still, "I will tell her."

"And what do you think she will say?" he asked, in an altered tone.

"What *can* she say but—*Come!*"

"Hurrah!"

The stranger caught her out of her chair as if she had been a child, and kissed her.

"Don't—oh, don't!" she cried out. "I am Sam's Maria!"

"Well—I am Maria's Sam!"

Off went the dark wig and the black whiskers—there smiled the dear face she had never forgotten! I leave you to imagine the tableau; even the cat got up to look, and Bowse sat on his stump of a tail, and wondered if he was on his heels or his head. The widow gave one little scream, and then she—

But, stop! Quiet people like you and me, dear reader, who have got over all these follies, and can do nothing but turn up our noses at them, have no business here. I will only add that two hearts were very happy, that Bowse concluded after awhile that all was right, and so laid down to sleep again, and that one week afterwards there was a wedding at the house that made the neighbors stare. The widow had married her First Love!

little bed, puts out a foot for a moment into the chilly expanse of sheet that stretches away from the warm nest in which he lies, and then pulls it swiftly back again, enjoying the cosey warmth the more for this little reminder of the bitter chill. Here, where the air is cool, pure, and soft, let us think of a hoarding round some old house which the laborers are pulling down, amid clouds of the white, blinding, parching dust of lime, on a sultry summer day. I can hardly think of any human position as worse, if not intended directly as a position of torture. . . .

"Think of being to-day in a stifling counting-house in the hot, bustling town. I have been especially interested in a glazed closet which I have seen in a certain immensely large and very crowded shop in a certain beautiful city. It is a sort of little office partitioned off from the shop; it has a sloping table, with three or four huge books bound in parchment. There is a ceaseless bustle, crush, and hum of talking outside; and inside there are clerks sitting writing, and receiving money through little pigeon-holes. I should like to sit for two or three days in a corner of that little retreat, and to write a sermon there. It would be curious to sit there to-day in the shadow, and to see the warm sunbeams only outside through a distant window, resting on sloping roofs. If one did not get sea-sick, there would be something fresh in a summer day at sea. It is always cool and breezy there, at least in these latitudes, on the warmest day. Above all, there is no dust. Think of the luxurious cabin of a fine yacht to-day. Deep cushions; rich curtains; no tremor of machinery; flowers, books, carpets inches thick; and through the windows, dim hills and blue sea. Then, flying away in spirit, let us go to-day (only in imagination) into the courts of law at Westminster. The atmosphere on a summer day in these scenes is always hot and choky. There is a suggestion of summer-time in the sunshine through the dusty lanterns in the roofs. Thinking of these courts, and of all their belongings and associations, here on this day, is like the child already mentioned when he puts his foot into a very cold corner of his bed, that he may pull it back with special sense of what a blessing it is that he is not bodily in that very cold corner."

It cannot be surprising that manifestations of this kind of spirit should make some people feel as Hotspur did at Holmedon:—

"He made me mad
To see him shine so brisk and smell so sweet . . .
And telling me the sovereign'st thing on earth
Was parmaceti for an inward bruise,
. . . and but for these vile guns
He would himself have been a soldier."

It is also tolerably evident that the author has less fellow-feeling than he would wish to have for modes of life and character very different from his own, and this want of fundamental sympathy is the reason why his popularity finds a definite limit. We cannot fancy that a very poor, or miserable, or struggling person would find much comfort in most of these essays. There is nothing very bracing about them. To this remark we must allow that the one on "Giving Up and Coming Down" is an exception; but it is the only one in the two volumes. We do not depreciate the value of the essays in general, as we have observed at the outset, by saying that they are addressed to a limited class. But we regret that the class should be limited, as we think it is, not only by intellectual development, but by worldly circumstances.

Nothing we have said, however, is meant to deter any one from reading the book, which is tolerably certain to be liked by those who like such reading at all. A very few pages will be sufficient to show its quality, for almost any page is characteristic enough to display the author's idiosyncrasy and power of expression. The essays are, of course, not all of the same merit. The one on "Scylla and Charybdis" was much admired at the time of its appearance, but a great part of it is rather commonplace, and the one good point—that on "Secondary Vulgar Errors"—appears to be due to Archbishop Whately. The "Dignity of Dulness" has some truth, but it is put in a very exaggerated way. The extent to which people believe in dulness and its cognate qualities is far too broadly stated, and the amount of justice which such belief involves is missed. "You cannot but feel an inconsistency," says A. K. H. B., "between the ideas of Mr. Disraeli writing *Henrietta Temple*, and Mr. Disraeli leading the House of Commons. You feel that somehow it costs an effort to feel that there is nothing unbefitting when the author of *The Caxtons* becomes a secretary of state. . . . How can a man befit a dignified office who has interested and amused you so much?" He explains the feeling by saying that because the jackpudding amuses us, we have a tendency to think that any one who does the like must partake of the character of the jackpudding. This is shallow. There is a real reason for preferring a man with literary antecedents like Sir Cornewall Lewis, or one with no literature at all, to a novelist or poet. The one has been exercising quite a different set of faculties to the other, and has accustomed himself to the approval of a different audience. A man who has been encouraging his imagination, fancy, and style, with the reward of immediate applause, is less likely to be cool and cautious in his measures, less disposed to have faith in the future, to wait the gradual ripening of a policy, less alive to the dead weight of custom and prejudice, too prone to deal wild strokes, to bear down opposition with contempt, to aim at an impracticable symmetry, and to hurry on the development of events. We do not, of course, mean that an imaginative man must have these defects, but they are such as, *primâ facie*, he may be expected to have; and this substantial ground for distrust is a point which Mr. Helps would have brought out very forcibly, but which seems quite to have escaped the essayist before us.

The best essay in the present volume is the one on "Giving Up and Coming Down," which contrasts the behavior, under failure, of men who accept the position without losing heart, and of those who consider all lost because one favorite object has not been attained. Another very good essay is the one on "Growing Old;" but we do not think that any are superior to the paper in the former volume on "The Way of Putting Things," which is the one we should place before a reader to whom we desired to recommend the Country Parson's work.

THE MYSTERIES OF TRADE.—In the intelligence from the Brazils, last week, we meet in one of the papers with the following curious paragraph:—

"Dry Germans opened at 59 1-2 reals, but declined to 58 for half ox half cow, and 60 for ox, this quotation being merely nominal."

The above is a complete mystification. Of course, in our travelling experiences, we have met with many "dry Germans," but we little suspected that they ever formed an article of commerce. Besides, who could care about purchasing a "dry German"? Then the question arises, how do you dry a German? or does he dry himself in his own tobacco-smoke? After this comes the further mystery of his being "opened." It is rather undignified to talk in this way of a "dry German," as if he were no better than a dried haddock, or a cured herring, or a Teutonic mummy, that had had the accumulated dust and cobwebs of centuries upon him. However, we are so far pleased as to notice that "dry Germans" fetch so good a price in the dry-goods market. It is more than we should feel inclined to give for such a specimen of dried metaphysics and transcendentalistic Kantism.

Another puzzle that bewilders us still more is the revelation that your "dry German" is "half ox, half cow." We have heard of an Irish bull, and of a *Vache Espagnole*, and of other curiosities belonging to the animal kingdom; but we must confess that such an ethnological specimen as a "dry German," that had the head of an ox and the tail of a cow, never, fortunately for us, crossed our scientific path before. We are so mystified that we must write to Professor Owen on the subject, though it looks very suspiciously as though Barnum, under a strong attack of animal spirits, had had a hand in stitching this new hybrid together for the enrichment of his New York Museum. We suppose that the "half ox" is a delicate compliment to the obstinacy of Prussia, and the "half cow" a graceful allusion to the calf-like attributes of Austria. However, our Foreign Office, that always evinces such a strong sympathy for German interests, should take the matter up. If slavery is abolished, why, we want to know, are "dry Germans" thus offered publicly for sale?—*Punch.*

SOCIETY FOR THE PREVENTION OF CRUELTY TO HUSBANDS.—In cold winter, when a horse's bit is full of frost, never put it (we are told) into his mouth without previously warming it. You shouldn't treat your husband with less kindness than you would your horse. Therefore, during the winter, put none but warm bits into the dear creature's mouth. Not to do so is very cruel, as it is very well known that the husband's mouth is much more sensitive in cold weather than at any other period of the year. It only makes him restive, and snappish, and spoils his temper, so much so that it is almost dangerous, at times, to go near him. Hence, whatever you do, avoid cold mutton.—*A Future Benedick.—Punch.*

From The Examiner.

Autobiography, Letters, and Literary Remains of Mrs. Piozzi (Thrale). Edited with Notes and an Introductory Account of her Life and Writings, by A. Hayward, Esq., Q.C. In two volumes. Longman and Co.

Mr. Salusbury, who possesses the record entitled "Thraliana" in which the experience of thirty-three years of Mrs. Piozzi's life (from 1776 to 1809) were faithfully chronicled by herself, will, no doubt after reading these volumes open his stores freely to Mr. Hayward. He has supplied interesting extracts, but considers the whole chronicle "of too private and delicate a character to be submitted to strangers." Henceforward in face of these volumes no member of Mrs. Piozzi's family can be justified in treating Mr. Hayward as a stranger. They give to her whom Doctor Johnson, even in the day of his discontent, characterized as "gracious, mild, and good," much of the reputation she deserves, and they make it tolerably evident that there can be nothing in the six volumes of "Thraliana" that ought to be withheld from the knowledge of a genial and considerate biographer. Few are the people for whom good-will does not strengthen upon closer knowledge, and Mrs. Thrale assuredly is not one of the exceptions. With the woman's heart opened to him more fully by the unrestricted reading of a frank record of experiences, not made without reference to the interest it would have for posterity, Mr. Hayward would know how to reconcile all apparent incongruities of character. At present there is still room left for speculation, and without any indiscreet publication, even without much addition of facts hitherto reserved, by help of the "Thraliana" fresh insight has yet to be given us into Mrs. Piozzi's character. We trust, therefore, that Mr. Hayward, after a full reading of that journal, will be enabled to add largely to the value of all future editions of a book that is now being read widely, as the pleasantest book of the season, and that will retain its interest for all students of literary history as a trustworthy collection of notes illustrating an important period.

The autobiographical and other writings of Mrs. Piozzi here first published are rich in anecdote, and they are set forth by an editor who has himself the happiest way of enlivening with anecdote all that he writes. Their editor knows how to win the ear even of the whole idle public, as a well-read gossip as well as a man basing his judgments upon sound thought and good feeling. Mr. Hayward's own sketch of Mrs. Piozzi's Life and Writings, in itself almost a volume, is followed by the first publication of some Autobiographical Memoirs written by her for the late Sir James Fellowes, who was one of her executors: of letters addressed to Sir James Fellowes, to the Rev. Daniel Lysons and to Mr. Samuel Lysons; of MS. notes by her from the margin of Boswell's Johnson, of Wraxall's Memoirs, and of her own printed works, the notes serving almost wholly to give more exact knowledge of facts; of extracts and information supplied from the "Thraliana," and finally of fugitive compositions of her own, new to the public, with a few reprinted pieces. The conclusion to which we are brought by the new information set before us is one that only a close study of the "Thraliana" could fully confirm. We are disposed to think that the lively Mrs. Thrale was a sad woman; that the queen of a blue-stocking coterie, the brisk and social Mrs. Thrale, was a domestic woman. With the sallies of a quick wit and the womanly tact that is amiable in all its forms, she doubled, indeed, the cheer of the Streatham dinner-table, and relieved the gloom of many years of Johnson's life; but even to the admiring Johnson all her heart could not be opened. The true wife for whom the husband's ear is dull is condemned to a silence that oppresses her not least when she is in a social crowd, talking among the talkers. It is for her, if for any sorrower, to stand aloof and murmur, "Res est sacra miser: noli mea tangere fata," and to give her outward life up to that hypocrisy of woman's triviality which is so often, when we hold it mean in her, a woman's heroism.

That she celebrated her eightieth birthday at Bath with a ball and led the dance, her death in the year following being the result of accident, not of disease, was no sign of a natural frivolity, though it was evidence of a confirmed habit of living in society. The old woman's fancy for Mr. Conway libelled in the American issue of "Love-letters of Mrs. Piozzi, written when she was eighty"—when surely we may remember with Mr. Hayward that *l'age n'a point de sexe*—represents a relation of warm friendship that is of every-day occurrence between youth and age that is not crabbed. With reversal of the ages and the sexes the same thing occurred also in the strong friendship of her girlhood for her preceptor, Doctor Collier, whose memory was sacred to the last with her. Sophy Streatfield, who supplanted her in the esteem of Mr. Thrale, followed her in her girlish friendship for the Doctor, and invited public applause for the sentiment by wearing black for him annually on the date of his death. The happiest days known to Mrs. Piozzi were those of the second marriage, against which her daughters, her friends, and the newspapers took up arms. Piozzi was by no means penniless. When yielding to the storm of opinion and assenting to abandonment of the intended marriage we find that he lent a thousand pounds to the rich widow who was then in debt, she was in debt still when they married, and her debts were paid in three years through his prudence in management of her property by which, when he died, it did not appear that he added to his own possessions. The estrangement of her daughters was the only grief during these years. Piozzi adopted her Welsh country and her creed, and left her nothing to desire. Her first marriage had not been one of love. She says in her Memoirs that Mr. Thrale, who had been chosen for her, "deigned to accept her undesired hand," and that he proved "much kinder than she counted on to a plain girl who had not one attraction in his eyes, and on whom he never had thrown five minutes of his time away, in any interview unwitnessed by company, even till after our wedding-day was done." He had offered himself to several women before her, she was told, but she was the first who would consent to live in the Borough. Thrale was handsome, affected fashion, and seems to have been, away from his own hearth, stupidly gay. His wife's confidence he took no trouble to win, and once when she was ill he insulted her at his own table by requesting her to yield her place at its head to his favorite Sophy. When, physically weakened, she burst into tears and left the room, Johnson and Burke sat on each side of her and said not a word in her support. Mr. Thrale was given to good eating; the gluttonous taste grew on him, and was associated painfully with his last illness. In the face of death he was inquiring about the next lamprey season. But the wife who graced his rich table was not to think of the kitchen, and says:—

"Driven thus on literature as my sole resource, no wonder if I loved my books and children. From a *gay* life my mother held me fast. Those pleasures Mr. Thrale enjoyed alone; with *me* indeed they never would have suited; I was too often and too long confined. Although Doctor Johnson (now introduced among us) told me once, before *her* face, who deeply did resent it, that I lived like my husband's kept mistress,—shut from the world, its pleasures or its cares.

"The scene was soon to change. Fox-hounds were sold, and a seat in Parliament was suggested by our new inmate as more suitable to his dignity, more desirable in every respect. I grew useful now, *almost* necessary; wrote the advertisements, looked to the treats, and people to whom I was then unknown, admired how happy Mr. Thrale must be in such a *wonder* of a wife.

"I wondered all the while where his heart lay; but it was found at last, too soon for joy, too late almost for sorrow. A vulgar fellow, by name Humphrey Jackson, had, as the clerks informed me all in a breath, complete possession of it. He had long practised on poor Thrale's credulity, till, by mixing two cold liquors which produced heat perhaps, or two colorless liquors which produced brilliancy, he had at length prevailed on him to think he could produce beer too, without the *beggarly elements* of malt and hops. He had persuaded him to build a copper somewhere in East Smithfield, the very metal of which cost £2,000, wherein this Jackson was to make experiments and conjure some curious stuff, which should preserve ships' bottoms from the worm; gaining from government money to defray these mad expenses. Twenty enormous vats, holding one thousand hogsheads each—costly contents! Ten more holding one thousand barrels each, were constructed to stew in this pernicious mess; and afterwards erected on, I forget how much, ground bought for the ruinous purpose.

"That *all* were spoiled, was but a secondary sorrow. We had, in the commercial phrase, no beer to start for customers. We had no money to purchase with. Our clerks, insulted long, rebelled and *ratted*, but I held them in. A sudden run menaced the house, and death hovered over the head of its principal. I think some faint image of the distress appears in Doctor Johnson's forty-eight letter, 1st vol. But God tempers every evil with some good. Such was my charming mother's firmness, and such her fond attachment to us both, that our philosophical friend, embracing her, exclaimed, that he was equally charmed by her conduct, and edified by her piety. 'Fear not the menaces of suicide,' said he; 'the man who has two such females to console him, never yet killed himself, and will not *now*. Of all the bankrupts made this dreadful year,' continued he, 'none have destroyed themselves but married men; who would have risen from the weeds undrowned, had not the women clung about and sunk them, stifling the voice of reason with their cries.' Ah, Sir James Fellowes, and have not I too been in a ship on fire, not for two hours, but for two full weeks, between the knowledge of my danger and the end on't?

"Well! first we made free with our mother's money, her little savings! about £3,000—'twas all she had; and big as I was with child, I drove down to Brighthelmstone, to beg of Mr. Scrase £6,000 more—he gave it us—and Perkins, the head clerk, had never done repeating my short letter to our master, which only said, 'I have done my errand, and you soon shall see returned, *whole*, as I hope—your heavy but faithful messenger, H. L. T.'"

She not only canvassed electors for her husband, but when taken into confidence as to the state of his business, worked faithfully for him, as this note to the chief clerk, Mr. Perkins, testifies.

"Mr. Thrale is still upon his little tour; I opened a letter from you at the counting-house this morning, and am sorry to find you have so much trouble with Grant and his affairs. How glad I shall be to hear that matter is settled at all to your satisfaction. His letter and remittance came while I was there to-day. . . . Careless, of the 'Blue Posts,' has turned refractory, and applied to Hoare's people, who have sent him in their beer. I called on him to-day, however, and by dint of an unwearied solicitation (for I kept him at the coach side a full half-hour) I got his order for six butts more as the final trial."

The boy for whom both she and her husband longed was lost by premature birth after exertion made by her to quell a riot among the brewery clerks. After Thrale's death she still worked in the counting-house.

"On Mr. Thrale's death I kept the counting-house from nine o'clock every morning till five o'clock every evening till June, when God Almighty sent us a knot of rich Quakers who bought the whole, and saved me and my coadjutors from brewing ourselves into another bankruptcy, which hardly could, I think, have been avoided, being as we were five in number, Cator, Crutchley, Johnson, myself, and Mr. Smith, all with equal power, yet all incapable of using it without help from Mr. Perkins, who wished to force himself into partnership, though hating the whole lot of us, save only *me*. Upon my promise, however, that if he would find us a purchaser, I would present his wife with my dwelling-house at the Borough, and all its furniture, he soon brought forward these Quaker Barclays, from Pennsylvania I believe they came,—her own relations I have heard,—and they obtained the brewhouse a prodigious bargain, but Miss Thrale was of my mind, to part with it for £150,000; and I am sure I never did repent it, as certainly it was best for us five females at the time, although the place has now doubled its value, and although men have almost always spirit to spend, while women show greater resolution to spare.

"Will it surprise you now to hear that, among all my fellow executors, *none* but Johnson opposed selling the concern? Cator, a rich timber merchant, was afraid of implicating his own credit as a commercial man. Crutchley hated Perkins, and lived upon the verge of a quarrel with him every day while they acted together. Smith cursed the whole business, and wondered what his relation, Mr. Thrale, could mean by leaving him £200 he said, and such a burden on his back to bear for it. All were well pleased to find themselves secured, and the brewhouse *decently*, though not *very*, advantageously disposed of, except dear Doctor Johnson, who found some odd delight in signing drafts for hundreds and for thousands, to him a new, and as it appeared delightful, occupation. When all was nearly over, however, I cured his honest heart of its incipient passion for trade, by letting him into *some*, and *only* some, of its mysteries."

Of what griefs she suffered from the sickness and death of many children we have only here and there a touching glimpse. It was the clever kindly woman putting a good face over the secret sorrows of her heart that the world saw. Inevitably her quick conversational power was accompanied with pleasure in its exercise; she found pleasure in society, but behind her social life there was that hidden which gave the character to her intercourse marked by her friend Johnson's love of her as "gracious, mild, and good," and by the turn given to the definition of her among other notable ladies celebrated in verse by a writer to the *Morning Herald* as—

"Thrale, in whose expressive eyes,
Sits a soul above disguise,
Skilled with wit and sense t' impart
Feelings of a generous heart."

"Amongst Miss Reynolds' 'Recollections' will be found: 'On the praises of Mrs. Thrale he (Johnson) used to dwell with a peculiar delight, a paternal fondness, expressive of conscious exultation in being so intimately acquainted with her. One day, in speaking of her to Mr. Harris, author of "Hermes," and expatiating on her various perfections,—the solidity of her virtues, the brilliancy of her wit, and the strength of her understanding, etc.,—he quoted some lines (a stanza, I believe, but from what author I know not), with which he concluded his most eloquent eulogium, and of these I retained but the last two lines:—

"'"Virtues—of such a generous kind,
Good in the last recesses of the mind."'"

Although we are not yet fairly admitted to "the last recesses of her mind," it is certain that the force of the material here brought together, and not only the kindliness of its editor, tends altogether towards confirmation of impressions such as these. In many respects she was in a false position. The false position of her first marriage she sustained with an unblemished dignity and worth. The artificial life in which she was thrown, the public flattery and public scandal that beset her, could not be without hurtful influence upon her mind. If she had written fewer books, or none, it would have been well, for she was misled into a false sense of literary power. There can be no doubt that the influence of Doctor Johnson went far, and the influence of her first disappointment as a wife and mother went farther, towards the conversion of Mrs. Piozzi, in her second marriage, into the sort of happy woman sketched in the next extract.

"Towards the end of 1765, Mrs. Piozzi left Streatham for her seat in North Wales, where (1800 to 1801) she was visited by a young nobleman, now an eminent statesman, distinguished by his love of literature and the fine arts, who has been good enough to recall and write down his impressions of her for me:—

"'I did certainly know Madam Piozzi, but had no habits of acquaintance with her, and she never lived in London to my knowledge. When in my youth I made a tour in Wales,—times when all inns were bad, and all houses hospitable,—I put up for a day at her house, I think in Denbighshire, the proper name of which was Bryn, and to which, on the occasion of her marriage I was told, she had recently added the name of Bella. I remember her taking me into her bedroom to show me the floor covered with folios, quartos, and octavos, for consultation, and indicating the labor she had gone through in compiling an immense volume she was then publishing, called "Retrospection." She was certainly what was called, and is still called, blue, and that of a deep tint, but good humored and lively, though affected; her husband, a quiet civil man, with his head full of nothing but music.'"

But we must cease from speculation, and illustrate, by a few of the anecdotes found among Mrs. Piozzi's annotations upon books, the pleasant character of the best piece of fireside reading that has been published for many a day.

"Mr. Keep, when he heard I was a native of North Wales, told me that *his* wife was a Welch woman, and desired to be buried at Ruthyn. 'So,' says the man, 'I went with the corpse myself, because I thought it would be a *pleasant journey*, and indeed I found Ruthyn a very beautiful place."

"Lord Thurlow was storming one day at his old valet, who thought little of a violence with which he had been long familiar, and 'Go to the devil *do*,' cries the enraged master; 'Go, I say, to the devil.' 'Give me a character, my lord,' replied the fellow drily; 'people like, you know, to have characters from their acquaintance.'"

"Lord Sandwich had trained up a huge baboon that he was fond of, to play the part of a clergyman, dressed in canonicals, and make some buffoon imitation of saying grace. Among many merry friends round the table, sat a Mr. Scott, afterwards well known by the name of Antisejanus; but then a mere dependent servitor at college, and humble playfellow of young Hinchinbroke. The ape had no sooner finished his grimaces, and taken leave of the company, than Scott unexpectedly, but unabashed, stood up and said:—

"'I protest, my lord, I intended doing this duty myself, not knowing till now that your lordship had so *near a relation in orders*.'

"I must add that Lord Sandwich praised his wit and courage without ever resenting the liberty."

"I don't know whether this Lord Harry Powlett, or an uncle of his wearing the same name, was the person of whom my mother used to relate a ludicrous anecdote. Some lady with whom *she* had been well acquainted, and to whom his lordship was observed to pay uncommon attentions, requested him to procure for her a pair of small monkeys from East India—I forget the kind. Lord Harry, happy to oblige her, wrote immediately, depending on the best services of a distant friend, whom he had essentially served. Writing a bad hand, however, and spelling what he wrote for with more haste than correctness, he charged the gentleman, to send him over *two* monkeys, but the word being written *too*, and all the characters of one height, 100—what was poor Lord Harry Powlett's dismay, when a letter came to hand, with the news that he would receive fifty monkeys by such a ship, and fifty more by the next conveyance, making up the *hundred* according to his lordship's commands!"

Our space is exhausted, but we might easily fill ten columns with anecdote from Mr. Hayward's store.

LIMITED PERFECTION.—Mr. William Peer, of the Theatre Royal, was an actor at the Restoration, and took his theatrical degree with Betterton, Kynaston, and Harris. Though his station was humble, he performed it well, and the common-comparison between the stage and human life, which has been so often made, may well be brought out upon this occasion. It is no matter, say the moralists, whether you act a prince or a beggar,—the business is to do your part well. Mr. William Peer distinguished himself particularly in two characters, which no man ever could touch but himself. One of them was the speaker of the prologue to the play which is contrived in the tragedy of Hamlet, to awake the consciences of the guilty princes. Mr. William Peer spoke that preface to the play with such an air, as represented that he was an actor, and with such an inferior manner, as only acting an actor, as (that he) made the others on the stage appear real great persons, and not representatives. This was a nicety in acting, that none but the most subtle player could so much as conceive. I remember his speaking these words, in which there is no great matter but in the right adjustment of the air of the speaker, with universal applause:—

"For us and for our tragedy,
Here stooping to your clemency,
We beg your hearing patiently."

Hamlet says, very archly, upon the pronouncing of it, *Is this a prologue, or a posy of a ring?* However, the speaking of it got Mr. Peer more reputation than those who speak the length of a puritan's sermon every night will ever attain to. Besides this, Mr. Peer got great fame upon another *little* occasion. He played the apothecary in *Caius Marius*, as it is called by Otway, but Romeo and Juliet as originally in Shakspeare. It will be necessary to recite more out of the play than he spoke, to have a right conception of what Peer did in it. Marius, weary of life, recollects means to be rid of it, after this manner:

"I do remember an apothecary
That dwelt about this rendezvous of death:
Meagre and very rueful were his looks,
Sharp misery had worn him to the bones."

When this spectre of poverty appeared, Marius addresses him thus:—

"I see thou art very poor,
Thou mayest do any thing;—here's fifty drachmas,
Get me a draught of what will soonest free
A wretch from all his cares."

When the apothecary objects that it is unlawful, Marius urges,—

"Art thou so base and full of wretchedness,
Yet fear'st to die? Famine is in thy cheeks,
Need and oppression stareth in thy eyes,
Contempt and beggary hang on thy back;
The world is not thy friend, nor the world's laws;
The world affords no laws to make thee rich,—
Then be not poor, but break it and take this."

Without all this quotation, the reader could not have a just idea of the visage and manner which Peer assumed, when, in the most lamentable tone imaginable, he consents, and delivering the poison like a man reduced to the drinking it himself, if he did not vend it, says to Marius:—

"My poverty, but not my will consents,
Take this and drink it off, the work is done."

It was an odd excellence, and a very particular circumstance, this of Peer's, that his whole action of life depended upon speaking five lines better than any man else in the world. But this eminence lying in so narrow a compass, the governors of the theatre observing his talents to lie in a certain knowledge of propriety, and his person permitting him to shine only in the two above parts, his sphere of action was enlarged by the addition of the post of "property-man."
—*Guardian, No.* 82.

From The Examiner.

Works and Correspondence of Alexis de Tocqueville. Edited by Gustave de Beaumont, Membre de l'Institut.*

We close our notice of this work with a couple of translated extracts, for which we had last week no space to spare:—

A Fortnight in the Desert.—(1831.)

"... In the midst of a society continually occupied with questions of morality and philanthropy, a complete insensibility, a cold and implacable egotism exists, as concerns the indigenous races. The inhabitants of the United States do not hunt the Indians with horn and hound as the Spaniards did in Mexico; but the same unpitying instinct animates Europeans towards them. How often in the course of our journeys have we not met honest countrymen who remarked, quietly sitting in their chimney corner, 'Every day the number of Indians is decreasing. It is not that we make war on them; but the cheap brandy we sell them does it. This world, in fact, belongs to us. God, in denying to the original race the power of becoming civilized, destined them to annihilation. The real proprietors of this continent, are those who know how to make the most of the riches it produces.' Satisfied with this reasoning, the American goes to his chapel, where he hears a minister of the Gospel repeat that all men are brothers, and that the Eternal who made all on the same model has given all the same duty to assist each other.

"The 19th of July, at ten in the morning, we went on board the boat going to Detroit; there was a fresh breeze from the north-west, which made the waters of Lake Erie like the waves of the sea. On our right extended a boundless horizon, to the left we kept near the southern banks of the lake, which we sometimes approached within hail. These banks are perfectly flat, and unlike, in that respect, all I have seen in Europe; neither do they resemble the borders of the sea: immense forests shade and make a thick and continuous belt around them. Suddenly the whole aspect of the country changes; on turning the corner of a wood a graceful spire, dazzlingly white houses and shops appear; two steps beyond the primitive forest recommences, apparently impenetrable, casting its deep shadow on the waters.

"Those who know the United States will find in this picture a striking emblem of American society. All is sudden — unexpected. Everywhere extreme civilisation and nature abandoned to herself meet face to face. In France this cannot be understood. For my own part, full of the illusions of a traveller, I had imagined something very different. I had remarked in Europe that the greater or less isolation of towns and cities exercised on the inhabitants a marked difference, even of several centuries, and in the New World I thought this would be even more apparent, and that a country peopled incompletely and successively like America, would offer an aspect of society representing all the ages of the earth, and I considered that America was the only country in which might be followed, step by step, all the transformations that the social state entails on man, and where it would be possible to perceive, as it were, a vast chain descending link by link from the opulent patrician of the city of the savages of the desert. In fact, I expected to find, between certain degrees of longitude, the whole history of humanity framed. There is no particle of truth in this view of the case; and of all portions of the globe America is least capable of affording the experience I came to seek. In America there is but one society; rich or poor, humble or brilliant, commercial or agricultural, all is formed of the same elements. The level of an even civilization has passed over the land, the man you left in the streets of New York you will find again in the western solitude; the same dress, the same spirit, accent, habits, amusements. Nothing rustic, nothing simple, nothing that tells of desert life, nothing even that resembles village life in Europe. The reason of this singular state of things is easy to comprehend. Those portions of territory, inhabited the first and the most completely peopled, have arrived at a high degree of civilization. Instruction has been profusely scattered; the spirit of equality has cast a singularly uniform hue over the interior habits of life. Now, observe, it is always the *same men* who go every year to people the desert. In Europe every one lives and dies on the soil that gave him birth. In America nowhere do we meet the representatives of a race which has multiplied itself in solitude, after having long lived ignorant of the world, and dependent on its own efforts. Those whom you find living in isolated spots arrived there, as it were, only yesterday: they come with the manners, the ideas, the wants of civilisation. They give to savage life no more than imperious necessity demands of them, and hence the most absurd contrasts. One passes without transition from a desert to the street of a city, from the wildest scenes to the liveliest pictures of social society. If night, surprising, does not force you to repose under a tree, you are likely to arrive

* The other part is at p. 11, No. 879, *Living Age*.

at a village, where you will find all you can require, even to French fashions and the caricatures of the Boulevards. The merchant of Buffalo or of Detroit is quite as well provided with all this as he of New York. Lyons weaves for one as much as for the other. . . . The hut of an American is only a momentary asylum, a temporary concession to the necessity of circumstances. As soon as the fields which surround him have yielded their produce, and the new settler has time to occupy himself with the pleasures of life, a mansion more spacious and more appropriate to his requirements will replace the log-house, and give space to numerous children, who in their turn will, at some future day, create for themselves a dwelling in some new desert.

". . . His whole mind centred in one end alone, that of making his fortune; the emigrant has succeeded in creating for himself an individual existence; even his family feelings resolve themselves into a vast system of egotism, and he hardly knows whether in wife or children he acknowledges more than a detached portion of himself. His hospitality is given with so much constraint and coldness, you perceive such profound indifference as to the effect it may produce, that your gratitude is frozen at its birth: he seems to afford it merely as a condition of his position, not as any thing that can give him pleasure. The settler is the representative of a race to which belongs the future of the new world, a race restless, reasoning, adventurous, which coldly performs acts which are usually explained only by the passions: a nation of conquerors which submits to a savage life without any feeling for its attractions, which cares for civilization and enlightenment only as they are useful to his own good, and who shuts himself up in the solitudes of America with his hatchet and a newspaper. An immense people! which, like all great peoples, has but one thought, and which marches on to the acquirement of riches, the only goal of its labor, with a perseverance and contempt of life which might be considered heroic if the term belonged to any other efforts but those of virtue. A wandering people whose progress no lakes nor rivers can arrest, before whom forests fall and meadows are covered with shade, and which, having reached the Pacific Ocean, will return, retracing its steps in order to disturb and destroy the society which it has formed behind its course."

M. de Tocqueville's opinion of liberty in Prussia is expressed in the following letter to Louis de Kergorlay:—

". . . The journey you are about to take interests me peculiarly, not only on your own account but on mine. All that you will see excites my curiosity most vividly. After England the country I have always most desired to visit is Prussia. All I have heard of it convinces me that it is a country which deserves to be examined with care: that which strikes me amongst other things is this: the Prussian Government, whether following out a principle or obeying an instinct, endeavors, it seems, to make its subjects forget that they are deprived of *real political liberty*, by liberally according such secondary liberties as may be compatible with absolute monarchy: so that it is preparing the people, either voluntarily or unknowingly, to do without it, and, without violent measures, reach the point of self-direction. It appears to me to be very curious to study this indirect influence exercised by the Free States of the West of Europe on the great despotic monarchies of the East and North.

"It comes to something similar to that which happened in the sixteenth century when the Reformed States modified the catholicism of those which remained Catholic. I indicate this subject in general to your observation, not perhaps as the most interesting, but as that which occupies me the most. Entering into detail, I would ask you to take note, as carefully as you can, of the Prussian *provincial* and *communal* system, as well as of their limits of centralization. I attach much importance to this. It is not by means of arguments, drawn from what passes amongst republican or semi-republican people, that we may hope to attack French centralization with advantage. It is only reason, taken from the subject, of an absolute government that will make a lasting impression on the anti-liberal mass. . . . As for general advice regarding your journey, remember that the most important thing is to mix with as many individuals as possible, and by putting every man upon the subject that he understands the best, to draw from him all he can give. To attain this the best way is to lead men to speak of each other: this kind of information is precious, and as you do not seek it to give it to the public, it is perfectly innocent to collect such.

"Your name and your letters are sufficient to introduce you to the aristocracy, but all your efforts should be directed to make you acquainted with the middle and literary classes. I recommend you also, as an old traveller, to listen to all sides without taking any in particular. You are a stranger, and are not obliged to give an opinion of what passes in Prussia: only, therefore, say enough to lead the interlocutor to develop his own thought. Be careful never to indulge in a custom which you are apt to carry to excess in France, of never frequenting the society of those who morally displease you. Write much; you cannot do so too much. In writing you become aware of the obscurity of your ideas, and of those of others, and you discover the causes of this. Write to me frequently, and I need scarcely say put under cover to me all the *sealed* letters you please. As you have so well said, the remarkable and truly moral and elevated part of our friendship is the great independence of thought and action we mutually allow each other in the midst of so strict an intimacy. I think this is all I have to say, adding however, as a matter of course, that you must vigorously shake off during your journey any disposition to *nonchalance*, which is apt to take possession of travellers, and of you, perhaps, more than another, because you are a dreamer. Act as much as you can. Never lose an opportunity of seeing, and above all of becoming acquainted with mankind. . . ."

MISUSE OF THE PARTICIPLE.—

"He would *have spoke*."—Milton, P. L. x. 517.

"Words *interwove* with sighs found out their way."—P. L. i. 621.

"Those kings and potentates who *have strove*."—Eiconoclast. xvii.

"And to his faithful servant *hath* in place
Bore witness gloriously." Sam. Ag. ver. 1752.

"And envious darkness, ere they could return,
Had stole them from me." Comus. ver. 195.
Here it is observable, that the Author's MS. and the first Edition have it *stolne*.

"And in triumph *had rode*." P. R. iii. 36.

"I *have chose*
This perfect man." P. R. i. 165.

"The fragrant brier *was wove* between."—Dryden, Fables.

"I will scarce think you *have swam* in a Gondola."—Shakspeare, As you like it.

"Then finish what you *have began*;
But scribble faster, if you can."—Dryden, Poems, Vol. II. p. 172.

"And now the years a numerous train *have ran*;
The blooming boy is ripen'd into man."—Pope's Odyss. xi. 555.

"Which I *had* no sooner *drank*, *but* I found a pimple rising in my forehead."—Addison, Tatler, No. 131.

"*Have sprung*." Atterbury, Serm. I. 4. "*had spake*—*had began*—"—Clarendon, Contin. Hist. p. 40, and 120. "The men *begun* to embellish themselves."—Addison, Spect. No. 434.

"Rapt into future times the bard *begun*."—Pope, Messiah,
And without the necessity of rhyme:

"A second deluge learning thus *o'er-run*,
And the Monks finished what the Goths *begun*." Essay on Criticism.

"Repeats you verses *wrote* on glasses."—Prior.

"Mr. Misson *has wrote*."—Addison, Preface to his Travels. "He could only command his voice, which *was broke* with sighs and sobbings, so far as to bid her proceed."—Addison, Spect. No. 164.

"No civil broils *have* since his death *arose*."
Dryden, on O. Cromwell.

"Illustrious virtues, who by turns *have rose*."—Prior.

"*Had* not *arose*."—Swift, Battle of Books: and Bolingbroke, Letter to Wyndham, p. 233.

"The Sun *has rose*, and gone to bed.
Just as if Partridge were not dead."—Swift.

"This nimble operator will *have stole it*."—Tale of a Tub, Sect. x.

"Some Philosophers *have mistook*."—Ibid. Sect ix.

"That Diodorus *has* not *mistook himself* in his account of the date of Phintia, we may be as sure as any history can make us."—Bentley, Dissert. on Phalaris, p. 98.

"Why, all the souls that were, were forfeit once:
And He, that might the 'vantage best *have took*,
Found out the remedy." Shakspeare, Meas. for Meas.

"Silence
Was took ere she was ware."—Milton, Comus.

"Into these common-places look,
Which from great authors I *have took*."—Prior, Alma.

"A free Constitution, when it has *been shook* by the iniquity of former administrations."—Bolingbroke, Patriot King, p. 111.

"Too strong to *be shook* by his enemies."—Atterbury.

"Ev'n there he should *have fell*."—Prior, Solomon.

"Sure some disaster *has befell*."—Gay, Fables.
Bishop Lowth's Grammar. 1762.

They say it out sells Tristram Shandy.
Bishop Hurd's Letters.

THE CHORUS OF THE UNION.

See the concluding paragraph of the President's Inaugural Address.

Ye sons of patriot sires!
List to your country's call,
Nor cherish those unholy fires
Which will but light her fall:
Hold to the glorious Union yet,
Nor sever it in two;
Our fathers' prayers would ye forget?
Ye know not what ye do!
Firm and united let us stand,
Nor madly, rashly sever
The golden links our fathers planned—
Planned to endure forever!

We're bound by mutual ties;
No hostile hands are ours,
From where Maine's snowy mountains rise,
To the fair land of flowers.
Lo! we are ONE, from sea to sea—
One League binds State to State;
Why haste to break such amity?
Pause, ere it be too late!
Firm and united let us stand, etc.

From every battle-field,
From every patriot's grave,
By whose warm blood the past was sealed,
Who died his land to save,
Are solemn, warning voices heard,
Of mingled grief and fear:
What soul so dead that 'tis not stirred
Those warning tones to hear?
Firm and united let us stand, etc.

From every hallowed spot
Stretch memory's mystic chords,
To heart and hearth, to hall and cot,
And yet shall swell the words
Of love and peace, the chorus grand
Of Union and the Free,
When by our better angel's hand
Once more they touched shall be.
Firm and united let us stand, etc.

Though passion may have strained
Affection's holy band,
Oh! break it not, nor be profaned
The genius of our land?
For friends and brothers still are we,
ONE flag will wave o'er all;
Or, o'er the corse of Liberty
Be spread a funeral pall!
Firm and united let us stand,
Nor madly, rashly sever
The golden links our fathers planned—
Planned to endure forever!

WM. L. SHOEMAKER.

Georgetown, D. C., March 8th, 1861.

—*North American.*

THIRTY-FIVE.

BY HENRY MORFORD.

HALT on the road a little space!
Pull up your team, old charioteer!
You're hurrying along at a slapping pace;
Suppose we stop and consider here!
If our lives are three score and ten—
If my count is all to be told—
The half-way house we are passing, then,
Thirty-five long winters old!

How has the ride been, charioteer?
Plenty of dust and a little of mire?
Cold North winds on the hills severe,
And the air of the valley thick with fire?
Horses balking, then running away—
Linch-pins lost, and axle down?
Creeping, crippled, at close of day,
To a night of rest at tavern or town?

More than this, O charioteer!
We have rounded the hills in the flush of morn,
Heard the sunrise bird sing loud and clear,
And snuffed the breeze on the blue waves born,
We have caught such glimpses of Eden vales,
Heard such sounds by wood and stream—
Drank such sounds by wood and stream—
As made all life an Elysian dream!

Rough and loud have voices been—
Pelting and bitter missile and storm;
But ever at last have we hurried in
And found some shelter snug and warm.
Kind, sometimes, have been word and fare;
Strong and steady the hand;
And erring roads had many a prayer
Breathing o'er them from the better land!

How much further, charioteer,
To the end?—and he shakes his head.
No, to the eyes of an older seer,
Peril is looming near and dread!
Tell me not, O charioteer!
Bold and blind let me meet my fate!
Only thus our journey steer—
So that we wreck at the Beautiful Gate!

Onward, now, but tighten rein!
Downward, now, our journey lies!
Weakened soon will grow hand and brain!
And the mist comes o'er the failing eyes!
God be with us, charioteer!
Keep us with heart and hope alive!
Sad and short is our stoppage here—
At the half-way house of thirty-five.

—*Charleston Courier.*

MINISTERING ANGELS.

I SEE no light, I hear no sound,
When midnight shades are spread;
Yet angels pitch their tents around,
And guard my quiet bed.

JANE TAYLOR.

THE LIVING AGE.

No. 881.—20 April, 1861.

CONTENTS.

NEW BOOKS.

Autobiography, Letters, and Literary Remains of Mrs. Piozzi (Thrale). Edited with Notes and an introductory account of her Life and Writings. By A. Hayward, Esq., Q.C. Boston: Ticknor and Fields.

The Sable Cloud: a Southern Tale, with Northern Comments. By the author of "A South-side View of Slavery." Boston: Ticknor and Fields.

The National Controversy; or, The Voice of the Fathers upon the State of the Country. By Joseph C. Stiles. New York: Rudd & Carleton.—Boston: Crosby, Nichols, Lee & Co.

Union, Slavery, Secession. A Letter from Governor R. R. Call, of Florida, to John S. Littell, of Pennsylvania. Philadelphia: C. Sherman & Son.

The South: a Letter from a Friend in the North. With special reference to the effect of Disunion upon Slavery. Philadelphia: C. Sherman & Son.

The Five Cotton States, and New York; or, Remarks upon the Social and Economical Aspects of the Southern Political Crisis.

The Flag of our Union. An Oration in Schuylkill County, Pennsylvania. By Robert Patterson Kane, Esq. Pottsville.

PUBLISHED EVERY SATURDAY BY

LITTELL, SON, & CO., BOSTON.

VIRGINIA TO THE NORTH.

THUS speaks the sovereign Old Dominion
To Northern States her frank opinion.

FIRST.

MOVE NOT A FINGER: 'tis coercion,
The signal for our prompt dispersion.

SECOND.

WAIT, till I make my full decision,
Be it for union or division.

THIRD.

If I declare my ultimatum,
ACCEPT MY TERMS, as I shall state 'em.

FOURTH.

THEN, I'll remain, while I'm inclined to,
Seceding when I have a mind to.

TO THE HON. ANDREW JOHNSON, SENATOR FROM TENNESSEE.

THE spirit in which most of the speakers in Virginia address the United States, is not unfairly exhibited in the epigrammatic verses, copied above from *The New York Commercial Advertiser.*

How different is the attitude of the States which refused to call conventions! It is said that "the woman who deliberates is lost;" and every State which takes into consideration whether it will revolt or no, stains its own character in some degree. "Touch not, taste not, handle not the unclean thing."

The people of the United States wait the progress of events with burning vexation, though willing to "let patience have her perfect work," and confidently trusting to the administration. But we are anxious to be *doing something* ourselves, and can hardly bear entire inaction while the "confederates" are sending their emissaries to propagate treason in the Border States and Territories. To sit still is to allow them to take us at disadvantage. "When bad men conspire, good men should write." Can we not organize a patriot band of brothers all over the country, whose fundamental principle shall be that our national government is one and indestructible, and that secession is only a new name for treason?

How is it that the loyal men of Virginia and some other of the Southern States, speak with bated breath of the revolutionists; and when they would defeat Secession, feel obliged to set up some middle ground instead of the Constitution? All the while they speak in this tone they are drifting away from their duty, and making their hearers familiar with disloyalty. We are mortified at such *contingent* patriotism.

How are we to know how far the virus of Calhounism has penetrated, unless we take some action against it? Let such a band of loyal men as I have suggested be formed in every State, and when they have ascertained their own strength let them call upon the Legislatures thereof, to "put the foot down firmly," proclaiming their adherence to "The Union and the Constitution." When we have thus ascertained what is sound, we can let the unsound go,—and proceed anew with the blessing of God, on our way to peace and renewed strength.

It seems a small thing, and yet it may be that a very great part of the success of the doctrine of "State Sovereignty"—and its descendant, Secession—has been, owing to our not having, *in one word*, a name for the nation like England, France, Spain.

I would propose as a name for the political brotherhood of private men—the title of *Washington Republicans.* Under this banner let us gather loyal men of every former denomination. Republicans, Democrats, Whigs, Union-men; holding no man obliged to give up his opinions upon the points which have formerly divided us; and pledged only to support our country as "one perfect chrysolite" against the men who are endeavoring to break and destroy it.

Your voice in the Senate sounded like a trumpet of defiance to Treason, and it was paralyzed before you! Let us hear it again, brave and faithful Senator! Marshal the patriot hosts, and lead us to the rescue of our insulted nationality!

E. LITTELL.

Living Age Office, Boston, 3 *April,* 1861.

From The Dublin University Magazine.

AN ONLY SON.

BY THE AUTHOR OF "ARTIST AND CRAFTSMAN."

CHAPTER I.

"CAPITAL! But it wasn't on a live boy's head, though?"

"What odds if it had been?"

"All the odds in the world, Ned. Funk makes a fellow's hand shake."

"Stop a bit, then, and I'll try again with Tommy Wilmot. Here! Tommy! Tommy!"

But when it was explained to Tommy, the gardener's son, that he was to stand blindfold whilst Master Locksley shot a bolt at an apple on his head, he manifested an unaccountable repugnance. In vain was he shown two apples spitted in succession by the marksman's skill: in vain was he made acquainted with the story of the gallant Switzer's boy: in vain was an offer made to dispense with the brass ferule on the bolt.

Then bribes were tried, a new sixpence and a bag of marbles. Then came hard words: "he was a muff;" "he was a monkey." Lastly, I am sorry to say, came threats, whereat he threw himself upon his back on the turf, kicking and screaming for "Mammy!"

"Ugh! the little toad!" said both his tormentors, with the most ingenious indignation.

"I have it, though," said the earl, after a pause. "Let's get Mrs. Locksley's big china jar out of the back drawing-room, stick it on a stool with the apple atop. Its no end of funky to shoot at."

It was indeed. Even Ned's recklessness quailed.

"A nice boy you are," quoth his lordship; "risk Tommy Wilmot's life or eyes and funk the crockery! Well!"

This was more than Ned could stand. Indoors he went, and brought out the jar in one hand, a tall stool in the other. On the lid squatted a grinning dragon with a smooth round pate. Thereon a pippin was then craftily poised, and the earl stepped off the distance at which they had been shooting before. Their weapon was a cross-bow, their bolt of wood tipped with a brass ferule.

Ned took aim so steadily that his companion muttered, "He'll do it, now." So, perhaps, he would, but for a saucy may-fly and a hungry swallow. The may-fly danced right in the line of aim; the swallow darted, snapped at and seized her. The gleam of the bird's glossy back dazzled Ned's eye too late to check the finger on the trigger.

Off went the head of the golden dragon of the dynasty of Ming.

"O Ned, Ned, we've been and done it," was the earl's generous exclamation.

"I've been and done it, not you, Phil!" was Ned's no less generous disclaimer.

"I put you up to it and bullied you into it, so the mischief's mine as much as yours: and that I'll stick to. But talk of sticking, Ned, couldn't we stick the vile brute's head on again?" said Philip, transferring, as we all do sometimes, a share of his annoyance to the victim of his misdeed.

"Perhaps we could," answered the marksman, ruefully. "It's a good job it wasn't Tommy's eye."

"That's the provoking part of it; the obstinate little toad will think he was right to refuse. What are you going for now, Ned?"

"Only the cement bottle in mammy's cupboard."

Very good cement it was; and, soon set hard, the Ming monster showed his grinders as well as ever. The ingenious earl bethought him of some gold shell in Ned's paint-box, and dapping therewith the line of fracture made it almost disappear.

"Repairs neatly done gratis for parties finding their own cement. The jar's as good as ever, Ned, put it away and there's an end of it."

Not so, Ned's uncompromising honesty would not allow it. His father soon after came up the lawn where the boys were still lounging under the cedars. At his approach, Tommy Wilmot, who was hovering about, took to speedy flight. Who could say but some vague charge of complicity might affect and endanger him? The earl, who was peeling a willow wand, was rather startled at hearing Ned begin—

"Papa, dear, I've been and done it again."

"More mischief, Ned?" asked Mr. Locksley, laying his hand upon the curly head, and looking down into the boyish eyes which sought his in perfect confidence.

"Yes. You know mammy's big china

jar. It's a mercy it aint atoms, I can tell you. But I knocked the monster's head off with a cross-bolt."

"Accident or purpose, Ned? That makes all the difference you know."

"Well, I shot at it on purpose, but cut the dragon over by accident," and Ned's look drooped at remembering the wantonness of his exploit.

"I haven't time to hear it out just now, Ned; you must tell me in my study after tea. Lady Cransdale wants you both up at the house. She told me to send you if I came across you; so be off at once."

As they went along, Philip asked of the other,—

"Do you always tell him things straight out that way, Ned?"

"To be sure I do. Don't you tell Lady Cransdale every thing?"

"Well, I do sometimes. Constance does always. But I say, Ned, will there be much row about this vile beast of a griffin?"

"You're hard on the poor griffin, Phil. He didn't ask to be shot at, yet he didn't object, like Tommy."

"Well, but what will your father do to you for breaking him?"

"Not knowing can't say. But if I catch it, it's a case of serve me right. The jar is mammy's and she'd have been monstrous sorry to have it smashed. Holloa! what's that? Your mother and Lady Constance on the walk, with the new pony! Cut along, Phil, and bother the griffin till after tea!"

In two minutes more they were up to the countess and her daughter with a rush and a shout which set the pony plunging.

"Isn't he too spirited, Con?" said Lady Cransdale. "One of the boys had better ride him first."

"Oh, please no, dear mamma. I like spirit in a pony. He's gentle enough with it, I'm sure."

She stepped up to the startled creature, which eyed her with its large, deerlike eyes, and with quivering nostril sniffed at her outstretched hand. Then, as if re-assured by her gentleness and fearlessness together, it stood quite still and suffered her to pat its crested neck.

"There now, mamma dear, Selim and I are friends for good and all. Do let me have the saddle on. It's only three o'clock, and the boys' half holiday; we could have such a canter. Do, there's a dear!"

"Then James must go too. I can't trust you with the boys alone the first time."

Old James, the head groom, touched his hat.

"I'd better ride the old brown hunter, my lady, he's as steady as a house."

No wonder that Lady Constance had both frame and face instinct with grace and beauty, for all she were as yet a wild slip of a girl. For she was daughter to that beautiful and stately mother, whose motherly beauty widowhood had saddened into a sweet serenity owning a special loveliness.

The children ran in at open windows on the ground floor. Lady Cransdale mounted the terrace-steps. There was a marble vase upon the balustrade, with heavy handles. Clasping one of these with both her hands, she leant her cheek upon them, and looked out wistfully, first upon the landscape, then heavenward.

"Ah, Philip dear," she sighed, "I wonder can you see the children now? Do you still halve the care of them with me?"

By and by the trample of skittish hoofs were heard upon the gravel. The boys looked up and bowed to her with chivalrous grace. Lady Constance cried, "See how I have him in hand, mamma!" But she was too prudent to look off Selim's ears as yet. The countess smiled to see them go,—a sweet smile and bright. She stood too high for any of them to have seen that its brightness sparkled through tear-drops.

The precise details of Ned's confessional conference that evening with his father have not been handed down. The penance imposed included, apparently, satisfaction to Tommy Wilmot's injured feelings, for he laid out a bright sixpence next day in "candy-rock" and toffy, and was in possession of a bag of marbles envied by the whole village school.

CHAPTER II.

BARREN of its chief blessedness is the boyhood of him that has no mother. But Edward Locksley's boyhood had been blessed with almost a double mother-love. Lady Cransdale had more than half adopted him to sonship. There was hereditary bond of friendship and esteem between the house of

Cranleigh and the Lockaleys. The grandfathers of the two boys who played under the cedars had tightened it. They were brother soldiers in one regiment during the American War of Independence. Either had contracted close obligation to the other for life or liberty in the vicissitudes of that adventurous struggle.

John, Earl of Cransdale, then Viscount Cransmere, left the army before the outbreak of the ensuing great continental wars. His friend, Edward Locksley, followed the profession of arms until the day of Corunna. There he fell, in command of a regiment of Light Infantry, under the eyes of his noble chief, doomed to death on the selfsame day.

His brother soldier did more than a brother's part for his children. Young Robert Locksley, our Edward's father, owed, in great measure, to the earl the completion of his school career, his entrance at the university, and his early admission to a post of confidence and wealth. He had been now for years under the elder lord, and then under his son, the late Earl Philip, manager of the Cransdale estates, intimate counsellor and friend of all at Cransdale Park.

Earl Philip had been a statesman, and had filled important offices abroad.

"I could hardly have gone upon that Indian governorship," he used to say, "if I had not had Locksley to leave here in my place. But with him here, I believe the country gained by my turning absentee."

Robert Locksley made a wise choice when he chose the old rector's daughter, Lucy Burkitt, to his wife. "Meek-hearted Lucy" was her distinctive title in her own family. She was pretty; she was gentle; she was tender; a true helpmeet for him every way. Knowing, for instance, better than he could, all the folk on the estates, among whom she was born and bred. Gently born and gently bred, moreover; for she was county-family, too, and the dames of the loftiest county magnates need not disown her.

"What a comfort," said Lady Hebblethwaite, at the manor-house, Sir Henry's wife, to Mrs. Mapes, of Maperley, "to have the old archdeacon's granddaughter at the Lodge, at Cransdale. The Locksleys, too, were always gentle folk, and the late colonel a distinguished soldier. But I had my fears lest Robert, in his peculiar position, might look us out some vulgar rich woman."

"In his position, dear. How so? The Cransdale agency must be an excellent thing, I fancy."

"Excellent, indeed; but still precarious. Any day a quarrel with the earl, you know, or with the guardians, should a life drop and a minority ensue, eh?"

"Well, to be sure, I never thought of that. And, as you say, a quarrel or a change of dynasty: but Lucy Burkitt is Lucy Locksley now. A dear good little girl she always was, and I had a vast respect for her grandfather, the late archdeacon; and I shall drive over to the Lodge and call on Tuesday."

And Mrs. Mapes, of Maperley, did call. So did Sir Henry and Lady Hebblethwaite. So did the Very Rev. the Dean of St. Ivo and his wife. So did some greater and some lesser personages than these, until the social position of the Locksleys was indisputably and most honorably defined.

Their Edward was born in the same week as Lord Cransdale's heir, and both babies were christened on the same day. The earl, who stood godfather to little Ned, would say, laughingly, that he and Phil were twins, and often brought one on each arm to be nursed as such by his countess. Lady Constance, in the full dignity of some two years' seniority, called them both "ickle baby brothers." She herself had first seen the light in the Government House of an Indian presidency, whence a change of Cabinet at home recalled her parents some months before the birth of Philip. Edward Locksley proved to be an only child, so the earl insisted upon his being playmate with his own children. One governess taught the three at first; later, there was one tutor for the two boys.

"Kate," said the earl, some time before his death, "Kate, let the boys grow up together. Philip will want a brother. Locksley will make a man of his own boy if any father can. And if they grow up as brothers, he will be a kind of father, of course, to poor Phil. You are a woman of women, Katy dear; but a boy wants a man's hold over him."

Her dying husband's wish became to her a sacred law. The Lodge, as the Locksleys' dwelling-place was called, stood not far from the great house, and within the precincts of its park. The boys had rooms in either, where all things were ordered for them as for brothers of one blood. Their little beds, their bookshelves, their desks, all in duplicate, save in so far as individual character will stamp differences even on the very features of very twins.

But the time was come when both boys must leave home. From father to son, for many generations, all Cranleighs had been Etonians. Catherine, Countess of Cransdale, spite of the desperate hug in which her widowed heart held her boy, was not the woman to let her weakness falter from the manly educational traditions of his race. Philip must go to Eton, and Edward must go with him, of course. The boys were eager to confront the adventures of that new world. Had not each himself, and each the other, to rely upon?

But that eagerness was hard for two mothers' hearts to note. It is not only when prodigals insist on leaving home that parent hearts are wrung; dutiful and loving children wring them sometimes by their cheerful parting smiles. Poor Lady Cransdale! She wished in her secret soul she could detect, in Philip's laughing eyes, a passing trace of that feeling which it was costing herself such heroic effort to conceal. Lucy felt a touch of the same anguish, but between her noble friend and her there was a world of difference. Lady Cransdale had been a happy wife; Lucy was one. Neither, however, would betray to her son the keenness of her inward pang. It was left to Lady Constance to do this. She was indignant at what she thought their heartlessness, and did her best to punish them both for it. She went pricking about with sharp words to find a soft spot of cowardice or of tenderness in either, but with little enough success at first. She racked her brain to think of all the cruelties she had heard or read that big bullies inflicted upon luckless youngsters. But this bugbear startled them not. They were country-bred lads, bold, active, and hardy. Moreover, they declared it would take a strapping big fellow to lick them both together, and they would fight for one another to the death. Lady Constance thought that was likely enough to be sure.

She tried an appeal to Phil's possible fastidiousness.

"You know you're nice enough about things at home, Philip. How shall you like to boil your big boy's eggs, and bake his toast, and fry his sausages, and, maybe, black his boots."

"Prime!" he retorted, "specially the cooking. You've a taste that way yourself, Con, or had, at least. Don't you remember the row you got into with mademoiselle, for warming veal 'croquettes' on the school-room shovel once!"

"Years ago, when I was a little girl," she said, firing up with the conscious dignity of a lady in her teens. "No Lady-bird nor Lightfoot, nor Selim for you, Phil; not one gallop the whole dreary half! Oh, dear!"

This was an artful and unexpected stroke. It told upon his lordship evidently, whose face lengthened, till Ned came to the rescue with a suggestion of "capital fun in boats."

"Boats, indeed! As if either of you could row a bit. Nice blisters you'll have on both your hands!"

This was a relapse into the Cassandra vein, and was accordingly derided.

"Oh, ah! blisters. Much we should mind them, I suppose. Maybe we didn't blister our hands with pickaxes when we dug out the badger in Cransmere wood."

"Selfish creatures boys are, to be sure!" she said again, after a pause. "Neither of you seem to care a bit for leaving me here all alone. No one to ride with but old James, pounding behind! No one to go fishing with up on the moor. No one to walk with as far as the 'Long Beeches' or over to Cransmere wood, where your badger was."

"Why, Con, you know we shall be very sorry to leave you, and all that, you know: but fellows must go to school. There's Hebblethwaite minor, in the 'lower fourth' at Eton, and even young Mapes, from Rugby, conceited monkeys, that try to lord it over us whenever we come across them."

"It's not so strange of Ned, perhaps, not to care for leaving me," she continued, with a slight flush, perhaps indicative of Junorian resentment after all; "but for you, Phil, my own, own, only brother;" and here her voice began to tremble, and Philip to feel queer again.

"How can you talk of being left alone, Con? Wont there be Mrs. Locksley left and mammy too, whom you pretend sometimes to love much more than I do. As if a fellow could help go-go-going to schoo-oo-ool;" he answered with an approach to a downright whimper.

"No, indeed," exclaimed her ladyship, brightening up in view of the adversary's faltering, "but you needn't talk so much about its being 'precious jolly' to go."

"When did you ever hear me call it precious jolly?" demanded luckless Philip, with some asperity.

"After tea, on Monday, before the lights were brought into the library," she replied at once, with that fatal female accuracy in the record of minor events. The reminiscence was too precise to be gainsaid.

"Mrs. Locksley heard it, and felt it too, I could see by her face." Here Ned's valiance began oozing out, and he quietly left the room.

"Yes," she continued, "and so did poor dear mammy too. I saw her face, by the firelight, looking so pale and sad. You might have some feeling, Phil, for her at least."

"O Con, how dare you say that I don't feel for her, my own poor darling mammy!"

As he spoke he heard his mother's footfall close behind him, and turning, the boy's bravery gave way at sight of her. He ran and threw his arms around her with a sob.

Ned, meanwhile went home, whistling, to the Lodge. But Lady Constance's word had pricked his heart also. His father and mother were out and would be back late to tea, the servant said.

"Good thing, too," muttered he, striding up-stairs to his own room; "time for a think, and I want one." Ned's ways were quaint occasionally. He bolted the door, shut the shutters, and lit a pair of candles. Then he took down a slate, and tilting it up upon a Latin dictionary, proceeded to write, as if taking down the data of a problem in arithmetic. "If Philip goes to Eton, but my mother don't like me to go so far from home, why need I?"

Plunging both hands into his curly brown hair, and propping both elbows on the table, he glared at the slate, and thought.

When the tea-bell rang, he washed his hands and face with scrupulous nicety, brushed and combed his tumbled locks, returned the dictionary to its shelf, the slate to its peg, extinguished the candles carefully, and went very deliberately down-stairs.

"I say, pappy dear," he began soon after tea was done, "I've a favor to beg; important too."

"Well, Ned, what is it?"

"I want to go to school at St. Ivo."

"To school at St. Ivo, Ned!" cried his father in amazement, and his mother dropped her knitting to stare at him.

"There's a firstrate master," he said, "at the cathedral school."

"Pray, Ned, who told you that?"

"Oh, I heard the dean say one day, at the Park, that the new man there, Mr. Ryder, had put a new life into the whole concern."

"Well, I believe he's done wonders, but not made an Eton of St. Ivo; eh, Ned?"

"Hardly; but it's a deal cheaper, you know," insinuated artful Edward.

"That's more my look-out than yours, my boy. I wonder what's put this freak in your head?"

Lucy was not so strong of heart, perhaps, as Lady Cransdale; at least, she had not known the cruel need to brace it, which the countess knew so well. The boy's freak flashed a gleam of hope upon her. St. Ivo was not ten miles off: Eton close on two hundred. At St. Ivo she might have weekly, daily sight of Ned, if she were minded. No need for mother lips to thirst so many weary months for kisses. It was a sore temptation.

With an effort to conceal her eagerness, she asked:—

"Should you, then, really like St. Ivo better, Ned!"

He looked her full in the face, and the boy, too, was tempted by the craving tenderness which gleamed in her soft eyes. But his father's look was on him also, full of manful help.

"I didn't quite say that, dear mammy."

"What did you say, then?"

"Only that I wanted, if pappy would allow, to go to the cathedral school."

"You are not afraid of facing so many strangers as at Eton, surely," said his father.

"The more the merrier," he bounced out inadvertently; "I like a jolly lot of fellows!"

He caught the fall upon his mother's countenance, and was acute enough to see that he had betrayed once more to her the feeling which Lady Constance said had hurt her.

Lucy seemed to lose again the clue she thought to hold. The fledgling's wing was not so weak as she had almost hoped. It was ready for a long flight from the nest. She plied her knitting again, part sorrowful, part proud, to note the spirit of her boy. Presently she put the knitting by for good and all. Her head ached a little, and she was going early to bed. Ned ran after her for another parting kiss before she reached her room. It sent her to sleep happy.

"What put this notion of St. Ivo in your head?" asked Mr. Lockaley once more, when the boy returned.

"If you don't mind, I'd rather say no more about it," answered Ned, discomfited.

"But if I do?"

"Of course, then, I shall out with it."

"Out with it, then, my boy," said Mr. Lockaley.

So he told his father how Lady Constance "went on" at him and Philip about their obdurate cheerfulness in face of approaching departure; and how her ladyship had given them to understand, among other things, that their respective mothers were pining at the prospect.

"Then, to put the question as your mother did herself just now, you wouldn't like St. Ivo better?"

"Oh, my! Better! What? St. Ivo, with thirty fellows in the poky little close, better than Eton with hundreds, and the playing-fields, and the river, and 'Pop,' and Montem, and all that! I should think not just about."

"But if your mother should wish to keep you nearer home, you're ready to give it up?"

He nodded assent.

"You'll have to give up Phil, too, remember. He wont go to St. Ivo."

Ned gave a sigh; but said, resolutely, "She's more to me than Phil, or half a dozen. I'll do what she likes, please."

"Well, sleep on it to-night, Ned; we'll talk it over again to-morrow."

Lady Constance, proud of having crushed her brother into contrition, looked anxiously the next day for signs of relenting in Master Ned. Perhaps she wished, perhaps she feared, to know whether, amongst other things, the boy would care a little for leaving her. Some say, to use a dyer's simile, that jealousy must be the mordant to fix any tint of true love, even be it only sisterly. I fancy that with women it is almost always so—much more invariably than with our less sensitive brotherhood. But Ned gave no sign. His countenance was imperturbable when, in the afternoon, as the ponies came round, his father told him that he must walk home with him, instead of riding with the others. There was a whole catechism of questionings in Lady Constance's eyes as she rode off with Philip; but Ned went, whistling and incurious, with his father.

"Don't, Ned. It worries me," said Mr. Lockaley. "I want to have a reasonable talk with you."

"All right, then," and he ceased his whistling.

"One good turn deserves another, doesn't it, my boy?"

"To be sure, and more."

"Why more?"

"Because the first's the first, and done out of mere good-will."

"Right, Ned. Saint John has said it: 'Herein is love, not that we loved God, but that he loved us.' Love's nobler than gratitude. The second turn wants multiplying to come up to the first."

"Ah! just about," said Ned, relapsing into a whistle to ease the overcharge of seriousness.

"Don't, boy; but listen."

Trust begets trust, which little else has power to beget. Locksley knew this much of the secret to win a son's heart well. He therefore told his boy far more explicitly than ever yet what were his obligations to the Cransdale family. How he had found a father in the old earl when the Frenchman's bullet had made him fatherless; how his relations with the late lord had but increased the debt. "I say nothing, Ned, of what his widow has ever been to you yourself."

"No need, pappy. No fear I shall forget it."

"Well, now, supposing you had set your heart on staying here at home—"

"Which I haven't, mind," interpolated Ned.

"But if you had, and we into the bargain, but Lady Cransdale wanted a friend for her boy Phil at school?"

"Why, what a father owes, a son owes; I should have to go."

It was a singular saying for a boy. Locksley turned it over in his mind aloud.

"'What a father owes a son owes,' eh? That's not a thought with which my own life ever set me face to face. But you're right about it, Ned, quite right."

Then, after a bit, "You needn't speak again about St. Ivo to your mother."

"Wasn't going to," quoth Edward.

"For better or for worse you go with Phil to Eton."

"For worse, indeed! You silly pappy! Floreat Etona!"

And up went Ned's hat, with a whoop, into the air.

CHAPTER III.

"We shall have a 'tuft' in the class-list, for a wonder, this term," said a student of Christ-church to another undergraduate of that stately house of learning.

"High up?"

"A safe 'second.'"

"What, Royston a safe second?"

"First, perhaps."

"Oh, nonsense about that."

"Will you give me two to one in half-crowns against him?"

"Willingly."

"Done with you, then."

"Done. But, I say, what makes you risk your small cash that way? Royston's too dressy to be cut out for a 'first.'"

"Well, Grymer, who 'coaches' me too, says he's lots of logic in him for a lord. And he was a bit of a 'sap' at Eton all along, they say."

This logical lord, Baron Royston, of Rookenham, was a distant kinsman of the Cransdale family, and their near neighbor in the county. He was like Philip, his own son, as they say; but had lost both parents in early life. He was undoubtedly of a studious and thoughtful turn of mind, and had made the best of Eton and of Oxford. A parliamentary career was his ambition. The dressiness wherewith his depreciatory fellow-student had reproached him was but an indication of a certain real indifference to his personal appearance, combined with a great horror of slovenliness in any matter. He happened to employ the best tailor in town and to have a judicious valet. Their judgment and his own methodical tidiness bestowed on him his unexceptionably fine clothing.

But the student's confidence in Grymer's "coaching" acumen was not misplaced. He pocketed his unbelieving friend's half-crowns, for when the class-list was out, there stood in the distinguished fore-front, among the few names in "the first," "Royston, Dominus de, Ex Aede Christi."

Among all the congratulations which reached him, none were more grateful than those which came from his kinswoman, Lady Cransdale. As a small indication of his gratitude, he ran down to Eton, took Phil out for the afternoon and "tipped" him.

"A regular brick is Royston," cried that young nobleman to Ned, whom he met later, coming up from "out of bounds."

"Here's something like a tidy tip, look," and he unfolded crisp and crackling, a new bank-note.

"He's been and got a first at Oxford, Royston has. I know they'll be no end of glad at home."

But Ned did not seem sympathetic.

"We'll have such a sock," ran on Philip. "I'll ask all the fellows in the ten-oar, and all of our cricketing eleven at my dame's. Come on, Ned. We'll have sausage-rolls, and raspberry puffs, and champagne! Hooray!"

Still Ned was apathetic, and excused himself. He'd a copy of verses to show up, and must go and grind at them.

"Verses be blowed! I'll tell you what, Ned; you're always rusty about Royston now-a-days. I can't conceive what ails you. It wasn't always so. I think he's an out-and-outer, and so they do at home, I know."

Ned knew it also. Perhaps "at home" the expression might have been other. Countesses and their lady-daughters don't scatter slang with the graceless ease of their noble young relatives at Eton. But the sentiment was the same; and the sweet breath of their praise of him was just, perhaps, what turned to rust upon the true steel of Edward's feelings. The boys were doing well upon the whole at Eton. They took their removes in due season regularly, and were "sent up for good" a satisfactory number of times. Ned was the steadier reader of the two; but Philip was very quick-witted, and held his own. They were never many places apart in school. They were firm friends still; indeed, almost as brotherly as ever. But in the little world of a public school, it was impossible for the old identity of taste and pursuits to live on unimpaired. Ned cricketed, Phil boated; thus one was thrown among the wet "bobs," one among the "dry." Ned was a careless dresser, Phil followed at humble distance, the sartorial splendors of Lord Royston. Phil's chums were chosen from the rattlepates, Ned's from the more earnest sort in mischief or in better things. Phil's mind was set on a commission in the Guards, Ned—those were not Crimean days, good reader—would hazard a sneer at Windsor campaigners now and then.

Casual circumstances, too, began to hint at the divergence inevitable even between brothers' paths as boyhood closes. Three vacations had been spent asunder. Twice the Cransdales had been on distant visits; once the Locksleys had spent summer holidays from home. That was a memorable period in Edward's history, for it was then that he first made acquaintance with his first-cousin by the mother's side, Keane Burkitt; then also that he first fell in with Colonel Blunt.

Lucy Locksley's eldest brother, James Burkitt, had been some years dead. In his lifetime he had been a solicitor in the flourishing seaport of Freshet. He had been a successful man of business, and had known successes in other ways. For instance, he had won, to his surprise, and some said to her own, the hand of Isabella Keane, the reigning beauty of that watering-place. There was a glitter in that showy young lady's eyes, which might have portended greed and hardness, and a restless temper. She made him, on the whole, however, a better wife than many had expected; but did little towards counteracting by her influence such faults of the same character as existed naturally in her husband, and were fostered by the peculiar temptations of his calling. When he died he left his widow a reasonable provision, partly realized and partly charged upon the profits of the firm. For, of course, as I may almost say, James Burkitt, Esquire, Solicitor, was in partnership. Burkitt and Goring was the firm. A very confidential firm indeed; in whose tin boxes, and more ponderous iron safes, the title-deeds, and wills, and acts of settlement of half the families in Freshet were in safe-keeping, to say nothing of documents and debentures affecting the interests of its commercial class.

It was stipulated and secured that in due course of time, his son, Keane Burkitt, should, if so inclined, claim a desk in the firm's office, and ultimately assume in its inner sanctum his father's former place of pre-eminence.

Keane Burkitt was not sent to a public school. His widowed mother had not Lady Cransdale's self-sustaining firmness, nor the help from without which Lucy's momentary weakness found. She sent her son as day-boarder to the so-called Academy-House, at Freshet. There he had few of the advantages of a public school education, none of those which strictly domestic training may afford. He had the manifest disadvantage of becoming presently head boy, without the ordeal of a sufficiently powerful antagonism to have made the upward struggle to the post heroical in mind or body. Nevertheless, he had more than average abilities, and in mere intellectual acquirement suffered no great loss by the classical and mathematical curriculum of Academy-House.

When two self-wills, a male and female, are pitted against each other, it is the latter most times which is driven to compass its ends by artifice, and to rule by feigned submission. But in the earlier years of conflict between Keane's temper and his mother's, the rod of power being necessarily in her hand, her son perforce served an apprenticeship to feminine subterfuge and craft. Mother's love, however, will often wax, as son's love wanes. The growing lad grew in his widowed mother's fondness as time went on, and in the natural weakening of her direct authority her fond weakness gathered growth also. Little by little Keane began to feel his way from servitude to tyranny. Yet the outward deference in which he had been schooled sat on his manner still—velvet still gloved the iron grip. A stranger might have thought him a dutiful son, nor would a careless observer, upon longer acquaintance, have thought otherwise. He was now about twenty years of age, senior by a couple of years only to his Cousin Edward. His mother's more judicious advisers spoke of the university, but she could not face the sacrifice of parting with him. He neither could nor would stay on at school, and manifested no kind of readiness to put on business-harness under Mr. Goring. His mother's persuasions failed to move the dead weight of his inert opposition; an attempt at imperative remonstrance had not only failed, but after such fashion as to make her feel that she had born and bred a despot over her. So Mrs. Burkitt taxed her brain to find some other influence which might be brought to bear upon him. Her kinswoman's husband, Robert Locksley, was a notable man of business. To judge by his success in training his own son and Lord Cransdale, he must have some power for governing or guiding boys. Besides which, Mrs. Burkitt had never been forgetful of the fact that Mr. and Mrs. Locksley were people in a position to make some intimacy between them socially desirable. Occasional letters to Lucy, occasional hampers of fish from Freshet, occasional meetings felicitously contrived, had kept the sense of kinsmanship from dying out. One morning, therefore, shortly before the summer vacation at Eton, Lucy found a letter from her sister-in-law in the Cransdale post-bag.

Mrs. Burkitt deplored the circumstance that their two sons should be growing up apart, and utter strangers to each other. Her Keane had left school for good and all, yet was too young to be expected at once to enter upon the drudgery of office-work. He had earned a holiday. The reverend principal of the Academy-House reported favorably of his attainments. Pupils of that establishment could hardly vie with classical Etonians, yet she should be curious to know how far behind his Cousin Edward her Keane had come from his books at last. He had purchased himself a half-decked boat, a miracle of sailing, the pride of Freshet Bay. He was wild to show his cousin such kind of boating as the Thames at Windsor, could not boast. She herself knew well that a fond mother grudged to lose one week of an only son's holiday. So she wished dear Lucy to come with her boy and visit them. She was well aware of the numerous and important claims upon Mr. Locksley's time; but if at any period of the season he, too, could join them, he would confer upon her a greater favor than even the mere honor and pleasure of his presence. He would, perhaps, understand better than her happy sister-in-law on how many points the mother of a fatherless boy, just touching manhood, might require the guidance and advice of such a person as himself.

"I shall write and refuse, of course," said Lucy to Robert, handing him the letter across the breakfast-table.

"Why refuse, dear?"

"Because I can't bear going away from you, you know."

"Well, but you've been out of sorts of late, and still look rather pale. Freshet is famous for its bracing air. You'd better go."

"Ned wont like spending the holidays from home, perhaps."

"Wont he? That sailing-boat, and the fishing in the bay, are likely to prove attractions, I should think."

"Ah, but we sha'n't have you, Robert, I am afraid. Ned wont like that any more than I shall, I know."

"But I don't know that you wont, Lucy. We're in want of timber for the new farms out by Cransmere, and there are always Norway ships at Freshet. I might combine a stroke of business with a pleasure-trip. Then there's something in what she says about her boy, poor woman. I think I'll take you down there, and come again, perhaps, to bring you back."

And so the Locksleys, in due time, went on a sea-side trip to Freshet.

CHAPTER IV.

The sailing-boat was, indeed, a triumph of build and rig. A trimmer and tauter never swam the still waters of Freshet harbor—never skimmed the surf outside in Freshet Bay. Ned was charmed with her. Yet when he read, in dainty golden letters on the stern, the name of "Lady Constance," he frowned—a slight frown only—sharp eyes were wanted to catch its momentary contraction on his forehead. But Cousin Keane's eyes were sharp, and caught it. They saw the lips just tighten, as the brow relaxed, to keep in a question which they would not ask.

"She had none till we knew that you were coming. Then my mother said your mother would like this one; and you too, perhaps."

Keane peered into his cousin's countenance, which at this warning was on its guard and imperturbable. So they stepped on board the "Lady Constance," whose owner slipped the moorings.

"Can you steer, Ned?"

The Etonian fixed the tiller, smiling.

"All right, then; I'll mind the sheets."

She was covered with white canvas in no time. There was a light breeze and a sunny ripple on the wave; the boys were soon standing out across the bay.

Mr. and Mrs. Locksley, as befitted seniors, paced solemnly the Esplanade, with Mrs. Burkitt. She judiciously dispensed familiar nods or statelier courtesies to numerous acquaintances and friends whom the breeze that cooled the summer evening brought out to enjoy its freshness upon the favorite public walk. By and by they met a tall, thin gentleman, upright of carriage, firm of tread. He wore a single-breasted blue coat, buttoned to the throat, which was encased in a black silk stock. The quick sharp click of his boot-heels as he brought his feet together, and the regulated precision of his bow could scarcely be mistaken.

"Colonel Blunt," said the widow; "Mr. and Mrs. Robert Locksley."

He gave another precise bow to Lucy; and, looking hard into her husband's face, he said,—

"Locksley! Why, bless me, Locksley! A thousand pardons, sir! But your features along with that name seem to come back to me so forcibly. Have I the honor of speaking to a brother officer?"

"No, not exactly," said Robert, good-humoredly; "unless you count for such an ex-lieutenant of the Cransdale Yeomanry."

"Well, excuse me, sir. I thought you hadn't quite the cut of our cloth. But—Locksley—let me see—Locksley? Had you an elder brother or relation in the service, sir, may I make bold to ask?"

"Neither, colonel. But my poor father fell at Corunna. He commanded the Welsh Rangers in the Light Division, all through Sir John Moor's campaign."

"Good heavens, Mr. Locksley! That explains it all; and accounts for the extraordinary impression made at once upon me by your name and face. I carried the colors of the Rangers at sixteen, sir. I stood not twenty paces from your father when he fell. A gallant soldier, sir!"

He held out his hand, which Locksley took with genuine emotion.

"How very delightful! and how very strange!" said Mrs. Burkitt. "I had no notion, colonel, that you had served under Mr. Locksley's father. You must follow up this chance introduction, gentlemen. We dine at seven, colonel, and shall hope to see you at dinner to-morrow at that hour."

"With greatest pleasure, madam."

He shook Locksley once more cordially by the hand, bowed to the ladies, and passed on. His tramp on the curbstone was firm and measured as of a sentry in the Guards. He had served in other than "light divisions" since the day when, at Moor's word, the Rangers turned to bay on Soult.

With military punctuality, his peal on Mrs. Burkitt's door-bell overtook the second stroke of seven on her hall-clock.

The colonel belonged to the old school of soldierly modesty, and was chary of emblazoning achievements on the left breast-flap of his evening coat. But this evening, in honor of his old chief's memory, and in compliment to the presence of his son and grandson, his many-clasped Peninsular medal hung there beside his Companion's badge of the Bath. Colonel Blunt was too courteous a gentleman to pour forth upon the ladies a flood of campaigning stories. He had too much manly reserve to have opened upon his male auditors, unprovoked, the sluices of his recollections. But no sooner had Mrs. Burkitt and Lucy gone up to the drawing-room, and the fresh bottle of claret been uncorked, than Locksley's desire to hear of his father and Ned's more exacting eagerness applied winches and levers to the hatches which penned his memories back. Then came, indeed, a rush and swirl of narrative and anecdote. Good listeners make good talkers; and upon such the veteran had chanced. "We," and "us," and "ours," studded the sentences. Who that has heard such glorious talk would wish it otherwise? If there be a grain of egotism in that soldierly pride of brotherhood in arms, who will be forward to censure it? The brotherliness is such pure gold that it suffers not by the imperceptible alloy. Nay, the amalgam gains its own special qualities—takes sharper character in the die—gives clearer ring upon the counter of conversation. Robert Locksley was profoundly touched by the respectful admiration which breathed so lifelike, after so many years, in the colonel's reminiscences of his father. It was as if he saw with his own eyes a new growth of laurel spring up over the far-off soldier-grave in Spain. War and weather had so marked and grizzled the man, the civilian scarcely remembered that, after all, the soldier was not by many years his senior. Whereas the soldier, as he talked, was suddenly grown young again—gone back in fancy to his beardless boyhood—to the day when he carried the colors of the famous Rangers under a Locksley, less his comrade than his chief.

"Ned," he would say; "Ned Locksley!" looking wistfully from the Etonian's face to his father's; "the name seems more at home in my ear, boy, than in my mouth. The men who called your grandfather 'Ned Locksley!' were even then 'mine ancients,' as Jack Falstaff hath it. They fell at Talavera, Salamanca, Vittoria, Quatre Bras, and Waterloo—generals, some of them, poor fellows! when their names figured in their last 'Gazette.' Some few are going still whom I know better now, such as hook-nosed Napier."

The colonel's talk kindled in Ned's eye a strange light, which the old campaigner noticed though his father did not. As for Cousin Keane, he relished the stories, too; but not quite so much, apparently, as he did the first ripe summer fruit of the dessert.

"Ha, youngster! a sweet tooth for early plums, I see. Puts me in mind of Corporal Chunk of 'ours.'"

"Corporal Chunk! well, that's a queer name, colonel, let's hear about him, pray."

"'Twas in the south of France. Know the country at all, Mr. Locksley? Ah! Well, there are some sandy roads there, and, what's more, choking hot dusty marches along them, as in all southern countries."

The old campaigner mopped his temples, worn bare by the shako, as if the southern sun were actually glaring on them still.

"One sultry evening I had an advanced picket, and, just after sundown, halted and turned the men into a fruit orchard on a grassy sward. That was something like refreshment after a long day's march along a French 'chaussée.' Mr. Locksley, the wine's with you. Corporal Chunk, youngsters, was 'Zummerzetsheere.' What brought him among Welsh Rangers I never could make out. He'd no Celtic liveliness about him, for certain. A steady soldier, but stupid. Arms were piled—knapsacks off. Some men lay down, wallowing in the soft green grass; some went swarming up into the trees. I took a couple of knapsacks for a pillow, and, stretched on my back, lighted the remnant of a part-smoked cigar. Those were not wasteful times, youngsters; we were saving of our minor luxuries. I think I said it was after dusk. Well, the season was too early for any ripe fruit; but the hard stomachs of our 'light-bobs' took kindly to the stony green plums. As the men rifled the boughs it was pleasant to hear the rustle of the leaves. Presently came the voice of Corporal Chunk, calling to a comrade in another tree.

"'I zaay, Bill! han't Vrench plooms wings?'

"'Wings, you blockhead! No, not no more nor English uns.'

"'Doan't 'ee zaay zo, Bill; now, doan't 'ee!' cried the corporal; 'else I've a bin atin' cockchaafers more nor this 'aalf hour!'

"After that, youngsters," quoth the colonel, "we had better go up to the ladies, if Mr. Locksley don't object."

Up-stairs, the drawing-room windows were wide open—the night wind could scarcely stir the light muslin curtains. There was a little balcony where Edward carried out a chair and sat down, leaning his arms on the rail, his chin on his arms. A broad path of heaving silver, laced with dark shadow-lines, as wavelets rose and fell, led his sight out, across the bay, to sea. Whither led it his thought and fancy? The "Lady Constance" lay at her moorings, right across the silvery track. The voices of father and mother both were audible in the room behind. Once he looked back, and thought his own heart rode at moorings, fast by their love. As he looked out again a long, glassy swell came rolling in from the bay. The fairy craft courtesied with dancing grace as it slipped under her. What a shame to tie that lifelike thing to moorings! Soft as the breeze was, her exquisite canvas would catch every breath, if hoisted. What dreamy delight to sail, and sail away, and yet away, beyond the sight-line, all along that heaving silver!

"Looking for the Skerry, Ned, or sentimentalizing?" broke in, unpleasantly, the voice of Keane.

"The moonlight lies just about in line for

it; but it's so far off one can't always make it out. We must sail over there and have a day's rifle-practice at the gulls."

It was not exactly to the Skerry to shoot gulls that Ned's fancy had been travelling along the shining seaward path; nevertheless he jumped at the notion—literally, off his chair, no less than figuratively. The old colonel's ear had also caught the well-known word.

"What's that about rifles, youngster; can you handle one, pray?"

"O colonel," cried both the boys, "come with us; that would be prime. We're going to the Skerry to shoot gulls."

"What? in that gim-crack boat of Burkitt's. The next major on the purchase-list would chuckle to see me get on board."

"Indeed," exclaimed her indignant owner, "you've no notion what a sea-boat she is. Stands as stiff as the lighthouse under half a gale of wind. You needn't be afraid, colonel. Ask any boatman in the bay."

"Impudent imp! So I needn't be afraid of going to sea in a washing-tub with two monkeys for ship's company. Thank you kindly. But as there's arms on board I think I will go, just to give you two a chance for your lives."

"Hurrah, colonel!" cried the monkeys, tolerant of insult at the prospect of his joining them.

When he did step on board with them, he was concerned to find how little stowage-room there was for his long legs.

"They've worried me many ways, these long legs of mine, and got me taken prisoner once."

"Prisoner! colonel. One would have thought that long legs, if ever of use, would have been useful to keep one out of that scrape."

"Well, I don't know. Little, stumpy legs beat long shanks at running most times. But I didn't get a chance to run."

"Go about, Ned!" cried his cousin. "It's your head you must mind this time, colonel, or the boom will take you overboard."

The tack successfully made, the boys begged for the story.

"'Twas on the retreat from Madrid, in 1812. We had the rear-guard, and were all higgledy-piggledy with the French van. Into villages and out of them, like 'puss in the corner.' One night a party of ours came on an old fonda. Grand old places some of those, with great vaulted ceilings to the stables and granaries overhead. The owners were gone, and all their goods with them. We ransacked cupboard and corner with no result but fleas, dust, and dead crickets. They had made clean sweep of all but the dirt."

"Luff, Ned, luff a bit," said Keane. "Go on, colonel."

"In despair I went out to rummage the stables. I had known a muleteer in a hurry leave a crust and a garlicky sausage-end in the hay. And even a handful of horsebeans don't come amiss in starvation-soup, youngsters. It was a great big stable—fifty mules might have stood at bait in it; but rack and manger were as bare as cupboard and shelf. I had a bit of lighted candle and went searching along. At the furthermost upper end of the last trough I came upon a little pile of lentils. It looked so neat and undisturbed that I thought it must have been formed after the general clearance. I looked up and saw a grain or two on the rack-beam. Looked right up to the ceiling and perceived a crack. A lentil dropped. There was, then, a store-room overhead. I climbed up on the rack-beam and went along till I saw a trap-door in the ceiling. 'I'm in luck for once,' thought I. I could reach the trap with my sword-point; so I gave a shove. Open it went and fell back, inside, with a bang. To spring up and into the gaping hole with the candle-end in my teeth was soon done; but as I was in, the candle-end was out. I groped onwards in the dark. I could hear the rats squeak and scamper in amaze; but they were not as amazed as I was at hearing—there was no mistaking it—a French cavalry bugle in the courtyard. To make things worse I felt something give under my left foot. Sure enough; crack went treacherous lath and plaster. I made a blundering attempt to right myself: crack and crash, both heels went through! I was astride upon a cross-beam and both legs dangling down. Vain was the struggle to loose one lanky limb and then the other. There was a fix! Then hoofs clattered, scabbards clanked, spurs jingled underneath. The French Chasseurs were in the stables."

"Beg pardon, colonel, but we must go about again."

Having bobbed under the boom again,

and seated himself to windward, he went on.

"There were only some ten or twelve of them, and the stable was very long. My best hope was they might keep down to the stalls by the door.

"'Mon sergent,' quoth a trooper, 'did we catch any of 'em?'

"'Catch, indeed! We couldn't boil up a trot between us. Poor Cocotte here has had three handfuls of chopped straw in her stomach since yesterday, and a stone under her shoe since this morning on the Sierra. That's not the way to catch English "Voltigeurs," eh?'

"'Geux de pays va. They talk of chateaux in Spain: when I'm "Marèchal Duc de N'importe quoi" I'll take care to build mine out of it.'

"'En attendant, François, as thou art only Marèchal des Logis, let's look out for the hay-loft.'

"To my discomfiture they lit a lantern and came upwards.

"'Mille Tonnerres, mon sergent!' cried François, gaping at the ceiling. 'Here's something now, for example! Here's a pair of legs dangling down like cobwebs.'

"'Ah, bah! thou art pleasanting.'

"'Pleasanting! To the contrary. Look at the boots and trousers!'

"'Drolls of legs!' cried the sergeant, holding up the light. 'Farcers of legs! Are they live, François?'

"I heard the hilt clang preparatory to 'draw swords'—I wanted neither prick nor scratch—and fell to kicking vigorously.

"'Tiens mon vieux!' said François. 'They're not only live but lively.'

"'Ah ca!' shouted the sergeant, apostrophizing my nether limbs. 'To whom are you? and what make you there? Allons donc répondez de suite.'

"There was nothing for it but to confess in such French as I might.

"'Tiens c'est un Anglishemanne!' they roared with loud laughter, and soon were up in the loft with a lantern.

"'Pardon, mon officer! C'est la chasse aux oignons qui a fait vot' petit malheur!'

"Sure enough, there was a noble string of onions swinging just over the heap of lentils; and a capital stew the Chasseurs made of them that night, I remember."

When laughter abated, Ned asked,—

"Were you prisoner long, colonel!"

"Oh, dear, no. One of our flank companions—I told you we were all higgledy-piggledy—burst in upon the fonda just before daybreak. There was no spare nag for me, and Cocotte couldn't carry double; so they left me behind when they scuffled away."

"Keep her a point away from the lighthouse rock, Ned," said Kéane, for the Skerry was full in view, looming large.

The sea-mews had a bad time of it. The colonel, besides his old experience of the rifle, had made fur and feathers fly all round the world, from almost as many species as the cases of the British Museum boast. Ned's accuracy of eye and steadiness of hand had increased since the day when grief came to the dragon of Ming. Keane, like most seaport lads, was a practised enemy of seabirds. Tired of slaughter, and sharp-set for luncheon, they presently moored the "Lady Constance" far out enough to get off at ebb-tide, and hailing a coble sculled by the lighthouse keeper's boy, got ashore, to the infinite relief of the colonel's legs. The Skerry was throughout a tilted table of chalk—on top, a slanting down of thymy grass, close-cropped by sheep, whose backs, as they grazed, made steep inclines. Shade was not attainable, but the breeze was fresh, though the sun was bright. It was pleasant enough, when the midday meal was done, to lie upon that short, crisp turf, and gaze landward. Day-dreams are dreamy enough, I allow. The shapes that haunt them are vague and ill-defined. The very coast-line of the firm land itself seemed to dance and quiver in haze as Edward looked on it. But indistinctness under broad sunbeams, looking landward, is other than vagueness under weird moonbeams, looking seaward. The sense of the indefinite and of the infinite are not one. The trickeries of the former work not the tender passionate longings of the latter. So Ned turned flat on his back, by and by, gazing into the unfathomable heaven. But a seabird came, poising herself on broad, lithe wing, right over him. Her clanging cry seemed fraught with reproach. Ned fancied he could discern a blood-spot on the snow of her downy breast. Would she arraign him of cruelty for the death of her mates under the cliff? "Pshaw, nonsense." He jumped up; the bird's wings quivered, and she went screaming out to sea. To and fro, musing, he paced some fifty yards; then forgot what had brought him to his feet, and found himself laughing at the remembrance of the colonel's long-legged misadventure.

"I'll go and get another story out of the old campaigner."

He found him stretched at full length, his face towards the ground, his head propped on both hands, his eyes on a little open book. Ned started, for staining the white margin was a rusty spot about the size of the blood-spot on the sea-mew's breast.

"Ha, youngster!" said the colonel, without looking up, "think it odd to find an old soldier poring over a prayer-book, eh?"

"Colonel, what is that stain upon the margin?" was the answer.

"A drop of a brave man's blood, boy," said the colonel.

He turned round, sat up, and sent a solemn, searching look into the lad's countenance. It was also solemn, and he was moved to speak when otherwise he had kept strict silence.

"Sit down, and I'll tell you how I came by it."

Edward sat down.

"It's in Latin, you see," holding the book towards him; "but the name on the fly-leaf"—turning to it—"is in German."

"Gretli Steiner" was written there in a thin-pointed female hand; underneath, in strong, awkward, masculine characters, "Muss oft gelesen seyn," "Must often be read."

"I was on divisional staff, in 1815, at Quatre Bras and Waterloo. Late on the latter day, when the French game was up, I went galloping with a message to the Prussians in pursuit. None but the chiefs—and they not always—know at the time the importance of even great victories. Yet, somehow, that evening, as I rode back over the field, thick-strewn with dead and dying, I felt that I had played my little part in one of the great events of history. A desire seized on me to carry some memento from that bloody battle-ground. I dismounted, threw the bridle over my arm, and went picking my way through piteous obstacles. I thought, at first, of taking a cross or medal for a keepsake, but could not bring myself to tear from a defenceless breast what its brave owner would have defended at cost of life itself. Presently I came upon a group of men and horses overthrown in confusion: corpses of them I mean, of course; three slain lancers of the Polish Guard, and, evidently their slayer with them. You remember I said 'a brave man's blood'?"

He nodded assent.

"His horse had fallen first: perhaps that alone lost him. He had not been killed outright, for he was sitting propped against the poor brute's carcass. By the skull and crossbones on its trappings and his uniform, I knew him for a Death's-head Brunswicker. Poor fellow! he was cold and stiff—his dying grip fast on this little book, open at this very page. He had a wound, among others, on his forehead. This drop must have fallen as he bent over the book. I took it, put it in my sabretasch, mounted, and rode fast away. For days and days I was uneasy, as if I had robbed the dead. I did not once take out or open the little book of prayers. When at last I did, the sentence on the fly-leaf read like an absolution and a pious bequest. 'Must oft be read!' Ay, boy, I have read and read, learnt and repeated these old Latin prayers, till I fancy sometimes some of their spirit has passed into mine. At war, in peace, in camp, at home, I have treasured and carried the dead Brunswicker's book. They shall put it in my shroud with me. I wish I could take it bodily with me into 'kingdom come' to return it to the Brunswicker. Pray God I may meet him there, with 'Gretli,' too, to thank them for the loan of it."

Then uprose the colonel, and whistled "The British Grenadiers." That is not a devotional tune, nor is whistling a good vehicle for church music; nevertheless, Edward Lockaley felt as if he listened to a solemn psalm.

"Now, Ned, look alive! Come along, colonel!" cried Keane, from below. "Time to be going aboard."

They descended to the beach. The boy with the coble was there, and his father, too.

"Neap tides this a'ternoon, gen'l'men," holloaed the latter, though he stood within a yard of them. He was wont to lose one-half his words, blown down his throat, upon that windy Skerry.

"Boat's aground, seemin'ly: can't'ee wait till't turns again?"

"Not if we're to make Freshet before sundown," said the owner. "What sort of bottom is it?"

"Soft and sandy, master; ye mought pole her out into deep water wi'out harmin' her keel, easily."

"Well, we'll try it, anyhow."

"Send boy back for me, to help shove, if she's very fast, master!"

"Ay, ay," cried Keane, as they put off in the coble.

Fast she was, sure enough. The boy went back, and brought his broad-shouldered sire to assist. Up to the waist in water, he applied the strength of those board shoulders to the bow. A few strains, and a few grunts, walruswise; then she began to slide, ever so little.

"Yeo ho, heave ho!" and off she goes at last.

Keane was in the bows, pole in hand, and one foot on the sprit. A few words passed between him and his helpers, which for the flapping of the sails that the colonel was hoisting were not heard by Ned. He was at the helm again. They were soon out of shoal water, and had all on board shipshape. Ned called out to his cousin,—

"Did you 'tip' those fellows, Keane?"

"No. Why should I?"

"They took a deal of trouble to get us off."

"Well, why shouldn't they?"

"I don't say they shouldn't; but we should have 'tipped' them."

"Bother them, they'll do well enough."

"That's more than we've done."

"Don't seem to see it," argued Keane. "The shilling's as well in our pocket as theirs. What's the use of shillings at the Skerry? The sea-mews don't keep shops: ha, ha, ha!"

Keane laughed at his own joke, but the laugh grated on his cousin's ear.

This was but one day of many spent in the colonel's company. He took as kindly to the youngsters as they admiringly to him. Keane said he thought him good fun. Ned secretly resented this off-hand expression. He relished the fun to the full as much as his cousin; but owned, in the very fibre of his heart, that some better thing than fun might be gotten out of the old soldier's company. The colonel would laugh, himself, at camp jokes and anecdotes till his sides seemed in danger of splitting the close-buttoned military frock. But under the straining cloth, Ned's eye seemed ever to discern the squared edges of the Brunswicker's prayer-book. "Old colonel," as the boys might call him, he was hard and hale and active yet. His stories came down to the most modern military times. He was home on a year's furlough from India, where his regiment was likely to remain some time. He would often say that he could bear no longer the slip-shod scuffle of promenaders on the Esplanade, that his ear pined for the measured thunder of a regiment's tramp. He declared that the "Gazettes" in the *Times* put him in terror twice a-week, lest he should read his own name amongst unfortunates "shoved upon the major-general's shelf."

"I don't want to lay by just yet, boys. I've neither chick nor child, and can't feel at home but in camp or barrack-yard."

Ned's great delight was to get him upon Indian ground—the only true field for a soldier's energy, as it then appeared.

"Tell you what, colonel, if I take a shilling, I shall take it from John Company sooner than from her gracious majesty."

The old "queen's officer"—king's officer that had been so long—would shake his head at this, and purse up his mouth; nevertheless, Ned's reasonings were not easily gainsaid.

"Take the company's shilling!" cried Keane, contemptuously; "what's the good? India's used up. Nothing but dry sticks come rattling down, now-a-days, for shaking the Pagoda tree. Better stop at home, and feather your nest at Cransdale, Ned, my boy."

"Stop at home I shall," Ned answered, somewhat ruffled; "but as for feathers, I'd sooner have them on my wings than in my nest."

"Well said, youngster," quoth Colonel Blunt.

The vacation drew to a close. The elder Locksley came down again to Freshet, for no timber ships had been there when he first came with his wife and son. Ned had advised him now that two Norwegians had at last appeared. They were at anchor far from the fashionable promenade, opposite a crazy old pier, whence a flight of steps, slippery with tangle, led down to a strip of beach. The shingle had long since disappeared under layers of broken bottles and fragmentary crockery, lobster claws, and oyster shells, battered tea-kettles and sodden cabbage stumps. Not even daily ebb and flow could clear the melancholy "detritus" away. Thither came Robert Locksley, with his son, to hail the nearest Norwegian for a boat. But, looking downwards, Ned perceived the coble from the Skerry, with her nose on that unsavory strip of sea-beach, and the boy asleep in her.

"Holloa, boy, put us aboard the barque there."

"Ay, ay, sir," said the boy, trained by his father, the old coastguardsman, to obey at once a voice of authority; but there was a sulkiness about his deference for all his practical obedience.

"Hold on alongside, we sha'n't be long aboard."

"Ay, ay, sir," with a grumble and a scowl.

But the scowl vanished in a pleasurable grin, and the grumble into the cheeriest of "Thank'ee, sirs," as the coble touched the slimy steps, and Ned handed over three half-crowns.

"You must be flush of money, Ned, to pay such wages for such work. Easy earnings, seven and sixpence for five hundred yards!" his father said.

"Do you remember Tommy Wilmot and the bag of marbles, pappy?".

"Can't say I do. Did you give him seven and sixpence for it?"

"It was a practical discourse of yours on compensation, pappy dear, that little affair of Tommy's. But never mind; it's another man's secret why the boy there got seven and six. Come along."

Away they went, arm in arm, happy father and happy son, trusting and trustworthy in a great matter or in a small.

The next day was to be their last at Freshet. Mr. Locksley and the colonel were both to accompany the ladies in a carriage drive to some ruin on a headland, which Ned had visited, and did not care to see again. He, therefore, and Keane took a farewell cruise. They sailed westward to a rocky islet half way between the mainland and the Skerry. They had both fowling-piece and rifle aboard, though Ned said he would shoot no more at sea-mews. The rock was reached and rounded without adventure. On the return, however, they came across a large, rare, diving-bird. It kept swimming, ducking, disappearing and re-appearing right in front of them, in the most persevering and tantalizing manner. Ned's vow was against purposeless murder of sea-mews; but the securing of such a specimen could not fall under its provisions. Forbid it science! to say nothing of sport. Ned was as eager as Keane to get a fair shot at it. Bang! and bang! went both barrels at last. But the saucy diver must have witnessed experiments with Eley's patent cartridges before that afternoon, so accurately did it calculate their utmost range, and keep just out of it.

"It's not a bit of use, Ned," said Keane, "shot wont touch him: you must try the rifle."

He took it in hand, and waited with patient, deliberate aim till the bird rose up once more in the water, flapping his finlike wings in a sort of mockery. "Crack!" "No go!" said both boys as, true to his kind, the diver dived.

"You've winged him, though!" cried Keane, breathless with excitement, as the bird, once more on the surface, took to churning the water with piteous flaps.

"Haul a bit on the mainsheet! I'll steer down on him!"

The Lady Constance skimmed the water as if the steersman's eagerness had quickened her very frame. The bird seemed unable to dive again but swam fast away. Not so fast, however, as the Lady Constance, which was soon up with and almost over it. Keane let the rudder go and made a clutch at the bird as it passed under the stern. The Lady Constance broached and fell away. Keane was overboard, with an agonizing cry for help. Born by the seashore, and at home from boyhood on its waves, the lad, like so many of his breeding, could not swim a stroke. The Etonian was more truly amphibious. Coat and shoes were off in a twinkling, lithe as otter or seal, he was in the water to the rescue.

"All right, old fellow! Here you are! Don't catch at me! don't splash so! tread water gently and I'll keep you afloat."

He had him tight by the collar from behind. So far so good. The mischief was, that the current was not strong enough to keep the Lady Constance from drifting before the wind, though strong enough to make pushing Keane against it no joke.

Ned saw the distance increasing with dismay. To save himself was but a sport of swimming; but this widow's only son—to think of losing him! He struck out with steady but desperate force. A great floating rack of sea-weed came happily down the current, plump against the broadside of the boat, and stopped her way a little. Ned had presence of mind to note the slackening, and redoubled efforts. Thus both lads' lives were saved. But when they had hoisted themselves by main force over the gunwale on board again, he was exhausted, and for a few minutes lay on his back.

When he got breath again he sat up and took the tiller-bar in hand.

"Mind the sheets, Keane, haul the jib closer home."

He put the boat's head seaward.

"What on earth are you after, Ned? Let's make for the pier-head quick," said the other dripping lad.

"After the puffin, to be sure," he answered, imperturbably. "A little tauter; that will do."

The bird was once more overtaken, and this time secured in safety. Neither then nor thereafter did one word touching Keane's rescue cross the lips of Ned Locksley, which was characteristic of him. But not one word crossed Keane's lips either, which was also characteristic of him.

CHAPTER V.

It was after Easter the following year. New men were in office. Their first measure of importance had been carried by a narrow majority in the Commons. Upon its reception "in another place" might hang the fate of Government. An animated debate: perhaps a close division, would enliven the decorous monotony of the Upper House. To make matters worse, the noble earl who led for ministers was feverish and in bed. Much would depend upon a very young debater, and still younger official, under secretary to the department which the Bill more immediately affected.

"Nervous thing for Royston," said one junior peer to another coming in from the lobby. "Does he funk it much?"

"I don't know whether he does; but I should think Government did." They looked up at the ladies mustering in force already.

"Any thing worth looking at?" asked one hereditary legislator, who wore an eye-glass because he really was near-sighted.

"Nothing particular, except the Cransdale girl," quoth his compeer, superciliously.

"Well she is particular. And how well her mother wears."

"Ah! to my mind, she beats Lady Constance hollow."

"Hardly that; but she's a grand type, certainly. There's Royston up now, isn't he? Hear, hear?"

Lord Royston was up, and, luckily for him, without suspicion that the eyes of Lady Cransdale and her daughter were upon him. His opening sentences were firm and self-possessed. He was well on in his speech when, during an interruption on a point of statistics, he first became aware of it. The discovery during an oratorical period might have thrown him off his balance; but having a blue book in hand and a string of figures in mouth to confute his noble interrupter, time was given him to recover before launching out again. His argument was precise and clear, and as he came to the wider political and moral aspects of the measure, enthusiasm roused him to eloquence. Cheers with the chill off, somewhat rare in that senate of patricians, greeted his winding up. When he sat down he had earned a genuine and honorable success. Several distinguished elders came across and shook hands with him. The subsequent debate was lively, but the division favorable. And Lady Constance had been looking on.

Her mother's presence with her was a stronger instance of interest in their young kinsman than even he had dared to reckon upon. Lady Cransdale had not been at a debate since her own dear Philip had spoken on his return from India, those weary widowed years and years ago.

It was happy for such interests of the British Empire as the business of Lord Royston's under-secretaryship might affect that nothing complex or important was on hand next morning. Choice between horns of one dilemma at a time is sufficient for the mind of any budding statesman. And the noble under-secretary was sorely exercised by the momentous question: "Should he call or not upon the Cransdales to thank them for their presence?" To do so might savor of vanity; not to do so, of indifference. It would not do to look ungrateful, nor would it do better to look like fishing for compliments. As he docketed papers and scrawled signatures mechanically, determination went swinging to and fro. The question ended, as so many do, by settling itself. Riding up through St. James' after office-hours, he met the Cransdale carriage, and the countess beckoned to him.

"Well, Royston, I congratulate you. We were in the House last night."

"Almost to my discomfiture."

"Civil! when we took so much interest in your success."

"True, though. Friends make the worst audience."

"Then why do they go to back a man up and cheer him?"

"Oh, party friends, that's quite another thing. Yet they would be nothing but for party enemies."

"Do you really mean," said Lady Constance, "that you would sooner face enemies than friends?"

"Than some friends, certainly," he answered, flushing to his hat brim.

"But last night," said her mother, "the interest must have been too keen to let you care for individual hearers, friend or foe."

"Keen enough, but there are keener."

He was afraid of his own boldness, and did not dare to look up and sun his triumph in Constance's soft eyes, when her mother assured him that many of the first men in the House had spoken of it in the highest terms.

"Have you heard from Philip?" he asked, to turn off the conversation and escape from its delicious pain.

"Oh, yes! And the boys have whole holiday on Thursday, so I'll have up him and Ned to town. Come and dine with us to meet them."

"Delighted!" said the under-secretary, bringing his spurs, in unadvised ecstasy, so near his spirited horse's flanks that he started off and went plunging up Constitution-hill in wildest fashion.

"Royston's been and done it just about, Ned," cried Philip, bouncing into Locksley's room, the *Times* in one hand, and his mother's letter in the other. Unconsciously merciless, he threw down the newspaper and insisted upon inflicting Lady Cransdale's account of her visit to the House upon his friend. "I've a scrap of a note from Con, too, and she says it was 'out and out.'"

"I don't believe it," blurted out Ned, beside himself.

"Don't believe what? Not what Con says of Royston's speech? Read it in the *Times*, then, and you'll see 'twas an out and outer."

"Perhaps it was, but she never talks slang," said Ned, catching at a means of extricating himself.

"Oh, bother, Ned, we're mighty particular all of a sudden, eh? Anyhow, Constance says she thought it fine and eloquent. And we shall have an opportunity of patting him on the back for it. Mammy says we may go up to town on Thursday."

Close conflict was in Ned's heart, between delight at the thought of seeing Lady Constance, and pain at seeing Lord Royston in her company. Young "grown men" have an irritating way sometimes of making young "ungrown men" feel their distance from their immediate elders; but Lord Royston had never so dealt by Ned. He liked the lad, and respected him; and, in his own undemonstrative way, had shown him that he did. Now, ingratitude was Ned's abhorrence, yet there is a gratitude most ungrateful to him that pays it He owned obligation, but felt its withes cut to the bone the wrists it bound. For, as my readers have seen long since, the poor lad's heart had yielded to the mastery of that passion which makes boys men—and men, boys. He knew not—how should he?—at what precise period Constance had lost her sisterly character, and stood out robed before his eyes in all the royalties of love; but early jealousy of Royston had long since taught him how to the word "passion" the old Latin meaning clings—how truly it is "a suffering." Yet Lady Constance's manner towards himself was less reserved and more affectionate than towards the other. Ned would exult in this sometimes, and sometimes quail at it. Sometimes his own lifelong intimacy with her would be counted gain, and sometimes loss. They stood upon such different footings that nothing fairly showed her judgment as between them.

"If I, too, were a distant kinsman, or he, too, were the close companion of her childhood, perhaps I might conjecture what she feels concerning us!" As for Lord Royston's feeling concerning her, spite of his equable demeanor, Ned had with unerring instinct conjectured it by countless subtle tokens. He knew that one name lay hidden in his own heart and in her kinsman's, and the knowledge was his daily disquieting.

It never troubled him that Lady Constance was his elder. For, first, the difference was no great one at the most; and, next, man's conscious manliness carries a consciousness of headship with it which takes little account of difference in age. The feeling takes an ugly shape at times. An urchin in the nursery, who cannot reach up to the father's knee, will class himself with him, and say, "We, men," in full disdain of mother, nurse, and elder sisters. Yet purge it of its arrogance, as fire of love can purge it purest, and the feeling is manly and worthy of a man. Younger men are wont to set their heart on older, older men on younger, women than themselves. Experience of life has not yet shown me that the older man's is always, or often, the truest ideal of what is love-worthy in woman. But, in truth, it did trouble Ned right sore that the man whose rivalry he had divined should be his elder. Such a lady's wooers must prove their worth, and Royston was proving his worthily; that could not be denied. Royston's were a man's efforts and a man's successes; his own, mere schoolboy struggles, and their meed a schoolboy's prize. His thought was ever fretting at the contrast—ever fretting, and ever devising how best to burst upon a sudden the boundary, which fences boyhood off from man's estate. Oh, for one single day of battle! That would alter all! A beardless ensign carries the flaunting silk into the storm of bullets, and comes out a veteran, with the torn flag in his hand. The countless deaths that have resulted have aged him in honor and esteem. There be days of fight which count for years of service, not in the army-list alone, but in the common account of men's opinion. No soldiering was afoot in Europe; but India was a frequent field of battle. One day of Hindostan might put a badge of manhood on his breast at which old men should bow.

Such were the floating fancies in his mind, which a few chance words were soon to fix. There was no party at the Cransdales on the Thursday; only another cousin besides Royston, one Katey Kilmore, godchild and namesake of the countess. Of course, then, the under-secretary gave his arm to Lady Cransdale; Philip his to Cousin Katey; Ned his, with tremor of delight, to Constance. Poor boy! the dainty white hand on his arm, the hand which had clasped his a thousand times in careless, childish play, now sent a thrill to his heart's core at every touch.

"Phil tells me, Lady Constance, you went to the debate."

He could not keep himself from speaking of what it vexed him sore to think of.

What a strange contrast between "Phil," the old familiar word, and that formal "Lady Constance." Once it had been "Con," and "Phil," and "Ned," at all times; but an awe was creeping over him against which the oldest intimacy could not prevail. She did not seem to notice it.

"Oh, yes; and I liked it wonderfully. I wish it had been in the Commons though."

That was well; it was not all for Royston's sake she had enjoyed it.

"Why rather in the Commons!"

"Because of the more lively stir and action, to be sure. Great questions are decided there, nine times out of ten. Royston says he wishes his seat were in that House."

This dashed the cup of comfort from his lips, all the more cruelly that the young lord turned at hearing his own name, and looked his pleasure at her giving weight to words of his.

It cost Ned something to continue.

"So you like stir and action?"

"To be sure I do; don't you?"

"What do you think of soldiering then, Lady Constance?" he next asked, nerving himself as a gambler against his nervousness by calling a higher stake.

"Come, Con," cried her brother, overhearing this, though Ned had not spoken loud, "say your say about soldiering, then we'll have Katey's."

"I don't care for red coats and gold epaulettes, Phil, anyhow; and bearskins are my bogies."

"You're a muff, Con," he retorted. "Now, Katey, what say you?"

She had one brother in the "Coldstream," and one hoping for the "Fusiliers," so she cried, "The Guards forever! Phil."

"Bravo, Katey; you shall be vivandière to our battalion."

Whilst they were laughing at their own fun, Ned said very gravely and quietly to Constance, "Of course I didn't mean the Guards, they only play at soldiers now-a-days; but real soldiering in camps and colonies; what do you think of that?"

"Better, at all events; but all soldiering is dangling idle work in time of peace."

"Not everywhere. Not in India for instance."

"India, I grant you; that is a field for a man's career. It should be mine if I were one. Soldier, statesman, missionary—there are endless roads to greatness there."

She wondered, as she looked at him, what the rush of blood to his forehead should mean—what the blaze that kindled in his eyes.

"Since when have you thought over Indian careers, pray?"

"Since when have I not, Ned? Have you forgotten that I am a Hindoo girl myself—that dearest pappy's official greatness was all Indian? I have read all his despatches that are in print, and some in manuscript besides, and every book of Indian travel or adventure I can lay my hands upon."

"How strange of me to have forgotten it?" said Ned.

Thereupon he fell into dead silence. She wondered all the more at him. She little knew her sweet lips had spoken doom of exile against a playmate from the cradle. Her wonder did not outlive the day; but thenceforth dated a new manner of intercourse between herself and Ned. Down at Cransdale in the midsummer holidays, under the cedars at noontide, on horseback in the long soft evenings, they would hold continuous and grave conversations. Phil voted them prodigious bores. "A talk with you two is about as lively as an hour up to Hawtrey in Thucydides. I wish I'd Katey Kilmore to run wild a bit upon the moor with me."

Boys on their way to manhood will pass through certain heroic moods, such as more callous—shall I say trivial?—elders mock at. Silly scorn! The tone and color of the finished life-picture may recall but faintly, by and by, the prismatic hues of the first "study" for it; the grouping may be strangely varied, the firmest outlines show "repentings," yet each worthiest work must needs retain indelible impress of that first conception.

"Heroic moods, indeed!" say some. "Walking on stilts, you mean: the lad's best friend is he that soonest brings him to his legs again." "Not if he break them in the breaking down," I say. And I would rather, when the stilts are dropped, see the boy stride, or even strut, than lounge and shuffle.

Scorn boy-heroics or not, good reader, you will agree with me that since a female figure must needs haunt them, it is huge advantage to the man that shall be when its proportions of worth and beauty are truly just and noble—are genuine realities, not figments of his fancy. Come of his green passion what may, 'tis well for him that she who kindles it be one for whose love "a world" were indeed "well lost." And such was Lady Constance. She was nearly twenty now; her girlish grace and freshness not worn off, but ripening into womanly glories. Two seasons' experience of the great London world had left her untainted, but not undisciplined. Her conversation fed and sustained the loftiest of the lad's aspirations. Had he but counted her as truly sister as she held him brother, all had been well, and this fresh intimacy had proved to him an unalloyed advantage. As it was now, the very mind was saturated with the sweet poison wherewith the heart was sick. But he put strong constraint upon himself, and hid this from her. That would have been perhaps impossible could she but once have gained a sight of him at distance, so to speak. However, she suspected nothing. He stood as he had always stood—too near.

Those were blissful holidays. No Royston was there to be a fly in amber. His very triumph had brought him tribulation. His department had to undergo remodelling in virtue of the very Bill that he had helped to pass, and he was chained to his under-secretary's desk. School-days were over, too, for good and all. Neither Phil nor Ned was to return next half to Eton. The former expected his commission daily, the latter was entered at Christ-church. That troubled him, however, so there was a fly in his amber after all. His repugnance against any but a soldier's career grew daily, yet he had not imparted it to his father—a second cause of inward disquiet.

His reserve on this one point was foreign to all their life-long relation to one another, a new growth, not rooted in any strange undutifulness or new mistrust; but only in excessive tenderness and lingering self-devotion. He must not follow the promptings of a dream, pushing him out of the beaten track of duty. How could an Indian soldier—gone in quest of name and fame to find both or neither, perhaps on a field of death—play an only son's part to such dear parents in their quiet English home? What vexed him most in brooding on his love for Lady Constance was this double-facedness. Sometimes it seemed the essence of unselfishness, it won him so far out of his inner self; sometimes it seemed a selfishness in quintescence, so utterly did it seduce him into forgetfulness of them. And when either parent spake, as parents will, of that coming Oxford life to which he could not feel heartily resigned, he hated the half-hypocrisy which shut his lips or opened them with words of little meaning.

Robert Locklsey took little if any notice of such symptoms of inner conflict as might sometimes have been perceptible in the outward bearing of his son; nor would perception of them have set him on conjecture. Ned's confidence was certain to be given him in good time; no fear of that. But meek-hearted Lucy had more misgivings: meek hearts look out at clear eyes oftentimes. She would not question, she could hardly bear to watch him, and indicate or even entertain suspicion thus against his trust in her. But it is hard to keep a mother's hungry watchfulness of love from off her only one. Following with delicate acuteness the boy's dreamiest glances, her own glance found itself carried, more than once, into a corner of the sitting-room, where the grandfather's sword hung. The blue steel seemed to pierce her own heart then. She thought of last year at Freshet, how quick and close an intimacy had sprung up between her son and the old soldier, how Ned had relished his campaigning stories, grave or gay. But she could hardly bring herself to accept that interpretation of her boy's unrest. His will had ever been too steadfast, his very fancy too self-controlled to be moved lightly to some novel scheme of life.

The Recreations of a Country Parson. Second Series. Parker, Son, and Bourn.

We are not at all surprised at the success of these essays. They are rambling, and diffusive, and now and then a little tedious, but they present in many ways a very favorable contrast to much of the periodical writing of the day. In the first place, they are the writing of a man who has thoughts of his own and communicates them to his readers. They are not written to order. It is evident that the writer has selected subjects which have a natural interest for him; and fortunately these subjects are of a kind that interest also most cultivated persons. He has an earnest, unaffected interest in human life, in natural scenery, in literature, and this gives a force and a charm to what he says about them, even when it is not new or remarkable. Then the mind of the writer is sufficiently "strung" and sufficiently refined to prevent his candid, comprehensive, unreserved discourse from degenerating into flippancy and impertinence on the one hand, or into twaddle on the other. The dying out of the old familiar "essay" like Lamb's or Hazlitt's, or Leigh Hunt's, is sometimes spoken of as a mere change of fashion in literature; but we believe the fact to be that such essays would be as popular now as ever, if only the proper sort of man could be got to write them. The success of these before us, inferior as they are (and we are sure the writer would be the first to admit it) to any of those just named, goes far to prove this. There is a very large class of people who like to read about "Growing Old" or "The Worries of Life" better than Iron-Plated Vessels or the prospects of the Rebellion in China; but they must have familiar themes treated by the right sort of persons. They will not stand "cockney clatter" about them; or the inflated eloquence of boys; or the maundering of well-intentioned but weak old gentlemen. The essayist must be, at least, a man of more than average thoughtfulness, of good education, and good taste, and the deserved success of these pleasant essays shows how welcome to a considerable section of the reading public these by no means exorbitant qualifications prove, when brought to bear upon familiar subjects of perennial interest.—*Economist.*

From Chambers's Journal.

SCHAMYL IN CAPTIVITY.

In the struggle of Russia to subdue the Caucasus, Schamyl Imam was the last of the powerful free chiefs who held out. Prince Dadian, the prince of Abbasia, and one or two others, may indeed preserve their shadowy rank, but they are in reality only splendid vassals of the czar. The embers of war may still be here and there smouldering sulkily, as among the Shapsoughs; but the flame which only a few months ago burned so fiercely is extinguished; and when Schamyl at last laid down his arms, the long, hopeless struggle of the warlike tribes who acknowledged him as their chief was felt to be ended.

There is no doubt that a great deal of the personal importance which attached to Schamyl was in the first instance attributable to the ignorance of his enemies. A man perhaps of very little previous account among his tribe is often at once raised to supreme power when messengers from a victorious general are sent to treat with him. But the priestly soldier whose wars have just closed so gallantly was no drivelling marabout or fanatic dervish. Though it is difficult to see clearly through the thick haze which shrouds political events among the wild mountains and defiles of the Caucasus, we know enough to excite our interest, and even our respect for him. By paths unknown to European ambition; by dauntless courage, an austere simplicity, rare self-denial, great firmness of purpose, and promptitude in action; by some intrigues, and some cruelties, he raised himself from the humble rank of groom to the Imam Kasy Moullah, to a position of unexampled authority among his countrymen; and he was even believed to possess that saintly character which is usually ascribed by the populace to the possession of supreme power in the east.

A touching and romantic incident made us first acquainted with his personal appearance and manner of life when at home among his mountains. It is a story of as chivalrous an act as that said to have passed between Richard the Lion-hearted and Salaheddin in the time of the third Crusade: a tale of generous enmity on one side, and noble trust upon the other. Many years ago, the Imam's eldest son, Djemmal Eddin, was taken prisoner by the Russians. His mother, Patimate, died of grief for his loss; but the boy was carefully educated by the late czar, and loaded with favors. He grew up with all the ideas of a Russian noble and a courtier. But at last his father obtained his exchange for the Princesses Orbeliani and Tchawchawadzé, whose romantic imprisonment at Veden made so much noise. The young man returned to his native mountains, but soon sickened there. He fell into a state of hypochondria, which puzzled all the medicine-men and charm-chanters; so at last Schamyl sent a messenger to ask aid of the Russians. Colonel the Prince Myrsky was fortunate enough to receive this knightly request, and to his undying honor, immediately despatched Dr. Petroffsky, the best surgeon of his regiment, to the young man's aid; but in vain.

According to the most trustworthy information obtainable, Schamyl is now probably about sixty years of age, though he himself not knowing exactly, this is mere conjecture. He does not look more than forty. He is tall in stature. His countenance is soft, calm, imposing. Its principal characteristic is melancholy; but when the muscles of the face contract, it expresses great energy. His complexion is pale, his eyebrows strongly marked; his eyes are of a dark gray, and usually half shut, like those of a lion reposing. His beard is dyed a reddish brown by henna, and very carefully kept; his mouth is good; lips red; teeth small, even, white, and pointed; his hands small, white, and scrupulously attended to. His walk is slow and grave. He looks like a hero.

When at Veden, his ordinary costume was a Lesguian tunic, white or green; a high-pointed cap of sheep-skin, white as snow, round which was wound a turban of white muslin, the ends falling behind. The point of the cap was in red cloth, with a black tassel. Embroidered gaiters, and boots of yellow or red leather, covered his legs and feet. On Fridays, when he went to the mosque, he wore a long white or green robe over his ordinary dress; and in winter, a crimson pelisse, lined with black lamb-skin, protected him from the cold. In war time, his arms were a sword, a dagger, a pair of pistols, and a gun. Two attendants also rode beside him, each carrying another pair of pistols and a gun for the Imam's use. This post was looked upon as one of high honor among the mountaineers; and if one of these attendants was killed, another immediately replaced him. Schamyl was said to be the best horseman among a race of horsemen, and his horses were the strongest and fleetest which could be procured.

The qualities of the Imam's mind belong to the very highest kind of Asiatic excellence. He prided himself upon his truthfulness. He was sparing of words, patient, sagacious, clear-sighted, politic, charitable; cold in his bearing, but tender-hearted, when his affections were roused. He used no titles, but gave and took the "Thee and Thou" with the simplest peasant. He was abstemious, and always ate alone. His food was flour, milk, fruit, rice, honey, tea; he rarely touched meat. He tried to suppress every kind of luxury; and his influence, where that of the greatest potentates of the earth have been proved powerless, was still supreme. Smoking was long as much a necessity to the Circassian as to the Turk; but Schamyl forbade it, and ordered that the money hitherto spent in tobacco should be used to purchase gunpowder. He was obeyed. His morals were pure, and he would not tolerate any weakness in others. A Tartar woman, a widow, and childless, lived with a Lesguian who had promised her marriage. She became pregnant. Schamyl had her interrogated, and the truth being made clear, he cut off the heads both of the woman and her paramour. The axe which did execution on this occasion is kept as a curiosity, and is in possession of Field-marshal the Prince Bariatinsky, viceroy of the Caucasus.

Schamyl had four wives; but of these Patimate died in 1839, and another he repudiated, because she bore him no children. He allowed his wives no mark of rank or distinction. He was a master rather than a husband.

From 1834 to 1859—for twenty-five years—this mountain-chief waged war with the most distinguished captains of Russia, and made the country over which he ruled one of the sternest military schools in the world. His enmity was one which no defeats, losses, or privations could diminish, which no offers, however splendid, could lull to sleep. Till at last, chased from one fastness, hitherto deemed impregnable, to another fondly thought more inaccessible still, he looked his farewell at hope from the heights of Ghounib, and surrendered, to save the lives of a mere handful of devoted followers, whom misfortune and disaster had left still true to him. Happily, even warfare has long ceased to be wantonly cruel or vindictive. The captive Imam has been allotted an ample pension and a residence in the town of Kalouga.

Kalouga pleased Schamyl, on account of the woods, hills, and ravines, which remind him of the Caucasus. The house hired for him has three stories. He has kept the upper story for himself, given the middle story to one of his sons, and the lower to another. Of the six rooms on the upper story, four are occupied by his daughters, who live with him—that is, two rooms are occupied by each young lady. These six rooms are very simply furnished with large sofas or divans, and are not ornamented with a single picture or even a looking-glass. The Imam's private room, serves as study, oratory, and bedroom. A large divan, an arm-chair, a writing-desk, a card-table, a book-stand, a basin, and a cushion to kneel on at prayer-time, complete its furniture. The middle story, destined for Rasy Mahomet and his wife Kerimate, who is said to be very beautiful, is adorned with glasses, draperies, carpets, and bronzes; its mistress has not yet arrived, but Schamyl has reclaimed Prince Bariatinsky's intercession to obtain permission for her to join her husband. On his arrival at Kalouga, Schamyl visited some of the authorities, conversed much with the archbishop, interested himself in the daily details of the life of Russian soldiers, and visited with much attention the barracks of the regiment in garrisons. The contact of this son of nature, endowed with a vast and lucid mind, kept in check only by native superstition, with our artificial life, is very interesting, as are also his patriarchal manners, and his curious sympathies and antipathies. Strange to all things, knowing nothing of the circumstances which surround him, he shows much tact in his actions; and the words he addressed to M. Rounovsky (to whom we are indebted for some of these particulars), when that officer was entering on his functions, are curiously illustrative of the tone of his mind. "When," said the Imam, "it pleases God to make a child an orphan, to replace its mother is given to it a nurse, who ought to feed, dress, wash, and keep it from harm. If the child remains in good health, gay, clean, and happy, every one praises the nurse: it is said the nurse does her duty, and loves the child. But if the orphan is ailing, dirty, slovenly, it is not the child we blame, but the nurse who has neglected it, left it untaught, and who does not love it. I am an old man; but I am a stranger here. I understand neither your language nor your customs; and so I fancy that I am no longer the old man Schamyl, but a little child, become, through God's will, an orphan, having need of a nurse. You are this nurse, and I pray you to love me as a nurse loves her child. For my part, I will love you not only as a child loves his nurse, but as old Schamyl can love a man who does good to him."

He frankly shows his sympathies and antipathies. He is very fond of music, and when asked out, first inquires whether any one will play the piano at the house to which he is invited. M. Rounovsky bought him an organ, which delighted him exceedingly. But a conjuror is the person who seems to interest him more than can be conceived. An individual of this class having apparently changed a piece of money, enveloped in a pocket-handkerchief, into a plume of feathers, the Imam was so impressed that he declared the mere remembrance of the trick had troubled his thoughts even at prayers. "Nevertheless," he added, "had the man been brought before me at Veden, I would have had him hanged."

A crab, which the Imam saw for the first time in his life at Kalouga, excited his utmost aversion. Taking it in one hand, he examined it attentively, till the crab seized a finger in its claws. He then threw it down, but continued to watch it eagerly. Having remarked the animal's mode of walking, he became indignant, kicked it from before him, and ordered Khadjio, one of his suite, to drive it out of the room. It was long before he recovered from the disagreeable sensation produced on his mind by the crab. "I never saw such a cowardly animal," he said; "and if I ever fancied the Devil, it was in that likeness."

At first, he went a great deal into society, and liked balls, though he disapproved of the dress-coats worn by European gentlemen, and also of the bare shoulders exposed by ladies; the latter being a temptation which mortal man, says the Imam, is too weak to look upon. He liked the theatre, too, and especially the dancing; but the uncovered faces of so many women troubled him, and he soon ceased his attendance. Now, when invited anywhere, he asks if ladies will be present. If the reply is affirmative, he refuses. His religion, he says, teaches him to object to unveiled women. But he is not bigoted on the subject, and is quite willing to discuss it.

The captive Imam still excites some curiosity, but it is rapidly dying away; and he will soon be as little talked of or thought about as Timour Meerza, or Abd-el-Kader.

Next Thing to an Angel upon Earth.—A gentleman walking through Knightsbridge on Sunday overheard the following conversation between a man and a woman, who appeared as if just come from some pleasure trip into the country: Woman—"Blow me, Bill, how tired I do feel! I'm as miserable, too, as a starved herring. What a miserable world is this! I wish I'd never been born, that I do; and now that I am born I wish myself dead again." Man—"Why, Bet, what's the matter with you now? What are you grumbling about?" Woman—"Why, don't I tell yer I am as miserable as a rat?" Man—"Miserable, indeed! Why, what on earth would yer have? You was drunk Monday, and you was drunk again Wednesday, and I'm blessed if you haven't had pretty near enough to-day. If that ain't enough pleasure for yer I don't know what is. I suppose you wants to be a downright hangel here upon earth."—*English Paper.*

Dr. Johnson on Pekin.—"What is Pekin? Ten thousand Londoners would drive all the people of Pekin; they would drive them like deer."—*Boswell's Johnson.*

From The Examiner, 16 Feb.

OCEAN TELEGRAPHS.

THE Geographical Society, popular and very prosperous (for at each of its fortnightly meetings a score of members are added to the 1,400 already enrolled), met last Monday. The main subject discussed was the North Atlantic Electric Cable. We may offer a few observations on this subject. The discussion arose out of papers read at the preceding meeting by the persons who conducted the survey by land and sea from Scotland to Labrador, when we say that those persons were Sir Leopold McClintock, Captain Allan Young, and Dr. Rae, it is the same as saying that it was performed with skill and intrepidity. But the practicability of connecting the Old and New World by an Electric Cable is a very different matter from a survey. Schemes as feasible, and even a good deal more so, have totally failed;—but the reader shall judge for himself when we enumerate a few of them.

First, then, the Great Atlantic Cable has been a great failure, and has cost the subscribers, as far as we understand, £450,000: the pounds and cable are equally at the bottom of the Atlantic. The next attempt was a greater, because a more costly failure. This was the Red Sea and Indian affair. It was to have brought the Nile and the Indus almost within hail of each other, although the distance between them was little short of 1,700 miles. For this adventure the government has given a guarantee of four and a half per cent on a million sterling for half a century, or, in other terms, the nation is for that long time to pay an annuity of £45,000, without receiving the smallest consideration in return. It never conveyed even a single message throughout, so that, as far as the nation is concerned, the million sovereigns might as well have been consigned to the sea that swallowed up Pharaoh, his horses, his chariots, and his horsemen. In the debate which took place in the Commons on Thursday last, an honorable member naïvely and drolly ascribed the failure "to certain occult causes at the bottom of the sea, which could not be provided against."

Our next speculation was meant to connect England with Spain by Falmouth and Gibraltar, aud the government bargained in this case for a firstrate cable at the cost of some £400,000, but the Atlantic being deemed too deep for it, it was transferred to Rangoon and Singapore, a distance of 1,200 miles, embracing the best part of the Bay of Bengal and the whole of the Straits of Malacca, among a hundred isles, islets, and coral reefs. The ship bearing it was wrecked in Plymouth Harbor, when the cable was discovered to be damaged by the corrosion of the iron and the decomposition of the gutta percha. It was not therefore deemed good enough for the Indian Ocean, and it is now destined to connect Malta with Alexandria; all the cables of the Mediterranean, whether English or French, having already failed. If we include the cable which was to have connected Malta with Spezzia, through Sardinia and Corsica, and that which was to have connected Malta with Corfu, both of which have failed, we have spent not less than two millions in experimenting upon oceanic cables.

But we are not the only people who have failed in the matter of long cables. The cable that was to have connected Algeria with France will not work, although it embraces but the breadth of the Mediterranean. The Dutch laid down a cable between Batavia and Singapore about six months ago. The distance is six hundred miles and it conveyed, like the great Atlantic cable, a few messages, when it stopped. Ships' anchors and coral reefs were fatal to it; it has broken a score of times, and has been finally given up as a hopeless project.

Such, then, being the result of our experience of Oceanic Electric Cables, what chance of success can there be with a cable that proposes to bring the Old and New World together by the route of Scotland, the Faroe Islands, Iceland, Greenland, and Labrador, over seas infested by icebergs, and along ice-bound coasts? We fear none whatever. The distance is little short of that across the South Atlantic. There are sea-gaps of eight hundred and of five hundred miles, and the inhospitable land is rather a hindrance than an advantage. We are, then decidedly of opinion that a North American Cable is a hopeless project that will not be, and ought not to be, attempted. The government, goaded on by the press and the public, has been already severely bitten, and will assuredly not guarantee a farthing. Without its guarantee there will as assuredly be no subscribers. Until some great discovery is made which no man at present even dreams of, our electric cables must be confined to the narrow seas, and the wafting of "sighs from India to the Pole" must be still an achievement known only in the domain of poetry.

From Chambers's Journal.

HOW DUMAS WROTE "MONTE CRISTO."

PEOPLE are always very anxious, says M. Alexandre Dumas, in a recent pamphlet, to know how my works were composed, and above all, who wrote them, and naturally, those works that have attained the greatest success have had their paternity most obstinately questioned. It is generally believed that *The Count of Monte Cristo* was written by Fiorentino.

Let me here relate how I came to write that romance, a work which to this day still continues to be reprinted.

In 1841, I was living in Florence. In that year, Prince Jerome Napoleon was also living there, in the charming villa of Quarto, where every Frenchman was desirous of being presented on his first arrival at the "City of the Medicis." This formality had been gone through by me in 1834, so that, on my second visit to Florence in 1840, I found myself, as it were, on the footing of an old friend of the exiled family. I was in the habit, indeed, of going every day to visit the prince at Quarto.

One day, Prince Jerome said to me, alluding to his son: "Napoleon is leaving the service of Würtemberg, and is returning to Florence. He does not wish, as you can well understand, to run the risk of serving against France. So directly he arrives, I shall introduce him to you, that you may not only tell him all about France, of which he is ignorant, but also, if you have time, make with him some slight expeditions in Italy."

"Has he seen the island of Elba?" I inquired.

"No."

"Well, I will take him there," I said, "if your highness thinks proper. It is but right that the nephew of the emperor should finish his education by a historical pilgrimage like that."

Therefore, when the Prince Napoleon arrived, he found every thing arranged between his father and myself, and after a few days devoted to his family and friends, we set out in the prince's carriage for Leghorn. I was at that time eight-and-thirty, and the prince scarcely nineteen.

The next morning, at about five o'clock, we landed in a small boat in Porto-Ferrajo, in Elba.

After having thoroughly wandered over the island, we resolved to make a shooting expedition to Pianosa, a low island scarcely elevated ten feet above the level of the sea, abounding in rabbits and red partridges. Unfortunately, we had forgotten to bring a dog. A man, however, the happy possessor of a black and white cur, offered himself, in consideration of the sum of two pauls, to carry our game-bag, and to lend us his dog besides. By its assistance, we were enabled to kill a dozen partridges, which the owner of the dog very conscientiously picked up. As he put each partridge into his bag, the good man kept exclaiming, glancing with a sigh towards a magnificent rock two or three hundred feet high: "Ah, your excellencies, if you went there, you would have capital sport."

"Well, what is there to be got there, after all?" I asked him at last.

"Whole herds of wild-goats: the island is full of them."

"And what is the name, then, of that happy island?"

"It is called *The Island of Monte Cristo*."

This was the first time that I ever heard the name of Monte Cristo.

The next day we set out for the island. The weather was beautiful, with just enough wind to fill the sail, which, seconded by the oars of our two sailors, made us do the three leagues in less than an hour. As we advanced, Monte Cristo seemed to rise from the bosom of the sea, and increase gradually in size, like the giant Adamastor. At about eleven o'clock, we were within two or three pulls of the centre of a little port. We held our guns in our hands, ready to jump out, when one of the two rowers exclaimed: "Your excellencies are doubtless aware that the island of Monte Cristo is deserted, and that at whatever port we enter after we have touched here, we shall be liable to five or six days of quarantine."

"Well," I said to the prince, "what do you say to that?"

"I say," he replied, "that this man has done well to warn us before landing; but he would have done still better if he had warned us before setting out."

"Then you don't think the five or six goats we may kill are worth suffering five or six days' quarantine?"

"And you?"

"I? Oh, I have no great passion for goats, and I have a great dislike for quarantine, so that if you don't object—"

"Well?"

"We will simply make the circumference of the island."

"For what purpose?"

"To settle its geographical position."

"Settle its geographical position," said the prince, "if you like; but what good will it do you?"

"It will serve," I said, "in memory of the voyage I have had the honor of making with you. It will serve to give the title of *The Island of Monte Cristo* to some romance I may hereafter write."

"Let us make, then, the circuit of the island," he replied; "and send me the first impression of your work."

Eight days afterwards, we retured to Florence. Towards the year 1843, being in France, I entered into an agreement with Messrs. Bethune and Plon to write a work in eight volumes, called *Wanderings in Paris*. I had at first intended to have done the matter very simply, commencing at the Barrier du Trône, and finishing at the Barrier de l'Etoile; touching with the right hand the Barrier de Clichy, and with the left the Barrier du Maine; when one morning Bethune came to tell me, in his name, and in the name of his partner, that he did not intend to have a mere historical and archæological production, but that he meant to have a romance—about any thing I liked, it is true, so long as it was interesting, but provided also that the wanderings in Paris formed no part of it. He had had his head turned by the success of Eugene Sue. As, however, it was just as easy for me to write a romance as to write my *Wanderings in Paris*, I set about to find materials for this work of Messrs. Bethune and Plon.

I had some time previously read in *The Police Unveiled* of Peuchet a story about twenty pages in length, called, I believe, "The Diamond and the Revenge." Whatever it was, it was very foolish, and those who doubt it, had better read it. Nevertheless, at the bottom of that oyster there was a pearl—a rough pearl, without shape or value, it is true, but a pearl merely requiring the hand of the jeweller. I resolved to apply to the *Wanderings in Paris* the plot which I might draw from this story; so I set myself down, in consequence, to that work of the brain which with me always precedes the mere manual labor. The first outline of the plot was this:—

A nobleman, very rich, dwelling in Rome, calling himself the Count of Monte Cristo, was to do some great service to a young French traveller, and, in exchange for the service, was to ask him to be his guide when he in his turn should visit Paris. The object of this visit to Paris was to have for appearance curiosity, but in reality revenge. In the course of his stay in Paris, the Count of Monte Cristo was to find out his secret enemies, who had condemned him in his youth to a captivity of six years. His fortune was to furnish him with the means of vengeance.

I commenced the work in this form, and I finished about a volume and a half of it. In that volume and a half are comprised all Albert de Morcerf's adventures in Rome, and those of Franz d'Epinay until his arrival in Paris.

I was just there when I happened to speak to Maquet, with whom I had already worked in collaboration. I told him what I had done, and what I still intended to do.

"I think," he said, "that you are passing over the most important part of the life of your hero—that is to say, over his amours with the Catalan, over the treason of Danglars and Fernand, and over the ten years in prison with the Abbé Faria."

I answered: "I intend to relate all that."

He replied: "You cannot tell it all in five or six volumes, and you have but five or six volumes left."

"Perhaps you are right," I said. "Come and dine with me to-morrow, and we will talk about it."

During that evening, that night, and the next morning, I thought over Maquet's remarks, and they appeared so true, that they prevailed over my previous intentions. So, when he came the next day, he found the work cut out into three distinct parts—Marseille, Rome, Paris.

That same evening, we made together the plan of the first five volumes: one of them was to be devoted to the introduction, three to the captivity, and the last two to the escape and recompense of the Morells. The remainder, without being entirely finished, was quite planned out.

Maquet believed he had done me only a friendly service; I maintain that he did the work of a *collaborateur*.

Thus *The Count of Monte Cristo*, commenced by me in my *Wanderings in Paris*, turned by degrees into a romance, and found itself at last completed by Maquet and myself together.

Every one, though, is yet at liberty to find in *The Count of Monte Cristo* any other source than I have said; but he will be very clever if he finds one.

Thus is briefly told, by the author himself, the origin of the most remarkable romance of our time; and we waive our ordinary rule against the admission of translations, in order that, by its publication, the fame of M. Dumas may be cleared from certain charges of plagiarism in the eyes of many whom his own statement would never reach.

MR. MATHIEU, surgical instrument maker, has produced a vegetable grease, which is both viscid and elastic. He calls it *Heveone*, to indicate that it consists principally of essence of caoutchouc, or of very pure caoutchouc, extracted from the *hevœa guyaniensis*, or india-rubber tree of Guiana, and that it is prepared at a very elevated temperature. This new preparation possesses very remarkable properties, and will render important services to many branches of industry. It adheres strongly to the surfaces to which it is applied; it never becomes oxidized under the influence of atmospheric agencies; but renders unoxidizable, and preserves from rust, all kinds of iron, copper, and steel implements, etc., and polished metals generally, upon the surface of which it forms a film of extreme thinness. Surgical instruments, domestic utensils, machines, arms, weapons, etc., can by its means be kept always clean and bright. The lubricating properties of *Heveone* are even more astonishing: applied to pistons, axles, hinges, pumps, pivots, screws, etc., it diminishes friction, rendering their action quite free and smooth. It never loses its viscidity, or becomes dry, nor oxidizes or combines with the metal. *Heveone*, as a coating impermeable to water, powerfully contributes to keep leather, and articles manufactured of it, intact and clean; boots, harness, straps, etc, it protects from the extremes of dryness and moisture, communicating to them the greatest suppleness, and preserving them from decay. Its salutary effects extend also to wood exposed to the weather, as in gun carriages; and not the least of its important applications is that to the interior of guns and rifles, rendering them much easier to clean, and to require cleaning less frequently.—*Welcome Guest.*

EDGAR A. POE.—A great deal has been written of the life and character of this erratic and erring son of genius, and a good deal that is supposititious and incorrect. An English writer, a Dr. Maudsley, has made Poe the subject of an article in the *Journal of Medical Science*, in which I find this sentence respecting Poe's parentage:—

"So David Poe [the father of Edgar] bade farewell to law, of which he had been a student, and with Elizabeth Arnold, the beautiful actress, went forth into the wide, wide world."

David Poe was an actor before he ever saw his wife. He was a young lawyer or student of law in Baltimore, who, with one or two other young men of that city, about the year 1803, became, as the phrase is, "stage-mad." They came to Richmond soon after, and Poe was a regular actor in the Virginia company of comedians. At that time, belonging to the same company, were Mr. and Mrs. Hopkins, an English actor and actress, he an admirable comic actor, she a sweet, pretty, modest little woman, very good, and a great favorite in the walks of minor comedy, such as *Rosina*, etc. Not long after Poe's appearance on the Richmond boards, Hopkins died, and a year or so after that Poe married the widow, of which marriage Edgar was the offspring, the only one, I believe. I knew them all well. Hopkins was a man of classical education and of much wit; the elder Poe was educated, clever, and agreeable. I have no recollection of the career or fate of Poe and his wife, as I left Virginia a year or two after their marriage. The *Philadelphia Bulletin* says "they died in utter destitution."—*National Intelligencer.*

SLAVERY, AS VIEWED BY A SLAVE.—We reported lately, on the authority of a Georgia journal, that an essay on slavery by a Georgia slave was in press. The result is before us in a pamphlet. "Slavery and Abolitionism, as Viewed by a Georgia Slave," by *Harrison Berry* the slave of L. W. Price, of Covington, Ga.

It is printed by Wood, Hanleiter, Rice, and Co., Atlanta, Ga., and will be furnished for 25 cents per copy.

It is a remarkable work and shall be noticed more fully.—*Charleston Courier*, 16 *March*.

From Bentley's Miscellany.

RECOLLECTIONS OF G. P. R. JAMES.

"Should auld acquaintance be forgot?"

WHEN the writer of "Richelieu," encouraged by the frank praises of Sir Walter Scott, commenced his long career of authorship, I was travelling in Italy, and engaged in studies which made me more familiar with the middle ages than with modern literature. And, on my return to England, I was but slowly overtaking his rapid powers of production, when I had the pleasure of knowing him as my friend and neighbor.

We were both residing on one of the most beautiful portions of the south coast, and I certainly never enjoyed splendid scenery in more agreeable companionship. He was at that time occupied—as usual—in writing a new romance; or rather in dictating it—a practice which he informed me he had adopted at the recommendation of Sir Walter Scott, who (as a piece of authorcraft) thought it both expeditious and economical. With a regularity rarely departed from, he was steadily at work with his amanuensis from soon after an early breakfast till two o'clock. He then walked for about two hours; and I was fortunate when he made me his companion by taking my home in his way. Pleasant was often our talk while

"High o'er the hills, and low adown the dale,
We wandered many a wood, and measured many a vale;" *

or looked from some well-known steep upon the line of picturesque and rocky coast which lay before us in almost Italian beauty. It is only in this way that a natural and easy intercourse can be enjoyed with one who feels that something not too common is expected from him; and those walks will be long remembered. On his return he dictated or corrected till near dinner-time, and in the evening (when not in society) he looked over his manuscript copy. This, till he saw "daylight" (to use his own phrase) in the progress of his story, was generally his daily routine.

But I am not about to become his Boswell. It is because the notices which have appeared since his death, while doing justice to him in every other respect, have been very chary in their acknowledgment of his talents, that I am induced to devote a page or two to his memory. His qualities of disposition have been dwelt upon as they deserved. His active friendship, his kindly feelings, his generous hospitality, could not be overrated. And why should not his talents have been as frankly praised? Who has replaced him? There was a time when one or two *three-volume* works of fiction yearly from his pen, seemed to be thought so absolute a necessity by the public, that it might have been supposed the machinery of society would stop whenever the supply should cease. *Punch* might smile at the two cavaliers who had so often appeared at the commencement of a romance, or might have represented him, pictorially, as grinding his works out of a mill; but in how few of our writers can we now look for the same unaffected style, or easy narrative, or for the pure and unobtrusive moral tone that distinguished every thing he wrote? Of how few works of fiction can we say, as of his, that we rise from their perusal without any perversion of our feelings or principles. He had, also, that power of productiveness which has, in itself been considered an attribute of genius. Like Scott or Voltaire, he could have sat in a library of his own creation; and if he had not the power which the former so eminently possessed of giving life and actuality to the personages he brought before us, he occasionally followed closely upon his great master in his descriptions of natural scenery and events. I only write from memory; but I may mention, *inter alia*, the thunderstorm, in "Margaret of Burgundy;" the trial scene, in "Corse de Leon;" the burning forest, in "Ticonderoga;" the Italian lake, in "Pequinello;" the battle of Evesham, in "Forest Days;" the attack on Angoulême and the battle of Jarnac, in the "Man at Arms;" and the revolt at Barcelona, in "De L'Orme;" a very incomplete list, but all that I at present recollect.

There was one quality in which he was peculiar. It was the natural and easy introduction into his narrative of reflections and remarks that often show great knowledge both of the world and of human nature.

When we were in habits of daily intercourse, I mentioned to him that this had always struck me, and that it was my intention to make a collection of them. It at once involved me in one of the embarrassments frequently consequent upon his gen-

* Spencer.

erosity; for in the course of the day he made me a present of half a dozen of his works, at the same time wishing me, as he thought proper to express it, a less dry and laborious occupation. If it had not, he said, been for the awkwardness of a writer's selecting his own "beauties," he should probably have undertaken it himself. He even fixed upon a publisher. A variety of occupations, however, local and political, prevented me from proceeding with my task beyond sufficient matter for one small volume: and from this I make, at hazard, a few brief extracts.

"Eloquence consists not in many words, but in few; the thoughts, the associations, the images may be many; but the acme of eloquence is in the rapidity of their expression."

"It unfortunately happens that talent is less frequently wanted than the wisdom to employ it."

"Let not people speak lightly of lovers' quarrels. Lovers should never quarrel, if they would love well and love long."

"In the awful struggle which has gone on for ages between good and evil, the eye of man has looked upon a mass of agony, sorrow, and despair which—could it all be beheld at once, or conceived even faintly—would break man's heart for the wickedness and cruelty of his own nature."

"The mirror, like every other invention of human vanity, as often procures us disappointment as gratification."

"In the sad arithmetic of years, multiply by what numbers you will, you can never produce *one-and-twenty* more than once."

"Thought loads the heart and does but little good, when our resolutions are once taken."

"'Providence,' says a powerful but dangerous author of another land, 'has placed Disgust at the door of all bad places.' But, alas! she keeps herself behind the door as we go in, and it is only as we come out that we meet her face to face."

"Servants have a wonderful pleasure in revealing useful information when it is too late; though they take care to conceal every thing they see amiss while their information can be of any service to their masters."

"Apprehension is to sorrow what hope is to joy,—a sort of *avant-coureur* who greatly magnifies the importance of the personage he precedes."

"Trust a woman's eye to discover when a man is insincere. She can always do it when her own heart is not concerned."

"Cast that man from your society forever who does or says a thing in your presence which you would blush to have said or done yourself."

"How often do idle words betray the spirit within. They are the careless gaolers which let the prisoner forth out of his secret dungeon. They have cost, if history be true, many a king his crown, many a woman her reputation, and many a lover his lady's hand."

"The great mass of a man's mind, like the greater part of his body, he takes care to cover; so that no one may judge of its defects, except they be very prominent."

"If we miss the precise moment, whether it be by a minute or by years matters not, we have lost the great talisman of Fate forever."

But it is not by such fragmentary specimens as these that we can judge of Mr. James' talents. If any one is unacquainted with his works, and wishes to estimate him as he deserves, let him read his "Attila;" which, as an historical romance, has rarely —except by the Great Master himself—been equalled; and having read it, he may say of him in the words used by his guide and friend on a different occasion, that few writers have so well "succeeded in amusing hours of relaxation, or relieving those of langor, pain, or anxiety," as the author of "Richelieu" and of "Attila."

In the usual intercourse of society he was rather an agreeable companion than a brilliant diner-out; and even the brightest, amongst these, are stars that have their periods of obscuration. I have seen the elder Matthews in a state of depression which might almost have threatened suicide. In an hour or two he was

"The life of pleasure and the soul of whim,"

the best toned and most gentlemanly of humorists. One of our opium-eating celebrities would suddenly become silent as if he had been shot; nor did he soon recover. And we are told of a party of wits—one of them no less a personage than Theodore Hook—that having been invited by a city notability to amuse his guests, they became, *en revanche*, solemnly stupid, reserving their talents for an after-symposium of their own. But whatever he may have been generally,

I remember how much the friend we have lost contributed to one of the most brilliant evenings I have ever witnessed at any dinner-table, from Albemarle Street to my own. He was unable, in the first instance, to accept my invitation, in consequence of the expected arrival of a visitor. On the morning of the day, he wrote me a note to say that if I had still a vacant place he would be happy to come. I need not mention how I answered it. He entered the drawing-room with an evident determination to be agreeable. Amongst the guests was one of the "best hands" of the *Quarterly Review*, who was an admirable talker. There were others of some mark. And for five hours the ball never fell.

But *œctus dulces valete!* I must bring these reminiscences to a close. If it was thought by the Romans to have been an act of piety to preserve from desecration the tombs of the departed, we may hold it to be a still higher duty to guard their memories from wrong; and, above all, when the wrong is done to one of whom we may say, in the language of *Bassanio*, that he was

> "—*The kindest man,*
> *The best conditioned and unwearied spirit*
> *In doing courtesies . . .*
> That e'er drew breath."

I am glad to have the privilege of speaking as he merits of one whom I so much esteemed. We rarely flatter the dead; and I never gave expression to praise with more sincerity than now.

On the Impediments to the Introduction of the Decimal System of Weights and Measures, and the best Way to remove them. A Lecture delivered Dec. 13, 1860, in the Hall of the Society of Arts, Adelphi, London. By Frank P. Fellows, Esq. London: Smith, Elder, and Co.

The introduction of a decimal system of weights, measures, and coinage is one of those improvements the desirableness of which is all but universally acknowledged, while scarcely any serious effort is made to secure its adoption. Mr. Fellows' lecture is an earnest and sensible attempt to overcome the general apathy on this subject. Even those who are most alien to the inconveniences of the existing system will be astonished at his statements of the inextricable confusion which has resulted from it; and few, after reading the evidence which he has collected on this point, will question the accuracy of his conclusion, that the introduction of the decimal system would shorten the time necessary for the acquisition of arithmetic by at least one-half. He points out that, our system of arithmetic being a decimal one, it is only natural that our weights and measures should be arranged on the same principle. He attempts to meet the objection that it would be very difficult to bring into familiar use a number of terms derived from Greek and Latin, by suggesting—not, we think, very successfully—a series of abbreviations, which might be substituted for these terms. But we are inclined to believe that the importance of this difficulty has been considerably overrated. No doubt the introduction of the decimal system would be immediately followed by a period of considerable confusion; but this inconvenience would only be of temporary duration, and would be far more than counterbalanced by the advantages which would surely follow. Russia has declared that she is only waiting for the adhesion of England to this system in order to adopt it herself; and there can be no doubt that our adoption of it would be the signal for the introduction of a uniform system of weights, measures, and coinage throughout the whole continent of Europe.—*Spectator.*

An ecclesiastical Censure.—Latimer having claimed free reading in English of the Scriptures for the English people, Doctor Buckingham, Prior of the Black friars, denounced his pernicious error, saying, "If that heresy prevail, we shall soon see an end of every thing useful among us. The ploughman reading that if he put his hand to the plough, and should happen to look back, he was unfit for the kingdom of heaven, would soon lay aside his labor; the baker likewise, reading that a little leaven leaveneth the whole lump would give us a very insipid bread; the simple man also, finding himself commanded to pluck out his eyes, we should soon have the nation full of blind beggars."

Naval Fashions.—Steel corsets are beginning to be worn by frigates, but do not, in the last novelty, come up to the bows in front or descend quite to the other extremity. The sides are pierced with holes for the arms, forming a stylish openwork. Canvas is less employed than formerly, which, during the prevalence of March winds, is not to be regretted.—*Punch.*

From Once a Week.

MY ADVENTURE IN SEARCH OF GARIBALDI.

The ass, which bore my portmanteau and bag, was a sturdy, well-conditioned ass, with plenty of red tassels and brass bells about its bridle, and a stout peasant lad to ensure with his cudgel that the pace was a fair one. Much of the summer heat was over, and though the air was rather heavy and oppressive, we made very good progress for about seven miles or so. At about that distance from Foudi lies a group of cottages, a mere hamlet, too small to possess a church, and where, to my disgust, no hospitable bush, hanging over a door, told of purple wine within. I was very thirsty. My mouth was an oven, and my tongue painfully parched, and I would have given its weight in gold for a tumbler of frothing Bass; but even country wine seemed denied me. The peasant boy who drove the ass talked patois, and my Italian was chiefly learned out of Dante and other classics of the Arno, so we were not very intelligible conversationists; but he seemed to indicate that if I could hope to get refreshments anywhere, it would be at a solitary wayside dwelling, about a hundred yards ahead. On I went, and there, sure enough, was an open door, and a leafy bush above it.

In a chair outside sat an old man, apparently enjoying the evening sun.

"*Buon giorno!*" I called out; "let me have some wine, and iced-water, too, if you have it, for I'm—"

Here I was cut short by not knowing the Italian word that stands for thirsty. The old man never moved. Asleep? I drew nearer. Yes, asleep, but in that last long sleep that none can break,—the solemn sleep of death. I started back with an involuntary cry. I had been addressing a dead man. The occupant of the chair was an old —probably a very old—man, for his wrinkled skin was yellow as an antique parchment, and the long but scanty locks that fell from under his black skull-cap were as white as snow. The hollow cheeks, the sunken features, told of gradual decay, and though the glassy eyes were open, the jaw had been carefully tied up, and a fair white linen cloth was folded around the breast of the corpse, while the hands were decorously disposed upon the lap, the withered fingers extended as if in prayer. On a nearer scrutiny, I observed that a small wooden platter was between the hands of the dead man, and in it lay several small coins of silver, and a much larger heap of copper. I now breathed more freely as I recollected to have heard of a singular custom which prevails in Italy, and with which all old residents are acquainted. When a death takes place in an indigent family, it is very usual to deposit the body, dressed in its holiday clothes, and with a plate between its hands, either at its own door, or in some public place, and to compel, as it were, this dumb and insensible mendicant to solicit alms of the charitable. The money obtained in this strange way goes to pay the expenses of the burial, *not* for the coffin, since bodies are buried uncoffined, but for masses, flowers, professional mourners, consecrated candles, and a sort of funeral-feast. This custom explained the presence of this ghastly guardian of the threshold, but still I shrank from it.

We northern folks cannot but feel shocked at the callous manner in which death, that dim, solemn mystery, is greeted by the natives of South Europe, and I admit that I felt a very great inclination to pursue my way with thirst unslaked, when a comely dark-haired woman, wearing the square kerchief of the Neapolitan peasantry of that province, came courtesying out to ask what could be done for my excellency's service. Ashamed to run away from the presence of a dead body, I conquered my repugnance, entered the cottage, and asked for what refreshments I needed. The hostess, a buxom young matron, with a picturesque jacket of some bright color and an immense rosary instead of the usual golden ornaments, was very chatty and pleasant, and told me that the Royalists had passed by that very afternoon on their foray for beasts of burden, but that she had no doubt but that, at Gavlaglio, or some such place, I should procure a carriage. I drank my wine and water, munched a few delicious grapes, and treated my guide to wine and the ass to water, all for a few carlini, and was taking my leave when the hostess asked, with an apologetic smile, if I "would bestow a trifle on grandfather?"

"On grandfather?" said I, turning to where the rigid figure sat, propped with cushions in its arm-chair; "do you mean that that is your grandfather, that—"

"*Si Signor*," answered she, "the best of parents, the dearest, kindest old soul—so pious too—ah! what a loss! Ah me!"

Wonderful how the moods of those Italians change! She was actually sobbing, that smiling, sunny-featured woman, who had seemed, while tripping about to fetch me a cool flask of the best, or playing between whiles with her two plump-cheeked children, perfectly happy and content. But how little can we judge from mere outward show, and how often do we find the face a sorry index to the heart! She was evidently much affected by the mention of the old man —her husband's father, she said—who had died that very morning about dawn, at a great age. The platter was to collect money to buy masses for his soul, she said, "not that he had many sins, poor dear;" and then she sobbed again. I am as good a Protestant as any, but whatever I might think of masses in the abstract, I felt that here was a case where all the logic of Exeter Hall would be wasted—these poor simple folks—it was plain that nothing but the ceremonies of the church they were bred in could carry balm to their bruised hearts, and I felt that I should be a brute if I were to deposit less than a dollar in the plate. I laid down a dollar, accordingly, said a kind word or two in my broken Tuscan, and departed, but not before the grateful woman had insisted on kissing my excellency's generous hand, and wishing my excellency a prosperous journey.

We stepped vigorously out along the dusty road, the boy, the ass, and I, and though night was falling, I cared little; now we were among the blue hills, and out of the Pontine marshes, where the night air is deadly, blowing as it does over many a foul morass. For a league we pushed on gayly enough, but then came a broad blue flash, and then a roll of thunder, and then a burst of hail and heavy rain, while the flash and roll were incessant, and the sky grew pitchy dark. Wet, and blinded by lightning, there was no chance of making our way to the next town; indeed, the road was no longer to be seen, except when a flash showed it; so, after a short council of war, back we scampered to the little wayside hostelry that we had so lately left, and where alone, according to the boy, we could hope for shelter. Soon did British traveller, donkey, and lad, stand before the porch of the small house of entertainment, but though less than two hours had elapsed, a change had come over us all. The donkey shook his dripping ears, and hung his sleek head wretchedly, the boy was wet and alarmed, and I was a draggled object to look upon, but eagerly bent on obtaining shelter and a fire to dry my clothes. Of course we found the door shut, and the arm-chair and its mute occupant removed into the house. Nay, but for the drenched bush that the wind was buffetting backwards and forwards, we should not have known the house from any other cottage, seeing it as we did by the transient glare of the blue lightning. I lifted the latch, and, flinging wide the door, entered without ceremony. I found a family group assembled around their supper-table. There was my buxom friend of the afternoon, with her two little ones nestling close to the maternal apron, there was a stout, bronzed peasant, her husband, and a tall, black-haired girl, who might have been the sister of husband or wife, and three sturdy younger brothers, in brown jackets and crimson sashes, eating brown bread and fried beans in a way calculated to have given Lord Chesterfield a heartache.

I must not forget the other member of the family—the dead man—whose chair stood now in the chimney-corner, which no doubt had been his place during life, and whose blank gaze and wan face were turned towards the crackling fire of sticks. The platter had been removed from between the stiffened hands, the linen-band untied from the jaw; this I noticed, but in no other respect had the body been disturbed. Not a look, as far as I could well see, was turned towards the inanimate member of the company. The careless Neapolitans were laughing over their meal as if there were no such thing as death at all. But my arrival created a sensation I was at a loss to account for. The family jumped from their seats, with confused and terror-stricken faces, uttering a profusion of imprecations more or less pious, or the reverse, and seemed more perturbed than they ought to have been at the arrival of a chance traveller. I accosted the hostess as an acquaintance, mentioned the raging storm, and announced my intention of staying all night, if they could accommodate me. I cannot say that they seemed anxious to house so distinguished a guest! Indeed, they gave me a clear idea that, but for shame's sake, they would have pushed me out again into the rain. Of course they were too humble—their poor little hut was not fit for such as my excellency, nurtured in palaces, etc., but at last they gave way, and promised to make me up a bed in one of the little rooms up-stairs. The boy and donkey they absolutely refused to shelter. No plea of mine or entreaty of his prevailed: boy and ass were ruthlessly denied accommodation, and I was obliged to dismiss them, with double pay, into the howling storm, to reach Fondi as they might. Then the door was shut and locked, and a wooden bar put across it. Sticks were thrown on the fire, and I stood before it, drying myself as best I might, my baggage lying at my feet. The people went on with their supper, but not quite as light-heartedly as before; their mirth was not so loud, and I thought they often cast a look askance at me. Then the hostess remembered her courtly manners, and deferentially asked if she could have the pleasure of setting any thing before the Signor Inglese. It was not to be supposed that his English excellency could eat beans, but perhaps an egg? *so* fresh, or some milk and chocolate? or a rasher of winter bacon? But his English excellency, though he was hungry, said not a word in reply. I could not have spoken, had my life depended on my oratory. My heart leaped, and then stood still; my hair rose bristling, my brow grew damp with fear, my eyes were riveted with horror and half incredulous marvel on the white-haired, venerable corpse of the patriarch in the arm-chair. And no wonder! *I saw the dead man move!* The glossy eyes rolled horribly in their wrinkled orbits, the jaws relaxed into a yawn, the arms were stretched as the arms of one awakening from sleep, and the old man's body rocked and quivered in the arm-chair. The sight of that yawning, glaring, moving corpse was almost too much for my nerves. I clutched the arm of the hostess; with a shrinking hand I pointed to the horrid sight—the hallucination—as I deemed it, of my fatigued senses. Ha! she sees it too, but I see no fear on her face. Some annoyance, perhaps, and a covert smile; surely, I am mistaken; but—no, those dead lips move, work, speak! Audibly fall upon my agonized ear the hollow accents of the departed. What are those words that break the silence? What fearful revelation to the living necessitates such a breach of the laws of nature? What secrets of the prison-house are about to be dragged into light? Let me listen to the dead man's awful speech.

"*Che ora è?*"

"What's o'clock?" that was all he said, upon my honor, as a gentleman. "What's o'clock?" A disembodied spirit bursting the gates of night, and intruding on the living, to ask what o'clock it was! They heard it. They all heard it. And my tortured ear was next insulted by such a peal of hearty horse laughter, begun by one, chorused by the rest, as I had seldom listened to. My brain reeled. Here was I, in presence of a corpse that demanded to know what o'clock it was, and the whole company were laughing like a menagerie of hyænas! "*Che ora è?*" repeated the dead man, into whose eyes there gradually stole more speculation than becomes the defunct, on the Swan's authority. And still the peasants laughed, and the deceased patriarch became more and more palpably alive. I gasped for breath, so utter was my amazement. I had read of trances and apparent deaths, and resuscitations, during funerals or after interment, but never had I heard of the dead alive being welcomed back into the bosom of their family, amid peals of uproarious laughter, as if their revival was a rare joke. But when the old man made an effort to rise, I could bear it no longer, but rushed to the door. To my surprise, one of the young men sprang up and set his back against it, grinning but resolute. Another jumped from his chair to reinforce.

"Scusa! signor!" said the landlord, "but you cannot go just yet."

I insisted, tried to force my way, and was good-humoredly baffled. I got into a towering passion, but in vain. They were four to one, and they swore by all the saints that I should not stir a step. I had come for my own pleasure. I should stay for theirs.

"Do you want to rob me, you villains?" I shouted.

"Gracious signor, the idea!"

"Are you brigands?"

"Signor, what a blunder! We are poor, but honest."

Then why would they not let me pass? "Signor, grandfather," — that word explained all. I turned; the old man was actually seated at supper, affectionately waited on by his two daughters, and playing a capital knife and fork for one who had shuffled off this mortal coil.

"Then," said I, as I viewed the hoary humbug, who I now saw was as completely alive as myself, "your precious parent was not dead, after all?"

They confessed that he was not.

"And his pretended death was produced by—"

"By this, signor carissimo," said the hostess, opening a cupboard and exhibiting a bottle labelled chloroform.

"And this atrocious deception," I began, but was again interrupted with,—

"Signor Excellency, have a little pity! We are poor industrious folks; we farm and we sell wine; but we have many mouths to feed, and there are debts. This is a harmless plan we have devised of raising a trifling sum to buy seed-corn and oil for winter. If grandfather were really dead, nobody would grudge a few carlini for his burial, and those kind souls who give under the belief that a dead hand holds out the platter, will be all the better for it in purgatory. The worst of it is, that your excellency cannot go—"

"Cannot go!" I boiled over with wrath.

"If your excellency could make shift with very poor accommodation until Friday!"

"Until Friday!" I could only repeat the impudent proposal. But the landlady and her spouse, with one accord though many words, proceeded to lay down before me the following propositions: imprimis, that I had most inconveniently popped behind the scenes and pried into a Blue Beard chamber I had no right to know the secrets of; secondly, that unless the delusion were kept up, no profit could be expected, but rather popular vengeance; thirdly, that the two next days would be marked by a concourse of pilgrims to Fondi, for the festival of the holy and miracle-working St. Somebody, and a plentiful crop of small coin was expected. The fourth proposition was, that I should remain with them till the festa was over and the pilgrims gone home, that I should be fed, cherished, and lodged as well as could be expected, for the moderate remuneration of one scudo per day, and that then I should be permitted to depart, on giving my promise not to say a word about my unlawful detention, while within the kingdom of Naples.

Who would not have stormed in such a case of false imprisonment? I flew into a passion, and threatened dreadful revenge. I would go to the judge, and the intendant; and the archbishop, I believe; and the British consul, I am certain. Her Majesty's Secretary of State for Foreign Affairs should hear of it, and so should Garibaldi's Englishman. What did they think Lord Palmerston would say? To my chagrin, they had never heard of Lord Palmerston at all. They were obdurate, for their profits were at stake. After an hour's fiercely verbose argument, and five minutes' wrestling with one of the stout young cubs who held the door, I was forced to surrender at discretion, and accept the terms of the conquerors. *Væ victis!* What a miserable three nights and two days did I spend under that roof-tree, guarded like a prisoner of war, in spite of my parole, for there were always a couple of young peasants at my elbow, and they watched lest I should reveal the secret to any stray pilgrim! I slept in a little cock-loft, well garnished by an interesting colony of mosquitoes; my bed was not a very bad one, with its clean brown linen and its ticking stuffed with the husks of maize; they waited on me—the womankind, that is,—civilly enough, and they fed me with the best they had for my scudo a day, not too high a price, when one considers their enforced monopoly of my custom. I was not very uncomfortable, physically speaking, and had I chosen to stay for my own pleasure, should have been content. But upon compulsion! I roared inwardly with bitterness of spirit, as I saw the humble devotees troop by to the shrine of St. Somebody, and seldom fail to drop a few baiocchi, at least, into the platter of the venerable old scamp, who sat outside in his chair, as rigid and senseless as chloroform could make him. And then, the torment of seeing that aged impostor, as it were, off duty, and in the family circle, nightly to witness his recovery from the stupor due to the drug, to see him yawn and stretch, with a vivid remembrance of my original terrors, and then to lose my own appetite in witnessing his abominable performances as a trencherman. I never thought, when I heard that every one had a skeleton in his cupboard, that I should ever be forced into intimacy with such a grisly piece of property, that I should breakfast and sup every day with the family skeleton occupying the head of the table, and generally demeaning itself as the founder of the feast.

He was not a bad old man either; a cackling, child-petting old grandsire he seemed, when desisting from his praiseworthy exertions for the benefit of his relatives. His third appearance before the public was, I am happy to say, the last. The pilgrims had ceased to flow past, and the carlini to rattle in the plate, and the Dead Alive had already obtained a hatful of money. Besides, the old gentleman's health might suffer from further chloroforming, his affectionate relatives being resolved to postpone his final and legitimate exhibition as long as filial pity could contrive it. For these various reasons the show came to an end, and my imprisonment along with it. The neighbors were called to witness the happy recovery of grandpapa, who had been three days in a trance, and suddenly awaked amid the congratulations of his kindred. All incredulity was repressed by the presence of the four sturdy peasants who were ready with cudgel and fist to maintain, if necessary, that their progenitor had been as dead as Julius Cæsar, and was now as living as Mazzini. And the timely gift of a brace of dollars brought in the alliance of the church, the curé of the next village publicly avowing the resuscitation as a pure miracle, not wholly unconnected with the Immaculate Conception, nor entirely divested of reference to the future triumph of papal authority over heretics and red shirts; by which we may guess that the curé was of the reactionary party.

I departed in sullen silence, answering no word to the salutations and blessings of the Phœnix and his offspring. And they wished my excellency a good journey, and called me their preserver, the hyprocrites! I got somehow to Naples, through the burned and pillaged country, but the time lost was irrevocable: my holiday was spoiled. I went to the front. I plunged into the midst of Garibaldi's ragged heroes, and I nearly got hit by a shell or two from the fortress, but skirmish or battle royal saw I none. Brief as was my stay, I missed the homeward-bound steamer, had to wait a week for another, and finally reached Dover just on the last day of the vacation.

JOHN HARWOOD.

Paris, Friday, March 1st, 1861.

The precious objects found in the summer palace at Pekin are now on exhibition in one of the pavilions of the palace of the Tuileries. They are well worthy the curiosity that has been attracting such crowds to visit them. There are several gigantic vases with brilliant enamelling, a magnificent pagoda of gilded bronze exquisitely chiselled and adorned with jewels, whimsical divinities of enamelled gold. A splendid costume of the emperor of China is displayed upon a manikin. Various robes are superposed one above the other, mostly of silk laminated with gold, overrich in embroidery. The whole is surmounted by a helmet, steel and gold, that rather resembles a tiara. It is very delicately worked—light and ornamented with pearls.

The two sceptres of which so much has been said, are shaped like a very elongated *C*, or rather as a broad bow, the ends curved in and much flattened out, to admit the settings of jade, green and white, that precious stone of which Chinese poets are so lavish in their verses.

Two enormous chimeras weighing each above six hundred pounds, present every possible writhing of form, and prove that the Chinese even surpass the western world in delicacy of casting. There are besides various monsters which it would be hard to characterize. Such utter departures from the forms of nature can only be the result of a civilization in which the arbitrary has usurped the place of free art. There is enough of imagination or rather fancy displayed in all. But it seems like the sickly creations of a feverish dream in which all shapes mingle and run confusedly into each other giving rise to whimsical, grotesque combinations.

The admirable porcelain cups, etc, compare more favorably with the productions of Sevres. —*Daily Advertiser.*

From The Spectator.

SEASONS WITH THE SEA-HORSES.*

MAN is a pursuing and destroying animal. In all ages of the world he has distinguished himself by the amount of game that he has run down or rode down, that he has slaughtered with javelins, trapped in pits, slain with arrows, shot with muskets, or otherwise secured. Wherever there is any thing to catch there is pretty nearly always a man to catch it; and if there be not one close at hand, there very soon will be. There is a rapture in adventure, a delight in danger, a pleasure in acquisition, a satisfaction in killing any thing with your own gun, or getting any thing off your own hook, which redouble the locomotive powers, and give men a proud consciousness of their superior dignity. In the old days this war with the noble savages of forest and jungle had something heroic in it; and the praise of being a mighty hunter before the Lord, if literally understood, is a fine tribute of poetic commendation in which even Nimrod himself might exult. Civilization diminishes and even destroys the opportunities for practising this kind of heroism. In Europe, and in England especially, the dastardly battue is a favorite resource of the degenerate sons of the old wolf-slaying, boar-spearing Celts and Normans. This kind of killing made easy, however, does not always satisfy the more adventurous of our English sportsmen. Hence, in late days, we have heard of a famous crusade against the lion in Africa, while a raid on the sea-horse, in the north of Europe, just now provokes the enterprise, taxes the powers, and stimulates the ingenuity of the sporting manhood of England.

Foremost among the occupants of this new hunting-ground is Mr. James Lamont, a gentleman who appears to have been very nearly everywhere; that is, everywhere where a gentleman ought to have been. He has not only employed his old battered opera-glass, he tells us, in its legitimate occupation of gazing at the collective loveliness of London, Paris, Florence, Naples, and New York; he has not only seen with it great races at Epsom, great reviews in the Champ-de-Mars, great bull-fights in the amphitheatre at Seville; he has not only used it to stalk red deers in the Highlands, and scaly crocodiles on the sand-banks of the Nile, to read hieroglyphics on the temples of Thebes and Karnak, to peer through loopholes at the batteries of the Redan and the Malakoff, to gaze over the splendid cane-fields of the West Indies from the mountain peaks of Trinidad and Martinique, over Cairo from the tops of the Pyramids, over the holy city of Jerusalem from the top of Mount Calvary —but he has taken the measure of a polar bear with it, and explored through its lens the geological, zoölogical, and botanical characteristics of the frozen North.

Mr. Lamont made his first trip to Spitzbergen in 1858; and, notwithstanding his cool reception, he was so delighted with the promise of physical and intellectual recreation, that he soon made up his mind to have another trip to the region of the bear and walrus. Before he set out he was requested by the Liberal party of a Scottish county to become a candidate in the approaching election. "The result, by a very narrow majority proved unfortunate for—the walruses;" and the liberated patriot, accompanied by his friend Lord David Kennedy, a renowned Indian sportsman, got on board a clur little tub of a sloop, the Anna Louisa, abot thirty tons British measurement, sailed from Leith Roads on the 6th June, 1859, and after being nearly run down by a tug-steamer during a dense fog off Aberdeen, and beating through the middle of the Orkney Islands on the 9th and 11th, with a heavy sea and the wind desperately ahead, ran up the noble Vamsen Fiord on the 16th, and finally reached Hammerfest on the 23d.

Walrus-hunting with all its wild excitement soon began. Mr. Lamont's animated narrative tells us how the boat, propelled by five pairs of oars, flies through the water, while a hundred walruses roar, bellow, blow, snort, splash, and "make an acre of the sea all in a foam before and around her;" it describes the harpooner standing with one foot on the thwart, and the other on the front locker, with the line coiled and the long weapon balanced for a dart; it pictures first, a hundred grisly heads and long gleaming white tusks appearing momentarily above the waves, to get a mouthful of fresh air, then a hundred brown hemispherical backs, then "a hundred pair of hind-flippers flourishing, and then they are all down."

* *Seasons with the Sea-Horses; or, Sporting Adventures in the Northern Seas.* By James Lamont, Esq., F.G.S. Hurst and Blackett.

The walrus, sea-horse, or morse, is an inoffensive beast, if let alone; but hunted, it becomes infuriated and dangerous. It staves in boats with its tusks, or charges and upsets them. A poor fellow, the harpooner of a boat thus capsized, was selected by one of these enraged beasts out of the number of those precipitated into the water, and nearly torn into halves with its tusks. In hunting the walrus, the calf should always, if possible, be struck first, for the old sea-horses have a "curious clannish practice" of coming to assist a young one in distress, and its little plaintive grunting cry brings the whole herd round the boat in a few seconds, rearing up breast high, with frightful menace of deadly aggression.

Let us now say a word of the general equipment, implements, and tackle of walrus-hunting, gathering our information from the vigorous, dashing, and business-like narrative of Mr. Lamont. A good walrus-boat for five men should be twenty-one feet long by five feet beam, having her main breadth about one-third from the bow. She should always be carvel-built, because this description of boat is less liable to damage from the ice and the tusks of the walruses. Each man rows with a pair of oars hung in grummets to stout single tholepins; the steersman rowing with his face to the bow, and the harpooner always taking the bow oars. Then there must be five enormous lances, with shafts nine feet long, to lie on the thwarts, with the blades protected in a box; two axes for decapitating the dead walrus, five or six sharp knives for stripping the skin and blubber off the animal, an ice-anchor, a compass, a telescope, rifle, ammunition, certain provisions, and various implements and utensils. These are the absolute necessaries. One *luxury* is allowed —a bag of mackintosh cloth lined with fur, to crawl into in severe weather. We understand Mr. Lamont to have had two walrus-boats built in Hammerfest, and to have engaged two skilful harpooners and a crew, natives of the North, English sailors being of little or no use in the walrus-boat service. The walrus is sometimes killed with the harpoon, sometimes with the lance, and sometimes with the rifle. The rifles Mr. Lamont and his friend used were elliptical four-barrelled Lancasters, of 40-guage; with a charge of five drachms of powder and a bullet hardened by an admixture of tin, they generally succeeded in smashing the walruses' skulls. Our adventurers had capital sport, killing, in Spitzbergen, in the summer of the year 1859, forty-six walruses, eighty-eight seals, eight polar bears, one white whale, and sixty-one reindeer; total, two hundred and four head.

Spitzbergen, if we except the settlement of Smeerenberg, or Blubbers Town, has never been inhabited. Discovered in 1596 by William Barentz, a Dutchman, it became in the early part of the seventeenth century the seat of the most flourishing whale-fishery that ever existed. Permanent colonization was contemplated, and merchants offered rewards to their crews to make the perilous attempt to support human life there during the winter, but none could be prevailed on to make the hazardous experiment. At length, "an English company hit upon the ingenious and economical idea of trying it upon some criminals who were under sentence of death in London; but so terrified were they at the cheerless prospects which awaited them, that when the fleet was about to depart, after conveying them to this region of north-east winds and early snows, they entreated the captain to take them back to London, and let them be hanged, in pursuance of their original sentence." A similarly unfavorable impression of the Spitzbergen climate seems to have been entertained by at least one of Mr. Lamont's crew. One day some of the sailors were heard discussing the respective merits of hot and cold countries, and in answer to the remark that although "neither rum nor tobacco grew in Spitzbergen, still the continual 'blow out' of fat reindeer might be considered a point in its favor, the dissentient replied, 'Well, Bob, all I can say is, that I would a deuced sight rather go to the West Indies and be hanged there, than die a natural death in this here —— country.'"

Hard and dangerous as is the life of the Spitzbergen walrus-hunters, the hides, the ivory, and the oil are a rich material compensation for the privations and perils which these reckless and energetic adventurers have to encounter. Under the inducements offered by the merchants of Tromsoe and Hammerfest, the best seamen and boldest spirits of the north of Norway, "true descendants and successors of the gallant Vikings and Berserkars," are generally found in the Spitzbergen sealers.

Besides his vivid accounts of the sports of the North, his descriptions of scenery, and record of grave or amusing incidents, Mr. Lamont gives us occasional notices of men and manners, or jots down facts of natural history that came under his own observation. Thus, the clannish practice among the walruses of coming to assist a calf in distress already mentioned, received actual illustration before his own eyes. It is said that this practice arises from the habit of combination to resist the attacks of the polar bear. If tempted by hunger and opportunity, Bruin is so ill-advised as to snap a calf, the whole herd seize him, drag him under water, and tear him to pieces with their long sharp tusks. The first bear Mr. Lamont secured was found bird's-nesting, in a low, black, rocky island; multitudes of gulls, fulmars, eider-ducks, and alcas being "in a state of great perturbation at Bruin's oölogical researches." A strange prejudice prevails among the people in most parts of Norway. They never allude to a bear by his name, but adopt some appropriate eupheucism, as, "old Eric," or "the party in the brown jacket," or "the old gentleman in the fur cloak," on the same principle, we suppose, on which our ancestors avoided directly speaking of the fairies, or on which the old Greeks called the Furies Eumenides, or well-meaning persons.

There are many passages on climate, geography, geology, and other cognate subjects in Mr. Lamont's briskly written and racy volume, on which we would willingly comment, but we must limit ourselves to one or two points only. We have long understood, to use the words of a splendid expositor in science and philosophy, "that the vast tracts of snow which are reddened in a single night owe their color to the marvellous rapidity in reproduction of a minute plant (*Protococcus nivalis*)." Mr. Lamont, however, who is certainly a man with eyes in his head, and the gift to use them, states "that all the red snow which has come under his observation has been simply caused by the coloring matter contained in the droppings of millions of little ants," and, while allowing that minute reddish fungi afterwards grow on the droppings, expresses his total unbelief in fungi growing on the snow *per se*. We neither accept nor reject Mr. Lamont's explanation, but in our zeal for communicating facts observed, or thought to be observed, we take pleasure in reporting this.

One more report takes us "into the deep waters of controversy at once," or, rather, takes our author there, for we have no intention of defending any hypothesis. It is our part to record hypotheses, and to adduce the facts that make for or against them. Mr. Lamont, then, after an attentive study of the arctic animals, declares himself favorably inclined to "the theory of progressive development, first suggested by the illustrious Lamarck, and since so ably expounded and defended, under somewhat modified forms, by the author of the 'Vestiges of Creation,' and by Mr. Charles Darwin." Accordingly, the more he observes nature, and the more he reflects on the subject, the more he is "convinced that Almighty God always carries out his intentions with regard to the animal creation, *not* by 'direct interpositions' of his will, not by 'special fiats of creation,' but by the slow and gradual agency of natural causes." We wish we could exhibit the argument which Mr. Lamont employs, to show that the polar bear is only a variety of the bears inhabiting Northern Europe, Asia, and America; or the evidence which he contends we have to superinduce the belief that the great seal or the walrus, or some allied animal, now extinct, has been the progenitor of the whales and other cetaceans. One fact only we will cite in favor of the theory that creation is the result of "slow and gradual causes, and in opposition to that of abrupt, unnatural, and uncalled-for interpositions of the Divine will." In a district of South Africa, not larger than Britain, says Mr. Lamont, "there are well known to exist nearly thirty varieties of antelopes, from the huge eland of six feet in height, and two thousand pounds in weight, to the diminutive bluebuck of eight pounds or nine pounds weight, and twelve inches high." Now that each and all of these numerous varieties or spècies of antelopes were originally brought into being separately and distinctly, as we see them now, Mr. Lamont refuses to believe. He refuses to believe that one variety was specially created for this petty locality, and another for that; that there was a special interposition of Providence to create a variety about the outskirts of the desert, which should only drink water once in three or more days, and other varieties which should be absolute non-drinkers.

Our author, it should perhaps be said, expresses himself interrogatively, while we have taken the liberty, without, as we conceive, altering his meaning, to translate his questions into affirmation. Modestly disclaiming the title of scientific naturalist, Mr. Lamont knows how to observe, and not only knows how to observe, but *has* observed. He has seen vast portions of South Africa undergoing a rapid desiccation, a desiccation which he thinks sufficient to account for the various antelope transformations; he has seen the white bear dive for a short distance like the walrus, that "plain and unmistakable link between animals inhabiting the land and the cetaceans, or whales," and he conceives the polar bear to have *become* a polar bear by living on seals, and therefore supposes that the seal and the walrus were originated *first*.

Though acknowledging that he follows Mr. Darwin in these remarks, Mr. Lamont claims for the chapter in which he vindicates the theory of natural selection an independent inspiration, the substance of the chapter having been written in Spitzbergen before the "Origin of Species" was published.

An appendix containing a list of fossils, etc., sent to the Geological Society, and an illustrative map of the north of Scotland, Denmark, Norway, Spitzbergen, etc., complete in a volume which we have found entertaining, thoughtful, and spirit-stirring. One special merit it has: there is no attempt at rhetoric in it. Mr. Lamont tells his story in a nervous, direct, intelligent, and manly way. We recommend every one to read his *Seasons with the Sea-horses.*

EARLY CARLYESE. "There be some that in composition are nothing, but what is rough and broken: *Quæ per salebras altaque saxa cadunt.* And if it would come gently, they trouble it of purpose. They would not have it run without rubs, as if that style were more strong and manly, that struck the ear with a kind of unevenness. These men err not by chance, but knowingly and willingly; they are like men that affect a fashion by themselves, have some singularity in a ruff, cloak, or hat-band; or their beards specially cut to provoke beholders, and set a mark upon themselves. They would be reprehended, while they are looked on. And this vice, one that in authority with the rest, loving, delivers over to them to be imitated; so that ofttimes the faults which he fell into, the others seek for; this is the danger, when vice becomes a precedent."—*Ben Jonson's Discoveries.*

THE RIGHT USE OF BOOKS.—"Let us consider how great a commodity of doctrine exists in books—how easily, how secretly, how safely they expose the nakedness of human ignorance without putting it to shame. These are the masters that instruct us without rods and ferulas, without hard words and anger, without clothes or money. If you approach them, they are not asleep; if investigating, you interrogate them, they conceal nothing; if you mistake them, they never grumble; if you are ignorant, they cannot laugh at you."—*Philobiblon, Richard de Bury, Bishop of Durham,* 1344.

"Read not to contradict and confute, nor to believe and take for granted, nor to find talk and discourse, but to weigh and consider."—*Bacon,* Essay on Studies.

"Few have been sufficiently sensible of the importance of that economy in reading which selects almost exclusively the very first order of books. Why should a man, except for some special reason, read a very inferior book at the very time he might be reading one of the very highest order!"—*Foster's Essays.*

EARLY TIPPERARY JOBS.—"*Eudoxus.* You are no good friend to new captains; it seems, Ireneus, that you bar them from the credit of this service; but to say truth, methinks it were meet that any one before he came to be a captain should have been a soldier; for *parere qui nescit, nescit imperare.* And besides, there is a great wrong done to the old soldier, from whom all means of advancement which is due unto him, is cut off, by shuffling in these new captains into the place for which he hath long served, and perhaps better deserved."—*Spenser's State of Ireland.*

From The Saturday Review.

THE GREATEST OF ALL THE PLANTAGENETS.*

It was a great day for Hume when Mr. Hallam spoke of him as "the first writer who had the merit of exposing the character of Edward I." So far as the compliment is deserved, Hume was guided to the truth, not by the light of industry and historical criticism, but by that of Scotch prejudice against the invader of Scotland. The value of his critical researches into this period of history is settled at once by his countenancing the story of Edward's massacre of the Welsh bards—a piece of carelessness, or rather of indolent injustice, singularly disgraceful, since not only is the story unsupported by any shadow of contemporary evidence, but it also happens that no centuries were more prolific of the nonsensical rhapsodies of the bards than those which followed their alleged extirpation. However, time and labor enough—and more than enough—have been spent in confuting Hume. He is honored far above his deserts in having his loose notions combated, as they are, expressly or tacitly, through a considerable portion of Mr. Hallam's *Constitutional History*. The time is come when, due credit being allowed him for the purity and gracefulness of his style, he may be set down in other respects as simply worthless, and ignored in all future discussions. A century hence, probably even the University of Oxford will remove him from the list of standard writers which she recommends to students. About the same period she may be expected to discover that England had a history before the Norman Conquest.

Mr. Augustus Clifford undertakes to clear the memory of Edward I., not only from the charge of injustice and cruelty in the cases of Scotland and Wales, but also from that of arbitrary tendencies in his domestic government. As regards Scotland and Wales, we are disposed, to a great extent, to accept the vindication; and even as regards the charge of domestic tyranny, though we cannot go the whole length with Mr. Clifford, we admit that some impression has been made. The substance of his case, as regards Wales, is that Llewellyn, as a great vassal of the English Crown, had been guilty of repeated acts of contumacy in refusing to attend the lawful summons of his suzerain, that he had justly forfeited his fief according to the international law of that age, and that he was treated by Edward with great mildness and forbearance. More than two years were employed in endeavors to bring Llewellyn back to his duty as a vassal by gentle and courteous means. War was then declared against him; but when he had been reduced to sue for peace, not only were mild terms granted, but much was abated even of those mild terms by the generosity of the conqueror. The fine of £50,000 was remitted, the stipulated tribute for Anglesea given up, the hostages restored. Hume suggests that the fine was remitted because "the poverty of the country made it impossible that it should be levied." But Mr. Clifford observes, with great truth, that a designing conqueror would have retained Llewellyn as his debtor, and exacted a cession of territory on default of payment of the debt. No Welshman will agree with us, but we are disposed to think, with Mr. Clifford, that "Edward's real purpose was to make Llewellyn his royal vassal and friend." It seems to us a just observation, though pressed rather too far, that when Llewellyn's brother and enemy, David, was brought by the king to England, and created an earl, with a great estate and an earl's daughter in marriage, so as to make him, by interest and connection, an English noble, proof was given that the king had no sinister design of playing off one brother against the other. Had there been such a design, David would have been subsidized no doubt, but he would have been left in Wales, instead of being thus taken out of Llewellyn's way. Celtic levity, unveracity, and belief in prophecies, ultimately drove the two brothers on their ruin. The cause for which David was condemned and executed would have seemed sufficient to any jurist or moralist of those times. The complicated punishment of hanging, disembowelling, and quartering, to which he was sentenced for his various offences of treason, murder, sacrilege, and conspiracy, would seem as natural and regular then as it seems revolting now. It is absurd to fix on Edward, individually, a charge of peculiar barbarity on this account. On the other hand, it is not rational to cite

* *The Greatest of all the Plantagenets.* An Historical Sketch. By Augustus Clifford. London: Bentley. 1860.

the separate interment of different parts of Queen Eleanor's body as a parallel to her fond husband's dismemberment of his rebellious vassal. It will be argued by Mr. Clifford's opponents that he assumes the feudal obligation on the part of Llewellyn to have been somewhat more distinctly admitted than it was, and that he generally treats the Celtic principality too rigorously as a territory governed, as to the rule of succession and otherwise, by the principles of the feudal law. Hume probably calls David "a sovereign prince" at a venture. But we apprehend he might very well have been accepted by the Welsh as their sovereign, even though his elder brother "had not died childless." The settlement of Wales, after its annexation to England, was conducted in a statesman-like and beneficent spirit, and after a careful inquiry into the native laws and customs of the people. None but very fanatical devotees of "nationality" can doubt that the annexation itself, putting an end to incessant raids on the one side and retaliatory invasions on the other, while it was a benefit to the stronger, was an unspeakable benefit to the weaker nation.

As to the matter of Scotland, it has always seemed to us that, regard being had to the circumstances and sentiments of that age, Edward's conduct was as defensible as his ambition in desiring to unite the whole island and put an end to border wars was rational and beneficent. The most questionable feature in it is his taking advantage of his position as an arbiter to obtain *pendente lite*, from the suitors for the Scotch crown, a recognition of his doubtful claim to the feudal sovereignty of Scotland. The arbitration itself was certainly not undertaken by him without due invitation. The Bishop of St. Andrew's the first of the four guardians and representatives of the kingdom, wrote to him "entreating him to approach the Border, to give consolation to the people of Scotland, to prevent the effusion of blood, and to enable the faithful men of the realm to preserve their oath, by choosing him for their king *who by right ought to be so.*" The "great army" which Hume asserts Edward to have carried with him to the meeting at Norham—thus "betraying the Scottish barons into a situation in which it was impossible for them to make any defence"—vanishes, under the critical examination of Mr. Clifford, into the elements of which Hume's facts are commonly composed.

The acknowledgment of the feudal supremacy of the king of England was not made by the Scottish barons under duress, though it was made in expectation of his award, and is somewhat tainted on that account. No satisfactory proof can be adduced of any intention on the part of Edward to disturb the continuance of the Scottish royalty, which he left unmolested for four years, and with which he then interfered on sufficient feudal grounds. The justice of his decision as arbiter in favor of Baliol is not questionable; and that he should have decided justly is a considerable proof of his good faith in the whole transaction. Had his designs been sinister, his policy would have been to set up a usurper, whose only title would have been the protection of his patron, or even to have embraced the doctrine that the kingdom of Scotland was partible between the three female lines, and to have weakened it fatally by division.

We presume Mr. Clifford will never think of venturing his person north of the Tweed after his handling of Robert Bruce and "Walleys, or Wallace." He, however, makes out a strong case for pronouncing Bruce, who was the first to acknowledge the feudal superiority of Edward, not the patriot leader that our fancy has painted him, but a Norman adventurer on the look-out for a kingdom, which he most gallantly and skilfully won. It is a still unkinder cut to make out that the victor of Bannockburn was more a Yorkshireman than a Scotchman. The magnitude of Wallace's glory had already been considerably reduced by the criticism of Lingard. The "Lion" appeared in only two battles—that of Stirling, which he won, with small exertion of military genius, through the insane presumption of the English commanders—and that of Falkirk, in which he was utterly defeated, and sank to rise no more. He is more than once compared by Mr. Clifford to Nana Sahib, and unquestionably the atrocities laid to his charge will bear a comparison with those of Cawnpore. In Wallace's raid on the northern counties of England, neither age nor sex was spared. English men and women were made to dance naked before the "hero," while he pricked them with swords and lances; infants were slain at their mothers' breasts, and a whole schoolful of boys was burnt alive. Priests and monks were involved in the general massacre. Hume speaks philosophically of these exploits as "some acts of violence committed during the fury of war," but Scottish minstrelsy celebrates them in a simpler strain. The death of Wallace in the national cause has naturally exalted his name and extenuated his atrocities in the eyes of his compatriots; yet to treat him as a national hero is to condemn the Scottish nation, who unquestionably left him, in the crisis of his fate, without sympathy or support. In excepting this bloodthirsty "patriot" from his magnanimous clemency, Edward was certainly justified by the sentiment of his own age. We expect some Scottish champion to take up his pen against the iconoclast of Scottish heroism, and in the mean time hold our judgment somewhat in suspense.

The garrison of Stirling, under Oliphant, held out against Edward for three months after the complete submission of the rest of the kingdom and its authorities, as private adventurers; and after a difficult and expensive siege, were compelled, by the imminence of an assault, to surrender at discretion. Edward spared the lives of the whole garrison, with the exception of one English traitor found among them, and only ordered them into temporary confinement, "without chains." History may contemptuously permit prejudice to stigmatize this conduct as "ungenerous." What would be said if the governor of Messina were to hold out for several months on his private account, and cause great expense and effusion of blood, after the flight or abdication of Francis II.?

With regard to domestic affairs, Mr. Clifford fails to convince us that Edward did not display some arbitrary tendencies and do some despotic acts, or that those who withstood his encroachments, even though they may have been actuated by somewhat narrow motives, did not deserve well of their country. It would have been strange indeed if a ruler and legislator called upon to contend with a very anarchical state of things had not sometimes, in quelling anarchy, laid a threatening hand on liberty, or if a man inspired with vast and, on the whole, beneficent designs, had, in carrying his designs into effect, always respected the forms of a half-settled constitution. Mr. Clifford does not fail to convince us that Edward on the whole showed a true and noble sympathy with open councils and the spirit of free institutions, and that he is entitled at least to divide the political glory of Simon de Montfort as the founder of a national representation. The greatest blot on his escutcheon is his application to the Pope for a bull cancelling the concessions respecting the royal forests to which he had perhaps improvidently bound himself in 1301. In this instance perhaps alone, amidst a treacherous and intriguing generation, he was false to his own indignant motto, *Pactum serva.* Mr. Clifford, while disclaiming any intention of justifying this proceeding, does, in effect, justify it as a "conscientious" and "honest" action according to the measure of moral and religious light which Edward, in a papal age, possessed. But this is to resign the claim to a morality and a sense of honor superior to those of his age which Mr. Clifford has advanced on behalf of the great object of his admiration, and, as we think, justly advanced.

We should not do justice if we were to conclude without a general acknowledgment of the value and interest of this work, which will take its place among the best essays (it is rather an essay than a "sketch") on special periods of English history.

Miss Burdett Coutts, a lady who is foremost in every benevolent undertaking, has erected in London a number of dwellings for the poor. These houses are large and convenient, while the rents are fixed at a sum which will yield three per cent on the outlay. Up to the present time the results have been most satisfactory. The buildings are always tenanted, while the tenants are orderly in conduct and regular in paying their rents.

From The Dublin University Magazine.

FROUDE'S HISTORY OF ENGLAND.

History of England from the Fall of Wolsey to the Death of Elizabeth. By James Anthony Froude, M.A., late Fellow of Exeter College, Oxford. Vols. v. and vi. London: John W. Parker and Son, West Strand. 1860.

With so large an instalment of Mr. Froude's work as the public now possess, it may be advisable for us, before entering upon a detailed examination of the present volumes, to give some answer to the question, which has lately been captiously asked, and not over-candidly answered; viz., is Mr. Froude a great historian, or, at least, high in the rank of those who nearly approach that distinction? And in making this attempt we shall refer more than once to the notices of Mr. Froude's last two volumes which appeared in the *Times* of August 31 and September 1, 1860. The writer of those notices endeavors, as we think, in an unworthy spirit, and with insufficient knowledge, to damn Mr. Froude with faint praise. His own brilliant but superficial sentences have derived all their lustre from the pages at which he sneers. He runs on, column after column, with words and thoughts which recall the history so exactly, that one is often inclined to wonder that the reviewer should have omitted to insert the usual formula of quotation. We have been unable to discover more than *one fact* (the price of wheat per quarter in 1556) which has not been borrowed from Mr. Froude's copious treasury. And if the susceptibilities of the historian be wounded by the criticisms of the writer in the *Times*, we would remind him of the brilliant lines in which Byron expands the thought which was originally introduced into English poetry by Waller, of the wounded eagle's pang in feeling that "she nursed the pinion which impelled the steel."

The reviewer — whose delineation of the character of Mary, and general conception of the causes of the reactionary movement in English society, which at first so perfectly fell in with her religious bigotry, are copied, touch after touch, from the sixth volume of the history — seems to consider that Mr. Froude has three capital deficiencies.

The first of these may be expressed by the ugly barbarism—"non-eventuality"—which is, we believe, employed by the critic himself. The charge is certainly not without some foundation. We remarked, about a year ago, that Mr. Froude's power lies more in the delineation of individual character than in unwinding the sequence of events. His book is a table covered with miniatures in jewelled cases—a gallery hung with portraits. It is an album of detached landscapes, rather than a true and complete chart. Faces sad or cheerful, brave or mean —the young and holy Jane Grey, the superstitious Mary, the profligate Courtenay; Cranmer, beautiful through all his weakness; Latimer, the stout and good; Pole, the slave of Rome and the rebel against England, dying amidst the wreck of all his hopes—look upon us in rapid succession. Each is painted with a master's band, and once seen can never be forgotten, the study is so finished and the lines so firm. Mary, in especial, has never been so well drawn; never, perhaps, so kindly delineated by a Protestant pen, yet never made so heavy a burden for Romanism to bear. It is instructive, and almost amusing to read the closing summary of Mr. Froude's sixth volume, with its intense yet suppressed indignation, and its unerring vigor of conception and expression, beside the faint and vacillating apologetic of Lingard. Yet, it must be admitted, that while we gaze with pleasure at these admirable sketches, we are sometimes apt to be confused. Time and place are recovered by the aid of awkward commonplaces, rather than in virtue of the smooth unwinding of the thread which the historian holds to guide us through the labyrinth. He has not the art of introducing naturally, openings through which the reader can take in the lie of the position, as Cardinal Perron praised a painter for the introduction of a window into a picture of a palace, through which the stretch of woods into the distance could be hinted to the eye. But this want of dramatic purpose in the narrative is supplied, in all essentials, by copious and accurate summaries, enriched by well-chosen citations from contemporary documents, in many cases hitherto unpublished. Let it be considered, also, that inferiority in bringing out the sequence of events is not so considerable a drawback in a historian of that period, if it be supplied by a marked superiority in the delineation of character. The lives of the great men in the reigns of Edward and Mary are history in a sense which the lives of the notables of Queen Victoria can never be. How small a part of the real history of the last twenty years would be covered by the best delineation of its most remarkable men. Lord Palmerston and Sir R. Peel in politics; Spurgeon, Whately, and Pusey, in theology; in philosophy, Hamilton; in engineering, Stephenson; in science, Airey and Sir William Hamilton; in political economy, Mill and Ricardo; in military history, Outram and Clyde—are great and varied names. Yet all these cover but a small portion of the field. They are but a few waves of a vast tide of life, with crests somewhat higher than the rest, yet almost lost in the multitudinous billows that are surging up around them. But at the period of the Reformation the whole field of English history is wellnigh covered with a few portentous shadows; or, to allude to the other figure already employed, the fountains of the great deep of English life are just being broken up, and he who can observe and paint the first great rollers, has given something like an adequate picture of the crisis.

The second objection which the reviewer makes to Mr. Froude is connected with his style and manner, although here he contradicts himself so curiously that it would seem as if he allowed his pen to run at random, and after a few sentences forgot the thought with which he started. The article in the *Times* speaks almost at the outset of "the charm of Mr. Froude's manner," and informs us that "his style is graceful, often *picturesque*, and generally interesting." Yet after a brief interval it is asserted that Mr. Froude has, with the death of Henry VIII., got over a factitious theory, the polemical interest of whose logical development has diverted attention from his artistic deficiencies; so that "the duty of criticism is limited to a question of style. Unhappily for Mr. Froude this is a question which, in his interest, ought to be deferred as long as possible. He has *no talent for the picturesque*; and, after Prescott's highly colored narrative, his page seems poor and tame." Now, we never defended Mr. Froude's style from the charge of occasional haste and awkwardness. In a former article we pointed out a few blemishes which disfigured his earlier volumes. As we write, our eyes rests upon a vigorous and dramatic chapter, headed "Calais," in which the word *said* occurs thirteen times within seven pages, in taking up the turns of certain dialogues between conspirators against Queen Mary, in 1556.

We must remonstrate once more against the clumsy pivot for bringing us from one place to another, "The scene changes;" and we dislike such questionable expressions as "bad patriotism" (vol. vi., 460), which is simply a barbarism. Yet we should be ashamed if we did not feel the noble and careless charms of a style which is at once so tender and so manly, so picturesque without mawkish affectation of coloring, and so strong without the ostentation of strength. The cobbler in the old story set a great master right: but it was on the fit of a shoe. The Turk, to whom was exhibited the great picture of the Decollation of the Baptist, dwelt with severity of animadversion on the fact that the skin did not shrink from the wounded part of the neck. From the shoemaker's and butcher's point of view the criticisms were, no doubt, unexceptionable. But after all they were the petty remarks of a cobbler and a headsman. If genius has been rightly defined as the faculty of adding to the existing stock of knowledge by new views and new combinations, as originality in intellectual construction, Mr. Froude's style is the vehicle of genius. The shoes in his picture may not fit with irreproachable accuracy; the skin of his sentences may not always wrinkle precisely at the orthodox line; yet the critic who is displaying the extent of his acquirements by disparaging remarks may be exhibiting at the same time the depth of his littleness. We do not think that the epithet *picturesque* conveys the very highest order of praise. In some respects painted are superior to written or spoken signs; in a thousand other, they are inferior—inferior in precision, in pliancy, in delicacy of association. The writer who is *picturesque*, and nothing more, may be deficient in all the highest mental capacities. Women, who are more subtly observant than men, can almost always write picturesquely when they have the slightest technical mastery over language. To be picturesque, and nothing more, is to paint with words and not with colors; and, therefore, to draw with an inferior pencil. But, in truth, we know few historians who in this department can compete with Mr. Froude. We need only quote a few sentences almost at random. In the history of Wyatt's rising, Wyatt examines London Bridge on a dark February night in 1554. His survey is described in these words:—

"On Sunday or Monday night Wyatt scaled the leads of the gatehouse, climbed into a window, and descended the stairs into the lodge. The porter and his wife were nodding over the fire. The rebel leader bade them on their lives be still, and stole along in the darkness to the chain, from which the drawbridge had been cut away. There, looking across the black gulf, where the river was rolling below, he saw the dusky mouths of four gaping cannon, and beyond them, in the torchlight, Lord Howard himself, keeping watch with the guard."

When the supposed symptoms of Mary's pregnancy pass away, the processions, in which the priests kept up the farce, are hit off with a few racy touches, happily tinted with a laughing light of rough old English humor:—

"Mary assured her attendants that all was well, and that she felt the motion of her child. The physicians professed to be satisfied, and the priests were kept at work at the litanies. Up and down the streets they marched, through city and suburb, park and square; torches flared along Cheapside at midnight behind the Holy Sacrament, and five hundred poor men and women from the almshouse walked two and two, telling their beads in their withered fingers. Such marching, such chanting, such praying, was never heard or seen before or since in London streets. A profane person ran one day out of the crowd and hung about a priest's neck, where the beads should be, a string of puddings; but they whipped him, and prayed on."

The condition of the unhappy queen, in May, 1555, is told in some inimitable sentences, which are the more admirable for the accuracy of the ground colors, derived as they are from some dull sentences in a despatch of Noailles to Montmorency—

"Her women now understood her condition: she was sick of a mortal disease; but they durst not tell her. And she whose career had been painted out to her by the legate as especial and supernatural, looked only for supernatural causes of her present state. Throughout May she remained in her apartments waiting—waiting—in passionate restlessness. With stomach swollen, and features shrunk and haggard, she would sit upon the floor, with her knees drawn up to her face in an agony of doubt; and, in mockery of her wretchedness, letters were again strewed about the place by an invisible agency, telling her that she was hated by her people."

The following portrait of Latimer is as true, yet as grand, fresh, and simple as that of Foxe himself:—

"Latimer was then introduced—eighty years old now—dressed in an old threadbare gown of Bristol frieze, a handkerchief on his head, with a nightcap over it; and over that again another cap, with two broad flaps buttoned under the chin. A leather belt was round his waist, to which his Testament was attached; his spectacles, without a case, hung from his neck. So stood the greatest man, perhaps, then living in the world, a prisoner on his trial, waiting to be condemned to death by men professing to be the ministers of God. So it was in the days of the prophets, so it was in the Son of man's days; as it was in the days of the Son of man, so was it in the Reformer's days."

Here, too, is a picture of a warrior, Lord Grey:—

"Grey was a fierce, stern man. It was Grey who hung the priests in Oxfordshire from their church towers. It was Grey who led the fiery charge upon the Scots at Musselburgh, and with a pike wound, which laid open cheek, tongue, and palate, he 'pursued out the chase,' till, choked by heat, dust, and his own blood, he was near falling under his horse's feet."

The bestowal of the epithet *picturesque* must, in the long run, be left to the adjudication of taste. But the standard of literary taste is not quite as capricious as that of the taste for claret or *Dindon-aux-truffes*. The critic who should read Keat's "Eve of St. Agnes" with that shuddering concentration of cold—

"The owl, for all his feathers, was a-cold,"

with those lines descriptive of the casement and the diamonded panes, that literally seem to blush with deep, damasked tints—with that matchless Alexandrine,—

"And the long carpets rose along the gusty floor;"

or who should turn to "Hyperion," and unconverted by—

"Forest on forest hung about his head
Like cloud on cloud;"

or,—

"Where the dead leaf fell, there did it rest,"

should maintain that this varied power of coloring, this capacity of seizing salient points and compressing the essence of whole descriptions into a touch or two, was accidental, and that "Mr. Keats had no talent for the picturesque;"—such a critic might be an accomplished gentleman, but he would preach to us in vain. And similarly in Mr. Froude s case: his pencil is equally at home, and his lights and shadows equally natural, however varied the subject may be. The conspirator grimly peering over the black gulf of night, the river rolling below, the dusky culverins on the far side, and the plumed and booted figure in the light beyond; the priests marching with their mummeries in the procession; the hysterical queen, the brave old martyr, the fierce knight, with his gashed face—each is struck out from musty parchment and dry volume, like a photograph, by the sunbeam of historic genius; and to say that "Mr. Froude has no talent for the picturesque," is to maintain a silly and spiteful paradox.

The reviewer has a third and more "architectonic" objection to Mr. Froude.

"We at once leap," he says, "to the conclusion that there were people of simple faith and noble aspiration in those days, who were raised high above the petty concerns which trouble nations now. They thought more of the remission of sins than of the reduction of taxes. The Bible supplied the place of consols in public regard. The rate of wages and the price of mutton were matters of indifference; but the sermon preached at Paul's Cross and the last bull from the pope were affairs of the highest moment. Whether the revenue of the year was short and the expenditure of the country was excessive were inquiries completely overshadowed by questions relating to the religious nurture of the boy-king, or the religious sentiments of the queen's betrothed. We observe that the whole nation is intent on mighty speculations as to faith and free-will, the real presence, the pope's authority, and justification by faith; and it is only when we come to the appendix that we find huddled together a few scraps of information as to the state of the currency, the price of wheat, and the amount of the public income. That three hundred years ago a nation which now grovels in pursuit of gain, and aims at physical perfection, was all for romances and spiritual profit, is a fallacy which we leave to the poet, but deny to the historian. With regard to our own history, a purifying criticism is required similar to that which the German scholars have applied to the early legends of Greece and Rome."

In the same smart, but we venture to think superficial, strain, Mr. Froude's censor deals with the whole reign of Mary. He reminds us of the long list of material evils that darkened those unhappy years. In the year 1555 the crops failed, and there was a famine, during which the queen gave up a fifth part of her revenue to the Church. In 1556, there was another dearth; the commonalty in some counties were grouting like hogs for acorns, and in London mothers were leaving their infants at the doors of wealthier neighbors. In 1557 there was, indeed, a golden harvest; but prices were deranged and capital disturbed. On the back of this fell a heavy war. Then we read of lists of landed and moneyed men being made out for the purpose of a compulsory loan, and of an income-tax of twenty per cent. The reviewer's logic from these premises is singular. "These were the real troubles," he triumphantly exclaims, "that gave a bad name to Mary and her rule. She entered upon her rule with an exhausted treasury. She had to encounter two years of famine. *Therefore* it is that the blood of the martyrs has left an indelible stain upon her memory. *Therefore* it is that the fires of Smithfield have burned black upon the page of history the record of her short, disastrous reign." A notable discovery!—it was not persecution but political economy which has given Mary so unfortunate a character. The epithet which attaches undying infamy to her name, and which can never be washed white short of the judgment-seat, should be commuted for some appellative which might indicate a dear loaf, or famine prices, or a twenty per cent income-tax.

We are not those who would affect to despise political economy. But we cannot consent that the fundamental moral and spiritual laws which hold society together, should be sneered away by plausible Sciolists. Let us remind the clever writer of the extracts which we have cited, of some very old-fashioned, but, as we fancy, most undeniable, truths.

In the first place, then, a consideration of the nature of man, may render it not so perfectly mythical, as he appears to think, that "the remission of sins" should, at least for a season, occupy as much of the popular attention as "the reduction of taxes," and that "the Bible" should be quoted as well as "Consols." The question has not to be decided here of the true character and permanent utility of the movements called Revivals; but it is a simple fact, of which Mr. Froude's critic may convince himself, that so lately as four years ago, hundreds and thousands of American merchants were literally in the condition which he seems to consider an impossibility. For a time, at least, the Bible, the sermon, and the prayer-meeting, were as prominent subjects as cotton and consols. If, then, he will apply his lively imagination, on the one hand, to the principles of human nature which underlie such phenomena as Revivals, and will, on the other hand, remember, that in the reigns of Edward and Mary the most profound questions which can agitate the breasts of men had been flung broadcast among the English people, he may be led to suspect that it is not quite so clear that there is nothing in Mr. Froude's view.

In truth, it is all very well for a historian like Gibbon, to reduce all the springs of human conduct to two—the love of pleasure and the love of action. It follows, smoothly enough, to say that to one of these may be ascribed the agreeable, and to the other the useful, qualifications. And if it be so, the consequence appears plausible enough, that the primitive Christians, to whom pleasure was a peril and action an impertinence, were of an inactive and insensible disposition, incapable of producing either private happiness or public benefit. But this "half-stoic, half-Epicurean homily," as it has been well called, is founded upon an imperfect draught of our nature. It takes no account of conscience, of the moral and religious sentiments. "We know," says Burke, "and it is our pride to know, that man is, by his constitution, a religious animal." The progress of natural history gives these words a meaning beyond that which was attached to them even by their illustrious author. What is the argument on this subject of one of the first philosophers of Europe, who may be well taken as the representative of Natural History? It is substantially this: man forms a reign by himself, the human kingdom. What, then, are the special *differential* phenomena which entitle him to this distinction? They do not exist in the organization which he has in common with the *mammiferæ*, and especially the ape, muscle by muscle and nerve by nerve. Experiments upon dogs, rabbits, and frogs, are ever reflecting light upon the human organism. Nor can the *os sublime cœlumquetueri* of Ovid constitute this *differentia*, since ducks and other birds possess this qualification. Even the mental faculties can scarcely be considered the special attribute of humanity, since some faint and rudimental images, at least, of these can be found in other tribes. "Articulately speaking men," is the beautiful and profound epithet of Homer. Yet some animals have a voice. The patient watchers in fields and forests have learned to speak of the *language* of birds and beasts. Agassiz goes so far as to affirm that the growls of some species of bears might be derived from those of other species, by the same process which a linguist like Max Müller would employ to trace the affiliation of Greek to Sanscrit. And as this differential peculiarity cannot be found in organization, in mental capacity or in language, neither is it to be traced in the sentiments and emotions, such as love, hatred, and jealousy, which exist among animals in a wild and rudimental shape. These distinctive facts are consequently and exclusively to be found in the moral region, in the notions of deity and immortality, in morality and religion. This great religious and theistic argument cannot be overthrown by the allegation of languages in which no moral terms occur, as is said to be the case with some Australian dialects, any more than from the absence of certain generic terms, such as *tree*, *fish*, *bird*, we can conclude that the Australian knows no such things. The supposed atheism of the Hottentots and Caffres has vanished upon a closer acquaintance; and Dr. Livingstone vouches for the momentous fact, that the existence of God, and a future life, are universally recognized among the most degraded populations of Africa. A strictly philosophical definition of man, after the fashion of Linnæus, will therefore bring us round to the sentence of Burke. Linnæus characterizes vegetables as "living, non-sentient, organized bodies." He terms animals "living, organized bodies, sentient, and moving themselves spontaneously." On the same principle, the zoölogical characteristic of man, in Linnæan language, ought to be, "an organized being, living, sentient, endowed with spontaneous movement, with morality and religion." Thus, we come round again with deeper insight to Burke's words, "Man is by his constitution a religious animal;" and see more scientifically the inadequacy of Gibbon's analysis. The mind of Mr. Froude's reviewer must be saturated with that analysis, or it would not seem to him a thing so utterly incredible that at certain crises the moral and religious sentiments, which are actually man's *differentia*, should manifest their existence above those economical and secretive qualities which he possesses in common with the ant and magpie. Mr. Froude believes, that "man shall not live by bread alone," and his censor attacks him for so old a prejudice.

We would further remind the reviewer, that one feeling strongly at work among the English in Mary's reign was, that all the miseries which darkened over the throne and kingdom were the shadow of God's anger. Not all the processions of priests in London; nor the gaudy symbolism of the restored rights; nor the half-simulated, half-hysterical emotion which ran round the Houses of Parliament at the ceremonial of the reconcilement to Rome, and national absolution, pronounced by Pole, could persuade the people that the conduct of Mary was not under a curse. From a false creed, and from the ashes of the martyrs, rose a blight which blackened the golden fields, and visited the queen with the dry breast and miscarrying womb. Possibly this feeling may seem superstitious to the reviewer; and the ways of God in history are to be traced with reverence. Yet, if we read the Apocalypse, not as a compendium of European history by anticipation with the dreamers of the day, but as a magnificent symbolical representation of the principles of universal history, we may be fain to excuse the impression. He who sits on the white horse with the bow and crown, conquering and to conquer, is not Trajan; but One whose name is not to be lightly spoken. The opening of the first seal is not past and gone, but continuous. The red horse of battle tramples ever and anon upon our hills. The black horse sweeps from century to century through the blighted corn and mildewed wheat; and the voice is heard in every famine year, "A measure of wheat for a penny, and three measures of barley for a penny." Possibly, in the eyes of him who saw the vision at Patmos, the peasants and artisans of Mary's reign might be better philosophers than even a writer in the *Times*.

But it is time for us to pass on to a more direct examination of Mr. Froude's volumes; and we will refer to those points which seem to us most worthy of study.

First, then, there is much important truth in the statement, which is brought out with such consistency and clearness, that the English people, on the whole, were discontented with the progress of the Reformation so far, and entertained hopes of Mary. A trail of corruption had followed its pathway over England. A reaction set in upon the extreme Puritanic views, which then were agreeable to an influential and noisy minority, but distasteful to the strong, quiet, common-sense instincts of the most powerful portion of the people. Some of the best men in England occupied the same theological position which we have been assured is now occupied by Garibaldi himself. They had no very strong objection to the ancient ceremonial. They were willing to be Catholics, even Roman Catholics—so far as a moderate theoretical recognition of the primacy of the Roman See—but not Papists by a single inch. One of the great merits of the volume is the strong way in which this is put; and then the stern, chorus-like indignation with which the historian places before us the divine Atè that drove the guilty Church and her miserable tools to lose the great game which lay in their hands. Every section which treats of the papal legate, or Philip and Mary, and of Paul IV., seems to be haunted by a voice chanting *Quos Deus vult perdere prius dementat*. In so ardent a Protestant, and with the key to Mr. Froude's words, the reader will not misinterpret this bitter summary:—

"The deliverers of England from the Egyptian bondage of the Papacy had led the people out into a wilderness, where the manna had been stolen by the leaders, and there were no tokens of a promised land. To the universities the Reformation had brought with it desolation; to the people of England it had brought misery and want. The once open hand was closed; the once open heart was hardened; the ancient loyalty of man to man was exchanged for the scuffling of selfishness; the change of faith had brought with it no increase of freedom, and less of charity. The prisons were crowded, as before, with sufferers for opinion, and the creed of a thousand years was made a crime by a doctrine of yesterday; monks and nuns wandered by hedge and highway, as missionaries of discontent; and pointed, with bitter effect, to the fruits of the new belief, which had been crimsoned in the blood of thousands of English peasants. The English people were not yet so much in love with wretchedness that they would set aside, for the sake of it, a princess whose injuries pleaded for her, whose title was affirmed by Act of Parliament. In the tyranny under which the nation was groaning, the moderate men of all creeds looked to the accession of Mary as to the rolling away of some bad black nightmare."—Vol. vi. p. 28.

And here we may indicate what seems to us a change in Mr. Froude's point of view. It is not the first in his restless intellectual career. The day was, when his brother's memory hung about him—when a dim, sweet blinding spell came over him—when a pomp of ritual attracted him, with its charm of chants and intoxicating incense. This was succeeded by the disenchantment described in the *Nemesis*. After a season of doubt, he began once more to wrestle his way to belief. But his convictions were weak and hesitating. A passionate hatred of priestcraft and dogmatism was the strongest article of his creed. In this mood the first volumes of his history were written. Anglicanism, with its moderate and compromising spirit, was then his abhorrence. But thought, and a deeper acquaintance with the life and writings of Cranmer and Ridley especially, have altered the position of the glass once more. He now sees that compromise is not cowardice, and that the mean, abhorred of youth and passion, is the quiet road by which Truth and Wisdom are wont to walk, scared by the crowd and gabble to the right hand and to the left. This beautiful passage on the Prayer-book could not have stood in the earlier volumes. It expresses a conviction which has been slowly arrived at:—

"As the translation of the Bible bears upon it the imprint of the mind of Tyndal, so, while the Church of England remains, the image of Cranmer will be seen reflected on the calm surface of the Litany. The most beautiful portions of it are translations from the Breviary; et the same prayers translated by others would not be those which chime like church bells in the ears of the English child. The translations and the addresses which are original have the same silvery melody of language, and breathe the same simplicity of spirit. So long as Cranmer trusted himself, and would not let himself be dragged beyond his convictions, he was the representative of the feelings of the best among his countrymen. With the reverend love for the past which could appropriate its excellence, he could feel, at the same time, the necessity for change. While he could no longer regard the sacraments with a superstitious idolatry, he saw in them ordinances divinely appointed, and therefore especially if inexplicably sacred. In this temper, for the most part, the English Church Services had now, after patient labor, been at length completed by him, and were about to be laid before Parliament. They had grown slowly. First had come the Primers of Henry VIII., then the Litany was added, and then the first Communion book. The next step was the Prayer-book of 1549; and now at last the complete Liturgy, which survives after three hundred years. In a few sentences, only inserted, apparently, under the influence of Ridley, doctrinal theories were pressed beyond the point to which opinion was legitimately gravitating. The priest was converted absolutely into a minister, the altar into a table, the eucharist into a commemoration, and a commemoration only. But these peculiarities were uncongenial with the rest of the Liturgy, with which they refused to harmonize, and on the final establishment of the Church of England were dropped or modified. They were, in fact, the seed of vital alterations for which the nation was unprepared—which, had Edward lived two years longer, would have produced first the destruction of the Church as a body politic, and then an after-fruit of reaction more inveterate than even the terrible one under Mary. But Edward died before the Liturgy could be further tampered with; and, from amidst the foul weeds in which its roots were buried, it stands up beautiful—the one admirable thing which the unhappy reign produced. Prematurely born, and too violently forced upon the country, it was nevertheless the right thing—the thing which essentially answered to the spiritual demands of the nation. They rebelled against it, because it was precipitately thrust upon them; but services which have over-lived so many storms speak for their own excellence, and speak for the merit of the workman. As the Liturgy was prepared for Parliament and people, so for the convocation and the clergy, there were drawn up a body of articles of religion—forty-two of them, as they were first devised—thirty-nine, as they are now known to the theological student. These also have survived, and, like other things in this country, have survived their utility and the causes which gave them birth."

But the central figure of this portion of the history is of course Mary herself. It has been drawn by Mr. Froude with care as well as genius; and his notes, brief and unostentatious as they are, sufficiently attest the assiduity with which contemporary manuscripts have been examined. She is exhibited to us as she was: a woman not naturally or disinterestedly cruel; but with that peculiar mental and moral constitution which seems capable of being saturated with the spirit of Roman superstition. What she became she was made by pope, cardinal, and priests. There is a mixture of irony, pity, and indignation in the delineation of the middle-aged devotee, chanting *Veni Creator* before the Host for a young and royal husband; tricking out her wan face to catch his fancy; waiting for the loiterer with hysterical longing; then protruding her lean and ghastly figure to make peers, Parliament, and people sensible of the hope with which she was pregnant; and finally, her love withered by Philip's profligacy, and her proud expectation of royal and Catholic issue changed into the sober certainty of disease and sterility, waiting for death, not without patience and firmness. Two sermons were preached at her obsequies, one by White, Bishop of Winchester, the other by Feckenham, Abbot of Westminster. White, who had a florid style, and whom Camden admits to have been a "tolerable poet," chose the curious text, "A living dog is better than a dead lion." It was drily remarked, that "one not present at the place might easily tell whom he made the lion and whom the dog." Yet, while "he strewed all the flowers of his rhetoric on Queen Mary deceased, leaving not so much as the stalks to scatter on her surviving sister," it must be admitted that some of the flowers were not wholly undeserved. "Take Queen Mary in herself," writes Fuller, "abstracted from her opinions, and secluded from her bloody counsellors, and her memory will justly come under commendation. Indeed, she knew not the art of being popular, and never cared to learn it; and generally (being given more to her beads than her book) had less of learning (or parts to get it) than any of her father's children. She hated to equivocate in her own religion; and always was what she was, without dissembling her judgment or practice for fear or flattery; little beloved of her subjects, to whom though once she remitted an entire subsidy, yet it little moved their affections; because, though liberal in this act, she had been unjust in another—her breach of promise to the gentry of Norfolk and Suffolk. However, she had been a worthy princess, had as little cruelty been done under her as was done by her. Her devotion always commended her profit, and oftentimes did fill the church with the emptying of her own exchequer." We will only add another personal touch from Fuller: "Queen Mary's person was no gainer (scarce a saver) of affection, having her father's features,—a face broad and big, with her mother's color—a somewhat swarthy complexion." We may now hang up Mr. Froude's portrait beside that of the quaint old historian.

"No English sovereign ever ascended the throne with larger popularity than Mary Tudor. The country was eager to atone to her for her mother's injuries, and the instinctive loyalty of the English towards their natural sovereign was enhanced by the abortive efforts of Northumberland to rob her of her inheritance. She had reigned little more than five years, and she descended into the grave amidst curses deeper than the acclamations which welcomed her accession. In that brief time she had swathed her name in that horrid epithet which will cling to it forever; and yet from the passions which generally tempt sovereigns into crime she was entirely free; to the time of her accession she had lived a blameless, and in many respects, a noble, life, and few men or women have lived less capable of doing knowingly a wrong thing. Philip's conduct, which could not extinguish her passion for him, and the collapse of the inflated imaginations which had surrounded her supposed pregnancy, it can hardly be doubted, affected her sanity. Those forlorn hours, when she would sit on the ground with her knees drawn to her face; those restless days and nights when like a ghost she would wander about the palace, rousing herself only to write tear-blotted letters to her husband; those bursts of fury over the libels dropped in her way, or the marchings in procession behind the Host in the London streets,—these are all symptoms of hysterical derangement, and leave little room, as we think of her, for other feelings than pity. But if Mary was insane, the madness was of a kind which placed her absolutely under her spiritual directors; and the responsibility for her cruelties, if responsibility be any thing but a name, rests first with Gardiner, who commenced them; and secondly, and in a higher degree, with Reginald Pole. The revenge of the clergy for their past humiliations, and the too natural tendency of an oppressed party to abuse suddenly recovered power, combined to originate the Marian persecution. The rebellions and massacres, the political scandals, the universal suffering throughout the country during Edward's minority, had created a general bitterness in all classes against the Reformers; the Catholics could appeal with justice to the apparent consequences of heretical opinions; and when the Reforming preachers themselves denounced so loudly the irreligion which had attended their success, there was little wonder that the world took them at their word, and was ready to permit the use of strong, suppressive measures to keep down the unruly tendencies of uncontrolled fanatics.

"But neither these, nor any other feeling of English growth, would have produced the scenes which have stamped this unhappy reign with a character so frightful. Archbishop Parker, who knew Pole and Pole's doings well, called him Carnifex et flagellum ecclesiæ Anglicanæ—the hangman, and the scourge of the Church of England. His character was irreproachable; in all the virtues of the Catholic Church he walked without spot or stain, and the system to which he had surrendered himself had left to him of the common selfishness of mankind his enormous vanity alone. But that system had extinguished also in him the human instincts—the genial emotions by which theological theories stand especially in need to be corrected. He belonged to a class of persons at all times numerous, in whom enthusiasm takes the place of understanding; who are men of an idea, and unable to accept human things as they are, are passionate loyalists, passionate churchmen, passionate revolutionists, as the accidents of their age may determine. Happily for the welfare of mankind, persons so constituted rarely arrive at power; should power come to them, they use it as Pole used it, to defeat the ends which are nearest to their hearts.

"The teachers who finally converted the English nation to Protestantism were not the declaimers from the pulpit, nor the voluminous controversialists with the pen. These, indeed, could produce arguments which, to those who were already convinced, seemed as if they ought to produce conviction, but conviction did not follow till the fruits of the doctrine bore witness to the spirit from which it came. The evangelical teachers, caring only to be allowed to develop their own opinions, and persecute their opponents, had walked hand in hand with men who had spared neither tomb nor altar; who had stripped the lead from the church roofs, and stolen the bells from the church towers; and between them they had so outraged such plain, honest minds as remained in England, that had Mary been content with mild repression, had she left the pope to those who loved him, and had married, instead of Philip, some English lord, the Mass would have retained its place, the clergy in moderate form would have resumed their old authority, and the Reformation would have waited for a century. In an evil hour, the queen listened to the unwise advisers who told her that moderation in religion was the sin of the Laodiceans; and while the fanatics, who had brought scandal on the reforming cause, either truckled like Shaxton, or stole abroad to wrangle over surplices and forms of prayers, the true and the good atoned with their lives for the crimes of others, and vindicated a noble cause by nobly dying for it; and while among the reformers, that which was most bright and excellent shone out with a preternatural lustre, so were the Catholics permitted to exhibit also the preternatural features of the creed which was expiring. Although Pole and Mary could have laid their hands on earl and baron, knight and gentleman, whose heresy was notorious, although in the queen's own guard there were many who never listened to a Mass, they durst not strike where there was danger that they would be struck in return. They went out into the highways and hedges, they gathered up the lame, the halt, and the blind; they took the weaver from his loom, the carpenter from his workshop, the husbandman from his plough; they laid hands on maidens and boys, who had never heard of any other religion than that which they were called on to abjure, old men tottering into the grave, and children whose lips could but just lisp the articles of their creed, and of these they made their burnt-offerings, with these they crowded their prisons; and when filth and famine killed them, they flung them out to rot. How long England would have endured the repetition of the horrid spectacles is hard to say. The persecution lasted three years; and in that time something less than three hundred persons were burnt at the stake.

"'By imprisonment,' said Lord Burleigh, 'by torment, by famine, by fire, almost the number of four hundred were in their various ways, lamentably taken off.' Yet, as I have already said, interference was impossible, except by armed force. The country knew from the first, that by the course of nature the period of cruelty must be a brief one, it knew that a successful rebellion is at best a calamity; and the bravest and wisest men would not injure an illustrious cause by conduct less than worthy of it, so long as endurance was possible. They had saved Elizabeth's life and Elizabeth's rights, and Elizabeth, when the time came, would deliver her subjects. The Catholics, therefore, were permitted to continue their cruelties till the cup of iniquity was full, till they had taught the educated laity of England to regard them with horror, and until the Romanist superstition had died amidst the execrations of the people of its own excess."

But we should omit some leading features of this portion of the work, if we did not dwell for a moment upon Mr. Froude's representations of Pole and Cranmer.

Of Mr. Froude it may be said that he realizes Johnson's wish—he is emphatically, "a good hater." The intensity of his abhorrence of Pole is something almost personal. An enthusiastic Oxford logician, of some twenty years ago, is said to have been startled by some heresy upon the "predicables," into exclaiming, with warmth: "If I met that ass, Porphyry, upon a coach, I should tell him that he was an ass." Certainly Mr. Froude is never wearied of telling us that Pole is "an ass," and something worse. According to him, the papal legate is the stormy petrel of his own party, ever boding ruin and disgrace to the cause which he loved so passionately. He it was who fed fat the queen's hysterical desire for the Spanish match. He it was who, more than Gardiner or Bonner, was responsible for the Marian persecutions. We differ from Mr. Froude, with the submission which belongs to our inferior knowledge. Bishop Short, in his jejune but very accurate History of the Church of England, gives it as his opinion, that "it should never be forgotten that the side of reason and mercy found an advocate in Cardinal Pole." It is recorded by Burnett, in the third book of his History of the Reformation, that when Bonner, in 1557, condemned sixteen persons to be burned, Pole obtained the pardon of two, the only pardon of the kind issued in that reign. A man's moderation may be inferred from the accusations of zealots of his own party. Pole lost the Papacy partly from the imputation of holding Lutheran views on the subject of justification; indeed, he is known to have sympathized with the Reformers rather than with the extreme opinions of such Romish divines as Osorius; and Haddon attributes to him a saying, little less noble than that of Cardinal Bellarmine, which has been quoted by Hooker: *Non potest viribus humanis nimium detrahi, nec addi Divinæ gratiæ.* "Too much cannot be taken from human strength, nor too much attributed to Divine grace." It is, indeed, impossible to exonerate Pole from the guilt of the blood which was shed by Thornton, his suffragan, and Hapsfield, his archdeacon, in the city and neighborhood of Canterbury; but he seems to have contented himself with burning the bones of dead, rather than the corpses of living, heretics; and he was probably always actuated by a desire of wiping away the imputation of Lutheranism rather than by the genuine spirit of papal intolerance.

Into the mind and character of Cranmer, Mr. Froude enters with fine psychological insight. His summary of the motives which might probably have weakened Cranmer's resolution in the hour of need, reminds one of Lord Bacon's saying that among the chief *desiderata* for rewriting history is a complete collection of "characters." Cranmer has been coarsely branded by Protestant as well as Roman Catholic. To Lingard he is, of course, the weak and cowardly author of the "seven recantations," published after his death, with Bonner's approbation; the subtle heretic who went to the stake with a speech retracting his doctrine on the eucharist, if he were pardoned, while if he were condemned a section could be slipped in, to disappoint his adversaries of the sweetest portion of their triumph, and to furbish up his tarnished name among the adherents of the Reformation. Protestants generally have passed by the subject with a sigh—perhaps reluctantly confessing with Bishop Short "that his fall takes off from the whole of the glorious dignity of his martyrdom"—perhaps, as Lingard says, "defending his memory by maintaining that his constancy at the stake had atoned for his apostasy in the prison." Yet is it not better to say of him, as our good old historian of Jewel's prevarication, "The most orient Jewel on earth hath some flaws therein. To conceal this his fault had been partiality; to excuse it, flattery; to insult over him, cruelty; to pity him, charity; to be wary of ourselves, in the like occasion, Christian discretion"? All men are not physically brave; and every man, perhaps, who has adopted a creed different from that of his nursery and schoolroom, and alien to the medium in which his spirit has lived up to manhood, has had misgivings of the heart, even while his will was unshaken, and his intellect unclouded. Let us hear the eloquent historian.

"The exact day on which this letter reached the archbishop is uncertain, but it was very near the period of his sentence. He had dared death bravely while it was distant; but he was physically timid. The near approach of the agony which he had witnessed in others unnerved him; and in a moment of mental and moral prostration, Cranmer may well have looked in the mirror which Pole held up to him, and asked himself whether, after all, the being there described was his true image—whether it was himself as others saw him. A faith which had existed for centuries; a faith in which generation after generation have lived happy and virtuous lives; a faith in which all good men are agreed, and only the bad dispute; such a faith carries an evidence and a weight with it, beyond what can be looked for in a creed reasoned out by individuals; a creed which had the ban upon it of inherited execration, which had been held in abhorrence once by him who was now called upon to die for it. Only fools and fanatics believe that they cannot be mistaken. Sick misgivings may have taken hold upon him in moments of despondency, whether after all the millions who received the Roman supremacy might not be more right than the thousands who denied it; whether the argument on the Real Presence which had satisfied him for fifty years might not be better founded than his recent doubts. It is not possible for a man of gentle and modest nature to feel himself the object of intense detestation without uneasy pangs; and as such thoughts came and went, a window might seem to open, through which there was a return to life and freedom. His trial was not greater than hundreds had borne and would bear with constancy; but the temperaments of men are unequally constituted, and a subtle intellect and a sensitive organization are not qualifications which make martyrdom easy. Life by the law of the Church, by justice, by precedent, was given to all who would accept it on terms of submission. That the archbishop should be tempted to recant, with the resolution formed notwithstanding that he should still suffer, whether he yielded or whether he was obstinate was a suspicion which his experience of the legate had not taught him to entertain. So it was that Cranmer's spirit gave way; and he who had disdained to fly, when flight was open to him, because he considered that having done the most in establishing the Reformation, he was bound to face the responsibility of it, fell at last under the protraction of the trial. So perished Cranmer. He was brought out with the eyes of his soul blinded, to make sport for his enemies; and in his death he brought upon them a wider destruction than he had effected by his teaching while alive. Pole was appointed the next day to the See of Canterbury. But the court had overreached themselves by their cruelty. Had they been contented to accept the recantation, they could have left the archbishop to die broken-hearted, pointed at by the finger of pitying scorn, and the Reformation would have been disgraced in its champion. They were tempted by an evil spirit of revenge into an act unsanctioned even by their own bloody laws, and they gave him an opportunity of redeeming his fame and of writing his name in the roll of martyrs. The worth of a man must be measured by his life, not by his failure under a single and peculiar trial."—Vol. vi. 413–416; 429, 430.

It is a very interesting suggestion of Mr. Froude, that one sentence of Cranmer's speech—"One word spoken by a man at his last end will be more remembered than the sermons made of them that live and remain"—was in Shakspeare's mind when he wrote these wonderful lines for the dying Gaunt—

"Oh! but they say the tongues of dying men
Enforce attention, like deep harmony:
Where words are scarce, they are seldom spent in vain;
For they breathe truth that breathe their words in pain.
More are men's ends marked than their lives before;
The setting sun, and music at the close,
As the last taste of sweets is sweetest last;
Writ in remembrance more than things long past."

There is yet another qualification which Mr. Froude possesses as the historian of the period which he has chosen. A poet requires humor *negatively*, that is to say, in sufficient quantity to make him conscious when he is ridiculous. But the historian of England, under the Tudors, requires humor *positively*, to render him capable of entering into the character of the times and the people with full appreciation. This was, perhaps, partly owing to the religion which was then dominant. There is more carelessness and indolence, more of the outward tumultuous life, less introversion and concentrated thought, among Roman Catholics than Protestants. Ceremonies and festivals collect the people in throngs. The intense belief in the remission of sins, as dependent upon the priest's *absolvo te*, prevents spiritual anxiety. Religious duty is not meditation upon a book, but the performance of certain functions. In all Roman Catholic countries, a light and jesting way of speaking of holy things is encouraged, which to us would seem very profane. This prevalent *humorousness* of the Tudor times was also, no doubt, in measure owing to the recklessness which constant exposure to danger engenders among a people so brave as the English. As a matter of fact, laughter and terror, the ridiculous and the sorrowful, are strangely intermingled in the chronicles of those days. Bright spray-drops of fun hang from the great mill-wheel of history. Acts of Parliament—witness that of Henry VII. on "sturdy and valiant beggars"—have a kind of grim playfulness. The Cardinal Legate must surely have been chuckling to himself when he uses the funny comparison, which we proceed to quote in his pastoral letter to the citizens of London, admonishing them to give back some part of the goods of the church, with which they had been indulged for a time: "It was left in your hand, as it were an apple in a child's hand given by the mother, which she, perceiving him to feed too much of, and knowing it should do him hurt if he himself should eat the whole, would have him give her a little piece thereof; which, the boy refusing, and whereas he would cry out if she would take it from him, letteth him alone therewith. But the father, her husband, coming in, if he shall see how the boy will not let go one morsel to the mother that hath given him the whole, she asking it with so fair means, he may, peradventure, take the apple out of the boy's hand, and, if he cry beat him also, and cast the apple out of the window." Nor is it only about gear and lands that those iron men can laugh. They can sport with the King of Terrors himself. The accusations which brought Ferrars, Bishop of St. David's, to the stake at Carmarthen, run riot with humor and bear witness to an inventiveness, which, in milder times, might have made a Thackeray or an Albert Smith. There is a richness in the picture of the right reverend prelate: "Espying a seal-fish tumbling in Milford Haven, and creeping down to the rocks by the water side, where he continued whistling by the space of an hour, persuading the company, that laughed fast at him, he made the fish to tarry there:"—which is only diminished when we remember the trifling fact that the object of this innocent joke was to burn a good man alive with insult and agony unutterable. We all remember how—

> "More's gay genius played
> With the inoffensive sword of native wit,
> Than the bare axe more luminous and keen."

But the rarest specimen of all is connected with Wyatt's rising, and we record it more willingly as it is not to be found in Mr. Froude's narrative or notes. The scene is Sir Thomas Wyatt's residence at Allingham Castle, on the Medway. The time is January, 1554. The wild winds are whistling through the leafless woods, and the yellow river rolls on with a dull and leaden gleam. Inside the castle all is commotion: outside, wild hope, and wilder terror. A few days will decide whether the master of the castle, and many a gallant gentleman, shall lose his head by a traitor's death, or drive out Philip and popery from England. A few days, and every church bell from Tunbridge to Maidstone, and from Maidstone to Rochester, will be ringing out an alarm, over farm and grange, and London itself be in arms. In this state of affairs, while the pear of rebellion is ripe, and the first touch may make it drop into the lap of death, a royal herald, in his gorgeous coat, booted and spurred, gallops up to the deeply moated house. The drawbridge was up. But one part of the moat appeared to be fordable. Just beyond that spot walked a retainer in Wyatt's livery. The herald shouted to inquire whether the place afforded a safe passage, to which came a shout of "Yea, yea!" In went horse and man, heavily accoutred as they were; the horse sank nearly up to the bridle. Had it not been for his prodigious strength, the magnificent animal would have been buried in the ooze, and his rider with him. Shivering with cold, his gilded and richly colored surcoat daubed with mud, his plume draggled with wet, the herald stood in the presence of Sir Thomas, and passionately complained of the danger and insult to which the queen's messenger had been exposed. Wyatt protested his innocence, and summoned his establishment together that the culprit might be discovered. The herald at once challenged the offender. "Alas!" said Sir Thomas, "he is a mere natural, as will appear, if you examine him." "Why, sirrah," asked the herald, "did you direct me to come over where it was hard to pass without drowning?" "The ducks came over not long before you," replied the fellow, "and their legs, I wot, were shorter than your horse's." Angry as the herald was, the joke was too racy of English soil at that time not to obtain pardon; he only smiled, and said, "Sir Thomas, hereafter let your fool wear the badge of his profession that he may deceive no more in this kind." The whole stern battlements of English history at this period are starred and dotted with rough flowers of this kind, peeping out between the loopholes behind which the armor gleams, and smiling in crannies under the scaffold and below the headsman's stroke. It is among Mr. Froude's subordinate, but real, claims to be a faithful exponent of the period, that he can recall the peculiar coloring of the lichens and wall-flowers as well as the massive framework of the building itself. The perusal of such sections as "Philip's Virtues," "The Wet Ride to Winchester," and "The Hot Gospeller," will prove that the praise which we accord is not beyond the truth.

We have now examined the chief accusations of Mr. Froude's severest critic, and given some analysis of the salient points in his recent volumes. On the whole, our conclusion must be, that while his narrative might be smoother, better joined, and more naturally continuous—and while his style is occasionally careless and redundant—these blemishes are more than atoned for by his peculiar capacity of hitting off the smallest lines of individual character; by his intense moral earnestness; by the laborious accuracy, whose rough materials are fused into the white glow of his eloquence; by his power of sympathizing with various and apparently irreconcilable forms of opinion, and of throwing himself into the very spirit and effervescence of the age. That his tendencies are spiritual rather than material; that his modes of thought are those of the poet and ethical philosopher rather than of the political economist; that he is at the antipodes to Comte and the positive school must be admitted. But we are not sorry to escape from the icy, transcendental region of laws and abstractions into the warmer range, which is inhabited by men and women of like passions with ourselves. And the fact of belonging to the spiritual school of historians is surely no grave accusation against him who chronicles the era of the English Reformation—the spring-tide of England's intellectual and religious new birth; the battle-field of contending principles; the age of bold doers, bolder thinkers, and sufferers bolder again than either.

The great moral lesson which these volumes contain is, we think, of a semi-theological character. It is that which has been expressed by Wordsworth—

> "High and low,
> Watchwords of party on all tongues are rife;
> As if a Church, though sprung from Heaven must owe
> To opposites and fierce extremes her life:
> Not to the golden means and quiet flow
> Of truths that soften hatred, temper strife."

An appearance of rushing wildly into extremes, with a deep, powerful undercurrent running quietly against this apparent tendency, and gradually overbearing it and sucking it down, is one great lesson of church history in England. So was it at the Revolution and at the Restoration—so is it with the Evangelical and Church revivals—so is it now—so was it on the accession of Mary—so again at her death. One great characteristic of our Church—and her characteristic it must remain, if she is to represent the life of this great people—is the comprehensiveness of her toleration. When she was but a small sapling the word was carved upon her rind by the strong hands of Ridley and Cranmer, and the letters have grown and lengthened upon the bark of the majestic tree, beneath whose shadow the nation reposes. Can it be otherwise with a church from whose lay members no other test seems to be exacted than the apostles' creed; while the Articles which her ministers are required to sign are (whatever Mr. Froude may please to say) framed to embrace rather than to exclude. Sneered at as a "compromise," taunted with "the stammering lips of her ambiguous formularies," wanting, as she is, in the cast-iron precision of the dogmas of Trent, and in the dogmatic narrowness of some of the reformed communions, she has yet the modesty of truth and the moderation of wisdom. As the Constitution of England is based upon the harmonious interworking of two opposite principles, the principle of order and the principle of freedom—without the former of which there would be a perpetuation of antiquated abuses, without the latter, no bulwark against the mutations of ignorant caprice—so in the Established Church, we find two classes of men mainly influenced by one or the other. Since the Reformation the representatives of these two principles have existed within her bosom. Occasionally they have come into fierce collision; occasionally one or other has stepped over the line of demarcation. The conciliation of these opposite tendencies may not appear to be going on now with a very accelerated pace; yet we may hope that practically impossible schemes of conciliation from without are soon to be exchanged for efforts after union within. Let men remember that the mountains must be of different outlines and of varying hues, but it is the one light of heaven which streams upon their uplifted brows.

A yet higher lesson, with which we conclude our notice, is eloquently taught. The Church could only be purified by her Lord's way of suffering. The iron bar, however massive, has a tendency to *crystallize* in severe frost, when it snaps and crumbles at a touch. Prosperity is the time of the Church's *crystallization*; but if the bar be removed, heated, and made incandescent in the furnace, it is restored to its original strength. So was the Church strengthened by her plunge into the fiery furnace of martyrdom. It is the highest merit of Mr. Froude's work that it shows us, walking among our faithful witnesses, a form like the Son of God.

VULGAR APPLAUSE.—"Praise is the reflection of virtue, but it is as the glass or body which giveth the reflection; if it be from the common people, it is commonly false and naught, and rather followeth vain persons than virtuous: for the common people understand not many excellent virtues: the lowest virtues draw praise from them; the middle virtues work in them astonishment or admiration; but of the highest virtues they have no sense or perceiving at all; but shows and species virtutibus similes serve best with them. Certainly fame is like a river that beareth up things light and swollen, and drowns things weighty and solid; but if persons of quality and judgment concur, then it is (as the Scripture saith) a good name is like sweet smelling ointment; it filleth all round about, and will not easily away."—*Bacon.*

STYLE.—"A man with a clear head, a good heart, and an honest understanding, will always write well; it is owing either to a muddy head, an evil heart, or a sophisticated intellect, that men write badly, and sin either against reason, or goodness, or sincerity. There may be secrets in painting, but there are none in style. When I have been asked the foolish question, what a young man should do who wishes to acquire a good style, my answer has been, that he should never think about it, but say what he has to say as perspicuously as he can, and as briefly as he can, and then the style will take care of itself.' —*Southey.*

A correspondent of the *Courier* aptly quotes the following lines in speaking of Mr. Bouligney, the Union representative from Louisiana:—

"faithful found
Among the faithless, faithful only he,—
Among innumerable false, unmoved,
Unshaken, unseduced, unterrified,
His loyalty he kept, his love, his zeal;
Nor number, nor example, with him wrought,
To swerve from truth, or change his constant
mind,
Though single."

From The Saturday Review.

LIFE OF MRS. EMILY C. JUDSON.*

We little thought, when a recent discussion in these pages on the moral philosophy of love-making was printed, that we should so soon have an opportunity of studying a case in point, and of discovering that after all it was quite possible to reconcile the mundane and the supersensual views both of the theory and practice of erotics. We now find out that the misletoe bough and "the plain Christian" are by no means so incongruous as might be supposed. We have before us what, in these days, is called a life-history which shows that it is possible for a young woman to be of the most gushing and susceptible nature, pecking at the waxy berries of the pleasant parasite which rains kisses, and at the same time quite ready, "when a Christian gentleman offers her his heart and home," to whisk off with him from New York to India, though he is fifty-seven, and a strict Baptist minister, who has already buried two wives. What we said was that eclecticism was the right thing; and as principles are best tested by extreme cases, the argument is a good one which is supported by the practical example of Mrs. Emily C. Judson. If we wanted a single sentence in which to describe the fair Emily's character, it would be afforded in the couplet in which Pope gives the last touch to his Narcissa:—

"A very heathen in her carnal part,
Yet still a sad, good Christian at her heart."

Miss Emily Chubbuck, subsequently the third wife of Dr. Judson, who attained a considerable name as a Baptist missionary in Burmah, was the daughter of poor cottagers, and born in 1817, at Eaton, in the State of New York. The record of her early life is extremely interesting, not only as displaying the energy of a seriously active mind—a sort of Americanized Charlotte Brontë,—but as illustrating the strange character of American institutions. If we could fancy Currer Bell divested of nine-tenths of her intellect, and glazed over with a superficial vanity and sentimentalism, we should understand what Fanny Forester (the literary name of Miss Emily Chubbuck) was like.

* *The Life and Letters of Mrs. Emily C. Judson.* By A. C. Kendrick, Professor of Greek literature in the University of Rochester, United States. London: Nelson and Sons. 1861.

Fanny Forester, however, was only the butterfly stage of Mrs. Judson. It was at the ripe age of seventeen that she emerged from the chrysalis of Emily Chubbuck into this alliterative soubriquet. The poor child's earlier history is very curious. Before she had completed her fifteenth year she had been a factory girl and a farm help. At the age of thirteen she asked the prayers of all the meetings for her conversion, although she believed that "she had acquired a hope in Christ when she was eight years old;" and then she took "lessons in rhetoric and natural philosophy of Miss L. W. F.," "who introduced her to the study of Gibbon, Hume, Voltaire, and Tom Paine." She became mistress of four several schools, which, as might have been expected, she shut up in succession,—was dipped, and acted as teacher or mistress in seven other schools,—"scattered abroad many gems of beautiful thought," that is to say, wrote about three hundred weight of nonsense verses,—and in her twenty-third year was admitted as a sort of pupil teacher in a tremendous "educational establishment," the Utica Female Seminary, of which Miss Urania Sheldon was the principal, Miss Cynthia having charge of the "executive and financial departments," which we suppose is the American for mending the stockings and making out the bills. In this temple of the Muses, Emily was at last at home; and it is the counterpart to Miss Brontë's Belgian domicile. Here, chiefly for the sake of getting new clothes (for she taught for her board), Miss Chubbuck began to write children's books, most of which seem to have been failures, and of which a considerable stock, in the shape of unsalable MS., of prose and verse, remained on hand. An accidental visit to New York, in 1843, fired the train of fame. The sight of certain smart bonnets and pretty gowns in Broadway so inspired the sacred flame of acquisitiveness and authorship, that the fair Emily offered herself—that is, her literary self—for sale to Mr. N. P. Willis, editor of the *Mirror*, in the following letter, which is too good to be lost, for it is not often that one gets a specimen of what the Greek professor who is Miss Chubbuck's biographer is pleased to call "the wantoning of this *naive* and unsophisticated child of nature in the creations of a genius that was just revealing itself to her virgin consciousness:"—

"*To the Editor, etc.*,—You know the shops in Broadway are very tempting this spring. *Such* beautiful things! Well, you know (no, you don't know that, but you can guess) what a delightful thing it would be to appear in one of those charming, head-adorning, complexion-softening, hard-feature-subduing neapolitans; with a little gossamer veil dropping daintily on the shoulder of one of those exquisite *balzarines*, to be seen any day at Stewart's and elsewhere. Well, you know (this you *must* know) that shopkeepers have the impertinence to demand a trifling exchange for these things, even of a lady; and also that some people have a remarkably small purse, and a remarkably small portion of the yellow 'root' in that. And now, to bring the matter home, *I* am one of that class. I have the most beautiful little purse in the world, but it is only kept for show: I even find myself under the necessity of counterfeiting—that is, filling the void with tissue-paper in lieu of banknotes, preparatory to a shopping expedition.

"Well, now to the point. As Bel and I snuggled down on the sofa this morning to read the *New Mirror* (by the way, Cousin Bel is never obliged to put tissue-paper in her purse), it struck us that you would be a friend in need and give good counsel in this emergency. Bel, however, insisted on my not telling what I wanted the money for. She even thought that I had better intimate orphanage, extreme suffering from the bursting of some speculative bubble, illness, etc., etc.; but did not I know you better? Have I read the *New Mirror* so much (to say nothing of the graceful things coined 'under a bridge,' and a thousand other pages flung from the inner heart), and not learned who has an eye for every thing pretty? Not so stupid, Cousin Bel; no, no!

"However, this is not quite the point, after all; but here it is. I have a pen—not a gold one, I don't think I could write with that, but a nice, little, feather-tipped pen, that rests in the curve of my finger as contentedly as in its former pillow of down. (Shocking! how that line did run down hill! and this almost as crooked! dear me!) Then I have little messengers racing 'like mad' through the galleries of my head, spinning long yarns, and weaving fabrics rich and soft as the balzarine which I so much covet, until I shut my eyes and stop my ears, and whisk away, with the 'wonderful lamp' safely hidden in my own brown braids. Then I have Dr. Johnson's Dictionary—capital London edition, etc., etc.; and after I use up all the words in that, I will supply myself with Webster's wondrous quarto, appendix and all. Thus prepared, think you not I should be able to put something in the shops of the literary caterers? something that, for once in my life, would give me a real errand into Broadway? Maybe you of the *New Mirror* PAY for acceptable articles—maybe not. *Comprenez-vous?*

"Oh, I *do* hope that beautiful balzarine like Bel's will not be gone before another Saturday! You will not forget to answer me in the next *Mirror*; but pray, my dear editor, let it be done very cautiously, for Bel would pout all day if she should know what I have written. Till Saturday,

"Your anxiously waiting friend,

"FANNY FORESTER."

To which Mr. N. P. Willis, Editor, etc., gallantly replies:—

"Well, we give in! On *condition* that you are under twenty-five, and that you will wear a rose (recognizably) in your boddice the first time you appear in Broadway with the hat and balzarine, we will pay the bills. Write us thereafter a sketch of Bel and yourself, as cleverly done as this letter, and you may 'snuggle down' on the sofa, and consider us paid, and the public charmed with you."

The progress of this literary amour illustrates Mr. N. P. Willis' tact and discrimination. He accepted the playful frolic of the pretty kitten, but declined to pay for her frisking. The fair Fanny was to be made famous, but only by Mr. Willis' praise. The coin that was current in the *Mirror* was only flattery. However, the arrangement was successful. Fanny Forrester became famous, as fame goes in New York, and was, in the judgment of literary America, bracketed with Mr. Willis' sister, whom he had contrived to puff into some sort of similar notoriety as Fanny Fern.

From the few specimens of Miss Chubbuck's genius which are furnished in this volume, we should say that Fanny Forester was a silly, flippant, empty-headed person, of the calibre of the Della Crusca celebrities who were put down by Gifford in the beginning of the century. In much the same way Mr. Willis goes on "glorifying his new-found star," till Fanny gets all sorts of "literary engagements" at piece work, which enable her to indulge in all sorts of bonnets. Meanwhile, though, as we are assured, the editor and contributor had not at present met, the literary flirtation between the two goes on till the following enigmatical passage occurs in the correspondence. It is from the gentleman editor:—

"I am writing while 'proofs' are coming—interruptedly and carelessly, of course. I was pleased and displeased at ——'s changing her opinion of me—displeased at the suspicion that my *inner-self* had ever committed its purity to the world, or had ever been on trial in a pure mind. My dear friend, you know, though you have never perilled your *outer* mind by laying it open to all comers, that there is an inner sanctuary of God's lighting which brightens as the world is shut out, and which would never suffer profanation. It is in this chamber of my better nature that you are thought of—but I have no time to explain.

"The pain that you are suffering from the *exposure of fame* is a chrysalis of thought. You will be brighter for it, though the accustomed shroud of seclusion comes off painfully."

For eighteen months "the chrysalis of thought was shedding its shroud;" or, in the language of common sense, Miss Emily Chubbuck was writing innumerable trashy articles in all sorts of trashy magazines and newspapers, which brought in a few hundred dollars. A selection of her writings was at last published under the fantastic title of *Trippings in Authorland.* At this time, to use the sonorous language of her biographer, "The glittering bow of promise, fame, arched the heaven of our literary neophyte." We are told that "in little more than one short year, Fanny Forester achieved a permanent shining-place in the clustering firmament of genius." But in what we have seen of them, we see very little indeed of the strict Baptist. Even her admirers admit that in her literary culmination "never had heaven receded into so dim a distance, and the powers of the world to come held so feeble possession of her soul." It was at this period that she at last made the personal acquaintance of her friend and patron, Mr. N. P. Willis, who at the moment became a widower. To the disconsolate and bereaved one the fair Fanny, now twenty-eight years of age, addressed a letter, which unfortunately is not extant, but whatever its hints might have been, it was replied to in the following choice epistle:—

"You ask me whether you shall marry for convenience. Most decidedly, no. What convenience would pay you for passing eighteen hours out of every twenty-four, for the rest of your life, within four walls, in company with a person not to your taste? I judge of you by myself. I would not pass one year thus for any fortune on earth. The private hours of one single month are too precious for any price but love. Think how little of the day poverty can touch, after all. Only the hours when you are out of your chamber. But the moment your chamber door is shut on you alone, all comparison between you and the richest is at an end. Let the majority of women marry for convenience if they will; but *you* are brimful of romance and delicacy and tenderness; and a marriage without love for you would be sealing up a volcano with a cobweb. You must love—you *must* and *will* love passionately and overpoweringly. You have as yet turned but one leaf in a volume of your heart's life. Your bosom is an altar on which there is a fire newly lit—lit by the late and sudden awakening of your genius. Your peculiarity is that your genius has its altar on your heart, and not like other people's in the brain. Take care how you throw away the entire music and beauty of a life for only a home that will grow hateful to you. I warn you that you *must* love sooner or later."

From this we gather that Fanny Forester had no particular objection to change her name, though it does not appear that Mr. Willis was disposed to assist on the occasion. But the hour and the man were approaching. "Providence had in store for her a different destiny." The distinguished author of *Pencillings by the Way* and the lovely authoress of *Trippings in Authorland* were not to come together in closer bonds than those of literary flirtation and epistolary coquetry. The plain Christian was "at hand in the person of the Rev. Dr. Judson," "a veteran hero of the Cross," who "had been obliged to leave India by the alarming illness of his wife—the lovely widow of the sainted Missionary Boardman." She died upon the passage; and after an absence of twenty-four years, the great Baptist missionary trod his native shores. Besides his duties to the Church, the Rev. Doctor had not been backward in cultivating the social and domestic relations. The lovely widow of the sainted Boardman had been the second matrimonial adventure of the hero of the Cross; but though fifty-seven, he was not yet converted to Dr. Primrose's views of monogamy. A slight railroad accident detained the reverend divine at a station where Fanny Forester's *Trippings* fell in his way. "The book is written with great beauty and power. Is the authoress a Baptist? I should like to know her." "Promptly, on the next day, he came over to Mr. J.'s. Emily was submitting to the not very poetical process of vaccination. As soon as it was over, Dr. Judson conducted her to the sofa, saying that he wished to talk with her. He discussed the *Trippings*. He wished to meet with a person to write the memoir of his departed wife. He named the subject to Emily. The consequences of the coming together of two persons respectively so fascinating were what has often occurred since the days of Adam and Eve."

Here we pause, and beg leave to suggest a doubt whether, since the days of Adam and Eve, any elderly widower of fifty-seven ever did engage a female to write the memoir of his second wife, and make her an offer on the spot. We quite agree with the hero of the Cross, "who finds in it a combination of circumstances which clearly mark supernatural agency." The "notion of her not only writing the life, but taking the place of the sainted deceased," no sooner presented itself to his "impassioned character," than he pressed the subject "with all the energy of his nature." The place of the lovely widow of the sainted Boardman must be filled up. Like the king of France, Mrs. Judson never dies. "It was not," as we are funnily told, "in Emily's nature to resist the force of such arguments from such a pleader, falling from lips wet with Castalian dews that descend upon the mountains of Zion"—a mixture which we are glad to hear of, because we should have suspected the influence of other spirits and water in such a case. The plain Christian had come, and Miss Emily Chubbuck, *alias* Fanny Forester, felt it to be her duty to accept this ardent suitor. The world laughed; the literary world of New York scoffed; and the religious world of Boston stood aghast. Here is the form in which the "plain Christian" makes his offer. Mrs. Judson's biographer says, "that it is half like a sacrilege to lift the veil upon a thing so sacred as a marriage proposal," and most people would agree with him; but when he goes on to remark, that "this interweaves so ingenious and graceful a memorial of his former wives, and illustrates so admirably the delicate playfulness of Dr. Judson's character," we accept his reason, though we own that we could not quite forget a somewhat similar marriage present made by Bluebeard to his succession of spouses:—

"I hand you, dearest one, a charmed watch. It always comes back to me, and brings its wearer with it. I gave it to Ann, when an hemisphere divided us, and it brought her safely and surely to my arms. I gave it to Sarah during her husband's lifetime (not then aware of the secret), and the charm, though slow in its operation was true at last.

"Were it not for the sweet sympathies you have kindly extended to me, and the blessed understanding that 'love has taught us to guess at,' I should not venture to pray you to accept my present with such an note. Should you cease to 'guess,' and toss back the article, saying, 'Your watch has lost its charm; it comes back to you, *but brings not its wearer with it*'—oh, first dash it to pieces, that it may be an emblem of what will remain of the heart of

"Your devoted, A. JUDSON."

We must say, that if a plain Christian always comes in this epigrammatic form, he comes in a very nice way; though it is very odd that Dr. Judson made "Sarah" an offer during her husband's lifetime. One of two things must be certain—either that it is the custom of Baptist missionaries to make love to their brother missionaries' wives, or, as seems to have been the case with Mr. and Mrs. Boardman, that they sometimes keep their marriage secret. Is this the case—and was it done for the sake of the scriptural example, Dr. Judson playing Abimelech to Mr. Boardman's Abraham? To turn to the plain Christian's offer of his heart and hand. We much doubt whether, in the way of a love-letter, an old boy of fifty-seven does not beat the conceited puppies of twenty-five. At any rate, amongst all the *Lettres Edifiantes et Curieuses* which missionaries have ever published, Dr. Judson's are not the least amusing. The couple were married; Fanny Forester became Emily Judson; and the surprise was, that "he who had been the husband of Ann Stephenson and Sarah Boardman should take as the successor to that sainted pair" a young woman figuring only as a magazine-writer, of very doubtful religious principles, and of no social position. All that we can say is, that when a plain Christian comes with lips rendered humid by the remarkable half-and-half in which Dr. Judson indulged, literary ladies must surrender at discretion or indiscretion. It is enough to add that Emily survived the husband of three wives, and has had her own "life-story" written by a Greek professor.

THE WORLD'S LAST HOPE.

'Tis gone! the glorious dream is past,
The work by sages wrought undone,
The brightest trophy, and the last,
In Freedom's cause, by patriot's won.

In vain have warriors toiled and bled,
And statesmen schemed the work to rear;
In vain the counsels of the dead,
Their country has no ear to hear.

Beneath their rule unceasingly
The forest fell, the valley glowed
With golden sheaves—from sea to sea
The land with milk and honey flowed.

Peace reigned supreme—on every hand
The miracles of art were wrought,
And countless sails from every strand,
The hourly gifts of commerce brought.

Secure abroad, at home, around,
With naught their growing strength to mar,
Like exhalations from the ground,
State rose on State, and star on star.

'Tis lost! On Europe's troubled shore,
With arms outstretched and eager eyes,
The wronged and helpless watch no more
The light of hope in western skies.

The despot, with his marshalled host,
Exults and points with scornful cry,
Where hopelessly the pride and boast
Of Freedom's cause in fragments lie.

'Tis gone! but curst the lips that spoke
The baleful words of hate and strife,
The selfish aims and acts that broke
The mystic tie—a nation's life.

Hard as their granite hills, and cold
Their hearts, as icy pools that feed
Their thirst for gain, and only bold
When onward urged by endless greed.

The vampires of the State that steal
Its blood—the teachers that alone
The pricks and stings of conscience feel
For others—easy with their own.

Prompt to parade, in speech and song,
Their claims to truth and warlike feat—
Their truth, a creed of crime and wrong,
Their boasted battle, a defeat.*

Accursed! Yes—in States unborn,
The specious plea of falsehood vain,
The millions with indignant scorn,
Shall brand them with the mark of Cain.

They talk of arms!—their open hate
For treacherous love we gladly hear,
The threatened war we calmly wait—
Their friendship is the foe we fear.

—*Charleston Courier.*

* The Puritan creed and practice bore no nearer relation to Christian love and charity than the battle of Bunker Hill to a great victory.

JACK'S VALENTINE.

BY FITZ-JAMES O'BRIEN.

Ah! Maggie, would that I could send
To you some sweet and tender line,
To tell you that your sailor lad
Still claims you for his valentine.

But all around is lonesome sea;
The unseen fingers of the wind
Clutch at the ropes and tear the sails
And heap the billowy hills behind.

Yet watching on the dismal deck,
Through midnight hours so drear and black,
My heart still sings its valentine,
But who will bear the message back?

Clouds scudding by the watery moon,
Go bless her cottage from above,
And shed from high in mystic dews
This lonely utterance of my love!

And you, dark ocean, myriad-tongued,
Wave following wave with ceaseless beat,
Seek you the beach she walks at eve,
And lay my message at her feet.

Fly, white-winged sea-bird, following fast,
That dips around our foamy wake,
Go nestle in her virgin breast,
And kiss her pure lips for my sake!

Winds howling through the shapeless night,
Unkennelled hounds that hunt the sea,
Hush your hoarse voices to a song,
And sing the love that lives in me.

Tell her, ye all through midnight dark,
In heat and cold, through storm or shine,
The sun-burned, honest sailor lad
Still thinks about his valentine.

—*Knickerbocker.*

NOW, AND THEN.

Birds are singing on bush and tree,
Singing a thousand loves and joys;
Once, it was music sweet to me,
Now, it seemeth only noise.
Ah! life's music fled with him!

Roses are blooming—once they were
Fairest of wonders that Nature weaves;
Now, their perfume makes faint the air,
And, to me, they are just—red leaves.
Ah! life's beauty faded with him!

Daylight dies, and the stars arise,
Not as of old with hope-giving light;
Then, they looked loving, like human eyes,
Now, they are pitiless, cold, and bright.
Ah! the brightest star has set!

Anna Hagedon.

—*Once a Week.*

THE LIVING AGE.

No. 882.—27 April, 1861.

CONTENTS.

PUBLISHED EVERY SATURDAY BY

LITTELL, SON, & CO., BOSTON.

In the Table of Contents, the political articles take up much room, but they are short, not averaging two pages each. We have not included in this calculation, the answer to the article entitled "Secession from another Point of View," copied from the *Examiner*, into No. 875. This answer is written by a Virginian now of Philadelphia, and extensively engaged in manufactures. He exposes some of the errors of fact and inference into which Mr. Cowell has fallen; and shows the great changes which have taken place since the visit of that gentleman to this country. A part of the answer may serve as a good refutation of what was called "The Forty Bale Theory." This was an odd notion of Mr. McDuffie's, which was extensively believed in South Carolina, and has had much to do with creating "dissatisfaction." At the time he wrote, the average rate of the tariff was, or he assumed it to be, forty per cent. Then it was found that the exportation of cotton was equal to all our importations from abroad. And the next step in the argument was to say, that the forty per cent on importations was a tax on the South equal to forty bales in each hundred of her cotton crop. Now if the whole of the importations, had been consumed in the South, this would have been correct. But in truth only a small part was so consumed. Perhaps a tenth or a fifth.

The South sells cotton to the Northern merchants—and gets pay for it in a large assortment of articles. A small part [illegible] European goods; a larger part in domestic manufactures of cotton, wool, iron [illegible] large amount in wheat, flour, Indian corn and meal, hay, pork, West India goods, Chinese tea and silks. The Western merchant buys a bonnet for his wife of the Northern dealer; and the latter asks him to send in payment, some hams down the Mississippi to the cotton planter, to whom the Northern dealer is in debt for some cotton. In fact, we believe the hams are often sent before the cotton is shipped. Probably the bonnet goes first, then the hams, and lastly the cotton. But the order of events is not material.

We are glad to see that in the writer's opinion: "If this tariff shall be found to have greatly increased the duties, this will no doubt be corrected." We fear it will prove a misfortune that so great a change should have been made at this inauspicious time; an experiment which we deprecated in advance. We already discover that it has lessened the sympathy of Europe for the United States, at a time when that good-will is especially important. It may prove a weak point in our controversy with the "confederates."

Alterations in the trade of a nation should be made with great caution, and be spread over a considerable course of time. This tariff was made up in haste, perhaps without expectation of its being passed so soon. As it is now the law, we must make the best use of it we can, and endeavor to modify it as time and experience shall make its faults apparent. So far as a tariff is to be "protective," it can only be *permanent* by being *moderate*. And without permanence it does no good to our manufacturers.

So far as we have heard, the cotton manufacturers in New England desired no change. They were in full prosperity under the more moderate tariff, and are wise enough to "let well alone."

It has been said that the new scale does not so much raise duties by a higher rate, as by preventing fraud. While it is certainly very desirable that this should be done, the comparative extent of the duty must be measured by the actual increase of payment. And if this statement about falsification of invoices is true, it had been good policy to lower the nominal rate, so that the actual payment should have been very little increased.

SUNSET.

BY THE ART-GOSSIP MAN OF THE "HERALD."

Behold! as Phœbus, with his car,
  Into the earth goes down,
How chromotyped his features are
  With mellow Cobalt Brown!

Oh! mark the saffron-purple sky,
  The Cadmium sapphire pool!
In mackerelescence bathed, they lie—
  Oh! my, how beautiful!

The quintessential bars that streak
  With Solferino Red,
Yon pyrotechnic mountain peak,
  Shed perfumes on my head.

The radiant shadows on the rock
  Each other, swift, pursue
In mad career, as if to mock
  The force of Madder Blue.

The topazescent clouds that glance
  Athwart the festive sky,
And by the woofy margins dance
  Are green—and so am I.

—*Vanity Fair.*

From Bentley's Miscellany.

OF STORM-BREWING, AND SKYEY INFLUENCES.

WAS there ever, I wonder, a novel written without a thunder-storm in it? A novel without a hero we have all heard of; but where is there a novel without tempest or hurricane?

Fictions just a few there may be, with this minus sign,—but then they are, depend upon it, of the dullest of domestically dull drab patterns,—without plot, or movement, or any such thing. Unless, indeed, they be the productions of that rare genius which can excite and sustain interest by the delineation of character alone.

It is half sublime, half ridiculous, to observe the everlasting recurrence of a thunder-storm, whensoever the novelist has occasion for a crisis or a catastrophe. He, with consummate ease and assurance, brings heaven and earth together to make two lovers happy, or the reverse. He gets up a tempest, regardless of expense in fire and water, to rescue his hero in the nick of time. He brews a storm, at a moment's notice, wherewith to whirl his arch-villain into present perdition. Whenever his ravelled skein of incidents is becoming knotted into Gordian complexity,—as soon as, or a little sooner than, the *nodus* appears to be really *vindice dignus*,—immediately the solution is evoked *deus interest*, in the lurid advent of a storm. Sometimes, however, a good smart pelting shower will serve his turn.

Not that this system of wholesale brewing is the monopoly of novelists by profession. Poets and playwrights go shares with them in the business. Epics and tragedies divide the profits with them. We might commence a series of illustrations long prior to Virgil and his—

> "Interea magno misceri murmure cœlum
> Incipit; insequitur commixtâ grandine nimbus,*

—on the day so critical to Dido and Æneas, when torrents poured down the hills, and the conscious air flashed with lights, and resounded with sobbing wails. But *passons au* (or rather *from* that) *deluge*, and, instead of beginning at the beginning, and submerging ourselves in the antediluvian times, or paulo-post-diluvian, let us take cursory note, here and there, of some more modern instances, to exemplify our theme.

* Æneidos, l. iv.

A gentle knight was pricking on the plain, who bore upon his breast a bloody cross, and a lovely lady rode him fair beside,—even thus opens, not one of Mr. James' novels, but Spenser's Faerie Queene; and before we have got through the sixth stanza of that first canto, the poet finds or forges occasion for nothing less than a "hideous storm of rain," threatening to wash out the colors of the Red Cross Knight.

> "Thus as they past,
> The day with clouds was sudden overcast,
> And angry Jove an hideous storm of rain
> Did pour into his leman's lap so fast,
> That every wight to shroud it did constrain;
> And this fair couple eke to shroud themselves were fain."*

No parallel passage to the Virgilian pairing off, however; but only a good drenching shower, and there an end. Contrast with so mild an effusion that storm-scene in the Temptation in the wilderness, of Milton's painting,—when either tropic

> "'Gan thunder, and both ends of heaven; the clouds,
> From many a horrid rift, abortive poured
> Fierce rain with lightning mixed, water with fire
> In ruin reconciled: nor slept the winds
> Within their stormy caves, but rush'd abroad
> From the four hinges of the world, and fell
> On the vexed wilderness, whose tallest pines,
> Though rooted deep as high, and sturdiest oaks,
> Bow'd their stiff necks, loaden with stormy blasts
> Or torn up sheer." †

Or, with the piled-up horrors of Lear's midnight wanderings—when we see the discrowned king, unbonneted too, contending with the fretful element, and tearing his white hair, "which the impetuous blasts, with eyeless rage, catch in their fury, and make nothing of"—striving to outscorn the to-and-fro conflicting wind and rain.

> "This night, wherein the cub-drawn bear would couch,
> The lion and the belly-pinchèd wolf
> Keep their fur dry, unbonneted he runs,
> And bids what will take all. ‡

The winds may blow, and crack their cheeks, for him,—cataracts and hurricanes spout, till they have drenched the steeples all around; lightnings "sulphurous and thought-executing," "vaunt couriers to oak-cleaving thunderbolts," are welcome to singe his white

* Faerie Queene, c. i. st. 6.
† Paradise Regained, b. 4.
‡ King Lear, Act III. Sc. 1.

head, and "all-shaking thunder" he bids, in his frenzied appeal, "strike flat the thick rotundity of the world," and annihilate the race of man. Lear taxes not the elements with unkindness: he never gave *them* kingdom, called *them* children; *they* owe him no obedience; so he bids them let fall their horrible pleasure on him their slave,—a poor, infirm, weak, and despised old man. And yet he calls them servile ministers, that have with two pernicious daughters joined their "high engendered battles, 'gainst a head so old and white," as his. Leal-hearted Kent bears record that since he has been man, "such sheets of fire, such bursts of horrid thunder, such groans of roaring wind and rain," he never remembers to have heard,—yet in vain implores his distracted master to seek a covert from the storm. Alack, bareheaded the houseless king bows to the "dreadful pother" o'er his head, and moralizes on trembling guilt and quaking crime, that "cry these dreadful summoners grace." Lear's wits are not turned yet; but, consciously (appalling consciousness!), they begin to turn now. What intensity of indignant pathos in Gloster's reproach of Regan, describing her father's outcast fate:—

"The sea, with such a storm as his bare head
In hell-black night endured, would have buoyed up,
And quenched the stellèd fires: yet, poor old heart,
He holp the heavens to rain.
If wolves had at thy gate howled that stern time,
Thou should'st have said, good porter, turn the key."

Of which fine stroke there is a fine paraphrase, later in the tragedy, when Cordelia exclaims:—

"Was this a face
To be exposed against the warring winds?
To stand against the deep dread-bolted thunder?
. . . Mine enemy's dog,
Though he had bit me, should have stood that night
Against my fire." *

There is no such storm in the wide, wide world of books, as that.

Other storms there are, however, of Shakspeare's brewing, not without their awe and grandeur. There is that in the "Winter's Tale,"† when the old shepherd finds babe Perdita on the sea-shore, just after Antigonus has left her with his—

"——Farewell!
The day frowns more and more; thou art like to have
A lullaby too rough: I never saw
The heavens so dim by day."

There is that, again, on the eve of Cæsar's death, when the conspirators are arranging their last plans—when Casca, out of breath, and wild-eyed, and sword in hand, being questioned by Cicero, in the public street, what all this may mean, replies, amid peals and flashes overhead,—

"Are you not moved, when all the sway of earth
Shakes, like a thing infirm? O Cicero,
I have seen tempests, when the scolding winds
Have rived the knotty oaks; and I have seen
The ambitious ocean swell, and rage, and foam,
To be exalted with the threat'ning clouds:
But never till to-night, never till now,
Did I go through a tempest dropping fire.
Either there is a civil strife in heaven;
Or else the world, too saucy with the gods,
Incenses them to send destruction." *

Cassius, as accords with his creed, or no creed, may make a merit of baring his bosom to the thunder-stone, and, when the cross blue lightning seems to open the breast of heaven, present himself "even in the very aim and flash of it;"—but Casca, who never knew the heavens menace so, is otherwise minded, and thinks it the part of men to fear and tremble, "when the most mighty gods, by tokens, send such dreadful heralds to astonish us." On such a night is Brutus summoned by anonymous appeals to awake, speak, strike, redress; and these letters he needs no taper to read at midnight:—

"The exhalations, whizzing in the air,
Give so much light, that I may read by them."†

Then again there is the opening scene of "Macbeth," devoted to that unhallowed congress of weird sisters, in thunder, lightning, and in rain. And another opening scene there is in a play to which the Tempest of that prologue gives its very name, as well as determines its plot.

The third act of Ben Jonson's "Catiline" closes, and the fourth commences, amid the

* King Lear, Act III. Sc. 2 and 7; Act IV. Sc. 7.
† Act III. Sc. 1.

* Julius Cæsar, Act I. Sc. 3.
† Act II. Sc. I.

crash and glare of Heaven's artillery. Into a street at the foot of the capitol, "Enter the Allobrogian Ambassadors. Divers senators pass by them," after the stage direction, "quaking and trembling." Whereupon one of the envoys disdainfully remarks:

> "Of all that pass, I do not see a face
> Worthy a man; that dares look up and stand
> One thunder out; but downward all, like beasts,
> Running away from every flash is made." *

Cato and Catulus, meanwhile, adopt a more reverent reading of the storm, believing that the "good heavens and just" are even now urging their anger against the sins of Catiline and his crew, and are telling guilty men what powers are above them; for, "in such a confidence of wickedness, 'twas time they should know something fit to fear." But to fear nothing is a practical maxim with Catiline and his crew.

Dryden gets up a tolerable bit of sea storm in his "Cymon and Iphigenia,"—where the transmuted lover is steering to Candy with his conquered prey, and all at once the winds arise, the thunders roll, the forky lightnings play, and the giddy ship labors and creaks in dread extremity—whereby is made to hang a new crisis in the tale.

Cowper evokes a storm, expressly to smite young Misagathus, "atheist in ostent."

> "A storm was near,
> An unsuspected storm. His hour was come.
> The impious challenger of power divine
> Was now to learn, that Heaven, though slow to wrath,
> Is never with impunity defied." †

The Christian poet, we may be sure, bent as he was on vindicating eternal Providence, would have strenuously maintained, if questioned upon this episode, that never was a rule *Nisi*, in the law *Nec Deus intersit*, more properly taken and made use of, than here.

When Miss Sindall, in Mackenzie's tale, ‡ is taking flight from her persecutor, "'Twill be a dreadful night," remarks her humble companion ("for it began to rain, and the thunder rolled at a distance"). The storm is a bad one, accordingly, and makes Mr. Bolton lose his way, and thereby light on an important stranger. When Edie Ochiltree and Dousterswivel § have their strange rendesvous in the ruined priory, of course the night sets in stormy, with wind and occasional showers of rain. The bride of Lammermoor becomes Ravenswood's guest at Wolf's Crag in virtue of a lowering and gloomy sky—and anon the storm-cloud bursts over the castle, with "a peal so sudden and dreadful, that the old tower rocked to its foundation, and every inmate concluded it was falling upon them. . . . Whether the lightning had actually struck the castle, or whether through the violent concussion of the air, several heavy stones were hurled from the mouldering battlements into the roaring sea beneath." * It might seem as if the ancient founder of the castle were bestriding the thunder-storm, and proclaiming his displeasure at the reconciliation of his descendant with the enemy of his house.

Night closes around Mrs. Shelley's modern Prometheus † near the Alps—the darkness and storm increase every minute; the thunder bursts with a terrific crash over his head; vivid flashes of lightning dazzle his eyes—and presently one flash discovers to him, too plainly, the gigantic stature and the deformed aspect, "more hideous than belongs to humanity," of the "filthy dæmon" to whom he has given life. A later apparition ‡ of the fiend is similarly ushered in by a heavy storm—title-page as it were to a tragic volume.

As Lear on the deluged heath bids the "all-shaking thunder"—

> "Crack nature's moulds, all germens spill at once,
> That make ingrateful man,"

so does Schiller's fisherman in the storm-scene on the lake, bid them, in his fury of aggrieved patriotism,—

> "In the germ
> Destroy the generations yet unborn." §

How the wind whistles and the whirlpool roars! exclaims the fisher-boy; and his elder interprets the tempest to mean Heaven's wrath at the apple-archery doings, just come off in Gesler's presence—a special performance by command.

> "To level at the head of his own child!
> Never had father such command before.
> And shall not nature, rising in wild wrath,
> Revolt against the deed?"

* Catiline, IV. 1.
† The Task, book vi.
‡ The Man of the World, ch. xvi. sq.
§ The Antiquary, II. 4.

* The Bride of Lammermoor, II. 2.
† Frankinstein, ch. vii.
‡ Ibid, ch. xxiii.
§ Wilhelm Tell, IV. 1.

The stage directions for managing the storm, prefixed to this scene, are characteristically German.

The atmosphere was heavy, and masses of low black clouds were gathering in the horizon, when young Werther called on Charlotte, and thereby inaugurated his celebrated Sorrows. There is company, and a dance; * but the dance is not finished when the lightning becomes vivid, and the thunder is heard above the music, and the ladies' shrieks considerably above both. When, in after days, Werther tore himself from Charlotte, with an "adieu, forever!" be sure the night was dark and stormy—it rained and snowed. "He reached his own door about eleven. His servant perceived, as he entered the house, that he was without a hat, but did not venture to say any thing; and as he undressed his master, he found that his clothes were wet. His hat was found afterwards upon the point of a rock which overhangs the valley; and it is inconceivable how he could have climbed to the summit on such a dark, tempestuous night without losing his life." † But how could a young man of Werther's mettle leave the world, except amid attendant associations of bad weather —the harmonies of storm discords—one of nature's voluntaries or symphonies, to the manner born?

But among Germans, commend us to Klingemann, not only for magic-lantern transparencies, death's-heads, fire showers, plush cloaks, etc., ‡ but for thunder and lightning—the former well brewed, the latter equally well bottled. In him you find enough and to spare of "churchyard and chapel scenes, in the most tempestuous weather,"—which to those who like to be out in such, is as uncomfortably charming as bad taste could desire.

Adept at this sort of brewing as Herr Klingemann may have been, there is a non-dramatic writer of our own who is equally productive in the same trade, and whose tap is more to the mind of native consumers. A thirsty soul may drink his fill of Thomas Ingoldsby's storm-brewing. There is that night, that horrible night, in the Witches' Frolic ("folks ever afterwards said with affright, that they never had seen such a terrible sight"), when, after the sun had gone down fiery red, and left behind him a lurid track of blood-red light upon pitch-dark clouds,—

"There came a shrill and a whistling sound,
Above, beneath, beside, and around,
Yet leaf ne'er moved on tree! . . .
And then a hollow moaning blast
Came, sounding more dismally still than the last,
And the lightning flashed, and the thunder growled,
And louder and louder the tempest howled,
And the rain came down in such sheets as would stagger a
Bard for a simile short of Niagara." *

So in that German wedding scene, between Sir Rupert and Lurline, at the altar rails:—

"With a gracious air, and a smiling look,
Mess John had opened his awful book,
And had read so far as to ask if to wed he meant?
And if he knew any just cause or impediment?
When from base to turret the castle shook!
Then came a sound of a mighty rain
Dashing against each storied pane,
The wind blew loud,
And a coal-black cloud
O'ershadowed the church, and the party, and crowd;
How it could happen they could not divine,
The morning had been so remarkably fine! †

Then there are the haunted ruffians in the Drummer-boy legend, whose colloquy is thus interrupted, just as it becomes exciting on the topic of a ghost:—

"'A what?' returned Bill,—at that moment a flash
More than commonly awful preceded a crash
Like what's called in Kentucky 'an almighty smash.'—
And down Harry Waters went plump on his knees," etc. ‡

Or again there is that more imposing example in the wedding progress of Edith and Sir Alured:—

"Now it seems that the sky
Which had been of a dye
As bright and as blue as your lady-love's eye,
The season in fact being genial and dry,
Began to assume
An appearance of gloom
From the moment the knight began fidget and fume,
Which deepened and deepened till all the horizon

* The Sorrows of Werther, b. i.

† Ibid., b. ii.

‡ See Carlyle on German Playwrights. (1829.)

* Ingoldsby Legends: The Witches' Frolic.

† Sir Rupert the Fearless: A Legend of Germany.

‡ The Dead Drummer.

Grew blacker than aught they had ever set eyes
on,
And soon, from the far west, the elements rumbling,
Increased, and kept pace with Sir Alured's grumbling.
Bright flashes between,
Blue, red, and green,
All livid and lurid began to be seen;
At length down it came—a whole deluge of rain,
A perfect Niagara, drenching the plain,
And up came the reek,
And down came the shriek
Of the winds like a steam-whistle starting a train;
And the tempest began so to roar and to pour," *

that in short, consequences ensued too numerous and critical for present mention. After which specimens, instead of citing others in addition, let us admit the appropriateness of Mr. Barham's parenthesis, in another stormy wind and tempest legend,—

" You don't want me, however, to paint you a Storm,
As so many have done, and in colors so warm;
Lord Byron, for instance, in manner facetious,
Mr. Ainsworth, more gravely,—see also Lucretius." †

Else we might tell how the Dutch packet was overtaken, " with the sands called the Goodwin's a league on her lee "—and how, by degrees, " still rougher it grew, and still harder it blew, and the thunder kicked up such a halliballoo, that even the skipper began to look blue, while the crew, who were few, looked very queer, too, and seemed not to know what exactly to do,

" And they who'd the charge of them wrote in the logs,
' Wind N.E.—blows a hurricane—rains cats and dogs.'
In short it soon grew to a tempest as rude as
That Shakspeare describes near the still-vext Bermudas,
When the winds, in their sport,
Drove aside from its port
The king's ship, with the whole Neapolitan Court,
And swamped it to give ' the king's son, Ferdinand,' a
Soft moment or two with the Lady Miranda."

Of Ingoldsby's three exemplars in the art of storm-brewing, Lucretius we need say nothing about, so trite and hackneyed is become his now proverbial picture. Byron's splendid sea-piece in the " Don Juan " neither needs quotation, nor will bear abridgment. Mr. Ainsworth's example we presume to be that where Roland and Darrell struggle by night on the black flowing river —an elaborate description of what is said, historically, to have been the most disastrous hurricane that ever ravaged the city of London.

* A Lay of St. Romwold.
† The Bagman's Dog.

But our examples embrace a wider range than the Ingoldsby triad. Hardly a name of note but supplies a good rattling storm of its own particular brewing—nay, has them ready by the half-dozen or more. If you don't fancy one tap, try another: there's plenty to choose from. Treble X is to be had, for strong stomachs, and for others a sliding scale of qualities, descending to the smallest of small beer.

Dip—and that is, perhaps, about as much as the run of light readers can be expected to do—dip into Mr. Plumer Ward's " Tremaine," and even in that placid model of didactic fiction you will not escape storm-free. The author wants to get his heroine inside the house of a *noli me tangere* recluse, who will hold parley with nobody in the neighborhood. And how is an entrance to be made? By a thunder-shower, of course. Georgina, besides having lost her way, has just had the door slammed violently in her face. But no matter. The author's brewery is at work, and all will go well. " Georgina was now in a real dilemma, not at all lessened by the change in the sky, in which large and heavy clouds had been gathering, and were now ready to burst over her head in all the drenching force of a summer storm. At length a thunder-cloud broke with a dreadful crash, and the rain descending in a torrent which in one instant soaked both the lady and her groom through and through." * Again, therefore, she seeks admittance at the inhospitable cottage, and in that opportune thunder-cloud her Open Sesame is found.

By the same agency is Abel O'Hara, in John Banim's romance, made acquainted with the Nowlans. Black clouds gather over his head, lightning quivers, thunder crashes and bellows above and around, and a torrent of rain rushes down, that in a trice drenches him to the skin. " To proceed four or five miles further during such a storm, or even supposing it should pass off, in such a trim, was a madness against which my guide warmly remonstrated," † of course

* Tremaine, ch. lii.
† The Nowlans, ch. i.

with success, or where would the story of "The Nowlans" be, at all at all? And not only must the storm bring him to their house, but keep him there. So, when his clothes are restored as dry as chips, he buckles his Bramah again across his shoulder, and puts on a resolute face of departure; but the storm is more resolute than he; the sky frowns back his challenge; and his hosts assure him that, even should the thunder cease, there will not be a dry half-hour that day among the mountains. Another and worse storm,* with one "tremendous clap" in particular, is of essential service to a subsequent chapter of the tale.

So, too, when Mr. Carleton's Hanlon hurries to his appointment with Red Roddy, to secure the tobacco-box that will convict a murderer, it is through rain and wind, on a dark night, with lightning flashes from a funeral canopy of clouds, that he makes his way. The same night the murderer is watched by his daughter, visiting the murdered man's grave; and when he, for her and our convenience muttering his thoughts aloud, incidentally moots the query whether there *is* a Providence, the next sentence is an inevitable sequitur: "The words had barely proceeded out of his mouth, when a peal of thunder, astonishing loud, broke, as it were, over their very heads, having been preceded by a flash of lightning, so bright that the long, well-defined grave was exposed, in all its lonely horrors, to Sarah's eye."† *Post hoc, ergo propter hoc*, thinks the wild Irish girl to herself, not in Latin, but, by intuition, more pithily still.

Again in that powerful Irish story of Gerald Griffin's, which a popular dramatist has just made so familiar to playgoers by his adaptation of it as "The Colleen Bawn," it is a dreadful night on which Eily O'Connor leaves the cottage in the gap. Meanwhile there is a drinking party at Kyrle Daly's: the thunder clatters close overhead, the rain falls in torrents, and the reflection of the frequent lightning-flashes dance upon the glasses and bowl, round which the company are seated in the little parlor.‡

The wind roars amid the pines of the Boehmer Wald, and a furious blast shakes the casements of the Giant's Castle, on the night of the Consuelo's arrival—"the storm," says Count Albert, who ought to know, "drives a stranger to our castle."* A storm, during which the rain burst down in a sheeted cataract, and at once swells every half-visible rivulet among the mountains to a strong and turbid river, is made the medium of Anthelia's introduction to, and rescue by, Sir Oran Haut-ton.† A storm is raised to bring about the shipwreck that shall facilitate the finale of "My Uncle the Curate." Abruptly a storm is got up, to produce that scene on the lake, in which a sudden squall avails to convince Miss Ferrier's Edith‡ that she is as nothing to Sir Reginald, and that Florinda is all. And what else effects the dénouement of the Two Old Men's first Tale? One moment we see Lord Louis proudly and happily receiving the congratulations of his tenantry, on coming of age. "The next moment—a crash of thunder, loud, terrible, rattled through the sky, and one bright flash penetrated, for a second, the horrible gloom. One flash—and a cry, a universal cry, rent the air—Lord Louis! Lord Louis!—the thunderbolt had fallen—and struck him dead at his mother's feet."§ Far more impressively, though (or because) with less of spasmodic effect, is wrought out the dénouement of Galt's best novel,‖ in that memorable storm-scene off the north coast of Scotland.

The prodigy of the tempest at Bertram's shipwreck, in Maturin's tragedy, elicited not a few strictures from Coleridge,¶ on the management and meaning of it, as a mere supernatural effect, without even a hint of any supernatural agency,—it being possible, in fact, for every event and every scene of the play to have taken place just as well, if Bertram and his vessel had been driven by a common hard gale, or from want of provisions. But to the dramaturge a dash of the miraculous in his storm-brewing, a soupçon of the supernatural, is so tempting, while he is about it. And that novelists are liable to the same weakness, witness some foregoing illustrations from Carleton and Mrs. Marsh.

Leaving that question alone, let us briefly

* The Nowlans, ch. vii.
† The Black Prophet, ch. xix.
‡ The Collegians, ch. xxxii.

* Consuelo, ch. xxiv.
† Melincourt, ch. x.
‡ Destiny, ch. xxi.
§ Two Old Men's Tales. The Deformed.
‖ The Entail.
¶ Biographia Literaria, II. ch. i.

renew our passing acquaintance with storm and shower literature, in its most miscellaneous aspect. Here is Bothwell, for instance, recalling, in his prison-fortress of Malmoe, the scene and circumstances of Rizzio's murder:—

"'Twas night—murk night—the sleet beat on,
The wind, as now, was rude,
And I was lonely in my room
In dreary Holyrood." *

An example, this, of the art of investing poetic narrative with picturesque accompaniments—little touches that add color and relief to surface painting. Of a wholly different and superior order, both in degree and in kind, is such a picture as that which closes Mr. Tennyson's second Idyl of the King—though in the moral of it, analogous to some of the preternatural examples already cited from humbler prose. Vivien, false and fair, protesting her single-hearted devotion to Merlin, appeals to high Heaven, as it darkens over them, to "send one flash," that, missing all things else, may make her scheming brain a cinder, if she lies:—

"Scarce had she ceased, when out of heaven a bolt
(For now the storm was close above them) struck,
Furrowing a giant oak, and javelining
With darted spikes and splinters of the wood
The dark earth round. He raised his eyes and saw
The tree that shone white-listed thro' the gloom.
But Vivien, fearing Heaven had heard her oath,
And dazzled by the livid-flickering fork,
And deafened with the stammering cracks and claps
That followed, flying back and crying out,
'O Merlin, though you do not love me, save,
Yet save me!' clung to him, and hugged him close.
. . . And ever overhead
Bellowed the tempest, and the rotten branch
Snapped in the rushing of the river rain
Above them; and in change of glare and gloom
Her eyes and neck glittering went and came;
Till now the storm, its burst of passion spent,
Moaning and calling out of other lands,
Had left the ravaged woodland yet once more
To peace." †

We were all but italicizing some lines and half-lines in this superb bit of word-painting, but the expenditure of italics would have been extravagant, and, more wisely, the word-painting is left to speak in plain type for itself.

Owen Meredith is another word-painter, even luxuriant in power. Here is the storm that overtakes Lucile and her gay cavalcade on the way to Bigorre:—

"After noontide, the clouds, which had traversed the east
Half the day, gathered closer, and rose and increased.
The air changed and chilled. As though out of the ground,
There ran up the trees a confused hissing sound,
And the wind rose. The guides sniffed, like chamois, the air,
And looked at each other, and halted, and there
Unbuckled the cloaks from the saddles. The white
Aspens rustled, and turned up their pale leaves in fright.
All announced the approach of the tempest.
Ere long,
Thick darkness descended the mountains among;
And a vivid, vindictive, and serpentine flash
Gored the darkness, and shore it across with a gash.
The rain fell in large heavy drops. And anon
Broke the thunder.
* * * * *
And the storm is abroad in the mountains.
He fills
The crouched hollows and all the oracular hills
With dread voices of power. A roused million or more
Of wild echoes reluctantly rise from their hoar
Immemorial ambush, and roll in the wake
Of the cloud, whose reflection leaves livid the lake.
And the wind, that wild robber, for plunder descends
From invisible lands, o'er those black mountain ends;
He howls as he hounds down his prey; and his lash
Tears the hair of the timorous wild mountain ash,
That clings to the rocks, with her garments all torn,
Like a woman in fear; then he blows his hoarse horn,
And is off, the fierce guide of destruction and terror,
Up the desolate heights, 'mid an intricate error
Of mountain and mist.
There is war in the skies!
Lo! the black-wingèd legions of tempest arise
O'er those sharp splintered rocks that are gleaming below
In the soft light, so fair and so fatal, as though
Some seraph burned through them, the thunderbolt searching
Which the black cloud unbosomed just now.
Lo! the lurching
And shivering pine trees, like phantoms, that seem
To waver above, in the dark; and yon stream,

* Aytoun's Bothwell, i. 22.
† Idyls of the King: Vivien.

How it hurries and roars, on its way to the white
And paralyzed lake there, appalled at the sight
Of the things seen in heaven." *

We might quote a worse-pendant, or parallel passage (poetical and topographical both), to this riotous *phantasiestück*, than Hood's proem to his Romance of the Iron Age, which begins,—

"Like a dead man gone to his shroud,
The sun has sunk in a coppery cloud,
And the wind is rising squally and loud
With many a stormy token,—
Playing a wild funereal air,
Thro' the branches bleak, bereaved, and bare,
To the dead leaves dancing here and there—
In short, if the truth were spoken,
It's an ugly night for anywhere,
But an awful one for the Brocken!
* * * * *
However, it's quite
As wild a night
As ever was known on that sinister height
Since the Demon Dance was morriced—
The earth is dark, and the sky is scowling,
And the blast through the pines is howling and growling,
As if a thousand wolves were prowling
About in the old Black Forest!
Madly, sadly, the Tempest raves
Through the narrow gullies and hollow caves,
And bursts on the rocks in windy waves,
Like the billows that roar
On a gusty shore
Mourning over the mariners' graves—
Nay, more like a frantic lamentation
From a howling set
Of demons met
To wake a dead relation.
* * * * *
The lightning flashes,
The thunder crashes,
The trees encounter with horrible clashes,
While rolling up from marish and bog,
Rank and rich,
As from Stygian ditch,
Rises a foul sulphureous fog,
Hinting that Satan himself is agog—
But leaving at once this heroical pitch,
The night is a very bad night in which
You wouldn't turn out a dog." †

That, we reckon, Yankee-(weather-)wise, is the genuwine article, raal grit.

Nor be overlooked the same sterling artist's narration of Miss Kilmansegg's last night here on earth—she absorbed, as usual, in golden dreams, while storm-fiends without are up and doing:—

"And still the golden light of the sun
Through her golden dreams appear'd to run
Though the night that roared without was one
To terrify seamen or gypsies—
While the moon, as if in malicious mirth,
Kept peeping down on the ruffled earth,
As though she enjoyed the tempest's birth,
In revenge of her old eclipses." *

In prose fiction, too, has Thomas Hood turned out some stingo samples of storm-brewing. For instance, the story of Raby's death, by the hands of the Creole, in "Tylney Hall,"—where the corpse is met, borne along on a litter of branches, by some of the Hall servants, one of whom remarks, in whispered interchange of misgivings with his mate, "Look up west, lad, at the sun settin',—he's like a clot o' blood, be'ant un? and the light's more like hell-fire, as the ranter talks on, than what's natural,—there's been summut done to make God Almighty angersome,—mark my words on it." Accordingly, we are told, to bear out honest Sam's weather-wisdom in matters ethical, that the western sky had really assumed an awful and ominous appearance: the glowing sun, as if a visible type of the all-seeing Eye, "red with uncommon wrath," slowly withdrew behind a stupendous range of dense, pitch-black, mountainous clouds, from whose rugged crests ascended jets of blood-red flame, and causing a lurid glow up to the very zenith, whilst enormous breaks and fissures in the dark volcanic mass, served to disclose the intense ardent fires that glowed within, suggesting a comparison with those nameless flames to which the rustic had alluded. "Fantastic clouds of a lighter texture, and portentous colors, in the mean time ascended rapidly from the horizon, and congregated overhead in threatening masses. Peals of distant thunder muttered from all quarters at once, as unintermitting almost as the roar of the ocean. The wind, rushing in fitful gusts through the forest, filled the air with unearthly moans, and sighs, and whisperings; and the dead leaves rose and whirled in rings, as if following the skirts of the weird beings who are said to dance at the approach of tempest and human desolation." † All this while the storm has been brewing only; presently it breaks forth in wasting and withering fury.

Need we remind the readers of "Barnaby Rudge" of the prominence given in that story to elemental strife—of the tone imparted to the whole tale from its opening

* Lucile, part i. canto iv.
† Hoods Poem, The Forge.

* Miss Kilmansegg and her Precious Leg: Her Death.
† Tylney Hall, vol. iii. ch. i.

scene, that stormy night at the old Maypole? Or how the scene is repeated, stormy night expressly included, just five years later, with a keen knowledge of story-book effect? The *tempest* chapter in "David Copperfield" is perhaps the author's masterpiece in highly wrought description—to say nothing of the art with which it is inwrought with a personal catastrophe. In "Bleak House," and elsewhere, we have "incidentals" in the way of shower and storm, comparatively faint in their coloring, but aptly timed, and effectively introduced.

Sir Bulwer Lytton is an eminent brewer of storms, in all their varieties of strength. The night that Eugene Aram's accomplice makes his attempt on Lester's premises, while the sisters, as the clock strikes one, are discussing dearest Eugene by the firelight,—"how loud the winds rave! And how the heavy sleet drives against the window!" Again, on the night of Aram's secret expedition, to confer with Houseman at the cavern, the rain descends in torrents, and the thunder bursts over their very heads, and, with every instant, the lightning, darting through the riven chasm of blackness that seems suspended as in a solid substance above, brightens the whole heaven into one livid and terrific flame, and shows to the two men the faces of each other, rendered deathlike and ghastly by the glare. At the time of Ernest Maltravers' tête-à-tête with Valerie, the hail comes on fast and heavy, the trees groan, and the thunder roars. When the orphan brothers in "Night and Morning" make their escape, a storm overtakes and obstructs them, dazzling them with forked lightning, confusing them with else utter darkness, and drenching them with pitiless rain. But Sir Edward's most momentous storm-piece, in the guise of a *deus ex machinâ*, is probably that which forms the conclusion of "Godolphin;" and involves the fate of that ambitious hero.

When Mr. Kingsley's high-and-dry vicar, in "Yeast," returns from his visit to Luke, ill at ease in his orthodoxy, though putting so bold a face on the matter, the author takes care to have the wind sweeping and howling down the lonely streets, and to lash the rain into his face, while gray clouds are rushing past the moon like terrified ghosts across the awful void of the black heaven. As he staggers and strides along the plashy pavement, the roar and tumult without him, we are told, harmonize strangely with the discord. And therefore, artistically speaking, are that roar and tumult upraised.

With thunder and lightning Mr. Wilkie Collins environs the acquaintance-making of Basil and his evil genius, mysterious Mr. Mannion. It is the pursuit of tea-table talk and tea-drinking under difficulties, considering that the hail is rattling vehemently against the window, and the thunder seeming to shake the house to its foundations. But Mr. Mannion sips on, and makes no sign—nothing by word, or look, or gesture, to show that the "terrible glory of the night-storm" has either a voice for his heart, or a sound for his ear; and therefore does Basil begin to feel strange, unutterable sensations creeping over him, and the silence in that little chamber becomes sinister and oppressive.

With thunder and lightning does Currer Bell make way for her Professor into the modest lodgings of Frances the lace-mender. "The clouds, severing with loud peal and shattered cataract of lightning, emptied their livid folds in a torrent, heavy, prone, and broad. "'Come in! Come in!' said Frances, as, after putting her into the house, I paused ere I followed: the word decided me; I stepped across the threshold, shut the door on the rushing, flashing, whitening storm, and followed her up-stairs to her apartment." * It is in a hailstorm that Lucy Snowe loses her way, and her senses, in the narrow streets of Brussels. † In a storm it is that she leaves Madame Walravens' inhospitable saloon ‡—a storm that seems to have burst at the zenith; it rushes down prone; the forked, slant bolts pierce athwart vertical torrents; red zig-zags interlace a descent blanched as white metal; and all breaks from a sky heavily black in its swollen abundance. And it is in a storm §—one that has roared frenzied for seven days, and strewn the Atlantic with wrecks—that M. Emanuel is lost.

* The Professor, ch. xix.
† Villette, ch. xvi.
‡ Ibid., ch. xxv.
§ Ibid., ch. xlii., Finis.

CHAPTER VI.

PASSING years bring growth and development to sons of peasants as of peers. Tommy Wilmot also was bordering upon man's estate. He likewise, had his ambitions and aspirations after a dreamy future. His good father hoped, I doubt not, that he would succeed himself as gardener at the Lodge, just as at the Lodge, Mr. Locksley looked to Ned's succeeding him in the agency of the estate. But Tommy's mind was gone afield like Ned's, only there was in his case, neither reluctance nor inward struggle.

"I wun't have nuffin to do wi' spades and rakes, veyther, no longer nor I can help, mind." Such had been his early and loud determination. "Vur and vethers vor I, veyther, none o' year cabbige and lattices!"

To be a "kipper," even undermost of "underkippers," was his practical desire. In its tricksiest moments fancy would conjure up a long green vista of over-arching trees, a barn door studded with clenched carcases of stoats and weasels, hawks and pies; a comfortable house, with kennels appurtenant, hencoops upon a green sward, with clucking hens and pheasant poults by dozens pecking ant-eggs; and, moving about among them, a sturdy figure in velveteens and leather leggings—no longer "Tommy," but "Muster" Wilmot, "head-kipper" of Cransdale park! And, O John Wilmot, gardener, progenitor of Tom, to think all that should come—all those wild aspirations, and their lawless venting—from an honest, innocent desire of thine, that Lucy Locksley, thy meek mistress, should fill jam-pots by the dozen with current jelly!

"Them blackbirds and thrushes wun't lave us narra mossel o' vruit to year! There, Tommy, buoy, couldn't 'ee manage to vire thic roosty gun?"

Fire it, indeed! There was a pie baked soon in the gardener's oven, wherein the "four-and-twenty blackbirds" of the nursery rhyme might have been counted when it "was opened;" but if they "began to sing," it was in Tommy's ears only; siren songs, for all they were no water birds, decoying Tommy's youthful yearnings into woody coverts where birds breed. Not blackbirds only, nor missel-thrushes; but long-tailed pheasants and plump partridges. Rabbits burrow there likewise, and hares crouch in form.

Dread Nemesis of the blackbirds!

O John Wilmot, gardener! Was there not wilfulness, like unto Tommy's, rife in thee? Zeal for "Missus'" jam-pots might have been very well, had not the murderous manifestation of it against the sweet-throated pilferers been made in flagrant disobedience to her will.

"A pound of currants more or less, John, cannot signify. I never grudge them to the blackbirds. Don't scare the pretty creatures, banging at them."

So said meek-hearted Lucy; but John shook his head—and all the answer that he gave was that suggestion to Tommy, when she was out of hearing:—

"Couldn't 'ee manage to vire thic roosty gun?"

It became his fetish, that rusty fire-arm—soon no longer rusty. With affectionate pride and care, with tow and train oil, and rottenstone, he worked up its old steel at last to brighter than silvery polish. "Muster Watson," the present incumbent of the "head-kipper's" benefice, was not a man to favor or to wink at any boy's possession of fire-arms on the estate.

"I can't abide to see them 'crow kippers' wi' guns, my lord," he often said to Philip. "Scarecrows is too much neglected; then there's clappers as makes a wery pretty noise, my lord, and is safer than guns for little chaps now, as I allays tells them farmers."

But the precincts of the Lodge garden were sacred, and Tommy's possession, within those limits, undisturbed. Nay, there were Saturnalia rook-shooting, for instance, or when great flights of "questies" or wood pigeons, were blazed at in the woods; when Tommy, bold, but with misgiving, would risk his all, and venture, gun in hand, within eyeshot of Muster Watson. In those early days, he himself eyed that great man with veneration rather than defiance. It really went against his grain to elude his observation; he could have wished to carry gun and shot-belt in his presence openly, with that proud submission wherewith worthy subalterns wait on the bidding of a truly noble chief. Upon underkeepers, even upon occasional watchers, he still looked as a spirited cadet might upon tried lieutenants of his corps. He was fraternal even with mere beaters when the coverts were shot in later autumn, and had carried an ash stick, not without distinction, in their ranks. All minor sporting servitudes were reckoned offices of honor and of love. It was no mean pleasure to bear the bag of ferrets when my lord and Master Ned went rabbiting; supreme felicity to follow with the landing-net, and to officiate at the securing of a two-pound trout. O foolish father, John! Why thwart so pronounced and so promising a call?

"There, I bees a gardener, and the son of a gardener, and I wants to be veyther to a gardener too."

But Tommy shook his head, and reiterated his declaration:—

"None o' yer cabbige and lattices for I."

Jane Wilmot, his mother, was for a compromise, of which the terms were wide; all but one article, which was close and stringent. Imbued with the wisdom of that folk lore, which tells that horses led to ponds, cannot, therefore, be made to drink, she was urgent with her John, that their Tommy should not be forced to follow the horticultural career of his sire. He was a smart lad, and could "turn his hand a'most to any thin'; let him try it on any other callin' as he can gi' his mind to." Any other, that is, save one.

Jane was a "kipper's" daughter, and a "kipper's" sister; and was so far from having her good man's love of caste, as to dread above all things becoming a kipper's mother. Well she might, poor woman! She was not from the Cransdale county at all. She had been born and bred in one where society was split into two hostile factions, of gamekeepers and gamestealers. There, in every grassy field, staked thorn bushes gave token of defence against the sweep of poaching nets. There mastiffs and blood-hounds fetched high prices as savage and sagacious helpers to such as must track or encounter nightly depredators. There one magistrate after another was continually "retiring from the bench during the hearing of this case," to let his impartial brethren condemn "a trespasser in pursuit of game" on his grounds, returning to sit in judgment on the next case, committed on the grounds of his brother magistrate, who, in his turn, "retired."

There, the lower class of public houses in the purlieus of country towns saw formidable conspiracies against the game on this or that estate, knit among groups of dissolute, and often desperate, men. There, not seldom, whole bands of these associated plunderers would sweep the country side, and grimly defy the protective forces of the squires. Jane Wilmot well remembered the sickening anxiety which looked ever and anon out of her own mother's haggard eyes. She well remembered how often, wakened by the soughing of the wind upon nights when murky clouds went scudding across the moon, she had lain in her childish crib, gazing at the white figure which sat with folded arms by the hearthstone, starting at the cry of every night-bird, jumping up and crossing the room a-tiptoe—lest she should waken the waking child—peering out through the lattice into the half darkness, venturing even sometimes to unbolt the door and raise the latch, and put out her head, and make sure that no sound of terror was borne upon the night wind.

But Jane remembered worse than this. The events of one fatal night were stamped with minute and terrible distinctness upon the tablets of her brain. That was the night when her sleep was broken suddenly, not by the long moan of the wind in the cottage chimney, nor by its hurtling rush among the tree-tops; but by the loud and sharp report of fire-arms in the thicket hard by. Angry bark of dogs, and angrier shouts of men, mingled in wild confusion. Then came an agonizing scream, distinct and piercing, above all the mingled noise. The mother, who was standing upright in her night-gown—her heavy black hair, streaked with gray, hanging loose upon her shoulders—changed her look of racking eagerness to one of blank dismay, clasped her hands together bitterly, and sank into the arm-chair by the hearth:—

"O Jenny, Jenny! yon scream was our Bill's!"

The mother-heart's foreboding was too true. Four men soon brought in a ghastly corpse, whose whole left side seemed to have been torn away by the heavy charge of shot poured into it at close quarters from the muzzle of the poacher's gun. The agony upon the white face of the murdered man was a fearful thing to look upon; but not so fearful, Jane thought even then—and thought continually in after years—as the horror and the hate, the misery and the vengefulness, which could be read plainer than printed words upon her father's face, as he came in behind his dead son. Since then Jane had lived for years in the quiet Cransdale district, where such tragedies were happily unknown—where poaching offences were peccadilloes, never crimes—where Muster Watson and his subordinates were in no danger of losing life in game preserving, otherwise than by having it "woritted out o' them by them poachin' chaps," as that functionary would often lament that his hard case was. But the haunting impressions of early childhood were not weakened by succeeding years. "Keeperin' and poacherin'" were equally her dread and her aversion. She went along with John in forbidding her son to indulge his sporting propensities in the legitimate way, and was as blind as he to the danger of throwing the lad back upon the unlawful alternative for their indulgence. I do not plead this opposition of his parents in excuse for Tommy, but state the facts; for upon that unlawful alternative, it must be confessed, he did fall back. His offences were tenderly dealt with by Watson, when occasionally detected, partly from consideration for his parents, partly from the known good-will towards the lad of my lord and Master Ned. Yet the head keeper would purse his mouth and shake his head, and say how much he feared John Wilmot's lad wouldn't "come to no good neither arter all."

Intricate is the woof of human life. All Mr. Watson's indulgence to Tommy's infractions of statutes for protection to game and fish, did not avail to save him from a serious scrape. Old school rivalries, and the institution of a county police, brought the thing about. Jim Hutchins was Tommy's schoolmate at the "National" in the old days, when he got the bag of marbles from Master Ned in satisfaction for his wounded feelings in the matter of William Tell. There was a close contest between the two boys in school and out, for mental and for physical mastery. It was a fair match mentally, and they took each other "down" in class turn and turn about. Physically the advantage lay at first with Hutchins, who was a full year older than his adversary: but he was a spindle-shanked youth, and as he shot upwards lost his superiority over Tommy Wilmot, whose active, sturdy build gained strength as surely as the other's lost it year by year. Presently their fights degenerated into simple threshings administered by Tommy as occasion arose; and Jim was driven to call in his "big brother" to redress the balance of power. He certainly did turn the tables upon the aggressor, but at cost of so much effort that Wilmot conceived the hope of being "square wi' un" at some future day. Before that day dawned the great institution of rural police had found its way into the secluded neighborhood of Cransdale. Jim's big brother donned the blue coat with lead buttons, and girt his wrist with the striped cuff of authority. Thenceforth, he figured in the local journal as that efficient and active officer, P. C. Hutchins, and regarded Tommy—whose delinquencies by flood and field were but too well known to him—with official reprehension, spiced by personal antipathy.

It was no wonder, therefore, that upon a certain morning, during the course of that memorable last vacation, the earl should appear in the breakfast-parlor at the Lodge, and thus accost young Locksley:—

"I say, Ned, Tommy Wilmot's been at it again. He's in the Cranston lock-up, and likely to go to gaol at St. Ivo's, unless matters can be mended."

"What matters, Phil?"

"Peeler Hutchins' head, among the foremost; that's the most material object broken."

"What's he broken Hutchins' head for?"

"Can't exactly say; but I heard what he broke it with, and you may guess by that."

"Well, what was the weapon?"

"The butt-end of a fishing rod."

"The old story—'Fur, feather, and scales,'—will bring Tommy to permanent grief some fine morning. Why don't you make an underkeeper of him, Phil, and give him his swing in a lawful way?"

"Why don't I, indeed? All along of your turnip-headed old John and his Jane, that wont hear of it, else we'd have had him under Watson years ago. Tell you what, Mr. Locksley, I hope you'll take warning yourself, and not thwart Ned's inclinations here if he takes to gibbing, and starting from a regular professional line after all."

"Ned won't play pranks, never fear!" said his father, smiling.

He knew not what a bounding pang went through the lad's heart as he lightly uttered the words.

"Well, we must ride over, I suppose, and see about plaistering the peeler's head with a five-pound note, and bailing out Tommy, or something; for his mother's been up to mine as tearful as Niobe, and I promised to do what I could for him. Come along, Ned; I ordered horses round."

"The worst of those perpetual poaching scrapes," said Mr. Locksley, "is, that one never knows how far astray they mayn't lead a lad. Tommy's a good fellow at bottom, I believe; but I'm afraid of his going to the bad at last. Can't you 'list him in your battalion when you join, my lord, and take him out of harm's way down here altogether?"

"He's three inches under our standard," answered Philip, as they went out; "and not likely to grow much more, I fear."

Tommy they found sulky, if sorrowful, in durance vile. The inspector and the head keeper had both visited him, endeavoring, in vain, to persuade him into repentance and submission. As to the cracked crown of P. C. Hutchins, it was worse than useless to dilate upon that feature in the case. Mention of it served only to spirit up the culprit.

"I've paaid off that 'ere 'Utchins any 'ows!"

He was somewhat softened, when my lord himself and Master Ned were ushered into his place of confinement, announcing themselves as having ridden over to try and effect a compromise. The fact that the pilfered trout were my lord's, put on an uglier aspect in the eye of conscience.

But when Philip suggested that an ample apology to the policeman was an indispensable preliminary to negotiations, he relapsed into savage sulkiness.

"That is a good 'un. That 'ere 'Utchins spiles my fishin', puts I in quod; and now I'se to apologize to he! No, my lord, not if I know it; there now!"

"For shame, Tommy! The man did his duty, as you would in his place, or you're not the man I take you for."

"Policeman!" said the earl, "I am ashamed to think an old acquaintance of mine, whose father and mother I have known ever since I can remember, isn't man enough to own he's in the wrong when he knows it. As Wilmot wont apologize himself to you, I hope you'll take an apology from me for him."

"Now don't 'ee my lord; don't 'ee, now!" almost whimpered Tommy, whom this unexpected move of Philip confounded utterly; "I beant a going to stand that 'ere, I beant. Tell 'ee what, perleeceman, I 'umbly ax your pardin, so as my lord wunt: and if five shillin' 'ood goo fur a 'pology' now—"

"There now, Thomas, there now; that will do," quoth Hutchins, in whose breast pocket was crackling a crisp new bank-note of the earl's. "We wont take no further notice of it, not for this once; but don't you let us see you here again, no more, Thomas, like a good lad now."

It must be owned that P. C. Hutchins was kickably pompous as he uttered this exhortation. Tommy winced, but contained himself.

"That's good advice of the peeler, notwithstanding, Tommy," said Philip to him outside, as the liberated captive held his stirrup at mounting.

"Better to give nor take, my lord. There, them live critters is like bird lime to I; I'se always at 'em, though I 'aint no right to be. And I'm sure I don't mean no offence to 'ee a killin' of them wot's yourn, my lord."

"Well, I wish we could let you stick to them in the way of business, Tommy, to keep you out of harm; but your father wont hear of it, nor your mother either."

"No! wuss luck, my lord!" said Tommy.

"Mr. Locksley said this morning, I had better take you soldiering along with me; but you're not tall enough for the Guards, you know."

"I've thought o' takin' a sergeant's shillin' scores o' times, I has;" and he touched his hat as Philip and Locksley rode away.

"Fine stroke that, Phil," said the latter, "bringing him to his knees by apologizing for him."

"Trúe for you, Ned, but it's only a copy. Her ladyship brought me round out of a towering tantrum that way once."

"I say, Phil, we've had just about a brace of mothers, eh?"

"Just about, indeed! Fellows talk of being tied to mammy's apron-strings.

There's one more of mine's to cut when I join. Well, the snip of the scissors will make my heart bleed. Whoop!"

In went the spurs. Both boys were glad of the long smooth stretch of turf which gave excuse for a furious gallop.

"What a thundering shame! Such weather as this!" cried Ned, when they pulled up, after "taking" the sunk fence into the park. They rode home at a foot's pace, under the shady trees.

"Shall you dine with us?" said Philip, as the other was presently turning down towards the Lodge.

"No; they expect me home this afternoon to dine early."

"Well, walk up later in the evening. You haven't seen her ladyship or 'Con' today?"

CHAPTER VII.

On the western side of Cransdale House was a slope of ground never subjected to the tyranny of terrace-makers. In that unkempt corner their childish gardens had been made, in the moss and among bushes. Such flower-beds as Constance had occasionally laid out had been cut by cabbage plots, and variegated by young cucumbers, grown under cracked tumblers. Whole tracts had been given up at times to the cultivation of milk thistles for the rabbits. So-called cavalry charges from the romping boys had periodically trampled all into a wilder confusion, and certain spots had been charred and blackened by bivouac-fires, lighted to roast birds' eggs. Varied styles of savage architecture had been atempted there; African huts, when they first read Mungo Park—Huron wigwams, when presently they made acquaintance with Fenimore Cooper.

By and by the long absences of the boys at school brought lengthened periods of sole occupation, and a title began to grow to exclusive possession. "Our" garden became "mine;" and change of name confirmed restricted ownership in "Constance's corner." As its fair owner grew, not only in grace and beauty, but in the sense of them, so grew her corner in the expression of both. Trees and shrubs, ferns and flowers, all there were choicest of the choice, some for exquisite rarity, some for loveliest simplicity.

At the summit of the slope was a carpeting of softest moss, on which showed the chiselled lip of a smooth white marble basin. A jet of water shooting skywards against the west seemed to Ned to fall back in a spray of living gems, as he came up the sward, and caught, far off in the stillness, the plash of its murmurous music. As he walked and watched the dancing crystal, a figure came across the sky-line. It stood between him and the sunset, looking out upon it. Intercepting thus the light it seemed carven in dark porphyry; but for iridescence, as of gleaming opal, made by the slanting sunbeams along its faultless outline. She stood, with one foot on the mossy carpet, the other poised on the marble rim. At that distance he could not tell exactly what was the motion of her hands; but it seemed to him that from time to time she dropped something into the water. In simple truth, her taper fingers, as those of thoughtful, or of thoughtless maidens will, were rifling a gathered rosebud and showering down its leaves. Soon she went forward, and over the slope, away. Ned, quick as thought, pressed upward from the other side. He reached the top. Her footprint was yet fresh upon the moss. He knelt down and kissed it passionately twice or thrice, gathered a few shreds of the moss where his lips had touched her footmark; picked a few floating rose-leaves from the water, and put both tenderly into his breast.

"Ned!"

He turned at the dear voice of one who was almost his mother too. Lady Cransdale sat on a marble seat close by, where she had been in conversation with her daughter.

"Ned! dear Ned! Come here, and let me know at once what meaning there is in what I have just seen you do?"

So he sat down beside her, and forced himself to speak, and told her what it meant, in the simplest, strongest words that he could find. He was so frank and manly, in his genuine and deep emotion, that it cut her to the quick; for she dearly loved the lad. Her long-lost Philip's early tenderness for him, her own obedient adoption of it, all her indulgent motherliness in proof—to think that all should end in having toiled him thus! The meshes were self-wrought, perhaps; but what of that? She felt that they were wrought in with living fibres of a true loving heart. No unravelling was possible; they must be rent. Her mournful firmness was the only consolation she could give him. She put on no idle affectation that his hurt was slight: she was no fool to think nor hypocrite to feign it. She had known and loved him all his life long as a boy, and had held him, up to that hour, for no more. But when he had opened out his heart in its honesty, she saw and owned him for a man—with a man's capacity to suffer, she prayed it might be with a man's strength to bear.

"You have been dreaming, Ned. So, indeed, have I; dreaming or blind. But open your eyes, as mine are open now, and see for yourself that you have dreamt what cannot be."

"What cannot be! You say so, too! I have said it myself a thousand times, but would not—could not, keep to it."

It was moonlight by this time, and Lady Cransdale saw the figure of Constance returning in search of her. She took her determination in an instant.

"I say, dear Ned, you have dreamt what cannot be. You may mistrust me, for I too was blind. But here comes Constance. I will leave you face to face with her. I trust you to speak out as manfully to her as you have done to me; and I trust her for the answer she will give."

She was gone before Constance reached them.

"You here, Ned!" She held out her hand and clasped his, so sisterly, that he foreknew his fate.

He held hers firm, and turned her gently, that the moonlight might come full upon her features; then he looked her in the face, and said:—

"Tell me, dear Lady Constance, can you think of ever loving me?"

"Loving you, Ned? Of course I can. I do love you with all my heart. You know I do—as I have always done."

The calm of her voice convinced him. He dropped her hand, and covered his face with both his own, lest she should see the anguish on it. Then the shock went through her that something was strangely wrong with him.

"Ned—brother Ned! Mine and Phil's! What ails you? Speak to me!"

"O Constance! you will think me mad. It is that word 'brother' hurts me. I have no sister but yourself; yet it is not brother's love with which I love you—heart and soul, out of all speech, sweet Constance!"

Ah! she understood him now; and her heart, as her mother's, was pierced through with pity; because, in very truth, she did love him as a brother.

"Lady Cransdale says that I have dreamt a dream; and that you will tell me true whether or not it is a dream of what cannot be. I know it cannot. But let me hear it from your own lips, Constance. Say, it cannot!"

Hers was a strong soul too, though very tender. Every syllable thrilled clear.

"No, dear brother Ned, it cannot."

"Then forgive me. But before I go, seal the grave of my dead hope, in token of forgiveness, with a kiss."

She knew his nobleness, and trusted him to know her own. He would understand, once and forever, that only upon a grave could she consent to put such seal so freely. So, as he knelt before her, she stooped and put a kiss upon his forehead. He spoke not another word; but rose, and walked rapidly down from the slope over the moonlit sward; and she watched him as he went.

All that sultry summer's night his own mother that bare him, Lucy Locksley, lay awake. It was late when he came in. Prayers were over, and she had gone to her own room. He opened the door as he passed, and kissed her hurriedly, and said "good-night." And she had only said, "God bless you, dearest!" but she had noted upon his features a handwriting of some strange grief to be spelt out on the morrow: so she lay sleepless, guessing at sadnesses. The nightingale sang all night. Lucy wondered whether it were a mere conceit of poets that the melodious complaint was for a nest left empty. But when the morning birds began to pipe—the thrush and ouzel—their very joyousness was wearisome, she fell into a short sleep, whence she awoke unrefreshed and anxious.

Ned was not at breakfast. The servants said he must be gone fishing. No one had seen him go, but his rod and basket were missing in the hall.

Presently was heard a man's footstep craunching the gravel outside the open windows of the breakfast-parlor.

"Ned back again," said Locksley, without looking up from his *Times*; "I thought it was nonsense fishing such a sunshiny morning."

The mother smiled to think her husband's ear should be so dull.

"That's not the dear boy's footstep, Robert. How can you think so?"

It was not. Through the window, which opened to the ground, Philip marched in, followed by a long-bodied terrier, whose tangled hair hid all his legs, and moving as he went, gave him the look of a monster centipede.

"'Morning, Mrs. Locksley. How nice and cool you are in here. It's grilling hot outside already. 'Morning, Mr. Locksley. Where's Ned?"

"Gone fishing early."

"Early! He'd better; unless he went before sunrise he might as well have stayed to fish in the teacups. What a nuisance! It's now or never with those rats."

"Rats?" cried Lucy.

"Yes, they are taking up the barn flooring at the Home-Farm to-day. It's full of them. And my new Skye, here, is to show his talents for the first time on the 'varmint.' Isn't he charming, Mrs. Locksley? He only came last night. Macphail, a fellow in our form at Eton, sent him down from the island direct. Ned hasn't seen him yet. Why didn't he come up to the house last night? he said he would."

"Why, surely, he was up there till long past ten," said Lucy.

"I never set eyes on him, at all events. No, sir," to Skye, begging with a bit of dry toast upon his nose; "how dare you? There now, good dog—catch! Ned grown mysterious, Mrs. Locksley?" She made no answer. After a few more dry toast exercises, Philip and Skye marched out again at the same open window. Locksley soon went off to his daily duties, and Lucy was left to brood over her undefined apprehensions.

Her household orders given and arrangements made, she was again in the cool breakfast parlor, working at a piece of embroidered muslin, when she heard another lighter step on the gravel. Her quick ear knew it at once for Lady Cransdale's. Something on the face of the countess told of a weighty matter on her mind, and, the first trivial salutation over, she asked, in obedience to an irresistible impulse—

"Did you see Ned last night, Lady Cransdale?"

"I did, indeed, my dear, dear Mrs. Locksley."

As they sat down together on the sofa, the countess took both Mrs. Locksley's hands in hers; and meek-hearted Lucy, seeing more plainly some grave sorrow in her friend's eyes, trembled and grew faint.

"Tell me, dear Lady Cransdale, what has happened? Philip was here just now, and said Ned was not up at the house last night. He came in late, and only spoke a word with me. This morning he was out before any one was up."

"Dear Mrs. Locksley, dear Lucy, my old friend, that has happened which I should, yet scarcely could, have foreseen. Last night the poor boy confided to me that he has set his heart, not boyishly, but with a great love, upon Constance. A sad thing, indeed!"

Lucy's meek heart was human, and had, as other human hearts, its own mysterious inconsistencies. It gave a bound within, which sent the red blood angry to her forehead. She drew her hands with quick motion from between those of the countess, and fixed on her a look of almost startling fierceness.

"A sad thing? Pray, for whom?"

"For Ned," said Lady Cransdale, firmly, though sympathizing fully with the roused heart of a mother.

"Lady Constance is very nobly born, my lady; she is very beautiful; she will be very rich—at least"—and there was a tremulous scorn in Lucy's voice—"at least, compared with such folk as we. But our Ned, Lady Cransdale—"

"Is worthy—that is, he will be—of any girl, however noble, fair, or good. I count the wealth for nothing;" broke in the countess. Fine mother-soul! She would not take offence at Lucy's sudden loftiness; but loved her all the more for her passionate pride in the boy.

"Why do you say he will be? What is wanting to his worth?" said Lucy, not yet disarmed.

"Years only, my dear friend! Ah, do not be unjust to me by thinking I would be unjust to our Ned. For he is ours. You let me love him from his cradle. I cannot forget it, nor be ungrateful for it, trust me."

The power of a soft answer to turn away wrath wrought upon Lucy; the anger died in part out of her eyes.

"If Constance had a younger sister," continued Lady Cransdale, "on whom he should have set his heart, it might have been otherwise."

"Age does not always go by almanac," the other answered.

"No! but Constance is a full ripe woman, mind and body. Ned will be a true man, I would pledge my life. But he himself asks time and scope to prove his manhood."

"What time? What scope?" cried Lucy, with a new flush of increased excitement. "What has he told you that he has never breathed to me? I saw the unquiet of his heart, and dreaded a confidence to come. But I am robbed, it seems, of the first place in his trust as in his love." She said it with returning bitterness.

"No, Lucy, no. He did well to keep his secret, in generous delicacy, even from yourself. I surprised it, and forced from his honesty what I shall tell you now."

Then she told her how the lad had dreamt, among other things, of snatching premature distinction upon a military field.

"Then is my doom sealed," said Lucy; "I have lost my son."

She folded her hands upon her lap, and fixed her gaze as if to look out into the far years to come.

Lady Cransdale still sat beside her; but for a space neither woman ventured upon a word. Little by little the widowed lady's eyes began to fill with tears. The strange quiet of Lucy, and the strong constraint she put upon herself, seemed to weaken the governance of her friend's will over her own emotions. She gave a sob at last; and when the other heard it, she turned round and said,—

"Leave me, dear Lady Cransdale; I shall have to beg your pardon for that and for my former abruptness—but I cannot just now."

So she kissed Lucy, and went out.

And then the wounded mother rose up from her seat, and went walking to and fro, her arms folded on her breast; but ever and anon unfolding to let her hands twitch, with convulsive motion at her throat. She did not cry. She could not; but the passionate heat that flushed her to the forehead, seemed to gather and glow round the orbits of her so gentle eyes.

"They have robbed him of his brave heart's love; and now they say, 'how sad for him!' Sad for me, too! But what of that? O my poor boy. My Ned! Yes, mine. 'Ours,' she said; but I say mine, my Ned; not ours!"

"Not ours! not ours! What are you saying, darling wife? What moves you?" asked that only one voice dearer than even her dear boy's.

"Ah, my own Robert! Yes, with you I will say 'ours;' our own poor Ned!"

She threw her arms about the father's neck, and laid her head upon his breast, and clung there, and gave way, and shook, as the tears rained down.

He would not break her grief with any question or foolish exclamation of surprise, but let this strange storm sweep across the unaccustomed sky of his Lucy's even temper. Presently he drew her towards the sofa, where they both sat down, his arm around her, her hands in his, and the dear head upon his shoulder still.

Then, of her own accord, she told him, almost word for word, what had been said between the countess and herself.

"And now, my own dear husband, promise me this one thing. By all the love which knits us, either to other, and both to our only child, promise me not to thwart him!"

"Not to thwart him, my sweet wife! What power have you or I to thwart or humor him in this? We cannot give him Lady Constance. His heart, poor boy, must wean itself from her. There is no help for it."

"Yes, I suppose—that is, I know—well, yes! Ah, my poor Ned!—it must. But do not let us make the weaning harder, Robert, dear."

"The Lord forbid! I don't quite understand you, Lucy."

"Yes, yes, you surely must. This is a double secret, and we hold both threads now."

"How so, a double secret?"

"Yes, a double longing. One for this Lady Constance who thinks light of him. It will be long before she finds another such to love her, Robert!"

"Well, Lucy; but the second?"

"For the life of a soldier."

"No, dearest, surely not. He has done very well at Eton. He will do well at Oxford. This soldiering was but a means to an impossible end, which he would not own for such, poor fellow!"

"Robert, do not deceive yourself; but look there, in the corner: what do you see there?"

"See? Nothing but my father's regulation sword."

"And that is every thing. I could not tell what ailed the boy these many days. And yet I caught his looks upon the sword a dozen times."

"It was a chisel only," said her husband, smiling sadly, "with which to carve a pedestal for his fair idol. The idol broken, no more need of pedestal."

Lucy gave back the sad smile, yet with a woman's archness who smiles at a man's clumsiness in guessing heart-riddles.

"Idols are easier broken than the hope of them. Empty pedestals seem to promise that they shall stand upon them yet. But you spoke of weaning. One must wean upon some kind of food. Such a spirit as Ned's will hunger ten times more for action and adventure now."

"I had not thought of that, dearest: perhaps it may. But Ned's is a dutiful and loving spirit. He will not leave us lightly."

The sad smile was still upon her countenance; but a subtle change came over it. Through its sadness gleamed a strange exultation: its sorrow irradiated by some mystic joy. The father loved his boy well—loved him better than life. But Lucy was his mother. The self-sacrificing mystery of mother-love was hers. Initiation in it, pangs of motherhood alone can purchase. Her sad smile was not arrogant, and yet it was a smile of conscious triumph; for the sense was on her of that supremacy in love, which it is a woman's joy to find so real, seeing how dear her weaker nature buys it.

"Yes, Robert, we have a dutiful and loving son. Love and duty might teach him to make a costly sacrifice. But it is anticipated. We have made it. For you will make it with me, dearest Robert. Perhaps he would not leave us of himself;—but we will bid him go."

Meekness is not one with weakness: who thinks so greatly errs. The man's manliness reeled at the shock which came so mighty from the meek heart of his wife.

"Bid the boy go, dear Lucy: bid him go! Send him away? Send Ned away, and with him all the fond hopes we have had of him?"

Great beads of tears stood in his eyes, and then came rolling down; and then his great sobs shook him. She put her gentle hands upon his shoulders and seemed to steady the strong frame that quivered.

"Just so, dear Robert, we will forego the fond hopes *we* have had of him. Remember, they were not his but ours. Why clutch them selfishly? We had our own hopes of ourselves, and have found them true in one another. Let him seek his, and pray God he may find them no more false than we have done!"

He folded her to his breast, and pressed her to his heart, as on the first day they were wed.

"We will make his hopes ours, my own Robert. We will not let him know but what ours are his."

Oh, mighty mother-love, and mighty consciousness of might!

She forbore to ask a promise, to entreat or plead. But in the silence made full conquest of her husband's will.

He pressed her once more to his breast, and kissed her tenderly, and said,—

"You are his mother, Lucy. I can have but one heart with yourself in this as in all else on earth. Do as you think best, love, and the good Lord comfort us."

CHAPTER VIII.

NED meanwhile was up upon the moorland. Waking from feverish and broken sleep to heaviness of heart, the thought of the fresh wilderness had beckoned him out. Mindful of his mother's possible anxiety, he had taken with him his fishing-rod and basket, that their absence might account for his. It was so early, and he went so fast, that the whin bushes had not yet caught a single gilding beam when he had reached the higher levels.

"Ex oriente lux," he said, as the bright sun-rim came up on the horizon. "After sunset one looks eastward for another sunrise. So must I."

Then his heart smote him to think that facing eastwards he had put his home behind him. So he turned to look back on it; but his treacherous eyes hot swerved and struck,—not upon the eaves under which his mother's head was pillowed; but upon the pinnacles of Cransdale House.

"A man shall leave his father and his mother, and shall—" No, boy, no. Not even if they reckoned thee a man. Art thou not even yet awake from that dream of what cannot be?

A flush of anger heated him. Without looking upon the house where he was born, he turned right round again, and walked over the moor, scanning eagerly its blue-brown ridges. That is no longer one of them on which his eye rests at last. Yon long level line is surely not a line of straggling moorland bushes? Those are the tree-tops of some long formal avenue,—the great avenue at Rookenham.

He set his teeth, and looked about him. Amidst the big boulders, between which the moorland stream came foaming, he spied a large, flat stone, so massive that he had much ado to raise it at arms' length above his head. And yet he hurled it with such force against one of those smooth-pated boulders that it shivered into fragments, one of which struck and cut him on the rebound. His excitement was too fierce to let him feel the cut. When blood began to trickle on his forehead he thought it water, splashed up in his face by the shivered stone. He went striding up-stream moodily, making savage cuts with his fishing-rod at tall thistles, or other lusty weeds.

Was this the same lad that had borne himself so gently with Lady Cransdale and her daughter over-night?

The very same. A young man's heart is fitful in its waywardness. And he was in a wilderness alone. He that is so may often encounter with a fiend. So on he went: the hot sun baking into clots the blood upon his angry forehead. He saw a trout basking in a quiet basin, shut out from the brawling stream by two big stones. He hurled his rod, in wanton wrath, at it so violently, that as the creature turned its side it showed a murderous rent among the flashing scales.

Butcherly done, not soldierly, Ned! In outrage of the laws of sport,—the mimic war!

But his anger burnt fiercely; and still he struck out savagely with the rod at every tall weed or flower as he went along.

He that will not wrestle with the tempter in the wilderness is driven of him. It was going ill with Edward until he encountered an angel and minister of grace in the strangest and most unlikely form.

He had reached a spot upon the course of the stream where the ground made an abrupt rise, above which the water was swollen by the inflow of two lesser burns, and so came tumbling in a miniature cataract over the fall. Beneath it rose, in front, a solitary shaft of stone, squared as if by human hands, and set up in mid-stream. It was known as the Pixie's pillar to the folk of the country side. To reach it required the nicest equilibrium; for the neighboring stones stood at a steeper dip, showing only thinnest edges, or tooth-like points above the water which eddied wildly round, or formed deep pools on either side. The capital of this strange natural pillar was a platform some three feet square, at such a sharp incline that it required the sure foot of a goat to stand on it; over all waved a little rowan ash rooted in the fissures of the stone. About its slender trunk a child had twined its left arm, and was grasping with the right hand at green berries on the outer boughs hung over the basin into which the tumbling waters fell. Ned fairly sickened to see the sapling bend with the child's weight, and sway to and fro with its eager outstretch. Its face was from him, and he did not dare to call, lest the rash little one, startled by the sudden cry, should lose its hold. Putting together two joints of his fishing rod, he advanced with its help as far along the chancy stepping-stones as he could make his footing good; there he waited till the child's face should turn his way. But the outmost bunch of berries seemed to have fascinated the urchin. Loosing the left hand from the trunk, he kept sliding it ever further along a projecting branch, edging his eager feet nearer and nearer to the brink of the steep stone. His fingertips just touched the dangling prize once, and then caught at it again, till the foothold slipped; and the right hand clutching the same branch with the left, the child hung for a moment at arm's length over the pool.

Ned dashed in. The water was low; so he found footing under the Pixie's pillar, and caught the urchin in his arms as it fell. It was an impish creature, and made hideous faces at him as he set it down safe upon the bank. Then it burst into fits of hysterical laughter.

"What's your name, little one," he asked, when this at last subsided.

A vacant stare was the only answer.

"How do they call you boy, then?"

The child opened its mouth wide, and gaped upon him.

"Can't you speak, little boy? Whose child are you?"

"Mammy's."

This was more hopeful; but it soon appeared to be the whole extent of information to be gained. No questioning, coaxing, wheedling, or threat, could discover mammy's whereabout. The more trouble Ned took to extract an answer, the more resolute grew the urchin to give none; indeed he soon ceased to listen to his questioner, or look at him, absorbed in the process of weaving rushes with the right hand between the outspread fingers of the left.

"Here's a pretty fix," thought Ned, as he threw himself also down upon the grass in the full blaze of the sunshine, to dry his clothes dripping from his dash into the pool. "Is the brat sulky or idiotic? And what on earth am I to do with it, anyhow?"

The moorland was wide and wild. He could not think of any village for miles whence the child might have come. He unslung his fishing basket, and threw it carelessly down between himself and his impracticable charge. By and by he remembered the lower joints of his rod which he had thrown away to plunge into the water. He got up and went out upon the stepping-stones to look for it. The child, who had eyed him with stolen glances all along, pounced upon the basket the instant that his back was turned. It held a fly-book and a spare winch. The former was at once tossed aside; the latter, new and bright, excited curiosity and desire. The child began to pull at the end of the coiled line: crrr—whrr—went the winch. What a wondrous and delightful toy!

Having some hazy notion of ownership, and vague apprehension of the dangers of theft, he looked round for Ned, whose back was turned and bent over the stream, out of which he was trying to fish the joints of his rod. The boy started up, hid the reel in his shirt breast, and scampered off.

When Ned turned again, he saw the urchin many hundred yards ahead, running as if for life.

"Cutting home again, I suppose; but there's no knowing, I'd better follow the monkey." So he slung his basket, without missing the winch, and set off at a trot in pursuit.

They ran half a mile at least, the child scudding on before wild and swift as a moorland hare. Presently, in a sudden fold of the ground, appeared a solitary human dwelling, into which it ran.

It was a long, low cottage, built of stonework as rough as if the builders had piled up stones and boulders off the moor without attempt to sort, or face, or dress them. The thatch was a mass of ling and heather kept down by heavy stones. There was no upper story; the two rooms, with a sort of barn or cow-shed, being on the ground floor. A plot of stunted cabbages, and of potatoes with weak haulms, were the only signs of cultivation.

When Ned came up, the door of rude oakslabs, stood ajar. No voice answered his knocking; so he went in.

The furniture of the kitchen, or keeping-room, was scanty, but very clean. It was, however, in complete disorder, as if the wayward underwitted child had been suffered to work his will upon it. There was a wide open chimney, and a big black iron cooking-pot hung over the white ashes of a dead fire. A small wooden Dutch clock hung in one corner; but its pendulum was still, and its click hushed. On a dresser were the fragments of a loaf apparently broken by the child. A kitten, not given to bread-eating, was sniffing at them, mewing starveling mews. There was an air of desolation over all.

"Holloa here! Any one at home?" cried Ned. Though he could not feel quite sure of it, he thought he heard a feeble answer to his hail.

"Where are you, then?" he cried again; "sing out a bit, if there's any one there!"

"Here, i' bedroom," the voice rejoined, a little louder, though very feeble still.

He pushed open the bedroom door. There was a poor tent bedstead without curtains, whose counterpane, though tossed and tumbled, was scrupulously clean. On the pillow lay the feverish head of a woman, with large dark eyes. In a corner stood a smaller truckle-bed, still more disordered; and down beside it crouched the child, pulling the line again to hear the "crrr—whrr" of the reel.

"Thank God sum 'un be coom at last!" the woman said, as Ned went up to the bedside and asked what ailed her. "I thought I should a died afore any one 'ud coom anighst me: and then what 'ud coom o' Benjy?"

"So that little fellow is yours, is he? I couldn't make out from him who his 'mammy' was."

"There, sir, I knows he aint ezackerly not as other folk's children; but kind o' lost most times. But there aint no harm in my poor Benjy nohow, neither."

"Well, I found him on the Pixie's pillar, off of which he tumbled, and I caught him; and when he cut away, I ran after him, for fear he should get into mischief again."

"God bless 'ee, sir; he must a sent'ee, sure enough, to save poor Benjy's life, and, maybe, his mother's. I've a lain here three days wi' a sort o' chill. I wur out a hay makin' a Saturday and wur cotched in thic starm as coom on arternoon, ye mind."

"What, were you out in that thunderstorm? I can't remember such a downpour this long time."

"'Ees sure, sir; an' it's a main step up here from Rookenham; t'wur in the park we wur haying. I wur that wet and coold afore I gotten our bit o' supper, and gotten Benjy to bed; there, I wur fit to bite my tongue off wi' my teeth a chatterin'."

"And then, I suppose, it turned to fever heat?"

"Coom all over wi' flushes and hets, till I feeled liker a coal; I wur sort o' wanderin' and light by night."

"And have none of the neighbors been near you?"

"Naighbors! why, bless 'ee, sir, there aint none lives nigher nor the kipper at Rookenham-gate."

"What! have you laid here without medicine, or food, or drink, these three days! Couldn't you send the child down to let some one know how ill you were?"

"That's where 'tis, sir; Benjy's quite sensible-like by times, and 'ull run arrands as well as other children a'most; leastways when he's a mind to 't. But fust he took on a cryin' to see mammy abed so long. Then he wur offended like as she 'udn't bile 'un no 'taters; then he tuk an' started on the moor, and left I all alone."

"Is there any thing in the house that I can give you," said Ned, in great concern, "before I go down to Rookenham to fetch the doctor? Whom I shall tell about you down there, who'll see to you and the child whilst you're so ill?"

"Well, if you could mak' me a drop o' tea now; but it's troublin' you."

"Oh, confound the trouble; but there's no fire, you know, and the water will take no end of time to boil; and it's a good step down into Rookenham. I'll tell you what, I'll light a fire, and put the kettle on, and cut down after the doctor whilst it's boiling, eh?"

"Well do 'ee now; and God bless 'ee for being kind to a poor widder 'ooman."

Assisted by Master Benjy, who brightened up at what he conceived to be preliminaries for boiling "taters," Ned soon had a blazing fire on the kitchen hearth. He was under some apprehension at leaving the idiot boy in charge, lest he should set fire to the cottage, and bring about a more hideous calamity for his sick mother. But she assured her new-found friend that Benjy might be trusted to tend the fire without danger to himself or her.

"And when ye've warned the doctor, good genelman, do 'ee call in at Park cooming back, and tell Mrs. White, the housekeeper, how 'tis wi' I. She's been biggest o' friends to me and my Benjy ever since I wur left a widder."

"Benjy," said Ned, as he went out, "do you know what peppermints are?"

"'Ees, goodies," quoth he, licking his lips with unmistakable intelligence.

"Well then, you mind the fire and take care of mammy, and don't run out upon the moor till I come back, you know, and I'll bring you some peppermints; do you hear, Benjy?"

"'Ees, goodies," he repeated, and licked his lips again.

So Ned went hurrying down towards Rookenham, forgetful of his own troubles, having gained a precious respite in his conflict with the fiercer spirit that had urged him on before this unexpected visit to the fatherless and widow in their affliction.

He chanced upon the doctor a mile before

reaching the village close by one of the Park lodges. He promised to go up at once to the sick woman; but would drive Ned up the Park avenue, to convey her message to the friendly housekeeper. Mrs. White, a motherly kind of woman, was much concerned at hearing of Rizpah Cottle's trouble. She would go to her at once; but must put up a little parcel of comforts whilst the Shetland ponies were being harnessed. She would give Mr. Locksley a lift over the moor on his way back. My lord's little study was the only room where the things were uncovered, as no one was at Rookenham just now; perhaps Mr. Locksley would step in there and sit down.

He sat down at a writing-table in the centre of the room, and looked round. It was plainly furnished, and but for the blue books and official papers, presented the appearance of a studious man's sitting-room in college. By the fireside was an armchair, whose shape and cover seemed to announce that it had strayed from a lady's boudoir; and on the mantel-piece, between two very common spill-holders, was an exquisite vase of old Dresden. Both were cherished souvenirs of Lord Royston's mother. That never came into Ned's mind; which fastening at once upon their presence, and perceiving their incongruity with all else in the study, looked forward for an explanation, instead of backward; setting down to anticipation what was indeed a retrospect. Hot and bitter came back the flush of jealousy.

"What? Is he so sure of her? Shall she sit there, and snip his red tape fot him, as he dockets his papers and fingers his blue books?"

He went striding up and down the room, his fingers twitching nervously with the play of an impulse, which almost mastered him, spite of his shame, to seize the Dresden vase and dash it into splinters, as he had done by the big stone on the moor.

"He counts already on seeing her dainty fingers coax the flowers into perfect grouping of form and color. I've half a mind to smash the—"

"Please Master Ned, the ponies is to, and I've put up Rizpah's parcel. We'd better be going before it's any later. But bless me, what have I been thinking about? I do believe the rheumatics affect my head at times. You've come over all the way from Cransdale, this forenoon, and I'll be bound to say you've never had a morsel of lunch. I beg a thousand pardons; you shall have a tray in five minutes."

"Not a bit—not a morsel!" cried Ned, with savage emphasis.

"Oh, deary, deary me! I beg your pardon humbly. It's more than my lord would easily forgive me, being so unhospitable; it's not Rookenham ways, by no means," quoth Mrs. White, much distressed. "We can't have nothing hot in so short a time, Master Ned—that is, Mr. Locksley; but if a cold fowl with a cut of ham and a grouse-pie, and—"

"Not a single morsel—I mean no thank you—I really beg your pardon. I am very sorry—that is, I didn't mean—in fact, I don't feel hungry. Thank you very kindly all the same, Mrs. White; but, as you said, it's late, and a long drive over the moor," stuttered out Ned. In his wrath he would have neither bite nor sup under his rival's roof, nor out of his rival's larder; yet he was in terrible and ridiculous confusion at having let that wrath burst out upon hospitable Mrs. White. He seized up his hat and hurried out, in spite of her entreaties. In the passage they met the still-room maid, whom she, with ready presence of mind, despatched for a bag of biscuits; but before even that dry fare could be provided, Ned had bustled the discomfited housekeeper into the pony-chaise, and with an unjustifiable cut at either Shetlander, had set them galloping down the avenue towards the lodge.

There was a trifle of asthma about the good stout lady sometimes no less than a touch of those "rheumatics" at which she had glanced in her apologies. So the Long Avenue was passed, and the stretch of high-road beyond the lodge; and it was the ponies' turn to be shortish of breath, tugging up the hill-side, before she had recovered hers sufficiently to enter upon conversation. Ned had been silently grinding his teeth, partly to confine his fury—partly, perhaps, to curb involuntary remonstrances of certain inward feelings against his sentimental refusal to satisfy their imperious and legitimate cravings.

"I'm so sorry my lord wasn't down at Rookenham, Mr. Locksley—Master Ned I was a-going to say. Then this sad business, maybe, wouldn't have happened."

"How could Lord Royston have kept poor Rizpah—that's her name I think you said—from getting a sun-stroke?"

"La, Master Ned. I beg pardon, Mr. Locksley. I wasn't a thinking of that poor creature, but of your going without your lunch now."

"Not another word about it, pray, Mrs. White. It's my own doing. No one who knows your heartiness could doubt it."

"Ah, Master Ned,—it *will* come more natural than Mr. Locksley—I mind the time when you'd have made something like a luncheon. Mussy on me! how fast time goes. It seems like yesterday, yet it's some years now, since I seen you three come tearing down the hillside and up the avenue a horseback; you, and the young earl, and Lady Constance, with her beautiful hair all fleering in the wind ahead of both of you. How she did gallop, to be sure! It's often made my blood run cold to see such a lovely child as she was running wild with you boys! I don't know when you've all three been over at Rookenham. Last time she came here you wasn't with her, not the earl nor you. She came with Lady Cransdale and my lord in the barouche."

Ned ground his teeth the harder; but Mrs. White, who rather liked to have the conversation to herself, went on,—

"She's altered very much, is Lady Constance, more grandlike and stately to look at; but just as beautiful as ever, I think; and quite as kind-spoken. She took one hand of mine in both of hers, she did, and says she—'You dear old Mrs. White, it's an age since I set eyes on you.' I'll tell you what it is, Master Ned, now," persisted the good housekeeper, edging nearer to the luckless driver and sinking her voice to a confidential whisper, "you should just a seen 'em standing side by side, my lord and Lady Constance, and you'd a thought as I did, 'Well, there wouldn't be such another couple to be found in England, if so be, as ever they were to *be* a couple,' as I'm sure I wish they might."

"Too steep for the ponies," was all Ned's answer, jumping down from his seat beside her as if she scorched him.

When the tug up-hill was over, he jumped in again, and began at once, determined not to let Mrs. White select the topic of conversation,—

"Who's this Rizpah Cottle, Mrs. White? What on earth brought her up there on the moor?"

"Well, she's a poor lone widow, Master Ned, and it's her Benjy brought her up upon the moor."

"Lone widow, sure enough; but she must have an extra turn for loneliness, spite of having Benjy to keep her company, if she lives up there of her own accord."

"Ah, Master Ned, you don't know what a mother's heart is! How should you?"

"Don't I, Mrs. White? You forget what a mother of my own I have."

"Not I, neither. I known her afore you were thought of, as they say. I lived housekeeper at her grandfather, the archdeacon's, years afore he got me my present place, in old Lord Rookenham's time. She were a sweet young lady, were Miss Lucy, so gentle and loving-like; there was the makins of a mother in her long before she had ever a child."

"Well, but what has Rizpah's motherly heart to do with living up all alone upon the moor with Benjy? I should have thought it safer for the child to have been down with other little 'uns at Rookenham. Is he mischievous? Would he bite 'em?"

"Lor, Master Ned, how can you? No, poor little fellow; he's mischievous by times, but not spiteful that ever I hear tell. I'd better begin at the beginning, perhaps, and then you'll understand all about it."

"All right, Mrs. White, fire away then."

"You know the quarries at Garlige, the other side of Rookenham village?"

"To be sure I do."

"Ralph Cottle—that was Rizpah's husband—was one of the quarrymen. Fine men they are mostly; but given to drink, which I never heard say as Ralph was, neither, Master Ned. But he was very careless and masterful about keeping in harm's way, as them quarrymen always have been, that I can mind."

"Careless about the powder-bags, eh?" threw in Ned considerately, for the conflict between the short wind of the asthmatic patient and the long wind of the story-teller, seemed to demand the occasional intervention of the listener. "I suppose he came to grief in blasting, quarryman fashion, too,"

"Just so, Master Ned, dear, just so. He was a walking unconcerned-like, with both hands in his pockets, when he should have been running; which, indeed, it was said at the coroner's inquest, he ought to have been out of harm's way two minutes afore the blast came at all—when off it goes, like any thing, and a sharp piece cut like a skull-cap right off his head, poor fellow, and scattered his brains, as it was awful to see, though they did tie it up with a handkerchief afore they carried the corpse right in to poor Rizpah, that was expecting him home to dinner, poor thing, a sitting by the fire, to watch a bit of fresh pork she had roasting, as she's told me scores of times since."

"What a ghastly sight for the poor woman! I wonder it did not turn her brain to look on it."

"No, she never gave so much as a screech they say; but sat stony-like, and said, quite quiet and composed: 'Please lay 'un out on the bed, poor fellow!' 'But there, Mrs. White,'—she've a told me scores o' times—'I feeled jist so as if my heart had given two turns wrong, and then bid still, you know.' Her baby was born not six weeks after, and though *her* brain wasn't turned, *his* was; for that was her Benjy. I've heard tell that she wanted to call him 'Benoni, the son of sorrow,' when he was christened, like Rachel a-dying; but our rector down at Rookenham persuaded her to alter it, like Jacob, you know, sir."

"Was the child an idiot from its birth, then?"

"I thought so myself, so soon as ever I set eyes on it; not as I said so to Rizpah, poor thing, for 'twas plain to see she didn't think so for a long time."

"Poor creature! I dare say she found it hard to face the fact."

"Hard! Bless you, it was heartless to see her watch for any sign of sense like in her baby. I have seen her sit with it upon her knees and nurse it, and sing, and talk to it, and look, look, look, into its restless eyes as if to fix the sense into them."

"Well, but Mrs. White, all this don't tell me what brought her and her Benjy up here upon the moor."

"Don't it though? Wait a bit, sir, and you'll find it does. She gave her life up to Benjy from the first. How she ever managed it, I've never rightly understood. Many were kind to her; but Rizpah had a proud spirit of her own, and never would beg while she could work. Work! I believe ye. She's done wonders to find time for work and to wait upon her child as well. She never neglected him for one half-hour, seemingly; and yet she'd earn enough to keep herself and him."

"But living up upon the moorland, so far off, must have increased her difficulties tenfold. They didn't live here in the father's time, did they?"

"No, Master Ned; no more they didn't in the first years of little Benjy's life. It was along of a foreign doctor, that came once to my lord's, that Rizpah left the village and took the cottage here."

"A foreign doctor?"

"Yes. He was a Swish, I think, leastways a German sort of gentleman with spectacles, as smelt of smoke. And he saw Benjy; and told his mother that pure air up on hill-tops, was likeliest for such as that poor child to thrive in. He said there was a plenty such where he lived, and they put them up in hospitals a-top of mountains. Christians, I think, he called 'em; though it's poor sort of Christians such as Benjy's like to make—not but what some persons *do* call them *Innocents*."

"Oh, crétins! Yes, I see the whole thing now. I've heard of those mountain hospitals. So Rizpah came up into the wild, to give to her idiot boy the best chance of thriving? Brave heart, indeed!"

"Only a mother's, Master Ned!" said Mrs. White.

"Only a mother's!" Ned kept repeating the words to himself aloud, long after he had parted at the cottage-door from Mrs. White.

O Mary, they have closed the Mill,
The looms are silent now;
And we must stoop with heavy souls
Beneath the rod to bow.
I feel a throbbing in my heart—
A chill within my breast—
And long to lay my weary form
Within the grave to rest;
For life has been a ceaseless strife
With cares that ever grew;
We slaved, and starved, and NOW, alas!
O God! what shall we do?

I've seen thee weep, when thou didst think
Thy tears I could not see;
And seen thee put aside thy food
That baby fed might be;
While oft thou forced a loving smile,
Although thy heart was sore;
And kissed my pale and bloodless cheek,
And bade me grieve no more.
But now thou canst not hide thy tears;
Thy lips they quiver, too;
Thy hand, it trembles in my own;
O God! what shall we do?

Thy fingers they are thin and worn
With needlework so cheap;
Thy eyes are red, thy brow is cold,
For want of rest and sleep.
Our little infant, fevered, droops,
And soon will be no more:
It had not starved had I been rich,
But I alas, am poor.
I wonder if the wealthy great
Would help us if they knew
Our wretched fate? The thought is vain;
O God! what shall we do?

For never shall these lips of mine
A pauper's pittance crave
While I have life, though after death
I fill a pauper's grave.
My soul grows fierce. Oh! that my voice
Could ring throughout the land,
And breathe the cares, the wants, and fate,
Of Labor's starving band;
And bid the Lords of Gold beware,
Lest they, like us, may sue,
When Revolution comes, and cry—
"O God! what shall we do?"

—*Songs of Labor, by John Plummer.*

THE QUIET ROOM.

I am with thee in this quiet room,
Dearest, I am with thee.
The church-bells ring, and the bird's sweet chaunt
Quivers around this lonely haunt
Of ancient piety;
But I can see, and I can hear
A sweeter song, and a scene more dear,—
And I am again with thee!

I am with thee in this quiet room.
The vine looks in at the casement old:
Through the old casement, diamond-paned,
Wander the vine-leaves, golden veined:
Low in the garden the roses bloom,
Loading the air with a rich perfume:
In quiet I sit, and the quiet room
Is half in shadow and half in gloom;
As I sit in the shadow my hands I fold,
My very breath I measure and hold,
Lest I trouble and scare
The spirits of air,
And memory leave her tale half told.

I am alone in my quiet room,
And alone with thee no more;
My heart is heavy, my heart is chill,
With a dull faint shiver of coming ill,—
Oh, spare me! spare this quiet room!

There have been times when it was to me
A prison of deadly gloom,
A den of sickness and of pain,
And so it yet may be again;
But now, it, and the garden deep,
Where the summer sunbeams quiver and brood
Over the purple flowers that sleep
In bliss beneath,—the trim green lawn,
And the dark cedar boughs that throw
A veil between the sunset's glow,—
Even the old house that I so often
Have thought so dull and drear, doth soften
Into a home of Old Romance,
Where one, who, like me, has suffered mischance,
May win all rare and lovely things
To soothe the soul's imaginings;
A twilight temple of repose
From the outer world of strife and woes.
A quiet cross, a blessed way,
Through peaceful paths of shadowy gloom,
To pass at length from this quiet room
Into the silence of the tomb.
Yes, it were lovely and sweet to pass
Down the old staircase and out by the grass,
Silent and chill as the night-bedewed flower,
Out of the dust of this life, and the power
Of sorrow to blight, and of joy to betray,
Out of "the burden and heat of the day!"

—*Lyrics and Idyls, by Gerda Fay.*

ONE O'CLOCK.

A SONNET.

Another stroke upon Time's anvil struck!
Another hour drawn hot from out the heart
Of silence; that within lone aisles, apart,
And hollow belfries, homesteads of the rook,
And this my cloister of the lamp and book,
Upwards the same dim Cyclop arm might dart,
Swing the same shadowy sledge, and mortals start
With the same brazen blow!—Sure man mistook
His own endurance, when he tongued the bells
To prophecy against him from their towers!
The high sun speaks not. Ocean's ebbs and swells
Rock through a silent calendar. All powers
Of life and death muffle their peals and knells:—
Why arm with thunder the avenging hours?

—*Dublin University Magazine.*

From The Christian Observer.

BASHAN; AND THE CITIES OF MOAB.*

Uses of far deeper value and moment than were formerly contemplated, are now subserved by the researches of travellers in Scripture Lands. Until quite recently it was thought enough if they were employed to confirm the accuracy, or to explain the allusions of an inspired writer: the interpreter's concern with them was ended when he could bring forward the place, or the custom alluded to in an obscure passage, and when he thus enabled us to read this intelligently and confidently, with a clear perception of the spiritual lessons that might be educed from it. And so extensive have these researches been, and so diligently have they been thus made use of, that in fact, very few pages of the Holy Volume have been left unexplained by this kind of illustration.

With great diligence have they been gathered, and most profitably have they been so employed. Still this use of them only enabled us to look on the sacred delineations at a distance. We saw clearly, and perhaps vividly, the occurrences related in the Bible: the import of the sacred narrative was unfolded, and it grew lifelike, and became familiar, as we gazed on it. Still it stood before us only as a picture, and it lay in remote distance. So far as living intercourse with the objects and beings brought forward in Scripture was concerned, it seemed that we must necessarily stand apart from the scenes which it unfolded. And now, indeed, some of our recent biblical interpreters have told us that just so it was intended that we should look on the inspired delineations. According to these teachers, such delineations *are* only pictures, or pictorial embodiments of thought: historical ideas, or theological conceptions, are depicted in these Eastern forms: they were not, nor were they ever intended to be, recognized as actual events and living men whom we have been looking on. This has been affirmed; and as the so-called historical philosophy has advanced, its professors have boasted that they, one after another, had divested our sacred records of its literal significance. Now, against statements of this kind, the confirmatory, illustrative use which the old commentators made of travellers' researches was wholly ineffective. All they had accomplished was to prove the accuracy of the sacred narrative, and its true adjustment, as if it were authentic history, with the framework that surrounded it. But not only was this view compatible with the sceptical theory, it even strengthened the confidence with which that theory was put forward. Another use, one far more deep and searching, of observations in Bible lands was needed, and this has been made opportunely, we may say providentially, just as this new form of scepticism has become most threatening and destructive. For now our Bible travellers, with deeper views of their work, and with far greater facilities of investigation, aspire rather after the reproduction of Scripture life, than its simple illustration: they now give us in colored stereographic views, rather than in surface pictures, the result of their investigations. We no longer look on Scripture scenes at a distance, but we actually live amongst them: their vicissitudes of climate, the changing aspects of their sky, the hues and shadows of their landscape, the objects seen by the men of Scripture, the sounds they heard, are known to us: we not only witness, but almost share in, the life of Bible times and men: our "newly awakened historical consciousness" is in the very scene and platform of its movements. No one who has familiarized himself with Dr. Robinson's exact descriptions, with Stanley's glowing illustrations of them, and especially with Mr. Grove's recent contributions to the topography of Scripture, can fail to recall numerous examples in illustration of these remarks. And in each case this vivid realization has been effected with no purpose of mere vindication, or even with the set design of illustrating the Bible history in the accustomed form. The truth of Scripture has been assumed, and it has been read trustingly on the scene of its occurrence. An "evidence of congruity" has hence arisen. The sense of agreement and conformity with facts has been so strongly felt, such an intense consciousness of the presence of truth has been awakened, that, while a deeper insight into the meaning of the

* Scripture Lands in Connection with their History, etc. By G. S. Drew, M.A., Incumbent of St. Barnabas, South Kennington. Smith, Elder, and Co. 1860. Five Years in Damascus. By Rev. J. L. Porter. Murray. 1855.

sacred writers has also been obtained, their historical verity, the literal and objective accuracy of their statements, has been so established, that the myth professor, the "philosophical historian," might as well attempt to vaporize the substantial facts around us, as to convert into the thin exhalations of his theory these historical details of the Scripture narrative which have been thus illustrated and confirmed.

The importance of this use of biblical travel, and its providential adaption to our present need, will be instantly recognized by all who understand the ground on which the biblical controversy has lately moved. As Mr. J. Taylor, the editor of Dr. Traill's Josephus, has remarked, "What seems just now to be needed is, not so much any new presentation of the Christian argument, as the bringing back upon the mind of the educated classes a firm, healthy, rational regard to the certainty of history,—a deference to evidence as opposed to the baseless theories, the myths, the mystifications, by means of which, of late, the public mind has been abused, and the edge of the most conclusive reasoning turned aside. There is needed an every-day familiarity with the scenes, with the persons, and usages, and costumes, with the minor incidents, as well as with the leading events of the Christian epoch. The times of the gospel history are indolently thought of by many, as if the clouds and mists of the remotest ages had settled down just upon that spot of time, or as if the rolling flood of years had there taken a sweep through an impenetrable gloom; and hence they have allowed themselves to listen to the wild conjectures of erudite pantheists." These remarks are even more applicable at the present time than when they were first published; and we may here observe, that few have done more than this accomplished writer himself in meeting the need which he has so forcibly expressed. His "Notes" in the above-named work abound with the means of that vivid realization of Scripture incidents which he has described. They suggested some of the uses which, in a former number of this journal, we made of the knowledge that has recently been collected respecting what we called the "subterranean Jerusalem." And now, it is from the same point of view, and with the purpose of subserving the objects which he has so clearly indicated, that in this article we propose to give some detailed account of another field of discovery recently explored, which furnishes means of vivid realizations of Scripture history that are not less remarkable than those above alluded to, though they are less familiarly and accurately known.

The regions to which we now allude are the provinces of the ancient Bashan, and the widely extended plains immediately on the south of them. They are still comparatively unfamiliar; and this may be explained by the form in which descriptions of them have hitherto appeared, as well as by the comparative brevity of those portions of Scripture which they illustrate. Neither Burckhardt, nor Porter, notwithstanding their high merit as accurate observers, have attempted any of that scenic picturing which gives the pages of Stanley and Grove their great charm and use. And the late important researches of Mr. Graham in this region are only known from the detached and hastily written papers in which he has attempted nothing more than an outline of his discoveries. Those who have given us our stereographic revivals of Bible life have hitherto employed themselves on the more familiar incidents of Holy Writ which occurred in the better-known and more frequently trodden paths of Western Palestine. Yet none of their delineations are more impressive than those which pens like theirs, guided by their methods and in their spirit, may present us with in the country we have just indicated; and the following outline may, at all events, indicate the nature and the amount of the materials which can in this manner be so employed.

It was in the beginning of the present century that the modern investigations, from which we obtain our only trustworthy accounts of these regions of Eastern Palestine, were commenced. Seetzen, the Russian consul, at Damascus, was the first explorer, but he only reached the towns on the northern borders; and the chief use of his journey was to stimulate Burckhardt, who, in the year 1810, penetrated into the interior, and reached the southernmost border of this then unknown land. Burckhardt's researches were carried forward with his usual care and accuracy; and his report of them, edited in 1822 by Col. W. M. Leake, still forms one of our best sources of information. In the year 1819, Buckingham followed him, and afterwards published an account of his observations. But it is disfigured by frequent inaccuracies, and little more of value was added to Burckhardt's narrative until the year 1853, when the Rev. J. L. Porter, then residing as missionary at Damascus, took advantage of the favoring circumstances of the country to examine it even more thoroughly than Burckhardt had done. He has given the results of his journey in his "Five Years in Damascus." No new ground, however, was explored by him, nor had any fresh discoveries been made since Burckhardt's time, until the year 1857. In the autumn of that year, Mr. Graham, with a rare union of enterprise and of good fortune, explored the country as far east of the limit which Burckhardt had reached, as that limit is itself distant from the mountain boundaries of the Jordan and its lakes. No discoveries of greater importance than his have been made in Scripture lands since Dr. Layard's excavations in Nineveh. In fact, he has just doubled our information respecting the country we are now speaking of; so that the mountain range which had formerly been regarded as its eastern boundary, should now be figured on the maps as running through the middle of it; as again, in its south-western regions, he was the first to visit and examine some of the many towns that come in view from the castle of Bozrah, not one of which had been previously examined.

From those sources an extensive and, in some degree, an exact knowledge of the region in question may be obtained. And here, for the purpose of giving some definiteness to our description of it, we cannot do better than imagine ourselves placed on the upper tower of the castle of Sûlkhad, which is built on the southern slopes of that Haurân range that runs north-west and south-east through about the middle of the scene of our inquiries. There we are somewhat north of the middle point of its lower boundary. South and south-west, as far as the eye can reach, the country extends in an undulating fertile plain, and at intervals are many deserted towns and villages:—

"To the south-east runs an ancient road, straight as an arrow, across the fine plain. . . . Our guide informed us that this road extends to Bûsra on the Persian Gulf: the same statement I afterwards heard from others; and the historian Ibn Said, cited by Abulfeda, says that from this castle a king's highway ran to Irak, and that by it Baghdad may be reached in ten days. (Mr. Graham followed the road for about ten miles.) On the plain extending from the south to the east, I counted fourteen towns or villages, none of them more than twelve miles distant, and almost all of them, so far as I could see by the aid of a telescope, still habitable, like Sûlkhad, but completely deserted. (All these towns Mr. Graham visited.) The houses in some of them I could distinctly see standing perfect, as when recently finished; and those strange square towers, so conspicuous in all the ancient villages of the Haurân, are here too." *

This is the southern view from the commanding point we are supposed to occupy. And now turning round, and looking first on our left side, i.e., north-westwards, the whole of Bashan lies before us. Due west, its furthest boundary is the high ground rising up into the mountain wall, which comes in view on the other side of Jordan, and this is about one hundred miles from the Haurân range, at the extremity of which we are now standing. The whole of the southern portion of this surface is made up of undulating downs, whose fertility is attested by the numerous ruins which, in this direction, also come within our furthest range of sight. Looking up along the mountain slopes on this side the Haurân range, we see traces of numerous forests, thick with the Bashan oaks, which are as characteristic of this region as the cedars are of Lebanon. Volcanic traces are everywhere discernible; and just beyond the limits of our prospect, is the dark waving line of the southern boundary of a district that lies almost midway in the upper provinces of Bashan, and which might be regarded as the fortress of that ancient kingdom. This is now called the Lejah. It is the Argob of the Old Testament, and the Trachonitis of the New; and is one of the most remarkable districts in the world. It appears to be the deposit of a great volcanic eruption, in an extremely remote period; and it may be described as a volcanic island of an oval shape, being about twenty-two miles long by twelve wide:—

"Its general surface is elevated from twenty to thirty feet above the surrounding

* Porter's Damascus, Vol. ii. p. 188.

plain; . . . and its border is almost everywhere as clearly defined as the line of a rocky coast, which, indeed, it very much resembles, with its inlets, bays, and promontories. . . . It is wholly composed of black basalt rock, which, in past ages, appears to have issued from innumerable pores of the earth in a liquid state, and to have flowed out on every side until the plain was almost covered. Before cooling, its surface was agitated by some fearful tempest, or other such agency; and it was afterwards shattered and rent by internal convulsions and vibrations. In many places there are deep fissures and yawning gulfs (especially on the western side), and so rough and rugged is the country, so deep the gullies and ravines, and so lofty the overhanging rocks, that the whole is a wild labyrinth, which none but the Arabs can penetrate." *

Both the nature of this district, and its central position in the Bashan kingdom, marked it as the fortress settlement of the inhabitants, and it is accordingly filled with towns, where they were—as in fact the present inhabitants of the same place are—inaccessible to ordinary invaders. The country beyond this district, on the west and north-west, subsides into the plain that stretches away towards Anti-Lebanon, as on the north and north-east, it melts into the desert country that encloses the Ghûtah, or valley of Damascus.

Such is the western side of the province towards which we look from our station on Sûlkhad. Another and very different prospect spreads out before us on the north-east. This half (speaking roughly) of the region in question presents an aspect utterly sterile and repulsive, and, in fact, it soon passes into the desert regions which reach to the Euphrates. Yet, barren as this side of the country is, it is neither trackless nor uninhabited. There are two broad roads, evidently formed at great cost and labor, running straight across it; one, to which we have before alluded, running south-eastwards from our position to Bûzra, on the Persian Gulf, and the other towards Palmyra, connecting Bozzah with that city. Numerous towns are scattered over the country through which these roads pass in the outset of their course; and while, in its stern bareness, it is wholly unlike the country on the west of our dividing range, it resembles that country in enclosing a volcanic district remarkably similar to the Lejah, which we have just described. This is called the Safâh, which is marked, even on recent maps, as a single tell, or eminence, but which, in fact, is a long mountainous range, extending lengthways, almost due north and south, for upwards of forty miles, and being in some parts between twelve and fifteen miles in breadth. While its elevation is far greater than that of the Lejah, in its physical formation and its aspect, it is said to be almost identical with that district. Mr. Graham describes it as "a sea of basalt, intersected with cracks and fissures which are often quite impassable." The country on the north of it melts into and blends with the desert region above described as surrounding the Damascus valley, while on the east it is soon lost in the wastes which border the Euphrates.

It would be across those wastes, and moving in a south-westerly direction, that the first company of emigrants from the primeval settlements in Western Asia made their way towards those rich provinces of Syria and Egypt, of which they might have heard from some adventurous explorer, or which, even more probable, their antediluvian traditions may have made known to them. In those early ages the stream of emigration would continually pour itself across the upper fords of the Euphrates, through the Tadmor oasis, and over the rich Damascus plain; and one company after another would stay and settle on the resting-places which they found in their long way. Thus were formed the communities at Tadmor and Damascus; and, later, the region we are now concerned with came to be occupied by races designated as the Emim, the Zuzim, and the Rephaim. We are unable to locate these races accurately on their respective settlements; and, in fact, except in some undeciphered characters found by Mr. Graham in the neighborhood,* no traces exist which give any intimation who they were that occupied the towns around the Safâh, and in the region called El Harrah, which extends into the desert on the east of it. With this part of the region we have been reviewing, history is connected only by suggestions or by inferences. But of the Rephaim (i.e. Giants), we know that, as might have been expected,

* Porter's Damascus, Vol. ii. pp. 240–242.

* In *Jour. Asiat. Soc.*, Vol. xvii., Mr. Graham has given some specimens of these inscriptions.

they established themselves and built their dwellings in that fortress settlement, as the Lejah may be called, which indeed none but such a race could then have occupied. It is plain that, if ever inhabited at all, it could only have been by people of gigantic prowess, who had reasons for establishing themselves in such an inaccessible position, and who had immense force at command for the erection of their dwellings in it. Such would be our conclusion, supposing no traces remained of the dwellings they actually erected. But many of them are still extant, and have been carefully described by the explorers of this region. In some instances they are covered over by the works of later occupants of the territory; in others they stand as they were originally built; and they present the most ponderous and massive instances of domestic architecture of which we have any knowledge. Their solid walls, upwards of four feet in thickness, are raised of large blocks of squared stones, placed one on the other without cement; their roofs are formed of enormous slabs of the same material, the black basaltic rock of the country, which is almost like iron. So also are their doors and gates, some of them being nearly eighteen inches thick, and secured by ponderous bars, the recesses for which can still be seen. "They are just such structures," says Mr. Porter, "as a race of giants would rear up; and are in every way characteristic of a period when architecture was in its infancy, when manual labor was of little comparative value, and when strength and security were the great requisites." And Mr. Graham, who visited the country shortly after an extensive tour in Upper Egypt, and after he had examined some of the most remarkable specimens of the massive Phœnician structures around Mount Hermon, remarks: "They are unlike any other buildings we have seen or even heard of. . . . If we had known nothing of their history, we should have been forced to the conclusion, that the people who had constructed them were not only a powerful and mighty nation, but that, individually, they were of greater strength than ourselves."

Now the unerring Record tells us that the original colonists of these regions were just such men; and, entrenched in their fortress homes, they would soon subject all the adjacent country to their control. It is probable, however, that their number was not considerable when Abraham passed on the west of them in his journey along the borders of their settlement. After emerging from the Damascus valley, he would descry their gloomy and inaccessible abodes far away on his left hand, and hurry on, as we may imagine, as quickly as he could, from their dangerous neighborhood. But that they were then few in number, may be inferred from the defeat which they soon afterwards suffered from the Chaldean forces, "which smote the Rephaim in Ashtaroth Karnaim," one of the border towns that were built as above described. It is indeed possible that this discomfiture of the Giants took place in some outpost skirmish, and that Chedorlaomer's troops did not venture to attack these formidable men in their rocky fastnesses. Be this, however, as it may, they soon became the paramount tribe in that region, as might have been expected, and as may be unmistakably inferred from the Egyptian monuments. And when, long after the time of Abraham, his two grandsons met at Mahanaim, they, too, were on the very borders of this territory of the Rephaim. Jacob had doubtless paid them the customary tribute exacted from the caravans which travelled past their settlements; while Esau, the powerful chieftain of the Seir mountains, was probably the only prince in the neighboring provinces who could venture to come so near them.

For nearly three centuries after that conference between the two brothers, history is silent respecting the country. It appears, however, to have been traversed during this time by the Egyptian armies, whose successes and frequent conquests over the Rephaim, and in their neighborhood, had hindered this mighty race from subjecting the surrounding nations to their rule.* The Ammonites, on the south of them, had been replaced by the Amorites (i.e., mountaineers) from the other side of Jordan; while the Moabites and Edomites, still further south, yet held peaceful possession of their territory. So far as can be ascertained, the Giants were confined to their rocky enclosure, while, at the same time, they held sway over the provinces immediately bordering upon it on the south, and the forest region which stretches on the south-east as far as

* Osborn's "Egypt," etc.

the slopes of the Haûran. In their inaccessible retreats, protected there by the mighty bulwarks which the volcano had built up around them, they were a continual occasion of dread to all the neighboring tribes, even to those who were yet exempt from their control. Og, and his chiefs, armed with iron missiles, and entrenched behind those mighty bulwarks, in those intricate and inaccessible fastnesses, were indeed terrible neighbors, and enemies dreadful to encounter in aggressive war. Nor had any of the adjacent powers ventured to assail them. Indeed it is probable that all which even the Egyptian armies had accomplished in their much-vaunted exploits against the Rephaim was to drive them within their fortresses. But now they hear of approaching hosts which awaken unwonted fears in them. For these hosts are in possession of all the Egyptian implements of war; and, besides being stronger and more valiant than the mightiest of the neighboring tribes (for had they not just vanquished the powerful Amorites, who had held their own for so many generations?) they had all, from their youth up, been severely trained by generals to whom the modes of Egyptian warfare were familiar.

On the Paran uplands they had received that soldierly training and discipline from men who were well able to conduct it. Joshua and Moses, and the nobles of the people, were familiar with the warlike science that had won such famous victories for the dynasty which was then supreme in Egypt. They had resources which enabled them to obtain from that country the war implements and machines which its science had invented. When they left their settlement in Paran, they marched forward under the inspiration of the loftiest hopes and promises. And half-way on their journey, their army had been purged of those who would have discouraged and encumbered them. Moreover, when they reached the borders of Og's territory, they were flushed and exultant with re-animated hopes, for the mountaineers of Gilead had just been defeated by them. And so, as the history intimates, they advanced without any misgivings to their encounter with the terrible chieftain, and with the mighty forces that were controlled by him.

We know the Presence which was advancing with them, and whose aid furnishes the reason why, in this instance also, they proved irresistible. Their divine Helper, however, wrought through and by means of their own valor and strenuous exertions; and as no visibly miraculous interposition is mentioned in this instance, we may confine our attention to the secondary causes that may be discovered in their defeat of the Bashan chieftain and his forces. All which the researches we are now dwelling on, has disclosed of his power, and of the strength of his position, may be accepted as testimony to the valor and discipline of the Israelites, and to the resources in their possession at this time. They must surely have been very different from a mere wandering host of Bedouin shepherds, as they are sometimes represented, when we find them going forward to the attack of such a formidable adversary, so entrenched and guarded. And their reasons for their valiant confidence were justified. They "smote Og and all his people:" "none" of all his gigantic force "was left to him remaining." "All his cities," also, which were fortified "with high walls, gates, and bars," built of that same basaltic rock, and on the same scale of massiveness, which is now visible in the private dwellings, "they took" at that time. There was not one of the "three-score cities (of which the ruins of thirty are now visible from Tell 'Amârah, on the south of the Lejah') which they took not," besides the unwalled towns on the undulating plain south of their main settlement. And there, in those gloomy massive homes, the Manassites at once established themselves. For the defence of their families, in such a position, it was sufficient for them to leave a small detachment from their tribe; while the great body of them went, in fulfilment of their compact with the brethren by whom they had been just aided, to help in the completion of the conquest on the other side of Jordan.

And if now, or if immediately after their return, they had perfectly finished their work, and wholly extirpated the foes whom they had defeated, they would have been impregnable in their new settlement. But, like their brethren on the west, they allowed many of the people whom they should have utterly driven out, to remain among them. All the forces of Og were vanquished, as the sacred writer expressly states. "But," it is added, "they did not expel the Geshurites, nor the Maachathites: but the Geshurites and the Maachathites dwelt among the sons of Israel" (i.e. in the north-east corner of the volcanic district above described), and in time the Manassites, like their brethren on the west, reaped the fruits of their short-sighted policy. Mingled with these heathens in their dwellings, they "learned their works." And their children were plundered and subjected by the very people they had defeated. This same region was among those which had to be recovered, and restored to Israel, by David in his conquests. And we must picture to ourselves another conflict here between his valiant troops and the dwellers in these wild retreats, that he might reinstate the faithful Manassites in their settlement. These rock cities, with those around the Safâh,* would then form some of the strongest fortresses by which David held his eastern dominions in subjection. There, too, were those garrisons of Solomon which protected the extensive commerce he carried forward by means of the frequent caravans to Damascus and Palmyra, and which added so much to his renown and opulence. And meanwhile another aspect would be gradually thrown over the rude stern dwellings. Midway between the architectural splendor of Jerusalem, and the luxurious dwellings of Damascus, some of their iron ruggedness would be clothed, softened, and adorned by the luxurious culture of the people.

Such was the condition of the country during the brief period of the Hebrew ascendency; and, as it gradually passed away, while the Syrian power was encroaching on the territory which yet remained to Israel, this was one of the positions of which the Damascus monarch would naturally strive to get possession. This he soon accomplished, and here in fact he was garrisoned, and established as on a fortress outpost, during his control over the trans-Jordanic tribes. In fact, it was one of the chief defences of the Syrian king on the south-west of his territory, as the Lebanon ranges were on the north and direct west, and as the Great Desert was on the east. His territory was not extended southward beyond this limit, except perhaps once for a brief period. For now, advancing towards this southern border was the enlarging kingdom of the Moabites. While Syria was encroaching on the province of Manasseh, Moab was absorbing those of Gad and Reuben, and this power was in its zenith when the rule of Assyria was paramount. Thus Moab held all that territory which, increasing in richness as we approach the west, comes in view on either side of the southern prospect from Sülkhad. No part of Syria is more fertile; none was more thickly peopled than those wide-spreading downs which stand blank and naked on our maps; and the Moabite kingdom, which included it at the period we have now reached, must have been exceedingly powerful and wealthy. It was this kingdom which was the subject of Jeremiah's denunciations; and one of the most interesting results of Mr. Graham's researches is found in his account of Um-el-Jemâl, "the ancient Beth Gamul, a very large city, and to be compared almost with the modern Jerusalem. It was very perfect" Mr. Graham continues; "and as we walked about among the streets, and entered every house, and opened the stone doors, and saw the rooms as if they had just been left, and then thought that we were actually in the private dwellings of a people who, for two thousand years had ceased to be a people, we felt a kind of awe, and *realized*, in a manner that we never perhaps could feel elsewhere, how perfectly every title of God's word is carried out. . . . These cities of Moab, which are still so perfect that they might again be inhabited to-morrow, have been during many centuries unpeopled. The land about them, rich and fruitful as any in Syria, has long ceased to produce aught but shrubs and herbs, the food of the camel and the antelope.*

If Um-el-Jemâl may be taken as a specimen of the numerous cities on the south which come in view from Sülkhad, we gain an impressive conception not only of the Moabite kingdom at this time, but also of the previous opulence of the Hebrew tribes who had owned this territory and occupied these cities, while at the same time they had exercised rule, as lords paramount, over the Moab and Edomite communities in their neighborhood. Let us fix our attention

* See Mr. Graham's account of them in Jour. Geog. Soc. Vol. xxviii. p. 287.

* Camb. Essays for 1858. See also Jour. Geog. Soc. Vol. xxviii. pp. 250-252.

steadfastly on their numbers and extent, on the ample resources of their vast provinces, and then connect with this view of them the strong fortresses on the north, which were held by their compatriots, and our conceptions of the national importance of the Israelites, and of the fitness of the ground chosen for the transactions of their great history, will be indefinitely heightened. This ground was over its whole extent, what the highland country on the other side of the Jordan valley was only in its choicest provinces. Rich streams of commerce were continually pouring through the cities built on it, as they flowed on from the Red Sea ports to Damascus and Palmyra, or again from the west, through Bozra, along the road which, as we have seen, led thence to the Persian Gulf. Here, on those broad and fertile pastures, on those richly wooded hills, beside those sparkling streams, with those great highways running through their cities, was the richest portion of Israel's inheritance. Here some of the most momentous parts of its "mission in the world" were to be fulfilled. Provinces like these were needed for the development of some of the characteristics of the Hebrew nature, for the fulfilment of some of its appointed work. And the entire significance of the history of the chosen people cannot be understood, if they are not distinctly taken into account in our survey of the scene where that history was carried forward.

In this point of view all these regions are full of the deepest interest, and we may gladly welcome the recent additions to our knowledge respecting them. Another use of them is found in the illustrations which they furnish of some of the predictive portions of Scripture; but this use must be made in a method differing from that which has been customary. And it must be borne in mind, that we rather infer the fulfilment of those predictions from the general aspect of the country, than actually witness it in what is seen by us. This distinction will go far to remove many of the difficulties which have recently been suggested (as in Stanley's Sinai and Pales., chap. vi.) in respect of the uses which some expositors of prophecy have made of the actual condition of Scripture Lands as illustrative of the inspired predictions. Let it be granted that the ruins and desolations we now look upon are not those which were in view of the inspired seer —and this must be acknowledged, for they betoken the overthrow of races far later than those to whom his denunciations were addressed—yet his words are illustriously verified by them. The existing ruins imply, or we may say they exhibit, the very overthrow which he predicted. As we have already intimated, much of that massive ponderous architecture which we assign to those early days the Scriptures speak of, does not meet us on the surface: the works of later ages are superimposed on them. The Roman builders, for example, who afterwards wrought here, frequently erected their princely structures on what was a field of ruins when their works were carried forward; and in those ruins, the waste and desolation, amidst which their temples and palaces and theatres were raised by them, we discern the fulfilment of the inspired predictions. We think there is reason to regret that commentators on prophecy have not observed this distinction; an element of weakness will be withdrawn from their argument when it is regarded.

For their use, as well as for the help of those who apply themselves to the embodiment and vivification of the history of Scripture, abundant materials are supplied by these late researches upon ground which was formerly almost unknown. It is true that, at present, it has only been roughly and generally surveyed, and indeed more than this has been hitherto impossible. Travel in some parts of this country is still impracticable, and it cannot be accomplished in any part except with risk and peril. It is now overrun by the most lawless of the Bedouins, and for many generations it will be liable to their incursions. As the "corsairs of the wilderness," they will hang upon its coasts for a long period. But under that improved government of Syria, which cannot be delayed much longer, the land itself must be reclaimed from them, and the traveller will be as secure against these outrages as he is now in Western Palestine. Those roads which run directly through their territory show that their ancestors were tamed, or at least made amenable to discipline, as indeed the present generation of them was, in a large measure, during the late Egyptian occupation of the country.

When this is again the case, and the country is thrown open to the deliberate inspection of observers, duly accomplished and gifted like those we have above named, we shall have its history revived, as that has been which was transacted in the familiar scenes of Judæa and Samaria. And thus will be completed a proof overwhelming in its power of demonstration on him who daily investigates it, that the sacred writers wrote what they knew, and testified what they had seen; and that no historical record in our possession is more authentic than that through which we have received the revelation of the mind and will of God.

From The Spectator.

CULTURE *VERSUS* EFFICIENCY.

ENGLISHMEN are not yet prepared to believe with Yeh that knowledge of Taoli is equivalent to merit, but they are fast approaching the stage next to that imbecile condition. They are beginning to believe culture the first requisite of efficiency, to look upon taste as a component of capacity, and style as the best evidence of power. The statesman who has re-organized a department is condemned if he utters a false quantity, and the general who has saved a province must write despatches in which De Quincey could find no flaw. Lord John Russell, while expressing the precise thought of the nation, is ridiculed because his sentences are involved, while Lord Derby is pardoned for calling the Italians dogs, because his quotation was so very "apt." Strength and fortitude, judgment and valor, no longer weigh against the power of writing well. The most menacing speech made in our day is well received because the speaker has developed unexpected oratorical power, and manifestoes of revolt are praised because they are written with the "weighty moderation" English writers have been taught to prize. Half Victor Emmanuel's popularity is due to the exquisite style of the penmen of his suite, half the disgust at Austria to the crass dulness of her official manifestoes. It is becoming time to examine the justifications for this drift of opinion, a drift which is very apt to accompany the falling vigor of a state. It was not till literature began to decay that style became the object of a Roman writer. The Augustan age of French style was an epoch in which despotism was only tempered by the epigrams it punished, and the English classics of style flourished in the most torpid period of our national history.

Is there, then, any evidence that this special variety of culture, this power of apt speech or clever writing which we demand from everybody, is a fair proof of power? The English mind has still a healthy reverence for fact and precedent, and fact and precedent alike are opposed to the idea. The greatest men of earth have not as a rule been men who possessed the literary faculty. One or two of the very highest capacity, men like Julius Cæsar and Xenophon, have added to practical ability a taste for clear and sonorous description, and Napoleon's bulletins entitle him to be classed, if not among the literati, yet among the successful orators of the world. But the mass of the efficient men of earth have been men to whom literature was unfamiliar or distasteful. Alexander, who first broke up the organization of the old world, and who planted kingdoms as meaner men plant oaks, was a drinking debauchee. Diocletian, who re-organized the Roman polity, could barely write. Mahomet, who changed not only the polity but the nature of a sixth of the human race, talks, in the Koran, nonsense it has tasked a generation of commentators to understand. His only imitator in modern times was a Joe Smith who could barely write, who stole a rubbishy novel, and called it a revelation—and founded among Anglo-Saxons a despotic creed. Charlemagne, who moulded Western Europe, signed his name with difficulty, and though he protected learned men, was not one of them. The first pope who ever lost Rome a kingdom, was perhaps the most cultivated man who ever adorned the chair. It is the same in modern history. Cromwell was "inarticulate." Peter the Great was an indecent boor. Macaulay's asthmatic hero scarcely possessed a book, and Frederick the Great could not spell in any of the three languages he mispronounced. Bolingbroke, the scholar statesman, fled from England a ruined exile, while Walpole, who could not understand literature, and whose only notion of wit was *double entente*, held power for twenty years. Sir Robert Peel, whose speeches were often the heaviest of platitudes, and whose quotations were usually from the Eton grammar, reversed our financial policy, regenerated Ireland, and died with the blessings of all Englishmen on his head. Disraeli, whose speeches are often a literary luxury, has never laid down a single principle of policy, foreign or domestic, never brought forward a great measure which was not ignominiously scouted. The professors who filled the Frankfort Diet made themselves the laughing-stock of Europe, and with sixty millions of brave men behind them were snuffed out without a struggle.

The literary class in France held power for seven-and-twenty years without a break: through the whole reign of Louis Philippe the successful essayist became a prefect, the successful journalist a minister. Yet, what have the men of 1831 ever founded, or what legacy has the world enjoyed from the victors of 1848? Half the "hommes de lettres" were maniacs for freedom, and France, after a generation of their government, is under a military despotism, without a press, and with a silenced Parliament. The other half were maniacs for "glory," and the only province added to the territory of France has been made by the man who puts his heel upon them all. Even in the sciences, where the literary faculty would appear the *sine quâ non* of success, the greatest achievements have been made by men with very deficient culture. Military discipline was revolutionized by Leopold of Anhalt-Dessau, as great a boor as his relative George the Third, who defeated the cultivated Whig aristocracy. Brinsley, who made our canal system, occupied himself at a theatre with counting the words; and Stephenson, who invented railways, had less than the culture of many an artisan. We might carry our illustrations over a still wider range. Who cultivates best, the Lombard peasant proprietor who cannot read, or the Dorsetshire gentleman educated at Eton? Which is the most efficient in life, the Prussian peasant who has been trained like a national schoolmaster, or the Scotch feuar with nothing but mother wit? But the education of races is too incomplete to afford a datum for argument, and we can but point to the fact that as yet no perceptible increase of efficiency has been acquired from instruction.

The truth is, and it is one we are in danger of permanently forgetting, that the higher kinds of culture have often an enervating effect. There are minds, and those amongst the most valuable, which much learning tends only to enfeeble. The polish is only obtained by planing away the wood. There is a rough-strength, a determined energy, which seems to be the attribute only of the half-educated. Men of great culture are apt to give their imaginations too much play, to desire harmonious impossibilities, to foresee the difficulties so clearly that action is foregone. They have put microscopes to their eyes, and cannot drink for fear of the animalcules. Mr. Gladstone, for example, we do not hesitate to affirm, would be the most capable administrator in Europe if he could only forget one-half of his cultivation. As it is, he worries England and delights his foes by theories too harmonious to be of the slightest use, and an insight too keen to suffer him to take one long step in advance. How often has the rough intellect of the premier enabled him to cut straight to the core of a matter of which his far abler colleague could only nibble at the rind?

It is only natural that it should be so, for the work of the world is done by qualities over which culture has no power. Courage is not developed by mathematics. Creative power is not increased by literary training. Insight is an instinct, not a product of education. That strange faculty of dominance which seems to stand apart from the other powers of the mind, which enables races as stupid as the Turk to subjugate races as subtle as the Greek, is not increased by polished cultivation. Ferdinand of Naples, who talked in a patois, utterly outwitted an intelligence like Poerio. Every day we see the scholar distanced in the race of life by the adventurer who can barely spell, the polished scion of a cultivated race defeated hopelessly by an orator innocent of Greek. Force, the true motive power of events, rests in the character, not the intellect, and it is only the latter high cultivation can improve.

From The Saturday Review, 2 March.

ITALY.

It is, perhaps, fortunate for Italy that the task of becoming a nation continues to require both military and political efforts. The South, as well as the North, is now for the first time interested in transactions which will hereafter form the material of a common history. The fall of Gaeta was celebrated as a triumph at Naples, though the operations were conducted by Piedmontese and Lombard troops; and the impending capture of Messina will remind the Sicilians that they also need the assistance of their distant countrymen. When Garibaldi first landed at Marsala, it was foreseen that the citadel on the Straits would probably defy the efforts of any force but a regular army. He was compelled to leave a hostile garrison in the island when he commenced his continental expedition, and circumstances have never since allowed of a reduction of the last Bourbon stronghold. In 1848, the insurgents held every other point on the island; but in the following year the possession of the fortress enabled Ferdinand to reconquer his lost dominion. Even within a few weeks, his son has thought it possible to cajole the people of Sicily into permitting a restoration, which could scarcely have been suggested if he had not retained a footing at Messina. It is now absolutely necessary that the anomaly of a hostile flag should disappear from the soil of the Italian kingdom. As long as Francis II. remained within the limits of his former dominions, the struggle might be regarded as a civil war, but since the fall of Gaeta and the departure of the ex-king, General Fergola has sunk into the position of a rebel engaged in maintaining the hopeless cause of a pretender. No military commander has a right to continue resistance on a particular spot when the fortune of war has positively declared itself against the possibility of his ultimate success. General Fergola has it in his power to inflict great injury on the city of Messina, and for some days or weeks he may perhaps be able to hold his own against a besieging force; but in default of reinforcements, his capitulation is only a question of time, and even if he were left unmolested, he would have no means of extending his master's authority in Naples. It might perhaps be difficult for those who continue the enterprise of Garibaldi to insist too strongly on the maxims of international law; but in strictness, a general who is not commissioned by a *de facto* government must be regarded as a private and unauthorized adventurer. It is certain that in Sicily there is no chance of a reaction which could plausibly assume the character of a civil war.

The annexation of Rome, while it is more doubtful and remote, occupies more seriously the thoughts of every true Italian. It is a curious fact, that while zealous Ultramontanists in foreign countries are using their utmost exertions to support the temporal dominion of the holy see, Italy itself scarcely contains any papal party. The peasantry in some remote districts may possibly be influenced by reactionary priests, but a large part of the clergy supports the national cause, and active politicians are either friendly to the king's government, or more anxious than Count Cavour himself for a total rupture with the Vatican. The opposition in the Parliament leans to Garibaldi or Bertani, and not to Antonelli and Merode. If the question were to be decided either by popular suffrage or by a vote in the Chambers at Turin, the pope would scarcely be allowed to retain the palace and the garden which are ridiculed as inconsistent with his dignity by French journalists and bishops. The project of a vicariat to be administered by Victor Emmanuel, though it dates only a few months back, has already become absurdly obsolete. The obstinacy of Pius IX. has been one of the most effective instruments of Italian unity, and there seems to be every probability that the reformation of the national Church will be practically effected without the inconvenience and danger of a schism. The vigorous suppression of monasteries in Naples is recommended by precedents in many Roman Catholic countries, and if a reasonable proportion of the vacant revenues is distributed among the secular clergy, the measure will be universally popular. The pontifical court, which avows itself irreconcilably hostile to the political improvement of Italy, will perhaps gradually lose even its spiritual supremacy. It may be hoped that the process of alienation will not be checked by the ill-timed zeal which invites the priesthood and people of Italy to adopt the doctrine and discipline of the Anglican Church. The introduction of theological quarrels into the national movement would probably revive the reactionary spirit which seems at present to be extinct.

The tone in which Italian questions are discussed by different French parties is not complimentary to an independent nation. It is universally assumed that the permanence of the new kingdom, as well as the settlement of the Roman question, depends wholly on the will of the Emperor Napoleon. The bishops and the Legitimists demand that the sovereignty of the pope shall be maintained or re-established, while more liberal politicians recommend that French generosity should confer as a boon the unity and independence which are already established in fact and in right. The campaign of Solferino was an invaluable service, but it constituted no perpetual relation of protection and vassalage. Having been relieved from the Austrian yoke in the hope that half a dozen petty States would take refuge under the patronage of France, Italy has, in defiance of remonstrance and opposition, consolidated herself into a kingdom which ranks among the Great Powers in wealth and population. The diplomatic recognition of the king's newly assumed titles is a matter of secondary importance. Victor Emmanuel governs Italy, though half Europe may shut its eyes to the fact; and he may be well assured that sooner or later the ceremonial attributes of his position will attend the substance. The United Provinces waited for seventy years before they were recognized by Spain; and the pope gave the title of King of England to the last pretender when he was living on a pension allowed him by George III. The king of Italy and his minister will not be so unwise as to purchase a formal concession at the cost of any promise which may impede the completion of their great enterprise. Their interest in the designs of France depends on the more substantial difficulty of the army which continues to occupy Rome. The attempt to expel the foreign garrison would be impolitic and hopeless; and the ulterior purposes of the emperor are utterly obscure, and perhaps they are yet undecided. It is not easy to decipher the meaning either of the imperial speech at the opening of the session, or of the not less official addresses which have been drawn up by the Senate and by the Legislative Body. M. Troplong is as faithful an adherent of any policy which may be adopted by the government as M. de Laguerronnière himself; and his composition is even more ambiguous than the language of the recent pamphlet. The unctuous phrases which offend the less orthodox members of the Senate appear to be regarded by the Ultramontanists as hypocritical inconsistencies; and it is not unreasonably thought that pious professions of attachment to the holy see imply a disposition to leave it to its fate. The address of the Legislative Body goes further, in a distinct reference to the unwise resistance offered by the pope to the counsels of France. The withdrawal of the garrison from Rome may not be immediately contemplated, but the emperor can scarcely intend to adopt the policy of a party which he puts off with elaborate and empty apologies. The papal supporters in France by no means affect to conceal their utter want of confidence in the government. The Bishop of Orleans attacks the emperor himself, in the person of M. de Laguerronnière, and taunts him with his ingratitude for the interested sycophancy of the bishops and clergy. It is difficult to ascertain whether the priesthood has any considerable influence over political opinion in France. The policy of intervention and dictation which it at present recommends is always acceptable to popular vanity, and a prelate who, in defiance of history, represents Charlemagne as a French king, will be easily allowed to draw the inference that the pope shall not be consigned to the protection of an Italian sovereign.

In the mean time, the government of Italy can only wait for the progress of events. Whether the French remain for one year or for ten, the reversion of Rome is vested in the nation and not in the pope. Every day of foreign occupation diminishes his claim to the sympathies and consideration of his countrymen, and the excitement of opposition is rapidly alienating from his rule even the inhabitants of his capital. The Austrians on their side are careful that Venice shall not forget the liberty which prevails on the other bank of the Mincio. Instead of relying exclusively on community of race, the advocates of unity offer good government in the place of stupid and meddlesome tyranny. The hardening of the hearts, or rather of the brains, of their enemies ought to satisfy the wishes of all good Italians.

FRANCE AND ROME.

(From The *Presse*.)

DOCUMENTS relative to the affairs of Rome show clearly two things—first, that the French government in the relations with the pontifical court has gone beyond all the bounds of patience; secondly, that the cardinals, if they had not considered this patience to be inexhaustible, would have shown themselves less intractable. In speaking to them loudly and firmly, and in coupling acts with words, they are always found to be made of very plastic materials. The history of France gives more than one proof of this. We will only instance one.

On the 29th of September, 1797, Bonaparte wrote to his brother Joseph, ambassador at Rome: "It is only with the greatest firmness, with the greatest expression in your words, that you will cause yourself to be respected by those persons. Timid when you show them your teeth, they are haughty when you are too delicate with them." The event did not fail to show that Bonaparte was right. So long as the French had been at a distance from Rome, the pontifical court had insulted and provoked the Republic. On learning the approach of the army commanded by Berthier, it changed its tone. The pope issued, on the 9th of February,

1798, a proclamation, in which he said—"Full of confidence in the uprightness and generosity of the French Republic."

Berthier entered Rome, the republic was proclaimed, and the pope stripped of his temporal power. The Sacred College bent its head, acknowledged the republic, and fourteen cardinals were present at the *Te Deum*—which was chanted to celebrate its establishment—that is to say, the deposition of the papal sovereign. Had the French government been inspired with the counsel given by Bonaparte to Joseph in 1797, it would not now deplore the uselessness of the efforts it has been making for ten years to save the pontifical court.

The spirit of vertigo, attested by all the despatches on the affairs of Rome, surpasses all that experience permitted us to expect from the counsellors of the Papacy. It is impossible to behold the boasting of Cardinal Antonelli, and the strange revelations made by M. de Grammont to M. Thouvenel, without thinking of the edicts in which the Emperor Honorius talked of the happiness and eternity of the Roman empire, at the very moment when this empire was crumbling to pieces on all sides. Notwithstanding those visible ruins, which increased every day, the writers of the time had the intimate conviction that the power of imperial Rome would only end with the world. We now find again the same blindness in the clergy, who, confounding the pope, head of the Church, with the pope-king, affirm that the Papacy is eternal, and that the destinies of the world are attached to its duration. But the first empire of Rome perished, and the world regenerated itself; the second is bending beneath the weight of its decrepitude and faults, and the world is renovating itself.

An earthquake can in a few minutes convert an immense city into a heap of ruins, but several ages are required to undermine the political and religious edifices that it has taken several centuries to develop and strengthen. Revolutions are the earthquakes of these edifices, and when they are strongly established, only one shock is necessary to overthrow them. The temporal papacy is a human institution, that was founded and augmented by the favor of circumstances. It represents the work of eighteen centuries; it took five to lay the foundations, five to raise up the structure, five to defend it, three to destroy it bit by bit, and now it is struggling in the last throes of death.

In the space of sixty years the temporal papacy has been seven times in peril; in 1798, it was overthrown by the French revolution; in 1800, the confederate kings walked over its ruins, devising how to render them irreparable, and only diverted from their projects by the victories of our armies. Raised again in 1801, the papacy was once more overthrown in 1809; in 1814 it owed its existence to Napoleon, for it is very doubtful, if the captivity of Pius VII. had been prolonged, whether the holy alliance would have restored to him all his states; in 1817, two Italian sovereigns came to an understanding for the partition of the Pontifical States, and the combination failed by the succeeding revolutions of the Roman State, which threw the kings into the arms of the priesthood. The temporal power, overthrown in 1848, and restored in 1849, is now nothing more, as proved by the despatches of M. de Grammont, than an embarrassment for every one—than an element of counter-revolution—than a monument of ingratitude.

It was owing to the French army that the pope was able to return to Rome in 1849; it is by the French army that he has maintained himself there for eleven years, and Rome is nothing less than a focus of intrigues and conspiracies against France. In a despatch (Feb. 8, 1860), very moderate, very curious, and in every respect most remarkable, M. Thouvenel establishes the fact that the pontifical court has failed in all its engagements, in every diplomatic usage, that it has systematically mixed up religious with political questions, refused all concession, all reform, and "allowed the state of things to get worse, to that degree when the malady often becomes irremediable."

Struck with so much obstinacy, and wearied out by so much bad faith, M. de Grammont ended by telling Cardinal Antonelli (despatch of March 3, 1860): "I begin to believe that you desire a catastrophe . . . You refuse to take a middle course of safety, and you invoke the tempest, as if you were speculating on the waifs of the shipwreck. . . . You might at least show a little desire of conciliation. You might promulgate the reforms agreed upon, and thus facilitate the task of the government of the emperor, whose most ardent wish it is to extinguish the fire of discord that is kept up between the holy father and his people."

To advice so wise, to demands so moderate, what is Cardinal Antonelli's reply? Here is its text: "I can only repeat what I have said. The pope will not act. He has bound himself to the Catholic world by his encyclical letter. He will do nothing, absolutely nothing." M. de Grammont was not discouraged; he endeavored to show to Cardinal Antonelli the danger he was causing the Papacy to incur by the obstinacy of his refusal. "But," said he, "I soon perceived the inutility of my efforts. I found myself in presence of a fixed resolution, and which may be briefly stated thus—the pope will never acknowledge the approval any thing short of the complete restitution of the state of things to what it was *ante bellum* in the duchies and the states." Then he insisted no longer, and withdrew with this remark to Cardinal Antonelli, "Your eminence, I leave you deeply grieved at the inutility of my efforts, and very uneasy at the dangers into which the holy see seems to be going with its eyes shut."

These dangers that terrified all sensible Catholics, the court of Rome affects either not to see or to despise. It receives with affected pomp the thin legions which the counter-revolutionary party sends it from France and Belgium; and if, among the "crusaders," there happen to be any that dislike repudiating all sentiment of nationality, the "influential crusaders," says M. de Grammont, take them soundly to task in these terms: "Sir, a man is the pope's subject before being a subject of his sovereign; if you do not entertain these ideas, what do you come here for?"

The reader sees that the court of Rome speaks and acts as it would have spoken and acted in the time of Innocent III.; it feeds upon illusions and pride; even since Castelfidardo it dreams of triumphs and meditates conquests. It openly makes religion subordinate to policy, not perceiving that this subordination is precisely that which has most contributed to the decline of pontifical power.

To preserve this power to the head of the Catholic Church it is necessary to sacrifice the sacerdotal kingship, to take from him temporal power, and put an end to this amalgam formed out of a sacred ministry and a political power that has corrupted all the heterogeneous elements of which the pontifical power consists. Wishing to secure to the pope an existence independent of all parties, liberated from all diplomatic influence and exclusively acknowledged in its ecclesiastical attributes, the French government would have desired (despatch of M. Thouvenel, April 7, 1860) "That the Catholic powers, each in proportion to its population, should offer to the pope a subsidy which they would inscribe at the head of their public debt, the interest of which would be paid at the regular periods into the hands of the representative of his holiness."

The pontifical government replied, that it will only accept tribute "under the form of compensation for first fruits and the ancient canonical rights over vacant livings, rights long disputed and finally abolished in all the states of Europe."

These pretended rights—these ecclesiastical privileges—were a remnant of feudalism destroyed by the French revolution, and which a few states, Piedmont for instance, made for a long time the mistake of forgetting in the midst of modern institutions. To have at the present day the pretension to resuscitate and maintain clerical feudalism, when the political and military feudal system has utterly disappeared, is an act of folly that appears incredible, even when we find it attested by official documents. And since the pope's advisers are afflicted with such incurable blindness, the time is not distant when they will be glad if we should be willing to be satisfied with the concessions that they now reject with so much arrogance. But then they will be told,—as all powers are told when irrevocably lost,—"It is too late."

From The Spectator, 16 Feb.

"THE ROMAN QUESTION."

"The people of Rome," says a recent letter from Italy, "believe that their deliverance is near at hand;" but the belief seems to most Englishmen only one of those fond illusions with which men are apt to deprecate despair. "In these days of jubilant nationality," says Mr. Disraeli, not without a suspicion of triumph in his tone, "the Gauls are still in Rome!" and who, asks the practical Englishman, is to remove the Gauls? Yet a careful review of the documents recently given to the world leaves little room to doubt that the instinct of the Romans is correct; that, like fevered patients, they feel the breeze before the doctors are aware of its approach. The obstacles which two months since seemed so numerous and so insuperable, are resolving themselves steadily into one, and that one, far less invincible than it may appear. There are but four powers whose resolves can influence the fate of Rome, and three of them are already in accord. The fourth, though still obstinate, is liable at any moment to a compulsion no obstinacy will be valid to avert. If a long series of utterances may be trusted, the emperor of the French, the Parliament of Italy, and the British government are at last in harmony upon the fate of Rome. The pope alone resists, but the pope has ceased to be master of the situation.

The position of the British government upon this section of the great Italian question has always been well defined. During an entire year, they have not ceased to press upon the emperor of the French the necessity of bringing the occupation to an end. Their remonstrances, at first reserved, at last assumed a tone almost of acerbity. "What becomes," wrote Lord John Russell, in November, "of this boasted independence, when it is only maintained from day to day by twenty thousand foreign bayonets. There is little use in preserving the name of the temporal sovereignty when the thing itself has ceased to exist." The object of the British government, then, is to effect the destruction of the temporal power of the pope without removing the Papacy from Rome.

The reply of the emperor, in the despatches published in Parliament and in the *Moniteur*, is invariably the same. He cannot leave Rome until assured that the holy father is safe alike from menace and from undue control. The pope must be able to perform his inestimable functions in tranquil independence. The impediments in the way of that happy condition of affairs are the excited condition of the Italian mind, and the spirit of revolution so obviously abroad. It must not be forgotten in considering this answer, that it is possible to distrust even a treacherous intellect too far. If the utterances of the emperor have ever been consistent, they have been so upon this occupation. The act was no act of his. For years he persistently threatened the Papacy with the withdrawal of his troops. In his first manifesto on the Italian question, he declared that the happiest hour for the Papacy would be when its temporal power ceased to be an obstacle to the good government of Italy. He has barely disapproved the absorption of the States of the Church into the Italian monarchy. He is even now publishing despatches which expose the court of Rome to that most deadly of assaults, the ridicule of France. He has affirmed over and over again that on the day on which Italy is reconciled to the pope his interest in Rome will cease. It may be of course that he is merely dissembling; it may be that the bitter scorn of Rome which crops out so often in the gravest of his Italian speeches is assumed for some hidden end. But when all antecedents, all professions, and all acts are for years in accord, even Napoleon is entitled to the poor honor of belief. The emperor, we submit, is anxious to escape from an untenable position by any act which the Catholic world is unlikely to resent.

The opportunity of verifying his professions is likely to be speedily afforded. The Italian elections, which have disappointed so many animosities, have been fatal to the hopes of Rome. A Mazzinian majority might have lent new vigor to the Papacy. The Italian Reds, whatever their other variations of opinion, are unanimous in their hatred of the pope. Left to themselves they would probably adopt the short course pursued by the convention with the priests. Even if fettered by the necessity of acting through Piedmont, they would have demanded Rome as the capital of Italy, and the immediate expulsion of the pope. The Parliament which the good sense of Italy has selected has widely different ideas.

M. Mauteucci, senator of Italy, writes to the *Nord*, on the 11th instant, to explain to Europe the policy that majority is decided to enforce. In a long and exhaustive letter, every line of which is worthy the careful study of English politicians, he defines most clearly the attitude of Parliament to Rome. Rome must be free, but not of necessity, or immediately, the capital of the monarchy. "We cannot submit," he says, "to parcel Italy—and Rome is the noblest, the most illustrious of our sections; but it is our interest not to exile from Italy one of our glories, and one of the great influences of the world. The contact and infiltration of liberty may, as we ardently wish, as we even venture to hope, renew the youth of the Church, and God knows how long that Church may yet once more be able to bless a multitude of faithful souls. . . . We cannot seriously believe that a small territory, subject to the same provincial and municipal laws as the rest of the monarchy, garrisoned by our soldiers, represented by its deputies and its senators, surrounded on all sides by the spirit of liberty and national feeling, could become a focus of despotism simply because the holy father and the sacred congregations made it their residence."

As to Rome as a capital, it is doubtful if, "with its monuments, its churches, its Transteverini, and its malaria," Rome can be changed into the metropolis of a great military state. The work of the Parliament will not be affected by its residence. "By leaving, as public opinion has decided, a large part of administrative authority to the municipalities and the provinces—by decentralizing as much as possible without weakening the unity of the national power—by preserving to the ancient capitals of the Italian provinces certain attributes of the central government, without creating political centres or menacing the legislative authority of Parliament, which *must* be supreme and absolute,—we shall succeed in establishing a regime of liberty, in harmony with our manners, and spare Italy the evils of an excessive concentration towards the heart of the state—a concentration contrary to our nature, and to all history. Finally, we have time to reflect on the choice of the capital of the new kingdom. Turin does not prevent us any more than Rome from the organizing our military forces, restoring our finance, or applying o… …stitutions to the development of local freedom." The Papacy, then, in the opinion of M. Mautecucci, may remain at Rome, yet be reconciled to the nation, and gain in security and spiritual vigor what it will lose in temporal authority. If these be really the ideas of the Italian Parliament, in what do they differ from those of the emperor of the French? That they are not those of the people of England is but little to the point. A little more hostility to the Papacy, a little more of the true revolutionary *verve*, would seem to Englishmen and Protestants to argue better for the Italian future. But even they will scarcely question that this moderation, so little expected from a popular body—this statesman-like patience so little hoped for from a southern people—render the solution of the eternal "Roman question" at least a possibility.

There remains the fourth power yet to be conciliated, but even here there is still ground for hope. The pope, it is true, has declared the patrimony of St. Peter an inalienable appanage of his see. But the subtle statecraft of the Papacy has been overpraised indeed if it cannot loose a knot tied in so light a cord as a bull of its own framing. Fifty expedients may be devised to leave the inalienable heritage intact. No Catholic prince is degraded by holding from the pope, and the sovereignty of the king of Italy would not be impaired by the addition to his titles of Vicar-General of Rome. The pope himself is an Italian, restive under the foreign assistance he implores, in his heart as contemptuous of the foreigner as the lowest lazzarone. His cardinals seem bitter, but they know that they are playing a dangerous game. Even Antonelli may well consider complete immunity, a seat in the Italian senate, and security for his wealth cheaply purchased by the surrender of a power which now yields him only the poor privilege to protest. The pope is weak, but he is also pious, and the serene headship of a Church which still seems to him universal, may well attract a man whom even the Romans declare not personally bad. Or in the last resort, the power of compulsion rests with the emperor of the French. With the pope formally acknowledged by the Italian Parliament, a strong Sardinian garrison in Rome, and the statute of Northern Italy the law of the land, the bitterest of Catholics could scarcely tremble for the safety of the Catholic Church. There would remain no excuse for French occupation, and the pope, willing or unwilling, would be compelled to subside into the spiritual head of the Catholic Christians of the world. The Romans, we submit, are not dreaming when they assert that their deliverance is at hand.

From The Press, 9 March.

THE DRAMA OF EUROPEAN POLITICS.

"What is nearest, touches us most," said Dr. Johnson when explaining the fact that "the passions rise higher in domestic than in imperial tragedy." The truth which holds good in the scenic representations of imaginary life is not less applicable to the real and grander drama of national politics. There need be no apprehension that domestic questions will fail to arouse a due amount of interest in the public mind; yet the time is manifestly approaching, step by step, when the grand movements of external European life,—movements reacting upon, and which ere long must directly implicate, the interests of England,—will for awhile overshadow all minor or factitious differences in domestic politics, and unite the hearts of the nation in the single desire to uphold the menaced power of the British empire. This week the curtain which seemed destined to remain undrawn for another year upon the stage of European politics, has been partially lifted up, as if a new act of the imperial drama were about to commence. The oration of Prince Napoleon in the Senate of France,—the disturbances at Warsaw,—the co-operative action of Russia and France in the Eastern question,—the obstinate attitude of the Separatist party in Hungary, and the fabrication in this very city of millions of Kssouth notes with a view to open revolution,—are events which appear to indicate that 1861 will witness the commencement of troubles which of late seemed relegated to 1862.

The British public, insulated from immediate contact with other countries, is ever slow to appreciate the bearing and tendencies of continental politics. But every new month will more and more lift the veil from their eyes. It is hardly possible any longer to ignore the fact that Europe is drifting down the rapids which lead to a catastrophe, and to changes second only, if second, to those inaugurated by the French Revolution of 1793. It is no longer possible to ignore the fact that all Europe, from the Rhine to the Bosphorus, from Smolensko to Venice, is agitated by conflicting passions of nationality, and that the imperial government of France is ready to avail itself of those distractions for the purposes of its ambition. Nice and Savoy have been declared by the emperor himself to be "righteous revendications," which it would be justifiable to imitate and repeat; and his cousin points to Italy as a power whose co-operation is to be expected in the further developments of the Napoleonic policy. Prince Napoleon speaks with fearless frankness of the objects of the imperial policy. "There never was a more just and glorious cause than that of the annexation of Savoy and Nice. . . . The glory of the emperor consists in having torn up the iniquitous treaties of 1815, which placed the foot of Europe on the throat of France." And addressing the Italians with reference to Venice, in words equally intended for all the "oppressed nationalities," he says: "No imprudence: come to an understanding with France. When we assist a people, it is not with weapons stolen in an arsenal; it is in the open day, and not in a surreptitious manner; it is with the cannon and flag of France, and loudly calling upon people to recover their liberties."

Such is the renewed announcement of the programme of Napoleonic policy. It does not surprise us: it is simply a further proof of the justness of our early anticipations. But what does England think of the prospect thus set before her? Certainly there has not been a time within the memory of the present generation when it has been so incumbent upon the statesmen and people of this country to consider maturely the aspect of continental affairs and the line of foreign policy which it becomes England to adopt. In the discussion on the Italian question on Friday week, the Earl of Malmesbury, in a speech alike eloquent and statesman-like, gave admirable expression to views which are as applicable to the future as to the past. Familiar with Italy and the Italians at a time of life when enthusiasm is most lively, and sympathy most readily evoked, the noble earl shares to the full the sympathy which the English public has so freely accorded to the aspirations of the Italians after liberty and independence. But it would ill become a British statesman to permit sentiment to usurp the place of judgment,—he cannot indulge a personal sympathy at the expense of international rights, upon which rests the whole fabric of order and peace in Europe. There are two things which the British government must not do,—two things which are forbidden alike by the present interests and by the traditional policy of this country. The British government must in all circumstances abstain from fomenting revolution in the dominions of foreign powers with which we are at peace; and it ought never officiously to stamp with its approval the conduct of any government which sets at naught existing treaties and the laws of nations. We may condone such acts, if they be done under the pressure of exceptional emergencies,—it ill becomes us, either as regards our interests or our duty, to recognize them as legitimate precedents.

Such is Lord Malmesbury's view of the true policy of England. The French government proceeds upon an entirely different principle. It is ready to excite embarassments in other States, in order that it may intervene with the sword to tear up the treaties of 1815 and remodel Europe in the interests of France. Such can never be an honorable or a safe policy for this country either to pursue or to support. Military intervention for such a purpose no ministry would be permitted to employ; but it is incumbent that respect for treaties, and the principle of non-intervention in the domestic affairs of other states, should likewise be observed in our diplomacy, and that we should not be chargeable with attempting timidly and covertly what we shrink from doing openly by force of arms. The adoption of any other course must unnecessarily embroil us in the European conflict, and moreover weaken our position, in the face of coming events which threaten to be sufficiently menacing to not a few of the imperial interests of England.

Italy is united—the fact is accomplished. Even if we grudged Italy her unity,—which we do not,—it is useless to say any more about it. But the past conduct of the court of Turin, as an index of its future policy, cannot be disregarded. It is not the accomplished facts which now either disquiet or concern us. So far as the unification of Italy satisfies the wishes of the Italians themselves, we rejoice at it. And so far as regards the interests of England, a united Italy would, in the ordinary condition of affairs, be a check upon the ambition of France. Unfortunately, this condition of affairs, does not at present exist. The independence which ought to be the result of a united Italy is prevented, in consequence of the court of Turin being bent upon further war, and being willing to become the vassal of France in return for further assistance from the French arms. The Italians have a greater liking for constitutional England than for so formidable a neighbor as despotic France. But they are bent upon having Venetia on the instant. If they would wait till Austria has re-organized herself, we believe Venetia would be peacefully resigned to them, as a province which cost Austria more than it is worth to her, and which her free Parliament would refuse to keep; but as long as Hungary threatens to rebel, and looks to the Garibaldians for support, for Austria to abandon the Quadrilateral would simply be to place her Hungarian rebels in direct communication with their Italian "sympathizers." Victor Emmanuel told his Parliament that "there is a time to wait, as well as a time to dare:" we believe if the Italians were wise enough to wait, they would have no occasion to dare. But too probably their impatience will be greater than their wisdom. They are unwilling to wait till the pear drops ripe into their mouth: and there are others beyond the Alps who are equally disinclined to wait for a pacific solution of the Venetian question.

A united Italy, so far as France is concerned, means war. If, while driving out the Austrians, and seizing Savoy and Nice, the emperor of the French could have left Italy in the condition of a weak and discordant federation,—as he desired to do,—he might have been content. But now, in spite of him, Italy has grown so united and powerful as, with the return of ordinary times, to become wholly independent of France. Now, then, before the return of quiet times, is France's opportunity. Napoleon has still three-fourths of his programme to accomplish—he needs allies—and his game is, while helping Italy anew, to involve her on his side in a contest with nations with whom willingly she would not go to war. Were the Venetian question once fairly settled, Napoleon would lose all hold over the Italians: therefore his object must be, not to permit the settlement of that question save in a way which will necessarily involve the fortunes of Italy with those of France for several years to come—in fact, until he has completed his "mission." His enemies must be made her enemies. The Germans —as was shown by the recent vote of the Prussian Chambers—cherish good-will towards the Italians; the Italians reciprocate that feeling, and will be most reluctant that the first act of their own united national life should be to help France in an attack upon the freedom and integrity of Germany. But we cannot help thinking that to accomplish this unnatural act is the object of the emperor of the French; and that, whenever the contest is renewed on the Mincio, he will complicate it by a war on the Rhine, in which he will be aided by the Italians, but which he will close, *more suo*, without the least deference to the wishes of the allies who have fought by his side.

We see no prospect of settled peace to Europe for several years to come. Turkey disintegrates steadily,—the lapse of the Mires loan will aggravate her dilemma,—French troops are in Syria, a Russian army is gathering at Tiflis,—under the joint action of these powers the internal troubles of Turkey assume formidable proportions,—and the threatened landing of Garibaldi in Illyria would complete the ruin of that once great empire. Venice, Hungary, Poland—each is a subject of grave disquiet, and two of them at least of prospective war. But it is seldom that the heavens fall in upon us all at once, and it is still less the desire of the grand schemer of the Tuileries that they should do so. Europe must not collapse with a crash, but bit by bit, in manageable fashion, so that the eagles may everywhere preside over the spoil. Nevertheless the Revolution and the Coalition are slowly yet steadily coming face to face. It will require a strong hand to keep them from meeting in a terrific strife. *Vive Napoleon III.!* has been shouted in the streets of Warsaw; and if the movement of Polish nationality continue, not even the Napoleonic predilections of Prince Gortschakoff can suffice to preserve the cordial understanding which has existed between the imperial governments of France and Russia since the close of the Crimean war. This much, however, is to be remembered: if a *mot-d'ordre* from Paris can postpone the Polish movement, the crisis will assuredly be delayed; for it is not the policy of the emperor of the French to bring on a rupture with Russia at present, or, until he has made further use of the Muscovite alliance in his scheme of aggrandizing France and weakening the powers of Germany. Therefore it is that he sends his imperial voice across Europe, to the disaffected everywhere,—"No imprudence: bide my time."

From The Spectator, 9 March.

THE DRY BONES STIRRING.

THE Napoleonic "idea" of nationalities is producing fruit. Italy is free already, Hungary has long been menacing insurrection, and now, after thirty years of acquiescent submission, the Poles are once more astir. Europe reads once more that the White Eagle has been paraded, and that "order reigns in Warsaw," and, remembering the last time those words were uttered, almost expects another outburst of Russian vengeance. The times, however, have changed, and the *émeute* differs from all which have preceded it alike in its features and its consequences. Two separate stories have reached Western Europe, the first of which we may dismiss as an astute but demonstrably false invention. According to this account, the Agricultural Society of Warsaw passed an unanimous vote conceding to the Polish serfs their land. As this vote was opposed to the imperial proposal, which only concedes to the peasants five acres of land a head, the people became fiercely excited, rose, and tried to get up a national demonstration, which was put down by force. As the *émeute* was created by the citizens of Warsaw, who are not serfs, and directed against the emperor, who is the friend of the serfs, the story carries absurdity on its very face. It has probably been circulated to anticipate the sympathies of Europe, even Liberals thinking, with not unnatural inconsistency, that slaves should receive their freedom from above.

The other and more probable story links the *émeute* with the new revolution. The citizens of Warsaw, inspired it is said by narratives of the resurrection of Italy, or more probably excited by the hope of French assistance, resolved to hold a grand national demonstration on the field of Grochow, the scene of the last great Polish victory. The government, with that sardonic intelligence which often marks Russian official acts, quietly ordered the garrison to hold *their* celebration on the same spot, to mourn for the Russians who had perished in the conflict with the Poles. Diverted from their original intention, the leaders organized a procession, the population poured into the streets, and the White Eagle was received with the mad enthusiasm only Poles and Irishmen can display. The police were "insulted," but the mob appears to have had no design beyond a demonstration. The police, however, resisted, and at last mounted gendarmes attacked the people, killed several persons, and "restored the circulation of the streets." In former years the affair would have ended here, the city would have been declared in a state of siege, and after a week of police outrages and military executions, Warsaw would have been pronounced once more in order. Circumstances, however, as yet unrevealed, have given the Poles nerve and cohesion. The garrison bivouacked in the squares and streets, but the Poles on the 27th organized a second demonstration, carrying the bodies of the slain up to the French consulate, and shouting "justice." Again, but this time on the order of a single general, the soldiery fired, and lives were taken apparently in pure wantonness. Formerly the soldiers would have been upheld, but the days of Nicholas are passed. The towns-people appealed to Prince Gortschakoff, the governor, inquiry was ordered into the conduct of the soldiers, the officer who gave the order was threatened with a court-martial, and the security of the town entrusted to the citizens themselves. The latter, headed by their nobles, arranged a public funeral, to which the Russian pickets presented arms, and an unpopular prefect of police was replaced by a nominee of the *émeutiers*. The people were still dissatisfied, and a petition, bold as that of the Hungarian Comitats, was drawn up for presentation to the emperor. In it the Poles demanded the restitution of their nationality, pure and simple. No desire of freedom, or constitutional government is openly expressed; all feeling is centred on the single point of separate nationality. Local disturbances are breaking out in the provinces, and all accounts allude admiringly to the fusion of classes which has taken place. There can be no doubt that the demonstration evinced the existence of a national feeling of the most unexpected intensity. Enslaved for a hundred years the sight of the national emblem still throws the Poles into a fever of enthusiasm. The traditions of Kosciusko are still alive, and the dream of 1823 is still the idol of the national imagination.

Poland is stirring, but the result of her movements is not so easily ascertained. The action of the Russian government has been throughout the recent affair so opposed to the traditional notions of Russian policy, as to be for the moment almost inexplicable. The governor behaved just as a lord-lieutenant of Ireland might have done, trusted the citizens with the care of order, promised inquiry into military offences, allowed a huge popular demonstration to expend itself in ceremonial, and himself promised to present a petition which ten years since would have cost its framers their heads. The emperor, instead of declaring the state of siege, promises the serfs emancipation, and Russia a constitution. Is Russia, then, becoming liberal? Or is the government really too weak to face the Poles in the field? Or is it true, as the organ of the Russian party in Berlin affirms, that the Russian Cabinet has purchased support from France for its policy in the East at the price of concessions to Polish nationality? Each and all of these explanations are beset with difficulties. The last promise addressed by Alexander to the Poles, warned them that he would hear of no disunion; that he could, if necessary, be as stern as his father Nicholas. Russia, though weakened by the war, is still more than a match for Poland, even if Poland were really prepared to bring the question to the test of arms. The known tendencies of the Napoleons towards Poland, the avowed desire of the emperor to raise the nationalities, the intriguing character of modern French policy, all lend an air of probability to a story which in any other time than the present would have been called a silly canard. In spite of all these concurrent circumstances, it is still to us simply incredible. The Russian government has striven for a century not to enslave Poland, or even to injure Poland, so much as to make Poland Russian. Favored by identity of race and social order, the czars have succeeded in making the Poles useful soldiers and submissive tax-payers. They will hardly give up their object now, or replace a quiet province by a turbulent nationality. Poland may share in the constitution if one is really to be granted, but the revival of Polish nationality is as impossible as a repeal of the Union.

In this view we cannot but regard the *émeute* of the 25th February as a most untoward event. The Russian government, occupied with the emancipation of the serfs, will, we doubt not, avoid to the utmost collision with the Poles. Their complaints will be heard, their pride soothed, perhaps their municipal arrangements left more exclusively in their hands. But the spirit of nationality is of necessity a spirit opposed to moderation, and the emperor, if driven to the wall, must fight as strenuously as his father. He is backed by the cordial support of a race treble their adversaries in number, animated by an inextinguishable dislike for a nation which has contended with them for five hundred years, and bearing in social character about the relation Scotchmen bear to the Irish. The victory is not doubtful, and the only result of movement must be a return to reaction, a revival of the old repressive spirit, the resumption by the czars of their detestable task as the armed champions of autocracy and silence. The battle may be a severe one, for the Poles are the Irish of the Continent, and their political imbecility is only equalled by their courage; but they are over-weighted and unless emancipation shatters Russian strength to the ground, an armed struggle can end only in one way—a severe, perhaps fatal, blow to the freedom of Eastern Europe. It is with the Russians, not apart from them, that the Poles must extort their freedom from the throne.

But, we may be told, Poland is not alone. She will be supported in her demands by all the weight of France, with money, arms, and diplomatic influence. Doubtless the sympathy of Louis Napoleon, however reserved, is a strong aid to any country in insurrection. Doubtless, also, a movement among the Poles would be most convenient if Hungary sprang to arms, and French troops appeared upon the Rhine. But Louis Napoleon is not about to repeat his uncle's blunder, to cross the Vistula, or even bind the Polish cause inseparably with his own. Short of this his assistance can only avail to make the ultimate retribution a little more moderate and just. The Polish question touches too many empires, affects too many nationalities, for a prince who avowedly dreads only a European coalition, seriously to embrace. The Poles must fight their own battle, and even with Austria paralyzed, and Prussia engaged by France, they are no match for their great hereditary foe.

From The Saturday Review, 9 March.

POLAND.

It is now exactly thirty years since Europe was convulsed with the news that the Poles had not only challenged the czar to a fair fight, but had actually withstood, on two hard-fought fields, a Russian army greatly superior in numbers, and commanded by a renowned veteran. The history of Poland during the spring of 1831 is one of the most exciting passages in the annals of the modern world; and it is not surprising that the Poles, although trodden underfoot by their conqueror, should cherish the memory of a time when they sent such noble troops to fight under the White Eagle against overwhelming odds, and when the gallant spirit of the nation was rivalled by the sagacity, the prudence, and the courage of its leaders. Nicholas determined to root out Poland from the face of the earth. There was to be no more Poland and no more Poles. In a Russian province the descendants of the rebellious Pole were to forget the fame, the language, the loves, and hates of their fathers. Whatever cruel, stern, unflinching determination could do to effect this was done. All that existed before 1830 to remind the Poles of their lost place in Europe—a national army, a national constitution, a local ruler, a vernacular education—were wholly suppressed. The Poles were ordered to become Russians. But a conqueror cannot always change the feelings and blot out the memories of millions of people. The war they had waged had been too glorious, the sympathy they had excited too manifest, the traditions of their race too illustrious, to make oblivion possible. Poland still longs as ardently as when she was first divided to have a separate and independent existence. The spirit of nationality has never died out since the days of Kosciusko, and Posen and Galicia long as ardently to quit Prussia and Austria as Warsaw longs to quit Russia. It is not the heavy punishment to which Russian revenge has exposed them that has stirred the heart of the Poles—it is the never-dying indignation at the extinction of a nation once the bulwark of Europe against barbarism. The Poles of Posen have been governed as mildly by Prussia as the Prussian theory of government admitted, and certainly Galicia has had little to complain of in the later days of Austria. Nothing will satisfy the Poles except that the old work of the Partition Treaties should be set aside, and that the dead kingdom of Poland should live again. For many years this longing has been stifled beneath the presence of the triumphant absolutism that has reigned at St. Petersburg.

But times are now changed. Italy has won her freedom by urging her case in the court of European opinion, by drawing the sword at the proper moment, and by engaging the assistance of France. The Poles seem to think that the time has come when they may do as the Italians have done; and the first symptom of this reviving hope has been an outbreak at Warsaw, to which it is impossible not to attach considerable importance.

The facts of the case appear to be these. Last November, the thirtieth anniversary of the commencement of the last revolution was celebrated by the patriots of Warsaw, without any violent opposition on the part of the government. Emboldened by this success, the leaders of Young Poland determined to arrange a still more striking ceremony in celebration of the anniversary of the battle of Grochow, where the Poles first showed that they could hold their own against the Russians. A procession was to be made to the site of the battle, which is near Warsaw; but it was discovered that the Russians also intended to hold a funeral service there in honor of the dead who fell on their side; and the Poles accordingly abandoned the project, and returned to the city, and a torchlight procession was substituted. A vast crowd collected, and was wrought to the highest pitch of enthusiasm by the display of the national ensign—the White Eagle. A collision with the soldiery was the result, and some lives were lost. Two days afterwards a crowd again collected to do honor to the funeral service of those who died in this first collision. All might have passed off well, as the funeral service had been performed, and the crowd was beginning to disperse, when unluckily a funeral procession, totally unconnected with the events of the day happened to pass along a main street. A troop of Cossacks mistook this for a political demonstration, and immediately adopted what appears the strange and summary remedy of horsewhipping the priests. The indignation of the mob was raised, and the officer in command of the troops, in order to quell all insubordination, ordered his men to fire. They obeyed, and several Poles fell dead at the first discharge. No further violence was used on either side. Prince Gortschakoff, the viceroy, acted with a forbearance that could hardly have been expected. The troops were immediately confined to their barracks, and the municipal authorities were told to keep the peace. The officer who had ordered his men to fire is to be brought to a court-martial, and the viceroy has not only consented to forward to the emperor a petition framed by the leading Poles, but is understood to have expressed an opinion that its prayer ought to be granted. Their petition asks for nothing less than the revival of the Constitution of 1815, and in fact for the restoration of Russian Poland to the position it occupied before the revolution of 1830. Poland once more asks to show that she is alive, and a Russian viceroy informs his master that it will be dangerous to deny the request altogether.

We may well ask how this can be. Poland, crushed for thirty years beneath the heel of its master, cannot hope to defy Russia in arms. It has got no national army, no national assembly, no recognized national existence, as it had when it braved the anger of Nicholas, and yet its utmost efforts were ineffectual then, and must be still more ineffectual now. If it came to a question of military strength, Poland would be absolutely powerless. But there are influences at work which prevent its being a question of military strength, and the might of Russian absolutism has been invaded by subtler dissolvents than the sword and the bullet. Russia has become in the last thirty years a part of Europe. She has learned to feel the force of European opinion, and to shrink before the blast of European censure. Political liberty is at least the dream of many Russians, and a most sincere desire widely prevails not to be behindhand in the arts of good government. To crush Poland still more, to drown petitions in the roar of cannon, and to deluge the streets of Warsaw with blood, is a task which would seem to the modern Russian at once too shocking to European feeling, and too inconsistent with the aspirations of the Russian people. The great social change which the emperor has matured with such infinite difficulty must also have its share in teaching forbearance. The introduction of entirely new relations between the owners and the cultivators of the soil is too nice and dangerous an innovation to bear the complication of military interference on a large scale with the freedom of the people. Russia must gain breathing-time and enjoy a little quiet, or the emancipation of the serfs will be almost impossible; and now that freedom has been promised them, it is equally impossible to retrace the steps that have been taken, and to prolong their bondage. Lastly, the state of Europe may make even the emperor of Russia feel very reluctant to engage in the invidious task of crushing an ancient nation by a dragonnade. The Poles confidently expect that France will help them. It was to the French consul they went to declare the wrongs that the soldiery had done them. They call to mind that Count Walewski has the ear of the Second Emperor, and that the First Emperor deeply regretted the mistake he made in not restoring the kingdom of Poland. That the emperor of the French would really send troops to the Vistula is exceedingly improbable; but it is by no means improbable that he may do something to secure a favorable hearing for the Polish petition, and there is nothing which would better suit both the imaginative and the practical side of his character than to win the reputation of befriending Poland, and to win it at so very cheap a rate as that of exercising a little diplomatic pressure. Little doubt can exist that France and Russia are working together in Turkey, and that Russia will claim to share the lucrative privilege of defending the Christians against the cruel Turks. By assenting to this claim France may gain an opportunity of earning the gratitude of Poland at the same time that she carries out her own policy in the East. Undoubtedly the concession of a Polish Constitution, which means the revival of Polish nationality, would be pregnant with the gravest consequences, and would alarm Prussia most seriously, and Austria as much as any thing can alarm her now. Perhaps, in the long run, Germany has more to gain than to lose by the creation of an independent state between herself and Russia, and this must be accepted as some consolation at Berlin and Vienna, even if the unfolding of the banner of the White Eagle is the beginning of a change which will one day end in the restitution of Posen and Galicia.

From The Spectator, 9 March.

THE PLAN OF MR. JEFFERSON DAVIS.*

MR. JEFFERSON DAVIS the new President of the Southern Confederacy, has delivered what it pleases the Americans to call his "inaugural" address. It is a windy speech, full of affected moderation, and of phrases about rights, freedom, progress, and social order, which sound oddly when uttered to such an audience by such a man. In the midst of the verbiage occurs, however, one sentence which, read by the light of the history of secession, lets us deep into the secrets of Mr. Davis' heart. "For purposes," he says, "of defence, the Confederate States may, under ordinary circumstances, rely mainly on their militia, but it is deemed advisable, in the present condition of affairs, that there should be a well-instructed, disciplined army, more numerous than would usually be required on a peace establishment."

In plain English, or American, the Republican President of the South recommends to the Republican Convention at Montgomery the creation of a standing army. With an administration not yet organized, and a treasury still unfilled, with the rebellion not yet acknowledged by diplomacy, and some fifty thousand militia to preserve order, Mr. Davis still demands that money and energy shall be devoted to the creation of a larger military force. What for? It cannot be to crush the slaves, for the slaves have not shown any new symptom of agitation. It cannot be to resist the North, for the North, if resisted at all, must be resisted *en masse* and at once, before the standing army can be organized. It cannot be to face invasion from the East, for the maritime powers, if not slaves to cotton, are still not likely wilfully to interrupt their own supply; and, for a maritime contest, a fleet, not an army, is required. Such a force can be destined only for conquest, and conquest by land; and as conquests to the North and West would be as difficult as profitless, the intended aggression must be towards the South. In short, the project confirms to the full the design long since attributed to the South of invading Mexico, and building, with that magnificent territory and their own possessions, a vast slave empire round the Gulf. The project is a large one even for the eighteenth century, which has lost the faculty of surprise, and for the New World, which has seen in this generation an illiterate boor found a city in the Salt Desert as the metropolis of a theocracy. In Europe, the conspiracy will probably be pronounced absurb. So completely has the hatred of slavery permeated the English feeling, that men refuse to believe political strength can co-exist with the institution. So thoroughly has the sense of justice which springs from the balance of power been implanted in the national mind, that a great and successful crime, a conquest of the old Pizarro stamp, is regarded as something incredible. The South will be stopped somehow, by internal disunion, or a slave insurrection, or European interference, or by some means undiscovered, but none the less certainly relied on.

We regret that we cannot join in these pleasing but vague anticipations. The maxim that injustice never succeeds may be true of long cycles, but Prussia still holds Silesia, and the power of Russia has been doubled since Poland was trampled under foot. It pleases Providence sometimes to let crimes like the Mahometan invasion be triumphant for centuries, and we feel no security that the ordinary march of events will be changed to arrest the victory of Mr. Jefferson Davis. The battle is still to the strong, and we fear that of the strength of

* Perhaps the considerations suggested in this article may explain the rumor of a speedy arrival in the Gulf of a combined British, French, and Spanish squadron.—*Living Age.*

the South, for external aggression, there can be no doubt whatever. There may be causes at work no observer can perceive, but of visible powers the only one which can check the march of the Southern President is his half-reluctant rival of the North.

Mr. Davis has the materials for a magnificent army in his hands. The poor whites, or white trash of the six States who acknowledge his authority, number 800,000 fighting men, the very material for soldiers. Poor, unscrupulous, and habituated to violence, they will crowd in thousands round any leader who offers them license for the present and a gilded idleness for the future. Thousands of them have been carefully drilled as militia, as minute men, and as conspirators towards this very invasion. They will be led by at least half the officers of the army of the United States, by the volunteers who shared in the last Mexican campaign, and by the foreign soldiers of fortune, reckless but able adventurers, who swarm about the cities of the South. The criminal complaisance of Washington has provided them with artillery, arms, and the foundation of a military chest. No large sum of money will be indispensable. It is the misfortune of Mexico that she is still a country in which war can be made to support war. With her treasury bankrupt, her credit annihilated, and her government in the hands of savages, she is still a country which can be plundered, still retains some large remains of the product of a decaying agriculture and abandoned mines. There is little native resistance to expect. The old Spaniards, even if numerous enough, will neither fight for Juarez nor be employed by him, and the wretched half-castes, mestizoes, brown, yellow, and parti-colored races, who now concede to a savage the title of President and the power of torture will go down before Anglo-Saxons like so many Cherokees.

The negroes may struggle, and perhaps will, if they comprehend the fate which awaits them; but the negroes have never displayed capacity for any military enterprise higher than a massacre. Mr. Davis, if unopposed except by Mexican arms, must, we fear, reach the capital, and, with Mexico in his hands, found an administration which, if it produces nothing else, will, in American hands, yield at least cotton and silver. The white race will be added to his strength, the Indians contemptuously relegated towards the Pacific, and the blacks supply that slave labor for which the "white trash" who swell his army are athirst. Master of the six States and Mexico, he will be in possession of a country larger than Europe, rich with every variety of soil and climate, abounding in mineral wealth, tilled by a race working at the word of command, and ruled by the fiercest dominant class the world has ever seen—millions in number, and every man by necessity a soldier.

What is there to impede the prospect we have sketched, and which now inflames every imagination in the South—European interference? What can Europe do? Spain even, if Mexico in her despair once more united herself to the parent state, could find no army competent to contend with fifty thousand acclimatized Anglo-Saxons. England and France might, both possessing light horse, whose agile courage would be all-powerful on those broad, arid plains. But neither England nor France can afford to cut off their own supply of cotton; neither are on friendly terms with Mexico; neither, however much opposed to slavery, are disposed to maintain the evil anarchy which, in the Spanish states of America, is officially styled government.

Or is it slavery which is to render conquest practically impossible? We must beware lest we allow our hatred of a crime to delude our judgment as to the probability of its continuance. The slaves, Mexico once conquered, would probably outnumber the whites, but history teaches us that no disproportion of numbers is sufficient to shake off a really dominant race. A hundred thousand veteran Rajpoots, fighting with the energy of despair, could not the other day shake off the yoke of eighteen thousand Englishmen. A million of "mere Irish" failed even to arrest less than fifty thousand Cromwellians; and the Irish were whites, and as brave as they are now. Slavery endured in the Roman empire fifteen hundred years, and the slaves, wholly outnumbering their masters, recruited from the most warlike races, and with eighty thousand gladiators in their ranks, still sank back time after time into abject submission and toil. There is nothing in the negro which should deprive intellect and organization of their accustomed strength, doubled as it has recently been by the invention of the weapons of civilization. The slaveholders, if history is not worthless, can hold down five times their own number, or if they consent to make their rule a little less strict, to turn slavery into serfage, twenty times. There is nothing to be hoped from slavery, while, till they rebel, the possession of slaves smooths away half the difficulties of ordinary armies.

The sole hope for Mexico is in the interference of the North, and it remains to be seen if the North will arrive in time at a sense of the value of the balance of power. It must be remembered the North, and more especially the border population, cannot at once lose their national sympathy with their compatriots. Long after the disruption, New York will wish victory to Carolina rather than to Mexico. The wilder spirits, too, who would at once urge on the Northern government, and supply it with the means of interference, are expected to be drawn away by the more glittering attractions offered by the South. Undoubtedly, if the North is really in earnest, if the men of New England and the border are prepared to invade the South, Mr. Davis will be unable to move. The strength which would ensure his conquest of Mexico will be wasted in a futile resistance to a power superior to his own. We confess we doubt whether the North is prepared for sacrifices which can bring her only future security at the price of a present civil war. But willing or unwilling, the only human prospect of averting the foundation of a slave empire on the Gulf, is to be sought, we feel assured, in the resistance of the North. Without that resistance, the extension of slave institutions over a territory as large as the whole United States, a crime as unexampled in its magnitude as its consequences, is, we sorrowfully fear, almost inevitable.

WITH the Border States preserved, the losses of the Union, though large enough to create a bitter feeling in every American heart, scarcely impair the permanent resources of the Republic. They are less at all events, both in population and territory, than England at the close of the American war endured and survived. The Cotton States are gone, but the Cotton States only cover a certain extent of ground. Their white population is less than a ninth of that of the Union, less than the mere increase since the census of 1851. The North retains a population of twenty-four million of whites, and a territory which could support five times that number, all the eastern seaboard, and just as much of the Southern traders she ever possessed. The revenue is unaffected, for the South, as a speculation, did not pay. The fleet is still in Northern hands. The army can be readily restored to its old level. Egress to the Pacific still remains under control, and the position of the Union among the nation is only impaired by the loss of the cotton supply, formerly the best defence against a coast blockade. Ten years more will, at the present rate of increase, repair all losses, and enable the States to present to Europe a front sustained by a population as large, wealth even greater than at present, and a frontier relieved of its only seriously weak points.

But we may be told the presence of a powerful republic in the South, still more the presence of a slave empire, is, of itself, a new source of weakness for the Union. That is not so certain. If the balance of power should become so important as to compel the Union to maintain an army and a fleet equal to her resources, Mr. Bright's boast of the cheap government of republics will indeed be signally falsified. But the Union, as a great political state, would be only the stronger for the necessity. The neglect of the fleet has already impaired the weight of the Republic in the world, and its reconstruction would enable her to become what Mr. Webster so often declared she ought to be—a maritime power competent to raise a voice in the European family. Even in internal affairs the existence of a strong army would not be without its compensations. The curse of the American government has been the weakness of the executive, its dependence on an opinion which varied every hour. With an effective army at his back, and a majority in both Houses, no future President is likely to treat rebellion with the meek forbearance of Mr. Buchanan. The new Union, relieved of a heavy drag in the shape of a question which exhausted all energies yet defied a settlement, may commence a career before which the whole history of the past will seem futile and inglorious.—*Spectator*, 16 *March*.

From The North American.

"SECESSION FROM ANOTHER POINT OF VIEW."

THE British press has recently exhibited an unwonted interest in the affairs of the United States, and it has shown itself also better informed than heretofore. In both respects this progress is gratifying to us and creditable to it. We cannot, however, accord any part of this credit to an article, with the title above, which appeared in the *Examiner* on the 26th of January last, but which only met our eye a few days ago in the *Living Age*, No. 875. It has the advantage of being written and signed by a gentleman (John W. Cowell) who spent in this country the years of 1837, 1838, 1839, as the agent of the Bank of England. The knowledge gained in those years entitles the author, in his estimation, to hold very decided opinions about what is now passing in this country, and imposes upon him the obligation to give the public the advantage of his opinions.

We should not think it needful to notice this article, had it not attracted some attention in England. The *Times* does not adopt its opinions, but other journals give them some credit. In this country there are enough who partake, in part, at least, of the same notions to gi e some color in the eyes of foreigners to the positions assumed.

According to this writer, the Southern people have not the slightest natural connection with the Northern people. England receives cotton from the South, and makes payment chiefly in her own manufactures, and he thinks this trade should be direct not circuitous; that it is intrusively diverted from its proper direct channel by New York and the Northern States, whose intervention is wholly unnecessary, and alike detrimental to the South and to England. The single object and business of the South is to grow cotton for England; the natural action of England is to send its ships to bring home the cotton to her shores, loaded with English manufactures to pay for it.

The idea that the Southern people, who speak the same language; are of the same lineage; who are far more homogeneous with those of the North than the inhabitants of the British isles with each other; who live side by side, with a common boundary of thousands of miles, with a domestic trade greater than that of any other people, have no natural connection with the Northern States, but have such with the people of England, from whom they are separated by over three thousand miles of ocean, is a rather startling proposition. But this writer states it broadly, and adds that the single object and business of the South is to grow cotton for England. This seems, in his view, to be a part of the eternal fitness of things. Now, although the Southern people have favored this policy of growing cotton for England alone, and giving that country the monopoly of its manufacture, the tendency of trade has been to prevent the complete success of this monopoly. The Northern States now manufacture as much cotton, and sell goods as cheap as England did in 1837, when this writer came to the United States, and made up his mind that the single business of the South was to grow cotton for England.

If the Southern statesmen had clearly understood their proper industrial policy they would have promoted the manufacture of their staple first among themselves, next in the Northern States, and then on the continent of Europe. Great Britain having the start in this growing business needed no stimulus. This policy would have given the planters four great markets for their cotton, and the competition of the purchasers would have given them a control over the price they have never had. But the whole policy of the leading men in the South has been to increase the power of British manufacturers over their rivals in this country and in Europe, thereby making Liverpool the great cotton market, and giving a control of prices to English purchasers which they could not otherwise have obtained.

The true policy of the cotton States was to favor the manufacture everywhere; the policy of England was to crush it everywhere else, and to this English policy the Southern people gave their support under the specious title of free trade. For, with the advantage possessed by the English manufacturers in skill and in machinery, they needed only the prevalence of free trade to extinguish every rival manufacture of cotton in the world. They could then have had the raw material at the lowest price at which the planter would make it. Fortunately for the Cotton States, the Northern States persisted in the policy of raising a portion of the national revenue by duties upon imported cotton goods, and of building up a domestic cotton manufacture already able to work up a full fifth of the whole cotton crop, and thereby to keep nearly a million bales off the English market. They thus maintain prices by increasing the number of purchasers.

It is evident, then, whatever may be the view of the writer in the *Examiner*, that the "single object and business of the South" is not to grow cotton for England, but to grow it for whoever will give the best price for it, and to increase the number of purchasers by all proper means.

The position of this writer, that there is "not the slightest national connection" between the Southern and Northern States of this country, can scarce be surpassed for absurdity and want of foundation. The domestic trade carried on between them is not equalled by that of any equal population in the world. The mutual accommodation in the way of business and credit has nowhere any parallel. It is not in any degree the incompatibility of their business relations, which has produced the recent rupture. This rupture is due to the movements of disappointed partisans, aided by the excitement of slavery discussions. Apart from political excitement, the business between North and South has been not only large and harmonious, but mutually beneficial. This mutual business, instead of being restricted by any thing unnatural in its materials, its progress, or in the relative position of the parties, has always tended to swell beyond its proper channels. The South has for the most part taken a credit in its purchasers beyond what has been allowed to other dealers. But this has had no tendency to discredit Southern purchasers, who up to the date of the disruption maintained a favorable position with Northern creditors.

It is a matter of constant wonder to Southern politicians why they receive their supply of foreign goods mainly from New York. The cotton goes directly, they know, from their ports, and it seems to them that European goods should come directly to their ports in return. They think they are injured, but, on the contrary, it is a benefit. The reason is a purely commercial one, and it governs the Southern merchants as well as those of New York. The quantity of foreign goods which could be sold in any Southern port is not great enough to warrant that large and varied importation which would fully meet the tastes and demands of all purchasers. A merchant of Charleston would have to ransack Europe, Asia, and Africa, to find the assortment he wants, if he should undertake direct importation. It could not be to the profit of Charleston importers to keep such a stock of goods as would fit out the retail shops of that city or the country depending on it. Foreign merchants and manufacturers, forming their opinion of the best point for the sale and destination of their commodities, have selected New York as the place, and they have made it the depository of vast quantities of goods. The merchants of this country having formed the same opinion of the advantages of the position, they have congregated there, and the joint operation of these parties has made New York not only the chief receptacle of foreign goods in our country, but, perhaps, equal, if not superior, to that of any country. The merchant of any Southern city can, in one day's time, select there a greater variety of foreign goods than he could in three months, or, perhaps, a year, if he were to undertake to resort to the sources whence they come. In this way Northern cities have lost some of their shipping business, but the natural operations of trade have produced the result. The same reasons which induce the merchants of the North to purchase foreign goods in New York influence those of the South. It is the interest of both.

But New York does not derive its wealth all or even mainly from the importation of foreign goods. Having become the grand receptacle of commodities from abroad, and, of course, the resort of many purchasers, it became also the depository of domestic goods of fivefold the value and quantity. This great aggregation of merchandise at New York, however it may in some respects draw some business from other cities which do business there, is yet the result of individual action on the part of the people of these cities. It is a commercial advantage to have an entrepot for the exhibition and sale of commodities, whether imported or made at home. Such markets are found in every country, and on a smaller scale in every district. They are not without their disadvantages, and the power they obtain over trade and industry is often wielded more for their own special benefit than for those of commerce or industry. They are a special result of free internal trade like that which has prevailed in the United States. Before the war of navigation acts and tariffs for protection of industry commenced, the commerce of the world was chiefly carried on by one or two cities, or countries, taking the lead, and for a time absorbing nearly the whole trade of the world. Such were Tyre and Carthage in ancient times, and Venice and the Hanseatic cities in modern days.

The reason why Southern merchants purchase their supplies of foreign goods in New York may be found in the simple fact that they find it for their advantage so to do. These goods would have been charged with no higher rates of duty at Charleston or New Orleans than at New York, and might of course have been imported at Southern ports with a saving of New York profits, and expenses and freights thence southward. The real state of the case has been that the south does not consume European goods enough to make it worth while or profitable to import them directly. The largest amount of importations made in a Southern port is at New Orleans, and it is well known that a large portion of these are by merchants of St. Louis, Louisville, and Cincinnati.

The writer in the *Examiner* is mistaken, then, when he alleges that the Southern trade with Great Britain "is intrusively diverted from its proper direct channel by New York and the Northern States," whose intervention he avers to be "wholly unnecessary, and alike detrimental to the South and to England." Nothing can be said of this trade more truly than that it has found its own channels by the free choice of those most interested in it. The markets of Europe were as free to the Southern as to the Northern importer, and the duties at all our ports were the same. Why did not the Southern merchants avail themselves of this, and of the fact that the South produced all the cotton, which is the chief item in the payment of our exports? What possible advantage had the North, originally, by which it could intrude into this business and divert it to New York? In the view taken of this subject by this writer, and by many Southern politicians, no sound reason or explanation can be assigned why there is so little direct trade between Europe and the South. If the Southern people had to pay duties in proportion to their consumption of foreign goods, the Northern people had to pay in the same proportion. The Southern merchants, guided certainly by their interests, have purchased the supplies needed by their customers at the North, and chiefly consisting of Northern manufactures, although foreign goods could have been imported by them if interest or advantage had dictated that course. Whilst merchants of the South and their customers were pursuing this mode of supplying their wants, Southern politicians and speculative writers upon political economy were insisting that a grievous and special wrong was done to that section. They urged that all the Northern manufactured goods were affected by the high duties upon foreign commodities, and that of course the extra price was a burden upon the South. But this burden fell also upon the Northern people, and as each party would incur it only in proportion to what was consumed, at least eight-tenths would fall on the Northern people as the chief consumers, from their greater number, their colder climate, more varied industry, and the absence of slaves.

At no time could it occur that the South would have to pay more than in proportion to its consumption, whether of the burden of duties or of increased prices; and the choice of purchasing at home or abroad was always open; the same choice which was free to the Northern people, that of purchasing the foreign article with the duty imposed, or the domestic article at the manufacturers' prices. The only ground of complaint, then, for the South would be that the tariff discriminated against the South by imposing heavier duties upon the special articles consumed chiefly by the Southern people, or that the duties were heavier than necessary to raise the required amount of revenue. Our tariffs have contained no duties discriminating against the South, and none which did not lean more heavily upon the Northern people who were not manufacturers than upon those of the South. It is true that the strict line of revenue duties has not been pursued in constructing our tariffs, the deviations being intended to promote the growth of such departments of production as were most important to our national independence. But this burden fell most strongly upon the population of the North, not only as much the largest, but also as being the largest consumers *per capita*.

We say, then, that the tariffs have inflicted no burden upon the South, but that which has fallen more heavily upon the North, and in no instance more than the proper share of the public revenue, and that the merchants of the South have better understood the interests of the South than the politicians and writers upon political economy. It was well known to the merchants as well as to many of the planters themselves, that a large proportion of the commodities procured at the North could not be obtained at all in foreign countries, or not of equal quality, and as well suited to the tastes and wants of the South. Cuba and other Southern agricultural regions, which have as free access to other markets, as ours import largely from this country, Cuba alone taking to the value of upwards of eleven million of dollars.

But we do not rest on such considerations as these our denial that the "intervention of New York and the Northern States is unnecessary and alike detrimental to the South and England." It is a very narrow and inadequate view of this business which suggested such a remark, and the other already quoted, that the "single object and business of the South is to grow cotton for England—the natural action of England is to send ships to bring home the cotton, laden with English manufactures to pay for it." Now this is so far from being true or correct, that the Cotton States, with their seven million of inhabitants, nearly one-half of whom are slaves, do not and cannot take English manufactures for their cotton. The manufactures with which England pays for the cotton she takes are consumed by the twenty-four million of our people who do not live in the Cotton States, and mainly by the nineteen million who inhabit the North and West. Those people residing out of the Cotton States furnish the cotton planters with food, agricultural implements, furniture, and innumerable articles of the product of men, labor, skill, and machinery, on terms as favorable, all things considered, as they could be obtained for elsewhere, and nearly to the full extent of the whole production of cotton. To pay for this purchase of commodities from their sister States, they turn over their whole product of cotton, one-fifth of which is retained for manufacture in the Northern and Middle States, one-fifth is sent to the continent of Europe, and three-fifths are sent to England, in payment for which England returns an amount of commodities suitable chiefly to the supply of the Northern markets. This indirect mode of paying for the cotton taken by England adds nothing to the price of the raw material, for that goes direct from the Southern ports, whilst it gives to England a market for the very kind of goods which afford the most profit, amongst a population three times greater than that of the Cotton States, a people who are thus made large consumers of the best and finest products of English skill in manufacture. If a direct trade between England and the Cotton States were attempted, by no possibility could purchasers be found there for English goods in sufficient quantity to pay for the cotton. This trade has long since found its proper channels—those which are most satisfactory to the mass of the parties concerned, and especially to those who best understand its operation.

A glance at the list of articles furnished by the Northern to the Cotton States shows that a very large proportion is in fact wholly unaffected by the duties of the national tariff, whilst the prices are greatly reduced by severe domestic competition. And it must be kept in mind that when there is competition between a foreign and domestic article, the foreign always rises in price when the domestic competition is extinguished or removed. There is no more effectual mode of keeping down foreign prices than by establishing a competition at home.

We deny, then, most distinctly, and in full view of the facts, that the trade between the United States and England, in so far as the Cotton States are concerned, is either detrimental to them or to England, or that there has been any unnecessary intrusion on the part of New York or the Northern States. This trade has taken its whole shape, course, and proportions from the combined action of the parties actually concerned, governed as they have been by what they regarded as their interest. This upon the principles of free trade should be regarded as conclusive. The duties imposed by the national tariffs never deprived the Cotton States of their right to supply their wants by importation from foreign countries; nor were the duties heavier on the average than were needful for the purpose of levying the national revenue. Besides the duties upon iron, and woollen and cotton goods, although at times greater than if imposed for revenue alone, fell upon a larger population out of the Cotton States who were not manufacturers of iron, nor of woollen nor cotton goods, nor in fact manufacturers at all, than the whole population of the cotton-planting region. The population employed in agriculture out of that region is more than twice as great as that in it, and individually they consume double as much iron, and woollen and cotton goods. The Northern people have imposed no heavy duties upon those of the South of which they have not borne by far the heaviest share, nor any the policy of which would not have greatly favored the Southern people if they had availed themselves of it.

The cities of Pittsburg, Wheeling, Cincinnati, Louisville and other towns in the States lying on the Ohio River, furnish the Cotton States on the Mississippi with an immense variety of manufactures suitable for their use, which could not, taken altogether, be obtained from England and distributed to them at a less rate and of equal quality, even if free of duty. This is equally true of a large proportion of the commodities furnished to the Cotton States on the Gulf of Mexico and on the Atlantic by the manufacturers of Virginia, Maryland, Eastern Pennsylvania, New Jersey, New York, and New England. Whatever may be said of the higher prices of American manufactures, such as are furnished from those States to the Cotton States, their very existence and success has much reduced the commercial prices of the corresponding European articles, and thereby greatly diminished the burden of the duties by lessening the costs of the articles on which the duties are imposed.

It is grossly absurd, then, in the writer of the article in the *Examiner* to contend that the import of cotton into England should be direct in regard to the English exports which pay for the cotton. The trade, as we have seen, is now in the shape which is most for the advantage of those directly interested; and if the present disturbed state of these relations shall continue, England will find that more than one-half of the cotton she imports will have to be paid for in gold, making a heavy drain upon the basis of her currency. The Northern States are quite prepared to manufacture for themselves, if their present trade with the South is taken from them, and as soon as this occurs the British goods will, to a large extent, be shut out of the Northern ports. This is already foreshadowed by the shipment to this country of larger amounts of gold than can be demanded by any balance of trade, by the actual diminution of the import of British goods, and by the passage of a tariff increasing the duties and making them specific.

Not less grossly absurd is this writer's assertion in respect to the disruption of the Cotton States that "slavery has nothing to do either with its origin or continuance. The *causa causans* from the beginning and throughout has been the tariff." * Now whatever may be the opinions of the small number of politicians who have participated and conducted this revolution, whether chiefly actuated by ambition, or by the disappointment of defeat, or jealousy of the overshadowing power of the North, or differing opinions on commercial policy, or whatever motives stimulated them personally in their rash movement, the instrument by which they effected it was slavery alone. Without this the disruption could not have been accomplished, and without it the rebellion could not be sustained an hour. And whenever the masses of the people in the se-

* See "The Philosophy of Secession" in No. 878.

ceding States are entirely satisfied that their rights as slaveholders are secure from invasion by the North, nothing will keep them from taking their position again in the Union.

The assertion that slavery had nothing to do with the recent political disturbance, stands in striking contrast with the floods of verbal, oratorical and printed discussions upon the subject which has been poured upon the country for the last three months for legislatures, conventions, public meetings, from pulpits, from the public journals, from books, pamphlets, and from the tongues of all talkers, male and female, in all places, high and low. If that writer had been doomed to hear and read what has been said and printed on the subject of slavery in connection with secession in this country, during the last few months, he would have been in no condition of body or mind to make such rash assertions—he would have been a used-up man.

How little he appreciates the tendencies of the present agitation is evinced by his prophecy, that in proper time the Southern people will, if secession takes place, be led to adopt the policy just going into effect in Russia, where the serfs, by millions, are now receiving their liberty. The present race of masters in the South assert that African slavery, as it exists in this country, is the very foundation of sound and pure society, the very acme of civilization. They assert that society, as it exists in those parts of this country where slavery does not prevail, is a failure, and that society as it is constituted in the Slave States is a model. According to their view the African is rightly, morally, religiously, socially and politically destined to perpetual servitude as property. They scout the idea of emancipation, however remote, as a thing at no time desirable, and not to be aimed at either in the interests of master or slave.

The writer in the *Examiner* concludes by remarking that "Owing to the monopoly which the tariff has conferred on the North, all the transactions of the South are liquidated at New York, and there the English houses have established their great agencies;" and he cautions the English public against the tendency of the "public organs to take their tone of opinion from these sources." Now it is quite possible that these great agencies in New York are as well informed and as disinterested as the writer in the *Examiner*. One thing, at least, they may be presumed to understand, and that is the proper place to establish their agencies. They know that the cotton shipped to England goes upon Northern account, and that the proceeds of cotton sold in England go to pay for commodities purchased by the cotton planters in the States north of them; and they know that these proceeds come over in English goods, nine-tenths of which are consumed north of the Cotton States. They establish their agencies in New York because it is the natural centre of this great trade, determined by the natural operation of unrestricted free trade in the United States.

England cannot mend this matter so far as the interests of her trade are concerned. The inclination of the people of the Northern and Middle States is to manufacture not only for themselves, but for others; and whilst they have succeeded in supplying the Southern people with commodities manufactured expressly for them, the influence of the South has kept open in the North for English goods a market far more important than the South itself could offer. The alarm exhibited about the tariff just enacted has no foundation. The intention was to return to specific duties, and not considerably to increase the burden. It has, doubtless, been prepared with too much haste, as most of the previous tariffs were, and it may be necessary to correct such errors as time and experience may show to exist. It is very easy to prove that specific duties are very heavy by selecting special articles for that purpose; but merchants knowing the operations of the duty take care, in their importations, to avoid the particular articles thus affected. As the experience of Europe is in favor of specific duties where the object is revenue, it is natural that, in this country, we should desire to return to a system to which England, France, Germany and other nations are indebted for their revenue by customs.

Not less than three-fourths of the British customs are the product of specific duties. If this tariff shall be found to have greatly increased the duties upon particular articles, this will no doubt be corrected; but no amount of clamor can bring about a return to the system of custom-house valuations as it has existed, with its multiplied abuses during the past fifteen years. But we believe there will be no hesitation in adjusting the duties by specifics when they are applicable upon the average prices of the articles for the last ten years. We know that many of the rates in the Morrill tariff were so adjusted, the object being not to increase the duty but to render it steady.

From The Examiner.

The History of England from the Accession of James the Second. By Lord Macaulay. Vol. V. Edited by his Sister, Lady Trevelyan. Longman and Co.

EXCEPT account of the preparations for a new contest with France, a few points of minor detail, and a summary, if summary was needed, of the character of his chief hero, Lord Macaulay lived to complete his History as far as to the death of William the Third. The posthumous volume now before us, which includes a full general index to the whole work, continues the narrative from the 2nd of December, 1697, Thanksgiving Day for the Peace secured by the Treaty of Ryswick. We have in it the spirit of the debates of three sessions of Parliament, together with the concurrent foreign policy of the king, told in three chapters that are, like their predecessors, bright with antithesis. Here we may again enjoy all that abrupt contrast of light and shade in the depiction of character, which has secured for Lord Macaulay's masterpiece a lasting popularity, but has deprived it of at least some part of the confidence due to the results of inquiry by an acute mind into facts collected with a bookworm's industry, and grouped with a rare sense of their value in relation to each other. The first break in the thread of the narrative occurs at William's abrupt prorogation of the Parliament, that had passed from a warm contest between the two Houses to a second attack upon Lord Chancellor Somers and on other friends of the king. This is succeeded by a finished account of the death in the following year, 1701, of James the Second, of the recognition by Louis of the Pretender, and of the feeling aroused in England by that act. In the midst of the ensuing general election the revised part of the History ends. It is followed by Lord Macaulay's first sketch for his narrative of William's death in 1702. These are its closing paragraphs :—

"The king meanwhile was sinking fast. Albemarle had arrived at Kensington from the Hague, exhausted by rapid travelling. His master kindly bade him go to rest for some hours, and then summoned him to make his report. That report was in all respects satisfactory. The States General were in the best temper; the troops, the provisions, and the magazines were in the best order. Every thing was in readiness for an early campaign. William received the intelligence with the calmness of a man whose work was done. He was under no illusion as to his danger. 'I am fast drawing,' he said, 'to my end.' His end was worthy of his life. His intellect was not for a moment clouded. His fortitude was the more admirable because he was not willing to die. He had very lately said to one of those whom he most loved: 'You know that I never feared death; there have been times when I should have wished it; but, now that this great new prospect is opening before me, I do wish to stay here a little longer.' Yet no weakness, no querulousness, disgraced the noble close of that noble career. To the physicians the king returned his thanks graciously and gently. 'I know that you have done all that skill and learning could do for me: but the case is beyond your art; and I submit.' From the words which escaped him he seemed to be frequently engaged in mental prayer. Burnet and Tenison remained many hours in the sick-room. He professed to them his firm belief in the truth of the Christian religion, and received the sacrament from their hands with great seriousness. The antechambers were crowded all night with lords and privy councillors. He ordered several of them to be called in, and exerted himself to take leave of them with a few kind and cheerful words.

"Among the English who were admitted to his bedside were Devonshire and Ormond. But there were in the crowd those who felt as no Englishman could feel, friends of his youth who had been true to him, and to whom he had been true, through all vicissitudes of fortune; who had served him with unalterable fidelity when his Secretaries of State, his Treasury and his Admiralty had betrayed him; who had never on any field of battle, or in an atmosphere tainted with loathsome and deadly disease, shrunk from placing their own lives in jeopardy to save his, and whose truth he had at the cost of his own popularity rewarded with bounteous munificence. He strained his feeble voice to thank Auverquerque for the affectionate and loyal services of thirty years. To Albemarle he gave the keys of his closet, and of his private drawers. 'You know,' he said, 'what to do with them.' By this time he could scarcely respire. 'Can this,' he said to the physicians, 'last long?' He was told that the end was approaching. He swallowed a cordial, and asked for Bentinck. Those were his last articulate words. Bentinck instantly came to the bedside, bent down, and placed his ear close to the king's mouth. The lips of the dying man moved; but nothing could be heard. The king took the hand of his earliest friend, and pressed it tenderly to his heart. In that moment, no doubt, all that had cast a slight passing cloud over their long and pure friendship was forgotten. It was now between seven and eight in the morning. He closed his eyes, and gasped for breath. The bishops knelt down and read the commendatory prayer. When it ended William was no more.

When his remains were laid out, it was found that he wore next to his skin a small piece of black silk riband. The lords in waiting ordered it to be taken off. It contained a gold ring and a lock of the hair of Mary."

The period included in this volume yields two subjects peculiarly suited to Lord Macaulay's vivid manner of depicting history, the visit of Czar Peter to England, and the tale of Paterson's unhappy Darien scheme. The state of Muscovy before the days of Peter the Great is represented by a few clear touches :—

"The English embassies had historians whose narratives may still be read with interest. Those historians described vividly, and sometimes bitterly, the savage ignorance and the squalid poverty of the barbarous country in which they had sojourned. In that country, they said, there was neither literature nor science, neither school nor college. It was not till more than a hundred years after the invention of printing that a single printing-press had been introduced into the Russian empire; and that printing-press had speedily perished in a fire which was supposed to have been kindled by the priests. Even in the seventeenth century the library of a prelate of the first dignity consisted of a few manuscripts. Those manuscripts too, were in long rolls: for the art of bookbinding was unknown. The best-educated men could barely read and write. It was much if the secretary to whom was entrusted the direction of negotiations with foreign powers had a sufficient smattering of Dog Latin to make himself understood. The arithmetic was the arithmetic of the dark ages. The denary notation was unknown. Even in the imperial treasury the computations were made by the help of balls strung on wires. Round the person of the sovereign there was a blaze of gold and jewels: but even in his most splendid palaces were to be found the filth and misery of an Irish cabin. So late as the year 1663, the gentlemen of the retinue of the Earl of Carlisle were, in the city of Moscow, thrust into a single bedroom, and were told that, if they did not remain together, they would be in danger of being devoured by rats.

"Such was the report which the English legations made of what they had seen and suffered in Russia; and their evidence was confirmed by the appearance which the Russian legations made in England. The strangers spoke no civilized language. Their garb, their gestures, their salutations, had a wild and barbarous character. The ambassador and the grandees who accompanied him were so gorgeous that all London crowded to stare at them, and so filthy that nobody dared to touch them. They came to the court balls dropping pearls, and vermin. It was said that one envoy cudgelled the lords of his train whenever they soiled or lost any part of their finery, and that another had with difficulty been prevented from putting his son to death for the crime of shaving and dressing after the French fashion."

Of Peter himself, as he appeared in England, Lord Macaulay's account recalls by its bright coloring and faultless grouping a picture by Mr. Maclise. His majesty, who to ensure to himself a strictly private view of a debate in the House of Lords, climbed to the leads and peeped through a small window :—

"Heard with great interest the royal assent given to a bill for raising fifteen hundred thousand pounds by land tax, and learned with amazement that this sum, though larger by one-half than the whole revenue which he could wring from the population of the immense empire of which he was absolute master, was but a small part of what the Commons of England voluntarily granted every year to their constitutional king.

"William judiciously humored the whims of his illustrious guest, and stole to Norfolk Street so quietly that nobody in the neighborhood recognized his majesty in the thin gentleman who got out of the modest-looking coach at the czar's lodgings. The czar returned the visit with the same precautions, and was admitted into Kensington House by a back door. It was afterwards known that he took no notice of the fine pictures with which the palace was adorned. But over the chimney of the royal sitting-room was a plate which by an ingenious machinery, indicated the direction of the wind; and with this plate he was in raptures.

"He soon became weary of his residence. He found that he was too far from the objects of his curiosity, and too near to the crowds to which he was himself an object of curiosity. He accordingly removed to Deptford, and was there lodged in the house of John Evel[illegible], a house which had long been a favorite resort of men of letters, men of taste, and men of science. Here Peter gave himself up to his favorite pursuits. He navigated a yacht every day up and down the river. His apartment was crowded with models of three deckers, and two deckers, frigates, sloops, and fireships."

Evelyn did not think much of his tenant:

"It was, indeed, not in the character of tenant that the czar was likely to gain the good word of civilized men. With all the high qualities which were peculiar to himself, he had all the filthy habits which were then common among his countrymen. To the end of his life, while disciplining armies, founding schools, framing codes, organizing tribunals, building cities in deserts, joining distant seas by artificial rivers, he lived in his palace like a hog in a sty; and, when he was entertained by other sovereigns, never failed to leave on their tapestried walls and velvet state beds unequivocal proof that a savage had been there. Evelyn's house was left in such a state that the treasury quieted his complaints with a considerable sum of money."

No man is treated in these pages with more scorn than Sunderland. His son, Lord Spencer, after a word of respect for his love of books, appears only as a too passionate Whig who could see no danger to liberty except from kings; and the romantic story of his daughter's faithfulness to her proscribed husband, Clancarty, who was hunted down by her brother and dragged from her arms to his prison in the Tower, is, of course, one of the episodes that Lord Macaulay knew how to employ to the best advantage.

The desire for reduction of the standing army, warmly expressed by the country, and which at one time drove William into a determination to resign the English crown, could not be flatly opposed by Somers, although action upon it was moderated by his tact. The dread of a Prætorian guard is extinct in England, but faith in the power of a national militia is reviving. Lord Macaulay, however, in his most emphatic way dwells on the fact "that the occasional soldier is no match for the general soldier." Against the pleas for a standing army, men urged the patriotism and the prowess of a national militia. But, says the historian:—

"The finest militia that ever existed was probably that of Italy in the third century before Christ. It might have been thought that seven or eight hundred thousand fighting men, who assuredly wanted neither natural courage nor public spirit, would have been able to protect their own hearths and altars against an invader. An invader came, bringing with him an army small and exhausted by a march over the snow of the Alps, but familiar with battles and sieges. At the head of this army he traversed the peninsula to and fro, gained a succession of victories against immense numerical odds, slaughtered the hardy youth of Latium like sheep, by tens of thousands, encamped under the walls of Rome, continued during sixteen years to maintain himself in a hostile country, and was never dislodged till he had by a cruel discipline gradually taught his adversaries how to resist him.

"It was idle to repeat the names of great battles won, in the middle ages, by men who did not make war their chief calling; those battles proved only that one militia might beat another, and not that a militia could beat a regular army. As idle was it to declaim about the camp at Tilbury. We had indeed reason to be proud of the spirit which all classes of Englishmen, gentlemen and yeomen, peasants and burgesses, had so signally displayed in the great crisis of 1588. But we had also reason to be thankful that, with all their spirit, they were not brought face to face with the Spanish battalions. Somers related an anecdote, well worthy to be remembered, which had been preserved by tradition in the noble house of De Vere. One of the most illustrious men of that house, a captain who had acquired much experience and much fame in the Netherlands, had, in the crisis of peril, been summoned back to England by Elizabeth, and rode with her through the endless ranks of shouting pikemen. She asked him what he thought of the army. 'It is,' he said, 'a brave army.' There was something in his tone or manner which showed that he meant more than his words expressed. The queen insisted on his speaking out. 'Madam,' he said, 'Your Grace's army is brave indeed. I have not in the world the name of a coward; and yet I am the greatest coward here. All these fine fellows are praying that the enemy may land, and that there may be a battle; and I, who know that enemy well, cannot think of such a battle without dismay.' De Vere was doubtless in the right. The Duke of Parma, indeed, would not have subjected our country; but it is by no means improbable that, if he had effected a landing, the island would have been the theatre of a war greatly resembling that which Hannibal waged in Italy, and that the invaders would not have been driven out till many cities had been sacked, till many counties had been wasted, and till multitudes of our stout-

From The Examiner.

The Medical Missionary in China; a Narrative of Twenty Years' Experience. By William Lockhart, F.R.C.S., F.R.G.S., etc. Hurst and Blackett.

DURING the score of years which he spent in China, Mr. Lockhart had peculiarly favorable opportunities for studying the habits of the people. He had representatives of almost every class of society under his medical eye, and they, with the gratitude of cured patients, opened to him many ways of intelligence. Thus, in addition to the special matter which he wishes to make public, he gives on many other subjects more complete information than has hitherto been afforded.

Of the tea-houses he writes an amusing description. Every Chinaman goes to his tea-house, either to talk with his friends, or to discuss political matters, or to listen to a lecture of some sort, and after an evening spent in drinking tea and cracking melon seeds and smoking, he has seldom to pay more than the equivalent of a halfpenny for the entertainment. In a country where there are no other newspapers than the dry official gazettes, the tea-shops are more necessary centres of intelligence than clubs in England. There are also tea-jars, after the fashion of our drinking fountains. Wealthy persons join to set up on the roadside large jars filled with weak tea from which any wearied passer-by may drink without charge.

In the bathing-houses the practice is more sensible than that of the Turkish bath now in vogue. Under large troughs of water fires are lighted, and on rafters placed across the troughs the bathers sit or lie exposed to the rising steam. The process is considered pleasant unless the rafters give way, as is not uncommon; and then the bather will be either boiled or half boiled. With or without the boiling, the cost of the bath is just a farthing. If a cup of tea and a pipe of tobacco be added, the charge is half as much again. To these cheap baths is attributed much of the Chinese cleanliness and freedom from disease.

Notwithstanding the overcrowding of houses and the absence of proper sewerage, illness is comparatively rare among the Chinese. But when they do fall ill they have little science by which they can be cured. Sometimes the native doctors make wise use of their individual experience; but the only written code of medicine is a small, defective manual prepared by Jesuit teachers. Mr. Lockhart speaks with proper pride of the help which Englishmen and Americans, within the present century, have given to the Chinese. Many valuable treatises on medicine and kindred sciences have been translated and thankfully received by the people. Youths eagerly present themselves at the English hospitals for instruction in the art of healing; and, with their new knowledge, they travel over the land, sure of honor and reward by reason of the power which they hold. Patients also come from all parts of the country and beg to be cured. One man journeyed a thousand miles, and when his health had been restored, announced, "I shall write the names of Jesus and God on cards, and will widely disseminate them among all the people in order to make some return for their great favors." Another wrote this letter: "Let the merits of Jesus, the Saviour of mankind, be promulgated throughout the world. You deliver from all diseases, and, by extraordinary means, save myriads of people. Lin-Lien-Man presents his compliments." In this way Mr. Lockhart calculates that the largest and best sort of missionary work is being done.

Mr. Lockhart spent fourteen years at Shanghai, and during his twenty years' service he attended personally upon more than two hundred thousand people. As the result of this large experience, he speaks more highly than we have been accustomed to hear concerning Chinese gratitude and good-heartedness. There is generally, he tells us, a kindly feeling between the people, and a lasting desire to show thankfulness to those foreigners who have done them good. Injustice and selfishness are more commonly displayed by the officials, whose great aim is to rise to higher place; but amongst them he found readiness to meet kindness with kindness.

ing on the diagrams which illustrated the newly discovered laws of centripetal and centrifugal force, writing little copies of verses, and indulging visions of parsonages with rich glebes, and of closes in old cathedral towns; had developed in him new talents; had held out to him the hope of prizes of a very different sort from a rectory or a prebend. His eloquence had gained for him the ear of the legislature. His skill in fiscal and commercial affairs had won for him the confidence of the city. During four years he had been the undisputed leader of the majority of the House of Commons and every one of those years he had made memorable by great parliamentary victories, and by great public services. It would seem that his success ought to have been gratifying to the nation, and especially to that assembly of which he was the chief ornament, of which indeed he might be called the creature. The representatives of the people ought to have been well pleased to find that their approbation could, in the new order of things, do for the man whom they delighted to honor all that the mightiest of the Tudors could do for Leicester, or the most arbitrary of the Stuarts for Strafford.

"But, strange to say, the Commons soon began to regard with an evil eye that greatness which was their own work. The fault indeed was partly Montague's. With all his ability, he had not the wisdom to avert, by suavity and moderation, that curse, the inseparable concomitant of prosperity and glory, which the ancients personified under the name of Nemesis. His head, strong for all the purposes of debate and arithmetical calculation, was weak against the intoxicating influence of success and fame. He became proud even to insolence. Old companions, who, a very few years before, had punned and rhymed with him in garrets, had dined with him at cheap ordinaries, had sat with him in the pit, and had lent him some silver to pay his seamstress' bill, hardly knew their friend Charles in the great man who could not forget for one moment that he was First Lord of the Treasury, that he was Chancellor of the Exchequer, that he had been a Regent of the kingdom, that he had founded the Bank of England and the new East India Company, that he had restored the currency, that he had invented the Exchequer Bills, that he had planned the General Mortgage, and that he had been pronounced by a solemn vote of the Commons, to have deserved all the favors which he had received from the crown. It was said that admiration of himself and contempt of others were indicated by all his gestures and written in all the lines of his face. The very way in which the little jackanapes, as the hostile pamphleteers loved to call him, strutted through the lobby, making the most of his small figure, rising on his toe, and perking up his chin, made him enemies. Rash and arrogant sayings were imputed to him, and perhaps invented for him. He was accused of boasting that there was nothing that he could not carry through the House of Commons, that he could turn the majority round his finger. A crowd of libellers assailed him with much more than political hatred. Boundless rapacity and corruption were laid to his charge. He was represented as selling all the places in the revenue department for three years' purchase. The opprobrious nickname of Filcher was fastened on him. His luxury, it was said, was not less inordinate than his avarice."

Yet a few sentences we must add to this.

"The name of Mæcenas has been made immortal by Horace and Virgil, and is popularly used to designate an accomplished statesman, who lives in close intimacy with the greatest poets and wits of his time, and heaps benefits on them with the most delicate generosity. But it may well be suspected that, if the verses of Alpinus, and Fannius, of Bavius and Mævius, had come down to us, we might see Mæcenas represented as the most niggardly and tasteless of human beings, nay, as a man who, on system, neglected and persecuted all intellectual superiority. It is certain that Montague was thus represented by contemporary scribblers. They told the world in essays, in letters, in dialogues, in ballads, that he would do nothing for anybody without being paid either in money or in some vile services; that he not only never rewarded merit but hated it whenever he saw it; that he practised the meanest arts for the purpose of depressing it; that those whom he protected and enriched were not men of ability and virtue, but wretches distinguished only by their sycophancy and their low debaucheries. And this was said of the man who made the fortune of Joseph Addison, and of Isaac Newton."

The absence of notes, references, and other accessories of a grave history is rightly suffered to remind us that we are in this volume parted from its author. But the five volumes now before the world are more than a fragment. Essentially the history is here complete, the few omissions of detail, the few marks of technical imperfection, and the fragmentary ending, will be to all posterity, considering what they express, a more impressive close to the whole work than could have been furnished by the best skill of the rhetorician.

I cannot tell you all,—tears dim my sight,
And the hand trembles as I strive to write.
Our deepest feelings words can ne'er reveal,
The *tongue* may falter, but the heart can feel.

Friends, whom on earth I may not meet again,
If word or deed of mine has caused you pain
When heavy clouds hung darkly o'er the soul,
If I have spurned thy wise and mild control;
With needless cares the burthened mind perplexed,
With many a fancied ill, annoyed and vexed—
Forgive, forgive! thy friendly task is o'er,
Thy strength, thy patience I shall try no more.

Far from them now, no scornful lip can say
That fear or favor guides my pen to-day;
Within my hand no glittering bribe I hold;
The praise I render is not bought with gold;
Unswayed by interest, unawed by fear,
'Tis the just tribute of a heart sincere.

Ye, to whose daily, hourly care, are given
Disordered minds, by wave and tempest driven,
Whose part it is to smooth their darkened way;
A strict account to render day by day;
Read not these simple lines with scornful eye,—
Ye may be better, wiser far than I.
The hand that traced them may be small and weak,
Yet true and earnest are the words I speak.
Ofttimes to eyes shut from the glare of day,
God gives, to light the soul, a purer ray.
That higher, deeper knowledge that he hides
From wisdom's children, he to babes confides.
How useful is the path your feet pursue!
How solemn is the trust reposed to you!
Be kind and gentle, faithful, wise, and just—
Prove not unworthy of that sacred trust!
For listen to the words I speak: If you
Are to that trust in word or deed untrue,
When at the dread, eternal bar ye stand,
God will require it of your careless hand!

Open and truthful as the light of day,
Fear not the arm of power, the face of clay.
Bring to thy work a spirit pure and high—
Ye serve one Master, him, whose sleepless eye
Can pierce the thickest wall, the darkest night,—
Oh, act as ever in his holy sight!
And oh, may he, whose holiest name is *Love*,
With power divine each word and action move;
Through every trial be your shield and stay,
And give you strength and patience day by day,
From those, whose skilful fingers guide the helm
When dangers threaten, and when waves o'erwhelm;
Whose strong and willing arms from wrong protect,
Whose wisdom governs, and whose hands direct,
To those, to whom the humblest duties fall,
God give his strength, his peace to each and all!

Source of all truth, Author of every good!
Our Guide and Guardian by land and flood!
Whose watchful care the lonely orphan bless;
Judge and Defender of the fatherless!
The heavy debt, I have no power to pay,
With trembling hands, low at thy feet I lay;
Where'er their future paths and homes may be,
Deal thou with *them* as they have dealt with me.

M. G. H.

AN OLD MAN'S MUSINGS.

He dwelt in solitude; his brain grew rife
With thoughts of ancient years, which came to him
Old, old traditions, cobweb'd, faint, and dim,
As from another life.

What is the past but a tradition,—far,
Far and half hidden in deep memory's cell?
What are the thoughts which used to rise and swell,
But banners stained in war?

Stained in the many conflicts from their birth,
Losing their lustre in the course of time;
We deemed in youth they'd rise to heights sublime,
We see them fall to earth.

Oh, racking thought, the highest genius lent
But makes the man to suffering more prone,
That which he deems his greatest good, alone
Brings its own punishment.

For knowledge yearns for knowledge, till desire
Becomes a passion, but the straining mind
Within its body prison all confined,
Finds it can rise no higher.

Is this what I have lived for, but to know
My past *a night filled full of idle dreams*,
Vague visions, fancy flittings, paltry schemes,
The sum of all below?

Thus mused an old man till the morning light
Banished the darkness:—with the rising sun
There came a voice, "Thy life is but begun
If thou wilt act aright.

"Old as thou art, and though earth's shadows close
Around thee now, yet may a morn be nigh;
Another sun rise in a nobler sky,
E'en as but now *I* rose.

"Then each desire, each thought, however grand,
Shall find its full expansion, if whilst here
Thou strivest to the light which full and clear
Gleams from that other land."

—*Once a Week.*

THE LIVING AGE.

No. 883.—4 May, 1861.

CONTENTS.

NEW BOOKS.

CURRENTS AND COUNTER-CURRENTS IN MEDICAL SCIENCE. With other Addresses and Essays. By Oliver Wendell Holmes. Boston: Ticknor and Fields.

PUBLISHED EVERY SATURDAY BY

LITTELL, SON, & CO., BOSTON.

DESTRUCTION OF FORT SUMTER.

In vain has been all the prudent, gentle, brotherly care of the President of the United States to avoid bloodshed. Patience and forbearance were carried to their utmost limits. Major Anderson, by orders of James Buchanan, unresistingly suffered the rebels to build a wall of fire round him. Had he used his guns, they could have raised none of the forts from which his walls have been battered down. Encircled by his enemies he was perfectly quiet. When his provisions were nearly exhausted, he proposed to the insurgents to withdraw all the troops but a sergeant and two men,—but this was refused. Indeed, it would have been impossible for the smallest force to have been less aggressive than these eighty men had been.

Not until the last moment did the government move, by giving notice of its intention to send mere provisions to those starving men, peaceably if permitted. Then came the premeditated outrage; eight thousand men poured their fire upon this little band, which had never by word or deed offended them. The *object* was to make war, and thus spread the contagion of rebellion to Virginia. Thank God! that not even an indiscretion can be charged upon the President, who will now have the support of every loyal heart.

16 *April*, 1861.

From The New York Sun, 13 April.

There is a God who governs the world, and the passions of bad men are among the leading instruments by which he "coerces" states and empires to fulfil his inscrutable decrees. Human passion is the "rod of iron" with which he is said to rule the nations. It moves at his touch, or rather—like certain pieces of machinery, which a controlled spring is permitted at the proper moment to actuate of itself—whenever it suits the all-wise Ruler to modify or remove the pressure which he keeps upon human depravity, it springs forth with the blind fury of a demon, to execute whatever work of destruction and change had been decreed.

It is but a stolid impiety, to live in a time like this, unconscious of the plain evidence in current events, of a grand and awful plan of Providence relative to both the good and the bad institutions of our country. For four months past, every day has afforded fresh demonstration that for Divine purposes the elements of disloyalty, violence, and passion that predominate in the Southern character, have been deprived of all restraint, and the people given over to the madness which makes them at once the blindest and the most destructive implements of a Providence of whose ends they know nothing. Every object which the States now in revolt have proposed to themselves, could have been secured, peaceably and lawfully, had prudence, instead of passion and blind self-will, controlled their councils. Even up to yesterday, supposing their people actually fixed in the desire for a separate nationality, a little time, calmness, and patience would have gained it, with peace, prosperity, and security. But on the contrary, every step of this atrocious revolt has proved the madness which rushes on destruction, and eagerly does all that common prudence would forbid. The solemn portent of the hour, like a flaming sword hanging over the doomed States and institutions of the South, is that they are thus bereft of all good influences, rational or divine, and given over to monstrous delusion and frenzy, such as poor human nature falls under only when utterly forsaken of God.

The world already stands amazed at the unmixed folly of their crimes—and when it learns that they have this day crowned all the rest by wantonly, viciously and gratuitously commencing unprovoked war upon the forbearing and pacific government they have rebelled against, their doom, and that of all that depends on them, will be written high and plain before the eyes of all mankind. Such another preternatural instance of judicial blindness and self-destruction can scarce be found in history; if, perhaps, we except the fanatical and terrible obstinacy of that revolt which ended in the destruction of Jerusalem and the extinction of the Jewish nationality.

While we stand in awe at the visible "finger of God" in the great events of the hour, the Christian, at least, should watch the paternal Providence with strengthening hope and solemn cheer. Mercy and judgment are mingled in the storm. We shall not come out of this conflict where we went in, nor as we went in. The love of liberty, of country, of the rights of man, of truth and honor, of law and justice, had sunk too low in the corruption and venality of our times, for any resuscitation less violent and convulsive than this. When the heavens are rolled together as a scroll, and the earth on fire shall be dissolved, and the elements shall melt with fervent heat, then look we according to his promise, for a new heaven and a new earth in which dwelleth righteousness. So in the minor convulsions that prefigure and prepare for the last great change, we may find the same promise and a like result—a new and better country.

From The Welcome Guest.

THE LAWYER'S SECRET.

BY M. E. BRADDON.

CHAPTER I.

IN A LAWYER'S OFFICE.

"It is the most provoking clause that was ever invented to annul the advantages of a testament," said the lady.

"It is a condition which must be fulfilled, or you lose the fortune," replied the gentleman.

Whereupon the gentleman began to drum a martial air with the slender tips of his white fingers upon the morocco-covered office table, to which the lady beat time with the point of her narrow foot.

For the gentleman was out of temper, and the lady was out of temper also. I am sorry to have to say it of her, for she was very young and very handsome, and, though the angry light in her dark gray eyes had a certain vixenish beauty in it, it was a species of beauty rather alarming to a man of a nervous temperament.

She was very handsome. Her hair the darkest brown, in rich waving masses, that fell into extemporary curls under her elegant Parisian bonnet. Her eyes, as I have said, were gray—those large gray eyes, fringed with long black lashes, which are more dangerous than all other eyes ever invented for the perdition of honest men. They looked like deep pools of shining water, bordered by dark and shadowy rushes; they looked like stray stars in an inky sky; but they were so beautiful, that, like the signal lamp which announces the advent of an express upon the heels of a luggage train, they seemed to say, "Danger!" Her nose was aquiline; her mouth small, clearly cut, and very determined in expression; her complexion brunette, and rather pale. For the rest, she was tall, her head set with a haughty grace upon her sloping shoulders, her hands and feet small, and delicately shaped.

The gentleman was ten or fifteen years her senior. He, too, was handsome, eminently handsome; but there was a languid indifference about his manner, which communicated itself even to his face, and seemed to overshadow the very beauty of that face, with a dark veil of weary listlessness, that extinguished the light of his eyes and blotted out the smile upon his lips.

That any one so gifted by nature as he seemed gifted, could be as weary of life as he appeared, was, in itself, so much a mystery, that one learned to look at him as a man under whose quiet outward bearing lay some deep and stormy secret, unrevealable to common eyes.

He was dark and pale, with massively cut features, and thoughtful brown eyes, which rarely looked up from under the heavy eyelids that shrouded them. The mouth was spiritual in expression, the lips thin; but the face was wanting in one quality, lacking which it lacked the power which is the highest form of manly beauty, and that quality was determination.

He sat drumming with his white, taper fingers upon the table, and looking down, with a gloomy shade upon his handsome forehead.

The scene was a lawyer's office in Gray's Inn; there was a third person present, an elderly lady, rather a faded beauty in appearance, and very much dressed, who took, however, no part in the conversation, but sat in an easy-chair by the blazing fire, turning over the crisp pages of the *Times* newspaper, which, every time she moved it emitted a sharp, crackling sound, unpleasant to the nervous temperaments of the younger lady and the gentleman.

The gentleman was a solicitor, Horace Margrave, the guardian of the young lady, and executor to her uncle's will. Her name was Ellinor Arden; she was sole heiress and residuary legatee to her uncle, John Arden, of the park and village of Arden, in Northamptonshire, and she had this very day come of age. Mr. Margrave was a trusted and valued friend both of her father, dead ten years before, and of her uncle, only lately dead; and Ellinor Arden had been brought up to think, that if there was truth, honesty, or friendship upon earth, those three attributes were centred in the person of Horace Margrave, solicitor, of Gray's Inn.

He is to-day endeavoring to explain and to reconcile her to the conditions of her uncle's will, which are rather peculiar.

"In the first place, my dear Ellinor," he says, still drumming on the table, still looking down at his desk, and not at her, "you had no particular right to expect to be your uncle, John Arden, of Arden's heiress."

"I was his nearest relation," she said.

"Granted; but that was no reason why

you should be dear to him. Your father and he, after the amiable fashion of brotherly love in this very Christian country, were almost strangers to each other for the best part of their lives. "You, your uncle never saw: your father living on his wife's small property in the north of Scotland; you brought up in that unknown and unpleasant region until your father's death, ten years ago; after your father's death sent to Paris, to be there educated under the surveillance of your aunt, and never once introduced to John Arden, of Arden, your father's only brother."

"My father had such a horror of being misinterpreted; had he sought to make his daughter known to his rich brother, it might have been thought—"

"That he wanted to get that rich brother's money. It might have been thought? My dear girl, it would have been thought! Your father acted with the pride of the Northamptonshire Ardens; he acted like a high-minded English gentleman, and he acted, in the eyes of the world, like a fool. You never, then, expected to inherit your uncle's money?"

"Never! Nor ever wished it. My mother's little fortune would have been enough for me."

"I wish to Heaven you never had a penny beyond it!"

As Horace Margrave said these few words, the listless shadows on his face swept away for a moment, and revealed a settled gloom, painful to look upon.

He so rarely spoke on any subject whatever in a tone of real earnestness, that Ellinor Arden, startled by the change in his manner, looked up at him suddenly and searchingly. But the veil of weariness had fallen over his face once more, and he continued, with his old indifference,—

"To the surprise of every one, your uncle bequeathed to you, and to you alone, his entire fortune. Stranger as you were to him, this was an act, not of love for you, but of duty to his dead brother; but the person he really loved, was unconnected with him by the ties of kindred, and he no doubt considered that it would be a crime to disinherit his only niece in favor of a stranger. This stranger, this *protégé* of your uncle's, is the son of a lady who once was beloved by him, but who loved another, poorer and humbler than Squire Arden, of Arden, and who told him so, candidly, but tenderly; as a good woman should tell a man of that which she knows may shiver the whole fabric of his life. She married this poorer suitor, George Dalton, a young surgeon, in a small country town. She married him, and three years after her marriage, she died, leaving an only child, a boy. This boy, on the death of his father, which happened when he was only four years old, your uncle adopted. He never married, but devoted himself to the education of the son of the woman who had rejected him. He did not, however, bring up the boy to look upon himself as his heir; but he educated him as a man ought to be educated who has his own path to make in life. He had him called to the bar, and Henry Dalton had pleaded his first cause a year before your uncle's death. He did not leave him one farthing.

"But —"

"But he left his entire fortune to you, on condition that you should marry Henry Dalton within a year of your majority."

"And if I marry any one else, or refuse to marry this apothecary's son, I lose the fortune?"

"Every farthing of it."

A beautiful light flashed from her eyes, as she rose hurriedly from her chair, and, crossing the room, laid her hand lightly upon Horace Margrave's shoulder.

"So be it," she said, with a smile. "I will forfeit the fortune. I have a hundred a year from my poor mother's estate—enough for any woman. I will forfeit the fortune, and"—she paused for a moment, "and marry the man I love."

We have said that Horace Margrave was a pale man; but as Ellinor Arden said these words, his face changed from its ordinary dark pallor to a deadly ashen hue, and his head sunk forward upon his chest, while his strongly marked black eyebrows contracted painfully over his half-closed eyes.

She stood a little behind his chair, with her small gloved hand resting lightly on his shoulder, so she did not see the change in his face. She waited a minute or two, to hear what he would say to her determination, and, on his not speaking, she moved away from him impatiently, and resumed her seat on the other side of the large office table.

Nothing could have been more complete in its indifference than Mr. Margrave's manner, as he looked lazily up at her, and said,—

"My poor romantic child! Throw away a fortune of three thousand a year, to say nothing of Arden Hall, and the broad lands thereto appertaining, and marry the man you love! My sweet, poetical Ellinor, may I venture to ask who is this fortunate man whom you love?"

It seemed a very simple and straightforward question, emanating, as it did, from a man of business, many years her senior, her dead father's old friend, and her own guardian and trustee; but, for all that, Ellinor Arden appeared utterly unable to endure it. A dark flush spread itself over her handsome face; her eyelids fell over her flashing eyes; and her lips quivered with an agitation she was powerless to repress. She was silent for some minutes, during which Horace Margrave played carelessly with a penknife, opening and shutting it absently, and not once looking at his beautiful ward. The elderly lady by the fireplace turned the crackling sheets of the *Times* more than once during this short silence, which seemed so long.

Horace Margrave was the first to speak.

"My dear Ellinor, as your guardian, till this very day possessed of full power to control your actions—after to-day, I trust, still possessed of the privilege, though, perhaps, not the right, to advise them—I have, I hope, some claim on your confidence. Tell me, then, candidly, as you may tell a middle-aged old lawyer, like myself, who is it you love? who is it whom you would rather marry than Henry Dalton, the adopted son of your uncle?"

For once he looked at her as he spoke, she looking full at him; so it was that their eyes met; a long, earnest, reproachful, sad look was in hers; in his a darkness of gloomy sorrow, beyond all power of description.

His eyes were the first to fall; he went on playing with the handle of the penknife, and said,—

"You are so long in giving me a candid and straightforward answer, my dear girl, that I begin to think this hero is of rather a mythic order, and that your heart, is, after all, perhaps free. Tell me, Ellinor, is it not so? You have met so few people—have passed so much of your life in the utter seclusion of a Parisian convent—when away from the convent you have been under the Argus-like guardianship of your respected aunt, that I really cannot see how you can have lost that dear, generous heart of yours. I suspect that you are only trying to mystify me. Once for all, then, my dear ward, is there any one whom you love?"

He looked at her as he asked this decisive question, with a shrinking upward glance under his dark eyelashes—something like the glance of a man who looks up, expecting a blow, and knows that he must shiver and close his eyes when that blow falls.

The crimson flush passed away from her face, and left her deadly pale, as she said, with a firm voice,—

"No!"

"No one?"

"No one."

Horace Margrave sighed a sigh of deep relief, and proceeded in his former tone—entirely the tone of a man of business.

"Very well, then, my dear Ellinor, seeing that you have formed no prior attachment, that it is your uncle's earnest request, nay, solemn prayer, that this marriage should take place; seeing, also, that Henry Dalton is a very good young man—"

"I hate good young men!" she said, impatiently. "Dreadfully perfect beings, with light hair and fresh colored-cheeks; dressed in pepper-and-salt suits, and double-soled boots! I detest them!"

"My dear Ellinor! My dear Ellinor! Life is neither a stage play nor a three-volume novel; and, rely upon it, the happiness of a wife depends very little on the color of her husband's hair, or the cut of his coat. If he neglects you, will you be happier, lonely and deserted at home, in remembering the dark waving curls clustering round his head, at that very moment, perhaps, drooping over the green cloth of a hazard table in St. James' Street? If he wrings your heart with the racking tortures of jealousy, will it console you to recall the flashing glances of his hazel eyes, whose looks no longer meet your own? No, no, Ellinor, dispossess yourself of the schoolgirl's notion of Byronic heroes, with turn-down collars, and deficient moral region. Marry Henry Dalton; he is so good, honorable and sensible, that you must ultimately learn to esteem him. Out of that esteem will grow, by and by, love; and, believe me, paradoxical as it may sound, you will love him better from not loving him too much."

"As you will, my dear guardian," she said. "Henry Dalton, by all means, then, and the fortune. I should be very sorry not to follow your excellent, sensible, and business-like advice."

She tries to say this with his own indifference; but she says it with a sneering emphasis, and, in spite of herself, she betrays considerable agitation.

"If we are to dine at six—" interposed the faded lady by the fireplace, who had been looking over the top of the newspaper every three minutes, hopelessly awaiting a break in the conversation.

"We must go home directly," replied Ellinor. "You are right, my dear Mrs. Morrison, I am most inattentive to you. Pray forgive me; remember the happiness of a life," she looked not at Mrs. Morrison, but at Mr. Margrave, who had risen and stood lounging—tall, graceful, and indifferent—against the mantel-piece, "the happiness of a life, perhaps, trembled on the interview of to-day. I have made my decision, at the advice of my kind guardian. A decision which must, no doubt, result in the happiness of every one concerned. I am quite at your service, Mrs. Morrison."

Horace Margrave laid his hand on the bell by his side.

"Your carriage will be at the entrance to the Inn in three minutes, Ellinor. I will see you to it. Believe me, you have acted wisely; how wisely, you may never know."

He himself conducted them down the broad panelled staircase, and, putting on his hat, led his ward through the quiet Inn gardens to her carriage. She was grave and silent, and he did not speak to her till she was seated with her elderly companion and chaperone in her roomy clarence, when he leaned his hand on the carriage door, and said,—

"I shall bring Henry Dalton to Hertford Street this evening, to introduce him to his future wife."

"Pray do so," she said. "Adieu!"

"Only till eight o'clock."

He lifted his hat, and stood watching the carriage as it drove away, then walked slowly back to his chambers, flung himself into a luxurious easy-chair, took a cigar from a costly little Venetian chest, standing on a tiny table at his side, lit it, wheeled his chair close to the fire, stretched his feet out against the polished steel of the low grate, and prepared for a lazy half-hour before dinner.

As he lit the cigar, he looked gloomily into the blaze at his feet, and said,—

"Horace Lionel Welmorden Margrave, if you had only been an honest man!"

CHAPTER II.

IN WHICH A SECRET IS REVEALED, BUT NOT TO THE READER.

THE hands of the ormolu clock, in the little drawing-room in Hertford Street, occupied by Ellinor Arden and her companion, protectress, and dependant, Mrs. Morrison, pointed to a quarter past eight, as Horace Margrave's quiet brougham rolled up to her door.

Horace Margrave's professional position was no inconsiderable one. His practice was large and eminently respectable; lying principally amongst railway companies, and involving transactions of a very extensive kind. He was a man of excellent family, a perfect gentleman, elegant, clever, and accomplished; too good for a lawyer, as everybody said, but a very good lawyer for all that, as his clients constantly repeated. At five-and-thirty he was still unmarried; why, no one could guess; as many a great heiress, and many a pretty woman, would have been only too proud to say "Yes," to a matrimonial proposition from Horace Margrave, of Gray's Inn, and The Fir Grove, Stanleydale, Berkshire. But the handsome lawyer evidently preferred his free bachelor life, for if his heart had been very susceptible to womanly graces, he would most inevitably have lost it in the society of his lovely ward, Ellinor Arden.

Ellinor had only been a few weeks resident in London; she had left the guardianship of her aunt in Paris, to launch herself upon the whirlpool of English society, sheltered only by the ample wing of an elderly lady, duly selected and chartered by her aunt and Mr. Margrave. The world was new to her, and she came from the narrow circle of the convent in which she had been educated, and the quiet coteries of the Faubourg Saint

Germains, in which her aunt delighted, to take her position at once in London, as the sole heiress of Mr. Arden, of Arden.

It was then to Horace Margrave—to Horace Margrave, whom she remembered in her happy youth among the Scottish mountains, a young man on a shooting expedition, visiting at her father's house—Horace Margrave, who had visited her aunt, from time to time, in Paris, and who had towards her all the tender friendship and respectful devotion of an elder brother—to him, and to him alone, did she look for counsel and guidance; and she submitted as entirely to his influence as if he had indeed been that guardian and father whom he by law represented.

Her cheek flushed as the carriage wheels stopped below the window.

"Now, Mrs. Morrison," she said, with a sneer; "now for my incomparable *futur*. Now for the light hair and the thick boots."

"It will be very impertinent of him if he comes in thick boots," replied her matter-of-fact protectress. "Mr. Margrave says he is such an excellent young person."

"Exactly, my dear Mrs. Morrison,—a young person. He is described in one word, 'a person.'"

"Oh, my dream! my dream!" she murmured, under her breath.

Remember, she had but this day passed wisdom's Rubicon, and she was new to the hither bank She was still very romantic, and, perhaps, very foolish.

The servant announced "Mr. Margrave and Mr. Dalton."

In spite of herself, Ellinor Arden looked up with some curiosity to see this young man, for whom she entertained so profound a contempt and so unmerited an aversion. He was about three years her senior: of average height, neither tall nor short. His hair was, as she had prophesied, light; but it was by no means an ugly color, and it clustered, in short curls, round a broad, low, but massive forehead. His features were sufficiently regular; his eyes, dark blue; the general expression of his face was grave, and it was only on rare occasions that a quiet smile played round his firmly moulded lips. Standing side by side with Horace Margrave, he appeared any thing but a handsome man; but, to the physiognomist, his face was superior in the very qualities in which the dark beauty of the lawyer was deficient; force, determination, self-reliance, perseverance; all those attributes, in short, which go to make a great man.

"Mr. Dalton has been anxiously awaiting the hour that should bring him to your side, Miss Arden," said Horace Margrave. "He has been for a long time acquainted with those articles in your uncle's will which you only learned to-day."

"I am sorry Miss Arden should have ever learned them, if they have given her pain," said the young man, quietly.

Ellinor looked up in his face, and saw that the blue eyes, looking down into hers, had a peculiar earnestness all their own.

"He is not so bad, after all," she thought. "I have been foolish in ridiculing him; but I can never love him."

"Miss Arden," he continued, dropping into a chair by the sofa on which she was seated, while Horace Margrave leaned against the opposite side of the fireplace,—"Miss Arden, we meet under such peculiar circumstances, that it is best for the happiness of both that we should at once understand each other. Your late uncle was the dearest friend I ever had; no father could have been dearer to the most affectionate of sons than he was to me. Any wish, then, of his must to me be forever sacred. But I have been brought up to rely upon myself alone, and I am proud in saying I have no better wish than to make my own career, unaided by interest or fortune. The loss, then, of this money will be no loss to me. If it be your will to refuse my hand, and to retain the fortune, to which you alone have a claim, do so. You shall never be disturbed in the possession of that to which you, of all others, have the best right. Mr. Margrave, your solicitor, and executor to your uncle's will, shall to-morrow execute a deed, abnegating, on my part, all claim to this fortune; and I will, at one word from you, bid you adieu this night, before," he said, with an earnest glance at her beautiful face, "before my heart is too far involved to allow of my being even just."

"Mr. Dalton," said Horace Margrave, lazily watching the two from under the shadows of his eyelashes, "you bring Roman virtues into May Fair. You will purify the atmosphere."

"Shall I go or stay, Miss Arden?" asked the young man.

"Stay, Mr. Dalton!" She rose as she spoke, and laid her hand, as if for support, upon the back of a chair that was standing near her. "Stay, Mr. Dalton. If your happiness can be made by the union, which was my late uncle's wish, let it be so. I cannot hold this fortune which is not mine; but I may share it. I will confess to you, and, I know, your generous nature will esteem me better for the confession, that I have dared to cherish a dream in which the image of another had a part. I have been foolish, mistaken, absurd; as schoolgirls often are. The dream is broken. If you can accept my uncle's fortune and my own esteem; one is yours by right, the other has been nobly won by your conduct of this evening."

She held out her hand to him, he pressed it gently, and, raising it to his lips, led her back to the sofa, and reseated himself in the chair by her side.

Horace Margrave closed his eyes as if the long-expected blow had fallen.

The rest of the evening passed slowly. Mr. Margrave talked, and talked brilliantly; but he had a very dull audience. Ellinor was *distrait*, Henry Dalton thoughtful, and Mrs. Morrison eminently stupid. The lawyer repressed two or three yawns, which he concealed behind an embroidered fire-screen, and when the clock, on which an ormolu Pan reclined amidst a forest of rushes, announced half-past ten, he rose to depart, and Ellinor was left to ponder over the solemn engagement into which she had entered on the impulse of the moment.

"I had better take a cab to the Temple," said young Dalton, as they left the house. "I'll wish you good-night, Mr. Margrave."

"No, Mr. Dalton, I have something to say to you that must be said, and which, I think, I'd rather say at night than in the day: if you are not afraid of late hours, come home with me to my chambers, and smoke a cigar. Before you see Ellinor Arden again, I must have an hour's conversation with you. Shall it be to-night? I ask it as a favor, let it be to-night."

Henry Dalton looked considerably astonished by the earnestness of the lawyer's words; but he merely bowed, and said,—

"With great pleasure. I am entirely at your service; if I returned to my chambers, I should read for two or three hours, so pray do not be afraid of keeping me up."

Henry Dalton and Horace Margrave sat talking for nearly three hours in the chambers of the latter; but no cigars were smoked by either of them, and though a bottle of Madeira stood on the table, it was entirely untouched. It was to be observed, however, that a cellaret had been opened, and a decanter of brandy taken out; the stopper lay beside it and one glass, which had been drained to the dregs.

The clocks were striking two as Horace Margrave himself opened the outer door for his late visitor: on the threshold he paused, and laying his hand, with a strong grasp, on Dalton's arm, he said, in a whisper,—

"I am safe, then! Your oath is sacred!"

Henry Dalton turned and looked him full in the face. Looked full into the pale face and downcast eyes, completely shrouded by the white lids and shadowy black eyelashes.

"The Daltons, of Lincolnshire, are not an old family, Mr. Margrave, or a rich family; but they keep their word. Good-night!"

He did not hold out his hand at parting; but merely lifted his hat, and bowed gravely.

Horace Margrave sighed as he locked the doors, and returned to his warm study.

"At least," he said, "I am safe! But then I might have been happy. Have I been wise to-night? have I been wise, I wonder?" he muttered, as his eyes wandered to a space over the mantel-piece, on which were arranged a couple of pairs of magnificently mounted pistols, and a small dagger, in a chased silver scabbard. "Perhaps, after all, it was scarcely worth the trouble of this explanation; perhaps, after all, '*Le Jeu ne vaut pas la chandelle!*'"

CHAPTER III.

AFTER THE HONEYMOON.

THREE months had elapsed since the midnight interview in Horace Margrave's chambers—three months, and the Opera House was opened for the season, and three new tenors, and two sopranos, and a basso-baritone had appeared under the classic proscenium of her majesty's theatre; the novel of the season had been circulated by Mudie; Rotten Row was gay with Amazonian equestrians and *blasé* lifeguardsmen, with long amber whiskers, as yet untrammelled by red tape; moss roses were selling on the dusty pavements of the West End streets; and Covent Garden was all a-bloom with artistically arranged bouquets of rich tropical flowers, gorgeous in color and delicious in perfume;—London, in short, was in the full flood-tide of the season, when Mr. and Mrs. Henry Dalton returned from their honeymoon visit to the Cumberland Lake district, and took up their abode in the small house in Hertford Street, furnished by Ellinor before her marriage.

Hers has been a short courtship; all the sweet uncertainties, the doubts, the dreams, the fears, the hopes, which make up the poetical prologue to a love-match, have been wanting in this marriage ordained by the will of her late uncle—this marriage, which is founded on esteem and not on affection; this marriage, into which she has entered on the generous impulse of an impetuous nature that has never learned to repress emotion.

Is she happy? Can this cold esteem, this calm respect which she feels for the man chosen for her by another, satisfy the ardent heart of the romantic girl?

She has been already married six weeks, and has not seen Horace Margrave, the only friend she has in England, except, of course, her husband, since her wedding-day. Not since that sunny May morning on which he took her icy hand in his and gave her, as her guardian and the representative of her dead father, into her husband's arms. She remembered that on that day when his hand touched hers it was as cold and powerless as her own, and that his listless face was even paler than usual under the spring sunshine streaming in at the church windows; but after all, that he had done the honors of the breakfast-table, toasted the bride and bridegroom, complimented the bridesmaids, and fascinated everybody, with all the finished grace and marvellous ease of the all-accomplished Horace Margrave; and if she had ever thought that she had a right, for auld lang syne, for her dead father's sake, or for her own lovely face, and her tender respect for him, to be any thing more or dearer in his eyes than the most indifferent of his clients, that thought was dispelled by the gentlemanly *sang-froid* of his adieu to her on the carriage steps, as the four pawing bays started off to the rail for Windermere.

It is the end of June, and she is seated in the small drawing-room, awaiting the advent of morning visitors. They have been a week in town, and Horace Margrave has not yet called upon them. She has a weary air this morning, and she seems to seek in vain for something to occupy her. Now she strolls to the open piano, and plays a few chords, or a brilliant run, or softly touches the notes of some pensive air, and sings some Italian words; now she takes up an uncut novel from the table, and reads a page or two here and there, wherever the book opens; she walks to an embroidery frame, and takes a great deal of trouble in selecting and comparing wools, and threading needles, but when this is accomplished, she does not do three stitches; then she loiters listlessly about the room, looking at the pictures, chiefly valuable engravings, which adorn the pale silver-gray walls; but at last she is so utterly weary, that she flings herself into a deep easy-chair close to the open window, and sits idly looking down across a lilliputian forest of heliotropes and geraniums into the hot, sunny street.

She is looking very lovely; but she is not looking at all happy. The rich masses of her dark brown hair are swept away from her broad, low brows, and secured into a coil of superb plaits at the back of her head; her simple white morning dress is only ornamented by large knots of broad violet ribbon, and she wears no jewellery whatever, except a tiny, slender gold chain, which she twists perpetually in and out of her white fingers.

She sits for about half an hour, always looking down across the plants in the balcony at the pavement opposite, when she suddenly starts, and wrenches the thin chain off her fingers in her agitation.

She has seen the person for whom she has been waiting. A gentleman, who lounges lazily along the other side of the street, crosses the road beneath the window, and knocks at the door.

"At last!" she says; "now, perhaps, this mystery will be explained."

A servant announces "Mr. Margrave."

"At last!" she says again, rising as he enters the room. "O Mr. Margrave, I have been so anxious to see you."

He looks about on the crowded table to find, amongst its fashionable litter, a place for his hat, fails in doing so, and puts it down on a chair, and only then looks listlessly up at her and says,—

"Anxious to see me, my dear Ellinor; why anxious?"

"Because there are two or three questions which I must ask—which you must answer."

That peculiar expression in Horace Margrave's eyes, which was as it were a shiver of the eyelids, passed over them now; but it was too brief to be perceived by Ellinor Dalton. He sank lazily into a chair near her own, but not opposite to it. A chair placed with its back to the light, and then said,—

"My dear Ellinor, my dear Mrs. Dalton, what questions can you have to ask me, but questions of a purely business character? and even those, I imagine, your husband, who is quite as practical a man as myself, could answer as well as I."

"Mr. Dalton is the very last person to whom I can apply for an answer to the questions which I have to ask!"

"And why the last person?"

"Because those questions relate to himself!"

"Oh, I see! My dear Mrs. Dalton, is not this rather a bad beginning? You appeal from your husband to your solicitor."

"No, Mr. Margrave. I appeal to my guardian!"

"Pardon me, my dear Ellinor, there is no such person. He is defunct; he is extinct. From the moment I placed your hand in that of your husband on the altar steps of St. George's, Hanover Square, my duties, my right to advise you, and your right to consult me, expired. Henceforth you have but one guardian, one adviser, one friend, and his name is Henry Dalton."

A sad shade fell over Ellinor Dalton's handsome face, and her eyes half filled with tears as she said,—

"Mr. Margrave, Heaven forbid that I should say a word which could be construed into a reproach to you. Your duties of guardianship, undertaken at the prayer of my dying father, have been as truly and conscientiously discharged as such duties should be discharged by a man of your high position and unblemished character; but I will own that sometimes, with a woman's folly, I have wished that, for the memory of my dead father, who loved and trusted you, for the memory of the departed childhood, in which we were companions and friends, some feeling a little warmer, a little kinder, a little more affectionate, something of the tenderness of an elder brother, might have mingled with your punctilious fulfilment of the duties of guardian. I would not for the world reproach you—still less reproach you for an act for which I only am responsible—yet I cannot but remember that, if it had been so, this marriage might never have taken place."

"It is not a happy marriage, then?"

"It is a most unhappy one!"

Horace Margrave is silent for a few moments, and then says, gravely, almost sadly,

"My dear Mrs. Henry Dalton,"—he is especially scrupulous in calling her Mrs. Dalton, as if he were anxious to remind her every moment how much their relations have changed,—"when you accuse me of a want of tenderness in my conduct towards yourself, of an absence of warm regard for the memory of your dead father, my kind and excellent friend, you accuse me of that for which I am no more responsible than for the color of my hair, or the outline of my face. You accuse me of that which is, perhaps, the curse of my existence, a heart incapable of cherishing a strong affection, or a sincere friendship, for any living being. Behold me, at five-and-thirty years of age, unloved and unloving, without one tie which I cannot as easily break as I can pay a hotel bill or pack my portmanteau. My life, at its brightest, is a dreary one. A dreary present, which can neither look back to a fairer past, nor forward to a happier future!"

His deep musical voice falls into a sadder cadence as he says these last words, and he looks down gloomily at the point of the cane he carries, with which he absently traces a pattern upon the carpet. After a short silence he looks up, and says,—

"But you wished to make some inquiries of me?"

"I did. I do. When I married Mr. Dalton, what settlements were made? You told me nothing at the time; and I, so utterly unused to business matters, asked you no questions. Besides, I had then reason to think him the most honorable of men."

"What settlements were made?" he repeats her question, as if it were the last of all others which he expected to hear.

"Yes, my fortune! How much of it was settled on myself?"

"Not one penny!" She gives a start of surprise, which he answers in his most *nonchalant* manner. "Not one penny of it! There was no mention whatever of any thing like a settlement in your uncle's will. He left his money to you; but he left it to you only on condition that you shared it with his adopted and beloved son, Henry Dalton. This implies not only a strong affection for, but an implicit faith in, the young man. To tie up your money, or to settle it on yourself, would be to nullify your uncle's will. The man that could be trusted by him, could be trusted by you. This is why I never suggested a settlement. I may have, perhaps, acted in rather an unlawyer-like manner; but I do believe, my dear Ellinor, that I acted in the only manner consonant with your late uncle's affectionate provisions for the two persons nearest and dearest to him!"

"Then Henry Dalton is sole master of my—of the fortune?"

"As your husband, decidedly, yes."

"And he may, if he pleases, sell the Arden estate?"

"The Arden estate is not entailed. Certainly he may sell it, if he wishes."

"Then, Mr. Margrave, I must inform you that he does wish to sell it; that he does intend to sell it."

"To sell Arden Hall?"

"Yes!"

An angry flush lights up her face, as she looks eagerly into the lawyer's eyes for one flash of surprise or indignation. She looks in vain.

"Well, my dear Mrs. Dalton, in my opinion he shows himself a very sensible fellow, by determining on such a proceeding. Arden is one of the dreariest, coldest, and most tumbledown old piles of building in all England. Magnificent oak panelling, contemptible servants' offices; three secret staircases, and not one register stove; six tapestried chambers, and no bath-room; a dozen Leonardo da Vinci's, and not one door that does not let in assassination in the shape of a north-east wind; a deer park, and no deer; three gamekeepers' lodges, and not game enough to tempt the most fatuitous of poachers! Sell Arden Hall! Nothing could be more desirable; but, alas! my dear Ellinor, your husband is not the man I take him for, if he calculates upon finding a purchaser!"

She looks at him with not a little contempt, as she says:—

"But the want of feeling; the outrage upon the memory of my poor uncle!"

"Your poor uncle will not be remembered a day the longer through your retaining possession of a draughty and uncomfortable house. When did Dalton tell you that he meant to sell Arden?"

"On our return from our tour. I suggested that we should live there,—that is, of course, out of the season."

"And he?"

"Replied, that it was out of the question our ever residing there, as the place must be sold."

"You asked him his reasons?"

"I did. He told me that he was unable to reveal those reasons to me, and might never be able to reveal them. He said, that if I loved him, I could trust him and believe in him, and believe that the course he took, however strange it might appear to me, was, in reality, the best and wisest course he could take."

"But, in spite of this, you doubt him?" he asks, earnestly.

"How can I do otherwise? Of the fortune which I have brought to him, he refuses to allow me a penny. He, the husband of a rich woman, enjoins economy—economy even in the smallest details. I dare not order a jewel, a picture, an elegant piece of furniture, a stand of hothouse flowers; for, if I do so, I am told that the expenditure is beyond his present means, and that I must wait till we have more money at our command. Then his profession; that is a thousand times dearer to him than I. No briefless, penniless barrister, with a mother and sister to support, ever worked harder than he works, ever devoted himself more religiously than he devotes himself to the drudging routine of the bar."

"Ellinor Dalton, your husband is as high-minded and conscientious a man as ever drew the breath of human life. I seldom take the trouble of making a vehement assertion; so believe me, if you can, now that I do! Believe me, even if you cannot believe him!"

"You, too, against me," she said, mournfully. "Oh, believe me, it is not the money for which I wish! it is not the possession of the money which I grudge him; it is only that my heart sinks at the thought of being united to a man I cannot respect or esteem. I did not ask to love him," she added, half to herself; "but I did pray that I might be able at least to esteem him."

"I can only say, Ellinor, that you are mistaken in him."

At this very moment they hear a quick, firm step on the stairs, and Henry Dalton himself enters the room. His face is bright and cheerful, and he advances to his wife eagerly; but, at the sight of Horace Margrave, falls back, with a frown.

"Mr. Margrave, I thought it was part of our agreement that—"

The lawyer interrupts him,—

"That I should never darken this threshold. Yes."

Ellinor looks from one to the other, with a pale, frightened face.

"Henry, Henry, Mr. Dalton, what, in Heaven's name, does this mean?"

"Nothing that in the least can affect you, Ellinor. A business disagreement between myself and Mr. Margrave, nothing more!"

His wife looks away from him, scornfully, and turning to Horace Margrave, rests her hand on the scroll work at the back of the chair in which he is seated.

It is so small an action in itself; but it says, as plainly as words could ever speak,—

"It is he whom I trust, in spite of you, in spite of the world."

It is not lost on Henry Dalton, who looks at her with a grave, reproachful glance, and says,—

"Under these circumstances then, Mr. Margrave—"

"I had no right to come here. Granted! and I should not have come, but—"

He hesitated a moment, and Ellinor interrupted him,—

"I wrote to my guardian, requesting him to call on me. Mr. Dalton, what is the meaning of this? What mystery does all this conceal? Am I to see my best and oldest friend insulted in my own house?"

"A married woman has no friend but her husband, and I may not choose to receive Mr. Margrave as a visitor in *our* house," Henry Dalton says, coldly and gravely.

"You shall not be troubled any longer with Horace Margrave's society, Mr. Dalton." The lawyer rises as he speaks, and walks slowly to the door. "Good-morning." He has his hand upon the lock, when he turns, and, with a tone of suppressed emotion in his voice, says to Mrs. Dalton, "Ellinor, shake hands with me." She extends both her hands to him. He catches them in his, bends his dark head over them for a moment, as he holds them in his grasp, and then says, "Forgive me, Ellinor, and farewell!"

He is gone. She rushes out on to the landing-place, and cries after him,—

"Mr. Margrave, guardian; Horace, come back—if only for one moment, come back!"

Her husband follows her, and catching her slender wrist in his strong hand, leads her into the drawing-room.

"Ellinor Dalton, choose between that man and me. Seek to renew your acquaintance with him, or hold any communication whatever with him, that does not pass through my hands, and we part forever!"

She falls sobbing into her chair.

"My only friend," she cries, "my only, only friend, and to be parted from him thus!"

Her husband stands at a little distance from her, earnestly, sadly watching her, as she gives passionate vent to her wild outburst of emotion.

"What wretchedness, what utter wretchedness!" he says aloud. "And no hope of a termination to it, no chance of an end to our misery!"

CHAPTER IV.

HORACE MARGRAVE AT BALDWIN COURT.

Henry Dalton prospered in his beloved profession. Gray-headed old judges talked over their after-dinner port of the wonderful acumen displayed by the young barrister in the most important and difficult cases. One, two, three years passed away, and the name of Dalton began to be one of mark upon the northern circuit. The dawn often found him working in his chambers in Paper Buildings, while his handsome wife was dancing at some brilliant assembly, or listening to the vapid platitudes of one of her numerous admirers and silent adorers. With Ellinor Dalton, to be unhappy was to be reckless. Hers was that impulsive and emotional nature, which cannot brood upon its griefs in the quiet circle of a solitary home. She considered herself wronged by her husband's parsimony, still more deeply wronged by his cold reserve, and she sought, in the gayest circles of fashionable London, for the peace which had never dwelt at her cold and deserted hearth.

"His profession for him," she said: "there is at least the world left for me; and, if I cannot be loved, I will prove to him that, at any rate, I can be admired."

In many of the houses to which she was a constant visitor, Horace Margrave was on intimate terms. The fashionable and wealthy bachelor lawyer was sure of a welcome where mamma had daughters to marry, or papa money to invest, or mortgages to effect. To him her manner never underwent the slightest shadow of a change.

"You may refuse to admit him here; you may forbid my correspondence with him. I acknowledge the right you exercise so harshly," she would say to her husband; "but you cannot shake my faith in my dead father's friend. You cannot control my sentiments towards the guardian of my childhood."

But, by degrees, she found that Horace Margrave was to be seen less frequently every day at those houses in which she visited; it was growing a rare thing now for her to see the dark, handsome head proudly over-topping the crowd in which the lawyer mingled; and even when she did meet him, though his voice had still its old gentleness, there was a tacit avoidance of her in his manner, which effectually checked any confidence between them. This was for the first two years after her marriage; in the third year she heard accidentally that Horace Margrave was travelling in Switzerland, and had left the entire management of his very extensive business to his junior partner.

Three years, the autumn of the third year from that of her marriage, and Ellinor and her husband were staying at the country-house of his friend, Sir Lionel Baldwin. Since that day on which the scene with Horace Margrave had taken place in the little drawing-room in Hertford Street, Ellinor Dalton and her husband had had no explanation whatever. On that day the young man had fallen on his knees at the feet of his sobbing wife, and most earnestly implored her to believe in his faith and honor, and to believe that, in every thing he did, he had a motive, so strong and so disinterested, as to warrant his actions. He begged her to believe, also, that the marriage, on his part, had been wholly a love-match; that he had been actuated by no mercenary considerations whatever; and that, if he now withheld the money to which, in all appearance, she had so good a right, it was because it was not in his power to lavish it upon her. But he implored in vain. Prejudiced against him from the very first, she had only trusted him for a brief period, to doubt him more completely than ever at the first suspicion that suggested itself. Wounded in her affection for another,—an affection whose strength, perhaps, she scarcely dared to whisper to her own soul,—her feeling for Henry Dalton became one almost bordering on aversion. His simple, practical good sense; his plain, unpolished manners; his persevering, energetic, and untiring pursuit of a vocation for which she had no sympathy,—all these jarred upon her romantic and enthusiastic temperament, and blinded her to his actual merits. The world, which always contrives to know every thing, very soon made itself completely acquainted with the eccentric conditions of Mr. Arden's will, and the circumstances of Henry Dalton's marriage.

It was known to be a marriage of convenience, and not of affection. He was a very lucky fellow, and she was very much to be pitied; this was the general opinion, which Ellinor's palpable indifference to her husband went strongly to confirm.

Mr. and Mrs. Dalton had been staying for a week at Baldwin Court, when the young barrister was compelled, by his professional pursuits, to leave his wife for a few days under the protection of his old friends, Sir Lionel and Lady Baldwin.

"You will be very happy here, dear Ellinor," he said; "the house is full of pleasant people, and you know how great a favorite you are with our host and hostess. You will not miss me," he added, with a sigh, as he looked at her indifferent face.

"Miss you! Oh, pray do not alarm yourself, Mr. Dalton! I am not so used to usurp your time or attention. I know, where your professional duties are concerned, how little I am ever a consideration to you."

"I should not work hard, were I not compelled to do so, Ellinor," he said, with a shade of reproach in his voice.

"My dear Mr. Dalton," she answered, coldly, "I have no taste for mysteries. You are perfectly free to pursue your own course."

So they parted. She bade him adieu with as much well-bred indifference as if he had been her jeweller or her haberdasher. As the light little phaeton drove him off to the railway station, he looked up to the chintz curtained windows of his wife's apartments, and said to himself, "How long is this to endure, I wonder?—this unmerited wretchedness, this most cruel misconception!"

The morning after Henry Dalton's departure, as Sir Lionel Baldwin, seated at breakfast, opened the letter bag, he exclaimed, with a tone of mingled surprise and pleasure, "So the wanderer has returned. At the very bottom of the bag I can see Horace Margrave's dashing superscription. He has returned to England, then."

He handed his visitors their letters, and then opened his own, reserving the lawyer's epistle till the last.

"This is delightful! Horace will be down here to-night."

Ellinor Dalton's cheek grew pale at the announcement; for the mysterious feud between her guardian and her husband flashed upon her mind. She would meet him here, then, alone. Now, or never, might she learn this secret,—this secret which, no doubt involved some meanness on the part of Henry Dalton, the apothecary's son.

"Margrave will be an immense acquisition to our party,—will he not, gentlemen?" asked Sir Lionel.

"An acquisition! Well, really now, I don't know about that," drawled a young government clerk from Whitehall. "Do you know, S'Lionel," all the young men under government called the old baronet S'Lionel, any other pronunciation of his name and title involving a degree of exertion beyond their physical powers, "do you know it's my opinion, S'Lionel, that Horace Margrave is used up? I met him at—at what-you-may-call-it—Rousseau and Gibbon, Childe Harold and the Nouvelle Héloise. You know the place," he said, vaguely; "somewhere in Switzerland, in short, last July, and I never saw a man so altered in my life."

"Altered!" exclaimed the baronet. Ellinor Dalton's face grew paler still.

"Yes, 'pon my honor, S'Lionel. Very much altered, indeed. You don't think he ever committed a murder, or any thing of that kind—do you?" said the young man, reflectively, as he drew over a sugar basin, and deliberately dropped four or five lumps into his coffee. "Because, upon my honor, he looked like that sort of thing."

"My dear Fred, don't be a fool. Looked like what sort of thing?"

"You know; a guilty conscience, Lara, Manfred. You understand. Upon my word," added the youthful official, looking round, with a languid laugh, "he had such a Wandering Jew-ish and ultra-Byronic appearance, when I met him suddenly among some very uncomfortable kind of chromo-lithographic mountain scenery, that I asked him if he had an appointment with the Witch of the Alps, or any of those sort of people?"

One or two country visitors tried to laugh, but couldn't; and the guests from town only stared, as the young man looked round the table. Ellinor Dalton never took her eyes from his face, but seemed to wait anxiously for any thing he might say next.

"Perhaps Margrave has been ill," said the old baronet; "he told me, when he went to Switzerland, that he was leaving England because he required change of air and scene."

"Ill!" said the government clerk; "Ah, to be sure, I never thought of that. He might have been ill. It's difficult, sometimes, to draw the line between a guilty conscience and the liver complaint. Perhaps it was only his liver after all. But you don't think," he said, appealingly, returning to his original idea; "you don't think that he has committed a murder, and buried the body in Verulam Building—do you? That would account for his going to Switzerland, you know; for he couldn't possibly stop with the body—could he?"

"You'd better ask him the question yourself, Fred," said Sir Lionel, laughing; "if everybody had as good a conscience as Horace Margrave, the world would be better stocked than it is with honorable men. He's a noble-hearted fellow, Horace; I've known him from a boy."

"And a crack shot," said a young military man, with his mouth full of buttered toast and anchovy paste.

"And a firstrate billiard player," added his next neighbor, busy carving a ham.

"And one of the cleverest men in the law," said a grave old gentleman, sententiously.

"Extremely handsome," faltered one young lady.

"And then, how accomplished!" ventured another.

"Then you don't think, really now, that he has committed a murder, and buried the body in his chambers?" asked the Whitehall employé, putting the question to the company generally.

In the dusk of that autumnal evening, Ellinor Dalton sat alone in a tiny drawing-room leading out of the great saloon—a long room, with six windows, two fireplaces, and with a great many very indifferent pictures in extremely handsome frames.

This tiny drawing-room was a favorite retreat of Ellinor. It was luxuriously furnished, and it communicated, by a half-glass door shrouded by heavy amber damask curtains, with a large conservatory, which opened on to the terrace walk that ran along one side of the house. Here she sat in the dusky light, pensive and thoughtful, on the evening after her husband's departure. The gentlemen were all in the billiard room, hard at work with balls and cues, trying to settle some disputed wager before the half-hour bell rang to summon them to their dressing-rooms. The ladies were already at their toilettes; and Ellinor, who had dressed earlier than usual, was quite alone. It was too dark for her to read or work, and she was too weary and listless to ring for lamps; so she sat with her hands lying idly in her lap, pondering upon what had been said at the breakfast table of her sometime guardian, Horace Margrave.

Suddenly a footstep behind her, falling softly on the thick carpet, roused her from her reverie, and she looked up with a startled glance at the glass over the low chimney-piece.

In the dim firelight she saw, reflected in the shadowy depths of the mirror, the haggard and altered face of her guardian, Horace Margrave.

He wore a loose, heavy great-coat, and had his hat in his hand. He had evidently only just arrived.

He drew back on seeing Ellinor, but as she turned round to speak to him, the firelight behind her left her face in the shadow, and he did not recognize her.

"I beg your pardon," he said, "for disturbing you. I have been looking everywhere for Sir Lionel."

"Mr. Margrave! Don't you know me? It is I—Ellinor!"

His hat fell from his slender hand, and he leaned against a high-backed easy-chair for support.

"Ellinor—Mrs. Dalton—you here! I—I—heard you were in Paris, or I should never—that is—I—"

For the first time in her life Ellinor Dalton saw Horace Margrave so agitated, that the stony mask of elegant indifference and gentlemanly *sang-froid*, which he ordinarily wore, entirely dropped away, and left him—himself.

"Mr. Margrave," she said, anxiously, "you are annoyed at seeing me here. Oh, how altered you are! They were right in what they said this morning. You are indeed altered; you must have been very ill?"

Horace Margrave was himself again, by this time; he picked up his hat, and dropping lazily into the easy-chair, said, "Yes; I have had rather a severe attack—fever—exhaustion—the doctors, in fact, were so puzzled as to what they should call my illness, that they actually tried to persuade me that I had nerves; like a young lady who has been jilted by a life-guardsman, or forbidden by her parents to marry a country curate with seventy pounds per annum, and three duties every Sunday. A nervous lawyer! My dear Mrs. Dalton, can you imagine any thing so absurd? Sir James, however, insisted on my packing my portmanteau, and setting off for Mont Blanc, or something of that kind; and I, being heartily tired of the courts of Probate and Chancery, and Verulam Buildings, Gray's Inn, was only too glad to follow his advice, and take my railway ticket for Geneva."

"And Switzerland has restored you?"

"In a measure, perhaps; but not entirely. You can see that I am not yet very strong, when even the pleasing emotion of meeting unexpectedly with my sometime ward is almost too much for my ultra-lady-like nerves. But you were saying, my dear Mrs. Dalton, that they had been talking of me here."

"Oh, at the breakfast-table this morning. When your visit was announced, one of the gentlemen said he had met you in Switzerland, and that you were looking ill—unhappy!"

"Unhappy! Ah, my dear Mrs. Dalton, what a misfortune it is for a man to have a constitutional pallor, and a head of dark hair! The world will insist upon elevating him into a blighted being, with a metaphysical wolf hard at work under his waistcoat. I knock myself up by working too hard over a difficult will case, in which some tiresome old man leaves his youngest son forty thousand pounds upon half a sheet of note paper; and the world, meeting me in Switzerland, travelling to recruit myself, comes home and writes me down—unhappy! Now, isn't it too bad? If I were blessed with red hair, and a fat face, I might break my heart once in three months, without any one ever troubling himself about the fracture."

"My dear Mr. Margrave, I am really now"—her voice, in spite of herself, trembling a little as she said—"I am really now quite an old married woman; and, presuming on that fact, may venture to speak to you with entire candor—may I not?"

"With entire candor, certainly." There is the old shiver in the dark eyelashes, and the white lids droop over the handsome brown eyes, as he looks down at the hat which swings backwards and forwards in his listless hand.

"Then, Mr. Margrave, my dear guardian, for I will—I will call you by that old name, which I can remember speaking for the very first time on the day of my poor father's funeral. Oh!" she added, passionately, "how well—how well I remember that dreary, wretched, terrible day! I can see you now, as I saw you then, standing in the deep embrasure of the window in the little library, in the dear, dear Scottish home, looking down at me so compassionately, with dark, mournful eyes. I was such a child then. I can hear your low, deep voice, as I heard it on that day, saying to me, 'Ellinor! your dead father has placed a solemn trust in my hands. I am young. I may not be as good or as high-principled a man as to his confiding mind I seemed to be; there may be something of constitutional weakness and irresolution in my character, which may render me, perhaps, by no means the fittest person for so responsible an office; but so deeply do I feel the trust implied in his dying words, that I swear, by my hope in Heaven, by my memory of the dead, by my honor as a man and a gentleman, to discharge the responsibilities imposed upon me, as an honest man and an honorable gentleman should discharge them!'"

"Ellinor! Ellinor! for pity's sake!" he cried, in a broken voice, clenching one white hand convulsively over his averted face.

"I do wrong," she said, "to recall that melancholy day. You did—you did discharge every duty, nobly, honestly, honorably; but now—now you abandon me entirely to the husband—not of my choice—but imposed upon me by a hard and cruel necessity, and you do all in your power to make us strangers. Yet, guardian, Horace, you are not happy!"

"Not happy!" he raises his head, and laughs bitterly. "My dear Mrs. Dalton, this is such childish talk about happiness and unhappiness—two words which are only used in a lady's novel, in which the heroine is unhappy through two volumes and three-quarters, and unutterably blest in the last chapter. In the practical world, we don't talk about happiness and unhappiness; our phrases are, failure and success. A man gets the woolsack, and he is successful; or, he tries for it all his life, and never gets it —well, he is unfortunate. But a happy man, my dear Ellinor,—did you ever see one?"

"You mystify me, Mr. Margrave; but you do not answer me."

"Because, Mrs. Dalton, to answer you I must first question myself; and, believe me, a man must have considerable courage, who can dare to ask himself, whether, in this tiresome journey of life, he has taken the right or the wrong road. I confess myself a coward, and implore you not to compel me to be brave."

He rose as he finished speaking, and, looking down at his dress, continued,—

"The first dinner-bell rang a quarter of

an hour ago, and behold me still in travelling costume; the sin is yours, Mrs. Dalton. Till dinner-time, adieu!"

Ellinor, left alone, sank into a gloomy reverie. "What—what can be the mystery of this man's life?" she murmured to herself; "If I dared—but no, no, I dare not answer that question?"

It was difficult to recognize in the brilliant and versatile visitor seated at Sir Lionel's right hand, whose incessant flow of witty *persiflage* kept the crowded dinner table in a roar of laughter, the gloomy and bitter Horace Margrave of half an hour before. Ellinor, charmed in spite of herself, beguiled out of herself by the fascination of his animated conversation, wondered at the extraordinary power possessed by this man. "So brilliant, so accomplished!" she thought; "so admired, prosperous, and successful, and yet so unhappy!"

That evening, the post brought Ellinor a letter which had been sent to her town house, and forwarded thence to Sir Lionel's.

She started on seeing the direction, and taking it into the little inner drawing-room, which was still untenanted, she read it by the light of the wax candles on the chimney-piece. She returned to the long saloon after refolding her letter, and, crossing over to a small table at which Horace Margrave sat, bending over a portfolio of engravings, she seated herself near him, and said,—

"Mr. Margrave! I have just received a letter from Scotland."

"From Scotland!"

"Yes. From whom, do you think? The dear old minister, James Stewart. You remember him?"

"Yes; a white-headed old man, with a family of daughters, the shortest of whom was taller than me. Do you correspond with him?"

"Oh! no. It is so many years since I left Scotland, that my dear old friends seem one by one to have dropped off. I should like so much to have given them a new church at Achindore, but Mr. Dalton of course objected to the outlay of money; and as that is a point I never dispute with him, I abandoned the idea; but Mr. Stewart has written to me this time for a special purpose."

"And that is—" he asks.

"To tell me that my old nurse, Margaret Mackay, has become blind and infirm, and has been obliged to leave her situation. Poor dear old soul! she went into a service in Edinburgh, after my poor father's death, and I entirely lost sight of her. I should have provided for her long before this; but now there is no question about this appeal, and I shall immediately settle a hundred a year upon her, in spite of Mr. Dalton's rigid and praiseworthy economy."

"I fancy Dalton will think a hundred a year too much. Fifty pounds for an old woman in the north of Aberdeenshire would be almost fabulous wealth; but you are so superb in your notions, my dear Ellinor; hard-headed business men, like Dalton and myself, can scarcely stand against you."

"Pray do not compare yourself to Mr. Dalton," said Ellinor, with quiet scorn.

"I'm afraid, indeed, I must not," he answered, gravely; "but you were saying—"

"That in this matter I will take no refusal; no pitiful and contemptible excuses or prevarications. I shall write to him by to-morrow's post. I cannot get an answer till the next day. If that answer should be either a refusal or an excuse, I know what course to take."

"And that course—"

"I will tell you what it is, when I receive Henry Dalton's reply. But I am unjust to him," she said; "he cannot refuse to comply with this request."

Three days after this conversation, just as the half-hour bell had rung, and as Sir Lionel's visitors were all hurrying off to their dressing-rooms, Ellinor laid her hand lightly on Horace Margrave's arm, as he was leaving the large drawing-room, and said,—

"Pray let me speak to you for a few minutes. I have received Mr. Dalton's answer to my letter."

"And that answer?" he asks, as he follows her into the little room communicating with the conservatory.

"Is, as you suggested it might be, a refusal."

"A refusal!" He elevates his dark, arched eyebrows faintly, but seems very little surprised at the intelligence.

"Yes; a refusal. He dares not even attempt an excuse, or invent a reason for his conduct. Forty pounds a year, he says, will be a comfortable competence for an old woman in the north of Scotland, where very few ministers of the Presbyterian church have any more. That sum he will settle on her immediately, and he sends me a cheque for the first half-year. But he will settle no more, nor will he endeavor to explain motives which are always misconstrued. What do you think of his conduct?"

As she speaks, the glass door, which separates the tiny boudoir from the conservatory, swings backwards and forwards in the autumn breeze, which blows in through the outer door of the conservatory; for the day having been unusually warm for the time of year, this door has been left open.

"My dear Ellinor," says Horace Margrave, "if any one should come into the conservatory, they might hear us talking of your husband."

"Every one is dressing," she answers, carelessly. "Besides, if any one were there, they would scarcely be surprised to hear me declare my contempt for Henry Dalton. The world does not, I hope, give us credit for being a happy couple."

"As you will; but I'm sure I heard some one stirring in that conservatory. Never mind; you ask me what I think of your husband's conduct in refusing to allow a superannuated nurse, of yours more than forty pounds a year? Don't think me a heartless ruffian, if I tell you that I think he is perfectly right."

"But to withhold from me my own money! To fetter my almsgiving! To control my very charities? I might forgive him, if he refused me a diamond necklace, or a pair of ponies; but in this matter, in which my affection is concerned, to let his economy step in to frustrate my earnestly expressed wishes,—it is too cruel."

"My dear Mrs. Dalton, like all very impetuous and warm-hearted people, you are rather given to jump at conclusions. Mr. Dalton, you say, withholds your own money from you. Now, your own money, with the exception of the Arden estate, which he sold on your marriage, happens to have been entirely invested in the three per cents. Now, if,—mind, I haven't the least reason to suppose that such a thing has ever happened, but for the sake of putting a case—now, if Henry Dalton, as a clever and enterprising man of business, may have been tempted to speculate with some of your money?"

"Without consulting me?"

"Without consulting you. Decidedly. What do women know of speculation?"

"Mr. Margrave, if Henry Dalton has done this, he is no longer a miser, but he is,—a cheat. The money left to me by my uncle's will was mine. To be shared with him, it is true, but still mine. No sophistry, no lawyer's quibble, could ever have made it his. If, then, he has, without my consent or knowledge, speculated with that money, I no longer despise him as a miser, but I detest him as a dishonest man. Ah! Horace Margrave, you with noble blood in your veins; you a gentleman, an honorable man; what would you think of Henry Dalton, if this were possible?"

"Ellinor Dalton, have you ever heard of the madness men have christened gambling! Do you know what a gambler is? Do you know what he feels, this man who hazards his wife's fortune, his widowed mother's slender pittance, his helpless children's inheritance, the money that should pay for his eldest son's education, his daughter's dowry, the hundreds due to his trusting creditors, or the gold entrusted to him by a confiding employer, on the green cloth of a west-end gaming-table? Do you think that at that mad moment, when the gas-lamps dazzle his eyes, and the piles of gold heave up and down upon the restless green baize, and the croupier's voice, crying, Make your game! is multiplied by a million, and buzzes in his ear like the clamor of all the fiends; do you think at that moment that he ever supposes he is going to lose this money which is not honestly his? No; he is going to double, to treble, to quadruple it; to multiply every glistening guinea by a hundred, and to take it back to the starving wife or the anxious children, and cry, 'Was I so much to blame, after all?' Have you ever stood upon the Grand Stand at Epsom, and seen the white faces of the betting-men, and heard the noise of the wagers upon the final rush of the winning post? Every man upon that crowded stand, every creature upon that crowded course, from the great magnate of the turf, who stands to win a quarter of a million, to the wretched apprentice lad, who has stolen half a crown from the till to put it upon the favorite, believes that he has backed a winning horse. That is the great madness of gaming; that is the terrible witchcraft of the gambling-house and the ring; and that is the miserable hallucination of the man who speculates with the fortune of another. Pity him, Ellinor. If the dishonest are ever worthy of the pity of the good, that man deserves your pity."

He had spoken with an energy unusual to him, and he sank into a chair, half exhausted with his unwonted vehemence.

"I would rather think the man, whom I am forced to call my husband, a miser, than a cheat, Mr. Margrave," Ellinor said, coldly; "and I am sorry to learn, that, if he were indeed capable of such dishonor, his crime would find an advocate in you."

"You are pitiless, Mrs. Dalton," said Horace Margrave, after a pause. "Heaven help the man who dares to wrong you."

"Do not let us speak of Henry Dalton any longer, Mr. Margrave. I told you that if he should refuse this favor, this—this right, I had decided on what course to take."

"You did; and now, may I ask what that course is?"

"To leave him."

"Leave him!" he exclaimed, anxiously.

"Yes; leave him in the possession of this fortune which he holds so tightly, or which, supposing him to be the pitiful wretch you think he may have been, he has speculated with, and lost. Leave him. He can never have cared for me. He has denied my every request, frustrated my every wish, devoted every hour of his life, not to me, but to his beloved profession. My aunt will receive me. I shall leave this place to-night, and leave London for Paris to-morrow morning."

"But, Ellinor, the world—"

"Let the world judge between us. What can the world say of me? I shall live with my aunt, as I did before this cruel fortune was bequeathed to me. Mr. Margrave—guardian—you will accompany me to Paris, will you not? I am so inexperienced in all these sort of things, so little used to help myself, that I dare not take this journey alone. You will accompany me?"

"I, Ellinor?" Again the dark eyelashes shiver over the gloomy brown eyes.

"Yes; who so fit to protect me as you, to whom, with his dying lips, my father committed my guardianship? For his sake, you will do me this service, will you not?"

"Is it a service, Ellinor? Can I be doing you a service in taking you away from your husband?"

"So be it then," she said, scornfully. "You refuse to help me; I will go alone."

"Alone?"

"Yes; alone. I go to-night, and alone."

A bright flush mounted to Horace Margrave's pale face, and a vivid light shone in his handsome eyes.

"Alone, Ellinor? No, no," he said, "my poor child, my ward, my helpless orphan girl, my little Scotch lassie of the good time gone, I will protect you on this journey, place you safely in the arms of your aunt, and answer to Henry Dalton for my conduct. In this, at least, Ellinor, I will be worthy of your dead father's confidence. Make your arrangements for the journey. You have your maid with you?"

"Yes; Ellis, a most excellent creature. Then to-night, guardian, by the mail train."

"I shall be ready. You must make your excuses to Sir Lionel, and leave with as little explanation as possible. *Au revoir!*"

As Ellinor Dalton and Horace Margrave left the little boudoir, a gentleman in a great coat, with a railway rug flung over his shoulder, strode out on to the terrace through the door of the conservatory, and lighting a cigar, paced for about half an hour up and down the walk at the side of the house, thinking deeply.

CHAPTER V.

FROM LONDON TO PARIS.

WHILE dressing, Ellinor gave her maid orders to set about packing, immediately. Ellis, a very solemn and matter-of-fact person, expressed no surprise, but went quietly to work, emptying the contents of wardrobes into imperials, and stowing silver-topped bottles into their velvet-lined cases, as if there were no such thing as hurry or agitation in the world.

It was a long evening to Ellinor Dalton. Every quarter that chimed in silvery tones from the ormolu timepiece over the chimney seemed an entire hour to her. Never had the county families seemed so insufferably stupid, or the London visitors so supremely tiresome. The young man from the war office took her in to dinner, and insisted on telling her some very funny story about a young man in another government office, which brilliant anecdote lasted, exclusive of interruptions, from the soup to the desert, without drawing any nearer the point of the witticism. After the dreary dinner, the eldest daughter of the oldest of the county families fastened herself and a very difficult piece of crochet upon her, and inflicted on her all the agonies of a worsted work-rose, which, as the young lady perpetually declared, would not come right. But however *distrait* Ellinor might be, Horace Margrave was not one whit the less the elegant and accomplished Horace of the West-end world. He talked politics with the heads of the county families; stock exchange with the city men; sporting magazine and Tattersall's with the country swells; discussed the last *débuts* at her Majesty's Theatre with the young Londoners; spoke of Sir John Herschell's last discovery to a scientific country squire; and of the newest thing in farming implements to an agricultural ditto; talked compliments to the young country ladies, and the freshest May-fair scandal to the young London ladies; had, in short, something to say on every subject to everybody, and contrived to please everybody, without displeasing any one. And let any man, who has tried to do this in the crowded drawing-room of a country house, say whether or not Horace Margrave was a clever fellow.

"By the by, Horace," said Sir Lionel, as the accomplished lawyer lounged against one corner of the long marble mantle-piece, talking to a group of young men and one rather fast young lady, who had edged herself into the circle, under cover of a brother, much to the indignation of more timid spirits, furtively regarding Admirable Crichton Margrave, as his friends called him, from distant sofas; "by the by, my boy, where did you hide yourself all this morning? We sadly wanted you to decide a match at billiards, and I sent people all over the house and grounds in search of you."

"I rode over to Horton after lunch," said Horace. "I wanted a few hours there on electioneering business."

"You've been to Horton?" asked Sir Lionel, with rather an anxious expression.

"Yes, my dear Sir Lionel, to Horton. But how alarmed you look! I trust I haven't been doing any thing wrong. A client of mine is going to stand for the place. But surely, you're not going to throw over the county electors, and stand for the little borough of Horton, yourself!" he said, laughing.

Sir Lionel looked a little confused, and the county families grew suddenly very grave; indeed, one young lady in pink, who was known by about seven fair *confidantes* to have a slight *tendre* for the handsome lawyer, clutched convulsively at the wrist of a younger sister in blue, and listened, with an alarmed face, to the conversation by the chimney-piece.

"Why, how silent every one has grown!" said Horace, still laughing. "It seems as if I had launched a thunder-bolt on this hospitable hearth, in announcing my visit to the little manufacturing town of Horton. What is it—why is it—how is it?" he asked, looking round with a smile.

"Why," said Sir Lionel, hesitatingly, "the, —the truth of the matter—that is—not to mystify you—in short—you know—they, they've a fever at Horton. The—working classes and factory people have got it very badly, and—and—the place is in a manner *tabooed*. But of course," added the old man, trying to look cheerful, "you didn't go into any of the back streets, or amongst the lower classes. You only rode through the town, I suppose; so you're safe enough, my dear Horace."

The county families simultaneously drew a long breath, and the young lady in pink released her sister's wrist.

"I went, my dear Sir Lionel," said Horace, with smiling indifference, "into about twenty narrow back streets in an hour and a half, and I talked to about forty different factory hands, for I wanted to find which way the political current set in the good town of Horton. They all appeared extremely dirty, and now, I remember, a good many of them looked very ill; but I'm not afraid of having caught the fever, for all that," he added, looking round at the grave faces of his hearers; "half a dozen cigars, and a sharp ten miles' ride through a bleak, open country must be a thorough disinfectant. If not," he continued, bitterly, "one must die sooner or later, and why not of a fever caught at Horton?"

The young lady in pink had recourse to her sister's wrist again, at this speech.

Horace soon laughed off the idea of danger from his afternoon's rambles, and, in a few minutes, he was singing a German drinking song, accompanying himself at the piano.

At last the long evening was over, and Ellinor, who had heard nothing from her distant work-table of the conversation about the fever, gladly welcomed the advent of a servant with a tray of glistening candlesticks. As she lit her candle at the side table, Horace Margrave came over and lit his own.

"I have spoken to Sir Lionel," he said, "a carriage will be ready for us in an hour. The mail does not start till one o'clock. But, Ellinor, it is not yet too late; tell me, are you thoroughly determined on this step?"

"Thoroughly," she said. "I shall be ready in an hour."

Mrs. Dalton's apartments were at the end of a long corridor: the dressing-room opened out of the bedroom, and the door of communication was ajar as Ellinor entered her room; her boxes stood ready packed. She looked at them hurriedly, examined the addresses which her maid had pasted upon them, and was about to pass into the dressing-room, when she stopped abruptly on the threshold, with an exclamation of surprise.

Her husband, Henry Dalton, was seated at the table, with an open portfolio spread before him, writing rapidly. On a chair, by the fire, lay his great coat, railway rug, and portmanteau.

He looked up for a moment, calmly and gravely, as Ellinor entered; and then continued writing.

"Mr. Dalton!"

"Yes," he said, still writing; "I came down by the 5.30 train. I returned sooner than I expected."

"By the 5.30 train?" she said, anxiously; "by the train which leaves London at half-past five, I suppose," she added.

"By the train which arrives here at half-past five," he said, still not looking up; "or should reach here by that time, rather, for it's generally five minutes late."

"You have been here since six o'clock?"

"Since ten minutes to six, my dear Ellinor. I gave my valise to a porter, and walked over from the station in a quarter of an hour."

"You have been here since six, and have never told me of your arrival; never shown yourself in the house!"

"I have shown myself to Sir Lionel. I had some very important business to arrange."

"Important business?" she asked.

"Yes, to prepare for this journey to Paris, which you are so bent upon taking."

A crimson flush suffuses her face, as she exclaims,—

"Mr. Dalton!"

"Yes," he says, quietly, folding and sealing a letter as he speaks, "it is very contemptible, is it not? Coming unexpectedly into the house by the conservatory entrance, which, as you know, to any one coming from the station, saves about two hundred yards, I heard, involuntarily, a part of a conversation, which had so great an effect upon me as to induce me to remain where I was, and, voluntarily, hear the remainder."

"A listener!" she says, with a sneer.

"Yes, it is on a par with all the rest, is it not? An avaricious man, a money-grubbing miser; or, perhaps, even worse, a dishonest speculator with the money of other people. O Ellinor Dalton, if ever the day should come (Heaven forbid that I should wish to hasten it by an hour) when I shall be free to say to you about half a dozen words, how bitterly you will regret your expressions of to-day. But I do not wish to reproach you: it is our bad fortune, your's and mine, to be involved in a very painful situation, from which, perhaps, nothing but a rupture of the chain which unites us could extricate us. You have taken the initiative. You would leave me, and return to your aunt in Paris—so be it. Go!"

"Mr. Dalton!" something in his manner, in spite of her long-cherished prejudices against him, impresses and affects her, and she stretches out her hand deprecatingly.

"Go, Ellinor! I, too, am weary of this long struggle! this long conflict with appearances which, in spite of myself, condemn me! I am tired to the very heart of these perpetual appeals to your generosity and confidence—tired of trying to win the love of a woman who despises me."

"Mr. Dalton, if—if—I have misconstrued"—she says, with a tenderness unusual to her in addressing her husband.

"*If* you have misconstrued—" he exclaimed, passionately. "No, Ellinor, no! it is too late now for explanations; besides, I could give you none better than those you have already heard—too late for reconciliation; the breach has been slowly widening for three long years, and to-night I look at you across an impassable abyss, and wonder that I could have ever thought, as Heaven knows I once did, of ultimately winning your love."

There are tears in his voice as he says these last words, and the emotion, so strange to the ordinary manner of the young barrister, affects Ellinor very much.

"Mr. Dalton! Henry!"

"You wish to go to Paris, Ellinor. You shall go! But the man who accompanies you thither must be Henry Dalton!"

"You will take me there?" she asks.

"Yes, and will place you under your aunt's protection; from that moment you are free of me forever. You will have about two hundred a year to live upon. It is not much out of the three thousand, is it?" he said, laughing bitterly; "but I give you my honor it is all I can afford, as I shall want the rest for myself." He looked at his watch. "A quarter past twelve," he said. "Wrap yourself up warmly, Ellinor, it will be a cold journey. I will ring for the people to take your trunks down to the carriage."

"But, Henry," she took his hand in hers. "Henry, something in your manner to-night makes me think that I have wronged you. I wont go to Paris. I will remain with you. I will trust you!"

He pressed the little hand lying in his very gently, and said, looking at her gravely and sadly, with thoughtful blue eyes,—

"*You cannot*, Ellinor! No, no, it is far better, believe me, as it is. I have borne the struggle for three years. I do not think that I could endure it for another day. Ellis," he said, as the lady's maid entered the room in answer to his summons, "you will see that this letter is taken to Mr. Horace Margrave, immediately, and then look to these trunks being carried down-stairs. Now, Ellinor, if you are ready!"

She had muffled herself hurriedly in a large velvet cloak, while her maid brought her her bonnet, and arranged the things which she was too agitated to arrange herself.

She stopped in the hall, and said,—

"I must say good-by to Horace Margrave, and explain this change in our plans."

"My letter has done that, Ellinor. You will not speak one word to Horace Margrave while I am beneath this roof."

"As you will," she answers, submissively.

She has suddenly learned to submit to, if not to respect, her husband.

Henry Dalton is very silent during the short drive to the railway station, and when they alight, he says,—

"You would like to have Ellis with you, would you not?"

She assents, and her maid follows her into the carriage. It seems as if her husband were anxious to avoid a *tête-à-tête* with her

Throughout the four hours' journey, Ellinor finds herself involuntarily watching the calm, grave face of her husband under the dim carriage lamp. It is impossible to read any emotion on that smooth, fair brow, or in those placid and thoughtful blue eyes; but she remembers the agitation in his voice as he spoke to her in her dressing-room.

"He is capable of some emotion," she thinks. "What, what if after all I should really have wronged him? if there should be some other key to this strange mystery than meanness and avarice? If he really love me, and I have misconstrued him, what a wretch he must think me!"

The next evening, long after dark, they arrived in Paris, and Ellinor found herself, after an interval of nearly four years, once more in her aunt's little drawing-room in the Rue Saint Dominique. She was received with open arms. Henry Dalton smoothed over the singularity of her arrival, by saying that it was a visit of his own suggestion.

"Every thing will explain itself at a future time, Ellinor; for the present, let ours be thought a temporary separation. I would not wish to alarm your poor aunt!"

"You shall have your own old bedroom, Ellinor," said her aunt. "Nothing has been disturbed since you left us! Look!" and she opened the door of a little apartment leading out of the drawing-room, in which ormolu looking-glasses and pink curtains very much preponderated over more substantial articles of furniture.

"But you are looking very ill, my dear child," she said, anxiously, as Ellinor pushed away the untasted plate of cold chicken, which her aunt had persuaded her to try and eat. "You are really looking very ill, my dear Ellinor!"

"My journey has tired me a little; if you

will excuse me, aunt. It is nearly eleven o'clock—"

"Yes, and rest will do you more good than any thing. Good-night, my darling child. Lisette—you remember Lisette—shall wait upon you exclusively, till your own maid gets accustomed to our foreign ways. I dare say the poor creature is protesting against frogs in the kitchen. I'll go and see whether they can make her comfortable."

Wearied out with a night and day of incessant travelling, Ellinor slept soundly, and, waking the next morning, found her aunt seated by her bedside.

"My dear girl, you look a great deal better after your night's rest. Your husband would not disturb you to say 'Good-by;' but has left this letter for you."

"Mr. Dalton gone!"

"Yes; he said he had most important business on the something, and a circuit," said her aunt, vaguely; "but his letter will no doubt explain all. He has made every arrangement for your comfort during your stay with me, my dear Ellinor. He seems a most devoted husband."

"He is very good," said Ellinor, with a sigh. Her aunt left her, and she opened the letter—opened it with an anxiety she could not repress. Her life had become so entirely changed in these few eventful days; and in spite of her indifference, nay, dislike for Henry Dalton, she felt so helpless and unprotected now she found herself abandoned by him, that she could not refrain from hoping that this letter might contain some explanation of his conduct—some offer of reconciliation. But the letter was very brief, and did neither:—

"My dear Ellinor,—When you receive these few lines of farewell, I shall be on my way back to England. In complying with your wish, and restoring you to the home of your youth, I hope and believe that I have acted for the best. How much you have misunderstood me, how entirely you have mistaken my motives for the line of conduct which I have been compelled to adopt, you may never know. How much I have suffered from this terrible misunderstanding on your part, it would be impossible for me ever to tell you. But let this bitter past be forgotten; our roads in life henceforth lie entirely separate. Yet, if at any future hour you should ever come to need an adviser, or an earnest and disinterested friend, I must implore you to appeal to no one but,
—Henry Dalton."

The letter fell from her hand. "Now—now I am indeed alone. What have I done," she said, "that I should have never been truly and sincerely beloved? The victim of a marriage of interest! It is very bitter. And the man—the only man I could have loved—no, no, the thought of his indifference is too painful."

CHAPTER VI.

HORACE MARGRAVE'S CONFESSION.

Life in the Faubourg St. Germain seemed very dreary to Ellinor after the brilliant London society to which she had been accustomed since her marriage. Her aunt's visiting list was very limited. Four or five old dowagers, who thought that the glory of the world had departed with the Bourbons, and that France, in the van of the great march of civilization, was foremost in a demoniac species of dance, leading only to destruction and the Place de la Grève; two or three elderly but creditably preserved aristocrats of the ancient *régime*, whose political principles had stood still ever since 1783, and who something resembled ormolu clocks of that period, very much ornamented and embellished, but entirely powerless to tell the hour of the day; three or four very young ladies, educated in convents, and entirely uninterested in any thing beyond M. Lamartine's poetry, and the manufacture of point lace; and one terrifically bearded and moustachoied gentleman, who had written a volume of poems, entitled "Clouds and Mists," but who had not yet been so fortunate as to meet with a publisher—this was about the extent of the visiting circle in the Rue St. Dominique; and for this circle Ellinor's aunt set apart a particular day, on which she was visible, in conjunction with orange-flower water, *eau sucrée*, rather weak coffee, and wafer biscuits.

The very first day of Ellinor's visit happened to be the day of her aunt's reception, and it seemed to her as if the tiresome hours would never wear themselves out, or the equally tiresome guests take their departure. She could not help remembering how different every thing would have been, had Horace Margrave been present. How he would have fought the battle of the *tiers étât* with the white-headed old partisans of the departed noblesse; how he would have discussed and critically analyzed Lamartine's odes with the young ladies from the convent; said a word or two of encouragement to the bearded poet; and regretted the Bourbons with the faded old dowagers. But he was away—gone out of her life, perhaps, entirely. "I shall never see him again," she said; "that dear and honorable guardian, in whose care my dead father left me!"

The next day she went with her aunt to the Louvre, and to the Palais Royal. The pictures only wearied her; the very coloring of the Rubens' seemed to have lost half its glowing beauty since she had last seen them; and Marie de Medici, florid and resplendent, bored her terribly. Many of the recent acquisitions she thought frightfully overrated, and she hurried her aunt away from the splendid exhibition before they had been there half an hour. In the Palais Royal she made a few purchases; and loitered for a little time at a milliner's, discussing a new bonnet; and then declared herself thoroughly tired out with her morning's exertions.

She threw herself back in the carriage, and was very silent as they drove home; but suddenly, as they turned a corner, they passed close to a hackney coach, in which a gentleman was seated, and Ellinor, starting up, cried out, "Aunt! my guardian, Mr. Margrave! Did you not see him? He has just this moment passed us in a hackney coach." She pulled the check-string violently as she spoke, and her aunt's coachman stopped; but Horace Margrave was out of sight, and the vehicle in which he was seated lost among the sinuous turnings of the neighborhood.

"Never mind, my dear Ellinor," said her aunt, as Ellinor, letting down the carriage window, looked eagerly out; "if you are not mistaken in the face of the person who passed us, and it really is Horace Margrave, he is sure to call upon us immediately."

"Mistaken in my guardian's face! No, indeed. But of course he will call, as you say, aunt."

"Yes, he will call this evening, most likely. He knows how seldom I go out."

"What can have brought him to Paris?" thought Ellinor. "I know he would rather shun me than seek me out; for, since the coolness between himself and my husband, he has always seemed to avoid me; so I can have nothing to do with this visit. But surely, he will call this evening."

All that evening, and all the next morning, she constantly expected to hear the lawyer's name announced, but still he did not come. "He had important business to transact yesterday, perhaps," she thought; "and he may still be employed this morning; but in the evening he is sure to call."

After dinner she sat by the low wood fire in her aunt's little drawing-room, turning over the leaves of a book which she had vainly endeavored to read, and looking every moment at the tiny buhl clock over the chimney; but the evening slowly dragged itself through, and still no Horace Margrave. She expected him on the following day, but again only to be disappointed; and in this manner a week passed, without her hearing any tidings of him.

"He must have left Paris!" she thought; "left Paris, without once calling here to see me. Nothing could better testify his utter indifference," she added, bitterly. "It was no doubt only for my father's sake that he ever pretended any interest in the friendless orphan girl."

The following week, Ellinor went with her aunt once or twice to the Opera, and to two or three réunions in the Faubourg, at which her handsome face and elegant manners made some sensation; but still no Horace Margrave! "If he had been in Paris, we should have seen him, most likely, at the Opera," said Ellinor; "he, who is such a connoisseur."

That week elapsed, and on the Sunday evening Ellinor Dalton sat alone in her own room, writing a packet of letters to some friends in England, when she was interrupted by a summons from her aunt. Some one wanted her in the drawing-room immediately.

Some one in the drawing-room, who wanted to see her! Could it be her guardian at last?

"A lady or a gentleman?" she asked of the servant who brought her aunt's message.

"A lady—a sister of charity."

She hurried into the drawing-room, and found, as the servant had told her, a sister of charity in conversation with her aunt.

"My dear Ellinor, this lady wishes you to accompany her on a visit to a sick person; a person, whom you know, but whose name she is forbidden to reveal. What can this mystery mean?"

"A sick person, who wishes to see me?" said Ellinor. "But I know so few people in Paris; no one likely to send for me."

"If you can trust me, madame," said the sister of charity, "and if you will accompany me on my visit to this person, I believe your presence will be of great service. The mind of the invalid is, I regret to say, in a very disturbed state, and you only, I imagine, will be able, under Heaven and the Church, to give relief to that."

"I will come," said Mrs. Dalton.

"But, Ellinor,—" exclaimed her aunt, anxiously.

"If I can be of any service, my dear aunt, it would be most cruel, most cowardly, to refuse to go."

"But, my dear child, when you do not know the person to whom you are going."

"I will trust this lady," answered Ellinor, "and I will go. I will throw on my bonnet and shawl, and join you, madame," she added to the sister of charity, as she hurried from the apartment.

"When these girls once get married, there's no managing them," murmured Ellinor's aunt, as she folded her thin white hands, bedecked with a great many old-fashioned rings, resignedly one over the other. "Pray do not let them detain her long," she continued aloud, to the sister of charity, who sat looking gravely into the few embers in the little English grate. "I shall suffer the most excruciating anxiety till I see her safe home again."

"She will be perfectly safe with me, madame."

"Now, madame, I am quite at your service," said Ellinor, re-entering the room.

In a few moments they were seated in a hackney coach, and rattling through the quiet faubourg.

"Are we going far?" asked Ellinor of her companion.

"To Meurice's Hotel."

"To Meurice's? Then the person I am going to see is not a resident in Paris?"

"No, madame."

Who could it be? Not a resident in Paris. Some one from England, no doubt. Who could it be? Her husband, or Horace Margrave? These were the only two persons who presented themselves to her mind; but in either case, why this mystery?

They reached the hotel, and the sister of charity herself led the way up several flights of stairs and along two or three corridors, till she stopped suddenly at the door of a small sitting-room, which she entered, followed by Ellinor.

Two gentlemen, evidently physicians, stood talking in whispers, in the embrasure of the window. One of them looked up at seeing the two women enter, and to him the sister of charity said,—

"Your patient, Monsieur Delville?"

"He is quieter, Louise. The delirium has subsided; he is now quite sensible; but very much exhausted," replied the physician; and then he added, looking at Ellinor, "Is this the lady?"

"Yes, Monsieur Delville."

"Madame," said the doctor, "will you favor me with a few moments' conversation?"

"With pleasure, monsieur. But first, let me implore you, one word. This sick person, for mercy's sake, tell me his name!"

"That I cannot do, madame; his name is unknown to me."

"But the people in the hotel?"

"Are also ignorant of it. His portmanteau has no address. He came here most probably on a flying visit; but he has been detained here by a very alarming illness."

"Then let me see him, monsieur. I cannot endure this suspense. I have reason to suppose that this gentleman is a friend, who is very dear to me. Let me see him, and then I shall know the worst."

"You shall see him, madame, in ten minutes. Monsieur Leruce, will you prepare the patient for an interview with this lady?"

The other doctor bowed gravely, and opened a door leading into an inner apartment, which he entered, closing the door carefully behind him.

"Madame," said Monsieur Delville, "I was called in, only three days ago, to see the person lying in the next room. My colleague had been for some time attending him through a very difficult case of typhus fever. A few days ago the case became still more complicated and difficult, by an affection of the brain which supervened, and Monsieur Leruce, not feeling himself strong enough to combat these difficulties, considered it his duty to call in another physician. I was therefore summoned. I found the case, as my colleague had found it, a most extraordinary one. There was not only physical weakness to combat, but mental depression—mental depression of so terrible and gloomy a character, that both Monsieur Leruce and myself feared that should we even succeed in preserving the life of the patient, we might fail in saving his reason."

"How terrible! how terrible!" said Ellinor.

"During the three days and nights which I have attended him," continued the doctor, "we have not succeeded until this evening in obtaining an interval of consciousness; but throughout the delirium our patient has perpetually dwelt upon two or three subjects, which, though of a different character, may be by some chain of circumstances connected into the one source of his great mental wretchedness. Throughout his wanderings one name has been incessantly upon his lips."

"And that name is—"

"Ellinor Dalton!"

"My own name!"

"Yes, madame, your name, coupled with perpetual entreaties for pardon; for forgiveness of a great wrong done—a wrong done long since—and scrupulously concealed—"

"A wrong done! If this is the person I suspect it to be, he never, never was any thing but the truest friend to me; but, for pity's sake, let me see him. This torture of suspense is killing me."

"One moment, madame. I had some difficulty in finding you; but mentioning everywhere the name of the lady of whom I was in search, I fortunately happened to make the inquiry of a friend of your aunt. This good, devoted Louise, here, was ready to set out immediately on her errand of mercy, and I thought that you might feel, perhaps, more confidence in her than in me."

At this moment, the door of communication between the two apartments opened softly, and the other doctor entered.

"I have prepared the patient for your visit, madame; but you must guard against a shock to your own feelings in seeing him. He is very ill."

"In danger?" asked Ellinor.

"Unhappily, yes—in very great danger!"

Throughout the brief interview with the physician, Ellinor Dalton had said to herself, "Whatever it is that must be endured by me, I will bear it bravely—for his sake I will bear it bravely." Her handsome face was white as death—the firm, thin lips rigidly locked over the closely shut teeth—the dark and mournful gray eyes tearless and serene; but her heart knocked against her breast, so loudly, that she seemed to hear the heavy throb of its every pulsation in the stillness of the room.

Her worst presentiments were realized.

Horace Margrave lay with his head thrown back upon the piled-up pillows, and his attenuated hand stretched listlessly upon the eider-down counterpane which was wrapped about him. His head was bound with wet linen, over which his nurse had tied a handkerchief of scarlet, whose vivid hue made his white face seem by the contrast still more ghastly. His dark brown eyes had lost the dreamy expression usual to them, and had the bright and feverish lustre of disease. They were fixed, with a haggard and earnest gaze, upon the door through which Ellinor entered.

"At last!" he said, with an hysterical cry. "At last!"

She pressed her hand tightly over her beating heart, and, falling on her knees by his bedside, said to him, very quietly,—

"Horace—Horace! what is this? Why—why do I find you thus?"

He fixed his great, lustrous eyes upon her, as he answered,—

"What is it, Ellinor! Shall I tell you?"

"Yes—yes! if you can tell me without unnerving yourself."

"Unnerving myself!" he laughed, with a bitter, unnatural cadence. "Unnerve myself—look at that!" he stretched out one thin, half-transparent hand, and it trembled like an aspen leaf, till he let it fall lifelessly upon the quilt. "For four years, Ellinor, I have been slowly burning out my life in one long, nervous fever; and you tell me not to unnerve myself."

He gave a restless, impatient sigh, and, tossing his weary head back upon the pillow, turned his face to the wall.

Ellinor Dalton looked round the room in which this brilliant, all-accomplished, ad mired, and fascinating Horace Margrave had lain for eleven dreary days—eleven painful nights.

It was a small apartment, *au quatrième*,

comfortably furnished, and heated by a stove. On the table by the bedside a Missal lay open, with a rosary thrown across the page, where the reader had left off. Near this was an English Testament, also lying open. The sister of charity who had been nursing Horace Margrave had procured this Testament in his own language, in hopes that he would be induced to read it. But the sick man, when sensible, spoke to her in French; and when she implored him to see a priest, refused, with an impatient gesture, which he repeated when she spoke to him of a Protestant clergyman, whom she knew, and could summon to him.

The dim lamp was shaded from the eyes of the invalid by a white porcelain screen, which subdued the light, and cast great shadows of the furniture upon the walls of the room.

He lay for some time quite quietly, with his face still turned away from Ellinor, but by the incessant nervous motion of the hand lying upon the counterpane, she knew that he was not asleep.

The doctor opened the door softly, and looked in.

"If he says any thing to you," he whispered to Ellinor, "hear it quietly, but do not ask him any questions; and, above all, do not betray agitation."

She bowed her head in assent, and the physician closed the door.

Suddenly Horace Margrave turned his face to her, and looking at her earnestly with his haggard eyes, said,—

"Ellinor Dalton, you ask me what this means. I will tell you. The very day on which you left England, a strange chance led me into the heart of a manufacturing town—a town which was being ravaged by the fearful scourge of an infectious fever; I was in a very weak state of health, and, as might be expected, I caught this fever. I was warned, when it was perhaps not yet too late to have taken precautions which might have saved me, but I would not take those precautions. I was too great a coward to commit suicide. Some people say a man is too brave to kill himself—I was not —but I was too much a coward. Life was hateful, but I was afraid to die. Yet I would not avert a danger which had not been my own seeking. Let the fever kill me, if it would. Ellinor, my wish is fast being accomplished. I am dying!"

"Horace! Horace!" She fell on her knees once more at the side of the bed, and taking the thin hand in hers, pressed it to her lips.

He drew it away as if he had been stung. "For Heaven's sake, Ellinor, if you have any pity—no tenderness! That I cannot bear. For four years you have never seen me without a mask. I am going to let it fall. You will curse me, you will hate me soon, Ellinor Dalton."

"Hate you, Horace—never!"

He waved his hand impatiently, as if to wave away protestations that must soon be falsified.

"Wait," he said; "you do not know." Then, after a brief pause, he continued,— "Ellinor, I have not been the kindest or the tenderest of guardians, have I, to my beautiful young ward? You reproached me with my cold indifference one day, soon after your marriage, in the little drawing-room in Hertford Street."

"You remember that?"

"I remember that! Ellinor, you never spoke one word to me in your life which I do not remember; along with the accent in which it was spoken, and the place where I heard it. I say, I have not been a kind or affectionate guardian—have I, Ellinor?"

"You were so once, Horace," she said.

"I was so once? When, Ellinor?"

"Before my uncle left me that wretched fortune."

"That wretched fortune—yes, that divided us at once and forever. Ellinor, there were two reasons for this pitiful comedy of cold indifference. Can you guess one of them?"

"No," she answered.

"You cannot? I affected an indifference I did not feel, or pretended an apathy which was a lie from first to last, because, Ellinor Dalton, I loved you with the whole strength of my heart and soul, from the first to the last."

"O Horace! Horace! for pity's sake!" She stretched out her hands imploringly, as if she would prevent the utterance of the words which seemed to break her heart.

"Ellinor, when you were seventeen years of age, you had no thought of succeeding to your uncle's property. It would have been, upon the whole a much more natural thing for him to have left it to his adopted son, Henry Dalton. Your poor father fully expected that he would do so; I expected the same. Your father entrusted me with the custody of your little income, and I discharged my trust honestly. I was a great speculator; I dabbled with thousands, and cast down heavy sums every day, as a gambler throws down a card upon the gaming-table; and to me your mother's little fortune was so insignificant a trust, that its management never gave me a moment's thought or concern. At this time I was going on in a fair way to become a rich man; in fact, was a rich man; and, Ellinor, I was an honorable man. I loved you—loved you as I had never believed I could love—my innocent and beautiful ward; how could it well be otherwise? I am not a coxcomb, Ellinor; and if there is one person I hold more in contempt than another, it is that of a lady-killer; but I dared to say to myself, 'I love and am beloved again.' Those dark and deep gray eyes, Ellinor, had told me the secret of a young and confiding heart; and I thought myself more than happy—only too deeply blest. O Ellinor! Ellinor! if I had spoken then."

Her head was buried in her hands, as she knelt by his pillow, and she was sobbing aloud.

"There was time enough, I said. This, Ellinor, was the happiest period of my life. Do you remember our quiet evenings in the Rue St. Dominique, when I left business, and business cares, behind me in Verulam Buildings, and ran over here, to spend a week in my young ward's society? Do you remember the books we read together? Good heavens! there is a page in Lamartine's 'Odes,' which I can see before me as I speak! I can see the lights and shadows which I taught you to put under the cupola of a church in Munich, which you once painted in water-colors. I can recall every thought, every word, every pleasure, and every emotion, of that sweet and tranquil time, in which I hoped and believed that you, Ellinor, would be my wife."

She lifted her face, all blinded and blotted by her tears, and, looking at him for one brief instant, let it fall again upon her hands.

"Your uncle died, Ellinor, and the fair elevation of this palace of my life, which I had built with such confidence, was shivered to the ground. The fortune was left to you on condition that you married Henry Dalton. Women are ambitious. You would never surely resign such a fortune. You would marry young Dalton. This was the lawyer's answer to the all-important question. But those tender, gray eyes, looking up from under their veil of inky lashes, had told a sweet secret, and perhaps your generous heart might count this fortune a very small thing to fling away for the sake of the man you loved. This was the lover's answer, and I hoped still, Ellinor, to win my darling. You were not to be made acquainted with the conditions of your uncle's will until you attained your majority. You were, at the time of his death, barely twenty years of age; there was, then, an entire year in which you would remain ignorant of the penalties attached to this unexpected wealth. In the mean time, I, as sole executor (your uncle, you see, trusted me most entirely), had the custody of the funded property John Arden of Arden had left.

"I have told you, Ellinor, that I was a speculator. My profession threw me in the way of speculation. Confident in the power of my own intellect, I staked my fortune on the wonderful hazards of the year 1846. I doubled that fortune, trebled, quadrupled it, and, when it had grown to be four times its original bulk, I staked it again. It was out of my hands, but it was invested in, as I thought, so safe a speculation, that it was as secure as if it had never left my bankers. The railway company of which I was a director was one of the richest and most flourishing in England. My own fortune, as I have told you, was entirely invested, and was doubling itself rapidly. As your uncle's trustee, as your devoted friend, your interests were dearer to me than my own. Why should I not speculate with your fortune, double it, and then say to you, "See, Ellinor, here are two fortunes, of which you are the mistress; one, you owe to Henry Dalton, under the conditions of your uncle's will; the other is yours alone. You are rich. You are free, without any sacrifice, to marry the man you love; and this, Ellinor, is my work'? This was what I thought to have said to you at the close of the great year of speculation, 1846."

"O Horace, Horace! I see it all. Spare yourself, spare me! Do not tell me any more."

"Spare myself? No, Ellinor, not one pang, not one heart-break. I deserve it all. You were right in what you said in the boudoir at Sir Lionel's. The money was not my own; no sophistry, no ingenious twisting of facts and forcing of conclusions, could ever make it mine. How do I know even now that your interest was really my only motive in the step I took? How do I know that it was not, indeed, the gambler's guilty madness only, which impelled me to my crime? How do I know? How do I know? Enough! the crash came; my fortune and yours were together ingulfed in the vast destruction; and I, the trusted friend of your dead father, the conscientious lawyer, whose name had become a synonym with honor and honesty; I, Horace Welmorden Margrave only lineal descendant of the royalist Captain Margrave, who perished at Worcester, fighting for his king and the honor of his noble race; I, Ellinor, was a cheat and a swindler,—a dishonest and dishonorable man!"

"Dishonorable, Horace? No, no; only mistaken."

"Mistaken, Ellinor? Yes, that is one of the words invented by dishonest men, to slur over their dishonesty. The fraudulent banker, in whose ruin the fate of thousands, who have trusted him and believed in him, is involved, is, after all, as his friends say, only mistaken. The clerk, who robs his employer in the insane hope of restoring what he has taken, is, as his counsel pleads to a soft-hearted jury, with sons of their own, only mistaken! The speculator, who plays the great game of commercial hazard with another man's money, he, too, dares to look at the world with a pitiful face, and cry, 'Alas! I was only mistaken!' No, Ellinor, I have never put in that plea. From the moment of that terrible crash, which shattered my whole life into ruin and desolation, I have, at least, tried to look my fate in the face. But I have not borne all my own burdens, Ellinor. The heaviest weight of my crime has fallen upon the innocent shoulders of Henry Dalton."

"Henry Dalton, my husband?"

"Yes, Ellinor, your husband, Henry Dalton, the truest, noblest, most honorable, and most conscientious of men."

"You praise him so much," she said, rather bitterly.

"Yes, Ellinor, I am weak enough and wicked enough to feel a cruel pain in being compelled to do so; it is the last poor duty I can do him. Heaven knows, I have done him enough injury!"

The exertion of talking for so long a time had completely exhausted him, and he fell back, half-fainting, upon the pillows. The sister of charity, summoned from the next apartment by Ellinor, administered a restorative to him; and, in low, broken accents, he continued,—

"From the moment of my ruin, Ellinor, I felt and knew that you were forever lost to me. I could bear this; I did not think my life would be a long one; it had been hitherto lit by no star of hope, shone upon by no sunlight of love. *Vogue la Galère!* Let it go on its own dark way to the end. I say, I could bear this; but I could not bear the thought of your contempt, your aversion; that was too bitter. I could not come to you, and say, 'I love you, I have always loved you; I love you as I never before loved, as I never hoped to love; but I am a swindler and a cheat, and you can never be mine.' No, Ellinor, I could not do this; and yet you were on the eve of coming of age. Some step must be taken, and the only thing that could save me from this alternative was the generosity of Henry Dalton.

"I had heard a great deal of your uncle's adopted son, and I had met him very often at Arden; I knew him to be as noble and true a hearted man as ever breathed the breath of human life. I determined, therefore, to throw myself upon his generosity, and to reveal all. 'He will despise me, but I can bear his contempt better than the scorn of the woman I loved.' I said this to myself, and one night—the night after Henry Dalton had first seen you, and had been deeply fascinated with the radiant beauty of my lovely ward, that very night after the day on which you came of age—I took Henry Dalton into my chambers in Verulam Buildings, and, after binding him with an oath of the most implicit secrecy, I told him all.

"You now understand the cruel position in which Henry Dalton was placed. The fortune, which he was supposed to possess on marrying you, never existed. You were penniless, except, indeed, for the hundred a year coming to you from your mother's property. His solemn oath forbade him to reveal this to you; and, for three years, he endured your contempt, and was silent. Judge now of the wrong I have done him! Judge now the noble heart which you have trampled upon and tortured!"

"O Horace, Horace! what misery this money has brought upon us!"

"No, Ellinor. What misery one partial deviation from the straight line of honor has brought upon us! Ellinor, dearest, only beloved, can you forgive the man who has so truly loved, yet so deeply injured you?"

"Forgive you!"

She rose from her knees, and smoothing the thick, dark hair from his white forehead, with tender, pitying hands, looked him full in the face.

"Horace," she said, "when, long ago, you tell me you thought I loved you, you read my heart aright; but the depth and truth of that love you could never read. Now, now that I am the wife of another, another to whom I owe so very much affection in reparation of the wrong I have done him, I dare tell you without a thought which is a sin against him, how much I loved you, —and you ask me if I can forgive! As freely as I would have resigned this money for your sake, can I forgive you for the loss of it. This confession has set all right. I will be a good wife to Henry Dalton, and you and he may be sincere friends yet."

"What, Ellinor, do you think that did I not know myself to be dying, I could have made this confession? No, you see me now under the influence of stimulants which give me a false strength; of excitement, which is strong enough to master even death. To-morrow night, Ellinor, the doctors tell me, there will no longer be in this weary world a weak, vacillating, dishonorable wretch, called Horace Margrave."

He stretched out his attenuated hands, drew her towards him, and imprinted one kiss upon her forehead.

"The first and the last, Ellinor," he said. "Good-by!"

His face changed to a deadlier white than before, and he fell back, fainting.

The physician, peeping in at the half-open door, beckoned to Ellinor:—

"You must leave him at once, my dear madame," he said. "Had I not seen the dreadfully disturbed state of his mind, I should never have permitted this interview."

"O monsieur, tell me, can you save him?"

"Only by a miracle, madame. A miracle far beyond medical skill."

"You, yourself, then, have no hope?"

"Not a shadow of hope."

She bowed her head. The physician took her hand in his, and pressed it with a fatherly tenderness, looking at her earnestly, and mournfully.

"Send for me to-morrow," she said, imploringly.

"Your presence can only endanger him, madame; but I will send you tidings of his state. Adieu!"

She bent her head, once more, and without uttering another word, hurried from the room.

The following morning, as she was seated in her own apartment, she was once more summoned into the drawing-room.

The sister of charity was there, talking to her aunt. They both looked grave and thoughtful, and her aunt glanced anxiously at Ellinor, as she entered the room.

"He is worse?" said Ellinor, to the sister, before another word had been spoken.

"Unhappily, yes. Madame, he is—"

"Oh, do not tell me any more! For pity's sake! for pity's sake!" she exclaimed. "So young, so gifted, so admired; and it was in this very room we passed such happy hours together, years ago."

She walked with tearless eyes to the window, and, leaning her head against the glass, looked down into the street below, and out at the cheerless gray of the autumn sky.

She was thinking how new and strange the world looked to her now that Horace Margrave was dead!

They erected a very modest tomb over the remains of Horace Margrave, in the cemetery of Père la Chaise. There had been some thoughts of conveying his ashes to his native country, that they might rest in the church of Margrave, a little village in Westmoreland, the chancel of which church was decorated with a recumbent statue of Algernon Margrave, cavalier, who fell at Worcester fight; but as he, the deceased, had no nearer relations than a few second cousins in the army, and the church, and a superannuated admiral, his great uncle, and, as it was furthermore discovered that the accomplished solicitor of Verulam Buildings, Gray's Inn, had left not a penny behind him, the idea was very quickly abandoned, and the last remains of the admired Horace were left to decay in the soil of a foreign grave.

It was never fully known who caused the simple tablet, which ultimately adorned his resting-place, to be erected. It was a plain block of marble; no pompous Latin epitaph, or long list of virtues, was thereon engraved; but a half-burned torch, suddenly extinguished, was sculptured at the bottom of the tablet, while from the smoke of the torch, a butterfly mounted upwards. Above this design there was merely inscribed the name and age of the deceased.

The night following the day of Horace Margrave's funeral, Henry Dalton was seated, hard at work, at his chambers in the Temple.

The light of the office lamp falling upon his quiet, fair face, revealed a mournful and careworn expression not usual to him.

He looked ten years older since his marriage with Ellinor.

He had fought the battle of life, and lost. Lost in that great battle which some hold so lightly, but which to others is an earnest fight. Lost in the endeavor to win the wife he could so tenderly and truly have loved.

He had now nothing left to him but his profession. No other ambition,—no other hope.

"I will work hard," he said, "that she, though separated from me forever, may still at least derive every joy, of those poor joys which money can buy, from my labor."

He had heard nothing of either Horace Margrave's journey to Paris, his illness, or his death. He had no hope of being ever released from the oath which bound him to silence,—to silence, which he had sworn to preserve so long as Horace Margrave lived.

Tired, but still persevering, and absorbed in a difficult case, which needed all the professional acumen of the clever young barrister, he read and wrote on, until past eleven o'clock.

Just as the clocks were chiming the half-hour after eleven, he heard the bell of the outer door ring, as if pulled by an agitated hand.

His chambers were on the first floor; on the floor below were those of a gentleman who always deserted them at six o'clock.

"I do not expect any one at such an hour; but it may be for me," he thought.

He heard his clerk open the door, and went on writing without once lifting his head.

Three minutes afterwards, the door of his own office opened, and a person entered unannounced. He looked up suddenly. A lady dressed in mourning, with her face entirely concealed by a thick veil.

"Madame," he said, with some surprise, "may I ask—"

She came hurriedly from the door by which she stood, and fell on her knees at his feet, throwing up her veil as she did so.

"Ellinor!"

"Yes. I am in mourning for Horace Margrave, my unhappy guardian. He died a week ago in Paris. He told me all. Henry Dalton, my friend, my husband, my benefactor, can you forgive me?"

He passed his hand rapidly across his eyes, and turned his face away from her.

Presently he raised her in his arms, and, drawing her to his breast, said, in a broken voice,—

"Ellinor, I have suffered so long and so bitterly, that I can scarcely bear this great emotion. My dearest, my darling, my adored and beloved wife, are we, indeed, at last set free from the terrible secret which has had such a cruel influence on our lives! Horace Margrave—"

"Is dead, Henry! I once loved him very dearly. I freely forgive him the injury he did me. Tell me that you forgive him too."

"From my inmost heart, Ellinor."

From Once a Week.

RECENT EXPLORATIONS IN AUSTRALIA BY JOHN MACDOUALL STUART.

An obscure surveyor employed by the colonists of Australia to mark out the limits of their "runs," has recently merged into fame by the astounding and dauntless explorations he has made into the interior of that vast continent. We allude to John Macdouall Stuart. Leading a precarious life on the outskirts, this explorer has evinced his nationality of character as a Scotchman, by persevering in the endeavor to be the first to cross Australia from south to north; and besides dissipating the geographical error as to its Sahara-like interior, has greatly enlarged the Adelaide territories by discovering new fields of pasture, springs, and waterholes in that dry and parched land.

Unfortunately, Stuart had been an unsuccessful settler, and hitherto his explorations have been made on behalf of Messrs. J. and J. Chambers, large stockholders in South Australia, who are generally believed to have reaped the fruits of so much daring. Small as the results are when compared with those realized by Livingstone in Central Africa, we have no hesitation in saying (after years spent in the Adelaide bush) that the party who, under the leadership of this fearless man, penetrated to 18° 47′ S., underwent far greater sufferings than the celebrated African traveller. With the thermometer ranging from 90° to 135° Fahr., travelling over burning sands and stony deserts, going without water sometimes for three or four days together, reduced to drinking from muddy and salt pools, or the more stern necessity of living on the blood of their horse, escaping often as if by a miracle (the mere chance of coming upon a native well, or a "clay pan" full of rain water) from the miserable deaths which have overtaken Leichardt, Gellibrand, Coulthard, and others, and swelling the number of those whose bones at the present day lie whitening where they fell, Stuart and his party, who planted their flag on the Central Mount, and actually travelled the extreme distance from south to north, though they did not reach the shores of the Gulf of Carpentaria, have earned for themselves the imperishable fame of having crossed Australia.

Smallest and least favored of the many colonies which fringe the outline of that continent, this niggardliness of nature, like the law of necessity in individuals, has aroused the energies of the Adelaide colonists, and forced them to put forth more than their share of exertion to increase their habitable territory, which consists merely of the coast-line extending along the margins of St. Vincent's and Spencer's Gulf, Yorke's Peninsula, and a pasture country stretching for about two hundred miles in from Port Augusta.

What a goodly tale has this colony to tell of the dauntless efforts of her adopted sons! Who has not heard of Stuart, long called *par excellence* the father of Australian exploration, who reaching unexpectedly the unknown waters of the Murray, allowed himself to be borne along on its bosom till he arrived at the sea through its embouchure into Lake Alexandria: who, in 1844, started from Adelaide at the head of a large party, on an expedition into the interior, and reached the then unprecedented distance of 26° S.; a journey which, though profitless in its issue, occupied many months, and exposed them to unheard-of dangers, and for which endeavors on their behalf the people of that colony allotted him a pension of £700 a year? Or of the hair-breadth escape of Eyre, who, conceiving that if a river entered the sea anywhere between South and West Australia, he must necessarily cross it by travelling along the coast from Adelaide to King George's Sound, actually accomplished the feat, though his fellow-explorer perished, and he was rescued from impending death by accidentally attracting the notice of a whaler, standing in towards the shore? Nor must we forget the names of Brown and Cadell, the one an enterprising and successful colonist, the other the spirited navigator of the Murray. In 1853, the latter, accompanied by Sir H. Fox Young, then governor of South Australia, steamed up the Murray for a distance of thirteen hundred miles in the "Lady Augusta," and since then has been indefatigable in his efforts to establish navigation on the Darling, Gundagai, and Murrumbidgee, besides assisting in the formation of a fleet of Murray steamers, and clearing the bed of that river of its many snags.

But the fame and endurance of all these pioneers of the Australian wilds sink into insignificance when compared with the renown and daring of Mr. Stuart. Long residence on the outskirt runs, where he gained a scanty livelihood by mapping out their boundaries for individual settlers, had inured him to hardship and privation, more especially to scarcity of water, that curse of South Australia, which has led to its meriting the name of Deserta, in contradistinction to Victoria, formerly called Australia Felix. So little indeed was thoroughly known of the immense tract marked out in the face of New Holland as the Adelaide territory, and of that little, so scanty a portion was available for depasturing flocks and herds, that the Colonial Government had been continually fitting out one expensive expedition after another, under the charge of Goyder, Babbage, Freeling, and others, in the hope of being able to relieve the already overstocked runs, and find new fields of enterprise for the increasing number of stockholders. Here, however, as in other parts of the world, private efforts have far outstripped government research, and all the discoveries that have of late been made have issued from individuals, who, penetrating into unknown country at their own risk, have carved out sheep-walks for themselves, and added materially to the interests and prosperity of the colony.

In the month of July, 1857, at a period of the year corresponding to our winter, when rain is more likely to be met with, and the "clay pans" to remain full for a time, the Messrs. Chambers, finding themselves, like many other large stockholders, cramped for room, despatched Mr. Stuart on an exploring expedition to the westward of Lake Torrens, that mythical inland sea which drains the flat country forming Central Australia, and empties itself into Spencer's Gulf, but which the researches of this traveller, coupled with the observations of Hack, Babbage, and Warburton, have proved to be a series of disconnected lakes of brackish water. Leaving the western bank of the mighty swamp, Stuart, in this his first expedition which brought him into notice, kept towards the north and west, sweeping round the Gawler Range, and though furnished with provisions for only three weeks, he and his companion remained out for six, suffering great hardships from the inclemency of the weather, and from living on reduced allowance; nor were the privations they endured in any measure recompensed, since the country they passed through proved quite unavailable for pastoral purposes.

It had been often noticed in the account given by Eyre of his perilous journey, that cool breezes and flocks of birds always came from the north; and though the design on which he planned his route did not allow of his taking advantage of this fact, it bore fruit in the course followed by future explorers. In 1856, Mr. Babbage, prosecuting a government research in the north, came upon a tract of country comparatively well watered, which he designated Blanche Water in honor of Lady Macdonnell, but here, with the exception of one or two, the runs put up to auction found no bidder. In 1857, a large and very stony piece of country was made known by Mr. Swindon, but so badly grassed, and so ill supplied with water, as to repel the idea of occupying it for pastoral purposes. In 1858, however, Mr. Stuart, acting on information gathered while resident at Oratunga, a station belonging to Mr. Chambers, situate four hundred miles from Adelaide, in what is termed, the far north, and again provisioned and supplied by that gentleman, set out on a second expedition, keeping to the north and west from the head of Spencer's Gulf, the direction from which Eyre had noticed the occurrence of cool breezes and flocks of parrots.

On this occasion he was eminently successful, discovering a tract of 16,000 square miles of new and available country, together with a large creek now known by his name, and many immense water-holes. After shaping his course for three or four weeks to the north-west, he, fearing that the water in his rear might be dried up, turned nearly due south, and made for the stations situated on Streaky Bay, near the eastern end of the Great Bight. It was on his return from this trip that we had an opportunity of hearing the details from his own mouth, while present at a conversazione in Government House, given by Sir R. G. Macdonnell to the members of the Adelaide Philosophical Society.

As the law then stood with regard to the waste lands of the crown, Mr. Stuart was quite entitled to put in a claim for lease of the whole, or part of this new territory; accordingly, he or his patron forwarded an application to government, praying to be permitted to occupy fifteen hundred square miles of it on the usual form of tenure.

Unable to ignore the great services he had rendered to his adopted country, the Legislative Assembly granted him a fourteen years' lease of one thousand square miles, to be selected from any part of it.

It may give some idea of the paucity of results earned by the government expeditions, as compared with those of private enterprise, to say, that at the same time that Stuart in six weeks had made these astounding discoveries, Mr. Babbage had spent six months at the head of an expedition costing an immense sum, and had hardly got beyond the settled districts, or sixty miles from Port Augusta. In the succeeding year (1859), this indefatigable traveller still prosecuted his researches, backed, of course, by the inexhaustible funds advanced by Messrs. Finke and Chambers; and though he added further to the revelations of good pastoral country already made known by his exertions, the crowning effort was reserved for the Australian winter of the present year (1860).

In the month of March, Stuart and his two companions—Kekwick and Heed—started from Oratunga, situated on Chambers' Creek, and returned after an absence of five months, having in the interval crossed the continent nearly on the mesial line, and attained to within one hundred miles of the sea-coast on the Gulf of Carpentaria. It was his intention to have kept more to the north-west, and have reached the Victoria River, made known to us by the travels of Mr. Gregory, the surveyor-general of Moreton Bay (Queensland), but all his efforts in this direction were checked by an extensive plain, devoid of grass, and covered with nothing but spinifex and gum-trees. Three times he endeavored to cross it, and was driven back, being saved the loss of his horses, which had been three days without water, solely by the accidental discovery of a native well.

Nothing daunted he made two more attempts to round this "horrid plain" to the eastward, but with similar want of success. He then withdrew, and observing, from the top of the central Mount Sturt (a hill situated about three miles to the north of the centre, and named after that celebrated explorer whom Stuart accompanied on the expedition of 1844), that there were ranges of hills to the north-east, giving indications of better country in that direction, he resolved to shape his course accordingly. Having reached latitude 19° 32′ S., by longitude 134° 18′ E., he determined to make one more effort to fall in with the Victoria River; but after journeying to the north-west for several days over a heavy, sandy soil, exposed to a burning sun, and losing three horses, owing to their being without water for a hundred and eleven hours, was obliged to abandon that project as hopeless. Stuart now changed his plan, and decided on pushing towards the Gulf of Carpentaria. With this intent he reached latitude 18° 47′ S., and had already got into excellent country, well grassed and watered, when his further progress was stopped by bands of savages, who, attacking him and his party, and endeavoring to cut off their pack-horses, necessitated a precipitate retreat.

These natives are described as being the most powerful and muscular yet met with on the Australian continent, and so fearless that it was not till they had been repeatedly fired upon, and several of their number killed, that Mr. Stuart and his two companions could retire unmolested. Opposed by such a dangerous enemy in front—having sustained the loss of three or four horses, being themselves much weakened by such long exposure, provisions, too, getting low, and the dry season coming on when possibly the water might be evaporated at the camping places where he had previously stopped on his journey—Stuart very unwillingly turned his horses' heads homewards, and arrived at Chambers' Creek, after having spent five months in a country hitherto unknown.

During this period he had travelled (including the various detours) upwards of three thousand miles—had all but reached the sea-coast—had overlapped in latitude the track of Gregory on the Victoria by a hundred miles, and had approached it, both on the east and west side, to within two hundred miles.

From March till August 26th scarcely any rain fell, at least, to use Mr. Stuart's own words, "not so much as would wet a shirt through," consequently, we can easily imagine that the sufferings of both men and horses, from the want of this necessary element, must have been very great, and owing to the lateness of the winter rains, many of the water-holes at which he had stopped on his journey northwards were so much evaporated on his return as barely to furnish a drink for the horses. The rations requisite for men going so long an expedition, and who must almost entirely depend on what they carry with them, have to be reduced to the smallest possible bulk, and at the dinner given to our old friend at Adelaide, the attorney-general made a most amusing comparison between the sumptuous repast just laid before them and a piece of gelatine belonging to Mr. Stuart's stock, about the size of an exaggerated cigar, estimated to form the food of thirty men for one day. It was owing to the sameness and scantiness of diet that Mr. Stuart became attacked with scurvy, and so debilitated in body that he could scarcely sit on horseback, while the movements of his companions (who were not above five-and-twenty years of age) became so enfeebled as to resemble those of men upwards of a hundred years old.

So incredible indeed did the fact seem, that three men should traverse the continent from south to north, return again, and, in so doing, journey upwards of three thousand miles in five months' time, that many of their neighbors in Victoria at first refused to place credence in the assertion, but the character of Stuart as an explorer, established under Sturt, and the corroborated authenticity and accuracy of his previous discoveries, leave no doubt as to his having achieved this great feat.

The expedition having been fitted out entirely at the expense of Messrs. Finke and Chambers, the Colonial Government had to make some arrangement (to us unknown) before they would deliver up the information gained by Mr. Stuart, which being settled, his journal and documents were locked up in the government offices. Owing to this transfer of services from the employ of Mr. Chambers to that of the government, as well as to the discretionary wisdom of the latter in concealing the various geographical points of Mr. Stuart's route, until he shall be again well advanced into the interior, lest the Victorian expedition under Burke, or any private party should rob him of the laurels all but won, we are kept much in the dark as to the minutiæ of this extraordinary journey. The existence of a large salt lake, supposed to be of great depth, the presence of the potato, and the Australian-like contradiction of the natives consuming the apples instead of the tubers, form some of the most striking features of this as yet unrevealed narrative. The party at the head of which Stuart is now no doubt far advanced on his previous route, consists of twelve persons well armed, with thirty-five pack and saddle horses, fitted out by a parliamentary vote of £2,500; and in order to anticipate the liberality of being outstripped by Mr. Burke at the head of his camels and horses, Mr. Chambers kindly placed all his stores at Oratunga at the disposal of the government, so as to save the time which would have been expended in forwarding the necessary rations from Adelaide.

Apart from the geographical interest connected with Mr. Stuart's journey, one cannot fail to see how important is the bearing of the few facts made known to us on the establishment of communication, whether telegraphic or otherwise, across the continent with India. Nor can we portray this in a stronger light, than by quoting the statement of his excellency Sir R. J. Macdonnell, that whereas the cost of a telegraphic wire carried all round the coast, whether east or west, would amount to upwards of £800,000, one carried right across, besides being more easily repaired, and having no marine cables, would not amount to more than £400,000.

The journals of the day have amused themselves at the expense of the petty rivalry of the South Australian government in concealing the details of Stuart's narrative from their more powerful neighbor of Victoria, but the poor colony has done more than that, she is applying for territorial extension northwards to the seaboard, with an eye no doubt of including the future line of transit. It has been pointed out to Stuart that, in the present exploration, his great aim must be to connect his most northerly point with the Victoria River. Should he succeed in doing so (of which there seems to be but little doubt) a settlement would soon spring up in the fertile territory around the mouth of that stream, and communication and transit being ere long established across the continent, Adelaide would be in the most favorable geographical position to reap the lion's share.

Federation, so often mooted by the various colonies, will one day obliterate all these petty rivalries; meantime it must be the ardent wish of every scientific man, that this dauntless traveller may accomplish the rest of his journey, and return in safety to enroll his name among other distinguished travellers—Bruce, Park, and Livingstone.

TO THE EDITOR OF "ONCE A WEEK."

SIR,—In your excellent article on the recent exploration in Australia by Mr. Stuart, in the 86th Number of *Once a Week*, you speak of the Victoria River being made known by the travels of Mr. Gregory.

This, I beg to inform you, was *not the case*, as you will find by referring to vol. ii. page 40 of my account of "H.M.S. Beagle's Exploratory Voyage in Australia" (published by Boone, Bond Street), during which the Victoria was the most important of several rivers discovered in that ship between the years 1837 and 1843.

Mr. Gregory's further exploration of this noble river quite bears out my anticipations of the extent it penetrates into the interior.

The discovery of the Victoria I have this reason to remember, that it nearly cost me my life, through being speared in the lungs by a native.

I am, Sir, your obedient servant,

J. LORT STOKES, Captain R. N.

MR. H. C. SELOUS' pictures of "Jerusalem in her grandeur" and "Jerusalem in her Fall" are now on view at the Gallery in Waterloo-place. In the first, Mr. Selous aims at conveying an idea of the actual aspect of the city of the three hills in the days of our Saviour. To attain this end he has carefully consulted every available and reliable authority. A morning sun illumines the ancient city which stretches out far away at the feet of the beholder, who is supposed to view it from the western side of the Mount of Olives. The Temple with its gates, courts, and towers, and resplendent with gold and marble, is its most conspicuous feature. Herod's three towers, his palace and amphitheatre,—the Proctorium,—the Tower of David, and the Garden of Gethsemane, are all shown, with many other buildings, and places of biblical, and historical interest. The foreground is occupied with numerous figures embodying the incident of Christ's triumphal entry into Jerusalem. The second picture is, of course, in direct contrast to the former, and depending as it does rather on facts than on legendary research for its interest, is more artistically and thoroughly complete. The point of view is much the same in both works, the lines of the landscape have undergone little change, but where the Temple once stood now rises the Mosque of Omar. The palaces and towers of former days are supplanted by narrow and deserted streets. English travellers wrangle in dispute with an Arab escort about the price of his services on the spot once trodden by the feet of the Redeemer. Both pictures are large in size, being some twelve feet long exclusive of their frames. Though in painting they partake somewhat of the "panoramic" quality, they yet are full of able and skilful workmanship, and more than average ability. Great labor and research, and much time, have been devoted by Mr. Selous to these paintings. The long perspective lines of the buildings, the general arrangement and composition, are very ably managed. The color is pleasing, and the effect of the one scene is brilliant without garishness, while the sombre tones of the other are free from blackness or opacity. A small pencil drawing of "Jerusalem," as seen coming from Bethany, by Sir David Wilkie, which hangs in the same gallery, strongly corroborates the truth of Mr. Selous' delineation of the present aspect of the fallen city. Both pictures are in process of engraving by Mr. Charles Mottram. With all students of scriptural history and topography the prints will be deservedly popular.—*Spectator*, 16 *March*.

M. HUC.—Perhaps it may not be generally known that M. Huc, the well-known author of "The Chinese Empire," and other popular works, was one of those who lost their lives at Pekin last September. It is however asserted that his death arose from a mistake, as the Chinese were very partial to him, and had even dignified him with the sobriquet of "Tai tai yat'sin sang,"—literally "Nineties one Teacher."

M. Huc was certainly impartial in his estimate of the national character of the Celestials. He painted their follies with inimitable humor, while doing every justice to their virtues, and he avoided the error of many of our own writers on the subject, whose sketches are too often mere distorted caricatures, and as unlike the reality as the Great Mogul on a pack of cards to the potent sovereigns so called. The robust, industrious, and intelligent Chinaman from Penang eastward is a very different person from the effeminate and grotesque type which has been a standard butt amongst us for so long. Absurdities, social and political, are not peculiar to our neighbors; and when we ridicule Tartar customs, and inveigh against bad faith, we should not altogether forget the subjects of *Punch*, and the more serious fact that it was we ourselves who first set the example by carrying on the opium trade, which had been declared contraband in the original treaty.

From Chambers's Journal.

WINTHROP MACKWORTH PRAED.

It is the compensation of all men who die young, that they are recorded by the generation that survives them as of great promise. Envy no longer attends *them*; and their renown is a convenient and unanswerable missile with which to crush a living aspirant after the laurel. "Verses, my good friend? Ah, pretty enough; but you should have seen poor Jones' lines upon the same subject. *He* had the real divine faculty, sir, had Jones. If he had but lived—but it was not to be so—there is no knowing what pinnacle he would not have reached. The broken column in the churchyard fitly tells his tale. You were too young to know him as we knew him; but enough to say that he was king of us all."

Who has not heard some vague eulogium of this sort, delivered by one not usually given to panegyric, over a dead contemporary of his youth? Without some evidence beyond the *ipse dixit* of such a speaker, we might well doubt the genuineness of his assertion; and, indeed, most hearsay reputations, used for the purposes of suppression and detraction, may be set down as by no means really formidable. A generous-natured man, too, will undesignedly magnify the talents of a departed genial spirit.

"You might have won the Poet's name,
If such be worth the winning now,
And gained a laurel for your brow,
Of sounder leaf than I can claim,"

says our greatest living poet of his dear dead friend; but we don't believe him, nor would he perhaps be better pleased if we did. The past will always win a glory from its *being* far, and orb into the perfect star we saw not when we moved therein, as he himself confesses.

On the other hand, it is certain that, now and then, at college or elsewhere, a young man will outstrip in many things the whole of his contemporaries in a very surprising manner; will coruscate and glitter in their firmament after a fashion impossible to a more middle-aged "body," however luminous, and then die; leaving perhaps nothing behind him save a shining track in the sky, discernible only by the eyes which beheld his living course. The generation that knew him perceive it, but not the next.

Thus was it especially with the late Winthrop Mackworth Praed. When a mere boy at Eton, he edited the school-magazine (*The Etonian*), and wrote poems in it such as were scarcely to be found in the most ambitious of the grown-up periodicals of that day. At Cambridge, where he obtained an unprecedented number of classical prizes, he was the most brilliant debater at the *Union* save one, and the very best writer of epigram. Moultrie, Sydney Walker, and Babington Macaulay, were contemporaries with him, and Praed was their favorite and their chief. It was there that he began to write (in *Knight's Quarterly*), those *vers de société* which have placed him at the head of all "fashionable" poets, and with no rival within sight; verses that not only deserve to occupy the space filled by the Hon. W. Spencer in the cyclopædias, but which may dispute for precedence with far greater names. Macaulay and he were of adverse politics, and in their songs of the Civil Wars they, of course, took opposite sides. One of Praed's subjects was *Marston Moor*:—

"To horse! to horse! Sir Nicholas, the clarion's note is high!
To horse! to horse! Sir Nicholas, the big drum makes reply!
Ere this hath Lucas marched, with his gallant cavaliers,
And the bray of Rupert's trumpets grows fainter in our ears.
To horse! to horse! Sir Nicholas! White Guy is at the door,
And the raven whets his beak o'er the field of Marston Moor.

"Up rose the Lady Alice from her brief and broken prayer,
And she brought a silken banner down the narrow turret-stair;
Oh! many were the tears that those radiant eyes had shed,
As she traced the bright word 'Glory' in the gay and glancing thread;
And mournful was the smile which o'er those lovely features ran,
As she said: 'It is your lady's gift; unfurl it in the van!'

"'It shall flutter, noble wench, where the best and boldest ride
'Midst the steel-clad files of Skippon, the black dragoons of Pride;
The recreant heart of Fairfax shall feel a sicklier qualm,
And the rebel lips of Oliver give out a louder psalm,
When they see my lady's gewgaw flaunt proudly on their wing,
And hear her loyal soldiers shout, "For God and for the king!"'

"'Tis soon. The ranks are broken, along the royal line
They fly, the braggarts of the court! the bullies of the Rhine!
Stout Langdale's cheer is heard no more, and Astley's helm is down,
And Rupert sheathes his rapier, with a curse and with a frown,
And cold Newcastle mutters, as he follows in their flight:
'The German boar had better far have supped in York to-night.'

"The knight is left alone, his steel-cap cleft in twain.
His good buff jerkin crimsoned o'er with many a gory stain;
Yet still he waves his banner, and cries amid the rout:
'For Church and King, fair gentlemen! spur on, and fight it out!'
And now he wards a Roundhead's pike, and now he hums a stave,
And now he quotes a stage-play, and now he fells a knave.

"God aid thee now, Sir Nicholas! thou hast no thought of fear!
God aid thee now, Sir Nicholas! for fearful odds are here!
The rebels hem thee in, and at every cut and thrust,
'Down, down,' they cry, 'with Belial! down with him to the dust!'
'I would,' quoth grim old Oliver, 'that Belial's trusty sword
This day were doing battle for the Saints and for the Lord!'

"The Lady Alice sits with her maidens in her bower,
The gray-haired warder watches from the castle's topmost tower;
'What news? what news, old Hubert?'—'The battle's lost and won:
The royal troops are melting, like mists before the sun!
And a wounded man approaches—I'm blind, and cannot see,
Yet sure I am that sturdy step my master's step must be!'

"'I've brought thee back thy banner, wench, from as rude and red a fray
As e'er was proof of soldier's thew, or theme for minstrel's lay!
Here, Hubert, bring the silver bowl, and liquor quantum suff.
I'll make a shift to drain it yet, ere I part with boots and buff—
Though Guy through many a gaping wound is breathing forth his life,
And I come to thee a landless man, my fond and faithful wife!

"'Sweet! we will fill our money-bags, and freight a ship for France,
And mourn in merry Paris for this poor land's mischance:
For if the worst befall me, why, better axe and rope,
Than life with Lenthal for a king, and Peters for a pope!
Alas! alas! my gallant Guy!—curse on the crop-eared boor
Who sent me, with my standard, on foot from Marston Moor!'"

This has the true clank of the war-ballad, and breathes, through fiery nostril, the true Cavalier spirit, but it is no shame to our author to say, that it is scarce a match for his friend's *Naseby*. Where Praed was not to be approached by any one, before or since, was in graceful humor, as in *The Belle of the Ball*:—

"Years—years ago—ere yet my dreams
Had been of being wise and witty;
Ere I had done with writing themes,
Or yawned o'er this infernal Chitty;
Years, years ago, while all my joy
Was in my fowling-piece and filly;
In short, while I was yet a boy,
I fell in love with Laura Lilly.

"I saw her at a country ball;
There when the sound of flute and fiddle
Gave signal sweet in that old hall,
Of hands across, and down the middle,
Hers was the subtlest spell by far
Of all that sets young hearts romancing:
She was our queen, our rose, our star;
And when she danced—O Heaven, her dancing!

"Dark was her hair, her hand was white;
Her voice was exquisitely tender,
Her eyes were full of liquid light;
I never saw a waist so slender;
Her every look, her every smile,
Shot right and left a score of arrows;
I thought 'twas Venus from her isle;
I wondered where she'd left her sparrows.

"She talked of politics, or prayers;
Of Southey's prose, or Wordsworth's sonnets;
Of daggers, or of dancing-bears,
Of battles, or the last new bonnets:
By candle-light, at twelve o'clock,
To me it mattered not a tittle,
If those bright lips had quoted Locke,
I might have thought they murmured Little,

"Through sunny May, through sultry June,
I loved her with a love eternal;
I spoke her praises to the moon,
I wrote them for the Sunday Journal.
My mother laughed; I soon found out
That ancient ladies have no feeling;
My father frowned; but how should gout
Find any happiness in kneeling?

"She was the daughter of a dean,
Rich, fat, and rather apoplectic;
She had one brother just thirteen,
Whose color was extremely hectic;
Her grandmother, for many a year,
Had fed the parish with her bounty;
Her second-cousin was a peer,
And lord-lieutenant of the county.

"But titles and the three-per-cents,
  And mortgages, and great relations,
And India bonds and tithes and rents,
  Oh, what are they to love's sensations?
Black eyes, fair forehead, clustering locks,
  Such wealth, such honors, Cupid chooses;
He cares as little for the stocks,
  As Baron Rothschild for the muses.

"She sketched: the vale, the wood, the beach
  Grew lovelier from her pencil's shading.
She botanized: I envied each
  Young blossom in her boudoir fading.
She warbled Handel; it was grand—
  She made the Catalina jealous.
She touched the organ: I could stand
  For hours and hours, and blow the bellows.

"She kept an albnm, too, at home,
  Well filled with all an album's glories;
Paintings of butterflies and Rome,
  Patterns for trimming, Persian stories:
Soft songs to Julia's cockatoo,
  Fierce odes to famine and to slaughter:
And autographs of Prince Leboo,
  And recipes of elder-water.

"And she was flattered, worshipped, bored;
  Her steps were watched, her dress was noted,
Her poodle-dog was quite adored,
  Her sayings were extremely quoted.
She laughed, and every heart was glad,
  As if the taxes were abolished.
She frowned, and every look was sad,
  As if the opera were demolished.

"She smiled on many just for fun,—
  I knew that there was nothing in it;
I was the first, the only one
  Her heart had thought of for a minute;
I knew it, for she told me so,
  In phrase which was divinely moulded;
She wrote a charming hand, and oh!
  How sweetly all her notes were folded!

"Our love was like most other loves,—
  A little glow, a little shiver;
A rosebud and a pair of gloves,
  And 'Fly Not Yet,' upon the river;
Some jealousy of some one's heir,
  Some hopes of dying broken-hearted,
A miniature, a lock of hair,
  The usual vows,—and then we parted.

"We parted: months and years rolled by;
  We met again four summers after;
Our parting was all sob and sigh,—
  Our meeting was all mirth and laughter;
For in my heart's most secret cell,
  There had been many other lodgers;
And she was not the ball-room belle,
  But only Mrs.—Something—Rogers."

Praed could write fairly, and even freshly upon any subject, and when, at the university, some ladies sent him this inexplicable jargon,—

"A dragon's tail is flayed to warm
  A headless maiden's heart,"

for the text of a poem, he produced two charming cantos upon it, called *Lillian*. After such a feat as that, it is not likely that he would fail when he had real flesh and blood to paint from, nor did he. Among his *Everyday Characters*,—who, however, are, alas! by no means too often met with, —his *Quince* will ever stand forth to combine the truthfulness of Crabbe with the wit and pathos of Thomas Hood.

The *Vicar* is quite as excellent a portrait, but that also is too full-length for hanging here, and besides, has not wise Miss Mitford already embalmed it in her own amber?* She dug Praed's poems forth from the old American edition, as we are now doing from the new,† two loosely compiled and ill-edited volumes, some of the errors of which are, however, unavoidable. It is a shameful thing that no Englishman has been ever intrusted with the task of collecting these "remains," scattered over the periodicals of twenty years ago, and under a multitude of pseudonyms, but each to be recognized without much difficulty by a genial and true critic. As it is, the work has been unsatisfactorily done: there should have been one volume instead of two; the juvenile and local poems should have been left out; and every first sketch of an afterwards finished poem (for, like Macaulay, Praed often wholly re-wrote his compositions) should, in common fairness, be expunged. We are thankful, however, for much good ripe grain, notwithstanding the chaff among which it lies. *Josephine* is a bold and original poem, upon a subject, however, which we wonder to behold in modest American type. *Schools and School-fellows* is at least as good as Hood's *Ode to Clapham Academy*:

"Where are my friends?—I am alone,
  No playmate shares my beaker—
Some lie beneath the churchyard stone,
  And some before the Speaker;
And some compose a tragedy,
  And some compose a rondo;
And some draw sword for liberty,
  And some draw pleas for John Doe.

"Tom Mill was used to blacken eyes,
  Without the fear of Sessions;
Charles Medler loathed false quantities,
  As much as false professions.
Now Mill keeps order in the land,
  A magistrate pedantic;
And Medler's feet repose, unscanned,
  Beneath the wide Atlantic."

* *Recollections of a Literary Life.* By Miss Mitford.

† *The Poetical Works of Winthrop Mackworth Praed.* New and enlarged edition. New York.

The reference to those "before the Speaker" would apply to Praed himself. He was at various periods member for St. Germain in Cornwall, for Great Yarmouth, and for Aylesbury; and in 1835 he was Secretary of the Board of Control. In 1839, he died of consumption, at the age of thirty-seven.

The *Red Fisherman*, one of the best of Praed's serious pieces, makes us lament its length—as no reader of it ever did—since that precludes its quotation; and the same may be said of the *Chant of the Brazen Head*, from which, however, we must cull two verses:—

"I think that friars and their hoods,
Their doctrines and their maggots,
Have lighted up too many feuds,
And far too many fagots;
I think while zealots fast and frown,
And fight for two or seven,
That there are fifty roads to town,
And rather more to heaven.

* * * * *

"I think that Love is like a play
Where tears and smiles are blended,
Or like a faithless April day,
Whose shine with shower is ended;
Like Colnbrook pavement, rather rough;
Like trade, exposed to losses;
And like a Highland plaid, all stuff,
And very full of crosses."

How many of Praed's excellent poems are known to our readers? Some half a dozen, perhaps, to some of them, but to the great majority, none. Even that simple song of his, beginning, "I remember, I remember how my childhood fleeted by," sung by so many young ladies in white muslin, is not awarded to its legitimate owner. Praed, who has long been a favorite author with the educated American public, is, in short, only known in his own country as the best poetical charade writer of his day, and as that, perhaps, only because Sir Walter Scott pronounced him to be so. With a very beautiful effort of that kind—although it is mere waste of wealth—we will therefore conclude this paper; nor, since it is very easy to be guessed, will we insult our readers, as is the manner of some periodicals, by promising "the answer in our next."

"Come from my First, ay, come!
The battle dawn is nigh;
And the screaming trump and the thundering drum
Are calling thee to die!
Fight as thy father fought,
Fall as thy father fell;
Thy task is taught, thy shroud is wrought;
So—forward! and farewell!

"Toll ye, my Second, toll!
Fling high the flambeau's light;
And sing the hymn for a parted soul,
Beneath the silent night!
The wreath upon his head,
The cross upon his breast,
Let the prayer be said, and the tear be shed:
So—take him to his rest!

"Call ye my Whole, ay, call!
The lord of lute and lay;
And let him greet the sable pall
With a noble song to-day;
Go, call him by his name;
No fitter hand may crave
To light the flame of a soldier's fame
On the turf of a soldier's grave."

The Foot and its Covering.—By James Dowie. Robert Hardwicke.—Mr. Dowie is a practical shoemaker, who is keenly alive to the fact that a badly-fitting shoe is the cause of no inconsiderable proportion of the ills that flesh is heir to, and very anxious that an evil which is so easily preventable should not be tamely submitted to any longer. This object he hopes to attain by the publication of the present volume, which consists of a translation of Dr. Camper's treatise on *The Best Form of Shoe*, accompanied by a commentary, which is at once much longer and more practically useful than its text. His book is mainly adapted for the use of gentlemen of his own profession, to whose notice we heartily recommend it; but his fundamental principle, that it is worse than folly to sacrifice not only comfort, but health also, to the requirements of an arbitrary fashion, is one that can scarcely be too strongly urged or too widely disseminated. Mr. Dowie holds, with Lord Bacon, that "every man is a debtor to his profession;" and in his case the debt is not only acknowledged, but fully and conscientiously discharged.—*Spectator*.

From The Press.

AUTOBIOGRAPHY OF MRS. PIOZZI.*

The position that Johnson holds in public estimation is the most singular that has ever been occupied by a literary man. The author of "The Rambler" and the "Vanity of Human Wishes" might well have followed Churchill, his superior in poetry, and Richardson, at least his equal in prose, into comparative obscurity. But whilst Churchill was diminishing his genius by a course of profligacy and excess, and Richardson was trifling away his time amidst a bevy of admiring blue-stockings, Johnson was the centre and moving spirit of a circle of great men, with Boswell at his elbow. Those conversations so literally recorded are the corner-stone of his fame. It was a strange thing to see those glorious satellites, Burke, Goldsmith, Reynolds, Gibbon, and Garrick, revolving round the slovenly, rugged, scrofulous old Jupiter, yielding to force of character the homage which genius alone could not have won, and unconsciously gaining fresh claims to remembrance as units in that friendly band. We see the whole man drawn out before us; we seem to see his inward thoughts without the sickly coloring of Rousseau's Confessions. His political prejudices, his outbreaks of temper, his roughness of manner, his fits of dejection, all conduce to make us feel that we know him. It is Cromwell painted with all his pimples. These private troubles mitigated by religious faith, this love of domesticity, and these personal failings, have made Johnson's every word and action a subject of study and pride to Englishmen, and have ennobled the associates who sympathized with and forgot his eccentricities.

Of these associates Mrs. Thrale was one of the most intimate, and the most unfortunate in her friendship. In fact, the present work has essentially the character of a justification. Of all Johnson's friends Hester Thrale had the least reason to boast, "Je ne suis pas la rose, mais j'ai vecu d' elle." The story of their intimacy is striking. It is evident that the wife and not the husband was the connecting link between the man of letters and Streatham. It was her task to guide the pen and soothe the superstitious terrors of genius at a crisis in which sickness and mental disease maintained a doubtful conflict with a mind that had lost its balance, and a system that had worn out its youthful vigor. And this without ties of friendship or calls of duty—not the tender nurturing of weeks or months, but the constant watching of many years. Surely, such a tenderness must have met with a due return in the hour of restored health and renewed strength. We find, outwardly at least, little but persevering rudeness and a constant disregard for the feelings of the kind entertainer. Not that we impute this as blame to Johnson, for the fault lay in early privations, defective education, and a diseased body, not in his heart. That was true enough. But it made the sacrifice all the more precious in one who with little effort could have raised herself to the highest place in the world of fashion and pleasure. Johnson was scarcely a pleasant guest. His manners at meals were rather those of a wild beast than of a man; at table his looks remained riveted on his plate, and he ate with a will that caused the veins of his forehead to swell and a strong perspiration to break out; on his travels he was even known to have attacked a dish of stewed carp with his fingers. So superstitious was he, that one day when late for dinner he was found vainly endeavoring to pass a particular spot in the ante-room. He tried the health of his friends and the patience of the servants by his love for late hours, and highly resented any attempt on their part to restrain this inconvenient habit. Few ladies would have borne with equanimity his turning the candles with their ends downwards, when they did not burn brightly, to the certain destruction of the carpets, almost reminding us of the man who would burn a house to roast his eggs. Still harder was it to expose one's friends to the criticism, often brutal, of a man whose temper was as uncertain as it was dangerous. The most innocent remark, the thinnest piece of badinage, might draw down a storm of personalities and invective on some sensitive and unwitting head. That Mrs. Thrale under this cloud of unattractive qualities and habits could discern the real merit of the sage speaks more for the soundness of her head and heart, than can be effaced

* Autobiography, Letters, and Literary Remains of Mrs. Piozzi (Thrale). Edited with Notes and an Introductory Account of her Life and Writings, by A. Hayward, Esq., Q.C. Two Vols. London: Longmans.

by the bitterness of a rival biographer and the unfairness of a brilliant essayist.

Boswell's Life and the "Autobiography" exhibit Johnson's character under two different phases. Whilst in the former we have drawn to the life the autocrat of the "Club," the wit and devotee, in the latter we find the social philosopher and the man of gallantry. No one has more fully shown the falseness of Rochefoucauld's maxim,—"Young women who do not wish to appear coquettes, and men of advanced years who do not wish to appear ridiculous, should never speak of love as a thing in which they take part." No one could discourse more wisely and pleasantly of love than Johnson; and his faithfulness to the memory of the "pretty charmer," whom he married in her forty-eighth year, displays one of the most pleasing traits in his character. What picture can be more charming than the uncouth old man fondling the little Burney on his knee? We can hardly explain his popularity with the other sex on the principle which makes them patronize lap-dogs and Chinese monsters; though possibly his personal peculiarities enhanced their admiration. They recognized his genius, and he understood their ways. It is sad that such a friendship as that between Johnson and Mrs. Thrale ended untimely. Mr. Thrale died 1781, Towards the latter part of his life he seems to have been a neglectful husband and a dull companion. Three years later Mrs. Thrale, after vainly striving with her passion, married Piozzi the singer. He seems to have been in every way a gentleman, and by his conduct fully attested the wisdom of his wife's choice. But he was a foreigner—and Johnson hated foreigners; he was a singer—and years afterwards Byron stigmatized Naldi and Catalani as "amusing vagabonds;" she had a large jointure—and the world termed her new husband a fortune-hunter. We do not give any credit to the suggestion that Johnson wished to marry Thrale's widow himself; and we think it an injustice to his memory to impute other selfish motives. The whole pith of the book before us, the justification of Mrs. Piozzi, is contained in the correspondence just prior to the marriage, which space alone prevents our quoting, to the signal discomfiture of Boswell, Macaulay, and Johnson,—of the last especially; for we venture to say that no man has ever shown less regard for the feelings of the veriest stranger, than Johnson shows there for the feelings of one who loved and honored him. The ease and completeness with which Mr. Hayward demolishes the ill-natured satire of Lord Macaulay, and chases him from one position to another, is at once amusing and instructive; for if the brilliant historian discover inaccuracy so gross in a comparatively small matter, it seems rather probable that he brings the same fault to the discussion of weightier subjects. To have led him so completely by the nose is also another feather in Boswell's cap. It is a remarkable instance of retributive justice that the same writer who reviled Mr. Croker with savage captiousness for ascertaining that Miss Burney had misrepresented her age, should be found guilty of defaming the reputation of a virtuous and tender-hearted woman.

Mrs. Piozzi was an active little woman—not exactly pretty, but with an expressive countenance. She says of herself, "I never was handsome; I always had too many strong points in my face for beauty:" and this statement is borne out by the portraits that exist of her from the hands of Reynolds and Hogarth. Though not gifted with genius, she possessed, by the confession of her contemporaries, great conversational powers, and, by the testimony of her writings, considerable literary talent. Her "Streatham Portraits" are good in themselves, and still more interesting in an historical point of view. Mr. Hayward has executed his task of editor with praiseworthy fidelity to the cause which it was his part to advocate. No man, as regards knowledge and mechanical skill of style, was more qualified for the task; and we think no man would have done it better.

From The Saturday Review.

HIDDEN ROMANCE.

Many persons are more or less misunderstood in this world, but the most misunderstood of all persons are middle-aged men. Other people have injustice done them by scattered individuals, but middle-aged men are misunderstood by a whole class. No one from twenty to twenty-five has the remotest notion of doing justice to another person ten or twelve years older. The young enthusiast has sympathies for every other description of person—adores children, sees heaven in infancy, reveres old age tottering to the grave, clings even to what Germans call the mother element in portly matrons. But he or she feels wholly and absolutely cut off from the middle-aged man. What are moonlight walks, and quotations from poets, and secret plans for a world-arousing novel, and confidential intimacies, and the embarrassments of love, to a stupid, prosaic, well-to-do creature, who wraps up before setting out in the night air, who wishes to have his dinner regular and well cooked, who talks politics or shop, and who has secured a wife as uninteresting as himself? The young heart is gushing with its first perusal of *Maud*, of Shelley's *Skylark*, or *Childe Harold*, and is exulting in a dim belief that it, too, is a poet. In comes the misunderstood one, talks not very willingly about *Maud*, thinks it has beauties, but great defects, pronounces Shelley rather vague, and *Childe Harold* in a great part elaborated by the simple machinery of finding the rhyme first, and then the sense to fit in. These remarks fall like sleet on a young plant. The impetus of romantic enthusiasm is checked, and the wounded spirit would refuse to believe, even on the oaths of two credible witnesses, that not many years ago this critic was full of romance, loved the moonlight, kept an album of quotations, and had a weakness for the tenderest passages of the most tender poets—that even now memory keeps the past tolerably fresh to him, and that he prizes a few favorite authors above land and goods. The solution of the apparent discrepancy is one which young people cannot apprehend. When persons have read and felt much, they in time begin to take the deeper emotions for granted. They are too far advanced to need or give the assurance that Shakspeare understood the human heart, that Byron expresses the ordinary and superficial emotions raised by scenery as well as they can be expressed, and that *Maud* is a wonderful exhibition of the affection of a morbid mind. People who are accustomed to things about which they have long ago given vent to their first feelings dwell naturally on the slighter points on which a difference of opinion can reasonably be expected, and as to which it is worth while to say something. The young forget that it is only their rosy cheek, and beaming eye, and pretty excitement that prevent the expression of their most cherished convictions sounding like a string of platitudes.

It is true, however, that much of romance fades away as life goes on. It will fade away in the life of the romantic youth or maiden just as it has faded away in the life of their elders. This is because romance is in a large degree personal. It takes the form of an imaginary shaping of our own careers. The young man who reads *Maud* pictures himself standing in the garden, and calling a real Maud to come to him. If he reads of adventures, of expeditions, of chivalry, of feats of arms or endurance, he likes to place himself in the position of those of whom he is reading, and do their acts, or outrival them, in fancy. The life of the young is a long happy dream, with successive pictures of excitement, of fame, and perhaps of religious ecstasy. The youth feels himself capable of doing or being any thing under the sky, and appropriates to himself as his bare due the most splendid rewards, and especially the reward of a romantic love. After a certain time of life, to dream such dreams is impossible. They are, we are aware, incapable of being realized. A man who knows he has made a sensible, happy, and tolerably prudent match with a young lady of his own station, cannot believe that he will go to Fairy-land and marry a princess. He knows that his Maud will come into the garden at any time he likes during the day, and that therefore it would be absurd to ask her to go there by night. He is aware of the possibilities before him. He will make so much or spend so much, if he is lucky, and so much less if he is unlucky. He knows that emotions end. He is aware that after the most sublime scenery bedtime must come, and that if the bed is damp or dirty, the scenery cannot make up for the inconvenience. He has also many realities to think about, many annoyances to endure or avert, many persons probably to care for. It is therefore unlikely that he can busy himself with the dreams of the imagination, for he has little spare thought for what is dreamy, and as dreams can no longer appear to him as the index of his own lot, he does not think it worth while to make time for them, and to control his thoughts so as to give them play.

Happily, however, the path of man through life is embellished with continual compensations. If we lose one thing we get another. Those who have done with personal romance for themselves gradually acquire it in a manner through others, and learn to take a vicarious enjoyment in the bursts of youthful enthusiasm. It is only slowly that this feeling takes possession of the mind, and at first we fight against a mode of regarding life which reminds us that so much of the flowery part of our own time is gone forever. But gradually we succumb to the pleasures—and they are very pure pleasures—of that vicarious romance. As life goes on, parents are absorbed in the destinies of their children. A mother watches over her daughter's engagement with almost as much interest as she once took in her own. A father is glad at heart that his boy likes the noble words of a noble poet, and spouts them by the seaside or in the wood. He exults when he finds the lad thinks that his partner at the last ball was perfection, and hints that she would perhaps come into the garden. But before this period of life arrives—before parental affection has made parents once more romantic—the time comes when the heart that has ended its own personal romance delights in the romance of those who are still in the morning of their years. The middle-aged man secretly heaps coals of fire on the head of the young and romantic being who despises him as prosaic. He returns good for evil. He loves the romance which is exhibited to shame him, and dreams for others what he cannot dream for himself. The engagements, or inclinations, or disappointments of his young friends are matters of moment to him, and he takes an interest in all their doings. As a pair of lovers turn out for their evening stroll among lilies and roses, they feel a contempt, which they do not much affect to conceal, for him, as they see him turn in to his quiet cigar or rubber. But he has really the best of it; for while this slightly unenviable prejudice blinds them, he blesses them in secret, and watches their receding forms with a smile of amusement and a tear of regret and sympathy. Whether this is to be called romantic in him or not is not very important. It comes near enough to romance to show that to be unromantic is not his chief characteristic.

It is also to be remarked that a very large portion of romance is not personal. Perhaps what is meant by "romance" and "romantic" may be expressed by saying that they convey the notion of a power, and a delight in the use of the power, of transporting ourselves into imaginary scenes of a tender or heroic kind. It is quite possible that one of the chief elements in the pleasure of romance may lie in fancying that we could personally go through these scenes; but it is also possible that there may be a pleasure in romance even if we do not for a moment suppose that we could be mixed up in reality with what we are thinking of. The highest poetry is very often distasteful to young people, for the precise reason that they cannot bring it within their range. They cannot see how it is connected with themselves. Their elders have a great advantage over them here. They do not want to see this connection. It is also a great advantage, in enjoying and judging many of the highest works that have embodied tender and romantic feelings, to be indifferent to love. As long as people are anxious to have their amatory instincts gratified in literature, they cannot bring themselves to care much for that species of poetry which is based on the other great phases of human feeling, or deals with the more permanent interests of man. Probably few persons under thirty like *Paradise Lost*. Young people know it is a fine poem, and full of magnificent imagery; but it is all about things that are very uninteresting as compared with *Maud* and the *Princess*. Wordsworth, again, is a writer who is seldom relished until his quiet melancholy is congenial to the mind that has lost its own early spring. It is true that Wordsworth once was the fashion even among young people, but that was because the great authorities of the day recommended him, and fashion made him popular. But he is, we believe, far less read now. He is merely one of the poets of the past, and he is not one that those who are now beginning to read poetry care to select. The poetry of action, like the *Iliad* and most of Shakspeare's plays, is equally welcome at all times of life to those who care for poetry at all; and therefore the chief change that years bring is the substitution of a delight in poetry of a grand, or religious, or melancholy, or reflective kind, for a delight in poetry addressed to the passions. No one who has tried both kinds of enjoyment will acknowledge that this is a change from better to worse. But it is a change which makes those who have undergone it very little inclined to speak of it, or to be enthusiastic in the expression of their admiration when they admire. People of sense and experience are generally inclined to keep their quiet melancholy and their spiritual aspirations to themselves; and therefore the romance of the middle-aged, even when most characteristic and intense, is usually hidden.

There is also a tendency in a large portion of the literature of the present time which has the effect of doubling the veil under which this hidden romance is concealed. Criticism acts on many persons as a stimulant to disobey it. They think it only shows a want of fine feeling and proper enthusiasm to test what is written by a high standard, to exercise reserve, and to praise in moderation. Accordingly, they pile up the tallest words they can find, speak of every thing in superlatives, overflow with enthusiasm, and put every thing on a grand footing, such as the whisperings of eternity, or the beatings of a nation's heart, or the mission of humanity. Writing of this kind, although it charms the writer and the gushing portion of the public generally, excites the disgust and contempt of those who have learned to control, and perhaps in some measure to forget, their own feelings, who wish that words when used should have as definite, clear, and apt a meaning as possible, and who regard all grandiloquence as a mere trick of style. They are constantly on their guard to avoid giving any color for the supposition that they could be romantic in the way in which those whose taste is to them simply execrable are romantic; and they thus hide their own romance more carefully and consciously than would otherwise be natural to them. There is no way of avoiding this. The time is far distant when there will no longer be two sets of people in the world—the one prone to criticism and the other prone to grandiloquence. We are entirely on the side of the critics, but we must acknowledge that there are some evils attaching to the habit of constantly keeping the expression of feeling within bounds. Romance may be so hidden as to fade away beneath the obscurity that hides it. This would take place very rapidly were it not that it is secretly fed by the communion with a few favorite and great authors; but even this may not altogether suffice, and romance, we must acknowledge, requires occasionally a little airing in order to be vigorous. How this is to be done is so much a matter of individual taste and character, of circumstances and opportunity, that it would be impossible to lay down any general rule that would be of much use as a guide. These occasional bloomings of hidden romance are as delicate as they are precious, and must be left to spring up in their own way.

Atterbury, the celebrated Bishop of Rochester, in the time of Queen Anne, happened to say in the house of Lords, while speaking on a certain bill then under discussion, that he had prophesied last winter this bill would be attempted in the present session, and he was sorry to find he had proved a true prophet. Lord Coningsby, who spoke after the bishop, and always spoke in a passion, desired the House to remark that one of the right reverend had set himself forth as a prophet; but, for his part, he did not know what prophet to liken him to, unless to that furious prophet Balaam, who was reproved by his own ass. Atterbury, in reply, with great wit and calmness exposed this rude attack, concluding thus: "Since the noble lord has discovered in our manners such a similitude, I am well content to be compared to the prophet Balaam; but, my lords, I am at a loss how to make out the other part of the parallel; I am sure that I have been reproved by nobody but his lordship!"—*King's Memoirs.*

From The Athenæum.

The History of England from the Accession of James the Second. By Lord Macaulay. Vol. V., Edited by his Sister, Lady Trevelyan. Longman and Co.

OVER that grave in the great abbey which the historian so warmly coveted and so nobly won, it would be the desire of every man of sense and sensibility that there should now be peace. But this will hardly be. The writer is at rest. The applause of his readers, the censure of his critics, can delight or exercise that gladiatorial brain no more. The strong and passionate heart which seemed to glow and sparkle in the fire of controversy, has done with all its loves and hates. But the written word remains; a word emphasized with power and scorn; a word announced with no misgiving and with no reserve; yet assailing characters the most revered, opinions the most cherished, institutions the most respectable. Around this word we cannot hope for truce. The war of evidence, of sarcasm, of vituperation, which already rages, will, we fear, burn out afresh and with greater violence. It is not, as in Lord Macaulay's earlier time, a war in which the reprisals were personal and the conquests easy. Against John Wilson Croker, Macaulay could defend himself. He had no great need to dread the wrath of Robert Montgomery. But no man can hope to outrage a nation and get off scot free. Personal ire exhausts itself very soon: a squib, an insult, or a literary victory may disarm resentment and allay rancor. But the passion of a party like that of the High Church,—of a community like that of the Quakers,—and of a nationality like that of Scotland, suffers no exhaustion and no fatigue. A succession of combatants will replace the retiring gladiator: Croker is followed by the Bishop of Exeter, Foster by Jannay and Paget, Napier by Robert Chambers.

We cannot hope to extinguish these controversies, seeing how much in the present volume is adapted to excite and inflame them. Those Quakers who have heretofore been scandalized by the picturesque caricatures of Penn and Fox, will, in the lesser degree, reject the story, as here told, of the fair Quaker who is supposed to have been in love with Spencer Cowper. The Scotch will be moved, and some of them maddened, by the elaborate representation of the Darien disaster. Admirers of John, Duke of Marlborough, will be offended by the continued maltreatment of that great officer. But we shall not ourselves to-day take part in these inevitable debates. We leave Mr. Bowden to defend the Stout family, and Mr. Chambers, or any other good Scot, to explain the impugned sanity and honesty of his countrymen who went out with William Paterson to found a new Tyre, or Venice, in the Isthmus of Darien. Marlborough is sufficiently taken care of. Of Montrose, of Dartmouth, of William Penn, enough has been said; but until many of the historical discussions which are still open shall have been closed, no final opinion on the value of Lord Macaulay's "History of England" can be pronounced. Popular judgments on books are liable to much revision. About a century ago, a work was announced in the newspapers under the title of a "History of England from the Accession of James the First to the Elevation of the House of Hanover," by Catherine Macaulay. The expectation was great, for Catherine Macaulay was a violent partisan, and the success enormous, for her book was clever, piquant, disputatious and calumnious. Everybody read it: the Whigs and Republicans to admire, the Tories to abuse and denounce. It was, indeed, a magnificent party pamphlet in five volumes. For several years the historian was a toast at Whig banquets, and the dismay of Tory and Jacobite politicians, male and female. The copyright of her history brought her several thousand pounds, so that compared with her revenues the literary gains of Goldsmith, or Savage, were below contempt. Goldsmith envied her many editions, and even Johnson's masculine understanding was disturbed by her success. The book was left a fragment. While Catherine Macaulay was drawing the attention of the reading world to her exaggerated views of the character of Charles, of Strafford, and of Cromwell,—doing good service, let us say, by her occasional insight into character and motives, and even by the violence and vituperation which compelled a closer searching into the sources of historic fable,—Edmund Gibbon was preparing his "History of the Decline and Fall of Rome." Five years after Catherine Macaulay published her fifth volume, Gibbon brought out his first. Its success, though great, fell below that of his female rival in popularity; and but for the controversial character of his fifteenth and sixteenth chapters, the public interest in his pages would have been considerably less than it was. Yet no one reads Catherine Macaulay now, and everybody reads Gibbon.

It was in the nature of Lord Macaulay's genius to consider the past as a politician rather than as a philosopher. He cared little for the past as the past, for fact as fact; he cared only for the lessons to be derived from history,—for the immediate uses to be made of truth. With all his apparent fervor, the seventeenth century was to him attractive and important only in so far as it helped him to understand the nineteenth. "History" was in his eyes a marble muse "teaching by example," enunciating wise saws and ancient instances, drawing the moral out of this and that act, and under great energy of expression, keeping her temper sedate and cold. Hence, there is discernible in each of his three separate publications of the "History" manifest references to the controversies raised by passing events. His account of the Revolution closed with a lecture to the English Chartists and the Paris Socialists of 1848. His third and fourth volumes abound in allusions to events in progress at the time he wrote them. He never fails to improve the occasion,—and in his new volume this vice is more frequent and conspicuous than in the former volumes. It opens with an elaborate view of the best defence of nations—*àpropos* to an imaginary invasion by the French—in which the excellence of professional soldiers, as compared against occasional soldiers, is insisted on with all the energy implied in Lord Lansdowne's well-remembered saying. He could not help instituting these comparisons and drawing these utilitarian conclusions. Of the morals which lie in every true story, he seems to have had considerable doubts. He would not rely, as the poet or the dramatist relies, on truth and on the detective and exploring sensibilities of mankind. If he saw a sermon in a stone, he would break the stone to get it out. If he spied a lesson in a tale, he stopped the tale to point the moral. Of sympathy with life merely as life, that sympathy possessed to perfection by women, by young children, by poets, by dramatists, he had none at all. Books were to him life. If he studied his species, it was that he might better comprehend his books. Men and women were to him organizations, orders, varieties of a system, things endowed with qualities, faculties, aptitudes, capacities, passions. Where he felt any keen sympathy it was with the intellect, not with the humanity. If he had a boundless admiration for William, or an inexpressible scorn of Marlborough, his feeling was excited by the politician not by the man.

As the question of defence is one still in agitation, and, indeed, likely, despite our Warriors, and Black Princes, our militias and volunteers, to be in agitation, so long as the guns of Dover and Calais frown at each other across the Channel, and the principles of the Saxon are unlike the principles of the Gaul, our readers will like to see what Lord Macaulay thought of recommending to his countrymen. The discussion which invites him to display his views on this topic, arose on the question of what should be done, after the peace of 1697, with that gallant army which William commanded, and which had so powerfully contributed to bring the peace about. England had never submitted to maintain a standing army. The whole nation was then more or less trained to the use of arms; every gentleman wore his rapier and practised with his pistols. Shooting and sword exercise were the delights of every class of the population. For six hundred years there had been no successful invasion of this country; and the levies, though suddenly raised and only half disciplined, had never met the French in a fair field without breaking and scattering them. The confidence and security of the people were consequently supreme. As they could not imagine a use for a permanent army other than that of supporting a despotic government in power, the whole nation was for disbanding the English regiments and for sending the Dutch guards home again. In the House of Commons, and in numerous pamphlets, the question was debated on general principles. Lord Macaulay puts the case in this way:—

"No man of sense has, in our days, or in the days of our fathers, seriously maintained that our island could be safe without an army. And, even if our island were perfectly secure from attack, an army would still be indispensably necessary to us. The growth of the empire has left us no choice. The regions which we have colonized or conquered since the accession of the house of Hanover contain a population exceeding twenty-fold that which the house of Stuart governed. There are now more English soldiers on the other side of the tropic of Cancer in time of peace than Cromwell had under his command in time of war. All the troops of Charles II. would not have been sufficient to garrison the posts which we now occupy in the Mediterranean Sea alone. The regiments which defend the remote dependencies of the crown cannot be duly recruited and relieved, unless a force far larger than that which James collected in the camp at Hounslow for the purpose of overawing his capital be constantly kept up within the kingdom. The old national antipathy to permanent military establishments, an antipathy which was once reasonable and salutary, but which lasted some time after it had become unreasonable and noxious, has gradually yielded to the irresistible force of circumstances. We have made the discovery, that an army may be so constituted as to be in the highest degree efficient against an enemy, and yet obsequious to the civil magistrate. We have long ceased to apprehend danger to law and to freedom from the license of troops, and from the ambition of victorious generals. An alarmist who should now talk such language as was common five generations ago, who should call for the entire disbanding of the land force of the realm, and who should gravely depict that the warriors of Inkerman, and Delhi, would depose the queen, dissolve the Parliament, and plunder the bank, would be regarded as fit only for a cell in St. Luke's."

The case was, however, very different in the seventeenth century. The people knew nothing of a domestic army, but the evil of it,—the license of Goring's crew, or of James' Hounslow regiments. As Lord Macaulay says: "One class of politicians was never weary of repeating that an Apostolic Church, a loyal gentry, an ancient nobility, a sainted king, had been foully outraged by the Joyces, and the Prides: another class recounted the atrocities committed by the Lambs of Kirke, and by the Beelzebubs and Lucifers of Dundee; and both classes, agreeing in scarcely any thing else, were disposed to agree in aversion to the red-coats."

Trenchard and Somers took the opposite sides in a violent paper war which preceded the debates in Parliament. Lord Macaulay undertakes to demonstrate that William's desire to retain his great army was, though an unprecedented, a reasonable and patriotic, wish. He first states, fairly, the argument of Trenchard; but with an eloquence and conciseness to which Trenchard made no claim:—

"Invasion was the bugbear with which the court tried to frighten the nation. But we were not children to be scared by nursery tales. We were at peace; and, even in time of war, an enemy who should attempt to invade us would probably be intercepted by our fleet, and would assuredly, if he reached our shores, be repelled by our militia. Some people, indeed, talked as if a militia could achieve nothing great. But that base doctrine was refuted by all ancient, and all modern history. What was the Lacedæmonian phalanx in the best days of Lacedæmon? What was the Roman legion in the best days of Rome? What were the armies which conquered at Cressy, at Poitiers, at Agincourt, at Halidon, or at Flodden? What was that mighty array which Elizabeth reviewed at Tilbury? In the fourteenth, fifteenth, and sixteenth centuries, Englishmen who did not live by the trade of war had made war with success and glory. Were the English of the seventeenth century so degenerate that they could not be trusted to pla the men for their own homesteads, and parish churches?"

To all this, and to much more of the same class, Lord Macaulay replies:—

"It must be evident to every intelligent and dispassionate man that these declaimers contradicted themselves. If an army composed of regular troops really was far more efficient than an army composed of husbandmen, taken from the plough, and burghers, taken from the counter, how could the country be safe with no defenders but husbandmen and burghers, when a great prince, who was our nearest neighbor, who had a few months before been our enemy, and who might, in a few months, be our enemy again, kept up not less than a hundred and fifty thousand regular troops? If, on the other hand, the spirit of the English people was such that they would, with little or no training, encounter and defeat the most formidable array of veterans from the Continent, was it not absurd to apprehend that such a people could be reduced to slavery by a few regiments of their own countrymen? But our ancestors were generally so much blinded by prejudice that this inconsistency passed unnoticed. They were secure where they ought to have been wary, and timorous.

where they might well have been secure. They were not shocked by hearing the same man maintain, in the same breath, that, if twenty thousand professional soldiers were kept up, the liberty and property of millions of Englishmen would be at the mercy of the crown, and yet that those millions of Englishmen, fighting for liberty and property, would speedily annihilate an invading army composed of fifty or sixty thousand of the conquerors of Steinkirk and Landen. Whoever denied the former proposition was called a tool of the Court. Whoever denied the latter was accused of insulting and slandering the nation."

It is impossible not to see that these arguments are addressed to Mr. Bright and the Peace party of our own day. We do not imagine that the sophism on which they proceed requires any particular refutation. It is perfectly certain that a prætorian guard which was absolutely useless for defence, might be a formidable instrument of domestic repression. James' Hounslow regiments were not at all terrible to the enemy, but they were exceedingly terrible to their fellow-subjects. In the case of a foreign invasion, the people would act together, with the law on their side and the government at their back. But for resistance to a despotic king, they would have the law, in appearance, at least, against them, and they would have to face the compact organization of the government before they were themselves armed and trained. The positions are so different, that one is amazed to find a politician arguing from one to the other. Take the instance of our own volunteers. With the help of government and by the sanction of law, a magnificent army has been organized, which in five or six weeks of campaigning would become fit to face any troops in the world; but a word from the government, and the staves of a dozen constables, might have prevented that magnificent army from ever being formed.

The views of Somers are thus set forth :—

"The evil of having regular soldiers, and the evil of not having them, Somers set forth and compared in a little treatise, which was once widely renowned as the 'Balancing Letter,' and which was admitted, even by the malecontents, to be an able and plausible composition. He well knew that mere names exercise a mighty influence on the public mind; that the most perfect tribunal which a legislator could construct would be unpopular if it were called the Star Chamber; that the most judicious tax which a financier could devise would excite murmurs if it were called Ship money; and that the words standing army then had to English ears a sound as unpleasing as either Ship-money or Star Chamber. He declared therefore that he abhorred the thought of a standing army. What he recommended was, not a standing but a temporary army, an army of which Parliament would annually fix the number, an army for which Parliament would annually frame a military code, an army which could cease to exist as soon as either the Lords or Commons should think that its services were not needed. From such an army surely the danger to public liberty could not by wise men be thought serious. On the other hand, the danger to which the kingdom would be exposed if all the troops were disbanded was such as might well disturb the firmest mind. Suppose a war with the greatest power in Christendom to break out suddenly, and to find us without one battalion of regular infantry, without one squadron of regular cavalry; what disasters might we not reasonably apprehend? It was idle to say that a descent could not take place without ample notice, and that we should have time to raise and discipline a great force. An absolute prince, whose orders, given in profound secrecy, were promptly obeyed at once by his captains on the Rhine and on the Scheld, and by his admirals in the Bay of Biscay and in the Mediterranean, might be ready to strike a blow long before we were prepared to parry it. We might be appalled by learning that ships from widely remote parts, and troops from widely remote garrisons, had assembled at a single point within sight of our coast. To trust to our fleet was to trust to the winds and the waves. The breeze which was favorable to the invader might prevent our men-of-war from standing out to sea. Only nine years ago this had actually happened. The Protestant wind, before which the Dutch armament had run full sail down the Channel, had driven King James' navy back into the Thames. It must then be acknowledged to be not improbable that the enemy might land. And, if he landed, what would he find? An open country; a rich country; provisions everywhere; not a river but which could be forded; no natural fastnesses such as protect the fertile plains of Italy; no artificial fastnesses such as, at every step, impede the progress of a conqueror in the Netherlands. Every thing must then be staked on the steadiness of the militia; and it was pernicious flattery to represent the militia as equal to a conflict in the field with veterans whose whole life had been a preparation for the day of battle.

The instances which it was the fashion to cite of the great achievements of soldiers taken from the threshing-floor and the shopboard were fit only for a schoolboy's theme. Somers, who had studied ancient literature like a man,—a rare thing in his time,—said that those instances refuted the doctrine which they were meant to prove. He disposes of much idle declamation about the Lacedæmonians by saying most concisely, correctly, and happily, that the Lacedæmonian commonwealth really was a standing army which threatened all the rest of Greece. In fact, the Spartan had no calling except war. Of arts, sciences, and letters he was ignorant. The labor of the spade and of the loom, and the petty gains of trade, he contemptuously abandoned to men of a lower caste. His whole existence from childhood to old age was one long military training. Meanwhile, the Athenian, the Corinthian, the Argive, the Theban, gave his chief attention to his oliveyard or his vineyard, his warehouse or his workshop, and took up his shield and spear only for short terms and at long intervals. The difference, therefore, between a Lacedæmonian phalanx and any other phalanx was long as great as the difference between a regiment of the French household troops and a regiment of the London trainbands. Lacedæmon consequently continued to be dominant in Greece till other states began to employ regular troops. Then her supremacy was at an end. She was great while she was a standing army among militias. She fell when she had to contend with other standing armies. The lesson which is really to be learned from her ascendency and from her decline is this, that the occasional soldier is no match for the professional soldier."

We cannot but think that if Lord Macaulay had lived to see that our issue out of those painful discussions of 1857 and 1858, caused by the invasion panic, was a return to the citizen-soldiership of our ancestors, he would have greatly modified his views on this subject as here expressed. As the resource of Whig politicians in those years was a large augmentation of the regular army, the historian pressed his historical readings into their service, just as he would have thought it his duty to do in the House of Commons. Thus, he lends the authority of his name to that version of the history of Sparta, which Somers, in a party pamphlet, made to tell on his side of the argument:—

"The first great humiliation which befell the Lacedæmonians was the affair of Sphacteria. It is remarkable that on this occasion they were vanquished by men who made a trade of war. The force which Cleon carried out with him from Athens to the Bay of Pylos, and to which the event of the conflict is to be chiefly ascribed, consisted entirely of mercenaries,—archers from Scythia and light infantry from Thrace. The victory gained by the Lacedæmonians over a great confederate army at Tegea retrieved that military reputation which the disaster of Sphacteria had impaired. Yet even at Tegea it was signally proved that the Lacedæmonians, though far superior to occasional soldiers, were not equal to professional soldiers. On every point but one the allies were put to rout; but on one point the Lacedæmonians gave way; and that was the point where they were opposed to a brigade of a thousand Argives, picked men, whom the state to which they belonged had during many years trained to war at the public charge, and who were, in fact, a standing army. After the battle of Tegea, many years elapsed before the Lacedæmonians sustained a defeat. At length a calamity befell them which astonished all their neighbors. A division of the army of Agesilaus was cut off and destroyed almost to a man; and this exploit, which seemed almost portentous to the Greeks of that age, was achieved by Iphicratus, at the head of a body of mercenary light infantry. But it was from the day of Leuctra that the fall of Sparta became rapid and violent. Some time before that day the Thebans had resolved to follow the example which had been set many years before by the Argives. Some hundreds of athletic youths, carefully selected, were set apart, under the names of the City Band and the Sacred Band, to form a standing army. Their business was war. They encamped in the citadel; they were supported at the expense of the community; and they became, under assiduous training, the first soldiers in Greece. They were constantly victorious till they were opposed to Philip's admirably disciplined phalanx at Chæronea; and even at Chæronea they were not defeated, but slain in their ranks, fighting to the last. It was this band, directed by the skill of great captains, which gave the decisive blow to the Lacedæmonian power."

The Inns of Court Volunteers will easily dispose of this history and of this inference. We must pass on.

Next to the vein of political moralizing which runs through Lord Macaulay's new volume, as through the former volumes, giving to the whole work on superficial view this air of passing and almost local interest, the most prominent feature, perhaps, is the gallery of portraits. In portraiture Lord Macaulay is popularly considered strong and striking, and in this the popular voice is just. But even in the exercise of this fascinating part of an historian's craft, we may see that Lord Macaulay follows the peculiar bias of his mind. His figures are not men, but qualities and circumstances. Mr. Carlyle, when he presents you to Mirabeau, to Cromwell, to Frederick, seems to have lived with his original; for he gives you the glance of his eye, the tone of his voice, the shade on his brow, the twitch of his nostril. Lord Macaulay tells you an anecdote or two, and describes a few facts and surroundings of the man. These presentations are always made with an immense verbal dexterity, though the one type is followed in all. Take, for example, this very clever portrait of Lord Spencer:—

"The precocious maturity of the young man's intellectual and moral character had excited hopes which were not destined to be realized. His knowledge of ancient literature, and his skill in imitating the styles of the masters of Roman eloquence, were applauded by veteran scholars. The sedateness of his deportment and the apparent regularity of his life delighted austere moralists. He was known, indeed, to have one expensive taste; but it was a taste of the most respectable kind. He loved books, and was bent on forming the most magnificent private library in England. While other heirs of noble houses were inspecting patterns of steinkirks and sword knots, dangling after actresses, or betting on fighting cocks, he was in pursuit of the Mentz editions of Tully's Offices, of the Parmesan Statius, and of the inestimable Virgil of Zarottus. It was natural that high expectations should be formed of the virtue and wisdom of a youth whose very luxury and prodigality had a grave and erudite air, and that even discerning men should be unable to detect the vices which were hidden under that show of premature sobriety. Spencer was a Whig, unhappily for the Whig party, which, before the unhonored and unlamented close of his life, was more than once brought to the verge of ruin by his violent temper and his crooked politics. His Whiggism differed widely from that of his father. It was not a languid, speculative preference of one theory of government to another, but a fierce and dominant passion. Unfortunately, though an ardent, it was at the same time a corrupt and degenerate, Whiggism; a Whiggism so narrow and oligarchical as to be little, if at all, preferable to the worst forms of Toryism. The young lord's imagination had been fascinated by those swelling sentiments of liberty which abound in the Latin poets and orators; and he, like those poets and orators, meant by liberty something very different from the only liberty which is of importance to the happiness of mankind. Like them, he could see no danger to liberty except from kings. A commonwealth, oppressed and pillaged by such men as Opimius and Verres, was free, because it had no king. A member of the Grand Council of Venice, who passed his whole life under tutelage and in fear, who could not travel where he chose, or visit whom he chose, or invest his property as he chose, whose path was beset with spies, who saw at the corners of the streets the mouth of bronze gaping for anonymous accusations against him, and whom the Inquisitors of State could, at any moment, and for any or no reason, arrest, torture, fling into the Grand Canal, was free, because he had no king. To curtail, for the benefit of a small privileged class, prerogatives which the sovereign possesses and ought to possess for the benefit of the whole nation, was the object on which Spencer's heart was set."

This character is brilliantly done, but we do not think it very fair or just. Another personage is painted with consummate skill and audacity—Cardinal Portocarrero, the minister of Charles the Second, king of Spain. We quote the material part:—

"Portocarrero was one of a race of men of whom we, happily for us, have seen very little, but whose influence has been the curse of Roman Catholic countries. He was like Sixtus the Fourth and Alexander the Sixth, a politician made out of an impious priest. Such politicians are generally worse than the worst of the laity, more merciless than any ruffian that can be found in camps, more dishonest than any pettifogger who haunts the tribunals. The sanctity of their profession has an unsanctifying influence on them. The lessons of the nursery, the habits of boyhood and of early youth, leave in the minds of the great majority of avowed infidels some traces of religion, which, in seasons of mourning and of sickness, become plainly discernible. But it is scarcely possible that any such trace should remain in the mind of the hypocrite who, during many years, is constantly going through what he considers as the mummery of preaching, saying mass, baptizing, shriving. When an ecclesiastic of this sort mixes in the contests of men of the world, he is indeed much to be dreaded as an enemy, but still more to be dreaded as an ally. From the pulpit where he daily employs his eloquence to embellish what he regards as fables, from the altar whence he daily looks down with secret scorn on the prostrate dupes who believe that he can turn a drop of wine into blood, from the confessional where he daily studies with cold and scientific attention to the morbid anatomy of guilty consciences, he brings to courts some talents which may move the envy of the more cunning and unscrupulous of lay courtiers; a rare skill in reading characters and in managing tempers, a rare art of dissimulation, a rare dexterity in insinuating what it is not safe to affirm or to propose in explicit terms. There are two feelings which often prevent an unprincipled layman from becoming utterly depraved and despicable, domestic feeling, and chivalrous feeling. His heart may be softened by the endearments of a family. His pride may revolt from the thought of doing what does not become a gentleman. But neither with the domestic feeling nor with the chivalrous feeling has the wicked priest any sympathy. His gown excludes him from the closest and most tender of human relations, and at the same time dispenses him from the observation of the fashionable code of honor. Such a priest was Portocarrero; and he seems to have been a consummate master of his craft."

Here, too, we have an assemblage of particulars, well chosen, well contrasted, full of interest, yet the man Portocarrero nowhere appears. How would Mr. Ward or Mr. Maclise set about a cartoon of which Cardinal Portocarrero was to be the central figure from the foregoing description?

We have spoken of Lord Macaulay's story of Spencer Cowper as likely to displease a certain religious community. This story is of deep interest; in its day it shook society like the case of Yelverton *versus* Yelverton:—

"At Hertford resided an opulent Quaker family named Stout. A pretty young woman of this family had lately sunk into a melancholy of a kind not very unusual in girls of strong sensibility and lively imagination who are subject to the restraints of austere religious societies. Her dress, her looks, her gestures, indicated the disturbance of her mind. She sometimes hinted her dislike of the sect to which she belonged. She complained that a canting waterman who was one of the brotherhood had held forth against her at a meeting. She threatened to go beyond sea, to throw herself out of window, to drown herself. To two or three of her associates she owned that she was in love; and on one occasion she plainly said that the man whom she loved was one whom she never could marry. In fact, the object of her fondness was Spencer Cowper, who was already married. She at length wrote to him in language which she never would have used if her intellect had not been disordered. He, like an honest man, took no advantage of her unhappy state of mind, and did his best to avoid her. His prudence mortified her to such a degree that on one occasion she went into fits. It was necessary, however, that he should see her, when he came to Hertford at the spring assizes of 1699. For he had been entrusted with some money which was due to her on mortgage. He called on her for this purpose late one evening, and delivered a bag of gold to her. She pressed him to be the guest of her family; but he excused himself and retired. The next morning she was found dead among the stakes of a mill-dam on the stream called the Priory River."

The coroner's jury found that Miss Stout had destroyed herself in a fit of temporary insanity; but the Stout family was not satisfied with their verdict. As Lord Macaulay puts it, "her family was unwilling to admit that she had shortened her own life, and looked about for somebody who might be accused of murdering her." At all events, their suspicions fell upon the man who had last been with her, who was suspected of having been her lover, and who certainly could not have been her lover without being also a villain. They got some evidence, such as it was:—

"It chanced that two attorneys and a scrivener, who had come down from town to the Hertford assizes, had been overheard, on that unhappy night, talking over their wine about the charms and flirtations of the handsome Quaker girl, in the light way in which such subjects are sometimes discussed even at the circuit tables and mess tables of our more refined generation. Some wild words, susceptible of a double meaning, were used about the way in which she had jilted one lover, and the way in which another lover would punish her for her coquetry. On no better grounds than these, her relations imagined that Spencer Cowper had, with the assistance of these three retainers of the law, strangled her, and thrown her corpse into the water. There was absolutely no evidence of the crime. There was no evidence that any one of the accused had any motive to commit such a crime; there was no evidence that Spencer Cowper had any connection with the persons who were said to be his accomplices. One of those persons, indeed, he had never seen. But no story is too absurd to be imposed on minds blinded by religious and political fanaticism. The Quakers and the Tories joined to raise a formidable clamor. The Quakers had, in those days, no scruples about capital punishments. They would, indeed, as Spencer Cowper said bitterly, but too truly, rather send four innocent men to the gallows than let it be believed that one who had their light within her had committed suicide. The Tories exulted in the prospect of winning two seats from the Whigs. The whole kingdom was divided between Stouts and Cowpers. At the summer assizes, Hertford was crowded with anxious faces from London, and from parts of England more distant than London. The prosecution was conducted with a malignity and unfairness which to us seems almost incredible; and, unfortunately, the dullest and most ignorant judge of the twelve was on the bench. Cowper defended himself and those who were said to be his accomplices with admirable ability and self-possession. His brother, much more distressed than himself, sat near him through the long agony of that day. The case against the prisoners rested chiefly on the vulgar error that a human body, found, as this poor girl's body had been found, floating in water, must have been thrown into the water while still alive. To prove this doctrine, the counsel for the crown called medical practitioners, of whom nothing is now known except that some of them had been active against the Whigs at Hertford elections. To confirm the evidence of these gentlemen, two or three sailors were put into the witness-box. On the other side, appeared an array of men of science whose names are still remembered. Among them was William Cowper, not a kinsman of the defendant, but the most celebrated anatomist that England had then produced. He was, indeed, the founder of a dynasty illustrious in the history of science, for he was the teacher of William Cheselden, and William Cheselden was the teacher of John Hunter. On the same side appeared Samuel Garth, who, among the physicians of the capital, had no rival except Radcliffe and Hans Sloane, the founder of the magnificent Museum which is one of the glories of our country. The attempt of the prosecutors to make the superstitions of the forecastle evidence for the purpose of taking away the lives of men was treated by these philosophers with just disdain. The stupid judge asked Garth what he could say in answer to the testimony of the seamen. 'My lord,' replied Garth, 'I say that they are mistaken. I will find seamen in abundance to swear that they have known whistling raise the wind.' The jury found the prisoners Not Guilty; and the report carried back to London by persons who had been present at the trial was that everybody applauded the verdict, and that even the Stouts seemed to be convinced of their error.

"It is certain, however, that the malevolence of the defeated party soon revived in all its energy. The lives of the four men who had just been absolved were again attacked by means of the most absurd and odious proceeding known to our old law, the appeal of murder. This attack, too, failed. Every artifice of chicane was at length exhausted; and nothing was left to the disappointed sect and the disappointed faction except to calumniate those whom it had been found impossible to murder. In a succession of libels, Spencer Cowper was held up to the execration of the public. But the public did him justice. He rose to high eminence in his profession: he at length took his seat, with general applause, on the judicial bench, and there distinguished himself by the humanity which he never failed to show to unhappy men who stood, as he had once stood, at the bar. Many who seldom trouble themselves about pedigrees may be interested by learning that he was the grandfather of that excellent man and excellent poet William Cowper, whose writings have long been peculiarly loved and prized by members of the religious community which, under a strong delusion, sought to slay his innocent progenitor."

In a note to this passage, Lord Macaulay expresses his surprise that no one of Cowper's many biographers, nor even Cowper himself, refers to this story about his grandfather—a fact at which we cannot pretend to share in any part of his lordship's surprise. Cowper himself would be extremely unlikely to recall such a circumstance as that his grandfather had been tried for murder. Southey, Chalmers, and Co. probably never heard the romantic and unpleasant tale.

No less romantic is the story of Lord Clancarty and his young wife, which is told by Lord Macaulay in his best style:—

"In the case of one great offender there were some circumstances which attracted general interest, and which might furnish a good subject to a novelist or dramatist. Near fourteen years before the time, Sunderland, then Secretary of State to Charles the Second, had married his daughter Lady Elizabeth Spencer to Donough Macarthy, Earl of Clancarty, the lord of an immense domain in Munster. Both the bridegroom and the bride were mere children, the bridegroom only fifteen, the bride only eleven. After the ceremony they were separated; and many years full of strange vicissitudes elapsed before they met again. The boy soon visited his estate in Ireland. He had been bred a member of the Church of England; but his opinions and his practice were loose. He found himself among kinsmen who were zealous Roman Catholics. A Roman Catholic king was on the throne. To turn Roman Catholic was the best recommendation to favor both at Whitehall and at Dublin Castle. Clancarty speedily changed his religion, and from a dissolute Protestant became a dissolute papist. After the Revolution he followed the fortunes of James; sate in the Celtic Parliament which met at the King's Inns; commanded a regiment in the Celtic army; was forced to surrender himself to Marlborough at Cork; was sent to England, and was imprisoned in the Tower. The Clancarty estates, which were supposed to yield a rent of not much less than ten thousand a year, were confiscated. They were charged with an annuity to the earl's brother, and with another annuity to his wife: but the greater part was bestowed by the king on Lord Woodstock, the eldest son of Portland. During some time, the prisoner's life was not safe. For the popular voice accused him of outrages for which the utmost license of civil war would not furnish a plea. It is said that he was threatened with an appeal of murder by the widow of a Protestant clergyman who had been put to death during the troubles. After passing three years in confinement, Clancarty made his escape to the Continent, was graciously received at St. Germains, aud was entrusted with the command of a corps of Irish refugees. When the treaty of Ryswick had put an end to the hope that the banished dynasty would be restored by foreign arms, he flattered himself that he might be able to make his peace with the English government. But he was grievously disappointed. The interest of his wife's family was undoubtedly more than sufficient to obtain a pardon for him. But on that interest he could not reckon. The selfish, base, covetous father-in-law was not at all desirous to have a high-born beggar and the posterity of a high-born beggar to maintain. The ruling passion of the brother-in-law was a stern and acrimonious party spirit. He could not bear to think that he was so nearly connected with an enemy of the Revolution and of the Bill of Rights, and would with pleasure have seen the odious tie severed even by the hand of the executioner. There was one, however, from whom the ruined, expatriated, proscribed young nobleman might hope to find a kind reception. He stole across the Channel in disguise, presented himself at Sunderland's door, and requested to see Lady Clancarty. He was charged, he said, with a message to her from her mother, who was then lying on a sick-bed at Windsor. By this fiction he obtained admission, made himself known to his wife, whose thoughts had probably been constantly fixed on him during many years, and prevailed on her to give him the most tender proofs of an affection sanctioned by the laws both of God and of man. The secret was soon discovered and betrayed by a waiting woman. Spencer learned that very night that his sister had admitted her husband to her apartment. The fanatical young Whig, burning with animosity which he mistook for virtue, and eager to emulate the Corinthian who assassinated his brother, and the Roman who passed sentence of death on his son, flew to Vernon's office, gave information that the Irish rebel, who had once already escaped from custody, was in hiding hard by, and procured a warrant and a guard of soldiers. Clancarty was found in the arms of his wife, and dragged to the Tower. She followed him and implored permission to partake his cell. These events produced a great stir throughout the society of London. Sunderland professed everywhere that he heartily approved of his son's conduct: but the public had made up its mind about Sunderland's veracity, and paid very little attention to his professions on this or on any other subject. In general, honorable men of both parties, whatever might be their opinion of Clancarty, felt great compassion for his mother who was dying of a broken heart, and his poor young wife who was begging piteously to be admitted within the Traitor's gate. Devonshire and Bedford joined with Ormond to ask for mercy. The aid of a still more powerful intercessor was called in. Lady Russell was esteemed by the king as a valuable friend; she was venerated by the nation generally as a saint, the widow of a martyr: and, when she deigned to solicit favors, it was scarcely possible that she should solicit in vain. She naturally felt a strong sympathy for the unhappy couple, who were parted by the walls of that gloomy old fortress in which she had herself exchanged the last sad endearments with one whose image was never absent from her. She took Lady Clancarty with her to the palace, obtained access to William, and put a petition into his hand. Clancarty was pardoned on condition that he should leave the kingdom and never return to it. A pension was granted to him, small when compared with the magnificent inheritance which he had forfeited, but quite sufficient to enable him to live like a gentleman on the Continent. He retired, accompanied by his Elizabeth, to Altona."

Such stories as the above sample make this volume of fragments very pleasant reading.

On the Darien scheme, and on the Scottish character in connection with it, we have this stately and elaborate paragraph:—

"That the Scotch are a people eminently intelligent, wary, resolute, and self-possessed is obvious to the most superficial observation. That they are a people peculiarly liable to dangerous fits of passion and delusions of the imagination is less generally acknowledged, but is not less true. The whole kingdom seemed to have gone mad. Paterson had acquired an influence resembling rather that of the founder of a new religion, that of a Mahomet, that of a Joseph Smith, than that of a commercial projector. Blind faith in a religion, fanatical zeal for a religion, are too common to astonish us. But such faith and zeal seem strangely out of place in the transactions of the money market. It is true that we are judging after the event. But before that event materials sufficient for the forming of a sound judgment were within the reach of all who cared to use them. It seems incredible that men of sense, who had only a vague and general notion of Paterson's scheme, should have staked every thing on the success of that scheme. It seems more incredible still that men to whom the details of that scheme had been confided should not have looked into any of the common books of history or geography in which an account of Darien might have been found, and should not have asked themselves the simple question, whether Spain was likely to endure a Scotch colony in the heart of her Transatlantic dominions. It was notorious that she claimed the sovereignty of the isthmus on specious, nay on solid, grounds. A Spaniard had been the first discoverer of the coast of Darien. A Spaniard had built a town and established a government on that coast. A Spaniard had, with great labor and peril, crossed the mountainous neck of land, had seen rolling beneath him the vast Pacific, never before revealed to European eyes, had descended, sword in hand, into the waves up to his girdle, and had there solemnly taken possession of sea and shore in the name of the crown of Castile. It was true that the region which Paterson described as a paradise had been found by the first Castilian settlers to be a land of misery and death. The poisonous air, exhaled from rank jungle and stagnant water, had compelled them to remove to the neighboring haven of Panama; and the Red Indians had been contemptuously permitted to live after their own fashion on the pestilential soil. But that soil was still considered, and might well be considered, by Spain as her own. In many countries there were tracts of morass, of mountain, of forest, in which governments did not think it worth while to be at the expense of maintaining order, and in which rude tribes enjoyed by connivance a kind of independence. It was not necessary for the members of the Company of Scotland trading to Africa and the Indies to look very far for an example. In some highland districts, not more than a hundred miles from Edinburgh, dwelt clans which had always regarded the authority of king, Parliament, Privy Council and Court of Session, quite as little as the aboriginal population of Darien regarded the authority of the Spanish viceroys and audiences. Yet it would surely have been thought an outrageous violation of public law in the king of Spain to take possession of Appin and Lochaber. And would it be a less outrageous violation of public law in the Scots to seize on a province in the very centre of his possessions, on the plea that this province was in the same state in which Appin and Lochaber had been during centuries."

The dishonesty of the Scotch is still further exposed:—

"So grossly unjust was Paterson's scheme; and yet it was less unjust than impolitic. Torpid as Spain had become, there was still one point on which she was exquisitely sensitive. The slightest encroachment of any other European power even on the outskirts of her American dominions sufficed to disturb her repose and to brace her paralyzed nerves. To imagine that she would tamely suffer adventures from one of the most insignificant kingdoms of the Old World to form a settlement in the midst of her empire, within a day's sail of Portobello on one side and of Carthagena on the other, was ludicrously absurd. She would have been just as likely to let them take possession of the Escurial. It was, therefore, evident that, before the new Company could even begin its commercial operations, there must be a war with Spain and a complete triumph over Spain. What means had the Company of waging such a war, and what chance of achieving such a triumph? The ordinary revenue of Scotland in time of peace was between sixty and seventy thousand a year. The extraordinary supplies granted to the crown during the war with France had amounted perhaps to as much more. Spain, it is true, was no longer the Spain of Pavia and Lepanto. But, even in her decay, she possessed in Europe resources which exceeded thirty-fold those of Scotland; and in America, where the struggle must take place, the disproportion was still greater. The Spanish fleets and arsenals were doubtless in wretched condition. But there were Spanish fleets; there were Spanish arsenals. The galleons, which sailed every year from Seville to the neighborhood of Darien, and from the neighborhood of Darien back to Seville, were in tolerable condition, and formed, by themselves, a considerable armament. Scotland had not a single ship of the line, nor a single dockyard where such a ship could be built. A marine sufficient to overpower that of Spain must be, not merely equipped and manned, but created. An armed force sufficient to defend the isthmus against the whole power of the viceroyalties of Mexico and Peru must be sent over five thousand miles of ocean. What was the charge of such an expedition likely to be? Oliver had, in the preceding generation, wrested a West Indian island from Spain; but, in order to do this, Oliver, a man who thoroughly understood the administration of war, who wasted nothing, and who was excellently served, had been forced to spend, in a single year, on his navy alone, twenty times the ordinary revenue of Scotland; and, since his days, war had been constantly becoming more and more costly. It was plain that Scotland could not alone support the charge of a contest with the enemy whom Paterson was bent on provoking. And what assistance was she likely to have from abroad? Undoubtedly the vast colonial empire and the narrow colonial policy of Spain were regarded with an evil eye by more than one great maritime power. But there was no great maritime power which would not far rather have seen the isthmus between the Atlantic and the Pacific in the hands of Spain than in the hands of the Darien Company. Lewis could not but dread whatever tended to aggrandize a state governed by William. To Holland the East India trade was as the apple of her eye. She had been the chief gainer by the discoveries of Gama; and it might be expected that she would do all that could be done by craft, and, if need were, by violence, rather than suffer any rival to be to her what she has been to Venice. England remained; and Paterson was sanguine enough to flatter himself that England might be induced to lend her powerful aid to the Company. He and Lord Belhaven repaired to London, opened an office in Clement's Lane, formed a Board of Directors auxiliary to the Central Board at Edinburgh, and invited the capitalists of the Royal Exchange to subscribe for the stock which had not been reserved for Scotchmen resident in Scotland. A few moneyed men were allured by the bait: but the clamor of the city was loud and menacing; and from the city a feeling of indignation spread fast through the country. In this feeling there was undoubtedly a large mixture of evil. National antipathy operated on some minds, religious antipathy on others. But it is impossible to deny that the anger which Paterson's schemes excited throughout the south of the island was, in the main, just and reasonable. Though it was not generally known in what precise spot his colony was to be planted, there could be little doubt that he intended to occupy some part of America; and there could be as little doubt that such occupation would be resisted. There would be a maritime war; and such a war Scotland had no means of carrying on. The state of her finances was such that she must be quite unable to fit out even a single squadron of moderate size. Before the conflict had lasted three months, she would have neither money nor credit left. These things were obvious to every coffee-house politician, and it was impossible to believe that they had escaped the notice of men so able and well informed as some who sate in the Privy Council and Parliament at Edinburgh. In one way only could the conduct of these schemers be explained. They meant to make a dupe and a tool of the Southron. The two British kingdoms were so closely connected, physically and politically, that it was scarcely possible for one of them to be at peace with a power with which the other was at war. If the Scotch drew King William into a quarrel England must, from regard to her own dignity which was bound up with his, support him in it. She was to be tricked into a bloody and expensive contest in the event of which she had no interest; nay, into a contest in which victory would be a greater calamity to her than defeat. She was to lavish her wealth and the lives of her seamen, in order that a set of cunning foreigners might enjoy a monopoly by which she would be the chief sufferer. She was to conquer and defend provinces for this Scotch Corporation; and her reward was to be that her merchants were to be undersold, her customers decoyed away, her exchequer beggared. There would be an end to the disputes between the old East India Company and the new East India Company; for both Companies would be ruined alike. The two great springs of revenue would be dried up together. What would be the receipt of the customs, what of the excise, when the vast magazines of sugar, rum, tobacco, coffee, chocolate, tea, spices, silks, muslins, all duty free, should be formed along the estuaries of the Forth and of the Clyde, and along the border from the mouth of the Esk to the mouth of the Tweed. What army, what fleet, would be sufficient to protect the interests of the government and of the fair trader when the whole kingdom of Scotland should be turned into one great smuggling establishment. Paterson's plan was simply this, that England should first spend millions in defence of the trade of his company, and should then be plundered of twice as many millions by means of that very trade."

We have spoken of Lord Macaulay's tendency to moralize and sermonize, not so much by way of objection as by way of characterization. The sermon, when we get it, is always eloquent, and the moral is very often sagacious and suggestive. We have a capital example in the whole presentation of Charles Montagu, Earl of Halifax. At the moment when this favorite of fortune is about to fall before his enemies, we are told:—

"Great wealth, suddenly acquired, is not often enjoyed with moderation, dignity, and good taste. It is therefore not impossible that there may have been some small foundation for the extravagant stories with which malecontent pamphleteers amused the leisure of malecontent squires. In such stories Montague played a conspicuous part. He contrived, it was said, to be at once as rich as Crœsus and as riotous as Mark Antony. His stud and his cellar were beyond all price. His very lacqueys turned up their noses at claret. He and his confederates were described as spending the immense sums of which they had plundered the public in banquets of four courses, such as Lucullus might have eaten in the Hall of Apollo. A supper for twelve Whigs, enriched by jobs, grants, bribes, lucky purchases and lucky sales of stock, was cheap at eighty pounds. At the end of every course all the fine linen on the table was changed. Those who saw the pyramids of choice wild fowl imagined that the entertainment had been prepared for fifty epicures at least. Only six birds' nests from the Nicobar Islands were to be had in London: and all the six, bought at an enormous price, were smoking in soup on the board. These fables were destitute alike of probability and of evidence. But Grub Street could devise no fable injurious to Montague which was not certain to find credence in more than half the manor houses and vicarages of England."

Of course, this hatred of Grub Street towards the great financier has to be explained, and the morals of such an antagonism between the wretched scribblers and the man of genius has to be put in a powerful light, which is done very much to the disadvantage and dismay of Grub Street:—

"It may seem strange that a man who loved literature passionately, and rewarded literary merit munificently, should have been more savagely reviled both in prose and verse than almost any other politician in our history. But there is really no cause for wonder. A powerful, liberal, and discerning protector of genius is very likely to be mentioned with honor long after his death, but is very likely also to be most brutally libelled during his life. In every age there will be twenty bad writers for one good one; and every bad writer will think himself a good one. A ruler who neglects all men of letters alike does not wound the self-love of any man of letters. But a ruler who shows favor to the few men of letters who deserve it inflicts on the many the miseries of disappointed hope, of affronted pride, of jealousy cruel as the grave. All the rage of a multitude of authors, irritated at once by the sting of want and by the sting of vanity, is directed against the unfortunate patron. It is true that the thanks and eulogies of those whom he has befriended will be remembered when the invectives of those whom he has neglected are forgotten. But in his own time the obloquy will probably make as much noise and find as much credit as the panegyric. The name of Mæcenas has been made immortal by Horace and Virgil, and is popularly used to designate an accomplished statesman, who lives in close intimacy with the greatest poets and wits of his time, and heaps benefits on them with the most delicate generosity. But it may well be suspected that, if the verses of Alpinus and Fannius, of Bavius and Mævius, had come down to us, we might see Mæcenas represented as the most niggardly and tasteless of human beings, nay, as a man who, on system, neglected and persecuted all intellectual superiority. It is certain that Montague was thus represented by contemporary scribblers. They told the world in essays, in letters, in dialogues, in ballads, that he would do nothing for anybody without being paid either in money or in some vile services; that he not only never rewarded merit, but hated it whenever he saw it; that he practised the meanest arts for the purpose of depressing it; that those whom he protected and enriched were not men of ability and virtue, but wretches distinguished only by their sycophancy and their low debaucheries. And this was said of the man who made the fortune of Joseph Addison and of Isaac Newton."

Of course, there is a splendid exaggeration in all this. Many of those who attacked Montagu were his equals in parts and learning; and it is quite gratuitous to say, that Montagu made the fortunes of Joseph Addison and Isaac Newton. He was certainly open to the attacks of his malignant and unrelenting enemies. But, in Lord Macaulay's eyes, some men can do no wrong, other men can do nothing right. Somers is all light; Churchill all shade. We see them in these pages as we find them in the party pamphlets of their day; for Lord Macaulay was a politician before he became an historian; and he fights for his side like the hottest writer in the contemporary newspapers. King William's coarseness, cruelty, and sensuality are passed without reproof. When Louis proposes to himself to offer William a pension, on condition of his entering into a new treaty of Dover and dismissing his troublesome and niggardly Parliament for good, Lord Macaulay considers it "a significant circumstance." He spends no withering sarcasm on the long descent in virtue which laid William open to the suspicion of being capable of such an act of political treachery and personal corruption. Suppose the French king had proposed to himself to buy up Marlborough!

This volume, which suggests so many topics of interest, closes with a carefully prepared sketch of William's death—finished, or nearly finished, we think, as regards the mere literary art. This sketch we transfer to our pages:—

"Meanwhile reports about the state of the king's health were constantly becoming more and more alarming. His medical advisers, both English and Dutch, were at the end of their resources. He had consulted by letter all the most eminent physicians of Europe; and, as he was apprehensive that they might return flattering answers if they knew who he was, he had written under feigned names. To Fagon he had described himself as a parish priest. Fagon replied, somewhat bluntly, that such symptoms could have only one meaning, and that the only advice which he had to give to the sick man was to prepare himself for death. Having obtained this plain answer, William consulted Fagon again without disguise, and obtained some prescriptions which were thought to have a little retarded the approach of the inevitable hour.

"But the great king's days were numbered. Headaches and shivering fits returned on him almost daily. He still rode and even hunted; but he had no longer that firm seat or that perfect command of the bridle for which he had once been renowned. Still all his care was for the future. The filial respect and tenderness of Albemarle had been almost a necessary of life to him. But it was of importance that Heinsius should be fully informed both as to the whole plan of the next campaign and as to the state of the preparations. Albemarle was in full possession of the king's views on these subjects. He was therefore sent to the Hague. Heinsius was at that time suffering from indisposition, which was indeed a trifle when compared with the maladies under which William was sinking. But in the nature of William there was none of that selfishness which is the too common vice of invalids. On the twentieth of February he sent to Heinsius a letter in which he did not even allude to his own sufferings and infirmities. 'I am,' he said, 'infinitely concerned to learn that your health is not yet quite reestablished. May God be pleased to grant you a speedy recovery. I am unalterably your good friend, William.' Those were the last lines of that long correspondence. On the twentieth of February William was ambling on a favorite horse, named Sorrel, through the park of Hampton Court. He urged his horse to strike into a gallop just at the spot where a mole had been at work. Sorrel stumbled on the mole-hill, and went down on his knees. The king fell off, and broke his collar bone. The bone was set; and he returned to Kensington in his coach. The jolting of the rough roads of that time made it necessary to reduce the fracture again. To a young and vigorous man such an accident would have been a trifle. But the frame of William was not in a condition to bear even the slightest shock. He felt that his time was short, and grieved with a grief such as only noble spirits feel, to think that he must leave his work but half finished. It was possible that he might still live until one of his plans should be carried into execution. He had long known that the relation in which England and Scotland stood to each other was at best precarious, and often unfriendly, and that it might be doubted whether, in an estimate of the British power, the resources of the smaller country ought not to be deducted from those of the larger. Recent events had proved that, without doubt, the two kingdoms could not possibly continue for another year to be on the terms on which they had been during the preceding century, and that there must be between them either absolute union or deadly enmity. Their enmity would bring frightful calamities, not on themselves alone, but on all the civilized world. Their union would be the best security for the prosperity of both, for the internal tranquillity of the island, for the just balance of power among European states, and for the immunities of all Protestant countries. On the 28th of February the Commons listened with uncovered heads to the last message that bore William's sign manual. An unhappy accident, he told them, had forced him to make to them in writing a communication which he would gladly have made from the throne. He had in the first year of his reign, expressed his desire to see an union accomplished between England and Scotland. He was convinced that nothing could more conduce to the safety and happiness of both. He should think it his peculiar felicity if, before the close of his reign, some happy expedient could be devised for making the two kingdoms one; and he, in the most earnest manner, recommended the question to the consideration of the Houses.

"It was resolved that the message should be taken into consideration on Saturday the 7th of March. But on the 1st of March humors of menacing appearance showed themselves in the king's knee. On the 4th of March he was attacked by fever; on the 5th his strength failed greatly; and on the 6th he was scarcely kept alive by cordials. The Abjuration Bill and a money bill were awaiting his assent. That assent he felt that he should not be able to give in person. He therefore ordered a commission to be prepared for his signature. His hand was now too weak to form the letters of his name, and it was suggested that a stamp should be prepared. On the 7th of March the stamp was ready. The lord keeper and the clerks of the Parliament came according to usage, to witness the signing of the commission. But they were detained some hours in the ante-chamber while he was in one of the paroxysms of his malady. Meanwhile the Houses were sitting. It was Saturday, the 7th, the day on which the Commons had resolved to take into consideration the question of the union with Scotland. But that subject was not mentioned. It was known that the king had but a few hours to live; and the members asked each other anxiously whether it was likely that the Abjuration and money bills would be passed before he died. After sitting long in the expectation of a message, the Commons adjourned till six in the afternoon. By that time William had recovered himself sufficiently to put the stamp on the parchment which authorized his commissioners to act for him. In the evening, when the Houses had assembled, Black Rod knocked. The Commons were summoned to the bar of the Lords; the commission was read, the Abjuration Bill and the Malt Bill became laws, and both Houses adjourned till nine o'clock in the morning of the following day. The following day was Sunday. But there was little chance that William would live through the night. It was of the highest importance that, within the shortest possible time after his decease, the successor designated by the Bill of Rights and the Act of Succession should receive the homage of the Estates of the Realm, and be publicly proclaimed in the Council; and the most rigid Pharisee in the Society for the Reformation of Manners could hardly deny that it was lawful to save the state even on the sabbath. The king meanwhile was sinking fast. Albemarle had arrived at Kensington from the Hague, exhausted by rapid travelling. His master kindly bade him go to rest for some hours, and then summoned him to make his report. That report was in all respects satisfactory. The states-general were in the best temper; the troops, the provisions and the magazines were in the best order. Every thing was in readiness for an early campaign. William received the intelligence with the calmness of a man whose work was done. He was under no illusion as to his danger. 'I am fast drawing,' he said, 'to my end.' His end was worthy of his life. His intellect was not for a moment clouded. His fortitude was the more admirable because he was not willing to die. He had very lately said to one of those whom he most loved: 'You know that I never feared death; there have been times when I should have wished it; but, now that this great new prospect is opening before me, I do wish to stay here a little longer.' Yet no weakness, no querulousness, disgraced the noble close of that noble career. To the physicians the king returned his thanks graciously and gently. 'I know that you have done all that skill and learning could do for me: but the case is beyond your art; and I submit.' From the words which escaped him he seemed to be frequently engaged in mental prayer. Burnet and Tenison remained many hours in the sick-room. He professed to them his firm belief in the truth of the Christian religion, and received the sacrament from their hands with great seriousness. The antechambers were crowded all night with lords and privy councillors. He ordered several of them to be called in, and exerted himself to take leave of them with a few kind and cheerful words. Among the English who were admitted to his bedside were Devonshire and Ormond. But there were in the crowd those who felt as no Englishman could feel, friends of his youth who had been true to him, and to whom he had been true, through all vicissitudes of fortune; who had served him with unalterable fidelity when his Secretaries of State, his Treasury and his Admiralty had betrayed him; who had never on any field of battle, or in an atmosphere tainted with loathsome and deadly disease, shrunk from placing their own lives in jeopardy to save his, and whose truth he had at the cost of his own popularity rewarded with bounteous munificence. He strained his feeble voice to thank Auverquerque for the affectionate and loyal services of thirty years. To Albemarle he gave the keys of his closet, and of his private drawers. 'You know,' he said, 'what to do with them.' By this time he could scarcely respire. 'Can this,' he said to the physicians, 'last long?' He was told that the end was approaching. He swallowed a cordial, and asked for Bentinck. Those were his last articulate words. Bentinck instantly came to the bedside, bent down, and placed his ear close to the king's mouth. The lips of the dying man moved; but nothing could be heard. The king took the hand of his earliest friend, and pressed it tenderly to his heart. In that moment, no doubt, all that had cast a slight passing cloud over their long and pure friendship was forgotten. It was now between seven and eight in the morning. He closed his eyes, and gasped for breath. The bishops knelt down and read the commendatory prayer. When it ended William was no more. When his remains were laid out, it was found that he wore next to his skin a small piece of black silk ribbon. The lords in waiting ordered it to be taken off. It contained a gold ring and a lock of the hair of Mary."

There is little more to say of these splendid fragments from an unfulfilled design. Lady Trevelyan has done very wisely in leaving them to speak for themselves. The form in which they appear is peculiar—text wholly detached from notes or references, as if they had a separate and independent existence in space. Thus, the statements now made are unsupported by any thing like originals. Lord Macaulay's plan was, to compose his narrative without having his authorities open before him, and, when his story was told, to stick in the references here and there. Our glimpse into the secrets of his plan of composition may help us to understand some of the peculiarities of his text. There is a good index, and, altogether, this "History of England" is in as perfect a state as it is now capable of attaining.

The bronze effigy of the great Napoleon, in cocked hat and great-coat, standing in his jack-boots on the pinnacle of the column in the Place Vendome, is doomed to descend from that lofty eminence. The original design of that pillar was strictly in accordance with classic precedent, and as Trajan and Antonius, in their imperial corslet or civilian toga, stood forth amid the monuments of Roman grandeur proudly surveying the aggregate of magnificence and looking down on the busy Forum swarming with citizens over whom they kept watch and ward, there was some congruity in the conception. The statue of Napoleon I., as erected in the first instance, was of marble, and robed in the folds of Roman imperialism. On the entrance of the Cossacks, and of Blucher in 1814, a gang of returned *émigrés* from London, pot valiant under the allied flag, procured a rope and with a long and strong pull, extending to Rue Rivoli, hauled off the marble from its exalted pediment to be smashed on the square below. Louis Philippe, with a taste as questionable as the policy, stuck him up in his present shape, the modern costume destroying all the ideal, and changing an apotheosis into a sort of pillory. It was remarked years ago, that seen from the environs of Paris the emperor looked like a benighted tiler that had lost his way on the roofs of the houses. Napoleon III. inspected on Wednesday, in the studio of M. Dumont, the new marble figure, modelled on the antique, which is to replace the present incumbent, or encumbrance.—*Globe Paris Correspondent.*

The *Journal of Rome*, of the 27th ult., announces that the sum received for Peter's Pence, from all parts of the Catholic world, amounts to 2,500,000 scudi (the scudo is 5f. 35c.). But it adds, that this sum is far outweighed by the vast number of prayers that have been offered up by the faithful "for the triumph of the Church over her enemies."

From Chambers's Journal.

HOW THE MONEY WEARS.

Of the way in which money "burns a hole in the pocket," it is unnecessary to speak; but there is a more imperceptible vanishing than this, of which none of us are aware of while it is going on, and which can only be detected by cumulative results. Whenever one coin rubs against another, a small portion of metal leaves each; we can never find, in our pockets, purses, or hands the minute fragments thus abraded, but *there they are*, whether we can see them or not. They do wear away, and they will wear, though the action is too slow to attract our notice. It is not an important point in our every-day life. A pound is a pound, a shilling is a shilling, so long as it will pass for a pound's worth or shilling's worth; nor does it matter to us whether the coin, when we part with it, weighs a few grains less than when we obtained it. But when the Bank of England, as is the case now and then, finds it expedient to weigh all the gold taken over its counter, and to deduct something for the sin of "light gold," then we obtain an idea of the practical depreciation of the rubbing process.

The first occasion on which the attention of the bank authorities was directed to this subject appears to have been in 1787. The silver coins were then in a wretched state, battered, crooked, thin, and their devices almost illegible. Taking some of the specimens at random, it was found that one Troy pound of shillings required 78 to turn the balance, whereas a pound of new shillings numbered only 62. A pound weight of sixpences, in a similar way, required 194—instead of 124—thus showing how very large a quantity of silver had gone, somewhere or other, from each coin. The loss in the sixpences was greater than in the shillings, partly because those coins were thinner, and because they changed hands more frequently in the operations of retail commerce. The crowns and half-crowns, being less in use, had suffered less; the former had lost, on an average, about 1 in 30, and the latter 1 in 14; whereas the shillings had lost weight in the ratio of 1 in 5, and the sixpences 1 in 3. The coins were allowed to run their usual course, changing hands in the wonderfully rapid way which English commerce illustrates, for a further period of eleven years. Large quantities, taken promiscuously, were weighed in 1798. It was now found that the shillings had suffered in the usual way from this hard work; 83 of them were needed to make up a Troy pound, instead of 78, as at the former weighing; while 201 sixpences were required, instead of 194. The crowns and half-crowns had also suffered, though in a smaller degree. Taking into account the whole amount of diminution since the first issue of the bright new coins, it was found that the crowns had, on an average, lost 3 per cent of their weight, the half-crowns 10 per cent, the shillings 24 per cent, and the sixpences 38 per cent.

It must not be inferred that the whole of this loss was due to legitimate wear and tear; in fact, the bank directors knew that it was not; and one of the objects they had in view was, to determine in how large a degree they and the people were robbed by knavery. Such things are not so much done now; but in those days the current coin of the realm was clipped and "sweated" in an audacious way. It was punched through the middle, scraped round the edge, and otherwise shorn of its proper dimensions and value. There were many reasons for wishing to know how much of the lessening in weight was due to such causes, and how much to legitimate wear and tear. A committee was appointed by the Privy Council, "to take into consideration the state of the coins of this kingdom; having, among other circumstances, remarked the considerable loss which the gold coin appears to have sustained by wear within certain periods; and being desirous to ascertain whether this loss was occasioned by any defect, either in the quality of the standard gold, or in the figure or impression of the coins." The committee, whose labors were confined to the gold coinage only, invited the co-operation of Mr. Cavendish and Mr. Hatchett, two distinguished Fellows of the Royal Society; and those *savants* were engaged on the inquiry from 1798 to 1801.

The first problem undertaken for solution was this: Does very soft and ductile gold, or gold made as hard as is compatible with the processes of coining, suffer the most by wear, under the various circumstances of friction to which coin is subjected in the course of circulation? The two philosophers prepared a very large series of alloys of gold with baser metals. Arsenic, antimony, zinc, cobalt, nickel, manganese, bismuth, lead, tin, iron, platinum, copper, silver—all were tried, combined in various proportions with the precious metal. They next exposed these alloys to all kinds of vicissitudes, to find which bore themselves most bravely. Some of the metals evaporated too much when heated; some were badly colored; some too brittle; some too soft. The worst of all the alloys were found to be those in which the gold was combined with bismuth, lead, or antimony; while the best of all was that which the united opinions of the governments of Europe had already determined as the most appropriate—namely, a small admixture of silver with the pure gold. The philosophers rubbed away for months, to see which alloy bore the ordeal most unflinchingly. They fixed twenty-eight pieces in a frame, and rubbed them with twenty-eight similar pieces fixed in another frame. This rubbing was continued for the enormous number of *half a million times*, with pieces or discs made of the several kinds of alloy above enumerated. The result was, that standard gold, consisting of twenty-two of pure gold to two of silver, suffered less by the abrasion than any other alloy, and also less than pure gold itself—a satisfactory result, showing that accumulated experience had taught the right thing to the money-makers. Lest it should have happened that this systematic sort of rubbing failed to imitate the various kinds of friction to which coin is usually exposed, the philosophers resolved to toss about their experimental pieces more indiscriminately. They prepared a box, so adjusted upon a pivot that it could be rotated. Into this box they put forty blanks of pure gold, forty of standard gold, forty in which the alloy was copper, and forty in which the gold was alloyed both with silver and copper—all the pieces having been first carefully weighed. The box was then rotated more than seventy thousand times, causing the pieces to rub against each other in every possible direction. The result confirmed that which had before been arrived at—the standard gold suffered less by the friction than any other combination.

In 1807, the authorities at the Mint, satisfied as to the fitness of the standard, recurred to the subject of wear and tear, and sought to inquire how much the coin had really been depreciated in value during its busy course in the scenes of commerce. One thousand guineas, taken from a banker's, were found on an average to be 19*s.* per £100 short in value. Of one hundred guineas obtained from a retail tradesman, the average deficiency was 23*s.* per £100. Of six hundred half-guineas, it was 42*s.*; but on three hundred seven-shilling pieces—a coin very little in use—it was only 17*s.* per £100. Mr. Jacob, a great authority on all matters relating to the precious metals, was of opinion that the gold coins thus examined had been in average circulation about ten years; and from further considering the proportion which the half-guineas bore to the guineas, and the relative wear of each, he stated his belief that the average *annual* loss of the coins by abrasion, consequent on the usual commercial dealings, was about 1-950th part of the whole.

Many years elapsed before any further inquiry took place into this curious matter. In 1826, the Mint authorities wished to ascertain how much loss by abrasion had been occasioned in gold and silver coined subsequent to 1816. One odd result of weighing was, that the *dirt* on three hundred pieces of money amounted to seven grains, if the coins were half-sovereigns; to twenty-two grains, if they were half-crowns; and to intermediate amounts, if other coins were experimented on. It was next found that gold coined in 1817 had lost about 5*s.* per cent on an average of sovereigns and half-sovereigns; while that coined in 1825 had suffered an average loss of 2*s.* per cent. Mr. Jacob, commenting on these results, expressed a belief that the coins had been in use about two years and a half on the average, and that they indicated a wear 1-800th part per annum. This was a greater ratio than that (1-950th) which he had before observed; but he accounted for it thus: that the annual average wear for two years and a half is greater than that for ten years; because it has been found that sovereigns lose more in the first than in any subsequent year, probably on account of the numerous sharp projecting points of the device. The shillings had lost from 5*s.* to 46*s.* per cent in value, according as they had been one year or ten years in circulation. The sixpences had lost more than this, the half-crowns less. Mr. Jacob, not choosing to be beaten by the complexity of the subject, examined all the results which had been obtained on all the coins, and in all the years; and he arrived at a conclusion that, under the usual conditions of English commerce, *silver* coins depreciate 1-200th part every year; that is, four or five times as much as *gold* coins. Some persons believe the loss to be still higher, but Mr. Jacob was very careful in his calculations. All agree that silver coins wear more than gold, because the same degree of friction will produce a greater diminution in weight, and because silver coins are more incessantly in circulation than those of gold.

Nothing further, so far as we are aware, occurred in relation to this subject until the year 1859, when, in accordance with a wish expressed by the governor of the Bank of England, Mr. W. Miller, first-assistant cashier, and Mr. J. Miller of the Gold Weighing Office, made an investigation into the condition of the gold and silver coinage, so far as concerned loss of weight by wear and tear. In order to test this matter carefully, it was considered desirable to select coins issued in a particular year, that each year's work of destruction might be duly measured. Mr. J. Miller collected, from parcels sent to the Bank on different days and from different places, one hundred sovereigns of the date 1820, all of which had therefore been knocking about the world for nearly forty years; he found the loss of weight by rubbing, estimated in money, to be £1, 6*s*. 7*d*.—somewhat more than three pence per sovereign on an average. Mr. W. Miller made a very elaborate series of experiments on two kinds of gold coin, and three of silver. He collected a large number coined between the years 1817 and 1825, and considered that 1822 would present about the average date of the whole. They had thus been in use somewhat more than thirty-six years. Then he determined how much weight of each denomination of coin was equivalent to £100 at the time of coining, and how much weight was equivalent to the same sum in 1859, from whence he easily deduced the amount of loss. The reader would not thank us for overloading the page with figures; but there is a mode of stating the matter which will appeal to the eye and the judgment at once. Mr. Miller said, in effect: "These coins have been playing their part in commerce during a period of thirty-six years; if they continued wearing at the same rate for a whole century, how much would they lose in value?" He answered his own problem thus: "£100 worth of sovereigns would lose about £3, 10*s*. in value and weight; of half-sovereigns, £6, 12*s*.; of half-crowns, £13, 12*s*.; of shillings, £36, 14*s*.; and of sixpences, £50, 19*s*.—that is to say, these last would be a little less than half their proper weight, after passing from hand to hand for a hundred years."

In a letter addressed by Mr. W. Miller to the deputy-governor of the Bank towards the close of 1859, the following interesting remarks occur touching the coinage generally: "Sovereigns issued from the Mint in different reigns, or at different times, do not wear equally well. They wear more or less, according to the difference in the alloy, in the impression, or in the temper of the metal. The sovereigns of George III. were much better than those of subsequent reigns, from their being alloyed with silver [without any copper?]. When the impression is simple, without many minute prominences, which soon rub off, the coin wears much better. The milling, too, round the rim, loses much by wear; a plain rim, with letters round it, would wear better. If the metal of a coinage should happen to be more soft or brittle than usual, the coins would not wear so well. The first coinage of a new reign will, after a long period, be found in better condition that one of two or three years subsequent, from the fact of many coins of the former being hoarded as curiosities. The wear of the coin depends on the manner in which it is used in circulation. A sovereign passed at the west end of London meets with better usage in such shops as jewellers' or milliners', than it does when rung with a strong arm on the counter of a potato-salesman, where it would be rubbed by the sand. In commercial towns, the coin becomes light sooner than in other places, not only from its greater circulation, but in consequence of the rough usage it undergoes in being so often thrown into bankers' scales and drawers. During a time of great commercial activity, as the coin would be used more, of course its wear would be greater than at other times. It is probable that the coin issued during the last ten years has become light more quickly than that issued in the preceding ten years, and it might perhaps be found that our coin becomes light more rapidly than the coin of other countries. I do not know whether the old process of sweating the coin by shaking it in a bag be ever practised now; but we have constant evidence of the sovereigns being reduced by acid, and also by being filed in many ingenious ways."

This is how the money wears!

DEATH OF JUDGE MCLEAN.

It is with extreme regret that we record that Hon. John McLean, one of the associate justices of the Supreme Court of the United States, died at Cincinnati on Thursday.

Judge McLean was born in Morris County, New Jersey, in the year 1785. Four years later his father emigrated to Virginia, whence he removed to Kentucky, finally settling in what is now the State of Ohio. Here his son received such education as the country then afforded, laboring on the farm meanwhile, and refusing to allow his education to be a burden to his father. The son, when eighteen years old, procured a place in the county clerk's office in Cincinnati, and studied law under Arthur St. Clare, once governor of the North-west Territory. In the fall of 1807 he was admitted to the bar, and began to practise law at Lebanon, Ohio, having in the previous spring married a daughter of Dr. Edwards, formerly of South Carolina. In 1812 he was elected to Congress as a supporter of Mr. Madison's administration, was re-elected in 1814, and in 1816 resigned to accept a seat on the Supreme bench of Ohio, being succeeded in Congress by General Harrison. He remained on the bench six years, evincing those high judicial qualities for which he has since been distinguished. He was appointed Commissioner of the Land Office in 1822, the Postmaster General in 1823 by President Munroe, and continued in the latter office through the administration of John Quincy Adams.

It has always been understood that General Jackson was desirous of obtaining McLean in his Cabinet, and that the latter if he had chosen might have had a place of higher rank, but that his feeling of delicacy and his native independence prevented. However that may be, it was early found that he could not be retained in the Cabinet, and the President therefore offered him the place then vacant upon the Supreme bench of the United States, for which Mr. Crittenden had been nominated by Mr. Adams but rejected by the Senate.

Judge McLean accepted the nomination, was confirmed and took his seat at the January term in 1830, and continued until his death one of the leading members of the court, preeminent for indefatigable industry, fidelity, courage, judicial acumen and research. He was the contemporary of Marshal and Story, and was at the time of his death the senior member of the court. The extraordinary growth of the states composing his judicial circuit (Ohio, Indiana, Illinois, and Michigan) caused such a vast increase of business in the United States courts, that the later years of his judicial life were extremely laborious, and taxed his great powers, both physical and mental, to the utmost. To the vast amount of labor devolved upon him, must also be added the fact that the exigencies of western progress, and especially the development of admiralty practice on the lakes, called for the decision of great numbers of original and perplexing questions. In the discharge of these duties and of his great responsibilities as a judge in the court of appeals, Judge McLean was always prompt, untiring, judicious and conscientious. It is to be feared, however, that the incessant labor of his position materially shortened his days.

Judge McLean probably occupied a more conspicuous position in political affairs than has fallen to the lot of any other member of the court of which he was a judge. In the time of the Whig party he was often looked to as a possible candidate, although neither then nor at any other time did he transgress the proprieties of his station by entering into political strife. His sound views upon the slavery question, and his well-known moderation and acknowledged devotion to the Union made him a leading candidate for the Republican nomination in 1856, and subsequent events indicate that had he received it Mr. Buchanan would never have been President. His firm stand in the case of Dred Scott and his subsequent resolute adherence to his position made him one of the most popular men in the Northern States, and in 1860 he was again prominent as a candidate for nomination. His name, however, is now no longer to be remembered in connection with political warfare, but as that of a great and good judge. Thirty-one years of upright official conduct and stainless private life have made the country rejoice that he has lived, and cause it to mourn sincerely at its loss now, when he has died, full of years and of honors.—*Daily Advertiser*, 6 *April.*

THE LIVING AGE.

No. 884.—11 May, 1861.

CONTENTS.

PUBLISHED EVERY SATURDAY BY

LITTELL, SON, & CO., BOSTON.

THE HUNTERS OF KENTUCKY.

YE gentlemen and ladies fair,
  Who grace this famous city,
Just listen, if you've time to spare,
  While I rehearse a ditty;
And for the opportunity;
  Conceive yourselves quite lucky,
For 'tis not often that you see
  A hunter from Kentucky.
Oh, Kentucky, the hunters of Kentucky,
  The hunters of Kentucky.

We are a hardy free-born race,
  Each man to fear a stranger,
Whate'er the game, we join in chase,
  Despising toil and danger;
And if a darting foe annoys,
  Whate'er his strength and forces,
We'll show him that Kentucky boys
  Are "alligator horses."

I s'pose you read it in the prints,
  How Packenham attempted
To make Old Hickery Jackson wince,
  But soon his scheme repented;
For we with rifles ready cocked,
  Thought such occasion lucky,
And soon around the general flocked
  The hunters of Kentucky.

You've heard, I s'pose, how New Orleans
  Is famed for wealth and beauty—
Its girls are of all hues, it seems,
  From snowy white to sooty;
So Packenham he made his brags,
  If he in fight was lucky,
He'd have their girls and cotton bags,
  In spite of old Kentucky.

But Jackson, he was wide awake,
  And wasn't scared at trifles;
For well he knew what aim we take,
  With our Kentucky rifles;
He led us down to Cypress Swamp,
  The ground was low and mucky;
There stood John Bull, in martial pomp,
  And here was Old Kentucky.

A bank was raised to hide our breast,
  Not that we thought of dying,
But then we always like to rest,
  Unless the game is flying;
Behind it stood our little force—
  None wished it to be greater,
For every man was half a horse,
  And half an alligator.

They did not let our patience tire,
  Before they showed their faces—
We did not choose to waste our fire,
  So snugly kept our places;
But when so near we saw them wink,
  We thought it time to stop them;
And 'twould have done you good, I think,
  To see Kentucky pop them.

They found, at last, 'twas vain to fight,
  Where lead was all their booty,
And so they wisely took to flight,
  And left us all the beauty.
And now, if danger e'er annoys,
  Remember what our trade is,
Just send for us Kentucky boys,
  And we'll protect you, ladies.
Oh, Kentucky, the hunters of Kentucky,
  The hunters of Kentucky.

—*Poetical Works of Samuel Wordsworth.*

RUTH'S MEDITATIONS.

[*Kneeling and rocking the cradle.*]

WHAT is the little one thinking about?
Very wonderful things, no doubt,
    Unwritten history!
    Unfathomable mystery!
Yet he laughs and cries, and eats and drinks,
And chuckles and crows, and nods and winks,
As if his head were as full of kinks
And curious riddles as any sphinx!
    Warped by colic, and wet by tears,
    Punctured by pins and tortured by fears,
Our little nephew will lose two years;
    And he'll never know
    Where the summers go—
He need not laugh, for he'll find it so!
Who can tell what a baby thinks?
Who can follow the gossamer links,
  By which the manikin feels his way
Out from the shore of the great unknown.
Blind, and wailing, and alone,
  Into the light of day?—
  What does he think of his mother's eyes?
What does he think of his mother's hair?
  What of the cradle roof that flies
Forward and backward through the air?
  What does he think of his mother's breast—
  Cup of his life and couch of his rest?
What does he think when her quick embrace
Presses his hand and buries his face,
Deep where the heart-throbs sink and swell
With a tenderness she can never tell,
  Though she murmurs the words
  Of all the birds—
Words she has learned to murmur well?
    Now he thinks he'll go to sleep!
    I can see the shadow creep
    Over his eyes, in soft eclipse,
    Over his brow, and over his lips,
    Out to his little finger-tips!
    Softly sinking down he goes!
    Down he goes! Down he goes!
[*Rising and carefully retreating to her seat.*]
See! He is hushed in sweet repose!

From The Christian Remembrancer.

1. *Autobiography and Correspondence of Mrs. Delany.* London: Bentley.
2. *Autobiography, Letters, and Literary Remains of Mrs. Piozzi.* London: Longmans.

THERE is at least an apparent propriety in taking the works at the head of our article together. They belong to the same class of literature, and thus seem to give one another importance and a purpose. They may be said exactly to divide the gossip of the eighteenth century between them, and to give us a picture of its social life, such as only women can give, and which very materially adds to our power of realizing its tone and aspect; by turns modifying, correcting, and strengthening our previous impressions, and giving life to the whole. Diffuse and often trifling as both works are, full of superfluous and unnecessary matter, they yet leave us with ideas enlarged; we feel that we have learned something; yet both seem to require apology, and need to be accounted for. We are disposed of each in turn to ask why it is published now. What circumstances then can at the same time have brought to light letters and documents which, having slumbered so long, might seem to have passed the period of possible resuscitation? Each editor has no doubt a good and different reason to give for the intrusion upon the latter half of our century of a name of such mild lustre even in her own day as Mrs. Delany's, and of such questionable celebrity as that of Mrs. Piozzi, and may establish a distinct claim on public attention; but one thing is certain, that if the obsolete system of buying books before we read them still prevailed we should have no such coincidence. Neither of these old ladies could possibly have appeared again upon the scene. Public libraries generally, and Mr. Mudie in particular, must be the occasion of such publications as those before us; and we recognise something even judicial in the three enormous volumes, two thousand ample pages in all, which embody Mrs. Delany's experience. It must be for Mr. Mudie's sins that a woman's private letters of more than a hundred years old should be given to the world in such unmeasured unexampled profusion. No person whose name and family does not occur in the select and aristocratic circle of her friends and intimates, would dream of buying a mass of correspondence, half of which was devoted to trifles so perfectly immaterial and unimportant at the time, except to the person addressed, that no lapse of years can make it curious, or give it adventitious value. But every reader of the literature of the day will want to see the books which hold in solution a great deal that is both curious and interesting. It is just the work to be in universal demand; not to be read through, page by page,—though after all that is the best way if people have the art of reading quickly,—but to be dipped into for the chance of a well-known name, a telling anecdote, a trait of obsolete manners, a glimpse of old-world splendors. Mr. Mudie is pledged to a supply in proportion to the demand wherever his sectarian convictions do not interfere with the liberality of his scheme—he must therefore have had to order a very large and costly supply of Mrs. Delany's correspondence. Again the prestige that still attends Dr. Johnson's name makes it a necessity that every one should know the last facts that can possibly be told of him from a reliable, or at any rate a genuine source, if it can be done without loading our shelves with more books about him; for his sake therefore the reader willingly skims the poor remains and gleanings of long-ago gathered recollections; and submits to follow the details of Mrs. Piozzi's sprightly, but not very reverent old age, for the chance of passing allusions and fresh combinations of names whose sole interest now lies in their association with the great social wonder of his time. Probably these volumes will lie but a short time within each one's reach—the suggestions therefore of a more systematic reading may supply some of the deficiencies of a passing and careless perusal.

The attempt to revive the more than half-forgotten names of two old ladies, will at least have a temporary success. Both books are suggestive, as the picture of any life whatever must be, but these had both a distinctness and a vigor in their several ways, and were passed under such circumstances of note and observation as fit them particularly for subjects of speculation. Regarding life not as a probation, but as a performance, they show us some of the elements of success and of failure in a marked manner. While a certain parallel may be drawn between the external position of these two women, the events of their lives, the place they once held, the notice and admiration they once excited, and the intellectual superiority attributed to them; the mode in which they used the advantages and met the difficulties of their lot, constitute as strong a difference as can well be found. Their portraits as old women, which stand at the opening of their works, prefigure and define this difference—though thirty years' distance in date may possibly diminish its full significance. Mrs. Delany, in coif and hood, comely and venerable, model of a wise, pious, decorous, acquiescent old age: Mrs. Piozzi, at nearly the same time of life, in hat and plumes, and false flaxen curls, to which her chronicler in candor bids us add, cheeks violently rouged. Each face is the type of a character and a career: in Mrs. Delany, of a harmony which is the characteristic of her life, adapting her to every successive stage of existence, causing her to fit in with every change and be always in keeping with the seasons of life as they came and passed by, from the tearful April and glowing May of her youth to the fall of Autumn and December snows: in Mrs. Piozzi's of exactly opposite characteristics—of a total want of this harmony and of the resolute hitch in her nature which disturbed all proportions; telling of a precocious womanhood, a girlish middle life, and a frivolous and fantastic old age. The one picture represents the gift of self-government, founded on a calm and modest self-reliance, the other that total incapacity for self-guidance, which so often is seen where vanity holds possession in the place of self-respect—the craving for the approbation or admiration of others rather than a wish to satisfy the individual judgment.

We are not attributing these differences wholly to an intrinsic superiority in one over the other. Circumstances seem to have been in the elder lady's favor, as they were against Mrs. Piozzi. It is not many people who know how to manage a borrowed and reflected consequence, or who, being once raised above their merits, can either be judicious under the fictitious elevation, or descend gracefully into obscurity. Probably Mrs. Delany's view of what she owed to herself, would under any circumstances have withheld her from devoting herself to a great name or a great man of any kind; she would not have disorganized her household, or deranged her hours, or broken her habits, for any colossus under the sun. She would have fully estimated Dr. Johnson, and given him a fair share of her respect, time, and affection; but no monopoly, nothing to derange the completeness and consistency of her own life, as to detract from the rights of other friends and other claims. But we can hardly blame Mrs. Thrale for the zeal of her devotion for a man at once so great and so dependent as Dr. Johnson, an object of such joint admiration and compassion. He was as it were a charge committed to her by her husband, by society, and by himself; and yet there is no doubt that her own life was unhinged by it. The necessity of soothing his wayward moments, of cheering his melancholy hours; the inevitable longing for his approval, the constant strain to meet his intellect, to answer his expectations, to entertain him by wit and readiness; to win his flattery; to avoid his blame; the perpetual stimulants to vanity, on the one hand, and on the other, the wounds to self-respect which he could not help inflicting on those around him, and which had to be borne with a mixture of noble and mean, high and low motives; the subservience, in fact, in which all had to live who lived much with Johnson, all inevitably disturbed the right balance, and unfitted those subject to it to a wise conduct in their own affairs. Besides, we must believe that a life of talk of any kind, a life of conversation, a life spent in hearing and saying wise things, or witty things, or silly things—perhaps it does not so much matter which, as may at first be supposed—a life where the tongue is kept going, and the ears are on the alert, and the spirits are excited, and the showy faculties kept on the stretch for immediate display—is in itself and for the things neglected by it demoralizing; it cannot be done with impunity—self-restraint and reasoning power, vigor of mind and strength of will are impaired by it. We cannot wish that Johnson had talked less; that gigantic effort and long silent labor, his dictionary, seems to justify a gigantic relaxation, but we suspect the readers of his wonderful talk have been greater gainers by it than those who hung day after day upon his lips: certainly Boswell ever since has been a proverb for a fool, and Mrs. Thrale, after enjoying this supreme pleasure and privilege for twenty years, fell desperately in love, as soon as she was her own mistress, with a singing master, who had nothing to say, and said that nothing in vile broken English, and who did not even understand what she said to him in reply. So much had the long stream of exquisite thought in exquisite language poured into her ear in such wealth and profusion as never woman was regaled with before, done for her, in the way of educating her mind, refining her taste, and ennobling her heart.

Mrs. Delany's course offers a very different spectacle; there are no mistakes, no lapses, no blunders. She never shocked her friends by a departure from their previous conception. Indeed, a certain halo played round her which we hardly understand. Ballard, for instance, chose her as the woman in England to whom to dedicate his "British Ladies," without any personal knowledge, simply from her reputation as fulfilling the ideal woman of her own time. And here we recognize that good fortune which distinguishes her from Mrs. Piozzi. Her qualities essentially fitted her for her own age; she could hardly have made so great a stir in ours, though such a nature would adapt itself to all circumstances. She was one of those wise persons who make the best of their own times, without too violent an effort to mend them. Reformers are a very useful and necessary class, but they do not attract the praise and veneration of those who have most to do with them, and they are apt to acquire embarrassing and provoking habits, if they do not start with them. There are, it is true, in these volumes mild protests against the vices of the time; we find excellent reflections on its peculiar vanities and follies: but she, nevertheless, takes the general view of things for granted, and makes the best of it, as of all the circumstances arising out of this view which befall herself, which, in her opening life, were very trying and awkward indeed. But she was was always able to see them exactly for what they were. She had no romance to exaggerate evil, or to raise impossible schemes for emancipation. She could, in the heyday of youth, take the good with the bad, and make the best of compensations. She never felt herself the sport of circumstances, as impulsive natures under misfortune are apt to do. She had self-possession in the fullest sense of the word, and was mistress of herself; realizing herself as something separate, distinct, her own—which no one could take from her—which she must defend, protect, and develop; not, of course, that she knew or thought all this, but she acted upon a class of impressions which belong to some persons, and not to others—which constitute a very marked, fundamental difference in those who are actuated by them. As an instance of what we mean, this Mary Granville, daughter of the second son of a noble family, is compelled at seventeen, to marry "Gromeo," as her autobiography calls him —in other words, Mr. Pendarves, a Cornish squire, sixty years old, of large, unwieldly person, crimson countenance, repulsive manners, and intemperate habits. Her uncle, Lord Lansdowne forces her to it. Clear-sighted beyond her years, of a noble, truthful nature, conscious, we do not doubt, of her own merits, he has the power to subdue her resistance, and to induce her to conceal her shuddering repugnance—not from the bridegroom, to whom she is careful by manner, at least, to convey her real feelings, but —from her parents, who are summoned to the wedding. The lax view of marriage prevailing at that time, which regarded it as a mere bargain in which inclination had no part, was pushed to its extreme in her case. She knew she was sacrificed, she felt herself a victim, and she must soon have learned that the transaction had not her future prospects in view so much as her uncle's political interests; for, with the habitual carelessness of selfishness, he trusted to the bridegroom's promises and professions, and the great fortune which had been promised her, and which was the avowed motive for the match, went to the heir-at-law. But none of this produced any useless resentment; she probably thought that *noblesse oblige;* she realized the advantage of high birth, took the penalty, and remained always on respectful and affectionate terms with her uncle to the day of his death. Her deportment to her husband and acceptance of her lot are in the same spirit. He takes her to his castle in Cornwall—a great tumble-down place, probably very romantic, but of which the parlor-floor was rotten and the ceiling falling in. The poor girl's heart for a moment fails her; she bursts into tears, which is a departure from the demeanor she had prescribed to herself. Poor Gromeo is really concerned, and allows her to repair and furnish the old place as she pleases.

This was the best form of relief that could have been prescribed; she owns that it helped to amuse her greatly. Congenial surroundings, a suitable atmosphere, was always necessary to her, as it is to the natures with whom we class her. She made the best of her position and of Gromeo; but she never deluded herself about him. She never worked herself up into any frame of mind. She never pretended to see things in a colored light. She obeyed him scrupulously; she submitted to his caprices she carefully respected his not unnatural jealousy. She was a model of propriety in a lax age, and under unusual temptations. She nursed him; she read to him for hours at a time, shivering in the winter cold, when the fires of the gout made him endure no other fire; but she never pretended, either to him or to herself, to *care* for him. He knew when he married her that it was against her will, and in the teeth of a violent repugnance; all the seven years of their married life, we gather that he might, and probably did, know the same. She took care, on the one hand, to conceal her *tears;* but, on the other, was as resolute to "show no delight in his company." "Gromeo," she writes, "who really loved me, was much concerned to see me so melancholy on the loss of my father, but that was no consolation to me." For two years he abstained from the bottle, possibly with some hope of favor, and then relapsed into old habits with old companions; and finally, after a bout with his old set, was found one morning dead by her side. He had the very night before shown some presentiment of what was coming; commended her as a good wife, and proposed to her to ring for witnesses to his will made in her favor. But hers was no sordid nature; she saw he was ill and low, and persuaded him to wait till the next day. Nor does she ever show any regret for the loss of a large estate. She writes to her friend the Duchess of Portland, who had asked for these details of her early life: "After being married seven years, I became a widow—a state, you may believe, not unwelcome," though the shock of such a death told for a time, but "my natural good spirits, time, and finding myself free from many vexations, soon brought me to a state of tranquillity I had not known for many years. As to my fortune, it was very mediocre, but it was *at my own command.*" The italics are her own.

Such a person did not need wealth to assert her right position; she only wanted independence, for which in her case the state of widowhood was essential. Henceforward she was never guided but by her own judgment. She resided first with an uncle and aunt, Sir John and Lady Stanley, afterwards in a house of her own; and from this time took her place amongst the women of highest rank, fashion, and reputation of the day. Her letters give us a glimpse of the society, and especially of the women, of the period between the respective dates of the "Spectator," and "Rambler," and Richardson's novels, as far as we can accept the last as a picture of fashionable life.

There is an impression of sweetness and choiceness thrown over the coterie who form her immediate friends and allies which is very attractive: they group themselves into fine combinations—the magnificence in which they lived or shared sets them off. We are convinced that they were lovely, graceful, elegant, after a distinct and distinguished fashion which our more levelling days will not admit of. Gorgeous to look upon, in their hours of state they wore their glittering attire with a sweeping grace which no width of crinoline can achieve now. To be observed and admired, to drive in coaches and six, to be attended by a bevy of devoted fine gentlemen, was so much their birthright, that notice influenced and moulded every movement, without making them vain. In this particular set, under Mrs. Pendarves' genial pen, we find no envy, jealousy, or meanness: they enhance one another's charms by a mutual adoration; they seek one another's society with constant friendship; they write volumes in absence; they consult one another's interest, and further each other's ends; they pursue pretty labors together; they sympathize, are merry, and sad together. There is no apparent affectation,—it was before the age of blue-stockings,—no straining after what is not theirs; but the serene content, the undoubting repose, induced by the knowledge that all that the world or society has to give is theirs already. They are evidently a set, a clique; they have names, grotesque, fanciful, or poetical, for themselves, and a cipher to express the outer world of their acquaintance. "Penny," "Pipkin," "Colly," "Fidget," the "Twopennies," are the Duchess of Portland's names for her friends and children. The "Pearl" and "Pearly-dews" are the epithets for Mrs. Delany's darling sister, Mrs. Dewes, to whom her letters are mainly addressed. Her cousins are, "Violet," "Primrose," "Daisy;" while the pretty, clever, lively, accomplished Duchess of Portland, the centre of this group, is "Our duchess," "Our sweet duchess," "Our well-beloved duchess," "Our lovely queen." Herein, however, Mrs. Delany rather conforms to a fashion than invents one; for, except under the pressure of some unusual excitement, her style is grave; she treats what are now called trifles seriously. For she, no doubt, perceived that they were very far from trifles in the influences they possessed over the success of society and of individuals. The topic of dress, for instance, is treated with the gravity which its importance no doubt demanded, but which in our times no woman would have the courage to use. She might say as much about it, and betray a deeper personal interest, but she would disguise it by an affectation of contempt for her theme. The subject of "*clothes*" with Mrs. Delany never meets with this injustice. It was, in fact, with her one of the fine arts. She had, probably, an exquisite taste in it, and in her early days, like the hapless Clarissa, exercised her invention, and struck out new thoughts. We see by the short and distinct directions she gives her sister in the country, that her judgment was final, and her authority law, as far as ladies' attire was concerned; for she says —and it is characteristic of her main sympathies lying with her own sex—she never can remember men's clothes which made quite as bold a claim to attention in brightness of colors and splendor of material; sometimes dismissing them summarily with "The men in general not remarkably fine," or the reverse.

When ladies by their *head* meant not the throne of intellect and the seat of expression, but the bit of lace that surmounted and presided over them, we can hardly wonder that the vocabulary of the art generally should be weighty. "Gauze heads," we are told, "are now the top mode;" and our prudent heroine does not think she is wasting her money when she gives fifty pounds, which would teach a language or an accomplishment, for a "Brussels head." There are pages of elaborate description of brocades of gold, and silver, and flowers, which read like more than mortal splendor, always written with the quiet conviction that they are as well worth describing as a fine picture. The very term *clothes* is a sort of voucher. "He saw my clothes," she writes of a beau who calls on her,—"The queen commended my clothes,"—"My clothes were grave, a great pennyworth I happened to meet with; they cost me seventeen pounds," —"There were many old clothes at court." Very rarely is there allusion to the effect of her magnificent get-up on others. She dresses in the mode due to herself and to the occasion. Only once do we notice excitement, a touch of levity, a momentary head-turning. It is at a time when she was receiving assiduous court from "Herminius"—i.e., Lord Baltimore, the man who presumed to trifle with our fair young widow's feelings, to make love for five years, and to draw back so soon as he had fully satisfied himself that he had won her heart. Then she announces to her sister, "I dressed myself in all my best array, borrowed Lady Sunderland's jewels, and made a tearing show. There was a vast crowd, and my Lady Cartaret got with some difficulty to the circle, and, after she had made her courtesy, made me stand before her. The queen came up to her, and thanked her for bringing me forward; and she told me she was *obliged to me* for my pretty clothes, and admired my Lady Carteret's extremely: she told the queen they were my fancy, and that I drew the pattern. Her majesty said, she had heard I could draw very well. . . . I suppose you will have some odd account of me. Let me know what they say of me behind my back." This last sentence, betraying a little sheepish, feminine vanity, is the only instance of the kind in these volumes. The court then must have been a more satisfactory arena for such displays than it can be in the crush, bustle, and mixture of ranks a drawing-room is described to be now. At the public court receptions then there was intercourse; it was society in a grand stately way. Everybody knew everybody. There was space to move in, to show clothes in; there was gossip with friends, and even with royalty itself. "The king," she writes, "asked me many questions." He was aware of her comings and goings. The queen had even little pleasantries about her admirers. We are amused and surprised, now and then, by a tone and airs which imply a more easy state of things still. The Duchess of Queensberry was Mrs. Delany's contemporary cousin, — Prior's "Female Phaëton," that "Kitty beautiful and young," who "set the world on fire," on her first appearance in it. These letters introduce her to us in the heyday of her beauty, which, indeed, seems to have been dazzling and altogether exceptional. Her caprices now and then draw upon her a notice of tender criticism. It seemed like vanity to Mrs. Delany, that she should "discard the borrowed aid that dress supplies," and choose to appear, on occasions of splendor, in studied simplicity of attire, without a jewel about her. Writing of George the Second's coronation, she says, "The Duchess of Queensberry depended so much on her native beauty, that she despised all adornment, nor had not one jewel, riband, or puff to set her off; but everybody thought she did not appear to advantage." But the duchess had her own view of things, and took her own way in most matters, which brought upon her amusing consequences. She chose to take up Gay, when his sequel to the "Beggar's Opera" had brought him into disgrace with the court, as seeming to reflect on the government. In spite of this, she pleaded his cause; asked the king and queen for subscriptions for him, and got herself forbid the court in consequence,—a thing never heard of to one of her rank. The vice-chamberlain was sent with the royal message, and returned with the following answer. We doubt whether duchesses, now-a-days, could express their feelings more readily, or more clearly. They might possibly keep to the *third* person throughout, but it would be at more cost than consistency is worth; for the heart refuses to speak in that indirect, back-handed, coldly grammatical method.

"*February* 27, 1728–9.

"The Duchess of Queensberry is surprised and well pleased that the king hath given her so agreeable a command as to stay from court, where she never came for diversion, but to bestow a civility on the king, and queen. She hopes, by such an unprecedented order as this is, that the king will see as few as he wishes at his court, particularly such as dare to think or speak truth. I dare not do otherwise, and ought not; nor could have imagined that it would not have been the very highest compliment that I could possibly pay the king to endeavor to support truth and innocence in his house, particularly when the king and queen both told me that they had not read Mr. Gay's play. I have certainly done right then to stand by my own words, rather than his Grace of Grafton's, who hath neither made use of *truth*, *judgment*, *nor honor*, through this whole affair, either for himself, or his friends.—C. QUEENSBERRY."—*Autobiography and Correspondence of Mrs. Delany*, Vol. i. p. 194.

The grave comment on this effusion is, "that though it shows spirit, it is not worded as her friends could have wished." But the fair Kitty knew her own value. The loss of its greatest beauty, and most daring and lively spirit, was no trifle to the court. "My Lady Harvey told her with a sneer, that now she was banished, the court had lost its chief ornament." "I am entirely of your mind," replied the duchess, and probably she was right, as point is often made of her entertaining qualities. She lived to be banished from court again, something about an apron she chose to wear, and which she flung in the lord-in-waiting's face; and also to shine there a dozen years later "in all the magnificence of dress," according to the poet's programme in such matters. Some one writes after describing the workmanship of her gown: "Allowing for her age (then forty), I never saw so beautiful a creature." We read of her later still, in the anguish of her eldest son's violent death almost before her eyes, and again with recovered spirits calling daily on Mrs. Delany to mix her medicines for her. But there was little in common between this erratic genius and the set we are particularly introduced to, the head of which, the Duchess of Portland, "was to bring virtue into fashion if any one could."

The picture of this lady and her family, which these letters present, is certainly a very agreeable one. The mixture of splendor and simplicity of manners could hardly be in our time, and characterizes an age.

Rank, in some respects, was a more evident and glaring possession then. Great people had monopolies of certain sensations; they figured in a more particular way before men's eyes; they, as it were, *wore* their coronets. Thus, when the Duke of Portland and his family migrated from Bulstrode to London, which they would now do by rail no faster, and in no greater privacy, than their neighbors, Mrs. Pendarves, who accompanied them, writes:—

"We set out from Bulstrode at eleven, and were in town by half an hour after two, over fields of snow and heaps of ice, but our horses flew as if each had been a Pegasus; four coaches and six with twelve horsemen attending, besides apothecaries, bakers, and butchers that joined in the procession to escort us part of the way."

A certain retinue, state, and publicity accompanies all their acts and movements; but the occupation of time and the family life is all simple and domestic—the children are brought up under the mother's eye; their education and dispositions are constantly in her mind. In the midst of constant necessary company, entertained with due splendor, the duchess is always busy with her own little schemes of fancy and usefulness. Her mind is stored with recipes and nostrums. She delights in being out of doors. She observes flowers and mosses and insects, and contrives all manner of devices to indulge her innate turn for work and invention. She and her friends are indeed alike in this, all are active spirits, full of business, occupied in their own affairs, taking a part in all the work going on about them, contriving, directing, managing, exhibiting the especial virtue of "notableness" so often commended, and uniting in their persons "the excellence of a good economist with the elegance of a fine lady," both qualities alike indispensable. It is wonderful where the good ladies of these books, but more especially Mrs. Delany, found time for all they did; but it was before the intellectual and dreaming age. Reading was not regarded by any of them as the business of life: it came in by the by. They were read to now and then, or they reserved certain evening hours, between tea and cards; but the prime hours of the day, such as were not passed with the visitors who came early and stayed long, and which were devoted to sitting at all, were spent in painting, *turning*, which was the duchess' hobby, and needlework, which was one of Mrs. Delany's numerous specialities, as well as spinning, which seems to have been a favorite occupation with her and her mother; the fineness of the thread testifying to the quality of the spinster. We cannot doubt that if the claims of rank and society had not stood in the way, these ladies, in our own time, would have made a bevy of authoresses. All the cravings after expression which found satisfaction in painting and shell work, and feather work, and grottoes, and quilts, and beds, and curtains, and fringes, and patterns, and neat and appetizing bills of fare (an admitted subject for arrangement and invention), would have found another vent—would have resulted in tales—moral, didactic, romantic—in poems, in essays, in scientific dialogues, in educational treatises, in tracts, by which the ladies of our own time confer such benefits on the world. Grottoes, for instance—what a world of romance which the mind and customs of that aspect of society kept down, found room to expatiate in the construction of a grotto. In our youth we remember wondering at the age which could have found any thing to please in the dank little dens, which, in gardens and ornamental grounds, were still considered points of attraction by the superannuated guide. Mean, childish, insignificant to our uneducated eyes—suggestive not of hermits and serene contemplation, but of spiders, newts, and sore-throats, we took a shuddering survey of the damp, dingy walls, the pitiful decorations, the miserable *tout ensemble*, and congratulating ourselves on the developed taste of the nineteenth century, returned to the cheerful day as quickly as we could. We should have looked on all with a different and more intelligent eye had we known the feelings which had been excited—the class of faculties set to work—in the creation of this little gloomy solitude; how it had been glorified as so many of our works are by a sentiment in the outset, which struggled for expression, and must find its way into some, however inadequate, action. If we had known that fine ladies had left the stiff grandeur of their drawing-rooms, and had laid aside their costly silks to indulge their fancy here, and work out a little dream of a pure primitive, quiet life, as remote in all its circumstances as they could devise it from the one they daily lived, where poetry, friendship, and religion should hold a perennial sway; where it should be always spring; where goodness, simplicity, wisdom, and philosophy should be inspired with the air; where the rustic cross, the scallop shell, the sandals, the staff, and the maple bowl, which actually formed the furniture of a firstrate grotto, should all be realities and suit somebody, though probably the precise person to enjoy this contemplative elysium might never be exactly defined. But altogether it afforded an idea of repose in a *busy* practical life, and thus was a poem. We can only guess that the Duchess of Portland's and Mrs. Delany's grottoes would resemble in their general character those we have seen. They would be sure to be the best of their kind, for the duchess had a fine spirit, and collected shells and stones regardless of cost from all parts of the world; and Mrs. Delany had really a fine taste, and was the undisputed head of all feminine works of fancy and invention of her time. It was one of her secrets of success, as we have said, that she never got quite beyond its tastes and aspirations; that she was always guided by its estimate of things, only setting these in their best and purest light. We are led to infer that she really was a very fair artist. She delighted to copy the works of great artists. Sir Joshua Reynolds warmly commended her copy of Correggio's Sigismunda, and her friends write with enthusiasm of all her performances, but she never doubted the fashions of her day even in their extremes of unreasonableness; and she who could expatiate on a Vandyke and a Raphael, and spend weeks and months reproducing them on her easel, writes quite nervously on hearing that her brother was following some adventurous spirits in wearing his own hair! "You said not a word to me," she writes, "about Bunny's wearing his own hair. I had a letter yesterday from Lady Carteret. She writes me word that he looks *very well* with his new adorned pate. Tell me what you think? I *fancy* a wig became him better; what provoked him to cut *so bold a stroke?*" Happily for her she had an innate love of simple pleasures, and the customs of the time, even in the fashionable world, were in many respects, in favor of them. Their hours admitted of being much out of doors, and of *al fresco* entertainments. There are continual allusions to meals out of doors, to expeditions with a Watteau touch of Arcadia about them. Thus, visiting, while in Ireland, Mr. Wesley, the grandfather of the Duke of Wellington, she writes:—

"Mr. Wesley (alias *Paris*) has provided every one of us with a walking staff whereon is fixed our Parnassus name. Mr. Usher is *Vulcan*, Young Nemmy, *Mars*, and Mr. Kit Don (the Revd.) is *Neptune*. Our staffs are white, and when we take our walks we make a most surprising appearance, somewhat like the sheriff's men at the assizes! Yesterday we walked four miles before dinner, and danced two hours in the evening."—*Ibid.*, Vol. i. p. 406.

The family of Wesley, by the way, seem to have been wonderful dancers. Mr. Wesley plays the fiddle, and dances with his children and guests at one and the same time, with something of the simple enjoyment Mr. Thackeray attributes to George the Third in his youth, who, he says, would dance country dances three or four hours together to the same tune. She entertains a friend at the home of her second marriage, and writes:—

"My garden is at present in the high glow of beauty, my cherries ripening, roses, jessamines, and pinks in full bloom, and the hay, partly spread, partly in cocks, complete the rural scene. We have discovered a new breakfasting place under the shade of the nut-trees impenetrable to the sun's rays, in the midst of a grove of elms, where we shall breakfast this morning; I have ordered cherries, strawberries, and nosegays to be laid on our breakfast table, and have appointed a harper to be here to play to us during our repast, who is to be hid among the trees. Mrs. Hamilton is to breakfast with us, and is to be cunningly led to this place *and surprised.*"—*Ibid.*, p. 558.

Or she describes a water party; and London and a Thames wherry answer excellently for Venice and a gondola. The Lord Tyrconnell mentioned had lately been refused by Mrs. Pendarves on the ground of want of sense:—

"After drinking tea Lady Mary went away: Capel proposed going on the water: we accepted the offer, took up Mr. Wesley on our way, drove to Whitehall Stairs, took the boat we liked best, and rowed away very pleasantly—the water smooth, the sky serene, the company in good humor. Philomel was soon called upon to make use of her sweet pipe, which she did; a boat with two ladies and one gentleman was immediately attracted and pursued us. As soon as they were near enough to see their faces, who should we behold but the Duchess of Ancaster, an odd woman with her, and my Lord Tyrconnell! I was not a little diverted at the interview, but much more so when he opened his wise mouth, and told Mrs. Donnellan her singing was 'the finest water language he ever heard, nay, the finest language he had ever heard by land or by water;' and many more polite speeches we had. They were in an open boat, ours was covered; it would have diverted you to see how the wretch peeped to look at us, which was no easy matter. My companion's voice charmed them so much that they did not quit us till she had sung several songs. Capel asked the Duchess of Ancaster to sing; which she did very readily; at last they agreed to sing a duetto out of the Beggar's Opera, but such catterwalling never was heard, and we all laughed."—*Ibid.*, p. 276.

The Thames of the London in 1861 has altered since June, 1731, when these people sung so merrily on its pure and undisturbed waters, which they seem to have had pretty much to themselves. On another occasion she describes a country walk at Welbeck, which the Duchess of Portland had recently inherited. We are not a little impressed with the cortége necessary to explore the country at a couple of miles from the great house:—

"Last Wednesday (Sept. 1856) we took a walk to a place called Creswell Craggs with the duchess and her fair flock. D. D. Mr. Smallwall, Lord Titchfield's tutor, and one of the duke's stewards to show us the way, and two pioneers to level all before us. At least a dozen stiles were laid flat, paths cut through thickets and brambles and briers, and bridges made in swampy places; the length of the way computed at about two miles and a half. A resolution was taken on setting out not to delay the walk by *simpling*, so we only snatched at any curious grass or flower in our way and stuffed it in our black apron pockets to observe upon at our return round the tea table."—*Ibid.*, Vol. iii. p. 441.

This *simpling*—"culling of simples"—was an unscientific botany. Every thing that was beautiful or curious in nature attracted their notice, though they seemed left very much to their own unassisted observations, and had none of those long Latin names, which modern science puts at our modern ladies' finger-ends, with which at once to dignify and to identify their discoveries. The duchess writes:—

"I have looked all over my collection of moss and can't find any thing like yours. That which most resembles it is the *small flowering green stone moss* and *the beard of brier*, but the first is a deeper green and not scarlet, and the other is not near so beautiful as yours. I found to-day a very odd fly—the body black, the legs red, and the tail half an inch long; the whole fly rather larger than a gnat."—Vol. i. p. 618.

There is something quite touching in this simple treatment of things, which learned men have now taught every lady to define "with a clumsy name;" but the love for them tells more as a characteristic before classification gave facilities and zest to such pursuits, and brought them into fashion. We find Mrs. Pendarves wondering at the insensibility of mankind to the beauty of shells, for which she had a passion, which was ministered to by friends and strangers till she had specimens from all parts of the world. At its commencement she writes to her sister:—

"I have got a new madness. I am running wild after shells. This morning I have set my little collection of shells in my cabinet, and they look so beautiful that I must by some means enlarge my stock; the beauties of shells are as infinite as of flowers, and to consider how they are inhabited enlarges a field of wonder that leads one insensibly to the great Director and Author of these wonders. How surprising is it to observe the indifference, nay (more properly), the *stupidity*, of mankind, that seem to make no reflection as they live, are pleased with what they meet with because it has beautiful colors or an agreeable sound; there they stop, and receive but little more pleasure from them than a horse or a dog."—Vol. i. p. 485.

It is a symptom of an unscientific age, and of an age, too, in which the canons of taste had as yet to be laid down, that this love for the pretty things of nature led to strange experiments of adapting them to domestic ornamentation. People did not care merely to look at them as specimens (very few do now), they must be made to do man a service, to minister, as it were, to his luxuries and whims. Thence resulted prodigious labors, of which we can only guess the effect. Not only were shells embedded in the walls of grottoes, but they are festooned into cornices for rooms and chapels —and positively painted over to one tint—and cemented round a framework for chandeliers; in every instance exciting intense interest in the progress of the work; and, what is much more surprising, satisfying the artist in the result, and causing an enthusiasm amongst her friends. What is new and neatly executed has a temporary triumph with us all.

The manual industry of these ladies is something to wonder at, and elicits from the editress some very pointed contrasts between past and present fine ladies. The duchess, besides her "cave," and her ivory and amber turnings, had twelve "toilettes" in hand at one time, whatever these may be; besides the more modern interests of a *virtuoso*, in making a fine collection of pictures and curiosities; and the work executed and turned out of hand by Mrs. Delany surpasses our ideas of the credible. The real value of most of these labors must always have lain in their effect on the worker. We know that they assisted to keep mind and body in health, serenity, and vigor to an extraordinary age. It is a further testimony to her model character that all this business does not seem to have induced a fussy, bustling manner, to which notable women are subject. A charming, graceful, easy serenity is spoken to by her friends.

She herself owns to ranking a good-manner, in her own sex at least, next to religion and pure morals, and perhaps *the* lesson to to be learned from this book is the value and importance of good manners. We feel that we have been to school. There is no doubt that (according to the approved phrase), we rise from its perusal with an added sense of the desirableness and pleasantness of being well mannered ourselves, and of all our friends being so gifted. We see a moral in a courteous and gracious deportment, and have an insight into the education that forms it. It is a subject on which Mrs. Delany thought a good deal: she practised all she preached, and no doubt was herself an authority. It enters into her primary ideas of education.

"Next to inculcating right religious principles, the most material work is to make brothers and sisters *perfectly well bred towards one another*. I see many sad disagreements arise in families, merely from want of *good manners!*"—Vol. iii. p. 58.

"There is nothing I wish so much for Mary, *next* to right religious principles, as a *proper* knowledge of the polite world. It is the *only means* of keeping her safe from an immoderate love of its vanities and follies, and of giving her that sensible kind of reserve which great retirement converts either to awkward sheepishness, or occasions the *worst evil of the two, a forward pertness.*"—*Ibid.*, p. 227.

"Mary (her niece) has had *uncommon* advantages at home for the improvement of what is *most* material, and a foundation is laid by her excellent, kind instructors, that will make her happy beyond this earthly tabernacle: but this is not all that is requisite, unless she is to turn hermit. There is *grace* and *manner*, which cannot be attained without conversing with a variety of well-bred people, which, well chosen, cannot efface what is certainly more necessary, but will give a polish, and by an agreeable recommendation, render all the good part more useful and acceptable to those she converses with."—Vol. iii. p. 537.

"About Mary I *cannot* think it necessary to the accomplishment of a young lady that she should be *early* and *frequently* produced in public. I would rather see a little awkward bashfulness, than a daring, forward genteelness. Good company and good conversation, I should wish to have my niece introduced into, as soon as she can speak and understand; but for all public places, till *after fifteen* (except a play, or an oratorio), she should not know what they are, and then *very rarely*, and *only* with her mother or aunt."—*Ibid.*, p. 92.

She is gravely solicitous about Mary's dancing:—

"Dunoyer is now, I believe, the best dancing-master in London: his price is high, but he will give the Pauline a better air in a month, than a less skilful dancing-master would in three. I believe Lady Cooper has good interest with him, and that may make him take more pains."—Vol. iii. p. 585.

She criticises her own manner in the tone of one who speculates on the subject, on occasion of giving her impressions of Irish society, in her first visit there, paid to restore her usual serenity, after the wound her spirits had received from "Herminius'" behavior. Dublin, it should be noted, was a much more courtly place while it had its parliament than it is now:—

"As for the generality of people I meet with here, they are much the same as in England—a mixture of good and bad; all that I have met with behave themselves very decently according to their rank; now and then an oddity breaks out, but none so extraordinary but that I can match it in England. There is a heartiness about them that is more like Cornwall than any I have known, and great sociableness. I apprehend, from that way of living, there must arise a good deal of tittle-tattle, but I have not heard much yet. Wherever I go I meet with great civilities. I don't take it as paid me on my own account, but that of those I am with, who are here highly regarded, and indeed, their friendliness and kindness to me increases every day. They study to entertain me, and I have no uneasiness on their account, but that they may think I am not so cheerful as they would have me; but, as I grow older (she is thirty-one), though I feel as much warmth as ever, I have not got so lively a way of showing it. I attribute it a great deal to the fear I have always had of appearing too gay; a wrong notion. I am now convinced it hurts the temper. Our spirits ought to have their full career when our inclinations are innocent, and should not be checked, but where they would exceed the bounds of prudence."—Vol. i. p. 291.

She was fastidious in her judgment of others on this point. In speaking of the young Lady Mornington, mother of the Duke of Wellington, we read:—

"I believe Mrs. Hill has been very careful, in the common way, for the education of her daughters; they are in very good order, and civil. What I think L. M. may be wanting in, is what few people have attained at her age, who have not some real superiority of understanding, and a little experience of the manners of the world; nor could she learn from her mother that politeness of behavior and address, which is not only *just* but *bright*. She is pretty, and excessively good-natured and happy in her present situation; but I own I think my godson required a wife that had more the punctilios of *good breeding*, as he is much wanting in them himself; and those things *should not* be wanting to men of rank and fortune. Indeed, I *carry it further*, and I think that nobody can do so much good in the world who is *not* well bred, as those that *are*. In truth, it is only a modern phrase (according to my notion of that virtue) for that '*charity*' emphatically expressed by St. Paul."—Vol. iii. p. 546.

She is a warm admirer and friend of Richardson, and sheds torrents of tears over Clarissa; still, it is well known that the fine ladies of that time were forced to admit solecisms in the manners of these admired and cherished volumes. A certain Miss Mulso comes in for some of the blame. She writes:—

"D. M. commends Miss Mulso's letters, but she does not so well like the young woman; that is, she admires her sense and ingenuity, but thinks her only second-rate as to *politeness of manners*, and that Richardson's *high admiration* for her has made her take her for a model for his genteel characters, and that is the reason they are *not so* really polished as he thinks them to be."—*Ibid.*, iii. p. 60.

"Genteel" then was a choice and expressive word, far from the disgrace into which it is now fallen. Women might pass very well; they might have rank and the habits of society, but not deserve to be called genteel. The writer pronounces of the belles of Bath, that they are very "ungenteel;" and Lady Betty Hastings was modest and civil in her manner, but not "genteel." Her strong notions of the duty of keeping up society gives the question of manners a moral aspect:—

"Three days together spent abroad is being a downright rake, but the sobriety of my own dwelling is much pleasanter to me than all the flirtations of the world, though the society of it I will always keep up *to the best of my power*, as it is a duty incumbent on us to live sociably; and it is necessary to keep up good-humor and benevolence in ourselves, or the qualities of the heart contract and grow useless, as our limbs would do without any proper exercise."—Vol. ii. p. 418.

She has a great respect for rules. "No ceremony," she says of a friend, "subsists between us,—

"Though ceremony is proper, to keep those at a distance that otherwise might be troublesome."

And in speaking of her dear friend, Letitia Bushe, whose perfection as a companion she very happily defines, saying, "She will be a great loss to me; she is one of the few who is perfectly qualified for an agreeable companion in a domestic way; her sweetness of temper makes her give in to all one's ways, as if she chose to do whatever is proposed;"—she writes, after parting with her, when her friendship was most needed:—

"My ingenious and agreeable companion, Mrs. Bushe, was obliged to return to Lady Austin, and I would not let her run the risk, by staying any longer, of disobliging her; it is not *honorable* to *monopolize*."—Vol. ii. p. 193.

And of all graceful attentions she says,—while hinting that, as a housekeeper, she could have dispensed with a dinner-party Dr. Delany (or D. D. as he is always called), arranged on her birthday:—

"Though I have too much regard for *les petits soins* of those I love not to value every mark of affection: but if people only keep upon the *great road of loving*, and neglect the little paths of friendship, many delicate pleasures are lost."—Vol. iii. p. 120.

A certain Lady Bell Monck seems to have greatly exercised the forbearance of this polite circle by her constant deviations from their high standard. Her name never occurs without some allusion to them; but we have a perfect confidence that this sensitiveness was never allowed to betray itself. This was the age, especially, for good manners and politeness to have their martyrs. Lady Bell and her husband are staying at Bulstrode, and spoiling a long-planned visit.

"L. B. M. is a sad check upon our pleasures; they have named three different days for going away, and yet they are here, and I fear will be, as long as we stay in the country, which is truly a mortification. The duchess behaves herself in the most obliging and proper manner that can be towards her, but it is much thrown away; however, it becomes her to do so, though *her pearls* are disregarded."—Vol. ii. p. 523.

The restraints of good-breeding a hundred and more years ago were, we suspect, of a more stringent character than modern habits would tolerate. They were a real discipline of which we think we perceive the fruits in more important points. These volumes, no doubt, introduce us to most favorable examples of the rank and fashion of the eighteenth century. Mrs. Delany and her friends were complimented on all hands as models for their sex's imitation and examples of virtue and piety; but theirs was essentially the religion of the day, and therefore tells of more than the habits of mind of one circle; and what strikes us in them, is a consistent resignation to the orderings of Providence, such as we miss in even the good people of our own time. They accepted the inevitable without grumbling or repinings. Modern inventions have cleared away so many hindrances, that we seem the more impatient of those that remain. We rail at every passing inconvenience, at every delay or stoppage in the social machinery, and, above all, at the one power which we cannot master, which we must submit to, whose caprices and severities are utterly beyond our control. How many Christians are practical atheists with regard to the weather! How many have contracted a habit of what we might call decent blasphemy against rain and cold, fog and damp, as though Providence had no concern with them—as though the check they offer to our plans and pleasures were the design of the evil principle! As far as we can judge, these things were better borne a century ago. The inconveniences of travelling, for instance, were enormous. It is a matter of surprise and congratulation to Mrs. Delany, that the high-road from London to Dublin was so good that they did not once come to a dead stand, so as to have to alight from the coach. After parting from her sister at Gloucester, on her return to London, she writes, in 1728:—

"I believe you have some curiosity to know how I was entertained during my journey. At the end of the town some part of the coach broke, and we were obliged to get out, and took shelter at an ale-house: in half an hour we jogged on, and about an hour after that, flop we went into a slough, not overturned, but stuck. Well, out we were hauled again, and the coach with much difficulty was heaved out. We then once more set forward, and came to our journey's end without any other accident or fright, and met with no waters worth getting out of the coach for."—Vol. i. p. 176.

It always took her three days to get from London to Gloucester, and she begs her sister not to ride to meet her on account of the intolerable dirt. From Oxford she writes:—

"We got to Euston about one: were delayed half an hour on the road, by the car *wheels breaking*; no overturn, but Smith was obliged to be hoisted up behind Bennet without any pillion, and James came wabbling on with the broken equipage, his *fribbleship* much ruffled. I feasted at Euston on your good provisions, but not very hungry; we staid about two hours. About three miles from Oxford, we had like to have lost one of our *fore-wheels*, but, fortunately saw our danger before any bad accident. The coachman very soon repaired the loss, and we arrived at Oxford about six."—Vol ii. p. 505.

She mentions it as a point of superiority in Ireland:—

"A comfortable circumstance belonging to this country is, that the roads are so good, and free from robbers, that we may drive safely any hour of the night."—Vol. ii. p. 686.

The passage to Dublin involved infinite delays and trials of patience, such as no modern temper could stand. To be at the water-side was nothing. Days had to be passed with no other employment than watching and waiting for the "yacht" and for the wind, and waiting with a long voyage, as it often proved to be, before them. But, supplied with a due amount of needlework and patience, the time passes serenely, —the dean, perhaps, deserving the greater praise, for he has the patience without the needlework,—and there is never a murmur; it is taken hardly as a trial, simply as an event. No grumblings even about sea-sickness, which is now and then touched upon as an inevitable accompaniment of a ship, without one word of vituperative description. All the eccentricities of the post are borne with equal philosophy. From Dublin she writes to her sister in England:—

"Your last letter was dated 27th January, and came to me in seven days. Could our letters always make as swift a passage, it would be charming."—Vol. ii. p. 421.

Letters were often a month on the way. Nor is it only this class of inconveniences that are borne with serenity. The same spirit of quiet gentle pious endurance supports our heroine in all the delays of a painful lawsuit which hangs over D. D. for years. She accepts suspense as the one trial of a happy lot, and strikes the balance in her own favor when things look their worst. London workmen, it is true, sometimes threaten to exhaust her patience, and once, she says, that if it were not that her friend was with her, she should be downright cross; but this exception only proves the rule. We are equally struck with the conduct of all concerned, when sickness or lesser ailments invade their circle. Mrs. Delany shows it in the prompt unmurmuring re-arrangement of all her plans, when those belonging to her, either nearly or remotely, fall ill. Nothing is ever called provoking or ill-timed; no disappointment is ever expressed. But we are particularly edified by the department of the Duchess of Portland and her family, when small-pox breaks out at Bulstrode. We have just been entertained with a pretty scene of the eldest daughter's first presentation:—

"Our duchess and Lady Betty came to town on Thursday, and we have been very full of business, in settling the jewels and clothes for the birthday. The Duchess of Portland's is white and silver ground, flowered with gold and silver, and a stomacher of white satin, covered with her fine *colored* jewels, and *all* her diamonds. Lady Betty is to have a very fine sprig of pearls, diamonds, and turquoises, for her hair, by way of pomponne, loops and stars of diamonds between, on blue satin, for her stomacher; her clothes white and silver, mosaic ground, flowered with silver, intermixed with a little blue. She *rehearsed* her clothes and jewels yesterday, and practised dancing with her train. She looks mighty well, and is a very genteel figure." . . .

And afterwards she reports of the scene:—

"I don't believe there was a more engaging figure than Lady Betty. She looked so modest, so composed, and, though glittering with diamonds, showed no sort of consciousness of any superior finery. . . . Lord Stormont, nephew to Mr. Murray, danced with Lady Betty. Never was such heat and crowding; but *she* says it '*was delightful for all that*;' she has the spirit one would wish a young thing to have, *great enjoyment* of the diversions allowed her, and no manner of regret when they are not thought proper for her."—Vol. iii. p. 303.

Within a few weeks, one of the sons is taken ill. The duchess, always ready with her recipes, prescribes for him, and sends for the doctor, who pronounces it small-pox of a middling sort, neither the best nor the worst.

"*Dec.* 25.—The duchess' spirits are more composed; her good sense and sweetness of temper make her exert and do all she can to keep up her spirits. It is a vast satisfaction to me that I am with her at this time, and so I am sure it is to you. She has given the young ladies *their choice*, to stay in the house or go to Whitehall; and they have so much fortitude that all *begged to stay*, and say they shall be miserable to leave her. I cannot help being anxious, though I trust in

God he will protect them, and he only can reward such filial tenderness. . . .

1*st Jan.*—Thank God, Lord Edward is quite out of danger of his late distemper. He has had a better sort than at first apprehended; it turned before the ninth day: he is the patientest little creature I ever saw. The young ladies still hold up most heroically; they have been taught to depend on Providence, and they credit their good teachers. The duchess says it would be unpardonable ingratitude in her not to be most cheerfully resigned to God's will, who has been so gracious and merciful in the recovery of her son. It will be very extraordinary if the young ladies escape the infection. . . . All the family were at church, and received the Sacrament last Sunday. Dr. Markham read prayers, and the Dean officiated at the communion table. . . . Dr. Markham has been here ever since Monday was se'nnight. He is master of Westminster School; he is reckoned a very agreeable man; the duchess and I think him dull, but he seems composed and steady, which may become his station more than vivacity. . . .

"15*th Jan.*—Last Monday, at dinner, Lady Margaret Bentinck was taken ill: everybody imagined all infection over. Yesterday morning she complained of giddiness in her head, and great pain in her back. The doctor was instantly sent for from Windsor, but the apothecary, who was in the house, felt her pulse, saying it was absolutely necessary to *bleed her* without staying for the doctor. She was let blood. She says, 'She is very glad,' when she can speak, that she 'has got the small-pox.' Her sisters are determined *not to leave her*, unless the duchess forbids them, but she is silent on that point, so that, in all probability, here will be the same succession as was in your family. . . . Lord Edward is quite well again, and expresses joy that his 'dear Peggy' has got the small-pox.

"17*th Jan.*—The small-pox has come out very favorably with Lady Margaret. Lady Betty was taken in the night of Tuesday. No bad symptoms appear. . . . We are in daily expectation of Lady Harriet. She continues well, but will not quit her sister's room all day. The duchess loves Babess extremely, and is always glad of her company; but as I can stay with her she will have nobody else, for she finds she must keep herself very quiet, and that the least hurry overcomes her. . . .

"20*th Jan.*—Lady Betty rested very well last night (natural rest). Lady Margaret, I fear, has not a very good kind; I don't believe it will turn before the eleventh or twelfth day. She bears it with great composure, but her throat is very sore, and her eyes closed up. The duchess bears up as well as she can, but her anxious state you can much easier imagine than most people. Dear Lady Harriet still holds out, but certainly, if she is ever to have it, can hardly now escape. She is (or at least appears to be) in very good spirits, and prepared to receive it whenever it comes. The poor duchess looks every moment with affectionate examining eyes for some alteration in her."

There is allusion to the duke, who is too anxious himself to be much support to his wife. At length, Lady Harriet is taken, and anticipates the doctor's too ready lancet, by a violent bleeding at the nose.

"31*st Jan.*—I hope the worst is over with Lady Harriet. She is indeed a sweet creature; so patient under her pains; so cheerful, and so thankful for the least amendment. I always thought the duchess blest in her children, but I did not know their full worth (nor, I may say, hers), till this trial. . . . Dear Lady Harriet goes on as well as can be expected, considering she has not a good sort. She has vast resolution in bearing her present miserable condition, for surely there cannot be any thing more terrible to bear while it lasts! Between whiles she tries to make comical jokes upon her own figure, and keeps up everybody's spirits by her good-humor. Lady Betty is fair almost as ever; her eyes as sparkling, and in charming spirits. She has not known the danger her darling sister has been in. Lady Margaret comes on slowly, and her spirits are but indifferent at best. . . .

"*Feb. 5th.*—Lovely Lady Harriet is in a fair way of recovery, *which I could not say till now.* The duchess is better: I was under great apprehensions for her a few days ago; she had all the symptoms of a fever, but they are gone off. . . . As to their fair faces, I fear Lady Margaret will suffer a little, and Lady Harriet a great deal; but we are at present so glad to have her alive that we are not yet mortified about it. The duchess has ordered rotten apples to be distilled, and is much obliged to you for your kind attention."—Vol. iii. p. 313.

We have thought it not amiss to give this simple history of the visitation of a scourge, which was felt or feared in every household within the memory of some amongst us. The young ladies of our own time could hardly pass with more credit through such an ordeal, or do greater justice to their training. Indeed, it is a picture creditable to that period in every respect but its medicine; and the medical ideas and practices, which transpire in these volumes, do more than excite our contempt for the doctors of that day—they excite a suspicion of all doctoring whatever. To see a whole generation acquiesce as they did in the notion of "blood-letting," as the cure for all distempers, makes us mistrust our own judgment as well as theirs. Every day may have its favorite fallacy, and be the victim of some dangerous delusion. These letters show us how Mrs. Delany's beloved sister, Mrs. D'Ewes, was slowly (not so very slowly either) bled to death by her doctors. But for their interposition, there is no doubt that the correspondence would have extended through three more volumes of equal length with the present. The more the poor lady languished, the more necessary was it thought to bleed her. She became giddy, no doubt from loss of blood, but the symptom was interpreted into the need of more constant bleedings than ever. All the doctors agreed in this, and all the friends and relations, Mrs. Delany amongst them, believed in the doctors. If she has a moment's misgiving, as where her brother reports:—

"I had a letter from him yesterday; he tells me you have let blood whilst he was with you, and that your blood was very good. Do you think it was of any service to you? *I fear not*, as you had a giddy fit or two after it."

She returns to her allegiance in a few days, after consulting with her own doctor, and in the last letter she ever writes to her sister gives his opinion:—

"He is very earnest for your being *often blooded*, but never to lose more than four ounces at a time. He lays great stress upon it."—Vol. iii. p. 626.

There is a case of a cousin who had some affection of the chest, for which she was bled, till she exhibited an alarming picture of attenuation, and who broke in upon various ceremonies by different summonses to her supposed death-bed, who yet lived to a good old age. Indeed, we must assume, that there was a stamina in these good ladies which the women of our time are without. Their active habits, their brisk housekeeping, their daily visits to the kitchen and larder—"apple-chamber and cheese-room"—their persevering energetic dancing far into middle life, were strong counter influences, and carried them on, in spite of the doctors, to a good old age, and in spite, too, of domestic quackery, for all prescriptions are not as innocent as "rotten apple-water, snails, and spiders," or a morsel of stale bread taken before breakfast, from which so much is hoped. For example, Mrs. Delany somewhere prescribes for her little nephew a decoction of quicksilver, to be taken at all meals, with an utter ignorance of the hidden powers of that metal—to say nothing of chalk and tar-water, which was the fashionable panacea of the day.

We cannot study the familiar history of this time without observing what an important and recognized place match-making held in the class of feminine occupations. The term is now one of reproach. No woman likes to be called a match-maker; but Mrs. Delany, and all her most respected acquaintance, would have failed in their ideas of duty towards their friends, and their friend's children, if they had not busied themselves in their establishment in life. It was evidently part of the office of a godmother or *gossip*, as is gravely termed, to plan a good and suitable match for her charge. Mrs. Delany had far more sentiment on the question of marriage than most of those she lived with. She realized and acted upon the truth, that there must be union of feeling and moral worth to constitute happiness in this relation. We know that, in our time, it would be something not absolutely commonplace for a woman of fashion to act on the principles here expressed to her sister, on occasion of an offer she had received:—

"I think he has a great deal of merit, and I protest solemnly I am extremely sorry to give him any pain; and had I any inclination to marry, and a fortune double what I have, I would prefer him to any man I know; but to let you see *seriously* that *money without worth* cannot tempt me, I have refused my Lord Tirconnell. Lady Carteret asked me, the other day, if I would give her leave to proceed in it; that she thought I should be blameworthy to refuse so vast a fortune, a title, and a good-natured man. All that, I told her, was no temptation to me; he had the character, very justly, of being silly, and I would not tie myself to such a companion for an empire. She said I *was in the wrong.*" —Vol. i. p. 274.

We find her, too, lamenting on the necessity that existed of women marrying for the sake of a home; but in the main she recognized it as a necessity, and could never see a marriageable young woman without wishing her well settled, nor help regarding matrimony as a cure for most evils. "Poor Maria Barber is a melancholy, drooping young woman," she writes, "and I wish a prospect of her being well settled, but I hear of none." She busied herself with all her skill to bring about a match between young Lord Weymouth, who was taking to dissipated courses, and Miss Carteret, and congratulates herself much on her success, though under circumstances which would hardly, in our eyes, have warranted it, and which savors much more of the days of Richardson than of Miss Yonge and Miss Sewell; as does the sentiment gravely uttered on occasion of her goddaughter, "Sally Chapene's," difficulties in preferring the lover who did *not* come forward :—

"I think it very hard that a young woman should be kept in an uncertain state, and not at liberty to accept the addresses of another man, because a person she has a high value for is so mysterious in his behavior, that she cannot tell what his designs are."—Vol. iii. p. 394.

But all the instances to the point would inconveniently swell our pages; we will content ourselves with one specimen example, where the process is given in detail, in its most dignified form and characteristic words. Are our bishops ever "sent for" on such errands ?—

"I have been for some time in an odd situation about an affair that I have had in my head and at my heart. Our dear, worthy Violet's circumstances are such, that if it were now possible to settle her well it would be doing a good action, and I have had a hint given me that Mr. G——n, near Windsor, has thoughts of marrying, but is afraid of the fine ladies, and that it was not impracticable if a judicious friend could be met with, to have her character given him, that such a union might be compassed. I thought of the Bishop of Gloucester, who is the most intimate friend the gentleman has. I sent for him, told him frankly my thoughts, and begged his friendship and assistance, both which he promised me when an opportunity offered; but he feared the gentleman wanted *some money*, as the earl had not settled the fortune, though the *title* would come to him; but he approved of my scheme, and said he would do all he could, for he thought they were worthy of each other, and *he* bears as good a character as *she* does. This was three weeks ago, and I have not heard one word."—Vol. i, p. 269.

A fortnight later, the bishop reports progress :—

"The Bishop of Gloucester has just been with me; he has had an opportunity of talking to Mr. G. He asked him if he had ever had such a query proposed to him, that her fortune was *so and so*, and her character a most extraordinary one from everybody. The gentleman agreed she had an excellent character, said she never had been mentioned to him, and made no objection, but gave no encouragement for the bishop to say more."—Vol. ii. p. 276.

A few weeks further on, the negotiation comes to a stop :—

"The Bishop of Gloucester was with me three days ago, but with no good news; he has twice mentioned what was desired, but nothing was said that could be interpreted to her advantage. The bishop wishes there may be interviews this summer which perhaps (as he is unengaged) may bring about some resolution."—*Ibid.* p. 284.

There the affair ends, but not the friendly zeal for Cousin Violet, who evidently weighs on her mind; for, two years later, we find another suggestion :—

"I don't think it likely Lord North should marry Lady W., but don't wonder, where there is such an intimacy, there should be such a report. If he does marry again (as I think it very likely he should), I don't know any one so fitted to make him and his family happy as our Violet. Her *discretion and goodness of temper* would make her a jewel in a family so mixed as they are. . . . But it is to be feared he will be taken by some blooming thing that will marry him for his fortune and to make a show," etc.—Vol. ii. p. 393.

There is evidently no end to the judicious arrangements that a sensible woman might make for her friends; and though Cousin Violet happens not to be an example in point of success, we are not at all sure that the decline of matrimony, so feelingly regretted in our day, and the vast increase in the community of old maids, which calls for so many remarks from the press, is not to be attributed in a good measure to a radical change in the system of making marriages. A hundred years ago, all the matrons were engaged in disinterested plans for their female friends. Merit, however modest and retiring, was not allowed to pass unnoticed; attention was called to it. Men were not permitted to remain widowers or bachelors without being reminded of the duty they owed to society and to female worth. And, on the other hand, ladies were advised to keep fancy and inclination under control: it was taken for granted on all sides, that a vast number of men were equally eligible, provided all could offer the same easy circumstances. We read of an infinite number of matches in these volumes, but of very few begun and carried through by the parties themselves simply because they loved each other. Such a proceeding would have been regarded with suspicion, as savoring of wilfulness or other impropriety. People first determined to marry, and then cast about for a proper object. Thus, Dr. Delany, having lost his first wife two years, set himself to consider who should succeed that lady in his affections. Long before, he had met Mrs. Pendarves in Dublin, and all who enjoyed her society thought her charming. His choice fell upon her, and a very cool choice we must think it to have been in an Irish D.D. of fifty-eight, and looking older. When his decision was made, his plan was not first to renew his acquaintance with the lady whom he had not seen for ten years, but to make his offer at once, and thus announce his approach. And a very fair straightforward letter it is, though much too long for our space. It induced Mrs. Pendarves, now forty-three years of age, to consult her mother and sister, with the full purpose, no doubt, of deciding for herself. She knew him to be a man of worth and of learning, and with such a reputation for wit as the chosen friend of Dean Swift must possess. She weighed all the circumstances, saw that his character, fortune, and position —though the last not what her friends might have expected for her—were such as would conduce to her happiness, and in a very short time closed with his offer. His proposal was made April, 1743, and the wedding took place the 9th of June of the same year. Nothing could have answered better, and there can be no happier picture of married life in middle age. It is marked by a uniformity of tastes, which is seldom seen where people have grown from youth into one another's habits, and such sweetness of temper on each side as would have made them happy, even if such sympathy had been wanting. Nor was Ireland at all such a banishment for a woman of fashion, as it would now be regarded. She was subject to no violent change, either of society or social habits. She was of a nature to be always young, and we are led to believe her face, figure, and habits, to have all favored the agreeable deception. The happy couple mutually befriended one another: her interest soon got him the deanery of Down, and she tried philosophically and decorously for a bishopric. But this further promotion, though seemingly within reach, never came. Their pretensions never clashed. She was always the loving, obedient wife, reverencing his office, implicitly deferring to his opinions, and proud of his official and parochial labors when she has such to record; while he looked up to her with at least equal respect; gloried in her accomplishments, encouraged all her pursuits, devoted himself to her happiness, sanctioned her liberal and elegant hospitality, and was delighted to see her at the head of the best society Ireland afforded, always sought after and courted, always sensible, genial, and gracious. He was evidently a most creditable specimen of a church dignitary, literary, clerical, devout, and orthodox; but his duties were not so arduous as to interfere with long absences, not only from Down, but from Ireland altogether, when he accompanied his wife in her triennial visits to her friends in England.

It was a marriage which for itself and for the time in which it was contracted eminently suited her. She was one of the people made for friendship rather than more absorbing emotions. She had a reserve and self-reliance, which led her to choose the confidence and companionship of her own sex, and to repose on the calmer domestic affections, the love of family and home; such influences as offered no disturbing forces to the natural development of her own nature. These volumes show us a temper perhaps a good deal rarer than we would at first sight suppose, one which we are apt to assume for ourselves, as a matter of course—we mean the affectionate temper; that is, really a nature in which there is such a harmony of engaging qualities, of warmth, tenderness, kindness, indulgence, unselfishness, fidelity, and discretion, as may lead to the formation of many real attachments, and constancy in them. Most people can be affectionate to those immediately about them and belonging to them, as parts of themselves; or they can be affectionate so long as there is an identity of interests or frequency of intercourse; but it belongs to few to go on loving with unwavering regard—in spite of changes of place and fortune, and inevitable changes of character (we speak of change, not deterioration)—the same people throughout a life; to hold by the friends of youth to old age. We all must admit that it implies habitual forbearance, toleration, and justice, a constant sense of others' claims and submission of our own, a freedom from jealousy, and a general right balance of mind, to maintain friendships unimpaired through the innumerable trials and vicissitudes to which they are exposed, as it needs expansiveness and warmth of heart to form them. It is a subject which might be pursued to great length: we consider Mrs. Delany an example of the virtue, though the circumstances of her day befriended this natural capability.

In her day a large number of separating causes did not exist which affect us now. The grades of society were more fixed, opinion in religion and politics was more fixed, people were more tolerant, they more needed each other's society, and had ways of entertaining themselves which kept them clear of intellectual excitement. It is curious, in this vast mass of correspondence, how few sore subjects, or disputed points, or differences of opinion, are touched upon. And when they occur it is no personal matter, but some case in which the warmth and generosity of her friendship leads her from the usual calm charity of judgment. Minds now-a-days, separated by circumstances, are apt to drift from one another in spite of themselves; there are so many questions on which friends may split, such rapid transitions, so many opportunities for divergence; such a feverish activity of thought circulates about us, of which there is little indication in these volumes. We infer that an intellectual age, in which people are always probing into the depths of their own and other people's minds, does not encourage habits of friendly, sociable, affectionate constancy. But that, even in Mrs. Delany's day, the temper we have attributed to her needed guidance and self-restraint is evident, in the following early counsel to her sister:—

"I am of your opinion, that nothing requires more penetration than to be able to find out other people's characters; too candid, or too severe a way of judging, is apt to mislead one, though the first occasions less mischief than the latter. *That talent* seems to me as much a genius as music, or poetry, etc.: it may possibly *be acquired* by much experience and observation, but not often. I think one ought to be very cautious in declaring one's opinion either to the prejudice or advantage of any one; for if you commended upon a slight acquaintance, and they afterwards prove unworthy of it, one's judgment will certainly be called in question. I need not give you any caution against censure, for no one is less apt to run into it; but I find, upon the whole, that a proper silence gives one more the *character* of wisdom than speaking one's sentiments too openly, though ever so well expressed." —Vol. i. p. 460.

She had not only caution but this knowledge of character, and an instinct of perceiving who and what she liked; for we find her pronouncing, for once on a slight acquaintance, a certain Mrs. Hamilton, "as one that I should always feel happy to have within my reach," who, twenty years after, when she was within reach, exactly fulfilled her expectation, was a much valued neighbor, with whom she held constant, delightful intercourse. To account in some degree for this felicity, it must be observed that she had an absolute accordance with her own age; she was visited by no obstinate questionings; she served her friends in the approved way, as well as with zeal. And after all, zeal does a great deal more, and is a much firmer ally when it goes with the times than against them. These good ladies, for instance, had none of them any scruples about places and sinecures. Their notions of politics are circumscribed; they value statesmen as they can get from them pensions and appointments for their friends. If they fail in finding a husband for some fair cousin, they try to make her a maid of honor, or to get her a pension; and when success attends these efforts, the congratulation and applause are without a suspicion or a doubt of the intrinsic merit of the transaction. As for example:—

"I have a letter from my brother, with the good news of the Duchess of Portland having obtained a pension of £200 for Babess; she struggled hard for £300, but it is well this is obtained. She has been a zealous and kind friend, and has acted in this af-

fair as few in her station have inclination to do, or if they have will not give up their time and thoughts enough to bring it about."
—Vol. iii. p. 21.

There is not a pretence that this "Babess" has any other claim on her country than being a single lady of high birth and small means. We are not, however, censuring either the action or the applause bestowed upon it; these ladies accepted the ideas of their time, and did the best for their friends with them.

Our space will not allow us to touch upon much that is curious and interesting. Accidental scattered notices of persons and customs attract us as we turn over the pages which we must pass by. There is constant mention of Handel, who was on terms of friendship with her brother Mr. Granville, and patronized by her family. She was an enthusiast for his music, and attends every opera and oratorio, but we learn nothing new about the man. She knew Hogarth and the leading artists of the day, but only names occur. She corresponded with Swift, with whom she became acquainted only a short time before his loss of reason. His letters convey a favorable impression as far as they go; his compliments are not so unmeaning as the compliments of the time generally are, and there is too much spirit, point, and style in all that he writes for him ever to degenerate into that wonderful form of composition, the complimentary letter of the eighteenth century, which is a thing *sui generis*. We have in these volumes innumerable examples of them from all sorts of people, but not one conveys any idea beyond a certain cloudy incense of homage, not one contains a fact or a statement—any thing so definite as either would be felt to be an impertinence. It is eating in a dream, groping in the dark, fume, flourish, and emptiness. Fortunately, it is only a state dress, kept for state occasions. Mrs. Delany assumes it now and then, when her style is nearly as pompous, turgid, and destitute of interest as Dr. Young's of the "Night Thoughts" himself, and we might almost add, John Wesley, from the one letter given of his, which is so vague and wordy, that it is hard to believe it was from the man who was so soon to rouse his generation. Her ordinary style is more modern than her age, and singularly free from affectation, telling what she wants to say in few words and in the simplest manner. It was regarded as a model and wonder of grammatical propriety and elegance in her own time, when many women of fashion could hardly spell, and when Swift told her he could remember fine court ladies writing to him with the "scrawl and the spelling of a Wapping wench." It is often only by the obsolete use of a few words that we are reminded of the more than century that has elapsed since the pen wrote them. One of the most frequent of these, the word *clever*, which is uniformly applied to nimbleness of *limb*, not of wit. "Six couple of as *clever* dancers as ever eye beheld." "All the *clever* men (as partners) had gone to Newmarket." Also the superlatives of every age will change. "*Mightily*," was a word in constant use, and "*pure*," as we use "*fine*," for excessive. "I will show her," says pretty Lady Harriet, after her small-pox, "a *pure* spotted face." Let us further observe on an absolute freedom from slang and cant terms; such would no doubt have been impossible vulgarisms from the pen or the lips of a correct fine lady. We cannot help indulging a passing regret that they are not *as* impossible in the ladies of our own day.

But it is high time to turn to Mrs. Piozzi. The date of Mrs. Delany's last letters are 1761, within four years of the period when Mrs. Thrale took her place amongst the noted women of the time, through her intimacy with Dr. Johnson. The editor somewhere gives it as his opinion, that "in some respects, Johnson's character gains by these fresh disclosures; in others, it certainly loses." Here we entirely differ from him. Every thing trustworthy in these volumes is entirely characteristic of Johnson, and shows him in no new light. A trait or two more or less of bearishness, or even of self-indulgence, can make no material difference in our thoughts of him, for we have always respected and admired him in spite of bearishness and other ungracious drawbacks. However, we cannot help speculating on every fresh exhibition of this most singular and interesting character, doomed, it would seem, because the uncouthness of its defects made it especially unfit for close scrutiny, to the protracted survey of posterity. We are never allowed in his case to know the mind without the man — that lumbering body, those wild gestures, those insufferable habits, are protruded upon us with endless persistence. In a certain sense they only add to his *prestige*. What must that mind have been which reigned and ruled in spite of *every* point of figure and manner being against him?

Amongst the many marvels of Dr. Johnson, not the least is the tolerance that was shown to his bearishness, to the rudeness, not to say brutality, of his manners—sometimes wholly unprovoked. No person, as we have said, would be the better for enduring these wounds to self-respect; but we suspect that Dr. Johnson was in the main unconscious of his own misdeeds. He wrote well on the subject of manners. We find in the *Rambler* the reflection, curiously applicable to himself, that "wisdom and virtue are by no means sufficient without the fundamental laws of good-breeding, to secure freedom from degenerating into rudeness, or self-esteem from swelling into insolence; a thousand incivilities may be committed, and a thousand offices neglected, without any remorse of conscience, or reproach from reason;" but the context does not at all give the idea that he had himself in his eye. Because he was possessed of extraordinary powers of mind, it is virtually assumed that he must be endowed with adequate control over these powers, and that his faults were more blamable because of his great intellectual superiority.

But, in fact, there is nothing more disproportioned and unequal than men of genius,—nothing more unmanageable by the possessors than force. Human beings do not rightly know what to do with extra powers. It is god-like to have a giant's strength, but it is tyrannous to use it like a giant. In fact, the giant can hardly help himself; he does not know the weight of his hand or the force of his blows. We believe he was constantly ignorant how his sayings told. Borne on by the excitement and stimulus of society, his whole mind was concentrated on talking well, a state directly opposed to sympathy. He was intent on wielding his engine with effect, to the exclusion of any thought where it fell. It was a public performance. With Boswell's miraculous memory taking notes at his elbow, he had generations for his hearers. It was necessary he should do well; he was pledged to show his best; he must come off victorious. Thus urged, he might expect even his opponent to see only the justice, the truth, or the simple intellect his brain was charged with. People's feelings had no better chance to be considered in this state of mind, than was their taste and sense of propriety, who had to witness his dreadful feeding time; when, absorbed by the food on his plate, he gave way to the passion of hunger. In each case he was so intent on what he was about, that what people would *think* never entered his head. When such ideas did make their way, he could be sensitive. He objected to being drawn in a way to betray his shortsightedness. Sir Joshua might paint himself with his ear-trumpet if he pleased, but he, Johnson, would not go down to posterity as "Blinking Sam." He would no more have wished to go down to posterity as "Bullying Sam" or "Gobbling Sam" could he have *seen* the figure he made at dinner, or while demolishing some luckless opponent, and so have realized the danger. All persons gifted or afflicted with strength of expression are liable to the same error in degree. Strength is to them truth, which they expect every one to see and acknowledge. It carries them for the time right over all considerations of tenderness, not at all necessarily for insensibility, but that they are possessed by an idea,—that prolific source of so much unconscious cruelty. We have little doubt that Johnson often expected his victims to be gratified by his treatment of them, for he felt he was saying a good thing, of which they were the object. And Boswell's receptions of such favors might well strengthen him in the persuasion. Johnson's life in society was unparalleled as a trial; biography or experience gives us nothing to equal it. Most great talkers have a hint now and then in the weariness of their hearers. People tired of Coleridge's monologues, they ran away from Madame de Stael, and Macaulay's *flashes of silence* were visibly welcome; but Johnson conversed: men's minds quickened with him, and they never tired of hearing him,—except it be Goldsmith, who could not stand his entire obscuration. In all books about Johnson, an immense deal of time is spent in reconciling what is irreconcilable; as if all talkers—brilliant, versatile, and speculative, as a good talker must be—did not contradict themselves. His love of paradox and contradiction produces endless discrepancies, which are conned over, disputed, gravely discussed. We work questions in our brain; there we own two sides, and conflicting arguments. Is the flowing eloquent talker likely to give only his mature conclusions, and to be always on his guard against the shadow of an inconsistency? Silent people may suppress all but the convictions arrived at; but nothing would surprise us more than a record of eager and abundant talk, clear of inconsistencies; it would create a suspicion of suppression or want of genuineness, as failing in the constant accompaniment of an active working intelligence, and seething brain. How many do we all know,—honest men, too,—who may be made to say seeming opposites within the hour? There is something to be said for every view; every full, ready, discursive mind sees all sides, and, except under restraint, or giving only his conclusions with his pen, is apt to talk on both sides. The man, for example, who has written well on one side, is in the very position to talk on the other. He is irritated by the dull way in which others echo his view; justice is not done to his opponents; he finds himself misunderstood; viewed as they would view him, he is one-sided, uncandid, unfair; he turns round upon his partisans, and shows them how much may be said where they see not a point to stand on, and sends them off discomfited. Moreover, persons who pique themselves on accuracy of thought and expression cannot tolerate the loose talking of others; their comments are a running correction of other men's inaccuracies; they must set things straight as they go along, though the effect on their hearers be disappointment and perplexity.

We know that Dr. Johnson was so far from sharing the views of his friends on the question of his manners, that he piqued himself on his knowledge of good-breeding. He had excellent theories, as we have seen, on the subject, and was conscious of frequent efforts to put them in practice. Speaking of Dr. Barnard, Provost of Eton, lately dead, and eulogizing his good qualities, he added, quite seriously:—

"He was the only man, too, that did justice to my good-breeding; and you may observe that I am well bred to a degree of needless scrupulosity. No man," continued he, not observing the amazement of his hearers—"no man is so cautious not to interrupt others; no man thinks it is so necessary to appear attentive when others are speaking; no man so steadily refuses preference to himself, or so willingly bestows it on another, as I do; nobody holds so strongly as I do the necessity of ceremony and the ill effects which follow the breach of it; yet people think me rude: but Bernard did me justice."—Vol. i. p. 59.

Nor do the additional letters to Mrs. Thrale, on her second marriage, make any change in our previous impressions of Dr. Johnson's feelings and conduct, except so far as we have been taken in by Macaulay's sounding sentences. But, in fact, we have ourselves to blame if we ever give implicit trust to those fine rounded periods, which carry inaccuracy on the face of them. Truth of detail will never fit into that sort of writing; all that we ought to look for is a fairly correct, general impression: the facts of the case are clearly made subordinate to a striking effect. We are glad, then, to find that Johnson did not break utterly with his old friend; that in his last letter to her on this subject he expresses gratitude, which was certainly due, and writes:—

"Whatever I can contribute to your happiness I am ever ready to repay, for that kindness which soothed twenty years of a life radically wretched."—Vol. i. p. 128.

Nothing again can be made of the charge of inconsistency. His words and his conduct were perfectly natural, and to his honor. All the fluctuations of feeling between old affection and new displeasure, the resolutions never again to speak of the affair, that were broken; the renewals of former tenderness that came to nothing, were inevitable, where the past affection and the present indignation were both real. It was a struggle, and that was all. That indignation and even disgust were warranted, we think can hardly be disputed, though every indecorous and ridiculous marriage is defensible if we will not allow public opinion a voice. Mr. Hayward, the compiler and editor of these volumes, maintains, against some seemingly creditable evidence, that Mrs. Piozzi never regarded her second marriage as a degradation: we answer that to believe, as she did, that every other person regarded it in this light, was to believe it herself. It is universal, unanimous opinion which settles such questions; this is virtually the only appeal. But it is not very easy to know what the editor thinks on the question. It is a point of honor with biographers to whitewash their subject whenever it is possible; so he gravely defends Piozzi from Dr. Johnson's querulous attack on his books. "Why, ma'am, he is not only a stupid old dog, but he is an ugly dog, too," giving vouchers for passable good looks and suitable age. When it comes to the point, it is not only easy to find influential arguments to divert a person from a resolution to play the fool. She knew that Piozzi was a singing-master, and had been an opera singer; she knew that he was a foreigner, who could hardly make himself intelligible in English; she knew all the grave objections on the score of religion and station. Johnson might think disparagement of his person as good an engine of attack as he could devise, or he might find this readiest mode of venting his ill-humor on his own account, and that of the outraged first husband. The precise terms in which people express bitter disappointment on such startling occasions are really not worth discussing. Nor is it a great deal that self mingled with more generous sorrow, and interposed its own regrets. He had been comfortable at Streatham; good dinners, in good company, had contributed no doubt to his enjoyment; his feelings and his ease were invaded by the same blow.

The marriage with Piozzi turned out much better on the face of it than friends and enemies expected: many gloomy prophecies had the common fate of such prognostics. He was respectable in his conduct, attentive to his wife, and careful of her money; and we are led to agree with Lady Keith, the eldest Miss Thrale, in her subsequent judgment, that she could not blame a man for marrying a rich and distinguished woman who had fallen in love with him. But the marriage had its appropriate harvest of ill-fruits, notwithstanding—to be found in the general loss of respect, in the separation from her daughters, in the breaking of all old ties; but mainly in its effects upon herself. Mrs. Thrale had probably never possessed an affectionate nature; and her education as a clever, precocious, spoilt, paraded only child—a "fondled favorite," as she expresses it—while it developed her intellect, did not cultivate her heart: her character being further sophisticated by a strange tutor, a Dr. Collier, who at sixty seems to have had the art of making his young pupils in love with him. But this second marriage turned all to gall. The celebrity she had acquired as Mrs. Thrale and Dr. Johnson's friend, made public contempt intolerable to her; henceforth every consideration was sacrificed to self-defence, and to retorting upon those who had slighted her. To this she sacrificed the memory of her first husband, laying bare, and probably exaggerating, his faults and sins, and asserting their mutual indifference. To this she renounced every sentiment of a mother, speaking unlovingly of her children to every fresh acquaintance, and leaving a legacy of cold censure and faint praise, worse than blame, to perpetuate the bitterness of a lifetime after death.

Every action, every letter, every dealing, is colored by it; every old friend thrown over. She lived in the past, and yet hated it for its contrast with the present. As a proof, she had a most choice collection of portraits of the distinguished circle at Streatham, remarkable for the subjects and for the artist who drew them, for most of them were Sir Joshua's: not urged by want of money, but from mere spite at old times and old friends, she sold them all. Possessed of vigorous health, lively spirits, and a ready wit, she could not be unhappy; but ever after her false step there was a strain to seem happier than she was, to parade her felicity to the world, to write letters and books about it, to express it by flighty and out-of-the-way methods. We are allowed to see no regrets; but her praises of Piozzi have constantly the air of being dictated by a restless desire to justify the step she has taken; and a consciousness of failure, of having made a life-long mistake, is we think discernible through all. In her first marriage her position was dignified; her conversation brilliant; her manner, as we are told, charming. After her second marriage, every thing is effort: she sought out new friends; she lived in public; she assumed a tawdry dress; there was a restless desire for display, and for the old homage. She *would* not be put aside or forgotten.

It is hard for any one to live creditably on

a past reputation, even if they have not damaged it like Mrs. Thrale. Perhaps the trial is greatest to women; they cling with tenacity to the period when, in their own little sphere, they were famous. All the life they care for was there. How much that is ridiculous in old age may be traced to this! A woman looks back to the time when she was in the world's eye, and her only idea of remaining in it is to ignore time, and hold by the old ideal—painted cheeks, flippant talk; reiterated anecdotes, a memory ransacked, and old stories tossed over and over, being all that is left of what was once an attraction. It is well for all to have a past, but the way to keep it fresh is to have a present as well, and one that suits our condition and actual circumstances, and in which it is not painful to keep exact account of the years as they go by. Keeping pace with the time has its resigned religious meaning, which those miss who worship any part of their past existence. Not that Mrs. Piozzi did not especially pique herself on doing so; she eagerly kept herself *au courant*. These letters, written between her seventy-fifth and eighty-first years, are full of the news of the day: she would not willingly allow any topic to pass without a sharp comment, or miss any popular attraction. She was encouraged to write them by the compliments of her new friend, Sir James Fellowes; and the editor boasts of them as remarkable compositions. But the reader cannot but feel that to collect and transmit the scattered recollections and remains of a lively, coquettish old age is not a charitable office. The egotism that can no longer be held in check, the affectation which was once grace, the flippancy that once looked like ease, the jingle of verses, the false criticism which cannot take to what is new, the dim insight into self, and somewhat vapid reflections on time and death,—the old stories, old epigrams, old compliments, old impromptus, flowing at random from the facile but worn-out pen,—suggest but an unsatisfactory picture. A good memory is not set at its highest value when crammed with old *vers de société*. Nor is the elasticity found most attractive which intersperses an exact record of every new dancer, actor, and singer, with moral reflections and ejaculations on the fleetness of life and the impending grave—a favorite topic with Mrs. Piozzi, but curiously mixed up with ill omens for the world she is leaving, and with prophecies of its approaching dissolution, as though there was comfort in the thought, *après moi le déluge*. It is difficult to find every characteristic in one example, and in the following the gayeties and smaller entertainments of the day are not touched upon; but it expresses her habitual state of feeling, and shows her style:—

"(Jour de Naissance, 27th January.)

"*Tuesday night, 16th January*, 1816.

"My dear Sir James Fellowes will like a long independent letter about a thousand other people and things. When I am one of the family cluster, we can think only of you. Yet poor old Dr. Harington must be thought of: he will be seen no more. Was it not pretty and affecting, that they played his fine sacred music so lately, and, by dint of loud and reiterated applause, called him forward, as he was retiring, to thank him for their entertainment? He returned, bowed, went home, sickened, and ——! This was a classical conclusion of his life indeed; like the characters at the end of Terence's plays, who cry, *Valete omnes et plaudite!* But I would wish a less public exit, and say *Vale* to my nearest friend, *Voi altri applaudite* to the rest.

"*A propos*, did you ever read Spencer's long string of verses, every stanza ending with wife, children, and friends? I can neither find nor recollect them rightly; but too well does my then hurt mind retain my answer to a lady (one of the Burneys) who quoted a line expressive of contempt for general admiration, giving us in this passage, which I *do* remember:—

"'Away with the laurel; o'er *me* wave the willow,
Set up by the hand of wife, children, and friends.'

My reply was, 'No; for,' said I,

"'Should love domestic plant the tree,
Hope still would be defeated;
Children and friends would crowd to see
The neighboring cattle eat it.'"

* * * * *

Then follow four more stanzas, showing how transient is domestic regret, figured in the willow; how envious are friends, and the like; and concluding with praises of the laurel:—

"'And should the berries e'er invite
Some envious, nibbling neighbor,
A blistered tongue succeeds the bite,
And best repays their labor.'"

"Did you believe I could ever have expressed myself with so much bitterness?

But if people will break the heart even of an apricot, sweetest and most insipid of all fruits, the kernel will yield a harsh flavor.

"Poor Dr. Harington, like myself, has found the kindness that sweetened his existence always from without doors, never from within.

"My cough is no longer a bad one, but the hoarseness does not go off: and when I tried to tell old stories last night, to amuse, I found the voice very odious; so Sir James Fellowes is best off now, that has me for a correspondent. Don't you remember, in some of my stuff, how Johnson said, if he was married to Lady Cotton, he would live a hundred miles away from her, and make her write to him once a week? Added he, 'I could bear a letter from the creature, but it is the poorest talker, sure, that ever opened lips.'

"Well, if you asked the pretty girls to tell you the color of the wind, and explain to you the tint of the storm, they would say the storm rose, I imagine, and the wind blew. We used to spell the color so in my young days.

"Meanwhile, the geological maps of what is to be discovered underground are fine things, certainly; but I feel so completely expectant of going to make strata myself, that the science does not much allure me; although I am *deeply* concerned in it at seventy-five years old. Dear me! 'tis a silly thing to try to extract sunbeams from cucumbers, like Swift's projector in 'Gulliver's Travels.'

"Princess Charlotte has at length made her choice, it seems, of le Prince de Saxe-Coburg, a handsome man, and she thinks so. Without that power of making impression, beauty in either sex is a complete nihility. Find me a better word, and that shall be turned out by her who wishes to keep best in every sense for you.

"Your faithful,

"H. L. P."

—*Ibid.*, vol. ii. p. 146.

What she says is true. The pleasures of her life never came from within-doors, except the reservation she forgets this time to make—Mr. Piozzi himself. To please her husband, or to spite her daughters, she had adopted a nephew of his, when only a child of four years old. He was educated as an Englishman, and naturalized, assuming her maiden name of Salusbury. He seems to have turned out well and creditably to her; but she derived little satisfaction from the child whom she endowed with her fortune. There is a constant suspicion in her tone towards him, though they were good friends, and she gave up a great deal to him. She needed the flattery and the fuss of new friendship; she liked to have some one *fresh* to observe and report the compliments and fine things which her visiting circle bestowed upon her; for she was a lion and a wonder in her Bath set; and the politeness and deference of her admirers could be most securely reckoned on, and the little flutter of shamefaced vanity could indulge itself more easily with them. She could report naturally such agreeable homage, as—

"Did I tell you the conquest I made in Wales of the Bishop of St. Asaph, Luxmore? He says now, 'What has become of that little Mrs. Piozzi, who shone here amongst us like a meteor for a month or two, and then away? When will she return, do you know? We are very dull without her.' And so they are, sure enough; no cards, no music, nor no conversation, except the petty quarrels which infest all counties distant from the metropolis, round whose central globe we roll at different distances; and Denbighshire is Saturnian in every sense of the word: their sorrows and their joys are so stupid."—Vol. ii. p. 254.

Denbighshire, though her property lay in it, and she had lived much there in Piozzi's time, was not a natural home for such a spirit—we can excuse a lively old lady for preferring Bath—but there is something painful in the little contrasts she intimates between the cold attentions of her adopted son, whom she had established on her Welsh estate, and the flattery of general society. The Conway, whom she next mentions, was an actor, for whom she got up a violent fancy. This admiration gave rise to reports which we think hardly warranted. She knew quite well that she was eighty, and felt this a justification of any language or other mode in which she might choose to express her approval:—

"Kind Conway has promised me a proof mezzo-tinto of his likeness in the character of Jaffier, by Harlowe; he says yours by Pellegrini is alive with resemblance. What will Salusbury say, when he comes first to dinner at aunt's house? whom he considers as a superannuated old goose, while she is petted, and flattered, and fed with soft dedication, all day long."—Vol. ii. p. 288.

It is likely that the Bath world should be better pleased than those immediately belonging to her, with the vivacity of an old lady who chooses to celebrate her eighty-first birthday with a fête to seven hundred people, herself leading off the dance with "*astonishing* elasticity." We do not know how far the enjoyment was real, or had heart in it, interspersed as it is with such reflections as, "No matter! the farce must go on till the curtain drops; and if everybody left off their disguisings as they grew old, why age would appear still more a deformity than at present!" and, "Dear me! how sick, how thrice sick I am of these parties! so falsely called society: for one idea in common with them I possess not. Yet one must live among people one cannot care about, in order to serve those who really amuse and delight one." Again, after the theatre, "Music and dancing are no longer what they were, and I grow less pleased with both every hour,"—but it was all she was capable of, and whatever the amount of satisfaction, society, and talking, and a prominent place, were essential, as all habits must be in old age. When hoarseness silences her, she writes, "a mute Piozzi is a miserable thing indeed." No recollections were pleasant to her that could not be put in the form of an anecdote to be told. Solitary reflection had no charm; the neglect of her children, through whatever cause, was a continual sore, and so was the estrangement of early friends. She never names either without bitterness. Her daughters she pronounces to be worldly and utterly without heart; her old friends, from Johnson downwards, to have been influenced by merely selfish motives; so that she declares herself to have thought "that there existed not a human creature that cared for poor H. L. P. now she had no longer money to be robbed of." However, the friends made in her seventy-sixth year restored her to charity with her species—the friends who brought strangers to see her "as the first woman in England." To these friends she confesses, "*I* was selfish *once*, and but *once* in my life; and though they lost nothing by my second marriage, my friends (as one's relations are popularly called) never could be persuaded to forgive it." She had placed herself in the unhappy position of having constantly, and through a life, to defend herself at the expense of her friends, and hers was just the mind to satisfy itself with seeming candor; she was always taking her own side without any real apprehension of the other. That her daughters deserve the testimony to their worth the editor bestows on them, receives confirmation from the following letter on the death of Mrs. Piozzi:—

"*Hotwells, May 5th*, 1821.

"DEAR MISS WILLOUGHBY,—It is my painful task to communicate to you, who have so lately been the kind associate of dearest Mrs. Piozzi, the irreparable loss we have all sustained in that incomparable woman and beloved friend.

"She closed her varied life about nine o'clock on Wednesday, after an illness of ten days, with as little suffering as could be imagined under these awful circumstances. Her bedside was surrounded by her weeping daughters: Lady Keith and Mrs. Hoare arrived in time to be fully recognized. Miss Thrale, who was absent from town, only just before she expired, had but the satisfaction of seeing her breathe her last in peace.

"Nothing could behave with more tenderness and propriety than these ladies, whose conduct, I am convinced, has been much misrepresented and calumniated by those who have only attended to one side of the history; but may all that is past be now buried in oblivion. Retrospection seldom improves our view of any subject. Sir John Salusbury was too distant, the close of her illness being too rapid for us to entertain any expectation of his arriving in time to see the dear deceased.

"He only reached Clifton *last* night I have not yet seen him; my whole time has been devoted to the afflicted ladies. To you, who so well knew my devoted attachment to Mrs. Piozzi, it is quite superfluous to speak of my *own* feelings, which I well know will become more *acute*, as the present hurry of business, in which we are all engaged, and the extreme bodily fatigue I have undergone, producing a sort of stupor in my mind, subsides. . . .

"P. S. PENNINGTON."

We further learn that her death was calm; that her last words were, "I die in the trust and the fear of God." This letter not only places the daughters in an amiable light; it does more for the character of Mrs. Piozzi than all the work beside. Of course, written under excitement, every word must not be weighed; but we gather from it that Mrs. Piozzi was capable of inspiring a thoughtful and amiable person, as the writer shows herself to be, with a sincere and warm attachment. It sets us defending the poor old lady against her own picture of herself. She was better than her pen would show her to be,—more genuine, more attractive, more lovable. As we have said, many things in her career were against her, and the world was hard upon her. That she was a woman of uncommon talent, spirit, and energy, worthy of Dr. Johnson's companionship, when in her prime, we cannot doubt. But the celebrity his friendship brought, took up her time, and unfitted her in every way for a mother's first duties. Her children were secondary to a great many things, and she never learned to love them, or taught them to love her. She had a husband whom, it seems, she could not respect, and who, she asserts, bestowed on others the love that was her due. During his lifetime, Johnson's society was an alleviation as well as distinction. She had much to put up with in ministering to his habits, and enduring his peculiarities, but there were equivalents which largely counterbalanced these inconveniences. After her husband's death, he soon became a restraint. Her mind was one that could submit to the inevitable, but was restive against minor hindrances. She broke her way through what most women think impossibilities, and had spirit not to be crushed by the consequences of her own act. Certainly, the world was very insolent towards her. She was the theme of newspapers; all sorts of impertinences were let loose upon her, in a strain to lead us to congratulate ourselves in an improvement in social morals. Her self-assertion rose above all. She affected to find the society of her husband's friends in Italy fully equal to that she had left behind. She threw herself into the interests of their pseudo-literary circle, and caught the knack of impromptus and epigrams with the readiness which had always enabled her to take the lead; all which is recorded in her account of her visit to Italy. The sham cleverness seemingly satisfied her like the real she had left behind. Her vanity, at least, was satisfied by the pre-eminence given to her, and the compliments bestowed on her talents, her beauty, and her virtue. Even the conventional love-making, addressed to her at forty-five, though a joke, was yet a piquante one. She was still a centre of a circle, a necessity with her for the remainder of her life; there was still employment for her pen, herself the central figure. That she had an ingenious and ready pen, her celebrated "Three Warnings" prove. She could turn a verse very easily; her classical acquirements, though not constituting her a learned woman, yet improved her power over words. Still, nothing in these volumes, given as specimens of her style, are worth reading; and the edition can only hint with apologetic reserve at her latest work, "Retrospection," which seems to have been a *résumé* of the world's proceedings from the Deluge to her own day. It was during its composition that she is described by one (Lord Normanby, we believe) who spent a day with her at Brynbella, the name of her place in Denbighshire. She showed him her bedroom; the floor of which was covered with huge books of reference for this work. "She was," he says, "certainly, what was called, and is still called, blue, and that of a deep tint, but good-humored and lively, though affected. Her husband, a quiet, civil man with his head full of nothing but music."

The history of her second marriage may, we think, teach a lesson in prudence and charity. Both are generally set at naught on the first announcement of a strange and outrageous marriage. Society may protest, when its own reasonable code is broken; but the tone towards the offenders, too often, as it were, denies them benefit of clergy: they are treated as though nothing that was now said could do them good or harm; we take no account of their souls; the words of old friends and neighbors crush or harden as the case may be. Coldness and silent displeasure from those who had a right to show offence in Mrs. Thrale's case, and an absence of all comment in the press on a matter not within their province, would have told as effectually in the way of convincing her she had wronged her children, and done a foolish thing, and would not have injured her moral tone to the same degree. Every circle learns its experience in such matters. Mrs. Thrale's case furnishes a lesson to the world at large.

Here, at least, ends all the teaching of every sort Mrs. Piozzi has to give; her name can rise no more on the surface of current literature. She supposed her last remains important; she was constantly arranging matters to look best to posterity; but once glanced over, her celebrity falls back on its only claim to it—her association with Dr. Johnson, as the one woman he preferred for constant intercourse and most intimate confidence. We may not take the same final leave of Mrs. Delany. The three weighty volumes of her correspondence, already given to the world, are only an instalment. What remains behind, how many more are to follow, the editor gives us no intimation; and as many pages may be in store to exhibit a good woman in serene, pious, and honored old age, as have been spent in depicting stroke by stroke her life of action, spent in the world, but guided by higher rules,—religious, moral, and prudential—than, in any age, direct the conduct or form the habits of society at large.

CHAPTER IX.

The dinner dressing-bell was ringing, as Ned reached the Lodge, and he was glad enough to go straight to his own room without encountering either father or mother. Few lads spent less time at a looking-glass in general; but, on this occasion, few fair ladies would have spent more than he. In fact, the stone-splinter had left its mark upon his broad forehead pretty plainly; and he had much ado to master the unwonted task of coaxing one lock of his brown hair to hide it. When at last he came down-stairs, he was glad to find a fourth person in the drawing-room, with Mr. and Mrs. Lockaley. That would stave awkward questionings off a little.

"No fish, Ned," said his father, "I suppose?"

"Not a fin."

"Who left her without a kiss this morning?" said his mother, as he bent to her cheek over the back of her arm-chair.

The fourth person was a man of business come to confer with Locksley upon some matter concerning my lord's estate. He was a well-informed and chatty man, whose conversation made the dinner unconstrained and tolerable. Once only, Ned felt his mother's look seeking what lay beneath the lock upon his forehead. She lifted it with her soft fingers as she passed him on her way out of the room, but dropped it without a word. "Only a mother's heart!" thought Ned, "only a mother's heart!" whilst the man of business was endeavoring to enlighten his father on the nature and value of railway scrip, a new and not over important item yet in the catalogue of marketable "securities." Clouds had come up at sunset, in spite of the past brilliancy of the day; so it was darker than might have been expected for the time of year.

"Any more claret, Mr. Robins?"

"No, thank you."

"And you *must* leave to-morrow morning?"

"Early, to meet the mail."

"Then I'm afraid we must shut ourselves up in the study, spite of the pleasant coolness in the air after all this heat. It's an intricate business, that Colnbrook mortgage, and will take us some time to look well through."

"Entirely at your service, my dear sir."

"Ned, tell your mother to send us a cup of tea down-stairs later. I don't think she'll see us in the drawing-room again to-night."

He found her lying on a sofa, in an arched recess, by a window, the light from which went past, leaving her in half gloom. He was glad of that shadowy darkness; he sat down in it, close beside her on the floor, and would have taken her hand in his. But she laid both hers gently upon his head, and drew it down to her own breast. Then she lifted the concealing lock again, and said, almost in a whisper,—

"I fear the wound is deep, Ned."

"What! that scratch, mother?"

"No, Ned! not that wound; but the other!"

"What other?"

He disengaged himself from her hold on him, turned, faced her, and was sorry now for the deep twilight which lay upon her countenance, dimming the lights and lines whence he might have read an answer.

Both were silent. But, through the shadows, the soft light, streaming full of tenderness, grew luminous between her own eyes and her boy's. At last he saw, and saw that she saw. So he let his head sink, till it rested on her breast again, and said,—

"Yes, mother, very deep, indeed."

His ear lay so close that it heard the quick throb quickening, and the words once more came thrilling him, "Only a mother's heart!"

How could he think of wringing it by leaving her? He would carry out her hopes, as truly as his own regrets, for burial, to that far East, towards which his face was set? By what right would he do so?

"Did you guess it, then, dear mother?"

"No, Ned. Fool that I was; how can I forgive myself?"

He was startled by a bitterness so little like her usual gentle mood. He put his hand upon her heart as he withdrew his head again, and felt the bound.

"Are you angry, then, with me for this?"

"No, my poor boy, my darling; not with you. Angry with *you*, indeed!"

"With whom, then, dearest? Not with *her*?"

Lucy was half indignant at his eagerness to absolve, nay to battle for her, who had filched his heart from himself and from his mother. But, half ashamed at her own indignation, she said nothing.

"Who told you, then?"

"Her mother."

"Was *she* angry with me?"

"She said not; only sorry."

"Well that was kind of her."

"Ah, but it hurt *me* more! I never knew till now the cruelty of pity."

Then, again, both were for some time silent.

"How came the cut upon your forehead?"

"From a splinter of a stone I smashed."

"Then *you* were angry; that's an old angry trick of yours. Angry with her, or with her mother, Ned?"

"With neither."

"With yourself?"

"I *should* have been."

"But were not. Tell me, then, with whom."

"I was high up on the moor, and could overlook the tree-tops at Rookenham."

"O fool, and blind!" she cried, starting up. "Not you, Ned, no my darling, not you; but your mother, here. I never thought of Royston for her, no more than of you, my poor boy. Are you sure of it?"

"Almost. And I think Royston is."

Then he told her; for, somehow, he could keep nothing back just then, how near the Dresden vase on Lord Royston's mantelpiece had been to sharing the fate of the splintered stone. He told her also of Mrs. White's chattering surmises, and of the way in which her random words had stung him to the quick.

Lucy's purpose had not faltered during all the long hours of that day, which had seemed weeks to her, waiting for this heart-to-heart talk with her son. Had it done so, his last words would at once have steadied it.

"He must go," she thought, "since it is plain that Lady Constance will not. If Rookenham is to be her home for life, it is as if she were fixed life-long here at Cransdale. To be pricked to death with pin points is exquisite ignominy no less than exquisite pain. Severance may bring sadness; but continual contact, such as theirs would be, can only breed fretfulness or savagery. My Ned shall go, were pangs of parting to kill me."

Little wonder that the lad felt more and more as if the subtle, sympathetic stream between her eyes and his were searching out the very deep of the spirit within him. Part from her! It seemed as if the power to will—could he still wish it—were being drawn from out of him, by that strange magnetism of a mother's victorious love.

"But what took you, my dear boy, to Rookenham? I should have thought it the last place where you would have gone today."

Then came the story of the idiot child and his sick mother.

"Poor woman! only think how she must have increased the hardship of the struggle for a livelihood by living miles off from her work up there. What a magnificent self-sacrifice!"

Oh, what luxury to hear him say so! To hear him marvel and admire at what she had it in her own heart to outdo. It sent a thrill through her, almost too delicious to be lawful. Stay! was that so, or was it not? Could self-indulgence be blameworthy rising, unsought, out of self-sacrifice?

"Yes, Ned! But she did it to keep her boy."

"To keep her boy," thought Edward; "so that is full explanation is it, and dwindles down the marvel in a mother's eyes? To keep her boy? That then is full satisfaction for a self-devoted mother's heart—'Only a mother's heart!' Ah, yes, I see. 'Only a mother's heart!' very true!"

Again there was a long spell of silence. Edward looked out at the open window, where a thinning space upon the cloudy sky-field showed that the moon's forceful gentleness was melting the heat mists away. But he still felt his mother's look stream on him, and knew that her eyes did not go wandering forth into the summer night.

He was now sitting on the lower end of the sofa and she near the head of it. Presently she drew nearer him, and, laying her hand upon his shoulder, said,—

"When do you go, Ned?"

"Go, dearest; go where?"

"To India."

"O mother, mother!" He put his arms about her so manful tenderly. "I was selfish, ungrateful, cowardly. I will stay here."

This also was delicious, with deliciousness pure beyond suspicion. She paused to drink it in and savor it. They had not stolen *all* his love from her!

"My Ned, I cried this morning in my first pain. My Ned, yes, *mine*, for he will stay with me."

And he was hers. Yet,—ah, she was spared knowledge of the cruel yet!—yet, as she put her mother lips upon the spot where Constance's had been upon his forehead, there was a shiver in his heart, as if the newly buried love had stirred within its living grave, because the seal on it was touched.

"You stay here, Ned? Have you counted the cost?"

His was a very truthful soul; a few moments, therefore, passed before his answering,—

"Summed it up in the rough; but hardly looked at items."

"And you are ready to pay?"

"Cost what cost will."

The moon's disk by this time was clear of mists. A silver beam came slanting into the arched recess. Her son could see by the moonlight, as her husband had seen by the glare of day, that a mystic smile was making some sweet glory upon her face; but he was no better able than his father to spell its full meaning out.

She turned away from him on a sudden, passing her hands between the sofa and the angle of the wall. A clink as of brass rings and buckles, struck his ear; and a gleam, as of burnished metal, flashed on his eye when she turned again.

"See, Ned! I cannot give you your proud lady-love; but I can give you this instead. Does not the 'Sword Song' call it a 'steel bride'?"

"What is it, mother, dear?"

But the words were idle; for, as if a magnet drew his fingers, they had at once an iron grip upon the hilt.

"You know it well enough, Ned. Your grandfather's old sword."

One hand was upon the hilt, the other on the scabbard. He drew it—scarce an inch or two, thrust the steel down quick into the sheath again and held it back towards her.

"Do not tempt me, dearest. I said 'cost what cost will.'"

"God bless you for your will to make the costly sacrifice, my son. May he accept it!—in such sort as we do—your father and I—taking the will for the deed; for we are well resolved to take no more from you. I will not call your wound a mere boy's fancy, Ned. A sorrow piercing your heart wounds my own too deep for that. But young flesh and young spirit are akin, when both are pure and healthy as I joy to believe yours, my darling. Their wounds heal firm and clean when nothing frets and gangrenes. This home would be a sickly hospital for you. Here you would have a thousand petty throes to regain your heart's mastery; and you might fritter away in them a thousand times the strength which would give it you, wrestling elsewhere."

She had fixed her eyes again upon him, and the love-stream flowed from them; but not now as before. They were sitting upon the sofa, not side by side now, but almost face to face. Ned had both hands upon the hilt of the sword, which had its point upon the floor. His head was propped on them, and he was looking at his mother as if he would try to read her inmost thought. But living books can scarce be read save when their life is passive, or when its energy is not directed full on the would-be reader. And there was a might kindled in those soft eyes of his mother which forbade the attempt to sit and merely read their meaning. His heart and mind seemed fairly subdued to hers.

"Something strange has waked up in me, dear boy. A pride *for* you of which my old pride *in* you had not made me yet aware. You know that I am sorry—oh, how sorry, how sorry!—for you, Ned, and for me. Yet, I am glad. This quiet nest-life here, green summer life, snug winter life—it is no life for *you*, *your* pulse beats too quick for it."

She stretched out her hand, whose soft fingers felt along his wrist for the veined passage where she might time his young blood's bounding.

"How could I think—it must have been wishing, not thinking, all along—that it would flow so gently dull as ours! I don't say now that I would have chosen a soldier's calling for you. But I would have you live a strong life; and since you have chosen, be it so—a strong soldier's."

Then she drew near him, and passed her arm round his waist; and because she felt certain now that in herself and in her boy there was a strength that would not weaken nor grow soft, she drew his head once more upon her shoulder, and they sat silent and still. When her lips once more touched that same spot on his forehead no pang quivered within. Presently they heard the father's footsteps on the stairs, and the parting "good-night" of his business-guest. Then Locksley came in, and Lucy rose up with her boy and went across the room to meet him. She took one of his hands and laid it upon the hilt of the weapon, which Ned yet held in one of his, and said,—

"Robert, you give your own son—do you not—your gallant father's sword? He wants to carry one, and I have told him that we wish it too."

"Take it, Ned, as your mother says," was all his answer. The film had come again across the summer moon, so the son saw not the salt beads which rolled over and out of his father's eyes.

CHAPTER X.

"WHAT'S up at the Locksleys', I wonder," quoth his lordship, sauntering into the room where his mother and Lady Constance were, his hairy doggie close upon his heels; "Ned and his father drove over before breakfast to meet the London mail; and there's something queer about Mrs. Locksley's eyes."

A quick look passed between mother and daughter; but they were saved any need of speaking by the entrance of a servant with the post-bag.

"One for me," said Philip, opening it. "Scotch post-mark; that's from Macphail, I bet, to know whether Skye came safe. Beg, Skye, beg; here's news from your kennel! One for my lady. Royston's fist apparently." And he gave it to his mother.

"The next is a whopper!—official, as I'm alive! It must be my commission; and I'm a grenadier for good!—Hooray!"

Suddenly that "something queer" of his easy slang came into his own mother's eyes as well. No such need hers as Lucy's, to steel her heart against pangs of utter severance; still the boy was gone one step further from her side. She drew him to her, almost unconsciously, and with nervous fingers would help him to break seals and tear envelopes. But Lady Constance left the room, and presently the house.

She had seen the light quenched in her mother's looks as it kindled up in Philip's, and she could not rest for thinking of the blight which must have fallen upon Lucy's joy.

She wondered whether in her heart her old friend had begun to hate her. Next to her own mother, there was no woman whom she loved so well. At her knee, as at a second mother's she had grown to womanhood. Countless memories, countless endearments, a thousand trifles, which make a girl's life sweet, bound her to Mrs. Locksley. And she felt, with unerring instinct, that Ned's love for herself had cost that dear friend her son.

On her heart's knees she longed to crave for pardon—but for what? For being lovely? For being lovable? At least for having seemed to be such in an almost brother's eyes? The very thought of having such self-consciousness made blushes burn under her satin skin.

Wherein had she wronged Edward? Not the strictest search of self could herein convict her of a single willing fault.

Wherein had she wronged Lucy! That were as hard to say. Wronged was not just the word. But if Lucy's son had missed his footing on some towering cliff, and fallen, because Constance, clad in white, had neared him, all unknowingly, and he had taken her for some sad ghost—what then? Would she feel shriven of her guiltless guilt until his mother's very lips had spoken absolution?—No!

Therefore she must speak to Mrs. Locksley face to face. And because her heart was brave, as well as tender, she must needs speak at once. And when they were come face to face, either did seem ghostly to the other. Ghostly, not ghostlike, for it was broad daylight; and each stood revealed to the other in real shape and true proportion; but the ghostly element, the spirit which was in either, seemed to have unusual mastery over the outward frame and expression of them both.

They spoke and spoke plain to one another—neither uttering a word.

Lucy was sitting where Lady Cransdale had found her sitting the day before. The same bit of muslin-work in her hands; but both hands idle in her lap. She sat upright, and looked straight out—not on the green lawn, not at the feathery cedars, not over the brown moor, not up to the summer sky;

but miles and miles off by the thousand, into the far East and into the coming years, looking at what should befall her boy.

Lady Constance came straight to the open window, and stood opposite her; and yet, for a long time, did not intercept her straining sight; and seemed at last to shape herself and grow distinct upon its field, gradually, as when a spy-glass is shortened till the focus is come true. And as Lucy felt fully conscious of her presence by degrees, so she felt conscious of a pleading power of rebuke in Constance's lovely violet eyes, as they looked on her. Constance knew nothing of that; but Lucy felt it in her inmost soul.

How dared she call her, last night, "his *proud* lady-love." Such heart-entreaty, such strong humility, such noble pitifulness, withal such consciousness of right, as now confronted her, what could these have to do with vulgar pride! "Unjust!" said the spirit within.

Love-light is complex; and though the glories of the passionate ray were wanting, yet Lucy saw that beautiful countenance—as she had never seen before—in some rays of the light in all of which her son had seen its loveliness.

She shook her head, and said in a low voice, yet loud enough to fall on the girl's ear, "No wonder!"

As if the spell which had kept her across the threshold, were broken, Lady Constance came in, knelt down by Lucy's side, took her unresisting hands and kissed them, and murmured,—

"Forgive me for breaking in upon your sorrow, Mrs. Lockaley; but I could not keep away."

"Then, you know why he is gone?"

She hid her face in Lucy's lap, and said,—

"I fear, because of me."

"And tell me, Lady Constance, do you know where he is going?"

Something harsh vibrated in her voice, whereat Constance, though still kneeling, looked up as if to meet a challenge. Firm, in perfect gentleness, she looked her friend again in the face, and answered deliberately, though without hesitation,—

"I think so; but am not quite sure."

Great deeps had been broken up in that mother's troubled soul, and strange lightnings were still playing over their turmoil. Constance caught one flash of them; but did not shrink from nor resent its glare.

Yes! It was hard hearing, that she who would have none of his love should yet have known his life-secrets before herself, who loved him more than life. But, after all, the storm was even now retreating; and though the flash were seen, no roll of angry thunder came.

"Dear Mrs. Lockaley," said Lady Constance, rising and taking seat beside her, "I will hide nothing from you of what I know. It is only now, this moment, under your troubled glance, that I remember how words of mine may have influenced your son in any wish to leave you; if, indeed, as I gathered from what he told my mother the other day, he thinks of leaving you for India."

It was some sort of consolation to gather hence that the jealous surmise was not wholly true; that her boy's secret wish had not been long beforehand delivered into other keeping than her own.

"He is gone to town with his father to seek an appointment in the Indian Army; but he is gone, Lady Constance," she spoke with tremulous eagerness, "at my own earnest entreaty and request."

"Thank God for that at least," said Constance.

"Why so?"

"Because—because—perhaps I am selfish; but I should have found this sorrow much more hard to bear, had dearest Ned's sad heart turned to rebellion against you,—against a mother so loving, and I will answer for it too, so dearly loved."

"Why did you call that 'selfish, perhaps'?"

"Because in presence of your grief, and his, I had no sort of right to be thinking whether what sorrow I might have to bear were less or greater."

"That is very nobly said."

"Is it? I did not know, but spoke the simple truth."

"Then you are sorry, indeed?"

She had no need to speak in answer to the question. Lucy saw that, but persisted,—

"For whom are you sorry? For me?"

Constance raised her friend's hands to her lips, and kissed them, so tenderly.

A momentary gleam of a wild hope shot through Lucy.

"Look at me full once more, Lady Constance. Are you sorry,—ever so little,—sorry with ever so faint a shade of sorrow—for yourself?"

Her breath seemed cut off as she wrung the beautiful girl's hands in the agony of that inquiring, beseeching, almost despairing moment. It was like the failure of a dying person's grasp, to feel her fingers fall away, as she turned back her head from the truth-telling eyes of Constance.

"Ah, well! But you did say you were sorry for him, too. Have you none of that for him to which pity is kin? Do you not love him a little?"

"No, dear Mrs. Locksley, not a little. Because I do love him, as I told him, so very much. He is my brother, and must ever be so."

"Then you do not"—she hesitated, and her eye dropped before her younger's, and she felt a flush of shame at asking an unworthy question; but, there, it spoke as it had spoken in her heart: and it was better to let it cross her lips and kill itself with its own sound, perhaps. "You do not despise him?"

"I should despise myself if I could do so. There must be something tenderer in ties of blood than of the earliest and closest intimacy. So, of my two brothers, there is a sense in which I love Philip best; but I never was blind to the nobler loveworthiness of Ned."

Sweet pain to hear her say so. Sweetness in the true verdict; pain, in the passionless calm of the true judge.

"What were those words of yours, then, which may have influenced his longing for this Indian soldiership?"

"Indeed, indeed, I never thought of influencing him; but we have often talked of India, and of that great Eastern Empire, and I spoke as I think of it."

"And how may that be?"

"As a grand field for a great-hearted Englishman."

"So you have sent him to reap there with a sword!"

"I never meant it so: never dreamt of doing it. But if I have done it, I will not say that my sorrow for him,—for *him*, mind you, dear Mrs. Locksley,—is on that account."

"Why not?"

"Because great fields want reapers of great heart, and Ned is one."

"Thank you! How well you know him! Oh, could you but have loved him as he loves you. Well, well! Forgive me! That could not be. No! could not. I understand now, Lady Constance, dear: it could not."

She was conscious of the stir within of yet one other question, which she had no right to put. But the wrong of putting would be too wrongful. She would not let it look out at her eyes, much less take frame upon the threshold of her lips. She was a woman even before a mother, therefore she would not yield to the temptation of affronting the frank and beautiful girl's womanliness. Her voice sunk at the "could not," without insinuating "why not?"

Constance rose to go. Lucy rose too, and by a mastering impulse held out her arms, and they were locked in close embrace, murmuring, "Forgive me," and "I have nothing, no, nothing, to forgive."

Lucy's tears fell fast when she was once more alone: but calm was returning to her heart as the showery veil falling, leaves the blue vault bright again.

"Hallo, Con!" cried the earl, as his sister came back into the room where he and his mother were still in conference.

"Where on earth have you been all this time, and what the mischief makes you look so grave? Queer eyes seem all the go this morning."

There was no use in concealing what must so soon be known, so she answered,—

"I have been to Mrs. Locksley's."

"Oh, you have! Well, what's up with Ned?"

"He's gone to London with Mr. Locksley to make interest at once for a commission in the Indian Army."

"What! Ned gone for a sodger, and a sepoy, too! Are you gone cracked and crazy, Con, or is he?"

"Not I, for certain; and I should think not he."

"This *is* a rum start! No wonder Mrs. Locksley's eyes were queer!"

Lady Cransdale shook her head,—a shake which he rightly interpreted as against his own inveterate slang.

"No, don't mammy dear, don't and I wont. I'll use dictionary words all right. I can come out strong in that line at a pinch.

But you must allow that there is something catastrophic in this unexpected development of Mr. Edward Lockaley's predilections for a strategical career! Why, let me see, when was it? Only the day before yesterday, as we rode over about Tommy Wilmot in quod, —I beg pardon—to the locality of Mr. Thomas Wilmot's temporary detention by the constabulary authorities of the county—"

"Don't be silly, Phil."

"Well, there's no pleasing you both. Lady Cransdale wont have slang, and Lady Constance wont stand the dictionary. But anyhow, as we rode out together two days ago, this would-be 'griffin'—technical Indian term, my lady, not Eton slang,—was discussing his prospects as a Freshman at Christchurch, next October Term. So I've some right to call it a 'rum'—a remarkable catastrophic incident, I mean.

"There's something sudden about his determination," said Constance, since something further must be said, though she scarcely knew what: "but he must have turned his thoughts to India long ago, for we have often talked of it together."

Her brother looked at her sharply, with an expression of extreme surprise.

"What, Con! Is your finger in this pie? Have you been recruiting for the Honorable E.I.C? What next, I wonder?"

He jumped up, and was going out, when his eye caught a letter on the floor under the table.

"Let's see, what letter's this? Why, it's Royston's. Is that the way you pitch about your correspondence, my lady?"

Lady Cransdale had dropped it unperceived, in her agitation at the receipt of Philip's official communication. He picked it up, and as he gave it to her, said,—

"What says the under-sec., my lady?"

"Dear me!" cried his mother when the note was opened, "it's just as well the letter caught your eye, Phil. Ring the bell, will you, that I may tell some one to have the rooms in the east wing ready."

"What, is he going to 'cut' the office for a day or two? I mean, is the noble lord about to tear himself from his public avocations in favor of a temporary rustication here?"

"Yes. His chief is come to town, he writes, and has given him three days' run. He'll be with us at dinner this evening."

Trouble upon trouble. Constance felt what brought him, uninvited, to spend his three days' holiday at Cransdale rather than at Rookenham. It disturbed her deeply that he should have come just then. What would not Lucy's sore heart surmise, with its motherly pain to sharpen its womanly keenness? And poor dear Ned—Ned so truly dear—would he not think it cruel when he should hear that Royston was come, on the very day when he himself was driven from his childhood's home? Then, why did Philip eye her as he was doing,—as he had done from the moment she had owned to some knowledge of Ned's Indian inclinations,—as he had seemed to do with quickened inquisitiveness from the moment he had picked up Lord Royston's letter?

Did he suspect that she had wronged Ned? or did he fancy she would trifle with their kinsman? or, by what right did he imagine, if indeed he did, that there was any relation between her and him which could make trifling possible? or—but who can tell the million moods into which a maiden's heart will ripple under the breath of such thoughts and feelings as were moving Constance?

Firm and self-possessed as she was most times, she found it hard to keep an outward calm in this inward agitation. Do what she would the rising sob could not be kept from bringing teardrops up to hang on the long lashes of her eyes. As she left the room, still under inquisition of her brother's look, her mother followed and took her hand outside the door and pressed it, turning down the passage another way without a single word. What strengthening and consolation in that one gentle grasp of a mother's hand; what assurance of full understanding and pledge of hearty sympathy!

Small helps are great to strong spirits. Her nerves were strung again before Lord Royston came. Philip was at first full of his own affairs; so there was plenty of embryo guardsman's talk to keep conversation going. Then, in spite of the "not-a-soul-in-town" state of the metropolis, there were several somebodies about whose weal or woe, changes and chances, questions must be asked and answered, or information volunteered. Those were days before wires, and grand trunks were the only lines on which rails ran. Cransdale was remote from any such: the budget of London news was therefore fresher, and its unpacking less to be dispensed with than now-a-days.

"By the by, Lady Cransdale, there's been one official change in which you may take some little interest. Sir James Macfarlane has got a 'liver,' so Barrington goes out to India in his stead. You know Barrington, don't you?"

"What! old Lord Bamford's son? Of course I do. Why, Royston, he's a connection of yours, on your mother's side. Old Lady Bamford was a Fitzhugh."

"Was she? Well I had forgotten; but your word is as good as 'Burke's Peerage' for it. So Buffer Barrington's my cousin, is he? It's a pity I don't want any thing Indian, that I know of, or I would claim cousinship by the next post, and tender your ladyship in proof of pedigree."

Constance's heart leaped up at the words "Any thing Indian!" Could Barrington do "something Indian" for Ned Locksley? she wondered. And if he could, how bring herself to ask for Royston's interest with him? To ask a favor is, sometimes, to grant one, so great and so significant, that the giver, who has no misgiving as to the effect of the petition, has many touching the dangerous generosity of making it.

"But surely Barrington's young for such an appointment, Royston? And I don't know that he has ever distinguished himself so very much."

The under secretary laughed outright.

"It's rude of me, Lady Cransdale, but I can't help it, I declare."

"You silly fellow, what are you laughing at?"

"The notion of *young* Buffer Barrington! He's about the oldest fellow going, is the Buffer, I should have said."

"Just hear him!" retorted her ladyship. "There are no young people now-a-days. I suppose, in five years' time, you'll be sending Phil out to command in chief."

"A very sensible notion, mammy," cried that recruit of to-day. "I shall have mastered the goose step in its remotest intricacies long before then, and be quite fit for high command. Now, mind you book that hint, Royston. I shouldn't so much mind a turn of Calcutta, if I went 'in chief;' but I go for nothing under."

"Do provincial governors have aides-de-camp?" ventured Lady Constance, who felt as if, after all, it would be treason to let slip such an opportunity.

"By George! well thought of, Con!" bounced Philip, with a sudden energy that showed her there was no use in cautious approaches any longer.

"A shoal of them if they like, I fancy. Lady Cransdale knows best. Your ladyship must remember how it was. But why do you want to know? Guardsmen are, I take it, eligible; but Phil says he wont go under command-in-chief. Aides-de-camp are a trifle below that mark."

"St. John's Wood is jungle enough for me," said Phil. "I'm not the aspiring aide-de-camp."

"Who, then?"

"I'm not sure that there is any in the case. But we were thinking of Ned Locksley."

"But Christchurch men can't be aides-de-camp, any more than ensigns can command in chief, eh?"

"Ensigns, indeed! Ensign and lieutenant, Mr. Under Secretary. None of your civilian sauce, if *you* please."

"Excuse 'a pékin's' inadvertency," quoth the other, with mock solemnity. "But what on earth do you mean by mixing up Ned Locksley with Indian aides-de-camp?"

"Fact is, some freak has taken him; he's gone for a sodger; struck his friends all of a heap, in consequence."

"Phil! Phil!" said his mother.

"Oh, I beg your pardon. I wished to convey to your lordship intimation of the fact that Mr. Edward Locksley's embracing a military career has been somewhat precipitate, and productive of some perturbation in the circle of his immediate connections. That's right now, mammy dear, isn't it?"

"The long and the short of it is," said Lady Cransdale, "that Ned has determined to enter the Indian service; indeed, he is gone to London to settle about his commission; and we, of course, are on the alert for any thing which can forward his interests in India."

Constance understood with what skilful and kind interest her mother had thrown out that "we, of course." She sent her across the table a glance of gratitude in return. Her mother saw it and readily understood its meaning. She would clear Constance at once of a petitioner's responsibility.

"Now really, Royston," she therefore went on to say, "I should take it as a personal kindness to myself if you could make play with 'Buffer Barrington,' as you call him, whether 'young' or 'old.' That is, if Ned goes to his Presidency. We shall soon know that."

"I'll move heaven and earth, Lady Cransdale—that is, such portions of them as comprehend the Buffer's universe—to do your bidding. Indeed, I should be very glad to do what I could for young Locksley's own sake. I don't know a more promising boy anywhere, though, somehow, he never seemed to take to me much."

"Boy!" mocked Philip. "Here's Royston coming the Pater conscriptus with a vengeance!"

"Oh, ah! Young man, I mean, of course, Phil, begging ten thousand pardons. I forgot Ned was your senior."

"Boy!" thought Constance, in her inmost heart. "Ah, poor dear Ned! if he could have heard *him* say it!"

She thought, moreover, deeper still within, that she could furnish Royston with a clue to that "somehow" which seemed inexplicable.

After dinner—the evening was exquisite—they went walking on the lawns and terraces. Constance kept close to her mother's side, and seemed to cling with nervous apprehension to her arm. She was usually so frank and fearless in every step and gesture, that her evident shrinking from him could not escape Lord Royston. The wit and wisdom of that rising young statesman suffered in consequence intense depression.

"Tell you what," said Phil at last; "you're about as jolly as a walking funeral, the lot of you. Skye, man, come here; we'll have a weed together, and let those solemn parties stalk about without the pleasure of our company." So he sat down on the grass, lit his cigar, and proceeded to worry the poor doggie with puffing smoke into his nostrils, till he snapped at him in desperation.

Lady Cransdale, after this, managed to get Lord Royston to the side of her, where Phil had been—a manœuvre which by no means augmented the cheerfulness of that official nobleman, but for which Constance hugged the arm on which she was hanging. And so they went, in spasmodic conversation, up and down, and round and round, till they found themselves upon the rim of the marble basin of Constance's corner. Some of her rose leaves still swam on the water; some were sodden, and had sunk under it. A caddis grub, or some such creature, had rolled one up and plastered it slimily with bits of stick and small pebbles. Constance shuddered to see the crooked leglets of the wee crawling thing, moving it along the smooth bottom of the big marble cup.

"Are those your rose leaves, Con?" said her mother, she hardly knew why.

"I suppose they are. Let us go back, mammy dear."

As they turned to go, she saw that Royston did not at once turn with them; but, though his knees were not yet bent to reach the rim, she felt that he would do as Ned had done, and skim some of her pulled rose leaves off the pond.

Quick as thought, and with as quick a pang of pain and girlish shame, she left her mother's arm and turned towards him, and laid her hand upon his shoulder.

"Please not, Lord Royston!"

He looked more hurt even than startled.

"Why not, dear Lady Con——No! Dearest Constance, why not?"

She only shook her head; hurt, likewise, at having let herself be startled into doing as she had done.

"No answer, but your sweet will? Well, that is law for me."

There was such grace of manliness in his submission, that Constance could not leave it quite unrewarded, so she said,—

"You shall have an answer, but not now."

Then she went forward quickly, and linked her arm close into her mother's, as before. Royston was wise enough to take his place also where he had been, upon the other side of Lady Cransdale, and they went slowly towards the house, none making many words.

But Philip was ready to rattle away again when they came in, having to demonstrate, among other things, the urgent needfulness of a return to town with Royston, when his three days' leave should end. The new soldier togs and trappings must be bought and tried.

Lady Cransdale did not wish to part from him unnecessarily soon: she and Constance would go too. So Cransdale House stood empty by the time that Mr. Locksley returned with Ned, an officer in the Company's army.

CHAPTER XI.

"WELL, what sort are the 'griffs'?" asked Captain Rufford of Lieutenant Jones. "How many of 'em are there this time?"

"Three, seemingly," he continued, unhooking his sword-belt; "one's a milksop to look at; I didn't notice the others. Here! messman! kidneys with the coffee; and jump about a bit!"

"A little badger-bait's about the thing, then, eh? By way of introduction to barrack life?"

"Bait, by all means; but without a badger; unless the others are more 'varmint' than the one I noticed. He wouldn't snap if he were drawn out of a barrel by the bung-hole."

"Ugh! the sneaking animal! But there's no knowing, after all, my boy. Some sneaks will snap under judicious provocation."

"Ah, well, we'll see. Here! messman, bitter beer? But how about the major, Ruff, my boy?"

"Major's a muff. I'd give a trifle to draw that old humbug's den itself. He's gray enough to do the badger to the life, he is!"

"Gray enough? And grim enough, I believe ye. If he bit, he'd make the teeth meet, or I am a Dutchman."

"Wouldn't he?" re-echoed the captain, with a scowl, which showed pretty plainly that he looked upon his senior officer with some worse feeling than a mere "fast" man feels against a mere "slow coach."

"Did you hear the old rascal's remark about that business with the cards at the queen's depôt last Friday night?"

"Not I," said Jones, a cruder scamp than his companion, and more compunctious withal. "To tell you the truth, Ruff," and his voice lowered to the confidential pitch; "I've my doubts myself whether young Archer should have been allowed to play. He'd had an overdose of wine, you know."

"I can't say that, as a principle, it's a good plan, in the long run, to let 'green' parties drink so deep before they play; specially when they're green enough to make play pleasant without it, Jones, my boy. But then, one mustn't look a gift-horse in the mouth; and that amiable ensign's cheque for 'fifty' came at such a nick of time, that I couldn't afford to take the scrupulous view, do you see?"

"What nick of time? Any thing more amiss than usual?"

"Don't you remember the thirty guineas lost upon the Battery-nag that won the hurdle-race. That Artillery Jenkins had been dunning me most inconveniently."

"Oh, ah, well, I'm glad you've paid him something; stave him off me, perhaps, for I'm ten pound wrong with him on the transaction, I am."

"Humph! What's the milksop's name you mentioned?"

"Garrett, I think."

"A very nice name at the bottom of a cheque, no doubt. That sort of young man comes from home with credit at a bank most times. Quite as good a name as Archer, eh? Do quite as well for Artillery Jenkins?"

And Captain Rufford looked hard at Lieutenant Jones, half sounding, half suggesting.

"Perhaps he don't play."

"Perhaps not."

"But one might teach him. No! confound it, Ruff; that business of Archer's not blown over either!"

"Can't see that Archer's business is any of yours; excuse me, Jones; but I'm not prepared to say it's your downright duty to teach Mr. Garrett the use of his cards. He wont want for tutors, I dare say, should he wish for them."

"Certainly not; no, certainly not."

And the lieutenant kept moving his coffee-cup round and round, half way between the table and himself, peering at the grouts in it, as if consulting some cabalistic oracle. After a considerable pause he began with diffidence again,—

"Perhaps, if that's your game with him, we had better not have any badger-baiting?"

"Whose game with whom? You're coming out in the sphinx line, Jones."

"None o' that, Ruff; you know what I mean."

"Do I? Hum! Well, speaking abstractedly, mind you, and without personal or particular reference; but as a mere general speculative theory, I am inclined to think that badger-baiting, upon first acquaintance, is a doubtful means for captivating the shy confidence of a junior; but one can't be cock-sure of any thing. Some colts want rough handling at once when taken up from grass, some coaxing."

"Ah, very true," said Jones; "yours is what I call practical philosophy."

"Yes, very practical;" wherewith the captain took to reading *Bell's Life* with determination. Jones knew there wasn't a word more to be got out of him just then.

Presently came in Major Anderson, commanding the Honorable Company's depôt at Chatterham. The dust had powdered his undress frock almost as gray as Indian service had grizzled his sandy locks. His adjutant was on the sick-list, and he had taken that duty on him this dry morning as well as his own command. The very slightest and stiffest courtesies, consistent with military etiquette, passed between him and his juniors; and when he sat down at the long table, to his moderate refection of tea and toast, he availed himself to the utmost of the privilege its length afforded, of keeping at a considerable distance from them.

By and by, the messroom door again was opened, with sound of rattle and clank outside, and loud calls upon the messman's immediate attention. Then came in, pell-mell, a whole squad of hungry youngsters, for the more part noisy, laughing, and talkative, the one graver face and steadier step among them being Ned Locksley's.

"Sharp-set with drill, young gentlemen?"

It was a grating voice, with a rasp of drill-sergeant's hoarseness in it, but by no means unkindly; nor was it an unkindly twinkle which came from the small gray eyes, whose corners were fine drawn with crowsfeet.

"It's yourself I'd ate, major," answered an unmistakable brogue, "if it wasn't for the Mutinee Act and Coorts-martial."

"Poor pickings you'd have of it," quoth the threatened one, "to say nothing of bones to choke such a cannibal, should you fall foul of my carcase, Mr. O'Brien."

"Well, major, it's osseous iligance your figure displays, for certain, rather than fleshy dilivopment."

"Ah, well! Six months' cantonments at at Churrucknagore will strip some vascular superfluities even from your sturdy frame, youngster, to say nothing of six-and-twenty years' campaigning."

"True for you, major, dear; and I told me frinds to take a good look at me at parting; shure the better they'd know me now, the worse they'd recognize me whin home on lave again."

A laughing chorus of subalterns, easily pleased with a joke, was followed by a storm of shouts for the messman. He came in at last with a waiter in attendance, and three or four soldier-servants. A crash of knives and forks followed, with occasional pop of ale-cork or fizz from soda-water. Lieutenant Jones came down from the top of the table, and made his way out, nodding to one or two of the youngsters as he went. Captain Rufford sat where he was, not so wholly absorbed in his sporting oracle as not to keep his ears well open or not to send a searching glance round the corner of its broadsheet now and then.

"The military art stands on a praycarious footin'," began O'Brien, after the disappearance of a beefsteak of abnormal size.

"How so?" said the major.

"Shure the goose-step as raycintly practised by the present company—"

"Shop!" cried another, "let's adone with drill for to-day, Pat."

"With all me heart—for to-morrow too, and the day after, into the bargain, savin' her majesty's presence."

"Drill's better than dawdling," caught up another voice, "what's to be done till dinner-time?"

"There's cricketing somewhere down the Long Meadows," another answered.

"Cricket be blowed—it's too hot for out-of-door amusements, I say."

"Bedad, thin," broke in O'Brien, "if it's too hot for you here, Mansfield, it's little enjoyment you'll have of the major's cantonments at Chokerychore, or whatever the name is."

"Claret cup and cards, with a nigger to keep a wet flap flapping, might help," suggested Mansfield.

Captain Rufford looked sharp and hard round the corner of his paper at the utterer of such congenial sentiments. Major Anderson eyed the speaker also, with a very different expression, from his crowsfooted eyes. Mansfield was not a bad-looking boy, but of unwholesome complexion. There was an aping of premature manliness and an affectation of off-hand manner about him, which seemed to be a protest against his own evidently boyish appearance and age.

Men of the Rufford stamp read "possible dupe and probable confederate" on such countenances as plain as on a placard.

"Humph, young gentleman!" said the major; "if that's your notion of what an Indian officer's life should be in cantonments—"

"Ah, major dear," rattled in the Irishman, "if it's Tilimachus ye're coming over us now; shure drill itself is an aisier divarsion for youngsters."

"Telemachus, sir?" asked the major, rather sternly.

"Ten thousand pardons, major," he answered, quite unabashed, "it's Mintor I mane, to be shure now."

Roars of laughter, in which the senior had the good sense himself to join, greeted the blunder, and under cover of it the party broke up. The major and Locksley went out side by side, some of the others following. Three or four stayed on in the mess-room; among them young Mansfield and another subaltern, with whom Rufford was acquainted. The captain put down his newspaper, and as he sauntered by, said to his acquaintance, "Introduce me to Mr. Mansfield, will you?"

Meanwhile the major, whose gray peering eyes had scanned Ned's firm and handsome features closely as they crossed the barrack-yard together, made up his mind that their possessor was a lad worth looking after.

"Pray, Mr. Locksley, how do you think to kill time this afternoon? I didn't hear you say, when the other youngsters were in discussion."

"No use to murder such a determined suicide," said he.

"Well put, indeed. It's a foolish phrase for a more foolish thing. I'm glad you're of that mind, Mr. Locksley."

"My words are wiser than my wishes, I fear, major, this morning; for to tell you the truth, the latter are in the Long Meadows already."

"Oh! you're a cricketer?"

"I have been," answered Ned, with just the least unconscious touch of a very young man's assumption of old experiences.

"Belong to any club?"

"The Eton Eleven."

This, with a not unpleasant spice of the school pride, which an old soldier's "esprit de corps" could well appreciate. The major made half a salute, with a genial gravity very pleasant to the younger man.

"Indeed! I beg a thousand pardons. They must be praying for you down there then, if they suspect so great an acquisition to the garrison side. But what keeps you from them?"

"Well, I had meant to 'sap' a bit this afternoon, till those fellows talked about the match, sir."

"Sap a bit? I didn't know there were siege operations to-day. Besides which, you're not for the Engineers, you know, so—"

Ned laughed outright.

"It's a bit of old Eton slang I should apologize for, major; and being translated means to stick to one's books."

"So you read, do you?"

"A little."

"Of what, may I make bold to ask?"

"Well, of siege operations, I suppose;" and he laughed quietly once more. "I've bought a book on fortification, and begun it; and I have got as far as cutting the leaves of a Hindustani grammar."

"So!" said the major, whose self-esteem as a physiognomist rose many degrees forthwith. "I'm not much of an engineer myself; but a tolerable 'Moonshee.' If you want help with your Hindustani, I would do my best to give it you at any time."

"Really, major, you could hardly do me a greater favor."

"I'll tell you what it is, sir, you come and take a quiet chop to-night, at seven, with Mrs. Anderson and me, unless you'd rather not miss dinner at the mess; and we'll settle about the grammar lessons out of hand."

Ned thanked him heartily, saluted, and on the strength of such educational assistance in prospect, thought himself entitled to exchange his regimentals for a suit of "flannels," and to take his pleasure for that summer day where wickets stood or fell.

He stood longer than most men's; and when a fatal "twister" took the legstump at last, the "garrison" side, as well they might, cheered loudly the new champion, at whose score the "citizens" faces had been growing blanker and blanker still.

Mrs. Anderson was rather an insipid lady, not having perhaps always been destitute of vital savor; but having parted with much of it under fierce Indian suns. She was a well-bred woman, however, and received her husband's young guest as such an one should. Tasteless in the passive sense, she was not wholly without power of taste in the active. So Ned discovered when she roused herself to animation in praise of a certain Mrs. Grant, whose absence she regretted.

"How very provoking, major, really. Didn't you say the captain said his wife had promised him to be back by the early mail to-day?"

"Yes, I did, dear; for so he did," answered the major, in words of one syllable, like a child's primer.

"O Mr. Locksley, I can't tell you how disappointed I am. I feel confident you would appreciate Mrs. Grant. You've been brought up among great folk yourself, I hear, and so was she, poor thing, and is well worthy of any place among them now, for all you find her a poor paymaster's wife. I think her very beautiful still, though she's no longer so young as she was; and so does the major, I believe, after all, though I reproach him with his indifference to her good looks. I don't see that a wife should be jealous if her husband admires one of her friends—do you, Mr. Locksley?"

"What a silly woman?" thought Ned; but he, luckily, did not think aloud, and only bowed acquiescence.

"No, certainly not; indeed, if he fails to do so, in a reasonable degree, he slights the sex, and vexes me; major, I've often told you so."

"But Mrs. Grant's good looks, Mr. Locksley, faded or not, are nothing to her mind and manners, are they, major?"

"Old Grant coming up, ma'am," said the major. "Hear his bootheels on the stairs, better hush up!"

"O captain; you haven't brought her! how could you disappoint me so? She's been gone three weeks, the day before yesterday; and said when she went she wouldn't stay more than a fortnight."

"It is very kind of you, to miss her so," said Captain Grant, with a look of gratitude and satisfaction, which made Ned repent of his hasty judgment upon Mrs. Anderson. There must have been something better, on her part, than affected admiration of his wife, to make the captain speak and look thanks as he did.

"Well, and what has kept her?"

"Amy had a head ache; and, though her mother thought it of no great consequence, and would have come away, her aunt wouldn't hear of it; so the 'route' was counter-ordered."

"But we shall have them to-morrow?"

"I suppose so; but I don't know by which coach, late or early."

"I wont ask her to come up here to-morrow, then, if she comes by the late one; but will drop in upon her myself after tea. You must promise, however, to dine here the day after. I want to introduce Mr. Locksley to her. I dare say they have friends in common. Do you know Mr. Locksley? Allow me; Captain Grant, Mr. Locksley."

Then she turned to Ned, and said, "I hope you *will* dine with us after to-morrow?"

He was half inclined to excuse himself, being bored beforehand with Mrs. Grant; but the major's Hindustani was too precious to be jeopardized for a caprice. So he accepted. Captain Grant was likewise cordial enough upon a first acquaintance, when he had heard from his old friend, the major, of Ned's studious turn.

"I shall be glad to see you at my quarters, Mr. Locksley," said he, as they sat over their wine. "I only regret, as Anderson does, that it's so hard, here especially, for oldsters to get on with youngsters!"

"Why specially here?" asked Ned.

"Because we are like a sieve here, with holes so large that every thing goes through. We are a mere passenger depot, so to say."

"But don't you think the youngsters get younger now-a-days, Grant?" quoth the major. "More boyish, and more thorough rattlepates altogether?"

"I am not so sure of that, major; but I'm thinking it's more certain that the oldsters get older. I can mind you with chestnut curls, major, not to say red outright; and we are gray enough now, the pair of us."

"True man, very true; yes, very true indeed," said the major with a sigh, and a sip at the port. "There's one thing I will say for the credit of the modern griff; he don't drink as his forbears did."

"That's fifty per cent increase upon his chances of coming out right at last," said the other.

"So it is; but there's that gambling is

the curse of the garrison just now. I hope that's not one of your vices, Locksley?"

"'Tis a thing I hate and detest," said Ned.

"Ah, well; I needn't preach to you to be upon your guard on that score," said the major, who looked into Ned's countenance, and read again there that neither lie nor craft were kin to the nature of its owner. He turned towards the captain.

"Did you hear of that affair of Archer, Grant?"

He nodded a grim assent.

"I hate a bark without a bite; but if I could only fix the thing upon that 'leg' of a Rufford, I'd bring him to a court-martial as sure as —"

"Coffee, sir! Mrs. Anderson bid me say, was in the drawing-room, to-night."

When Edward, two days after, met the Grants at the major's, his estimation of Mrs. Anderson rose considerably. Admiration, so well placed, could not well be affected. Mrs. Grant was charming. Her "mind and manners" specially, little as Ned liked the term. As for her beauty, youngsters' eyes are less indulgent than oldsters' to that fading of charms which even Mrs. Anderson admitted. Ned's also were specially fastidious, having an image of rare perfection ever in them yet.

But there was no denying the grace of feature and expression, which gave a charm that would not fade to the face of the paymaster's wife.

There are some faces, winsome indeed of love; but which seem busier in giving than in winning it—faces on which the sorrow-lines show more of the sweetness wrought by sorrow than of the bitterness of its working-hours—faces on which the joy gleams are never insolent with selfish exultation; but ever radiant with a generous, unselfish glory. A brother that had lost a loving sister, might find on such a face a lifelike reminiscence of true sisterly sweetness. An orphan that had never known a mother, might almost spell out on it what mother's love may be. A lover, whose love should be thrown back on itself in deepest disappointment, might catch such consolation on it, as grows of learning how love looks, purified from passion. It was quite true, that, as Mrs. Anderson had phrased it, "she had been brought up among great folk;" not among them only, but of them. Her manners had all that admirable self-possession, which scarcely true self-forgetfulness can give without the added advantage of the best social discipline; yet she was so perfectly, and kindly, and naturally, at home, just where she was, that there was no sense of incongruity aroused between herself and what surrounded her; none of that uncomfortable consciousness that one of the company has come down from a pedestal, expressly to be put upon a footing with the rest. There was music in her voice when she spoke; melody, though little power, when she sang; what is rarer, melodious music in her laughter at the loudest.

Her mental cultivation was evident even in the interchange of chance conversation with one of so poorly furnished mind as Mrs. Anderson. She knew some persons whom Edward knew, more yet about whom he knew; so they were soon on almost intimate terms, though he had not yet accepted the captain's invitation to visit them at their quarters. Perhaps he waited till it should come from her; for she was the last lady in the world with whom, for all her sweetness, any one would venture to take a social liberty.

But Ned was often at the major's, who was as good as his word in the matter of Hindustani, and who for all his long familiarity with the spoken language, found it no child's play to satisfy the grammatical and scholarly queries of one who had stood second in the sixth form at Eton.

One afternoon, as he came out from the major's den, with grammar and lexicon under his arm, as he might have come erewhile out of the crusty presence of old Keate himself, he heard a childish voice exclaim, in tones, which, but for transposition into treble, might have been Mrs. Grant's,—

"What a big school-boy! With a soldier's coat on!"

"Oh, for shame, Amy!" answered Mrs. Anderson.

"Why for shame, Aunt Susie? I'm not ashamed; and I don't think he is. He looks like a good boy, too."

"And so he is Amy!" laughed the major's wife. "Go and shake hands with him."

She hung down her head, and shook a forest of golden curls over her face, out of which her large eyes scanned him, then she shook back the silken curtain, and with entire confidence went up to him, and put her tiny fingers into his outstretched hand.

"My name is Amy—pray, what's yours?"

"His name is Mr. Locksley," said Mrs. Anderson, before he could answer for himself.

"That's not a name at all," answered Miss Amy, pouting: "Nobody calls me Miss Grant; and I call you Aunt Susie, though you know you're not my aunt a bit; and other people call you Mrs. Anderson."

"My name is Edward—will that do better?" he said, not a little amused.

"Is that what your brothers and sisters call you?"

"I have none," he said.

"Oh, dear, that's just like me! Then you're an only child?"

"Just so."

"Then what does your mother call you?—you have a mother, I hope." She said these last words in a voice as silvery as her own mother's; and over her mobile face stole a sweet anxiety, as if, child as she was, she dreaded having set inadvertently some sad chord in vibration in another's heart.

"Yes, thank God, I have, Amy; and a very, very dear one."

"And she calls you?"

"Ned."

"Very well, so shall I."

"Dear me!" said Mrs. Anderson, looking up suddenly just then at the clock, "it's nearly half-past four. What shall I do to get you home, Amy? I promised your mother you should be home by this time. I can't take you myself, for I have to go elsewhere with the major, and my tiresome maid is not come in."

"Perhaps," said Ned, good-humoredly, "you would trust her with me, Mrs. Anderson."

"Well, if you would be so kind, I should be very much obliged to you."

So Amy's hat was tied on. and her gloves found, after considerable search, in possession of a tabby kitten, under a sofa; and after kissing Aunt Susie, who hugged her with the longing of a childless woman, unsoured by her childlessness, she set off in high spirits with her new friend. She insisted, however, upon his leaving the books behind; it looked so much more like a schoolboy than a soldier to have them under his arm, she said.

"I like all soldiers, even drummer boys, for I've always lived where there were soldiers. But I don't like schoolboys. There were three where we've been staying, mamma and me; and they were very rude to me; and tied knots in my hair; and one of them broke the nose of one of my dolls besides."

"That was a pity, certainly; but most dolls' noses get flattened some time or another, I believe."

"Yes, I believe they do. But then you know my dolls are not like most dolls—not a bit."

"Indeed! What are they like, then?"

"Oh, you shall see, since you are coming home with me. I like showing my dolls—to sensible people, that is—you know."

"And do you think I'm one?" he said, much amused with the child's grave way of saying it.

"I'm sure of it."

"Pray why? Because of the big dictionary?"

"Well, just a little bit for that, perhaps—not much though."

"For what else then, Amy? I should like to know."

"Should you? I'm not sure I shall say."

"Don't, if you don't like to."

They walked on for a minute, without a word from either. Then Amy shook her curls, and looked up at him, with her mother's own expression, and said,—

"Yes, I will, then."

"Will what?"

"Why, tell you why I am quite sure that you are sensible."

"Well, and what makes you sure?"

"Because you are so good-natured and good-humored; and yet your face is sad."

Ned winced a little under the diagnosis of the clever little physiognomist.

Presently he had another proof, as he took it, of her quickness at reading countenances.

"Who is that captain?" she asked, when two officers, coming the other way, had passed them.

"Which captain?"

"You know there was only one," she answered.

"Yes, *I* knew; but how did *you*?"

"How very silly! By the gold lace, to be sure. Didn't I tell you I had always lived where there were soldiers? Of course

I know one officer's uniform from another, else I should be a little goose, you know."

As he made no reply to this, she returned to the charge.

"You didn't tell me who the captain was, though."

"His name is Captain Rufford."

"Do you like him? *I* don't."

Again he took no notice of her remark, so she went on again.

"Mamma says I am not to talk about my likes and dislikes. Perhaps you are going to say so too. But I can't help it: I don't like that captain. He looks so greedy."

Ned smiled; she noted it; and said quickly,—

"We needn't talk about him any more, you know."

"This is Mr. Locksley, dear mamma," she said, taking his hand with graceful action, and leading him towards her mother, as they entered the little drawing-room of the paymaster's cottage.

"Yes, Amy, I know it is," answered Mrs. Grant, rising to shake hands with him.

"Oh, you know him, then?" cried Amy, disappointed. She had thought to have the whole credit of his first introduction at home.

"Yes, I have had the pleasure of meeting him at Major Anderson's."

"Perhaps, though," brightening up a little, "you don't know what his name is, mamma."

"His name, dear Amy! Why, Locksley, to be sure."

"That's not the name I mean; but his own name—what his mother calls him. He says he has a very, very dear mother, and she calls him Ned. So shall I."

"Amy, dearest, you must not be rude, and take liberties."

"No, darling, I wont; but I shall call him Ned. Of course he likes that name best, since his mother calls him so. Come into this corner, Ned, and you shall see my dolls."

Mrs. Grant was about to remonstrate, but guessed, from Ned's manner, that any remonstrance would be as much against his grain as Amy's. She took up the work just laid aside, and left them to their own devices.

"You see the doll's box is not like a common box for dolls to live in, is it?"

"Not at all. It's a Ceylon box, is it not? I have seen some like it before, but never one so large or handsome. How beautifully it is inlaid!"

"Yes, isn't it? It was given to me long before I can remember, by a brother officer of dear papa. I was quite a tiny baby, then, and the regiment lay at a place called Tricky? Trickery? I can't remember."

"Trichinopoly?"

"Ah, yes! that's it. Mamma has got a gold chain made by the native jewellers there."

Then she threw open the lid of her ivory chest, and drew herself back to let Ned look in; and perhaps to judge the better of the effect which the sight of its treasures might produce upon the mind of the beholder.

"Not like most dolls, are they?"

"By no means, Amy. How well dressed they all are: and all differently!"

"Yes! This, you see, is the poor Ayah. It was her delicate nose those rude boys broke. I've had it glued on again, and the seam painted; but you can see where it was done, if you hold her up against the light. The nose-ring was lost, you know, which was a pity. The bangles on her arms and legs are all right though, and they are real silver. My Ayah was dressed as like this one as possible."

"Indeed? Had you an Ayah then to nurse you?"

"Yes; for I was born in India."

"So was she!" said Edward, dreamily.

"Who? the Ayah? of course she was."

"No, not the Ayah; but a lady,—I mean some one I was thinking of." And he blushed up to the very roots of his hair, catching up the next doll to hide his confusion and escape further questioning.

"This is a Welshwoman, is she not, with the linsey-woolsey petticoat, and a man's hat on her head?"

"Oh, yes, she is the last of my family. Mamma dressed her for me not six months ago, when the regiment was at Pembroke. You see now what my plan is with the dolls. I have one in the costume of every station that we spend any time at. Here's a Greek from Corfu, I don't remember much about that though. And here's an Andalusian, that was copied exactly from a girl's dress at Gibraltar. But here's my pet of all, except poor Ayah." And she kissed the face so rudely mutilated by her enemies the schoolboys.

"And pray what dress is hers? Another Spanish one, I suppose, with that black mantilla."

"Dear me, no! that's not a mantilla, but a 'faldette.'"

"Well I am no wiser for knowing that. So tell me what countrywoman this little lady is, with the black silk hood, that's not a mantilla?"

"Why, she is a Maltese, to be sure; and that's why I am so fond of her. See, here's her Maltese cross, of real gold filigree. Oh, I remember Malta very well, and our little house at Sliema, and the orange trees at Bosco, and picking mushrooms out at Gozo—just as well as if it were yesterday. Were you ever at Malta, Ned!"

"No, never; but I shall go there on my way out, you know."

"Out where?"

"To India. I am not a queen's officer like your papa; but a soldier of the Indian Army."

"Shall you go soon?"

"Yes, very."

"Well, I am sorry for that; for I wanted to be great friends with you. I, say though, is India very large?"

"Very; what makes you ask?"

"Because you might meet Ayah if it wasn't: and I would give you a present for her. Mamma always says she was such a kind nurse to me."

Then she showed him the little drawers, inside the inlaid box, where there were a few spare dresses for the dolls, and other childish treasures. When all was inspected, and he was about to leave the corner, she put her hand again in his, and asked,—

"Are you going now, Ned?"

"Yes, I think I must; so good-by, Amy."

"Good-by, Ned. But I want to ask you one more thing before you go."

"What is it?"

"I want to know the name of the lady you were thinking of—the lady that was born in India, too."

He hesitated; had there been pertness in the child's face, he would not have answered, "Constance."

"Constance!—that's a very pretty name. And does she call you 'Ned'?"

"She used to."

"Oh, indeed! Well, good-by, Ned."

Fashions for Festivals.—The subjoined announcement, *mutatis mutandis*, that is to say with change only of names, lately appeared in the advertising columns of the *English Churchman*:—

"Surplices.—Surplices for Easter.—Messrs. Falderal & Son have prepared their usual large supply of Surplices of superior form and quality, so much admired."

There are supposed to be some old women among the clergy; but the above advertisement seems to indicate that there are also many young ladies. Here we have linendrapers announcing themselves as having prepared for Easter their usual large supply of surplices, and describing those surplices in just the very terms which the trade applies to silks and muslins. What is the material which forms the fabric of these surplices of "superior" form and quality, "so much admired." Is it chintz? Fancy a lot of young parsons collected together and staring in at Messrs. Falderal & Son's window, or being taken by female friends to the establishment of that enterprising concern, shopping. Imagine the assistants behind the counter saying, "Any other article to-day, sir?—allow me to tempt you with an alb. Sweet things in stoles, sir! Neat dalmatics, sir; very chaste! Pretty patterns for chasubles, sir; charming copes; last Spring fashions from Paris and novelties from Rome." Now that we see surplices advertised in the regular slang of milliners, we can quite understand the feeling with which a certain rector whose bishop had compelled him to relinquish his pretty robes, pathetically observed that he should never wear those beautiful vestments again. We suppose we shall soon have divines of this class sporting flounces on their frocks, and ecclesiastical emporiums and depôts puffing their "Crinoline for Cassocks."—*Punch.*

From Chambers's Journal.

LAST NEWS FROM DR. LIVINGSTONE.*

On the 10th March, 1858, the expedition to the Zambesi, under the command of Dr. Livingstone, left Liverpool in the screw-steamer *Pearl*, of two hundred tons burden, commanded by Captain Duncan, bound for Ceylon, but which had engaged to put us ashore at the mouth of the Zambesi. Our expedition consisted of Dr. Livingstone, Charles Livingstone, Dr. Kirk, Commander Bedingfield, R.N., Thomas Baines, Richard Thornden, and myself, the engineer. We were accompanied by Mrs. Livingstone and her youngest child, a fine boy of six years of age. On the deck of the *Pearl* was securely placed our little steam-launch, in three compartments, all fitted and in readiness to be bolted together on our arrival at the mouth of the Zambesi. We arrived all safely at the Cape of Good Hope, towards the end of April; but having, on my late voyage home, been shipwrecked, and lost my journal, I cannot now be certain of the correct dates. At the Cape, Mrs. Livingstone and her son left us, for the purpose of going with her father, the Rev. Mr. Moffat, to the missionary station at Kuraman. We left Simon's Bay on the 1st of May, and on the 15th, reached the mouth of the Zambesi, in lat. 18° long. 36° on the south-eastern coast, having steamed all the way.

My duties now commenced, and I immediately proceeded to get our launch out. This was a most anxious period for Dr. Livingstone; but as I had been planning during the whole voyage how we should get the launch over the ship's side, we lost no time, but at once erected a derrick, and succeeded in getting her safely into the water; and on the third day after, had steam up, and started in search of a navigable channel to the Zambesi.

Our first attempt was up the west Luabo, a distance of about fifty miles, which it took us three days to accomplish; and this apparent river terminated in a reedy marsh, where the mosquitoes were so plentiful and so hungry, that both my eyes were completely closed up in the morning; so we had nothing for it but about ship, and return to the *Pearl*. On reporting to Dr. Livingstone the failure of our search, he requested Captain Duncan to recross the bar, and attempt the Kongone. The *Pearl* then departed, leaving us in the launch, where we remained one week, until the arrival, outside the bar, of H.M.S. *Hermes*, Captain Gordon, which signalled us to come out, and enter the Kongone, where we found the *Pearl* lying at anchor inside the bar.

On communicating with the *Pearl*, we found that Dr. Livingstone and Mr. Skede had gone up the Kongone in the *Hermes'* cutter. Next morning, we started in the launch, and after steaming about thirty miles up the river, met the cutter coming down, they having succeeded in finding a good navigable channel. We returned in company to the *Pearl*, which then proceeded up the river a distance of about forty miles; and finding she could not with safety proceed further, on account of the shallowness of the water, we started again in our launch in search of a suitable island—of which there are many—on which to erect our storehouse. After mature consideration, our commander decided upon one about thirty miles above where we had left the *Pearl*, and which was named Expedition Island. And now we proceeded to erect an iron house, which we had brought with us for the purpose of serving as a depôt for our stores. It took us about four weeks to get all our stores safely conveyed up to the island and deposited in our storehouse.

The *Pearl* then left us to our own resources and proceeded on her voyage to Ceylon. Afterwards, our first step was to make out Mazoro, a Portuguese settlement, about fifteen miles further up the river. On arriving at this place, we found the natives at war with the Portuguese. They took us also in our launch for Portuguese, and were threatening to fire upon us, when Dr. Livingstone, without hesitation, at once went on shore, and having told them who we were, completely disarmed them, and made them our fast friends.

Dr. Livingstone being now certain that we were in the right river, and that there were no insurmountable obstacles between us and Tette, we returned to Expedition Island for a load of stores, which we purposed taking on to Sanna, a Portuguese

* This report of Dr. Livingstone's new expedition is from the pen of his engineer, Mr. Rae, who recently returned to England. We have concluded that, though but a sketch, it will gratify curiosity intermediately, without prejudice to the ampler accounts which may in time be looked for from the venerated chief of the enterprise.

town, situated about fifty miles above Mazoro. On our way up to Sanna, when about one mile above Mazoro, the morning being very thick and foggy, we were steaming along as usual, when it suddenly cleared up, and we saw the dead bodies of several natives, half-eaten by alligators, which are here very numerous and large. We called Dr. Livingstone's attention to this, and he said there must have been fighting going on; and immediately afterwards, on winding a sharp angle of the river, we came in view of a large encampment of the Portuguese, who had taken the field to quell a rebellion of the natives of the surrounding districts. Being hailed by the Portuguese officers, who had heard of our being in the river, and knew who we were, we drew close inshore, and were informed by them that their governor, who was commanding in person, was very sick of fever. They wished Dr. Livingstone to come on shore to see him, who at once consented, and accompanied them to the governor's quarters, whom he found very ill and much reduced. Dr. Livingstone proposed that he would remove him in the launch to Supanga, a distance of about thirty-five miles further up, on the opposite or right bank of the river. During this time, the fighting had recommenced, and great numbers of the Portuguese slaves were flying before the rebels, and tried to force their way on board of us, but were kept off by our own hands, principally Kroomen, armed with cutlasses, as, if they had got on board, they would undoubtedly have swamped us. Finding they could not get on board of us, they swam off for an island about a mile from the shore, and I here saw a Portuguese sergeant shooting at them while they were swimming. Several of the shots seemed to take effect, as some of the heads disappeared.

Becoming alarmed for the safety of Dr. Livingstone, I took my rifle and went ashore, and on reaching the top of the bank, about one hundred and fifty yards from the launch, saw Dr. Livingstone at the distance of half a mile assisting the governor towards the launch. I immediately sang out to our firemen to get up steam. The bullets were flying around them in all directions. The doctor, however, kept steadily on, and was enabled to reach us in safety, bringing with him his patient, who was so tall that while one half of him was on the doctor's back, the other half was trailing on the ground. As soon as we got under cover of the bank, the doctor said: "I am glad we have got this length, Rae, for I don't like those bullets whistling past my ears."

Steam being now up, we started at once for Supanga, where we arrived in safety about 5 P.M., and learned afterwards that the Portuguese had that day been defeated, losing all their stores. We now made several trips to and from Expedition Island, and got the most of our stores removed to Supanga, Sanna, and Tette; but our vessel being small and slow, much valuable time was lost in these journeys. Dr. Livingstone was very anxious to get all this work over, and worked himself night and day in order to get us all out of the lower part of the river, where fevers are so common; and this he happily accomplished about the end of September, when we arrived for the first time at Tette, and Dr. Livingstone met the Makolo, whom he had left there two years before, and who had all remained there, in the firm belief that he would return.

The meeting was truly a happy one—the men rushing into the water up to their very necks in their eagerness once more to see their white father. Their joy was perfectly frantic. They seized the boat, and nearly upset it, and fairly carried the doctor ashore, singing all the time that their white father was alive again, their faith in whom was quite unshaken. On inquiry, we found that thirty of them had died from small-pox, and six had been murdered by a drunken chief. They told us that they did not mourn for the thirty who had died, but that their hearts were bleeding for those who were murdered.

Up to this time, all the natives we had seen were slaves to Portuguese owners, with the exceptions of Dr. Livingstone's Makolo men, and the rebel party formerly mentioned, who were mostly runaway slaves fighting for their liberty under a chief named Mariana; and I have little doubt they would have succeeded in establishing their independence, had they been better provided with ammunition. I have since learned, from reliable sources, that about six hundred male and female prisoners, afterwards taken by the Portuguese, were by them sold as slaves to some other markets; and I myself saw a large party of them seemingly from four hundred to six hundred, on their way to the coast to be shipped.

After this, having with enormous labor and difficulty got our goods and stores into places of safety, and having found that our launch was insufficient for the purpose of further ascending the Zambesi, and Dr. Livingstone having written to her majesty's government, urging upon them to send out a more powerful steamer, he thought, while waiting replies from home, that instead of remaining idle, he would push up the Shire, which comes from the north, and joins the Zambesi about forty miles below Sanna. From this attempt, the Portuguese endeavored to dissuade us, stating that we should find it impassable, on account of the vast quantities of duck-weed with which they said it was covered. For a very short distance above its junction with the Zambesi we certainly met with considerable quantities, but not such as to stop us; and about three miles up the river became perfectly clear, and we proceeded onwards, where not even the Portuguese had ever been, they having spoken from report only; after steaming about forty to fifty miles up this noble river, finding never less than two fathoms' water, and the banks of the river very fertile land, we reached the base of a large mountain, called by the natives Moramballa, whose summit is nearly four thousand feet above the level of the sea. The inhabitants of the country, from the mouth of the river up to this point, are the natives who acknowledge the leadership of Mariana, and who were most friendly to us. We stopped here one day, and a party of us ascended the mountain, and thence saw the Shire stretching far away northward, through a magnificent valley, nowhere under twenty miles in breadth, as far as the eye could reach.

Starting up the river next day to explore this great valley, we steamed about one hundred miles, which it took four days to accomplish, and reached a series of rapids, preventing further progress in that direction; these rapids Dr. Livingstone named the Murchison Falls. We landed at several villages each day, and found the natives very friendly to us, and living in the enjoyment of their own liberties, and perfectly uncontaminated by the slave-trade. At first, they were rather afraid that we meant to fight for the purpose of subjecting them to our power, but Dr. Livingstone soon obtained their entire confidence. We were told by them that the Shire flowed out of a lake named by them the Shirwa, but we could not at that time proceed further. Returning again to Tette, for the purpose of refitting, but with the intention of returning to endeavor to reach Lake Shirwa, we found our comrades all well, and rejoiced to see us.

After remaining at Tette for two or three weeks, I erected the small sugar-mill, saw-mill, and stationary steam-engine, which we brought from Glasgow, and got all ready for a start in the sugar-making and wood-cutting lines. Having been supplied with a quantity of sugar-canes by Major Sicard, we set to work expressing the juice, to the great delight of the natives. But the wonder of wonders was the steam-engine and saw-mill, cutting the timber.

We started for the Shire once more on the 10th March, 1859, and proceeded again up to Murchison Falls, finding that the good character we had established on our former visit was now of very great service to us with the natives. This valley of the Shire we found abounding in cotton and large quantities of sugar-cane. The cotton the natives manufacture themselves into a coarse kind of cloth, and the sugar-cane they use as food, not knowing how to extract the sugar. We found also large numbers of the lignum-vitæ tree, of a great size, ebony and boaza trees. The bark of the last tree is of a fibrous nature, and is used by the natives for the manufacture of cordage. The river abounds in edible fish of various kinds, and hippopotami of a very large size frequent its banks. Ivory is very plentiful, and I have counted two hundred and two bull elephants in a single herd.

When we neared Murchison Falls, we met the head-chief of the valley, named Chibiesa, whom we had not seen on our former trip, but who now received us most kindly. He informed us that his favorite daughter had been stolen by the Portuguese about two years before our visit, and was, he understood, now living at Tette, in the house of the priest; he asked Dr. Livingstone if he thought there was any possibility of recovering her from them, as her mother's heart was always bleeding for her child. Dr. Livingstone replied, that provided he found her at Tette, he had little doubt of being able to procure her freedom and send her home. After Dr. Livingstone's return from Lake Shirwa to the mouth of the Shire, as he himself was not going up to Tette, but down to the mouth of the Zambesi, he redeemed his promise by writing to Major Sicard to have this young girl, only fourteen years of age, set at liberty, and returned at his expense to her parents, which was accomplished, and she safely returned, to their great joy.

Dr. Livingstone, accompanied by Dr. Kirk, proceeded northward, and discovered Lake Shirwa; while I remained in charge of the launch and the hands at the bottom of the Falls. Chibiesa having sent some of his own men to accompany Dr. Livingstone, he was everywhere kindly received and treated; but he found this Lake Shirwa not to be the source of the Shire, but a lake having no outlet, and consequently brackish; he was told by the natives that beyond Lake Shirwa there was another lake of immense extent, out of which Dr. Livingstone conjectured the Shire to flow; but he could not at present undertake this journey, his party returning all in good health, to the launch, after an absence of thirty-five days.

After a few days spent at Tette to refit, we started again towards the end of June, with intention of reaching the great lake. We arrived at Murchison Falls about the end of August, 1859, and leaving the launch there, started on our journey. The exploring party consisted of Dr. Livingstone, Dr. Kirk, Mr. Livingstone, and myself, with about forty Makolo, accompanied by four of Chibiesa's men to act as our guides. They knowing the way, we experienced little difficulties, except those presented by an unknown country, and got along at about the rate of twelve miles a day. The Murchison Rapids extend about thirty-five miles, after which we found a deep navigable river all the way to Lake Nyassa. The river falls during these thirty-five miles about one thousand three hundred feet, the scenery being grand, and the valleys very fertile. Above the Falls, the valley again spreads out to about eighteen or twenty miles in width, and the country abounds with the cotton and indigo plants, and the same useful woods that we had met with below the Falls—ebony, lignum-vitæ, etc. We also fell in with a soft wood, which I believe would be good for carpenter-work in general. It is also a well-watered country, very healthy. We were forty nights sleeping in the open air, and suffered no inconvenience, nor experienced any evil effects afterwards.

About three days' journey from the head of the Falls, being on the left bank of the Shire, we began to meet with slave-parties, bound for the coast of Mozambique; and all the way up to the lake we met parties of slave-hunters, and found villages deserted, the inhabitants fleeing to the woods at our approach, supposing us to be on the like errand. On finding this, Dr. Livingstone despatched two of Chibiesa's men in advance, to inform the natives we were Englishmen —the black man's friends—which had everywhere the desired effect of allaying their fears.

And here it may be well that I should give some account of the slave-hunters' usual mode of procedure when on a stealing expedition. The men who follow this nefarious trade are all half-caste Arabs, blackguard looking fellows, armed with muskets and cutlasses, and generally on foot. The hunting parties we met numbered from three to twenty or more, and were attended by a number of their own slaves. Stealing up during the night to some village marked as the scene of their depredations, they lurk about until morning, when the children and younger members of the community are beginning to move about; these they seize, one after the other, until they obtain a considerable number. The peaceful inhabitants having no fire-arms, are powerless either to defend or recover their stolen offspring. These are then secured by means of a long forked stick, the neck of the poor victim being placed between the prongs, and a piece of bamboo tied across in front of the throat. The slave-hunter then takes the extreme end of this cruel instrument of torture, and by means of it pushes them along, and should any of them prove refractory, a twist of his hand nearly strangles them. I have myself seen bands of them, four and five at a time —as we were told, newly captured—with their necks all chafed and bleeding, and their eyes streaming with tears, principally young men of ten to eighteen years of age, driven along in this inhuman manner. We also met a large party near Lake Nyassa on the 17th September, 1850—the same day on which we discovered the lake—consisting of between four and five hundred poor creatures, being led off to slavery, and lately torn from their peaceful homes.

We were told by a native chief named Massasoweka, that this party was in his neighborhood, and he was afraid they might do us harm. While he was yet speaking, five of the slave-hunters, having heard of our being there, came up to us, supposing us to be of the same profession, bringing with them six children, boys and girls, of six to eight years of age, wishing us to purchase them, and offered them to us for about a yard of calico apiece; but finding we were English, they at once decamped; and before daylight next morning the whole camp had disappeared, the mere mention of the English name being sufficient to put them all to flight. The slaves that we saw of this party were jaded and travel worn, and some of them reduced to perfect skeletons.

From the information we obtained in the lake district, we understand that the country, from the sea-coast inland to the Shire and Lake Nyassa, is almost depopulated; and the slave-hunters are now crossing the Shire to the west, for the purpose of procuring additional supplies for the slave-trade along the coast from Quillimane to Zanzibar. Colonel Rigby, the English consul at Zanzibar, told me that nineteen thousand slaves per annum to his knowledge, besides great numbers that he cannot obtain proper account of, are brought from the district near Lake Nyassa. It is the opinion of Dr. Livingstone and all our party—and in conversing with Colonel Rigby, he concurs with us—that a single steamer placed on Lake Nyassa, and manned by British subjects, would be sufficient to put an end to most of the traffic.

The first to set eyes on Lake Nyassa was Dr. Livingstone himself, who shouted out: "Our journey is ended! Hurrah, my boys!" His men had before this been anxious for a termination to their very arduous toils.

Arrived at the shores of the lake, observations were taken by Dr. Livingstone, when he found we were in lat. 14° 25″ S. The lake is of immense extent, the Shire flowing out of it to the south; and the rise and fall of the river does not exceed two feet, according to observations made for two years, showing that the lake must be of immense extent to maintain such an equal flow. The length of this piece of water we had no means of ascertaining; but on inquiring at Massasoweka, a very intelligent old chief, seemingly about a hundred years of age, how long we might take to travel to the head of the lake, his first answer was a derisive laugh, and said, "You can never travel to the end of this large water. Neither we nor our forefathers, after travelling four moons, could find or hear of the end, so white men need not try it."

The lake had every appearance of a great sea, for although the day was calm, there was a heavy deep swell setting in upon the shore. From all the information we could gather here and elsewhere, the whole of the slave traffic from the west side of the Shire and Lake Nyassa to the Zanzibar and Mozambique coasts passes through between the northern end of Lake Shirwa and the southern end of Lake Nyassa, a space of only about ten or twelve miles broad; and a single steamer running from and to the Murchison Falls and on Lake Nyassa must cut off the entire traffic.

On the 18th of September, we left the shores of Lake Nyassa, pleased and thankful that we had been the instruments in the hands of Providence to reveal to the civilized world this great and important country; and hoping that, ere long, we should be enabled to return to do something to advance civilization, and check the horrid traffic in human beings that prevails to such an enormous extent, well knowing that this was the object nearest our great leader's heart. On our return-journey, we were everywhere treated with the greatest kindness by the natives; and when about thirty miles south of Lake Nyassa, on the eastern side of the Shire valley, arrived at Mount Zombo, one of a range of mountains many miles in length, which, although fatigued with our long journey, Dr. Livingstone, Dr. Kirk, and myself determined to ascend. This task we accomplished after great difficulty; and found by the aneroid the height of the mountain to be about seven thousand feet above the sea. The view from the summit was grand beyond expression. Near the summit, winding through the ravines, we came upon a considerable river, as broad as the Leven above Dumbarton, and which seemed to flow into Lake Shirwa. The water we tasted, and found sweet and palatable. While resting on the top, we sent on two of our men to inform the chief of our being on his ground, and he immediately sent back an invitation to visit him; his messengers bringing with them a present for us, consisting of three goats, half a dozen fowls, three large wooden bowls filled with meal, and some vegetables, which were all acceptable. We were obliged, for the present, to decline his invitation, but promised to give him a call next time we were in the neighboroood. His head-man assured us he had plenty of honey and milk, and wished to get the news from the sea. We found on the summit of this hill heath in bloom exactly the same in appearance as that found upon our Scottish mountains, and also wild-brambles having the same flavor and appearance as those at home, only being rather smaller. Dr. Kirk, as botanist, examined both of them, and brought off specimens. Dr. Livingstone also cut and brought off a pepper-stick to make a walking-staff. We remained upon the top of the hill all night, sleeping in the open air, and in the morning woke up to find it extremely cold until sunrise, although this was the hot season. This was the greatest degree of cold I felt in Africa. We descended shortly after daybreak, and joined our party, the same day, at a village about four miles from the bottom of the mountain.

We then proceeded onwards, meeting everywhere with a hearty welcome from the natives, until on the 8th of October we again got in safety to our launch, at the bottom of the Murchison Falls, having been absent forty days on this exploring journey.

Dr. Kirk being now deputed by Dr. Livingstone to proceed overland from the Murchison Falls to Tette, I started with him on that journey on the 18th October, accompanied by thirty of the Makolo men. This being a part of the country never formerly traversed by Europeans, and very thinly inhabited, our journey proved to be the most toilsome and difficult that we had yet undertaken. Immediately upon leaving the valley of the Shire, we struck into the mountains lying to the south-west, and entered a barren country, through which we travelled three or four days without meeting any natives, or falling in with any of their villages, where we could purchase fowls or other food, so were entirely dependent upon the stock we carried with us, which consisted only of about a dozen pounds of salt pork. Water also was very scarce, we being sometimes a day and a half without getting any, and even what we procured was very salt and brackish, and in such very small quantities, that instead of quenching, it frequently only aggravated our thirst. On the fourth day, the man who carried our pork disappeared, having fallen behind our party, and we now experienced the pangs of hunger in earnest; but, most providentially, on the fifth day from leaving the Shire, towards midday, we reached a pretty large village where our wants were attended to, and where we remained the following night. In the morning, we purchased from these hospitable natives, a sheep—for which we paid about a fathom of calico; six or eight fowls, paying for them about a yard of calico; and some meal for our men, which cost us about ten of our glass beads; and being once more provisioned, we again set out upon our journey, and found the same scarcity of water still prevailing; we occasionally met herds of antelopes, but could not get near enough to them for a shot. By this time, we were drawing near to the Portuguese territory, and food was more easily procured, the country being here more thickly inhabited; and on the eighth day from our leaving Murchison Falls, arrived at Tette, where, after procuring supplies of provisions, and also some materials much wanted for the repair of our steam-launch, which we purposed executing at the mouth of the Kongone, where we could beach her, we started in the pinnace, early in November, to go down the Zambesi; and after fifteen days' sailing met our leader with the launch, at Kongone, where he had arrived nearly two weeks before us.

H.M.S. *Lynx*, Captain Barclay, was also lying off the bar, and with the assistance of her engineers, we got the launch patched up, and once more afloat; but after three days, had again to beach her, other leaks breaking out as fast as we could stop up old ones; so we now had no other resource but stop up her leaks with clay, finding it quite impossible to keep her afloat any other way. We once more started about the end of December, in the launch, for Tette, where we arrived after much difficulty and frequent stoppages to repair, about the beginning of February, 1860. It having been now decided by Dr.

Livingstone that I should be sent home to procure a more powerful and portable steamer, to be specially adapted for the navigation of the river Shire above the Falls, and also Lake Nyassa, we left Tette for the mouth of the river on the 18th of February, where we expected to meet, according to appointment, one of her majesty's ships, in which I was to return to England. But on our arrival at the bar, about the end of February, finding no ship due until the 15th of March, Dr, Livingstone sent me round to Quillimane, where we expected to find some ship in which I could get a passage home; but I had to remain there until the middle of June.

As the launch had by this time become perfectly useless, Dr. Livingstone, knowing that nothing could be done without a steamer, resolved to redeem his promise made to Seheletu on his former visit, by accompanying the Makolo men to their own country, a journey they of themselves could never have accomplished, on account of the dangers to which they would be exposed from neighboring tribes; and while I remained at Quillimane, I had letters from him, dated 15th May, in which he stated that on the following day he purposed leaving Tette, where he then was, accompanied by Dr. Kirk and Mr. Charles Livingstone, for that purpose. I also had letters from Major Sicard, in which he stated that he had news from Dr. Livingstone, then two days upon his upward journey, and that he had sent with him a number of natives to assist him in his progress. While I remained at Quillimane—as was to be expected from the low, marshy nature of the country—I had an attack of fever; and Dr. Livingstone being far away, I felt very much the want of that skill and attention which he was so well qualified, and always willing to give. On the 14th of June, H.M.S. *Lyra*, Captain Oldfield, arrived at Quillimane. Captain Oldfield informed me that on the 2d he stood off the Kongone, and sent in two boats, expecting to find me there; and most unfortunately, when crossing the bar, one of the boats was swamped, and the paymaster drowned, a circumstance which gave me great grief. I was taken on board the *Lyra* on the 14th, which left Quillimane the same evening, and towards the end of the month reached the island of Johanna, where we fell in with a small schooner bound for the Mauritius, on board of which we shipped the cases of botanical specimens, and confided to the care of her captain Dr. Livingstone's despatches; but for want of room he could not give me a passage. Captain Oldfield, indeed, was very much opposed to my risking a voyage in such a small vessel. After this, I cruised about on this station in the *Lyra*, whose particular duty was the prevention of the slave-trade, and whose captain was a terror to all the slave-dealers on the coast, and I had the good-fortune to assist in the capture of a slaver of three hundred tons, fitted up for one thousand slaves.

An American bark, the *Guide*, Captain M'Millan, having come into the port, bound for Aden, and as there was no prospect of my getting a passage to the Cape before December, I considered it the best way to carry out the wishes of Dr. Livingstone, and for the good of the expedition, that I should embark in her for Aden, and thence, per Peninsular and Oriental Co.'s steamers, to England, which I calculated would land me there by the middle of September.

We sailed from Zanzibar on the 30th August in the *Guide*, hailing from Salem. Our ship's company consisted, as nearly as I can now recollect, of twenty Americans, besides three Spanish ladies, passengers, and myself. On September 4, about midnight, the vessel struck, and went ashore at Rass Haffoon, near the Gulf of Aden. The boats were immediately lowered, the wind blowing fresh at the time, and we got biscuits and water put on board, and the passengers' private luggage, with the intention of pulling out to sea, so as to reach Aden; but the surf being very heavy, our boats were all swamped and knocked to pieces against the ship's sides, when we lost every thing of which we were formerly possessed. With great difficulty, we again scrambled on to the ship's decks; and as daylight was now just beginning to break, we could see the land about two hundred yards distant, the ship being forced ashore by the action of the surf. As daylight increased, the natives appeared in hundreds, and by eight A.M., they succeeded in boarding us. At first, they pretended to be friendly to us; but on seeing that we were perfectly helpless, and our boats all destroyed, they commenced plundering the passengers and ship, tearing the ear-rings from the ladies' ears, and flourishing their long knives, as if they intended to massacre the whole of us. We then dropped over the ship's side into the water, which was now a few feet deep, and escaped to the shore during the excitement consequent upon the plundering of the vessel, taking with us only the clothes in which we stood, and about 14,000 dollars in gold pieces, divided amongst us, for the purpose of aiding us to get away from the coast. We travelled along the shore towards the north-east, in search of water, and also to be out of the reach of ill-usage at the hands of the natives, who we now found were Sumalies with a mixture of Arabs, all well armed with asseghaies and long knives, and seemingly bent upon our destruction. On the first day we reached the rock of Rass Haffoon, where we wandered about for two days more, searching for water, and keeping a look-out, hoping to see some ship pass near us. On the evening of the third day from that of the wreck, five of the crew went off in search of water, which they expected to find near a green bush which we saw at a short distance. These men never returned, and we learned afterwards that they had all been murdered, and saw some of the natives wearing their clothes. Our sufferings at this time were indescribable, our tongues perfectly parched, and our voices so much altered, that we could scarcely understand what each other said. I scraped away the sand to fit my side, so that I might lie comfortably at night. On the third morning, Captain M'Millan and I started for the north side of the rock, in search of the men who had left us the preceding evening, and hoping also to fall in with fresh water. This, although only three miles distant, was, in our weakened condition, and with the hot glare of the sun reflected from the sand, a most painful and laborious journey; but our labor was in vain, as we could neither see nor hear of the missing men, found no water, and could see no ship.

On rejoining our companions in misfortune, despair was in every heart: six of the crew and the three ladies talked of destroying themselves by drowning. I was a few steps off when this was proposed. Captain M'Millan came to me, and said, "What do you think of the proposal?" My answer was: "I have not the slightest intention of doing so yet; as long as there is life, there is hope." By this time, we were now approaching the others; the ladies had got to their feet, and were walking off to the water. Some of the crew then asked me: "How long can we live, Rae, without food or water?" My reply was: "At least eight or ten days; and if you remain here at rest, you may probably live longer." The ladies stood still hearing this conversation, and wishing us all to go into the water and die together; but I opposed this, and said: "Come, let us try and get to the wreck." The men objected, saying: "Although we go to the wreck, we will just be killed—better die here than be murdered." I then said: "There is a chance of us not being murdered; and if we get back to the ship, we are sure of a drink of water, and perhaps some food."

The mate insisted that we should not go: "We will not be long a dying here; we will be dead by to-morrow night." After some more argument and talking of the same sort, we all sat down, and it was now proposed to kill the captain's dog, which had accompanied us from the ship. The dog was instantly killed by a blow from an axe, and some of the crew ate a small part of the flesh. I put a small piece over my lips, to keep them moist, they being severely cracked and very painful.

After some further persuasion on the part of Captain M'Millan and I, they were all got upon their feet; but the ladies still insisted on destroying themselves, and walked towards the water. I followed, and caught hold of one of them, and carried her along; the others then turned, and followed, and we all proceeded in the direction of the wreck, lying about seven miles distant, several of the crew shewing symptoms of mental aberration.

To the best of my recollection, we reached the wreck on the fifth day, but from this time I lost all recollection of the days of the week or month. We went straight to the ship's side, and tried to scramble up, but in our weak state, only a few of us succeeded. By this time the natives were again around us, and stripped us of our clothes, allowing us to retain only the shirt and trousers. I walked up to a tent made of our sails, where a pleasant looking old woman was standing at the door, from whom I begged as much water as would wet my

From The Examiner.

The Impending Crisis of the South; How to meet it. By Hinton Rowan Helper, of North Carolina. Hundredth Thousand. Sampson Low, Son, and Co. New York: A. B. Burdick.

Mr. Helper's book may almost be said to belong to the history of the present quarrel between the American States of the North and South. The author is a Southern Abolitionist, and his book was first published in 1857. He foresaw the impending crisis as one turning on the question of slavery. He amassed telling facts against the economy of the slave system, and compiled as "Testimonies" the arguments and opinions of men of note in North and South. It must be owned that he used no tenderness in dealing with the question, doing his work rather in the spirit of a warm-blooded partisan than of a statesman, for he seemed to think that it would be a gain to the slaveholders of the South, as much as it was their duty, to emancipate all the blacks and give them sixty dollars apiece to begin freedom with. Very soon after the publication of this book a suggestion came from the managers of the *New York Evening Post*, a paper of which an excellent American poet, Mr. Bryant, is known to be chief proprietor, for the gratuitous issue of a hundred thousand copies of a compendium of its facts. Political changes deferred action on the scheme until the spring of 1859, when the proposal to print a hundred thousand copies of such an epitome by subscription was endorsed by sixty-eight members of the House of Representatives, and is said to have been publicly approved by Mr. Seward, whose position in the Republican party gave significance to what he might do. The book was read on both sides, and violently protested against by the men of the South, who were entitled bitterly to resent its intemperate manner. Of the compendium one hundred and forty thousand copies passed into circulation. Of the original work, the copy before us, dated 1860, is declared on the title-page to be one of the Hundredth Thousand. We are sorry for it. In this day of a great national crisis nothing but evil can be expected from such wide acceptance of a book designed throughout in the spirit of the following extract. Advantage from the facts amassed is as nothing, in a day of controversy, to the evil of a way of dealing with the facts that we might fairly accuse of being deliberately calculated to inflame passion on both sides:—

"Waiving all other counts, we have, we think, shown, to the satisfaction of every impartial reader, that, as elsewhere stated, on the single score of damages to lands, the slaveholders are, at this moment, indebted to us, the non-slaveholding whites, in the enormous sum of nearly seventy-six hundred million of dollars. What shall be done with this amount? It is just; shall payment be demanded? No; all the slaveholders in the country could not pay it; nor shall we ever ask them for even a moiety of the amount—no, not even for a dime, nor yet for a cent; we are willing to forfeit every farthing for the sake of freedom; for ourselves we ask no indemnification for the past: we only demand justice for the future.

"But, sirs, slaveholders, chevaliers and lords of the lash, we are unwilling to allow you to cheat the negroes out of all the rights and claims to which, as human beings, they are most sacredly entitled. Not alone for ourself as an individual, but for others also —particularly for six million of Southern non-slaveholding whites, whom your iniquitous statism has debarred from almost all the mental and material comforts of life —do we speak, when we say, you must, sooner or later, emancipate your slaves, and pay each and every one of them at least sixty dollars cash in hand. By doing this, you will be restoring to them their natural rights, and remunerating them at the rate of less than twenty-six cents per annum for the long and cheerless period of their servitude, from the 20th of August, 1620, when, on James River, in Virginia, they became the unhappy slaves of heartless tyrants. Moreover, by doing this you will be performing but a simple act of justice to the non-slaveholding whites, upon whom the system of slavery has weighed scarcely less heavily than upon the negroes themselves. You will also be appl ing a saving balm to your own outraged hearts and consciences, and your children—yourselves in fact—freed from the accursed stain of slavery, will become respectable, useful, and honorable members of society.

"And now, sirs, we have thus laid down our ultimatum. What are you going to do about it? Something dreadful, of course! Perhaps you will dissolve the Union *again*. Do it, if you dare! Our motto, and we would have you understand it, is *The Abolition of Slavery, and the Perpetuation of the Union*. If, by any means, you do succeed in your treasonable attempts, to take the

From The Athenæum.

Poems, Sacred and Secular. By the Rev. William Croswell. Edited, with a Memoir, by A. Cleveland Coxe. Boston: Ticknor and Fields; London: Lowe and Co.

An accomplished editor's loving care has been worthily aided by publisher and printer, to make this a beautiful book; and the written remains of a mind that was lovely in life have been enshrined with a reliquary richness after death. William Croswell was born in November, 1804, at Hudson, in the County of Columbia and State of New York. In 1827, Croswell and Doane started the *Watchman*, which became "an influence" in the American Church. In 1829, Croswell was ordained to the priesthood, and entered on the rectorship of Christ Church, Boston. This church was an interesting old colonial fabric, one of the very few in America having a chime of bells. Its silver altar-service was a gift of George the Second. From its tower the chief men of Provence had watched the battle of Bunker's Hill. Mr. Coxe, the editor speaks very affectionately of his poet-friend. He appears to have been of a spirit singularly pure and faithful, and, after some two-and-twenty years of life spent in the Master's service, his death was singularly touching. On Sunday, the 9th of November, 1851, he baptized an infant, at the evening service, and preached to the children on the "little maid" whose fidelity led to the cure and conversion of Naaman. He joined in the singing, then knelt down at the rails of the chancel, and, looking towards the altar, began the prayer. The book fell from his grasp. The hand of death had been laid gently on the bowed head as he knelt in the white vestment of his priesthood. A blood-vessel had burst in his brain. We do not get the best of a nature like that of Croswell in books. Accordingly, the poetry will be found pale after the warm, bright word of his friend. But the goodness shines transparently through it, and his gentleness must be fully felt. There is manna in it for many, only it must fall into the right hands. The specimen we give will not do justice to the book in its higher aspect, but it is natural, and we like it:—

"TO MY FATHER.

"My Father, I recall the dream
Of childish joy and wonder,
When thou wast young as I now seem,
Say, thirty-three, or under!
When on thy temples, as on mine,
Time just began to sprinkle
His first gray hairs, and traced the sign
Of many a coming wrinkle.

"I recognize thy voice's tone
As to myself I'm talking;
And this firm tread, how like thine own,
In thought the study walking!
As, musing, to and fro I pass,
A glance across my shoulder
Would bring thine image in the glass,
Were it a trifle older.

"My Father, proud am I to bear
Thy face, thy form, thy stature,
But happier far might I but share.
More of thy better nature;
Thy patient progress after good,
All obstacles disdaining,
Thy courage, faith, and fortitude,
And spirit uncomplaining.

"Then for the day that I was born,
Well might I joy, and borrow
No longer of the coming morn
Its trouble or its sorrow;
Content I'd be to take my chance
In either world possessing
For my complete inheritance
Thy virtues and thy blessing!"

Indigestion from Irish Stew.—The disruption of the once United States was at first wholly attributed to difference of opinion on the subject of slavery, and next in part ascribed to diversity of views and interests respecting commercial legislation. Another and more powerful cause may also have contributed to produce a result so much to be deplored and blushed for by all the friends of representative government. During many years, a great emigration of disaffected Irishmen had been continually increasing the population of the American Republic. For a long time America digested them. Perhaps, however, the nutriment which she has gone on deriving from Ireland so long, may have at last disagreed with her, occasioning constitutional disturbance which is, in a great measure, nothing more than an outbreak of a suppressed Irish malady, the fever which, with a smouldering fire, has always burned for Repeal of the Union.—*Punch.*

From The Economist, 30 March.

THE COMMISSIONERS FROM MONTGOMERY AND THEIR MISSION.

THE veil is not yet removed from Mr. Lincoln's policy,—and eminent senators of the United States were engaged at the last advices in exchanging those dignified personalities on the subject, for which their debates are so remarkable. It seems to be generally believed that the President intends to abandon Fort Sumter to the South Carolinians, but to use all the force at his command to retain other United States' forts and property that he may think more tenable. But while Mr. Lincoln deliberates, Mr. Jefferson Davis acts. Besides pushing on with unusual promptitude the organization of the Southern Army, and the reinforcement of the Southern forts, he has imposed the agreeable task on Lord John Russell and M. de Thouvenel of explaining to three Southern Commissioners that, for the present at least, they must be regarded by foreign States as private persons,—able, doubtless, to communicate much that is interesting concerning the progress of events in the Southern States, but representatives of nothing that a government can yet recognize. The Hon. W. L. Yancey and his friends are coming, we hear, in the expectation of a cordial reception and of an immediate success. But in England, at least, they will be disappointed. We cannot, of course, go on forever on the diplomatic fiction that the Southern States are included in the Union, if they become independent. It has been our rule in all cases, after the lapse of a sufficient period to test the issue, to recognize *de facto* independence. But such time has not yet elapsed. It would be, in fact, an adhesion to the South for us to acknowledge its revolt before the United States' government have even explained their policy, or shown in a single instance how they intend to deal with the contumacious States,—and a step not in us the more respectable, but the more thoroughly ignominious, on account of the selfish tariff policy of the North. Nor is there any danger of such a false step with our present rulers. The American fanatics who wish to persuade themselves that in England the coarsest self-interest overrules every other consideration, are crying out that we shall grasp at the bribe offered us by the more rational tariff of the South. But, in fact, it would be the insanest as well as the most immoral policy to permit this consideration to influence us at all. For what would it amount to? To this,—that it is better for English interests to establish an independent nation round the Gulf of Mexico adopting the double policy of Slavery and Free Trade,—than that the States round the Gulf should be incorporated in a Union hostile to the extension of slavery, but more or less ruled by the foolish cry of protection. Of course this alternative does not really rest with England,—but if it did, no sensible man can doubt how she would decide, even as a matter of pure interest. The deeper delusions of protection can only be short-lived in an intelligent country. More or less they refute themselves. But the policy of slavery is insatiate: give it what it asks, and it asks more. Let the Southern States be independent and active for another seven years, and they will be planning descents on Jamaica.

It is not for us, then, to deviate a hair's-breadth from our usual course. Nay, even when it is generally acknowledged,—as no doubt sooner or later it will be,—that disunion is a *fait accompli*,—even then our acknowledgment of the Southern Confederation should be cautious and conditional. At present they have declared themselves against the Slave-Trade. But never let it be forgotten that the very men who planned secession, planned it with the avowed purpose of re-opening the Slave-Trade. The Hon. W. L. Yancey, who is now delegated by Mr. Jefferson Davis to negotiate a recognition with us, was the zealous, the shameless, the consistent advocate of its revival. He it was who contended against the injustice of a law which he described as saying: "*You of the South shall not import Negroes from Africa, though you of the North may import Jackasses from Malta*,"—and doubtless it is his own and many of his colleagues' intention to agitate for the repeal of the restriction, so soon as they shall have consolidated in one Confederation as many States as they are able to tempt out of the old Union. At present they are consulting the scruples of the feeble-minded, deferring to the weaker consciences of Virginia and Kentucky. The ordinance against the Slave-Trade is "milk for babes:" the meat will come later. Once let them see their way clear to independence and a Mexican extension, and then old-world scruples, as Mr. Yancey calls them, will be cast to the winds. Therefore, we think that in recognizing whenever we are compelled by common sense to recognize, the accomplished fact of their independence, we ought to give them fair warning that in case they ever repeal that ordinance, either actually or virtually, it will become a ground of serious difference with us: that we are prepared to enter into a close compact with the Northern Union to put an end to this shameful traffic forever,—and that their attempt to renew it, should they ever venture on it, would not be allowed to stand in our way.

From the Press, 30 March.

THE COLLAPSE AT WASHINGTON.

NOTHING has so much surprised us, in the present crisis of American affairs, as the total absence of energy and decision on the part of the people of the North. Ever since America was a Republic, it has been the loudest of all the nations of the earth in admiration of its own institutions, in exultation at its own achievements, and in eulogy of those whom it regarded, very often with justice as its great men. It was difficult to suppose that a profound sentiment did not lie at the root of this efflorescent and redundant patriotism. To believe in the American Republic, great, glorious, sacred, and indivisible, was the first—one might almost say the only—article of the national creed. Not only did the rightful leaders of opinion, whether statesmen, writers, diplomatists, or legal dignitaries, always appear to rest their surest claim to popularity on the vigorous and constant reiteration of this confession of faith, but the lowest stump orator could always command a cheer by an allusion in or out of season, to the star-spangled banner; the unconquerable, though possibly dirty and illiterate, son of freedom was always ready from his bright home in the setting sun to hurl a defiance at the despot and the tyrant. Like Mr. Pickwick in the quadrille, who was incessantly dancing in his place when there was no call whatever for his exertions, American patriotism, when nobody threatened it, indulged in all those restless and somewhat aggressive gesticulations which might be supposed to proceed from a superabundance of vigor and vitality.

A time has come for all these vaunts to be made good. In the heat of civil dissension all the froth will be evaporated, and we shall see what amount of sincerity and determination will remain at the bottom of the crucible. Certainly, to judge from present signs, the residuum will be insignificant. Everybody looked to the accession of the new President as the period that was to end doubt and discussion, and to inaugurate action. The most powerful section of a great community was supposed to be anxiously awaiting in that event the signal to put forth its might in defence of all that had lately been its pride. The President's speech was disappointing, but might, at any rate, be taken to indicate prudence, if it did not exhibit vigor. If no decisive means were at hand to coerce the refractory States, forbearance might for the moment be politic. If the appearance of weakness was only assumed to hold the wavering in suspense until the power of action should be matured, such a pretence might not only be pardonable but sagacious. But in the same speech the limits of forbearance were defined, and the reports tell us that no parts of the address were so emphatically delivered or so warmly cheered as those which asserted the determination to collect the revenue and to defend the property of the State. And when the next mail tells us that Fort Sumter—the very portion of State property which is most imminently threatened, and which has come to be regarded as the first test of strength of the rival parties—is now to be abandoned to the Secessionists, all reliance on the vigorous action of the government must go near to vanish.

Still it must be remembered that the President succeeded to office under conditions peculiarly disadvantageous to the prompt and vigorous exercise of power. The national troops, few in number, are dispersed over the wide horizon of Republican territory; while the strongest weapon which the government could wield—the naval power—has been rendered useless by the traitorous precautions of the late minister, who took care to put the fleet for a time beyond the reach of his successor in office. Thus it is impossible to convey reinforcements to Fort Sumter, as the troops could only be sent up the harbor and landed under the protection of powerful broadsides; and even if the garrison were strong enough in men and metal to oppose the extensive works in preparation for the attack, yet the failure of provisions will, it is said, soon render the withdrawal of the defenders a necessary measure of humanity.

In the interval necessary for the return of the naval squadrons and the establishment of the new ministry in office, it would be premature to pronounce the government incapable of dealing with the crisis. But the tranquillity or apathy of the people of the North remains unaccountable. It cannot be that they are waiting for the development of the government policy, because they are the most self-asserting population on the face of the earth, and much more likely to initiate and compel the action of the state than to follow it. It cannot be the repose of stubborn inarticulate resolve, because trifling political conjectures have generally evoked an inordinate manifestation of public feeling. It cannot be the want of an inspiring rallying-cry or of a decisive policy, for events are in progress which, if not arrested, will leave America without influence or credit as a nation. The right to secede being quietly yielded, no future confederacy of States can be sufficiently stable to command respect or to assert influence.

It will always be felt that the caprice of a majority * may at any moment dissolve any

* Or, of a *minority.—Living Age.*

Union, with all its institutions, its responsibilities, and its engagements. We should have expected the whole Republican party to be in a fever of patriotism. Never was there, since the Republic was established, such a field for the display of eloquence, of public spirit, and of united action. The old platitudes of Transatlantic oratory would acquire a new significance with the importance of the occasion; and even the well-worn shade of Washington might now be invoked with perfect propriety. There can be little doubt that the united action of the North would suppress the revolt. In intelligence and wealth it possesses an immense superiority. Its militia is far better than that of the South, and would be hampered in its action by no necessity of intimidating a slave population that might at any moment become the most formidable of hostile elements. Its climate, commerce, and productions render it far more independent, self-sustaining, and capable of a protracted conflict, without disorganization or exhaustion. Agitators and orators would find for once a noble field in rousing and directing enthusiasm. A free contribution of funds for the common object, followed by a general military training, such as a less imminent peril has called forth here, a concentrated movement of regular troops and militia to the frontier, and a blockade of the Southern ports, would end in reducing the revolted States to obedience. But the only step hitherto taken is a most impolitic one. Revenue is to be raised by an additional tax on imports from Europe. It is proposed thus to make the friendly foreigner pay the expense of the domestic crisis. That our sympathy with America should augment with her exactions is scarcely to be expected, even if there were other points in her conduct to command our respect. Meanwhile the North, with supine attitude and lack-lustre gaze, watches the energetic movements of the revolted South. What will arouse the American eagle? He has had his tail pulled out and his wings clipped—yet the meek bird now holds out his claws to be pared, with a resignation that would be degrading in the most henpecked of domestic fowls. The old despotisms of Europe, reputed so effete, have at least died fighting. The king of Naples on the ramparts of Gaeta was a more respectable potentate than the American President at his levee, smiling in his "black frock, vest, and pants," as the reporters graphically depict him, while half the Republic was in open revolt. Where shall mankind look for the stability necessary to its happiness and its development, if tyrannies and democracies are alike subject to such sudden and helpless dissolution?

The Comminuted States.—Who can say where Secession will stop? That is a question which is raised by Mr. Lincoln, in a part of his inaugural address, directed to enforce upon fools and madmen the necessity of acquiescence by minorities in the decision of majorities. The President tells the frantic portion of his fellow-countrymen that:—

"There is no alternative for continuing the Government but acquiescence on one side or the other. If a minority in such a case will secede rather than acquiesce, they make a precedent which in turn will ruin and divide them, for a minority of their own will secede from them whenever a majority refuses to be controlled by such a minority. For instance, why may not any portion of a new confederacy, a year or two hence, arbitrarily secede again, precisely as portions of the present Union now claim to secede from it? All who cherish disunion sentiments are now being educated to the exact temper of doing this."

The force of this simple reasoning will be seen by the lunatics to whom it is addressed, during their lucid intervals, if they have any. It may even be hoped that some of them may recover the use of their reflecting faculties so far as to be enabled to follow out President Lincoln's argument, and their own folly, into ultimate consequences and conclusions. Then they will see what is likely to be the end of Secession, for it is not quite true that there is no end to Secession, and the end of Secession will be for the Secessionists an end of every thing. Seceders will go on seceding and subseceding, until at last every citizen will secede from every other citizen, and each individual will be a sovereign state in himself, self-government personified, a walking autonomy, a lone star, doing business and supporting itself off its own hook.—*Punch.*

From The Saturday Review.

EARTH AND SUN.

Two clocks were once placed at a distance from each other, one of them being set going and the other not. After a time it was observed that the pendulum of the latter was also in full swing, and the clock ticking like its neighbor. The clock was intentionally stopped, but after a few hours it was observed again in action. The pendulums, in fact, of both clocks had been of the same length and oscillated in exactly equal times; the consequence was, that the impulses of the moving pendulum, transmitted through the air and solids which intervened between the clocks, so accumulated as to set the second pendulum in motion. Had the one pendulum been slightly shorter than the other the same accumulation could not have taken place. It is just the case of a boy upon a swing; by properly timing his impulses he can augment the amplitude of his oscillations. Precisely on the same principle, a stretched string is able to respond to a certain note. The aërial waves by which the note is transmitted strike upon the string, and if the rate of oscillation of the latter coincide with the recurrence of the waves there is finally such an accumulation of small impulses that the second string is actually rendered sonorous. Everybody has observed how one window-pane responds to notes of a certain pitch, while other panes remain silent. This is also a case of isochronism between the vibrations which the window-pane easily performs and those of the air which strikes against the glass.

And from the particles of oscillating air, which are concerned in the propagation of sound, we may pass to the particles of oscillating ether which are concerned in the propagation of light and heat. As regards light, the principle above indicated has recently received some splendid applications; and to illustrate these was in part the object of a most interesting lecture delivered by Professor Roscoe before the members of the Royal Institution, on the evening of Friday, March 1st. It has been long known that the salts of certain metals impart colors to flames; and on this property, indeed, many of the chromatic effects produced in theatres depend. The salts of copper, for example, color a flame green, the salts of strontium crimson, the salts of sodium an intense yellow, and so of other salts. Common salt, for example, when thrown into the flame of a lamp burning a mixture of alcohol and water, which flame itself possesses scarcely a trace of color, at once makes it a vivid yellow; and the purity of the color is attested by the fact that the hues of the most brilliant flowers or tissues, the tint of the rose, or of the lips—all colors, in fact, with the exception of yellow—disappear from bodies illuminated wholly by this light. A human face thus shone upon is the most ghastly object imaginable. By making use of a series of flames which of themselves possessed little or no color, Professor Roscoe showed, in a striking manner, how these flames were affected by the introduction into them of various metallic salts. Some were turned purple, others violet, others green, others red, others yellow, and others purple and crimson.

But the color is but a rough indication of the real state of the flame. To know the true character of the rays emitted, we must resort to prismatic analysis. Take, for example, the flame colored by common salt. We know that the light of an ordinary candle, the lime-light—the light, in fact, emitted by any solid brought to a high state of incandescence—gives us, when analyzed, a *continuous* spectrum, composed of the seven so-called prismatic colors. But the spectrum of the sodium light consists of a single vivid yellow band. The light emits rays of a specific refrangibility only; namely, such as are competent to produce the sensation of yellow. Other metals, when volatilized by heat, produce other bands—some two, others several. Strontium, for example, gives us a series of bands at the red end of the spectrum, and also a very brilliant band in the blue. Each metal, in short, emits one or more groups of rays of definite refrangibilities, between which gaps occur, which indicate that the volatilized metals are incompetent to emit rays of the refrangibility necessary to fill those gaps. To take a comparison from sound. The lime-light, or that of any *solid* raised to a state of incandescence, resembles an orchestra which sends forth notes of every possible pitch, whereas the light emitted by a *volatilized* metal, resembles an orchestra in which the instruments or voices consist of a finite number of groups, each of which emits notes of a single pitch only.

No matter where or how a metal may be concealed, no matter what the compound may be in which it is disguised, the rays which it emits, when the substance which contains it is volatilized, are perfectly constant. No matter where we meet sodium, whether in culinary salts, or in Glauber salts, or in any other of the many combinations into which it enters, we have always our bright yellow band. So also of the other metals—every one of them has a distinct band, or series of bands, which never alter, and which are perfectly characteristic of the metal. This has been proved by Bunsen and Kirchoff, the former a chemist, the latter a natural philosopher—two of the most eminent men of the present age in their respective lines of research. Having proved this constancy of the metals throughout a large range, these excellent investigators noticed a series of bands which were not produced by any of the known metals. They were not the men to indulge in a rash prediction; still they did predict that the earth's crust contained a metal which human eye had never seen nor human finger felt. They set to work, and found the substance. Professor Roscoe exhibited a quantity of one of the compounds of this metal, about the fifth part of a small thimbleful. It had been obtained by the evaporation of four tons of mineral water. This is an example of the labor which natural philosophers bestow upon the truths they follow. Bunsen and Kirchoff have quite recently announced the discovery of a second metal by the same means of analysis. The quantities of matter which may thus be rendered evident are of inconceivable smallness. A fraction of the millionth of a grain declares its presence by indications not to be mistaken. The air we breathe is thus proved to be full of substances of the existence of which in our atmosphere we had some time ago no notion; and bodies which have been hitherto regarded as of the rarest occurrence, are shown to be almost everywhere present in minute quantities. Here also is a mode of analysis placed within reach of the medical man which tells him infinitely more than he previously could know regarding the substances which his patients inhale day by day. In fact, the issues of these discoveries are incalculable. But not only do they shed light upon terrestrial things; by their means we are also enabled to extend our inquiries beyond our planet's verge, and investigate the character of the substances which enter into the composition of sun and stars.

It has long been known that the solar spectrum was intersected by shaded lines of lacking light, called Fraunhofer's lines, from the man who first thoroughly investigated them. They are invariable in position and appearance; they occur in solar light and in all the derivatives of solar light—in the light of moons and planets. They have been of infinite use in optical investigations. When, for example, the philosopher in this country wishes to speak to his brother on the Continent, or at the Antipodes, of light of a certain color or refrangibility, he defines it with mathematical precision by reference to one of the fixed lines in the solar spectrum. These lines of Fraunhofer indicate that certain rays are always failing in the light which reaches us from the sun—such rays being not at all emitted, or else somehow extinguished in their passage from the sun to the earth.

What is the true cause of the absence of the particular rays? Let us experiment and reason cautiously. We take a flame colored yellow by sodium, and behind it we place the far more intense Drummond-light. Let the beams from both pass through the same slit, and let the light issuing from this slit be decomposed by a prism. We have here the rays of the Drummond-light passing through the sodium flame, and afterwards reduced to their colored components. The following remarkable fact at once reveals itself. The spectrum of the lime-light is no longer continuous, but a dark line is found drawn across it exactly in the position occupied by the bright band of the sodium flame. Quench the lime-light, and the bright yellow band appears on the spot where a moment before was a dark line. This line is really only dark by contrast with the adjacent brightness—the sodium flame, in fact, has stopped that precise ray of the lime-light which it is itself capable of emitting. Exactly as a pendulum absorbs the vibrations of another of the same length, and disperses the motion thus acquired on all sides, so the atoms of the sodium flame have taken up those vibrations of the lime-light which are isochronous with their own, and thus prevented them from going straight on to their original destination. Let the same experiment be made with the flames of the other metals; in all cases where the intense rays of the lime-light are sent through a flame, those precise rays of the former are absorbed which the latter are capable of emitting; and in virtue of the greater intensity of the lime-light, the lines which appear bright when the flame alone is examined appear dark when both are experimented with.

Do, then, the dark lines of Fraunhofer in the solar spectrum coincide with the bright lines produced by any of our metals? They do. In a small space of the spectrum Kirchoff has already mapped seventy lines which correspond to a mathematical nicety with the bands of terrestrial metals. Fraunhofer's lines are, in fact, produced when the lime-light is caused to shine through the flames of these metals. There is absolutely no difference between them. Now the lines are perfectly characteristic of the metals, and the presence of the latter in the sun is thus reduced to demonstration. The sun, in fact, possesses a luminous atmosphere which bears the same relation to its solid nucleus as the sheet of flame does to the solid lime-light. And those lines that we observe in the solar spectrum indicate exactly the positions of those rays which the solar atmosphere itself would exhibit *as bright bands*, if there were no intense nucleus behind it. The conclusiveness of the reasoning here, and the real grandeur of these discoveries, will be best appreciated by those whose thoughts have been disciplined by such studies. But even the general reader cannot fail to be interested in such splendid intellectual achievements. Surely, the man of science has just reason to be content with a vocation which secures to him and to humanity such noble results.

CONCENTRATED ESSENCE OF THE MILK OF HUMAN KINDNESS.—*An ingenuous appeal to the aged, and persons about to die, or tired of life.*—Many who are on the point of leaving this world, or have lost their relish for its pleasures, are nevertheless blest with the means of conferring on others that earthly happiness which they themselves must soon relinquish, or are incapable of enjoying. Such are too often in the habit of seeking unattainable gratification in the exercise of benevolence by distributing large sums of money in small donations amongst the poor. The munificence which is thus spread over a multitude of objects is so attenuated that by each of its recipients it is scarcely felt. The charitable donor thus fails to obtain the exquisite satisfaction of reflecting that he has gladdened the heart of a fellow-creature. His bounty is as it were a loaf, vainly dispersed in crumbs among a famishing crowd, instead of being effectually applied to relieve the hunger of one starving sufferer. Those who are desirous really to taste the luxury of doing good should concentrate their generosity on particular persons. An opportunity is now offered to all who are anxious to secure the genuine article. A healthy young man, with a large appetite of every kind, is well-nigh destitute of the means of procuring any one pleasure. In order to subsist, it is necessary for him to work hard, which he very much dislikes, and to earn a precarious and scanty living by anxious labor. He is, in short, in want of a large and independent income. Oh, if he only had that how happy he would be! and though at present necessarily an unmarried man, he would very soon have a wife and perhaps ten children, whom, as well as himself, a certain affluence would render happy.

Let the wealthy who derive no enjoyment from their own riches, only think of the bliss which it is in their power to confer on this young man. Let them consider how much more sensible an amount of blessing they would impart by bestowing all their charity on him, than they can dispense by frittering it away upon a host of others. How much better to give him a large sum of money than to squander it on schools and institutions? It is in the power of every one, however humble, to contribute to his felicity, and thus be enabled to cherish the pleasing assurance of having performed an act of efficacious kindness. The smallest contributions will be thankfully received; for a sufficient number of farthings would insure the object so earnestly sought by this young man. Subscriptions, legacies, etc., to be sent to the Office, 85, Fleet Sreet; at which application may be made by any party or parties desiring to adopt an Heir.—*Punch.*

MARION BROWN'S LAMENT.

[Founded on the story told of Claverhouse, who, when he had shot her husband asked mockingly, "What think you now of your braw goodman?"]

"'What think you now of your braw goodman?'
Ah! woe is me!
My heart was high when I began,
My heart was high and my answer ran,
'More than ever he is to me.'

"Mickle thought I of my bridegroom brave,
Ah! woe is me!
Mickle I thought of him douce and grave,
When he waled me out among the lave,
Me a poor maiden his wife to be.

"But there on the greensward lying dead,
Ah! woe is me!
As I laid on my lap his noble head,
And kissed the lips that for Jesus bled,
More than ever he was to me.

"My heart was high when I began,
Ah! woe is me!
I was so proud of my brave goodman,
Never a tear from my eyelids ran,
Altho' they stood in my e'e.

"But when I laid him on his bed,
Ah! woe is me!
And spread the face-cloth over his head,
And sat me down beside my dead,
Oh, but my heart grew sair in me.

"And aye as I lookt at the empty chair,
Ah! woe is me!
And the Book that he left lying open there,
And the text that bade me cast my care
On the Father of all that cared for me.

"And aye as my Mary, and little Will,
Ah! woe is me!
Whispered, 'Father is sleeping still,
And hush! for Minnie is weary and ill,'
My heart was like to break in me.

"It's well for men to be heroes grand!
Ah! woe is me!
But a woman's hearth is her country, and
A desolate home is a desolate land;
And he was all the world to me."

—*Bishop's Walk, By Orwell.*

A LITTLE WHILE.

Beyond the smiling and the weeping,
I shall be soon:
Beyond the waking and the sleeping,
Beyond the sowing and the reaping,
I shall be soon.
Love, rest and home!
Sweet home!
Lord, tarry not, but come.

Beyond the blooming and the fading,
I shall be soon;
Beyond the shining and the shading,
Beyond the hoping and the dreading,
I shall be soon.
Love, rest and home!
Sweet home!
Lord, tarry not, but come.

Beyond the rising and the setting,
I shall be soon;
Beyond the calming and the fretting,
Beyond remembering and forgetting,
I shall be soon.
Love, rest and home!
Sweet home!
Lord, tarry not, but come.

Beyond the parting and the meeting,
I shall be soon;
Beyond the farewell and the greeting,
Beyond the pulse's fever beating,
I shall be soon.
Love, rest and home!
Sweet home!
Lord, tarry not, but come.

Beyond the frost-chain and the fever,
I shall be soon;
Beyond the rock-waste and the river,
Beyond the ever and the never,
I shall be soon.
Love, rest and home!
Sweet home!
Lord, tarry not, but come.

Rev. Dr. Bonar.

BITTERNESS.

We sat among the ripe wheat sheaves;
The western skies were golden red:
We had a book; we turned the leaves;
But not a word we said.

A sudden lull; a thrilling pause;
We seemed at once one thought to have.
We little could divine the cause
That such a moment gave.

A minute that comes once and goes;
That must be snatched at once or lost:
O foolish heart!—but something rose
In me. Our Fate was crossed.

We rose up from the shining sheaf;
We looked back at the setting sun;
We scarcely spoke; we seemed to grieve
The golden day was done.

And on the morrow I was gone,
Who could not speak for paltry fear,
The morrows will go gliding on,
And we find each a bitter one,
Nor meet for many a year.

—*Chambers's Journal.*

THE LIVING AGE.

No. 885.—18 May, 1861.

CONTENTS.

NEW BOOKS.

THE SEMI-ATTACHED COUPLE. By the author of "The Semi-Detached House." Boston: T. O. H. P. Burnham.

PUBLISHED EVERY SATURDAY BY

LITTELL, SON, & CO., BOSTON.

THE FLAG OF FORT SUMTER.

We have humbled the flag of the United States." —*Gov. Pickens.*

Our banner humbled!—when it flew
Above the band that fought so well,
And not till hope's last ray withdrew,
Before the traitor's cannon fell!

No! Anderson! with loud acclaim,
We hail thee hero of the hour,
When circling batteries poured their flame,
Against thy solitary tower.

Stood Lacedæmon then less proud,
When her three hundred heroes slain,
No road but o'er their breasts, allowed
To Xerxes and his servile train?

Or does New England blush to show
Yon hill, though victory crowned it not,—
Though Warren fell before the foe,
And Putnam left the bloody spot?

The voices of earth's noblest fields
With the deep voice within unite—
'Tis not success true honor yields,
But faithful courage for the right.

Keep, then, proud foe, the crumbled tower,
From those brave few by thousands torn,
But keep in silence, lest the hour
Should come for vengeance on your scorn.

Yet I could weep; for where ye stand,
In friendly converse have I stood;
And clasped, perchance, full many a hand,
Now armed to shed a brother's blood.

O God of Justice! smile once more
Upon our flag's victorious path;
And when a stern, short strife is o'er,
Bid mercy triumph over wrath!

Dorchester, April 20th, 1861. S. G. B.
—*Boston Transcript.*

"WHAT THE HAND FINDETH TO DO."

My true love laid her hand on mine,
Her soft and gentle hand,
'Twas like a wreath of purest snow
Upon the embrownèd land.

As white it was as snow new fallen,
Like snow without its chill;
And the blue veins marbled it sweetly o'er,
But left it snowlike still.

I looked at her hand, so white and soft;
At my own, so brown and hard:
"This is for strife and toil," I said;
"And that for love and reward.

"This is to keep the wolf of Want
Away from the hearth of home;
And this to welcome me tenderly,
When back to that hearth I come.

"This is to labor with tireless nerves,
Perchance at tasks that soil;
And this to greet with a loving clasp
The palm that is rough with toil.

"This is to win through rock and wood
A way, where way seemed none;
And this to chafe the poor proud limbs
That droop when the goal is won.

"This is to grasp in the world's long fight
The weapons that men must wield;
And this to bind up the aching wounds
Ta'en on the well-fought field.

"This is to put forth all its strength
In Earth's rough tasks and strife;
And this to kindle the sweet love-fires
That brighten the march of life.

"For labor, and sweat, and scars is this;
And this to scatter round
The flowers of beauty, and love, and hope,
On Home's enchanted ground.

"I would these fingers, for thy sweet sake,
Might a giant's strength command,
To toil for and guard thee worthily—
But Love will strengthen my hand.

"And if ever its weakness o'ercome its will,
And it fail in its toilsome part,
The fate that disables my fainting hand,
As surely will still my heart."
—*Chambers's Journal.*

LET HIM PASS ME SCORNFUL BY.

Let him pass me scornful by,
What care I?
To look as cold, I can try,
So for looks—what care I?
The pangs I feel he shall not know;
Nor sigh, nor tear my love shall show.

Another heart he may woo;
What care I?
He may court, and wed her too,
That he may—What care I?
So that my grief he doth not know,
Until in death my love I show.

Then he may his error find;
What care I?
Wish he had not been so blind;
Hopeless wish—What care I?
Though peace and rest no more I know,
A broken heart his grief shall show.
—"*Songs of Labor,*" *by John Plummer.*

INSCRIPTION FOR A SPRING.

Whoe'er thou art that stay'st to quaff
The streams that here from caverns dim
Arise to fill thy cup, and laugh
In sparking beads about the brim,
In all thy thoughts and words as pure
As these sweet waters mayst thou be,
To all thy friends as firm and sure,
As prompt in all thy charity.
—*Chambers's Journal.*

From The Westminster Review.

VOLTAIRE'S ROMANCES AND THEIR MORAL.

Voltaire's Romances and Novels. Romans de Voltaire.

In Goldsmith's story, our great lexicographer is represented as a candidate for a place in the chariot of Fame, which he claims by virtue of the ponderous Dictionary he bears under his arm. He is informed, much to his surprise, that Fame cares nothing for his *magnum opus*, and intends to assign him a place among those she honors only for the sake of the little romance he thought too trifling even to put forward. Whether right or wrong as regarded Johnson, the fable will apply to many eminent literary men who, laboring hard to overtake Fame in one way, were surprised to find her coming to meet them in a direction entirely unexpected. On what does the renown of Voltaire mainly rest? The vast philosophical dictionary has made but little mark upon the intellect of Europe. The "Henriade" is looked upon very much as people think of a college prize poem. The nations which possess a Shakspeare, a Schiller, an Alfieri, can scarcely warm into enthusiasm even over "Zaire;" and it is difficult to read the "Orphan of China" without a sensation of the ludicrous at the *petit maitre* love-making of the great Tartar conqueror. Even Voltaire the clear and vivid historian is quite overshadowed by Voltaire the satirist and the wit. Of that latter being, the best and most characteristic memorials possessed by posterity are the fantastic, humorous *nouvellettes* and satirical fables known as his romances. A man's true nature, says Goethe, is best divined by observing what he ridicules. In these romances we can study Voltaire's real nature; for in them we have set before us all he thought ridiculous in society around him and in the general systems of the world. In them he is not playing the philosopher or toiling to be an epic poet. In them we can discern him free of the personal weaknesses with which feeble health, much flattery, self-created vexations, and the injudicious humorings of friends, crusted over his better nature. A man who thoroughly and fairly studied these little stories would probably lay them down with a better knowledge of the real nature and genius of Voltaire than was acquired by Frederick of Prussia, by Madame du Chatelet, or by Madame Denis.

It was unfortunate for the development of Voltaire's special gifts that he should have been proclaimed, because of a few bold utterances, a prophet by one party of listeners, and a blasphemer by another. It is unfortunate for the true appreciation of his genius, that so many people still persist in regarding him as an audacious infidel philosopher, or a great progressive sage. The truth is, that nature, character, and circumstances quite disqualified Voltaire from becoming what can with any propriety be termed a philosopher of any kind. He was unable to take a large and general view of most subjects; to balance the good and the evil; to discern how much of either was accidental to a system, and how much was inherent and ineradicable; to trace out patiently the connection of effect with cause. Voltaire's was what Condorcet correctly termed an impatient spirit. The absurdities or the defects of any thing actually coming under his own notice, Voltaire could expose to ridicule and contempt as no man else could. If a system had a weak point, Voltaire could in the fewest possible words place its weakness in the most ludicrous light. But he was not a man whose opinion of the general character of the system should have been accepted unconditionally by any one. Few men of his day were less qualified to judge of Christianity as a system of religion; but no man could so effectively expose the errors and inconsistencies into which the professing Christians plunged when they set up their own self-conceit and prejudice as the interpreter and standard of Christian doctrines. It is amazing to observe the dread and horror with which many people even still shrink from the perusal of Voltaire's writings. Supposing him to have been an anti-Christian, a more harmless opponent Christianity has seldom encountered. That man must in our days indeed be simple whose Christian faith could be affected in the slightest by the keenest of Voltaire's arguments. Even where Voltaire had a clear view of the truth, he frequently failed to take a tenable position in its favor. He founded a variety of arguments against popery upon the contrast between the personal immortality of many popes and their supposed spiritual infallibility. But he seemed to forget that Roman Catholics do not claim personal infallibility for a pope acting merely as an individual; and that Roman Catholic doctrines, true or false, are no more affected by the blunders or the crimes of a single pope than the truths of any part of the Old Testament by the human errors of David. Voltaire is generally as weak in his theological arguments as in his famous explanation of the vestiges of shelly formations found in the Alps, by the hypothesis of pilgrims having let fall their cockleshells while crossing the Great St. Bernard. It is astonishing to find many people even still fall into the unspeakable absurdity of regarding Voltaire as an atheist, in ignorance of the fact that some of the only serious and dreary passages in his satires are those which he devotes to the superfluous labor of demonstrating the irrationality of atheism. Indeed, Voltaire all but detested atheists, and firmly believed he had himself given to the world some splendid confutations of their errors. Unfortunately, the individual who set up for an atheist must have been a very dull personage indeed if he could not answer some of the arguments which Voltaire pompously parades for his confusion in the dialogue between the pious Englishman, Freind, and the infidel companion of the youth who bears the peculiarly British prenomen of Ienni. The explanation is, that Voltaire really felt little interest in abstract truths of any kind. A genuine human grievance, a downright human folly, quickened him into intense animation; but he had not a nature which sympathized much with the mere maintenance of principle. His genius was altogether of the partisan order. He did not much trouble himself by a laborious investigation of both sides of a question; but where his instinct led him right, he could hit with a keen force which philosophy alone could never master. All his interests were thoroughly human, thoroughly wrapped up in the movements of ordinary life. Many of his philosophic sayings, and dogmas, which were received in his own day with reverent admiration or with shouts of denunciation, are universally recognized now as the mere commonplaces of truth, or as paradoxes whose extravagance needs no refutation. But the satirical wit which he brought to the exposure of some actual grievance or genuine folly remains immortal—keen and fresh as ever, although the grievance and the folly have long passed away. One popular idea of Voltaire is that of a mere scoffer at sacred things, a ribald reviler of the best human sentiments. Another common notion of him is that of a cold sceptic, who subjected every thing to the test of a narrow reasoning process; a man who cared nothing personally either for good or evil; who was all brain and no heart. If these romances fairly reflect the real nature of Voltaire, they exhibit the character of a very warm-hearted, sensitive, undiscriminating man, who sickened over human suffering and human persecution, and who employed, with an almost reckless prodigality, against the enemies he hated most, the instinctive weapon of wit which served him best.

As mere stories, these romances have little value. No reader can be warmed into any interest by their personages or their incidents. No one can for a moment forget that Voltaire is speaking to him, and not the princess of Babylon, or the luckless Candide. No child could care to read them. The very simplest student of fairy-tale literature could not be deceived into believing that they breathed the genuine atmosphere of the East. There is no rich coloring in them; no heightening of beauty, as Mary Wortley Montagu said, by the idea of profusion; very little simple pathos; scarcely a gleam of hearty, exhilarating good-humor. Some one said no pure mind could understand them. Taken in its literal meaning, the criticism was entirely unjust; but it was very correct indeed, if it merely meant to signify that no one, ignorant of the evil ways of the world in Voltaire's age, could appreciate or even comprehend them. They are simply the satirical hooks on which Voltaire gibbeted, for exposure to the world and posterity, all the evils of human origin which he saw crushing down humanity in France. His satire is often too comprehensive and sweeping; often, indeed, entirely unjust in its personal application. Whatever Voltaire did of his own impulse, he did earnestly, and sometimes extravagantly. He did not go to war for an idea; he embodied every opponent, and hated it like a personal enemy. The same headlong generosity and headlong animosity which characterized him in his dealings with individuals entered into his satirical review of events and systems. Right or wrong, Voltaire was thoroughly practical, and when he touched the shield of an opponent, hit fiercely and straightforward with the point of his weapon. What shortens the average lives of Frenchmen? what makes men poor, and keeps them so? what embitters domestic life? what renders children curses instead of blessings? what stifles free thought? what turns philosophy to a sham?—these were questions with which his sympathies tormented Voltaire. He thought that the state of society around him gave answers to many of them, which he determined to interpret into intelligible language. The satirical romances are valuable because they contain Voltaire's explanations of the condition of France in his day. War, religion, hypocrisy, religious intolerance, court domination and court intrigue, superficial or quack philosophy, idlers, soldiers, and priests—these Voltaire looked upon as the national evils of France; therefore his romances are simply satires directed unchangingly and perseveringly against all these enemies. But for the never-failing wit which makes the dullest theme sparkle with the most varying lights, they would be positively monotonous, so uniform is their pervading purpose.

War of any kind seemed to Voltaire a pure, unmitigated evil. He saw nothing in it but scenes such as he has described in "Candide"—slaughter and licentiousness, blazing roofs and mangled bodies. Religion he almost invariably identified with its professors, as Mr. Bertram in Scott's novel, could only think of the king's revenues as embodied in the persons of the guagers. Voltaire looked around society, and saw that bigotry and lazy priests were common there. He heard doctrines of the most savage intolerance promulgated as if they were gospel truths. He knew that men and women harmless, industrious, and moral people—had been turned out of house and home because they differed from the ruling Church on the question of Transubstantiation, or the unqualified supremacy of the pope. He had spoken with those who could tell him of the scenes which followed the Revocation of the Edict of Nantes. He saw that to persecute the religious opinions of others was very often accepted as an atonement for personal immorality and irreligion. After reading one of Voltaire's descriptions of a bigot and a priest, it is painful to have to believe that in many instances the strength of the satire lay in the unexaggerated correctness of its application. A man must not be charged with deliberate impiety, even if he sometimes was extravagant in his scorn of religious teaching which their own exponents maintained must necessarily conduct to the intolerance they practised. Voltaire was a nervous man, with a keen dread of physical pain. He quivered all over at the idea of bodily torture. He saw that throughout the course of history one point of resemblance had connected almost all the great religious sects of the world. Each, in its day of power, had, at some time or other, endeavored to enforce its views by the infliction of bodily torture. Voltaire was not sufficiently impartial to recognise the fact, that it was but the possession of unlimited power by arrogant human creatures which had led to the employment of such modes of persecution. A man of feeling rather than of reasoning power, it was enough for him to see that in France there was neither happiness nor freedom; that something calling itself religion presided ostensibly over society, and represented to the world the Divine Providence as a kind of exaggeration of the character of Louis XIV. It was sufficient for Voltaire to observe this; and, gifted with the most powerful weapon in the world, he used it like a partisan, and not like a philosopher.

Voltaire was particularly angry with some of those who invented consolations for men's misery. He flamed up especially against those who endeavored to satisfy unquiet minds with the shallow quibbles which passed for optimism, and whose whole secret consisted in calling a disagreeable thing by a fine name. The Lisbon earthquake, which took place in 1755, had, no one needs to be told, an especial effect on the mind of Voltaire. It seemed to him that such a calamity utterly confounded the self-satisfied dogmas of those who sought to philosophize a beneficent scheme out of the events of this world alone, without reference to any supplemental and higher state of being. Well-meaning persons furnish terrible weapons to a man like Voltaire, when they endeavor to vindicate God's providence by ingenious arguments about the fitness of things, and the physical and human good directly arising out of every thing. The Lisbon earthquake taken by itself—and Voltaire would not take it otherwise—appeared to him a mere destruction of human life, an uncompensated and unconditioned evil. It was idle to tell Voltaire that the earthquake which destroyed so many human beings must be regarded as a beneficent process, because a certain condition of physical nature or of society demanded a purgation. An intellect very much below that of Voltaire could not fail to perceive the absurdity of such an argument, or, indeed, of any argument which takes upon itself to interpret and explain the secrets of Providence. Few will forget that, in the town of Frankfort, a bright-eyed precocious child began to argue himself into infidelity because of that same Lisbon earthquake. A genius of a more exalted and poetic kind effaced the morbid impressions drawn out of this calamity more readily from the mind of Goethe than from that of Voltaire. The reasoning of Voltaire upon this and kindred subjects is not indeed a whit better than that of the moral philosophers who argued against him. Taken in Voltaire's point of view, a single twinge of toothache ought as distinctly to interfere with the belief in a beneficent Providence as the destruction of countless lives in Lisbon. If we accept Voltaire's reasoning, that physical suffering caused to a human being is nothing but evil, and that a beneficent Power cannot cause or tolerate evil, the momentary pang of a single individual is quite as efficacious for the argument, as the ruin of a city. But Voltaire's reasonings upon the Lisbon earthquake explain, in great measure, the character of the man, and excuse much that seems unmeasured in his satires. He looked only at the outside or shell of every thing, and weighed all questions by their relation to man's physical happiness. Optimism jarred most harshly against Voltaire's special ways of thinking. The romance of "Candide" contains in the person of Dr. Pangloss one of the strongest, coarsest caricatures satiric literature can produce. It is impossible not to be amused at the whimsically pertinacious manner in which Pangloss clings to his philosophy, despite of all external shocks: and at the naïve credulity and naïve scepticism of Candide, equally absurd when he believes and when he doubts. But the satire is extravagantly overdone, just because the satirist felt his subject warmly, and determined to draw his caricature in such thick deep lines that no one could fail to recognize the portrait. The story, too, is spun out beyond all reasonable endurance. Candide's travels want variety. Nobody could read the work merely as a story: and a satirical tale, whatever its merits, is so far a failure if it cannot be admired for its mere narrative. "Candide" cannot be read as people read "Gulliver's Travels," or "Gil Blas." It entirely lacks warm descriptive power, and shows little skill in the delineation of character. No man had a keener eye for human whims, weaknesses, and follies than the satirist of Cirey: but while he could set these off in the most ludicrous light, Voltaire could not draw a full individual character. He did not even trouble himself to develop whatever capability of that kind he may have possessed. His interest was not in the narrative he told, or the people he described, but in the follies and vices he satirized; and so long as he made his meaning plain and vivid, he was little concerned for the artistic perfection of the narrative. He concentrated his eyes upon the peculiar object he wished to satirize, until at length its proportions became magnified to his vision. Pangloss is a personage of preposterous absurdity; so extravagantly drawn that the traits sometimes fail to have any genuine satirical force of application. It is curious to observe how inartistic and ineffective Voltaire is when compared with Swift upon a parallel subject. Gulliver is about the size of a Brobdignagian's little finger. We can all see the relative proportions, and can appreciate the humor of the situations in which such a pigmy is placed when encompassed by such giants. We can at once conceive what Gulliver looks like on Glumdalclitch's knee. But of Voltaire's Micromegas, who is so large that he takes a whale upon his thumbnail, and requires a microscope to discern the shape of the leviathan, we can form no conception whatever. The extravagance of the disproportion renders it quite impossible to realize, and so deprives it of the power even to excite our wonder. What Micromegas is to the Brobdignagians, Pangloss is to Don Quixote.

Is it not a mistake to talk of the knowledge of human nature displayed in "Zadig" and "Candide"? Where is there in these stories a single personage like any ordinary man or woman? Where is there any capacity evinced for moulding and blending together the variety of traits which make up even the most insipid of human characters? To discern that some men were honest, and some hypocritical; that most woman of the age were over-fond of gayety and of pleasure; that priests were sometimes sensual and sometimes deceitful; that magistrates were occasionally corrupt; that courtiers were not uncommonly parasites; and that philosophers not unusually got into depths where they could neither stand nor float,—to discern all this surely required no very profound penetration of human nature. Yet the groundwork of all Voltaire's satires sinks no deeper than this. Even on some of his favorite themes Voltaire was occasionally quite incorrect in his general views of the human character. Hypocrisy was one of the vices he most delighted to satirize. Yet he never appeared to appreciate the fact, that scarcely any human being ever believed himself to be a hypocrite, and admitted himself to a full, bare knowledge of his own falsehood. Voltaire's idea of a hypocrite is the old stage villain who deceives others, but not himself. Voltaire delighted to expose bigotry, but his picture of a bigot was almost invariably that of a mere religious swindler,—a man cruel in the repression of antagonistic belief, but himself without either faith or morals. Indeed, Voltaire generally delineated human nature as a very much more simple and less complicated kind of thing than any really comprehensive observer would have drawn it. One of the commonest of errors is to ascribe to a man a profound insight into human nature because he is quick in ferreting out certain special foibles or vices. Ordinary individuals in gossiping conversation commonly display an abundance of this kind of penetration into the moral constitution of their neighbors. The majority of Voltaire's men and women are mere lay figures on which to hang his scraps of satire. The princess of Babylon is not distinguishable from Cunegonde or Astarte, except by the difference of the adventures. Even the adventures themselves are frequently flat and colorless in effect. Compare the travels of Candide with the voyages of Sinbad! Compare the sketches of gay life with those of Gil Blas! Compare the portraits of eccentric or humorous characters with those of Molière! Compare the extravaganza incidents with those of Swift! Compare the Oriental correspondence of Amabed with the "Persian Letters" of Montesquieu. Nowhere does Voltaire sink for a moment his own identity. Less egotistical than Rousseau so far as direct allusion to himself was concerned, he was far more so in the perpetual introduction of his own peculiar notions upon every subject. Other of the great charms of every species of fiction are also wanting to these stories. Scarcely a gleam of beauty, even of the sensuous kind, shines upon them. Beauty of style is not the thing wanting, for in their own way the style of these stories is incomparable. But no sensation is diffused by any one of them to show that their author thrilled with any emotion for beauty in nature or in art. Even a beautiful woman is only described by a dry catalogue of charms like that pronounced by Olivia in "Twelfth Night:"—"Item, two lips indifferent red; item, two gray eyes; item, one neck, one chin, and so forth." There is not so much of a recognition of the beautiful throughout the whole of these romances as is expressed in the few lines of the Roman satirist about the valley and springs of Egeria. There is little of human affection in them: little even of genuine human passion. For aught these satiric fables teach us, men and women might be only good from a sense of propriety or honor, bad because they happened to have no such feeling. Parting and death—those most pregnant themes of the story-teller of every age—have scarcely any real share in the interest of these romances. In the story of the Huron, L'Ingenu, and his beautiful and ill-fated mistress, Voltaire most nearly approaches to a sympathy with the pangs of parted lovers; and yet it may be very well questioned whether any human eyes ever moistened over the separation and sufferings of the pair he describes. It is only by observing the deficiency of Voltaire in so many of the great leading qualities of a story-teller and a satirist that it is possible to appreciate fully the surpassing power of the special attributes by which he became so successful in each capacity.

The purpose which animates almost every

one of these tales, and the wit which gives force and brightness to every one of them, are the characteristics for which they merit to be immortal. No cold sceptic, working with unimpassioned heart and bitter tongue, is discernible to the reader who gives them an impartial study, but a sensitive and impulsive man, whose earnest nature lent fire to his matchless wit. That weapon of wit which in these satires Voltaire wielded honestly for the sake of his fellow-men, was surely the very keenest of its kind ever employed in such a cause. Some of these romances preserve its finest achievements. Voltaire's wit is not like Molière's, for it never exuberates; or Pascal's, for it never acknowledges earnestness; or Le Sage's, for it is never sprightly and careless; or Goldsmith's, for it is never childlike, or Swift's, for it is never savage; or Sydney Smith's, for it never plays upon words; or Douglas Jerrold's, for it never outwardly exhibits bitterness. Time and change have indeed somewhat cooled much of the interest which the world felt in Voltaire's satire, as well as in that of Pascal. We no longer feel very keenly the evils against which those great masters of sarcasm lifted up their voices. Let us be glad to think that Father Fa Tutto is gone along with the intellectual supremacy of the Jesuits. We feel as little immediate and personal satisfaction in the humiliation of either, as in the exposure of Margaret of Navarre's detested Cordeliers. But Voltaire's wit is of a kind which owes nothing of its preservation to its subject. On the contrary, there could be no topic so ephemeral and trifling which, encased in the amber of that incomparable satire, would not remain preserved forever. It seems to have come to its author by instinct, and to have come from him without effort. None of the great humorists and satirists of the world's literature seem to have been gifted with a faculty of sarcastic expression at once so powerful and so easy. It sparkles forth so readily that it appears to have been spontaneous and out of its author's control. It is so full of meaning and so perfect, that long labor might have been given to its preparation, and that no further attempt at emendation or improvement could do any thing but spoil it. Half a dozen light, apparently careless words, and behold a whole generation's folly so completely turned inside out, that the dullest must see its drollery, and the gravest must laugh at it. One is reminded of the expert German executioners who boasted that they could sweep their sword-blade through the neck of the culprit so lightly and so dexterously that he died without feeling the thrill of his death-blow. What an admirable essay on the wisdom of the decree which sentenced Byng to die, is wrapped up in the immortal words carelessly let fall in "Candide:" "Dans ce pays-ci il est bon de tuer de temps en temps un amiral pour encourager les autres!" Probably since Voltaire wrote the lines no words have been more often quoted in his own country and in ours. People who never read one line of Voltaire, people who never bestowed a thought upon the source or the origin of the quotation, are every day repeating and applying its concluding phrase. Even the never-dying "Nous avons changé tout cela," and "que diable allait il faire dans cette galère," of Molière scarcely show themselves so often in print. Every page of these romances supplies a sentence just as pregnant with humor, just as whimsically effective in its application. Take, for instance, at random a page in "L'Homme aux Quarante Ecus"—that which describes the debate between the theologians concerning the soul of Marcus Antoninus. When all the chief reasons have been urged which sustained those who believed no worse fate than purgatory had befallen the great emperor, the argument is brought to a climax by adding, "Moreover, there is some respect due to a crowned head—'il ne faut pas le damner légèrement.'" In how many different shapes has this sentiment been imitated and reproduced, by how many different writers, and who ever made it half so true, telling, and humorous? The Oriental Amabed, describing in his letters one of the "vice-dieux," as he terms the popes, who has just expired in Rome, pictures him as "an old, turbulent soldier, who loved war like a madman; always on horseback, distributing blessings and sabre-cuts, damning souls and killing bodies," and adds, with a comic naïveté as untranslatable as irresistible, "Quel diable de vice-dieu on avait là!" In the "Travels of Scarmentado" we are told of a certain famous bishop whose boast was that he had decapitated, drowned, or burned ten millions of infidels in America. "I cannot help thinking," gravely adds Scarmentado, "that the bishop exaggerated; but even if we reduce his sacrifices to five millions, *cela serait encore admirable.*" Such illustrations might be multiplied through page after page. They need no searching and no selection. They lie, scattered by the prodigal hand of the great wit, everywhere over his lighter works. It must be added that many keen witticisms are couched in phrases which must not now be translated at all. Not all the adventures or the observations of Candide or Cunegonde or Charme-les-yeux will bear to be reproduced for any English readers of this day. Voltaire fell too freely into one of the errors of his age, and the seriousness of the error must not be treated lightly. But that age was not as ours is, and it is only fair to the memory of Voltaire to say, that he wrote but as others wrote and spoke—that his writings did not contrast with the literature of all the world besides, as the novels of Balzac, and Paul de Kock, and Dumas Fils, and so many of the *chansons* of Beranger more recently did. Many of the passages which no one now can read aloud were once recited by the lips of Voltaire himself to groups of accomplished and irreproachable women, who only laughed at their plain speaking and thought no harm. Possibly we are better than our great-grandfathers and grandmothers in this respect at least; but we must not anathematize Voltaire in especial. Voltaire's, too, let it be added, was only plain-speaking. He was not more plain-spoken than Fielding or Swift; and he never approached the corrupting, heartless, unmanly decency of Congreve or Wycherley. Even Addison, the pure and good, with "a sabbath shining on his face," will not bear to be read aloud now, unexpurgated and word for word, to a female audience. We must not condemn our authors by an *ex post facto* law; above all, we must not single any special one out, and while allowing all the rest to go scot free, apply the retrospective clause to him alone.

The story of "L'Ingenu" is that which bears the nearest resemblance to a romance, according to our English meaning. There is more of feeling in it than in any of its companions. Not thoroughly original itself, it has been the parent of many a romantic tale. A young Canadian savage, sprung from European forefathers, comes by chance to live with his surviving relatives in France, where his simple nature is opposed, startled, and thwarted at every turn by the meanness, hypocrisy, and falsehood of civilized ways. The young Huron is, of course, the famous "noble savage" of poets and romancists: the ideal being, endowed with all the best qualities of man in his most perfect condition, and free from any of the weaknesses and errors of civilization. Generous, truthful, temperate, loving, and brave, this Huron, it must be owned, in nowise resembles any of the dirty, lying, drinking, treacherous, and remorseless savages with whom some of Voltaire's countrymen made unhappy acquaintances at a day not much later. The Huron, who for his noble simplicity is styled "L'Ingenu" becomes a Christian; and, studying the Bible, is every day bewildered to observe how little the practices of Christians consort with their doctrines. He falls in love with the beautiful Mademoiselle de Saint Yves, and is loved in return. Chance throws him in the way of gaining an important victory for his countrymen over an invading band of Englishmen (all our heroes of the same day win wonderful triumphs over the French): he goes to court to seek some reward for his services, but falling in with some expelled Huguenots on the way, espouses their cause with an ardor and an openness which bring on him a *lettre-de-cachet.* Cast into prison, he becomes the companion of an old condemned Jansenist, Gordon. From him the Huron learns to appreciate and love literature, and acquires a knowledge of many arts and sciences. The friendship and companionship of this imprisoned pair have suggested to Alexander Dumas some of the most striking personages in his "Chateau d'If." The learning and the piety of Gordon teach the Huron to be a genuine Christian; but, on the other hand, the simple, unsophisticated views and thoughts of the redeemed savage win the Jansenist away from the narrow bonds of his own peculiar sect, and invite him to the broader and more genial paths of Christianity. Those who only associate the name of Voltaire with impiety and ribaldry, would fail to recognize their ideal in the clear, strengthening, and manly tone of thought which pervades many of these passages. But misfortunes crowd upon the poor Huron. His mistress comes in despair to seek him, and learning of his imprisonment, implores a powerful minister for his release. The old story of Lord Angelo or Colonel Kirke is repeated, but with a different catastrophe. A price is set upon the lover's liberation. Saint Yves struggles and resists long; but at last, betrayed by a treacherous friend, prompted by a base confesser, sacrifices herself to redeem her lover, and finally dies of grief and shame. A professional romancist might unquestionably have made a very charming and pathetic story out of these materials. Even as the tale stands written, although its satire is its most prominent part, it has many occasional glimpses of feeling and of tenderness. Gleams of a pathos not commonly belonging to such a style shine here and there through it. But Voltaire did not care to produce an affecting romance; the loves and the unmerited sufferings of L'Ingenu and his mistress were only invented to enable the author more vividly and effectively to satirize religious hypocrisy and priestly intolerance. But it is a satire such as only Voltaire could have produced. It has no playing upon words, and no extravagant caricatures. Quiet deep thrusts are so lightly given, that they seem at first mere punctures. Pascal might have written the dialogue in which Father Tout-à-tout endeavors to reconcile the conscience of the struggling St. Yves to the act forced upon her. With a quiet satirical power, wholly indescribable, we are told that the confessor was rewarded by his patron with "boxes of chocolate, sugar-candy, citron, comfits, and the Meditations of the Rev. Father Croiset and the Flower of Saints bound in morocco." Some indications, too, are in this story of a sympathy with more delicate shades of human emotion than those evoked by racks and gaol torments. "Ah!" exclaims the unhappy Saint Yves, when almost overpowered by the proffered generosity of her betrayer, "que je vous aimerais si vous ne vouliez pas être tout aimé!" L'Ingenu, the reader is told, never after her death alluded to her without a deep sigh—"et cependant sa consolation était d'en parler."

Perhaps, however, Voltaire's happiest style is to be seen in his shorter papers. His capacity for producing effective and precious trifles was something wonderful,—not mere curiosities, but condensed morçeaux of genuine satire, whose meaning grows and deepens as they are studied. What, for instance, can surpass the concise humor of Scarmentado's Travels? Or "The Blind Judges of Colors," with its whimsical conclusion, in which, after the recital of all the quarrels and battles which took place among the blind disputants, each of whom claimed to be an infallible judge of colors, we are gravely told that a deaf man, who had read the tale, admitted the folly of the sightless men in presuming to decide questions of color, but stoutly maintained that deaf men were the only qualified musical critics? Or Bababec and the Fakirs? A Mussulman, who is the supposed narrator of the tale, and a good Brahmin, Omri, visit the Fakir groups by the banks of the Ganges, at Benares. Some of these holy men are dancing on their heads; some inserting nails in their flesh; some staring fixedly at the tips of their noses, in the belief that they thus will see the celestial light. One, named Bababec, is revered for special sanctity because he went naked, wore a huge chain round his neck, and sat upon pointed nails which pierced his flesh. Omri consults this saintly sage as to his own chances of reaching Brahma's abode after death. The Fakir asks him how he regulates his life. "I endeavor," says Omri, "to be a good citizen, a good husband, a good father, and a good friend. I lend money without interest to those who have need; I give to the poor, and I maintain peace among my neighbors." "I am sorry for you," interrupts the pious Fakir, "your case is hopeless; you never put nails *dans votre cul.*"

Such specimens, however, are only like the brick which the dullard in the old story brought away for the purpose of giving his friends an idea of the beauty of the temple. Admirably as the French language is adapted for the expression of dry, satirical humor, Voltaire developed its capability in this way to a degree equalled by no other man. So much sarcastic force was, probably, never compressed into so few and such simple words as in many of these little fictions. The reader is positively amazed at the dexterity with which subjects are placed in the most ludicrous light possible, and the easy manner in which the legerdemain is performed. Sometimes Voltaire's ideas become extravagant, but his style never does. Sydney Smith frequently lacks simplicity, but

Voltaire is always simple, and never strains. What an admirable pamphleteer Voltaire would have made had he but been an Englishman! What inextinguishable ridicule he would have scattered over a ministry or an opposition! How irresistibly people would have been forced to think any thing he laughed at deserving of laughter! How he would have written up some measure of emancipation, and made a reluctant government afraid to refuse it! That Voltaire appreciated English freedom of speech no one needs to be told. Had he but understood the genius and the worth of our best literature as well, it would have been better for his critical, and, perhaps, for his dramatic, fame. Voltaire, of course, made fun of English ways now and then. My lord *Qu'importe*, or *What-then*, who said nothing but "How d'ye do" at quarter-hour intervals, is the prototype of many a caricature drawn by succeeding hands. But in the very chapter which contains this good-humored hit at our proverbial insular taciturnity, he calls the English the most perfect government in the world, and adds, with a truth which prevails at this day more than ever, "There are, indeed, always two parties in England who fight with the pen and with intrigue, but they invariably unite when there is need to take up arms to defend their country and their liberty; they may hate each other, but they love the State; they are like jealous lovers, whose rivalry is to see which shall serve their mistress best."

A noble weapon was that Voltaire owned, for one who used it rightly—who understood, as Sydney Smith said, how to value and how to despise it. It would be idle to deny that Voltaire sometimes used it unfairly. Fantastic, hot-tempered, sensitive, spiteful by nature, how could such a man have such a stiletto always unsheathed, and not sometimes give a jealous stab, and sometimes thrust too deeply, and sometimes wound those who were not worth piercing at all? He often imported petty personal spleens into his satires, and used his giant's strength upon some poor ephemeral pigmy,* some Freron, or some Boyer. But so did Horace, and Pope, and Swift, and so has Thackeray done even in our own milder days. Voltaire has got a worse name for meanness of this kind than almost any other man of kindred genius, and yet seems, after all, to deserve it less than most of the great satirists of the world.

Indeed, posterity has, upon the whole, dealt very harshly with Voltaire's errors, and made scant allowance of the praise which his purposes and efforts so often deserved. Few of the leading satirists of literature ever so consistently and, all things considered, so boldly turned his point against that which deserved to be wounded. Religious intolerance and religious hypocrisy, the crying sins of France in Voltaire's day, were the steady objects of his satire. Where, in these stories at least, does he attempt to satirize religion? Where does he make a gibe of genuine human affection? Where does he sneer at an honest effort to serve humanity? Where does he wilfully turn his face from the truth? Calmly surveying those marvellous satirical novels, the unprejudiced reader will search in vain for the blasphemy and impiety with which so many well-meaning people have charged the fictions of Voltaire. Where is the blasphemy in "Zadig"? It is brimful of satire against fickle wives and false friends, intriguing courtiers, weak kings, intolerant ecclesiastics, and many other personages tolerably well known in France at that day. They might naturally complain of blasphemy who believed themselves included in the description of the learned Magi who doomed Zadig to be impaled for his heretical doctrines touching the existence of griffins. "No one was impaled after all, whereupon many wise doctors murmured and presaged the speedy downfall of Babylon," was a sentence which probably many in Paris thought exceedingly offensive and impious. Possibly yet greater offence was conveyed to many minds by Zadig's famous candle argument. Zadig became sold to slavery, and fell into the hands of a very humane and rational merchant, named Setoc. "He discovered in his master a natural tendency to good and much clear sense. He was sorry to observe, however, that Setoc adored the sun, moon, and stars, according to the ancient usage of Araby. . . . One evening Zadig lit a great number of flambeaux in the tent, and when his patron appeared, flung himself on his knees before the illumined wax, exclaiming, "Eternal and brilliant lights, be always propitious to me!" "What are you doing?" asked Setoc, in amazement. "I am doing as you do," replied Zadig. "I adore the lamps, and I neglect their Maker and mine." Setoc comprehended the profound sense of this illustration. The wisdom of his slave entered his soul; he lavished his incense no more upon created things, but adored the Eternal Being who made them all.

Is it impious to satirize the glory of war, the levity of French society, the practice of burying the dead in close churchyards in the midst of cities, the venal disposed of legal and military offices? All these are the subjects on which the author pours out his gall in the "Vision of Babouc." The travels of Scarmentado simply expose religious intolerance in France, Spain, England, Italy, Holland, China, etc. The letters of Amabed denounce fanaticism coupled with profligacy. Any thing said against the manner in which the vices of Fa Tutto are exposed, must apply equally to Aristophanes and Juvenal, to Rabelais and Swift, to Marlowe and Massinger. The "History of Jenni" is a very humdrum argumentation against atheism; inefficacious, we fear, to convert very hardened infidels, and serving only to demonstrate the author's good intentions and his incapacity for theological controversy. "The White Bull," if it have any meaning whatever beyond that of any of Anthony Hamilton's Fairy Tales, means to satirize the literal interpretations of certain portions of the Old Testament in which very stupid theologians delighted. To accuse of blasphemy every man who refused to accept the interpretations which Voltaire in this extravagant parable appears to reject, would be to affix the charge upon some of the profoundest of our own theologians, some of the best and wisest of our thinkers. It is unquestionable that Voltaire was deficient in that quality which we call veneration. He had no respect even for what Carlyle terms the "majesty of custom." With all his hatred of intolerance, he was himself singularly intolerant of error. He did not care to *menager* the feelings of those whose logical inaccuracy he ridiculed. Frequently and grievously he sinned against good taste—against that kindly, manly feeling which prompts a gentle mode of pointing out a fellow-man's errors and follies. But there is nothing in these volumes, at least, which affords any real foundation for a charge of blasphemy, or wilful impiety; and these volumes more truly and faithfully than any thing else which remains of him reflect to posterity the real character and spirit, the head and heart, of Voltaire. In these we learn what Voltaire thought deserving of ridicule: and with that knowledge, on the great German's principle, we come to know the man himself.

What is the moral of all these satires? Voltaire gave them to the world with a moral purpose, and, indeed, marred the artistic effect of many of them by the resolute adherence with which he clung to it. Do they teach any thing else but that truth, unselfishness, genuine religious feeling, freedom, and love are the good angels of humanity; and falsehood, selfishness, hypocrisy, intolerance, and lawless passion its enemies and its curses? Why accept Juvenal as a moral teacher, and reject Voltaire? Why affix to the name of Voltaire a stigma no one now applies to that of Rabelais? Voltaire mocked at certain religious teachings unquestionably; and it is not, under ordinary circumstances, amiable or creditable to find food for satire in the religious ceremonial or professions of any man. To do so would now be unamiable, because it would be wholly unnecessary. Where each man has full and equal freedom to preach, pray, and profess what he pleases, nothing but malignity or vulgarity can prompt any one to make a public gibe of his neighbor's ceremonials of worship, even although his neighbor's moral practices may appear somewhat inconsistent with true worship of any kind. To satirize the practices or doctrines of the Established Church of any civilized country now argues, not courage, but sheer impertinence and vulgarity. There is no need to scoff at that which no one is constrained to reverence. But things were very different when Voltaire wrote. To set the world laughing at certain religious ceremonials was a very pardonable act when those who conducted them arrogated to themselves dominion over the worldly and the eternal happiness of any one who declined to join in their mode of worship. Where it might entail banishment, worldly ruin, or even death, to speak a free word of criticism upon the doctrines or the hierophants of the dominant church, it was not merely a very excusable, but a very necessary and praiseworthy deed to expose the folly of some of the teachings, the inconsistency and immorality of some of the teachers.

Gessler may wear his hat any fashion he chooses, and only ill-breeding would laugh at him so long as he does not insist upon any one performing any act of homage to his honor. But when he sets his beaver upon a pole in the centre of the market-place, and orders imprisonment or exile for every subject who will not fall down and worship it, that man does a brave and a wise act who sets the world laughing at the tyrant and his preposterous arrogance. The personages who sang comic songs and danced the clog-dance during the performance of divine service at St. George's-in-the-East were vulgar and culpable boors. Whatever they might have thought of the service, they were not compelled to attend it, and in our days theological differences are not decided by mobs and hobnailed shoes. But if the incumbent of the church had the power to bring down penal disqualification, or exile, or worldly ruin upon the heads of all who declined to acknowledge his ceremonials as their worship, the first man who raised a bold laugh at the whole performance might be very justly regarded as a hero. Something, at least, of this qualified character is to be said in palliation of the irreverence of Voltaire. Much which was stigmatized as blasphemy a century ago most people regard as plain truth now. Much even of the most objectionable of Voltaire's writings may be excused by the circumstances of the time, by the feelings with which he wrote, by the distorted and hideous form in which Christianity was presented in the dogmas of so many of its professional exponents. Much, indeed, may be admitted to be wholly inexcusable—for did he not produce the "Pucelle"? But no one claims for Voltaire an immunity from some severe censure. All that is sought for him is a more general and generous recognition of the praise he merited and the motives which impelled him, a mitigation of the sentence which so many have pronounced upon him. No other man from his own birth downwards, not even excepting Rousseau, has borne such extravagance of praise followed by such a load of obloquy. He was not a profound thinker; he was not a hero; he was not a martyr for truth; he was not a blameless man. But he had at least half-glimpses of many truths not of his own time, and which the world has recognized and acknowledged since. He has probably as much of the heroic in him as a man constitutionally nervous and timid could well be expected to have. No one would ever have relished less the endurance of the martyr's sufferings in his own person, but he made odious and despicable those who had caused or connived at their infliction upon others, and he did something to render any future martyrdoms impossible. For his time and his temptations his personal offences were not very many or very great. If people would but cease to think of him as a great philosopher either of free thought or of infidelity, and would merely regard him as a great political and social satirist, they would recognize in his satirical works not only the memorials of a genius unrivalled in its own path, but the evidences of a generous nature, an enlightened perception, and an earnest desire for the happiness and the progress of human beings.

In the middle of last year the railways in operation in the United Kingdom had 127,450 persons in their employment, and the railways in course of construction employed 53,923 more, making in all 181,373. On the railroads in operation there were 3,601 stations. There were 1,051 miles of railroad in course of construction, and upon them were employed 7,381 artificers and 42,126 "laborers;" but the word "navvy" does not seem to be admissible in these returns made to the Board of Trade.

Here be Truths.—M. Guillaumin, in the French Chamber, intending to be severe upon England, said England makes her *propaganda* with the Bible in one hand and a piece of calico in the other, but France bears her banner in one hand and the Cross in the other. Proper gander yourself, M. Guillaumin, for you have just hit it. England proffers enlightenment and the comforts of life. France comes with superstition and "glory." It strikes us that such orators should be choked off by their priests.—*Punch.*

From The Cornhill Magazine.

HORACE SALTOUN.

PART III.—VÆ VICTIS.

SOME little time after our last interview, Horace paid me a visit. I imagined from his manner there was something on his mind of which he desired to unburden himself; it soon came out.

"Paul, what should you say if you heard I entertained the wish to marry?"

"Say, Horace?" I replied, slowly; "I hardly know what I should say."

He began to talk with a little nervousness and rapidity. "I have been steady and in good health now for some years; I feel better than I ever did in my life."

"I'm glad of it, Horace: you look like it. Have you ever had any return of that morbid craving."

"I wont say I have had no sensations of the sort, Paul; but never with the same irresistible strength: never so strongly that I could not only resist it, but I felt I could do so; consequently, I nerved myself for the struggle, without that wretched despondency which used to overpower me."

"Well, Horace, I am far from saying you ought not to marry, for every man has a chance of becoming a better and happier one when he has a good wife; but much depends upon what sort of a woman she may be. What is she like?"

"She is like—" here he stopped, and took a long suck at his cigar. "Well, Paul, she is like a Juno without her severity. She gives me a sensation of rest only to stand near her. I'm a big fellow, but I don't look it beside her. She's a large, calm, gentle woman: there, Paul, don't laugh at the description. This is all a man could wish for to be his comfort and his better angel; to rule his home, and to be the mother of his children!"

"In love, Horace?" I said, jestingly.

"Well, I suppose I am; at least this looks like it," and he looked rather silly as he bared his arm, and displayed tatooed thereon in slender blue lines, the initials M. O., with an anchor and a cross, done in sailor fashion with gunpowder. "I ought to tell you her name, 'Margaret Oliver.'" He said it several times over, as if it sounded pleasantly to him.

"How old is she?"

"Thirty, or thereabouts: a year or two more than I have; but I'm not sorry for that. She has no one but herself to please: her father and mother are both dead. She lives at ——" (naming a place a few miles from town), "and an old lady, a sort of companion, resides with her."

I was silent.

"You don't think me wrong to marry, Paul? I tell you if any thing would keep me strong and happy, marrying such a woman as that would do it. Don't say it would be wrong, old fellow," he continued, in an agitated manner: "say any thing but that. In truth," he continued, sadly, "I don't think that I ought to be condemned to live forever hopeless and alone. I tell you I feel so lonely sometimes, I often think I shall cut my throat."

"Would you be insured against cutting your throat by marrying Miss Oliver?"

"I think there would be so much then to make life dear; at present why should I live to cumber the ground, and occupy the place of a better man on the earth? My parents had done well if they had smothered me as soon as I was born: if I am so cursed, better that I had never lived to see the light of day!"

"And in the face of that would you run the chance of becoming a father to a generation who might be as miserable as yourself?"

"I know what you are driving at, Paul, and I've thought of all that; but in the first place, both my father and mother were temperate people, and in the second, science and experience support us in the idea that the mother has in general more influence than the father on the cerebral development of her child. Margaret has such a perfect organization, such a calm, fine temper, it would be impossible to conceive of her failing to influence all near her."

I reflected. I didn't like to advise, and told him so.

"Why, Paul, it's enough to make a man go mad of himself, or take brandy indefinitely, to be isolated as I am: I could shed tears sometimes when those rough scampish fellows show the personal affection to me which they often do."

I still did not speak, but sat silent and pre-occupied.

"Well," he said, with an outburst of strong emotion, "then here goes my last chance of happiness. I'll have a grand funeral, and bear away and bury, with what pomp I may, the dead body of this dear hope, and set it round with faded good intentions and the ghost of a possible joy; for, being now dead and useless, it will be as odious in my nostrils as a corpse left to decay."

His features worked painfully, and he turned himself back in his chair. I could not bear this; I thought there was reason in what he urged.

"Not so fast, Horace; don't put opinions into my mouth. As to marriage, do that which you think right; but I think Miss Oliver ought not to be in ignorance of the circumstances of your history."

He looked distressed, but faced me at once.

"I think so too, Paul: as an honorable man I am bound not to conceal that from her. It may—probably will—cost me all I dared to hope for; but better lose her than win her by fraud. You are quite right; it must be done. But I have a boon to ask of your friendship—a friendship now of many years' standing; and for the sake of the youth and manhood which we have passed together, you will not refuse me: it is, that you will yourself tell it to Margaret."

"My dear Horace," I said, "consider: I am unacquainted with her; and she will reasonably think that a revelation of such matters should come from your own lips. It would be most officious, or appear so, in me."

"No, it would not, Paul. You can't think how I shrink from it. Besides, I wish her decision to be uninfluenced by compassion or kind feeling, and would have it the result of her judgment, apart from my presence."

I need not recount his persuasions and arguments; it will suffice to say that he prevailed: that I consented that he should send a letter to Margaret Oliver, which should procure me a private interview, and contain such partial explanation as might break the ground for me.

Two days afterwards I rode down and presented myself at Miss Oliver's residence, to perform my disagreeable mission. The room into which I was shown opened into a conservatory filled with rare exotics; a variety of trifles were about, indicating feminine occupation, and that harmony and good taste prevailed which characterize the presence of habitual refinement. The mellowed, softened tone, the fading light, and the delicious odor of the flowers, combined, threw me into a reverie; from this I roused myself by an effort when the servant entered to say that Miss Oliver would be with me in a few minutes, and begged that I would, meanwhile, walk into the conservatory.

When she appeared, I thought I had seldom seen a grander specimen of womanhood, both morally and physically. When Horace compared her to the Olympian queen divested of her severity, he did not describe her ill. She had large, calm, limpid eyes, with a singularly candid and tender expression, ample but finely formed limbs, somewhat heavily moulded lips and chin, and a quantity of dark hair folded about the head; and though, from the admirable proportions of the latter, the size did not appear inordinate, it was yet an unusually large brain for a woman. Her complexion was the marble, opaque tint which distinguished the old Roman women; and her walk, as she swept forward to me, I thought like herself, calm and undulating. When she spoke it was in a rich, low voice; and her smile was so full of benignity and goodness that I at once realized the truth of the sensation which Horace described her as inspiring; that of *rest*. A slight degree of embarrassment at meeting was perhaps inevitable, and it existed; but I am sincere enough to own that it was on my side alone.

After a little preliminary conversation, she told me at once that she knew I had come with a communication from Mr. Saltoun. I therefore entered on what I had to say, rather awkwardly and hurriedly, I fear; but I gathered calmness as I proceeded: it was perchance reflected from hers. I gave his history, as far as I knew it,—the antecedents of his father, the illness of his sister, his engagement to Cecile Otway. I did not look up, but I *felt* that she moved slightly here; then she bowed her head, and I continued. I praised, as indeed I justly could, his nature and disposition. I mentioned his professional fame. Then I gave the whole sad history, as delicately, truthfully, and tenderly as I could; omitting nothing, according to his directions. I glanced at her once; she was listening with averted head, and her hand shaded her eyes. I could hear a tremulous, heavy breath drawn now and then, but she made no other movement: feeling, and, I doubt not, suffering, but calm and stirless. I dwelt on his blameless life, his complete solitude, his lonely home, his genuine humility and distrust of himself, and, above all, on the noble truthfulness and confidence in her which he displayed by insisting on her being acquainted with these mortifying and humiliating occurrences in his life.

When I had finished, there was a pause. Miss Oliver remained for more than a minute so still she hardly seemed to breathe. Then she turned her face and person full towards me, as though te present herself unarmed to the foe,—her face tear-stained, though her eyes looked truthful and luminous as ever,—and she said solemnly, yet a little tremulously, "You are Horace Saltoun's friend, and you will, of all men, know that I do right. I will marry Horace; and if a wife's true heart can shield him from the horrors that have beset him, mine shall do so, and then I shall not have lived in vain. But if that may not be, I will still share his fate; preferring rather, if God will, to run some risk in sustaining a great and noble nature, than to marry some man who less needs comfort and succor."

What words of mine could shake a resolution so full of womanly feeling and generosity? I had neither the heart nor the wish to alter it. In fact, I could not speak, but wrung her hand, and left her.

I may hurry over this part of my history. Miss Oliver had, as Horace said, no one to please but herself; she had an ample fortune, and his income was very sufficient, so they were at once affianced, and were to be married at the close of one month. I saw them frequently during this interval, and was at each interview more and more convinced that she was of all women the one best suited to Horace.

But if he had done ill to marry at all? Alas, who can tell! Her cheerfulness was so serene, so pervading her whole being, that she seemed the visible expression of that fine sentiment of Herder. "The greatest treasure which God hath given his creatures is, and ever will be, genuine existence."

Now Horace, notwithstanding his powerful and energetic nature, had occasionally a certain melancholy on him; similar, I think, to that which Kant describes in a commentary on an observation of Saussure: "A species of sadness," he says, "belonging to the bracing emotions, and which bears the same relation to a relaxing sadness as the sublime does to the beautiful."

There was, I do not deny, a proportion of phlegm in Margaret's temperament, against which irritable and excitable spirits broke and fretted themselves in vain, and then, spent and exhausted, they returned to rest themselves on her, as though they thereby imbibed a part of that calm which seemed to know no disturbance. I have heard it said by small, acrid women, that her figure was clumsy and her movements slow; but the outward form corresponded to the inner nature: it knew no littleness, no scorn, no bitterness. She was born to become a man's stay. Such a woman would hardly have fulfilled nature's purpose if she had not been so placed as to impart some of her own equable happiness to one less fortunately constituted; and on such a tender and loving breast any man would be glad to rest a weary head and wounded spirit. Her characteristic was not intellect,—many men and women surpassed her in that; but in her moral strength, in the power of gentleness, in her exquisite tenderness, there were few who did not experience when near her a sensation of being cared for, and sympathized with, lulled, soothed, and borne away as though by the current of a mighty yet noiseless river.

They were married, and for several years enjoyed more happiness than usually falls to the lot of mortals. Between the terms of his lectures they resided at a small property of hers on the northern coast of Wales. Under her genial influence his intellect seemed to expand with fresh vigor, while her unswerving kindness and goodness of heart, added to her wonderful serenity, lent to his impulsive and unequal temper all that it most specially required.

Mrs. Saltoun became the mother of one little girl. The child lived, while the mother all but died. Fever supervened, and for nearly six weeks Horace hardly took off his clothes or left the bedside of his wife. The case was one of that exhausting nature which demands refreshments or stimulants every hour, or still more frequently, in order to retain the rapidly sinking vitality, and this service Horace insisted on performing unassisted. Now I need not say that to do this for such a length of time is a most frightful strain on both mind and body: it is similar in its nature to the often-attempted feat of walking one thousand miles in one thousand successive hours—a task in which not a few have broken down.

She recovered, but he did not escape so easily; though it was not until her convalescence that it told on him. I was myself ill at this period, and it was not until I was showing appearances of improvement that I was allowed to talk. The young surgeon before mentioned was in attendance on me, and one of my first questions was as to the Saltouns.

"Just what I was wanting to speak to you about," was the reply. "You have been wanted up there, and may go now, as soon as you like."

"What has gone wrong? Why did you not tell me before?"

"Which question am I to reply to first? Every thing has gone wrong; and you were to be kept undisturbed. When I am in possession of a patient, I take charge of mind as well as body."

"Give me some insight into the matter, for I shall start to-morrow."

"Saltoun has been drinking, or drugging, or something, and has had a touch of the horrors again: his wife bears it like an angel, they say. There now, I'll pack your carpet-bag."

I started, of course, immediately, and reached my destination the following day.

The house was an old, rambling building of gray stone; it was only two stories high, and was covered with creepers, moss, lichen, etc. One side faced the sea: it stood, in fact, at the end of a ravine which widened on to the shore; to the right and left the cliffs were very precipitous and rocky: altogether the scenery was wild and grand, and the situation one of great natural beauty.

I could hardly tell whether Saltoun was glad to see me or not. I know I thought him frightfully shaken, and irritable to the last degree. His memory, too, was much affected: he often forgot what he wanted to do, or the name of an article he required; and whether any one noticed it and tried to supply the omission, or whether it were passed over, he was equally impatient and angry. He evinced a pointed disinclination to enter on the subject of his illness with me, alleging that it was one most hateful to him. But I ascertained from other sources, that though he had constantly administered wine, brandy, etc., to his wife, he had never either tasted them, or appeared to wish to do so. Almost as soon as his wife was able to leave her room safely, however, he went out to take exercise, as he said; he came in wet, tired, and haggard, and went straight to his own room, where he drank himself into a state of stupor.

I had not been with him more than three days when he expressed his determination to go to town and recommence his lectures. His wife endeavored by instant acquiescence to let this intention die a natural death, and received the announcement with apparent equanimity; but when, in spite of this, he persisted, she became much disturbed, and expressed to me her distress. When soothing and argument had no effect, she tried, poor thing, to draw his attention to her delicate health, and begged him not to leave her. It was in vain. As for me, I heard it with consternation; but all I could say was useless; so we reluctantly abandoned the idea of preventing him, and prepared reluctantly to face the trial, which I could not conceal from myself would be a very serious one.

Margaret Saltoun was as yet but little altered in appearance, though her eyes had an air of languor about them, and I thought I could trace a few silver threads among the masses of dark hair. With her usual sweet temper she commenced making her little preparations to accompany him. At first he forbade this, but she laid her hand on his shoulder, and, bending over him, kissed his forehead: "Where you go, I go, Horace."

As she raised her head, I saw her eyes were brimful of unshed tears. No more was said, and we travelled together to town—not a very gleeful trio. . . .

I went with him to his class-room, and Horace Saltoun once more, amid the plaudits of the students, made his way up to his accustomed standing-place; but not with the confident, vigorous step of old. There was, however, no very visible want of nerve about his manner as he faced us. It was with a strange and painful sort of feeling I heard him announce that the subject on which he proposed that day to lecture was "*The Brain.*"

He proceeded, after a few brief remarks, to describe the anatomy of the cerebrum. I could detect no omission as he proceeded rapidly to dispose of one of the hemispheres, illustrating the different divisions by diagrams, which he drew as he went on; most exquisite specimens of anatomical drawing they were. Then he faltered a little, and his eye seemed to lose its intensity of gaze; by a violent effort he recovered himself, and went on:—

"Gentlemen, I need not recount to you the old superstitions. People have supposed that the principle of life, or the secret centre of intelligence, resided in this," laying his finger on one minute gland. "False, all these theories. Is the mind that which we can crush between our fingers, or resolve into phosphates or carbonates? No, this is not mind; this is not life. A child can live for a time without a brain, and a madman or an imbecile can drag on existence with a brain complete in all its parts." He said this with singular emphasis.

This was so unlike his usual style of lecture, curt, witty, and practical, that several men regarded each other inquiringly. He paused, essayed to begin, but stopped again, and I saw his memory failed him. He passed his hand over his forehead, with an inexpressibly troubled look; then he went on again, but this time with the anatomy of the heart; even in this he evidently forgot many of the terms, and several times left a sentence unfinished. He drew another diagram with entire success, then came another embarrassed pause. A most uncomfortable sensation stole over every one present. He referred to his diagram, and seemed to remember that he had left the brain unfinished; then—giving me one glance of such agony as I can never forget—he recommenced; but the treacherous memory again failed: he attempted to explain one part, and utterly lost the thread of the argument, and not only the name but the very idea. He drew himself up to his full height, looked at us steadily for a moment, and bursting into tears, hurriedly left the room. In all London there was perhaps no greater misery than that proud and sensitive heart endured that night.

Horace never entered this lecture-room again. For upwards of a year he travelled with his wife on the Continent; and I was told the mineral waters at some of the spas in Germany had done wonders for his shattered health. When they returned to this country they retired to the property I have before alluded to in Wales, and lived there in comparative seclusion. I saw him very seldom, and only for short periods, and then he seemed enjoying very fair health, though not the man he was when I first knew him: but I was informed that he still continued occasionally to make sad outbreaks; not by any means frequently, but that when he did get intoxicated it was to a terrible excess.

One bright, undimmed star still shone in their heaven amid these driving clouds and storms, and that was their mutual and passionate love. In this fact friends and foes agreed alike; so that I still hardly repented that I had not urged him to abjure marriage. . . .

One day a letter was placed in my hand, containing these words in Mrs. Saltoun's handwriting, "Come to me instantly."

In those days the network of railways did not exist as at present, and though I travelled all night it was morning before I drove up to the house. Margaret met me in the doorway, strangely saddened, and very pale. Her habitual calm was not the dogged submission of a fatalist, but the humble, softened confidence of one who believed that Heaven watched over all. She was by no means one of those women whom the smallest anxiety reduces to a skeleton, and therefore, though the pallor habitual to her had become more than ever marble in its hue, the blue veins more easily traced, and the large, full, lustrous eyes languid and heavy, yet, worn and tried as she looked, Margaret Saltoun was now, as ever, a most noble specimen of perfect womanhood; fined down, perhaps, through much suffering: but it has been finely remarked, "We predicate more nobly of the worn appearance of St. Paul than of the fair and ruddy countenance of David."

But few words were uttered: the consciousness of misfortune was on us both. As

I wrung her hand, my eye rested almost unconsciously, perhaps, on her black dress. She responded to the silent thought.

"God has taken my little one to himself: it is better, perhaps, so"—here her voice trembled exceedingly, and there followed a silence, which I, at least, had no words to break. At last she resumed, in her rich, pleading voice, "You know the worst, doctor, when you know that at this moment we are ignorant where Horace may be; or, indeed, whether he is alive or dead. Something in these letters has grieved him up to that point when he could no longer control himself. He has often told me—and it is even now my pride and joy to know—that no earthly sorrow touched him which he did not confide to me. You will read these letters" (she placed them in my hand); "you will judge how little he is to blame for what they record; and you will see in all this another proof that nothing has power to overthrow his strength of mind except anxiety of the heart, or grief and unkindness from those he loves."

I hurriedly mastered their contents. His sister was dead! In one were the certificated reports of the foreign authorities. Miss Saltoun had, in a fit of somnambulism, precipitated herself from a window, died, and was buried; that was the substance of the intelligence. Alas! somnambulism or delirium —who could tell? The other was a letter stamped with about fifty postmarks. It had apparently, through some ignorance in the writer of the proper address, made the tour of Europe. It was dated five weeks prior to the unhappy event: in it Mdlle. Justine sent in her resignation; "finding," she said, "that her young lady no longer required her services."

"When did Horace leave the house?" I inquired.

"He received this letter the day before yesterday, and appeared stunned rather than agitated by the news; then he swallowed a quantity of wine, and I fear spirits likewise, and lay down on his bed, feverish and restless. I lay by his side, and as he seemed to become more tranquil, I slept. When I awoke he was no longer by me. We sent messengers in all directions, and traced him down to the shore. Early this morning I myself found his clothes; they were thrown off in disorder, and soaked in dew, as if they had been there many hours."

She was deadly pale as she said this, and the tears rained down her face: there was no trembling, no loud cry, but a grief pure and noble, and yet chastened and resigned.

"Dear Mrs. Saltoun," I said, "I would not for worlds deceive you, but my impression is that Horace is not lost to us: first remember that he was a bold, and steady, and powerful swimmer; secondly, if, as I imagine, a brief delirium has seized him, strong physical exertion may prove most useful to him. It would be about four o'clock yesterday afternoon that he left you: no very great time has elapsed."

That day the country round was again scoured by men and horses, and the sea-shore carefully searched. I superintended the latter in person. The coast was very wild and picturesque at this point, forming a vast amphitheatre of crags and precipices, intersected in one place by a deep gully, and again further up by a torn and rent ravine, partially clothed with verdure in the cleft; a few pine-trees and dwarfed oaks sprang out of the fissures in the rocks, whose bent and twisted branches testified to many a long year of exposure to the drifting spray, and of struggle with the wind and tempest Several subterranean passages ran deep into the cliff, terminating in some fine caverns, formerly the resort of smugglers on this coast. No trace of the fugitive could I discover; but, knowing well the passionate attachment of Horace for the sea, I suspected strongly that he was concealed in some of these caves, and would probably prowl out as soon as he thought darkness would secure him from pursuit.

The bay was rather a large one, running deep inland, and the coast to the left extended so far out as to appear almost opposite. A broad tongue of black purple lay on the water's edge, and above it towered the snow-capped mountain of ——, at that instant warmed into rose color by the rays of the setting sun. As if to mimic this there ran out from the shore in a slanting direction, for above half a mile, a chain of rough rocks, which, being partially under water at high tide, were mostly covered with black sea-weed. From the extreme point it was a quarter of a mile in a straight line to the main land, and between it and this natural break-water the sea was in general as placid as a lake, but of very considerable depth. When I had fully mastered the chief points hereabouts, I returned to the house to give Margaret such scanty hope as was in my power. I insisted on her swallowing a sedative, and advised her to go to bed at once, and sleep if possible.

About eleven at night, I again took the path to the shore, and loitered about for upwards of an hour without seeing or hearing any thing that I sought for; I then took up my position in the mouth of one of the caves, which commanded a full view of the bay. For half an hour or more I continued my vigil without any result. I strolled out and perceived evident signs of a change of weather, but feeling reluctant to return to that unhappy lady without tidings of her husband, I again went under shelter.

Gradually the stillness grew ominously hushed, and for a quarter of an hour nothing was heard but the moan of the sullen wave as it broke on the sands. Another instant and the winds were loosed with irresistible fury; down came the storm-king from his throne, down drove the white mist, down drove the torrent, and the gray sea was a sheet of foam. The pine-trees ahead looked like isolated fragments of darkness, and the gnarled oaks creaked and strained to hold their own. The war of the elements continued with fury for upwards of an hour. I fancied I heard a voice, or voices, and indeed felt so persuaded of it that I ventured forth once; but the rain blinded me: the air was thick with spray, and the roar of the sea, which was perfectly invisible to me, made all else inaudible, so I was glad to return.

Almost as abruptly as the storm began, it ceased; leaving, however, a dense white fog, which moved capriciously, sometimes allowing the breakers to be visible, and the next minute gathering over the sea and clearing away to the cliffs. At length, it hovered in a heavy mass over earth and water, while the sky was no longer hidden, and I could see the moon attempting to emerge from a coil of rain-laden clouds. Suddenly as I stood straining my eyes into darkness, the mist, by some undercurrent of air I imagine, was raised as though by mechanism, and for a brief minute I saw the ocean, the bay, and the jutting-out reef of rocks. But I saw more than this: my eyes beheld distinctly at the extremity of the reef, touched as it was by the moonlight, a human figure pacing rapidly to and fro. Then by a vexatious caprice the current of air changed, the mist fell like a white pall, and I saw no more: but that was enough. Scrambling out, I made my way as rapidly as possible along the rough shingle, to gain if I could the command of the point in question.

The rocks were of great size, curiously massed together in grotesque position and outline, and being very slippery and full of deep fissures containing water, it was no easy work to make satisfactory progress along them in that uncertain light; so that when I had accomplished a quarter of a mile I was bathed in perspiration, and almost disposed to think that my eyes had deceived me, and that I was on a fruitless and foolhardy errand. Still I continued onward, and the chain grew more narrow; but though the sea was calm, I could hear nothing but the gurgle of its deep inky waters against the base. The fog cleared in a circle round me as I proceeded, the moon shone forth from a lake of deep blue sky surrounded by an almost transparent halo of fleecy silver clouds, while now and then the cliffs to my right, whitened by her beams, stood out in strong relief, and the sands lay beneath in a deep shadow of unbroken gloom.

I could now discern clearly a figure: it was, then, no spectre of my fancy: and I felt equally convinced that it was Horace, and none other: for who but a man distraught would be in such a place at such an hour? I resolved to proceed very cautiously, since the fog behind me was so whitened as almost to point me out; and if I could see him so plainly, there was no reason why he should not perceive me. I approached near enough to hear some one shouting, muttering, and laughing. Whenever the figure faced in my direction, I crouched behind the large rocks which were nearest to me, then made another spring, and again concealed myself. At last I stood within half a dozen yards.

I had not deceived myself; it was indeed Horace Saltoun. He was entirely naked, with the exception of a chaplet of black seaweed on his head, and a twisted rope made out of the root part of the same material, coiled round his neck, waist, and loins, and terminating in a fantastic knot which fell to his knee, his feet were cut and stained, and a thin streak of blood was visible from a cut on his forehead, from which it trickled slowly down his face. He was shouting, blaspheming, and gesticulating, and tearing the sea-weed violently from the rocks, and hurling it by great handfuls into the sea.

I stood hidden from his sight for a few moments, to regain my breath and consider what was my best course of action. To return for assistance would obviously be to lose the result of my labor; yet it was hardly probable that in his present excited state he would consent to accompany me of his own will. I was not near enough to spring upon him, and even if I could, holding a naked man by force is slippery work, and I did not feel disposed to place confidence in the strength of the sea-weed rope; there only remained a hand-to-hand struggle, the most likely termination of which seemed to be that we should both roll off into the sea. In this dilemma I resolved to try the effect of suddenly announcing my presence. His present condition was not a surprise to me: I had long expected that his increasing excesses in stimulants would bring on a maniacal attack; and I was aware that in that condition every thing may be hoped for, as far as management goes, by taking advantage of a timely diversion of attention. So I walked boldly forward, and said as calmly as I could, "It is very cold work out here, Horace."

He staggered back as if I had struck him, and then confronted me, shading his eyes with both his hands.

"What, you've come, have you?" he said, slowly.

"Yes," I replied, "and I want to help you in what you are about," and I made a few steps forwards.

"Then stand back," he yelled out, at the very top of his voice. "Stand back, or I'll twist your neck as soon as I get hold of you."

"Horace," I called out, in slow, distinct tones, "come home; your wife is ill,—very ill, and wants you."

"My wife ill?" he repeated after me: "Margaret ill?" and he bent forward, and peered curiously at me.

I kept my eye fixed on his, endeavoring to rivet his attention, and advanced close to him. He stood perfectly still. I touched him; he continued motionless, and a hard sinister smile stole over his face: my hand even glided up his arm; but as soon as it reached his shoulder, he burst into a loud, shrill, derisive laugh, made one bound backwards off the reef, and the sea closed silently over him. I leaned over the edge, keeping my eye on the spot where he disappeared; he rose to sight again nearly in the same place: and never, as long as I live, can I forget that singular scene. The white mist formed a clear ring of which we were the centre, the moon shone pale and cold on the murky waters, while each ripple made by the plunge bore a silver sparkle on its tiny crest. In the midst of these circling eddies, gleaming ghastly in the moonlight, the dripping hair swathed back from the forehead, floated this white human face with a strangely malign expression in the eyes. Even now I feel cold when I think of that moment: my blood curdled round my heart as I watched him. He smiled,—or seemed to smile, and then, rounding the point, disappeared; striking off, as far as I could judge, in a slanting direction, towards the shore rather than otherwise.

A good deal cast down by my ill-success, I began to retrace my steps. I had tried the boasted power of the human eye, and it had signally failed me. Perhaps it might be in some measure due to my long familiarity on equal terms with Horace; for, in cases of this description, former personal intimacy often militates against a physician's influence. Before I fairly quitted these unlucky rocks my foot slipped, and I managed to sprain my ankle severely; not enough to bring me to a standstill, but sufficiently so to impede materially the rapidity of my progress. Leaving myself in this untoward condition, I will relate what occurred meanwhile at the house.

Margaret had, according to my recommendation, swallowed the sedative, undressed, and retired to bed; where, overcome by fatigue and wretchedness, she sank into a heavy sleep. The bedroom in question, the one usually occupied by herself and her husband, was on the ground-floor, at the extremity of the right wing, and looked out on a small plot of grass and a thickly tangled shrubbery.

About five o'clock that morning, when dawn was breaking, she awoke with the feeling of something cold being pressed tightly on her throat. She opened her eyes, starting up mechanically from her pillow, and saw what might well have tried the nerves of the strongest man. There was poor Horace sitting calmly by her bedside, perfectly naked, his seaweed chaplet still on his head, and his arms folded on his breast, making conspicuously visible her own initials and the cross and anchor in pale blue, which he had so carefully punctured on himself in the days that were passed away. But in his hands he held the two ends of the coil of black sea-weed stalk, which he had twisted tightly round her neck; and it was the pressure of this deadly ligature upon her throat that roused her from sleep. Owing to her instinctive self-possession, and her wonderfully calm nature, aided, perhaps, in some measure by the effects of the opiate, she neither started nor screamed when she discovered her peril, but at once addressed him cheerfully, and tried to link one of his hands in hers; yet he still retained his hold on the coil, so that she knew she was helpless. She told me afterwards, how difficult it was for her to withstand the inclination to put her fingers to her neck and endeavor to rid herself of the ghastly necklace. But she did refrain.

"Yes, it is I, Margaret, love," he answered, dreamily. "I have come to enable you to die. It is necessary," he continued, with frightful calmness, "that you should be strangled. I've been a long time preparing this rope, and it is now thoroughly charmed."

She shivered a little.

"It is cold—is it not?" he said; "but that will not signify in the end. It seems almost a pity—does it not?" and he touched her full and finely moulded throat doubtfully with his fingers. "Don't be afraid, love," he added, almost tenderly, and proceeded to tighten the coil.

She made a desperate effort. "You know, Horace, I can have no objection, but I must have my hair properly dressed; you must dress it for me. You used to think my hair beautiful, you know."

He seemed puzzled for a moment. "Is it absolutely needful?" he inquired, sternly.

"I am sure it is," she replied, with a vague idea that it would be better to assign some reason, however absurd; "the corpse would otherwise look unseemly."

"Very well," he answered, gravely. He then assisted her out of bed, still keeping the detestable coil in his fingers.

She placed herself before the glass, biting her lips to bring back the color which had fled, and trying to smile; then letting down her long hair, she handed him the brushes. He took them, and began his task with the greatest gentleness, and to her inexpressible relief, she felt the coil relax as the two ends fell down on the floor; though, of course, it was still round her throat. Those moments seemed hours, and her agitation and suspense were fast growing intolerable. Meanwhile, poor lady, she praised his dexterity, which seemed to please him excessively, and stimulated him to new endeavors. He began to perform the most extravagant manœuvres, brushing her hair quite up, and letting it fall in a mass over her shoulders, then twisting it round his own neck, and laying it over his face: all this with immovable gravity.

It was precisely at this juncture that I arrived from the shore. Under the idea that the shortest path was by the shrubbery, I pushed my way through the tangled branches, and, standing on the lawn, I reconnoitred the house. I was naturally surprised to see Mrs. Saltoun visible at that hour from the bedroom window: it was low enough for me to have a view of part of the interior of the room; and I saw that she was sitting before her mirror, her face turned towards the window. She was excessively pale, and had a strange forced smile. Though she caught my eye, she neither moved nor made the slightest sign of recognition, but continued to gaze with such a stern, stolid, fixed expression, that I was moved with a nameless dread. I stepped back and looked again; yes, so it was! I saw plainly her mad husband standing behind her: I could see his head still crowned, and his naked shoulders. Though I was not aware of the critical nature of her peril, I knew there was danger, so, crouching down out of sight, I made my way instantly into the house. I encountered his own servant, a man much attached to his master; he inquired eagerly if I had tidings of him.

"Take off your shoes," I said, instantly, "and follow me; your master is in the house."

I paused outside the bedroom door and listened. I could hear nothing excepting the rustling of the brushes in the hair, and an odd low chuckling laugh. I then tried the handle of the door as noiselessly as possible: good; it was not bolted or locked inside, as I had feared to find. I instantly threw it wide open. Horace faced me, and with a terrible yell sprang upon me like a wild beast. Poor fellow! assistance was at hand, and he was quickly overpowered. When I turned to seek Margaret she had fainted.

That house still remains tenanted, but half of it is closed; and the brilliant lecturer, Horace Saltoun, is heard of no more. In one range of apartments you may see a fantastically attired, restless being, talking perpetually and incoherently. His smile is unmeaning, his restlessness incessant, his actions are aimless. In close attendance on him is his servant; but ever haunting his steps, clad in the plainest garb, performing almost menial offices for that poor, broken-down wreck who is still her husband, his noble-minded wife continues her cheerless task: and no one has the same influence over him which she possesses. Her cheeks are a little hollow and worn, there is a look of pain on her brow, and there are dark violet rings beneath eyes that are still pure and lustrous; but the same serene benevolence, the same tender, genial smile is ever there. She listens to all his long dissertations without point or sequence, in which scraps of anatomy are curiously mingled with exordiums on the necessity of her duty, and obedience, and gratitude to him: for he who used to be the most humble-minded and unselfish of men is changed as much morally as intellectually; and his arrogant and patronizing manner towards her would be laughable if it were not so very, very sad. Time to that blinded eye seems to stay his scythe. Poor Horace lives only in the present: he can neither remember the past, nor apprehend for the future. Sometimes he will make a brilliant metaphor, or begin to quote a fragment of some fine passage, but invariably relapses into vapid nonsense before he can finish it; the lightning flash only serves to reveal still more the blackness of the ruin.

Beggars in London a Century Ago.—"But notwithstanding we have so many excellent laws, great numbers of sturdy beggars, loose and vagrant persons, infest the nation, but no place more than the city of London and parts adjacent: if any person is born with any defect or deformity, or maimed by fire or any other casualty, or by any inveterate distemper, which renders them miserable objects, their way is open to London, where they have free liberty of showing their nauseous sights to terrify people and force them to give money to get rid of them; and those vagrants have for many years past removed out of several parts of the three kingdoms, and taken their stations in this metropolis, to the interruption of conversation and business. . . . As to those creatures who go about the streets to show their maimed limbs, nauseous sores, stump hands or feet, or any other deformity, I am of opinion, that they are by no means fit objects to go abroad; and considering the frights and pernicious impressions which such horrid sights have given to pregnant women (and sometimes even to the disfiguring of infants in the womb) should move all tender husbands to desire the redress of this enormity," etc.—*Propositions for Better Regulating and Employing the Poor*, chap. xxiii. 36, in *The Trade and Navigation of Great Britain Considered*, by Joshua Gee, 6th edit., Glasgow, printed and sold by R. and A. Foulis, 1760, 16mo. pp. 180.—*Notes and Queries.*

In 1859 the quantity of hops retained for home consumption was 67,143,652lbs.; in 1860, only 10,352,520lbs.—not a sixth of the previous year's crop. The quantity of malt also fell off from 47,746,289 bushels in 1859, to 41,754,050 bushels in 1860. British spirits from 23,878,688 gallons in 1859 to 21,404,088 in 1860. The quantity of paper increased from 197,684,847lbs. in 1859 to 207,182,013lbs. in 1860.

From Once a Week.

SIR JOSHUA'S PUPIL.

A YOUNG apprentice with very little heart in the study of his craft, after the manner of young apprentices, toiling in a watch and clock maker's shop in the town of Devonport, heard one day the fame of great Sir Joshua's achievements in London sounding through the county—became conscious that the good folks of the shire took pride in the son of the Rev. Samuel Reynolds, Master of Plympton Grammar School. Why should not he, the apprentice, become as great, or nearly so, a credit to Devonport, his birthplace, as was Sir Joshua to Plympton, *his* birthplace? Could one man only have art, abilities, and ambitions, and make for himself the opportunity to employ and gratify them? So the apprentice asked himself. And he must have been a clever fellow, that apprentice! He soon convinced himself—that was easy; but he convinced his family. He convinced several of his townsmen—difficult task, decidedly—that the best thing they could do with him was to send him up to town to study under his countryman, Sir Joshua, and to become, like him, a great painter. He had his way at last. In his twenty-fifth year he was painting in the studio of Reynolds, living under his roof.

After all, his dearest wishes gratified, perhaps the pupil was little better off. If cleverness, like fever, were contagious, it had been all very well. But the master was but an indifferent master. He could not, or would not, instruct. He was himself deficient in education—had few rules—only a marvellous love and perception of the beautiful, and an instinctive talent for its reproduction on his canvas. It was as certain as it was innate, but not to be expressed in words, or communicated or reasoned upon in any way. The deeds of genius are things done, as of course, for no why or wherefore, but simply because there is no help for it but to do them. So the pupils painted in the studio of their supposed preceptor for a certain number of years, copying his works; or, when sufficiently advanced, perhaps working at his back-grounds, brushing away at draperies, or such conventional fillings in of pictures, and then went their ways to do what they listed, and for the most part to be heard of no more in art chronicles. They had probably been of more use to the painter than he had been to them. Certainly our friend the clockmaker's apprentice was. For when there arose a cry of "Who wrote Sir Joshua's discourses, if not Burke?" this pupil could give satisfactory evidence in reply. He had heard the great man, his master, walking up and down in the library, as in the intervals of writing, at one and two o'clock in the morning. A few hours later, and he had the results in his hands. He was employed to make a fair copy of the lecturer's rough manuscript for the reading to the public. He had noted Dr. Johnson's handwriting, for *he* had revised the draft, sometimes altering to a wrong meaning, from his total ignorance of the subject and of art: but never a stroke of Burke's pen was there to be seen. The pupil, it must be said for him, never lost faith in his master. Vandyke, Reynolds, Titian—he deemed these the great triumvirate of portraiture. Comparing them, he would say, that Vandyke's portraits were like pictures, Sir Joshua's like the reflections in a looking-glass, and Titian's like the real people. And he was useful to the great painter in another way, for he sat for one of the children in the Count Ugolino picture (the one in profile with the hand to the face): while posed for this, he was introduced as a pupil of Sir Joshua to Mr. Edmund Burke, and turned to look at that statesman. "He is not only an artist, but has a head that would do for Titian to paint," said Mr. Burke. He served, too, another celebrated man. With Ralph, Sir Joshua's servant, he went to the gallery of Covent Garden Theatre, to support Dr. Goldsmith's new comedy, "She stoops to Conquer," on the first night of its performance. While his friends are trooping to the theatre, the poor author is found sick and shivering with nervousness, wandering up and down the Mall in St. James' Park. He can hardly be induced to witness the production of his own play. Johnson's lusty laugh from the front row of a side box gives the signal to the worthy *claque*, who applaud to an almost dangerous extent, in their zeal for their friend, because there runs a rumor that Cumberland and Ossian Macpherson and Kelly are getting up a hiss in the pit.

"How did you like the play?" asked Goldsmith of the young painter, who had been clapping his hands until they ached, in the gallery by the side of good Mr. Ralph.

"I wouldn't presume to be a judge in such a matter," the art-student answered.

"But did it make you laugh?"

"Oh, exceedingly."

"That's all I require," said Goldsmith, and sent him box tickets for the author's benefit night, that he might go and laugh again.

Sir Joshua's pupil was James Northcote, a long-lived man, born at Devonport in 1746, and dying at his London house, in Argyll Place, Regent Street, in 1831. If he had a Titianesque look in his youth, he possessed it still more in his age. Brilliant eyes, deeply set; grand projecting nose; thin, compressed lips; a shrewd, catlike, penetrating look; fine, high, bald forehead, yellow and polished, though he often hid this with a fantastic green velvet painting cap, and straggling bunches of quite white hair behind his ears. A little, meagre man, not more than five feet high, in a shabby, patched dressing-gown, almost as old as himself, leading a quiet, cold, penurious life. He never married. He had never even been in love. He had never had the time, or he had never had the passion necessary for such pursuits, or he was too deeply devoted to his profession. He was always brush in hand, perched up on a temporary stage, painting earnestly, fiercely, "With the inveterate diligence of a little devil stuccoing a mud wall!" cried flaming Mr. Fuseli.

He received many visitors in his studio. He was constantly at home, and liked to talk over his work, for he never paused on account of the callers. He never let go his palette even. He went to the door with a "Gude God!" his favorite exclamation in his west country dialect, "what, is it *you*? Come in:" and then climbed his way back to his canvas, asking and answering in his cool, self-possessed way, all about the news of the day. Yet he was violent and angry, and outspoken sometimes, was Sir Joshua's loyal pupil.

"Look at the feeling of Raphael!" said some one to him.

"Bah!" cried the little man. "Look at Reynolds: he was all feeling! The ancients were *baysts* in feeling, compared to him." And again: "I tell'ee the King and Queen could not bear the presence of *he*. Do you think he was overawed by *they*? Gude God! He was poison to their sight. They felt ill at ease before such a being—they shrunk into themselves, overawed by his intellectual superiority. They inwardly prayed to God that a trap-door might open under the feet of the throne, by which they might escape—his presence was too terrible!"

Certainly he was possessed by no extravagant notions of the divinity of blood royal.

"What do you know," he was asked, "of the Prince of Wales, that he so often speaks of you?"

"Oh! he knows nothing of me, nor I of him—it's only his *bragging!*" so the painter grandly replied.

He could comprehend the idea of distinction of ranks little more than old Mr. Nollekens, who would persist in treating the royal princes quite as common acquaintances, taking them by the button-hole, forgetful altogether of the feuds of the king's family, and asking them *how their father did?* with an exclamation to the heir-apparent of, "Ah! we shall never get such another when he's gone!" though there was little enough veneration for the king in this, as he proved, when he measured the old king, sitting for his bust, from the lip to the forehead, as though he had been measuring a block of marble, and at last fairly stuck the compasses into his majesty's nose. Even the king, who was not very quick at a joke, could not fail to see the humor of the situation, and laughed immensely.

Modern taste prefers Northcote's portraits to his more pretentious works. The glories of Mr. Alderman Boydell's Shakspeare Gallery have pretty well passed away. However, Northcote's pictures were among the best of the collection. His "Arthur and Hubert," and the "Murder of the Princes in the Tower," and "The Interment of the Bodies by Torchlight," were very forcible and dramatic works of art, and possessed more natural attractions than the pictures of many of his competitors. His pupilage with Sir Joshua prevented his falling into the washed leather and warm drab errors of tone that then distinguished the English school of historical painting. In the picture of the Burial of the Princes, Fuseli criticised:—

"You shouldn't have made that fellow holding up his hands to receive the bodies.

You should have made him digging a hole for them. How awfully grand; with a pick-axe, digging, dump, dump, dump!"

"Yes," Northcote answered; "but how am I to paint the sound of dump, dump, dump?"

The Boydell pictures were for a long time very popular, and the engravings of them enjoyed a large sale. Of course, Northcote despised Hogarth. Abuse of that painter seemed to be one of the duties of the British historical artist of that day. Yet he paid him homage: he painted a series of pictures, Hogarthian in subject, and proved to the satisfaction of everybody, one would think, the absolute superiority of Hogarth. Mr. Northcote's moral subjects, illustrative of vice and virtue, in the progress of two young women, are not to be mentioned in the same breath with the "Marriage à la Mode." Not merely were they deficient in expression—they were not equal in point of art-execution, though of course the more modern painter had planned to excel in both these qualities. But Northcote's portraits are really admirable—broad and vigorous—with much of Sir Joshua's charm of color, if not his charm of manner exactly.

For fifty years he lived in Argyll Place, passing the greatest part of that time in his studio—a small room not more than nine feet by twelve, crowded with the conventional articles of *vertu* that were then considered to be the indispensable properties of a painter. His maiden sister—"Northcote in petticoats," she was often called, she was so like him in face, figure, and manner—superintended his frugal household. Its economy was simple enough. The brother and sister were of one opinion. "Half the world died of over-feeding," they said. They went into an opposite extreme, and nearly starved themselves. When there was a cry in the land about scarcity of food, they did not heed the panic; they were accustomed to the minimum of sustenance, they could hardly be deprived of that. Fuseli, who sowed his satire broadcast, exclaimed, one day: "What! Does Northcote keep a dog? What does he live upon? Why, he must eat his own fleas!" But the painter did not attempt to force his opinions upon others, so the kennel and the kitchen fared better than the parlor. The servants were indulgently treated, permitted to eat as they pleased, and die in their own fashion—of repletion or apoplexy, if it seemed good to them.

If he was cold and callous and cynical to the rest of the world, he was ever good and kind to the pinched, elderly lady, his sister. By his will he gave directions that every thing in his house should remain undisturbed, that there should be no sale of his property in her lifetime. He was counselled by considerate friends to have all his pictures sold immediately after his funeral while his name was fresh in the memory of the public; it was urged that his estate would benefit very much by the adoption of such a course. "Gude God, no!" the old man would cry; "I haven't patience with ye! Puir thing! d'ye think she'll not be sufficiently sad when my coffin be borne away, and she be left desolate! Tearing my pictures from the walls, and ransacking every nook and corner, and packing up and carting away what's dearer to her than household gods, and all for filthy lucre's sake! No; let her enjoy the few years that will be spared to her; when she walks about the house let her feel it all her own, such as it be, and nothing missing but her brother. I'd rather my bones were torn from my grave, and scattered to help repair the roads, than that a single thing should be displaced here to give her pain. Ye'll drive me mad!"

One day there was a great crowd in Argyll Place. Not to see the painter, not even to see a royal carriage that had just drawn up at his door, nor a popular prince of the blood who occupied the carriage, but to catch a glimpse of one about whom the town was then quite mad—raving mad, a small good-looking schoolboy, a theatrical homunculus, the Infant Roscius, Master William Henry Betty. Of course rages and panics and manias seem to be very foolish things contemplated by the cool gray light of the morning after. It seems rather incredible now that crowds should have assembled round the theatre at one o'clock to see Master Betty play Barbarossa in the evening; that he should have played for twenty-eight nights at Drury Lane, and drawn £17,000 into the treasury of the theatre. He was simply a handsome boy of thirteen with a fine voice, deep for his age, and powerful but monotonous. Surely, he was not very intellectual, though he did witch the town so marvellously. "If they admire me so much, what would they say of Mr. Harley?" quoth the boy, simply. Mr. Harley being the head tragedian of the same strolling company—a large-calved, leather-lunged player, doubtless, who had awed provincial groundlings for many a long year. Yet the boy's performance of Douglas charmed John Home, the author of the tragedy. "The first time I ever saw the part of Douglas played according to my ideas of the character!" he exclaimed, as he stood in the wings: but he was then seventy years of age. "The little Apollo off the pedestal!" cried Humphreys, the artist. "A beautiful effusion of natural sensibility," said cold Northcote; "and then that graceful play of the limbs in youth—what an advantage over every one else." As the child grew, the charm vanished; the crowds that had applauded the boy fled from the man. Byron denounced him warmly. "His figure is fat, his features flat, his voice unmanageable, his action ungraceful, and, as Diggory says [in the farce of "All the World's a Stage"], 'I defy him to *extort* that d—d muffin-face of his into madness!'" Happy Master Betty! Hapless *Mister* Betty!

Opie had painted the Infant as the shepherd so well known to nursery prodigies watching on the Grampian Hills the flocks of his father, "a frugal swain, whose constant care," etc., etc. His royal highness the Duke of Clarence, who was a patron of the stage—or the people on it, or some of them—brought the boy to Northcote, to be represented in a "Vandyke costume retiring from the altar of Shakspeare"—rather an unmeaning ceremonial. But the picture was a great success, and the engraving of it published and dedicated to the duke. He was then about forty—a hearty, bluff gentleman, supposed to be free and breezy in his manliness from his service at sea, kindly and unaffected in manner, had not the slightest knowledge of art, but regarded Northcote as "an honest, independent, little, old fellow," seasoning that remark with an oath, after the quarter-deck manner of naval gentlemen of the period.

The prince sat in the studio while the artist drew the Infant. Northcote was not a man to wear a better coat upon his back for all that his back was going to be turned upon royalty. He still wore the ragged, patched dressing-gown he always worked in. The painting of Master Betty was amusing at first, but it seemed, in the end, to be but a prolonged and tedious business to the not artistic looker-on. He must amuse himself somehow. Certainly Northcote's appearance was comical. Suddenly the painter felt a twitching at his collar. He turned, frowning angrily, but said nothing. The prince persevered. Presently he touched lightly the painter's rough white locks.

"Mr. Northcote, pray how long do you devote to the duties of the toilet?"

It was very rude of his royal highness, but then he was *so* bored by the sitting.

The little old painter turned round full upon him.

"I never allow any one to take personal liberties with me. You are the first that ever presumed to do so. I beg your royal highness to recollect that I am in my own house."

He spoke warmly, glanced haughtily, then worked at his canvas again. There was silence for some minutes. Quietly the duke opened the door and left the room. The painter took no notice.

But the royal carriage had been sent away. It would not be required until five o'clock. It was not yet four, and it was raining!

The duke returned to the studio.

"Mr. Northcote, it rains. Will you have the kindness to lend me an umbrella?"

Calmly the painter rang the bell.

"Bring your mistress' umbrella."

Miss Northcote's umbrella was the only silk one in the house. The servant showed the prince down-stairs, and he left the house protected from the shower by Miss Northcote's umbrella.

"You have offended his royal highness," said some one in the room.

"*I* am the offended party," the painter answered with dignity.

Next day he was alone in his studio when a visitor was announced.

"Mr. Northcote," said the duke, entering, "I return Miss Northcote's umbrella, you were so kind as to lend me yesterday."

The painter bowed, receiving it from the royal hands.

"I have brought it myself, Mr. Northcote," the duke continued, "that I might have the opportunity of saying that I yesterday took a liberty which you properly resented. I am angry with myself. I hope you will forgive me, and think no more of it."

The painter bowed his acceptance of the apology.

"Gude God!" he exclaimed, afterwards telling the story, "what could I say? He could see what I felt. I could have given my life for him! Such a prince is worthy to be a king!"

More than a quarter of a century passed, and then the Duke of Clarence was the king of England—William the Fourth. The old painter was still living, at work as usual, though weak and bent enough now, but with his brain still active, his tongue still sharp, his eyes still very brilliant in his lined shrunken face. "A poor creature," he said of himself, "perhaps amusing for half an hour or so, or curious to see like a little dried mummy in a museum." He employed himself in the preparation of a number of illustrations to a book of fables published after his death. He collected prints of animals, and cut them out carefully; then he moved about such as he selected for his purpose on a sheet of plain paper, and, satisfying himself at last as to the composition of the picture, he fixed the figures in their places with paste, filled in backgrounds with touches of his pencil, and then handed the curious work to Mr. Harvey, the engraver, to be copied on wood and engraved. The success of the plan was certainly as remarkable as its eccentricity.

He employed his pen as well as his pencil, contributed papers to the "Artist," and published, in 1813, a life of Sir Joshua. A year before his death he produced a "Life of Titian," the greater part of which, however, was probably written by his friend and constant companion Hazlitt.

He was in his small studio, brush in hand, very tranquil and happy, within two days of his death. It seemed as though he had been forgotten. "If Providence were to leave me the liberty of choosing my heaven, I should be content to occupy my little painting-room, with the continuance of the happiness I have experienced there, even forever." He spoke of his works without arrogance. "Every thing one can do falls short of nature. I am always ready to beg pardon of my sitters after I have done, and to say I hope they'll excuse it. The more one knows of the art, and the better one can do, the less one is satisfied."

Sir Joshua's pupil—"Of all his pupils I am the only one who ever did any thing at all,"—died on the 13th July, 1831, in the eighty-sixth year of his age.

DUTTON COOK.

SHIPTONIANA.—Just after the Cato Street conspiracy, I called on my friend John Taylor, the editor of *The Sun* (then in its Tory meridian), when he exclaimed, "We have them now! one of their gang (Monument is the fellow's name) has peached; and he is lodged in the Tower for safe-keeping." "Ah! ha!" said I, "Mother Shipton's prophecy, word for word!—

"'When the Monument doth come to the Tower,
Then shall fall rebellion's power.'"

"Where did you find that?" cried Tory John, pretty considerably astonished. "There are several editions of Mother Shipton," I gravely replied; "I found it in mine." He insisted on a copy. Into *The Sun* it went that same evening, and in due time he showed me several provincial journals into which it had been copied. In fact, it went the round of the press. Over and over again he asked me to show him my copy, until I was obliged, in confidence of course, to confess, the impromptu.—*Notes and Queries.*

A PERFECTLY successful attempt has been made to illuminate the courts of the Tuileries and the Place du Carrousel by the electric light. The generating apparatus is placed in a cellar under Marshal Vaillant's apartments in the Tuileries, and the illuminating power is so great that the ordinary gas-jets seem absolutely lightless. The appearance of these localities every evening is that of an animated fair. The cost of the electric light is stated to be considerably less than that of gas.

From The Welcome Guest.

SAMUEL LOWGOOD'S REVENGE.

FROM the first to the last we were rivals and enemies. Perhaps it was on my part that the hatred, which eventually became so terrible a passion between us, first arose. Perhaps it was, perhaps it was! At any rate, he always said that it was so. I am an old man, and the past has much of it faded out; but that portion of my life which relates to him is as fresh in my mind to-night as ever it was fifty years ago, when his Gracious Majesty George the Second was king, and Christopher Weldon and I were junior clerks together in the great house of Tyndale and Tyndale, shipowners, Dockside, Willborough.

He was very handsome. It was hard for a pale-faced, sallow-complexioned, hollow-eyed, insignificant lad, as I was, to sit at the same desk with Christopher Weldon, and guess the comparisons that every stranger entering the counting-house must involuntarily make, as he looked at us,—if he looked at us, that is to say; and it was difficult not to look at Christopher. Good heavens! I can see him now, seated at the worn, old, battered, ink-stained desk, with all the July sunlight streaming through the dingy office windows, down upon his waving clusters of pale golden hair, with his bright blue eyes looking out, through the smoky panes, at the forests of masts, dangling ropes, and grimy sails, in the dock outside; with one girlish, white hand carelessly thrown upon the desk before him, and the delicate fingers of the other twisted in his flowing curls. He was scarcely one-and-twenty, the spoiled pet of a widowed mother, the orphan son of a naval officer, and the darling idol of half the women in the seaport of Willborough. It was not so much to be wondered at, then, that he was a fop and a maccaroni, and that the pale golden curls, which he brushed off his white forehead, were tied on his coat collar with a fine purple ribbon on Sundays and holidays. His cravat and ruffles were always of delicate lace, worked by his loving mother's hands; his coats were made by a London tailor, who had once worked for Mr. George Selwyn and Lord March; and he wore diamond shoe buckles and a slender court sword sometimes out of office hours.

I, too, was an orphan; but I was doubly an orphan. My father and mother had both died in my infancy. I had been reared in a workhouse, had picked up chance waifs and strays of education from the hardest masters, and had been drafted, at the age of ten, into the offices of Tyndale and Tyndale. Errand boy, light porter, office drudge, junior clerk—one by one I had mounted the rounds in this troublesome ladder, which for me could only be begun from the very bottom; and, at the age of twenty-one, I found myself—where? In a business character, I was on a level with Christopher Weldon, the son of a gentleman. How often I, the pauper orphan of a bankrupt cornchandler, had to hear this phrase,—the son of a gentleman. In a business character, I say, I, Samuel Lowgood, who had worked, and slaved, and drudged, and been snubbed, and in spite of all, had become a clever accountant and a thorough arithmetician—throughout eleven long, weary years—was in the same rank as Christopher Weldon, who had been in the office exactly four weeks, just to see, as his mother said, whether it would suit him.

He was about as much good in the counting-house as a wax doll would have been, and, like a wax doll, he looked very pretty; but Messrs. Tyndale and Tyndale had known his father, and Tyndale senior, knew his uncle, and Tyndale junior, was acquainted with his first cousin, who lived at the court end of London; so he was taken at once into the office, as junior clerk, with every chance, as one of the seniors told me confidentially, of rising much higher, if he took care of himself.

He knew about as much arithmetic as a baby; but he was very clever with his pen, in sketching pretty girls, with powdered heads, flowing sacques, and pannier hoops; so he found plenty of amusement in doing this, and reading Mr. Henry Fielding's novels behind the ledger; and the head clerks left him to himself, and snubbed me for not doing his work as well as my own.

I hated him. I hated his foppish ways and his haughty manners. I hated his handsome, boyish, radiant face, with its golden frame of waving hair, and its blue, beaming, hopeful eyes. I hated him for the sword which swung across the stiff skirts of his brocaded coat; for the money which he jingled in his waistcoat pockets; for the two watches which he wore on high days and holidays; for his merry laugh; for his melodious voice; for his graceful walk; for his tall, slender figure; for his jovial, winning ways, which won everybody else's friendship. I hated him for all these; but, most of all, I hated him for his influence over her.

She was a poor dependant upon the bounty of the house of Tyndale and Tyndale, and she had the care of the town residence belonging to the firm, which communicated with the offices.

People knew very little about her, except that she was the daughter of a superannuated old clerk, who had gone stone blind over the ledgers of Tyndale and Tyndale, and that she lived with her father in this dreary, old, deserted, unoccupied town house. Once or twice in a year, the brothers would take it into their heads to give a dinner party in this disused dwelling, and then the great oak furniture was polished, and clusters of wax candles were lighted in the twisted silver sconces, and the dim pictures of the Tyndales dead and gone, shipowners and merchants in the days of William and Mary, were uncovered; but, at other times, Lucy Malden and her blind old father had the great place, with its long, dark corridors, and its lofty chambers into which the light rarely penetrated, all to themselves. The house joined the offices, and the offices and the house formed three sides of a square, the dockside forming the fourth. The counting-house in which Christopher Weldon and I sat was exactly opposite the house.

I watched him the morning when he first saw her—watched him without his being aware of it. It was a blazing July day; and, when she had arranged her father's room, and her own, and the little sitting-room which they shared together, which formed a range of apartments on the second story, she came to her window, and, opening it to its widest extent, sat down to her needlework. She eked out the slender income which the firm allowed her father, by the sale of her needlework, which was very beautiful. A screen of flowers, in great stone jars, sheltered the window, and behind these she placed herself.

He saw her in a moment, and his pen fell from his listless hand.

She was not beautiful. I know that she was not beautiful. I think that many would have scarcely called her even a pretty girl; but to me, from the first to the last, she was the fairest, the dearest, and the loveliest of women, and it is so difficult to me to dispossess myself of her image, as that image shone upon me, that I doubt if I can describe her as she really was.

She was very pale. The dreary, joyless life she led in that dark, old house, in the heart of a dingy seaport town, had perhaps blanched the roses in her cheeks, and dimmed the sunlight in her thoughtful brown eyes. She had very light hair—hair of the palest flaxen, perfectly straight and smooth, which she wore turned back over a roll, and fastened in one thick mass at the back of her head. Her eyes, in utter contrast to this light hair, were of the darkest brown, so dark and deep, that the stranger always thought them black. Her features were small and delicate, her lips thin, her figure slender, and below the average height. Her dress, a little quilted petticoat, with a gray stuff gown, and a white apron.

His pen fell out of his hand, and he looked up at her window, and began to hum the air of a favorite song in the new opera, about thieves and ragamuffins, which had got Mr. Gay and a beautiful duchess into such disgrace, up in London.

He was such a conceited beau and lady-killer, that he could not rest till she had looked at the office window by which he sat.

The song attracted her, and she lifted her eyes from her work, and looked down at him.

She started, and blushed—blushed a beautiful, rosy red, that lighted up her pale face like the reflection of a fire; and then, seeing me at my desk, nodded and smiled to me. She and I had been friends for years, and I only waited till I should rise one step higher in the office, to tell her how much I loved her.

From that day, on some excuse or other, Christopher Weldon was always dangling about the house. He scraped acquaintance with her blind old father. He was a pretty musician, and he would put his flute in his pocket, after office hours, and stroll over to the house, and sit there, in the twilight, playing to the father and daughter for the hour together, while I hid myself in the shadow of the counting-house doorway, and stood watching them. Oh! how I hated him, as I saw, across the screen of plants, the two fair heads side by side, and the blind old father nodding, and smiling, and applauding the music. How I hated that melodious opera of Mr. Gay's! How I hated him, as they stood on the step of the hall door, between the tall iron extinguishers under the disused oil lamp, wishing each other good-night! I thought that I could see the little white hand tremble, as it fluttered an adieu to him, as he strode away through the dusky evening.

Should I dog his steps, and, when he got to a lonely place upon the narrow quay, dart suddenly upon him, and push him into the water?—push him in where the barges lay thickly clustered together, and where he must sink, under their keels, down into the black stream? Heaven knows I have asked myself this question!

For months I watched them. Oh, misery! what bitter pain, what silent torture, what a long fever of anguish and despair!

How could I do him some dire injury, which should redress one atom of this mighty sum of wrong which he had done me?—fancied wrong, perhaps; for if he had not won her love, I might never have won it. But I prayed,—I believe I was wicked and mad enough even to pray for some means of doing him as deadly an injury as I thought he had done me.

He looked up at me one day, in his gay, reckless fashion, and said, suddenly pushing the ledger away from him, with a weary sigh,—

"Samuel Lowgood, do you know what a tailor's bill is?"

I cursed him in my heart for his insolence in asking me the question; but I looked down at my greasy, white coat-sleeve, and said,—

"I have worn this for five years, and I bought it second-hand of a dealer on the quay."

"Happy devil!" he said, with a laugh; "if you want to see a tailor's bill, then, look at that."

He tossed me over a long slip of paper, and I looked at the sum total.

It seemed to me something so prodigious, that I had to look at it ever so many times before I could believe my eyes.

"Thirty-seven pounds, thirteen and fourpence halfpenny. I like the fourpence halfpenny," he said; "it looks honest. Samuel Lowgood, my mother's heart would break if she saw that bill. I must pay it in a fortnight from to-day, or it will come to her ears."

"How much have you got towards paying it?" I asked.

My heart beat faster at the thought of his trouble, and my face flushed up crimson; but he was leaning his forehead gloomily upon his hand, and he never looked at me.

"How much have I got towards it?" he said, bitterly. "This." And he turned his waistcoat pockets inside out, one after the other. "Never mind," he added, in his old, reckless tone, "I may be a rich man before the fortnight's out."

That evening he was dangling over at the house as usual, and I heard "Cease your Funning," on the flute, and saw the two fair heads across the dark foliage of Lucy Malden's little flower-garden.

I was glad of his trouble, I was glad of his trouble! It was small, indeed, to the sorrow and despair which I wished him; but it *was* trouble, and the bright, fair-haired, blue-eyed boy knew what it was to suffer.

The days passed, and the fortnight was nearly gone, but he said no more about the tailor's bill. So one day as we sat as usual at the desk, I working hard at a difficult row of figures, he chewing the end of his pen, and looking rather moodily across the court-yard, I asked him,—

"Well, you have got rid of your difficulty?"

"What difficulty?" he asked, sharply.

"Your tailor's bill. The thirty-seven, thirteen, and fourpence halfpenny?"

He looked at me very much as if he would have liked to have knocked me off the office stool; but he said, presently, "Oh, yes, that's been settled ever so long!" and he began to whistle one of his favorite songs.

"Ever so long!" His trouble lasted a very little time, I thought.

But in spite of this he was by no means himself. He sat at his desk with his head buried in his hands; he was sharp and short in his answers when anybody spoke to him, and we heard a great deal less of the "Beggar's Opera," and "Polly."

All of a sudden, too, he grew very industrious, and took to writing a great deal; but he contrived to sit in such a manner that I could never find out what he was writing.

It was some private matter of his own, I knew. What could it be?

Love-letters, perhaps; letters to her!

A fiendish curiosity took possession of me, and I determined to fathom his secret.

I left the counting-house on some pretence, and, after a short absence, returned so softly that he could not hear me, and, stealing behind him, lifted myself upon tiptoe, and looked over his shoulder.

He was writing over and over again, across and across, upon half a sheet of letter paper, the signature of the firm, "Tyndale and Tyndale."

What could it mean? Was it pre-occupation? mere absence of mind? idle trifling with his pen? The fop had a little pocket mirror hanging over his desk. I looked into it, and saw his face.

I knew then what it meant. My hatred of him gave me such a hideous joy in the thought of what I had discovered, that I laughed aloud. He turned round, and asked me savagely what I was doing? and, as he turned, he crumpled the paper in his hand, inking his pretty white fingers with the wet page.

"Spy! sneak! sycophant!" he said, "what are you crawling about here for?"

"I was only trying to startle you, Mister Weldon," I answered. "What are you writing, that you're so frightened of my seeing? Love-letters?"

"Mind your own business, and look to your own work, you pitiful spy," he roared out, "and leave me to do mine my own way."

"I would, if I were you. It seems such a nice way," I answered, meekly.

Two days after this, at half-past three o'clock in the afternoon, Christopher Weldon asked one of the senior clerks for a quarter of an hour's leave of absence. He wanted to see a fellow round in the High Street, he said, and he couldn't see him after four o'clock.

I felt my sallow face flame up into a scarlet flush, as my fellow-clerk made this request. Could it be as I thought?

He had been four months in the office, and it was the end of November. The end of November, and almost dark at half-past three o'clock.

They granted his request without the slightest hesitation. He left his desk, took his hat up, and walked slowly to the door: at the door he stopped, turned back to his desk, and throwing his hat down, leaned moodily upon his folded arms.

"I don't know that I care much about seeing the fellow, now," he said.

"Why, Chris," cried one of the clerks, "what's the matter with you, man? Are you in love or in debt, that you are so unlike yourself?"

"Neither," he said, with a short laugh.

"What, not in love, Chris? How about the pretty little fair-haired girl over the way?"

"How about her?" he said, savagely. "She's a cold-hearted little coquette, and she may go to—"

I slapped the ledger, on which I was at work, violently on to the desk, and looked up at him.

"Christopher Weldon!"

"Your humble servant," he said, mockingly. "There's a face! Have I been poaching upon your manor, Samuel?"

"If you want to see your friend before four o'clock, you'd better be off, Chris," said the clerk.

He took up his hat once more, twirled it slowly round for a few moments, then put it on his head, and, without saying a word to any one, hurried out of the office and across the courtyard.

She was standing at her open window opposite, with her forehead leaning against the dingy framework of the panes, and I watched her start and tremble as she saw him.

"If I'm to take these accounts into the Market-place, I'd better take them now, hadn't I, sir?" I asked of the senior clerk.

"You may as well."

There was a back way through some narrow courts and squares which led from the dock-side to the High Street, in which the house Tyndale and Tyndale banked with was situated. I was hurrying off this way, when I stopped and changed my mind.

"He'll go the back way," I thought; "I'll cut across the Market-place by the most public road."

In five minutes I was in the High Street. Opposite the bank there was a little tobacconist's, at which our clerks were accustomed to buy their pennyworths of snuff. I strolled in, and asked the girl to fill my box. I was quite an old man in most of my ways, and snuff-taking was a confirmed habit with me.

As she weighed the snuff, I stood looking through the low window at the great doors of the bank opposite.

One of the doors swung back upon its hinges. An old man, a stranger to me, came out.

Three minutes more.

"I am waiting for a friend," I said to the girl at the counter.

Two minutes more the doors opened again. I was right, and I was not surprised. Christopher Weldon came out of the bank, and walked quickly down the street.

It was too dark for me to see his face; but I knew the tall, slender figure and the dashing walk.

"I am not surprised; I am only glad," I said.

During my long service in the house of Tyndale and Tyndale, I had lived so hard as to have been able to save money from my scanty earnings. I had scraped together, from year to year, the sum of forty-eight pounds fifteen shillings.

"I will save a hundred," I had said, "and then I will ask her to marry me."

But the only dream of my life was forever broken, and my little hoard was useless to me now.

Useless to purchase love, perhaps, but it might yet bring me revenge.

I put every farthing I possessed into my pocket the next morning, and the first time I could find an excuse for going out, hurried down to the bank.

"One of our clerks presented a cheque here, yesterday," I said.

The man looked up with an expression of surprise.

"Yes, certainly. There was a cheque cashed yesterday. Your handsome, fair-haired junior brought it."

"Will you let me look at it?"

"Well, upon my word, it's rather a strange—"

"Request. Perhaps. On the part of Messrs. Tyndale and Tyndale, I—"

"Oh, he said, "if you are commissioned by the firm to—"

"Never mind," I said, "whether I am or not. As you think my request a strange one, I'll put it in another way. Will you be so good as to look at the cheque yourself?"

"Yes, certainly. Here it is," he added, selecting a paper from a drawer; "a cheque for forty. Payable to bearer."

"Look at the signature of the firm."

"Well, it's right enough, I think. I ought to know the signature pretty well."

"Look at the 'y' in 'Tyndale.'"

He scrutinized the signature more closely, and lifted his eyebrows with a strange, perplexed expression.

"It's rather stiff, isn't it?" I said. "Not quite old Tyndale's flowing calligraphy. Very near it, you know, and a very creditable imitation; but not quite the real thing?"

"It's a forgery!" he said.

"It is."

"How did you come to know of it?"

"Never mind that," I answered. "Mr. Simmonds, have you any sons?"

"Three."

"One about the age of Christopher Weldon, perhaps?"

"One pretty nearly his age."

"Then you'll help me to save this young man, wont you?"

"How is it to be done?"

"Cancel the cheque, and replace the money."

"My good young man, who's to find the money?"

I drew a little canvas bag out of my pocket, and turned out a heap of one-pound notes and spade guineas upon the clerk's desk.

"Here's the exact sum," I said, "forty pounds, ready money, for the slip of paper Christopher Weldon presented here at ten minutes to four yesterday evening."

"But who finds this money?"

"I do. Christopher Weldon and I have been fellow-clerks for four months and upwards. I have seen his mother. I know how much she loves her handsome, fair-haired, only son. I know a girl who loves him, and I don't mind forty pounds out of my savings to keep this matter a secret. Mr. Simmonds, for the sake of your own sons, let me have that slip of paper, and cancel the cheque."

The old man caught my hand in his, and shook it heartily.

"Young Lowgood," he said, "there's not another lad in Willborough capable of such a generous action. If I were not a poor old fellow, with a hard fight of it to get a living,

I'd be twenty pounds in this transaction; but I respect and honor you."

I burst out laughing as he let go my hand and gave me the forged cheque in exchange for the forty pounds I counted out to him.

"Laugh away, laugh away," said the old man, "you've need to have a light heart, Samuel Lowgood, for you're a noble fellow."

In the back office there was a great chest which had been disused for some years. The clerks let me have it for my own use, and inside it I had a smaller iron clamped strong-box of my own, which I had bought of a broker on the quay. Into this strong-box I put the forged cheque.

Christopher Weldon's high spirits entirely deserted him. It was such pleasure to me to watch him slyly as I sat beside him, apparently occupied only by my work, that I was almost tempted to neglect my business.

No more "Beggar's Opera," no more "Polly," no more flute-playing in the dusk of the evening over at the gloomy old house.

"That lad Weldon is leaving off his giddy ways, and growing industrious," said the clerks; "he'll get on in the world, depend upon it."

"Let him—let him—let him," I thought, "let him grapple, let him mount the ladder, and when he reaches the highest round—then—then—"

In the following March there were some changes made in the office. Tyndale and Tyndale had a branch house of business in Thames Street, London, and into this house Christopher Weldon was drafted, with a salary nearly double that he had received in Willborough.

The change came about very suddenly. They wanted some one of gentlemanly appearance and polished manners in the London office, and Weldon, they said, was the very man.

I hadn't spoken to Lucy Malden for upwards of two months; but I thought I would go and tell her this piece of news.

"I shall find out whether she really loves him," I thought.

She sat at her old place at the window, in the cold, spring twilight, when I followed her father into the house and bade her good-evening.

She was not paler, for she had always been pale; nor graver than usual, for she was always grave; but, in spite of this, I saw that she had suffered.

My presence had no more effect upon her than if I had been nothing more sentient than the clumsy, high-backed, oak chair, upon which I leaned as I stood talking to her.

She looked at me when I spoke, answered me sweetly and gently, and then looked down again at her tedious work.

I knew that I had come, coward as I was, to stab this generous and innocent heart, but I could not resist the fiendish temptation.

"So our pretty fair-haired boy is going to leave us," I said, by and by.

She knew whom I meant, and I saw the stiff embroidery shiver in her hand.

"Christopher?" she faltered.

"Young Mr. Weldon," I said. "Yes, the gentleman clerk. He's going away, never to come back here, I dare say. He's going into the London house to make his fortune."

She made no answer, nor did she ask me a single question. She sat, going on with her work, sorting the gay-colored silks, straining out her eyes in the dusky light over the difficult pattern; but I saw—I saw how deeply I had struck into this poor, pitiful, broken heart, and I knew now how much she had loved him.

Ten years from that day, I stood in the same room—she working at the same window—and asked her to be my wife.

"I do not ask," I said, "for the love which you gave to another, ten years ago. I do not ask for the beauty which those who speak to me of you, say is faded out of your mournful face. You will always be to me the most beautiful of women; and your gentle tolerance will be dearer to me than the most passionate love of another. Lucy Malden, will you marry me?"

She started up, letting her work fall out of her lap, and turning her face towards the window, she burst into a tempest of sobs.

I had never seen her cry before.

At last she turned to me, with her face all drowned in tears, and said,—

"Samuel Lowgood, ten years ago, day after day, and night after night, I waited for another to say the words which have just been said by you. I had every right to expect he should say them. He never did—he never did. Forgive me—forgive me—if it seems to break my heart afresh to hear them spoken by another!"

"He is a prosperous man, in London," I said; "Lucy Malden, will you be my wife?"

She dried her tears; and, coming slowly to me, put her little, cold hand into mine.

"Does that mean yes?" I asked.

She only bent her head in answer.

"God bless you! and good-night."

* * * * *

A year and a half after our marriage, we heard great news in the old Willborough house. Christopher Weldon had married a nobleman's daughter, and was about to become a partner in the house of Tyndale and Tyndale.

A night or two after we heard this news, there came a great rattling knock at the grim dragon's-head knocker of the house door. My wife and I lived in her old apartments, by permission of the firm, for I had advanced to be head clerk in the Willborough office.

I was sitting, going over some accounts that I had not been able to finish in the day; so she looked up at the sound of the knocking, and said,—

"I'll answer the door, Samuel—you're tired."

She was a good and gentle wife to me, from the first to the last.

Presently I started from my desk, and rushed down the stairs. I had heard a voice that I knew in the hall below.

My wife was lying on the cold stone flags, and Christopher Weldon bending over her.

"Poor little thing!" he said. "She has fainted."

"This decides me—this decides me!" I thought; "I'll have my forty pounds' worth before long."

Christopher Weldon had come down to the house to announce to us, its custodians, that he was about to occupy it, with his wife, the Lady Belinda Weldon.

He brought a regiment of London upholsterers the next day, and set them to work tearing the gloomy old rooms to pieces. My lady came too, in her gilded chair, and gave orders for a blue room here, and a pink room there; cream-colored panelling and gilt mouldings in this drawing-room—pale green and silver in the other; and a prim housekeeper came, after her ladyship's departure, to inform my wife that we must be prepared to leave the house in a week. In a week the place was transformed; and at the end of the week, Christopher Weldon was to give a great dinner party, at which Messrs. Tyndale and Tyndale were to be present, to inaugurate his entering into partnership with them. As senior clerk, I was honored by an invitation.

My enemy had mounted to the highest round of the ladder. Rich, beloved, honored, the husband of a lovely and haughty lady, partner in the great and wealthy house which he had entered as a junior clerk—what more could fortune bestow upon him?

My time had come—the time at which it was worth my while to crush him.

"I will wait till the dinner is over, and the toasts have been drunk, and all the fine speeches have been made; and when Tyndale senior has proposed the health of the new partner, in a speech full of eulogy, I will hand him the forged cheque across the dinner table."

The night before the dinner party, I was in such a fever of excitement, that I tried in vain to sleep. I heard every hour strike on the little clock in our bedroom. Tyndale and Tyndale had given us a couple of empty offices on our being turned out of the great house, and enough of their old-fashioned furniture to fit them up very comfortably.

One — two — three — four — five—there I lay, tossing about. The hours seemed endless; and I sometimes thought the clock in our room, and all the church clocks of Willborough, had stopped simultaneously.

At last, towards six o'clock, I dropped off into a feverish, troubled sleep, in which I dreamed of the forged cheque, which I still kept locked in the strong-box inside the great chest in the back office.

I dreamed that it was lost—that I went to the strong-box, and found the cheque gone. The horror of the thought woke me suddenly. The broad sunshine was streaming in at the window, and the church clocks were striking nine.

I had slept much later than usual. My wife had risen, and was seated in our little sitting-room, at her accustomed embroidery. She was always very quiet and subdued, and generally sat at work nearly all day long.

My first impulse on waking was to look

under my pillow for my watch, and a black ribbon, to which was attached the key of the strong-box. The key of the chest hung on a nail in the office, as nothing of any consequence was kept in that. My watch and the key were perfectly safe.

My mind was relieved; but I was in a fever of excitement all day. "I will not take the cheque out of its hiding-place till the last moment," I said; "not till the moment before I put on my hat to go to the dinner party."

My wife dressed me carefully in a grave snuff-colored suit, which I generally wore on Sundays; she plaited my ruffles, and arranged my lawn cravat with its lace ends. I looked an old man already, though I was little better than thirty-three years of age; and Christopher Weldon was handsomer than ever.

At four o'clock in the afternoon, the courtyard was all astir with sedan chairs and powdered footmen. My wife stood in the window, looking at the company alighting from their chairs at the great door opposite.

"You had better go, I think, Samuel," she said; "the Tyndales have just arrived. Ah! there is my Lady Belinda at the window. How handsome she is! How magnificent she is, in powder, and diamonds, and an amber satin sacque!"

"You've a better right to wear amber satin and diamonds than she," I said.

"I, Samuel!"

"Yes. Because you're the wife of an honest man. She is not."

I thought for love of him she would have fired up and contradicted me; but she only looked away and sighed.

"You will be late, Samuel," she said.

"I have something to fetch out of the back office, and then I shall be ready," I answered.

* * * * *

The fiend himself must be in the work. It was gone—gone, every trace of it. At first, in my blind and maddened fury, I blasphemed aloud. Afterwards, I fell on my knees over the open chest, and wept—wept bitter tears of rage and anguish. It was gone!

* * * * *

I had a brain fever after this, which confined me for nine weeks to my bed.

Christopher Weldon lived and died a prosperous and successful merchant—honored, courted, admired, and beloved.

My wife and I, childless and poor, used to sit at our windows in the dusk, and watch his children at play in the courtyard beneath us, and hear the innocent voices echoing through the great house opposite.

Thirteen years and five months after our wedding-day, Lucy died in my arms: her last words to me were these:—

"Samuel, I have done my best to do my duty, but life for me has never been very happy. Once only since our marriage have I deceived you. I saved you by that action, from doing a great wrong to a man who had never knowingly wronged you. One night, Samuel, you talked in your sleep, and I learned from your disjointed sentences the story of Christopher Weldon's crime. I learned, too, your purpose in possessing yourself of the only evidence of the forgery. I learned the place in which you kept that evidence; and, while you slept, I took the key from under your pillow, and opened the strong box. The cheque is here."

She took it from a little black silk bag which hung by a ribbon round her neck, and put it into my hand, "Samuel, husband, we have read the gospel together every Sunday evening through thirteen years. Will you use it now?"

"No, Lucy, no—angel—darling—no. You have saved him from disgrace—me from sin."

* * * * * *

Every clerk in the house of Tyndale and Tyndale attended my wife's funeral. Not only were the clerks present, but pale, mournful, and handsome, in his long black mourning cloak, Christopher Weldon stood amidst the circle round the grave.

As we left the churchyard he came up to me, and shook hands.

"Let us be better friends for the future, Samuel," he said.

"My wife, when she died, bade me give you this," I answered, as I put the forged cheque into his hand.

M. E. Braddon.

From The British Quarterly Review.

1. *Iceland: its Volcanoes, Geysers, and Glaciers.* By Charles S. Forbes, Commander R.N. London: John Murray. 1860.
2. *Northufari; or Rambles in Iceland.* By Pliny Miles. London: Longmans. 1854.
3. *Iceland; or the Journal of a Residence in that Island during the Years* 1814 *and* 1815. By Dr. Ebenezer Henderson. 2 vols. Edinburgh: Oliphant. 1818.
4. *Travels in Iceland.* By Sir George Stewart Mackenzie, Bart. New edition. Edinburgh: Chambers. 1842.
5. *Journal of a Tour in Iceland in the Summer of* 1809. By Sir William Jackson Hooker, F.L.S. 2 vols. London: Longmans. 1813.
6. *Visit to Iceland and the Scandinavian North.* By Madame Ida Pfeiffer. London: Ingram, Cooke, and Co. 1853.

THERE is an island on the borders of the Polar Circle where the Frost Giants and the Fire King are engaged in perpetual conflict. Which shall have the mastery is a question still unsolved, though centuries have been consumed in the strife. So equally matched are the rival powers, that neither of them can acquire any permanent ascendency. From its proximity to the North, we might expect that the furniture of this island would be of the wintriest description, and that its mountains would be covered with snow, its gorges filled with glaciers, and its streams congealed into "motionless torrents." But we find that some of its hills are smoking volcanoes, that others are fuming with sulphur, that many of its plains were recently flooded with molten lava, and that the soil is pierced in all directions with pools of boiling mud, and fountains of scalding water.

If St. Helena has been styled a volcanic cinder, Iceland may be called a great volcanic block. Its whole substance has been poured out of the earth's glowing entrails. There was a time when the sea hung over its site; but the bed of the ocean was ruptured, and a huge mass of matter forced its way upwards, spite of the enormous resistance it had to encounter, until its steaming head was lifted high above the waters. What a magnificent spectacle this must have been, had mortal eye existed to trace the grand acts of upheaval. In modern times we have known rocks rise from the womb of the deep, but who has ever witnessed any gigantic feats of parturition like those which gave birth to Iceland? In the year 1757 an islet, measuring a mile across, was thrown up about three miles from Pondicherry. In 1811, Sabrina was similarly formed in the neighborhood of St. Michael's (Azores), amidst terrible convulsions of land and ocean. Ferdinandea (or Graham's Island), near the Sicilian coast, Joanna Bogosslowa, in the sea of Kamtschatka, and several others, children of the submarine volcano, have also sprung up in the waters; but these have all been comparatively puny in their dimensions, and after a short sojourn at the surface, down they sunk into the depths from which they were so strangely protruded.

At what period the foundation-stone of Iceland was laid, and how many successive eruptions occurred before the whole forty thousand square miles were upreared, are matters which belong to the unrecorded past. But at no time could this vomit of the volcano be regarded as a tempting territory. Even at the present day not more than one-third of the island is available for agriculture, another third is fit only for the growth of heather, whilst the remaining portion is filled up with mountains, deserts, and lifeless tracts of lava. Looking at the interior, with its surface pimpled over with rugged hills and volcanic cones, its sandy solitudes where scarcely a blade of vegetation can be discovered, its horrible plains where the molten effusions of neighboring craters have congealed in the wildest forms, like a raging sea suddenly struck dumb, we should be disposed to say that, of all regions on the globe, this had been selected as the great battle-ground between Frost and Fire.

Now, that man should ever dream of settling in such an inhospitable place may well excite surprise. As a penal colony,—an insular gaol,—good. It is just the grimmer regions of the globe which ought to be set apart for the reception of rogues, instead of spoiling some of the fairer spots by copious importations of felonry. If the governments of Europe had been in want of a nice little convict isle, a cesspool for the overflowings of their scoundrelism, we fancy that Iceland might have struck them as an extremely eligible quarter for the purpose.

But its destiny has been more fortunate. On this forbidding soil men sprung up as if by magic, and, instead of contenting themselves with a shivering sort of civilization, they laid it out as a kind of literary garden, and stocked it with such flowers of fancy that it became almost as gay and verdant as an academic grove. Not that its first visitors were the most promising of personages. The discoverer of Iceland was a freebooter of the name of Nadoddr, one of those vikings who thought that plunder was a part of the duty of man, and that a descent upon an unprotected town was an honorable feat which would prove a sure passport to Valhalla. Sailing towards the Faroe Islands in the year 860, this marauder missed his mark, but came in sight of the land of Geysers, which, from its wintry look, he christened Snow Land. There being nothing to steal and nobody to slay, Nadoddr returned to richer seas, and four years afterwards was followed by a brother of the same craft, Gardar by name, who explored the whole coast, and repaid himself for his trouble by putting his door-plate (so to speak) upon the island —from thenceforth it was to be known as Gardar's-holm. Pirate the second was, however, speedily supplanted by pirate the third —Floki of the Ravens, as he was afterwards called; for, having taken three of these birds on board, he sent them out at different times to guide him on his course, and at length, reaching the isle, he gave it the title it has ever since carried, and spent ten years in investigating its shores. Was not this as rare an act of abstemiousness in a man who lived by picking and stealing, as it would be for an Algerine corsair to devote himself to a course of quiet geographical research?

It was clear, however, that Iceland was no place for men of buccaneering mould. Colonists of a higher quality speedily followed. Just about a thousand years ago certain Norwegians found themselves uncomfortable in their native country. Their king, Harold the Fair, had made himself so troublesome to his subjects by his tyranny and extortionate acts that many of them resolved to seek an asylum beyond the seas. Whither was the question? It was rumored that far away in the ocean there lay a peaceful little island where they might hope to escape the attentions of his troublesome majesty, and to live free, though self-banished. Under the leadership of a nobleman named Ingolf, but doubtless with heavy hearts, the exiles set sail in the year 874, and after a rambling voyage of seven or eight hundred miles, performed in slender skiffs, they reached what Arngrim Jonas, one of their chroniclers, styles "the Canaan of the North." A strange title to give to a country whose plains were scorched with fire, and whose mountain peaks were wrapped in snow. But an early visitor had told them in language worthy of a Scandinavian George Robins, that the streams were full of delicate fish, and that the very "plants dropped butter." Salmon and cod, indeed, they found in abundance, but the pastures which were to serve as natural dairies—the vegetables which were to churn them butter for the asking—were not to be discovered in any quarter of the island. Such, however, was the charm of independence, that the Norwegians flocked thither in troops, and at length his troublesome majesty Harold forbade any further emigration, being determined, like Louis XIV. on the revocation of the Edict of Nantes, that his discontented subjects should neither enjoy peace at home nor be permitted to seek it abroad.

It was in the year 874 (A.D.), then, that the history of Iceland commenced. "History, indeed," the reader will exclaim, "if such a functionary as a state annalist exists on that volcanic mound, will not his story be as brief as Canning's knife-grinder's, and his chapters as summary as Pontoppidan's on the snakes? What material could a Tacitus, a Gibbon, or an Alison find for his pen in a country which has had no kings with a host of vices to portray, and no warriors with a host of victories to record? What can a chronicler make of a region which even at the present hour has no fortresses to be taken by storm, and cannot boast of a single civilized park of artillery? A pretty place to think of having any history at all!"

Let us, however, overlook the presumption of the natives in this particular, and simply say, that for about half a century after Ingolf's settlement the colony subsisted under a species of patriarchal rule; but about the year 928 changes ensued, and the island was declared a republic. The new arrangements were admirable. Laws were carefully compiled; literature began to flourish; maritime discoveries (America included) were effected, and Christianity was established as the religion of the country. This was the golden age of Iceland. But, somehow or other, a golden age never lasts. In our weary world a lease of happiness, personal or political, never runs long. In the present case it was out in little more than three hundred years. Perhaps this might be a fair spell of national bliss, all things considered, but, at any rate, in the year 1261, King Hacon of Norway, who had frequently cast a longing eye upon the island, contrived to corrupt a number of its influential people, and to bribe them into a transfer of their allegiance. What wont men do to acquire a little gold or a little land? Verily, we believe there is scarcely an acre of enviable ground on the face of the globe which has not cost a soul or two at some period of its history. Handed over to Hacon in 1261, however, the island remained in the possession of the Norwegian sovereigns until 1380, when it was annexed to the crown of Denmark, and to the crown of Denmark it has ever since belonged.

But it is with the physical curiosities of the country, rather than with its history or its inhabitants, that we are now concerned. No sooner does an inquisitive traveller approach its shores than he feels an intense longing to visit its wonderful Geysers. Landing at Reykjavik, he finds himself in one of the funniest little capitals on the face of the globe. Iceland must of course have a metropolis. Why should it not, we should like to know? If it cannot exactly indulge in a London, Paris, or a Yeddo, there is no reason why it should not have a small chief town consisting mainly of two streets—with a small cathedral, capable of holding nearly one hundred and fifty persons—a small governor's palace, originally intended for a prison—a small house of Parliament, of ample calibre for nearly thirty senators—a small hotel, without either signboard or name; and, besides a few other public edifices, of a small number of private residences which look like warehouses; and of warehouses which look exceedingly like themselves. Nearly all these tenements are made of wood covered with tar, so that the capital of Iceland appears to be in deep mourning. Internally some of them are handsomely furnished, and Madame Pfeiffer discovered no less than six square piano fortes in the place, but she maliciously surmises that Liszt and Thalberg would never have recognized their own music when executed by Icelandic hands. Many of the houses possess small gardens, where small vegetables are cultivated; but the botany of the island is so wretched, that good turnips, according to Sir W. Hooker, are about the size of an apple; and the largest tree in the country, according to Mr. Miles, was one on the governor's premises, which did not exceed five feet in height. No monster gooseberries of course are ever produced (or rapturously reported), and it has been sarcastically affirmed that the gardens are kept clean simply because the weeds wont trouble themselves to grow. This small metropolis, too, has its small gayeties, for we hear of balls where the orchestra consisted of a violin, a rusty triangle, and a "half-rotten" drum; where ladies of fragile virtue appeared quite at home with the bishop of the island; where men walked about with tobacco-pipes in their mouths, and indulged in what Sir George Mackenzie politely terms the unrestrained evacuation of their saliva on the floor; and where waltzes were performed in such a funeral way that the spectator was reminded of soldiers stepping along to the music of the Dead March in Saul. Need we say further, that the population of Reykjavik scarcely exceeds that of many a British village—consisting as it does of about six hundred native residents, but increased by Danish traders and summer visitors from other parts of the country to about twelve hundred.

Having thus taken a hasty glance at the capital, let us start for those glorious steam-fountains which, were they transferred to British ground, would be sufficient to turn the head of the best English county. In Iceland you cannot hire a cab, coach, cart, or other vehicle, for the simple reason that there are none to be had. Nor can you travel on foot, for that would be considered almost as foolish as to proceed on all fours. Your plan is to purchase horses—some for yourself, some for the guides, and others for the baggage. There being no Golden Lions or Royal Hotels in the country, it is advisable to carry a tent, and to look after the commissariat as narrowly as if you were about to traverse the Great Desert. Milk may be procured; but as you may have to proceed fifteen or twenty miles without seeing a cottage, the best policy is to victual the expedition at the outset, though it involves you in the expense of a complete caravan. The difficulties of travel, indeed, are great. The country is such, that neither General Wade nor Mr. Macadam could have tamed its rugged paths into easy turnpike. In some places the road is like the bed of a Highland watercourse, in others your route might as well run through a stone quarry. Too frequently, the traveller picks his way over a sheet of lava, stretching for miles, unrelieved by trees or vegetables, except a few sickly bushes, which have found a nest in some hollow where the wind has deposited a handful of soil. He finds that this lava is broken up into sharp blocks, or gashed with fissures which are so teasing that constant attention is required to prevent accidents. Or he may have to cross swamps and marshes, where the yielding nature of the ground is scarcely less trying to the temper; and if encumbered with much baggage, the beasts of burden need constant supervision as well as their apathetic guides.

Approaching Thingvalla, on his way to the Geysers, the visitor is startled by arriving at the edge of a precipice. A deep but narrow chasm, extending to a distance of more than a mile, suddenly yawns before him, as if the ground had been torn open by an earthquake. No warning is given him of its vicinity until he finds himself standing and shuddering upon the verge of the abyss. This is the famous ravine of Almannagiâ, which is justly considered to be one of the most remarkable spots in Iceland. Its depth is about one hundred and eighty feet, its width may be the same in some parts, but in others it diminishes to a few fathoms. How to cross it is the question for the traveller. Told he must descend to the bottom, and, somehow or other, contrive to reach the opposing bank, he shakes his head, and thinks it a feat for a goat but not for a man. There is no help for it, however. Dismount, and you will find a sort of natural staircase, which conducts you giddily to the bed of the rift.

"Colossal blocks of stone, threatening the unhappy wanderer with death and destruction, hang loosely, in the form of pyramids and of broken columns, from the lofty walls of lava which encircle the whole long ravine in the form of a gallery. Speechless, and in anxious suspense, we descend a part of this chasm, hardly daring to look up, much less to give utterance to a single sound, lest the vibration should bring down one of these avalanches of stone, to the terrific force of which the rocky fragments scattered around bear ample testimony. The distinctness with which echo repeats the softest sound and the lightest footfall, is truly wonderful. The appearance presented by the horses, which are allowed to come down the ravine after their masters have descended, is most peculiar. One could fancy they were clinging to the wall of rock."

Not far from the village of Thingvalla, the vale of which is unrivalled in Iceland for its beauty, lies the most sacred spot in the whole country. This is the plain where the Althing, or General Parliament, held its annual sittings for nearly nine centuries. Here national affairs were discussed, public justice was administered, strangers met from all parts of the island, friendships were formed, marriages were contracted, quarrels were settled or originated, females convicted of child-murder were drowned in a neighboring pool, and culprits sentenced to be decapitated lost their heads on a little isle in the midst of the river. But in 1800 the Althing was abolished, or rather transferred to Reykjavik, and now this venerated seat of law consists of "a mere farm, and contains two huts and a very small church."

Two or three days are occupied in your jaunt to the Geysers. The scenery is singularly diversified, for there are charming meadows, and pleasant shrubberies, and beautiful lakes on the route, as well as frightful fissures and rugged tracts of lava.

At last, turning the flank of a mountain, you observe big clouds of steam curling into the air at a distance of about three miles; and if your pulse breaks into a transient gallop, how can you help it when told that you are now within sight of one of the greatest wonders of the world? Scampering across bog and stream, you arrive at the foot of a hill about three hundred feet in height, and find yourself amongst a colony of boiling springs and vapor fountains. Upwards of one hundred of these are collected within a space of little more than fifty acres. There is no difficulty in recognizing the chieftain of the group. Upon a mound seven feet in height there rests a basin which at first appears to be tolerably circular, its diameter being fifty-six feet in one direction and forty-six in another. The interior, from three to four feet in depth, is smooth and polished, and at the moment of your approach may be partially filled with water in a highly heated condition. Through the clear crystalline fluid a funnel in the centre of this gigantic saucer may be perceived. Its breadth at the top has been variously estimated at from eight to sixteen feet, but as it descends it narrows its bore, and when sounded—your time for this ticklish operation being just after an explosion—the pipe may be traced to a depth of sixty-three feet.

It may be necessary, however, to wait some time before the Gusher or Rager—that is the meaning of the word Geyser—will do you the honor to play. His movements are very fitful, and twenty or thirty hours frequently pass, nay as many as three days have been known to expire, without any hearty and emphatic eruption. Upon the curious traveller this interval of suspense has quite an exciting effect. When Sir George Mackenzie lay down for the night he could not sleep for more than a minute or two at a time, his anxiety compelling him to raise his head repeatedly to listen, and when the joyful notice was given, up he started with a shout, and bounded across the space which separated him from the Geyser. And what a spectacle it is when the explosion *does* commence! With a roar and a rush which are deafening—the earth trembling beneath you as if it were about to open and give birth to some strange monster—the boiling water is driven aloft in a huge column, which breaks into different ramifications, and then drooping as its impetus is lost, each separate jet falls back in graceful curves to the ground. At the lower part the ascending stream may appear to some eyes to be blue or green, but at the summit it is torn into the finest, snowiest spray. Volumes of steam accompany the discharge, and roll away in great clouds, which add to the sombreness and majesty of the scene. After raging thus grandly for a few minutes, the Geyser relaxes his fury, and then ceases to eject either water or vapor. The fluid in the basin rushes down the well in the centre, and slowly but surely this magnificent hydraulic machine begins to prepare for another eruption. Very different heights have been assigned to the jets. Olafson and Paulson, for example, estimated them at three hundred and sixty feet. Lieutenant Ohlsen took the measure of one by the quadrant, and found it two hundred and twelve feet; whilst Henderson saw some which he computed at one hundred and fifty feet; but other travellers have cut them down to one hundred feet at the utmost, and Forbes averages them at seventy or eighty.

So much for the Great Geyser. About one hundred and thirty or one hundred and forty yards to the south you will meet with, and might very possibly walk into, another of the principal fountains. This is the famous Strokr, or Churn, as that native name implies. Unlike the former, it has neither mound nor basin, and might easily be mistaken for an ordinary well, were it not for the furious bubbling of the water in its shaft. This shaft is about six feet in diameter, according to Forbes, with a depth of about forty-eight feet; but it is very irregular in its bore, and contracts considerably: it is also bent in its course, and therefore, as Mr. Miles suggests, resembles the Irishman's gun, which had the faculty of "shooting round a corner." The ejections of the Churn are more numerous than those of the Rager, occurring at least once or twice a day, and though its jets are less voluminous, they last for a longer period, and radiate in a still more tasteful manner.

Now Strokr possesses one interesting property. He can be made to discharge almost at pleasure; and not only so, but you may force him to extra activity, and extort an eruption of a much fiercer character than is his natural practice. The way to accomplish this is very simple. Collect a quantity of stones or sods, and shovel them into the pipe of the Geyser. Down they go, splashing into the fluid, which instantly ceases to boil, as if Strokr were astonished at your impudence. And well he may, for stones and sods are things he abominates to such a degree that, collecting all his strength, he soon vomits them forth, and hurries them aloft in a pillar of water, which sometimes appears to reach to twice the ordinary elevation. Henderson, who stumbled upon this discovery, states that some of the jets rose to a height of two hundred feet, and that fragments of stone were propelled to a still greater altitude, the column of water being succeeded by a column of steam, which lasted for nearly an hour. This experimentalist narrowly escaped punishment for his temerity; for, whilst examining the pipe, the insulted Spouter, boiling with rage, shot up into the air a hissing torrent, which swept within an inch or two of his tormentor's face. Need we be surprised if prankish visitors can hardly resist the temptation to tease the Geyser? Spite of the grandeur of the spectacle, you feel a strong propensity to laugh at the idea of rousing Strokr, and throwing him into a profound passion. Mr. Miles literally "made game" of the spring, and when the exasperated phenomenon sought to relieve himself, was quite delighted to see his waters—stained and blackened with the clods—rising wrathfully to a height of one hundred and thirty feet. Commander Forbes subjected poor Strokr to a still greater indignity, for he compelled the Geyser to cook his dinner. Having invited the neighboring curé and farmer to a meal, he packed up a piece of mutton in the body of a flannel shirt, and a ptarmigan in each sleeve, and then flung the garment into the Churn, which was previously primed with a quantity of turf. For some time Strokr took the transaction in such high dudgeon that he refused to eject; but finding that preparations were making for another dose of sods, he launched his waters into the air with unwonted fury, and the traveller soon beheld his shirt flying upwards, "with the arms extended like a head and tailless trunk." On its descent to the ground it proved to be in such a scalding state that it was necessary to wait a quarter of an hour before dinner could be served, and then it appeared that though the mutton was done to a nicety, the birds were torn to shreds. The Churn, in fact, was a sort of Papin's digester, where the very twigs of turf received such a soaking of caloric that they came out in a sodden condition. A drunken man once fell into the spring—so the legend runs—and after seething for a short time, was thrown up in a spray of human fragments.

Still further to the south—about one hundred and six yards from the Strokr—you arrive at the Little Geyser. It has a shallow basin like its big brother, but its pipe, thirty-eight feet in depth, is any thing but uniform in its shape. In the days of Mackenzie this fountain was not accustomed to cast up its contents to a greater altitude than four or five feet, but it made amends for its poverty of flight by spouting for an hour without intermission. When visited by Henderson the little fellow had raised his leaps to ten or twenty feet, and went through his gymnastics about twelve times in the course of the day. Mr. Miles (in 1852) found that he had shortened the intervals between his performances, and was then in the habit of exhibiting every half-hour, though the spectacle was limited to five minutes at a time, and the column did not exceed eight or ten feet in height.

These are the principal springs at Haukadal, but the ground is pierced in all directions, and puffs of steam, jets of water, and pools of seething fluid tell the visitor that he is standing on a great caldron, the crust of which might be torn to fragments in a moment, were the riotous vapors denied the means of escape. He feels that hundreds of safety-valves are at work around him, and naturally wonders whether Iceland would not burst like a boiler if these should happen to be clogged or destroyed.

The larger fountains generally give notice of their intention to play. This is only reasonable, for otherwise a curious traveller, venturing too near the basin, might be drenched with scalding water by a sudden eruption; or, worse still, whilst peering down a tube, might receive the jet in his face, and recoil parboiled at a blow. The New Geyser, however, declines to give any intimation of his movements, and therefore, as Sir George Mackenzie remarks, it is necessary to deal cautiously with him, unless assured from a recent outbreak that his hour is not yet come. The notice served upon the public, in cases where due warning is given, consists of a series of detonations, which break on the ear like the report of distant artillery. The Head Geyser makes the ground quiver under your feet, as if an infant earthquake were gambolling below. Gun after gun is thus fired at varying intervals, as much as to say that a grand performance is just about to commence, and then the water begins to bubble in the pipe or to heave in the basin. Very frequently, however, the visitor, who rushes up, panting and agitated, on hearing the subterranean signals, is doomed to disappointment, for, after rising a few feet in a column, the liquid retires into the well, and leaves the spectator to ascertain (if the point is not already settled) whether patience is one of the virtues he really enjoys.

In the other respects, too, as well as in the hours of display, these thermal fountains are somewhat capricious in their proceedings. The quantity of water ejected, the height to which it is propelled, the mode of evacuation adopted, differ according to circumstances which cannot be accurately explained. The Geysers, in fact, are rather whimmy phenomena. Gradual changes must necessarily ensue from the violent wear and tear to which they are exposed, as well as from the deposit of siliceous matter, and since earthquakes are incidents of common occurrence in Iceland, it is natural to suppose that their underground mechanism will frequently be disordered. Prior to 1789, there existed a lively rattling fountain, known as the Roaring Geyser, which flung out its contents every four or five minutes with unspeakable fury; but several shocks being experienced in that year, the Roarer was disabled, and in course of time subsided into a mild, tranquil pool, from which no noisy jet ever presumes to ascend. Sometimes, too, a concussion will open out new vents, as was the case in 1785, when thirty-five fresh springs were established at Haukadal, and the three leading performers began to play with augmented energy.

But how shall we account for the action of these intermittent fountains? Formerly it was supposed that steam was produced in certain subterranean cavities, and that it accumulated there until it became sufficiently powerful to expel all the liquid in the tube, and in the reservoir with which it was connected. But this theory, which might have suited a Geyser of regular habits, and with a certain amount of suavity in its manners, would not account for the spasmodic proceedings so frequently observed in the tribe. The underground boilers were therefore abandoned. Professor Bunsen in Germany, and Professor Tyndall in England, have advocated a more probable solution. Under ordinary circumstances, water flies off in steam at 212° F., because its elastic force is then sufficient to overcome the weight of the atmosphere. But let the pressure upon it be increased, and its passage into the gaseous state is proportionately resisted—in fact, if a quantity of liquid were enclosed in a vessel of adequate strength, it might be heated, under compulsion of its own steam, until it became red-hot. The moment, however, that the fluid is freed from this pressure, it will burst into vapor, and as steam occupies seventeen hundred times the space required by water, it will explode with a degree of violence exactly corresponding to the unnatural constraint it has endured—the same law prevailing in mechanics or pneumatics which obtains in morals and politics. Now, remembering that a Geyser is furnished with a long shaft which gradually fills with water, and that the pressure on the fluid at the bottom of this tube must therefore become very considerable, we have only to suppose that a large amount of heat is brought to bear upon the lower portion of the pipe, when the following consequences may be expected to ensue. A quantity of liquid will receive a much higher charge of caloric than it ought to carry. Some of this liquid, rising in the shaft, must flash into steam when it reaches a point where the pressure is sufficiently relaxed, and hence the excitement in the basin, and the abortive eruptions which so frequently tantalize the traveller. But when, in consequence of the increase of the temperature—the tube being now full—the fluid below can no longer restrain its gaseous propensities, it explodes violently, and drives the superincumbent water before it with resistless impetuosity. And as the declining pressure releases more liquid from its bondage, jet after jet is produced until the apparatus is emptied for the time, or until the falling floods are so cooled in their rush through the air that they check the further development of vapor for the time. The Geyser, in fact, is a species of steam-cannon, which fires round after round of liquid missiles, just as Mr. Perkins' steam-gun did leaden pellets. "Der Geyser [says Cotta] gleicht dann also einer grossen Dampf-Kanone welche statt mit Kugeln mit Wasser schiesst." Professor Müller, of Freiburg, contrived a little instrument which may serve as an artificial "Rager." Procure a metallic tube at least six feet in height, and surround it at the foot, and again at some little distance up the shaft, with wire cages capable of holding burning charcoal. The lowest cage should be the largest. Then fill the tube with water, light your fires, and in due time you will have a pretty little eruption from your miniature "Gusher." A basin attached to the top of the instrument to receive the liquid and return it to the pipe, will ensure a succession of discharges, and save you the trouble of a voyage to Iceland. So a cork lightly fastened into the mouth of the tube, and afterwards blown out by the steam, will qualify you to talk of Strokr as if you had dosed him with sods and stones in person.

All modern accounts seem to agree that the reputation of these fountains has not been overrated. Travellers of every temperament are astonished at the giant gambols of the Geysers,* and some resign themselves at once to literary despair, as if conscious that no language, however vivid, could adequately represent the magnificence of the scene. Even Mr. Pliny Miles declares that the first view of the Great Gusher excited him so much, although then in a quiescent state, that he shall never forget its appearance "whilst memory holds her seat," and that when in action, the spectacle was such as no words can describe, adding, that it even surpassed the Falls of Niagara in grandeur. But, alas! speedily relapsing into the dollar state of mind which is so characteristic of some Americans, he begins to speculate upon the uses to which all this native steam-power might be put, and wishes that Barnum "could collect the Mammoth Cave of Kentucky, the Niagara Falls, the Natural Bridge of Virginia, Fingal's Cave, and the Icelandic fountains within one fence," and "fury! what a show-shop he would open!"

Upon one race of people, however, the Geysers seem to make little impression. These are the natives themselves. Few of the inhabitants ever visit the spot, and those who live in the vicinity treat them with a *nonchalance* which is quite disgusting. Reversing the well-known Millerism, the miserable creatures refuse to exhibit any feeling because they *do* belong to the parish of the phenomenon. The Great Geyser is no hero to his Icelanders. He has not even a staff of showmen, a troop of parasites, to fatten upon his glories. It is singular, too, that all the early annalists of the island are silent on the subject, though the first historian of the north, Ari Frodi, was educated almost within reach of their spray (1075). The most ancient notice of them is supposed to be that of Saxo-Grammaticus in his *History of Denmark*; but this is a mere curt recognition of their existence, such as an English topographer might vouchsafe to the hot springs at Bath, or the dropping well at Knaresborough. Great alterations will, of course, have occurred in the course of centuries; but as in Iceland the "pot" is always "kept boiling," spouting springs in different localities must have long been amongst the prominent marvels of the region.

In other parts of the island as well as Haukadal, boiling springs abound. In the valley of Reykum, or Reykir, about forty or fifty miles from the metropolis of the Geyser system,—*vallis fontibus fervidis abundans*—upwards of a hundred may easily be counted within a circumference of a mile and a half. Some of these are, of course, mere Lilliputian pools, but many are caldrons of considerable bulk, from which the traveller may at any moment receive a scalding shower-bath, the water being occasionally spirted up without the least notice of coming hostilities. One of the head fountains in this region, the Little Geyser, was accustomed to erupt nearly every minute in Sir John Stanley's time; but having grown weary of this feverish work, it now contents itself with a blow-up every three hours, or, according to Madame Pfeiffer, only twice or thrice in the day. Another, the Badstofa, plays every five or six minutes, the jets lasting for about a minute; but as they issue from beneath a shelving rock, they assume an oblique direction, like an arched fan, and produce a magnificent effect.

Again,—Iceland has its springs of mud as well as of water. The fluid which darts from the Geysers is generally limpid, and

* At the British Association (1865) Dr. Stevenson Macadam proposed to explain the operations of a Geyser on the principle that liquids, on encountering a highly heated surface, assume a spheroidal form, and afterwards blow up when the temperature reaches a certain level. But his theory required a double cavity in the ground, and a more complicated machinery than Bunsen's, which is at once simple and competent.

has frequently excited astonishment from the fact that it contains a large quantity of silica in solution. How such a refractory substance as flint could be dissolved, and then precipitated on the simple cooling of the liquid, was considered a kind of chemical puzzle. It is, however, well ascertained from the experiments of Dr. Fuchs, M. Kuhlman, and Mr. Ransome, on the production of water-glass, that if silica is fused with potash or soda, under certain circumstances, it will readily dissolve in boiling water, or if flint be exposed to the action of a strong solution of either alkali in a boiler, under high pressure, it foregoes its right to be regarded as the emblem of obduracy.

From Dr. Black's analysis of the water of the Great Geyser,* it will be seen that silica is the largest mineral ingredient, and that soda exists in abundance both in a free and a wedded condition. When, however, the fluid cools, the flinty matter is deposited in the basins and channels, where it forms incrustations which are generally compared to cauliflower-heads of exquisite beauty. Not only stones but twigs, grass, mosses, and other delicate objects receive such a coating that they appear to have been perfectly fossilized.

In some cases the fluid of these wells is still more singularly charged. What does the reader say to springs of soda-water? Such there are in various parts of the island, but one of the most celebrated is at a spot about two miles to the north of Roudemelr. The liquid there occupies two cavities in the ground, and is kept in a state of constant excitement by the bubbles of carbonic acid which are always ascending. Frisky and pungent, it is tolerably agreeable, and from the stimulant powers of the gas, the place is known as the Ol Kilda, or the Ale Well. How many a thirsty Englishman would be delighted to have a spring of this description, or, still better, a genuine well of Bass or Allsopp on his own premises!

Frequently, however, as already stated, mud is the only liquor in which a spring will deal. And some of these mud springs profess to a little business as Geysers. Very clumsily and uncouthly, without doubt; for how can we expect a thick pasty fluid to shoot aloft in graceful columns, or to fall in light, elegant spray? Near the sulphur banks of Krisuvik, for example, there is a pretentious spring of this description, which Mr. Miles describes as "an enormous kettle, ten feet across, sunk down into the earth, and filled within six feet of the top with hot boiling liquid. There it kept boiling and spouting, jets rising from its pudding-like surface ten and fifteen feet, and is kept constantly going." It was into a vile caldron like this that a horse once fell, and was never seen or heard of again. Still more striking are the mud springs in the neighborhood of Mount Krabla, in the northeastern corner of the island. Dr. Henderson suddenly came upon the brink of a precipice, where he perceived below him a row of large caldrons, twelve in number, which were splashing, fuming, and thundering in such a hideous manner that he stood for a quarter of an hour as if petrified. The boldest strokes of fiction, the strongest flights of imagination, could not, in his opinion, describe half the horrors of that fearful spot.

There are places, too, where pure steam is emitted instead of water or mud. Amongst other curiosities of this kind, near Krisuvik a torrent of vapor, twenty feet in length, gushes out of the rock in a slanting direction, with a roar which may be compared to that of some monster locomotive when retiring from the toils of the day. Seen by Mr. Miles in 1852, and collated with the description given by Sir G. Mackenzie in 1810, this jet did not appear to have changed its physiognomy in the least, though for two-and-forty years it had probably been playing without intermission. At Hveravellir (famous for its thermal springs) there is a circular mound about four feet in height, from which a current of steam "escapes with a noise louder than that of the most tremendous cataract," and with a force so great that stones thrown into the aperture are shot out to a considerable height, as if fired from a mortar. The natives call it with justice the Roaring Mount.

Scarcely less striking than the boiling springs are the sulphur mines of Iceland. There are places where you seem to have literally strayed into a region of fire and brimstone. The most celebrated of these spots is a mountain about two or three miles

* He found that a gallon contained 31.58 grains of silica, 5.56 of soda, 14.42 of muriate of soda, 8.57 of sulphate of soda, and 2.80 of alumina.

from Krisuvik. The ascent has its own troubles. Toiling up a slippery bank of clay and sulphur, almost stifled by the exhalations which the wind probably sweeps full in your face, you arrive at a great hollow, where the banks are covered with a fine yellow crust or powder. The ground is pierced with holes through which steam and smoke are constantly ascending. To walk over this treacherous surface is a task of considerable peril, for if the coating gives way, the traveller's feet may sink deep into the hot clay or scalding mud. Mr. Bright suffered much pain from an accident of this description, and Dr. Hooker plunged up to his knees in a half-liquid mass of sulphur and clay, and was only saved from further immersion by throwing himself upon the ground, and stretching out his arms over firmer soil. In the basin of this valley lies the great caldron already mentioned, which is filled with blue mud always on the boil, and always emitting a thick, noisome vapor. Hot springs and steam jets abound in the mountain. The place, indeed, is prolific in horrors. "What between the roaring of this caldron," says Commander Forbes, though not in the choicest language, "the hissing of the steam jets, the stink of the sulphur, the clouds of vapor, the luridness of the atmosphere, the wildness of the glen, and the heat of the soil increasing tangibly at every inch, I could not help occasionally glancing around to assure myself that his satanic majesty was not present, and nestled up to my companions to be ready in case of any such emergency as 'Pull devil, pull governor,' arising."

Extending over a space of twenty-five miles in length (to say nothing of the soufrières and solfaterras at Namufiall, Mount Krabla, and in other northern parts of the country), it will be seen that Iceland possesses in this region one treasure of very salable importance. Living as we do in a world where a mixture of saltpetre, charcoal, and brimstone is the grand specific for all political diseases (coupled with copious bleeding), sulphur must of course take high rank amongst the necessaries of human existence. Talk of dispensing with it altogether? Certainly not! How could we carry on the business of the globe for a single year without the help of Schwartz's potent and persuasive compound? Surely, then, there is no probability that our stock of these ingredients will ever run out? Many a good Briton, moved by patriotism and fine grandfatherly feeling, becomes quite uneasy when he asks himself whether our coal may not possibly be exhausted in the course of a few generations, and whether the day may not arrive in which no steam-engine can be kept in fuel except at a ruinous price. But imagine the horror of a man like the first Napoleon, or of any other owner of a fire-eating army, were he told that, in a few years, the supply of nitre or brimstone might wholly cease. What groans that individual would utter!—what wailing there would be amongst his troops! Would not the poor planet, in their opinion, become quite bankrupt in glory? With our rifles all unloaded, and our cannon virtually spiked, should we have any more history worth narrating? It is difficult to believe. But let no hero despair. The military mind would make itself quite comfortable on this point could it survey the vast deposits at Krisuvik, and observe how the precious exhalations stream from the ground, as if there were a boundless magazine beneath. There is enough brimstone at this spot alone to fight fifty thousand battles. Such, indeed, are the sulphurous resources of Iceland, that it could supply all the armies of Europe, and enable them to take every town in the world if they liked.

Now, considering the commercial value of this mineral, it is surprising that the mines have been so languidly worked. The difficulty of transport, and the want of enterprise on the part of the natives, may, indeed, explain *their* indifference; but the Danes, who know more of the merits of gunpowder, might have been expected to turn the substance to lucrative account. A French traveller, M. Robert, not long ago called the attention of his countrymen to the subject, and hinted that it would be well to keep these valuable localities out of the hands of the British, lest they should furnish us with one of the great munitions of war—"Aussi doit il bien se garder de jamais accorder aux Anglais, qui l'ont sollicitée, la faculté d'exploiter ces soufrières." But, alas for poor M. Robert, Commander Forbes informs us that an Englishman, Mr. Bushby, has already purchased the sulphurous sublimations of the southern district, and obtained the refusal of those in the north.

But, in speaking of Iceland, it is necessary to speak of Hekla. This mountain is the Hamlet of the island, and must, on no account, be omitted from any survey of its physical phenomena. On the ground of stature it can make no great pretensions, as it is only about 5,700 feet in height; and, in regard to personal appearance, travellers sometimes feel unable to conceal their vexation at its want of majesty. But its northern position, its volcanic vivacity, and the peculiarity of its eruptions, have combined to bring it into sinister repute. Planted at a distance of about thirty miles from the southern coast, it forms a hill twenty miles in circumference at the base, and is crowned with three blackened peaks, which are sometimes spotted, sometimes covered with snow.

To reach these is a task of difficulty. From Nœfreholt, the Chamouni of the mountain, to the summit, is about seven miles, of which nearly four may be performed on pony-back. At first, you canter very pleasantly through green patches of pasture; then, threading a narrow gorge, you enter a great, silent, secluded amphitheatre, which forms, according to tradition, a gateway to the regions of perdition; for it is beneath this volcano that Hela (Death) torments the spirits of the lost; and here, time after time (if the peasantry may be believed), she has been seen driving the souls of the dead, particularly after some bloody battle has been fought. Next, passing over a long slope of volcanic sand, you dismount from the ponies, which the Icelanders tie head to tail, so as to form a living circle, and then address yourself to the real hardships of the ascent. Sometimes scrambling over the hard, sharp lava, which cuts the hands or knees like a knife; sometimes trudging, ankle deep, through the fine black sand and loose ashes: sometimes struggling over the slag, which slips from beneath the foot at every step, you reach the crater, which was scooped out of the mountain during the eruptions of 1845–6. As seen by Mr. Miles, its aspect was worthy of the grim goddess who is reputed to haunt the volcano:—

"What a terrible chasm! Indeed, it seemed like hell itself,—fire and brimstone literally,—dark, curling smoke, yellow sulphur, and red cinders appearing on every side of it. The crater was funnel-shaped, about one hundred and fifty feet deep, and about the same distance across at the top. This was one of four craters where the fire burst out in 1845. After the eruption they had caved in, and remained as we now saw them. In a row above this one, extending towards the top of the mountain, were three other craters, all similar in appearance. Our progress now was one of great danger. At our left was the north side of the mountain; and for a long distance it was a perpendicular wall, dropping off more than a thousand feet below us. A large stone thrown over never sent back an echo. The craters were on our right, and between these and the precipice on our left we threaded a narrow ridge of sand not wider than a common foot-path. A more awful scene, or a more dangerous place, I hope never to be in. Had it not been for my long staff, I never could have proceeded. The dangers and terrors of the scene were greatly increased by the clouds and cold wind that came up on our left, and the smoke and sulphurous stench that rose from the craters on our right. One moment we were in danger of falling over the perpendicular side of the mountain on the one hand, and the next of being swallowed up in the burning crater on the other. Our path was exceedingly steep, and for nearly a quarter of a mile we pursued it with slow and cautious steps. Old Nero saw the danger, and set up a dismal howl. A few moments after he slipped, and was near falling into the fiery pit. In five minutes an animal or a man would have been baked to a cinder. Pursuing our way by the four craters, our path widened, and half an hour more brought us to the top of the mountain. Our purpose was accomplished—we stood on the summit of Mount Hekla."

The view from this elevation is undoubtedly one of the most remarkable on the face of the globe. Such a mixture of beauty and desolation is not, perhaps, to be witnessed from any other mountain-top. Painted before you, as in a colossal panorama, lie green valleys threaded by silvery streams—plains speckled with peaceful lakes—slopes covered with purple heather—snatches of dark-looking shrubbery which represent the forests of the land—to the south, the rippling ocean, from whose bosom the tall cliffs of the Westmann Isles rise perpendicularly to a height of two thousand feet; whilst to the north, the eye wanders over an expanse of volcanic cones, smoking craters, domes of ice, fields of snow, hideous tracts of lava, streams of stones which once flowed like rivers—in fact, over a region so withered and shattered that it looks the picture of a "chaos in creation." It is here, indeed, that the giants of frost and the spirits of fire seemed to have joined battle, and fought like the Berserkers of old, until exhausted by fury, they laid themselves down to rest for a season, their weapons still in hand, and wrath, inextinguishable wrath, yet raging in their hearts.

The eruptions of this volcano have been chronicled since 1004 (A.D.). Twenty-four black-letter years appear in its calendar. There have been intervals of seventy-four, seventy-six, and seventy-seven years between its paroxysms; but few Icelanders who attained the ordinary term of life could expect to do so without hearing more than once that the terrible mountain was in labor. In 1300 the annalists assert that Hekla was rent in its agony from top to bottom—yes, down to its very centre, they say; but the awful gash, now marked by a deep ravine, was partially healed by the collapse of the rock and the falling in of stony masses. During the convulsions of 1766, Sir Joseph Banks states that ashes were carried to a distance of one hundred and eighty miles, that the cattle in the neighborhood were either choked by the noisome vapors or starved for want of food, and that when the stomachs of some were opened, they were discovered to be full of volcanic dust.

Besides Hekla, however, there are many burning mountains in this island, and some of them have played a still more mischievous part. From Krabla a stream of molten rock was ejected between the years 1724 and 1730, and rushed into the lake Myvatn, where it killed the fish, dried up the waters, and continued to burn with a blue flame for several days. But there is no eruption so darkly renowned in Icelandic history as that of Skaptar Yökul in 1783. Skaptar is a mountain in the south-eastern quarter of the island, or rather, it is a part of a cluster of mountains which seem to lay their heads together to bear up a huge snowy field apparently inaccessible to human foot. From an account published by Chief-Justice Stephenson, who was sent by the Danish sovereign to hold an inquest, as it were, over the disaster (though his narrative has been charged with some exaggeration), it appears that throughout the syssel, or county in which this Yökul is situate, the ground was seized with shivering-fits on the 1st of June, which increased in intensity from day to day, and seemed to forebode some hideous convulsion. On the 8th, pillars of smoke were seen to shoot up amongst the hills, and speedily formed a great black bank in the air, from which sand and ashes fell so profusely, that at Sida the light was quite obscured, and the ground in the neighborhood covered to the depth of an inch. Terrible were the subterranean noises which were then heard. The sounds were like the thunder of meeting cataracts. The inhabitants left their houses in affright, and pitched their tents in the open fields. On the 10th, jets of fire were observed amongst the peaks to the north, and then a torrent of glowing lava burst from the volcano. Rushing in a south-east direction, it approached the river Skaptar, and dashed into its bed. Imagine the conflict which ensued between the two streams! The struggle was fearful, but, hissing in his death-throes, the river god at last succumbed. In less than four-and-twenty hours that rapid torrent, swollen as it was, had ceased to exist. Its place was taken by the fiery invader. The lava not only rapidly filled the gorge through which the river ran, though in some places the banks were nearly six hundred feet high and two hundred wide, but flooded the adjoining lands, and at Aa swallowed up pastures and houses with merciless voracity. Sweeping along the channel of the stream with awful impetuosity, the molten matter issued from amongst the hills, and seemed as if it would deluge the whole plain of Medalland.

Fortunately, a great lake, or, as some say, an unfathomed chasm in the river, lay across its path. Into this it poured with a horrible noise for several days in succession; but when this reservoir was filled to the brim, the burning flood resumed its progress, and dividing into various currents, burned up a number of farms and woods as it ran its mad but magnificent race. Now and then it spread over certain ancient lava tracts, and penetrating every fissure and cavern, produced the strangest effects; sometimes driving out the air through the chinks with a horrible whistle, sometimes melting and firing the old deposits, and not unfrequently blowing up the crust and hurling great masses of rock to a considerable height. Huge blocks of stone, torn from their site and heated till they became red-hot, were seen floating in the stream. The water which came down from the fountains of the Skaptar, and from the melting snows, was intercepted on reaching the lava, and, boiling, overflowed many pastures and woodlands which the molten deluge had spared. Besides the river, numerous brooks and streams were dammed up by the torrents of lava, and many farms and buildings were consequently submerged. At Skal the people had seen the fiery tide approach, and waited breathlessly to learn whether it would be necessary to flee. To their great relief it passed at a short distance; but on the 21st of June, the rivulets, which were distended by rain and denied their usual outlet, attacked the church and village, and next morning the steaming waters were surging with violence over the drowned hamlet. In its attempts to reach Skal the lava ascended the slope of the hill to some distance, rolling up its covering of moss as if it were a large piece of cloth folded by human hands. Numerous eruptions from the volcano between the 18th of June and the 13th of July fed the fire-streams with new material, and as the older effusions were now becoming stiffer and more consolidated, the fresher currents were seen rolling above them, until in some places the lava attained a thickness of six hundred feet. The Stapafoss waterfall on the Skaptar River was dried up; but the molten matter came down in its stead, and swept over the precipice in a splendid cataract of fire, filling up the enormous cavity at its base before it proceeded on its deadly way. At the commencement of August, the lava, which had now choked up the Skaptar River and swamped the neighboring grounds, struck off to the north-east, and poured into the Hversfliot—a stream almost equal in size and nearly parallel in course. Great was the consternation of the people who lived on its lower banks to see it begin to fume, to find it grow excessively hot, and then to observe it disappear altogether. What could they expect? They knew what had happened in the adjoining district, and gloomily awaited the appearance of the enemy. Down he came. Heralded by lightnings and thunders, signalled by pillars of fire and smoke in the distance, he dashed furiously along the bed of the river, streaming over its banks, and then, having reached the open country, spread his glowing waves across the plain to the distance of four miles within the space of a single evening. Continuing to flow until the end of August, the invader licked up some farms, drove the inhabitants from others, and spread devastation wherever he appeared. For several years afterwards the vapor still arose from particular spots, as if the fury of the intruder were even then unsatiated. It was not until February, 1784, after ejecting a prodigious quantity of lava from its entrails, greater, perhaps, than ever issued from volcano before, that the mountain returned to its ordinary condition.

The effects of this calamity were terrible. The atmosphere was so filled with smoke, sulphur, and dust, that it was difficult for the healthy, and for asthmatic persons almost impossible, to breathe. The heavy rains which fell became charged with noxious materials, and incrusted the fields with an inky coating which poisoned the grass and polluted the streams. Vegetables of all kinds withered, and became so friable that they fell to powder with a touch. The mortality which ensued amongst the cattle of the island, not only in consequence of the scarcity of fodder and the fouling of the herbage, but also from the putrid state of the atmosphere, was prodigious. In the course of 1783 and 1784, it is calculated that 129,947 sheep, 19,488 horses, and 6,801 horned cattle fell victims to that terrible volcano. The fish in some of the fresh-water lakes were destroyed, and cast up dead on the beach, whilst those at sea were driven from the coast. Certain birds, swans amongst the rest, were expelled from the country. To the inhabitants the results were equally disastrous. Many fearful distempers arose, and amongst these was one which produced swellings in the limbs and contractions in the sinews, so that the sufferers became crooked in person, the teeth grew loose, and the gums mortified; the throat was covered with ulcers, and sometimes the tongue rotted entirely out of the mouth. In this, or in other ways, not less than nine thousand persons are supposed to have been murdered by Skaptar Yökul.

But the mountains of the island sometimes pour out water as well as fire. Clothed as many of their summits are in snow and ice, vast glaciers occupying their ravines, it is evident that if the subterranean fires should grow unruly, the overlying masses will melt, and there will be a rush of water into the hapless plains beneath. The volcano of Kötlugia (to the south-east of Hekla) is famous for the floods it has discharged. On one occasion the deluge of water, bearing huge blocks of ice and stone on its foaming tide, swept away the houses of Höfdabreka, and carried the wooden church out to sea, where it was seen floating for some time before it fell to pieces. On another, all the inhabitants in the immediate vicinity except two were destroyed by a fearful inundation. The most appalling, however, of these eruptions occurred in 1755, the year of the great earthquake which overthrew Lisbon, shook a large portion of Europe, upset towns in Africa, and even propagated its throes to Asia and America. From the 17th of October to the 7th of November the Yökul was in a state of tremendous excitement, pouring forth streams of hot water, which hurried ice and rock before them into the ocean, where the deposit became so great that it extended to a distance of more than fifteen miles, and even rose above the waves in some places, though the sea was previously forty fathoms deep. Mixed with these vomits of water were vomits of fire. Red-hot globes were hurled to a great height, and then shattered into a thousand pieces. The air was occasionally so darkened with smoke and ashes that a man could not see his companion's face at the distance of a yard, whilst at other times it was so brilliantly illuminated by columns of flame that midnight appeared to be turned into midday. The ground frequently rocked, and the unearthly noises which proceeded from the Yökul appalled the stoutest hearts. Fifty farms were laid waste during these and the other eruptions which happened in the following year, and, to crown all, the mephitic gases diffused through the atmosphere brought on a frightful mortality which ought to have appeased the wrath of the mountain demon for centuries to come.

Occasionally, too, the Yökuls give rise to what may be called travelling fields of ice. These move slowly forward, encroaching in many cases upon lands which were once cultivated, and even devouring a parish now and then, as if to emulate the appetite of the volcano. Sometimes they retrogade at certain periods, and afterwards advance. The Southern Skeidará is said to move backwards and forwards alternately for the distance of half a mile, and in 1727, during an eruption in the neighborhood, it was seen to oscillate, whilst numerous streams suddenly started from its base, and placed the spectators in great jeopardy. The Breidamark Yökul, however, affords the most remarkable sample of an itinerant field. Twenty miles long, by fifteen broad, with a maximum height of about four hundred feet, it covers what was once a fair and fertile plain. How was it formed? Not like the glaciers of a Swiss or a Norwegian scene, for there there are no burning mountains or scalding-hot springs to produce great floods of melted snow and carry down big lumps of ice. But in Iceland this does happen, and it will be seen that the blocks which are thus discharged into the valley will accumulate, whilst further accessions from the same source will gradually add to the extent of the sheet, and then the slope of the ground, the constant pressure *à tergo*, the lubricating of the soil by the snow streams, combined with other causes, will probably explain why the mass glides so regularly, with its stealthy ghost-like step, towards the sea.

But as our space is diminishing faster than the soil over which that icy wanderer is creeping, we must now be content to note a few more points of interest connected with the island in mere descriptive shorthand. Iceland has its Surtshellir caverns, extending for upwards of a mile underground, with chambers where beautiful stalactites, formed by the once fluid lava, or still superber icicles formed by the dripping water, hang from the roofs in the most "curious and fantastic shapes;" and from this cavern, which few natives will dare to enter, the people believe that Surtur, the enemy of the gods, will one day issue to set the universe on fire. Iceland, too, has its huge lava bubbles, which were produced in the material whilst plastic by the expansion of the gases, and now constitute caves—some fifty or one hundred feet in diameter—where frozen and vitrified pendants adorn the domes as they do in the Halls of Surtur. It has horrible passes also, like that of Bulaudshöfdi, where the track runs along the face of a nearly perpendicular mountain one thousand feet above the sea which is roaring at its base, and the traveller seems to cling like a fly to the side of the cliff; or again, as at Ennit, he must creep along at the bottom of a frightful rock two thousand five hundred feet in height, but only at low water, and with the chance of being crushed in a moment by the fall of great stones from the side of the precipice, numbers of natives having already been killed in the perilous passage. Iceland, again, is peculiarly a land of earthquakes, and during the paroxysms mountains have been cleft to their foundations, boiling springs have spouted from the soil, the wells have become white as milk, men and cattle have been tossed into the air, the darkness has become so great that all travelling was impracticable, the quiverings of the ground grew so incessant that service in the churches was suspended for weeks together, and in 1784 not less than one thousand four hundred and fifty-nine houses were overturned, whilst five hundred and thirty more were greatly damaged. The inhabitants, too, are seized upon by various forms of disease. Owing to their fishy food, scanty supply of vegetables, want of cleanliness, and many local disadvantages, they suffer severely if any epidemic should be abroad.

In the year 1707, sixteen thousand individuals, more than one-quarter of the whole population, perished from the small-pox. In 1797, six hundred persons were sent to the grave by that infantile complaint, the measles. The natives are peculiarly liable to the itch, and keep up a terrible scratching, though there is sulphur enough in the island to cure the whole human race, if it were thus vilely afflicted. But the most horrible of their distempers is the Icelandic leprosy, which converts the sufferer, with his seamed countenance, scaly skin, ulcerated body, fetid breath, and haggard looks, into a living corpse, too loathsome for his fellow-creatures to approach, and almost too burdensome for himself to bear. The climate of the country is not so harsh as its latitude might imply, though the summer is short, and during the long winter a native rarely travels further than his parish church. For eight months Dr. Henderson never ventured more than a quarter of a mile out of the capital, except on one occasion, when he paid a visit to a neighboring seat. Fortunately, the rigors of an arctic position are moderated by the beneficent Gulf Stream, which breaks upon the island, and, dividing into two branches, leaves it a grateful legacy of warmth. It is in a northern locality especially that we can best appreciate the generosities of that noble ocean-river; for, as the polar currents bring down such a quantity of ice (with a few bears occasionally for passengers) that it has been known to form a belt thirty miles in breadth, and the whole space between Iceland and Greenland has even been filled with frozen masses; so, but for that stream of heated water, the atmosphere of the country would be sadly lowered in tone, and the sea would be so cooled that the fisheries, on which the natives depend for subsistence, might be destroyed. Nor is this great current less remarkable for the driftwood which it kindly conveys from other quarters and deposits on the Icelandic shores. Without it the inhabitants would be sorely distressed for fuel. Coal like ours they have none themselves. Beds of Surturbrand exist, but these have probably been formed of drifted timber. Forests in this country are such ridiculous affairs, that it is difficult to contemplate one with a serious countenance. The trees may be about four or five feet in height. Some may reach six; Mackenzie mentions a few which ranged from six to ten; but where will you find many which can overtop a very tall man? A traveller feels quite merry when he discovers that he can crash through, stride over, or even trample an extensive wood underfoot, as if he were a Gulliver in a corn-field, or an elephant in a shrubbery. A boy who has often smarted under the rod would feel perfectly enchanted when he saw that the troubler of his soul—the tree from which the disciplinary twigs are always gathered—was here stripped of its strength, deprived of its pungency, and tamed down from a goodly piece of timber to a poor dwarf of a vegetable. It is the absence of wood, indeed, which gives a particularly naked look to the country, as if it were all shaven and shorn, and consequently, in the highest degree forlorn. Iceland, further, is a land whose interior is so little explored that the people believe its deserts and glacier regions are occupied by a race of outlaws; and though no traces of these Utilegu-menn have been discovered, yet their existence is assumed from the fact that multitudes of sheep vanish from the high pasture grounds, coupled with the circumstance that sometimes wanderers who have ventured too far into the bowels of the country have never returned.

"Truly a wretched island!" many of us cosily situated Englishmen may be disposed to exclaim. It is a place where no corn is regularly produced, and in Madame Pfeiffer's time, only one bakehouse existed in the country. The natives live chiefly on cod, and their principal beverage is milk; so that, should the fisheries prove bad, or the hay season unfavorable, a famine is almost certain to ensue. Unable to raise sufficient supplies, even for the scanty population, a war which should cripple their commerce for a few months, or simply cut off their imports of fishing-hooks, would reduce them to a state of lamentable destitution. There, if a peasant is ill, and needs a medical man, he may have to seek him at a distance of fifty, eighty, or one hundred miles; and in winter it may be requisite to open a road, and pioneer for the doctor with shovels and pickaxes. If a man wishes to attend divine worship, he may have to ride many miles to a church, twenty or thirty feet in length, which is used as a lumber-house by the incumbent, and as an hotel by travellers, the latter spreading their beds on the floor, and sometimes taking their meals from the altar; and when service is performed, it will be by a well-educated clergyman, who considers himself passing rich on ten to two hundred florins a year, and who shoes horses or makes hay, whilst his lady milks cows and tends sheep.

But the Icelander will tell us that his country has some splendid negative advantages at the least. It has no forts, no soldiery, no policemen (worth mentioning), no custom-house officers, no income-tax gatherers, and happily for its peace (so the general public may say), no professional lawyers! Neither has it had a single executioner for some time past, for it is remarkable that no native could be found to undertake this odious duty; and consequently, it has been necessary to export malefactors to the mainland, in order that they might be despatched. He will tell us also,—such is the strong attachment which man naturally conceives for his native spot, however uncouth and ungenial—that, though his country is blistered with lava and blanched with snow, though its hills may be without verdure, and its valleys without corn, though its atmosphere reeks with sulphur, and its streams may flow from boiling fountains, though he walks on a nest of earthquakes and sleeps amongst a host of angry volcanoes, and though, to all appearance, his little island might at any moment be blown up into the air, or let down into the sea; yet, after all, in his opinion, Iceland is the very "best spot on which the sun shines."

"Still, even here, content can spread a charm,
Redress the clime, and all its rage disarm.
Though poor the peasant's hut, his feasts though small,
He sees his little lot, the lot of all;
Sees no contiguous palace rear its head,
To shame the meanness of his humble shed;
No costly lord the sumptuous banquet deal,
To make him loathe his poor and scanty meal;
But calm, and bred in ignorance and toil,
Each wish contracting, fits him to the soil."

Just one point more. At the present moment Iceland possesses an additional feature of interest—one which may possibly render it of great service to the New World as well as the Old. The difficulties of laying an electric cable across the Atlantic, and of working it with the requisite vigor when laid, have made it expedient to break the length of the journey by establishing several intermediate posts. By fixing upon three stepping-stones, as it were, the ocean may certainly be overleaped by the galvanic fluid without much sense of resistance. Of these Iceland must be one. We conclude by giving Commander Forbes' opinion on the subject, at the same time expressing our obligations to him for his lively and interesting work. It is sketchy in character, and scarcely fulfils the expectations which its title and appearance excite. Nor is the language at all eminent for its polish; but taking it as a sailor's narrative, purposely written with a free-and-easy pen, the reader will find much in its pages to entertain and instruct.

"The manifest advantages of a North Atlantic telegraph would be, that four electrical circuits would be obtained, none of greater length than six hundred miles; and as submarine telegraphs now working at greater lengths demonstrate the possibility of complete insulation and retardation up to that distance, whereas, when we get beyond the thousand miles, all is doubt and conjecture, to say nothing of the hazard attendant on the enterprise, and the advantage of having to relay a portion instead of the whole length of the line, in the event of a fracture, the superiority of this route cannot fail to command attention. The honor of originating the North Atlantic line belongs wholly to Colonel Shaffner, of the United States, who, in 1854, obtained a cession from the Danish government of exclusive telegraphic rights in the Faroes, Iceland, and Greenland. His proposed route is as follows: From Scotland to the Faroes, two hundred and fifty miles; from Faroes to Iceland, three hundred and fifty miles; from Iceland to Greenland, five hundred and fifty miles; from Greenland to coast of Labrador, six hundred miles. Now with regard to the objections that may be advanced against this line there are only two worthy of notice; namely, the icebergs of these northern coasts, and the submarine volcanic line of the south-western extreme of Iceland. The latter may be easily avoided by landing the cable on any of the many eligible spots between Portland and Cape Reykianœs, and thence carrying the line across country to any part of Faxe Fiord. All this portion of the coast is free from icebergs, and the shore-ice occasionally formed in the winter is inconsiderable; and besides, it has been already demonstrated in the Baltic and American lakes that shore-ice does not interfere with the workings of submarine lines. With regard to any local electrical difficulties to be surmounted, it must be remembered that, as far as our present knowledge goes, they are only conjectural; and when it is added that the bottom in these regions is, for the most part, composed of sand and mud, and nowhere of a greater depth than two thousand fathoms,* the only wonder is that this North-about route was not first adopted."

* The expedition since employed to sound this line found much less depth of water than had been anticipated.

Mudie's—A Literary Institution.—Owing to the high price of books in England, few but the rich can buy. The multitude have either not to read or to go to the circulating libraries, where they can obtain whatever books they desire, either by annual subscription, ranging from one guinea a year to five, or by paying about eight cents a volume, with permission to retain it for a couple of days. The guinea subscriber is allowed one set of books, new or old, at one time. The five-guinea subscriber is allowed fifteen volumes of the best and newest works, at one time. One Select Library (Mudie's in New Oxford Street), purchases over one hundred and eighty thousand volumes of new books per annum. This is wholesale dealing. A recent announcement tells us on what scale new books are purchased by Mr. Mudie. Thus: The Mill on the Floss, three thousand copies; Macaulay's History of England, Vol. V., twenty-five hundred copies; The Woman in White, two thousand; Motley's History of the Netherlands, fifteen hundred; Autobiography of Mrs. Delany, one thousand; Hook's Lives of the Archbishops of Canterbury, one thousand; Atkinson's Travels in Amoor, one thousand; Paul the Pope, by T. A. Trollope, one thousand copies. Considering that, hitherto, an edition of any new work, except in the case of very great previous popularity, rarely exceeds, and frequently is less than, a thousand copies, some idea of Mr. Mudie's patronage of literature may be formed.

At intervals, when the freshness of a work has vanished, Mr. Mudie reduces his stock. Out of three thousand copies of The Mill on the Floss, there are probably not more than three hundred volumes remaining for circulation. Other books are treated in the same way. When novelty is over, the surplus copies are sold to minor circulating libraries in town or country, or to private persons, at reduced prices.

Mr. Mudie, purchasing so largely, is allowed great privileges. For example, the retail price of Macaulay's new volume is *twelve* shillings sterling to the public. It is given to "The Trade" at *nine*; but Mr. Mudie does not pay more than *six* for each of twenty-five hundred volumes.

The circulating library—which, by the way, was invented by Allan Ramsay, the poet,—would scarcely "pay" in this country, where books are so cheap. It is the offspring of high prices, to which, we fear, an international copyright treaty would gradually but inevitably conduct us.—*Philadelphia Press.*

From The Press, 23 March.

ENGLAND REGAINING HER AMERICAN COLONIES.

The contingency which we are about to set before our readers is bold and startling in its aspect; but it is by no means impossible, or even improbable. It is neither more nor less than a return of the Northern States of the American Republic to British allegiance.

The more solid and thinking portion of the Northern citizens are weary of "sensations," "rowdyism," "platforms," hard and soft conchology, and "grit" of divers degrees of consistency. They must be sick of elections, passing like moral earthquakes through the land,—tired of the "success of the ticket,"—fatigued with committees, "Franklin propositions," Chicago "conventions," and "caucuses" of every kind. The excitement produced by brandy cocktails and mint juleps leads to corresponding periods of depression, or, if continually kept up, to early decay and premature dissolution. American elections cannot fail to disgust the sober part of the community. They combine the morals of a horse-race, the manners of a dog-fight, the passions of a tap-room, and the emotions of a gambling-house. A general election in England is a series of merely local convulsions, as different from a presidential election in America as ploughing the land for a new crop is from an earthquake or volcanic displacement of the soil. A political sleep like that of Rip Van Winkle would be a national boon to our fast-going cousins on the other side of the Atlantic.

Again, it is certain that Old World institutions have greatly gained ground in American estimation. It has long been observable that, away from home, there is no monarchist or feudalist more apt and eager than your thorough Yankee. Who so venerates traditions, localities, institutions, and antiquarianism? Who makes a pilgrimage to Shakspeare's house, gazes with reverence on the Woolsack, admires Queen Victoria as the best of women, shakes hands with the Lord Mayor as a privilege, and everywhere delights in a nobleman? The American citizen. In the States themselves is there no pride of birth and family? Are there not the blue blood of Virginia, the Dutch descent of New England, and other and numerous distinctions? Is not "honorable" a coveted title?—and does not a man who deals in pistols, or any other sort of dry goods, call himself colonel or general, and perchance, if in a sufficiently inland district, commodore or admiral?

The tranquil virtues of the ruling sovereign of the old country, and the late happy visit of the Prince of Wales to the United States, have both done much to recommend his ancestral institutions and traditions to Jonathan of late. He has had his unchecked Republican swing, and it must be owned that externally his political experiment has been a marvellous and unblotted success. Possibly this has only assisted in the development of his internal difficulties. War without often strengthens union within. Both secessionists and anti-secessionists have been beguiled by the greed born of leisure and prosperity. Had the Northern and Southern States been forced to rally against a common enemy, they would not have had time and opportunity to plot against each other's prosperity, and wager cotton against hardware,—each strangling their own goose in the endeavor to snatch the golden egg from the other.

The division of the North and South, or North-North-West and South, according to Wyld's map before us, will probably, if it finally take place, hasten one of two things. Either British North America may join the Northern Confederacy, or some of the States of the Northern Confederacy will unite with the British provinces. This is a startling enunciation, but not more startling than events already passing before our eyes. It remains with Great Britain to prevent the former and invite the latter. This can only be done by the speedy union and consolidation of our North American provinces. This is no new proposition; but, much as it has been ventilated by far-seeing men, the plan still remains to be carried out, and stands invitingly forward to arrest the attention, employ the energies, and illustrate the career of some leading statesman of the age.

It is an ill wind that blows nobody good; and it is manifest that the British provinces, and their ports, their navigation, and their transit, their trade and their development, will derive a great benefit and receive a great stimulus from the closing of United States' ports and the increase of United States' tariffs. The importance, so frequently dwelt on by us, of opening a direct railway communication between Halifax and Quebec through British territory now forces itself on public attention. Hitherto Liverpool and Cunard, Rowland Hill and his patrons and satellites, the *Times* and what is called the moneyed interest, have combined to give the preference to Boston and New York over our own cities and stations. We have paid £200,000 a year to have even our letters carried by a circuitous route to Canada on

American railroads. It is time that all this should end. Mr. Lever and the Galway Company made a great mistake when they abandoned or falsified their proposition to maintain British interests by a direct route viâ Galway to and through our own possessions. Amongst others, Sir Allan M'Nab, a stanch and sturdy colonist, was deceived by these representations into an early co-operation with the adventure. Greedy speculation, coupled with shortsighted policy, is not always certain even of an immediate return. Before the Galway line is in full play, or properly established, it will be a question of a change of route, of which the speculators were fully forewarned.

If, again, our supposition of the greatest and strongest Union that the world has ever seen, including the whole of the Lake territory, and all the continent of North America, from New Jersey, Arkansas, and California northward, under British sway—if all this be a dream, and an insult to free and enlightened citizens (which last emphatically we do not mean), then there remains a second most important consideration before us. In British North America, as it is, there are room and resources for the most magnificent empire in the world. In British North America there exists that of which the united and disunited States cannot boast—a patent highway of communication and traffic between the Atlantic and Pacific oceans. Upon this, and its vast importance, we shall not now expatiate further than to say that it does exist. In 1850 a bulky volume was published by Messrs. Richards and Wilson, in which not only was the late royal visit to America and its good effects prefigured, but the union of our North American provinces dwelt upon at considerable length. The climate, fertility, resources, and facilities of an interoceanic communication within the limits of British North America were entered upon in this volume, which American journalism attributed to the British government, which sent Asa Whitney to this country, and which caused three separate explorations to be made of United States' territory, with a view of anticipating British enterprise in extending a broad belt of commerce and dominion round half the globe. In this country the progress of the idea has been sure though not rapid. Truth on so vast a basis cannot fail to erect some edifice, be it palace or mausoleum, workshop or tomb.

If the union of British North America be now accomplished, thus much is at least certain,—that annexation to the Northern States of America will not take place. On the other hand, we have sufficiently prefigured the possibility of a far different issue. The annexation of the Old Country has long been a favorite topic among our free-spoken kinsmen. Surely, there can be no harm in reversing the situation, and in making every thing ready for them, should they at any time be disposed to annex themselves.

From The Economist, 16 March.

THE COMPARATIVE *MONEYED* POWER OF THE SLAVE STATES AND OF THE FREE.

The present state of America suggests many questions which before now no one ever dreamed of considering, and consequently gives many collections of statistics a significance and value which were not anticipated by those who amassed them. We are now constantly discussing the relative power of the Free States and the Slave States,—we are continually estimating what the relative force of each will be in time of war, and what its capacity for commerce in time of peace. The vagueness of such speculations makes any accurate and systematic data very valuable, and it fortunately happens that we have one nearly complete set of figures which are exactly fitted to aid our understandings. In whatever respect America is defective, it is not defective in banking statistics. The Democratic government of the United States has exacted from the banks throughout its territory a degree of minute information which no despotism can exceed, and which seems the maximum of inquisitorial tyranny to an English banker.

These statistics will now be of use to us. The moneyed wealth of a State is a reasonably approximate index both of its efficiency in war and its capacity in peace. And of its moneyed wealth the deposits in its banks are a fair comparative test. These deposits represent the floating capital which it is able to embark in any pursuit it pleases: they are the *sinews* which it can apply as well to the task of creation as to that of destruction. If a nation is poor in these accumulated resources, its efforts, whether military or pacific, will probably be weak. If a nation is rich in these, we may reasonably expect that its exertions will be effective and powerful abroad both in war and commerce. What, then, is the comparative strength of the Slave States and of the Free when estimated by this significant and searching test?

The aggregate deposits of the *whole* American Union are a little more than £57,000,000, and of this a very little more than one-fourth belongs to the Slave States. The enumeration is as follows:—*

	Deposits. £
Alabama	1,091,509
Delaware	219,650
Florida	29,141
Georgia	1,066,115
Kentucky	1,274,150
Louisiana	4,450.008
Maryland	1,996,690
Missouri	755,364
North Carolina	334,636
South Carolina	937,263
Tennessee	973,079
Virginia	1,739,172
	14,866,777
Kansas Territory	606
	14,867,383

All the remainder of the floating capital of America belongs to the Free States. The deposits in the banks of the latter are as follows:—

Connecticut	£1,254,352
Illinois	156,833
Indiana	382,607
Iowa	118,659
Maine	542,479
Massachusetts	6,256,056
Michigan	84,464
New Hampshire	267,297
New Jersey	1,291,829
New York	23,415,811
Ohio	908,912
Pennsylvania	5,887,764
Rhode Island	799,448
Vermont	177,262
Wisconsin	694,307
	42,238,080

Not a very magnificent list of "deposits" according to the notions of an English banker, but indicative of far greater wealth than those of the Slave States.

There are no returns from Arkansas, Mississippi, or Texas, where the banking system seems to be very rudimentary and imperfect. California likewise is not included.

Nor does this comparison, instructive though it is, give us by itself an adequate impression of the exact nature of the unequal rivalry which has at length arisen between the North and the South. The most expressive parallel is to contrast the great Free State of New York with the Slave State of South Carolina, which already anticipates that its capital (Charleston) will be the "New York of the South." The figures are these,—

	Deposits. £
New York	23,415,811
South Carolina	937,263

A very hopeless comparison for the novel and boastful aspirant.

We arrive at the same result if we compare the accommodation given to trade in the South and in the North. The loans and discounts of the four Free States which had lent the most were as follows:—

	Loans and Discount. £
New York	45,079,500
Massachusetts	24,168,897
Pennsylvania	11,323,610
Connecticut	6,267,776

And of the four Slave States which had lent the most:—

	Loans and Discount. £
Louisiana	7,965,361
South Carolina	6,255.430
Kentucky	5,689,036
Virginia	5,619,553

The accommodation given by the whole four not being nearly equal to that given by the single Free State of New York.

There are two very important reflections which these statistics will at once suggest at the present moment to the mind of every Englishman. The first is, that the portion of America which will be injuriously affected by the highly stringent provisions of the new protective tariff is far richer than the part which will not be so affected. Our wealthiest customers are in the Free States, and, with an absurd infatuation, those States are endeavoring to exclude the commodities they could best purchase from us, and are fostering a costly system of unhealthy protection within their own boundaries. It is not likely that they will be successful. It is not likely that the great grain-growing States of the interior will be content to be taxed for the exclusive benefit of the manufacturing and mining interest of their Eastern neighbors. It is not likely, as we have elsewhere observed, that they will be able to establish a line of custom-houses over a great tract of country where such an institution is unknown. Still, for a time the infatuated effort may have a pernicious effect, and we cannot fail to observe with regret that it will tend to impair our profitable intercourse with our richest Transatlantic neighbors.

The second remark is of a different kind. The poorness of the Southern States in loanable capital will tend to attract that capital

* These figures are made up according to the return received nearest to 1st of Jan. 1860, the last date up to which the whole of them have been made public.

from hence. Already has this happened to some extent, and "cotton bills" have even now been discounted in Lombard Street, which in former times would never, by any chance, have found their way there. We may expect this call for our capital will largely augment. Cotton will still be grown in the Southern States, probably for many years in enormous and augmenting quantities, and, as capital is scarce there, and the difficulty of getting it at the North must for some time be greater than it has been, we may confidently expect that it will be sought after here. This emigration of capital is natural and inevitable, and if it were not for the peculiar structure of society in the Southern States of America it would not be a subject for regret. It is natural and proper that the capital of old and accumulating countries should be transmitted to assist the industry of young and rising communities. Raw cotton is the most pressing requisite of our manufacturing industry, and wherever it is to be raised probably English capital must go to raise it. Such an interchange of benefits between new countries and old is a principal instrument of commercial civilization, and if we are wise we should rather seek for its increase than desire its diminution. But the present social and industrial system of the Southern States of America is too inseparably bound up with slavery to make it possible for us to rejoice at an increased connection with them. We do not mean that there is any reason for apprehending a slave outbreak in consequence of present events; indeed, we do not believe that an abrupt termination to American slavery is very likely to happen speedily from any cause. But with such a basis as slavery, every social system must be unstable and unsatisfactory; and it must be with regret that we contemplate the evident probabilities of a new tie between us and any industrial system resting upon an essentially false and dangerous foundation.

From The Press,* 6 April.

ENGLAND AND THE SOUTHERN CONFEDERACY.

The hour is at hand when a new power will take its place among the states of Christendom. The British government has just made a formal recognition of the kingdom of Italy, and already commissioners from another new state are on their way to claim a similar recognition of accomplished facts. The government of the new Southern Confederacy of America has despatched three commissioners to obtain from the leading states of Europe the recognition of their country as an independent power and to negotiate with them commercial treaties on the footing of reciprocity. These commissioners are now crossing the Atlantic, and in little more than a week they will arrive to commence their important mission at the court of St. James. A new minister at the British court has at the same time been appointed by the Cabinet of Washington, to represent the views of President Lincoln, and he will arrive almost simultaneously with the rival mission from Montgomery.

The Southern States are confident as to the success of their mission, and their confidence is well founded. The principle of the British government is to recognize every *de facto* government, and the government of the Southern Confederacy is as much an accomplished fact as is the kingdom of Italy. The Northern States—the old Union—may not recognize the new Confederacy, any more than Austria recognizes the kingdom of Italy; but they have made no attempt to resist its establishment, and if they do make such an attempt they will assuredly fail. Our government has no choice in this matter. We have no desire to see any undue haste in the recognition of the new power. Our government, out of courtesy to the Cabinet of Washington, may delay its answer for a few days, until it is fully apprised of the views and intentions of President Lincoln. But any longer delay than is absolutely necessary is most strongly to be deprecated. We need not say it would be unseemly that England, who so readily recognizes all governments, should be behind France in acknowledging a state of her own kindred. It is enough for us that the Cabinet at Montgomery is a *de facto* government, and accordingly entitled to be recognized by us as an independent power, with whom diplomatic relations have to be established and commercial treaties negotiated.

The recognition of the Southern Confederacy cannot be avoided, nor do we desire to avoid it. The regret of the English people at the rupture of the American Union was a feeling most honorable to them, and which testified, in a most striking manner, the attachment and good-will of the parent nation to its noble offspring beyond the Atlantic. The regret was genuine and universal, and yet the calamity to the Union which we deplored was evidently favorable to our own interests, both political and commercial. When his house is divided against itself, Brother Jonathan can no longer bully us, as with generous patience we have so often permitted him to do. And also, with the establishment of a Confederacy of purely agricultural States in the South, the restric-

* *The Press* is D'Israelite—Tory.

tive tariff of the old Union, and the still more restrictive one recently adopted, will no longer suffice to prevent the entry of our manufactures into the American continent. Free-trade pure and simple—free-trade of the most absolute kind is opened to us by the new Confederacy; not as a bait—though it is a powerful one—but because such a commercial system is of all others most in accordance with its own interests. Even our shipping interest will benefit largely by this change in the political organization of North America; for the Cabinet of Washington will find it hard to maintain any longer its preposterous assertion that the maritime traffic between New York and California is a portion of its "coasting-trade."

From The Economist, 16 March.

THE USE OF THE FRENCH DEBATES TO THE EMPEROR.

We do not think the debates either in the Senate or the *Corps Legislatif* can be quite pleasant to the emperor. To hear himself denounced as the enemy of the Church and the tool of England must be far from agreeable. To hear it said that he has lost all hold over the Italian movement and weakly permitted France to be entirely surrounded by kingdoms of the first order, cannot be agreeable to any Frenchman, least of all to a Napoleon. But we think there are several counterbalancing advantages which so shrewd a politician as the emperor will not be slow to discern. And these we will attempt to point out.

In the first place, then, it will do much to set him right with the other governments of Europe—to exonerate him from the charge of having stimulated a selfish and greedy spirit in the French people. It is only candid to admit that the more we hear of the true political aspirations of the French people, the more highly we appreciate the difficulties of the French government, and the more credit we are disposed to give it for the generally liberal course it has taken in Italian affairs. It would certainly seem, not only that the emperor was driven on by the public opinion of France in the annexation of Savoy and Nice, for that we knew before, but that it exerted a great pressure upon him to carry out a thoroughly French policy in Italy,—that it would have obliged him, if it could have done so, to force the Villafranca treaty on the people of Italy, to defeat the plans of Garibaldi, to take an active part in the defence of the King of Naples, and to maintain by French arms the temporal authority of the pope. All this, as we learn by the divisions and debates in the French Chambers, would have been a highly popular policy in France,—would have gained for the emperor the enthusiastic support of all the women and all the priests, and, in consequence, the active if not the enthusiastic support of a very considerable number of the men. We cannot deny, in the face of the strong opposition which has manifested itself in both Chambers, that the emperor has at least represented a policy of a more moderate, a more statesman-like, and a far more liberal cast, than that which would have gained him the greatest popularity at home. Nor is it difficult to imagine that in acting as he did about Savoy and Nice,—nay, even in breaking, as he did, his pledge to give Chablais and Faucigny to Switzerland, he might have been carried away by a selfish tide of public opinion which he thought too strong to resist. Certainly, from the three most discreditable features of the French Opposition,—the dread of a United Italy, the hatred of England, and the subserviency to the Papal See,—the emperor's policy has shown itself far more free than the opinions of the nation at large would appear to be. In foreign policy at least, there has been far less divergence between the actual diplomacy of the empire and the views of such men as M. Jules Favre, than between the recommendations of the latter and those of the party represented by M. Plichon, or M. Keller. If the debates, then, were of no other use to the emperor, they would at least do much to explain the difficulties under which he has labored in attempting to reconcile the wishes of France and Italy. We do not suppose that it was disagreeable to him to annex Savoy and Nice, nor that he was glad to see the terms of the Villafranca treaty cast to the winds,—but we do now know that if such *had* been his feelings, he could scarcely have dared to express them openly and without *finesse* in the present condition of French opinion. There is so large a mass of that opinion far more illiberal than that of the emperor's government, that the actual p licy of his government seems benignant and wise in the comparison. Already the fruits of this debate are telling on the English press, and papers that have been for years pleading for the stifled opinion of France against the tyranny of the empire, are now,—not certainly deploring the new freedom,—but devoting all their strength to defending the policy of the empire against the opinion of France. A French Opposition that openly declares for war with England, cannot but in some measure gain over English opinion to the side of the French government.

Another advantage resulting from this

new freedom of invective will be, that it must soon evoke an unofficial party in defence of the more liberal acts of the French Government within the nation as well as outside; and nothing, we know, would strengthen the imperial government so much as some really independent support. Previously the true Liberals were too anxious for a still more liberal policy in Italy, —were too anxious for a still closer co-operation with England, to appear as advocates of the French government,—and they were, moreover, too much disgusted with the restrictive interior policy of the emperor for such a step. But it is of the essence of a violent Opposition to condense the ranks of the supporters of government, and the French Liberals cannot help giving far warmer support to the foreign policy of the empire than they have ever been disposed to give to its policy before, in the face of such assaults. No doubt, too, this advocacy of its foreign policy will to a certain extent induce the government to concede something to the same party in domestic policy, so that little by little the emperor may gain a band of really independent supporters, if the Papal and anti-English party are foolish enough to persevere in their invectives.

Again, it will be, we think, a very great advantage to the ministerial officials of the empire that they should be obliged to plead the cause of the government before a vehement French Opposition. Hitherto no cabinet in Europe has been more contemptible than the so-called French cabinet, which was indeed a mere staff of secretares. Often perhaps they have had no views of their own. Sometimes their views have been known to be at issue with those of their master. They have regarded themselves, and consequently have been regarded, as the mere tools of his will. This can scarcely remain the same,—or at least can scarcely remain so much so as before,— if once the ministers acquire the habit of identifying themselves with the government in an assembly where free discussion is permitted. The result is, and must be, to imbue them far more thoroughly with the policy they defend, than any of their purely official duties can be conceived to do. In the warmth of such argument a certain amount of genuine conviction is generated, even where it did not exist before,—and we are sure that the debates in the French Chambers will result in giving Louis Napoleon a better and more coherent-minded cabinet, if he choose to use it, than he ever had before.

MARY QUEEN OF SCOTS, HAD SHE A DAUGHTER?—By a strange coincidence I had just been reading Mr. Reid's curious paper on Mary and Douglas of Lochleven (*antè*, p. 50.) when I met with a bookseller's catalogue in which Castelnau's *Memoires* are spoken of as the only book containing an account of Mary's having given birth to a daughter by Bothwell. I was about on the instant to send off to "N. and Q.," a Query as to the fact; but on second thoughts first referred to its indices to see if it contained any thing upon the subject. I was rewarded for so doing (as one generally is for doing right) by finding a long and valuable Query by A. S. A., in the sixth volume of the present Series. A. S. A.'s paper seems almost to settle in the affirmative his own inquiry; but not so completely, I dare say, as to satisfy those who think the beautiful Scottish queen could do no wrong. A. S. A.'s Query has, however, not called forth a single reply. You have among your many learned correspondents one at least (I mean J. M., who has done so much in your columns to illustrate Early Scottish History and Literature) capable of throwing light upon this very curious point of history, and I hope you will indulge me with the small space necessary to recall attention to it by the present communication.—*Notes and Queries.*

PASQUINADES.—Would Cuthbert Bede, or some other correspondent who has turned his attention to the subject, furnish the readers of "N. and Q." with a list of the rival publications to *Punch*?

If the entire list should be too long for insertion, one supplemental to that in the *Quarterly*, would be most acceptable to many.—*Notes and Queries.*

ADAM WITH A BEARD.—Can you inform me if there is any picture or statue by old or modern artists and sculptors in which Adam is represented with a beard?—*Notes and Queries.*

From Chambers's Journal.

SCIENCE AND ARTS FOR FEBRUARY.

BUNSEN and Kirchoff's interesting experiments with the spectrum in chemical analysis have been repeated by Mr. Matthiessen, at a meeting of the Royal Society, to the gratification of all beholders, for, apart from the intrinsic value of the results, some of the effects are strikingly beautiful. The black lines seen in a solar spectrum, which are known to students as Fraunhofer's lines, appear white, as Mr. Matthiessen demonstrated, when the spectrum is produced by the spark from a galvanic coil. Seeing, then, that every different kind of light hitherto tried shows a different effect on the spectrum, the light of the stars is to be tested by the same apparatus, in the hope that conclusions may be arrived at concerning the physical condition of those distant bodies, and the nature of their atmosphere. Foucault showed, some years ago, that the ray D of the electric spectrum coincides with the same ray of the solar spectrum; if, therefore, the starlight spectrum present the same coincidence, it would be safe to infer an identity in the nature of the light. There seems something wonderful in the notion of thus making out the secrets of remote space by scanning an illuminated stripe within a small darkened box. With regard to the hygienic view of the question, readers of our former notice of this subject will remember what was said concerning sodium and dust; the vast amount of sodium in the atmosphere is derived from the sea by evaporation, and diffused by the action of winds and waves; each minute particle of water holds a still more minute solid nucleus of chloride of sodium, which remains floating in the air after the water has evaporated. Now, it seems reasonable to conclude, that these minute particles supply some minute forms of organic life with the saline element essential to existence, and that animal life generally is influenced by their presence in greater or lesser proportions. Hence, to quote from the *Journal* of the Chemical Society, "if, as is scarcely doubtful at the present day, the explanation of the spread of contagious disease is to be sought for in some peculiar contact-action, it is possible that the presence of an antiseptic substance like chloride of sodium, even in almost infinitely small quantities, may not be without influence upon such occurrences in the atmosphere." The test for this theory would be a constant and long-continued series of spectrum observations, noted hour by hour, as has been the case with magnetical and meteorological observations, whereby the increase or diminution of sodium in the atmosphere would be detected.

Among the experiments made by Loewel, a chemist lately deceased, there are some of singular importance, as appears from a work published in France. It was discovered, two or three years ago, that air filtered through a layer of cotton would not excite fermentation; that the freezing of water under cotton is less firm than when uncovered, and that crystallization is retarded by the same means: Loewel found that air, heated by friction or agitation, will not excite crystallization. If compressed air be allowed to escape in a jet from a receiver, and play upon a saturated solution, no crystals appear; but if only two or three bubbles of common air be permitted to pass, the solution will solidify. Air, in this passive condition, is distinguished as adynamic, and the filtered air would come under the same definition. What is the significance of this peculiarity? Does it apply on the large scale, and is the air of our atmosphere ever thrown into an adynamic condition by hurricanes and storms, and is the effect thereof on human beings in any wise different from that of undisturbed air? Again, is there in this adynamic air any support for the theory of spontaneous generation, or the reverse? To answer these and other inquiries which suggest themselves, would be an interesting course of research for some ingenious and diligent student.

Some years ago, Mr. R. W. Fox, of Falmouth, astonished the scientific world by showing specimens of artificial copper produced by electricity; we now hear of a German chemist who produces silver—sterling silver, not German—by artificial means, at a cost of about three shillings an ounce. We hear, moreover, that a snug company is forming to work the discovery on a profitable scale: the appliances required are certain chemical preparations and galvanic apparatus of sufficient power to act on them. Should the experiment succeed on the large scale, the profit will certainly be handsome, and additional weight will attach to the opinion, that all metals are resolvable into two or three elements.

The new telegraph company for London, to which we called attention last autumn, is making satisfactory progress, and the expectations formed of the usefulness of Mr. Wheatstone's simplified instruments are fully realized. They—the company have already erected a number of lines across the house-tops, and purpose extending the same system into all parts of the metropolis. Mr. Reuter, of multi-telegram reputation, rents more than a score of wires for his own especial use; the *Times*, for the present, has taken three; the city police avail themselves of the new system, as also certain manufacturing firms; and now, when a lady calls to ask when her piano will be ready, instead of being told that she will be informed by post next day, receives an immediate answer by telegraph from the factory in the suburbs. The rent charged for a wire is £4 a mile per annum, inclusive of maintenance; and in cases where it is not desired to purchase the instruments, they also may be rented. One economical advantage, which the company derive from the use of Mr. Wheatstone's instruments, is, that small wires are available for the transmission of messages; for as from thirty to fifty such wires can each be completely insulated in an india-rubber cord not thicker than a man's finger, it follows that in setting up a mile of cord fifty miles of wire are set up at once, which may be rented to as many different individuals. When set up, the cord is painted white, to check absorption of heat; and it is found that india-rubber is far preferable to gutta-percha as an insulator, inasmuch as it will bear extremes of temperature without any of that softening which allows the wires to shift their position in a gutta-percha coating. The india-rubber cord is manufactured by Messrs. Silver, at their works near North Woolwich; and it is worth notice that the central wire, which is thicker than the others, is the "hanging wire," and bears all the strain of suspension, whereby the conducting wires are left free from strain-disturbances, and have nothing to do but convey the messages. We hear that four hundred telegraph stations are to be established in Paris.

The late severe visitation of frost has occasioned the inquiry—Is it possible to announce the approach of a frost by telegraph, as it is to give warning of a cyclone? a question of vital importance to vine-growers in the south of France. The answer, which has however to be demonstrated by practise, is that it is possible, for cold currents in the atmosphere are commonly a day or a day and a half in travelling from the north of Russia to the Pyrenees: hence, if a message were flashed from Archangel or Stockholm, notifying a fall of the temperature to 20 degrees or to 0 degrees, which would be represented by 30 degrees or by 10 degrees in the south of France, the cultivators would have sufficient time to protect their vineyards by the usual means, which, as is well known, cost but little, and are easily applicable.

The Academy of Sciences at Naples offer a prize for researches in answer to the question: What are the circumstances in which the atmospheric oxygen is transformed into ozone? Is the cause of the change to be sought for in vegetation or electricity? Does the change take place by day or by night, and in what electric condition is the atmosphere at the time of the change?—Wolf, of Zurich, is pursuing his observations on the sun-spots, and is collecting all the tables of past observations which he can hear of for the purpose of corroborating his theoretical calculations. So far the verification is satisfactory; but he is particularly in want of observations for the years 1729 and 1748; and any one who can inform him where these may be found, will aid the cause of science. He finds by his investigations that a small defined spot crossed the solar disk in 1800, which seems to answer to one of the appearances of the intra-Mercurial planet, Vulcan, as ascertained by retrospective calculation.—Dr. Buijs Ballot, of Utrecht, who is also a sun-observer, with especial attention to solar rotation and temperature, is led to conclude that one-half of the sun is hotter than the other. In the photosphere, or atmosphere of light, which surrounds the mighty orb, he finds a movement from west to east in the equatorial region, thereby confirming the deductions of former observers, that trade-winds exist on the sun as well as on the earth.—M. Liais shows the perturbations of Mercury which have long puzzled astronomers, to arise from its exposure to a continual shower of aërolites, which of course affects its mass. Of this shower of aërolites, our earth occasionally receives a few wandering specimens; its quantity is enormously increased with nearness to the sun, and hence the ceaseless fall on Mercury. To it, as M. Liais remarks, we owe the phenomenon of the zodiacal light; and agreeing with other physicists, he believes it to be the source and support of the sun's heat: derived from without, and not from within.

These are among the most important questions in astronomical or in cosmical science, and we cannot therefore pass them by unnoticed. While one class of inquirers is occupied with their investigation, another is discussing that interesting geological question, which, in consequence of recent chemical discoveries, has once more revived—the debate between fire and water. The Neptunists, as the aqueous philosophers are called, are bringing forward more convincing arguments than before, which it will tax the ingenuity of the Vulcanists to confute. Granite cannot have been formed by the action of fire, assert the former, because that rock is constituted of minerals whose melting-point is so different that they could not have been formed at one and the same time;

and yet these minerals interpenetrate and cross each other, like the roots of neighboring trees. Again, mica and free silica exist in the same mass of granite; and some kinds of granite contain soft mica charged with from four to five per cent of water, which facts appear quite irreconcilable with the theory of a vulcanic origin.

A lively debate has also taken place among the members of the Academy of Medicine at Paris, on that highly important question —Life. The argument was carried on from three different points of view: that of the organicians; that of the animists; and that of the vitalists; and each party found much to say in support of their own opinions. The vitalists, who contend that life is a vital force entirely independent of physical influences, were triumphantly answered by M. Poggiale, who proved to demonstration that the phenomena of life are due to physico-chemical action. The chemist, applying his science to physiology, experiments on the living organism, and discovers the formation of sugar in the liver; that in respiration oxygen combines with the hydrogen and carbon of the blood, and produces animal heat; and that the gastric and pancreatic juice act upon alimentary substances enclosed in glass tubes with the same result as in the body. The result of the debate will probably be to give an impulse to the science which embraces the chemistry of life.

Dr. Hooker, who has recently returned from a scientific travel in the range of Lebanon, in company with Captain Washington of the Admiralty, has catalogued the plants collected by the naturalist of the yacht *Fox* in her recent North Atlantic surveying expedition. The number is one hundred and seventy, of which nearly one hundred are flowering-plants; and the doctor, after contrasting them with the plants of other arctic localities, and thereby widening the scope of geographical botany, adds, that he "is drawing up a general account of the whole arctic flora, which he shall have the honor of laying before the Linnæan Society." From the soundings made during this expedition, further confirmation has been gained that animal life can be maintained at very great depths. About midway between Greenland and Ireland, living star-fish were brought up from one thousand two hundred and sixty fathoms—nearly a mile and a half; and minute annelids were found at one thousand nine hundred and thirteen fathoms. Clearly the "zero in the distribution of animal life," referred to by the late eminent naturalist, Edward Forbes, is not yet arrived at.

At the instance of Mr. Tite, the Institute of British Architects have held a discussion "on the various processes for the preservation of stone," in which, as was hoped, available facts and principles were brought out, and trustworthy information given as to the actual condition of the walls of the Houses of Parliament, to which the preserving wash has been applied. The whole question of building materials is one of increasing importance; and while the present high price of bricks is maintained, experiments will be made to render stone durable, or to produce some artificial substitute. We noticed, some time since, the *béton*, a kind of concrete, manufactured in blocks at Paris, suitable for walls either above or below ground, and for factory cisterns, as it resists the action of acids, and, judging from late reports, it answers expectation. A builder at Reading, actuated by a close examination of the mortar which still binds the flint walls of the ancient abbey in that town, with almost irresistible tenacity, has recently patented a process for the manufacture of what he calls "Reading Abbey Rubble Stone," which resists moisture, heat, cold, and pressure, presenting a clean and smooth surface, capable of formation into mouldings, corbels, quoins, balustrades, and so forth, and acquiring an extraordinary degree of hardness within a few minutes after leaving the moulds. Seeing that ornamental blocks and slabs of any size can be produced, all the parts of a house, the steps, landings, basement-stairs and floors, sinks and window-sills, may be fashioned from this "rubble-stone," as well as blocks for the walls, and at a cost below that of bricks.

As meteorological reports come in from distant parts, it appears that scarcely any region of the globe has escaped the visitation of unusual weather: the continent of Europe, North Africa, North America, as well as England, had more clouds and rain than sunshine; and now we hear that Australia has experienced an unusual demand for umbrellas. In the middle of November last, about a month from their midsummer, the colonists of New South Wales were glad to sit by the fire; and from the beginning of the year, up to that time, more than five feet of rain had fallen.

From The Transcript.

DEATH OF HON. JOSEPH T. BUCKINGHAM.

JOSEPH T. BUCKINGHAM, the well-remembered editor and originator of the weekly *New England Galaxy*, and the daily *Boston Courier*, died at his residence in Old Cambridge this morning, at half-past two o'clock. There are very few men who, in their day and generation, have filled a larger space in the public eye, within and beyond their own community, than Joseph T. Buckingham occupied in the hey-day of his lifetime. He was a man of most indomitable energy, of highly moral character, of excellent scholarship,—which he attained, through natural taste, by severe labor and thorough reading—of acute discernment of all political affairs and political men, which came within his range, from the time when he entered active life, nearly unto that in which he passed away. He was a writer of great nerve and of exceeding vigor—a thorough master of the English language. In the field of controversy he was a terrible opponent,—in judgment of passing affairs, he was always quick and decided,—in many things humorous and satirical—in the office of paying tribute to the memory of departed friends, and in sketching the lives of men, as they actually were, he was unequalled in his truthfulness and lifelike descriptions.

Mr. Buckingham was born in Windham, a small town in the north part of Connecticut, Dec. 21, 1779. His father was a Revolutionary soldier. In his early days he was apprenticed to the printing business, which was the great object of his young desire, at what was then a somewhat celebrated printing-office, in Walpole, N. H., where he commenced his novitiate in 1796. He afterwards pursued his vocation in Greenfield, Mass., and in 1799, he came to Boston, a youthful, unknown, and unfriended adventurer. After some experience as a journeyman printer, he commenced the publication of the *New England Galaxy*, a weekly journal, which, under his auspices, with almost the single aid of his talent and industry, reached the highest rank, and the largest circulation of any secular journal of that day, and wielded more influence than any similar journal has ever attained in this country. The *Galaxy* was a terror to pretenders and mountebanks of all descriptions,—political, clerical, and miscellaneous—and was also always cheering to virtue and sobriety, to prudence, honesty, and truth. The paper had also the supplementary title of *Masonic Magazine*, as Mr. Buckingham was an early member of the Masonic Fraternity.

Mr. Buckingham had been previously engaged in other periodical publications, which, as they and the memory of them have almost passed away, among the multitude of such productions, it is not necessary to mention here. One of his earliest friends was the late Rev. Dr. Charles Lowell, who has so recently passed from life before him. He was of valuable assistance to the youthful struggler for subsistence and fame, by his introductions to eminent publishers of that day. A more intimate friend (Rev. Dr. Frothingham) was his own pastor at the First Church in this city, and was for many long years his intimate friend and correspondent.

In 1824, Mr. Buckingham came out, unscathed, from a bitter libel suit, which was instituted against him by Rev. John N. Maffit, a Methodist clergyman of much celebrity in which trial the character of the prosecutor was the principal point which was before the jury. The notoriety which this circumstance added to the fame and power of the editor of the *Galaxy*, called for the expression of such a man's opinions in a wider field, and the result was the establishment of the *Boston Daily Courier*, on the 1st of March of that year. He continued its publication, with much favor and success, though not with great profit, until 1848, when, from political reasons, he retired from newspaper publication, and finally left his long-occupied editorial chair, though he continued to write for various journals after that time.

In 1831, in connection with his son, Edwin, Mr. Buckingham commenced the publication of the *New England Magazine*, a monthly periodical of much literary ability; but the enterprise was discontinued two years afterwards, as he had no heart to continue it after the death of his much-loved coadjutor.

A man like Mr. Buckingham was, of course, a mark for political honor and corporation dignity. He was a member of the Massachusetts House of Representatives from Boston and from Cambridge; he was also a senator from Middlesex County for two years. He was President of the Massachusetts Charitable Mechanic Association for many years, and during his presidency, the Massachusetts Mechanic Association took up the business of finishing the Bunker Hill Monument, which at that time was only a heap of stones upon an open field. To no man more than to Joseph T. Buckingham belongs the credit of raising and finishing the Bunker Hill Monument. He started the idea,—he had with him such men as Edward Everett and William Sullivan, with Robert G. Shaw, and other patriotic men,—and completed the erection of the monument which is now before our eyes.

In speaking of the bright talent of the friend who has passed away from us, nothing has been said of his social and family qualities. No better man was ever known than Joseph T. Buckingham was at home. There he was supreme in his love and his affection. He was a most indulgent and careful father. The loving partner of his life passed away before him, to his great grief and his manifold sorrow. In his last days he looked only to the future which was beyond the tomb, in his quiet, composed, and entirely submissive manner. He looked forward to death as a relief from the burdens of life through which he had passed, as a shining light in his day. He had no desire to pass through them again. Peace be upon him, for he was a man, who, take him all in all, we ne'er shall look upon his like again.

I. W. F.

"Bogie:" what is it?—Your correspondent, Timon, derives this word from a villain of that name, who is reported to have pillaged Surat in 1664. This material Bogie may have alarmed the Dutch merchants of that place, although it appears from the story that he avoided coming to logger-heads with them; but I much question his authorship of the famous *spectrum*, which held our infant grandmothers in fear. The reign of nursery terror seems to have been universal: thus, it is said (see Gibbon), the Assyrian mothers scared their infants with the name of Narses; so did the Syrians, with that of Richard of the Lion-heart; and the Turks, with some version of the name of the Hungarian king I expect that *Lurdane* was a sound causing terror in its day; and our own Wellington is celebrated in song, in a sort of Anglo-French nursery-rhyme, which I do not remember to have seen in print, as being "tall and straight as Rouen steeple," and dining and supping, regularly of course, "every morning and at night," upon the never-failing supply of "naughty people." (A version of this little ode, of three or four stanzas, would be a pretty addition to the *Arundines Cami.*)

To apply this to *Bogie*, whom I can hardly conceive to have appeared in England, from the Dutch, only in the seventeenth century, the notion of terror conveyed in it points to *Boh;* who (as Warton tells us, *Diss.* i. p. xxviii.) was the fiercest of the Gothic generals, and son of Odin to boot, whose name was enough to spread a panic among his enemies. Then, passing onwards, we have the Russian word *bohg* (=*angel, or saint*); and in the sixteenth century we find *bugs*,* in the company of "goblins, fairies nightmares, urchins, and elves" (see Brand's *Pop. Antiq.*, "Robin Goodfellow, *alias* Pucke, *alias* Hobgoblin"); and also used for *terror* in the version of Psalm xci. 5., in Mathewes' Bible.

I would suggest, therefore, that *Bogie* has been received, among other vernacular legacies, from our northern ancestors,—derived from old *Boh*, through the Scandinavian *bohg*,—and is neither more nor less than *ghost;* and that this is also the origin of the name of the strange sect of Mystics, or Spiritualists, in the tenth century, who were styled in the Slavonian district, *Bogomiles.—Notes and Queries.*

Ονειροποιετικα.—When Coleridge awoke from his dream of "Christabel," he transcribed it *memoriter et in extenso:* rarely has the extravagant and erring spirit hied back to its confine with so precious an acquirement. Was Coleridge its author? If not, who was?

One night, I sat out the presentation of a drama: all whereof has escaped my memory, save the general impression of its excellence and the remembrance of four especial lines. I awoke repeating them:—

"The morning now, like to some potent lord
Making himself a king above his peers,
Puts off her meaner coronet of stars,
And takes the sun for her bright diadem."

Claiming none of their praise to myself, I wish to record them in "N. and Q."—*Notes and Queries.*

* Richardson gives *bug*, *bugbear*, *bugabo;* but not *Bogie*.

THE LIVING AGE.

No. 886.—25 May, 1861.

CONTENTS.

NEW BOOKS.

THE REBELLION RECORD: a Diary of American Events, 1860, 1861. Edited by Frank Moore, author of the "Diary of the American Revolution." New York: G. P. Putnam.

PUBLISHED EVERY SATURDAY BY

LITTELL, SON, & CO., BOSTON.

FOR Six Dollars a year, in advance, *remitted directly to the Publishers*, the LIVING AGE will be punctually forwarded *free of postage*.

Complete sets of the First Series, in thirty-six volumes, and of the Second Series, in twenty volumes, handsomely bound, packed in neat boxes, and delivered in all the principal cities, free of expense of freight, are for sale at two dollars a volume.

ANY VOLUME may be had separately, at two dollars, bound, or a dollar and a half in numbers.

ANY NUMBER may be had for 13 cents; and it is well worth while for subscribers or purchasers to complete any broken volumes they may have, and thus greatly enhance their value.

A NEW SONG OF THE SHIRT.

BY A LADY.

To the quiet nooks of home,
To the public halls so wide—
The women of Boston hurrying come
And sit down side by side;
To fight for their native land,
With womanly weapons girt,
For dagger, a needle—scissors for brand,
While they sing the song of the shirt.

O women with sons so dear,
O tender, loving wives,
It is not money you work for now,
But the saving of precious lives.
'Tis roused for the battle we feel,—
Oh, for a thousand experts,
Armed with tiny darts of steel,
To conquer thousands of shirts!

Stitch—stitch—stitch
Under the sheltering roof.
Come to the rescue—poor and rich,
Nor stay from the work aloof.
To the men who are shedding their blood—
To the brave, devoted band—
Whose action is honor, whose cause is good,
We pledge our strong right hand.

Work—work—work,
With earnest heart and soul—
Work—work—work
To keep the Union whole.
And 'tis, oh, for the land of the brave,
Where treason nor cowardice lurk,
Where there's all to lose or all to save,
That we're doing this Christian work.

Brothers are fighting abroad,
Sisters will help them here,
Husbands and wives with one accord
Serving the cause so dear.
Stand by our colors to-day—
Keep to the Union true—
Under our flag, while yet we may
Hurrah for the Red, White, and Blue.

—*Transcript.*

TO THE MEN OF THE NORTH AND WEST.

BY R. H. STODDARD.

Men of the North and West,
Wake in your might,
Prepare, as the rebels have done,
For the fight;
You cannot shrink from the test,
Rise! men of the North and West!

They have torn down your banner of stars;
They have trampled the laws;
They have stifled the freedom they hate,
For no cause!
Do you love it, or slavery, best?
Speak! men of the North and West!

They strike at the life of the State—
Shall the murder be done?
They cry, "We are two!" And you?
"*We are one!*"
You must meet them, then, breast to breast,
On! men of the North and West!

Not with words—they laugh them to scorn,
And tears they despise—
But with swords in your hands, and death
In your eyes!
Strike home! leave to God all the rest.
Strike! men of the North and West!

—*Transcript.*

A PATRIOTIC HYMN.

The choir of the Broadway Tabernacle Church, in New York, wishing to sing the *Marseillaise*, called upon the pastor, Rev. Dr. Thompson, to prepare a patriotic hymn. The following attempt to adjust inflexible English syllables to the tortuous notes of the French Air of Liberty, was the response. The hymn, such as it is, was sung with good effect at the Tabernacle on sabbath evening, 21 April,—the vast audience joining with great enthusiasm in the chorus:—

Arise! arise! ye sons of patriot sires!
A Nation calls! and Heaven speed your way.
Now Freedom lights anew her waning fires,
And spreads her banner to the day,
And spreads her banner to the day.
While to His throne our hearts are swelling,
Freedom and law and truth and right,
May God defend by his own might,
By his right arm the treason quelling!
Ye loyal sons and true,
Sons of the brave and free,
Join hearts, join hands, to strike anew
For God and Liberty.

With faith your all to him confiding,
Who crowned with victory your fathers' hand,
With courage in his strength abiding,
Go forth in Freedom's sacred band,
Go forth to save our native land.
Defend from faction's wild commotion
Our homes, our laws, our schools, and spires,
The names and graves of patriot sires,
Till freedom reigns to farthest ocean.
Ye loyal sons and true,
Sons of the brave and free,
Join hearts, join hands, to strike anew
For God and Liberty.

—*Transcript.*

MEMORY.

I think of thee when through the grove,
The nightingales their notes of love
Pour forth in harmony.
When dost though think of me?

I think of thee when twilight gleaming
By crystal founts I wander dreaming.
Where dost thou think of me?

I think of thee with wishes glowing
With timid fears with hot tears flowing.
How dost thou think of me?

Oh! think of me, until we meet,
In some glad star in union sweet,
Alas, nor time nor place may be,
When I think not of thee.

M. T. E.

From The Saturday Review.

THE MANSE OF MASTLAND.*

New scenes from clerical life are here laid open to the curious, and sketches both serious and humorous are drawn by the pen of a clergyman of the Dutch Established Church. The title of the work before us may suggest to many persons that it is a novel; but it is simply a reminiscence of parochial experience in a village near the Meuse, and contains photographic views of rural life in the Netherlands without fictitious coloring. To Mr. Keightly we are indebted for this translation from the Dutch. By chance he saw the original in an old book-shop; the title and its being a recent third edition, induced him to buy and read it; and he was so much pleased that he considered it worthy of being translated. He adds:—

"Not wishing, however, to rely on my own judgment alone, and happening to be then in correspondence with the bishop of St. David's on the subject of the Dutch language and literature, I begged of him to read the work. He did so, and wrote to me as follows:—

"'I have finished the Pastorij te Mastland, and am extremely obliged to you for the loan of it. It has to me more than justified your commendation. There is a good deal of quiet humor and pathos, and pleasant glimpses of the *buiten leven* ("rural life") not easily to be gained in the country itself by any but the native. To *me*, however, its chief interest consists in the view which it gives of the working of the Dutch Established Church, and of its strong and weak points. In this respect I have found it highly instructive and suggestive. I really think it likely that it would be attractive to a large class of readers, particularly such as take an interest in clerical matters. How very little is known in England of Dutch literature; which nevertheless is perhaps more congenial to our taste than either the German or the French.'"

From the dialect of the peasantry, the colloquial style, and the familiar tone of the *Manse of Mastland*, there must have been considerable difficulty to be surmounted by Mr. Keightley, who admits that he is not so familiar with the Dutch as with the German and other languages. It may be that a point here and there has been, as it were, blunted, if not destroyed, by translation. Idioms and proverbs are hard to render, for even when perhaps there are equivalent words to express the literal meaning, the humor or spirit is untranslatable. Mr. Keightley has appealed to Dutch authorities for explanations of the most obscure passages, and therefore we can fairly assume that his is a good version of the original. In the opinion of some persons, the unexciting must be dull, and a Dutch pastor's existence as monotonous as his dykes. As it has been said, the expression "seeing life" is always understood to mean a familiarity with scenes of vice and excitement, but, as a vast majority of mankind have little to do with either, it follows that those who see such life only glean their experience of one phase of existence. Books like this Dutch volume lead one to think of lives which pass away, and may be compared to days when the sky is of one even tone, luminous enough, but without brilliant sunshine or lowering clouds.

The circle in which the village clergyman moves is narrow indeed, with few social advantages, for his means do not allow of much intercourse with the world beyond. He is often the centre of intellectual light, which grows feebler when stimulating contact with equals is unusual and books are rare. With a perfect knowledge of these disadvantages our author forbids the public to look with compassion on lives hidden in country obscurity. People weigh, says he, our position in golden scales, and in them it proves of little value. "It is no doubt a certain income," says the trader, "but it's a scanty one indeed." And whenever the minister comes from his remote residence into the town, then his coat is rather threadbare, his hat out of the fashion, and his children gape and stare all about them, as if they had never known before that the world was so large. Some look on with pity, but others make a jest of him, and deem him nothing better than a peasant in a black coat. As the writer, however, insists, there are no more important professions than his, and, unknown to the busy or reading world, the village pastor can, by his quiet, undisturbed, continuous exertion, exercise a great and a lasting influence over a large portion of the

* *The Manse of Mastland.* Sketches, Serious and Humorous, from the Life of a Village Pastor in the Netherlands. Translated from the Dutch, by Thomas Keightley, Author of "Fairy Mythology," etc. London: Bell and Daldy. 1860.

population, and precisely over that part of it which is the firmest support of real prosperity, nationality, and morals. His objects are really as great as the part he plays on the world's stage looks small, and the author would enable the impartial reader to make acquaintance with the little circle in which he moves—not with an ideal representation of his mode of life, but with a simple description of it. To this purpose he faithfully adheres. He introduces himself in his study, where, on a Monday morning, he is indulging after his day of work in a well-earned holiday. He rises with the delightful feeling that he is not called upon to make any exertion :—

"In the full consciousness of my comfort I lay an extra half-hour peeping through the bed-curtains, and amused myself with the industry of my wife, whose day of rest was already over, while mine was but just beginning. So I fell again into a slumber, in that pleasant state of dreaminess in which we enjoy the repose of the sleeping, and yet have not altogether lost the consciousness of the waking, man, when I heard the well-known voice saying, 'Come, William, it's now high time. Breakfast has been waiting for you ever so long!'

"After breakfast I went out to take a view of my hotbeds; that is to say, of a couple of old frames, which, after three years' ample deliberation, had been taken by the ruling elders out of the front gable of the manse, and then, after three monthly meetings, had been cobbled up with old planks into the form of hotbed frames. I raised up one frame, and I was much gratified at the prospect of eating our first salad in about a fortnight; then the other also; but oh! the mole has not been caught yet. He had gone through the whole place once more, and in one night raised with his back and turned over the harvest of a month, and the only spot he had not visited was where the trap was. I then returned to the house, to communicate the doleful intelligence to my wife; and after mature consultation on what was to be done in this business, I went up-stairs to the garret to make an inspection of my apples; it looks as if they were ashamed of having lasted so long, now that the sun of spring was shining so pleasantly, so they were making all the haste they could to decay. Then I went down into the cellar, to make them tap a kilderkin of beer, and so rambled through all the rooms in my house except the best room, which was my Cornelia's own *sanctum;* and now I am sitting here mending pens, and putting books out of the way, and beginning a letter, which I do not finish, and from time to time taking a look at the boughs of the fruit-trees, from which the melted snow is trickling, like tears shed by winter at taking leave.

"Then I hear a cautious knocking at my room-door; but as it is Monday morning, it is opened at once, without waiting for an answer. It is my Keetye, with the dear little Minn in her arms."

He admits his wife into his confidence, and reads a plan which he has drawn up to be shown by a friend to a bookseller. He says that the form in which he intends to put his notes is that which he imagines will be most acceptable. Published letters belong to the eighteenth century. "Our times have been surfeited with essays." He hopes to adapt himself to the taste of the public, as he cannot expect it to adapt itself to him; and a work should not only be good, but *it* should be read. The conclusion is that "light sketches just suit the minds of most readers, who do not like any great effort, and are quite content with reading the half, provided they are not required to remember any part of it." From his induction at Mastland to his "call" to a more extended *field* of labor, we live with the pastor, and in one volume share the experience of his five years' duty, comprehending its pleasures without feeling the fatigue and disappointment which are inseparable from all high effort. The candor with which the writer admits us into his feelings, experience, aspirations, and failures is only exceeded by his manly reticence. At the end of five years, he says, he is little more than a novice; and to a fellow-student he ingenuously confesses, "To tell you the truth, I am full of observations and opinions; and I am longing, like every one else—especially like one whose knowledge is new—to hang them out to air."

After the forty years' service of their deceased Dominie, the Kirk-session had to give their first call; and they gave it with the expectation that it would be responded to by the ideal perfection which each had created in his own mind. Accordingly, "half a dozen probationers exhibited their gifts in the pulpit of Mastland," subject to the usual frivolous criticisms made by an ignorant and prejudiced congregation. The result was favorable to our author, though, as he heard the powerful and affecting sermon of his most formidable rival, he gave up all expectation; so he was the more astonished when a vote of one of the deacons determined the matter in these words: "Listen to me, gentlemen, when I was going round with the poor-bag, I looked up now and then, but mind me, it was not to be borne to see those spectacles of his! It is true he kept them off in general; but, mark what I say, it will be another guess matter, if once he gets the place; and it is not wise of us to take a man that is half blind, when we can get plenty of those who can see well." The congregation fully entered into this enlightened reasoning, and chose the man without spectacles. Upon the strength of his appointment our author gets married, and brings his wife in May to Mastland, where they are received with many demonstrations and ceremonies that seem strange to us. They make their entry, driving through the beadle-guarded street, which has been strewn with branches of palm and flowers. A dozen young girls were in waiting at the railing of the Manse, which was itself adorned with green boughs. The young peasants, ready to salute, formed a guard of honor; and Balyon, the schoolmaster, "wiped the perspiration from his brow, and every quarter of an hour read his verses over again, in which from time to time he amended a word or so with a black-lead pencil." They were received by the authorities, and welcomed by cheers from all the villagers who turned out for the occasion. The following Sunday the new-comer was ordained and inducted. The former ceremony he describes in words of real emotion and reverence. It is the custom of the Dutch Church to repeat the Ordination Service at each induction; and the writer, rationally objecting to the practice, asks, "Is the first consecration lost? Are the promises of life forgotten? Does not the minister bring with him the testimony of a parish? And is he likely to keep his second Yes, if he was not faithful to his first?" The crowding and bustling about at the Manse did not, as we might imagine, harmonize with his feelings; but such are the festive customs of the Netherlanders that the clergyman's wife was just as much perplexed about the hams and ribs of beef as her husband was about his induction discourse. Brother clergymen, with a whole train of woman and children, and mounted elders, college friends, relations, and acquaintance, "all pour in and out, so that it was not worth while to shut the door or to latch the outer gate." The womankind compliment the bride, and then repair to the rooms appointed for them, the men following their example. They smoke, and afterwards there is a general onslaught on the ham and ribs of beef. After the afternoon service, they drink tea, and then the party breaks up, to be succeeded by the village authorities and their wives, who remain till ten o'clock, when the burgomaster, with an expressive look, knocks the ashes out of his pipe; at which signal the company depart, leaving the Dominie and his wife in peaceful possession of the Manse of Mastland.

We are taken in turn to visit the village magnates. First, to the burgomaster, who lives in a house half-homestead, half-town-house, colored glaring yellow and strong green, with a garden close by, with box-hedges, tulips and marigolds growing in an English grass-plot. At the back, a barn with tarred sides, pointed, reed-covered roof, and small attic windows, together with a cheese-cellar, gives a rustic air in spite of the gentility of having a hall-door with marble steps, windows with Venetian blinds, and a handsome brass bell. The hall-door is opened with difficulty, as neighbors go in and out at the back. The parlor-blinds are equally unmanageable from disuse. The clergyman is introduced to Madame Van der Zanden by her husband, and then the ruddy and corpulent burgomaster smokes and drinks coffee with his visitor; and a dialogue on the origin of Mastland and other local subjects ensued, which was resumed, or rather repeated, whenever they met. The school comes next, with the old master, who "swayed his sceptre over the rising generation. He bowed low before every minister that came in." His hair had grown gray and his hand stiff, while he is forever teaching the first fragmentary elements of knowledge to little peasants. To his principles the pastor could not object, as he piously believed all that his predecessors had taught, and, by anticipation, all that he should be taught in future. Then a new doctor, with a French name, was established in the village. "His education, general knowledge, reading, and manners distinguished him completely from the rest of the people of the village; so that they were almost obliged to fall sick in order to have some point of contact with him." Du Meaux was a superficial free-thinker; and although they were on intimate terms, the writer acknowledges that he did not convert his friend; and the conclusion at which he arrived was, that when any one is resolved not to be convinced, argument is injurious, and that it is sufficient to excite ideas in the sceptic's mind "by means of which he may either convert himself or God may convert him—in my opinion, a matter of no great difference." That at last he succeeded in raising doubts as to the truth of his opponent's opinions was a sufficient triumph, and he never sought a confession.

A chapter is devoted to the *Rentenaer*, which Mr. Keightley translates *rentier*, as there is no synonymous term to indicate a man living on his property, be it large or small. The *rentier* is a person of consequence; yet the class seems to be unpopular in Holland, as there is an antipathy to idlers in trading towns. "There any one is a *rentier* who runs against you while you are busily employed." So the *rentier* prefers a cheap and retired village or miniature town, where he can get a position without spending too much of his substance. The clergyman's relations with the various members of his congregation, and the petty usages of the place, are all narrated by our candid Dutch author. The inhabitants of Mastland might find their counterparts in a remote English village; but we imagine there is greater dulness of comprehension amongst Dutch rustics, for they deeply resent a satirical remark, and, being too slow to make a repartee, they are equally slow in forgetting a jest.

To those interested in the working of a parish, the chapters on catechizing, visiting from house to house, receiving members, and the affairs of the poor, will be edifying, and also instructive to the uninitiated in the Presbyterian system of Holland and Scotland, where each parish has its deliberative and executive body. The "affairs of the poor" were most burdensome to the pastor, for, says he, in large parishes there are persons appointed to relieve the destitute, but in a village the management of the poor is altogether a matter belonging to the Kirk-session; and although the deacons are the acting power, in matters of the session the minister is every thing—the man who advises and projects, the man who carries on correspondence, and sets entangled matters right, and, in fine, the man on whom is laid the blame of every thing. Thus on us, he says, weigh all the annoyances of the poor, while the members of the session say, tranquil as death, "The Dominie has to provide for that; my time is up New Year's day." The writer is not in the least bigoted to religious forms, and the practice of visiting every house with an elder, and inviting Church members to the sacrament, seemed to him at first worse than useless; but having experience of its working, he now sees the advantage of a system that seemed merely a repugnant ceremony and waste of time. If faithfully carried out, he considers that such formal visiting facilitates intercourse, gives a right of access to all, and acquaintance with every one whom he ought to instruct.

What the preacher has to say on sermons deserves particular attention. At Mastland he found himself prepared with a precious collection of sermons, the result of much hard study in theology, and a number of very perfect and lifeless outlines, fruits of a severe composition course. He describes, not without a touch of humor, the infinite labor he expended during the first year on discourses which, when committed to memory, were delivered with effort, though he had been an active member of a debating society, and had always learned to move his eyes and hands skilfully, and should have learned to do the same with his feet if the pulpit had not been closed in at the bottom. The sermon was correct in form, yet the introduction fell unheeded. The demonstrative part sent almost every one to their sleeping corners, though the schoolmaster supplied all the ruling elders—a front row of women—with snuff. The word "application" aroused the dozing congregation, who stood up and saluted one another in odd country form, and listened with eyes and ears to the minister. After a long and disheartening probation, the Dominie gave up his theological disquisitions as a mistake, feeling quite certain "that if we must first make our hearers good theologians in order to make them good Christians, our blessed heaven will be wonderfully empty." The final success of the preacher was owing, not to his appeals to the sluggish intellect of his hearers, but to their consciences and heart, "from which several by-paths lead to the brain." He gives his opinion that the Church wants a regular transition from theory to practice, which cannot be obtained at a university, where colleges make divines but not ministers. In Mastland, many illusions have been destroyed, but the minister still holds to his faith in the higher qualities and aspirations of human nature, and he sees the world with the eyes of a philosopher and a philanthropist, who has arrived through experience at certain conclusions:—

"With regard to the notions and morals of the poor, perhaps they are rather better than worse than we are, but every thing has with them a ruder, more animal form. That way of thinking which we call great and noble is rare among them. They cannot even conceive it; it appears to them as extravagant and foolish as the sentimental and frantic does to us, which yet often originates in a good principle. Their religion, in like manner, is of a rugged nature; their faith is strong, but not pure; they may sometimes forget it, but they rarely desert it. The poor man is but half a Protestant; he has neither time, nor inclination, nor knowledge, for free inquiry, and he cannot raise himself above party prejudices. His natural feeling governs him therefore in religion, the voice of his conscience, the traditional notions of his forefathers, which you constantly hear repeated by him without alteration, and with that the greater or less reliance on your superior knowledge and your sagacity, though this last does not counterbalance with him the authority of the venerable traditions.

"In his way of living the poor man is nearer to the state of nature; not as imagination conceives it, but as we may observe it in children as well as among rude tribes. His passions are strong, and self-restraint is a stranger to him. He is given to uproarious laughter and wild delight. He names himself first, and boasts of his own talents and virtues; mock-humility is therefore utterly unknown to him. The virtue which is the least to be met with in him is the *love of truth*. As all tribes of savages are deceitful, so also is the poor man. The self-immolation demanded by truth is too great for him; for him the union of the harmlessness of the dove with the wisdom of the serpent is too elevated. Still he does not lie and deceive for the mere pleasure of the thing only, but for his own advantage. If then you are rich, he will bless you, but at the same time he will impose on you with the most innocent face and the deepest cunning. If you are his landlord, master, or employer, he carries on a covert war against you, a *tirailleur's* campaign of all sorts of little artifices, just as schoolboys do against the master."

Fully appreciating the quiet joys and usefulness of a village pastor's life, the writer refused his first offer of promotion; but the following year he accepted "a call" to a large town, though agitated by conflicting feelings. Change might not add to happiness, and he was warmly attached to Mastland and its sturdy inhabitants; but innate restlessness, repressed ambition, and prudence weighed heavily in the balance.

It is impossible to lay down this book without feeling a hearty liking for the pastor, who reveals himself with singular *naïveté*, and without an attempt at idealization. The author is anonymous, but his translator has learned that his name is Koetsveld, and he is a clergyman residing at the Hague. His own countrymen have, by buying numerous editions, appreciated the work of one who modestly asserts that he is neither novelist, poet, nor painter—simply a preacher, nothing more. We believe that his popularity will extend to this side of the Channel, for he has wisely restrained all temptation to enlarge too much on favorite or professional topics. The sketches of Tailor and Blacksmith, Winter in the Country, and the Visit from his Uncle—a Rotterdam tobacconist—will amuse from their originality and humor. The Dutch author may be assured that many people will gladly endorse Mr. Keightley's statement that the *Pastorij te Mastland* is a good book, and deserving of being read.

From The National Review.

M. DE TOCQUEVILLE.

Œuvres et Correspondance inédites d'Alexis de Tocqueville, précédées d'une Notice par Gustave de Beaumont. 2 vols. Paris, 1861.

It is a very difficult question to decide at what distance of time after a great man's death his biography should be given to the world. If it is put forth at once, as interest and affection would naturally dictate, while the world is yet ringing with his fame, and his friends yet grieving for his loss, when every one is eager to know more of a man of whom they had heard so much, the sentiments it excites will be more vivid, and the treatment it receives will be more gentle; it will be read more widely, and handled more tenderly; enmity will be silenced and criticism softened by the recency and the sadness of the severance. But, on the other hand, much must be sacrificed for the sake of those advantages. If the deceased has been a statesman, considerations of political propriety compel silence, or only half disclosures, in reference to transactions which perhaps more than most others would throw light upon his character; his reasons for what he did himself, and his judgments of what was done by others, have often to be suppressed out of generous discretion, or from obligations of promised secrecy: and thus only a mutilated and fragmentary account of his thoughts and deeds can be laid before the public. Or if, without being a politician, he has mixed largely with his fellows, as most great men must have done,—if he has lived intimately with the celebrated and the powerful, and poured out in unreserved correspondence with his friends his estimates of the characters and actions of those whom he has known and watched,—and if his abilities and opportunities rendered these estimates of singular interest and value,—we are doomed to a still severer disappointment. For these, which are precisely the things we most desire to learn, and for which we should most treasure his biography, are precisely the things which must be withheld. His contemporaries and associates, the objects of his free criticism, and it may be of his severe judicial condemnation, are still living; their characters must be spared, and their feelings must be respected; the work must be garbled and impoverished by asterisks and omissions, and all the richest and most piquant portions of it must be postponed to a more distant day. If, in order to avoid these inconvenient and enforced discretions, the publication of the life be delayed till the generation to which it belonged has passed away, the necessity for suppression will be escaped, but half the interest in the subject will have died out. The man, unless he belonged to the very first order of great men, will have become one of the ordinary figures of history; his memory may still be cherished by many, but his name will no longer be in every mouth. The delineation of his character may be incomparably more complete and perfect than it could have been at an earlier period, but comparatively few will care to read it; it may be infinitely more instructive, but it can never be half as interesting, for those who would especially have drawn interest and instruction from its pages are gone where all biography is needless. If the subject of the narrative were a public man, his life may still furnish valuable materials for the history of his times; if he were a great thinker, or philosopher, or discoverer, the details of his mental formation and operations may throw much interesting light upon psychology and morals; but if he were only, or mainly, a good man or a social celebrity, it is often hard to see why after so many years any account of him should be given to the world at all.

But these are not the only doubtful questions which those who contemplate biography have to consider. It is not easy to decide who would be the fittest person to undertake the delineation of the character and the narration of the career—a widow, a son, or a brother, or a bosom friend—or an unconnected literary man, capable of full appreciation, but not disturbed by too vivid sympathies. The family of the deceased may of course be expected to know him more thoroughly than any mere acquaintance could do; they have watched him more closely and more continuously; they alone have seen him in his most unbent and therefore most natural, though not perhaps his best, moments; they, more than others, can tell what he was in those private relations of life which, usually but not always, afford the clearest insight into the inner nature of the man. But, on the other hand, they will seldom have known him in his younger days

—his widow rarely, his son never; they will generally be withheld by reverence from any keen critical judgment of his attributes or actions; or, if not, their criticism will carry with it a semblance of unseemliness, and they will scarcely be able to estimate rightly the real space which he filled in the world's eye, the particular points which the world will wish to hear, and the degree and kind of *detail* which it will bear. They will be apt to fall both into indiscriminate and excessive eulogy, and into voluminous and wearisome minuteness. A very intimate and attached friend, especially if he be not also a man of the world, will be exposed to many of the same dangers, though in a less degree. On the other hand, if the materials are put into the hands of a professional writer, well chosen, and really competent by comprehension and just appreciation to treat the subject, the probability is that he will give the public what it wants to know, and will bestow that righteous and measured admiration which the general judgment can ratify; but it is certain that he will never satisfy the family, who will be pretty sure to condemn him as unsympathizing, critical, and cold.

Again: how, and on what principle, is the biographer to hold a fair balance between what is due to his readers and what is due to his hero? The real value of a biography consists in its fidelity, fulness, and graphic truth;—in displaying the character in all its weaknesses as in all its strength; in glossing over nothing, and painting nothing in false colors; in concealing nothing, and distorting nothing which can render the picture genuine as an honest delineation, or useful as a moral lesson, or instructive as a mental study. If, out of regard to the fame of the deceased, or the feelings of his family, events or materials are suppressed by which admirers are deceived as to their estimate, or psychologists misled in their philosophical inferences, integrity has been violated, and mischief has been done. The very facts concealed may be precisely those which would have explained the origin of perplexing anomalies in the character, and have thrown a luminous clearness on the dark places of metaphysic science. A "Life" that is not scrupulously faithful is a narrative only—not a biography, and fails of its highest purpose as well as of its implied promise. An analogous moral question relates to the discretion which the biographer is called upon to exercise as to the literary reputation of his friend. Here, as in the points first referred to, he has to discharge tacit engagements to two parties, whose respective claims he must reconcile. In determining what remains he shall give to the public, is he to consider first and mainly what will elucidate the writer's character, or what will enhance or confirm the writer's fame, or what will be interesting and useful to the world? Is he to withhold what is eminently distinctive, and what would be eminently impressive and instructive, because it had not received the last perfection which the author, had he lived, would have been careful to bestow upon it, and because in comparison with his other writings it would have seemed unfinished and undressed, pleading that his friend set special store on the polish and form of his productions? In a word, is he to be guided by the principles which would have actuated the writer himself while upon earth, or by those purer and more unselfish considerations which may be presumed to animate him *now*?

These various questions M. de Beaumont, in his *Life and Remains of Alexis de Tocqueville*, has had to deal with and decide; and, with the exception of last, we think he has solved them rightly. A close and loving intimacy with his friend for more than thirty years; association with him both in literary labors and in public life; a position which enabled him to know thoroughly what Tocqueville *was* in domestic intercourse, and what he was thought to be in the world; a superiority of mind which qualified him fully to comprehend and analyze that rich nature, combined with a tried and proved affection which made it easy for him to criticise and judge without incurring the faintest suspicion of a cold or depreciating temper—rendered him unquestionably the fittest person that could have been selected for the task he has performed so well. The "Notice" which he has prefixed to the correspondence and unpublished remains has few faults except its brevity. It is simple, succinct, and clear; it gives a sufficient outline of the principal events in Tocqueville's somewhat uneventful life, with the exception of his political career, of which it would perhaps be difficult at present to speak fully and boldly, and of which it certainly would not answer to speak timidly or obscurely; and it thoroughly displays, and makes intelligible, a character of unusual beauty, subtlety, and delicacy. In this, which appears to have been the biographer's single and steadfast aim, we think he has perfectly succeeded. It is impossible to lay down the "Life" without feeling that you *know* the man.

The only ground on which we feel disposed to join issue with M. de Beaumont has reference to the literary remains which he has *withheld*. We fully admit that the gallery of portraits of the public men with whom Tocqueville acted or whom he closely watched, and which we are delighted to hear is in a sufficiently completed state for eventual publication, could not, without indecorum and unkindness, be given to the world during the lifetime of his more notable contemporaries. It was, morever, his own special injunction that the publication of these "Souvenirs" should be delayed till the passing generation should, like himself, have gone to rest. We can even understand and respect, though inclined to regret, the motives which are assigned for the biographer's entire silence as to Tocqueville's speeches and proceedings during the ten years previous to 1848, when he was an active member of the Chamber, though some of those speeches were singularly interesting, and all those proceedings did honor to the actor. But he usually opposed, and often with earnestness and severity, those ministers who, as leaders of the old constitutional party, are now, along with his own more immediate friends, involved in one common proscription; and the circumstances were inopportune for what would have looked like a posthumous attack. It may even have been right to suppress the memoir which Tocqueville had prepared on the Indian Empire, though it must have been full of interest and suggestive value; since the author had himself appended a note to the MS. to the effect that the work would only be worth publishing in the event of his being able to resume and terminate the needful researches. But we cannot acknowledge the validity of the reasoning which has decided M. de Beaumont to withhold from us those portions of the second volume of *L'Ancien Régime et la Révolution*, which he himself describes as nearly, if not quite, finished. He tells us that the volume was within a few months of its completion; that the order of the chapters and the sequence of the ideas was arranged from first to last; that some chapters were not only entirely written, but had received the last touch of the master's hand; and that, by collating those materials, and adding here and there a page or two, here and there only a word or two, a volume might have been legitimately given to the public. He tells us further that the notes and documents which were to furnish Tocqueville's materials, all written by his own hand, are "an immense arsenal of ideas;" that from some of these notes alone other authors might draw the substance for whole volumes; and that some of the preparatory "studies"—such as those on Turgot, on the states-general, on England, and on some German publicists—*sont autant d'ouvrages tout faits*. Yet he has decided, irrevocably he says, that all this vast intellectual wealth, all this knowledge which the prolonged and patient industry of his friend had brought together, all this treasure-chamber of political sagacity, shall be sealed to the public now and forever!

The reasons given for this decision may be satisfactory to a Frenchman, but scarcely to an Englishman. We take leave to doubt whether they would have appeared satisfactory to the philosopher himself. All this invaluable matter, which Tocqueville had collected and digested for the enlightenment of the world, the world is to be denied access to;—and why? Because it would be "profanation to mingle an inferior style with the product of that glorious pencil," and inflict upon the author the responsibility of the faults and feebleness of his editor and continuator. In the first place, we would not have advised, and we are sure M. de Beaumont would have had far too much skill and taste to commit, the error of such intermixture. What was fragmentary we would have had given as a fragment, not cooked up into a finished article. Tocqueville was so precise a thinker, and so minute an investigator, that his detached *pensées* and *pièces justificatives* would have had more value, would have been more profound and suggestive, than the most maturely elaborated productions of almost any other man. We should have valued them as "remains," and should never have fallen into the ungenerous blunder of judging them as finished performances. And, in the second place, if we *had* so judged them, where would have been the harm? We should have been conscious of the casual imperfection while cherishing and admiring the inestimable jewel. The literary fame of so unrivalled a master of style as the author of the *Ancien Régime* could not have suffered in the eyes of any, because it was discovered that his condensed and pregnant phrases were not the *first* form that the thought had assumed in his mind. And even if it had so suffered in the fancy of some thoughtless reader, we say, what then? Is literary renown or public usefulness the weightier consideration? Is the first and paramount purpose of the statesman and the philosophic patriot, in handling these grave matters, to enhance his own reputation for genius and profundity, or to warn his countrymen, from the errors of the past, of the perils which await them in the future? Above all, what was Tocqueville's own estimate of these things? M. de Beaumont says: "Tocqueville ne comprenait une publication *qu'à la condition d'un accroissement de gloire pour son auteur:* il n'admettait pas qu'on fît un livre pour faire un livre." We believe that in saying this he has been guilty of great injustice to the high and unselfish nature of his friend. No doubt Tocqueville was about the last man to sit down to write a book for the mere pleasure of book-making, though he himself often tells us that one of the most effective causes that goaded him into literary activity was his incurable discontent and unrest whenever he had no great object of study and of work on hand. No doubt, too, he had too much of the genuine spirit and conscience of the artist to be content to turn out of his studio any piece of workmanship which fell below his severe standard of attainable perfection; and too sincere a respect for his readers to cast his thoughts before them in any but the most becoming dress and the most decorous attitude; and, more than all, too deep a sense of what was due to the great question he was investigating, and the pregnant principles he was laboring to elicit and enforce, not to spend his utmost strength to clothe them in the fittest words, and to give them forth in the most digested, polished, and effective shape. A slovenly sentence or a slipshod thought was equally his aversion: *ἀεὶ ἀριστεύειν* was his desire in every page he wrote—scarcely *ὑπείροχον ἔμμεναι ἄλλων*. At least we are sure that, though an *accroissement de gloire* from each new volume was far from indifferent to him, as proving that he had done his work well, and so far succeeded in his aim, yet it was by no means his actuating motive nor his prevailing and inspiring thought. He was an earnest and enthusiastic patriot, saddened to the very soul by the discreditable present and the gloomy future of his country, yet grieving less over her degradation than over the moral deficiencies and faults to which that degradation was attributable, and which, if not cured, would go far to insure its hopeless permanence; he saw that the roots of all that he deplored lay deep in the antecedent history and in the inherent nature of the people; he was bent upon penetrating to the very inner spirit and meaning of the Revolution, the causes to which it owed both its existence and its special features, and the enduring consequences it had left behind; and he was sanguine in his hopes that in a thorough comprehension of these things might be discovered some guiding light by means of which what was good in that mighty movement could be maintained and made productive, and what was evil modified and controlled. To this great work he resolved to vote those dark years of France's annals which condemned him, in common with all nobler and purer politicians, to retirement; and how, then, can we agree that any contribution towards its accomplishment which he had prepared ought to be suppressed merely out of deference to his credit as a consummate writer? We cannot believe that such considerations would have decided him while on earth: we are sure they will not influence him now.

However, it would be too much to hope that any arguments of ours can now influence M. de Beaumont to reconsider his decision on these points; though our regret is enhanced by the specimen he has given us to show what the work would have been had Tocqueville lived to complete it. *L'Ancien Régime et la Révolution* is in our judgment a far maturer and profounder work than the *Démocratie en Amérique,* deeper in its insight, graver in its tone, soberer, simpler and chaster in its style; and the two chapters now published, which would have formed part of the second volume of the *Révolution*, show an advance even on the first-named book in lucidity and in mastery of grasp. They are entitled respectively, "Comment la République était prête à trouver un maître," and "Comment la nation, en cessant d'être républicaine, était restée révolutionnaire;" and they depict, with a force and clearness which we never saw approached elsewhere, the profound lassitude, discouragement, and disenchantment which made the *coup d'état* of the 18th of Brumaire so easy and so welcome.

We wish our space would permit us to give an analysis of these two admirable fragments,— if, indeed, any thing so condensed is capable of analysis. But we can only find space for one paragraph,—the conclusion of the first chapter:—

"Quelque habitué que l'on doive être à la mobilité inconséquente des hommes, il semble permis de s'étonner en voyant un si grand changement dans les dispositions morales d'un peuple: tant d'égoisme succédant à tant de dévouement, tant d'indifference à tant de passion, tant de peur à tant d'héroisme, un si grand mépris pour ce qui avait été l'objet de si violents désirs, et qui avait coûté si cher. Il faut renoncer à expliquer un changement aussi complet et aussi prompt par les lois habituelles du monde moral. Le naturel den otre nation est si particulier que l'étude générale de l'humanité ne suffit pas pour le comprendre; elle surprend sans cesse ceux même qui se sont appliqués a l'étudier à part: nation mieux douée qu'aucune autre pour comprendre sans peine les choses extraordinaires et s'y porter; capable de toutes celles qui n'exigent qu'un seul effort, quelque grand qu'il puisse être, mais hors d'état de se tenir longtemps très haut, parcequ'elle *n'a jamais que des sensations et point de principes;* et que ses instincts valent toujours mieux que sa morale; peuple civilisé entre tous les peuples civilisés de la terre, et cependant, sous certains rapports, resté plus près de l'état sauvage qu'aucun d'entre eux; car le propre des sauvages est de se decider par l'impression soudaine du moment, sans mémoire du passé et sans idée de l'avenir."

["However we may be familiar with the unreasoning changeableness of men, we may be permitted to express our astonishment at seeing so great a change in the moral qualities of a people: so much selfishness succeeding to so much devotion, so much indifference to so much enthusiasm, so much fear to so much heroism, so great a contempt for that which had been the object of such violent desires, and which had cost so much. We must despair of explaining a change so complete and so sudden, by the general laws of the moral world. The nature of our nation is so peculiar that the general study of man will not enable us to understand it; it continually surprises even those who have made it their particular study: a nation better fitted than any other to understand readily, and take part in extraordinary affairs; competent to every thing which demands but a single effort, however great it may be, but not able to maintain a long elevation; because she has feelings and not principles; and because her instincts are always worth more than her *morale;* a people eminently civilized, which has yet in some respects remained nearer than any other to the savage state; for the characteristic of savages is to judge by the sudden impression of the moment, without memory of the past or thought of the future."]

The events of Tocqueville's life were neither many nor remarkable. He was the youngest son of an ancient and noble family of Normandy; his mother was the granddaughter of Malesherbes, and his father, himself a literary man of some pretensions, was at one time Prefect of Versailles, and peer of France. Alexis received but an imperfect education, embraced the judicial career, and at the age of twenty-two was appointed *Juge-auditeur*, or Assessor to the Court of Justice of Versailles,—a post which he held for five years, and then reigned in consequence of the dismissal of his intimate friend, M. de Beaumont. Charged by the French government to investigate the penitentiary system of the United States, he sailed to America in company with this same friend in 1831; and on his return, after presenting his official report to the authorities, devoted himself for some years to the preparation of his great work on the American Democracy. The first part of this book, which at once made him famous and placed him in the very first rank of political writers, appeared in 1835, and the second in 1840. In 1835 he married an English lady, than whom no one in mind and character could have been more worthy to be his companion through life; and in 1841 he was elected to the *Académie Française*. In 1839 he was chosen deputy for Valognes, and remained a member of all the successive Chambers till the *coup d'état* in 1851. He felt immense interest in all parliamentary struggles, and took part in them so far as his health permitted, but found himself obliged always to act with the liberal opposition. He felt painfully and indignantly that the narrow electoral basis on which the Chambers rested precluded the great body of the nation not only from exercising any legitimate influence on political proceedings, but from feeling any vivid interest in them; while the trivial and unworthy party conflicts which made up the chief portion of the parliamentary annals of that time taught the people to regard that arena as a mere stage for the display of personal ambition. To Louis Philippe, in the first place, and to Guizot and Thiers in the second, to the disgust created by the corruption of the one and the squabbles of the other, he attributed both the Revolution of 1848 and the discredit which overshadowed constitutional government in France. In a letter to Mr. W. R. Greg, dated 1853, he says:—

"The electoral system of the constitutional monarchy had one enormous vice, which, in my judgment, was the principal cause of the fall of that monarchy: it rested on too small a body of electors (there were about 240,000). The result was, that the electoral body soon became nothing but a small *bourgeois* oligarchy, pre-occupied with its special interests, and separated from the people, whom it neither considered nor was considered by. The people, therefore, ceased to have the slightest sympathy with its proceedings; while the ancient upper classes, whom it jealously kept out of the administration, despised it, and impatiently endured its exclusive supremacy. Nearly the whole nation was thus led to regard the representative system as a mere political contrivance for giving predominance to certain individual interests, and placing power in the hands of a small number of families—an opinion far from correct even then, but favoring, more than any other cause, the advent of a new government."

M. de Tocqueville did not speak often in the Chamber, for his voice was feeble, and the form in which he instinctively clothed his sentiments was philosophic rather than rhetorical, and was too terse and polished to be as effective as the matter of them deserved; but whenever he did appear in the tribune, he always excited interest; and one of his speeches, delivered just three weeks before the catastrophe of February, 1848, created an extraordinary sensation. He warned his audience, with all the earnestness of prophetic insight, that they were on the eve of a most formidable revolution; that notwithstanding the absence of *émeutes* and street-disturbances, a profound perturbation agitated men's minds to their inmost depths; that the passions which would predominate over the coming outbreak would be social rather than political, and would assail society itself more than particular governments and laws; and that the worst danger of the volcano on which they were sleeping consisted in the *contempt* felt by the lower classes for those above them, as unworthy and incapable at once. The Chamber protested against such conclusions; but in less than a month came the Republic, and in four months, the frightful and sanguinary struggle in the streets of Paris.*

When the revolution which he had predicted with such a rare sagacity broke out, he prepared himself to do his duty to his country in that perplexing crisis with a courage and a clearness of vision still more unique and admirable. He saw that society and liberty as well as government were in danger; he had little faith in a republic, and little sympathy with the sort of men with whom republican institutions would infallibly mix him up; and he had no sanguine hopes that it would be possible to steer France through the perils she had conjured up around her. But he felt that it would not be the part of a good citizen or an honorable man to desert the helm because the sea was stormy, or the vessel damaged, or the crew dirty or disreputable; he was convinced that the only chance for liberty and order lay in making the Republic *work*, if it were possible to do so; and for this object,

* Not long before, he had written to M. de Corcelle from his country-house in Normandy: "I find this country without political excitement, but in a most formidable moral condition. We may perhaps not be close upon a revolution, but assuredly it is thus that revolutions are prepared. The effect produced by Cubières' trial is immense. The horrible affair, too, which has filled every mind for the last week (the murder of the duchess and the suicide of the Duke de Choiseul Praslin) is of a character to create an undefined terror and a profound uneasiness. I confess it does so with me. I never heard of a crime which has shocked me more from its indications as to man in general and the humanity of our day. What disturbance in the consciences of men does not such a deed proclaim! How it shows the moral ruin which successive revolutions have produced!"

therefore, he sacrificed many of his own tastes and submitted to the defeat of many of his predilections and opinions. He sat in both the *Constituent* and the *National* Assemblies, and took an active part in framing the new and short-lived constitution. His opinion was to the last, that, if they had had fair play, there was wisdom and sober patriotism in those two Assemblies to have managed the political machine. In the letter from which we have already quoted he bears the following remarkable testimony to the working of universal suffrage, when perfectly free and genuine :—

"It must be admitted that the two general elections conducted under this system were the most honest and unfettered that have been seen in France since 1789. There was neither corruption nor intimidation of any kind. Intimidation was, indeed, attempted by the government, and by different factions, but without success. The great number of the electors, and especially their collection in great masses in the electoral colleges, rendered the action of the government absolutely unfelt. On the contrary, the system restored, in most provinces, to the clergy and the rich proprietors more political influence than they had possessed for sixty years,—and they nowhere abused it. This became apparent when the genuineness of the contested returns came to be discussed in the Assembly. It was unanimously recognized that the influence of the clergy and the great landowners had been considerable. But there was scarcely a single complaint of the peasants having been either bullied or bribed;—the truth being, that, in a country where wealth is as much *distributed* as in France, intimidation or corruption *by individuals* can never be pushed very far under any electoral system. The influence, therefore, which was exercised over the peasant by the rich proprietor was entirely a moral one. The peasant, himself a proprietor, and alarmed for his property by the doctrines of the communists, applied for guidance to men who were more enlightened than himself, and had still larger proprietary interests at stake. I cannot say that this would have always continued to be the case. I merely state the facts I witnessed; and I affirm that the Conservative majority which predominated, first in the Constituent and then in the National Assembly, contained more rich and independent landed proprietors, more of what you in England term *country gentlemen*, than any Chamber in which I have sat."

In June, 1849, Tocqueville consented to accept the portfolio of Minister for Foreign Affairs. He retained it only five months, when his disapproval of a step taken by the president on the 31st October compelled him to resign. But during his period of office occurred, we grieve to say, the expedition to Rome, and, we are glad to say, the support given in conjunction with Great Britain to Turkey in her resistance to the infamous demands of Austria and Russia for the extradition of the Hungarian refugees. From the time when Tocqueville left the ministry till the *coup d'état* in December, 1851, he sat sad and disgusted in the Assembly, watching its long agony, and waiting for the obviously preparing and inevitable stroke. He was one of the two hundred deputies who were seized and sent to Vincennes. His political life ended with the death of liberty in France. He retired to his beloved home, near Cherbourg—his ancestral Château de Tocqueville—and thenceforward till his decease occupied himself, as far as health permitted, in collecting materials for the great work which, to the regret of all, he was compelled to leave unfinished. Profoundly discouraged and sorrowful he certainly was; but he never altogether lost heart as to the final redemption of his country, and never for one hour ceased to ponder and to labor for it.

To the general world, however, Tocqueville is known not as the active politician, but as the profound and meditative writer on political science;—and as such he ranks, as at least an equal, with the three great modern masters in his own department, Machiavelli, Montesquieu, and Burke; possessing at the same time certain marked characteristics which distinguish him from each in turn. Machiavelli was a subtle and sagacious statesman, and his writings abound in ingenious deductions and suggestions; but his purpose in *The Prince* was mainly practical, and the ground ranged over in the *Discorsi sopra Tito Livio* was comparatively narrow. He was admirable in his faculty of large generalization and of penetrating insight; but his materials were deplorably scanty, being confined to one Roman history of very questionable accuracy, and of very unquestionable incompleteness, and to what he had himself learned at first hand, or heard from others, of the political annals of the small Italian states. The truth is, he drew far more from his own intuitive sagacity sharpened as it had been by active participation in political affairs and intimate intercourse with the ablest statesmen and generals of his age, than from any facts which the annals of other countries laid before him; and in reading his chapters we are perpetually disturbed by the contrast between his wide inductions and the apparently flimsy foundation on which they are made to rest.* Montesquieu, we confess, we have never been able to appreciate—at least, not to any thing like the degree of admiration expressed for him by his countrymen. The *finesse* and acuteness of his mind render his *Esprit des Lois* a most entertaining book; but it is impossible not to feel that you are dealing with an intellect too ingenious to be quite sound, and too distinct and positive in solving the great problems of society to have been fully conscious of their depth or difficulty; and moreover, the reader soon finds that no reliance can be placed on the facts adduced by the author to illustrate or to prove his positions. Any statement which answers his purpose is taken for gospel, however contemptible the authority on which it rests: if a philosopher or historian does not give him what he wants, a missionary or a traveller will do as well; the statistics of Meaco are quoted to exemplify doctrines which the statistics of France or England might have refuted; and any idle tale about Siam, Japan, or Timbuctoo which has reached his ears is eagerly pressed into the service if no solider materials are at hand. Both the *Esprit des Lois* and the *Grandeur et Décadence* are therefore rather clever disquisitions than works of real philosophical research. Burke was a mind of a very different order. He was not a systematic or analytic thinker, like Machiavelli or Montesquieu, nor probably did he meditate over all he saw and knew as patiently and searchingly as Tocqueville; but his memory was stored with wealth of every sort; his genius was perhaps the very loftiest and finest that has ever been devoted to political investigations; his wonderful imagination, though it sometimes led him astray, and often tempted him too far, yet gave him a profound and penetrating insight, and an almost prophetic intuition, which mere reason and observation could never attain; and his passionate sympathies with all that was good and noble or suffering and oppressed, while they frequently made him intemperate and occasionally made him unjust, throw over his works a fascination and a glow which belong to no other writer. The more we study him, the more are we compelled to rank him as at once the wisest and most lovable of political philosophers.

Tocqueville had two or three characteristics as a writer and thinker which distinguished him from all his three predecessors. He was not a learned man, though no one ever took greater pains to make all the investigations and to amass all the information requisite to form a conscientious judgment on the questions which he treated; he had all the clearness and precision of thought which belong to the French mind; he had a faculty of patiently "chewing the cud" of his reflections and materials which was almost German; he was a *ruminating* animal;* he revolved and meditated, as well as examined and reasoned; while he was peculiarly English in the eminently practical turn of his ideas, as well as in his almost solemn earnestness of purpose and in the predominance and constant activity of the

* It is interesting to see Tocqueville's estimate of his great predecessor. He writes to Kergolay: "The Machiavelli of the *History of Florence* is, to me, the same Machiavelli who wrote *The Prince*. I cannot understand the perusal of the first work leaving any doubt as to the object and meaning of the second. Machiavelli in his History often praises great and noble actions; but with him this is obviously an affair of the imagination. The foundation of his ideas is, that all actions are morally indifferent in themselves, and must be judged according to the skill they display and the success they secure. For him the world is a great arena, from which God is absent, in which conscience has nothing to do, and where every one must manage as well as he can. Machiavelli is the grandfather of M——. I need say no more."

* His mode of working is thus described in a letter to Duvergier d'Hauranne. "When I have a subject to treat, it is almost impossible to read any books that have been written by others on it: the contact of the ideas of other men disturbs and affects me painfully. But, on the other hand, I take incredible pains to find out every thing for myself in the original documents of the epoch I am dealing with; often I obtain in this manner with vast labor what I might have discovered much more easily by following a different line. When I have gathered in this toilsome harvest, I retire as it were into myself; I examine with extreme care, collate, and connect the notions I have thus acquired; and I then set to work to draw out and expound the ideas which have arisen spontaneously within me during this long effort, without giving a single thought to the inferences which others may deduce from what I write."

moral element within him. It is this last feature in his speculations, more even than their depth and astonishing sagacity, which lends them their greatest charm: you feel that you are dealing with a man who not only believes every word he says, and experiences every sentiment to which he gives expression, but to whom, in this crisis of the destiny of mankind, every thing is grave and nearly every thing is sad. Tocqueville had no taste for abstract reasoning; he abominated metaphysics; he found himself thrown into the arena of life, in a land, and at a time, where there was much to alarm and yet more to perplex and disgust both the patriot and the general philanthropist; he saw a tide setting in over the whole western world which seemed irresistible in its strength and perilous in its direction; and he set to work with his whole soul to study its nature and its origin, in the hope, which at length nearly ripened into a conviction, that what could not be checked might be modified and guided, so as to become comparatively harmless and almost beneficent. He believed that the democratic tendencies of the age, throughout Europe as well as in America, were omnipotent as against all antagonism, but that they might be mastered, and *ridden* as it were, if we could at once accept them as inevitable, understand their meaning and their foibles, and foresee and guard against the dangers and excesses inherent in their essence. This was the *idée-mère*, as he often calls it, of his great work on the *American Democracy*; this engrossed and colored all his thoughts and directed his course while an active politician; this dictated his last literary effort, *L'Ancien Régime*, and haunted him to his latest hour. In 1836 he writes to Kergolay:—

"Tout ce que tu me dis sur la tendance centralisante, réglementaire, de la démocratie européene, me semble parfait. . . . Les pensées que tu exprimes là sont les plus *vitales* de toutes mes pensées; ce sont celles qui reviennent, pour ainsi dire, tous les jours et à chaque instant du jour dans mon esprit. Indiquer, s'il se peut, aux hommes ce qu'il faut faire pour échapper à la tyrannie et à l'abâtardissement en devenant *démocratiques*, telle est, je pense, l'idée générale dans laquelle peut se résumer mon livre, et qui apparaîtra à toutes les pages de celui que j'écris en ce moment. Travailler dans ce sens, c'est à mes yeux une occupation *sainte*, et pour laquelle il ne faut épargner ni son argent, ni son temps, ni sa vie."

["All that you say about the centralizing, regulating tendency of European Democracy, seems to me to be perfect. . . . The thoughts which you there express are the most vital of all my thoughts. They are those which come back again, so to speak, every day and all the day to my mind. To point out, if I can, to men that which they must do, in order to escape from tyranny and abasement in becoming democratic,—this is, I think, the general idea of my work, and that which will appear in every page of that which I am now writing. To work with this object is in my eyes a sacred occupation, in which one should spare neither his money, his time, nor his life."]

To his friend Stoffels he explains his purpose more fully:—

"I wished to show what in our days a democratic people really was, and, by a rigorously accurate picture, to produce a double effect on the men of my day. To those who have fancied an ideal democracy, as a brilliant and easily realized dream, I undertook to show that they had clothed the picture in false colors; that the democratic government which they desired, though it may procure real benefits to the people who can bear it, has none of the elevated features with which their imagination would endow it; and moreover, that such a government can only maintain itself under certain conditions of faith, enlightenment, and private morality which we have not yet reached, and which we must labor to attain before grasping their political results.

"To men for whom the word 'democracy' is the synonyme of overthrow, spoliation, anarchy, and murder, I have endeavored to prove that it was possible for democracy to govern society, and yet to respect property, to recognize rights, to spare liberty, to honor religion; that if democratic government is less fitted than other forms to develop some of the finest faculties of the human soul, it has yet its noble and its lovely features; and that perhaps, after all, it may be the will of God to distribute a moderate degree of happiness to the mass of men, and not to concentrate great felicity and great perfection on a few. I have tried, moreover, to demonstrate that, whatever might be their opinion upon these points, the time for discussing them was past; that the world marched onwards day by day towards a condition of social equality, and dragged them and every one along with it; that their only choice now lay between evils henceforth inevitable; that the practical question of this day was not whether you would have an aristocracy or a democracy, but whether you would have a democratic society, without poetry and without grandeur, but with morality and order, *or* a democratic society disorganized and depraved, delivered over to a furious frenzy, or else bent beneath a yoke heavier than any that have weighed upon mankind since the fall of the Roman Empire.

"I wanted to lessen the ardor of the first class of politicians, and, without discouraging them, to point out their only wise course. I sought to lessen the terrors of the second class, and to curb their will to the idea of an inevitable future; so that, one set having less eagerness, and the other set offering less resistance, society might march on peaceably towards the fulfilment of its destiny. *Voilà l'idée-mère de l'ouvrage*."—Vol. i. p. 427.

It is obvious enough from this passage, as from many others, that Tocqueville's own opinions and predilections were any thing rather than democratic. He writes to Kergolay from the United States in 1831:—

"Nous allons nous-mêmes, mon cher ami, vers une démocratie sans bornes. Je ne dis pas que ce soit une bonne chose; ce que je vois dans ce pays ci me convainc au contraire que la France s'en arrangera mal; mais nous y allons poussés par une force irrésistible. . . . Dans les premiers temps de la république, les hommes d'état, les membres des Chambres, étaient beaucoup plus distingués qu'ils ne le sont aujourd'hui. Ils faisaient presque tous partie de cette classe de propriétaires dont la race s'éteint tous les jours. Maintenant le pays n'a plus la main si heureuse. Ses choix tombent en général sur ceux qui flattent ses passions et se mettent à sa portée. Cet effet de la démocratie, joint à l'extrême instabilité de toutes choses, au défaut absolu d'esprit de suite et de durée qu'on remarque ici, me demontre tous les jours davantage que *le gouvernement le plus rationnel n'est pas celui auquel tous les intéressés prennent part, mais celui que dirigent les classes les plus éclairées et les plus morales de la société*."

["We ourselves, my dear friend, are tending to an unlimited democracy; I do not say this is a good thing; what I see in this country convinces me, on the contrary, that France will make a bad business of it; but we are pressed to it by an irresistible power. . . . In the early times of the republic, the statesmen, the members of Congress, were much more distinguished than they are now. Almost all of them belonged to the class of persons of large property which dies out every day. Now the country is not so fortunate. Its choice now in general, falls upon those who flatter its passions and submit themselves to its will. This effect of democracy, joined to the extreme instability of every thing, and the absolute want which we notice of the spirit of persistence and fixedness, shows me more and more every day, that the most rational government is not that in which all who are interested take a part, but that which is managed by the most enlightened and most moral classes of society."]

The truth is, that Tocqueville had an essentially *judicial* mind; he adhered to no special political party; he had no political passion but that of liberty; and he had no political prejudice at all. His birth from an aristocratic family, and in a democratic age, made it, as he says in a letter to Mr. Reeve, easy for him to guard himself against the unreasonable likes and dislikes of both classes:—

"On veut absolument faire de moi un homme de parti, et je ne le suis point. On me donne des passions, et je n'ai que des opinions; ou plutôt, je n'ai qu'une passion, l'amour de la liberté et de la dignité humaine. Toutes les formes gouvernementales ne sont à mes yeux que des moyens plus ou moins parfaits de satisfaire cette sainte et légitime passion de l'homme."

["They insist upon making me out a party man; but I am not. They think I have passion; but I have only opinion; or rather, I have only one passion, the love of liberty and human dignity. All forms of government are in my eyes only means, more or less perfect, for satisfying this legitimate and holy passion of man."]

Alexis de Tocqueville had long been known over the world as one of the profoundest political thinkers of this or any age: it is only from his correspondence that those who had not the privilege of knowing him personally could learn how unique and how superior he was in his inner nature, and in all the relations of private life. This correspondence is extraordinarily rich and interesting; for to Tocqueville not only was constant intercourse with his friends, and a real interchange of sentiments and ideas, an absolute necessity, but it was a positive pleasure to him to develop his views and the workings of his mind in writing when he could not do it in conversation. He wrote, too, moreover, with the greatest openness as well as with singular clearness and care; and he

puisable de sentiments élevés et énergiques, de belles émotions, de résolutions généreuses, un monde à part, un peu idéal peut-être, mais où je me repose, non point comme un paresseux, mais comme un homme fatigué qui s'arrête un moment pour reprendre des forces et se jeter plus avant ensuite dans la mêlée."

["To make an end of this matter, I will tell you that nothing is more precious to me than our friendship. I see in it an inexhaustible source of high and energetic opinions, of beautiful feelings, of generous resolutions; a separate world, a little ideal perhaps, where I rest myself, not indolently, but like a weary man who pauses a moment to gather up his strength, and throw himself further forward in the struggle."]

His estimate of existence, its value, and its uses was as lofty and generous as religion and philosophy could combine to make it. Among his scattered manuscripts is found this sentence, which, as his biographer observes is in itself a *résumé* of his whole life: "La vie n'est pas un plaisir, ni une douleur; mais une affaire grave dont nous sommes chargés, et qu'il faut conduire et terminer à notre honneur."

["Life is neither a pleasure, nor a grief; but a serious business which has been committed to us, and which we must carry on and complete to our honor."]

Again, he writes shortly before his marriage:—

"I feel more and more as you do as to the joys of conscience. I believe them to be at once the deepest and the most real. There is only one great object in this world that deserves our efforts; that is the good of humanity. . . . As I advance in life, I see it more and more from that point of view which I used to fancy belonged to early youth; viz., as a thing of very mediocre worth, valuable only as far as one can employ it in doing one's duty, in serving men, and in taking one's fit place among them. How cold, small, and sad life would become if, by the side of this every-day world, so full of cowardice and selfishness, the human mind could not build for itself another in which generosity, courage, virtue, in a word, may breathe at ease! . . . Ah! (he concludes) que je voudrais que la Providence me présentât une occasion d'employer à faire de bonnes et grandes choses, quelques périls qu'elle y attachât, ce feu intérieur que je sens au dedans de moi, et qui ne sait où trouver qui l'alimente."

["Ah, how I wish that Providence would give me an opportunity to employ in doing great and good things (whatever dangers may go with them), this interior fire which I feel within me, and which does not know where to find food for itself."]

A quarter of a century later, about two years before his death, he writes to a friend who had dissuaded him from spending too much of his time in the solitude of a country life:—

"You know that my most settled principle is, that there is no period of a man's life at which he is entitled to *rest;* and that effort out of one's self, and still more above one's self, is as necessary in age as in youth —nay, even more necessary. Man in this world is like a traveller who is always walking towards a colder region, and who is therefore obliged to be more active as he goes further north. The great malady of the soul is *cold.* And in order to counteract and combat this formidable illness, he must keep up the activity of his mind not only by work, but by contact with his fellow-men and with the world. Retirement from the great conflicts of the world is desirable no doubt for those whose strength is on the decline; but absolute retirement, away from the stir of life, is not desirable for any man, nor at any age."

It is always extremely interesting to know the estimate formed of mankind in general by those who have studied them profoundly as well as acted with them in the most trying relations of life. Tocqueville's opinion of his fellow-men was indulgent, but not high. When a young man, he tried to love them, he says, but without much success. "I like *mankind;* but I constantly meet *individuals* who repel and disgust me by the meanness of their nature. It is my daily effort to guard against a universal contempt for my fellow-men. I can only succeed by a minute and severe analysis of myself; the result of which is, that I am inclined, as a rule, rather to condemn men's intelligence than their hearts." In 1840, when immersed in public life, he says to Stoffels. "I[illegible]
sad side of human[illegible]
We may say, with[illegible]
that nothing there[illegible]
or thoroughly disi[illegible]
generous, nothing[illegible]
There is no *youth,*[illegible]
est; and somethin[illegible]
meditated may be d[illegible]

apparently passionate proceedings." And, as the summary result of his experience, he speaks thus to a somewhat misanthropic friend:—

"You make out humanity worse than it is. I have seen many countries, studied many men, mingled in many public transactions; and the result of my observation is not what you suppose. Men in general are neither very good nor very bad; they are simply *mediocre*. I have never closely examined even the best without discovering faults and frailties invisible at first. I have always in the end found among the worst certain elements and *holding-points* of honesty. There are two men in every man: it is childish to see only one; it is sad and unjust to look only at the other. . . . Man, with all his vices, his weaknesses, and his virtues, this strange mixture of good and bad, of low and lofty, of sincere and depraved, is, after all, the object most deserving of study, interest, pity, affection, and admiration to be found upon this earth; and since we have no angels, we cannot attach ourselves to any thing greater or worthier than our fellow-creatures."

Our space is limited, and, as we have been chiefly anxious to display the character and inner nature of Alexis de Tocqueville as revealed in these volumes, we have been obliged to pass over nearly all his judgments and reflections on the events of his day both at home and abroad, though these are everywhere replete with interest and instruction. If we had been able, we should have wished to cite his views as to the change in the literary temper of his country; as to the moral retrogression since the epoch of 1789; his vivid picture, in a letter to Madame Swetchine, of the transformation of the young conscript from the peasant into the soldier, and *vice versâ;* his profound remarks on the mischief which in France religion has always suffered from the alliance between the Church and the government; and his sound and sagacious notions as to the peculiar perils and difficulties of our Indian Empire. But for all these we must refer our readers to the volumes themselves, of which an English translation by a most competent hand is about to appear. We must, however, be allowed to extract his remarks as to the "political selfishness of England," and the singular impressions on this head which prevail in every part of the world, and which so friendly and acute an observer as Tocqueville could not help avowing that he shared. He had noticed what few others on the Continent seem yet to have perceived:—

"The gradual change which has come over the English temperament, which is daily becoming more pacific, less irritable, and less proud, than at any previous period of modern history. This I believe to be only the result of the grand revolution which has been at work there, slowly indeed, but as irresistibly as everywhere else,—the predominance of the middle classes over the aristocracy, and of the industrial element over the agricultural and real-property one. Will this be a good, or an evil? Your grandchildren will discuss this question. A society calmer and duller, more tranquil and less heroic,—such, no doubt, will be the spectacle for our successors."

But in 1856 he writes to M. de Beaumont:—

"Mme. Grote nous envoie quelquefois des journaux anglais qui font ma joie. Ils ont une espèce de naïveté ravissante dans leur passion nationale. A leurs yeux, les ennemis de l'Angleterre sont tout naturellement des coquins, et ses amis de grands hommes. La seule échelle de la moralité humaine qu'ils connaissent est là."

["Mrs. Grote sends us occasionally English journals which are my delight. They have a kind of freshness in their national enthusiasm. In their eyes the enemies of England are all born scoundrels, and her friends, all great men. The only scale of human morality they know is that."]

And to Mrs. Grote herself he says:—

"Aux yeux des Anglais, la cause dont le succès est utile à l'Angleterre est toujours la cause de la justice. L'homme ou le gouvernement qui sert les intérêts de l'Angleterre a toutes sortes de qualités, et celui qui la nuit, toutes sortes de défauts; de sorte qu'il semblerait que le *criterium* de l'honnête, du beau, et du juste doit être cherché dans ce qui favorise ou ce qui blesse l'intérêt anglais. . . . En France, on a fait souvent en politique des choses utiles et injustes, mais sans que l'utilité cachât au public l'injustice. Nous avons même quelquefois employé de grands coquins, mais sans leur attribuer la moindre vertu. Je ne suis pas bien sûr qu'au point de vue moral cela vaut mieux, mais elle montre du moins une faculté plus grande de l'esprit."

["In the eyes of the English, that cause whose success is useful to England, is always just. The man or the government which serves the interests of England has all good qualities, and that which injures her, all sorts of evil ones; so that it seems, that the criterion of the honest, the beautiful, and the just, must be looked for in that which favors or injures England. . . . In France we have often done in politics things which were at the same time useful and unjust; but their usefulness has not blinded the public to their injustice. We have even sometimes employed great villains, but without attributing the least virtue to them. I am not quite sure that in the interests of morality that is the best way; but it shows at least more vigor of intellect."]

Finally, he calls the attention of M. Senior to the painful fact that the Indian crisis, even more than our sufferings in the Crimean war, showed how little sympathy and liking for England can be found among foreign nations. Our discomfiture in that fearful conflict, he observes, could have profited no one and no cause but that of barbarism; yet it was generally wished for. No doubt, he says, this universal sentiment was partly attributable to malice and envy, but also in part to a less discreditable reason,—"to a conviction felt by all people in the world that England never considers others except from the selfish point of view of her own grandeur; that all sympathetic sentiment for *what is not herself* is more absent in her than in any nation of modern times; that she never notices what passes among foreigners, what they think, feel, suffer, or do, except in reference to the advantage that England may draw therefrom,—occupied in reality only with herself, even when she seems most occupied with them. There is certainly some exaggeration in this notion, but I cannot say there is not much truth in it."

It is well, no doubt, that we should be aware what harsh things are thought of us, and especially that we should hear them from a man so candid and so fair, and usually so well inclined to admire and love England, as Tocqueville assuredly was;* for it is a proof that, however unjust the accusation, we must have given some grounds for it by our language and our manners, if not by our actions. But as to the charge itself, we must avow our conscientious conviction that it is monstrously overdrawn, if not utterly unfounded, and as coming from a Frenchman absolutely astounding. We may readily admit that England has often done unjust actions, and has shown curious ingenuity in blinding herself to their injustice; we may even allow that, like other nations, she is disposed to judge her friends and servants more leniently than her foes,—to

"Be to their faults a little blind,
Be to their virtues very kind;"—

we may confess, with shame, that the language of our statesmen, especially of late, when they have had occasion to explain or justify the measures of their foreign policy, has often been calculated to give an air of truth to this accusation of unsocial selfishness: and that, if we could consent to be judged by the coarse and ferocious manifestoes of Mr. Bright, we should not have a word to urge in our defence;—but that England in these respects has been worse than other nations, that she has not, more particularly during the last half-century, been much better than other nations, that she has not of late years been the one power which has habitually proclaimed the principles and held the language of generous sympathy and unselfish public morality,—we must emphatically and deliberately deny. She has hailed the progress of civilization and prosperity everywhere; she has expressed the warmest appreciation of the efforts and aspirations of liberty wherever they have broken forth; she has been the first to denounce the acts of injustice and oppression occasionally exercised by her own agents and proconsuls; and she has steadily opposed and protested against the grasping and intriguing iniquities of France, the cynical immorality and selfishness of whose public conduct has been written in sunbeams on every page of recent history. We need look no further than Italy to be able to form a comparative judgment of the relative capacity for disinterested sympathy displayed by the two nations. Republican France, without the faintest vestige of a just pretext, sent an army to crush the republican liberties of Rome, within eighteen months after she had

* His admiration of our country was earnest and sincere. On his return from England in 1857, he wrote to M. de Corcelle: "C'est le plus grand spectacle qu'il y ait dans le monde, quoique tout n'y soit pas grand. Il s'y rencontre surtout des choses entièrement inconnues dans le reste de l'Europe et dont la vue m'a soulagé."

turbulently seized her own; she replaced the worst government of Europe on its throne by force, and has acted as its sbirri ever since; she did this simply and avowedly to prevent Austria from gaining additional influence in Italy by forestalling her proceeding; and, we grieve to write it, she committed this enormous and unblushing crime while Alexis de Tocqueville was Minister for Foreign Affairs. Italy has now recovered her liberties, thanks to *Imperial* rather than *French* assistance; she has formed a united country under a constitutional monarch; she bids fair to be free, happy, and progressive. What does England say to the prospect?—she is wild with disinterested enthusiasm and delight. What does France say? Why, every French publicist or statesman, with scarcely a single exception besides the emperor,—Liberal, Orleanist, Despotic, Legitimist, Republican, Catholic, Protestant—are grinding their teeth with dishonorable envy and more dishonorable rage. "*It wont suit France,*" is their unanimous and shameful cry, "to have a great and independent Italy beside her; she may become our rival; and what title has Italy to be free while we are whining or fawning under despotism?"

We must draw to a close. The great charm of these volumes, as we have already said, lies in the complete and distinct picture they present of the real nature and being of the man, without drapery and without disguise. No man was ever more worth seeing in this unreserved disclosure than Tocqueville, and few men's characters could bear it so well. Every fresh revelation of his most intimate sentiments and thoughts only serves to make us love him better and admire him more. He was not exactly a perfect character, and yet it was impossible to wish any thing changed or any thing away. You might imagine something more absolutely faultless, but you could not imagine any thing more attractive or more noble. Perhaps his most unique and characteristic distinction was that, while perfectly simple, he was at the same time unfailingly high-minded. You felt at once that no sentiment mean, ungenerous, prejudiced, or shallow, *could* gain entrance into his mind or find utterance through his lips. A profound moral earnestness pervaded every thing he did, or thought, or wrote. He could not separate either public from private morality, or patriotic from personal affection. With all that delicate chivalry of honor which belonged to the purest of the old *noblesse* he blended a far loftier code and a far sounder judgment as to the truly right and good than the old *noblesse* ever dreamed of. He threw his whole soul into both his philosophic investigations and his political career. He loved his country as he loved his friends: its misfortunes grieved him like a domestic calamity; its crimes and follies weighed down his spirits like the sin and dishonor of a brother or a son; the clouds and dangers that hung over its future haunted him like a nightmare. Partly from this cause, and partly from a delicate organization and frequent suffering, he was often sad, and at times melancholy almost to despair. His intellect was sensitive and restless in a remarkable degree for one so sober and moderate in all his views; work, actual labor for some great aim, was absolutely necessary to his comfort and tranquillity, while, alas, it was often too much for his strength. To him every thing in life was serious; he felt too keenly and he thought too deeply not to be habitually grave, though his elegant taste, cultivated intelligence, and natural sense of humor prevented this gravity from ever becoming oppressive, except to the most frivolous and shallow minds. The grace of his manner and the charm of his conversation were, by universal admission, unrivalled in this day; while to the intercourse of daily life the exquisite polish of his spirit, mingled with a most affectionate and caressing disposition, lent a fascination that was strangely irresistible. In the midst, too, of all his rare refinement and maturity of wisdom there was a fund of enthusiasm which gave relief and animation to the whole; and there were few changes in France which he deplored more than the cold and passionless materialism which seemed to have absorbed all classes and all ages. In 1858 he describes a visit which he paid to an enthusiastic old Benedictine of ninety-six, who had shared in all the hopes and efforts of 1789; and then goes on to say to M. Freslon, his correspondent:—

"J'ai déjà remarqué qu'en France la quantité de calorique intellectuel et moral était en raison inverse du nombre des années. On est plus froid à mesure qu'on est plus jeune; et la température semble s'élever avec l'âge. Des hommes comme vous et moi paraissent déjà des enthousiastes bien ridicules aux sages de dix-huit ans. Suivant cette loi nouvelle, mon centenaire devait être tout feu. Et il l'était en effet quand il parlait des espérances de '89 et de la grande cause de la liberté. Je lui ai demandé s'il trouvait la France bien changée sous le rapport moral. 'Ah! monsieur,' m'a-t-il repondu, 'je crois rêver quand je me rapelle l'état des esprits dans ma jeunesse, la vivacité, la sincerité des opinions, le respect de soi-même et de l'opinion publique, le désintéressement dans la passion publique. Ah! monsieur (ajou-tait-il en me serrant les mains avec l'effusion et l'emphase du xviiime siècle), *on avait alors une cause: on n'a plus que des intérêts.* Il y avait des liens entre les hommes: il n'y en a plus. Il est bien triste, monsieur, de survivre à son pays.'"

["I have already said that in France the quantity of intellectual and moral heat, is in inverse proportion to age. We are cold in proportion to our youth, and our temperature seems to rise as we grow older. Men of your age and mine already seem ridiculous enthusiasts to sages of eighteen. According to this new law, my centenarian should be all fire. And in fact he was when he spoke of the hope of '89 and the great cause of liberty. I asked him if he found much moral changes in France. 'Ah, sir,' he answered, 'I think I am dreaming when I recall the state of mind of my youth, the liveliness and sincerity of opinions, the respect of one's self and of public opinion, the disinterested public feeling. Ah! sir,' added he, grasping my hands with the gush and the emphasis of the eighteenth century, 'we had then a *cause*, now we have only *interests*; then there were ties between men, now there are none. It is very sad, sir, to outlive one's country.'"]

We are naturally desirous to know the sentiments of a man at once so good, so wise, and so free, on religion—that great matter on which wise and free and good men differ so marvellously, if not so hopelessly. Neither the memoir nor the correspondence is very specific on this head. This much, however, appears clearly, that the subject was one that occupied his intentest thought, and that he held faith to be a possession of first necessity to individuals as to States. He often laments the indifference and infidelity of his countrymen, and their apparent inability to do as England had succeeded in doing,—to unite belief and liberty. Among memoranda and reflections written early in life and found among his papers, is the following: "Il n'y a pas de vérité absolue," and a little further on, "Si j'étais chargé de classer les misères humaines, je le ferais dans cette ordre: 1°. Les maladies; 2°. La mort; 3°. Le doute."

["There is no absolute truth. . . . If I were charged with the classification of human miseries, I should place them in the order: 1st Disease. 2nd Death. 3rd Doubt."]

Many years afterwards, when he was about forty-five years old, he writes to M. de Corcelle: "Je ne sais d'ailleurs si les dernières circonstances dans laquelle je me suis trouvé, la gravité plus grande que l'âge donne à la pensée, la solitude dans laquelle je vis, ou toute autre cause que je ne sais pas, agissent sur mon âme et y produisent un travail intérieur; la vérité est que je n'ai jamais plus senti le besoin de la base éternelle, du terrain solide sur lequel la vie doit être batie. Le doute m'a toujours paru le plus insupportable des maux de ce monde, et je l'ai constamment jugé pire que la mort."

["Besides, I don't know whether the later circumstances in which I am placed, the greater gravity which age gives to thought, the solitude in which I live, or some other unknown cause, acts upon my mind, and produces an inward labor. The truth is that I have never more felt the need of the eternal foundation, the solid ground, upon which life ought to be built. Doubt has always seemed to me the most insupportable of earthly evils, and I have always thought it worse than death."]

From this doubt, however, which he so deprecated, it was impossible for a spirit at once so searching and so honest as his ever quite to free itself; but it remained speculative merely, and though it might disturb his religious creed, it never for one moment weakened his religious sentiment; and in all that is essential, eternal, and indisputable, no sincerer Christian ever lived and died. In this, as in other matters, Tocqueville grew more tranquil with years, if not more happy. Serenity, indeed, could never be the portion upon earth of a temperament so tremblingly sensitive as his; and his later letters are filled with the most touching expressions of the growing sadness which gathered over him as he found himself becoming more and more isolated in feeling and opinion, in aspirations and in aims, from most of those around him. What his contemporaries worshipped and followed had no dignity or charms for him; he despised what they desired; he cherished what they had neglected and forsaken; they seemed hurrying down a steep incline of which he saw the inevitable abyss, but could not induce them to listen to his warnings. The past, containing so much that was beautiful and noble, was daily becoming more dead, more remote, and more forgotten; and in the immediate future, as far as human eye could penetrate, no dawn of hope was to be discerned. Much as we mourn for his untimely loss, deeply as we grieve over his empty place and his unfinished work, we can well believe that he would himself have discovered some consolation for all that he was leaving in the thought that he was "taken away from the evil to come." He died peaceably at Cannes on the 16th of April, 1859: the purest, noblest, truest gentleman it was ever our privilege to know. Over no death-bed might the lofty language of Tacitus be more fitly spoken: "Si quis piorum manibus locus; si, ut sapientibus placet, non cum corpore extinguuntur magnæ animæ, placidè quiescas: nosque, domum tuam, ab infirmo desiderio et muliebribus lamentis, ad contemplationem virtutum tuarum voces, quas neque lugeri neque plangi fas est; admiratione te potius et, si natura suppeditet, emulatione decoremus."

The Fall of Table Rock: by the last Man that stood on it.—I said I had something to do with the fall of Table Rock, that broad shell on the Canada Side, which in 1850 looked over the very caldron of the seething waters, but which tumbled into it on a certain day in the month of June of that, by me, well-remembered year. About noon on that day, I accompanied a lady from the Clifton House to the Falls. Arriving at Table Rock, we left our carriage, and as we approached the projecting platform, I pointed out to my companion a vast crack or fissure which traversed the entire base of the rock, remarking that it had never appeared to me before. The lady almost shuddered as she looked at it, and shrinking back, declared that she did not care about going near the edge. "Ah," said I, taking her hand, "you might as well come on, now that you are here. I hardly think the rock will take a notion to fall merely because we are on it."

The platform jutted from the main land some sixty feet, but, to give the visitor a still more fearful projection over the raging waters, a wooden bridge or staging, had been thrust beyond the extreme edge for some ten feet. This terminated in a small box for visitors to stand in, and was kept in its position and enabled to bear its weight by a ponderous load of stone heaped upon its inner ends. The day was very bright and hot, and it being almost lunch time at the hotels, but very few visitors were out, so we occupied the dizzy porch alone. We gazed fearfully out upon the awful waters, we stretched our heads timidly over the frightful depth below, and we felt our natures quail in every fibre by the deafening roar that seemed to saturate us, as it were, with an indefinable dread.

"This is a terrible place," said I. "Look under there and see on what a mere shell we stand. For years and years the teeth of the torrent, in that jetting, angry stream, have been gnawing at that hollow, and some day this plane must fall."

My companion shuddered and drew herself together in alarm. Our eyes swept the roaring circle of the waters once again, we gazed about in fearful fascination, when suddenly, turning our looks upon each other, each recognized a corresponding fear. "I do not like this place!" exclaimed I, quickly. "The whole base of this rock is probably disintegrated, and, perhaps sits poised in a succession of steps or notches, ready to fall out and topple down at any unusual perturbation. That fissure there seems to me unusually large to-day! I think we had better leave, for I do not fancy such a finish; and, besides, my paper must be published next week."

With these very words—the latter uttered jocosely, though not without alarm—I seized my companion's hand, and, in absolute panic, we fled as fast as our feet could carry us, towards what might be called the shore. We first burst into a laugh when we gained the land, and jumping into our carriage, felt actually as if we had made a fortunate escape. We rolled back toward the Clifton, but before we had proceeded two minutes on our way, a thundering report, like the explosion of an earthquake, burst upon us, and with a loud roar the ground trembled beneath our wheels. We turned to find that Table Rock had fallen. We were the last upon it, and it was, doubtless, the unusual perturbation caused by our flying footsteps that disturbed the exactitude of its equilibrium and threw it from its final poise. In a minute more the road was filled with hurrying people, and during the following half-hour we were told a hundred times in advance of the next morning journals, that a lady and gentleman who were on the Table Rock had gone down the falls. We are told that the trot of a dog would shake old London bridge from end to end, when it would not be disturbed by the rolling wheels of havily loaded trains. Table Rock had not been run upon in the way I have been describing for years—perhaps never, and therefore, whenever I hear it spoken of, I always shudder and feel as if I had something to do with its fall.

George Wilkes.

From Once a Week.

THE BEGGAR'S SOLILOQUY.

I.

Now, this, to my notion, is pleasant cheer,
  To lie all alone on a ragged heath,
Where your nose isn't sniffing for bones or beer,
  But a peat-fire smells like a garden beneath.
The cottagers bustle about the door,
  And the girl at the window ties her strings.
She's a dish for a man who's a mind to be poor;
  Lord! women are such expensive things.

II.

We don't marry beggars, says she: why, no:
  It seems that to make 'em is what you do;
And as I can cook, and scour, and sew,
  I needn't pay half my victuals for you.
A man for himself should be able to scratch,
  But tickling's a luxury:—love, indeed!
Love burns as long as the lucifer match,
  Wedlock's the candle! Now, that's my creed.

III.

The church-bells sound water-like over the wheat;
  And up the long path troop pair after pair.
That man's well-brushed, and the woman looks neat,
  It's man and woman everywhere!
Unless, like me, you lie here flat,
  With a donkey for friend, you must have a wife:
She pulls out your hair, but she brushes your hat.
  Appearances make the best half of life.

IV.

You nice little madam! you know you're nice.
  I remember hearing a parson say
You're a plateful of vanity peppered with vice;
  Yon chap at the gate thinks t'other way.
On his waistcoat you read both his head and his heart:
  There's a whole week's wages there figured in gold!
Yes! when you turn round you may well give a start:
  It's fun to a fellow who's getting old.

V.

Now, that's a good craft, weaving waistcoat and flowers,
  And selling of ribbons and scenting of lard:
It gives you a house to get in from the showers,
  And food when your appetite jockeys you hard.
You live a respectable man; but I ask
  If it's worth the trouble? You use your tools,
And spend your time, and what's your task?
  Why, to make a slide for a couple of fools.

VI.

You can't match the color o' these heath mounds,
  Nor better that peat-fire's agreeable smell.
I'm clothed-like with natural sights and sounds;
  To myself I'm in tune. I hope you're as well.
You jolly old cot! though you don't own coal:
  It's a generous pot that's boiled with peat.
Let the Lord Mayor o' London roast oxen whole:
  His smoke, at least, don't smell so sweet.

VII.

I'm not a low Radical, hating the laws,
  Who'd the aristocracy rebuke.
I talk o' the Lord Mayor o' London because
  I once was acquainted with his cook.
I served him a turn, and got pensioned on scraps,
  And, Lord, sir! didn't I envy his place,
Till Death knocked him down with the softest of raps,
  And I knew what was meant by a tallowy face!

VIII.

On the contrary, I'm Conservative quite;
  There's beggars in Scripture 'mongst Gentiles and Jews:
It's nonsense, trying to set things right,
  For if people will give, why, who'll refuse?
That stopping old custom wakes my spleen:
  The poor and the rich both in giving agree:
Your tight-fisted shopman's the Radical mean:
  There's nothing in common 'twixt him and me.

IX.

He says I'm no use! but I wont reply.
  You're lucky not being of use to him!
On week-days he's playing at Spider and Fly,
  And on Sundays he sings about Cherubim!
Nailing shillings to counters is his chief work:
  He nods now and then at the name on his door:
But judge of us two at a bow and a smirk,
  I think I'm his match: and I'm honest—that's more.

X.

No use! well, I mayn't be. You ring a pig's snout,
  And then call the animal glutton! Now, he
Mr. Shopman, he's naught but a pipe and a spout
  Who wont let the goods o' this world pass free,
This blazing blue weather all round the brown crop,
  He can't enjoy! all but cash he hates.
He's only a snail that crawls under his shop;
  Though he has got the ear o' the magistrates.

XI.

Now, giving and taking's a proper exchange,
  Like question and answer: you're both content.
But buying and selling seems always strange;
  You're hostile, and that's the thing that's meant.
It's man against man—you're almost brutes,
  There's here no thanks, and there's there no pride.
If Charity's Christian, don't blame my pursuits,
  I carry a touchstone by which you're tried.

XII.

—"Take it," says she, "it's all I've got:"
  I remember a girl in London streets:
She stood by a coffee-stall, nice and hot,
  My belly was like a lamb that bleats.
Says I to myself, as her shilling I seized,
  You haven't a character here, my dear!
But for making a rascal like me so pleased,
  I'll give you one, in a better sphere!

XIII.

And that's where it was—she made me feel
 I *was* a rascal: but people who scorn,
And tell a poor patch-breech he isn't genteel,
 Why, they make him kick up—and he treads on a corn.
It isn't liking, it's curst ill-luck,
 Drives half of us into the begging-trade:
If for taking to water you praise a duck,
 For taking to beer why a man upbraid?

XIV.

The sermon's over: they're out of the porch,
 And it's time for me to move a leg;
But in general people who come from church,
 And have called themselves sinners, hate chaps to beg.
I'll wager they'll all of 'em dine to-day!
 I was easy half a minute ago.
If that isn't pig that's baking away,
 May I perish!—we're never contented—heigho!

GEORGE MEREDITH.

"AH! WHO CAN TELL?"

BY ONE OF THE OFFICERS OF THE NIAGARA, ON THE HOMEWARD VOYAGE.

WE'RE nearing home—a few days more,
And upward from that sun-lined main,
Will slowly rise the blessèd shore
That we've so yearned to see again.
  But as we near
  That coast so dear,
And feel joy's pulse our bosoms thrill,
  The voice of fear
  Is whispering near,
And asks—are those we love there still?
Do *all* those eyes on earth still dwell,
To greet us home? Ah! who can tell?

Long months have passed in homeward flight,
Since news from those dear hearts beguiled;
And Time o'er noon oft brings a blight
To joys on which at morn he smiled.
  Thus as we near
  That land so dear,
With joy's emotion in our eyes,
  The voice of fear,
  In accents drear,
Asks, Is it well with those we prize?
And though hope's glance responds—
  All's well!
Fear whispers back, Ah! who can tell?

We're nearing home! The Eastern "Trade"
Still presses on our sails and spars,
Day's beams are still on ocean laid,
And night assembles yet her stars;
  Oh! in our flight,
  Beneath their light,
While in love's soul dear hope's the theme—
  While night's asleep,
  And watch we keep,
What happy scenes of home we dream!
Amidst their halo shall we dwell
Once more—once more? Ah! who can tell?

We're nearing home—*our native land!*
Those clustered States so blessed of Heaven!
Can *such* a gift from God's great hand
Be *lightly prized—be rashly riven?*
  Dark rumor's tongue
  Such dread notes rung
Before we left the Indian clime;
  But faith still smiles,
  And hope beguiles—
They sing to patriot hearts a chime!
While in the soul *such* anthems swell,
We'll cease to sigh: Ah! who can tell?

—*At Sea, Monday, April* 8, 1861.

MODERN CIVILIZATION.

AIR—"*The Vicar of Bray.*"

HIS holiness, the Pope of Rome,
 Has launched an allocution
At reform abroad and reform at home,
 Which he calls revolution;
He heaps abuse, pronounces blame,
 And deals out condemnation
Direct, without reserve, by name,
 On modern civilization.

For other times the pontiff sighs,
 And groans for other ages,
While he scolds and screams and shrieks and cries,
 And roars and raves and rages,
For the palmy days of interdict,
 And excommunication,
All which have been to limbo kicked
 By modern civilization.

'Tis likely Rome will grow too hot
 To hold the holy father:
He'll have to seek some other spot
 To rule and govern, rather.
Jerusalem some folks suggest;
 And that's a situation
Where he would not be much distrest
 By modern civilization.

'Twere better if to Jericho
 He went, with all his head men,
Or his cardinals and he might go
 Among the Indian red men;
The pope and conclave would amaze
 The native population;
Let them fly to the far Ojibbeways,
 From modern civilization.

—*Punch.*

From Fraser's Magazine.

CONCERNING FUTURE YEARS.

DOES it ever come across you, my friend, with something of a start, that things cannot always go on in your lot as they are going now? Does not a sudden thought sometimes flash upon you, a hasty, vivid glimpse, of what you will be long hereafter, if you are spared in this world? Our common way is too much to think that things will always go on as they are going. Not that we clearly think so: not that we ever put that opinion in a definite shape, and avow to ourselves that we hold it: but we live very much under that vague, general impression. We can hardly help it. When a man of middle age inherits a pretty country-seat, and makes up his mind that he cannot yet afford to give up his profession and go to live at it, but concludes that in six or eight years he will be able with justice to his children to do so, do you think he brings plainly before him the changes which must be wrought on himself and those around him by these years? I do not speak of the greatest change of all, which may come to any of us so very soon: I do not think of what may be done by unlooked-for accident: I think merely of what must be done by the passing on of time. I think of possible changes in taste and feeling, of possible loss of liking for that mode of life. I think of lungs that will play less freely, and of limbs that will suggest shortened walks, and dissuade from climbing hills. I think how the children will have outgrown daisy-chains, or even got beyond the season of climbing trees. The middle-aged man enjoys the prospect of the time when he shall go to his country-house; and the vague, undefined belief surrounds him, like an atmosphere, that he and his children, his views and likings, will be then just such as they are now. He cannot bring it home to him at how many points change will be cutting into him, and hedging him in, and paring him down. And we all live very much under that vague impression. Yet it is in many ways good for us to feel that we are going on —passing from the things which surround us —advancing into the undefined future, into the unknown land. And I think that sometimes we all have vivid flashes of such a conviction. I dare say, my friend, you have seen an old man, frail, soured, and shabby and you have thought, with a start, Perhaps *there* is Myself of Future Years.

We human beings can stand a great deal. There is great margin allowed by our constitution, physical and moral. I suppose there is no doubt that a man may daily for years eat what is unwholesome, breathe air which is bad, or go through a round of life which is not the best or the right one for either body or mind, and yet be little the worse. And so men pass through great trials and through long years, and yet are not altered so very much. The other day, walking along the street, I saw a man whom I had not seen for ten years. I knew that since I saw him last he had gone through very heavy troubles, and that these had sat very heavily upon him. I remembered how he had lost that friend who was the dearest to him of all human beings, and I knew how broken down he had been for many months after that great sorrow came. Yet there he was, walking along, an unnoticed unit, just like any one else; and he was looking wonderfully well. No doubt he seemed pale, worn, and anxious: but he was very well and carefully dressed; he was walking with a brisk, active step; and I dare say in feeling pretty well reconciled to being what he is, and to the circumstances amid which he is living. Still, one felt that somehow a tremendous change had passed over him. I felt sorry for him, and all the more that he did not seem to feel sorry for himself. It made me sad to think that some day I should be like him; that perhaps in the eyes of my juniors I look like him already, careworn and ageing. I dare say in his feeling there was no such sense of falling off. Perhaps he was tolerably content. He was walking so fast and looking so sharp, that I am sure he had no desponding feeling at the time. Despondency goes with slow movements and with vague looks. The sense of having materially fallen off is destructive to the eagle-eye. Yes, he was tolerably content. We can go down-hill cheerfully, save at the points where it is sharply brought home to us that we are going down-hill. Lately I sat at dinner opposite an old lady who had the remains of striking beauty. I remember how much she interested me. Her hair was false, her teeth were false, her complexion was shrivelled, her form had lost the round symmetry of earlier years, and was angular and stiff; yet how cheerful and lively she was! She had gone far down-hill physically; but either she did not feel her decadence, or she had grown quite reconciled to it. Her daughter, a blooming matron, was there, happy, wealthy, good; yet not apparently a whit more reconciled to life than the aged grandame. It was pleasing, and yet it was sad, to see how well we can make up our mind to what is inevitable. And such a sight brings up to one a glimpse of Future Years. The cloud seems to part before one, and through the rift you discern your earthly track far away, and a jaded pilgrim plodding along it with weary step; and though the pilgrim does not look like you, yet you know the pilgrim is yourself.

This cannot always go on. To what is it all tending? I am not thinking now of an out-look so grave that this is not the place to discuss it. But I am thinking how every thing is going on. In this world there is no standing still. And every thing that belongs entirely to this world, its interests and occupations, is going on towards a conclusion. It will all come to an end. It cannot go on forever. I cannot always be writing sermons as I do now, and going on in this regular course of life. I cannot always be writing essays for *Fraser*. The day will come when I shall have no more to say, or when the readers of the Magazine will no longer have patience to listen to me in that kind of fashion in which they have listened so long. I foresee it plainly, this evening,—the time when the reader shall open the familiar cover, and glance at the table of contents, and exclaim indignantly, "Here is that tiresome person again with the four initials: why will he not cease to weary us?" I write in sober sadness, my friend: I do not intend any jest. If you do not know that what I have written is certainly true, you have not lived very long. You have not learned the sorrowful lesson, that all worldly occupations and interests are wearing to their close. You cannot keep up the old thing, however much you may wish to do so. You know how vain anniversaries for the most part are. You meet with certain old friends, to try to revive the old days; but the spirit of the old time will not come over you. It is not a spirit that can be raised at will. It cannot go on forever, that walking down to church on Sundays, and ascending those pulpit steps; it will change to feeling, though I humbly trust it may be long before it shall change in fact. Don't you all sometimes feel something like that? Don't you sometimes look about you and say to yourself, That furniture will wear out: those window-curtains are getting sadly faded; they will not last a lifetime? Those carpets must be replaced some day; and the old patterns which looked at you with a kindly, familiar expression, through these long years, must be among the old familiar faces that are gone. These are little things, indeed, but they are among the vague recollections that bewilder our memory; they are among the things which come up in the strange, confused remembrance of the dying man in the last days of life. There is an old fir-tree, a twisted, strange-looking fir-tree, which will be among my last recollections, I know, as it was among my first. It was always before my eyes when I was three, four, five years old: I see the pyramidal top, rising over a mass of shrubbery; I see it always against a sunset-sky; always in the subdued twilight in which we seem to see things in distant years.

These old friends will die, you think; who will take their place? You will be an old gentleman, a frail old gentleman, wondered at by younger men, and telling them long stories about the days when Queen Victoria was a young woman, like those which weary you now about George the Third. It will not be the same world then. Your children will not be always children. Enjoy their fresh youth while it lasts, for it will not last long. Do not skim over the present too fast, through a constant habit of onward-looking. Many men of an anxious turn are so eagerly concerned in providing for the future, that they hardly remark the blessings of the present. Yet it is only because the future will some day be present, that it deserves any thought at all. And many men, instead of heartily enjoying present blessings while they are present, train themselves to a habit of regarding these things as merely the foundation on which they are to build some vague fabric of they know not what. I have known a clergyman, who was very fond of music, and in whose church the music was very fine, who seemed incapable of enjoying its solemn beauty as a thing to be enjoyed while passing, but who persisted in regarding each beautiful strain merely as a promising indication of what his choir would come at some future time to be. It is a very bad habit, and one which grows unless repressed. You, my reader, when you see your children racing on the green, train yourself to regard all that as a happy end in itself. Do not grow to think merely that those sturdy young limbs promise to be stout and serviceable when they are those of a grown-up man; and rejoice in the smooth little forehead with its curly hair, without any forethought of how it is to look some day when overshadowed (as it is sure to be) by the great wig of the Lord Chancellor. Good advice: let us all try to take it. Let all happy things be enjoyed as ends, as well as regarded as means. Yet it is in the make of our nature to be ever onward-looking; and we cannot help it. When you get the first number for the year of the Magazine which you take in, you instinctively think of it as the first portion of a new volume; and you are conscious of a certain though slight restlessness in the thought of a thing incomplete, and of a wish that you had the volume completed. And sometimes, thus looking onward into the future, you worry yourself with little thoughts and cares. There is that old dog: you have had him for many years; he is growing stiff and frail; what are you to do when he dies? When he is gone, the new dog you get will never be like him; he may be, indeed, a far handsomer and more amiable animal, but he will not be your old companion; he will not be surrounded with all those old associations, not merely with your own by-past life, but with the lives, the faces, and the voices of those who have left you, which invest with a certain sacredness even that humble but faithful friend. He will not have been the companion of your youthful walks, when you went at a pace which now you cannot attain. He will just be a common dog; and who that has reached your years cares for *that?* The other, indeed, was a dog too, but that was merely the substratum on which was accumulated a host of recollections: it is *Auld lang syne* that walks into your study when your shaggy friend of ten summers comes stiffly in, and after many querulous turnings lays himself down on the rug before the fire. Do you not feel the like when you look at many little matters, and then look into the future years? That harness—how will you replace it? It will be a pang to throw it by, and it will be a considerable expense too to get a new suit. Then you think how long harness may continue to be serviceable. I once saw, on a pair of horses drawing a stage-coach among the hills, a set of harness which was thirty-five years old. It had been very costly and grand when new; it had belonged for some of its earliest years to a certain wealthy nobleman. The nobleman had been for many years in his grave, but there was his harness still. It was tremendously patched, and the blinkers were of extraordinary aspect; but it was quite serviceable. There is comfort for you, poor country parsons! How thoroughly I understand your feeling about such little things. I know how you sometimes look at your phaeton or your dog-cart; and even while the morocco is fresh, and the wheels still are running with their first tires, how you think you see it after it has grown shabby and old-fashioned. Yes, you remember, not without a dull kind of pang, that it is wearing out. You have a neighbor, perhaps, a few miles off, whose conveyance, through the wear of many years, has become remarkably seedy; and every time you meet it you think that there you see your own, as it will some day be. Every dog has his day; but the day of the rational dog is overclouded in a fashion unknown to his inferior fellow-creature; it is overclouded by the anticipation of the coming day which will not be his. You remember how that great though morbid man, John Foster, could not heartily enjoy the summer weather, for thinking how every sunny day that shone upon him was a downward step towards the winter gloom. Each indication that the season was progressing, even though progressing as yet only to greater beauty, filled him with great grief. "I have seen a fearful sight to-day," he would say, "I have seen a buttercup." And we know, of course, that in his case there was nothing like affectation; it was only that, unhappily for himself, the bent of his mind was so onward-looking, that he saw only a premonition of the snows of December in the roses of June. It would be a blessing if we could quite discard the tendency. And while your trap runs smoothly and noiselessly, while the leather is fresh and the paint unscratched, do not worry yourself with visions of the day when it will rattle and creak, and when you will make it wait for you at the corner of back streets when you drive into town. Do not vex yourself by fancying that you will never have heart to send off the old carriage, nor by wondering where you will find the money to buy a new one.

Have you ever read the *Life of Mansie Wauch, Tailor in Dalkeith*, by that pleasing poet and most amiable man, the late David Macbeth Moir? I have been looking into it lately; and I have regretted much that the Lowland Scotch dialect is so imperfectly understood in England, and that even where so far understood its raciness is so little felt; for great as is the popularity of that work, it is much less known than it deserves to be. Only a Scotchman can thoroughly appreciate it. It is curious, and yet it is not curious, to find the pathos and the polish of one of the most touching and elegant of poets in the man who has with such irresistible humor, sometimes approaching to the farcical, delineated humble Scotch life. One passage in the book always struck me very much. We have in it the poet as well as the humorist; and it is a perfect example of what I have been trying to describe in the pages which you have read. I mean the passage in which Mansie tells us of a sudden glimpse which, in circumstances of mortal terror, he once had of the future. On a certain "awful night" the tailor was awakened by cries of alarm, and, looking out, he saw the next house to his own was on fire from cellar to garret. The earnings of poor Mansie's whole life were laid out on his stock in trade and his furniture, and it appeared likely that these would be at once destroyed.

"Then [says he] the darkness of the latter days came over my spirit like a vision before the prophet Isaiah; and I could see nothing in the years to come but beggary and starvation—myself a fallen-back old man, with an out-at-the-elbows coat, a greasy hat, and a bald brow, hirpling over a staff, requeeshting an awmous: Nanse a broken-hearted beggar-wife, torn down to tatters, and weeping like Rachel when she thought on better days; and poor wee Benjie going from door to door with a meal-pock on his back."

Ah, there is exquisite pathos *there* as well as humor; but the thing for which I have quoted that sentence is its startling truthfulness. You have all done what Mansie Wauch did, I know. Every one has his own way of doing it, and it is his own especial picture which each sees; but there has appeared to us, as to Mansie (I must recur to my old figure), as it were a sudden rift in the clouds that conceal the future, and we have seen the way, far ahead,—the dusty way,—and an aged pilgrim pacing slowly along it; and in that aged figure we have each recognized our own young self. How often have I sat down on the mossy wall that surrounded my churchyard, when I had more time for reverie than I have now,—sat upon the mossy wall, under a great oak, whose branches came low down and projected far out,—and looked at the rough gnarled bark, and at the passing river, and at the belfry of the little church, and there and then thought of Mansie Wauch and of his vision of future years! How often in these hours, or in long, solitary walks and rides among the hills, have I had visions clear as that of Mansie Wauch, of how I should grow old in my country parish! Do not think that I wish or intend to be egotistical, my friendly reader. I describe these feelings and fancies because I think this is the likeliest way in which to reach and describe your own. There was a rapid little stream that flowed, in a very lonely place, between the highway and a cottage to which I often went to see a poor old woman; and when I came out of the cottage, having made sure that no one saw me, I always took a great leap over the little stream, which saved going round a little way. And never once, for several years, did I thus cross it without seeing a picture as clear to the mind's eye as Mansie Wauch's,—a picture which made me walk very thoughtfully along for the next mile or two. It was curious to think how one was to get through the accustomed duty after having grown old and frail. The day would come when the brook could be crossed in that brisk fashion no more. It must be an odd thing for the parson to walk as an old man into the pulpit, still his own, which was his own when he was a young man of six-and-twenty. What a crowd of old remembrances must be present each Sunday to the clergyman's mind, who has served the same parish and preached in the same church for fifty years! Personal identity, continued through the successive stages of life, is a commonplace thing to think of; but when it is brought home to your own case and feeling, it is a very touching and a very bewildering thing. There are the same trees and hills as when you were a boy; and when each of us comes to his last days in this world, how short a space it will seem since we were little children! Let us humbly hope that in that brief space parting the cradle from the grave, we may (by help from above) have accomplished a certain work which will cast its blessed influence over all the years and all the ages before us. Yet it remains a strange thing to look forward and to see yourself with gray hair, and not much even of that; to see your wife an old woman, and your little boy or girl grown up into manhood or womanhood. It is more strange still to fancy you see them all going on as usual in the round of life, and you no longer among them. You see your empty chair. There is your writing-table and your inkstand; there are your books, not so carefully arranged as they used to be; perhaps on the whole less indication than you might have hoped that they miss you. All this is strange when you bring it home to your own case; and that hundreds of millions have felt the like makes it none the less strange to you. The commonplaces of life and death are not commonplace when they befall ourselves. It was in desperate hurry and agitation that Mansie Wauch saw his vision; and in like circumstances you may have yours too. But for the most part such moods come in leisure,—in saunterings through the autumn woods,—in reveries by the winter fire.

I do not think, thus musing upon our occasional glimpses of the future, of such fancies as those of early youth,—fancies and anticipations of greatness, of felicity, of fame; I think of the onward views of men approaching middle age, who have found their place and their work in life, and who may reasonably believe that, save for great, unexpected accidents, there will be no very material change in their lot till that "change come" to which Job looked forward four thousand years since. There are great numbers of educated folk who are likely always to live in the same kind of house, to have the same establishment, to associate with the same class of people, to walk along the same streets, to look upon the same hills, as long as they live. The only change will be the gradual one which will be wrought by advancing years.

And the onward view of such people in such circumstances is generally a very vague one. It is only now and then that there comes the startling clearness of prospect so well set forth by Mansie Wauch. Yet sometimes when such a vivid view comes it remains for days, and is a painful companion of your solitude. Don't you remember, clerical reader of thirty-two, having seen a good deal of an old parson, rather sour in aspect, rather shabby-looking, sadly pinched for means, and with powers dwarfed by the sore struggle with the world to maintain his family and to keep up a respectable appearance upon his limited resources; perhaps with his mind made petty and his temper spoiled by the little worries, the petty malignant tattle and gossip and occasional insolence of a little backbiting village? and don't you remember how for days you felt haunted by a sort of nightmare that there was what you would be, if you lived so long? Yes; you know how there have been times when for ten days together that jarring thought would intrude, whenever your mind was disengaged from work; and sometimes, when you went to bed, that thought kept you awake for hours. You knew the impression was morbid, and you were angry with yourself for your silliness; but you could not drive it away.

It makes a great difference in the prospect of Future Years if you are one of those people who, even after middle age, may still make a great rise in life. This will prolong the restlessness which in others is sobered down at forty; it will extend the period during which you will every now and then have brief seasons of feverish anxiety, hope, and fear, followed by longer stretches of blank disappointment. And it will afford the opportunity of experiencing a vividly new sensation, and of turning over a quite new leaf, after most people have settled to the jog-trot at which the remainder of the pilgrimage is to be covered. A clergyman of the Church of England may be made a bishop, and exchange a quiet rectory for a palace. No doubt the increase of responsibility is to a conscientious man almost appalling; but surely, the rise in life is great. There you are, one of four-and-twenty, selected out of near twenty thousand. It is possible, indeed, that you may feel more reason for shame than for elation at the thought. A barrister unknown to fame, but of respectable standing, may be made a judge. Such a man may even, if he gets into the groove, be gradually pushed on till he reaches an eminence which probably surprises himself as much as any one else. A good speaker in Parliament may at sixty or seventy, be made a Cabinet Minister. And we can all imagine what indescribable pride and elation must in such cases possess the wife and daughters of the man who has attained this decided step in advance. I can say sincerely that I never saw human beings walk with so airy tread, and evince so fussily their sense of a greatness more than mortal, as the wife and the daughter of an amiable but not able bishop I knew in my youth, when they came to church on the Sunday morning on which the good man preached for the first time in his lawn sleeves. Their heads were turned for the time; but they gradually came right again, as the ladies became accustomed to the summits of human affairs.

Let it be said for the bishop himself, that there was not a vestige of that sense of elevation about *him*. He looked perfectly modest and unaffected. His dress was remarkably ill put on, and his sleeves stuck out in the most awkward fashion ever assumed by drapery. I suppose that sometimes these rises in life come very unexpectedly. I have heard of a man who, when he received a letter from the prime minister of the day offering him a place of great dignity, thought the letter was a hoax, and did not notice it for several days. You could not certainly infer from his modesty what has proved to be the fact, that he has filled his place admirably well. The possibility of such material changes must no doubt tend to prolong the interest in life, which is ready to flag as years go on. But perhaps with the majority of men, the level is found before middle age, and no very great worldly change awaits them. The path stretches on, with its ups and downs; and they only hope for strength for the day. But in such men's lot of humble duty and quiet content there remains room for many fears. All human beings, who are as well off as they can ever be, and so who have little room for hope, seem to be liable to the invasion of great fear as they look into the future. It seems to be so with kings, and with great nobles. Many such have lived in a nervous dread of change, and have ever been watching the signs of the times with apprehensive eyes. Nothing that can happen can well make such better; and so they suffer from the vague foreboding of something which will make them worse. And the same law reaches to those in whom hope is narrowed down, not by the limit of grand possibility, but of little; not by the fact that they have got all that mortal can get, but by the fact that they have got the little which is all that Providence seems to intend to give to *them*. And indeed there is something that is almost awful, when your affairs are all going happily, when your mind is clear and equal to its work, when your bodily health is unbroken, when your home is pleasant, when your income is ample, when your children are healthy and merry and hopeful,—in looking on to future years. The more happy you are, the more there is of awe in the thought how frail are the foundations of your earthly happiness: what havoc may be made of them by the chances of even a single day. It is no wonder that the solemnity and awfulness of the future have been felt so much, that the languages of Northern Europe have, as I dare say you know, no word which expresses the essential notion of futurity. You think, perhaps, of *shall* and *will*. Well, these words have come now to convey the notion of futurity; but they do so only in a secondary fashion. Look to their etymology, and you will see that they *imply* futurity, but do not *express* it. *I shall* do such a thing means *I am bound to do it, I am under an obligation to do it*. *I will* do such a thing, means *I intend to do it, it is my present purpose to do it*. Of course, if you are under an obligation to do any thing, or if it be your intention to do any thing, the probability is that the thing will be done; but the Northern family of languages ventures no nearer than *that* towards the expression of the bare, awful idea of future time. It was no wonder that Mr. Croaker was able to cast a gloom upon the gayest circle, and the happiest conjuncture of circumstances, by wishing that all might be as well that day six months. Six months! What might that time not do? Perhaps you have not read a little poem of Barry Cornwall's, the idea of which must come home to the heart of most of us:—

"Touch us gently, Time!
Let us glide adown thy stream,
Gently,—as we sometimes glide
Through a quiet dream.
Humble voyagers are we,
Husband, wife, and children three—
One is lost,—an angel fled
To the azure overhead.

"Touch us gently, Time!
We've not proud nor soaring wings:
Our ambition, our content,
Lies in simple things.
Humble voyagers are we
O'er life's dim, unsounded sea,
Seeking only some calm clime:—
Touch us gently, gentle Time!"

I know that sometimes, my friend, you will not have much sleep if, when you lay your head on your pillow, you begin to think how much depends upon your health and life. You have reached now that time at which you value life and health not so much for their service to yourself, as for their needfulness to others. There is a petition familiar to me in this Scotch country where people make their prayers for themselves, which seems to me to possess great solemnity and force when we think of all that is implied in it. It is, *Spare useful lives!* One life, the slender line of blood passing into and passing out of one human heart, may decide the question whether wife and children shall grow up affluent, refined, happy, yes, and *good;* or be reduced to hard straits, with all the manifold evils which grow of poverty in the case of those who have been reduced to it after knowing other things. You often think, I doubt not, in quiet hours, what would become of your children if you were gone. You have done, I trust, what you can to care for them, even from your grave: you think sometimes of a poetical figure of speech amid the dry technical phrases of English law: you know what is meant by the law of *Mortmain;* and you like to think that even your *dead hand* may be felt to be kindly intermeddling yet in the affairs of those who were your dearest: that some little sum, slender perhaps, but as liberal as you could make it, may come in periodically when it is wanted, and seem like the gift of a thoughtful heart and a kindly hand which are far away. Yes, cut down your present income to any extent, that you may make some provision for your children after you are dead. You do not wish that they should have the saddest of all reasons for taking care of you, and trying to lengthen out your life. But even after you have done every thing which your small means permit, you will still think, with an anxious heart, of the possibilities of Future Years. A man or woman who has children has very strong reason for wishing to live as long as may be, and has no right to trifle with health or life. And sometimes, looking out into days to come, you think of the little things, hitherto so free from man's heritage of care, as they may some day be. You see them shabby, and early anxious: can *that* be the little boy's rosy face, now so pale and thin? You see them in a poor room, in which you recognize your study chairs, with the hair coming out of the cushions; and a carpet which you remember now threadbare and in holes.

It is no wonder at all that people are so anxious about money. Money means every desirable material thing on earth; and the manifold immaterial things which come of material possessions. Poverty is the most comprehensive earthly evil; all conceivable evils, temporal, spiritual, and eternal, may come of *that.* Of course, great temptations attend its opposite; and the wise man's prayer will be what it was long ago—"Give me neither poverty nor riches." But let us have no nonsense talked about money being of no consequence. The want of it has made many a father and mother tremble at the prospect of being taken from their children; the want of it has embittered many a parent's dying hours. You hear selfish persons talking vaguely about faith. You find such heartless persons jauntily spending all they get on themselves, and then leaving their poor children to beggary, with the miserable pretext that they are doing all this through their abundant trust in God. Now this is not faith, it is insolent presumption. It is exactly as if a man should jump from the top of St. Paul's, and say that he had faith that the Almighty would keep him from being dashed to pieces on the pavement. There is a high authority as to such cases, "Thou shalt not tempt the Lord thy God." If God had promised that people should never fall into the miseries of penury under any circumstances, it would be faith to trust that promise, however unlikely of fulfilment it might seem in any particular case. But God has made no such promise; and if you leave your children without provision, you have no right to expect that they shall not suffer the natural consequences of your heartlessness and thoughtlessness. True faith lies in your doing every thing you possibly can, and *then* humbly trusting in God. And if, after you have done your very best, you must still go, with but a blank out-look for those you leave, why, *then* you may trust them to the Husband of the widow and Father of the fatherless. Faith, as regards such matters. means firm belief that God will do all he has promised to do, however difficult or unlikely. But some people seem to think that faith means firm belief that God will do whatever they think would suit them, however unreasonable, and however flatly in the face of all the established laws of his government.

We all have it in our power to make ourselves miserable, if we look far into future years and calculate their probabilities of evil, and steadily anticipate the worst. It is not expedient to calculate too far ahead. Of course, the right way in this, as in other things, is the middle way; we are not to run either into the extreme of over-carefulness and anxiety on the one hand, or of recklessness and imprudence on the other. But as mention has been made of faith, it may safely be said that we are forgetful of that rational trust in God which is at once our duty and our inestimable privilege, if we are always looking out into the future, and vexing ourselves with endless fears as to how things are to go then. There is no divine promise that if a reckless blockhead leaves his children to starve, they shall not starve. And a certain inspired volume speaks with extreme severity of the man who fails to provide for them of his own house. But there *is* a divine promise which says to the humble Christian, "As thy days, so shall thy strength be." If your affairs are going on fairly now, be thankful, and try to do your duty, and to do your best, as a Christian man and a prudent man, and then leave the rest to God. Your children are about you; no doubt they may die, and it is fit enough that you should not forget the fragility of your most prized possessions; it is fit enough that you should sometimes sit by the fire and look at the merry faces and listen to the little voices, and think what it would be to lose them. But it is not needful, or rational, or Christian-like, to be always brooding on that thought. And when they grow up it may be hard to provide for them. The little thing that is sitting on your knee may before many years be alone in life, thousands of miles from you and from his early home, an insignificant item in the bitter price which Britain pays for her Indian Empire. It is even possible, though you hardly for a moment admit *that* thought, that the child may turn out a heartless and wicked man, and prove your shame and heart-break; all wicked and heartless men have been the children of somebody; and many of them doubtless the children of those who surmised the future as little as Eve did when she smiled upon the infant Cain. And the fireside by which you sit, now merry and noisy enough, may grow lonely—lonely with the second loneliness, not the hopeful solitude of youth looking forward, but the desponding loneliness of age looking back. And it is so with every thing else. Your health may break down. Some fearful accident may befall you. The readers of the magazine may cease to care for your articles. People may get tired of your sermons. People may stop buying your books, your wine, your groceries, your milk and cream. Younger men may take away your legal business. Yet how often these fears prove utterly groundless! It was good and wise advice given by one who had managed with a cheerful and hopeful spirit, to pass through many trying and anxious years, to "take short views:" not to vex and worry yourself by planning too far ahead. And a wiser than the wise and cheerful Sydney Smith had anticipated his philosophy. You remember Who said "Take no thought" —that is, no over-anxious and over-careful thought—"for the morrow; for the morrow shall take thought for the things of itself." Did you ever sail over a blue summer sea towards a mountainous coast, frowning, sullen, gloomy; and have you not seen the gloom retire before you as you advanced; the hills, grim in the distance, stretch into sunny slopes when you neared them; and the waters smile in cheerful light that looked so black when they were far away? And who is there that has not seen the parallel in actual life? We have all known and anticipated ills of life—the danger that looked so big, the duty that looked so arduous, the entanglement that we could not see our way through—prove to have been nothing more than spectres on the far horizon; and when at length we reached them, all their difficulty had vanished into air, leaving us to think what fools we had been for having so needlessly conjured up phantoms to disturb our quiet. Yes, there is no doubt of it, a very great part of all we suffer in this world is from the apprehension of things that never come. I once remember well how a dear friend whom I (and many more) lately lost, told me many times of his fears as to what he would do in a certain contingency which both he and I thought was quite sure to come sooner or later. I know that the anticipation of it caused him some of the most anxious hours of a very anxious though useful and honored life. How vain his fears proved! He was taken from this world before what he had dreaded had cast its most distant shadow. Well, let me try to discard the notion which has been sometimes worrying me of late, that perhaps I have written nearly as many essays as any one will care to read. Don't let any of us give way to fears which may prove to have been entirely groundless.

And then, if we are really spared to see those trials we sometimes think of, and which it is right that we should sometimes think of, the strength for them will come at the time. They will not look nearly so black, and we shall be enabled to bear them bravely. There is in human nature a marvellous power of accommodation to circumstances. We can gradually make up our mind to almost any thing. If this were a sermon instead of an essay, I should explain my theory of how this comes to be. I see in all this something beyond the mere natural instinct of acquiescence in what is inevitable; something beyond the benevolent law in the human mind, that it shall adapt itself to whatever circumstances it may be placed in; something beyond the doing of the gentle comforter Time. Yes, it is wonderful what people can go through, wonderful what people get reconciled to. I dare say my friend Smith, when his hair began to fall off, made frantic efforts to keep it on. I have no doubt he anxiously tried all the vile concoctions which quackery advertises in the newspapers, for the advantage of those who wish for luxuriant locks. I dare say for awhile it really weighed upon his mind, and disturbed his quiet, that he was getting bald. But now he has quite reconciled himself to his lot; and with a head smooth and sheeny as the egg of the ostrich, Smith goes on through life, and feels no pang at the remembrance of the ambrosial curls of his youth. Most young people, I dare say, think it will be a dreadful thing to grow old: a girl of eighteen thinks it must be an awful sensation to be thirty. Believe me, not at all. You are brought to it bit by bit; and when you reach the spot you rather like the view. And it is so with graver things. We grow able to do and to bear that which it is needful that we should do and bear. As is the day, so the strength proves to be. And you have heard people tell you truly, that they have been enabled to bear what they never thought they could have come through with their reason or their life. I have no fear for the Christian man, so he keeps to the path of duty. Straining up the steep hill, his heart will grow stout in just proportion to its steepness. Yes, and if the call to martyrdom came, I should not despair of finding men who would show themselves equal to it, even in this commonplace age, and among people who wear Highland cloaks and knickerbockers. The martyr's strength would come with the martyr's day. It is because there is no call for it now, that people look so little like it.

It is very difficult, in this world, to strongly enforce a truth, without seeming to push it into an extreme. You are very apt, in avoiding one error, to run into the opposite error; forgetting that truth and right lie generally between two extremes. And in agreeing with Sydney Smith, as to the wisdom and the duty of "taking short views," let us take care of appearing to approve the doings of those foolish and unprincipled people who will keep no out-look into the future time at all. A bee, you know, cannot see more than a single inch before it; and there are many men, and perhaps more women, who appear, as regards their domestic concerns, to be very much of bees. Not bees in the respect of being busy; but bees in the respect of being blind. You see this in all ranks of life. You see it in the artisan, earning good wages, yet with every prospect of being weeks out of work next summer or winter; who yet will not be persuaded to lay by a little in preparation for a rainy day. You see it in the country gentleman, who, having five thousand a year, spends ten thousand a year; resolutely shutting his eyes to the certain and not very remote consequences. You see it in the man who walks into a shop and buys a lot of things which he has not the money to pay for, in the vague hope that something will turn up. It is a comparatively thoughtful and anxious class of men who systematically overcloud the present by anticipations of the future. The more usual thing is to sacrifice the future to the present; to grasp at what in the way of present gratification or gain can be got, with very little thought of the consequences. You see silly women, the wives of men whose families are mainly dependent on their lives, constantly urging on their husbands to extravagances which eat up the little provision which might have been made for themselves and their children when he is gone who earned their bread. There is no sadder sight, I think, than that which is not a very uncommon sight, the care-worn, anxious husband, laboring beyond his strength, often sorrowfully calculating how he may make the ends to meet, denying himself in every way; and the extravagant idiot of a wife, bedizened with jewellery and arrayed in velvet and lace, who tosses away his hard earnings in reckless extravagance; in entertainments which he cannot afford; in giving to people who do not care a rush for him; in preposterous dress; in absurd furniture; in needless men-servants; in greengrocers above measure; in resolute aping of the way of living of people with twice or three times the means. It is sad to see all the forethought, prudence, and moderation of the wedded pair confined to one of them. You would say that it will not be any solid consolation to the widow, when the husband is fairly worried into his grave at last—when his daughters have to go out as governesses, and she has to let lodgings—to reflect that while he lived they never failed to have champagne at his dinner parties; and that they had three men to wait at table on such occasions, while Mr. Smith next door had never more than one and a maidservant. If such idiotic women would but look forward, and consider how all this must end! If the professional man spends all he earns, what remains when the supply is cut off; when the toiling head and hand can toil no more? Ah, a little of the economy and management which must perforce be practised after *that*, might have tended powerfully to put off the evil day. Sometimes the husband is merely the care-worn drudge who provides what the wife squanders. Have you not known such a thing as that a man should be laboring under an Indian sun, and cutting down every personal expense to the last shilling, that he might send a liberal allowance to his wife in England; while she meanwhile was recklessly spending twice what was thus sent her; running up overwhelming accounts, dashing about to public balls, paying for a bouquet what cost the poor fellow far away much thought to save, giving costly entertainments at home, filling her house with idle and empty-headed scapegraces, carrying on scandalous flirtations; till it becomes a happy thing if the certain ruin she is bringing on her husband's head is cut short by the needful interference of Sir Cresswell Cresswell? There are cases in which tarring and feathering would sooth the moral sense of the right-minded onlooker. And even where things are not so bad as in the case of which we have been thinking, it remains the social curse of this age, that people with a few hundreds a year determinedly act in various respects as if they had as many thousands. The dinner given by a man with eight hundred a year, in certain regions of the earth which I could easily point out, is, as regards food, wine, and attendance, precisely the same as the dinner given by another man who has five thousand a year. When will this end? When will people see its silliness? In truth, you do not really, as things are in this country, make many people better off by adding a little or a good deal to their yearly income. For in all probability they were living up to the very extremity of their means before they got the addition; and in all probability the first thing they do on getting the addition, is so far to increase their establishment and their expense that it is just as hard a struggle as ever to make the ends meet. It would not be a pleasant arrangement that a man who was to be carried across the straits from England to France, should be fixed on a board so weighted that his mouth and nostrils should be at the level of the water, and thus that he should be struggling for life, and barely escaping drowning all the way. Yet hosts of people, whom no one proposes to put under restraint, do as regards their income and expenditure a precisely analogous thing. They deliberately weight themselves to that degree that their heads are barely above water, and that any unforeseen emergency dips their heads under. They rent a house a good deal dearer than they can justly afford; and they have servants more and more expensive than they ought; and by many such things they make sure that their progress through life shall be a drowning struggle. While if they would rationally resolve and manfully confess that they cannot afford to have things as richer folk have them, and arrange their way of living in accordance with what they can afford, they would enjoy the feeling of ease and comfort; they would not be ever on the wretched stretch on which they are now, nor keeping up the hollow appearance of what is not the fact. But there are folk who make it a point of honor never to admit that in doing, or not doing any thing, they are actuated for an instant by so despicable a consideration as the question whether or not they can afford it. And who shall reckon up the brains which this social calamity has driven into disease, or the early paralytic shocks which it has brought on?

When you were very young, and looked forward to Future Years, did you ever feel a painful fear that you might outgrow your early home affections, and your associations with your native scenes? Did you ever think to yourself, Will the day come when I shall have been years away from that river's side, and yet not care? I think we have all known the feeling. O plain church to which I used to go when I was a child, and where I used to think the singing so very splendid: O little room where I used to sleep; and you, tall tree, on whose topmost branch I cut the initials which the readers of *Fraser* know; did I not even then wonder to myself if the time would ever come when I should be far away from you—far away as now, for many years, and not likely to go back—and yet feel entirely indifferent to the matter? and did not I even then feel a strange pain in the fear that very likely it might? These things come across the mind of a little boy with a curious grief and bewilderment. Ah, there is something strange in the inner life of a thoughtful child of eight years old! I would rather see a faithful record of his thoughts, feelings, fancies and sorrows, for a single week, than know all the political events that have happened during that space in Spain, Denmark, Norway, Sweden, Russia, and Turkey. Even amid the great grief at leaving home for school in your early days, did you not feel a greater grief to think that the day might come when you would not care at all; when your home ties and affections would be outgrown; when you would be quite content to live on month after month far from parents, sisters, brothers; and feel hardly a perceptible blank when you remembered that they were far away? But it is of the essence of such fears, that when the thing comes that you were afraid of, it has ceased to be fearful; still it is with a little pang that you sometimes call to remembrance how much you feared it once. It is a daily regret, though not a very acute one (more's the pity), to be thrown much, in middle life, into the society of an old friend whom as a boy you had regarded as very wise; and to be compelled to observe that he is a tremendous fool. You struggle with the conviction; you think it wrong to give in to it; but you cannot help it. But it would have been a sharper pang to the child's heart, to have impressed upon the child the fact, that "Good Mr. Goose is a fool, and some day you will understand that he is." In those days one admits no imperfection in the people and the things one likes. You like a person; and *he is good. That* sums the whole case. You do not go into exceptions and reservations. I remember how indignant I felt as a boy, at reading some depreciatory criticism of the *Waverley Novels*. The criticism was to the effect that the plots generally dragged at first, and were huddled up at the end. But to me the novels were enchaining, enthralling; and to hint a defect in them stunned one. In the boy's feeling, if a thing be good, why there cannot be any thing bad about it. But in the man's mature judgment, even in the people he likes best, and in the things he appreciates most highly, there are many flaws and imperfections. It does not vex us much now to find that this is so; but it would have greatly vexed us many years since to have been told that it would be so. I can well imagine that if you told a thoughtful and affectionate child, how well he would some day get on, far from his parents and his home, his wish would be that any evil might befall him rather than that! We shrink with terror from the prospect of things which we can take easily enough when they come. I dare say Lord Chancellor Thurlow was moderately sincere when he exclaimed in the House of Peers, "When I forget my king, may my God forget me!" And you will understand what Leigh Hunt meant when, in his pleasant poem of *The Palfrey*, he tells us of a daughter who had lost a very bad and heartless father by death, that,—

> "The daughter wept, and wept the more,
> To think her tears would soon be o'er."

Even in middle age, one sad thought which comes in the prospect of Future Years is of the change which they are sure to work upon many of our present views and feelings. And the change, in many cases, will be to the worse. One thing is certain, that your temper will grow worse if it do not grow better. Years will sour it, if they do not mellow it. Another certain thing is, that if you do not grow wiser, you will be growing more foolish. It is very true that there is no fool so foolish as an old fool. Let us hope, my friend, that whatever be our honest worldly work, it may never lose its interest. We must always speak humbly about the changes which coming time will work upon us, upon even our firmest resolutions and most rooted principles; or I should say for myself that I cannot even imagine myself the same being, with bent less resolute and heart less warm to that best of all employments which is the occupation of my life. But there are few things which, as we grow older, impress us more deeply than the transitoriness of thoughts and feelings in human hearts. Nor am I thinking of contemptible people only when I say so. I am not thinking of the fellow who is pulled up in court in an action for breach of promise of marriage, and who in one letter makes vows of unalterable affection, and in another letter, written a few weeks or months later, tries to wriggle out of his engagement. Nor am I thinking of the weak, though well-meaning lady, who devotes herself in succession to a great variety of uneducated and unqualified religious instructors; who tells you one week how she has joined the flock of Mr. A., the converted prize-fighter, and how she regards him as by far the most improving preacher she ever heard; and who tells you the next week that she has seen through the prize-fighter, that he has gone and married a wealthy Roman Catholic, and that now she has resolved to wait on the ministry of Mr. B., an enthusiastic individual who makes shoes during the week and gives sermons on Sundays, and in whose addresses she finds exactly what suits her. I speak of the better feelings and purposes of wiser if not better folk. Let me think of of pious emotions and holy resolutions, of the best and purest frames of heart and mind. Oh, if we could all always remain our best! And after all, permanence is the great test. In the matter of Christian faith and feeling, in the matter of all our worldly principles and purposes, *that* which lasts longest is best. This indeed is true of most things. The worth of any thing depends much upon its durability—upon the wear that is in it. A thing that is merely a f… flash and over, only disappoints. The highest authority has recognized this. You remember Who said to his friends, before leaving them, that He would have them bring forth fruit, and much fruit. But … even *that* was enough. The fairest profession for a time, the most earnest labor for a time, the most ardent affection for a time, would not suffice. And so the Redeemer's words were, "I have chosen you, and ordained you, that ye should go and bring forth fruit, and that *your fruit should remain*." Well, let us trust that in the most solemn of all respects, only progress shall be brought to us by all the changes of Future Years.

But it is quite vain to think that feelings as distinguished from principles, shall not lose much of their vividness, freshness, and depth, as time goes on. You cannot now by any effort revive the exultation you felt at some unexpected great success, nor the heart-sinking of some terrible loss or trial. You know how women, after the death of a child, determine that every day as long as they live, they will visit the little grave. And they do so for a time, sometimes for a long time; but they gradually leave off. You know how burying-places are very trimly and carefully kept at first, and how flowers are hung upon the stone; but these things gradually cease. You know how many husbands and wives, after their partner's death, determine to give the remainder of life to the memory of the departed, and would regard with sincere horror the suggestion that it was possible they should ever marry again; but after awhile they do. And you will even find men, beyond middle age, who made a tremendous work at their first wife's death, and wore very conspicuous mourning, who in a very few months may be seen dangling after some new fancy, and who in the prospect of their second marriage evince an exhilaration that approaches to crackiness. It is usual to speak of such things in a ludicrous manner, but I confess the matter seems to me any thing but one to laugh at. I think that the rapid dying out of warm feelings, the rapid change of fixed resolutions, is one of the most sorrowful subjects of reflection which it is possible to suggest. Ah, my friends, after we die, it would not be expedient, even if it were possible, to come back. Many of us would not like to find how very little they miss us. But still, it is the manifest intention of the Creator that strong feelings should be transitory. The sorrowful thing is when they pass, and leave absolutely no trace behind them. There should always be some corner kept in the heart for a feeling which once possessed it all. Let us look at the case temperately. Let us face and admit the facts. The healthy body and mind can get over a great deal; but there are some things which it is not to the credit of our nature should ever be entirely got over. Here are sober truth, and sound philosophy, and sincere feeling together, in the words of Philip van Artevelde :—

"Well, well, she's gone,
And I have tamed my sorrow. Pain and grief
Are transitory things, no less than joy;
And though they leave us not the men we were,
Yet they do leave us. You behold me here,
A man bereaved, with something of a blight
Upon the early blossoms of his life,
And its first verdure—having not the less
A living root, and drawing from the earth
Its vital juices, from the air its powers:
And surely as man's heart and strength are whole,
His appetites regerminate, his heart
Re-opens, and his objects and desires
Spring up renewed."

But though Artevelde speaks truly and well, you remember how Mr. Taylor, in that noble play, works out to our view the sad sight of the deterioration of character, the growing coarseness and harshness, the lessening tenderness and kindliness, which are apt to come with advancing years. Great trials, we know, passing over us, may influence us either for the worse or the better; and unless our nature is a very obdurate and poor one, though they may leave us, they will not leave us the men we were. Once, at a public meeting, I heard a man in eminent station make a speech. I had never seen him before; but I remembered an inscription which I had read, in a certain churchyard far away, upon the stone that marked the resting-place of his young wife, who had died many years before. I thought of its simple words of manly and hearty sorrow. I knew that the eminence he had reached had not come till she who would have been proudest of it was beyond knowing it or caring for it. And I cannot say with what interest and satisfaction I thought I could trace, in the features which were sad without the infusion of a grain of sentimentalism, in the subdued and quiet tone of the man's whole aspect and manner and address, the manifest proof that he had not shut down the leaf upon that old page of his history, that he had never quite got over that great grief of earlier years. One felt better and more hopeful for the sight. I suppose many people, after meeting some overwhelming loss or trial, have fancied that they would soon die; but that is almost invariably a delusion. Various dogs have died of a broken heart, but very few human beings. The inferior creature has pined away at his master's loss; as for *us*, it is not that one would doubt the depth and sincerity of sorrow, but that there is more endurance in our constitution, and that God has appointed that grief shall rather mould and influence than kill. It is a much sadder sight than an early death, to see human beings live on after heavy trial, and sink into something very unlike their early selves and very inferior to their early selves. I can well believe that many a human being, if he could have a glimpse in innocent youth of what he will be twenty or thirty years after, would pray in anguish to be taken before coming to *that!* Mansie Wauch's glimpse of destitution was bad enough; but a million times worse is a glimpse of hardened and unabashed sin and shame. And it would be no comfort—it would be an aggravation in that view—to think that by the time you have reached that miserable point, you will have grown pretty well reconciled to it. *That* is the worst of all. To be wicked and depraved, and to feel it, and to be wretched under it, is bad enough; but it is a great deal worse to have fallen into that depth of moral degradation, and to feel that really you don't care. The instinct of accommodation is not always a blessing. It is happy for us that though in youth we hoped to live in a castle or a palace, we can make up our mind to live in a little parsonage or a quiet street in a country town. It is happy for us that though in youth we hoped to be very great and famous, we are so entirely reconciled to being little and unknown. But it is not happy for the poor girl who walks the Haymarket at night that she feels her degradation so little. It is not happy that she has come to feel towards her miserable life so differently now from what she would have felt towards it had it been set before her while she was the blooming, thoughtless creature in the little cottage in the country. It is only by fits and starts that the poor drunken wretch, living in a garret upon a little pittance allowed him by his relations, who was once a man of character and hope, feels what a sad pitch he has come to. If you could get him to feel it constantly, there would be some hope of his reclamation even yet.

It seems to me a very comforting thought, in looking on to Future Years, if you are able to think that you are in a profession or a calling from which you will never retire. For the prospect of a total change in your mode of life, and the entire cessation of the occupation which for many years employed the greater part of your waking thoughts, and all this amid the failing powers and flagging hopes of declining years, is both a sad and a perplexing prospect to a thoughtful person. For such a person cannot regard this great change simply in the light of a rest from toil and worry; he will know quite well what a blankness, and listlessness, and loss of interest in life, will come of feeling all at once that you have nothing at all to do. And so it is a great blessing if your vocation be one which is a dignified and befitting one for an old man to be engaged in. one that beseems his gravity and his long experience; one that beseems even his slow movements and his white hairs. It is a pleasant thing to see an old man a judge. his years become the judgment-seat. But then the old man can hold such an office only while he retains strength of body and mind efficiently to perform its duties; and he must do all his work for himself; and accordingly a day must come when the venerable chancellor resigns the great seal: when the aged justice or baron must give up his place; and when these honored judges, though still retaining considerable vigor, but vigor less than enough for their hard work, are compelled to feel that their occupation is gone. And accordingly I hold that what is the best of all professions, for many reasons, is especially so for this, that you need never retire from it.

In the Church you need not do all your duty yourself. You may get assistance to supplement your own lessening strength. The energetic young curate or curates may do that part of the parish work which exceeds the power of the ageing incumbent. while the entire parochial machinery has still the advantage of being directed by his wisdom and experience; and while the old man is still permitted to do what he can with such strength as is spared to him, and to feel that he is useful in the noblest cause yet. And even to extremest age and frailty—to age and frailty which would long since have incapacitated the judge for the Bench—the parish clergyman may take some share in the much-loved duty in which he has labored so long. He may still, though briefly, and only now and then, address his flock from the pulpit, in words which his very feebleness will make far more touchingly effective than the most vigorous eloquence and the richest and fullest tones of his young coadjutors. There never will be, within the sacred walls, a silence and reverence more profound than when the withered kindly face looks as of old upon the congregation, to whose fathers its owner first ministered, and which has grown up mainly under his instruction; and when the voice that falls familiarly on so many ears, tells again, quietly and earnestly, the old story which we all need so much to hear. And he may still look in at the parish school, and watch the growth of a generation that is to do the work of life when he is in his grave: and kindly smooth the children's heads; and tell them how One, once a little child, and never more than a young man, brought salvation alike to young and old. He may still sit by the bedside of the sick and dying, and speak to such with the sympathy and the solemnity of one who does not forget that the last great realities are drawing near to both. But there are vocations which are all very well for young or middle-aged people, but which do not quite suit the old. Such is that of the barrister. Wrangling and hair-splitting, browbeating and bewildering witnesses, making coarse jokes to excite the laughter of common jurymen, and addressing such with claptrap bellowings, are not the work for gray-headed men. If such remain at the bar, rather let them have the more refined work of the Equity Courts, where you address judges and not juries; and where you spare clap-trap and misrepresentation, if for no better reason, because you know that these will not stand you in the slightest stead. The work which best befits the aged, the work for which no mortal can ever become too venerable and dignified, or too weak and frail, is the work of Christian usefulness and philanthropy. And it is a beautiful sight to see, as I trust we all have seen, *that* work persevered in with the closing energies of life. It is a noble test of the soundness of the principle that prompted to its first undertaking. It is a hopeful and cheering sight to younger men, looking out with something of fear to the temptations and trials of the years before them. Oh! if the gray-haired clergyman, with less now indeed of physical strength and mere physical warmth, yet preaches, with the added weight and solemnity of his long experience, the same blessed doctrines now, after forty years, that he preached in his early prime; if the philanthropist of half a century since is the philanthropist still,—still kind, hopeful, and unwearied, though with the snows of age upon his head, and the hand that never told its fellow of what it did, now trembling as it does the deed of mercy:—then I think that even the most doubtful will believe that the principle and the religion of such men were a glorious reality! The sternest of all touchstones of the genuineness of our better feelings, is the fashion in which they stand the wear of years.

But my shortening space warns me to stop; and I must cease, for the present, from these thoughts of Future Years. Cease, I mean, from writing about that mysterious tract before us; who can cease from thinking of it? You remember how the writer of that little poem which has been quoted asks Time to touch gently him and his. Of course he spoke as a poet, stating the case fancifully; but not forgetting that when we come to sober sense, we must prefer our requests to an Ear more ready to hear us, and a Hand more ready to help. It is not to Time that I shall apply to lead me through life into immortality! And I cannot think of years to come without going back to a greater poet, whom we need not esteem the less because his inspiration was loftier than that of the Muses, who has summed up so grandly in one comprehensive sentence all the possibilities which could befall *him* in the days and ages before him. "Thou shalt guide me with Thy counsel, and afterward receive me to glory!" Let us humbly trust that in that sketch, round and complete, of all that can ever come to us, my readers and I may be able to read the history of our Future Years!

A. K. H. B.

From The Examiner, 13 April.

THE WRONG END OF A QUARREL.

An article in the *New York Tribune* upon an article in the New Orleans *De Bow's Review*, is in these days a choice example of the outcry of the pot against the kettle. We speak in this country so temperately of the quarrel between North and South, that we need help from the transatlantic papers if we would have fair understanding of the blindness of the passions that, in all good political forecast, must enter into calculation of the chances of the future. *De Bow's Review* is the most reputable organ of the Southern States. Its articles are confidently appealed to by writers, North and South, for statements and statistics that may fairly be taken to represent the case of the slaveholders. There is not much literature in the Southern States; libraries and reading-rooms are at a discount in their half-civilized towns, but the mind of New Orleans has hitherto, we believe, considered itself fairly represented in the pages of De Bow. It happens now that transatlantic writers of the North and South are on the high ropes; and what are we to say of either, unless it be what Joseph Scaliger said of Scioppius, that when he got into his altitudes he was like a monkey getting up a pole. The higher he went the more he displayed his tail, and confined observation to the wrong end of himself.

The Northern critic on the Southern politicians, while he quotes De Bow for censure, finds the men of the South guilty of national madness, victims to an insane fanaticism surpassing any thing ever before known in the civilized world; men uttering propositions of mingled atrocity and absurdity at which the rest of the civilized world is struck aghast with horror and astonishment. But, he says, "it is only when the natural results of characters formed under the influence of such a monstrous perversion of truth and right show themselves in treason, rebellion, and public robbery, that we are startled and disgusted."

Yet we must admit that this kind of political discussion is a mere sprinkling of rose-water compared with the writing from De Bow's review, which it is designed to introduce. The Southern reviewer who is the nearest representative of an English writer in the Edinburgh or Quarterly that can be furnished by the seceding States, says that the women and clergy of the South are the chief promoters of the disunion movement. The women who are "all conservative, moral, religious, and sensitively modest, abhor the North for its infidelity, gross immorality, licentiousness, anarchy, and agrarianism." In this way De Bow explains the election of Mr. Lincoln: "The stupid, sensual, ignorant masses of the North, who are as foolish as they are depraved, could not read the signs of the times, did not dream of disunion, but rushed on heedlessly as a drove of hungry hogs at the call of their owners."

The writer very properly points out that there is an antagonism of temper between the descendants of the Cavaliers and of the Puritans. If that which he himself shows us be the temper of the modern transatlantic Cavalier we can believe any thing we have heard about ruffianly duelling, and other signs of bad blood in the Southern gentlemen.

"The Cavaliers, Jacobites, and Huguenots, who settled the South, naturally hate, contemn, and despise the Puritans, who settled the North. The former are master races,—the latter a slave race, the descendants of the Saxon serfs. The former are Mediterranean races, descendants of the Romans; for Cavaliers and Jacobites are of Norman descent, and the Normans were of Roman descent, and so were the Huguenots. The Saxons and Angles, the ancestors of the Yankees, came from the cold and marshy regions of the North, where man is little more than a cold-blooded, amphibious biped."

The notion of the Roman origin of the Northmen who came to England after settlement in France arose perhaps from an impression founded on the Roman nose of an aristocratic hero, of which there may have been mention in some old novel of the Minerva Press that the reviewer had found in a New Orleans circulating library. Out of the same reading comes no doubt the following boast:—

"We are the most aristocratic people in the world. Pride of caste, and color, and privilege, makes every white man an aristocrat in feeling. Aristocracy is the only safeguard of liberty, the only power watchful and strong enough to exclude monarchical despotism."

In the North, on the contrary, each several State, given up to anarchy, infidelity, and free love, is to become the centre of its own petty military despotism.

Something has been heard in Europe of the violence with which every man is attacked who, while in the Southern States, can be suspected of a word tending to the abolition of slavery. The nightly patrols; the stringent laws for the capture of slaves who are found anywhere beyond bounds without a permit; the burning alive of defiant slaves that terror may be struck into the black population; even the dread of insurrection that thrilled from the South about a twelvemonth since, rise to our memory while the bold Southern writer says: "Slaves are the only body-guard to be relied on. Buonaparte knew it, and kept his Mohammedan slave sleeping at his door; all history proves it."

It is well for the Southern planter that the black slave is still sleeping at his door; teacher and preacher are forbidden to awaken him. Truly there would be need of little help to raise him to the level of his master, if the mind of his master be at all represented by such writing as we find here quoted from *De Bow's Review*. Another of the reviewers thinks it probable that New York City will adopt Mayor York's proposition and secede. "It is practical and feasible," he says, "as it is classical." And the second writer, as he mounts, exhibits the wrong end of himself no less conspicuously than the first. "Gypsies," he says,—

"Gypsies and free negroes have many amiable, noble, and generous traits; Yankees, sourkrout Germans, and Canadians none. Senator Wade says, and Seward, too, that the North will absorb Canada. They are half true; the vile, sensual, animal, brutal, infidel, superstitious democracy of Canada and the Yankee States, will coalesce; and Senator Johnson of Tennessee will join them. But when Canada and Western New York, and New England, and the whole beastly, puritanic 'sourkrout,' free negro, infidel, superstitious, licentious, democratic population of the North become the masters of New York—what then? Outside of the city, the State of New York is Yankee and puritanical; composed of as base, unprincipled, superstitious, licentious, and agrarian and anarchical population as any on earth. Nay, we do not hesitate to say, it is the vilest population on earth. If the city does not secede and erect a separate republic, this population, aided by the ignorant, base, brutal, sensual German infidels of the North-west, the stupid democracy of Canada (for Canada will in some way coalesce with the North), and the arrogant and tyrannical people of New England, will become masters of the destinies of New York."

We do not condemn a people for these frothy outpourings of its passions. But we, who stand apart, have to remember that in the midst of such wild talk, not wholly without its influence upon action, the men whose forefathers were our forefathers, are battling with a crisis in their history that may prove even more momentous than their separation from the parent state.

From The Spectator, 13 April.

THE LAST PHASE IN AMERICA.

The tendency of the last intelligence from America is to re-assure commercial men, and disgust politicians. The probability that the dismemberment of the Union will be peacefully effected increases daily. The Lincoln Administration is as imbecile, or we might perhaps more justly say as powerless, as that of his predecessor. The President, after pledging himself solemnly to carry out the laws, occupies himself with the distribution of the spoils, and suffers the last remnants of national authority to rot away piecemeal. Fort Sumter is to be evacuated. Fort Pickens, it is announced, cannot be defended. No effort has been made to reappoint Federal officers in any of the seceding States. No preparations have been made or discussed to collect a force able to carry out the ultimate resolution of the Executive, or even to submit the whole subject to the free choice of the people. No attempt is talked of to reinforce the Union party in States in which it is palpably able to make some head against its foes. In Texas, for example, the governor, supported by a moiety of the people, declares for the Union, but he is left unsupported to fight his battle with the seceders, while the troops in the State who might have turned the scale in favor of the Federal Government are withdrawn. And now, after a month of irresolution, it is discovered that the laws the President intended to carry out do not permit him to levy revenue in the harbors, and he must consequently either march an army, which he has not at his command, into the resisting States, or abandon the attempt to perform any one function of an Executive Government. The latter alternative, it is stated, is the one preferred by the more influential members of his Cabinet. The Secretary of State, it would seem, quite prides himself upon the energy with which he advocates a "peaceful solution" of the difficulty, by surrendering every thing for which the Confederate States contend. To European ideas, a household might as well plume himself upon his skill in "peacefully solving" the questions raised by a burglar by the surrender of his cash and spoons. Even Mr. Chase, a Republican of Republicans, is supposed to have gi en way, and the Southern leaders regard their prospects, in their own quaint slang with "considerable cheerfulness of mind." They may well be cheerful, for they have exhibited precisely the qualities Northern Americans appear to lack —decision, unity, and statesman-like foresight. While a nation of nineteen millions of brave men confesses its inability to raise a force for its own defence, a nation of two and a half millions places an army in the field. While the old-established Republican Government gropes blindly about to find a policy, lets its treasury run dry from simple want of financial skill, and declares commercial war with Europe, a new Government, scarcely elected, frames a new and improved constitution, adopts a new system of finance, and tempts all European trade to enter its own ports. The local minority is restrained with the mixed judgment and unscrupulousness usually displayed by far better established powers. The people of South Carolina wish to revive the slave trade, but the President vetoes the bill which changes the offence from piracy to misdemeanor. Half the people of Louisiana are hostile to secession, but the Convention first decrees that the State shall secede, and then refuses to submit the proposition to the mass. The Germans everywhere are supporters of the Union, but they are enrolled as minute men, and employed to defy the Free States, as easily as if they were not free-soilers in opinion. The action of the South is in fact the best demonstration of the official imbecility of the North. Whatever the five States who secede can do, the twenty-seven States who remain could have done better. If Mr. Jefferson Davis could extemporize an army so could Mr. Lincoln. The President of the South never chatters about legality, but states quietly that the South intends to secede, and if necessary to carry out her intention by the sword. The North has five times the population, and twenty times the wealth of the South, while her yeomanry lay claim to fighting qualities at least equal to those of the planting chivalry. Yet she submits through want of organization to an ignominious defeat from men with whose policy not one Northern man in ten even professes sympathy. The internal Government of the North is as weak as its external policy. The treasury is empty, and the Secretary offers a loan at six per cent. At the same time the victorious party, powerless to retain the Union together, is strong enough to perpetrate a gigantic job which buys an interested support at the price of national solvency. Pennsylvania at the last election was believed to be divided in opinion. To ensure victory to the Republicans, their leaders offered the ironmasters protection, and were rewarded by a majority of ninety thousand votes. To keep the engagement, they passed a bill authorizing a tariff so heavy as to cripple the customs' revenue, and so complicated as to be unworkable. The moment the bill is passed they discover that one essential element in success has been forgotten. The South adopts a lower tariff, and the North finds that to construct a line of frontier custom-houses would be to acknowledge the seceding States as foreign powers. Consequently, they must bear to see trade transferred to the Southern ports, without being able to tax it *en route* to their own cities, and so lose by one brilliant stroke of party statesmanship commerce and revenue together. The Americans are fond of deriding the slowness of the Old World, but European statesmen are apt to succeed. In America a great policy is enforced by a surprise, and then given up because its supporters had not considered so ordinary a condition of success as the position of their frontier. The Morrill Bill must either be abandoned or ruin the Northern treasury, demonstrating in either case that aristocracies are not the only rulers who prefer personal interests to the welfare of the state.

The events, however, which prove to politicians the feebleness of American institutions, tend at the same time to the benefit of commerce. The peaceful separation of the States may be ruinous to American prestige, but it is favorable to the abundance and consequent cheapness of cotton. The tax imposed by the South of a half-cent a pound will not diminish the supply half so much as an invasion from the North, or an effective blockade of the Southern ports. The States separated are as valuable customers as the States when combined, while the tax on cotton falls as heavily on the Northern manufacturer, who has a long land carriage to pay, as on his English rival. The political imbecility which while passing the Morrill Tariff neutralizes its effect, is a direct gain to Great Britain, for every such bill keeps prices up, while the open frontier annuls the duties which were to restrict supply. The stagnation of business, moreover, has made money for the moment plentiful in New York, to the relief of the English market, which has been oppressed for months by a drain to the West. Whether the movement will ultimately be favorable to commerce may reasonably be doubted. A Republic devoted, as the Confederacy will be, to the extension of its dominions, is not likely to keep up its production, or keeping it be able to avoid the taxation which is as injurious as a diminution of supply. For the present, however, the tendency of events, though unfavorable to the prestige of American statesmen, is decidedly beneficial to the prospects of the British commerce.

From The Economist, 18 April.

THE TRUE ISSUE BETWEEN NORTH AND SOUTH.

We are waiting with deep anxiety the next news from America, which will probably decide the question as to peaceable severance or hopeless civil war. It is idle to speculate now, and the best-informed people both here and there seem in complete uncertainty as to the result. For ourselves —menacing as was the aspect of affairs at the date of the last accounts—we adhere to the opinion we formed at the outset; viz., that there will be no reunion and no fighting; and we hold this view because we believe that no really practical ground for compromise exists, and that the Americans are too sensible to shed each others' blood without a clear reason and an adequate object. The only ostensible and sufficient justification for an attempt at coercion would lie in the knowledge that reunion was desired by a large and respectable minority in the South, who were intimidated, silenced, and overborne by mere numbers. But of any such fact there seems no indication.

Meanwhile, do not let us deceive ourselves by permitting the controversy between the old Federation and the seceding States to be placed, even in our own minds, upon false issues. As the matter at present stands, both parties seem wedded to a grievous economic error and to a sad social injustice and moral wrong. The North is bent upon a Protective Commercial policy, which will injure themselves and wrong the Western States; and the South is bent upon perpetuating and extending slavery, which will be fatal to their future prosperity, and is a shameful iniquity against the African race. We do not mean for one moment to put the two follies and the two wrongs *on a level* as regards either their social gravity or their moral heinousness,—especially as the one must soon be abandoned, while the other may be persisted in for generations. But, in the lines they have respectively taken, each of the two confederations, while conciliating one of our predilections, have done grievous violence to another. The Northern States are Freesoilers and Protectionists: the Southern States are Slaveholders and Free-traders. We can, therefore, contemplate their relative position with some degree of calm impartiality. Do not, then, let us mistake their several aims and principles, and give our sympathies under mistaken pleas. If, indeed, the Northern Federation were prepared heartily, resolutely, and unanimously—as no doubt a few of their citizens are—to take their stand on the solemn principle of prohibiting and preventing the extension of Slavery to any States and Territories where it does not now exist, then such a ground might be well worth an obstinate struggle and even a long civil war, if there were any reasonable prospect of ultimate success; because if slavery were strictly and forever confined within its present limits there is every hope that it must ultimately die out. An object like this, if attainable, would be worth fighting for, and might perhaps justify even civil war:—but what ground is there for assuming that any such distinct and noble aim is in the heart of Mr. Lincoln's government when they speak of coercion? Mr. Lincoln, indeed, contends for the right of Congress to make laws for all unannexed, unsettled, and unadmitted territories:—he has never, so far as we are aware, taken up the high ground of saying that slavery *shall not* be introduced into any new districts. This is the ground of the Abolitionists; but it is not the ground of the Republican party as a whole; still less is it the ground of the mass of the people in the Northern and Western States. On the contrary, nearly every compromise yet proposed—and *all the proposed compromises have come from the North or from the Border States*—has stipulated that slavery shall only be prohibited *north of a certain line* (north of which slavery cannot profitably exist, and consequently need not be prohibited);—but that south of this line, its introduction shall be left to the decision of the inhabitants themselves. Some of the suggested compromises, indeed, have contained a proviso that no new territory shall be acquired without the consent of the majority of all the States, both Slave and Free. But we can scarcely regard this as likely to be at all effective in *really* limiting the area of slavery, when we consider, first, the enormous space *already acquired* and peculiarly adapted for negro cultivation; and, secondly, that even the North and North-Western States have never yet, as a whole, shown the slightest reluctance to the extension of the dominion of the Republic in any direction or by any means. Do not, therefore, let us give our sympathies to those Northerners who would appear to be preparing to maintain the old Union by force, on the erroneous impression that they are about to fight on the grand, intelligible, and worthy ground of confining slavery forever within its present area. If it were so, and there were a fair prospect of success, we could almost wish them God speed, though a terrible civil war was the only means to their cherished end. But, alas! it is not so. Abhorrence of negro-slavery, as we feel it here, and determination at all hazards to clear their nation's fame and future from so foul a blot, are sentiments confined to but a small minority of the citizens of the Northern Federation. What *all* these are anxious for—and what some are meditating war in order to ensure—is that the vast and rich territories which are still unsettled or which may in future be acquired (and which chiefly lie to the south of lat. 36.30), shall not fall into the hands of slaveholders and planters, and thus give them a preponderance in the Senate and control over the policy of the Union. And this object we believe can scarcely be secured by war, and would not be worth a war even if it could.

The real issue between the North and South, then, is not the abolition or the extension of slavery, but the decision whether a free-labor or a slaveholding republic shall henceforth hold the reins and direct the policy of the Great American Federation, or the chief part of it—a vast question, no doubt, and a momentous one, but not rising to the moral magnitude of the other. And if it shall really appear that the future of the negro race is not at issue in this controversy, then there is much in the position and conduct of the seceding States to add strength to our hope and desire that no attempts at forcible reunion shall be hazarded, but that they shall be allowed to separate and to reorganize themselves without interference. They have evidently some sagacious heads as well as some resolute wills among them; and they seem scarcely more intemperate and much more wise than their Northern brethren. In the framing of their new Constitution they have laid their finger on nearly every blot of the old one, and seem resolved to profit by experience. They give their President a longer term of office and forbid his re-election. They provide, in a great measure, for the irremovability and independence of the judges, which had become so fatally impaired. They restore dignity and security to the civil service, by declaring virtually that all except the highest *employés* shall be considered to hold office for life, or during good behavior. And they empower the ministers (who have hitherto been excluded from Congress) to sit and speak there—but without votes. By these enactments they go far to rectify what were felt by all observers to have become most dangerous and spreading evils under the old system. They have adopted a moderate tariff, which will at least discourage smuggling, and bring some considerable and reliable revenue into their coffers; and, as they have not yet—any more than the Northerners—the nerve or the virtue to establish an onerous scheme of direct taxation, and yet *must have* funds, we are by no means sure that the plan of an export duty upon cotton is not open to as few objections as any other. Certainly, it is not deserving of the unmeasured condemnation which has been passed upon it. If the States were the *only* cotton-producing country in the world, then such a tax would obviously be the right one to impose: it would be analagous to the case of saltpetre in India, which the sagacity of Mr. Wilson at once fixed upon as fit to bear an export duty. America is not the only cotton-producing country, but it is the principal one; and so long as the duty is moderate and the demand brisk, it is not probable that it will perceptibly check exports, though it may prospectively encourage rivals. Of course, as the American cotton thus burdened will have to meet Indian and Egyptian cotton in the markets of the world, the duty will to a great extent come out of the pockets of the American producer; but then, if ten millions of dollars are wanted and *must be got*, how could they be extracted out of those buttoned pockets at once less noxiously and less vexatiously? It is as if the planter surrendered (say) every tenth bale to the State, to be sold and exported for the public benefit. We by no means say that it is a good financial measure, but if a property tax will not be endured, we do not know that any better could be substituted.

From The Economist, 20 April.

THE AMERICAN NEWS AND ITS LESSONS.

There is a painful sense of imbecility produced by all public criticism on a tide of events apparently so irresistible, and yet so uncertain in direction, as those which are rushing forwards in the United States. Even the American journals feel this: they comment on the stream of events without any hope of influencing it, and with little hope even of divining its immediate tendency. The truth is, that the time for criticism is past; and until some final act of the competing administrations either precipitates the country into civil war, or opens a definite prospect of peace, there is little to do but to bear the political suspense with as much patience as possible. The next mail may, it is feared, bring news of the disaster which we have so long feared, yet hoped to see averted—a collision between the seceding and non-seceding States. It was feared at the date of the last advices that such a collision had already taken place at Pensacola, as no telegraphic despatches had been received for several days from Fort Pickens; and three United States frigates were on the point of sailing under sealed orders, whether to succor Fort Pickens or to put down the Spanish filibustering attack on St. Domingo, was not known. Another mail must probably clear up the question of peace or war,—and it is only too probable in the worst way.

If we could look forward to even a civil war as decisive,—as likely to end soon, and without ulterior evil consequences, in the triumph either of Union or Disunion, we should not shrink even from that terrible remedy for a terrible malady. Unfortunately, we fear it would only result in the further disintegration of what remains of the Union, and in a new and grievous exacerbation of the hatreds and rivalries between the various fragments. At present, the six Northern Slave States that have not seceded, —Arkansas, Tennessee, North Carolina, Kentucky, and Virginia, —are waiting with suspended judgments to watch the steps of the rival administrations. On the course of these Border Slave States almost every thing depends. Their free population is double that of the seceded States, and far more adapted to military purposes. Should they ultimately join the South, the Confederated States would have a *free* population more than one-third of that of the Northern Union, and a government probably much more compact and formidable. But the chances are that the Border States will never join the South, though a civil war would in all probability ensure their recoil from the North. Their interests are in many respects different from those both of North and South. To a very large extent they are of course identified with slavery;—but they are not for the most part Cotton States; they have very large districts in which free-labor would be more effective than slave; and they are warmly interested in preventing any renewal of the slave-trade. The result, therefore, of any fresh impulse of disgust towards the North would probably be to cement them into a new Union of their own. And a still worse result of civil war would of course be the growth of that intense jealousy and mutual hatred of which American States seem but too susceptible.

From The London Review, 20 April.

[This is a weekly paper, edited by Dr. Mackay, who lately spent some months in the United States.]

AMERICAN PROBABILITIES.

We have often had occasion to remark that those politicians who boast, and with perfect truth, of "access to the best sources of information," are by no means always the best informed. At least, they are by no means the keenest estimators or the truest prophets. They may know the opinions and designs of those nearest to the scene of action, and, possibly, even of the actors themselves, but they usually assign far too much weight to these, and do not adequately consider how far less effectively operative are the wills of men—even eminent and able men—than permanent interests, the wishes of the general public, or that combination of hidden causes and remote influences which we are in the habit of somewhat loosely designating "the tendency of events." It is often far more easy to prognosticate the probable issue of any contest, the probable course of any set of occurrences, by looking at the whole question from a distance, and considering the great aggregate of considerations that bear upon it, than by gaining the most intimate acquaintance with the intentions, the views, or even the most fixed determinations, of leading men, although those men should be presidents, emperors, prime ministers, or mighty orators. This is simply a corollary of the statement often made, without any very definite meaning being attached to it,—"that circumstances are stronger than men." Confidence in this proverb has led us from the outset to a strong conviction, in reference to the probable course of American affairs, which, till of late, few Englishmen and scarcely any Americans were prepared to share.

We have for some time regarded the disruption of the great Transatlantic Republic as inevitable, sooner or later, and no less inevitable than desirable. But whenever we ventured to broach the opinion we were met, especially on the other side the ocean, with the assertion that it was about the most improbable of future contingencies; that the pride and patriotism of the United States would prevent such a catastrophe from ever taking place; that any serious attempt at it would bring about a desperate and bloody civil war; and that if successful it would be one of the most calamitous and deplorable of occurrences. A few months ago, when secession was first openly announced, and the first decided steps towards its practical realization taken by South Carolina, the general impression, the almost universal one in the Northern States of the Union, was that, somehow or other, no one pretended to say *how*, the breach would be healed, and the Union restored; that a compromise would be effected; that the seceding States only intended to bully their opponents into acceptance of their terms, and if possible to recover the command of the government of the Federation. As time passed on, however, and the resolution of the slaveholding provinces became more pronounced and their action more prompt and daring, the fact of a separation was reluctantly admitted: but the common opinion, especially among native Americans, was that force would be employed to bring them back, and that force would be successful. The wealth, and numbers, and potential strength of the North was believed to be so enormously preponderant, that few thought the slaveholders would be suffered to succeed; and the inaugural address of the new President appeared to confirm the notion that coercion would at all events be tried. We have never varied in our opinion, nor are we inclined to vary now. We are satisfied that there *will* be secession, and it may be accompanied with violence; but in spite of the warlike preparations on both sides, we will still indulge the hope, until the conflict shall have actually commenced, that the separation may be accomplished without the shedding of blood. If war shall thus happily be avoided, the disruption of the great Republic will prove the most auspicious of catastrophes; and for these reasons.

It had for some years been increasingly apparent that the union of the several States, which had formerly been a natural bond dictated by circumstances, was becoming an artificial one, which demanded much effort, vigilance, and mutual compromise to keep up. The area of the Republic had been quadrupled; the number of sovereign States had increased from *thirteen* to *thirty-three;* the population of the federation had swelled from four to thirty-one millions; and the garment which fitted the small and infant body politic was no longer suitable to the mature and overgrown commonwealth. Then, too, discrepant interests and still more discrepant feelings had sprung up with extension of territory, with divergency of occupations, and with lapse of time. One-half the Union had gradually come to regard slavery as an economic blunder, and was rapidly learning to regard it as a moral sin; the other half, which in earlier days used to speak of it as an institution to be regretted, and in time abandoned, was beginning to proclaim it the normal phase of society, and the only system of husbandry available in those climes. Between States which considered slavery a curse and a disgrace, and States which considered it a blessing and a right, there could be no permanent harmony of principles or action. Besides this, the Free States were most of them commercial, and some of them manufacturing, and these clung to the old fallacies of protection, and clamored for high duties on foreign goods. The Slave States were purely agricultural, were dependent on foreign trade for nearly all their luxuries. their utensils, and their clothing, and were anxious for as unrestricted exchange with Europe as was possible. Then, again, the South was always anxious for an increase of territory—for new virgin soils whereon the negroes might be located with advantage—as well as for conquests which should flatter their national pride, and supply space in which new Slave States could be formed. The North on the other hand, of late at least, had learned to look coldly upon this covetous and aggressive tendency, which not only alarmed their commerce by frequent misunderstandings and quarrels with foreign countries, but endangered their political preponderance.

Finally, and to complete these various causes of mutual alienation, the rapid and preponderating increase of the Free States, both in wealth and population, and their decided superiority in education, naturally gave them the conviction that with them ought properly to lie the control over the policy of the Union, while at the same time they saw as a fact that the Slave States, aided by a portion of the Northern Democracy, still, in spite of all efforts, retained the almost exclusive direction of that policy. The North had the command of the lower House of Congress, but the South kept the Senate and the presidential chair in their own hands. For some years there has been a ceaseless struggle for supremacy: up to 1860 the South had been successful; but this year the tide turned, and from that moment secession, long foreseen and prepared, became inevitable. The Slave States had long felt extreme irritation at the menaced, or rather at the dreaded possibility of interference on the part of the North with their cherished "domestic institution," as well as much envy of its superior prosperity and more rapid progress, but so long as they had the government in their own hands, they gained power and *prestige* by the extent of the Union, and were, therefore, willing to maintain it; but the moment the sceptre passed to their antagonists, the only motive (beyond barren pride) for continuing in the Federation was gone. They were willing to remain as masters and in a majority, but not as inferiors and in a minority. The Free States, too, felt that their connection with the slaveholding South had dragged them through mud and mire, and brought on them much obloquy; but they could not bear the idea of the loss of grandeur and the mortification of national vanity consequent on the severance of more than half the most fertile portion of their territory, and the reduction of their magnificent commonwealth to comparatively moderate dimensions, especially just as they had climbed into power, and attained that supremacy of rule to which they had long felt themselves entitled.

These considerations will explain both the resolute and unshakeable determination of the Southern States to secede, and the anxiety of the Northern States to ward off secession—the almost humiliating offers of compromise alternating with threats of coercion which we have witnessed on the one side, and the profound contempt and even insult with which both allurements and menaces have been listened to on the other. The truth is—and to those who could look calmly on the conjuncture, it seems to us it might have been clear from the beginning—the South has long made up its mind that it will remain in the Union only on condition of being the supreme arbiter of its policy; and the North, though willing to concede almost every thing else, cannot, without suicide and dishonor, concede *this*. There is, really, not the slightest desire for compromise or conciliation on the one side, nor any possible basis for compromise or conciliation on the other. And matters *must*, therefore, take their destined course.

LONDON FIRES: BLOWING UP HOUSES WITH GUNPOWDER.—

"Hark! the drum thunders; far, ye crowds, retire;
Behold the ready match is tipt with fire;
The nitrous store is laid; the smutty train
With running blaze awakes the barrelled grain.
Flames sudden wrap the walls; with sullen sound
The shattered pile sinks on the smoky ground," etc.
Gay's *Trivia*, book iii. p. 78; *Poems*, 1720.

The expedient of blowing up houses with gunpowder, in order to arrest the progress of the flames, is said to have been resorted to with success during the Great Fire of London, 1666; and from the above extract from Gay it may perhaps be inferred that the practice still continued in his days. Is there any well-authenticated instance of this?

To descend to more modern times. Is there any case on record during the last century in which the same plan has been adopted? At present (thanks to the multiplication and increased power of fire-engines, and to improved methods of building) there is no necessity for having recourse to such desperate expedients for the purpose of controlling the rage of the "devouring element."—*Notes and Queries.*

HOUSE OF GUELPH.—The error of the author of *The Antient and Present State of Germany* needs correction, in stating the name of Henry the Proud as Henry *Guelph*, A.D. 1135, whereas the Guelph family was extinct in the male line, A.D. 1055. The heiress of that house, Cunegonda, married Azo of Este, who left two sons, Guelph and Fulke, the former created Duke of Bavaria in 1070, who left two sons, Guelph and Henry the Black; and the last named left also two sons, Henry the Proud (Duke of Bavaria, 1127, and of Saxo, 1136) and Guelph (who gave name to the party opposed to the Guibelines).

In the house of Este, therefore, the name Guelph was a Christian or baptismal name, and not a family or surname. Henry the Proud was grandfather of Otto IV., emperor in 1209, and great-grandfather of Otto the Infant created the first Duke of Brunswick by the Emperor Frederick II. in 1285. Otto the Infant inherited the extensive territories of the house of Guelph in Lower Saxony; and he is the ancestor of the houses of Brunswick-Wolfenbüttel, of Brunswick-Luneburg and of Hanover.—*Notes and Queries.*

YOKUL.—Amongst the many names by which rustics are designated, or by which they designate each other, such as a Yokul, a Chopstick, a Chawbacon, a Tummas, a Mate, a Feller, a Chap, etc., there is only one which particularly puzzles me, and that is the first. What is the derivation of "Yokul," and what is its proper meaning?
PAUL PRY.

[As *yoke* seems plainly to be connected with the Latin *jugum*, we have always been disposed to derive *yokul* from the L. *jugalis* or *jogalis*, which signifies "pertaining to a yoke" (as of oxen or other animals). We would therefore submit that the term *yokul*, as applied to a rustic, primarily signified one who yoked or drove oxen, horses, etc.; and hence, generally, a peasant or countryman.]—*Notes and Queries.*

A JACK OF PARIS.—Does E. H. find an illustration of the phrase he quotes from Sir Thomas More, in

"And many a Jacke of Dover hast thou sold,
That hath ben twies hot and twies cold"?
Chaucer, *The Coke's Prologue.*

—*Notes and Queries.*

AMERICAN METEOROLOGY.—"Now boy, what are aërolites?" "Guess they're the remains of secedin' stars smashed to pieces, that have tumbled out of the sky."—*Punch.*

From The National Magazine.

THE MYSTERIOUS BEAUTY.

A Paris chronicler, writing of the opera ball in that capital of the fashionable world, says, We have been told that intrigue was dead, but it has come to life again recently, and in a singular fashion. The occurrence we are about to relate is not old, and we believe we are doing a service to the public in making it known.

One of our young friends, who has a good fortune and enviable position in society, attended an opera ball for the first time, without any definite object, prompted merely by curiosity, idleness, and that indefinable feeling which impels us toward any thing unknown and mysterious. At the entrance of the green-room, where the crowd was the thickest, the button of his coat became entangled in the lace of a domino so intricately that it was necessary to tear the frail texture in order to release it. The wearer of the lace gave her assistance very graciously, and took the accident in a lofty style, like one to whom the injury was a matter of entire indifference.

The young man was already weary of the ball; the intelligence the lady had displayed in the few words they had exchanged interested him. He offered her his arm — she accepted it with a nonchalance rather unpromising for the future of the adventure. When they had succeeded in releasing themselves from the crowd, he proposed that they should take a seat, not in a box, but in some part of the green-room, where they would not attract attention. She assented with the same carelessness, and he no longer doubted that he was in the company of some disdainful belle. The lady was tall, slender, and admirably dressed; her domino of black satin, her *camail* trimmed with exquisite lace, and tightly closed, her mask also of satin with thick *barbe*, which did not permit a single hair to be seen, nor allow the curious to divine even the color of her skin; her irreproachable white gloves, a little foot clad in a black open-work silk stocking and black satin slipper—every thing about her, in short, indicated the woman of good society, such as are not always to be found in these assemblies.

The conversation began with commonplaces: the domino seemed to wish to test her chevalier. Suddenly she changed her style, and our friend was astonished to hear himself called by name. He was not disposed to deny it — it would have been useless, indeed, as the lady knew it by heart. She sketched his character with the hand of a master, told the story of his life, pointed out his faults, and urged him to correct them. Every trace of hesitation or apathy had disappeared; she showed such sagacity, such refinement, such delicacy of feeling and expression, that he was stupefied. Handling all subjects, playing all parts with equal ease, she passed in review, society, literature, the opera; related a thousand anecdotes, and uttered sparkling witticisms with a grace of attitude and manner quite irresistible. The young man, dazzled by this brilliancy, could hardly utter a word; he looked, listened, wondered.

"Is it possible that I do not know you — you who know me so well?" he said, at length, impatient at his own passiveness.

"You do not know me, I assure you; if one should tell you my name it would sound perfectly strange to you; if I should show my face, you would see it for the first time."

"Where have you learned, then, what you have told me? Are you a sorceress?"

"Perhaps; or I may have divined what I have told by my knowledge of human nature. Do you fancy yourself the only subject of my study?"

Our friend did not dare to discuss this question, and the domino gave him no time. She changed the subject, opened another chapter, and showed herself under a new face. Never a chameleon changed more quickly, or more to the purpose. He was so engrossed in the conversation, that he did not heed the jests of the passers-by, nor reply to several direct attacks, and when the last of the merry-andrews had retired, he was startled by an intimation from the officials that they were about to close the hall, and that it was necessary to withdraw.

"Already!" exclaimed our friend.

They had been talking for five hours.

"Permit me to conduct you home," he said.

"Impossible."

"Am I not to see you again?"

"I will think about it."

"And will you not tell me who you are? This is cruel. You take possession of me, turn my head, and then abandon me, as a child throws away a toy of which he is weary. I shall not submit to it, I warn you; you forbid me to accompany you, but I will follow you, I will learn who you are, I will force you to avow yourself—to receive me—to love me. After an enchanted evening like this there must not be forgetfulness and indifference between us. Make your decision, and accept my company, if you would not have me impose it upon you."

"You would not do that, I am sure. If you did, I should succeed in evading you. On the contrary, you must leave me free, and give me your word of honor not to seek to know who I am; in that case I will make you two concessions greater than you could have hoped for, though, indeed, I had long since resolved to grant them when you had earned them."

"What are they?"

"I will return next Saturday, and I will give you my portrait. You can look at it when I am no longer near you. Do you consent?"

He made her repeat three times the promise to return, he received from her hand the card-photograph in a sealed and perfumed envelope, and hastened to a gas-light to tear it open. She profited by the moment to disappear. When he raised his eyes she was no longer there. The portrait represented the most beautiful, bewitching creature that one could ever dream of. Our lover remained for some moments stupefied by his own happiness. Such a face, and such an intellect! It was hardly to be believed, yet he could not doubt it now. He hastened home like a miser bearing his treasure, tried to sleep, but found it impossible; he gazed at the beautiful face, recalled the five hours passed so quickly, and concluded he could not wait a week to see his unknown — he must, at any price, discover her, and see her again, under penalty of losing his senses.

As soon as it was light and he could present himself with propriety, he went to see three somnambulists and as many fortune-tellers. Each one told him a different story, and sent him in a different direction for the mysterious beauty. This would not do—he must try elsewhere. The card which he had received did not bear, as usual, the name of the photographer, but it must have been done in one of the fashionable establishments. He would visit them all. He went first to that of Nadar. He was too much pre-occupied to observe all the miracles of the *atélier*, one of the wonders of Paris. He could see neither rocks nor cascades, nor works of art, all that the most refined taste can collect in a house like this—the true lover has no eyes but for his mistress. Our friend gave not a look to this art-palace; he drew the card from his pocket, asked the principal if it was his work, and if he could tell the name of the original.

"Monsieur," replied the artist, "if I made this photograph, and did not sign it as usual, I must have had reasons for abstaining; if I did not make it I ought not to claim the merit of it. You understand me—I cannot reply to your question. As to naming the person you desire to know, it would be still more impossible; we are a sort of father-confessors, and never reveal the secrets that are confided to us. I am unhappy that I cannot oblige you, but a little reflection will convince yon that I am obeying my duty."

He received nearly the same answer from Disderi, from Ken, from Dagron, and everywhere else. He returned home in despair, asking himself to what saint in the calendar he should address his vows to discover the mystery. His good star sent him one of his cousins, to whom he related his perplexities. The latter, after long discussion, finding himself unable to help him, introduced him to a gentleman well known in Paris for his perspicacity and intelligence, which amounts almost to a second-sight for the intellect, while his kindness is a second-sight for the heart. He heard the story, examined the picture, and uttered his oracle,—

"Go to-morrow to the *rendezvous*, and as soon as you shall see your domino, say, 'It pleases me. I am enchanted with it; present me.'"

This was another enigma; in vain the lover asked an explanation.

"I will be at the ball," was the only reply. "I will wait for you at three o'clock, in box No. 20; come there, tell me the effect you have produced, and you shall know all."

It was necessary to be content with this. Saturday came slowly, but it came. The impatient one was at his post, replying by monosyllables to a sultana, who persecuted him with compliments. The domino appeared, he recognized her immediately, and disengaging himself somewhat brusquely from his odalisque, he seized the hand of the unknown and led her aside, with a palpitating heart. He forgot the enigmatical phrase; it only occurred to him when she announced her intention of retiring early. He hoped to retain her by this "open sesame." He repeated it. The lady could not restrain a movement of surprise, and kept silent for a few moments.

"I do not comprehend you," she said, with a troubled voice.

"You seem, on the contrary, to comprehend me admirably; much better," he muttered inwardly, "than I comprehend myself. What do you reply?"

The answer was embarrassed—labored; it rendered matters more obscure, instead of enlightening them, and soon after, in a place where the compact crowd permitted individuals hardly to be distinguished, the lady wound suddenly, like a hare, through the groups, and disappeared. Of course our friend was eager to have the key of all this. He hastened to box No. 20, related to the *sage* his disappointment, and begged him to conceal nothing, if he would not drive him insane.

"My dear young friend," replied his counsellor, "you see that I was not mistaken, and you shall now comprehend my meaning. This woman who has captivated you is neither more nor less than a marriage-broker. She wishes to unite a poor young girl to a rich young man; she has intellect, the girl has beauty. She commences the fascination with her intellect, under a mask—the face will finish the work; by the aid of love you could be blinded to the deception till it was too late for a remedy. This is the whole mystery. I suspected it when you repeated the conversation; no girl of sixteen, such as that picture represents, could have the skill and knowledge of the world of your siren. I advised you to apply the test, and it succeeded. You cannot imagine what these elderly women of the world, disappointed as to matrimony, are capable of. When I made my *début* in society, a certain Italian countess gained her living by two doubtful Titians and an apocryphal Raphael. She lay in wait for English and Italian amateurs, intimating to them that she had three remarkable pictures for sale. They hastened to see them. She received them with the most charming manners, showed them the pictures by an indistinct light, then introduced them to some magnificent creature, who looked her part as well as the countess played hers. This often failed, or had a result different from her intention; but if it succeeded twice or thrice, it secured her a subsistence. Your domino belongs to this school. Be assured of that, and thank Heaven that your eyes are opened before it is too late."

We have thought it best to unmask this new method of getting an honest livelihood, to warn prospective victims against such snares. It is very disagreeable to a worthy man to find that he has married only a pretty fool, when he fancied he had got both beauty and intellect.

In Malcolm Flemyng's *Dissertation on Dr. James' Fever Powders* occurs the following passage:—

"... *Dr. Charleton*, a celebrated physician in Charles II.'s reign, who had the licensing of Quacks, told me on his death-bed, that all the useful and successful cures performed by the Mountebanks of his time were solely owing to preparations of Mercury and Antimony."

Is this the origin of the word "Charlatan."—*Notes and Queries.*

Hast thou found life a cheat, and worn in vain
Its iron chain?
Hast thy soul bent beneath earth's heavy bond?
Look thou beyond;
If life is bitter there forever shine
Hopes more divine;

Art thou alone, and does thy soul complain
It lives in vain?
Not vainly does he live who can endure.
Oh, be thou sure,
That he who hopes and suffers here can earn
A sure return.

THE RALLY.

I.

Off her bar of Charleston harbor our gallant vessels lay,
The dark north-easter swept its clouds of rain across the bay,
Beneath its gloomy veil a thick blue vapor heavenward curled,
Where the cannon of the batteries their deadly missiles hurled.

II.

And still when slacked the driving rain, and the thick smoke eddied by,
You might see the glorious stars and stripes against the murky sky,
Where, worn with care, and watching through the weary night and day,
Brave Anderson, in Sumter, held ten thousand foes at bay.

III.

Full thirty hours he held it against the traitor power,
And but sixty men to back him in that stormy opening hour,
There was Moultrie, iron Cummings, and seven batteries more,
The quick, fierce flashes lit the long low reach of sandy shore.

IV.

Full thirty hours he fought them in sunshine and in cloud,
Then first, before a traitor's flag, our country's banner bowed,
And Treason's Rubicon was passed, the Traitor's challenge given,
So manlike take the proffered gage, and rest your cause with Heaven!

V.

Hark! those guns have found an echo on mountain and in glen,
From farthest East to West, and in the hearts of valiant men,
And our Union's flag shall fly again where now it droops in shame,
And a hundred thousand heroes rally round her honored name.

VI.

There's a sound of coming footsteps, a trumpet's signal call,
Above the breaking of the seas along Maine's granite wall,
Wafted with murmur of the pines from far New-Hampshire hills,
And mingling with the music of the clear Green Mountain rills.

VII.

From the valleys of Connecticut the martial call is borne,
And the hills of Massachusetts have passed the signal on,
O'er the iron Adirondacks it echoes low and deep,
From Manhattan's sunny bay to where Ontario's waters sleep.

VIII.

From the Alleghany ridges borne northward by the breeze
That along fair Juniata wakes to life the sleeping trees,
And where the broad Atlantic breaks in showers of glancing spray,
Brave hearts are answering to the call on Narragansett Bay.

IX.

O'er the cornfields of Ohio in the new Spring's genial glow,
In the wash of Erie's waves, in the rivers stately flow,
From Wisconsin's sunny opening, from Indiana's fields,
Sounds the clashing of the weapons which many a warrior wields.

X.

From East to West the land is up to guard her ancient name,
And the Altar of the Commonwealth from foul disgrace and shame,
From the mountain and the valley they come with steady tread
To a victor's garland living or a nation's reverence dead.

XI.

They are coming, they are coming, for the memories of the Past!
For our Flag, against a traitor hand, to strike one blow at last,
For the love of their high duty, they are going to the fight,
God have them in his keeping, and God defend the right!

—*Vanity Fair.*

A SUNBEAM AND A SHADOW.

I heard a shout of merriment,
A laughing boy I see;
Two little feet the carpet press,
And bring the child to me.
Two little arms are round my neck,
Two feet upon my knee;
How fall the kisses on my cheek!
How sweet they are to me!

That merry shout no more I hear,
No laughing child I see;
No little arms are round my neck,
No feet upon my knee!
No kisses drop upon my cheek,
Those lips are sealed to me,
Dear Lord, how could I give him up
To any but to Thee!

From The National Magazine.

THE MISUNDERSTANDING.

> "There's somewhat in this world amiss,
> Shall be unriddled by and by."
> —*Tennyson.*

"WELL, aunty," said Lucy, looking dreamily at the red cinders of the comfortable fire, "I suppose

> "'It is better to have loved and lost
> Than never to have loved at all.'

I wish," she added, half shyly, "I wish you would tell me about yourself."

"Myself, my child! no, don't ask me; and yet, why should I not tell you? Had I not been so selfish—so utterly wrapped up in my own thoughts and sorrow, I must have seen, I might have prevented, much that your father and mother suffered; might have given happiness to those nearest and dearest to me. I will tell you, Lucy. I never thought to tell the tale again; I have never told all. Your father knew some part, but I never spoke to him save once, and once when we both heard the end together.

"Where shall I begin? Years ago, when I was two-and-twenty. My mother died when I was very young; I never thought my father was very fond of me. Nigel inherited my mother's beauty, which I did not; but he was rich, proud of his old family, and he wished me to make what would be called a good match. I did not much think about it, I had all I wanted at home; but I did care for one at last; I met him often, he was staying with some friends; he stayed here several times. His regiment was quartered at Carlisle, and the officers were asked everywhere. My father seemed to like him, too, and often told him he should be glad to see him at Littlecourt whenever he liked a day's shooting, and that was a great deal for him to say. I thought he liked me; I felt sure of it sometimes when he would bring me a flower, and bend down over me in a peculiar way as he gave it, and once, too, he said he wished we were not so rich. I felt so happy then, I only laughed.

"He sang, O Lucy, such a voice! I never heard one like his. I can hear it now. He sang without music at first, but after I had played for him once he used to ask me to accompany him, and ask me to sing, which I could not do; but he would say he thought I *must*, for I played his songs as no one else did, as if I felt them; I must have been dull indeed not to feel that voice, 'Oft in the Stilly Night,' 'The Land o' the Leal,' and some of the old Scotch and Irish ballads that thrilled through every one."

"Tell me what he was like, aunty," Lucy said, stroking Miss Beresford's thin hand.

"Taller than your father, Lucy; I could see his head above every one in the room; light hair, and he had a way of passing his fingers through it, and shaking a rebellious lock back that always fell over his forehead. His eyes were dark, I scarcely know what color, they changed and looked darker as he spoke. But he was so good and gentle, and I was so thoughtless then for any thing beyond this world. I remember his staying here over a Sunday, 20th April, 1832, and at the afternoon service there was a baptism, as there often was. I looked upon it as an interruption to the regular Prayers, and sat still, looking at the painted glass, or beautiful carving of our old church: but he stood or knelt according to the service. I never hear a baptism without seeing him standing so firm with his arms crossed, and hear his 'Amen' to those beautiful words, 'And to continue Christ's faithful soldier and servant unto his life's end.'

"As we walked home he asked me if I knew 'The Christian Year:' it was new then, but I had it, and though not understanding or valuing it as I do now, I admired many of the poems. It was a lovely evening, and we came across the fields and through the larch wood, then in all the beauty of its fresh bright green leaves, studded with small crimson cones, and great bunches of yellow primroses peeping out everywhere, the birds singing, every thing looking bright, bursting into leaf, making one feel gay and hopeful too. On reaching the brow of the hill we stopped to look at the sunset, so glorious it was, and a young girl of our party exclaimed,

"'Let us each take one of those feathery clouds for our own and see what happens to it. I will have that white feathery bit, and you, Mr. Armstrong, take that bit of bright gold.' So we each chose our little cloud, and watched their future destiny.

"*His* bright golden one moved swiftly straight on, on, on, and melted away in the great golden sunset in the west.

"'Your journey is soon over, Armstrong,' cried one, 'now look at Miss Beresford's, where in the world is she going?'

"It was said lightly, but I saw a look in his face—he did not take it lightly. My cloud afforded amusement for some time with its wanderings, but at last it also joined the glorious crimson sunset.

"We had all talked and laughed carelessly about it, but somehow I felt grave, and I said to Percy as we again moved on our way down the hill,—

> "'When the shore is won at last,
> Who will count the billows past.'

"'That is just what I was thinking,' he said eagerly. 'I could not help feeling there was something under those clouds deeper than we first thought.'

"I tell you all this, Lucy, because he did not forget it, and I often thought his bright cloud so soon being gathered into that glorious sunset was a warning—a shadow of his own early end; of his young pure spirit, which was soon, so very soon, to wend its way to the 'land that is very far off;' and mine, after all its wanderings, mine reached the same bright haven. So I hope, Lucy, I hope on.

"Those were very happy days; they went on for some weeks more, constantly meeting. Then my father went from home for a fortnight, taking me with him. We were to return for a ball at Warnham, and the house was to be full. I knew he would be there; he was to be at the Grange, and I thought he would come over to see us. I had not seen him for more than three weeks, and yet he did not come; I felt vexed, then hurt, then angry; I never mentally controlled my temper; I could conceal my annoyance from others, because I was naturally reserved; I had no mother or sister to be unreserved with, and my brother Nigel was much older than I was. How I thought of this ball—how I thought of my dress for it! I thought I looked my best that evening; I remember feeling satisfied with my own face and dark hair as I finished dressing; it was only with the hope of pleasing him—I cared for no one else.

"We drove to Warnham. The last ball I had been at he was on the stairs,—as I thought waiting for us, for he had taken me into the ball-room, and asked me to dance at once; but he was not there now. However, I saw his head as soon as we entered, and thought he would come to meet me; I saw him look at me, but he did not come. We were rather late; and as we edged our way to the far end of the room, I was one of the last, and there were several people between us. I felt him watching me, so I bowed; he did not come round to me at once, he only bowed again, and looked so grave—so pale; I could not go to him, I was too far off to speak. There were several gentlemen with us, and I knew I should be obliged to dance with them; how I hoped he would come and ask me, but he stood there, leaning against the corner of the bench as if he had forgotten where he was.

"'What has happened to Mr. Armstrong?' said Mrs. Biddulph, and she looked at me and smiled.

"'Who?' said Sir Henry Vivian.

"'That handsome young fellow, Percy Armstrong, of the —th. I call him my Hotspur.'

"'The Knight of the Sorrowful Countenance, *I* should call him,' said Sir Harry, putting up his glass. 'But do you really consider him good-looking, Mrs. Biddulph?'

"'Yes, remarkably so, and you would too, only you are so horridly conceited.'

"'Ah!' said Sir Harry, 'you always flatter me. Do you admire me, Miss Beresford?'

"How I hated him for asking me!

"'It is a well-known fact,' said Mr. Lane, 'that Armstrong and I are the handsomest men in the room. You are a stranger here, Sir Harry, so may be excused for not finding it out.'

"I could not help laughing, and felt grateful to kind, ugly little Mr. Lane for coming to my rescue, and saying what I dared not.

"'Well,' said Mrs. Biddulph, 'I shall go and ask him, and tell him we are all speculating on what can make him so unlike himself.'

"She moved towards Percy, she spoke to him in a rallying way, he looked at me; surely, she had not used my name! but I felt my color rise, for his face flushed, then he came straight towards me.

"'Were *you* laughing at me, too?' he said, bending down to catch my answer.

"'I! oh, no,' I said, and looked up at him, though my eyes were full; I held out my hand, he took it, and in the same low, sad voice said,—

"'I did not believe it; I knew you could not do that.' He pressed my hand in both his. 'God bless you,' he said, and turned quickly from me. I saw my father meet him, shake him heartily by the hand, and then Percy passed on through the room to the door. I watched him so eagerly I found Sir Harry Vivian asking me for the second time to dance. As Percy reached the ball-room door he turned, only to see me taking my place in the dance—only to think he was nothing to me, when my whole heart was his, and I felt as though I were dreaming a miserable dream.

"I tortured myself fruitlessly for years, thinking I might have said or done something different that dreadful evening. If he had only said one word—if he had only called me Helen, I could have spoken—could have followed him—could have told him that I was ready to follow him to the world's end.

"'Myself must tell him in that purer life,
But *then* it was too daring.'

I watched the door in vain, he did not return. I never saw him again, Lucy.

"I suppose I looked deadly pale, for some one asked me if I were ill; then I remembered I must not betray myself; I must dance and talk and smile through that horrible ball. Then came the drive home; no relief; not alone till I was undressed, my maid gone, and then I could think over all, and feel I was miserable, loving him utterly as I did. Why had he left me in that way? Was it possible after all he did not care for me? How humbled, crushed, broken I felt, as that idea forced itself upon me!

"How wretched I looked the next morning! but I had a part to act, and I acted it well, I believe. After breakfast my father called me to the library, and told me I had been much admired at the ball; had I money enough for all I wanted? if not, he would double my allowance; he liked me to be well dressed, etc., etc. At the end he said,

"'By the by, my dear, Armstrong's regiment is ordered to India, and he thanked me last night for all our attention and kindness to him; he was to catch the night mail, and sail from Liverpool next week, I think he said: he is a fine young fellow, a credit to any corps.'

"What could I say? I felt something rise in my throat—I could not speak. Then he had not really cared for me, and I had allowed myself to think of nothing—no one but him. I thought I never could be more miserable than I then was.

"A few months passed; it was the end of October. I had been so happy in October a twelvemonth ago. One morning at breakfast my father, reading the newspaper, exclaimed, 'Good heavens! the Berkshire lost with the —th on board! Let me see,' and then he read aloud,—

"'It is with feelings of deep regret we announce the total loss by fire of the ship Berkshire, on the 10th August, latitude 5 North, longitude 20 West, bound for Calcutta with the —th on board. Only five officers and one hundred and twenty men saved. The troops behaved nobly, obeying orders to the last. The flames gaining upon them in spite of every exertion, the boats were lowered, and the women and children all put in. Lots were then cast for the men in perfect silence; the captain and officers of the vessel declining to lessen the small number who could possibly escape. Shortly after the boats got off, the flames reached the gunpowder, and in a few moments scarcely a vestige remained of the ill-fated vessel. Names of the officers saved—Major Playfair, Captain Howard, Lieut. Edwards, Lieut. Atkinson [I hope that may be a mistake for our friend Armstrong], and Ensign Willis. ['Pon my word there must be some great carelessness about these transport vessels!] The boats were picked up by the Conqueror, homeward bound, on the 16th August, after great sufferings from heat and thirst, under which most of the children and many of the women sank.'

"I heard all; my tongue dry, my eyes burning, I tried to say something, but my voice did not come; my lips moved, but there was no sound. I reached my own room—my trembling limbs carried me so far—and I threw myself on the couch: I could not faint, I could not forget, I knew he was gone; I felt persuaded he was not one of the five saved; I never had any hope of that, and I must not appear to care: I had no right even to wear a black gown for him; and oh! the misery of bright colours when your whole heart is in such mourning!

"I don't remember how the time passed from that day until my father's death. Early in January, he was seized with paralysis one evening, and never regained consciousness. Nigel arrived too late to see him alive.

"Nigel left the army and came to live here; he had been left guardian to your mother, and her only remaining aunt dying about that time, she came to live with us. She was ten years old then; a dull home she found, poor child, as far as I was concerned; I was so selfishly bound up in my own sorrows, I did not do half I ought to have done for others. I often wonder how dear Nigel bore with me as he did. My father's affairs were complicated in some way, there was a difficulty about my fortune; it was never clearly ascertained what had become of it. Nigel took no end of trouble, and again went to London for me about four years after my father's death. When there he wrote to me to look for some papers which were missing. 'Do look in my father's bureau and send me all the papers you can find relating to Spanish Bonds.' I took the key and went to the library, with the melancholy feeling such a task gives one. I had never opened that bureau before. I searched one drawer after another; I could find nothing. At last I found an inner drawer; it looked as though the contents had never been touched—there was a bundle of papers tied up, headed 'Spanish Bonds.' I took it and untied the red tapes to see if Nigel would want them all; as I unfolded one I saw it was a letter, I saw the signature, 'Percy Armstrong,' there was a note enclosed, unopened, addressed to me. I read the letter to my father first; it was written just one week before that ball; he said my father must have seen how much he cared for me, but he was afraid would think him very presumptuous in asking for his consent to try and win me; he had little now, but he was to succeed to a small property on the death of an uncle, and he only asked to be allowed to hope. His regiment was under orders for foreign service, and he could not bear to go leaving me in ignorance of his feelings.

"On the other side of his letter was the rough copy of the answer he must have received.

"'MY DEAR ARMSTRONG, — I really am very sorry so disagreeable a duty devolves on me. We feel grateful for the feeling you express, which we hope however may not be very lasting, as my daughter could never think of a match which, much as we like you personally, would be, you are aware, not what I have every right to expect for her.'

"I will not tell you all he said. I have forgiven, I trust quite, quite forgiven; he was my father, and acted as he thought for the best; indeed, the joy of finding I might acknowledge I had loved him took away from me so much bitterness, that it was not until some time after, I felt I had something to forgive my dead father.

"The missing papers were never found; when I told Nigel, I told him, too, what I believe; he must have received them at the same time with Percy's letter, and by mistake must have burnt *them*, filing his letter with the other papers. What was all the money in the world to me, compared with what I had found?

"I would not keep that answer, I tore the sheet in half; there were no envelopes then, it was a sheet of letter paper. I burnt the half-sheet, watched the black, shrivelled page rise slowly up the chimney, and then returned to read *his* over again and again, with my own little treasured note clasped in my two hands. I forgot all that had passed —all those weary years; I felt as if he had only just written to me, that I might answer him, tell him he might come, speak to me, love me, sing with me!

"I saw him ride up to the door, and pat Selim ere they led him away—I heard his step in the hall, saw him pass his fingers through his hair as he came to the drawing-room—saw his smile, as I rose to meet him, both my hands in his—then it all came back upon me, sweeping away my happy thoughts into the deep, deep sea that rolled over him. I should never hear his step again, never see his smile, never touch his hand, never see those great dark eyes, that bright wavy hair, —never hear that voice again, never, never, —save in my dreams,—all, all gone!

"At last I opened my own little note. He entreated me to answer, but if he did not hear he should still go to the ball, just to see me once more. If I did not, could not care for him, would I only let him say a few last words, would I say one kind word to bid, 'God speed' him on his way. Lucy, I cannot tell you; read it for yourself," and Miss Beresford gave Percy Armstrong's first and last love-letter into the young girl's hand. Lucy's tears were quite ready as she read,—

"I will not annoy you, dearest; if you give me not a smile or a blush I shall know that the last few months have been a dream of joy not to be mine—a dream that I am not indifferent to you, but indeed, no one can ever love you more than I—and always must, my Helen. Mine or not? God bless you always.

"PERCY ARMSTRONG."

"And he thought I had received this when I bowed to him in that ball-room!"

"O aunty, you don't know how sorry I am," said Lucy.

Miss Beresford slowly replaced the letter, and stroking the girl's bright hair said, "Yes, my darling. I was too hard and cold; I needed such a blow to soften me; nothing is *too* much, no cross greater than we can bear;—and now I can think calmly, and see many mercies were granted me, even when I was most repining. One of the greatest—that in the first sharp pangs of visitation and pique I did not accept the first offer made me and marry. I shrink now when I think what I should have felt when I found his letter, had I been the wedded wife of another! Lucy, I was going to say, Never marry any one you cannot love; but, O my child, never on your knees before God vow to love, honor, and obey one man, when your whole heart is given—is worshipping another.

"And I had one unspeakable comfort. Some years after, I was going to London with Nigel; at Coventry a gentleman got into the same carriage; I saw 'Major Howard —th Regt,' on his carpet-bag. I should hear, I was determined to know the last. I said quite calmly to Nigel, 'I *must* ask him.' Poor Nigel, I little knew then how wretched he was himself; it was just before he went to India; but he instantly addressed the stranger, saying he wished much to hear of Percy Armstrong: could he tell him, did he see any thing of him at the last?

"'Percy Armstrong,' he interrupted, 'the best and bravest! no one knew what he was till that awful day. We had been becalmed for some days, the heat beyond expression. One morning, that awful 10th of August, something was evidently wrong; and soon the words were whispered from one to the other, "The ship is on fire." The captain came pale as death to our colonel, and said, "We have every hope of getting it under, but bring the women and children on deck, and keep all as quiet as possible." A short time after, he came again, and said, "The fire is raging fiercer than ever; it has now broken out among the stores. The boats are ready for lowering." There was no hope; our men behaved splendidly; and Percy, he was as calm as on parade. I saw him rush down for a child that its shrieking mother had been unable to save. I saw him hand it down to her in the boat, and heard her bless him for it. Then lots were drawn which of us should go in the boats. *He* was one of them; he might have been saved, if he had not been his own noble self. He saw another's agony at being destined to remain in the burning vessel. "O God," exclaimed the poor fellow, "my wife and children, what will become of them!" Percy Armstrong looked up to the blue sky above us for a moment, then in a calm, clear voice, "Take my place," he said, "I have no one to love me; I shall never be missed."

"'In the selfish clinging to life that man wrung his hand with a "God bless you," and followed into the boat.

"'I do not know how it was, but I seemed to see and hear every thing. I don't think I had any idea of surviving. I scarcely remember how I got into the boat. I know I felt as if I would gladly have been one of those two hundred and eighty fine fellows who met death in the glorious way they did. They all came to help, handing us down water, and such things as we might want; and William Rowlands, a fine young fellow in my company, son of my father's gamekeeper, called out to me, "Captain Howard, sir, you'll get my poor old mother the pay that's due to me; will you, sir? and tell her, sir, now when it's come to this, I'm right glad I went to church with her that last Sunday, and if I was to be on dry land again, I'd never go idling my Sundays, and doing the things I did do again—never, never; and tell her I remember the text that last Sunday: it was about the angels being glad when such as me repented, sir. I can't say the words exact, but you'll tell her when you get back safe, as I hope to God you will, sir; and if you please, sir, tell her to give Jane Wilkins my love." "I will, I will, my poor fellow," I answered, "if I live; so help me God, I will."

"'Then James Gray leant over; "My wife, sir, will be in trouble: will you look to her, sir, when you get home again? and tell her Jim is getting old enough, and I'd like him to join the old Regiment; no one need be ashamed of it I hope, sir. You'll tell her we did our duty, and I hope she'll want for nothing. I've got her Bible here, sir, going with me where we're going; God bless you, sir."

"'Then Percy Armstrong spoke to me for the last time. "Howard, my dear fellow, here's my Prayer-Book for you; God bless you, we're all steady." He stood up quite firm; passed his hand through his hair, as he always did, do you remember?—[oh, did I not remember *so* well!]—pointing to the blue heaven, "no sea *there*," he said.

"'I thought his face was like the face of an angel; then he turned away encouraging the men.

"'We had to row hard to get the boats away from the burning ship; but the sea was so calm, not a breath of wind, and such horror and awe among us all, not a word was uttered, and we could hear the voices of those left behind. I knew Percy's voice as he began the litany. I heard him say, "In the hour of death, and in the day of judgment;" then one deep full cry for mercy echoed over our heads, "Good Lord, deliver us;" then came the fearful explosion, and all was over.'

"He stopped a moment; then he added, 'Poor fellow! those awful days of suffering and thirst and death. I read his Prayer-Book as I never read before. I would give it to some of his friends, if I could find one who loved him.'

"I started forward then, 'Give it to me, oh, give it to me, for I *did* love him, and he loved me.'

"Look, Lucy," and she opened the fly-leaf. Under his name was written—

"When the shore is won at last,
Who will count the billows past."

"*Littlecourt, Sunday, April 20th,* 1832."

"If you are with me at the last, let it go with me to my grave. His note is in it; it is so bound up in my mind with all that is good and holy, I like to keep it there. I feel now that we shall meet, please God, in heaven, where all misunderstandings will have passed away,—

"'Where all will be ended, the hope, and the fear, and the sorrow,
All the aching of heart, the restless unsatisfied longing,
All the dull, deep pain, and constant anguish of patience,'

where love will be made perfect—'perfect through suffering.' If less sorrow would have sufficed for me, Lucy, less would have been sent.

"'Love weighs the cross of each in heaven,'

and sent me mine. Remember, Lucy darling, do'nt let his book be taken from me; put it with me into my coffin."

"I will, aunty," was all she said, with her arms round her neck as she kissed her.

And she did.

M. E. G.

From Once a Week.

STEER N.W.

THE FIRST OFFICER'S STORY.

About two years ago, I left the service. I was tired of it; and as I wanted some more exciting employment, I joined a whaler. We were unlucky—somehow, I bring no luck anywhere—and we were nearly empty. We were cruising up here to the north, and thinking of making for home, as the weather had changed: and the ice forms precious quick in those latitudes when it once begins. The captain naturally wanted to hang on to the last for the chance of another haul.

One bright afternoon, just after eight bells, I made up the log, and took it to the captain's cabin. I knocked at the door, and as nobody answered I walked in. I thought it odd the captain hadn't answered me, for there he was, sitting at his desk, with his back to me, writing. Seeing he was employed, I told him I had brought the log, laid it down on the table behind him, and as he made no answer, I walked out. I went on deck, and the first person I met was the captain. I was puzzled—I could not make out how he had got there before me.

"How did you get up here?" I said; "I just left you writing in your cabin."

"I have not been in my cabin for the last half-hour," the captain answered; but I thought he was chaffing, and I didn't like it.

"There was some one writing at your desk just now," I said; "if it wasn't you, you had better go and see who it is. The log is made up. I have left it in your cabin, sir," and with that I walked sulkily away. I had no idea of being chaffed by the captain, to whom I had taken a dislike.

"Mr. Brown," said the captain, who saw I was nettled, "you must have been mistaken, my desk is locked. But come—we'll go down and see about it."

I followed the captain into the cabin. The log was on the table, the desk was closed, and the cabin was empty. The captain tried the desk—it was locked.

"You see, Mr. Brown," he said, laughing, "you must have been mistaken, the desk is locked."

I was positive. "Somebody may have picked the lock," I said.

"But they couldn't have closed it again," the captain suggested; "but to satisfy you, I will open it and see if the contents are safe, though there is not much here to tempt a thief."

He opened the desk, and there—stretched right across it—was a sheet of paper, with the words, "Steer N.W." written in an odd, cramped hand.

The captain looked at the paper, and then handed it to me.

"You are right, Mr. Brown; somebody has been here. This is some hoax."

We sat there some time talking, and trying to guess what could be the object of such a joke,—if joke it was meant to be. I tried to identify the back of the man I had seen at the desk with that of any of the crew. I could not do it. It is true I had at first taken the man for the captain, but now points of difference suggested themselves. I had not looked very attentively at the figure, but still I was under the impression that the coat it had on was brown, and the hair, which appeared under the cap, seemed, as I remembered it, to have been longer and whiter than the captain's. There was only one man on board who resembled in the least the figure I had seen. I suggested to the captain that it might have been old Shiel, the boatswain. He did not like to suspect the old man, who was a great favorite; besides, what motive could he, or indeed any one else, have had in trying to change the course of the vessel.

Not to appear to suspect any one in particular, the captain determined to have up all the crew. We had them up, one by one. We examined them, and made all those who could write, write "Steer N. W.," but we gained no clue. One thing was very clear—it could not have been old Shiel, who was proved to have been forward at the time I was in the captain's cabin. The mystery remained unsolved.

That evening I sat drinking my grog with the captain in his cabin. We were neither of us inclined to be talkative. I tried to think of home, and the pleasure it would be to see old England again, but still, my thoughts always wandered back to that mysterious writing. I tried to read, but I caught myself furtively peeping at the desk, expecting to see the figure sitting there.

The captain had not spoken for some time, and was sitting with his face buried in his hands. At last, he suddenly looked up, and said,—

"Suppose we alter her course to Northwest, Mr. Brown?"

I don't know what it was; I cannot hope to make you understand the feeling in my mind that followed those words; it was a sense of relief from a horrible nightmare. I was ashamed of the childish pleasure I felt, but I could not help answering eagerly, "Certainly; shall I give the order?"

I waited no longer, but hurried on deck and altered the course of the vessel.

It was a clear frosty night, and as I looked at the compass before going below, I felt strangely pleased, and caught myself chuckling and rubbing my hands; at what, I cannot say,—I didn't know then, but a great weight had been taken off my mind.

I went down to the cabin, and found the captain pacing up and down the small space. He stopped as I came in, and looking up, said, abruptly,—

"It can do no harm, Mr. Brown."

"If this breeze continues," I answered, "we can hold on for thirty hours or so, but then, I should think—"

"But then—we shall find ice. How's the wind?"

"Steady, North by East."

We sat down and finished our grog. I had the morning watch to keep next day. I was too restless to sleep after it, so I kept on deck the whole of the day. Even that did not satisfy me. I was continually running up into the tops with my glass, but every time I came down disappointed. The captain was as unquiet as myself. Something we expected to happen, but of what it was to be we could form no idea. The second officer, I believe, thought us both crazy; indeed, I often wondered, myself, at the state I was in. Evening came, and nothing had turned up. The night was bright, and the captain determined to carry on under easy sail till morning.

Morning came; and with the first gray light I was on deck. It was bitterly cold. Those only who have seen them can form an idea of the delicate tints of the morning sky in those Northern Seas. But I was in no humor to appreciate the beauties of nature. There was a mist low down on the horizon: I waited impatiently for it to lift. It lifted soon, and I could not be mistaken,—beyond it I could see the shimmer of ice. I sent down to tell the captain, who came on deck directly.

"It is no use, Mr. Brown," he said; "you must put her about."

"Wait one moment," I said; "wait one moment, the mist is lifting more, it will be quite clear directly."

The mist was indeed lifting rapidly. Far to the north and west we could see the ice stretching away in one unbroken field. I was trying to see whether there appeared any break in the ice towards the west, when the captain, seizing my arm with one hand, and pointing straight ahead with the other, exclaimed,—

"Good Heaven! there is a ship there."

The mist had risen like a curtain, and there, sure enough, about three miles ahead, was a ship seemingly firmly packed in the ice. We stood looking at it in silence. There was some meaning after all in that mysterious warning, was the first thought that suggested itself to me.

"'She's nipped bad, sir," said old Shiel, who, with the rest of the crew, was anxiously watching our new discovery. I was trying to make her out with the glass, when the flash of a gun, quickly followed by the report, proved that she had seen us. Up went the flag, Union downwards. We needed no signal to know her distress. The captain ordered the second officer off into the boat. I watched him as he made his way over the ice with a few of the men towards the ship. They soon returned with eight of the ship's crew. It was a dismal account they gave of their situation. They might have sawed their way out of the ice, but the ship was so injured that she could not have floated an hour. The largest of their boats had been stove in, the others were hardly seaworthy. They were preparing, however, to take to them as a last resource when our welcome arrival put an end to their fears. Another detachment was soon brought off, and the captain with the remainder of his crew was to follow immediately.

I went down to my cabin, and tried to think over the singular fate which had made us the preservers of this ship's crew. I could not divest myself of the idea that some supernatural agency was connected with that paper in the desk, and I trembled at the thought of what might have been the consequences if we had neglected the warning. The boat coming alongside interrupted my reverie. In a few seconds I was on deck.

I found the captain talking to a fine old sailor-like looking man, whom he introduced to me as Captain Squires. Captain Squires shook hands with me, and we remained talking some time. I could not keep my eyes off his face; I had a conviction that I had seen him somewhere, where I could not tell. Every now and then I seemed to catch at some clue, which vanished as soon as touched. At last he turned round to speak to some of his men. I could not be mistaken—there was the long white hair, the brown coat. He was the man I had seen writing in the captain's cabin!

That evening the captain and I told the story of the paper to Captain Squires, who gravely and in silence listened to our conjectures. He was too thankful for his escape out of such imminent peril to question the means by which it had been brought about. At the captain's request he wrote "Steer·N.W." We compared it with the original writing. There could be no doubt of it. It was in the same odd, cramped hand. Can any one solve the mystery?

H. A. H.

From Chambers's Journal.

SCIENCE AND ARTS FOR MARCH.

Of noticeable facts in photography, one is that the exhibition of the Photographic Society is remarkably good, and that a fac-simile copy of *Domesday Book* is about to be taken under the direction of Colonel Sir H. James in the Photographic Office of the Ordnance Department at Southampton. We mentioned some time ago the process by which these copies could be taken and multiplied, and would take leave to suggest that it should be applied to any of our national archives that show signs of decay. We have seen copies of ancient documents which are under the care of the Master of the Rolls, differing in no respect from the originals, except that they are sound and fresh; and we may believe that Englishmen of the future who will look back on our times through as long a vista as we look back on the Conquest, will thank us for handing down to them a perfect image of William the Norman's wonderful book.

In a small work published at Paris, M. Testelin shows, while discussing the theory of the formation of the photographic image, that it is a physical, *not* a chemical effect, dependent on well-known physical laws which are recognizable in other phenomena. He considers "electric polarity" to be the exciting cause, and thus puts forth the question to undergo discussion by those photographers who have most studied the effects produced on their interesting operations by cosmical or meteorological causes.

A subject which seems likely to have an important bearing in investigations of atmospheric phenomena, has been treated of by Dr. Tyndall in lectures before the Royal Institution and Royal Society. Starting with some of the experiments made by the late Professor Melloni of Naples, he has examined the effects of heat-radiation, and obtained remarkable results demonstrative of the power possessed by certain transparent and impalpable media of absorbing or intercepting rays of heat. For instance, if olefiant gas be placed between the source of heat and the galvanometer by which the amount of heat is measured, an immediate check is observable, and scarcely a trace of heat passes. This result is the more surprising, because of the extreme transparency of the gas; and at first sight it appears hardly credible that the passage of heat should be stopped by something which is invisible. Similar results are obtained with sulphuric ether, and other kinds of gas, and Dr. Tyndall has tabulated them as a basis for further experiment. It should be explained that the heat-rays here in question are derived from an obscure, not an illuminated source—from, in fact, a small cistern of water kept at a boiling temperature. It is thought that meteorologists and astronomers will be able to turn these results to account when studying the phenomena of our own atmosphere, or that of remote planets.

The *Proceedings* of the American Geographical Society contain interesting particulars concerning the arctic expeditions which sailed last year from New London and Boston: Dr. Hayes, whose object was to search for the open Polar Sea which has long been supposed to exist in the highest circumpolar latitudes, and which was seen by the Russian explorer, Admiral Von Wrangell, in one of his adventurous journeys, had written from Upernavik that his prospects were encouraging, that he hoped to winter at Cape Fraser, Grinnell Land, latitude 79° 42′, and then carry forward his equipments and provisions as far towards the pole as possible, and there leave them, in readiness for travelling-parties in the spring of the present year, who are to push northwards, and, if possible, discover the mysterious sea. Possibly, they might have a chance of getting to the pole.

The other expedition is still more striking. Mr. C. F. Hall, a printer of Cincinnati, a man of dauntless spirit, who has taken especial interest in recent arctic voyages, impressed by the notion that Sir Leopold M'Clintock has not exhausted the search for relics of Sir John Franklin's unhappy party, sailed last June in a whaleship for Davis' Strait, where he intended to pass the winter at Cumberland Inlet, in acclimatizing himself, and acquiring, as far as possible, the habits and language of the Esquimaux. This accomplished, he purposed starting in the spring with a boat, convertible at pleasure into a sledge, accompanied by a few picked natives and a good pack of dogs, for King William Land; and having made certain explorations on the way, he will then devote himself to a careful and minute examination of the route taken by the crews of the *Erebus* and *Terror*, including the mainland about the mouth of Great Fish River. By this means, employing two or three years if desirable, and sojourning, from time to time, among the natives, Mr. Hall hopes to hear of or discover every trace and relic which may yet remain of the Franklin expedition; and we heartily wish him success. If, as we hope, he be alive and well, he is now probably thinking of his start, and making preparations. Excepting natives, he anticipated being quite alone, and he will need courage and endurance to carry him through his self-imposed task in so desolate a region, and to sustain him until he shall return to the shore of Davis' Strait, to watch for some whaler that will give him a voyage home. Should Mr. Parker Snow persist in his intention of exploring the same country, he may now calculate on meeting with a companion.

The culture of the vine is becoming more and more an object of attention in North America: the Academy of Science at St. Louis, Missouri, has published an able paper thereupon, in which it is shown that there are, in the southern parts of that state, along the banks of the Osage, the Niangua, and in lands bordering on the Missouri River, 5,000,000 acres of soil excellent for vineyards. It is a limestone region, and bears wild-grapes of good quality, and if we may judge from a lithographic drawing, has a striking resemblance to the scenery of the Rhine. The author of the paper shows that this extent of acres equals that of the grape-bearing districts of France, and that if planted with vines, it would employ 2,000,000 people, and yield 1,000,000,000 gallons of wine annually, worth 500,000,000 dollars. Besides the money value, there might be a promotion of sobriety, by the substitution of pure grape-juice for the villainous compounds so largely sold in the States as wine and brandy.

Some of our readers will be interested in learning that agricultural improvement is not neglected in the United or (Dis-united) States, as appears from an official Report which is published in the form of a stout octavo; the results are given of the operations carried on in the government experimental and propagating garden at Washington. fertilizers are treated of, breeds of sheep, plants used for food by man, the culture of vegetable fibre, and, for the benefit of the agricultural population, there is a well-written chapter on the best way of building farmhouses, and how to inhabit them without the slovenliness that too often appears in backwoods' dwellings. Acclimatization of animals and breeding of fish are largely noticed; and we commend to the attention of our newly formed Acclimatization Society, a passage concerning the golden-breasted agami of South America. "It is a bird," says St Hilaire, "that has the instinct and the fidelity of the dog; it will lead a flock of poultry, or even a flock of sheep, by which it will make itself obeyed, although it is not larger than a chicken. It is not less useful in the poultry-yard than in the field; it maintains order there, protects the weak against the strong, stands by young chickens and ducks, and divides among them their food, from which it keeps away others, and which, itself will not even touch. No animal, perhaps, is more easily taught, or naturally more attached to man." The society might, moreover, inquire for that Siamese bean, named ào-fao, which contains so much caseine that it can be made into cheese.

Layman officiating as Deacon at Mass.—In the life of Urban V., in the *Biographie Universelle*, it is stated that when the Emperor Charles IV. came to Rome in 1368, at the request of that pope, he crowned the empress on All Saints' Day at mass. The writer proceeds: "L'empereur y remplissait la fonction de diacre, mais il ne lut point l'évangile, ce qu'il ne pouvait faire que le jour de Noël." Is there any authority for this statement?—*Notes and Queries.*

From the Spectator.

THE POETICAL WORKS OF GERALD MASSEY.*

A NEW edition of the Poetical Works of Gerald Massey, the son of the canal boatman in Herts, and himself successively silk-mill worker, errand-boy, and journalist, will be welcomed by the less fastidious readers of poetry. Those who sympathize with fine feelings and delicate susceptibilities, who delight in profuse imagery and florid diction, will assuredly find much in this volume which they will regard, and which in some sense they will rightly regard, as poetry. But those who demand imaginative conception, who require, first, that the poet have something to sing, and then that he sing it with purity, simplicity, and *proportion*, will not find here the poetry which they seek. Mr. Massey is not an original writer. He is scarcely a copyist indeed, but he reproduces, perhaps unconsciously, the impressions which the poetry he admires have left on his sensitive nature. In the very first page of his book we read,—

"When Danaë-earth bares all her charms,
And gives the God her perfect flower—"

surely an echo of a line in *The Princess*, "Now lies the Earth all Danaë to the stars." In fact, the whole of the "Ballad of Babe Christabel," from which these verses are taken, perpetually suggests its great precursor, the *In Memoriam* of Tennyson, which we cannot but regard as, in this instance, the immediate source of inspiration to Mr. Massey's muse. We are far, however, from saying that this very poem is not instinct with beautiful thoughts and fancies clothed in melodious language. For instance,—

"When beauty walks in bravest dress,
And, fed with April's mellow showers,
The earth laughs out with sweet May-flowers,
That flush for very happiness;

"And Puck his web of wonder weaves
O' nights, and nooks of greening gloom
Are rich with violets that bloom
In the cool dark of dewy leaves."

In this last verse the picturesque expression of "greening gloom" would be more admired if it did not remind us of the "greening gleam" of one of Mr. Tennyson's fine psalms. And a little below, Mr. Gerald's "Song like a spirit sits i' the trees" is too like the greater poet's "The lark became a sightless song" for us to feel satisfied that it is not a resetting of the same thought.

Perhaps Mr. Massey's best poem is that which idealizes a sad experience, "The Mother's Idol Broken." It is graceful and touching; and once at least nobly pathetic.

"This is a curl of our poor 'Splendid's' hair!
A sunny burst of rare and ripe young gold,"

is a true and natural introduction to the "babe-wanderings and little tender ways," to "the wee wax face that gradually withdrew and darkened into the great cloud of death," to the three words of human speech

"One for her mother, one for me, and one
She crowed with for the fields and open heaven.
That last she sighed with a sweet farewell pathos
A minute ere she left the house of life,
To come for kisses never any more.
. . . .
And there our darling lay in coffined calm:
Beyond the breakers and the moaning now!
And o'er her flowed the white eternal peace:
The breathing miracle into silence passed:
Never to stretch wee hands, with her dear smile
As soft as light-fall on unfolding flowers:
Never to wake us crying in the night:
Our little hindering thing forever gone,
In tearful quiet now we might toil on.
All dim the living lustres motion makes!
No life-dew in the sweet cups of her eyes,
Naught there of our poor 'Splendid' but her brow."

We doubt if Mr. Massey has written any thing better than *that*. His "Craigbrook Castle" is often musical, and is prodigally fanciful. Fancy indeed is his most prominent attribute. The third section of the poem last mentioned contains a succession of mental coruscations that dazzle, rather than delight, "the wondering eyes of men."

Of Mr. Massey's political poems we say nothing. He does not value them highly himself, retaining them only "as memorials of the past, as one might keep some worn-out garment because he had passed through the furnace in it." One or two of his rhyming compositions are slightly humorous, that for example about the lion who "shook his incredulous head, and wagged his dubious tail." There is one, too, on England and an illustrious living personage, which, without going the whole way with the sarcastic poet, we can read with some degree of satisfaction. It begins,—

* *The Poetical Works of Gerald Massey*. A new edition with illustrations. Published by Routledge, Warne, and Routledge.

"There was a poor old woman once, a daughter of our nation,
Before the Devil's portrait stood in ignorant adoration.
'You 're bowing down to Satan, ma'am,' said some spectator civil,
'Ah sir, it 's best to be polite, for we may go to the Devil,
Bow, bow, bow,
We may go the Devil, so it s just as well to bow.' "

The edition of Mr. Gerald Massey's poems from which we are now quoting contains a biographic sketch, which is not without interest, and the poet's own preface to the *third* issue of "Babe Christabel." This poem, as now published, thus appears the fourth time—a proof of the auth popularity. If we admire his producti less than others, it is that our standard higher than that of others. Let Mr. Mas write more slowly, take more pains with versification, be less with Queen Mab, and dwell more among the great central facts of human life, with its perennial joys and griefs, and we shall not be backward to recognize his superiority. But let us have no more "stars and flowers," no more "Tita pulses" and "purple rondures." The highest poetry can *afford* to dress plainly.

"Spun" equivalent to "Pluckt."—When a man has failed in his examination at Woolwich, he is said to be "spun," as in the Universities he is said to be "pluckt." What is the origin of the former term? The latter is well known. A. B. M.

[*Spunt* in provincial English is *spurned*, and hence may be viewed as equivalent to *rejected*. Can it be in this sense that a person rejected at a competitive examination is said to be *spun?*

"Spunt, Spurned. *Suffolk.*"—*Halliwell.*

"Spunt, *part. p.* Spurned. *Suff.*"—*Wright.*

Spun for *plucked* is a term not restricted to any *one* of our great schools of learning, but is now very generally employed in the elegant vernacular of Young England.

We may as well add that "getting *toko*," a phrase used at schools when a young gentleman receives corporal correction, is apparently a sportive allusion to the Italian "tocco," a *stick*, *wand*, or *twig* (properly, the stick used at schools in pointing to the letters of the alphabet, from It. *toccare*). Cf. in Fr. and Romance, "toc," a blow. "Tan tost qu'es feritz d'un toc:"—"Aussitôt qu'il est frappé d'un coup."]—*Notes and Queries.*

Solar Eclipses.—I send you extracts from Motte's *Abridgment of the Philosophical Transactions*, 1700 *to* 1720, which would appear to relate to the "rose color," "corona," and "beads," which have excited so much interest in solar eclipses of late years. These passages in the *Transactions* may perhaps not have come under the eye of some of your readers, and may therefore interest them.

"At Bern Capt. Stannyan observed, May, 1706, on the sun's 'getting out of the eclipse, that it was preceded by a blood-red streak of light from its left limb, which continued not longer than six or seven seconds of time.'

"In April, 1715, Dr. Halley observed, during an eclipse, 'that about two minutes before the total immersion, the remaining portion of the sun was reduced to a very fine horn, whose extremities seemed to lose their acuteness and to become round, like stars. And for the space of about a quarter of a minute, a small piece of the southern horn of the eclipse seemed to be cut off from the rest, like an oblong star.' and which he attributes to inequalities of the moon's surface. 'A few seconds before the sun was all hid, there discovered itself round the moon a luminous ring, about a digit in breadth—of a pale whiteness or pearl color, and a little tinged with the colors of the Iris,' etc. 'During the whole time of the total eclipse, I kept my telescope constantly fixed on the moon,' etc. 'I found there were perpetual flashes of light which seemed for a moment to dart out from behind the moon—now here, now there, on all sides; but more especially the western side, before the emersion, and about two or three seconds before it. On the same western side, where the sun was just coming out, a long and very narrow streak of dusky but strong red light seemed to color the dark edge of the moon,' etc etc."—Motte's *Abridgment*, pp. 268, 273, 274, vol. i., from 1700 to 1720.—*Notes and Queries.*

Knights too Fat to Ride.—"In the oldest order of knighthood, a knight who became too fat to ride was rightly deprived of his spurs," p. 22.—*The Art of Riding*, London, 1710, 12mo. Which order, if any?—*Notes and Queries.*

THE LIVING AGE.

No. 887.—1 June, 1861.

CONTENTS.

PUBLISHED EVERY SATURDAY BY

LITTELL, SON, & CO., BOSTON.

THE HOUR HAS COME.

The hour has come; the cloud which slowly gathered
O'er heaven's blue,
Has thundered loudly, and with lightning flashes,
Is riven through.

E'en now it wraps its folds of darkness round us;
Along our shore
The trampling of the feet of many thousands
Sounds evermore.

Not vainly brave our fathers lived and suffered;
The holy dead
Speak now among us, and their glorious mantles
On us are shed.

When the first cannon woke the sleeping echoes
On Charleston Bay,
Men looked, and lo! the murky sky above them
Was streaked with gray.

And when the sculptured hand of him who saved us
In days gone by,
Held forth the flag, which in the roar of battle
Was lifted high,*

The cheer then raised by many hearts and voices,
Winds wafted far and wide,
And the valleys and the mountains and the forests
Of our free land replied;

And the wild waves which ever break in music
Along our shore,
Shook their white crests, and with the voice of thousands,
Mixed their exultant roar.

Though there is sadness, and a voice of mourning,
When men must die,
And tears are shed like rain, and hearts are bleeding
Where'er they lie,

Go forth! go forth! ye men of Massachusetts!
Go like true, noble men,
Though some may never see belovèd faces,
Dear voices hear again.

Go in the strength of God, of truth, of justice;
Tread where your fathers trod;
And look above, where o'er the darksome shadows,
Reigneth a loving God.

Salem, Mass., April 23, 1861.

—*Transcript.*

* At the immense Union meeting in New York, April 20th, Major Anderson was present, and the flag which was over Fort Sumter during its bombardment, was placed in the hand of the statue of Washington.

THE FLAG.

Why flashed that flag on Monday morn
Across the startled sky?
Why leapt the blood to every cheek,
The tears to every eye?
The hero in our four months' woe,
The symbol of our might,
Together sunk for one brief hour,
To rise forever bright.

The mind of Cromwell claimed his own,
The blood of Naseby streamed
Through hearts unconscious of the fire,
Till that torn banner gleamed.
The seeds of Milton's lofty thoughts,
All hopeless of the spring,
Burst forth in joy as through them glowed
The life great poets sing.

Old Greece was young and Homer true,
And Dante's burning page
Flamed in the red along our flag,
And kindled holy rage.
God's gospel cheered the sacred cause,
In stern, prophetic strain,
Which makes his right our covenant,
His psalms our deep refrain.

Oh, sad for him whose light went out
Before this glory came,
Who could not live to feel his kin
To every noble name:
And sadder still to miss the joy
That nineteen millions know,
In human nature's holiday
From all that makes life low.

—*Transcript.*

ARCHBISHOP LEIGHTON.

A frail, slight form — no temple he
Grand for abode of Deity;
Rather a bush inflamed with grace,
And trembling in a desert place,
And unconsumed with fire,
Though burning high and higher.

And with the fine pale shadow, wrought
Upon his cheek by years of thought,
And lines of weariness and pain,
And looks that long for home again;
So went he to and fro
With step infirm and slow.

A frail, slight form, and pale with care,
And paler from the raven hair
That folded from a forehead free,
Godlike of breadth and majesty—
A brow of thought supreme
And mystic, glorious dream.

Beautiful spirit! fallen, alas,
On times when little beauty was;
Still seeking peace amid the strife,
Still working, weary of thy life,
Toiling in holy love,
Panting for heaven above.

—"*Bishop's Walk*," by *Orwell.*

From The Edinburgh Review.

The Personal History of Lord Bacon. From unpublished MSS. By Wm. Hepworth Dixon. London: 1861.

It is not the first time that the pages of this journal have been devoted to an examination of the charges which weigh upon the character of Lord Bacon, and compel us to believe that the man who stands forth to all ages as the noblest representative of England's intellect, is not the noblest representative of her public virtue. The cause was argued at our assize long ago,* when no less a man than Basil Montagu was the advocate of the great chancellor, and no less a judge of historical evidence than Lord Macaulay rejected and refuted the defence of that enthusiastic biographer. It may well be that this great problem of the union of the highest intellectual powers with acts of incredible moral meanness and baseness, still exercises an irresistible attraction over the mind of many a student of history and of mankind; another generation has sprung up in the interval, and more accurate and extensive researches into the State Papers and Council Registers of Elizabeth and James, have somewhat augmented the evidence bearing upon Bacon's life. Mr. Hepworth Dixon, with this evidence in his hands, calls upon the world to reject its former conclusions, and to reverse our former sentence. It would be an idle and a presumptuous attempt to rewrite those brilliant pages of our late illustrious contributor, which stand recorded in English literature as the most complete summary extant of the grandeur of Bacon's genius, and of the deplorable failings of his character. But in justice to Bacon himself, and to his most recent champion, we have carefully re-examined the whole of the evidence, both old and new; and though we can find in this volume no sufficient reasons to alter our former convictions, we think our readers will not be unwilling to receive at our hands a more fresh and full account of the facts by which that conviction is sustained.

That Bacon should find another advocate among the men of letters of this day, is not a matter of surprise to us. Nor—although we object on many grounds to the undiscriminating eulogy before us—do we doubt that the real Bacon of history was very different from the harsh caricature which Pope originally gave to the world, and which several modern writers have amplified. It is evident from his letters and speeches, and from the testimony of most of his contemporaries, that Bacon not only was a statesman of deep insight and broad views, but that he had that large and humane ambition to accomplish social and political good which occasionally blends with the philosophic temper. His ideas respecting church government and toleration; his project of making the Law of England "the structure of a sacred temple of justice;" his admirable plan "of reducing Ireland to civility and right, to obedience and peace;" his thorough perception of the numerous mischiefs which a lingering feudalism was inflicting on England; and his full appreciation of the happy consequences which a union with Scotland was likely to produce, attest at once the comprehensiveness of his wisdom and the general kindliness of his disposition. If we measure him, too, by the standard of his age, reflect upon the circumstances of his life, and consider the various influences and temptations which operated on his acts and character, we believe that even those parts of his career which appear most worthy of blame and contempt admit of at least a partial vindication. That tame servility which shocks us so much, because so unworthy of his splendid powers, seemed probably only a graceful pliancy to the bishops and nobles of James and Elizabeth. His holding a brief for the Crown against Essex, and pleading against his unfortunate friend, we characterize as the blackest of treasons; but a lawyer trained in the courts of the Tudors, who had heard from the lips of living witnesses how Somerset had done his brother to death and Norfolk had sat in judgment on his niece, would certainly have been of a different opinion. Even the least defensible act of Bacon, his writing a posthumous libel on Essex, may, in some degree, be excused on the grounds that Elizabeth positively ordered the composition, and that disobedience to the Crown in those days would probably have been followed by punishment. So, too, precedent, usage, and reasonable authority sustain some passages in Bacon's attorney-generalship which we now condemn

* The article referred to was copied into The Museum of Foreign Literature, Oct. and Nov., 1837.

as cruel and iniquitous; and this defence may be partly urged to palliate the charge of judicial corruption of which we cannot believe him innocent. Notwithstanding all these allowances, however, the moral and intellectual nature of Bacon will still present a marked antithesis; and this, in fact, was his main characteristic. With his splendid energy and boldness in speculation, he was evidently timid and hesitating in action, with a natural tendency to yield to power, and not entirely superior to temptation. To use his own language, he had two sympathies, the sympathy for perfection and the sympathy for advancement; and to gain advancement he has told us plainly that he had no objection to creeping and obsequiousness. Place such a man, a giant in intellect and rich in every endowment of genius, yet weak, irresolute, and full of ambition in the court and closet of James and Elizabeth, and would the corrupting currents of the world be likely to leave him unsoiled by their contact?

That this was the real character of Bacon, and the only vindication it admits of, we think we shall prove to our readers' satisfaction. Mr. Dixon, however, proclaims the contrary; and insists that Bacon, the lawyer and politician, is, on the whole, as worthy of our reverence as Bacon the author of the "De Augmentis." He maintains that, even when tried by the test of modern social and political ethics, the conduct of Bacon can always be justified, and that certainly none of his public acts deserved blame in the seventeenth century. He contends that Bacon was nearly as conspicuous for dignity, rectitude, and disinterested patriotism, as he was for keen ability and wisdom, and that the man whom many have portrayed as a cowardly flatterer, libeller, and timeserver, was really one of the heroes of statesmanship. Impressed with this view, he not only brings out into much more than their fit prominence the fairer passages in the life of his subject, but he vindicates Bacon's conduct to Essex, applauds him throughout his career in Parliament, insists on his excellence as an officer of the Crown, and struggles to prove that his judicial integrity was as undoubted as his judicial ability.

Notwithstanding all these assertions, however, we decline to reject the former evidence on this subject; and, indeed, "demonstration" in the face of fact is, as Bacon has told us, "empty and futile." Our judgment upon this volume is, that it is throughout an unprofitable paradox, the ideal of vaporous fancy, as Bacon probably would have termed it. Nor do we think much the better of it because in this eccentric rhapsody Mr. Dixon has shown considerable diligence, and a true appreciation of some of the characters who rose to eminence in the history of the period. The Sophist in the "Clouds" was not always in the wrong, though his aim was to trifle with common sense; and Pangloss was often ingenious and learned in proving the ills of the world delightful. When the main idea of a work is unsound, it is little to the purpose that here and there it contains some new and original matter, and now and then some acute observations; but, even in these subordinate respects, Mr. Dixon can claim but little commendation. While we have no doubt that his theory is false, and that all he has said will not shake in the least the general opinion of Bacon's character; and while he has used all the artifices of an advocate in embellishing facts that tell on one side, and making enormous omissions and misstatements, we must also add that his original researches have not been fruitful in much new matter, on points at least of paramount importance. As for the manner, design, and style of this book, they appear to us to be in the worst possible state. A biography should be a portrait executed with manliness, simplicity, and truth, not a display of spasmodic rhetoric, tawdry ornament, and false effect: and we regret to have so soon to notice another distressing example of those extravagances and deformities of style with which Mr. Carlyle has infected the English language.

Before, however, we deal with the case which Mr. Dixon has here put forward, we would call attention to those parts of this volume which seem to us worthy of commendation. Mr. Dixon has given us some information upon the social relations of Bacon; and the letters of Anne Lady Bacon to her sons, which appear for the first time in his Appendix, are very characteristic and amusing. He has also collected a number of facts respecting the youth and the marriage of Bacon, which fill several agreeable

;es; while, as regards more important nts, he has thrown some new light on the lliers' match, and on the combination of rties which led to the fall of the great ancellor. We are also obliged to Mr. ixon for his account of the early career of acon in the last four parliaments of Elizbeth. He observes, justly, that Bacon's iographers have passed over his life in the louse of Commons between 1580 and 1593, nd only notice him in 1593, in reference to is opposition to Burleigh when bringing orward the double subsidy, and claiming he votes of the peers upon it. Even a cursory study of D'Ewes' Journal would convince any one that in these years the position of Bacon in Parliament was eminent; and it was only proper to dwell at some length upon this interesting phase in his history. The account of Mr. Dixon contains some facts which hitherto have not been generally made public. It appears certain that, even from youth, the mind of Bacon had matured plans at once bold, comprehensive and practical, for "ministering to the welfare of England," and that he seldom spoke in the House of Commons without commanding respect and attention. At this distance of time it is difficult to guess how far his scheme of resisting the change which was passing over the England of the Tudors—the conversion of arable land into pasture, and the slow decline of the able-bodied yeomanry—would have been capable of being carried out; but, although the scheme seems useless to us, and we smile at the mischiefs it aimed at removing, we should not forget that these mischiefs appeared most perilous to the statesmen of the day, and that Bacon down to the end of his life approved of his early efforts to redress them. We can better appreciate his youthful wisdom, by a reference to his noble designs, enunciated before he was thirty, of amending and consolidating our municipal law, and of doing away with the evils of purveyance, the most galling and ruinous incident of feudalism. In these respects we see plainly not only that he was far in advance of his time, but that his aims were thoroughly fixed and practical; and we feel amazed at the depth and power of a genius which so largely anticipated the future, and could shape out such magnificent improvements. In reference to the hackneyed charge, so often urged against Bacon at this time,—we mean that, in 1593 he opposed Burleigh from interested motives, and objected to the levy of a subsidy which in after years he warmly supported,—we fully admit that Mr. Dixon has done something to vindicate his hero; and in fact we think that until we know much more of the state of the England of Elizabeth, at the troubled close of the sixteenth century, than our actual means of knowledge disclose, we have little right to denounce a politician for a change of opinion on a matter of taxation.

This portion of Mr. Dixon's narrative is, however, open to several exceptions. It is overloaded with panegyric, and passes by some important matters which certainly should have received attention. As regards the grant of the subsidy in 1589, Mr. Dixon seizes a small opportunity of praising Bacon beyond his merits. He tells us that "Bacon's soul was *in the patriotic tug*, and that he moved to insert in the bill that the grant was extraordinary and exceptional." If we turn, however, to D'Ewes' Journal, we find that this was the act of "*divers* who were of opinion that meet words to that effect should be inserted in the Preamble," and that Bacon only "noted it in writing." This slip, perhaps, is of slight importance, except to show Mr. Dixon's tendencies; but other and graver errors occur in reference to what followed afterwards.

Let us waive the question whether Bacon was right in denouncing in 1593 the means by which the subsidy was levied, and in advocating in 1597 and 1601 an equal or greater amount of taxation. We will assume that the change of judgment was patriotic, that it was not caused by interested motives, and that it really may be attributed to events of which the clue is now lost to us. But why did Mr. Dixon omit to state that Bacon in 1595 apologized humbly for the speech of 1593, comparing it "to a variety in counsel as a discord in music to make it more perfect;" and taking care to remind Burleigh that "he had been the first to speak for the subsidy"? And is it fair in dealing with this subject to avoid alluding to the significant fact that Raleigh evidently in 1597 was sceptical as to Bacon's motives for having abandoned the opposition, and twitted him with some sharpness on his conduct? It is obvious, too, why Mr. Dixon takes care not to draw attention to the part which Bacon played in the Parliament of 1601, a part, we fear, expressive of his character. The question of the day was that of the monopolies, and the opposition contended strenuously, not only for the mischief of monopolies, but also for their absolute illegality. It is perfectly certain that Bacon was alive to the evils of this mode of traffic; and as a lawyer he must have known from D'Arcy's case, then actually decided, not to speak of a pregnant passage from Fortescue, that such restrictions were not lawful. What, however, did he say on the question? "He struck himself on the breast," writes D'Ewes, "and declared, that for his part "he allowed the prerogative of the prince, and hoped it never would be discussed, and that men should take care how they meddled in this business." Mr. Dixon of course rejects our solution of Bacon's conduct on this occasion,—that by this time he had made up his mind to take up the side of the court party; but, be the solution what it may, the scene should certainly have been noticed.

But our chief complaint against Mr. Dixon, so far as regards this part of his narrative, concerns his treatment of Bacon's relations with Burleigh, Cecil, Essex, and Elizabeth. To uphold the position that, in his career, every act of Bacon may be justified, that he had a lofty and generous spirit, and that such words as treachery and ingratitude can never be associated with his conduct, it was necessary to present a view of these relations very different from that in common acceptation. Mr. Dixon has elaborated a view of his own on this important subject, respecting which we shall only say, that if it displays some skill and cleverness, it is nevertheless essentially unfair, and cannot bear the test of inquiry. In order to lessen the weight of obligation which was certainly due from Bacon to Essex, we are told that Burleigh upon the whole was "a leal friend" to Bacon from the first; that Burleigh and Cecil pleaded "warmly" the claim of Bacon to the solicitor-generalship; that the queen was a gracious patron to him on all occasions, and in every instance; that she gave him a full remuneration for his services, in the shape of estates, fines, and places; and that Bacon, therefore, was pledged to her by every tie of duty and affection. With the same object Mr. Dixon informs us, that although Essex dou[illegible] exerted himself to obtain office for B[illegible] from the queen, he did so in such an [illegible] tunate way, that he caused his frie[illegible] lose the solicitor-generalship; that [illegible] made Bacon a present of an estate an[illegible] deavored to gain him a wealthy bride, [illegible] acts were more than adequately return[illegible] Bacon's legal advice and kindness; th[illegible] connection of Bacon with Essex cease[illegible] two years before the trial of the latter; [illegible] that Bacon, therefore, at the time of [illegible] trial, was not under any obligation to [illegible] Having thus completely inverted the r[illegible] tions which are usually supposed to [illegible] existed between the parties, Mr. D[illegible] paints in the blackest colors the treason[illegible] acts imputed to Essex, contends that he [illegible] tertained the design of murdering Eliza[illegible] and restoring "popery," and maintains [illegible] when made acquainted with these [illegible] Bacon only did what was perfectly righ[illegible] making his celebrated speech against [illegible] As for the trial of Essex, "there never [illegible] a fairer one:" "to have done more," [illegible] Mr. Dixon, "than Bacon did in the con[illegible] of this bad drama, might have been [illegible] and patriotic, to have done less would [illegible] been to act like a weak girl, not like a [illegible] man." However, before the treason of [illegible] sex had been completely disclosed to Eli[illegible] beth, we are told "that Bacon went to [illegible] extremest lengths of chivalry" to indu[illegible] the queen to forgive his friend; that "[illegible] offender never had such an advocate;" an[illegible] that even then "any man but Francis Bac[illegible] would have left the earl to his fate"—on the scaffold. In a word, Mr. Dixon's statement of the case is, that Bacon in his relations with Essex, was free from any obligations towards the earl; that he acted throughout with the finest feeling; and that in his conduct before and at the trial of Essex, "he took the only course open to an honest man."

Let us now compare this statement of the case with evidence from contemporary sources, supplied in the main from Bacon's own writings. We will grant that Burleigh secured for his nephew a place in reversion in the Star Chamber, and that after Bacon's humble apology respecting the speech of 1593, he made "constant and serious endeavors" to raise the apologist to the office of solicitor-general. We will also grant that on this latter occasion Cecil seems to have conded his father and cousin; and that possibly Bacon may have wronged him in suspecting "that he wrought in a contrary spirit." But that Burleigh was "a leal friend" to Bacon, or that Cecil ever supported him "warmly" in the sense of real and affectionate kindness that would bind Bacon to lasting gratitude, is, we think, disproved by the fullest testimony. "The time is yet to come," wrote Bacon, bitterly, when as yet a young though rising barrister, "that your lordship did ever use or command or employ me in my profession in any services or occasions of your lordship's own;" and the whole tone of his letters to Burleigh is that of a distant and suspicious suitor. As for Cecil, nothing can be more certain than that Bacon never acknowledged his friendship; and that Bacon thought himself wronged and neglected by both the Cecils, father and son, is clear from his deliberate statement "that they purposely suppressed all men of ability." And did Bacon in fact feel that Elizabeth had dealt kindly to him, had recompensed him according to his deserts, or had placed him under any real obligation? It is certain that in 1595 she had scorned his claim for the solicitor-generalship, although recognized fully by his profession, having told Essex, that "although Bacon had a great wit and an excellent gift of speech, yet in law he was rather showy" than otherwise. It is equally certain that Bacon suspected her of having thrown upon him the blame of "making her incensed against Essex," and thus having charged him with treachery alike disgraceful and ruinous to his prospects. These facts are against the supposition that Bacon felt any gratitude towards her, or had any good grounds to do so; and, as for his obligations to the queen, he says in a letter to James, before he had obtained any office from the king, "that he was bound to his majesty for trust and favor, and to his old mistress for trust only." Will Mr. Dixon deny that Bacon was able to estimate the kindliness of the Cecils, or the measure of the generosity of Elizabeth?

On the other hand, what were the obligations under which Bacon lay towards Essex, and did Bacon ever repudiate them? Mr. Dixon himself is forced to admit that Essex made the strongest efforts to procure the solicitor-generalship for Bacon, that he gave his friend a valuable estate, worth about £8,000 in our money, and that he seconded his suit to Lady Hatton with the most generous and honorable fervor. Did Bacon himself, at any time, even when it was his highest interest to do so, insinuate that "he owed to Essex the loss" of the legal promotion he was seeking; that the gift of Essex was merely a payment resembling the fee of a counsel or doctor; that his warm and gracious offices of friendship were "only the cheap generosity of words;" and that "the connection of Bacon and Essex was one of business and politics merely," that "imposed on Bacon no obligations"?

We shall not refer, as regards this question, to the mass of letters of Bacon and Burleigh respecting the interest Essex took in seeking the solicitor-generalship for Bacon, though these letters prove, as clearly as possible, that "the kind and wise" solicitations of the patron received the grateful acknowledgments of the client. But what did Bacon deliberately write several years after these passages were over, when he was striving to answer the bitter accusation of having betrayed and ruined his friend, and when, therefore, he would gladly have tried to relieve himself from the sense of obligation? "I must and will ever acknowledge," he writes in his Apology, "my lord's love, trust, and favor to me, and last of all his liberality. . . . After the queen had denied me the solicitor's place for the which his lordship had been a long and earnest suitor in my behalf, it pleased him to come to me from Richmond to Twickenham Park. . . . 'I die,' these were his words, 'if I do not somewhat for your fortune, you shall not deny to accept a piece of land which I will bestow on you.'" And what was the "cheap generosity of words," which Essex lavished on Lady Hatton when pressing her to accept Bacon? "My dear and worthy friend, Mr. Francis Bacon, is a suitor to my Lady Hatton, your daughter. What his virtues and excellent parts are you are not ignorant. If she were my sister or daughter, I would as confidently resolve to further it as I now persuade you." It is tolerably plain that Bacon, at least, never knew that Essex injured his prospects, never dreamed that his connection with him was only one of "business and politics," never sought to disclaim the obligations created "by love, favor, and liberality." And will Mr. Dixon venture to say that he knows more than Bacon on the subject?

We think it, therefore, clearly established that Bacon owed almost every thing to Essex, and little or nothing to the Cecils and Elizabeth. Such, therefore, being the state of the case, had Bacon "no other course as an honest man" but to prosecute Essex as counsel for the Crown, to go out of his way to speak against him,—the reply ought properly to have fallen to Fleming,—and to quicken the wrath of the jealous queen against his ruined and defenceless friend, by likening him to the Athenian tyrant, or to the destroyer of a contemporary sovereign? We will grant the truth of all the circumstances which Mr. Dixon sets round the subject; that for two years preceding the trial the intimate relations of Bacon and Essex had terminated "by the earl's own acts;" that after the expedition to Ireland "their prospects and affections lay widely apart;" that Essex did, in fact, conspire to kill the queen, and "restore the Smithfield fires;" that his trial was a fair and proper one, and that Bacon "received the queen's commands" to appear as a counsel against the culprit. We contend, even on these assumptions, not one of which can be sustained in fact, that the conduct of Bacon cannot be justified, and that if it can be partly palliated, this must be done by other arguments.

Are two years a period of limitation, to bar the rights of friendship and kindness, and to cancel the weight of immense obligations? If Essex were the most dangerous of rebels, was there any necessity to magnify his crimes by the most artful and cruel allusions, when he and every one of his associates lay already within the gripe of the executioner? If, in fact, according to Tudor rules, his trial was not conducted improperly, was Bacon bound as a prosecuting counsel to close the door of mercy against him by language far more deadly in meaning than any of Coke's intemperate effusions? And if Bacon received a retainer from the Crown, was he forced to thrust himself forward on this occasion, and to "prove how widely his prospects and affections lay" from those of his old benefactor and friend, by taking the place of the solicitor-general who, he knew well, was incapable of invective? We will put a case to Mr. Dixon which we think will show the flimsiness of the excuses which his zeal for Bacon induces him to make, and which, but for our sympathy with his client, would never mislead the most credulous person. It cannot be denied that the attempt of Monmouth against the life and crown of James the Second was at least as complete an act of treason as any thing done or thought of by Essex. Had Monmouth been brought before the High Steward, and one of his oldest and nearest friends and followers had lent his tongue to denounce his patron, as a plotter against the liberties of England, and bent on overthrowing the monarchy, would not Jeffreys himself have been surprised, and Sawyer and Williams whispered of conscience? Would any writer in this generation set up in behalf of such a man the defence Mr. Dixon has pleaded for Bacon? Would he say, respecting such an advocate, "that he followed the course of an honest man"?

Let us see, however, how the qualifying facts which Mr. Dixon puts confidently forward will bear the test of a strict examination. It is true that between 1597 and 1599 the friendship of Bacon and Essex had cooled, and possibly we may attribute this to Bacon having advised his patron not to undertake the government of Ireland. But from a letter, dated 1599, it is certain that Bacon wrote to the earl, referring to the splendor of the appointment, and that, too, in the most cordial language. It is also certain, when Essex had returned, that Bacon wrote affectionately to him; that he resumed his office of counsel to the earl; and that he sought to excuse himself from appearing at the investigation at York House, on the plea of his obligations to his benefactor. Is this consistent with the assertion that "for two whole years" the earl and Bacon "had met but once," to part in difference, and that the connection of the friends had ceased before by the earl's own conduct?

Again, where are the proofs of that black design of slaying the queen and reviving "popery" which Mr. Dixon makes the apology for Bacon's behavior at the Essex trial? It is all very well to rake together confessions made by such men as Blunt, reported hearsays of third persons with whom the prisoner had no connection, and loose inferences from doubtful acts which fairly bear a different construction, and to bid us, upon s kind of testimony, to convict Essex of eds of crime which were never laid to his arge when living, and certainly are ex- emely improbable. But why did Mr. ixon forget the reasons for an opposite onclusion, or did he choose advisedly to ppress them? If Essex were guilty of the onspiracy, the proofs of which Mr. Dixon forms us were in the hands of the Privy ouncil as early as January, 1600, why was e inquiry at York House, which took place n June, five months afterwards, entirely onfined to different accusations? Are we o suppose, if Elizabeth knew that the earl vas plotting against her life, or for the sub- ersion of Church and State, that she would ave studiously limited that inquiry "ad eparationem non ad ruinam," and not have ent him at once to trial? And when, in February, 1601, the earl really committed an act which made him technically guilty of high treason, — it would now-a-days proba- bly be treated as a riot,—we ask why none of the counsel for the Crown attempted to charge the prisoner with the crime of seek- ing the natural death of the sovereign, or of overthrowing the established faith, and carefully rested their case on the grounds of treason by implication and construction? It may be said that Coke, Fleming, and Ba- con believed that they had sufficient proofs to convict Essex without such allegations, and chose to rely on the minor accusations; and Bacon in fact asserted this in his tract subsequently written on the subject; but such a proceeding would be so inconsistent with every precedent of Tudor state trials that we cannot think such a motive sug- gested it. Nor should we forget, in judging of this case, that Essex throughout his trial and at his death expressly disclaimed any guilty purpose against the queen and the constitution, while he fully admitted his "legal transgression;" that at the accession of James I. the attainder against him was reversed; and that Bacon towards the close of his life, wrote in terms of high commen- dation about him. Such facts surely dis- prove the theory that Essex was a Fawkes or a Catesby.

As for the trial of Essex, the "fairness" of which Mr. Dixon thinks was a pattern for all ages, it was quite as fair as most instances of Tudor inquisitions for treason, — that is, the prisoner had no chance of escape, not having any legal assistance, and the rules of evidence being what they were. When we are told of its special "fairness," we wonder if Mr. Dixon remembers that two of the earl's most bitter enemies sat in judgment on him despite his protestations; that the evidence of one of the witnesses was suppressed; that Coke inveighed against the accused with more than his wonted bru- tal irrelevance; and that, according to a contemporary writer, the verdict of the Peers was given under the inspiration of "beer and tobacco," most admirable aids for a "true deliverance"! As for any spe- cial command from the queen to Bacon to prosecute Essex, which Mr. Dixon seems to insinuate, we defy him to prove that it ever was given; and we think that Bacon's own words on this point, "the service was merely laid upon me with the rest of my fellows," should satisfy any reasonable person.

We think, therefore, that the point of view which Mr. Dixon asks us to take in judging of Bacon's conduct to Essex, is cer- tainly set aside by the evidence. We are told however, that between the time when Essex returned to England from Ireland and actu- ally committed the crime he suffered for, Ba- con "went the extremest lengths of chivalry in his efforts to save him," and that "one voice alone dared to breathe to Elizabeth" excuses for the guilt of her favorite. Now we gladly admit, so long as the queen was not averse to expostulation, that is while Essex remained at large, though in half cap- tivity at Essex House, that Bacon did ex- ert himself honorably to revive Elizabeth's affection for his friend, and to win him again a place in her favor. We do not credit a hint of Cecil to which Bacon himself ad- verted, that the advocacy was all hypocrisy; nor shall we suggest that it might have been an interested speculation on the chance that Essex might regain his former ascen- dency. We think it certain that during this time Bacon did, in Mr. Dixon's language, "lavish wit, eloquence, and persuasion on this cause;" and, bearing in mind the char- acter of the queen, we feel assured that his mode of pleading, though somewhat eva- sive, was exactly that most calculated to move her. But it is equally clear from Ba- con's admissions, that when the mood of Elizabeth had changed into fixed hostility towards Essex — that is, after the inquiry at York House, but before the final act of treason, and when Bacon had satisfied his mind that his earnest pleading might injure himself, — he resolved to forego an arduous task, which possibly might involve danger, and certainly would contravene his interests. "Madam," he tells us were his words to the queen, in reference to her alienation from him, "for his speeches and courses on the side of my lord," — "if I do break my neck I shall do it in a manner as Mr. Dorrington did it, which walked on the battlements of the church many days, and took a view and survey of where he should fall." . . . . "Whereupon I departed *resting then determined to meddle no more in the matter*, as that that I saw would overthrow me and do him no good." Was this a proof of that noble chivalry which sacrifices itself for the sake of others, and is most conspicuous in the hour of peril, or was it a sign of prudent timorousness overcoming the sense of obligation, and the voice of a real yet selfish friendship? Besides, what was the conduct of Bacon in reference to the inquiry at York House, which Mr. Dixon conveniently suppresses? He begged, it is true, to excuse himself from attacking Essex before the Privy Council, but he wrote to the queen "that he knew the degrees of duties, and that no particular obligation could supplant or weaken the entireness of obligation which he owed to her and to her service;" and he added that, after he could not "avoid the fact which had been laid upon him, he did not handle it tenderly in delivery." These "extreme lengths of chivalry" we think—the mock reluctance to prosecute a friend, and doing the task with decorous harshness—approach the confines of cunning treachery, and are only the more to be condemned when they are purposely confused with the boundaries of duty.

How Essex died, and the pitying nation, who were not in the secret of his "popish" practices, made Elizabeth feel their indignation, and assailed his accusers "in common speech," is attested by every writer of the period. It is also well known to what the proud queen was compelled to resort on this occasion: to stay the ferment of the general ill-will, she caused "the treasons of the Earl of Essex" to be set forth in a public document, and chose Bacon to prepare the composition. Let us give him freely the benefit of his pleas that he had "express directions on every point," and that "many alterations" were made in his draught; but the fact remains that, whether from fear or from the pressure of royal urgency, he stooped to become the hired libeller of his slaughtered friend and benefactor.

How Mr. Dixon has dealt with this act, the most unworthy of Bacon's life, may be expressed in three words—he has not written a syllable on the subject — and, therefore, on this as on other charges, he has allowed judgment to pass against his client. As fair writers we cannot avoid to dwell for an instant on this conduct as an illustration of Bacon's character. Considering the time, the circumstances of the case, and the tone and contents of Bacon's "Declaration," we are bound to say that so cruel a publication was scarcely ever given to the world. Was it decent, exactly at the crisis when Ireland was up in fanatical rebellion, and the fleets of Spain were menacing Kinsale, to invoke the wrath of England on the dead, by a long detail of his Irish "treasons," not one of which can be proved against him? Was it honest, when the attainder of Essex had left his children destitute outcasts, to wage war against youthful innocence by exaggerating guilt which had been expiated on the scaffold? Was this the tribute of chivalrous "friendship"—to write an epitaph on a friend in a grave prepared for him by the writer's hands—which would probably sentence his house to ruin, and blacken his with perpetual infamy? Nothing more unjust, too, can well be conceived, than the statements and charges made in this document. Every act and turn of Essex in Ireland is tortured into a proof of treason. The most ingenious rhetoric is used to represent equivocal conduct in the colors which the queen and Cecil wished to affix to it. The inferences drawn from the slightest events, and all pointed in the same direction, are quite shameless from their perversion; and every kind of evidence is treated as certain truth to sustain the accusation. All the varied tricks and graces of phrase, exaggeration, metaphorical terms, and the different glosses of cunning sophistry are also used in full abundance; and nothing that skill can achieve is omitted to give effect and piquancy to the picture. We can well understand, as Bacon tells us, "that her majesty took a liking to his pen" for drawing such descriptions as these; but it is sad to think that such an intellect should ever have stooped to such a service. It must also be remembered that Bacon received a positive benefit from these state prosecutions. Twelve hundred pounds were given him by the queen out of a fine imposed on Catesby. This is rather an awkward fact as regards the "disinterested chivalry" of Bacon in this matter. Mr. Dixon appears to suppose he has brought this fact to light from the council register; it was already recorded in Mr. Foss' excellent volumes.* We protest against this idle attempt to elevate Bacon into a hero so far as regards his relations with Essex.

The next portion of Bacon's career embraces the years from the death of Elizabeth to his elevation to the attorney-generalship. Mr. Dixon's account of his hero at this time undoubtedly gives us some new information, but it overflows with idle panegyric, it suppresses many important facts and several necessary general considerations, and it gives an idea of Bacon's conduct, which is certainly not borne out by the evidence. Mr. Dixon tells us that Bacon's name was "dear" to the country at the accession of James, that at Court only "he was under a cloud;" and he urges, in confirmation of this, that Bacon entered the Parliament of 1604 as member for Ipswich and St. Albans, and that he was thought a fit candidate for the office of Speaker of the House of Commons. As for his parliamentary status at this period, we are told that it was more lofty and splendid, and more distinguished for pure patriotism, than that of any other English politician, and that all his acts are to be ascribed "to his height of view and round of sympathy." It was owing to "his reconciling genius which spanned the dividing stream of party," that he managed "to stand on good terms with a hostile Court and House of Commons." His unremitting "votes for supplies" which, the popular party suspected justly, "dropped into the pouches of Herbert and Carr," were "given to rescue James and his servants from the magnificent corruptions of the Spanish minister." His advocacy of the union with Scotland had nothing to do with the wishes of James and of his tribe of hungry parasites, who could not batten on English manors so long as in law they remained aliens, but "as a measure of defence" against Spanish aggressions. His opposition to wardship and purveyance was prompted wholly "by a desire to improve the old ways before improvement was too late," and had not the sidelong object of adding to the private revenues of the sovereign. As for Ireland, "the green and lustrous island" owed "nearly all that was gracious and noble, most wise and foreseeing in the policy of this reign, to Francis Bacon, after Arthur Chicester," because Bacon advised James to increase the number of Irish buroughs. If we add to this "that the principle of toleration was exercised as a virtue of Bacon's life;" that he aided the colonization of Virginia "as a branch of the great contest with Spain;" and that his one aim throughout this period was "to arm, to free, and to guide" his country, we may certainly admit that so noble a part was perhaps never fulfilled by a statesman.

As we stand before this picture, however, we have a right to criticise its truth and accuracy. Unquestionably Bacon, though very unpopular "in common speech" in 1603, regained the ear of the House of Commons, and rose to his former eminence in it before the close of the Parliament of 1604. This fact, however, may well be ascribed to the splendor of his reputation for genius—the "Advancement of Learning" was published at this time—to the power and brilliancy of his eloquence, to the gracious courtesy of his manners, much more than to the favor of his countrymen. It is possible, too, that Bacon's votes in behalf of subsidies for the Crown may have been justified by the occasion; most probable that he fully appreciated the advantages of the union with Scotland, and the danger from Spain to English freedom; and quite certain that he perceived the injuries wrought by a lingering feudalism, the necessity of a just government for Ireland, the value of toleration in the abstract, and the usefulness of the colonies to the empire. But what we complain of in this account is that, even supposing its facts to be true, they do not bear out a number of its statements; that in several parts its evidence fails; that it ascribes motives to Bacon's acts which are either guessed at or were not dominant; and that at best it is a series of half truths with immense suppressions.

* Foss' Judges of England, vol. vi. p. 72.

What proof have we that the politician who wrote to James that "he gloried in obsequiousness, and was flattering Cecil as a noble patriot," at the very time when he hated him in his heart, ever rose superior to political selfishness, and aimed at swaying the counsels of England in virtue of "his reconciling genius" and wisdom? If Bacon really voted the supplies in the Parliament of 1604, on account of a strong hostility to Spain, why did he take special credit with the king, who hated the Spanish war of all things, for having supported the bill for the subsidy which was given expressly for this purpose? It is true that Bacon advocated the Union; but that this was rather to gratify the king, and the crowd of Humes, Herberts, and Carrs, than with any particular reference to Spain, is proved not only by numerous letters, but by the fact that in 1603, when the Spanish war was as yet raging, he certainly thought the Union impolitic. As for the manifold evils of the feudal tenures, Bacon doubtless saw them in all their bearings, did good service in trying to abolish them, and showed considerable zeal on the subject; but, to quote his own words, he attributed his efforts not only "to the wish to improve the old ways," but to the hope that "the abolition would invest the Crown with a more ample dowry." That Bacon, too, approved of toleration is shown by his admirable essay on the subject; but that he attempted to put it in practice we think is contrary to much evidence; while as respects the government of Ireland, though we quite allow that he saw what it should have been, we deny that his courtly advice to James to augment the number of Irish boroughs was prompted by aught but regard for prerogative. And as for Bacon's having aided a scheme to relieve Virginia from Spanish aggression, we should think this was rather a frail foundation for Mr. Dixon's superstructure of eulogy.

On Mr. Dixon's own showing, therefore, we dispute the accuracy of this description of Bacon at this stage of his fortunes. It is singular, too, that he does not refer—though we think we can guess the reason why—to the chief evidence in favor of the assertion that Bacon was a mediator between the Commons and the Crown between 1604 and 1610. He does not tell us that Bacon insisted upon the prerogative of the Crown to impose customs' duties on the subject; and yet that in 1610 he was made the spokesman of the House of Commons in the great petition on this and other grievances. To have stated this, however, would have called attention to the subservient tone which Bacon adopted on this latter occasion,—comparing "the sound of the grievances of the Commons to the *gemitus columbæ*, the mourning of a dove,"—and which has made some writers suspect that he really was an agent of James while seeming to speak for his fellow-members. This omission, however, of Mr. Dixon is only one of numerous suppressions in reference to this part of the subject which he has chosen to make for the purpose of sustaining his theory, and to which we shall briefly advert.

In judging of Bacon's conduct at this time, it is surely necessary to bear in mind the character of the government of James, and the questions of politics then in agitation. The great contest of the seventeenth century—the struggle between a modern absolutism and the full development of our ancient institutions—was then rapidly coming to a crisis. A drivelling and half-foreign pedant, the feeblest and yet most galling of tyrants, was seeking, if not to enslave his people, to add indefinitely to prerogatives which the pretensions of the Crown made perilous to freedom. United to him were some of the nobility, very different from the Nevilles and Cliffords who had once sustained the cause of the nation, and a swarm of needy and profligate courtiers, who paid for the lavish grants of their master by spreading abroad the influences of despotism. The Church, also, with singular fervor, concurred in supporting her temporal head; and purchased the right of persecuting dissent, and binding the laity in odious fetters, by announcing doctrines of passive obedience, and of indefeasible hereditary right, which were so many libels on liberty. Even in the first years of the seventeenth century, the consequences of this movement displayed themselves, and became ominous of a dark future. Whitehall was not only disgraced by scenes which revived the days of Nero and Commodus, but resounded with notes of adulation, and with courtly and priestly arguments for despotism, which no Englishman should have uttered. The foreign policy of the great queen was set aside in spite of the nation; gross invasions of the Constitution were attempted under color of the prerogative. The settled right of enacting laws by king, Lords, and Commons only, was violated by numerous royal proclamations. The jurisdiction of the common law was encroached upon by spiritual tribunals, far more subservient than those at Westminster, because entirely independent of juries. The courts of the High Commission and Star Chamber committed excesses of arbitrary power which had never been attempted by Elizabeth; and the great right of the House of Commons—control over the national purse—was set aside by the novel doctrine that the king could tax all imports at pleasure. Meantime, every effort was made by the king, the Church, and the heads of the State to corrupt opinion in favor of absolutism; the legislature was alternately menaced and cajoled; the most submissive instruments of power were singled out for public trusts; the army, the navy, and the bench were filled with the flatterers of Carr and the minions of James; and the rising generation was educated in theories tending to Turkish despotism. The England of Henry VIII. and Elizabeth, that had hurled foul scorn at Parma and Spain, was threatened by an enemy from within more perilous than the League or the Armada.

A large majority in the House of Commons, and the great mass of the people of England, opposed steadily these noxious influences so perilous to their ancient liberties. How they boldly asserted their legal rights, denounced the doctrine of passive obedience, protested against the usurpations of the Crown, especially as regards taxation and proclamations, condemned the encroachment of the ecclesiastical tribunals, and insisted upon their share in the government, the records of the first Parliament of James have made sufficiently known to the reader. Mr. Dixon has carefully kept out of view the nature and character of this contest, and even most of its chief incidents, because, if he had referred to them, his picture of Bacon as a model of patriotism, wisdom, and disinterested purity, would have seemed at once untrue and incongruous. For what, in reference to this contest, was Bacon's attitude as a public man in the first year of the seventeenth century? We do not complain that he did not join the noble ranks of the Hydes and Hakewills, the predecessors of the St. Johns and Hampdens to whom we owe our actual liberties. He is not to be blamed for having elected to vote usually with the Court party, though, in his case, it is hard to believe that he did not foresee the drift of their policy. But why did Bacon at this period exhaust the language of adulation in favor of such a sovereign as James, comparing him to the "healing angel who stirred the waters in the pool of Bethesda," to the "breath of the law" and the "soul of justice," when he perfectly knew that sovereign's character? Did he, who thoroughly understood "the true state of the greatness of Britain," oppose, even in a single instance, the attacks of the Crown on the rights of the nation, or say a word in behalf of liberties which were being stealthily sapped and subverted? Did he, a profound constitutional lawyer, ever hint that a royal proclamation had not the binding force of a law, or allude to the usurpations of courts, especially under the influence of the Crown, upon the regular popular tribunals? Knowing full well, with the commerce of England expanding before his prophetic eye, that, if the sovereign could impose taxes by raising duties on foreign imports, the House of Commons would soon become a mere shadowy appendage of the Crown, why did he assert in the case of Bates that this "prerogative" was not to be questioned? And when delegated by the House of Commons to state their grievances to the sovereign, why did he so accomplish his mission as to make his conduct matter of suspicion? In a word, are these the proofs of a patriotism, more lofty than that of any of our statesmen, that Bacon in the first Parliament of James never once opposed the stealthy tyranny which was breaking down our institutions, but, on the contrary, always supported it? Can his frequent displays of a prescient-genius, and his general support of wise legislation on subjects not connected with the prerogative, and where he was left untrammelled in action, entirely atone, in the eyes of posterity, for these positive derelictions of duty, and raise him to the rank of our greatest patriots? Mr. Dixon evades an answer to this question by not noticing most of the instances of Bacon's partisanship at this time; but our readers, we hope, will not forget them, and will draw their own conclusions accordingly.

Let us own, however, that this panegyric is pitched in so much too high a tone, that it urges us to a contrary judgment, and makes us forget some commendation which is due to Bacon at this period. We know well that the large wisdom, and the tendency to benevolent schemes, for which his intellect was conspicuous, were not eclipsed in this Parliament; but their lustre is sullied by his weak subserviency to the meanest arts of despotism. It is only just, however, to add, that some passages in his conduct at this time,—for instance, his attitude towards the Crown when he brought forward the Great Petition,—may admit perhaps of an explanation which would reflect some credit upon him. It certainly is not a little strange—upon the supposition that after 1607 when he became solicitor-general of James he always acted in the interest of the Crown—that he should have been selected by the Commons to be the mouthpiece of their petition; and it may be that, although he had spoken in favor of some of the illegalities referred to in that important document, he afterwards changed his mind on the subject, and in 1610 was a real reformer. It is also not at all impossible that his public life in this Parliament may yet be set in a fairer light than our actual knowledge appears to warrant, and even that his seeming neglect to defend these high constitutional rights which were being assailed by James and his favorites, may be excused without discrediting him. It doubtless is a most singular fact that the man who, so far as the evidence goes, was covering James with flattery at this time, and advocating some of his worst actions, should have held the eminent position he did in the House of Commons of 1604–10; and this induces the reader to hope that gaps exist in the proofs on this subject which, if filled up, might alter his views so far at least as regards Bacon. But as yet the eulogy of Mr. Dixon remains only an idle guess, at present, at least, contradicted by the evidence; and we feel assured that no discovery will ever establish Bacon in the position of a model of pure and disinterested patriotism.

We pass on to consider Bacon as attorney-general of James and as lord chancellor. In dealing with this part of his subject Mr. Dixon has been a little more prudent than in the preceding chapter of his work, though his views are still essentially erroneous. He eulogizes justly the general decorum of Bacon as a public prosecutor, and his proved humanity in several instances; insists on his constitutional opinions as evidence of his constitutional conduct; and passes a well-deserved eulogium on the triumphs of his judicial genius. He calls attention properly to the facts that in the Parliament of 1614 Bacon was returned for three boroughs; that the House of Commons declared him duly elected, although the actual attorney-general, against existing usage and precedent; and that, even when condemned for corruption, he had still a considerable party in his favor. He stands, however, mainly on the defensive; and tries to obliterate, one by one, the various charges against Bacon in reference to his conduct at this period. We gladly admit that in doing this he has shown some ingenuity and acuteness; that he has brought to light some important facts which hitherto had not received due weight; and that he has given reasons at the bar of History for mitigating its adverse verdict on his client. But we must add that here, as before, Mr. Dixon has evaded considerations which should have entered into his estimate of this question; that he has omitted to notice several facts which bear against his view of the subject; and that, on the whole, his account of Bacon at this important point in his career, cannot abide the test of a scrutiny.

Between 1614 and 1621 what were the acts and character of the government of England, and what were Bacon's relations to it? The sceptre of the Plantagenets and Tudors was consigned by the meanest of faineants to the most worthless of mayors of the palace. The counsels of Burleigh and the valor of the Howards were superseded by the dictatorship of the cowardly, wasteful, and profligate Buckingham. The crimes, the sins, and the horrors of the palace broke through the cloud of dishonest incense which rose around the sovereign and his favorite, and revealed James pandering to adultery, interfering with the process of justice to cloak some unknown secret of infamy, and sullying the honor of the royal name by the most unmanly and vile self-abasement. This great empire became the prey of a fopling harpy, reckless, avaricious, and despicable as a Dubois or a Godoy, who, feeling that a summons of the national estates might bring on a day of national reckoning, kept England in ignominious repose, prostrated her at the feet of Spain, and abused her laws, her commerce, and her wealth, for the sake of a brief indulgence in tyranny. The nation protested, and its representatives were dispersed without a semblance of reason, and for some years were prevented from re-assembling. Every bad expedient of arbitrary power—in many instances absolutely illegal, in others barely sanctioned by precedent—benevolences, monopolies, proclamations, and impositions,—was resorted to, to replenish the exchequer and retard the meeting of the House of Commons; and any attempt at resistance was put down with unsparing harshness. By a dexterous ingenuity of oppression, the laws which had been enacted to support the cardinal institutions of the state—the national church and the courts of justice—were turned into instruments to relieve the Crown from responsibility to the people; enormous fines were laid on incessantly for the purpose of making a fund for the sovereign; and the High Commission and Star Chamber were made machinery for extracting revenue. In the mean time the efforts of the Court were applied steadily to the task of breaking down the Constitution; the patronage of the Church was confined to the most subservient advocates of monarchy; the judges were tampered with by the king, and some of them were convicted of corruption; the method of "undertaking" for Parliament was made a secret of the Privy Council; and the unmanly doctrine of passive obedience became the shibboleth of loyalty. Servility, tyranny, vice, and degradation were the characteristics of this reign, the most contemptible in the annals of England.

Now of this government it is unquestionable that Bacon was the principal adviser, though certainly not the chief administrator. What he must have thought of its character and acts, of its nominal head and real director, of its miserable policy at home and abroad, we know well from his own writings. He was a sober, chaste, and pure-minded man, and must have scorned the gluttony and sensuality, the coarse profligacy, and animal habits of James, Carr, Villiers, and their associates. He knew perfectly that the king was a dotard, "who asked counsel from the past and not from the future," to use his own significant euphuism, and that Buckingham was the most worthless of ministers. Having written well about the relations between a sovereign and his dependants, "if you flatter him you betray him and are a traitor to the state," he doubtless spurned the adulation which gathered round the puppet of Villiers. He must have detested the long abasement of England to the House of Austria; for in fact in 1614 he had the boldness to insinuate that "our peace is usque ad satietatem;" and in 1624, when war with Spain was the cry of the nation, he preached a vehement crusade in its favor. He has told us himself that "the greatness of Britain consisted in the temper of a government fit to keep subjects in good heart and courage, not in the condition of servile vassals." He said distinctly that "the use of parliaments in this kingdom was very excellent, and that they often should be called;" and therefore must have distrusted the attempt to govern England without their sanction. He declared also "let the rule of justice be the law of the land, and impartial arbiter, between the king and people and one subject and another;" and must accordingly have disproved illegal taxation and Stuart proclamations. "Let no arbitrary power be intruded," he said emphatically to the youthful Villiers; so he thought of course that benevolences, and edicts, the fines of the High Commission and Star Chamber, and attempts to pack and influence parliaments, were really acts of treason to England. As for levying money through penal laws, and by putting in force the arms of intolerance, we know that he often denounced these laws as the great blot on the English statute-book, and that persecution on religious grounds was with him "to deface the laws of society." Monopolies he termed "the cankers of trading," "not to be admitted under spurious colors;" so what must have been his real opinion as regards Mitchell's and Mompesson's patents? As for the state of the Church, as respects its government, its servile doctrines, and usurpations, his lofty genius scorned its pretensions; and must have loathed the mitred sycophants who compared James to Solomon and to Christ. What he must have felt in his heart, alas, as regards any tampering with judges and the least taint of judicial corruption, we set down in his own words: "by no means," he wrote to Villiers, "be you persuaded to interfere yourself, either by word or letter, in *any* cause depending in *any* court of justice, nor suffer any other great man to do it, when you can hinder it, and by all means *dissuade* the king himself from it." . . . "Be your hands and the hands of your hands, I mean those about you, clean and uncorrupt from *gifts*, from meddling in titles, and from serving on turns, be they of great ones, or small ones." . . . "The place of Justice is a hallowed place, and, therefore, not only the bench, but the foot pace, and precincts, and purprise thereof, ought to be preserved from scandal and corruption." Assuredly the author of these eloquent words understood the character of secret attempts to compel judges to warp their decisions, of screening criminals from public justice, and of tainting the judgment-seat with corruption.

Such were Bacon's *thoughts*, what his *acts* were we shall set down as briefly as possible. No beggarly courtier who knelt to James to buy the hand of a rich heiress, no priest who cringed at Buckingham's levies to crave a mitre or a benefice, surpassed the attorney-general and chancellor in servile flattery of the king and his favorite. We might fill pages with evidences of this fact, but we gladly pass from the mournful scenes of moral and intellectual prostitution. When the murder of Overbury cried for vengeance, and disclosed the hateful orgies of Whitehall, Bacon, evidently guessing at some fearful secret, lent his aid to attempts to suppress inquiry, and did this to gratify his master. In a number of letters he congratulated James upon the peaceful triumphs of his reign, meaning by the phrase his country's degradation. He proposed to influence the Parliament of 1614, and also that of 1621; and, though certainly not averse to parliaments, during six years he never insisted upon the necessity of convening one. He took part with more or less prominence in most of the illegal acts of the interim; assented to royal proclamations entrenching upon the domain of statutes, set the seal to the most disgraceful monopolies, and exulted in forcing a man to his ruin for having sharply denounced a benevolence, and reflected on its false-hearted exactor. In a very remarkable letter to the king, he tells him that his "*endeavors* with the recusants had been *no small spurs to make them feel his laws*, and that their penalties should be farmed, as a means of an increase of revenue;" believing of course that mulcts for conscience' sake "did not deface the laws of society." How well he worked the penal laws, and the stern process of the Star Chamber, as means of filling unfairly the exchequer, and how, no doubt, against his inclination, he engaged in divers cruel prosecutions, we know from several cases of this period; nor is there a proof that he ever deprecated the usurpations and exactions of the priesthood. As for his practising with the officers of justice, in every possible kind of case, against the protest, always of one of them, and of the whole bench on one occasion, this is evident from his own admissions; and the case of Peacham reveals too clearly his method of extorting confessions, and the part he played in assisting at torture. As for his conduct upon the bench, we shall here say only that his letters prove that he did repeatedly, when on the judgment-seat, "allow a great man to interfere" with his suitors; and that not once, but over and over again, in public and private, to friends and foes, he acknowledged that "neither his hands, nor his hands' hands, were free from corruption." In a word, during the whole of this period the language and conduct of this great man were as far apart as light and darkness; and we do not know a more memorable instance of the "law of sin which is in the members bringing into captivity" the law of conscience.

This, then, is our general charge against Bacon, that, being one of the first of intellects, having naturally a kind and humane disposition, being far beyond his age in civil prudence, and thoroughly comprehending our law and constitution, he should have identified himself with a government conspicuous for its meanness and tyranny, its cruelty, illegality, and rapacity, and should not only have sanctioned its acts, but in several instances, have encouraged it in a course of wrong and despotic innovation. Was it for Bacon, the glory of English intellect, to illustrate, by a number of examples, the truth of that deep and mournful saying that when the light within us is darkness, that darkness is very great and terrible? Was he to earn for his name the censure which attaches justly to those wrong-doers, who put bitter for sweet, and sweet for bitter, and evil for good, and good for evil? Could not he, engaged at this very time, at the noble work of endowing man with the "secret of the labyrinth of nature," have left to others the wretched task of packing parliaments, torturing prisoners, enforcing violations of the constitution, conniving at public fraud and robbery, and tainting the judgment-seat with corruption? Let us freely admit any mitigating facts which may be urged for him at this juncture—that in many instances he did display humanity as a public prosecutor—that he usually acted under the orders of the king, the Privy Council, and Buckingham—that at this period an officer of the Crown was more under the sovereign's control than he ever has been since the Revolution—that some traces of his wisdom and philanthropy, though not so many as in former days, appear in his correspondence at this time,—and that he fulfilled the duties of a chancellor with great despatch and commanding genius. Still the general charge remains unanswered; nor do we believe it possible for any one to meet it fairly in every particular, or to do more than excuse it partially. Mr. Dixon, however, has attempted this; and his efforts, although occasionally ingenious, and, in some respects successful, are as a whole, we think, a signal failure. He avoids entirely calling attention to the character of the government in these years, and to Bacon's close relations with it. He omits to allude to several of the facts which tell most heavily against his client—his influencing the Parliament of 1614, his efforts to stop the mouth of Somerset, and to stifle inquiry at the trial, his deep responsibility in the case of Peacham, his double confession of the charge of acts of bribery and corruption, and his extraordinary subsequent conduct so inconsistent with the hypothesis of his innocence. With respect to the residue of the charges, he avails himself of a well known artifice in common use among wary advocates—he evades the *cumulative* force of the proofs, discusses the charges one by one, and claims in this way an absolving verdict. That some of his pleadings may be admitted, we fully concede in justice to him, but, even as regards this part of his argument, we think his account in the main erroneous.

Let us first refer to the case of St. John, respecting which Mr. Dixon tells us that Bacon deserves rather praise than otherwise. In 1614, the Parliament, which the attorney-general had advised James to "influence" to his wishes, was most improperly closed by a dissolution, and some of its members were thrown into prison. James tried to supply his treasury by a "benevolence," an impost, which, if levied by coercion, contravened a celebrated popular statute,—though, if asked merely as a free gift, it was possibly just within the law,—but which, in whatever form or guise, was odious to the mass of the nation. It is not improbable that this benevolence was claimed in the shape of a voluntary offering,—the meaning of which is tolerably intelligible,—but it is certain that it aroused indignation, and that the first law authority of the day expressed for a time a doubt of its legality. In the angry state of the public mind, especially when the law was doubtful, it was surely the duty of the attorney-general to treat remonstrance with some deference, not to scan too harshly the language of protest, and not to punish with reckless severity even noisy vehemence on the subject. What, however, was Bacon's conduct on the occasion? He scorned the opposition to the benevolence, supported the king in his evil policy, reflected on Coke for questioning the law, and singled out an individual who had written a libel in reference to the subject, for the tender mercies of the Star Chamber,—that is for a fine of crushing amount, and imprisonment for an indefinite period. Let us admit every one of Mr. Dixon's pleas—that in fact coercion was not employed as regards the levy of the benevolence,—that St. John was a despicable character,—and that his language reflected bitterly on the king,—was Bacon, therefore, justified in urging the raising a fund by questionable means, in spurning public opinion on the subject, in setting aside the legal doubts of Coke, and in praying for such a tremendous judgment for the offence of writing a libel on the question? Mr. Dixon seems to think this was right—even by the rules of the present day;—we beg to protest against this conclusion.

We pass on to the case of Peacham, in allusion to which Mr. Dixon assures us "that the lawyer is happy who has no worse recollection," than the having imitated Bacon on this occasion. Let us take the case from the words of Judge Croke, a prerogative lawyer of the time of Elizabeth, and a contemporary witness of the highest value. "Edward Peacham was indicted for treason, for divers treasonable passages in a sermon which was never preached, *or never intended to be preached, but only set down in writing and found in his study.*" . . . "*Many* of the judges were of opinion that it was not treason." . . . "He was tried and found guilty, but not executed." These few words record a prosecution, disgraceful in the annals of English jurisprudence, and in which we think it impossible to relieve the conduct of Bacon from weighty censure. It appears from Bacon's letters and the state trials, that, on the discovery of Peacham's sermon, the royal jurist, whose meddling in law led him into several follies and infamies, insisted upon a prosecution for treason, and actually wrote an opinion on the subject. Many of the judges, however, servile as they were, presumed to doubt if unpublished writings could be an overt act of high treason; and although there is a passage in the Institutes, which appears to solve the doubt in the affirmative, it is certain that even at this period no precedent could be found for a view which contravened the plain words of the statute. In this state of affairs, Bacon undertook to seduce the judges to his master's wishes; that is, by private practising, and arguments, to lead them to wrest the law against their consciences, and not only to plan the death of a fellow-subject, but to lay down a rule for all time, destructive alike of reason and liberty. He went himself to the chief justice, and sent his colleagues separately to confer with the other judges of the king's bench, in the hope, as he tells us out of his own mouth, that Coke would not continue in opposition, "if put in doubt that he would be alone in it." This conduct is an interesting commentary on the precept that any interposition in any cause in a court of justice, is culpable in the highest degree, nor need we say a word of its morality. That, besides, it was a violation of the law, of which Bacon was the public defender, is proved not only by Coke's own words, "that such auricular taking of opinions was not according to the custom of the realm," but by a remarkable passage from the year books, which expressly declares that "in cases of treason which deserve so fatal and extreme a punishment, the judges ought not to deliver their opinions before-hand, in a case put, and proofs urged of one side in the absence of the accused," *because* "*that they cannot stand indifferent*, and *do right* between *the king and the people.*" We will do Bacon the justice to believe that shocking conscience and outraging law were not among his "happy recollections."

Nor was this the end of this disgraceful business. It was necessary, not only to garble the law, but to find evidence against the accused, and to force him to implicate others. For this purpose, a special commission, of which the attorney-general was a member, resolved upon the illegal crime of putting the wretched prisoner to torture, and wringing testimony from his agonies. It is sickening to think that Bacon the philosopher, the friend of humanity, the Plato of England, should have sat by while Peacham was "questioned before, after, and during torture," and actually should have written to the king to try again the hideous experiment. We will grant that he shared the guilt with others, and that possibly for this atrocious act the king and Council are primarily answerable. It is evident from his letters, however, that he felt himself a chief agent in this wickedness, and that his conscience accused him for it. "I wish it were otherwise," he wrote to James, "complaining that he was driven to the question." And as for the illegality of this act, we shall merely observe that, although there are proofs that torture was used in the Tudor age, the practice, even in the reign of Edward II., was declared expressly to be "abominable;" that Coke says in the plainest words, that "torture is not warranted in this land;" and that only a few years after this time all the judges gave a unanimous opinion against the lawfulness of this shameful cruelty. Nor do we remember a single instance, even in the iron age of the Tudors, excepting that of the infamous Rich, who lied Sir Thomas More to his scaffold, and watched the torments of Anne Askew, in which the first law officer of the Crown assisted personally at this barbarous inquisition.

We assert, therefore, in Peacham's case, that Bacon not only was guilty of deeds unsanctioned by the practice of the age, but that he wilfully broke the law, although its sworn and responsible supporter. What is the answer of Mr. Dixon to these grave and most evident charges? We pass by the irrelevant pleas that Peacham was a "libeller and a liar," that his sermon was full of treasonable matter, and that he wrongfully implicated others when in the mortal agony of the "question." As regards the charge of tampering with the judges, Mr. Dixon thinks that Bacon is absolved, because, in the case of the "heretic" Legate, the officers of the Crown consulted Coke in reference to the amount of the punishment. He tells us that this is a clear precedent in favor of the lawfulness of asking the judges to anticipate a trial, to declare beforehand the nature of a crime, and to give their opinion upon an act, the evidence of which is not before them! For a judge *after* a case has been heard, and *after* conviction has been obtained, and *after* all the proofs have been adduced, to listen to an attorney-general's suggestion respecting the sentence which is to follow, is the same thing as a judge being led *before* the accused has been brought to the bar, and *before* a word of the charge has been heard, to take his view of the law and facts from the secret prompting of the accusing party! To state the two cases proves that they differ as widely as any two cases can; and, even if Legate's case were a "precedent" in favor of this tampering with the judges, Mr. Dixon has scarcely a right to plead it, since Bacon was one of the law officers who sought for Coke's opinion on the sentence, and his own misdeed can never excuse him.

This defence of the "tampering," therefore, fails; and what is the plea to the second charge in reference to the torturing of Peacham? Mr. Dixon insists that the practice of torture was common in Europe in the sixteenth century, and was quite a custom in Tudor England. This assumes as true, in regard to England, what certainly is at best questionable; and keeps out of view the important facts, that torture was prohibited by law, and that the law officers of the Crown apparently shunned the countenancing the practice, the most telling circumstance against Bacon. He also contends, that throughout this business, Bacon acted under the orders of the Council, and was, at most, their consenting agent; a plea certainly true in part, and which we gladly receive in palliation. But Bacon's own letters show that he felt that he was highly responsible for the deed; nor should we forget, in reference to this point, that the attorney-general must have been the chief adviser of James and the Council, as regards the *lawfulness* of the proceeding. It is obvious, therefore, that, though at the time when the sentence was actually being inflicted, the king and Council were most guilty, the sin of advising this odious tragedy,—not to speak of that of assisting in it,—must rest mainly on the head of Bacon. It follows, therefore, that the attempt to shift the blame upon other persons is only very partially successful; and that Bacon, as he evidently felt, must bear the charge of being a principal in an act of gross and illegal cruelty. Would this be "a happy recollection," we will not say for a lawyer of this day, but even for a Finch or a Saunders?

As Mr. Dixon thinks that tampering with the judges was not a fault in a lawyer of that day, we shall scarcely refer to the case of "Commendams," in which Bacon tried to justify this practice, on principles evidently contrary to law, and declared that "he had no scruple in this service." We shall merely observe, that all the judges, dependent and slavish as they were, with the one exception of Sir Edward Coke, maintained that "notwithstanding the letter," which Bacon had written to order delay, "they were sworn to go forth and do the law;" and that Coke, when the rest of his brethren had succumbed, remained firm in his honest opposition. Mr. Dixon's account of this interesting scene, when James, with Bacon and the Chancellor Egerton, convened the remonstrant sages before them, and read them an angry lecture on their duties, is tolerably graphic and well narrated; but it purposely diminishes the figure of Coke, and it falls into the common error of ascribing the fall of Coke to this incident. The fact is, that Coke was disgraced for the active and energetic part which he took as regards the murder of Overbury, and which, for some reason at present unknown, but possibly not very difficult to guess, excited the king's indignation and terror.

We come next to the case of Somerset, in reference to which Mr. Dixon enlarges upon the "gentleness and mercy" of Bacon, in opening the charge for the prosecution, and on his kindliness and humanity in advising the pardon of Sir Thomas Monson. We accept these facts in Bacon's favor; but why did Mr. Dixon suppress the real circumstances of this terrible case, which perhaps disclose a different motive than that of humanity for Bacon's conduct, and certainly prove him guilty of abetting the checking inquiry in a great prosecution? It is quite evident from Bacon's letters that he knew that Somerset was privy to some secret which touched the honor of the king to the quick; that the secret had some reference to the circumstances bearing on Overbury's murder; and that he preferred, at his master's instance, to stay a thorough and searching investigation, to running the risk of some fearful disclosure. Else, what is the meaning of phrases like these: . . . "Your majesty will be careful to choose a steward of judgment, that may be able to *moderate* the evidence, and *cut off digressions*, for I may interrupt, but cannot *silence*." . . . "If my Lord of Somerset should break forth into any speech of *taxing* the king, be he not to be *presently* by the Lord Steward interrupted and *silenced?*" Couple these allusions with the fact that Somerset openly boasted that the king would not *dare* to bring him to trial: that James privately reviewed the evidence, and ordered Bacon to omit part of it; that the "restless motions" of the king in reference to the conduct of the cause was commented on by several observers; and that, most probably, the very "digressions" which Bacon was so eager to suppress would have given some clue to the dreadful crime; and we hardly can doubt that Bacon knew that Somerset's trial was delicate ground on which it behoved him to tread with care, and from which it was absolutely necessary to exclude the searching light of thorough investigation. This possibly might account for the lenity of his tone and behavior at Somerset's trial; and as for the case of Sir Thomas Monson, it is singular, too, that the mercy of Bacon concurred exactly with that of James, who insisted on stopping the trial of Monson for some reason we do not know, and never forgave the vehemence of Coke, who struggled to press the business forward. We do not affirm that these various facts disprove the lenity and mercifulness of Bacon as a prosecuting counsel for the Crown; but, unquestionably, they weaken the proof on the subject; and they plainly convict him of wrong connivance, if not of very criminal complicity. It is clear why Mr. Dixon omitted them when dealing with the cases of Monson and Somerset.

We now come to the important question, Was Bacon guilty of judicial corruption? Our charges against him are twofold: that although he well knew the impropriety of third persons interfering for suitors, he permitted the king and Buckingham to do so, not once or twice, but in common practice; and that, while he insisted on the necessity of "keeping the hands of judges pure," his own were certainly soiled with corruption. As regards the first charge, in itself a grave one, it is proved conclusively by Bacon's correspondence; and as Mr. Dixon does not refer to it, he has allowed judgment to pass against his client. As for the second, and more important charge, Mr. Dixon claims a triumphant acquittal; and although we cannot concur in this, and our general impression remains unchanged, we gladly admit that he has weakened the proofs against Bacon's judicial integrity. This, indeed, we think the best part of this book; it displays learning and acuteness; brings out several new facts which hitherto had not attracted notice; and relieves Bacon from the imputation of being a gross and wholesale seller of justice to the highest bidder, a character not unfrequently given him. Beyond this, however, it is not successful; and when Mr. Dixon asserts that Bacon was a perfect Aristides of justice, we can only smile at the "logic of his ideas."

Mr. Dixon's case on this subject is this: That it was a common practice for suitors at that period to give presents to the judges who decided their causes; that such presents were not in the nature of bribes, but rather in that of perquisites of office, if given after the suit had ended; that those presents only were bribes which were made with ill faith to procure a judgment, and therefore before the cause had been finished; that all the cases of presents to Bacon were either offerings made to him when he really thought that judgment had been pronounced, or were simply debts, or innocent gifts, entirely disconnected from litigation; and, consequently, that the charge against Bacon of taking bribes, and being corrupt, is a wicked libel upon his memory. Mr. Dixon also insists that Bacon was the victim of a determined conspiracy, got up by Buckingham and his agents, in which the king at least participated; that he was mercilessly assailed by vindictive enemies; that the Peers and most of the Commons were in a league to overwhelm the virtuous chancellor; that many of his friends believed in his innocence; that his full, complete, and minute confession was owing partly to the weakness of disease, in part to a credulous trust in James, and in part to a consciousness of judicial errors, though certainly not of a want of integrity; and, accordingly, that the judgment of Parliament, although hitherto unshaken by time, cannot stand the inquiry of the critic. This being reversed, it is easy to assure us that Bacon was not less upright as a judge than he was eminent as a philosopher.

Although plausible and partly sound, this defence, we think on the whole, must give way, and certainly does not protect Bacon from some of the facts which tell against him. It is doubtless true that, in Bacon's age, the system of feeing judges by presents was not obsolete nor very uncommon; and that such presents, when made after judgment, and not extravagant in point of amount, were not considered as bribes. But it is equally certain that honorable men had set their faces against the practice; that Sir Thomas More, nearly a century before, had pointedly shown his disapproval of it, and that a judge of Bacon's own time had expressly marked his sense of its impropriety. It is evident, too, that Bacon must have seen the flimsiness of the distinction between a bribe before and after a decision; and, although he drew the distinction himself, when making memoranda for his defence, it is very remarkable that his friends in Parliament appear to have laid little stress upon it. Nor should we forget that, although the system of post-judicial acceptance of gifts was not regarded in Bacon's time as precisely the same as taking bribes, this appears to have been upon the condition that such presents should be in proportion to the length, the difficulty, and the nature of the cause, and should be neither irregular nor immoderate.

It is evident, then, from these considerations, that even as respects this species of gifts, Bacon was not free entirely from corruption. What he did, if not completely illegal, had been denounced by upright magistrates, by no one more pointedly than by himself, and could not have cheated his own understanding into any misconception whatever. What he did, if at all justifiable in the view that such presents were in the nature of fees, assessed upon a reasonable scale, became grossly improper and wrong when carried on to the lavish extent to which he pushed this suspicious practice. If there are traces that Coke and Egerton accepted small post-judicial offerings, where is the trace, in the case of these magistrates or of any judge within the century, of such enormous presents as those which were swept into the lap of Bacon? It is plain, therefore, even as regards the class of post-judicial offerings, that Bacon was not free from culpability; that to take the most favorable view of his conduct, he exaggerated a very questionable practice until it became an intolerable evil; and that, knowing as he did, that absolute purity was one of the chief requirements in a judge, he enlarged vicious precedents which led directly to judicial corruption. Was the merely delaying the moment of venality "preserving the place of justice hallowed"?

If, however, a partial excuse may be urged for Bacon's conduct in these cases, what can be said as regards the instances in which he broke through his own distinction, and accepted money before giving judgment? Mr. Dixon, of course to maintain his thesis, denies the existence of such instances, or contends for Bacon's ignorance, or forgetfulness, in reference to the time of the acceptance. We join issue with him on this point; and taking Bacon's published confession—prepared evidently with great deliberation, and intended as a defence for posterity—we assert that the cases of Trevor and Wharton, of Egerton and Hansbye, of Montague and Reynell—six out of the twenty-eight charges alleged,—were clear cases of gifts before judgment,—that is, of plain and admitted bribery. We assert further, there is no proof—not even Bacon's *positive* assurance—of real ignorance or forgetfulness in the matter; and, although there is an *attempt* of this kind, we candidly own that it sounds to our ears a thoroughly "*non mi ricordo*" defence.*

* Notwithstanding the length of our comments

We maintain, therefore, that, though the defence ostentatiously urged by Mr. Dixon excuses Bacon in some degree, it leaves unanswered a grave charge of what we may call constructive corruption, and six charges of positive bribery. And what is the value and truth of the circumstances which Mr. Dixon sets round the trial, by means of which he would influence our judgment? Admit that Bacon had many enemies, that Churchill and Keeling were tainted witnesses, that the king and Buckingham threw him over,—do these facts establish his innocence? Could not such excuses be equally pleaded in reference to the case of Hastings, and do they atone for the slaughter of the Rohillas, or for the plunder of Oude and Benares? As for the animus of the Houses against Bacon, we appeal with confidence to the State trials, to show that although a majority in both were certainly very adverse to Bacon, he had still the offer of an impartial hearing, and every possible opportunity of defending himself. It is also true, that a number of persons appear to have clung to him to the last; but really a plea of this description is scarcely worth a moment's consideration. And as for the other assertions of Mr. Dixon, what weight have they, and can they be substantiated? If Bacon were ill, could he not have sought a longer time for answering the charges; and seeing what we see in the State trials, can we doubt that it would have been joyfully granted? Where is the proof that James and Buckingham seduced him into a weak confession, and what motive had James to do so? How can any thing be more idle than the supposition that if Bacon really had a defence he could have been led by any one to forego it? And in fact, as Lord Macaulay observes, the very idea of such a thing would argue a greater baseness in Bacon than his worst enemy ever charged him with. It is impossible to conceive a greater degree of servility than that which could induce an innocent man—and that man Bacon—to abandon his own defence, and allow judgment to go against him then and forever, merely to suit the convenience of his master,—that master being James I.

Besides, even if we partly admit the truth of these purely collateral circumstances, what value have they, when weighed in the scale against Bacon's positive confession: "I ingenuously confess I am guilty of corruption, do renounce all defence, and put myself on your lordships"? If we bear in mind that these memorable words were uttered after full time for deliberation,—that Bacon at first had meditated a defence, and afterwards chose advisedly to withdraw it—that he made a prior confession of the charges which the Peers rejected as too general—and that the confession actually put in bears every trace of minute elaboration—a series of facts omitted by Mr. Dixon—we hold it merely a waste of time to question that Bacon meant what he said, or to search for evidence beyond the confession. Add to this, that not once or twice, but repeatedly, he admits guilt in his subsequent

we quote the words which Bacon employed in these instances, which appear to us as conclusive as possible.

I. "I confess and declare that I received at New Year's tide £100 from Sir John Trevor; and because it came as a New Year's gift I neglected to inquire whether the cause was ended or depending: but since I find that though the cause was then dismissed to a trial at law, *yet the equity was reserved*, so it was in *that kind* pendente lite.

II. "I confess and declare that I did receive of the Lady Wharton, at two several times as I remember, in gold, £200 and 100 pieces; *and this was certainly pendente lite.*"

III. "I do confess and declare, that upon a reference from his majesty of all suits and controversies between Sir Rowland Egerton and Edward Egerton, both parties submitted themselves to my award by recognizances reciprocal in 10,000 marks apiece. Thereupon after divers hearings I made my award with the advice and consent of my Lord Hobart. The award was perfected and published to the parties, which was in February. Then some days after the £300 mentioned in the charge was delivered to me. *Afterwards Mr. Edward Egerton* flew off from the award. *Then* in Midsummer Term following *a suit was begun* in Chancery by Sir Rowland, to have the award *confirmed*; and *upon that suit* was the decree made mentioned in the article."

IV. Hansbye's case. "I confess and declare that there were two decrees, one as I remember for the inheritance, and the other for the goods and chattels, *but all upon one bill:* and some good time after the first decree and *before the second*, the said £500 was delivered unto me by Mr. Toby Mathew: *so as I cannot deny it was in the matter* pendente lite."

V. Montague's case. "I confess and declare there was money given, and, as I remember, to Mr. Bevis Thelwall" (an agent of the chancellor) "to the sum £700 mentioned in the article after the cause was decreed; *but I cannot say it was ended, for there have been many orders since.*"

VI. Reynell's case. "I confess and declare that at my first coming to the Seal, when I was at Whitehall, my servant Hunt delivered me £200 from Sir George Reynell, . . . and this was, as I verily think, before any suit began. *The ring* was received *certainly pendente lite;* and though it were at New Year's tide, *it was too great a value for a New Year's gift.*"

letters; that he never prayed for a reversal of the sentence on the grounds of surprise or error in the judgment, though he often did on the ground of its severity; and that his tone to James and Buckingham, before his pardon had been made out, is that of a man borne down by shame, and sinking under the load of misery, but not that of injured virtue: and we cannot hesitate as to our conclusion. Probability is the rule of life; and, when we have in one side of the scale, the evidence of the party most interested to lead the mind to an opposite conclusion, and yet thoroughly establishing his guilt in a long series of positive proofs, and in the other there only appear a mass of facts, in part irrelevant, and in part only raising a presumption, and a number of vague and dubious conjectures, we are bound not to shut our eyes to the balance.

As regards, therefore, the general charge of abetting a bad and treacherous government, and as regards the particular acts which we have examined in these pages, we cannot say "not guilty" for Bacon. The rule of criticism is that of law, enunciated in his pregnant words—"it were infinite to consider the causes of causes, and their impulsions one of another;" and in judging of the moral aspect of acts we must pronounce on the evidence alone, and not run to remote conjectures. Tried by this test, the conduct of Bacon in several phases of his career cannot escape the censure of history, and must reflect discredit upon him. But in judging his character as a whole—and we gladly do so "with charitable speech," to use the mournful phrase of his will—we may fairly consider several facts, and look into several probabilities which, though not sufficient to cancel wrong, nor justly admissible against proof—may fairly relieve his memory from some obloquy. We have already referred to the deep wisdom, and to the schemes of benevolence and philanthropy, which occasionally marked his public conduct; and these in justice should be set off against his faults, his sins, and his misdeeds. Brought up as he was in the air of prerogative, the son of a Tudor lawyer and judge, and the "young lord keeper" of Queen Elizabeth, we can scarcely appreciate the obligation of obedience which he felt was due to the Crown by its servants, and which led him into that habit of obsequiousness and most of those disgraceful acts which have cast indelible stains upon his character. Living as he did in an age of transition, when our polity was undefined and unsettled, he felt himself not bound down by rules which are now well recognized by statesmen; and although we naturally visit him with blame for not having been as advanced in political morality as we know that he was supreme in speculation, we must bear in mind that the former quality depends as much on courage as on wisdom, and that Bacon certainly was not courageous. Nor should we forget that history gives us the most offensive parts of his character; that while it records his errors and his fall, it is probably silent as to many of his good deeds; and that these should certainly be taken into account if we would see Bacon as he really was. At a distance, as Bishop Berkeley observes, the most magnificent building appears a speck of darkness upon the landscape; and only a close approach reveals the richness and majesty of its proportions. So, let us in charity hope, may have been the life of Francis Bacon could we examine it not from afar and only on its public side, but in all its social and private relations. Mr. Dixon appears to us not to have materially altered the aspect of the case; and certainly the declamatory vehemence and rhetorical artifices which he employs are altogether out of place. We still await with interest the more mature publication of the biographical volumes with which Mr. Spedding has promised to complete his magnificent edition of the works of Bacon: but we do not conceive that any fresh manipulation of historical evidence can change the moral conviction arising from a candid survey of Bacon's life.

From Once a Week.

THE DUNG-BEETLE.

(A NEW TALE, BY HANS CHRISTIAN ANDERSEN.)

Now the Emperor's Horse got shoes of gold—a golden shoe on each foot.

Why was it that he got golden shoes?

He was the handsomest of steeds; he had fine legs, his eyes were wise looking, and he had a mane that hung down like a silken veil over his neck. He had carried his master through the smoke of battle and through showers of bullets; he had heard the balls screech and sing; he had bitten, and pawed, and fought when the enemy pressed on; he had leapt with the Emperor on his back over the horse of the fallen foe; saved his Emperor's crown of red gold; saved his Emperor's life, which was more than red gold, and so the Emperor's horse got shoes of gold—a golden shoe on each foot.

And now the Dung-beetle crept out.

"First the great and then the small," he said; "but it isn't the size that makes the difference," and with that he stretched out his thin legs.

"What do you want?" asked the Smith.

"Gold shoes," answered the Dung-beetle.

"You must have a bee in your bonnet," said the Smith. "Must you have gold shoes, too?"

"Gold shoes!" said the Dung-beetle. "Am not I just as good as yon big beast, who must be groomed, and currycombed, and waited on, who must have food and drink? Don't I belong, too, to the Emperor's stable?"

"But," asked the Smith, "why did the horse get gold shoes? Don't you know that?"

"Know! I know why well enough," said the Dung-beetle. "It was to put a slight upon me. It is an insult—and so now I will e'en go out into the wide world."

"Sneak off with you," said the Smith.

"Rude fellow!" said the Dung-beetle, and so he went out of doors, flew a little bit, and now he was in a sweet little flower-garden, where there was such a smell of roses and lavender.

"Isn't it lovely, here?" said one of the small Ladybirds, which flew about with black spots on the red shield-strong wings. "How sweet every thing smells here, and how charming every thing is!"

"I am used to better things," said the Dung-beetle. "Call this charming! Why there isn't so much as one dung-heap!"

And so he went farther on, under the shade of a tall wallflower; there a Caterpillar crawled up to him

"How lovely the world is!" said the Caterpillar. "The sun is so warm—every thing is so delightful! and when once I fall asleep and die as they call it, I shall wake up and be a Butterfly."

"Any more fancies?" said the Dung-beetle. "Now we fly about as Butterflies—do we? I come from the Emperor's stable, but no one there, not even the Emperor's charger, who, after all, trots on my cast-off gold shoes, has such fancies. Get wings!—fly!—look at me, how I fly," and so the Dung-beetle flew away, saying, "I don't wish to be out of temper, but yet I am out of temper."

So he plumped down on a great grass-plot, and there he lay still awhile and fell asleep.

Heavens! what a downpour of rain fell! The Dung-beetle woke up at the patter, and tried to get under ground, but he couldn't. He rolled over and over, and swam on his belly and on his back; as for flying, it was no good thinking of that: it seemed as though he would never leave the grassplot alive, and so there he lay and lay.

When the shower held up a little, and the Dung-beetle had winked the water out of his eyes, he caught a glimpse of something white. It was linen put out to bleach, and he reached it, and crept under a fold of the wet linen. It was not, truth to say, just the same thing as lying in the warm dung in the stable; but there was nothing better, and so he stayed there a whole day and a whole night, and so long did the rain last. Next morning the Dung-beetle came out; he was so out of humor with the climate.

There on the linen sat two frogs: their clear eyes gleamed for very joy.

"This is blessed weather," said one: "how it freshens one up, and this linen holds the water so beautifully! I feel such a tickling in my hind legs, just as if I were about to swim."

"I'd like to know, now," said the other, "if the Swallow who flies so far about, if he, in all his many travels abroad, has ever found a better climate than ours—such drizzle and such wet! 'Tis for all the world like lying in a damp drain! If one is not glad at this, one can have no love for his own native land."

"Then you have never been in the Emperor's stable?" asked the Dung-beetle. "There it is both warm and balmy. That's what I have been used to, that's my climate; but then one can't take *that* along with one on one's travels. Is there no dung-heap in this garden where people of station like me can turn in and feel themselves at home?"

But the Frogs did not understand him, or did not choose to understand him.

"I never ask a question twice," said the Dung-beetle, after he had asked it three times and got no answer.

So he went on a bit farther, and there lay a potsherd. It ought not to have lain there; but as it lay it gave shelter. Here lived ever so many families of Earwigs. They don't want much house-room, but they must have company. The lady Earwigs are very tender mothers, and so the young ones of each were models of beauty and wisdom.

"Our son has gone and engaged himself," said one mother; "sweet little innocent! his highest aim in life is to be able, one day or other, to creep into a parson's ear. He is such a childish darling. And this engagement will keep him out of bad company. 'Tis such a pleasure to a mother's heart."

"Our son," said another mother, "was at his tricks as soon as ever he crept out of the egg; he is full of fun, and is putting out horns. What an immense joy for a mother, is it not, Mr. Dung-beetle?" for they knew the stranger by the cut of his jib.

"You are both of you quite right," said the Dung-beetle, and so he was asked to step up into the parlor, for so far one could go into the potsherd.

"Now you must see my little Earwigs," said a third and a fourth mother; "they are the dearest children, and so amusing. They are never naughty except when something pains them inside, but that is so common at their age."

And so each mother talked about her little ones, and the little ones talked too, and used the little fork that they have on their tails to pull the Dung-beetle's moustachios.

"Little rogues," said the mothers, bursting with tenderness, "how they make themselves at home with every thing!"

But that bored the Dung-beetle, and so he asked if it were far from thence to the Dung-heap.

"That is far, far out in the world, on the other side of the Drain," said the Earwigs; "so far I hope none of my bairns will ever get, else I should die outright."

"So far, though, I will try to get," said the Dung-beetle; and so off he went without leave-taking, for that is the politest way.

By the drain-side he met some more of his race—all Dung-beetles of that ilk.

"Here we live," they said, "and a jolly life, too. Mayn't we ask you to turn down into the fat soil? You must be tired after your journey."

"So I am," said the Dung-beetle. "I have lain on linen in rainy weather, and washing and cleanliness take it out of me more than any thing else. I have got the rheumatism, too, in one of my wing-joints by standing in a draught under a potsherd. It *is* really refreshing to come at last to one's own people!"

"You come, perhaps, from the dung-heap?" asked the others.

"Higher up," said the Dung-beetle. "I come from the Emperor's stable, where I was born with gold shoes on my feet; I am travelling on secret services, about which you mustn't ask me, for I wont tell you."

And so the Dung-beetle stepped down into the fat slush. There sat three young lady Dung-beetles, and they tittered, for they knew not what to say.

"They are not engaged," said their mother, and so they tittered again, but it was only out of bashfulness.

"I have never seen fairer young ladies than these, even in the Emperor's stable," said the travelling Dung-beetle.

"Don't deceive my daughters! and don't talk to them, unless you really have intentions—ah! I see you have, and so I give you my blessing."

"Hurrah!" shouted all the others, and so the Dung-beetle was betrothed. First betrothed, then bridal, and then—there was not much to look for.

The next day went smoothly by, the day after it was dull work, but when the third day came, it was time to think of getting food for his wife and perhaps for little ones.

"I have let myself be taken by surprise," said the Dung-beetle, "and so I may just as well take them by surprise, too."

And so he did. Gone he was; gone the whole day, gone the whole night—and there his wife sat a widow. The other Dung-beetles said it was an out-and-out vagabond that they had taken into their family, who had gone and left his wife a burden to them.

"Well!" said her mother, "let her go back and sit among the girls, sit as my child; fie upon that dirty wretch who deserted her!"

Meantime, he was on his travels. He had sailed on a cabbage leaf across the drain; towards morning two men came who saw the Dung-beetle, took him up, turned and twisted him about, and they were very learned men, both of them, especially the younger.

"'Allah sees the black dung-beetle in the black rock in the black mountain.' Stands it not so written in the Koran?" he asked, and translated the Dung-beetle's name into Latin, and gave a history of his genus and species. The elder was against taking him home, for he said they had just as good specimens, which the Dung-beetle thought was not politely said, and so he flew away from off his hand and fluttered a good way, for his wings were quite dry. And so he got to the hot-house, into which he could creep with the greatest ease, as one of the frames was open. As soon as he got inside, he buried himself deep down into the fresh dung.

"This *is* nice!" said the Dung-beetle.

Soon he fell into a slumber, and dreamt that the Emperor's horse had fallen and broken his neck, and that the Honorable Mr. Dung-beetle had got his gold shoes, and a promise of two more beside. That was pleasant, and when the Dung-beetle awoke, he crept out and looked about him. What splendor there was in that hot-house! Tall fan-palms spread out their leaves aloft. The sun made them transparent, and under them there were teeming beds of green, among which shone flowers red as fire, yellow as amber, and white as new-fallen snow.

"This is a matchless array of plants; how nice it will all taste when it falls into rottenness!" said the Dung-beetle. "This is a fine store-room. Some of the family live here, no doubt, so I will go out and explore, and see if I can find any one who is fit company for me. Proud I am, I know it; that is just my pride," and so he went about thinking of his dream about the dead horse and the gold shoes won at last.

Then, all at once, a hand caught hold of the Dung-beetle. He was squeezed, and turned, and twisted.

The gardener's little son and a playfellow were in the hot-house, and had seen the Dung-beetle, and were going to have some fun with him. Rolled in a vine-leaf, he went down into a warm trouser-pocket; he scratched and scraped, but he only got a pinch from the boy's hand, who went as fast as he could to the great lake at the end of the garden. There the Dung-beetle was put into an old split wooden shoe, off which the ankle was broken; into it a bit of wood was stuck as a mast, and to the mast our Dung-beetle was tied by a woollen thread. Now he was a skipper, and was to sail on the sea.

It was a very large lake; as for the Dung-beetle, he thought it was the ocean, and he was so scared that he fell on his back, and scrabbled with his legs up in the air.

So the wooden shoe sailed, for there was a current in the water, but when the boat got a little too far out, one of the little boys tucked up his trousers in a trice, and waded out and brought it in; but as it was drifted out again and again, the boys got cold, very cold, and they made haste home and let the wooden shoe be a wooden shoe. Then it drifted and drifted ever further and further from land, and it was fearful work for the Dung-beetle, for he could not fly, he was fast bound to the mast.

Just then a Fly paid him a visit.

"This is fine weather we have," said the Fly, "I can rest myself here—I can sun myself here. You must find it very pleasant here."

"You chatter according to your lights," said the Dung-beetle; "don't you see that I am tethered?"

"Well," said the Fly, "I am not tethered," and so it flew off.

"Now I know the world," said the Dung-beetle. "'Tis a base world. I am the only honest thing in it. First they refuse me gold shoes, next I must lie in wet linen, then stand in a draught, and last of all they fasten a wife on me. If I make a bold step out into the world and see how one can live and how I ought to live, there comes a man's whelp and throws me into bonds on the wild sea. And all this while the Emperor's Horse trots about on his gold shoes. That cuts me most to the heart. But one must not look for sympathy in this world. My adventures in life are very interesting, but what good is that when no one knows them? The world does not deserve to know them, or else it would have given me gold shoes in the Emperor's stable, when the charger was shod, and stretched out his legs. Had I only got these gold shoes, I should have been an honor to the stable, but now it has lost me, and the world has lost me; all is over."

But all was not over yet, for up came a boat with some young girls in it.

"There sails a wooden shoe," said one.

"There is a little insect fast tethered in it," said another.

They were then just alongside of the wooden shoe; they picked it up, and one of the girls took out a tiny pair of scissors, cut the thread of wool in two without hurting the Dung-beetle, and when they came to land, she laid him down in the grass.

"Creep, creep! fly, fly, if you can," she said. "Freedom is a lovely thing!"

And the Dung-beetle flew straight into the open window of a great building, and there he sunk wearily down into the long, soft, fine mane of the Emperor's Horse which stood there in the stable which had been the Dung-beetle's home. He caught fast hold of the mane, and sat awhile humming to himself, "Here I sit on the Emperor's charger! Sit as a knight! What do I say? Ah! now it is all clear. It is a good thought, and a true thought. Why did the horse get gold shoes? That was the very question that Smith asked me. Now I see it all! 'Twas for my sake that the Horse got his gold shoes.

And so the Dung-beetle got into a good-humor.

"Nothing like travel for clearing the brain," he said.

The sun shone in upon him, shone very brightly.

"The world is not so bad, after all," said the Dung-beetle. "We must only know how to take it."

So the world was lovely, for the Emperor's Horse only got his gold shoes because the Dung-beetle was to be his rider.

"Now," he said, "I will step down to the other beetles, and tell them how much has been done for me. I will tell them of all the pleasant things which befell me in my foreign travels; and I will add, that now I mean to stay at home till the Horse has worn out his gold shoes." G. W. D.

SECRET SOCIETIES IN IRELAND.—The following are some, and the dates attached:—

Hearts of Oak	1763
Hearts of Steel	1773
Whiteboys	1775?
Terry-alts	1830
Peep-o'day Boys	——
Ribbonmen	——

I shall feel obliged for the dates of the two last named, as well as any addition to the list. —*Notes and Queries.*

WE have been requested to publish the following correspondence. Whatever may have been our views heretofore upon the subject of allegiance, the altered condition of affairs—a revolution having been accomplished, and Virginia, by her own sovereign act having declared that she is no longer an integral part of the late United States, it becomes every citizen, native and naturalized, to acknowledge allegiance to Virginia alone. Self-preservation and the best interests of the State, require that there shall be no division of sentiment amongst us now on this important subject. We subjoin the correspondence.

"NELSON CO., VA., NEAR ALLEN'S CREEK P.O. "April 18, 1861.

"*J. R. Tucker, Attorney General of the State.*

"DEAR SIR,—There are a large number of Irishmen at work in this neighborhood, who wish to know your opinion, as regards their duty to the State of Virginia, when out of the Union —they having taken their oath to support the Constitution of the United States. Does the secession of the State absolve them from their oath? An early reply will much oblige your obedient servant, B. C. MEGGINSON."

"April 22, 1861.

"The oath to support the Constitution of the United States is duly binding so long as a man is a citizen of a State of the Union. When she secedes, he is no longer bound. He is a citizen of Virginia, which has ceased to be one of the United States, and his allegiance is due to Virginia.

"This is my well-settled opinion, and I act upon it. For I am sworn as an officer to support the Constitution of the United States. But when Virginia secedes I feel I am entirely absolved from my oath, and am bound only to support Virginia. J. R. TUCKER." —*Lynchburg Virginian.*

THE FLEUR-DE-LYS FORBIDDEN IN FRANCE. —The following has appeared in most of the newspapers during the past month. It is a curious illustration of the manners of the times in which we live. Please preserve it in "N. and Q.," as an item, valuable alike to the historian of art, and the chronicler of human error:—

"By a decision of the Paris Court of Cassation, jewellers and all manufacturers of fancy articles are fully informed that it is unlawful in France, in virtue of a Napoleonic decree, in 1852, against factious or treasonable emblems, banners, etc., to introduce the *fleur-de-lys* on any jewel, bracelet, cabinet-work, tapestry, or upholstery, and, accordingly, the tribunal at Riom, which, on the 28th November last year, gave a more lenient interpretation to the law was wrong, and is rebuked."—*Notes and Queries.*

OATHS.—In the papers of the 19th ult., reference is made to a lady appearing before one of the magistrates, and when requested to take the oath refusing to do so unless it was administered to her as a Presbyterian; and of a gentleman waiting upon the magistrate, and saying he would find the Act of Parliament. Is there such an act or such a form, or is the oath which is administered in Scotland to a Covenanter the oath alluded to? Where is the form of the latter, and under what Act of Parliament is it administered? Where is an account of the oaths as at present allowed to be administered to be found? S. O.

[It is not by Statute that a Presbyterian can swear in his own form of oath. But there have been decisions to the effect that any person objecting to a mere form of oath, and declaring himself to be bound by a particular form, may be received as a witness, and the penalty of perjury would follow on an oath so taken.—Manning *v.* Clement. For Forms of Oaths formerly administered, see *The Book of Oaths, and the Several Forms thereof, both Ancient and Modern*, 8vo. 1689. We are not aware where the oaths at present in force will be found recorded.]—*Notes and Queries.*

"CRY HAVOC, AND LET LOOSE THE DOGS OF WAR!"

They are straining in the slips—
  You may feel their sulph'rous breath,
As it steams from throats and lips
  That parch and pant for death.
You may hear their muffled bay,
  As against the leash they hang,
And churn and toss away,
  The foam about the fang,
They need no voice to tarre *
Them on, these dogs of war!

Again — again — again — !
  Is it a single sound,
By echo's doubling strain,
  Repeated all around?
Has East as well as West,
  Has North as well as South,
Its own erected crest,
  Hoarse throat and fangèd mouth?
I see them, near and far,
Those threatening dogs of war!

Where Po runs, brimming over
  His green and grassy mound,
Fierce bursting from his cover,
  See Italy's young hound —
Spite of tethers that impede,
  And hands that would restrain,
He has proved his fighting breed,
  And would prove his breed again,
And who has strength to bar
Italy's dogs of war?

In front, pent, fierce and foul,
  Behind their walls of stone,
The Austrian ban-dogs growl,
  Late baffled of their bone.
Licking their yet green wounds,
  Nursing old grudges warm,
The gaunt and grisly hounds,
  Hot for the quarry, swarm —
And hungry dogs they are,
Those Austrian dogs of war!

But ware your rearward foes,
  Where on the Theiss' plain
In spite of recent blows,
  And unforgotten pain,
The Magyar dogs are trooping,
  Defying slip and scourge:
Teeth set and sterns undrooping,
  Pesthward like waves they surge,
Nor least fierce the Magyar
'Mong Europe's dogs of war.

Neath Savoy's snowy Alp,
  On the pleasant banks of Rhone,
Hark! the French dogs they yelp!
  Well Europe knows the tone!
Friends for the moment's friend,
  Foes for the moment's foe —
So there's battle at its end,
  What odds the road they go?
With a ribbon and a star
You lead French dogs of war.

And see the sick man lying
  Almost in moral swound;
The bed where he is dying
  With his own pack girt round —
The Pariah dogs of Bosnia,
  The Rouman wolf-dogs grim,
Mouth their master ere he's dead,
  And claim, each hound, his limb.
Carrion to rend and mar
Befits such dogs of war.

And the Danish dogs are baring
  Their tushes sharp though small,
While the German mastiff's swearing
  To eat them, bones and all:
E'en the ill-used Polish turnspit
  That so long the buffets bore
Of the giant Russian bear-hound,
  Has shown its teeth once more —
As if Sirius his star
Had fired all dogs of war!

Ringed in with gathering growls,
  Fierce fangs on every hand,
'Mid defiant snarls and scowls,
  See Britain's bull-dog stand.
Not couchant, as the wont
  Is of the placid brute;
But legs set firm in front,
  With muzzle drenched and mute.
Ware all — who tempt too far
That peaceful dog of war! —*Punch.*

* *Tarre*: to set on dogs.—Shakspeare.

SHADE.

To-night, untasted be the cup,
  My lips refuse the wooing wine,
Whose restless spirits bubble up,
  Like laughter of its native Rhine.
I would not have young Bacchus tread,
  With jocund feet and noisy glee,
Where pensive memory rests her head,
  Nor wake her from the reverie,
That roams the past with murmuring low,
And twines sere florets round her brow.

Sing me no lightly-worded song,
  But tell me how, heart-sick and lone,
Some love-lorn maiden tarried long
  In some old castle, lichen-grown,
To hear the massy drawbridge clank,
  And mailed retainers outward roll,
Until her heart's forebodings sank
  Like rust into her weary soul —
While *he*, the theme of knightly story,
Lay couched in the ghostly arms of glory.

Or, better, wake a sterner note,
  How, on his own resources cast,
Some mental gladiator smote
  With earnest hand, and won at last
A victory from the world. I would
  Not feed my thoughts with trifling wiles,
For grief demands more solid food
  Than airy pleasure's simpering smiles,
To force the palsied heart through pain
And fill its veins with life again.

—*Once a Week*

From The Quarterly Review.

1. *Travels and Discoveries in North and Central Africa in the years* 1849–55. By Henry Barth, Ph.D., D.C.L., etc. London, 1857.
2. *Travels, Researches, and Missionary Labors during an Eighteen Years' Residence in Eastern Africa.* By the Rev. Dr. J. Lewis Krapf. London, 1860.
3. *The Lake Regions of Central Africa.* By Richard F. Burton, H. M. I. Army. London, 1860.
4. *Narrative of an Exploring Voyage up the Rivers Kwora and Binue (commonly known as the Niger or Tsadda) in* 1854. By William Balfour Baikie, M.D., R.N., F.R.S., in command of the Expedition. London, 1856.
5. *Narrative of the Niger, Tsadda, and Binue Exploration, including a Report on the Position and Prospects of Trade in those Rivers.* By T. J. Hutchinson, Esq., H. B. M., Consul for the Bight of Biafra. London, 1855.
6. *Sketches of the African Kingdoms and Peoples.* Society for Promoting Christian Knowledge. London, 1860.
7. *The Negro Land of the Arabs Examined and Explained.* By William Desborough Cooley. London, 1841.
8. *Inner Africa Laid Open.* By W. D. Cooley. London, 1852.
9. *Journal of the Royal Geographical Society*, vol. xxx. London, 1861.
10. *Missionary Travels in South-Eastern Africa.* By the Rev. David Livingstone, LL.D. London, 1859.
11. *Egypt, the Soudan and Central Africa, with Explorations from Khartoum on the White Nile to the Regions of the Equator.* By John Petherick, F.R.G.S., H. B. M. Consul for the Soudan. Edinburgh and London, 1861.
12. *Exploration and Adventure in Equatorial Africa.* By M. Du Chaillu. London, 1861.

Africa may, in one sense, be defined as a continent of the future. At least seven-eighths of the enormous area of one of the largest divisions of the globe have yet to acquire even the rudiments of true civilization. Although forming so considerable a portion of the earth, Africa has been almost entirely neglected by the nations of modern Europe since the discovery of America. They directed their attention and their enterprise almost exclusively towards the new regions which were so unexpectedly revealed. The tide of colonization long flowed in an uninterrupted stream to the West, where the hope of easy conquests and the expectation of boundless wealth attracted the most ambitious and energetic spirits of the age. If Columbus could have foreseen the effect which his great discoveries would have upon a large portion of the human race, the piety and humanity of the great navigator would certainly have recoiled from the spectacle. It is a melancholy reflection that one of the continents of the Old World should owe by far the greater portion of its sufferings to the discovery of the New. The conquerors and colonists of America, having used up an immense proportion of the population in compulsory toil, turned to the opposite continent for the supply of their industrial wants. The robust natives of Africa were found to be specially fitted for labor in hot countries, and the petty sovereigns of the coast were soon instructed in the art of replenishing their treasuries by the sale of their subjects, who were exported by hundreds of thousands to the remote and unknown regions of the West. Thus one-quarter of the earth has been left a prey to rapacity and violence disgraceful to humanity.

It was not before the close of the last century that any general interest was felt in the condition of Africa. No one supposed that it was endowed with resources little if at all inferior to those of the other continents, or that there existed within the intertropical zone a very dense population, with capacities altogether inconsistent with a theory that dooms them to a state of perpetual barbarism, or of essential inferiority to the rest of the great family of man. Shut out from almost all the influences of ancient civilization, its people have multiplied from age to age in a land which brings forth in prodigious abundance almost every thing that uncivilized man can desire. The clay hut, the slight raiment, coarse but ample food, rude music and the festive dance have, generation after generation, supplied their simple wants and filled up the measure of their enjoyment.

The only civilization which has penetrated to any extent the interior of the African continent, and left its stamp upon the indigenous races, was introduced by the Arabs. They are the only people who now possess, amidst the political and moral wilderness of intertropical Africa, any tolerable form of civil polity or bond of social organization. The origin of the intercourse between Arabia and Africa is lost in its remoteness, but a commerce between the two countries was carried on from the earliest ages. The conquest of Africa by the Arabs was first attempted by the Caliph Othman, in the year 647 of the Christian era. At the head of forty thousand Moslems, he advanced from Egypt into the unknown regions of the West; and a few years subsequently the Sultan Akbar marched from Damascus, at the head of ten thousand picked troops, and taking into his pay many thousand native Africans, just as England organized and armed the natives of India for its conquests in that country, swept every obstacle before him until his course was arrested by the Atlantic Ocean.* The Arabs speedily advanced by the aid of the camel across the sandy desert towards the centre of the continent, and along the two coasts, as far as the Senegal and the Gambia on the west, and Sofala on the east. From the latter place they not only explored the interior far beyond the limits of ancient discovery, but planted colonies at Mombas, Melinda, and Mozambique. They have since spread over almost every known part of Africa north of the equator, from the shores of the Red Sea to the Atlantic, mingled their blood with negro races, engrafted Mohammedan learning and ingenuity on the ignorance and simplicity of the native tribes, and introduced an Oriental splendor which gives to their governments at least the outward aspect of civilization.

To what extent the letters of Asia have penetrated into Africa it would be difficult to form an opinion, but that the Arab colonists brought with them from time to time many of the treasures of ancient learning there is every reason to believe. A recent traveller in the interior found in many of the Arab chiefs a considerable amount of literary cultivation, and an intellectual activity which invited discussion on some of the most important subjects of human inquiry. The disposition of the Arab chiefs towards England is generally most satisfactory. They are proud of being the objects of occasional diplomatic visits, and receive the compliments and presents with which the envoys are charged with undisguised satisfaction. The sultan of Sakotu in 1823 sent a body of horse, preceded by drums and trumpets, to escort Captain Clapperton into his capital. Dr. Barth owed his life to the protection of a noble sheikh, who risked every thing dear to him to protect his guest from the hostile designs of a fanatical party in Timbuctoo; and the sultan of Zanzibar has cordially assisted every exploring expedition which has started for the interior from the eastern coast.

When the Portuguese commenced their colonization of Mozambique they found the Arabs in possession of almost the whole of the coast. They dispossessed them of their settlements, converted the mosques into churches, broke up their trading establishments, and entered upon a war of extermination. Many Arab chiefs fled into the interior, beyond the reach of their oppressors, and easily induced multitudes of the indolent and voluptuous natives to embrace the faith of the Prophet. The Mohammedan Arabs settled in Eastern Africa chiefly in the character of traders, and the wealth of the prosperous merchants was lavishly displayed. The city of Melinda was long the pride of Eastern Africa: its gardens were celebrated for their delicious fruits, fountains, and groves, and its inhabitants arrayed themselves in silk and purple.

The rule of the Mohammedan Arabs has given to portions of Africa a certain unity, and imparted a degree of civilization. Some of their political institutions have been found not ill adapted to barbarous races, and their governments may be favorably contrasted with the negro monarchies which have been erected on the western coasts, in regions to which Arab influence has not extended. Egypt, and probably the coast of Africa bordering on the Indian Ocean, was better known to the Eastern nations of antiquity than any portion of Europe. The Carthaginians were, doubtless, well acquainted with the countries south of the Great Desert, for the elephant, which was in extensive use, must have been brought from the regions of Central Africa, as it is not known to have ever been an inhabitant of the Atlas region. When the Romans became masters of Northern Africa, they formed settlements to the south; and many beautiful monuments in the interior of Tripoli, of different periods of art, prove that the dominion of Rome in

* Gibbon, vol. ix., p. 463.

that district of Africa could not have been either of very limited extent or of short duration. The Romans are believed to have established their dominion as far south as Garana or Jerna; but there is in Pliny a distinct account of Suetonius Paulinus (A.D. 41) crossing the great mountains of the Atlas, and even proceeding some distance beyond them; and Ptolemy states that a Roman officer, who started from the neighborhood of Tripoli, went a four months' journey in a southern direction. This route probably brought him into the latitude of Timbuctoo and into the neighborhood of Lake Tchad. No detailed record, however, exists of any important exploration of the interior of Africa during the period of Roman dominion.

More has been accomplished in the last sixty years to make us acquainted with the geography and social condition of the interior of Africa, than during the whole period which has elapsed since the days of Ptolemy. The modern era of exploration may be said to have commenced when Park undertook his remarkable expedition. The celebrated travels of Denham and Clapperton excited a European interest. They added largely to our geographical knowledge, and made us acquainted with many interesting facts connected with the state of society in Africa. In 1823 Clapperton reached Lake Tchad, and the surrounding countries were explored as far as Sakatu on the west, and Mandara on the south. Major Laing reached Timbuctoo, but was murdered in the desert on his return. Lander descended the Niger from Yaouri to its mouth, and the result of that important event was the great Niger expedition of 1841, which terminated in a disastrous loss of life, and discouraged for a time any further exploration in that direction. The eastern and southern districts of Africa have been visited by numerous travellers. Many modern attempts have been made to discover the sources of the Nile, by expeditions originated or sanctioned by the pasha of Egypt. The territory in the vicinity of Abyssinia has been the seat of a Christian mission which has enlarged our knowledge of a very interesting country; but all that had been previously attempted or accomplished on behalf of scientific geography and African civilization sinks into insignificance when compared with the great discoveries of the last ten years. The penetration of Dr. Barth into the interior of the continent; the discovery, and successful navigation, of the upper course of the Niger; the travels of Dr. Livingstone in South-eastern Africa; the ascertained existence of great inland seas at, or in close proximity to, the equator; the steps which are being made towards a solution of the great geographical problem of the source of the Nile, and the recent remarkable discoveries of M. Du Chaillu in the west, indicate that Africa has at length obtained the serious attention of Europe.

The physical conformation of the African continent is in many respects remarkable. In one of his annual Presidential Addresses to the Royal Geographical Society, Sir Roderick Murchison predicted that the interior of Africa would in all probability be found to be a watery plateau of less elevation than the flanking hill ranges. He suggested that violent igneous action, extending along both sides of the continent, tilted up the lateral rocks, and that the energy and extended range of volcanic disturbance at remote periods have imparted to Africa its present very simple littoral configuration. Addressing Major Burton previously to his journey of exploration, Sir R. Murchison detailed his special reasons for believing the centre of Africa to be a vast region of lakes of some, but not considerable, elevation above the sea. The theory was based on a discovery, then recently made, in the Cape Colony, of fossil remains in a lacustrine deposit of the secondary age, and the well-known existence on the coast of lofty mountains of the primary period circling round the younger deposits. Sir. R. Murchison therefore inferred that a network of lakes would be found prolonged northwards from Lake Ngami towards the interior. But, carrying his induction still farther, he intimated that he saw no possibility of explaining how the great rivers could escape from the central plateau-lands and enter the ocean, except through deep gorges formed at some ancient period of elevation when the lateral chains were subjected to transverse fractures. This hypothesis, which was suggested in the Presidential Address for 1852, became known to Dr. Livingstone while he was in the act of exploring those very "transverse gorges" by which the river Zambezi escapes to the east and discharges itself into the Indian Ocean. The present century has thus witnessed two great triumphs of scientific induction by the same eminent philosopher: the prediction of the discovery of gold in Australia by rigid *à priori* reasoning, and an anticipation of the great lake discoveries in the interior of Africa by the application of geological science.

We proceed to notice the most important of the recent expeditions which have been undertaken for the exploration of Africa, to describe briefly the districts which they have succeeded in penetrating, and to enumerate the geographical, social, and political results of modern enterprise in that quarter of the globe.

The expedition of Mr. Richardson, with whom were associated Dr. Barth and Mr. Overweg, was organized for the purpose of concluding commercial treaties with the chiefs of Northern Africa, inhabiting the country extending from the frontier of Tripoli to Lake Tchad. These gentlemen left Tripoli in March, 1850, but, his two coadjutors having fallen sacrifices to the climate, the duties of the mission ultimately devolved on Dr. Barth, and he prosecuted his travels alone. Taking his departure from Tripoli, he traversed a country dotted for a distance of one hundred and fifty miles with many splendid Roman remains, and passing through the country of the Tawàrek, or organized plunderers of the desert, he extended his travels to the very borders of the Central African nations, three hundred and fifty miles to the south of any point previously reached by a European explorer. Denham and Clapperton reached the city of Kuka, the capital of the kingdom of Bornu, and discovered Lake Tchad—an event which created at the time a great sensation in England, but the importance of which has been much diminished by the discovery of the large inland seas lying to the south and east of Clapperton's explorations. Dr. Barth proceeded to Yola, in the Adámawa country, situate in about 8° N. lat. He describes the district as the finest he had seen in Central Africa, abounding in rich pastures, in valleys of very fertile land, and in mountains clothed to their summits with noble trees. It was his intention to have extended his researches as far as the equator, but the difficulties proved insurmountable, and he was obliged to return to Kuka, the seat of a comparatively stable government. The towns and cities of this portion of Africa are walled and respectably built; the markets are numerously attended, and a considerable trade is carried on. He found commerce radiating in every direction from Kano, the great emporium of Central Africa, and spreading the manufactures and the productions of an industrious region over the whole of Western Africa. The fixed population of this city he estimated at thirty thousand; but on the occasions of the great fairs, at sixty thousand; and he is of opinion that this capital will at some future day be one of considerable importance to the commercial interests of Europe. At present very little English merchandise finds its way to the great emporium of Negroland, British calico and muslin being almost the only articles displayed in the bazaars. The state of the contiguous countries is described as wretched in the extreme—all the petty governors and sultans habitually making predatory excursions for slaves, and even selling their own subjects for the liquidation of their debts.

The remarkable lake, the Tchad, Dr. Barth describes as an immense lagoon, enlarging or contracting its dimensions according to the amount of rain or evaporation: it was at the season of his visit only sixty miles in extent from east to west, although Clapperton has estimated it at one hundred and twenty miles. Its average depth was found to be from ten to fifteen feet. An eminent geographer has stated his opinion that the African lakes are, in more instances than one, merely the expansion of large rivers running through a level country during the period of the tropical rains.* This is doubtless the case with the Tchad. It was navigated by Overweg in a boat brought over the desert in pieces on the backs of camels. He passed seven weeks on its waters, displaying the British flag to the people on its banks, and startling the hippopotami from their haunts among the gigantic reeds. The population of the numerous islands he found considerable and comparatively prosperous in consequence of their being inaccessible to the slave-hunters, who are the curse of Central Africa.

Denham did not proceed beyond Logon in

* Mr. Macqueen. Journal Royal Geographical Society, vol. xx., p. 119.

the Bornu country; Dr. Barth entered the Bagirmi kingdom to the east, and reached its capital, intending to extend his travels in that direction and to penetrate to the region of the Nile. This having proved impracticable, he turned his steps to the south-west, and made what he considers the most important geographical discovery of the age; namely, the eastern branch of the Niger, eight hundred yards wide and eleven feet deep, at Tepi. The stream which Dr. Barth reached is the Benuwé, by which, if an uninterrupted navigation should be established between it and the lower Niger, a route will be opened by water into the very centre of Africa. At the spot where Dr. Barth discovered the Benuwé, another considerable river, the Faro, enters it with a strong current. The whole of the district traversed by Dr. Barth in this direction he found to be of extraordinary fertility, producing cotton, indigo, and sugar, and supplying ivory, rhinoceros' horns, wax, and hides, in the greatest abundance. It is satisfactory to find that in all the countries visited by Dr. Barth the desire for increased communication with Europe was strongly and unanimously expressed.

It is remarked by Mr. Cooley in his learned work, "Inner Africa Laid Open," that the popular belief of the great river of Negroland, the Niger, uniting with the Nile is of very ancient date, and may be traced back to the time of Herodotus. It is stated with more or less distinctness by all the Arab geographers, and they generally likewise asserted the connection of the Quorra or Niger with Lake Tchad. The geographical knowledge of Central Africa, even of those living on its confines, must have been very limited, since this delusion was only dispelled by the researches of a European traveller. The Tchad has no outlet; and the Quorra or Niger undoubtedly rises in a mountainous region, at no very great distance from the part of the river's course discovered by Dr. Barth; and it is fed by the same tropical rains, and subject to the same inundations, as many of the other rivers of Africa. The expectations of Dr. Barth have been completely realised by the voyage of the "Pleiad," undertaken by the direction of the British Government. The Tshadda and Benuwé have been ascertained to be the eastern branches of the great Niger, which pours its waters into the Atlantic through numerous mouths. The Nun channel being the most central, has been proved, by recent exploration, to be the best adapted for communication with the interior. To the town of Dolti, on the Benuwé, the distance is four hundred and forty-seven geographical miles from the sea; and the river up to that place has been found to offer no impediments to navigation. Want of fuel alone prevented the steamer from proceeding beyond; but with the rising waters, or a full flood, the river is believed to be navigable for vessels of considerable burden to a much higher point.

The Niger has acquired a bad notoriety in consequence of the lamentable loss of life resulting from several attempts to ascend it. The rank vegetation which clothes its banks, and the periodical subsidence of its waters, were found to generate miasma fatal to the European constitution. The mortality among the settlers on the model experimental farm established by the government on the left bank of the river has not unnaturally suspended the prosecution of similar enterprises. The successful result of the voyage of the "Pleiad," and the almost total immunity from fever enjoyed by her crew in consequence of some very simple hygienic precautions, have however been the means of again directing attention to this important region of Africa, from which the interior can be so easily reached. The river, it has been ascertained, if entered with the rising waters, is comparatively healthy. There are in the basin of the Niger immense tracts of rich and virgin soil and numberless localities well adapted for the formation of model cotton farms. Two facts strongly impressed themselves on Mr. Hutchinson's mind during his residence in Western Africa: one, that the negro race have a perfect knowledge and appreciation of the immense industrial resources of their country; the other, an apparent readiness to take advantage of them, together with an aptitude for imitation and a desire for instruction that are most hopeful indications of future progress. These favorable features were most conspicuous all along the banks of the Niger, the Tshadda, and the Benuwé,—a country that seemed to him fresh, as it were, from the hands of God, and only waiting the energies of man to bring to perfection the numerous products of its prolific soil.

There is an atmospheric phenomenon common to all the rivers of this coast that must exercise a very salutary influence. The trade-winds blow up the streams, and this is especially the case with the Niger while it is in flood. "For ten months in the year," says Mr. Macqueen, "but particularly from May till November, the prevailing wind in the Bights of Benin and Biafra is from the south-west, thus blowing right up all the outlets of the Niger." * This was fully confirmed during the passage of the "Pleiad." In the upper parts of the river, Mr. Hutchinson says, a "glorious breeze prevailed, and made the atmosphere cool and agreeable, and the vessel often had a breeze that would have been more than sufficient, had she possessed her canvas, to stem the current; and so strong was it when she was drifting down the stream that it offered quite an obstacle to her progress, and made her rock as though she were on the ocean." The northern branch of the Niger, flowing from Timbuctoo, has been successfully navigated to a distance of twenty miles above Rabba, or rather more than three hundred miles from the sea, where the river is broken into rocky and intricate channels. A few miles beyond Rabba is a waterfall, which presents an impassable barrier even to canoes at any season. Captain Bancroft, in 1845, successfully navigated one of the channels; but in 1857 the "Pleiad," in attempting the same passage, was lost on the rocks. Two important consequences may be said to have followed from the Niger expeditions, calamitous as some of them have been justly regarded: they have impressed both upon the population and rulers residing on the banks of this great river a knowledge not only of the commercial character of England, but of her thorough detestation of slavery in all its forms, and of her resolution to use every effort in her power to put an end to it.

The natural outlet for the commerce of Kano, and the immense district of which it is the emporium, is this eastern branch of the Niger, which it is to be hoped will, at no distant day, be opened throughout the whole of its course. In the mean time we are assured by Dr. Barth that the only commercial use which has been made of his important discovery is by American slave-dealers, who have opened a trade in those regions.

That Dr. Barth's mission to Central Africa has produced an excellent effect we have the assurance of a later explorer. In a recent expedition into the Niger country Mr. May found the population animated with the best feeling towards England, and when endeavoring to impress the natives with a sense of the efforts which the British Government were making to open a trade with their country, his remarks were always received with approbation, and a firm belief was expressed that the "white man had only to will it to do it." *

In reference to this portion of Africa we have to notice the discoveries of M. Du Chaillu, an American gentlemen of French descent, who was commissioned by the Academy of Philadelphia to proceed to the equatorial regions of Western Africa. The narrative of this gentleman, who but recently presented himself before the British public, has created an extraordinary sensation, and his work cannot fail in obtaining for its author a wide reputation. The importance of his discoveries is only equalled by their singular interest. M. Du Chaillu, after having prepared himself by acquiring the languages of the tribes among which he determined to reside, boldly pushed into the interior from the neighborhood of the Gaboon River. His first discovery was a range of mountains rising in a series of terraces to the height of six thousand feet, a spur from which approaching the coast was named by the Portuguese the Crystal Mountains. This range M. Du Chaillu found covered with dense and nearly impenetrable forests. It is now clearly established by this and the other discoveries of M. Du Chaillu that a great mountain chain, rising occasionally into eminences twelve thousand feet high, runs due east and west along the equator, and probably extends completely across the continent.

It has often been a subject of surprise that the Arab adventurers, having pushed their conquests so far to the south as they did, should not have proceeded farther and crossed the equator. The great mountain

* Macqueen's Geographical Survey of Africa.

* Mr. May's Journey in the Yòruba and Nùpe Countries in 1858. Journal Royal Geographical Society, 1860.

chain which M. Du Chaillu has discovered supplies the explanation. This region is almost devoid of animal life, and, consisting of thick jungle and of rugged steeps incapable of cultivation, and inhabited only by savage apes and a few human beings almost equally savage, has presented an invincible barrier to the farther progress of the Mohammedan tribes. In these mountains are the sources of the Muni, the Moondah, the Gaboon, the Nazareth, and probably the Congo and other rivers which empty themselves into the Atlantic. Some of these streams will doubtless be found adapted for commerce when more fully explored. In a commercial sense the most important discovery made by M. Du Chaillu is that of the great river, the Agobay, which he ascended to a distance of three hundred and fifty miles from the coast. It was there a noble stream five hundred yards wide, from three to four fathoms deep, and running with considerable force. If, as Dr. Barth is said to expect, this great river should prove to be the lower portion of one which he was informed ran westward, many days' journey south of Wadai, another immense stream will have been discovered connecting the central regions of Africa with the sea, and entering it at a spot from whence they can be most easily reached. The Agobay is certainly one of the most important rivers in Western Africa, and is formed in the interior of the country by two large rivers, the Rembo Ngourjai and Rembo Okanda. Until M. Du Chaillu traversed these regions the river Nazareth and its delta, the Mexias, and the Fernand Vaz, were thought to be three distinct rivers, rising in the mountain chain to the north, but he found that they communicated with each other. The Nazareth and the Mexias are formed by the Agobay, the latter river throwing the remainder of the water into the Fernand Vaz a few miles above its mouth. This river, although chiefly fed by the Agobay, is remarkable for following for forty miles the direction of the seashore, from which it is separated by a low, sandy prairie, six miles broad. The amount of fresh water poured into the sea by these rivers is enormous, but the navigation of the numerous channels is very intricate, and the Fernand Vaz communicating with the Agobay, is the only one that can be said to have a navigable channel.

Ascending the Npoulounay, a branch of the Agobay, M. Du Chaillu reached a fine lake, the Anengue—a sheet of water ten miles wide, dotted with wooded islands, and with water deep enough in every part for steamers of moderate draught. The whole country about this lake is covered with India-rubber vine and fine ebony trees, and is able to supply the best caoutchouc, an article of yearly increasing commercial value, in the greatest abundance. On a second visit, in the dry season, he still found the Npoulounay quite practicable for a steamer of light draught, but the lake was somewhat changed in appearance. Its surface was dotted with islands of black mud, on the slimy slopes of which crocodiles swarmed in incredible numbers: M. Du Chaillu says he never saw so horrible a spectacle. Many of the reptiles were twenty feet long, and, opening their monstrous jaws, seemed ready to swallow the canoes and their occupants without an effort.

The tribes which M. Du Chaillu visited are the most remarkable of intertropical Africa. The Fan people are undoubtedly cannibals, as are, it is believed, all the adjoining mountain tribes. They buy the dead for food, and the king alone is not eaten. Piles of human bones and skulls, fragments of the ordinary meals, met the eye at every turn. Human flesh is exposed in the public market for sale. It is the food of all, and is relished by all. Ordinary animal food is scarce. The Fans are of a lighter hue than any of the western tribes. They are well armed, and bear shields of elephant-hide, impenetrable as iron. The Ostreba, a neighboring tribe, are expert blacksmiths; and as iron ore is found in considerable quantities in the country, they make their iron weapons, and obtain by native skill a much better quality of steel than any brought from Europe or America. They have constructed a very peculiar pointed axe, which, when thrown from a distance, strikes with the point down. They use this weapon with great effect; and as the object aimed at is the head, the point penetrates the brain, and kills the victim immediately, and the round edge of the axe is then used to cut off the head. Their ingeniously constructed knives are sheathed in covers made of human skin. These people seemed to M. Du Chaillu the finest and bravest race he had seen in the interior of

Africa. They point to the east as the quarter from whence they migrated, describe it as a very mountainous country, and say that the people are cannibals like themselves. Domestic slavery does not prevail to any considerable extent among these tribes, but great numbers are sold every year to the traders, and M. Du Chaillu says that French "emigrant" ships have been recently filled with Fans, and that they have been thus transported from their country in great numbers.

The interest of M. Du Chaillu's work consists not only in the narrative of his geographical discoveries, and his description of the cannibal tribes in that region of Africa, but in the warfare which he carried on with the gorilla, the creature that divides and almost disputes with man the empire of this mountain tract. It has driven nearly all the other animals from the forest which it haunts. Neither the rhinoceros, the giraffe, the buffalo, the horse, the ox, nor the ass, is found where the gorilla dwells; even the lion has quailed and retired before a ferocious ape. The roar of the gorilla can be heard at an almost incredible distance, and is often mistaken for thunder. The native idea of this creature is, that it combines the intelligence of a human being with the savage nature of a brute. Its rage and exasperation are unbounded when brought face to face with man. It beats its chest with its enormous fists, and makes it resound like an immense drum. Its eyes flash defiance; its roar shakes the woods, and seems to proclaim its rightful dominion over the wilderness. In the first encounter which M. Du Chaillu had with one of these monstrous animals, it advanced boldly to within a distance of six yards to prepare for its deadly spring. It reminded him, he says, of some infernal dreamlike creature, half man, half beast, as pictured by the old masters in their representations of hell. However close the resemblance of the gorilla may be to man, we possess the satisfactory assurance of Professor Owen that it is distinguished by important differences which preclude the possibility of a "development" of the human being from the brute. The formation and setting of the great toe are essentially different, converting the foot into a grasping hand. It possesses thirteen ribs, whereas man has but twelve; and the brain-case is not larger than an infant's, although the weight of the immense head is seven or eight times as great as that of the human skull. M. Du Chaillu has brought to England upwards of twenty specimens of the gorilla which he shot, and also other apes, two of them of new kinds—the Kooloo Kamba, so called from the two distinct notes which it utters, and the Nsiega Mbouve, remarkable for the nest or bower which it builds on high trees, with branches to shelter it from sun and rain. The collections brought over by M. Du Chaillu, and especially the perfect skeletons and skulls of these apes, may throw important light upon one of the great controversies of the day; and we hope that a collection so valuable and instructive, and containing so many new species of mammals and birds, may be obtained for our National Museum.

While Central and Western Africa have thus been largely explored, and the courses of several great rivers which pour their waters into the Gulf of Guinea have been determined, Eastern Africa has not been neglected. The explorations in this quarter, which resulted in the discovery of the two great lakes, the Tanganyika and the Nyanza, may be said to have commenced when Dr. Krapf, of the Church Missionary Society, established himself at Rabba, near Mombas. Here he heard, from time to time, that there was in a part of the country to which the Arabs were in the habit of resorting a great inland sea, the dimensions of which were such that nobody could give any estimate either of its length or breadth. Their concurrent statements seemed to indicate a single sheet of water, extending from the equator down to 14° S. lat., which would form an inland sea, or African Caspian, of about eight hundred and forty miles in length, with an assumed width of two hundred or three hundred miles. "In fact," says Major Burton, who does full justice to the single-minded men who prepared the way for his discoveries, "from this great combination of testimony that water lay generally in a continuous line from the equator up to 14° S. lat., and from not being able to gain information of there being any terrestrial separations to this water, they naturally, and I may add fortunately, created that monster slug of an inland sea, which so much attracted the attention of the geographical world in 1855–56, and caused our being sent out to Africa."

Dr. Krapf's explorations were carried on principally in the East African mountain district, the features of which are described as being eminently picturesque. The country appears to be an extension of the Abyssinian highlands, diversified with hills, streams, and glens, rich in tropical productions, and partially covered with deep impenetrable woods. In proceeding towards Usambara from Mombas, "the higher we went," says Mr. Rebmann, the fellow-laborer of Dr. Krapf, "the more pleasant was the air. The cool water trickling from the granite rocks, the little hamlets rising above the mountain ridges, the many patches of Indian corn, rice, bananas, and sugar-cane, the numerous cascades, the murmur of the Emgambo, the mountain masses in the distance, all tended greatly to elevate the spirits of the wanderer, and I felt at a short distance from the equator as if I was walking on the Jura Mountains in the Canton of Basle, so cool was the air and so beautiful the country." * The characteristic of this portion of Eastern Africa seems to be an extensive plateau from which rises a series of isolated mountains and mountain groups.

The existence of mountains in Eastern Africa capped with perpetual snow has been keenly disputed. The alleged discovery by Dr. Krapf and Mr. Rebmann of two great mountain masses rising into the region of perpetual congelation close to the equator, and presenting the sublime spectacle of isolated peaks with an elevation of at least eighteen thousand feet, shone upon by the tropical sun, excited, as soon as it was announced, an extraordinary interest. The president of the Royal Geographical Society cautiously intimated his doubts, and suggested that the matter which two simple-minded and unscientific gentlemen at a distance mistook for snow, might be white quartz rock or a crystalline dolomitic formation, which, glittering in the rays of a brilliant sun or shone upon by the moon, would present a somewhat similar appearance. Mr. Rebmann positively affirms that in his first journey to Jagga, in 1848, he saw distinctly for the first time the snowy peak of Mount Kilimandjaro. Dr. Krapf states that on the 10th of November, 1849, on his first journey to Ukambani, he also beheld it when thirty-six leagues from Mombas, and from several elevations "the silver-crowned summit" of the lofty Kilimandjaro was plainly visible. He saw it again, he says, in 1851, when it was plainly discernible with the naked eye. Mr. Rebmann informs us that he slept at the foot of the mountain, and that by moonlight he could distinctly perceive snow. He conversed with many natives respecting the white matter upon the domelike summit, and was told that the "silver-like stuff" when brought down in bottles proved to be nothing but water. The second snow-capped mountain, which bears the name of Kegnia or Kenia, was seen by Dr. Krapf in December, 1849, when he observed "two large horns or pillars" rising over an enormous mountain to the north-west of Kilimandjaro, covered, he says, with a white substance. One of the people of the village at which he rested informed him that his tribe resided near the "white mountain;" that he himself had often been at the foot of it, but had not ascended it to any great altitude on account of the intense cold and the white matter which sometimes rolled down the mountain with a great noise. These facts, which the natives never could have invented or imagined, seem to us conclusive that the impressions of Dr. Krapf and Rebmann were correct, and that vast mountains crowned with perpetual snow undoubtedly exist in Eastern Equatorial Africa. There is no reason why the existence of snow in those regions should be doubted when it is found under the equator in America; and Dr. Krapf and Mr. Rebmann may, we think, justly claim the honor of having discovered the great snowy mountains Kilimandjaro and Kenia. When in Ukambani Dr. Krapf heard of the existence of a volcano in constant activity at some distance north-west of Kenia, probably forming a portion of the "Mountains of the Moon." A range of snowy peaks at the African equator, in volcanic action, would afford a striking parallel to the phenomena of Equatorial South America, and the Andes and the Mountains of the Moon would thus possess several points of resemblance. All doubt on these interesting questions will be speedily dissipated either by Captain Speke or by the Baron von Decken, a Hanoverian, who has recently

* Church Missionary Intelligencer, Sept. 1856.

sailed for Zanzibar for the purpose of fully exploring Kilimandjaro and its district.*

Dr. Krapf has collected a large amount of information relating to the forms of government and the state of society prevailing among the Eastern African nations. He is of opinion that these people were formerly in a much more settled and civilized condition. The ancient kingdom of Ethiopia may have extended, he thinks, as far as the equator, and even in its decline have afforded the neighboring African rulers a model of government on which they formed their political institutions. The most intellectual and energetic of the native races of Eastern Africa are the Gallas, who occupy a country extending from the eighth degree of north to the third degree of south latitude, and number from six to eight millions—a population which few other African states possess. They thus fill a large space in Eastern Africa. They call themselves "Oroma," or strong and brave men, have a manly bearing, are powerfully built, but "with savage features, made still more savage by their long hair, which is worn like a mane over the shoulders." They are held in high estimation as slaves. The weapons of this warrior-race are a spear, a sword, and a shield; they are mounted on horses, and the women gallop by the side of their husbands in battle. They are industrious tillers of the soil. The climate of the country, abounding in mountains, is remarkably healthy, the average temperature, according to Dr. Krapf, being 56° Fahrenheit; the highest being 70°, and the lowest 46°. The Gallas occupy plains which are verdant throughout the year, and afford pasture for immense herds of cattle. Their villages and hamlets are placed "in groves and woods, on heights, or on the sides of mountains and rivers," and the land is abundantly provided with springs and brooks fed by tropical rains. This powerful nation possesses, in Dr. Krapf's opinion, a purer faith than any of the heathen tribes of Eastern Africa. Throughout the whole of Eastern Africa, indeed, fetichism is unknown — a very remarkable peculiarity, which points to some previous instruction of the people in a religion which has preserved them from the grosser forms of Pagan idolatry. Dr. Krapf notes as some approximation to Jewish and Christian faiths, that many of the Galla tribes show great respect for Saturday and Sunday, on which days they do not work in the fields, terming Sunday "Saubatta gudda," or the greater sabbath, in contrast to the "Saubatta kenna," or the lesser sabbath. The territories now occupied by the Galla tribes are believed by Dr. Beke to have been once the possessions or dependencies of the Christian emperors of Abyssinia, a fact which, if correct, would sufficiently account for the fragments of Christian truth which are found mixed up with their religious system. There are traces of the worship of the Virgin Mary in the veneration paid to Maremma, "the mother of God;" and Balawald, the son of Maremma, is supposed to indicate our Saviour. The pantheon of the Gallas, however, possesses many deities; but Dábilos (the devil) is not one of them, his residence being in the desert, where he is believed to have "come of himself," without having been created. Siétan is a distinct person from Dábilos, and of a more malignant nature, being the author of death. His dwelling is "underground." The Gallas have neither churches nor priests.*

In strong contrast to this intelligent and comparatively advanced race are the two tribes, the Wakuafi and Masai. They occupy large plains in the interior of Eastern Africa, extending from two degrees north of the equator to four degrees south. Nomads, and living entirely on milk, butter, honey, and black cattle, they have a great dislike to agriculture, believing that cereals enfeeble the frame, while meat and milk alone give courage and strength. In this they bear a remarkable resemblance to the Kaffirs, and in another peculiarity they possess a strong family likeness. When cattle fail them, they make raids on their neighboring tribes. They are especially dreaded as warriors; but as they consider themselves the exclusive proprietors of the plains, they do not attack the inhabitants of the mountains, if the latter do not descend and attempt to cultivate the level country. These tribes constitute republics, with elective chiefs, and the orders and ranks in society

* See Earl de Gray's Address to Royal Geographical Society for 1860.

* See an interesting article on "Christianity among the Gallas," by Dr. Beke, in the British Magazine for December, 1847.

are well defined. Like the Kaffirs, they have many wives, and purchase them with cattle.* They are immoderately fond of tobacco, as well as of beads, and use copper wire for rings and armlets. There is another peculiarity in which they further resemble their South African brethren: they do not make slaves of their prisoners, neither do they traffic in slaves. Their deity (Engai) resides on a lofty mountain, the Olympus of Eastern Africa, "whence come the water and the rain to fertilize their fields and refresh their flocks and herds." There is in their theology a mediator between themselves and Engai, and it is to this mediator that they first address themselves to gain the favor of the great being who dwells on the "mountain of whiteness." Human sacrifices are not unknown in a portion of the country bordering on Abyssinia. In Senjero the slave-dealers throw a beautiful female into the lake Umo when they leave the country with their human merchandise; and a remarkable custom prevails of families offering up their first-born sons as sacrifices, because once, "when winter and summer were jumbled together in a bad season," and the fruits of the earth would not ripen, the priests enjoined it to propitiate the offended deity. The superstitions of Africa are always most freely indulged during periods of calamity. Dr. Krapf was himself in great danger of being sacrificed because he was suspected of being the cause of a long-continued drought; but as soon as the refreshing showers began to fall, the people were equally eager to deify him for his supposed interposition on their behalf.

The missionary prospects in this part of Africa appear to be far from encouraging. The king of Shoa, from whom Dr. Krapf met with a very honorable reception, having promised him six boys for the purpose of being educated in the Christian faith, afterwards receded from his engagement, declaring that he did not need spiritual teachers so much as doctors, masons, and smiths. We are glad to find so zealous a missionary as Dr. Krapf admitting that Christianity must be presented to these tribes, at once sensual, ignorant, and superstitious, not merely in the form of dogmatic teaching and exhortation, but realized and exemplified in family life. Christianity in Africa must spring out of civilization, not civilization out of Christianity.

The discoveries of Major Burton and Captain Speke in the interior of Africa are among the most important accessions to geographical knowledge which have been made during the present century. They have confirmed in a striking manner the anticipations of science, and have invested a long-neglected continent with fresh interest and attraction. The existence of great lakes in the interior was often asserted by the natives of the eastern coast, and the slave merchants of Mozambique, as early as the middle of the last century, informed Mr. Salt that seven months' journey from Mozambique a great lake of fresh water was to be seen; and that a few days' journey from Quiloa, or Kiloa in modern maps, another great lake existed which was spoken of as a fresh-water sea.* The second of these lakes is undoubtedly the Nyassi, ten days' journey from Kiloa; the first, either the great lake Tanganyika, or the Nyanza, but probably the former, which the Portuguese historian De Barros describes, from report, as a sea of considerable magnitude, containing an island capable of sending forth an army of thirty thousand men. These statements were long discredited by European geographers, and they were regarded merely as travellers' tales.

It was reserved for two British officers, animated by the love of adventure and by the desire of extending the boundaries of geographical knowledge, and supported by the liberal aid of one of the most eminent of our scientific associations, to withdraw the veil of mystery from the lake regions of Africa. Major Burton and his companion, Captain Speke, quitted Zanzibar in June, 1857, and after a journey of nearly eight months through a country of which the rank and luxuriant vegetation often teemed with miasma, and after having overcome moral and physical obstacles of no ordinary kind, they reached the great lake, which was the first object of their expedition. "What is that streak of light?" said Major Burton to one of his followers, while reposing, after a fatiguing march on a hill summit. "I am of opinion that it is *the* water," was the re-

* See Quarterly Review, No. 215, p 188.

* Malte Brun, vol. iv., p. 412.

ply. Advancing a few yards the lake burst suddenly upon his view, filling him, he says, with wonder, admiration, and delight.

At the town of Ujiji, the port of the lake, Major Burton fixed his quarters, and found it the ivory depôt of the district, and furnished with a tolerable market for the produce of the neighboring country. The direct longitudinal distance of Ujiji from the coast, Major Burton estimates at five hundred and forty geographical miles, which the sinuosities of the road prolong to nine hundred and fifty statute miles. The route, broken into short stages with necessary rests, occupied one hundred and fifty days. Ujiji was first visited by the Arabs in 1840, and their factors navigated the lake for the purpose of collecting slaves and ivory from the tribes resident on its shores. Major Burton found the bazaar supplied with sugar-cane, tobacco, and cotton, and with an abundance of coarse native grain (holcus) grown in the district. Herds of elephants wander in the bamboo jungles which surround the great inland sea; but the piles of ivory seen in the market of Ujiji were said to have been collected from an area of some thousands of square miles.

Major Burton gives an unfavorable report of the tribes resident in this region of Africa. Intoxication, the effect of "palm-toddy," is a prevalent vice, and it has produced a general demoralization. The principal tribe he describes as "a burly race of barbarians, with harsh and strident voices, and with manners independent even to insolence;" and the women, he says, often exceed their masters in rudeness and violence. These people, do not, however, appear to be dangerous to travellers.

The Tanganyika was navigated by Major Burton to within a few hours' voyage of its northern extremity; but he was provokingly prevented, by the impracticability of a chief, from proceeding to explore it. He learned, however, from intelligent natives, who were well acquainted with the upper reach of the lake, that a river *enters* the Tanganyika in that direction. If this information should be correct, which there is no reason to doubt, the notion of connection of this lake with the Nile is, of course, dispelled. Major Burton and his companion were also prevented from reaching the southern end of the lake. But it is the hard fortune of an African traveller to be often suddenly stopped in the career of discovery by obstacles which no courage can surmount.

The great inland sea Tanganyika was never before visited by a European. The sides of its basin rise to a height of two thousand or three thousand feet above the water-level. The lower slopes are described as beautifully wooded. The direction of the lake is due north and south, and its shape a long oval. Its total length has been roughly computed at two hundred and fifty rectilinear geographical miles, and its breadth at from thirty to thirty-five miles. Its waters are sweet and pure; its color is sometimes a soft, clear blue, sometimes a dull sea-green, but rarely, as far as Major Burton's observation extended, "deep and dark, like the ultramarine of the Mediterranean," and, "under a strong wind, the waves foam up from a turbid greenish surface, and its aspect becomes menacing in the extreme." Soundings could not be taken, but the Arabs declared that with lines of several fathoms' length they found bottom only near the shore. Land and sea breezes are as regular as on the shore of the Indian Ocean. "A careful investigation," Major Burton states, "leads to the belief that the Tanganyika receives and absorbs the whole river-system —the network of streams, mullahs, and torrents—of that portion of the central African depression whose watershed converges towards the great reservoir." But geographers doubt whether such a mass of water, situated at so considerable an altitude, can maintain its level unchanged without an effluent; and we accordingly find the noble president of the Royal Geographical Society questioning the correctness of Major Burton's conclusions. He characterizes it as a strange hydrological puzzle if a lake, situated in the damp regions of the equator, subject to a rainy season that lasts eight months, and supplied by considerable rivers, should have no outlet whatever. Captain Speke places the Tanganyika, by barometrical measurement, at 1,844 feet above the level of the sea, and Dr. Livingstone places the Shirwa, contiguous to the Nyassa, at two thousand feet: if these measurements are correct there can of course be no connection between them. But the accuracy of the measurement may, Earl de Grey says, fairly be doubted. Previous verifications had shown an occasional amount of variation in the barometer of Captain Speke; and as an error of 1° represents an altitude of five hundred and thirty-five feet, it is quite possible that the Tanganyika may be really on a slightly higher level than the more southern lakes. The Nyassa was found by Dr. Livingstone to be the exit of a fine river, the Shiré; and as the Shirwa is only separated from the Nyassa by a spit of sandy soil, it is far from improbable that they may be occasionally united, and a connection may be established through a chain of minor lakes between the Nyassa and the great Tanganyika, and therefore between the Tanganyika and the ocean.*

The honor of having been the first European who reached the great lake Nyanza is due to Captain Speke. While his companion was prostrated by illness at Kazeh, in the Unyambezi district, Captain Speke arranged a separate expedition to proceed to the north to explore the lake known to exist in that direction, and to enable him to reach which the Arab merchants had given him clear instructions. After a journey of sixteen days, through a country presenting no serious difficulties, and inhabited by a friendly population, Captain Speke attained the object of his hopes, and stood on the banks of that enormous inland sea to which he has given the proud name of the Victoria Nyanza. This lake, of which the extent is at present utterly unknown, is, according to barometrical measurement, 3,750 feet above the sea-level; its waters are fresh and clear, and it appeared to Captain Speke, from the nature and configuration of its shores, to be the receptacle of the surplus rainfall of the centre of the African continent. It does not lie in a deep hollow, like the Tanganyika, but, as far as his observation extended, spreads over a comparatively flat country, and its surface-level must be subject to considerable variations. What he at first believed to be two considerable islands at its southern extremity proved to be promontories connected by low spits of land with the neighboring country, but occasionally converted into islands by floods. The extent of the Victoria Nyanza is at present only a subject of conjecture. It probably reaches far beyond the equator; but no person could give Captain Speke any reliable information on that point. He was told that it extended "to the end of the world;" and one of the wives of the sultan whose territories form a portion of its southern shore, and whose native place was far up the lake, informed Captain Speke that she had never heard of there being *any* end to the lake, and that if any way existed of going round it she would certainly have known it. Its very great extension in a northerly direction must necessarily be inferred from these native statements.

* President's Address, 1860.

At its southern extremity, which constitutes a tortuous creek in which were numerous small rocky islands clothed with brushwood, the observed latitude of the lake was 2° 24′ S. The mean temperature of the elevated region on its banks during August, the hottest month of the year, Captain Speke found to be only 80°. Bordering on the lake, to the south-east, is an extensive iron-field which the natives work with success, making in large quantities the hoes which are used in African agriculture, and which are articles of considerable export from the manufacturing district of the Victoria Nyanza. Tropical produce in great variety, including rice, is raised on the rich soil of the southern bank, and to the east ivory is said to be abundant and cheap. The Karuqwa hills, overlooking the lake, are said to be cool and healthy, and to support herds of cattle with horns of stupendous size. All the necessaries of life are to be procured in abundance. Of the country beyond the equator Captain Speke states, that "rapturous" accounts were given him by the ivory traders, and it was represented as supporting a dense population who cultivate coffee and possess large flocks and herds.

Public attention is at the present time very much directed to this interesting portion of Central Africa, and we await with impatience the further discoveries which, should success attend his present expedition, Captain Speke cannot fail to make. These great lakes, which are placed in the very centre of the continent and have excited the wonder of Europe, are doubtless destined to figure conspicuously in the future of civilized Africa. It is possible that a connection may be found between the Victoria Nyanza and the Nile, the slope of the continent from the equator being undeniably towards the north. Engineering science and steam may overcome any obstacles,* and vessels of light burden may, perhaps, at no distant day, pass from the Mediterranean to the very centre of Africa, and the flag of all nations float on the Victoria Nyanza.

The region yet unsurveyed in which the source of the Nile must lie is now so circumscribed that there is every reason to expect a speedy solution of the great geographical problem which has maintained its interest for more than two thousand years. To the combined efforts of Captain Speke and her majesty's consul for Sudan, Mr. Petherick, we may hopefully and confidently look for this result. Mr. Petherick during a residence of fifteen years on the Upper Nile, has at various periods penetrated farther into the interior of that portion of Africa than any other traveller. The farthest point on the White Nile reached, until recently, was Gondokoro, in about 4° 30′ N. lat. and 31° 50′ E. long., nearly fourteen hundred miles above Khartum and more than three thousand from Alexandria. Mr. Petherick was the first European who attempted to ascend the Bahr-el-Gazal or south-western branch of the Nile, but he was prevented from landing on its banks by the hostile attitude of the people. In the year 1854, however, he succeeded in landing and forcing his way into the country. Since that period he advanced his posts farther and farther, until he arrived at a place called Mundo, among tribes suspected of cannibalism, and situate at, or very near, the equator.

Captain Speke alludes to a range of mountains in Eastern Africa running north and south across the equator; and since one of the watersheds of the mountainous districts visited by Dr. Krapf is towards the west, it is highly probable that the streams descending from Mount Kenia may find their way into the Victoria Nyanza. Dr. Krapf was informed that there are more than fifteen rivers running west and north from Kenia, one being, he was told, very large, and flowing in a northerly direction into a great lake on the banks of which a traveller might proceed for a hundred days without reaching its extremity. It is impossible to doubt that the lake thus indicated is the Nyanza.

A little above the point where the Sobat joins the Nile the principal stream expands into a series of lakes, more or less connected at different seasons of the year, and known as the Bahr-el-Gazal, or the Sea of the Gazelles. Mr. Petherick describes this sheet of water as one hundred and eighty miles in length, overgrown with reeds and lilies and full of hippopotami, and fed by many rivulets as well as by a large river running from the south-west, but covered with weeds. The depth and magnitude of the Nile, as well as of many large tributaries at the latitudes reached by Mr. Petherick, promise important results when this district shall be more fully explored. The Sobat, the first great tributary of the White Nile, drains a large extent of country to the east, and has been navigated for a distance of two hundred miles. At its junction with the Nile it is one hundred yards wide, and on the 2nd of December, while under the influence of the inundation, it was thirty feet deep. Its course is described as tortuous, with high banks. The channel of the lake Bahr-el-Gazal Mr. Petherick found to be twenty feet deep, with a sluggish stream of a quarter of a mile per hour. The interest of this traveller's recent contribution to geographical knowledge consists not only in his voyages up the White Nile, but in several remarkable journeys from its banks into countries previously altogether unexplored. He had some severe conflicts with the natives, and the manner in which he extricated himself more than once from very embarrassing situations proves him to be possessed of all the qualifications requisite for a successful explorer. Mr. Petherick's last expedition was from the extreme end of the Bahr-el-Gazal in a southerly direction inland, and in twenty-six days he reached the country of the Nyam-Nyam tribe, reputed to be cannibals. These people have discovered the use of that remarkable projectile the boomerang, supposed to be confined to the natives of Australia; but the African savage constructs it of iron and gives it a sharp cutting edge, and in the hands of a muscular race it must be a weapon of terrible power. That the Bahr-el-Gazal is connected with the Victoria Nyanza Captain Speke considers highly probable, for

* Such is the opinion of Mr. Petherick. He mentions the existence of rapids in the White Nile in 8° 30′ N. lat., but he thinks they would be no obstruction to steam power. The cataracts, or, as they may be more correctly termed, rapids of the Lower Nile might doubtless be surmounted by the same means, or avoided, as in the St. Lawrence, by canals.

in the place where Mr. Petherick crossed the latter piece of water, in 4° N. lat., it had its head directed to the south-east. The geographical problem is one of great interest, and the discovery of another great practicable highway into the very centre of Africa would be one of the triumphs of the age. It is to settle finally, if possible, a question now reduced to very narrow limits that Captain Speke has been empowered to proceed, in company with Captain Grant, to the field of his former explorations. He has been instructed to make the best of his way to the southern end of the Victoria Nyanza, and from thence to explore it to its northern extremity, and especially to ascertain whether it has a northern outlet. He is then to proceed to Gondokoro, where Mr. Petherick, proceeding up the White Nile, hopes to meet him in November next.

The discoveries of Dr. Livingstone in the south of Africa are too well known to need more than a very cursory notice. In the year 1849 he reached, in company with Messrs. Oswell and Murray, the lake Ngami, in 20° 20′ S. lat. and 23° 30′ E. long. From this lake he found a considerable river, the Zouga, flowing towards the east and south-east for a distance of three hundred miles, but, like many other African rivers, it had no outlet, but was lost in a desert sand. On returning to the examination of the district in the following year, and crossing the Zouga to the northward, he discovered the Chobe, a fine navigable river, in 18° 23′ S. lat. and 26° E. long., have penetrated the country to a distance of two thousand miles from Cape Town. The name of Livingstone will always be associated with that of the great Zambezi, the upper course of which he was the first to discover. It was in June, 1851, that Dr. Livingstone first saw the great stream—the future highway for the commerce of South Africa—at a spot marked by Portuguese geographers in their maps as an arid desert. He found it at Seheske, rolling its volume of deep flowing waters towards the east, and varying in breadth from three hundred to six hundred yards. At the period of its annual inundation it rises twenty feet, and floods fifteen or twenty miles of the adjacent country. The Zambezi, or Leeambye, denotes, in the native language, the river *par excellence*, and signifies the fact of its being the great drainage artery of the country. The river in its natural channel, is of great breadth, often a mile, and is broken by numerous islands, some of which are covered with timber. A portion of the course of the Zambezi is composed of a succession of rapids or cateracts, which oppose a barrier to its continuous navigation. The rapids do not exist when the water is high; but some of the cataracts must always be attended with considerable difficulty and danger in their descent, if they are not altogether impassable, their fall averaging from four to six feet. At one portion of Dr. Livingstone's route, it was necessary to take the canoes out of the water, and carry them a mile over land, the fall within that distance being thirty feet. The Barotse valley Dr. Livingstone estimated as a hundred miles in breadth, and it bears a considerable resemblance to the valley of the Nile, since it is inundated annually by the rise of the Leeambye exactly as Lower Egypt is flooded by the Nile. The inhabitants of this fertile district raise two crops of corn in a year, and the saying is common in the country, "here hunger is not known." One kind of grass grows to the height of twelve feet; but when the waters recede they leave behind them masses of decayed vegetation which produce malaria pernicious to the native constitution, and engender a fever that would be almost certainly fatal to Europeans.

The Zambezi offers no serious obstruction to navigation below Tete, a distance of more than three hundred miles from its embouchure; and steamers of light draught might ply on it with success. It is the largest river that enters the ocean on the eastern coast of Africa. So great is the volume of its waters and the rush of its floods from its seven mouths, that at a distance of ten miles from land the sea was found by Captain Owen perfectly fresh. Above the rapids the country, although abounding in various productions, does not, Dr. Livingstone thinks, present an immediate field for commercial enterprise. On the Leeba, a tributary of the Zambezi, the people have a strong commercial spirit and are enterprising merchants, bringing Manchester goods into the very heart of Africa from Loanda. To the Africans, Dr. Livingstone says, our cotton-mills are fairy dreams; and their productions look so wonderful that they cannot believe them to be the work of mortal hands.

"How can irons," say these people, "spin and weave and print so beautifully?" and an attempt to explain the manufacture was followed by the exclamation, "Truly ye are gods!"

The services which Dr. Livingstone has rendered to civilization consist in his having traced the course of a great stream, the existence of which throughout any very extensive district was unknown, and in having opened a large and most interesting portion of South-eastern Africa. No one can have perused the narrative of this remarkable man's travels without being impressed with his noble character. Heroism and humility are admirably blended in his nature; and he relates acts of courage and self-devotion without any consciousness of merit, or the faintest approach to obtrusive egotism. He will now pursue, in the double character of a consular representative of the British Government and a minister of the gospel, and with the advantage of enjoying the good-will of the natives, the career so successfully commenced. In his own little "Pioneer" he will stem the waters of the great Zambezi, making the British name and character known to millions, scattering the seed of a future commercial, moral, and religious harvest.

If Africa is distinguished more than any other quarter of the globe for its physical, ethnological, and moral peculiarities, it is equally remarkable for its political diversities. Almost every form into which human society can be thrown may be there found in its simplicity. Monarchy seems to be the primitive type of government among the negro tribes. The king of Dahomey is the most absolute sovereign in the world. Royalty modified by aristocracy prevails in the Arab political organization, and the rule of the great chief of Sakatu, with his numerous dependent sultans, may not inaptly be compared to that of the head of the old Germanic empire. In the district of Eastern Africa republics and democracies abound. In Northern Africa the Arab element predominates. The colonizing tribes carried the standard of Mahomet into almost the centre of the continent, and the Arab and the negro blood were freely intermixed. The original religion of nearly all the African tribes was, Dr. Barth thinks, a worship of the elements, of the sun and moon, and of the souls of their ancestors—a superstition common at the present day, it is believed, to almost all the African races. But if the opinion of the same distinguished traveller is correct, the forms of worship which now prevail are much more savage and grotesque than they were at a former period, the religious rites of the interior being, however, far purer than those near the coast.* We learn from a distinguished African geographer that when the Portuguese discovered and took possession of the western coast they found a negro king who had not only extended his conquests from the centre of Hausa to the border of the Atlantic, and from the pagan countries of Mosé, in 12° N. latitude, as far as Morocco, but governed his subjects with justice, and adopted such of the customs of Mohammedanism as he thought conducive to civilization.†

Europe, we fear, is chargeable with the change in the character of the negro governments which history thus seems to indicate has taken place in Africa. The negro races are naturally as full of the feelings of humanity, their family affections are as strong, and their sense of justice is as correct, as those of any other people or race; and in the few regions to which the slave-trade has not yet extended these virtues flourish. It is the man-traffic which has perverted the natural instincts, raised the arm of the native against his brother, converted rulers into the tyrants and kidnappers of their species, and made two-thirds of a vast continent one great market of human flesh and blood. This atrocious commerce has tainted the very sources of civilization, and forbids, while it lasts, all hope or possibility of improvement. The king of Dahomey's butcheries are still practised with impunity, and meet even with the approbation of the peoples.‡ The pride of some of these petty lords

* See Dr. Barth's Paper, "A General Historical Description of the State of Human Society in Northern Central Africa," in the last volume of the Journal of the Royal Geographical Society.

† See Cooley's "Negroland of the Arabs."

‡ The "West African Herald," published, only in February last, statements from eye-witnesses of the barbaric custom then recently perpetrated in Dahomey. In this fearful narrative we learn that the late sacrifice was one of the most revolting which had ever taken place. The number of persons slain on the occasion was estimated at two thousand; but another correspondent gives the number as seven thousand. He states that he was present by compulsion, and that the blood swept

of Africa is equal to their ferocity. They regard themselves as superior beings, proclaim their dominion over the elements, and demand divine honors as their due. They sell their ministers in fits of caprice, and bury their relations alive. The latest of our African travellers testifies to the continued prevalence of savage customs over the whole field of his late explorations. The king of Uganda's palace, a mile in length, is often burned down by lightning, and on such occasions the warriors are obliged to assemble and endeavor to extinguish the fire by rolling over the flames. There are two wants with which this sovereign always troubled his visitors: one, a medicine against death; the other, a charm to avert the thunderbolt. This chief fell in battle, pierced by an arrow, when riding on the shoulders of his prime minister. The Arab governments in Africa are free from most of the revolting usages of the negro dynasties. The foreign slave-trade, however, is their chief support. The only mode in which Dr. Barth could carry on his explorations to the south of Kuka was by joining two Mohammedan expeditions, of ten thousand men each, for the avowed purpose of capturing and selling into slavery unoffending tribes.

Changes of government are frequent in Africa, and out of a number of small hereditary sultans, each master of his separate province, one, either by intrigue or by conquest, attains supreme power. From the 20th degree of north latitude almost to the Cape frontier are tribes which are commonly classed as Ethiopic, although many are undoubtedly of mixed races. The most influential people in Africa are the Felatahs or Foulahs, supposed to be of Carthaginian origin, but probably descended from the Arabs who invaded Africa in the seventh century and mingled with the negro race. Throughout the whole of Negroland the Foulahs maintain a paramount influence. They are found, according to the authority of Mr. Hodgson, spread over a vast geographical region, extending from the mouths of the Senegal and Gambia on the west to the kingdoms of Bornu and Mandara on the east — a superficies containing more than seven hundred thousand square miles, equal to a fourth part of Europe, and embracing a tenth of the African continent.* The supreme sultan can bring into the field a force of ten thousand horse, and the contingents of his tributary sultans much exceed that number. There are a few isolated negro nations governed by native African kings, who live in secluded state, and disdain to visit even the wealthiest of the Arabs; and these native princes sometimes display a certain dignity of demeanor which indicates a mixture of foreign blood.† In the regions of Central Africa there is the greatest diversity of nations. In some the kingdom is hereditary, in others elective; but where the principle of hereditary succession prevails, the sister's son succeeds to the throne. Malte Brun mentions a singular institution of one of the negro states, which may be thought by some to provide as effectual a security for good government as a constitution. A council of grandees has the power of deposing the sovereign and putting him to death, and one of the regal relatives holds the office of royal executioner, his duty being to carry the judicial sentence into effect. It is a place of the highest distinction, and the individual who holds it is said to live on terms of perfect cordiality with the prince to whom he stands in so peculiar a relation.‡

European articles sometimes find at the African courts a use for which they were never designed. Dr. Krapf, who had presented a hospitable chief of Eastern Africa with a silver fork, saw it on the following day stuck in the woolly hair of his host, where it was proudly worn as a distinguished ornament during the remainder of his stay.

Travelling in Africa is attended with many hardships. The slowness of the rate of progress is not the least of the trials which an explorer has to bear. The *impedimenta* of the march are necessarily great. Bags of beads, rolls of brass wire, bales of cloth, supplies of food, tent equipages, cooking utensils, boxes for clothing, and cases for the more costly presents, require a large amount of carriage, consisting either of cam-

past him like a flood into a large reservoir. Another correspondent, referring to these inhuman butcheries, says, "I assure you it made me quite sick, and at the same time I felt stunned." The victims are said to have met their death with perfect indifference.

* Notes on Northern Africa. By W. B. Hodgson. New York.

† Burton's Lake Districts of Central Africa, vol. ii., p. 362.

‡ Malte Brun, vol. iv., p. 122.

els and horses or of the sturdy porters of the country. Major Burton, to give an idea of the relative cost of travelling, states the expenditure in Eastern Africa at half a crown per mile, while in most parts of Europe it does not now exceed one penny. The roads are a mere track which a party must traverse in single file, and it is soon overgrown by almost impenetrable brushwood. This mode of travelling differs materially from that of Northern or Central Africa, where the camel and the horse are employed. There is one source of expense common to the whole of Africa; namely, the kuhonga, or blackmail, which is extorted from all travellers by chiefs of every rank. It forms a considerable portion of their revenues, and is a recognition of their territorial rights. If any hesitation about the payment is made, the first question put to an objector will be, "Is this your ground or mine?" The chiefs have no conception of a right of free passage through their dominions. Dr. Livingstone found the custom universal in his journey between the Zambezi and Loanda, and he was repeatedly called upon to pay the transit duty, and was told that he might do it either with a bullock or a man.

The moral and political degradation of Africa is a subject of mournful interest. A modern geographer * estimates the population at one hundred and fifty million, of which three-fourths are in a state of slavery, and the other fourth constitutes a despotic governing power under which it is morally impossible that the people can make any important progress in civilization. Domestic slavery is interwoven with the state of society, and a complete moral revolution must take place before it can be abolished; but the foreign slave traffic constitutes the gigantic evil of Africa, and throughout vast regions man has no property but slaves, and no articles of merchandise but his fellow-creatures. The sultans regarded their people simply as a herd of cattle. The almost normal state of war which exists in Central Africa is maintained solely for the purpose of supplying foreign markets with the human commodity, and every crime is punished by a forfeiture of liberty and the immediate transfer of the offender to the slave-dealer. Accusations of witchcraft or adultery are always ready when more serious offences are wanting, and the population of a whole village is sometimes suddenly carried off in satisfaction of a debt. The effect of this commerce upon the African character is apparent to all who have penetrated into the interior. Dr. Livingstone states that he had never known an instance of a parent selling his own offspring, but Captain Speke says that, on the shores of the Tanganyika Lake, the women, for the consideration of a few loin cloths, readily parted with their little children and delivered them into perpetual bondage to his Belooch soldiers; and in Eastern Africa, Major Burton informs us that, in times of necessity, a man will sacrifice his parents, wives, and children, and even sell himself without shame.* It was stated long ago by an unexceptionable witness that mothers were frequently to be seen on the western coast selling their children for a few bushels of rice; but a stout African once took his little son to sell him to a European: the lad, however, well acquainted with the language of the foreigner, cunningly suggested that a man of the size and strength of his father must be of far more value than himself, and thus induced the slave-dealer to take his father in his stead, notwithstanding the vociferous protestations of the man that in Africa a son had no right to sell his own parent.†

This dark blot on the continent of Africa can only be effaced by proving to the sultans and chiefs how much more profitable it will be to employ their people in developing the natural riches of the soil and raising produce for which there will be a European demand, than to export them as the staple commodity of the country. Commerce must be the great regenerator of Africa. The Arab governors are unanimous in their desire for an increased intercourse with Europe, although they are perfectly aware that the slave-trade, in which they are deeply financially interested, cannot long survive a closer commercial relation with England. They doubtless feel that their revenues will greatly increase with the extension of legitimate trade, and that their position in the country will become more secure. With the cessation of the foreign slave-trade an era of real progress will commence. Native

* Mr. Macqueen.

* Burton's Lake Regions, vol. ii., p. 367.

† Travels in Africa by Mollien, quoted by Malte Brun.

merchants admit this, and declare their conviction that the country is capable of producing, in almost unlimited quantity, every commodity that Europe can desire from it. The greatest eagerness is shown to possess European productions; and recent travellers have been everywhere questioned as to the probability of a regular market being opened for English goods. An intensely commercial spirit pervades almost the whole of Africa. Sailing close in shore on a coasting voyage, south of the river Fernand Vaz, M. Du Chaillu was hailed by canoes full of negroes begging him to establish factories in their villages, and in some places he saw, from the sea, the large house already built, as he was told, for the *future* factory "which was to make everybody rich." It is satisfactory in the mean time to find a recognition in many quarters of the truth that commerce in Africa must be the pioneer of Christianity. Dr. Livingstone has given expression to a sentiment which, emanating from so zealous a minister of the Gospel, ought to be accepted as a maxim in our future dealings with heathen populations. "No permanent elevation of a people," he emphatically declares, "can be effected without commerce." We cannot but regard the commercial intercourse of nations as one of the appointed means of bringing them all into a closer union with each other, and of inculcating those great doctrinal and moral truths, without whose reception and influence civilization, however splendid, is little better than a polished barbarism.

The difficulties of imparting civilization to Africa are nevertheless exceedingly great. The idiosyncrasy of the negro race is peculiar. Indolence has long been the habit, and enjoyment the business, of their lives. The higher instincts of their nature have not been developed, and they have existed for ages under conditions entirely incompatible with human progress. There is doubtless some deficiency of energy in their original constitution. They have never shown themselves skilful in the hunt; they have not subdued to their use any of the nobler animals; and they are not addicted to riding except on the backs of their brother men. There was not in the time of Lopez, a Portuguese traveller in the eighteenth century, a single horse to be found throughout the whole of Congo. The mule and the ass are equally objects of disfavor, no true negro having ever dared to mount either the one or the other.* They are expert, however, in swimming and diving, and will face with resolution a stormy sea. Many of the arts are, nevertheless, carried on by the black population of Africa, and have been brought to considerable perfection. They show much skill in working in iron and gold; and in Kano, Timbuctoo, and Bornu they make swords, axes, knives, gold ornaments, and other articles. They have little taste for any but the coarsest food. They feed daintily upon the hippopotamus, and disdain not the flesh of the crocodile; the wolf is far from being unacceptable, but their greatest luxury is roasted dog; the elephant often supplies the *pièce de résistance* at a negro feast; the boa constrictor is laid under contribution for his fat; slugs as large as the human arm are served up as delicacies, and grasshoppers, beetles, and bees are esteemed as minor relishes. An African epicure, on hearing a description of the European *cuisine*, replied, "Ah! all very good; but you are not acquainted in England with the delicacy of white ants!"

That there is no inherent incapacity for civilization in the negro nature has been proved by the success of the free colony of Liberia, on the western coast of Africa, where the African has, under favorable circumstances, imitated with success the policy, the arts, and even the institutions, of Europe. "The progress of this colored settlement," to quote from an excellent little essay on the African kingdoms and peoples,† "during the last forty years has hardly been surpassed by any thing recorded in the history of civilization; and it may therefore be said with truth that the negro has given the lie to the assertion of the ethnological sciolists, who, presuming on his alleged natural inferiority, declared him incapable of taking care of himself. He *has* taken care of himself—has provided by acts of courage and self-denial for the growth of his prosperity, for the education of his children, and for his instruction in the truths of Christianity; and in so doing has forever solved and settled the question as to his capacity for self-government."

On the important subject of African com-

* Malte Brun states this.

† Published by the Society for Promoting Christian Knowledge.

merce our remarks must necessarily be brief. It is a startling fact that the whole existing commerce of the vast continent does not exceed that carried on by Hamburg alone.* The total exports from Africa at the present time are estimated at little more than £20,000,000, and the total imports at about £17,000,000. Assuming the population to be one hundred and fifty million, the exports of the country would average 2*s.* 6*d.* per head, whereas from Great Britain they amount to 86*s.*, the United States to 54*s.*, France to 41*s.*, and Russia to 7*s.*; but when the exports of North Africa, Cape Colony, Natal, and the African islands are deducted, the amount for the remainder of Africa is reduced to only 9*d.* per head. And yet this continent abounds in natural wealth. It possesses a population able and, with due encouragement, willing to develop the agricultural capabilities of a soil which, over enormous areas, although of superabundant fertility, is as much neglected as the sands of the Sahara. The commercial classes are anxious to barter the produce of their country for the highly prized and universally coveted commodities of Europe. Vegetable oils, cotton, coffee, tobacco, sugar, indigo, ivory, hides, timber, gums, and wax, might be produced in unlimited quantities, and are sure of commanding remunerative prices in Europe. Of one of the most important of the productions of Africa, namely, palm-oil, forty thousand tons are imported annually into Great Britain. The trade of England with Africa greatly exceeds that of any other nation; and if the great channels of communication are opened, it may be increased to an indefinite extent. The Niger, the Zambezi, and possibly the Nile, will doubtless, at no distant day, form the great highways into the interior, and millions of square miles will thus become accessible to European enterprise and afford an invaluable market for British commodities. The caravan routes through the desert are, as Dr. Barth has shown, too expensive and dangerous, and the quantity of goods thus exported and imported has of late sensibly decreased.† "But from whatever quarter," says this experienced traveller, "Europeans may endeavor to open intercourse and regular and legitimate trade with these nations, the first requisite seems to be the strictest justice and the most straightforward conduct, for almost all the natives of the interior of Africa are traders by disposition, and at least want to barter for beads in order to adorn their own persons and those of their women." This demand for beads is one of the characteristics of the present stage of African civilization, and will give way, we trust, speedily to the desire for more rational and useful importations. They constitute the trinkets and jewelry of Africa, and since the day that Vasco de Gama first visited the eastern coast thousands of tons have been poured into the interior without glutting the market or diminishing the steady demand. The natives rejected the gold and silver ornaments that were offered them by their first visitors, but grasped eagerly at baubles which had no intrinsic worth. Children then, the natives of Africa are children still. A string of bright scarlet porcelain beads excites the same tumultuous delight in Central Africa that a new diamond necklace does in more civilised regions. The passion is common to all classes and to both sexes. There are at least four hundred varieties of beads manufactured for Africa, each of which has its peculiar name, value, and local demand.

The uncertainty of a continued supply of cotton from America has recently been the subject of grave apprehension and of anxious inquiry. Its extensive production in Africa would give an immense impetus to the civilization of the continent. There land is cheap, the soil good, and free labor abundant. Cotton is indigenous in the fertile regions both of Eastern and Western Africa. In the country between Zanzibar and the Tanganyika Lake, according to Major Burton, the shrub grows wild, and the virgin soils of large districts are peculiarly adapted for its cultivation. In a letter which this distinguished explorer recently addressed to a public journal, he enters fully into the capacity of Eastern Africa to supply any demand for cotton that could be made upon it, and particularly specifies the territory lying to the north of Mozambique as far as the equator, and extending eastward from the Indian Ocean to the Ghauts or meridional range of mountains. Throughout the whole of this area the climate is hot and damp, the soil rich, and there is an industrious negro pop-

* Appendix to the Travels of Dr. Krapf on the Commerce of Africa.

† Paper on Northern and Central Africa.

From Once a Week.

THE HISTORY OF A LOVE-LETTER.

"FOUR letters for you, ma'am, to-day," said my maid Bridget, breaking in upon my solitude one morning as I sat busily at work upon a muslin frock, being a gift destined for my little godchild on the approaching auspicious occasion of her completing her third year.

"Four letters!" I re-echoed in surprise, letting the delicate piece of embroidery fall to the ground, while I took them from Bridget's hand. "Why I did not expect one!"

The damsel doubtless thinking that they would themselves be better able to account for their unexpected appearance than she, wisely forebore to attempt it, and, as she quitted the room, I proceeded, after a hasty glance at the handwriting and postmarks borne by the covers, to gratify my curiosity by opening my despatches.

"What can Martha be writing about again so soon?" was my soliloquy ere I commenced reading No. 1. Martha was my only sister, married some ten years before, and the mother of as many children. "Baby" had "cut his first tooth!" He had been longer about the business than any of his nine predecessor babies, and mamma had been fearful his darling gums were destined to prove a physiological wonder by remaining toothless forever! Her anxiety was now happily removed, and she wrote "in haste" to bid me rejoice with her. Although she spoke of haste, her letter consisted of eight closely written pages. She gave in an ascending scale the latest biographies of all her olive branches. Fanny (the destined possessor of the frock) was "growing such a sweet, affectionate child." She was "always talking of Aunt Mary. Did Aunt Mary remember next Thursday would be her birthday?" But I must cut sister Martha short.

Letter No. 2 was an intimation from my Aunt Betsy, a maiden lady, that she proposed shortly to spend "a week" with me, "if convenient." Now, although Aunt Betsy never evinced the slightest satisfaction in my society, though she found fault with every thing in my house and domestic management; yet her "week" was never less than a month, and kept recurring a good deal oftener than I liked; yet for the life of me I dared not say her visit was not convenient. No, Aunt Betsy knew perfectly well that her proviso was a safe one.

Letter No. 3 was soon despatched, being an appeal in behalf of missions to some distant Borioboola Gha.

And No. 4? Now, as a lady is always supposed, as a matter of course, to reserve her most important intelligence—the *crême de la crême*—for her P.S., so No. 4, though last, will be preconceived not least. And, in truth, No. 4 contained an offer of marriage. Scarcely could I believe my eyes. Hereby, suppose not, dear reader, that I had never received an offer before. Nor, although I acknowledge myself not so young as I had been, suppose not either that I thought it so impossible I should ever receive another. No, there was no gray hair in my head; there were no wrinkles on my brow; I might without vanity deem it possible I should have a lover yet to come. It was not the offer that astounded me, but that Mr. James Warrington should be the man to make it. A clap of thunder is often made the simile of a thing sudden and unexpected, yet the thunderclap is commonly preceded by some darkening of the heavens —some indications of the approaching storm. Mr. Warrington's offer, on the contrary, had been preceded by no sign whatsoever. There had been neither word nor look. I had given him my hand to shake, and had been sensible of no tender pressure. I had met him out walking, and he had passed me with a bow. I had spent many an evening in his company, and he had never offered to see me home. Yet the letter I now received was assuredly signed with the name of James Warrington. Who was James Warrington? Before transcribing his letter I must, to the best of my ability, answer this question for the reader's enlightenment.

Of Mr. Warrington's birth and parentage I knew nothing; of his worldly circumstances, likewise, nothing beyond what he now told me. He had never been a resident in the place whereof I write myself a citizeness, but about six months previously he had paid a visit of some length at the house of some acquaintances of mine in this city. Their respectability was received as a voucher for his. Mr. Warrington was handsome, gentlemanly in manner and appearance, lively and well informed, and he speedily became a favorite in our circle in C——. He was invited everywhere. Some few persons indeed there were who whispered, "Who is he?" "Where does he come from?" but the questions remained without an answer, and it might have been he had dropped from the clouds, and after inhabiting this lower sphere of ours for a period of some six or eight weeks, had been caught up again by the same elements. I knew of no *particular* bright eyes that strained their wistful gaze after his flight. I knew of no *one* tender heart that mourned its sun departed. Mr. Warrington had been universally liked by the ladies, and had appeared to like their society, but as far as my knowledge went, he had quitted C—— heartwhole. And now there came this letter for me by the post. It was dated from some street or square in London. Its style I thought singular. It had no formal commencement: thus it began:—

"I love you, Mary, with all my heart and soul, distractedly, devotedly, unchangeably. Forgive this abrupt and incoherent declaration. How long has all utterance been denied me! How often, in the time gone by, when I saw you day by day, and every day loved you more and more, did the words of passion rise to my lips, and I repressed them until my heart wellnigh burst. Did you never read my feelings, Mary? Ah yes, I think you must have done so, in spite of all my boasted self-control. Once, in particular, I wonder if you recall the time [No indeed, I do not], I felt almost sure you had discovered my secret, and there was a look in those dear blue eyes [my eyes are brown, he can never have looked at them well], those dear blue eyes which sent a thrill through me, and inspired me with a hope which has shone before me like a beacon through all this dark night of absence [more like an *ignis fatuus* than a beacon, I'm sure—the vain man—seen in my eyes, indeed]. Yes, Mary [he is very free with my name], I could remain no longer near you without speaking, I could not speak while my worldly prospects were so gloomy and uncertain. I had no fortune; you, too, I knew had none [well, £200 a year is not much, to be sure, but still I think it need not be called nothing by a penniless adventurer]. Poverty would have seemed a light ill to me with you by my side, but I could not bear the idea of your having to contend with all its trials and difficulties. So I tore myself away in silence from the place which your presence made like a heaven to me. Of the following six months I will not speak, save to say that never for one moment has your image been absent from my thoughts. Ah! has my Mary in all that time, I wonder, ever thought of me? [Very seldom, if the truth must be told.] At length, after disappointments numberless, and hopes deferred until my heart was sick, I yesterday received two letters. One was from an influential friend, and contained the information that he had succeeded in obtaining for me an honorable appointment, whereby a competent income was secured me. After a moment's pause of self-congratulation, I opened the second letter, and found myself most unexpectedly the inheritor of a considerable legacy by the will of an old friend of my father, just deceased. Thus was my tongue loosed from its fetters. Mary, I love you with all the fond, deep, and true affection of which a man's heart is capable. Say not, dearest, that the feeling finds no response in your own, suffer me at least to come and plead my cause by word of mouth. You have no parents from whom I must seek to obtain such permission; I do not consider that your aunt has any right to withhold it. I wait, therefore, but your own word to hasten on wings of love and joy to your side. Mary, my own, deny me not. It shall ever be the one dearest aim of my life to make you happy. Adieu.

"Most devotedly yours,
"JAMES WARRINGTON."

I have already said once I could scarcely believe my eyes, and I must say it again. Yet the lines were bold and free, and fair to read. I had had a note from Mr. Warrington once before, when he was staying at C—— (a few brief lines of thanks accompanying a book I had lent him), and I remembered the handwriting well. So well that I rejected the idea, which came across me for a moment, that this ardent epistle must be a forgery. Besides, who would play me such an ungentlemanly hoax? I had always lived at peace and charity with all mankind; I knew nobody who bore me any ill-will, and the matter could not be viewed as a simple joke. No, it must be true, Mr. Warrington must be really in love, or really fancy himself in love with me. Strange, very strange,—what could have inspired him with such a passion? Was it my brown, alias blue, eyes? There was a pier-glass over the chimney-piece. I got up to take a survey of my own image therein. What did I behold? A round face, shaded by dark-brown hair; two brown eyes as aforesaid; a nondescript form of nose, neither Roman, Grecian, nor aquiline, not very obtrusive, nor yet exactly a snub; a rather wide mouth; a set of regular white teeth; a complexion pale, neither brown nor fair. Item, rather a neat little figure. It was not altogether an ugly picture, yet very far from one I should have expected Mr. Warrington to admire. He always struck me as a man who would inevitably select a beautiful woman for his wife. Since to beauty, however, I could make no pretension, it must be some other charm which had procured for me this conquest, and I was utterly at a loss to decide what this might be. Accomplishments I had few to boast, my music was far below the average of a boarding-school miss, and though the walls of my drawing-room were profusely decorated with the works of my pencil, Mr. Warrington had never seen these masterpieces, so I could not owe my triumphs to those Italian skies, purple mountains, silvery streams, and green trees with the nymphs reposing beneath them. I rather prided myself upon my powers of conversation, but these had never seemed to possess much attraction in the eyes, or *ears* I should rather say, of Mr. Warrington. He talked more to old Mrs. Hearnaught, who could only be talked to through a trumpet, and to Miss Thickskull, whom nobody could talk to through any thing but the purest good nature, than he had ever done to me. Ever? No, once, and but once, I recollect my conversation did appear to interest him. It was when I was speaking of ferns. The book I lent him was on that subject. If I married Mr. W. I should certainly choose a bridal-wreath of ferns. Some species of the delicate *Adiantum* or *Maidenhair* seemed by its name peculiarly appropriate for such a destiny. If I married him did I say? Yes, that was the question. Here was I foolishly wasting time in idle guesses as to what could have induced him to ask me, and neglecting the great point whether I should say yes or no. I had no one to consult hereupon but myself. The course of love in my case "hung" not "upon the choice of friends." No, it might run on a smooth and rapid river without danger of meeting any obstacle to its current. Parents I had none. My Aunt Betsy, Mr. Warrington indeed but justly considered, had small right to be consulted; so small that I wondered it had occurred to him to mention her. I recollected, however, that she was spending one of her longest weeks with me while he was at C——, so that he might very probably think she resided permanently with me, or I with her. No, I had no need to ask Aunt Betsy any thing about the matter. But did I love Mr. Warrington? I could not say that I did, but I loved nobody else, and might it not be that I only did not love him because I had never regarded him in the light of a lover? Was not Mr. Warrington young, handsome, and every thing that a girl's fancy could desire? Were not his circumstances, according to his own showing, unobjectionable? Was I not often very lonely in my solitary dwelling? Was I not frequently sighing for some sweet companionship? I had lost my mother in infancy, I was but just emancipated from school when my only sister married, and a few months later death suddenly deprived me of my dear father, who was all in all to me. I had then accepted the home Martha offered me, but though always treated with the utmost kindness both by her and her husband, I could not help feeling myself somehow a stranger and intermeddler in their domestic happiness. At the end of a year, I determined to have a home of my own, however lonely and joyless it might be. I came to C——. Friends I had found and kind ones, and the years of my life here had not been unhappy; still I was conscious of something wanting, of sympathies unclaimed, of—of—might it not be in Mr. Warrington's power to make my lot happier? I had been romantic, I had had my dreams of ideal bliss, I was conscious that in all this self-questioning, this hesitation, there was wonderfully little romance. It was not the love I had dreamt of. But time and youth were fleeting, and such dreams becoming more and more unlikely ever to be realized. Still I hesitated what answer to return Mr. Warrington. I was not prepared to write "Come, I await you with open arms," but was it necessary either to do this or to bid him avaunt? Might I not choose a middle course,—the *happy* medium?

My mind was made up. It wanted a good many hours to post-time, but that was no reason why I should not write my letter at once. I took out my writing-case and a sheet of note-paper from it. No, five quires for a shilling might do very well for making out washing bills upon, or even for the ordinary purposes of letter-writing; but it was not worthy of bearing the transcript of an answer to an offer of marriage. I placed before me in its stead a sheet of superfine cream laid, and brought my pen to bear upon its smooth surface.

"My dear Sir,"—No, such a commencement was in too marked contrast to Mr. Warrington's passionate address. Those three words would of themselves suffice to give the death-blow to his hopes—he would dash my letter into the fire, having read no further. I took a second sheet, and wrote "My dear James." No, maidenly reserve would not permit me to use such familiarity to a man whom until that very morning I had regarded quite as a stranger. With my third sheet I succeeded better.

"MY DEAR MR. WARRINGTON,—Your letter, this morning received, has surprised me very much indeed. I am, however, deeply sensible of the honor you have done me, and although I cannot at present say that I return the sentiments you have been pleased to express for me, I do not feel that it is impossible I should ever be able to do so. I know you so little, and you, too, know so little of me, that I cannot feel certain that on further acquaintance you might not discover I was not at all what you thought me, that your sentiments for me and wishes might not change. Cannot we meet as friends, without further engagement on either side for the present? On these terms, I should be very happy to see you again at C——. Meanwhile believe me,

"My dear Mr. Warrington,

"Yours very sincerely,

"MARY HENDERSON."

Having read over this epistle, and found nothing to alter therein, I folded it in an envelope, sealed and directed it. Nothing further remained but to carry it to the post, which I purposed myself to do, while taking my usual morning walk before dinner. The next hour, however, put an end to this project. The sky had all the morning been threatening, it began to rain, and soon settled into a determined wet day. Well, no matter, I could stay in and finish little Fanny's frock, and Bridget could take the letter by and by. Talk or think of a certain person, and—my maid's journey to the post was scarcely settled in my mind, when there came a tap at the door of the room in which I was sitting, immediately followed by the appearance of her round, good-humored face within it.

"Please, ma'am, I came to ask if you'd be so good as let me go home this afternoon. Cousin Richard's just come to say mother wants to see me very much."

And Cousin Richard doubtless wants to walk home with you very much, too, I thought to myself. I had for some time had a suspicion that Bridget had an admirer, and the deepening flush in the damsel's at all times rosy cheeks, as she named the name of Cousin Richard, convinced me he was the man. I was never a hard mistress, and probably the having a love affair of my own on the way, made me look with a kindlier eye than usual on that of my domestic. So I said,—

"Very well, Bridget, I have no objection to your going to see your mother. I am afraid though you'll have a very wet walk."

Bridget's home was something more than two miles off.

I did not hear the damsel's answer very distinctly, but I am almost sure Cousin Richard's name was uttered again, together with something about a "big umbrella."

"Very well, Bridget," I resumed, "I have only to say further that I shall expect you back by nine o'clock in the evening, and as you pass the post-office in going, don't forget to post this letter."

Bridget acquiesced with a pleased smile and a courtesy, took the letter from my hand and departed. I then settled myself industriously to work, now and then letting my thoughts follow the rustic lovers under their big umbrella, but more frequently centring them upon Mr. James Warrington and his extraordinary passion for myself. At two o'clock I dined. I had but just finished this meal when there came again a rap at my door, and cook entered (there was no one else to play the part of waiting-maid, now Bridget was gone), bearing a note in her hand.

"Please, ma'am, a servant's brought this from Miss Morton, and is to wait for an answer."

"Miss Morton," I mentally ejaculated, "I trust she's not going to give one of her stupid tea-parties." The note was as usual in her niece's handwriting, but I soon discovered its purport was quite different to that I had so hastily deprecated. Thus it ran:—

"DEAR MISS HENDERSON,—The enclosed came by post this morning, in an envelope addressed to me, evidently by mistake. I hasten to forward it to you, and beg you, in case you should in like manner, as seems probable, have received a note intended for me, to be so kind as to send it by the bearer.

"Ever, dear Miss Henderson,
"Yours affectionately,
"MARY MORTON."

With a presentiment of what was to follow, I hastily glanced at the enclosure.

"Mr. Warrington presents his compliments to Miss Henderson, and would feel greatly obliged if she would kindly inform him of the name and publisher of the work on British Ferns she did him the favor to lend him on a former occasion. Mr. Warrington's uncertain recollection, and his wish to procure the book for a friend, must be his apology for troubling Miss Henderson."

Here was a pleasant mistake! What a simpleton I had made of myself! If it might have been but in my own eyes it would have been tolerable, though humiliating enough. But, alas! my letter to Mr. Warrington was already in the post. Both he and Mary Morton would laugh over my vain credulity. Where was his letter which had so deceived me? It was quickly found. I could have torn it to atoms in my impotent wrath, but the recollection that it belonged of right to Ma., Morton, that she had sent to claim it, restrained me. Enclosing it in an envelope in which I scribbled a line to Mary, telling her I should call to see her the next morning, I gave the letter to the servant who waited for it, and was then at liberty to indulge my own reflections, which it will be imagined were any thing but agreeable. I was not of an envious disposition, and could have given up the imaginary lover of some two or three hours without a grudge or a sigh. It was that idea of being laughed at I could not bear. Why had I not guessed the truth? Mary Morton was a very sweet, and moreover a very pretty girl, just the sort of girl I might have imagined Mr. Warrington would fall in love with. She had been a schoolfellow of my own, but was so much younger, that we had never been companions, and while she was Mary to me, I was always Miss Henderson to her. She was like myself an orphan, and a maiden aunt had taken her to live with her "out of charity." These were the words at least which the elder Miss Morton always used to everybody, although everybody had their own private opinion that never was soul less illumined by the divine light of charity than Miss Morton's, and that the home, food, and clothing Mary received were but poor payment for the labors which were daily and hourly imposed upon her, for the hard words and cruel taunts which were borne with such uncomplaining meekness. I had often thought how glad I should be if that pretty bird might be freed from its present cage, as now it would very probably be, but if these were the first steps towards such a deliverance, they were not at all such as I should have chosen.

Again I asked myself why I had not guessed the truth. But Mr. Warrington had, so far as my observation went, bestowed scarcely any more attention upon Mary Morton than he had upon Mary Henderson, and I could not blame myself for my want of penetration. No, Mr. Warrington was alone to blame. In a matter of such importance, why did he fail to assure himself he had put the letters into their right covers? Or why need he have written that note to me at all? He seemed pretty confident about the issue of his love suit, surely, that matter of the ferns might have waited a verbal settlement on his arrival at C——. He had spoken of travelling hither on "wings," which agents of locomotion it might be presumed would at any rate be not less expeditious than the railroad. A short time ago I had been debating with myself whether I could *love* Mr. Warrington, and now the question was whether I could help *hating* him.

After awhile this idea came into my head —might I not possibly arrest the progress of my letter? A friend of mine once told me she had effected such a purpose, but then that was in a small country village, where she was well known, and but few letters comparatively passed through the post-office. However, I could but try. It wanted yet nearly two hours to the time of closing. Regardless of the rain which continued to fall heavily, I donned hat and cloak, and soon reached the post-office, but it was a fruitless errand.

"A letter, madam," I was politely informed, "once posted becomes the property of the post-office, which is answerable for its being duly delivered as addressed."

"Well, then," I thought to myself, "there is no help for it. I must resign myself to ridicule, and try to put the best face on the matter, when I go to see Mary Morton to-morrow." All the way home, all tea-time, and all the time after tea, I was revolving in my mind what I should say to her, unable to arrange my thoughts in any satisfactory manner.

As nine o'clock struck, Bridget entered the room to announce her punctual return.

"Well, Bridget," I said, "I hope you have had a pleasant day, and found all well at home."

"Yes, thank you, ma'am," answered the damsel, smiling all over her round pleasant face.

"You put the letter I gave you into the post-office?" Bridget's memory was seldom or never in fault, and I put the question without any doubt of her reply. But, behold, the smile had fled from Bridget's countenance, and in its place was a look of confusion and dismay.

"Dear, ma'am, I am so sorry, but I quite forgot all about the letter."

"Bridget, I could have embraced thee on the spot. Cousin Richard, Cousin Richard, I owe this to thee. Thou hast been a good friend to me this day, and in very gratitude of soul, I will henceforth do all I may to favor thy suit. Bridget shall be half an hour on her errand to the grocer's shop, which is but just over the way, and shall meet no reprimand from me on her return. And should I ever again chance to find the back-door open, and imagine I behold the shadow of thy stalwart form behind it, I will hold my peace to the damsel on the subject of draughts as conducive to that neuralgia to which I am so often a martyr. And in due time (for I have heard thou bearest a good character, and art in receipt of good wages from thy master), I promise a wedding breakfast in this house, and that I will not let the bride depart without some suitable marriage gift." This jubilant apostrophe, I must remark, was in the way of self-communing, and was not uttered aloud in the ears of Bridget, whom after she had returned me the letter from her pocket, I suffered to depart with nothing beyond a consolatory assurance that the letter was of no consequence, and that she need not distress herself about it. When she was gone I immediately threw it into the burning grate, and viewed its speedy reduction to ashes with no little exultation.

Next morning directly after breakfast, I made my call on Mary Morton, having a motive for going early. I found her alone, and had never seen her look so beautiful. Her features, her form, and her complexion had always been faultless, but there was generally an air of depression and melancholy on her countenance (caused doubtless by the tyranny of her aunt), which was painful to look at. This had now given place to an expression of happiness which was perfectly radiant, and the beauty of her face was by no means lessened by the conscious blush which stole over it at my approach. I went up and kissed her.

"Mary, my dear," I said, "I hope you are not angry with me for having found out your secret. It was not my fault, you know."

"Oh, no! dear Miss Henderson," she returned in a voice which was music's self, "but you wont tell anybody else, will you?"

I vowed to be as silent as the grave. And then I added. "I need not ask, Mary, what the end of it will be, I see by your face that you have not told Mr. Warrington he must clip those 'wings' on which he promised himself such a delightful journey to C——. Don't be angry at my nonsense," I went on, as I saw the blush deepening on her cheek, "I am *so* glad, and I hope you will both be *very* happy. But have you sent your letter to Mr. Warrington yet?"

"No," she replied, "it was too late when I got *his*;" to hear her intonation of the pronoun was worth something. "Aunt wanted me to do something for her, and I had not time to write before the post went out."

"Then, Mary, I have a favor to ask of you. Don't tell him of the mistake he made. He might not like my having seen his letter to you, and I should very much prefer he should not know I had done so."

Mary readily promised. I saw, to my great satisfaction, it had never entered into her head to imagine I should have believed the letter really meant for myself.

"Didn't you guess," she asked, "as soon as you read it, that it was meant for me?"

I believe it was my turn to blush now, but had my cheeks, by nature pale, been like unto peonies, Mary would have had no suspicion what in truth I had "guessed." Perhaps she didn't remember that my own name was Mary. Doubtless also she would have deemed it an impossible thing to suppose that Mr. Warrington should be in love with *me*. After a moment's hesitation I answered,—

"Why no, my dear, I can't say I did. I had never seen any thing suspicious either in Mr. Warrington's behavior or in yours. And you see there was no clue in the name, as I know a dozen Marys in this town, at least half of whom have blue eyes, and Mr. Warrington's acquaintance might very possibly have a wider range than mine. So it was the wisest thing to keep the letter until the proper person sent to claim it."

I shall not report our conversation further. On my return home that morning, I wrote a brief note to Mr. Warrington, giving him the desired information about the ferns. Two days later he appeared at C——. Not only Mary, but Mary's aunt smiled upon the lover, which was perhaps as well, though in Mr. Warrington's opiniou it did not signify. That tantine smile made all the difference in Mary's trousseau, which was in consequence a very handsome one. The wedding took place within three months, I was was one of the bridesmaids, and I believe I may truly end my story in the eld-fashioned manner, by saying that the married pair lived happily ever afterwards. My own history has likewise since then been a happy one, but that has nothing to do with this "History of a Love-Letter."

WHAT A HUMBLE PHILANTHROPIST DID IN ENGLAND. — On Saturday the body of a well-known and useful philanthropist, always designated "Tommy" Brown, was interred in St. George's Church, Mossley. The body was preceded by the members of the Shepherd's Flock Lodge of the Loyal Order of Ancient Shepherds, of which the deceased was a member, and was followed by a large procession, including several clergymen. The deceased was born at Barrocks, near Spring Cottages, Car Hill, in 1829, and died on Monday morning. In his childhood he was subject to fits, and his intellect was somewhat afflicted. When eleven years of age he commenced, and has ever since continued, to solicit subscriptions on behalf of the poor, walking many miles, after his work, for that purpose, or for the still more gratifying one of relieving the distressed.

The deceased for many years kept an accurate account of his receipts and disbursements, which was regularly audited, and it cannot but be worth recording in the "simple annals of the poor," what may be done by a persevering person who has learned "the rich luxury of doing good." On an examination of the books of the deceased for two years ending January, 1861, it is found that he has collected no less a sum than £77 2*s*. 10*d*., in amounts of not less than 6*d*. nor above 5*s*.; but he has disbursed in charity the sum of £90 14*s*. 2*d*., the difference being made up by smaller sums received by him, and 1*s*. per week which he contributed from his own scanty earnings. Since the above date he had received, according to his last entries, £4 1*s*. 8*d*. and paid £4 2*s*. 4 1-2*d*.

MOUNTAIN SCENERY IN PERU.—As a general rule the mountain scenery in Peru is on too gigantic a scale to enable one to appreciate it. You have to travel over vast wastes before you come upon the lovely spots that nestle in the recesses of the great Sierra. Putting aside such limited scenes as those in the valley of Vilcamayu, or the campina of Arequipa, the most striking general view of the mountains that I can recollect, is from the middle of the desert of Islay. But let no one expect in a tropical climate the more varied effects of European mountain scenery. Out of the temperate zones is found no Monte Rosa "hanging there,"

"Faintly flushing, phantom fair,
A thousand shadowy pencilled valleys
And snowy dells in a golden air."

The traveller rises so gradually towards what appears to be the base of the gigantic range, that without being aware of it he has already passed out of the region of the most beautiful vegetation, and the scene has become bare, and cold, and desolate; whereas, among mountains on a smaller scale, you can approach their boldest passes before you have bid farewell to tree, and flower, and grass. But what is lost in beauty is gained in a conception of grandeur and vastness. Never till you have travelled painfully day after day over some small portion of the far-stretching Andes will you understand what a barrier they are; on what a scale the mountain masses are piled together; or that the vast and desolate pampas over which you have been riding, are simply the dreary gradients to mountain-tops that roll away as far as you can see. And as you ascend the highest passes, still far above you rise the snow-capped peaks untrodden and perhaps unapproachable forever.—*Vacation Tourists and Notes of Travel.*

From The Examiner, 27 April.

THE CIVIL WAR IN AMERICA.

It is impossible to foresee any other than a deplorable immediate issue to the war begun between the citizens of the United States in North and South by the attack on Fort Sumter. Were the consequences less serious we might smile at the details of the act itself: a terrible outpouring of noise and smoke from forts and batteries; a large assembly of ladies seated before the spectacle with opera glasses in their hands; a few stones broken but no bones, and daring services performed under the lively fire of guns that poured out any thing but deadly shot. There had been stir in the navy yards of New York. General Beauregard, therefore, anticipating the arrival at Charleston of six or seven transports with two thousand troops convoyed by three men-of-war, brought to an end Major Anderson's days of tolerance in Fort Sumter, by cutting off the supply of provisions that had been allowed to pass to him, and then calling upon him to surrender. As he could not in honor yield at a word, on the 12th of April—yesterday fortnight—Charleston harbor, which had for some time been arming to the teeth, opened fire on the major in his strong fort, under-garrisoned with about eighty soldiers and thirty workmen, besides being under-armed with only seventy-five out of its one hundred and forty guns. The fort replied to the fire from city and harbor, at first slowly, afterwards briskly, and maintained the duel until next day, Saturday, when the white flag was hoisted, and by the first easy victory of the Secessionists the States of the North were thoroughly provoked to battle.

The quarrel is in itself simply deplorable, an "affair of honor," in which region fights against region, instead of one man against another. If there was no peaceful way to union, surely, there was no way left of securing it by war. What could there be but weakness in the union of States partly composed of a beaten South forced into co-operation with a conquering North; the spirit of the South being, moreover, the haughtier?

It is a civil war without a noble cause to sustain either side; mere acting out upon a national scale, and as a national misery, of the old code of the duellist, who fastens on his friend a challenge for a fancied insult, and whose challenge must, as an affair of honor, be accepted. In the United States such feuds have been too often cruel and deadly between man and man, and we fear that they will not be less cruel when once the weapons are raised between State and State.

From The Economist, 27 April.

CIVIL WAR IN AMERICA AND THE ATTITUDE OF ENGLAND.

The fall of Fort Sumter must soon, we fear, if we may rely at all on the drift of the recent news, issue in civil war. The rumor that the Southern Confederation intends to anticipate an attack by moving upon Washington is scarcely likely to be true, for President Davis is too sagacious a man to take a step which would so enrage the North as to induce it to enter heart and soul into an internecine contest with the South. If he were wise, indeed, he would not have ventured any active collision at all, such as has taken place at Charleston. It would have been better to trust exclusively to blockade for the reduction of the Federal garrisons in the revolted States. The moral shock of any collision is most dangerous, as the accounts of the frantic excitement in Washington on the arrival of the news of the collision at Fort Sumter and the surrender of Major Anderson, sufficiently prove. It is true that American rage even at its highest pitch usually manages to stop short where policy would direct, and that we in England are exceedingly liable to be deceived by its effervescent symptoms. Still there is now the gravest reason to apprehend a serious civil war; indeed, all the Free States seem already to have intimated to the President, through the telegraph, their readiness to support a war policy; and, if it is prevented at all, it will only be by the unwillingness of the Northern statesmen to risk the adhesion of the Border States by an actual invasion. But if the Southern States should, as is rumored, be so foolish as to take the initiative by invading Washington, they would play directly into the hands of the extreme party in the North. All compunction would immediately be at an end, and in all probability the Border States would themselves be induced by such a step to fight with the North. The situation is very similar to the attitude of Austria and Sardinia. The neutrals will inevitably throw their influence into the scale of the party attacked. Mr. Lincoln, as far as his own popularity and political position is concerned, can wish for nothing better than to be relieved by his antagonist of the responsibility of a decision. His difficulty has hitherto been, that the great power and wealth of the North has been passive, and reluctant to foment a fratricidal strife. But let once the Slave States take the guilt upon themselves, as in some degree they have already done, and Mr. Lincoln would find his hands strengthened and his cause enthusiastically supported by a power such as does not exist in the Southern States at all. We do not believe, then, in the reported invasion of Washington. A course so blind and insane is utterly inconsistent with the general ability shown by the Southern Government. But we do fear that the strife and defeat at Charleston will render it very difficult for Mr. Lincoln, in the attitude in which he now stands, to evade some attempt at reprisal, and that thus a regular war may soon break out.

Under these grave circumstances it is that Mr. Gregory proposes to ask the House of Commons on Tuesday next to affirm the expediency of an immediate recognition of the Southern Confederation. We can imagine no course more disgraceful to England, or less likely to command the assent of the popular body appealed to. Not that we desire to see a civil war in America, even though the North should be completely triumphant. We have often said that unless there were a Union party in the Southern States considerable enough to make some head even without external assistance, the defeat of the newly confederated States by the North could scarcely lead to any good result. It would be mere military conquest; and a power like the American Union cannot hope to hold together its territory by military force. And seeing that there is, unhappily, but little trace of a powerful Unionist minority among the seceded States, we cannot wish to see a fratricidal strife which would multiply indefinitely the mutual hatreds of North and South, without solving the ultimate difficulty. But this is not the question for us to consider. It has been England's universal rule to acknowledge a *de facto* revolutionary government whenever it has established its practical independence by incontrovertible proofs,—then and not sooner. Whatever be the wisdom or folly of the war which there is but too much reason to believe is now declared between the Federal Government at Washington and the revolted States,—it is not yet begun, or is only just beginning. There can be no question whatever of the constitutional right of President Lincoln to treat the hostile Confederation as a treasonable rebellion, which, so far as it trenches on Federal property and laws, he may resist by force. This is his present attitude. He hopes, however little we may hope, to suppress the rebellion. He thinks, however little we may think, that he shall be able to enforce the laws enacted at Washington, and to redeem the United States property from the hands of the seceders. This may be sanguine; nay, it may even be a mere hallucination. With that we have nothing to do. We profess always to abstain from judging the rights of a quarrel between a people and its rulers, and to guide our conduct by the plain results of political fact. We are now on the eve of seeing what these results will be. Either war or compromise seems now inevitable. If it be compromise, we shall know how to act. If it be war, we are bound to await the results of that war. A premature recognition of the Southern Confederation would be a departure from the recognized course of England, and could not but therefore express a political *bias* in favor of the seceders.

Now, is it even *decent* to ask an English House of Commons to express such a bias in favor of such a power as that which has its seat of government at Montgomery—a power which is based on slavery as the very principle of its individual existence, and which, though it professes for the moment to have abolished the slave-trade, is worked by men many of whom have openly assailed the laws against that traffic as a gross violation of the rights of the South. The head of the Commission appointed to negotiate with the European powers for the recognition of the Southern Federation, the Hon. W. L. Yancey, of Alabama, has devoted a great portion of his public life to denouncing the obsolete views of Washington and the other great American statesmen of the last century on this subject. The men and the journalists who chiefly instigated secession were most of them deeply pledged to a repeal of the slave-trade laws. It is true that when secession was achieved, they found it necessary as a political measure to put forward more moderate men,—men like Mr. Stephen, of Georgia, who had done his best to arrest the secession movement—and to acquiesce in their counsels. But it remains certain that such papers as the *Charleston Mercury*, and such statesmen as Mr. Yancey were the motive power of the secession movement, and will again become the motive power of a slavery extension policy (which in its turn will require the slave-trade as its legitimate result), so soon as the ends of compromise have been answered by securing the recognition of the new power in Europe, and if it may be so, the adhesion of some of the wavering States. Under these circumstances, we earnestly rejoice to see that Mr. W. E. Forster has given notice of an amendment to Mr. Gregory's motion to the effect that "the House does not at present desire to express any opinion in favor of such recognition, and trusts that the Government will at no time make it without obtaining due security against the renewal of the African slave-trade." Such an amendment will come with the greatest weight from the representative of Bradford,—a town which, though identified more with the worsted than the cotton trade, still represents fairly the public spirit of our Northern manufacturing interests. The determination of England not to let interested motives interfere with the high principles which she has always shown on the questions of slavery and the slave-trade, could not be expressed more fittingly than by the member for Bradford.

From The Press, 27 April.

We regret to say that intelligence has arrived from America pregnant with strife and bloodshed. Deeply should we lament such a catastrophe, which we hope and trust may still be averted. It appears to us impossible to reconcile the divided States. Victory on either side will, therefore, be a barren and costly triumph. The Southern States, aware of their own deficiencies, have made great exertions; while the Northern are as yet somewhat supine in their feeling of superior strength, and possibly their consciousness of a better cause. We trust that Mr. Lincoln may be endowed by Providence with the wisdom and humanity to avoid civil war; but we must own that his presidential path is beset with greater difficulties and complications than ever were known even to Washington. Whatever be the issue, the present dark and threatening aspect of affairs in the States gives threefold weight and pressing importance to all that we have urged in this and former articles. And we may add, in reference to the bold enunciation of a contingency which had its birth in the columns of *The Press*—viz., that several of the Northern States may ere long proclaim their return under the sovereignty of these isles as the free choice of a people of a common language, ancestry, and race—that we have since seen many indications of the reality of the foundation on which our assumptions were based.

We are of opinion that war between the States—much and earnestly as we deprecate such a terrible event—will increase the chances of an offer on the part of the Northern States of America to unite with the consolidated Northern Provinces under the time-honored banner of Old England, and thus to defy the world. What honor would accrue from such event both to parent and to child! The States of America, in spite of Mr. Cobden's fallacies, are far more heavily taxed than our colonies. Their progress has tripped itself up in the universal race. Their intellect has not expanded as it should have done. The truth is, it has not had time. There is the raw material of genius, which has never yet been polished or worked up. A period of social and political repose would do wonders in this respect for our transatlantic kinsmen. This, however, is not a point which we have leisure to discuss at the present moment. All we wish to see is, that England should consolidate her own empire in North America, by taking steps which are not only wise but necessary in any and every case,—to defend and maintain her own, or to accept the opportunities of righteous and legitimate aggrandizement which may await her.

From The Saturday Review, 27 April.

AMERICA.

The attack on Fort Sumter may be explained by the strong interest of the seceding States in provoking a collision. Although the officer in command seems to have sustained the honor of his flag, the result of the struggle could not have been doubtful. The Government of Washington must have foreseen the occurrence, and it has throughout preserved the secret of its intentions with unusual firmness. The telegraphs and the newspaper correspondents have become so far aware of the change as to diversify their positive statements with occasional confessions of ignorance. A small force has been despatched southward, but it has for some time been understood that the Cabinet had abandoned all intention of relieving Major Anderson in Fort Sumter. The remaining alternatives were the occupation of posts on the islands of the southern coast, and the more formidable enterprise of reinforcing General Houston in Texas. In the absence of information, it may be safely assumed that Mr. Lincoln had never any intention of commencing hostilities, though it might be prudent to take up positions which might be serviceable in the event of a collision, while they would have a tendency to exercise a favorable influence on negotiation. Mr. Jefferson Davis has probably a defensive force greatly superior to any army of which the Northern States could dispose for purposes of invasion. On the other hand, he cannot hope to command the sea, and he must be well aware that foreign powers will not be hasty to quarrel on the subject of blockade with the United States. It is said, on doubtful authority, that there is a hope of reconquering the divided population of Texas. General Houston, after ratifying the vote of secession, has disputed the authority of the Convention which was elected for the special purpose of deciding for or against the maintenance of the Union. Northern politicians think that the quarrel between the rival authorities of the State indicates the existence of a strong party, perhaps of a majority, opposed to secession; yet it is clear that the Convention, according to American usages, represented the popular judgment, and the governor bimself, who leads the opposite, party, is pledged to the same policy. Even if a schism really exists, it will disappear as soon as either faction receives offers of assistance from the Government of the United States. The people of Texas are not of the straitest sect of political moralists, as they principally consist of daring adventurers, who are at the same time enamored of slavery and willing to carry on a desultory warfare with savages and with half-civilized Mexican neighbors. It is certain that few among their number will sympathize with the Republicans who at present hold office at Washington. General Houston, if he wishes to preserve his influence, will be the first to repudiate the armed alliance of the obnoxious North. Recent events have not encouraged projects for the employment of the United States army in Texas. The respectable Twiggs laid down his arms to the secessionists only a few weeks since, transcending the Floyds and their accomplices as far as a deserter is, in common estimation, regarded as worse than a simple traitor The astonishment and admiration which have been called forth by Major Anderson's discharge of a plain duty seem to show that little reliance is to be placed on the average officers of the army. The soldiers, who are for the most part either Irishmen or Germans, are not likely to show any patriotic enthusiasm in favor of the service. Any force which might be sent to Texas from the North would collapse and disappear before it could enter on a campaign for the restoration of the former Federal Government. The inhabitants of the State may perhaps require assistance against the Indians and Mexicans, who are said to have lately taken advantage of the distracted state of the Union; but the Southern Confederation will furnish numerous volunteers for a popular war, which may serve as a natural commencement of its meditated conquests in Spanish America. On the whole, it is highly improbable that Mr. Lincoln has sent his available force to a point far removed from the expected scene of hostilities. If the remainder of the South maintains its independence, it will evidently be impossible for Texas to resume its former connection with the Government of the United States.

The other Federal posts in the South will probably share the fate of Fort Sumter. Both the principal parties in the dispute are, with good reason, chiefly anxious to secure the support of the wavering Border States. Virginia and Kentucky can only be kept in the Union by pacific and conciliatory measures; and therefore Mr. Lincoln and Mr. Seward had every reason for postponing a collision as long as possible. Mr. Davis may perhaps have hoped to effect his object by a precisely opposite course. When blood has once been shed, alliances are determined by the preponderance of interests and sympathies, and not by a judicial estimate of the merits of the ultimate quarrel. Slave States, since the struggle has begun, will not desire to be at war with the supporters of their own institutions. In ordinary times, it would be highly inconvenient to Border slaveholders to live in the neighborhood of an imaginary frontier with free institutions beyond it, and without a fugitive slave-law; but if it is necessary to break with either party, Virginia, as a slave-breeding country, can no more dispense with the cotton districts than the Lincolnshire horse-dealer could do without a market in London. It was, therefore, the interest of the South, and not of the North, to bring about a state of affairs in which neutrals will be compelled to choose their side. For this purpose, it may have been worth while to accept the responsibility of being both really and apparently in the wrong. Another motive for a rupture may have been furnished by the existence of the minority which, according to the sanguine belief of Northern politicians, is inclined to revoke the act of secession. Mr. Jefferson Davis and his colleagues are themselves undoubtedly in earnest, and they must be well aware that a war would at once suppress all difference of opinion. At the time of the revolt against England, a large part of the American population was opposed to separation, but the more numerous or more vigorous section affected to speak in the name of the country, which has since almost forgotten a difference of opinion inconsistent with patriotic traditions. Whatever private hesitations may prevail, the fall of Fort Sumter will be celebrated by all South Carolina with unanimous shouts of triumph.

The English worshippers of American institutions are in danger of losing their last pretext for preferring the Republic to the obsolete and tyrannical Monarchy of England. Till within a few months, they were never tired of pointing to the harmony and perfect unity of a great empire without an army, a navy, or a peerage. When the disruption came upon them unawares, after an interval of surprise and disappointment, Mr. Bright's followers recovered their breath to express their admiration for the mode in which the secession had been accomplished. Industry, they said, went on as before—there was no quarrel, except in newspapers—and the peaceful euthanasia of the Union was the best proof of its sound constitution. Kingdoms and aristocratic Republics, with armed forces at their disposal, resisted with ruinous obstinacy, at the cost of unlimited bloodshed, the revolt of disaffected provinces. The American Government, on the other hand, had avoided the sin and danger of fighting, because, amongst other reasons, there was no army to fight. Twiggs himself, it might be added, obtained his commission as general, and his appointment to command in Texas, not from a parliamentary kinsman, but only from a Secretary at War who foresaw the necessity for an accomplice in treason. Ordinary politicians doubted whether facility of discerption was, in politics or in nature, characteristic of a high organization. There are reptiles or insects which grow into new units when they are cut in pieces, while warm-blooded animals are liable to die on the loss of any vital part of the system. It now appears that the peaceable completion of the secession has become impossible, and it will be necessary to discover some new ground of superiority by which Mr. Buchanan or Mr. Lincoln may be advantageously contrasted with Queen Victoria. The distinction is not to be found in commercial orthodoxy, for the Morrill Tariff shows that the Republican manufacturers can be as greedy of selfish advantage as the stoutest agricultural Protectionists who were formerly to be found in England. Until the present difficulty has passed away, perhaps it would be convenient to discontinue the standing contrast between English defects and American excellences. Even Mr. Berkeley recited his ballot performance without a single reference to his former transatlantic models.

From The London Review.

AMERICAN PROBABILITIES.

We explained last week why we felt satisfied that the secession of the Southern States was and had long been inevitable; and it was not difficult to find reasons why both parties, if they were wise, might separate in a friendly manner.

The Southerners dislike the New Englanders and New Yorkers as prigs; they despise them as snobs; they envy them as prosperous rivals; they are irritated by them as wealthy creditors. They resent their suspected interference with the institution of slavery, and they are mortified by their increasing preponderance in Congress. The Northerners, to a great extent, reciprocate the hostile feeling, and are scandalized, if not at the brutal and violent behavior of many of the Southern politicians, orators, and rowdies, at least at the disgrace which this brings upon the American name in the eyes of other nations. Then, again, the Southerners have their own grand dreams of empire — of an empire sustained and based, like the democracies of old, on the institution of domestic slavery — an empire reaching to the Isthmus, and including Cuba and the Antilles, in which all white men shall be chiefs and privileged rulers, and the only working classes shall be negroes. They wish to be at liberty and absolutely unfettered to carry out these gorgeous visions; and they feel that the Free States, especially as these become more and more powerful in the Legislature, would materially hamper their realization, as well as carry off, perhaps, the lion's share of the profits, and the pride of rule.

Under such circumstances, it is plain that the North would gain little by compelling the adherence to the Union of five or six millions of unwilling citizens, even if coercion on such a scale were possible. But coercion on such a scale never can be possible; and in no instance less than in the case before us, since such an attempt would at once swell the number of the Secessionists by the adhesion of all the Border States to the Southern Confederacy; and in the face of so equal a division, of course, the very idea of compulsion must be abandoned as absurd; while, even without such assistance, it is notorious that the Secessionists are at present much better prepared than their opponents for a conflict. They are united and resolute, while the Northerners are uncertain and divided. They have not only more men now under arms, but they have a far larger *idle* population to recruit from—the "mean whites," accustomed to fight and bully, inured to hardship, and greedy for plunder and for pay. The North certainly is far richer, and has greater resources in the background, but it is also more busy and more prudent; and, to complete the contrast, the South has over it the fatal though discreditable advantage which, in such cases, the debtor always has over his creditor. The slaveholding States, both publicly and privately, owe vast sums of money to Northern capitalists and merchants, of which, in case of civil war, they will assuredly withhold payment. We, therefore, felt sure that there would be no attempt at coercion on the part of the Northern States; since the mere attempt to coerce must bring on civil war; and since the citizens of the Northern States have too much good sense, to say nothing of good feeling, to encounter a civil war, which would cost them so much, and could profit them so little. If discomfited, they would be disgraced and damaged. If successful, they could reap nothing but a vast harvest of future and ceaseless embarrassment.

The reasons why the Southern States should desire to accomplish their secession peaceably were, in our eyes, not less valid than those which should operate upon the Northern States. And the most cogent of them may be inferred from the statements we have already made of the superiority in riches and eventual resources possessed by the North. Yet we saw that it was not impossible that the angry passions of the Southern politicians might break out in acts of violence; though we hoped for better things, if not from their good feeling, at least from their prudence. But the news brought by the mail, which has just arrived, has dashed those hopes to the ground. We learn that hostilities have actually commenced—that the army of the seceding States, which has long been threatening Fort Sumter, has attacked it with all the forms of war; heavy batteries battered its walls, and, for awhile, the guns of the fort replied with vigor, till at last the heavy cannon of the assailants set fire to the wooden buildings within the fort; then, after a resistance of something less than two days, Major Anderson, the officer in command, was forced to surrender with his garrison.

The secessionists were, naturally, greatly elated at this success; their army was increasing, and fresh troops were swarming into Charleston; the Southern Government had called on each secession State for additional troops; and it was hourly expected that they would proceed to the attack of Washington.

We learn at the same time that, though all business was suspended, and the citizens of the capital, as is natural, were in the greatest state of excitement, yet in the money-market the Government securities had not fallen. Even now we would hope that this may be taken as a sign that in the opinion of the sounder part of the population, it may still be possible to arrest the war before it proceeds to more formidable lengths, and the fact of success having attended the first efforts of the Secessionists may render such a termination of it more possible than if they had failed. Unless they have very able generals at their head nothing is more embarrassing than rapid success; and a large party will surely be found who will hesitate before they actually attack the capital, rendered sacred as it must be in the eyes of many of them by the venerable name of Washington; and the slightest division or vacillation will give time for the cooler heads on both sides to interpose. The greater the danger, the greater the credit to those who by their wisdom and public virtue may exert themselves to avert it. And American vanity, if, at such a solemn moment, there is any room for such a feeling, may take comfort in the idea that the question of the continuance or cessation of hostilities in these States is reckoned one of the greatest importance in every country in Europe. If England seems to take an especial interest in the question, it is not merely because of the extent to which our commerce is connected with that of America, but because, looking on them as our descendants, we feel our national credit in some degree at stake in the wisdom and dignity of their conduct. This consideration it was that enabled Anchises to speak to Cæsar on a similar subject with greater authority than to Pompey; and his words we, as the mother country, may apply to both the parties in the unnatural strife that threatens to divide them:—

> "Tuque prior tu parce genus qui ducis Olympo,
> Projice tela manu sanguis meus."

A MONTHLY review of journalism in France is a new feature in its periodical literature. The first number contains a full history of the *Siècle*, its management, and biographies of its editors. No less than twenty eminent writers are employed on it, each having an appropriate department. Some of the editors have secretaries to assist them. It has besides a large number of reporters, who are styled the rifle battalion. The leading journals of Paris are very ably edited, and their writers are generally learned and brilliant men, familiar with every thing worth knowing.

IN order to advance more readily into Germany, Russia has constructed a "quadrilateral" of fortresses, between the Vistula, the Narew, the Bug, and the Wreprz. The fortresses are Modlin, four leagues from Warsaw, Litouski, Tareuse and Demblin. Besides these is the citadel of Alexander, at Warsaw, one of the strongest military positions in the world.

BEAUTY'S ORDERS.

Three knights are bent at Laura's knee
And each his suit prefers;
But all unmoved will Laura be
To pay their love with hers.
"Away," she cries, "o'er sea and land,
Your deeds throughout a year,
Shall prove who best deserves a hand
He vows to prize so dear."
Now, 'tis a duty,
I have heard,
To take a beauty
At her word.

The first went forth with lance in rest,
And many a foeman found;
But proud as waved that foeman's crest,
Its plumage kissed the ground.
The next unmoored a gallant bark,
And wooed a favoring breeze;
He chased each pirate banner dark,
And swept it from the seas.
For, 'tis a duty,
I have heard,
To take a beauty
At her word.

The third, nor bark, nor sail took he,
Nor lance in rest he laid;
But daily swore, at Laura's knee,
That love his parting stayed.
And when their year of trial ceased,
Two champions homeward hied,
In time to grace a marriage feast,
To greet a rival's bride.
Still, 'tis a duty,
I have heard,
To take a beauty,
At her word.

—*Welcome Guest.*

A SAILOR'S WIFE'S SONG.

Oh, bonny is my husband's ship, the ship that well I love,
And welcome are its coming sails, all welcome sights above;
There's not a tarry rope, not a spar that there I see,
Not a deck-plank that he treads on, but it's oh, how dear to me!

Oh, bright, bright was the May-time through which he sailed away,
But to me more wan and dreary than November was the day;
O wintry winds, beat keen with sleet, O cold seas, rage and foam,
But calm will be, and bright to me, the day that brings him home.

O Katie, playing on the floor—O Jockie, at my knee,
When father sits beside the fire, how happy we shall be!
O babe unborn, that when he comes shall bless my happy breast—
God send my baby safe to me to kiss him with the rest.

And many a pretty thing he'll bring for little Kate and Jock—
Carved wooden man and funny beast, and shell and sparkling rock;
A monkey, perhaps, so clever, with Kate and Jock to play,
And a rainbow-colored parrot, that will chatter all the day.

Oh, never be a sailor, Jock, to make the angry foam
The terror of a loving wife and babes you've left at home;
And marry not a sailor, Kate, to be his weary wife,
Unless you get one dear as he who's dear to me as life.

Move swiftly on, O lonesome hours; tick quicker on, O clock,
And bring the hour when at my breast my baby I shall rock—
When in my arms my blessèd babe shall laugh and leap and crow,
And I shall teach its little eyes its father's face to know.

O Thou who guid'st the stormy winds—O Thou who rul'st the sea—
O God, look down in mercy upon my babes and me:
Through storms and perils of the deep, oh, hold him in thy hand,
That we may bless thy blessèd name when safe he treads the strand.

O wives who're blessed with plenty, how little do you know
The blessings that on such as I your riches would bestow.
O John, come back with half enough to keep you safe ashore,
And day and night I'll work, that you may go to sea no more.

—*Chambers's Journal.*

He. Violet, little one mine!
I would love thee, but thou art so small.

She. Love me, my love, from those heights of thine,
And I shall grow tall, so tall!
The pearl is small, but it hangs above
A royal brow, and kingly mind:
The quail is little, little, my love,
But she leaves the hunter behind.

Owen Meredith.

THE LIVING AGE.

No. 888.—8 June, 1861.

CONTENTS.

NEW BOOKS.

A NEW MONETARY SYSTEM. By Edward Kellogg. Edited by Mary Kellogg Putnam. New York: Rudd and Carleton.

A KEY TO THE DISUNION CONSPIRACY. The Partisan Leader. By Beverly Tucker, of Virginia. Secretly printed in Washington (in the year 1836) by Duff Green, for circulation in the Southern States. But afterward suppressed. New York: Rudd and Carleton.

PUBLISHED EVERY SATURDAY BY

LITTELL, SON, & CO., BOSTON.

For Six Dollars a year, in advance, *remitted directly to the Publishers*, the LIVING AGE will be punctually forwarded *free of postage*.

Complete sets of the First Series, in thirty-six volumes, and of the Second Series, in twenty volumes, handsomely bound, packed in neat boxes, and delivered in all the principal cities, free of expense of freight, are for sale at two dollars a volume.

ANY VOLUME may be had separately, at two dollars, bound, or a dollar and a half in numbers.

ANY NUMBER may be had for 13 cents; and it is well worth while for subscribers or purchasers to complete any broken volumes they may have, and thus greatly enhance their value.

From The N. Y. Evangelist, 16 May.

WISDOM, PATIENCE, AND FIRMNESS.

It is matter of devout gratitude to God, in this hour of our country's peril, that we have at the head of our armies a chief in whose great skill, long experience, and tried patriotism, we can place unbounded confidence. For half a century General Scott has been engaged in the service of his country. He has risen from one grade to another, till he now occupies the highest military rank ever given to an officer—that of lieutenant-general—a rank created for him, and filled by no other since Washington. He has been often engaged in war, has fought in hard battles, and conducted great campaigns with masterly skill and success; and yet he has been as much distinguished for humanity as for judgment and sagacity in the great movements of war.

General Scott is now an old man (seventy-six years), and is suffering physically from the infirmities of age. Yet we are assured by those who have been with him lately and have seen him intimately, that his mind is as clear as ever. And though he may not be able in person to take the field, he may render a far greater service in presiding at the centre, with his clear eye looking out as on a map over the whole theatre of war, ordering the combinations and directing the whole campaign.

His patriotism, too, is undoubted. Though a native of Virginia, he acknowledges no allegiance but that to his whole country. A few weeks ago, when Virginia seceded, and many of his officers, including even his own aids, fell away from their duty, there were those who trembled lest even *his* iron firmness might be shaken. Such was the sanguine hope of many at the South. It was even reported that he *had* resigned, and so confidently was it believed, that a commissioner came from Richmond to offer him the command of the armies of Virginia! But the man who dared to name the proposal received a reply which silenced him and sent him back humbled and ashamed. He has just renewed for the third time his solemn oath of allegiance to the United States, and is evidently determined to give his last days and his last strength to the service of his country. Such is the man who is now at the head of our armies. In this we recognize the same Providence which raised up Washington to be our leader in the war of Independence, and which has now preserved to us the greatest captain of the age to be the second deliverer of his country.

The prominent traits in the character of General Scott, as shown in all his military career, are great caution and wisdom in laying his plans, a sagacity which though it may seem slow, render success inevitable, and his humanity. The old hero is as gentle as he is brave, and never for the mere glory of a dashing feat of arms has he been known to sacrifice a single life. He is sometimes accused by amateur soldiers or flippant martinets of being *slow*, and so in one sense he is. In his whole history no one thing has been more often proved than that General Scott *cannot and will not be hurried*. He will take ample time to make all his preparations complete before he will hazard a step on which may depend the fate of an army. But if his advance is deliberate, how firm and sure! His step is slow, but it is the tread of a giant, and when he moves, every thing is swept before his irresistible march.

PRAYER FOR THE COUNTRY.

(SET FORTH BY THE BISHOP OF NEW HAMPSHIRE.)

Almighty and Eternal God, King of kings and Lord of lords, by whose judgment nations are cast down, and by whose mercy they rise again in strength and glory, we humble ourselves before thee in this great extremity and distress of our country. And while we confess our guilt and unworthiness in thy sight, and must own the justice of this visitation of thy wrath, we fervently implore thy forgiveness, and thy gracious intervention for our relief and protection. By thy merciful and mighty power uphold, we beseech thee, the Government of this land. Overrule the counsels of those who are enemies of union and peace. To all in authority over us give wisdom, energy, and courage, that through their faithful performance of duty and the resources committed to them by thy providence and made effectual by thy blessing, this Republic may be preserved in peace to many generations. Grant that our free institutions may stand as things that cannot be shaken, but which remain as monuments of thy protecting care and the patriotism of thy people. Stay the progress of insurrection and intestine war. Restore to our country union, peace, and prosperity,—and grant, that all of us, humbled and improved by these sore afflictions, may henceforth strive more faithfully to serve thee in this world, and may finally attain to everlasting life hereafter; through Jesus Christ our Lord. *Amen.*

From The Quarterly Review.

Life of the Right Honorable William Pitt. By Earl Stanhope. Vols. I. and II. London, 1861.

In undertaking to write the life of his distinguished kinsman, Lord Stanhope is not entering upon absolutely untrodden ground; but his predecessors have done their work so badly, that to the generality of readers a Life of Pitt will be absolutely new. Bishop Tomline's performance has been described, by a high authority, as having the honor of being the worst biography of its size in the world. The small portion of it that is original is undoubtedly distinguished by the solemn emptiness of which the bishop was an acknowledged master. But the sarcastic observation of a contemporary reviewer, that "the work was due less to his lordship's pen than to his lordship's sharp and faithful scissors," is really applicable in almost as great a degree to the work of his predecessor, Mr. John Gifford. Gifford's Life of Pitt was conceived on too large a scale, and drew too liberally upon Hansard, to be an attractive biography; and a biographer misses his chief function if his performance is not attractive. His business is to increase the fame of his hero, and no hero's fame was ever increased by being associated with a dull compilation. Lord Macaulay's essay in the "Encyclopædia Britannica" * is, indeed, as fascinating as any thing that ever issued from his pen; but he was necessarily limited to a very narrow space, and the sketch with which he was forced to content himself is too slight to rank as a biography. The field is, therefore, open to Lord Stanhope practically without competitors. Few persons could be better fitted to perform a task which every Englishman must wish to see done well. The biography of Pitt should not be abandoned, as the biographies of great men too often are, to writers who have no other title to literary fame. A life that was all public, a career so closely intertwined with English history that all its lights and shades correspond with the prosperity or the perils of the whole community, is most fittingly intrusted to the hands of one who holds the first rank among the living historians of England. Lord Stanhope's political position is also favorable to his undertaking. That Pitt's biographer should have been once a House of Commons partisan is almost indispensable to enable him to describe with fidelity a conflict which was carried on almost entirely within its walls; but a very keen interest in the party struggles of the moment would be incompatible with that judicial habit of mind which is of the first necessity in the chronicler of deeds which have been the subject of such embittered controversy. It is natural that high expectations should be excited by a work whose author possesses so many qualifications for his task; and the work itself will not disappoint those who have formed them. It is agreeable and lively in its style, and at the same time exact and ample in its details, without overtasking the reader's attention by the reprint of tedious state papers or of the jejune and lifeless abstracts which are all that is left to us of the oratory of those times. Its solid merits as an historical contribution will be generally recognized. The pleasantness of the style does not rob the narrative of its impartiality. In respect to transactions and questions some of which affect us very nearly even now, it may not be possible to maintain an absolute impartiality; but Lord Stanhope seems to have approached more nearly than any previous writer upon the same period to this unattainable ideal. Indeed, his gentleness of judgment often overshoots the requirements of equity; it amounts to optimism. He describes the proceedings of an age when political corruption had not died out, and faction was looked upon rather as a merit than a sin, with as large a charity and as unsuspicious a faith in the virtue of politicians as if he were writing of our own quieter and purer times. It is, undoubtedly, a fault on the right side. Readers will be more competent and more willing to temper Lord Stanhope's mercy with justice than to perform the opposite process; and his kindlier judgments and roseate views are very agreeable reading, and leave pleasant illusions on the mind, just as a Richmond head is pleasanter to look at than a photograph, though one may not be able to repress the consciousness that it overflatters the grim human reality.

The materials already in existence for the history of this period are very ample, and have been long before the world. Lord

* *Living Age*, No. 778.

Stanhope, however, brings to the common stock some new contributions of very considerable interest. Pitt's letters to his mother, his correspondence with his friend the Duke of Rutland, and the king's letters to him, have been committed to Lord Stanhope's care, and are either printed at length in these volumes, or worked up into the narrative. That they should introduce any new facts into a history which has been so exhaustively investigated was, of course, not to be expected; but they enable him to give fresh life to an old story, and, here and there, to throw a new light upon a controverted question. His suggestion, for instance, that Lord Temple's sudden retirement from office, two days after he had overthrown the Coalition, was due to his indignation at not being able to extract a dukedom out of George the Third, will probably be accepted henceforth as the solution of that mysterious episode. It is certainly more probable than the theory of that most inaccurate of chroniclers, Wraxall, which both Lord Macaulay and Mr. Massey have endorsed, that he retired in disgust because he could not procure an immediate dissolution. Lord Stanhope produces a letter of George the Third, hitherto unpublished, which proves that the king was very angry at Temple's desertion on this occasion, and stigmatized it as "base conduct;" yet no one pressed an immediate dissolution more anxiously upon Mr. Pitt than the king himself, and he was not likely to treat as "base conduct" an overzealous maintenance of the same opinion. On the other hand, Temple's later correspondence betrays that he had at some earlier period asked for a dukedom, and that he was very sore at having been refused.* The hint which is furnished by the worthlessness of the excuse which he instructed his brother, Mr. W. Grenville, to make in the House of Commons, deserves, too, to be taken into consideration. It was to the effect that Temple had resigned, in order to be in a better position for repelling the charges that had been made against him in that House. But the charges had been made before he took office, so that, if they were enough to induce him to resign it, they would have been enough to induce him never to accept it. Every one appears to be agreed that the reason thus publicly given was not the true one: but if there had not been something in his reason for retiring which he was ashamed of publishing, he never would have put forward a transparently false one in its stead. The most sensitive of men, which Temple was not, would hardly feel that it was disgraceful to have had his advice on a matter of mere tactics overruled; but most people would be rather ashamed of letting it be known that they had abandoned their sovereign in a grave emergency because an extra title had been refused them.

The letters of George the Third are the most interesting part of the new matter contributed by Lord Stanhope. They give a very different picture of the king from that which has been drawn by partisan humorists and pamphleteers. They show a shrewd and intelligent mind, thoroughly familiar with public affairs. The style of them is hasty, the grammar not always irreproachable; but the sound and practical character of the king's opinions would have done honor to persons who have far more opportunities of mixing with the world than can ever fall to the lot of monarchs. A taste for useless and costly wars has often been made the reproach of his policy. How ill those who make this charge have appreciated the real nature of his convictions and inclinations, the following extract will sufficiently prove. It is a letter written to Mr. Pitt on the occasion of the introduction of the sinking fund. Some portions of it read like selections from one of Mr. Bright's attacks upon foreign-office diplomacy:—

"Considering Mr. Pitt has had the unpleasant office of providing for the expenses incurred by the last war, it is but just he should have the full merit he deserves of

* A letter of Mr. W. Grenville, to which Lord Stanhope has not adverted, shows that about eight months before, while Temple was still in Ireland, he was scheming to obtain a step in the peerage, and was only withheld from pressing it on the king by the king's resolution to grant no patents while Fox was minister. It therefore strongly confirms the idea that he seized the first moment after Fox's fall and his own accession to office to urge his claim. The following is the passage, in a letter dated April 1, 1783:—

"You will observe that part of the king's ground is a resistance to advancements as well as to creations. This seemed naturally to throw so much difficulty upon your object that I thought there would be an indelicacy in pressing it at the time you were lamenting the unavoidable difficulties under which he already labors. This delay, I firmly believe, will be very short indeed."

having the public know and feel that he has now proposed a measure that will render the nation again respectable, if she has the sense to remain quiet some years, and not by wanting to take a showy part in the transactions of Europe, again become the dupe of other powers, and from ideal greatness draw herself into lasting distress. The old English saying is applicable to our situation: 'England must cut her coat according to her cloth.'"

The king's manner, like his style, never did justice to the sterling value of the shrewd thought and honest emotions that it concealed. Mankind, and especially literary mankind, are the ready dupes of a squib or of a caricature; and one ridiculous trait or habit will often outweigh in their judgment a whole catalogue of virtues. George the Third's celebrated "What, what?" has made a deeper impression upon the minds of the writers of the last thirty years than all the coarseness of his grandfather, or the still graver failings of his son. The letters published in these volumes will do something to restore to its proper place in public estimation the character of a monarch who may have committed errors, but who has been systematically maligned, not on account of those errors, but on account of his hostility to the profligate statesman whom the Whigs have delighted to honor.

Two volumes of the biography have been published, extending as far as the year 1796: two more, which will conclude the work, will shortly follow. The earlier portion of the biography, which deals with the brief interval that elapsed before he became a public leader, is enriched with a considerable number of Pitt's letters to his mother. They, of course, give a clearer insight into the character of the man than it is possible to obtain when once the possession of political power had made communicativeness a crime. As his life advanced, and both business and secrets multiplied upon him, his private correspondence became much more scanty. He could no longer speak freely on the subjects nearest to his heart. His whole life was given up to politics, and politics was precisely the subject on which he was bound to be discreet. Consequently, his letters come at rarer intervals, and are written in a tone which, though kindly, is obviously constrained.

We shall not accompany Lord Stanhope in the earliest stages of his biography. In a previous number of this Journal (No. 194),* we followed Pitt through his boyhood and earliest youth, and through his first political struggles—his acceptance of office under Lord Shelburne, when Fox resigned in pique at Lord Shelburne's appointment—his expulsion from power upon the question of the American peace by the coalition of Fox and North, who had opposed each other all their lives—and his recall to it as prime minister, when the king took advantage of the India Bill to dismiss the Coalition. We need not recount how the dismissed ministers defeated him in division after division —how his popularity grew rapidly in the country in spite of the most threatening resolutions of the House of Commons—how he closed the contest by an appeal to the country—and how the appeal was answered by a majority which secured his supremacy for life. A conflux of strangely mingled causes had combined to raise him to an eminence which no other English statesman has occupied since England ceased to be despotically ruled. To the measureless astonishment of his adversaries he had, at the age of twenty-four, scattered by his own single arm a combination of all that was eloquent and all that was powerful in the House of Commons. They had never dreamed of such an issue. It had occurred to them as a possibility that the king's undisguised dislike of Fox might break out into action and cause them a temporary reverse. Their letters show that they were not blind to the possible contingency of a short sojourn in opposition; but they never harbored a doubt that their huge majority would force the king to swallow his antipathies and submit to them again. In the House of Commons at least they thought that they were unassailable. The idea of danger there never crossed the mind of the most despondent. The numbers who, during the last ten years, had formed the opposing hosts in parliamentary campaigns were now united into a single phalanx. The debaters, who had so often in eloquent periods besought the nation to believe in each other's incapacity and treason, were now rallied under a common standard, and were prepared to combine their vituperations against any one who should attempt to dispute their supremacy. There was no visible power that could make

* *Living Age*, No. 604.

head against such an array in the existing House of Commons; and the leaders of the Coalition had persuaded themselves that an appeal to the constituencies would only add fresh strength to their position.

And yet when the trial came they were defeated by a mere youth, with no majority, no eloquent supporters, no organized party-following, no antecedent fame. He not only utterly routed them, but he captured all the standards under which they had fought. He proved himself the real owner of the watch-words they had stolen, the true champion of the various interests which they had once defended, and which by coalescing they had betrayed. Lord North had served the king obsequiously for years, had based his political position on the king's favor, and for the sake of retaining it had made himself the king's tool when the king was manifestly in the wrong. Fox had been the popular champion, railing at courtly corruption and royal power, and disdaining no arts of faction and no extravagance of invective to exalt the people and to degrade the king. Yet it was by the strength of king and people combined that Pitt overthrew their coalition. We should be inclined, in spite of Lord Macaulay's dictum, to place here at the very beginning the true culmination of Mr. Pitt's career. At a later period he gained a wider power, and was the object of a more unbounded adoration. But the greatness of an achievement is measured by the magnitude of the obstacles in the face of which it has been performed. To have gained this great power in the first instance was a more searching trial of strength than to have maintained it when it was gained. To estimate the difficulties which Pitt had surmounted when the nation at his appeal sent back an overwhelming majority to support him against all which had hitherto borne authority in Parliament, it is necessary to remember that North, Fox, Sheridan, and Burke were his opponents, that he had no single eloquent debater at his side, that he had no past performances to appeal to as his credentials for future trust, and that he took office in consequence of a transaction in which he indeed had no share, but which might well be looked on with disfavor by all who were jealous for the Constitution. To have conquered all these obstacles, to have reduced in the course of two months' debating a majority of one hundred and four to a majority of one, and to have so entirely converted public opinion in the course of that short struggle that his rivals never held up their heads again, was an achievement that no English statesman ever performed before, and no English statesman is ever likely to repeat.

Many explanations of a success so startling have been suggested by various narrators, according to their respective prepossessions. Fox himself used to attribute a large share of it to the wonderful popularity of the Carlo Khan caricature: Lord John Townshend, who was one of Fox's most intimate friends, referred it all to the "wrong-headed intemperance" of Mr. Burke. Mr. Wright, whose judgment is disturbed by a bias perhaps more violent than even that of Lord John Russell, talks of the power of the king, and of the slanders propagated by the Court-party. But the power of the king had not availed to save Lord Shelburne; and the party which could boast of the pen of Captain Morris and the pencil of Rowlandson ought not to have shrunk from a contest in which slander and ridicule were the weapons. Lord John Russell in much the same spirit refers it to the "perverse skill and fatal dexterity" of Mr. Pitt's partisans. Skill and dexterity are not rare qualities in politicians; but it is very rarely that they are rewarded by a triumph so overwhelming as that which condemned Fox to a life-long opposition. Lord Stanhope takes into account many combining causes. He allows for the halo of romantic veneration that still gathered round the memory of Chatham, for the young minister's own transcendent talents, and for the apprehensions of the terrified corporations whom no party-discipline availed to pacify when once they heard of the provisions of the India Bill, and Lee's unfortunate defence of it,—"What is a Charter? A parchment with a seal dangling at one end of it." But Lord Stanhope justly attributes the chief efficacy in producing that tremendous revulsion of national feeling to causes of far deeper and more permanent operation. The general support which Pitt obtained pointed to stronger influences than any merely temporary disgust. It was the judgment of the nation, pronounced at last, after long and patient forbearance, against the revolting factiousness of which their dearest interests had for so many years been made the sport. They had borne it long, seemingly acquiescent, as is the English custom, while faction wrestled with faction, and clique with clique, for the division of the rich spoil which then was the reward of power. The factions mistook the meaning of this apathy, and construed it as consent. They would not recognize the gradual accumulation of silent disgust which their acts were causing in the public mind. They imagined that every accession of numbers from whatever quarter was a help to office, and that every majority, no matter how gained, was a triumph. It is a sort of error not peculiar to the politicians of that day. It has infected almost every generation of parliamentary combatants since parliamentary government began. There is no blindness so unaccountable as the blindness of English statesmen to the political value of a character. Living only in and for the House of Commons, moving in an atmosphere of constant intrigue, accustomed to look upon oratory as a mode of angling for political support and upon political professions as only baits of more or less attractiveness, they acquire a very peculiar code of ethics, and they are liable wholly to lose sight of the fact that there is a stiffer and less corrupted morality out of doors. They not only come to forget what is right, but they forget that there is any one who knows it. The educated thought of England; before the bar of whose opinion all political conduct must appear, measures the manœuvres of politicians by no more lenient code than that which it applies to the affairs of private life. Ordinary men cannot easily bring themselves to pass over, as judicious tactics in a statesman, the conduct which in their next-door neighbors they would condemn as impudent insincerity. On the other hand, the politician cannot bring himself to believe that the party strategy and personal competition which are every thing to his mind, are trifles too slight to think about in the eyes of the nation he serves. He goes on with his game of chess, in which mighty principles and deep-seated sentiments are the pawns to be sacrificed or exchanged as the moment's convenience may suggest, in the simple faith that this is the real business which he has been sent to Parliament to transact. And thus we have had the spectacle, even in later days, of party leaders of considerable intellect laboriously and carefully ruining themselves in the esteem of the nation, and heaping blunder upon blunder from which the meanest of their followers would have been competent to warn them. They have failed because they have been blind to the elementary truth, that a character for unselfish honesty is the only secure passport to the confidence of the English people. Its place can never be supplied by fine speeches or dexterous manœuvres. Eighty years ago the error was commoner than it is now, in proportion as the morality of the governing classes was relatively lower in comparison with that of the nation at large. The combination of politicians whom the king had just driven from his councils were especially the victims of this delusion. At the crisis of their fate it never seems to have occurred to them that their past political conduct could possibly have injured their popularity with the nation.

Fox had begun life as a Tory, and had suddenly plunged in a moment of pique into the opposite extreme—had opposed the American war to turn out North, and had opposed the American peace to turn out Shelburne—and had then combined for the sake of office with the very man whom he had spent the flower of his political life in denouncing as treacherous and corrupt. The language in which he and Burke had denounced North up to the very eve of their junction far exceeded in acrimony what would now be tolerated in Parliament. Few things told so powerfully against the Coalition as a collection of the most abusive of these passages, published under the title of "Beauties of Fox and Burke." Only two years before the Coalition, Fox had told Lord North that he trusted that, "by the aroused indignation and vengeance of an injured and undone people, the ministers would hear of the calamities of the American war at the tribunal of justice, and expiate them on the public scaffold." Barely twelve months before he became Lord North's political ally, he told the House of Commons that, "from the moment when he should make any terms with one of them [the ministers], he would rest satisfied to be called the most infamous of mankind. He could not for an instant think of a coalition with men who, in every public and private transaction as ministers, had shown themselves void of every principle of honor and honesty. In the hands of such men he would not trust his honor for a minute."

The public naturally took him at his word, and believed him to be, what by anticipation he had named himself, the most infamous of men. Burke had made almost equal shipwreck of his good fame. His abuse of Lord North had scarcely been less violent, and his proceedings in and out of office were more glaringly in contrast. In opposition he had distinguished himself by his unsparing assaults upon the laxity, and worse than laxity, with which the public money was administered in those times. He was the great champion of economical reform. But the difference between theory and practice was very painful. One of his first acts, as member of the Coalition Government, was to restore to office two clerks who had been dismissed by Pitt, and were at the moment undergoing a criminal prosecution for embezzlement of public money. This was a sad commentary on much passionate declamation against ministerial corruption. Some of his old speeches upon Indian matters, too, were recalled to memory by his brilliant efforts upon Fox's India Bill. A short time before he had denounced a proposal for putting an end to the Charter of the East India Company with characteristic exuberance of language as "the most wicked, absurd, abandoned, profligate, and drunken intention ever formed." When the public saw the same rich vocabulary exhausted for the purpose of eulogizing a similar proposal, they naturally treated the praise and the blame as equally insincere. By the light of these contrasts they learned to look on the opposition to Lord North in the first instance, and the alliance with Lord North in the second, as nothing more than so many different leads in the game of which office was the stake. The later performances of the Coalition only confirmed the impressions which its formation had spread abroad. The shreds of character which these various transactions had left to it were torn from it by the discovery of the *coup d'état* which lurked in the machinery of the India Bill. Lord John Russell has attempted to defend this celebrated plot for "taking the crown off the king's head and placing it on Mr. Fox's," by pleading that the Board which was to wield in his interest irresponsible power over £300,000, worth of patronage, was only appointed for four years. Mr. Massey has justly replied that that circumstance would only make them more desperately eager to keep in office the ministry that was likely to re-appoint them. But Lord Stanhope suggests the real answer to modern admirers who attempt to represent this outrageous effort of faction as a misconstrued act of patriotism. If there had been in Fox's mind the faintest desire that the vast patronage of India should be used for any other purpose but to keep him in office, it would have been easy for him to have given effect to it by nominating a neutral Board. The composition of the Board was the real touchstone of the character of the Bill. That the new commissioners were, every one of them, thorough-going partisans, bound by every political and family tie to do the bidding of the Coalition, is the best proof that the Bill was proposed in order to secure the ends which they were best fitted to serve. The greediness of place, of which this intrigue convinced the most unsuspicious, stimulated the king to struggle against his captors, and disenchanted the nation of their last illusion touching the patriotism of the Rockingham Whigs. The sovereign and his people, after many differences, were at last of one mind in this, that they were sick at heart of the selfish ambition which the great revolution houses had masked for so long under patriotic phrases. When the empire was parting asunder, and the finances seemed collapsing under their colossal load of debt, they were weary of entrusting their destinies to men who fought the fight of principle in the spirit of political *condottieri*. This was the peculiar advantage which fortune threw into Pitt's hands, and which he improved with so much skill. Men were in a temper to yield themselves to almost any candidate for their favor who was untainted with the intrigues they had endured so long. They turned to Mr. Pitt, in spite of his youth and his apparent want of parliamentary support, as the only man who could free them from the dominion of selfish faction. His character stood high; his moral purity said something for his principle; his known pride was some guarantee for self-respect; and at least, if untried, he was unpolluted. His celebrated refusal of the clerkship of the Pells evinced that from the love of money he was absolutely free. This contrast between his character and that of his opponents was the true secret of the marvellous rapidity with which he rose to the head of affairs. Birth, eloquence, royal favor, would have done very little to secure him such a triumph, but for the blindness with which the Coalition laid bare to the public eye the meanness of motive and the hollowness of conviction which underlay the fiercely phrased patriotism of all existing statesmen.

The same contrast which raised him continued to be his chief support. Throughout his career it was a comparison of character, far more than of measures or of eloquence, that formed his great political strength. His opponents fell lower and lower in public esteem, and fully justified the national condemnation which the Coalition had provoked.

They still continued to possess all the powers of eloquence and all the social fascinations which had made them so powerful before. The masterpieces of oratory which constitute the fame of Fox, Burke, and Sheridan, were delivered during their long exile from office. But the old curse clave to them. They remained as blind as ever to the value of political character, and never compassed sufficient foresight to forego a single chance of inflicting a temporary embarrassment upon their rival's government.

They took the earliest opportunity of practising this suicidal strategy. One of the earliest objects that attracted Pitt's attention was the reform of the commercial code which, at that time, stifled the industry of the country. The system of prohibitions was maintained, not only towards foreign countries, in which case it was at least consistent with the extreme theories of protection then generally entertained, but towards Ireland, whose prosperity and progress were indissolubly linked with our own. Mr. Pitt —the first minister who entered at all into the philosophy of free trade, which modern Whigs are rather apt to boast of, as if they had first discovered it, and had never been particularly enthusiastic the other way—applied himself to remove this glaring financial evil. Of course, his proposals excited a violent panic among the Lancashire manufacturers, who were the great protectionists of those days. Their mills would be stopped, their hands thrown out of work; the cheaper labor of Ireland would inevitably drive them out of the English market. A proposal to allow Ireland to share in the benefits of the colonial trade was represented as a death-blow to the Navigation Laws, and as being certain to make Cork the emporium of the empire. This silly panic was an embarrassment to Pitt, but it was one which the party led by Fox and Burke were specially beholden to allay. In them, if in any one, should have been found the champions of the new truth against the ancient error, of the welfare of the nation against the vested interests of the few. Burke was bound to have supported the measure by every tie of honor as well as of patriotism. When he sat in opposition to Lord North he had supported with all his powers a similar measure of relief, and had resigned his seat at Bristol rather than give way to the self-seeking clamor of his mercantile constituents. But in 1785 he had lost all relish for a free-trade policy, when it was discredited by the advocacy of Pitt. Fox and Lord North were equally bound by their own previous measures to a temperate treatment of the differences between England and Ireland. It was under Fox's government that the supremacy of the British over the Irish Parliament had been abandoned; and this, though undoubtedly a necessary measure, had been the beginning of Irish troubles. It was under Lord North's administration that Ireland had been suffered to create the army of Volunteers, whose first act was to dictate their own terms to the Government of England. But, in spite of the responsibility thus incurred, none of these three statesmen shrank from using the antipathy of English and Irish as the lever of a factious opposition. They threw themselves alternately on one side and the other. First Fox tried to improve to the utmost the discontent of the manufacturers, urging for delay to enable them to agitate, and stigmatizing Pitt's proposal as "an attempt to make Ireland the grand arbitress of all the commercial interests of the empire." By these tactics he succeeded in forcing Pitt to recede from some of his original propositions, and to give a more English color to the scheme. No sooner was this effected than he changed his tone. He and his coadjutors now became keenly sensitive to Irish wrongs, and to the objections that might be taken from an Irish point of view; and though, of course, they were not likely by this manœuvre to injure the measure in London, they entertained well-founded hopes that their taunts and misrepresentations would damn it in Dublin. Fox, while he still described the plan as "a tame surrender of the manufactures and commerce of England," protested that Ireland, if she accepted it, would be "resigning her legislative independence;" Burke designated certain compensatory payments that she was to make as the tribute of a conquered country; and Sheridan dared the Irish Parliament to pass such degrading resolutions, and appealed to the Irish people to rise against them if they did. This reckless style of warfare did not fail of its effect. It has never been hard to goad the Irish into jealousy of English policy; least of all, when they were still in the fresh enjoyment of a newly achieved emancipation. A cry was raised against the measure far more furious than that which had greeted it in England, and the unblushing factiousness of the English opposition was rewarded by the abandonment of the Bill.

What they had done against Ireland it was too much to expect that they should not do, or attempt to do, against France. Burke had already swallowed his convictions upon free trade; and Fox, who openly avowed that he never could understand the science of political economy, had no convictions to swallow. They had no difficulty, therefore, in combining to resist the French treaty of commerce, of which the abandonment of the Methuen treaty was, as far as regards England, the main provision. At the present day, under our existing financial burdens, the very name of French treaty disgusts us. Like many of Pitt's measures, it has been discredited by the unintelligent mimicry of later imitators. But this was a scheme which really did fulfil its promise, of swelling revenue and stimulating trade. It was a measure beyond its age, and very much beyond the Liberal leaders of 1787. If they had based their objections to it on the same narrow ground as that which they adopted in opposing Pitt's Irish policy, they would simply have deserved the charge of being laggards in the march of progress of which they professed to lead the van. But this time they had no encouragement for the display of their intense protectionism. The manufacturers had learned to feel so much confidence in Pitt, that they did not venture to dispute his dicta on a matter of finance. It was no use, therefore, this time to talk of a "tame surrender of our commerce." Accordingly, they were driven to take a position in point of statesmanship more humiliating still. As they had succeeded before by a declamatory appeal to national antipathies, they hoped to succeed by the same means again. On the very first night of the session, Fox thundered against the idea of any concert or alliance with the French, long before he had an idea what that alliance was likely to be. When it was brought before the House he argued in the same strain. France was the hereditary foe of England, and it was incredible that she could have agreed to a treaty unless it concealed some device to injure us. Grey, who made his maiden speech on this occasion, reiterated the assertion, that no French assurances were to be believed. Burke maintained that the two nations had been established by nature to balance each other, and seemed to think there was something impious in converting them into allies. Francis invoked the shade of Chatham, and taunted Pitt with blasting the triumphs of his father's administration, and making friends of his father's foes. But topics of this kind were the last resource of desperation. The time had gone by when they could influence the House of Commons, or blind even a popular constituency to the advantages of a pacific policy. The French treaty passed both Houses by a large majority; and the opposition to it produced no other result than to furnish a new proof that in Fox's hands Whiggism meant the advocacy of all that was ignorant, antiquated, and narrow.

Such a policy as this, pursued by the advocates of peace and progress, only confirmed the general impression that there were no principles, however cherished, of which Fox would not cheerfully lighten himself in the race for office. He appears rather to have been guided by a passionate instinct of rivalry than by any definite calculation of the political benefit which his proceedings were likely to yield. But whether it was antagonistic impulse or blundering ambition that shaped his course, the utter absence of definite convictions was equally manifest throughout the whole of it. It is difficult to say exactly what he did seek, or whether his own exaltation or the humiliation of Pitt was nearest to his heart. But it is quite clear that what he did *not* seek was the triumph of any set of principles in which he believed. If proof were still wanting, his conduct on the Regency question supplied it. To construct Fox's distinctive creed is not a very easy matter from a modern point of view. In practice he was the antagonist of Pitt; in theory he professed to be a Whig. But he had very little in common either with the Whigs who went before him, or the Whigs who have come after him. Fox voted with Pitt on Reform, though he never introduced a Reform Bill himself, turned him out of office for supporting peace, and threw out his measure for securing retrenchment. There was one point, and one only, upon which any kinship of opinion can be established between his party, the Revolution Whigs, and the Whigs of our own day, and that was the desire, which all three professed, to exalt the authority of Parliament in relation to that of the Crown. He and Burke had supported Dunning's celebrated motion that "the influence of the Crown had increased, was increasing, and ought to be diminished." This language they had held with tolerable consistency up to the year 1788, and could point to it with pride as their solitary remnant of consistency. But an unfaltering opposition to a king who has declared himself to be your irreconcilable opponent is a very easy exhibition of political principle. Would he fold the cloak of his patriotism so closely round him when court sunshine began to warm him? He was never actually tried. The smiles of royalty never lightened his career from the beginning to the end. But on one occasion, for a few short weeks, he thought that he saw in front of him a faint glimmer of that invigorating ray; and the extraordinary metamorphosis which this distant gleam effected in his principles enables us to judge what sort of minister he would have been if fate had destined him for a court favorite. The Regency crisis was one of those sharp and searching ordeals which put men's principles to the test, and show how much of them is lacquer, how much genuine metal.

The illness of George the Third towards the end of 1788, while it seemed likely to arrest Pitt's career in the full tide of his success, offered a prospect of recovery to the desperate fortunes of Fox. Whether the king died or went mad, the Prince of Wales must succeed to the royal power; and the Prince of Wales was Fox's friend, bound to him by all the ties that unite men who have drunk at the same debauch, and gained at the same tables. The novelty of the prospect that burst on both the rival statesmen was startlingly sudden. To Fox it was an undreamed-of opening to power and fame; to Pitt it was the menace of irretrievable ruin. He had little or no private fortune; he was deeply in debt; and he had scorned to provide himself with any of the sinecures in which statesmen of limited means were wont to find a harbor of refuge. The contrast between the conduct of the two antagonists in this unexpected crisis was of a piece with the contrast that had marked their whole lives. The minister displayed the same singleness of purpose, the same lofty disregard of his private interests, that he exhibited throughout his whole career. He took precisely the course that was most just to the king and most salutary to the country, but which was also the course that seemed most fatal to himself. He could easily have saved himself from all risk, if he had chosen to do so. He might have imitated the conduct of the Coalition, and have used his present majority for the purpose of securing himself a long lease of power. Precedents were not wanting for such a course. There was no precedent of the appointment of a regent exactly in point to the present emergency; for the case of an insane sovereign, with an heir-apparent of full age, had never before occurred in English history. But the contingent appointment of a regent in case of the demise of the Crown during the heir's nonage was a precaution that had been frequently observed; and in such cases it had been usual to appoint a Council of Regency to control the executive power of the regent. Pitt might, with great show of reason, have acted on a precedent which would have prevented the Prince of Wales from disturbing a ministry to which he was known to be hostile, and to which the king was known to be attached. We know that the Opposition leaders entertained no doubt of his power of carrying some such scheme into effect. But Pitt had come to the conclusion that a more vigorous executive was necessary than a Council of Regency could be expected to furnish, and therefore he resolved that the regent should choose his own ministers as he liked, though he was aware that the first exercise of that power would be his own dismissal.

"The part of Pitt was promptly taken. It was, as his part was ever, straightforward and direct. He would listen to no terms for himself. He would consider only his bounden duty to his afflicted king. He would, by the authority of Parliament, impose some restrictions on the Regency for a limited time, so that the sovereign might resume his power without difficulty in case his reason were restored. What might be the just limits or the necessary period of such restrictions he had not yet decided, and was still revolving in his mind. But he had never the least idea, as his opponents feared, of a Council of Regency which might impede the prince in the choice of a new administration. On the contrary, Pitt looked forward to his own immediate dismissal from the public service, and he had determined to return to the practice of his profession at the Bar.

"Far different was the course of Thurlow. Under an appearance of rugged honesty he concealed no small amount of selfish craft. He was ready to grasp at an overture, and it was not long ere an overture came. Two gentlemen in the prince's confidence—the comptroller of his household, Capt. Payne, more commonly called Jack Payne, and Richard Brinsley Sheridan—had set their heads together. Was it not to be feared that Pitt would attempt to fetter the coming Regency with some restrictions? And by whom could that attempt be more effectually prevented than by the statesman holding the Great Seal? How important then, if possible, to gain him over!

"With these views, and with the prince's sanction, a secret negotiation with Lord Thurlow was begun. It was proposed to him that he should do his utmost to defeat any restrictions on the regent, and that in return he should become President of the Council in the new administration. But the offer of the Presidency was spurned by Thurlow; he insisted on still retaining the Great Seal. This was a more difficult matter, from the engagements of the prince, and indeed of the whole Fox party, to Lord Loughborough. Sheridan, however, strongly pressed that Lord Thurlow should be secured upon his own terms. The prince agreed, and the negotiation was continued without Lord Loughborough. The bargain was struck, or all but struck, awaiting only Fox's sanction when he should arrive from Italy.

"The perfidy of Thurlow in this transaction stands little in need of comment. To this day it forms the main blot upon his fame. Nowhere in our recent annals shall we readily find any adequate parallel to it, except indeed in the career of his contemporary and his rival, Loughborough.

"Lord Thurlow succeeded at first in concealing all knowledge of the scheme from Pitt. In this he was much assisted by the fact that from this time forward the cabinet councils were frequently held at Windsor, thus affording him good opportunities for slipping round in secret to the apartments of the Prince of Wales. But a very slight incident brought to light the mystery. His cabals were detected by his own hat. Thus used the story to be told by a late survivor from these times, my lamented friend Mr. Thomas Grenville. One day when a council was to be held at Windsor, Thurlow had been there some time before any of his colleagues arrived. He was to be brought back to London in the carriage of one of them, and the moment of departure being come, the chancellor's hat was nowhere to be found. After long search, one of the pages came running up with the hat in his hand, and saying aloud, 'My lord, I found it in the closet of his royal highness the Prince of Wales.' The other ministers were still in the hall waiting for their carriages, and the evident confusion of Lord Thurlow corroborated the inference which they drew.

"Thus might Pitt suspect, or much more than suspect, the chancellor's double dealings. But still he had no positive proof of them; and he might feel as the younger Agrippina, that in many cases the best defence against treachery is to seem unconscious of it. Thus, maintaining his usual lofty calmness, he forbore from all inquiry, all expostulation."

It was the second time that Pitt had been able to show, on a splendid scale, how mean a thing in his eyes was the possession of office, or even the attainment of a bare competence, compared to the furtherance of the public weal. The English, whatever other errors of judgment they commit, are seldom backward in expressing their admiration of disinterestedness; and they did not fail to recognize it in the present instance. All the brilliancy of his opponents failed to draw from the nation the smallest of those tokens of admiration which were readily yielded to Pitt's upright and loyal statesmanship. In 1784 the people testified their value for him by consigning one hundred and sixty of Fox's friends to private life. In 1790 a new batch of victims testified to their increased and settled esteem. In 1788 there was no question of elections, but the admiration that his conduct elicited was expressed, if possible, in a still more striking way.

"But during the interval he received a most signal token of the public esteem and approbation. It was well known by the public that Pitt would not be continued one hour in office by the regent. It was known that he had already taken measures for returning to his first profession. It was also known, perhaps, that his neglect of his private affairs had involved him in some debts, which he trusted to discharge by an industrious application of his talents at the Bar. At this very time, however, there was held, by public advertisement, a meeting of the principal bankers and moneyed men of London, anxious to tender him on his retirement from office a substantial mark of their esteem. The sum of £50,000 was first proposed, but so great was the enthusiasm that in the space of forty-eight hours this sum was doubled, and Mr. George Rose, as his Secretary of the Treasury, was requested to press upon him, in the manner most likely to be acceptable, a free gift of £100,000. But Mr. Pitt answered his friend as follows: 'No consideration upon earth shall ever induce me to accept it.'

"'Surely, it was not without reason, nor merely from the warmth of private friendship, that we find William Grenville, at almost the same date, exclaim to his brother, 'There certainly never was in this country at any period such a situation as Mr. Pitt's.'"

Fox and Sheridan, though certainly not less embarrassed in circumstances, were never exposed to the perplexity of having to refuse so tempting an offer. In proportion as the Regency debate raised the minister in popular estimation, it lowered his opponents. They availed themselves of the opportunity to convince the nation that they were still the heroes of the half-forgotten Coalition, unchanged by reflection, untaught by experience. As they then allied themselves with Lord North, whom it had been their main parliamentary occupation to denounce, so now, to humor the prince, they took under their protection the very principles which they existed as a party to oppose.

As soon as the king's illness had been ascertained by an examination of the physicians, Pitt proceeded, according to the usual course in any case of constitutional difficulty, to move for a committee to search for precedents. It was natural to expect that the motion would be unopposed. Common prudence, as well as common decency, should have suggested to Fox to observe punctiliously every formality in the process of transferring power from the sovereign who hated him to the regent of whose favor he was secure. But either the near prospect of the fruition of hopes so long deferred was too much for his self-control, or an instinctive distrust of the prince's good faith made him eager at once to secure himself in his patron's good graces by a striking display of devotion. Whichever was the motive, he refused to wait for Pitt's tedious though decorous forms. He insisted on it that there was no need for a committee of precedents. It was not a question of precedent. By virtue of the Constitution, by his own inherent right, the heir-apparent was entitled to assume the full regal power just as much as if the king had been dead; and it was nothing but his abundant courtesy that prevented him from acting upon all his rights the very moment that the king's incapacity was ascertained. It was the province of Parliament to ascertain that fact, but further than this Parliament had no right to interfere. Pitt listened with unconcealed triumph to this high prerogative doctrine—higher, as Grenville observed, than any thing that had been heard since the days of Sir Robert Sawyer. The minister turned round to a friend who was sitting next him on the treasury bench, and whispered, "I'll *unwhig* the gentleman for the rest of his life." He amply redeemed his promise in the debates that followed; but, in truth, the great Whig leader had unwhigged himself.

Since the Stuarts had disappeared, the only point of contact between the Whigs of the time of Rockingham and the Whigs of the time of Somers had been the desire to exalt Parliament above prerogative. And now their leader was exalting the inherent prerogative, not of the reigning sovereign, but of the heir-apparent, to such a height that the interference of Parliament in a case unforeseen by the Constitution was resented as impertinent the moment it proceeded beyond the formal duty of certifying to an incontestable fact. To make matters worse, Sheridan closed the debate by threatening the House with "the danger of provoking the prince to assert his rights." An inconceivable storm was raised in the House by this indecent menace. William Grenville, who had sat in Parliament during all the ferocious party struggles which succeeded the fall of Lord North's administration, writes to his brother that he never remembers to have witnessed such an uproar. Two or three days afterwards, Fox, who felt he had committed a blunder, made an awkward attempt at explanation; but it was impossible to do away the impression that had been created. Spite of all the disturbing influences which the near prospect of a new reign and a change of ministry would naturally exercise on a parliamentary following, Pitt kept his majority together. He was able without difficulty to pass his Regency Bill through the House of Commons, though it was a measure calculated to test the fidelity of any majority to the utmost. It contained restrictions which were known to be odious to the regent, though they did not lessen his opportunities of revenging himself. They were goading the tiger at the very moment they were opening his cage. The Regency Bill was a patriotic measure, but for party purposes it was a very unwise one. Its object was to enable the prince to govern, without enabling him either to trouble the king's present comfort, or to fix his own policy round the king's neck in case the king should recover. Thus he was to do what he liked with the ministry, but he was not to confer peerages or life-pensions, or to meddle with the Royal Household. The fear in Pitt's mind obviously was, that, if the regent's ministers should discover that the king was recovering, they would attempt to repeat the manœuvre of the India Bill, and make themselves safe against future accidents by filling the House of Lords with their own creatures. The Opposition were furious at the suspicion, in proportion as they felt it was deserved. They lost their tempers as completely, and blundered as recklessly, as they had done in the few eventful weeks that followed the fall of the Coalition. They abused Dr. Willis because he would not give as bad a report of the king's condition as they desired; they accused the queen of conspiring with him to keep the prince out of his just claims, by issuing false bulletins of the king's health; and they accused her of conspiring with Pitt to retain in his hands the patronage of the Household for the purpose of controlling Parliament. Pitt's answer to the last charge was simple,—that the Household commanded just seven seats in the House of Commons: the other charges needed no answer but disdain. Burke especially distinguished himself in this saturnalia of vituperation. He nicknamed Thurlow "Priapus," and gave a caricatured description of his face in the House of Commons; he called Pitt a "competitor for the Regency" and "the prince opposite;" and, when the division went against him, he threatened the House with the penalties of treason at the prince's hands for the resolutions they had passed. The "wrong-headed intemperance" of which Fox's friend Lord John Townshend feelingly complained, was never pushed to so extravagant a length as during these Regency debates. All these exhibitions very seriously damaged the Opposition out of doors. They contrasted ill with the minister's haughty, reserved, and manly bearing; and it happened, by a strange chance, that his high character for fidelity was enhanced by the reputation acquired by a colleague who in reality deserved it less than the meanest of the prince's parasites. Even Lord Stanhope, from whose pen words of condemnation flow reluctantly in the most obvious cases of guilt, loses something of his gentleness when he comes to speak of Thurlow. His description of the well-known scene in the House of Lords is a good specimen of the clear and easy narrative which is the charm of this biography:—

"The chancellor delivered himself of a temporizing speech, as though not yet fixed in his opinion. But he began to fear that he might be a loser instead of gainer by his projected act of treachery. The reports of Dr. Willis were in due course submitted to him. He might observe that day by day they expressed a confident hope of the king's recovery. He might observe that on the 13th the queen and the princesses, whom the king had not seen since the 5th of the last month, were brought into his presence without danger. He seized her majesty's hand, kissed it, and held it in his during the whole interview, which lasted half an hour. The little Princess Amelia, who from her infancy had been his favorite child, sat upon his lap.

"The chancellor felt that he could temporize no longer without great risk to his own position. With the new hopes of the king's recovery which Dr. Willis gave, he determined to take a bolder course on the next occasion in the House of Lords. That next occasion came on the 15th of December. Then the Duke of York made a good and sensible speech (his first in Parliament), disavowing most expressly in his brother's name any claim not derived from the will of the people. The chancellor upon this left the Woolsack and addressed the House. He began by expressing his great satisfaction that no claim of right was to be raised by the Prince of Wales. But as he next proceeded to the afflicted condition of the king, his emotion seemed to grow uncontrollable, his voice faltered, and he burst into a flood of tears. Recovering himself, he declared his fixed and unalterable resolution to stand by a sovereign who, during a reign of twenty-seven years, had proved his sacred regard to the principles which seated his family upon the throne. Their first duty, he said, was to preserve the rights of that sovereign entire, so that, when God should permit him to recover, he might not find himself in a worse situation than before his illness. The chancellor dwelt on his own feelings of grief and gratitude, and wrought himself up at last to these celebrated words: 'and when I forget my king, may my God forget me!'

"It seems scarcely possible to exaggerate the strong impression which this half sentence made. Within the House itself the effect was not perhaps so satisfactory. Wilkes, who was standing under the throne, eyed the chancellor askance, and muttered, 'God forget you! He will see you d—— first!' Burke at the same moment exclaimed, with equal wit and with no profaneness, 'The best thing that can happen to you!' Pitt also was on the steps of the throne. On Lord Thurlow's imprecation, he is said to have rushed out of the House, exclaiming several times, 'Oh, what a rascal!'

"But in the country at large the intrigues of Thurlow were not known—they were not even suspected. He was looked upon as the fearless assertor of his sovereign's rights —as a strictly honest man, prepared, if need should be, to suffer for his honesty; and the impressive half sentence which he had just pronounced fell in exactly with the current of popular feeling at the time. The words flew from mouth to mouth. They were seen far and wide in England, printed around portraits and wreaths, embossed on snuff-boxes, or embroidered on pocket-books. It can scarcely be doubted that in the parliamentary conflict they became a valuable auxiliary on the minister's side."

The truth was, that the intrigues of the prince and the prince's friends met with very little favor from the nation. All their sympathies were with the good old king and his homely virtues; and they looked forward with little less than consternation to the advent of a reign as dissolute as that of Charles the Second. Nor were they reconciled to the prospect by the fact that the change which admitted social profligacy to the Court could admit political profligacy to the Cabinet at the same time.

The Regency was the last throw of Mr. Fox's party. They narrowly missed an overwhelming victory; for George the Third afterwards declared that if, when he recovered, he had found the Regency established, nothing should have induced him to resume the reins of power. But they did miss it; and it was their forlorn hope. The passionate greediness with which they had rushed upon the spoil, even before it could be legally assigned to them had marked them rather as hungry adventurers than as statesmen. The impression which the Coalition had originally left became deeper and more permanent; and the nation centred its attachment more and more exclusively on Pitt. He never lost it up to the day of his death. It gathered itself more passionately round him as the clouds of the French Revolution collected over Europe, and his name was associated with the cause of law and order —his rival's with the bloodiest excesses that have ever been committed in the name of liberty. Every new danger that threatened —each successive phase of that great convulsion—was a support to the ministry, and a blow to the Opposition. The more the middle and upper classes were terrified by the spread of Jacobin doctrines, the more they clung to the minister who put down those doctrines with a strong hand. The greater their terror of the successes of the French armies, the more resolutely they turned away from the apologist of the Revolution and the admirer of Buonaparte.

A different explanation of Pitt's success is naturally popular with Whig historians. Lord Macaulay, whose affection for Lord Holland never left him free from bias in judging of the character of Lord Holland's uncle, prefers to exalt to a preternatural height the power of eloquence in the House of Commons, and then to attribute to Pitt a pre-eminence as a debater which his most ardent admirers have seldom claimed. That Pitt can have ruled by sheer eloquence in a

House where he was opposed by Fox, Burke, Sheridan, and Grey, is inconceivable. The early development of his eloquence was very remarkable; but it is never recorded to have produced the wonderful effect which is attributed to Lord Chatham's speeches. It was a quality which he, no doubt, possessed in great perfection, but which he possessed in common with many great statesmen before and since, who yet have not been able, with the help of it, to retain an undisputed ascendency over their countrymen during two-and-twenty years. The phenomenon requires some more adequate explanation. The peculiarity of his position—its strange and impregnable strength—lay in the contrast between his own character and that of his opponents. There have been many statesmen with worse characters than Fox; there may have been some as pure as Pitt. But the extremes have never been contrasted with each other as they were in that generation. There never was a time when the reputation of one rival stood so high, while that of the other stood so low. So long as the political and private character of Fox, Sheridan, and the Prince of Wales remained as a foil to his own unimpeached purity, Pitt was unassailable. This is the true key of his unparalleled success. No doubt he could not have maintained so lastingly his sudden elevation if his high character had not been reinforced by talents equally lofty. But a nation may easily underrate ability; it rarely misconstrues a high morality, or for any length of time, gives honor to motives that are really base. The secret of Pitt's popularity is betrayed by the utter absence of any reaction in favor of his opponent. Before his life closed England had passed through many vicissitudes of Fortune, good harvests and bad, peace and war, contentment and rebellion, victories and reverses—vicissitudes which, in other times, have constantly changed the current of public favor from one competitor for power to the other. But never during all that period, under any pressure of taxation, or in the face of any disaster, did the nation manifest the faintest ambition to be again governed by Mr. Fox. With the king the name acted as a spell to tame the will that had never been tamed before. In Mr. Pitt's hands it was a wand of power which many of Mr. Pitt's predecessors in office would have given much to possess. The simple intimation that Mr. Pitt must retire, or, in other words, that the possibility would be opened for the return of Mr. Fox, reduced the king to pliability in a moment on any subject not bearing upon religion. Even his affection for Lord Thurlow could not stand the strain. In fact to the end of Mr. Pitt's life, there was but one subject outside the domain of religion in regard to which he ever found the king impracticable, and that was the restoration of any portion of political power to Fox.

Many hard names have been flung at George the Third for his refusal in 1804 to come to any terms with the Whig leader. Lord Macaulay dismisses him with the gentle epithets, "dull, obstinate, unforgiving, and half mad." But, nevertheless, it is easy to see in Lord Macaulay's own essay, and in many other quarters, that on the subject of Fox's political career the opinion of our generation is gravitating toward that of the much-reviled monarch. The truth is, that affectionate and interested efforts have thrown an artificial halo round the fame of Mr. Fox. His personal fascinations were so powerful, that almost all who fell within the range of his influence felt bound throughout the rest of their lives to defend his memory against all comers. A political party who for the last thirty years have been powerful in politics and still more powerful in literature, being afflicted with a scarcity of heroes, have centred all their hero-worship on this single image. This political canonization has effected transformations in history as strange as any that were ever perpetrated by any *Acta Sanctorum*. The intrigues of a restless ambition, that never knew scruple, or worried itself about principle, have been converted into the struggles of a second Hampden against a court conspiracy for enslaving England. The phrases struck out in the heat of debate, or selected at random as the readiest missiles to fling at an adversary's head, have been cited as the profound maxims of a political philosopher. But all this is passing away, and a truer measure is beginning to be applied to the political conduct of Mr. Fox. Later revelations have tended to cloud his fame. His sagacity turns out to have been more limited, and his patriotism more dead, than any one had believed. Lord John Russell with sacrilegious hand has himself done much to disfigure his idol's beauty. To use Lord Stanhope's just though guarded language:—

"The familiar correspondence of Fox, as edited with ability and candor by Lord John Russell, has not tended on the whole to exalt his fame. Such, at least, is the opinion which I have heard expressed with sincere regret by some persons greatly prepossessed in his favor—some members of the families most devoted to his party cause. It seems to be felt that, although a perusal of his letters leaves in its full lustre his reputation as an orator, it has greatly dimmed his reputation as a statesman. There are, in his correspondence, some hasty things that are by no means favorable to his public spirit, as where he speaks of the 'delight' which he derived from the news of our disasters at Saratoga and at York-town. There are some hasty things that are as far from favorable to his foresight and sagacity. Take, for instance, a prophecy as follows, in 1801: 'According to my notion the House of Commons has in a great measure ceased, and will shortly entirely cease, to be a place of much importance.' Perhaps, also, after the perusal of these letters, we may feel more strongly than before it that many parts of Fox's public conduct—as his separation from Lord Shelburne, or his junction with Lord North—are hard to be defended."

But the king had special ground, beyond any that his subjects could have pleaded, for entertaining a strong dislike to Mr. Fox. He felt all that they could feel against him, for he entered keenly into public affairs during the last twenty years of his government. He sided thoroughly with his ministers, hated their foes, and loved their friends, and felt their triumphs as his own. His letters to Mr. Pitt show that he took as lively an interest in every division and debate as any party-whip could do. Consequently, he felt all the indignation Mr. George Rose himself could feel at each of Fox's discreditable manœuvres. The factiousness of 1783, the unfeeling ambition of 1788, the reckless, unpatriotic conduct of 1794, accumulated an amount of hatred in the king's mind which nothing but a strong necessity could have induced him to overcome. But there was another and a more personal cause of resentment never absent from his memory, which deepened in his eyes the dark hue of Mr. Fox's political offences. He had good grounds for attributing to Mr. Fox's advice and instigation the great affliction of his life—the scandalous habits, and, still more, the rebellious attitude of the Prince of Wales. To a certain extent this imputation was supported by the facts. To a still greater extent it was supported by appearances which there were then no means of testing, and from which the king could only have escaped by accepting an explanation of the most painful kind.

Of Mr. Fox's complicity in many of the prince's offences there can be no doubt. Their friendship in the first instance probably arose from the prince's discontent with the frugal fare and the rigid morality of Buckingham House on the one hand, and Mr. Fox's political calculations on the other. The king's health, like that of the Duke of Wellington and several other long-lived persons, was not reputed to be good in his middle age. The probability of his early death was eagerly reckoned, and was the subject of many a wager at Brook's club; and Mr. Fox early turned to the worship of the rising sun. Few people could withstand the charm of Mr. Fox's manner if he chose to undertake their subjugation; and he could offer to the prince the additional bait of an introduction to a paradise of new pleasure, unknown within the virtuous precincts of his father's court. A friendship soon sprang up of the closest kind. The prince used to address the statesman in all their correspondence as "Dear Charles;" and the statesman, though using more respectful language, always spoke his mind with the most unrestrained freedom to the prince. They lived on terms of the strictest intimacy, Fox combining in one the character of Mentor and of Falstaff, and supplying both jolly companionship and political advice. It is presumable that the former was of better quality than the latter, or the friendship would not have lasted very long. It was cemented on both sides by mutual services. Sixty thousand pounds a year were allowed by the king to the prince to support his petty court, a sum that ought to have been ample so long as he remained unmarried. He looked on it, however, as niggardly in the extreme, and insisted that it ought to be doubled. Fox strained every nerve to procure him this further supply of the sinews of debauchery. The effort to force it at all hazards on the king very nearly broke up the Coalition Ministry before its time; but the king knew tolerably well the purposes to which the increased allowance was destined, and stood firm. The demand naturally did not meet with more favor when Pitt was in power. Pitt was above all things anxious to reduce debt, and bring the finances into good order; and a hundred thousand pounds was a considerable sum in a peace expenditure which, exclusive of debt, did not exceed six million. Foiled in this application, the prince for some time had recourse to the simple expedient of not paying his bills, and lived at the rate of a hundred and twenty thousand a year with an income of sixty; but after a time the tradesmen became tired of this plan, and he was compelled to bethink him of another. At one time he was very much inclined to accept a large present of money from the Duke of Orleans, the notorious Egalité, who was reported to be the richest subject in Europe, and who felt a natural sympathy for the difficulties of a kindred spirit. Mr. Fox, who was wise enough to foresee the dangers of such a step, persuaded him to abandon the idea; but he suggested in place of it a device that was even more offensive to the king. It was to put down his court, give up all his outward show, sell his horses, dismiss his Lords of the Bedchamber, and thus come before the nation to sue *in formâ pauperis* for relief—to appeal to them by all the external signs of poverty against the rigor of an avaricious father. This did not mean that he was to abandon the substance of his pleasures, but only the show. Mr. Fox did not suggest to him that he should part from his mistress, or give up the Capreæ of Brighton, in order to pay his debts. In fact, the nine months during which this self-denying resolution was in operation were principally spent at that ascetic residence. He was only to give up the royal state, which he had received his income expressly to maintain. Naturally this peculiar mode of showing penitence did not excite much sympathy with the public. It was nothing less than a fresh act of hostility towards the king. The wits made themselves very merry with caricatures of the revels of the "Merry Beggars" at Brighton; but neither the prince nor his advisers increased their popularity by the manœuvre. Still less did he melt the heart of the unsympathetic prime minister. His friends did the best they could for him both in Parliament and out of it; but after a time he was compelled to moderate his demands, and to compromise his claim for a slight augmentation revocable at the king's pleasure.

In gratitude for these services, and generally for the honor of Fox's friendship, the prince threw himself without limit or reserve into the arms of Fox's party. In public that party acted in hostility to the king; in private he was the object of their unrestrained scurrility. But this peculiarity was in the prince's eyes no bar, probably it even added a zest, to their alliance. He certainly omitted no occasion for showing that he preferred their friendship to his father's. When he was but nineteen he openly took part in the Windsor election against the court. When the Coalition had overthrown Lord Shelburne, and the king was engaged in vainly attempting, by alternate entreaties to Pitt and North, to escape from his captors, the prince was heard to say aloud at the drawing-room "that his father had not yet agreed to the plan of the Coalition, but by God he should be made to agree to it." In the same spirit he voted for the India Bill against the king's known wishes, and took a public part in the Westminster election, decked out in Fox's colors.

This unconcealed enmity, painful and scandalous as it was, the king used freely to lay to the charge of Fox. Fox vehemently denied the imputation, and declared it to be a slanderous fiction of Thurlow. If there is any thing more probable than that Fox should have been guilty of the offence, it is that Thurlow should have invented the charge; but, at any rate, it is certain that, if Fox did not engender, he at least fostered the prince's hatred of his father, and built upon it all his hopes of political success. It is not just to vilify the king, as Lord Macaulay has done, because to the end of his life he cherished a peculiar aversion for Mr. Fox. It was no case of transient insult, or of common political hostility. Lord Macaulay asks why Grey and Erskine, who as politicians had been quite as violent, were not visited with a similar proscription. The answer is, that Grey and Erskine had not estranged from him his son's affection, his heir's allegiance, and had not tainted with the contagion of licentiousness the purest court in Europe.

We have dwelt a good deal upon the conduct of Mr. Pitt's opponents, because they really furnish the standard by which his public conduct ought to be judged. We should not appreciate his lofty public spirit as it deserves, except by comparing it with the self-seeking intrigues which were tolerated and practised by the statesmen among whose ranks he enrolled himself on his first entry into public life. We might look upon his prudence and foresight as matters of course, if they were not contrasted with the blind and greedy recklessness of those who, if he had fallen, must have occupied his place. Of his administration so long as England remained at peace,—and no man labored more hard to keep her at peace than he did,—there is not much to say. Like all prosperous histories, its evenness makes it uneventful. There is no difference of opinion among modern writers upon the skill with which the disordered finances were repaired, the disaffection pacified, which when he acceded to office was widely spreading, and the failing trade of the country stimulated. Under his wise and humane administration the English became both a wealthier and a more contented people; but this only lasted so long as the country remained at peace. When the French Convention forced England into war, there was a grievous change. Heavy taxes were laid on, harsh laws enacted, severe punishments inflicted. The era of prosperity was succeeded by a period of suffering and consequent discontent, and the discontent was repressed with an iron hand. This sinister change has with great injustice been laid to the charge of Pitt. It would be easy to show that the sacrifices both of resources and of liberty which England was undoubtedly forced to make, were only the sacrifices to which every country must be exposed which has an aggressive neighbor in a condition of frantic anarchy. But we have hardly left ourselves space to do justice to this subject. We shall be better able to treat it worthily, if we reserve it till the publication of Lord Stanhope's concluding volumes enables us to examine into Pitt's foreign and domestic policy as a whole during all that part of the revolutionary period which he lived to witness. It has been too fiercely criticised to be despatched within such limits as we can now afford to it.

But with respect to the excellence of his policy during the years of peace, there has been very little controversy in recent times. The only quarrel has been as to which political party has the right to appropriate his merits. For many years it was an historical axiom that Pitt was a Tory. He was regarded as the ideal of Tory ministers—the pattern of vigorous government and anti-revolutionary principles; and for some time accordingly Whig writers, with proper party spirit, abused his measures and depreciated his fame. As partisanship cooled, however, they were compelled to recognize his merits; but they indemnified themselves by the discovery that he was not a Tory but a Whig. The controversy is rather a difficult one to decide, from the want of a definition of the principal terms employed. There is no doubt, on the one hand, that when he entered Parliament he took his place among the Rockingham Whigs; and it is equally certain that he was a Reformer, a Catholic Emancipator, and to some extent a Free-trader. On the other hand, he was opposed from the beginning to the end by Fox and Grey, who are enshrined in the foremost niches of the Whig Pantheon; and his political pupils were Castlereagh and Canning, who were certainly supposed by their contemporaries to be Tories. Lord Macaulay lays down that Pitt was an enlightened Whig. Before we can say ay or no to that proposition we must ascertain what are the specific qualities which in all times and places distinguish a Whig from every other breed of politician. It is needless to say that no such differentia can be found. No principle cherished by the Whigs of any one generation can be named, which the Whigs of some other generation have not repudiated. Nor is this change of watchwords peculiar to the Whigs. The historical continuity of parties has a political as well as a sentimental value; but it is an absolute delusion if it is applied to measure the tendencies of a statesman in one age by the tendencies of another statesman in another age. It will only mislead if it is used to give a character of permanence to that which is in its nature fleeting. The axioms of the last age are the fallacies of the present; the principles which save one generation may be the ruin of the next. There is nothing abiding in political science but the necessity of truth, purity, and justice. The evils by which the body politic is threatened are in a state of constant change, and with them the remedies by which those evils must be cured. Such changes operate very rapidly in these days. The concessions that were salutary yesterday may be doubtful to-day, and infatuated weaknesses to-morrow. To insist that those who revere a great statesman's memory shall carry out, ay, and exaggerate, the policy which in his lifetime he thought prudent, is to forget that we live in an ever-changing scene. To measure Pitt by modern party-guages, to try to accommodate his views to any "platform" of the present day, is a folly no other in kind, and only less in degree, than that of those historians who have written the history of Greece and Rome from the "stand-point" of reformers of 1832.

The truth is that Pitt will always be a perplexity to those who love to classify the politics of bygone statesmen. He was far too practical a politician to be given to abstract theories, universal doctrines, watchwords, or shibboleths of any kind. He knew of no political gospel that was to be preached in season and out of season alike. When he thought reform wholesome, he proposed it: when he ceased to think it wholesome, he ceased to propose it. Whether his memory would be claimed by reformers or anti-reformers was a question upon which he troubled himself very little. In the same way he urged Catholic Emancipation, even at the cost of power, when he judged that the balance of advantages was on its side. He abandoned it with equal readiness as soon as the king's strong resistance and the necessity of avoiding intestine division in the face of foreign peril had placed the balance of advantage on the other side. The same untheoretic mind may be traced in all his legislation. The great merit of his measures, so far as they had a trial, was that they were admirably calculated to attain the object they had in view, with the least possible damage to the interests which any great change must necessarily affect. Their demerit was, if demerit it be, that they were justifiable on no single theory, and were often marred by what seemed to be logical contradictions, which damaged them in argument, though they did not hinder them in practice. The result was that they were difficult to pass, and that he often seemed to conceal by his dexterity as a debater the essential unsoundness of his doctrines. But when they were fairly passed they worked very well. Or if he did not succeed in passing them, the miscarriage of later adventurers in the same region enables us to see that they failed precisely in proportion as they disregarded the beacons which he had laid down. His India Bill was one of the happiest instances of this sort of prosaic sagacity. Fox's bill, setting aside the atrocious partisanship which marked the nomination of the commissionerships, was simple and systematic. Complete concentration of power and patronage in a single office, complete independence of the changing caprices of the Crown and the House of Commons, checked by a periodical liability to parliamentary supervision, combined to make a theorist's perfect structure. But the storm of hostility with which its appearance was greeted sufficiently foretold the fatal resistance it would have practically met with when it came into operation, if Lord Temple's manœuvre had not tripped it up in the House of Lords. Pitt's bill was in all points the very reverse. It was a double government; and double governments are generally found to be weak. It professed to correct the misgovernment of the East India Company; and yet it left all the details of administration into which misgovernment mostly finds its way at their disposal. It professed to leave inviolate the privileges of the East India Company; and yet in some of the most momentous questions of policy it superseded the Company altogether. Its whole motive power was the highly artificial contrivance, we may say the fiction, of the secret committee; not a fiction that had sprung up in the lapse of ages from the decay of old powers and the growth of new, but one which was freshly and elaborately constructed by an Act of Parliament. Yet the system which he projected succeeded beyond all hope. It conducted the government of India with glory and success through many a conquest and many a civilizing reform for more than half a century. Its complicated structure made it, no doubt, slow and cumbrous; but the secret of its success was that it worked absolutely without friction. At the cost of logical simplicity it conciliated all interests and disarmed all jealousies.

The same practical good sense, and the same contempt for the reproach of anomaly, were displayed, though on a smaller scale, in the famous Regency Bill. The difficulty was an exceptional one, and required an exceptional remedy. It lay in the youth, thoughtlessness, and friendships of the Prince of Wales. It was almost a matter of certainty, from the bearing he and his advisers had adopted, that if he acceded to the royal power in January, 1789, he would have reversed the whole of his father's policy, flooded the House of Peers with his own creatures, and distributed life offices and pensions among them with no sparing hand; so that when his father resumed the reign two months afterwards he would have returned to power with an overburdened Civil List and an intractable House of Lords. On the other hand, no one who wished well to the empire could have wished to intrust its affairs in a critical time to a Council of Regency. Pitt took a course between the two, giving to the prince only a limited portion of the regal power, but allowing him to exercise that portion without restraint. It was the only course which was practically safe; and so it was judged to be by the nation, which throughout the debates supported Pitt with enthusiasm. But it was equally evident that he was creating an officer unknown to the British Constitution—a sort of half-king, with all a king's irresponsibility and rank, but only half a king's power. A less self-reliant man than Pitt, or one more under the dominion of theory, would have shrunk from the anomaly of such a step, and still more from the difficulty of defending it in debate.

The same peculiar tact in dealing with the feelings and prejudices of those on whom his measures were to operate might be traced, if our remaining space permitted us to do it, in most of the beneficial legislation by which the peaceful half of his administration was distinguished. Within the limits of the great principles of the Constitution, he always preferred to sacrifice any amount of theory rather than make for his proposals a single needless enemy. But perhaps it was in the measure which he was not allowed to pass that this tendency was most strikingly displayed. In his Reform Bill, and his proposals for Catholic relief, many of his admirers have even thought that he went too far in this direction. But still this very excess shows how deeply rooted in his mind was that tenderness for minorities which Montalembert has eulogized as the salvation of our constitutional system. It seems an obvious political truism that a great change, however right in itself, is much less likely to be carried out successfully if a large number of persons are left whose prejudices incite them to hamper it. There was no truth of which Pitt was more convinced.

In respect to the question of Catholic relief there were difficulties on both sides. Mr. Pitt, as is well known, proposed to adopt some measure for the payment of the Irish priesthood, at the same moment that he admitted their nominees to sit in Parliament. Undoubtedly he saw the real danger of emancipation. It was a proposal in effect to admit to the councils of the nation those who thought, spoke, and acted as the subjects of a foreign and distant prince. Such a description was said in that day to be a slander; but we in our own day know by bitter experience that it is true. Mr. Pitt foresaw and wished to avert the dangers of "independent opposition." He judged that the concession must be made; but he wished to strip it of its terrors, by converting those who were to have the nomination to so many seats in Parliament from subjects of the pope into subjects of the king. And he wisely conceived that the shortest and simplest plan for effecting that object was a grant from the English Treasury. But the problem was in truth insoluble. To frame an acceptable solution of this great and perplexing difficulty was in the nature of things impracticable. Every thing that would have converted the Irish into loyal subjects would have alienated the religious feelings of the English. Matters had come to that pass, that it was a choice on which side of the water there should be disloyalty. The cure of the chronic discontent had become hopeless, because whatever was an emollient to one country was an irritant to the other. Among the Irish Roman Catholics themselves, as we learn from the diaries and correspondence of Lord Colchester*—a publication to which, as relating chiefly to a later period than that with which we are now dealing, we do not here allot the notice to which its importance entitles it—the state

* 3 vols. 8vo., London, 1860.

of feeling very soon after became such that no such Treasury grant would have been accepted.

Of Pitt's character, not as a statesman but as a man, these volumes will leave a very pleasant impression. It has been too much the fashion to regard him either as a blue-book on two legs, in whom facts and figures had smothered all human passion, or else as a joyless, loveless misanthrope, the incarnation of pure and unmixed ambition. It is impossible that any one can retain either of these impressions on rising from a perusal of Lord Stanhope's volumes. Wilberforce's diary, and the letters which Lord Stanhope prints for the first time, shows that there was nothing approaching to sullenness in his disposition. There is not a black thought or moody word in them from the first to the last. He was tried, spite of his success, by severe disappointments both at home and abroad. The Opposition harrassed him with an unscrupulousness of tactics, of which even we, who have seen some brilliant displays in that style, cannot form an idea; and his colleague Thurlow treated him with a mixture of insolence and perfidy compared to which open opposition was a luxury. Most of the darling schemes of his life were foiled by the anarchy of Ireland and France. And, to make all annoyances worse, the gout appears from his letters to have been a very frequent visitor. And yet not a word approaching to impatience ever appears in any one of them. The tone which prevails throughout them is that of a cheerful, contented, quiet man, with whom the world is going evenly. In point of manner their most striking feature is their extreme equanimity. There is no trace of depression at his first defeat at Cambridge, or of anger at the intrigue which drove him and Lord Shelburne out of office after peace. There is no trace of exultation at the marvellous success of his early speeches, or at his own unparalleled popularity in 1784. He announces his victories over the Coalition in the same unimpassioned tone in which he announces that he has been to the Duchess of Bolton's. There are none of those professions of indifference to good or evil fortune which belie themselves; there is no word indicating the existence of any feeling on the subjects of which he writes, except that of a calm complacency. When his letters appear, as they occasionally do, by the side of letters from some one of the colleagues who were standing by him in the fight, the contrast shows how wide an interval there was between Pitt's instinctive calmness and the self-control of ordinary men. His reliance appears to have been the result of no conscious effort. He rather writes as if he had the habit of regarding language as an unsuitable vehicle for the communication of feelings, and would have recoiled from any allusion to them as an impertinence. Even when he is forced to speak of them, as on the occasion of the death of his younger brother, he does so in a stiff and labored style which shows how much the effort cost him. His grief appears to have been very sincere; but the language in which he expresses it reads as if it were taken from the "Complete Letter-Writer."

His manners have been censured as "stiff, retired, reserved, and sullen." The accusation has been sufficiently refuted by Lord Wellesley, who spoke from close and intimate acquaintance in a letter addressed to the late Mr. Croker in 1836 (No 114):—

"His manners were perfectly plain, without any affectation, but he seemed utterly unconscious of his own superiority, and much more disposed to listen than to talk. He never betrayed any symptom of anxiety to usurp the lead or to display his own powers, but rather inclined to draw forth others, and to take merely an equal share in the general conversation: then, he plunged heedlessly into the mirth of the hour with no other care than to promote the general good humor and happiness of the company. . . . He was endowed beyond any man of the time whom I knew with a gay heart and a social spirit."

The volumes before us contain abundance of similar testimonials. The club at Goostree's, of which he was the life and soul, certainly do not seem to have thought him sullen; and when Wilberforce picked up the fragments of his opera-hat out of the flower-garden at Wimbledon, he probably did not complain of Pitt's manner as being too reserved. Nor was this gayety the mere ebullition of youthful spirits. Nineteen years of office did not wear it away. "Nothing," says Lord Fitzharris, writing in 1806, "could be more playful than Pitt's conversation. His style and manner were quite those of an accomplished idler." Equally unfounded is the charge that his heart was unaffectionate or cold. His tender affection for his nieces, the earnest and thoughtful regard for his mother which his letters constantly breathe, his deep attachment to his home, and interest in all that concerned it,—all negative the absurd assertion that "he had no domestic joys," and that he was a mere official machine unencumbered with a heart. Some of the greatest mistakes he committed were the mistakes of affection. His feelings misled him into making two appointments, which were not only the worst that he ever made, but almost the worst which it was possible for him to make—and those were the appointment of his brother, Lord Chatham, to the admiralty, and the appointment of his tutor, Dr. Pretyman, to a bishopric. Almost the only letter in which he departs for a moment from his habitual calmness is that in which he implores Secretary Dundas not to leave the ministry on account of the arrogant encroachments of the Duke of Portland, who had just joined it. The only occasion on which his self-possession deserted him in the House of Commons was when his old friend, Lord Melville, was condemned by the House for culpable laxity in his dealing with the public money:—

"I have ever thought," says Lord Fitzharris, "that an aiding cause in Pitt's death, certainly one that tended to shorten his existence, was the result of the proceedings against his old friend and colleague Lord Melville. I sat wedged close to Pitt himself, the night when we were two hundred and sixteen to two hundred and sixteen; and the Speaker, Abbot, after looking as white as a sheet, and pausing for ten minutes, gave the casting vote against us. Pitt immediately put on the little cocked hat that he was in the habit of wearing when dressed for the evening, and jammed it deeply over his forehead, and I distinctly saw the tears trickling down his cheeks. We had overheard one or two, such as Colonel Wardle (of notorious memory), say they would see 'how Billy looked after it.' A few young ardent followers of Pitt, with myself, locked their arms together, and formed a circle, in which he moved, I believe unconsciously, out of the House; and neither the colonel nor his friends could approach him."—*Lord Fitzharris' Note Book*, 1805.

These are lighter traits. It is no slight testimony to the matchless purity of his public character, that he has to be defended on questions such as these. If his eager detractors could have hunted out any other flaw, they would not have busied themselves with the graces of his manner, or the temperature of his emotions. It is not on issues so trifling that posterity will try the greatness of "the pilot that weathered the storm." The lapse of years only brings out in brighter lustre the grandeur of his intellect and the loftiness of his character. In the combined gentleness and firmness of his administration he was a typal English statesman. No man was ever so yielding without being weak, or so stern without being obstinate. In ordinary times he followed after peace more anxiously than Walpole, and often offended his friends by his willingness to compromise and concede. When revolutionary passions had made gentleness impossible, he could be as rigorous as Strafford or as Cromwell. As a legislator, the experience of years has tended more and more to confirm his wisdom. Most of the evils under which we suffer are evils of which he warned us; and where we have averted or softened them, it has been by remedies of his devising. The policy, both at home and abroad, in commerce and in government, which all parties now by common consent pursue, follows very closely the maxims which he laid down. He was the first parliamentary statesman, unless an exception be made in favor of his father, who represented not a section, but the whole of England — monarchical, aristocratic, agricultural, commercial. The king justly prized him, as his wisest and truest champion. The aristocracy, after he had overthrown the clique which had domineered over them for so long, rallied gradually round his standard. The country gentlemen long toasted him as the impersonation of loyal and patriotic statesmanship, and the commercial classes clung to him as their special protector. England may well cherish his fame, and look upon his greatness with an interest which no other single image in modern political history can claim. She owes it to him that she was rescued from the deep degradation into which corruption and imbecility had plunged her. She owes to him the policy which, planned and commenced by him, and perfected by his disciples, placed her on a pinnacle of greatness which no modern nation had attained before. But she owes to him a greater benefit than all these—an example of pure and self-denying patriotism, and the elevation of public feeling which it has worked. If corruption has been driven from our politics altogether,—if faction is being daily more discredited,—if our public men, even the worst of them, are more patriotic in their conduct than the statesmen of the Coalition, these results are in no small degree due to the spectacle with which Pitt's long career familiarized the nation's eyes, of stainless purity and lofty forgetfulness of self.

Color of Servants' Liveries.—Can any of your correspondents inform me whether there is any principle for the regulation of the colors of servants' *liveries?* They appear to be connected with the colors in coats of arms; and ordinarily the predominant color is, I believe, taken from that of the shield. But this cannot be universal, for nothing is more common than for the field or ground of the shield to be *or* (gold); yet yellow is seldom a predominant color in liveries; nor is red, although that tincture may sometimes be predominant in the shield. —*Notes and Queries.*

Remarkable Statements about the British Nobility.—If, as Lord John Manners sings, laws and learning, trade and commerce are matters of secondary importance compared with the preservation of "our old nobility," we must seek some other ground for preference than the antiquity of that institution, at all events as represented in the present House of Peers. It may be that the noble lords, when they ventured last year to usurp taxing powers in defiance of the ministers of the crown and of the representatives of the people, did so under some vague idea that, as descendants in some sort or other of the barons who came over with the Conqueror and afterwards wrung Magna Charta from King John, they had a right to make their will law, and override alike the theory of the British constitution and its practices for ages. Nothing can be more unfounded than such a pretext for their usurpation. John a Nokes and Richard Styles are just as much akin to those same domineering barons as any member of the present House of Peers. As regards the great majority of its members, "our old nobility" *is a mere mushroom aristocracy.* It consists of four hundred and forty members, of whom four hundred and ten members are temporal and thirty spiritual peers. Of the former there is only one whose patent of nobility dates so far back as the last eight years of the reign of Henry III.

Of the four hundred and ten temporal peerages, three hundred and eighty-one have been created within the last three hundred years; of these, one hundred and eighty-two date within the present century, eighty-eight between 1760, and 1809, seventy-five between 1660 and 1760, thirty-six between 1560 and 1660, fourteen between 1460 and 1560, seven between 1360 and 1460, eight between 1260 and 1360, and not one further back. The Saxon, Danish, and Norman nobility, and also the barons of Runneymede, are therefore without a representative in the British House of Peers. *Of the whole House there are only thirty-one members the nobility of whose families is of three hundred years' standing.* The following is a list of them, with the dates of their patents, as given in "Dodd's Parliamentary Companion," from which we have compiled these particulars:—

	Creation, A.D.	Temp.
Baron de Ros,	1264	Henry III.
Baron Hastings,	1289	Edward I.
Baron Audley,	1297	"
Baron Clinton,	1299	"
Baron Dacre,	1307	Edward II.
Baron Willoughby d'Eresby,	1313	"
Baron Camoys,	1383	Richard II.
Earl of Crawford,	1398	"
Baron Saltoun,	1440	Henry VI.
Earl of Shrewsbury,	1442	"
Baron Gray,	1445	"
Baron Say and Sele,	1447	"
Baron Stourton,	1448	"
Baron Saltoun,	1450	"
Earl of Errol,	1453	"
Baron Berners,	1455	"
Earl of Morton,	1458	"
Earl of Derby,	1485	Henry VII.
Baron Willoughby de Broke,	1492	"
Earl of Eglinton,	1507	"
Baron Conyers,	1509	Henry VIII.
Baron Elphinstone,	1509	"
Baron Vaux of Harrowden,	1523	"
Baron Wentworth,	1529	"
Earl of Huntly,	1529	"
Baron Lovat,	1540	"
Duke of Somerset,	1546	"
Earl of Pembroke,	1551	Edward VI.
Earl of Devon,	1553	Mary.
Baron St. John,	1558	Elizabeth.
Earl of Moray,	1561	"

The peers, as a body, cannot, therefore, plume themselves on their antiquity, or safely presume to take liberties with the prerogatives of the crown and the rights of the people on the strength of what was done by their ancestors.—*Liverpool Mercury.*

TO THE AMERICAN PEOPLE.

BY BAYARD TAYLOR.

I.

THAT late, in half-despair, I said:
"The Nation's ancient life is dead:
Her arm is weak, her blood is cold;
She hugs the peace that gives her gold—
The shameful peace, that sees expire
Each beacon-light of patriot fire,
And makes her court a traitors' den"—
Forgive me this, my countrymen!

II.

Oh, in your long forbearance grand,
Slow to suspect the treason planned,
Enduring wrong, yet hoping good,
For sake of olden brotherhood,
How grander, how sublimer far
At the roused eagle's call ye are,
Leaping from slumber to the fight
For Freedom and for chartered right!

III.

Throughout the land there goes a cry:
A sudden splendor fills the sky:
From every hill the banners burst,
Like buds by April breezes nurst;
In every hamlet, home, and mart
The fire-beat of a single heart
Keeps time to strains whose pulses mix
Our blood with that of Seventy-Six!

IV.

The shot whereby the old flag fell
From Sumter's battered citadel,
Struck down the lines of party creed
And made ye one, in soul and deed—
One mighty people, stern and strong
To crush the consummated wrong,
Indignant with the wrath, whose rod
Smites as the awful sword of God!

V.

The cup is full! They thought ye blind:
The props of State they undermined;
Abused your trust, your strength defied,
And stained the Nation's name of pride.
Now lift to Heaven your loyal brows,
Swear once again your fathers' vows,
And cut through traitor hearts a track
To nobler fame and freedom back!

VI.

Draw forth your million blades as one:
Complete the battle then begun!
God fights with ye, and overhead
Floats the dear banner of your dead.
They, and the glories of the past,
The future, dawning dim and vast,
And all the holiest hopes of man,
Are beaming triumph in your van!

VII.

Slow to resolve, be swift to do!
Teach ye the false how fight the true!
How bucklered Perfidy shall feel
In her black heart the patriot's steel;
How sure the bolt that Justice wings;
How weak the arm a traitor brings;
How mighty they who steadfast stand
For Freedom's flag and Freedom's land!

—*Independent.*

HOPE FOR THE BEST.

HOPE for the best, there is energy in it;
Courage will stand rough adversity's test.
Strive, strive for the palm, and you're certain to win it;
You *may* be tried now, but it's "all for the best."

Rough rain-clouds are gathering greater and greater,
Obscuring the heavens so recently fair;
There's a rainbow behind to come sooner or later,
And the watchword of wisdom is "Never despair."

Try again, try again, there is always a turning;
The lane may be long, but the end you must find.
Look firmly *before* you, all obstacles spurning,
For a fixed resolution will *not* look *behind.*

Fail at first. Never mind! Others did so before you.
Courage and prudence were never in vain.
The reward of your toil *must* be hovering o'er you.
Have patience and faith; try again, try again.

Hope for the best! It can *not* be forever.
The hardest of trials must all have an end.
Energy knows not the meaning of *never;*
Things may come to the worst, but they're certain to mend.

Hope for the best, there is fortitude in it;
Patience will triumph o'er poverty's test.
Strive, strive for the palm, and you're certain to win it,
And if you are tried now, why, it's "all for the best."

—*Welcome Guest.*

REMINISCENCES.

He. AND art thou wed, my Belovèd?
My Belovèd of long ago!

She. I am wed, my Belovèd. And I have given
A child to this world of woe.
And the name I have given my child is thine:
So that, when I call to me my little one,
The heaviness of this heart of mine
For a little while may be gone.
For I say not . . . "Hither, hither, my son!"
But . . . "Hither, my love, my belovèd!"

OWEN MEREDITH.

From Once a Week.

AN OLD BOY'S TALE.

In some people, and especially in those who live and die unmarried, there is a period before that of second childhood, frequent indeed in those who to the end of their days show no sign of childishness, which may be termed their second youth—a period at which they yearn to recall the loves and romances of former years, and dwell with a peculiar fondness on the beautiful or pathetic episodes of their early life. Happy is the boy, though snubbed by papa, and kept in jackets by mamma, whose bachelor uncle remembers his own sixteenth year, with its not trifling passions, ambitions, and sorrows. Happy is the maiden, though novels are forbidden and Byron a sealed book, who has some gentle friend in whom forty years of stern reality have not obliterated the image of some old ideal—an ideal of which the original might blush to know, so much have the coloring of love and the haze of time embellished and softened it. Happy I say, and happier far than tailcoats or Byron could make them; for from those worn weak hearts divine lessons of long suffering may be learned, more than a mere love-story, as we may many of us know by experience.

In his second youth died the man who left behind him the folllowing simple autobiography. He was like most of these men in their second youth, brisk, mild, and precise, with an unobtrusive flow of uninteresting talk; a man whom no one would accept an invitation to meet, or refuse one to avoid, essentially a *stop-gap* in society, and in private life the faithful friend of schoolboys.

And when he died, "So poor A— is gone," said Mr. Smith and Mr. Jones, but Tom, Dick, and Harry, their sons, lamented the "Old Boy."

I have no compunction in offering his tale for perusal, as from internal evidence it must have been at least meant for that of his friends, and a perhaps too partial recollection of him makes me think that his readers will become his friends for the time. I feel sure that any pleasure they may find in reading it will be far inferior to that with which he noted down the sentimental remembrance of the past. It fell into my hands through circumstances which, as they are quite unimportant, I need not relate.

The most difficult task I ever set myself is that of realizing that I am old. I measure my life by the public events I remember, and they carry me back to the last century; but Time and I have dawdled so quietly along, that I feel no fatigue. I look in the glass as I shave, and I try to find marks of age, but I do not see more wrinkles than I did last year, nor more gray hairs. Jones looks old, I know, and gets balder, but I cannot see that *I* do. Then I take out a coat I had made for a wedding near sixty years ago; I hang it on a chair, and contemplate its make; I do not wear a broad blue velvet collar now, nor brass buttons; just under my shoulders my coat is old—yes, certainly—but I cannot feel that *I* am. Then I look at my contemporaries: Halford, who played cricket with me in the year 1795, is a grandfather, and his wife, who was such a pretty girl, wears a wig; but I have no wife nor grandchildren. Where are the milestones on the road I have travelled? and I sigh—for tombstones mark the miles that I have trodden—but they cover the young, the fair; how should they make me feel old?

The events of my life have been of the most commonplace character. I went to school as a child, to college as a boy, into a banking-house as a young man. I had a moderate fortune to start with, and have been moderately successful in my business. I have lived within my income, and never married. But, like many other ordinary people who have not talent or force of character to make events for themselves, the circumstances that gathered round my early years were in some respects peculiar, and appear to me worth relating.

I was not more than five years old when I lost both my parents by a singular and dreadful accident. The house we inhabited was situate in a lonely but stormy spot on the north-east coast. A hill sheltered it from the north winds, and it basked in the noonday sun on the brink of the sea. A promontory bent its arm round our little bay, and breaking off abruptly re-appeared at a mile from the shores a group of rocks and small islands.

Even now but little has faded of the mystery and romance with which my childish imagination invested those islands, and none of the terror with which I regarded them, for among those rocks, one angry sundown, my father and my young mother found their grave. The early evening was lovely and calm. They started in their pleasure-boat, waving their hands and blowing me kisses on the perfidious breeze. Not two hours after did the distracted household watch from the windows the short and frightful tragedy of their end.

A fresh air rose as the sun went down, favoring the rising tide. The sea rushed swiftly and suddenly through the tiny straits between the rocks in foaming rapids, which met in whirlpools each moment deeper and fiercer, and the unwary little skiff, her sails useless among the opposite gusts through the rocks, her oars and rudder unavailing against the contending currents, was tossed for a few minutes on the waves, and then disappeared behind a crag. Boats had long before this left the shore, but the wind rose rapidly; with the night, rain came on in torrents; to venture among the rocks was mere frantic risk, and the pleasure-boat with its freight was seen no more.

I relate this as I was afterwards told it, for sleep rested on my unweeping eyes as my father and mother struggled for their last breath—but such accidents, to fishing-boats, were not unfrequent on our treacherous shore. I remember with vividness the waking next morning, to find myself fatherless and motherless, almost uncared for in the midst of bewildered and masterless servants.

We lived some miles from any town, and our only neighbors were the fishermen of the village; but in a few hours a friend of my father had been informed of the event, and came to fetch me from the home to which I have never since returned. I was too young to feel much besides excessive terror and wonder; in fact, it seems to me that I must have been to some extent stupefied by the sudden changes, though I so far understood that I should never see my mother again, as to beg to have for my "very own" a portrait of her that had been done a year or two before—a request that was kindly and wisely granted. I cried bitterly whenever I realized my loss, but that, at five years, was but seldom after the first burst was over.

Of any details succeeding these events I have no recollection, nor of how long I stayed with my kind friends; not long, I suppose, for I left them before my sixth birthday. Nor do I remember any preparation for my departure, beyond a leave-taking one evening, and falling asleep in my nurse's arms to awake in a stage-coach.

Dear me, can it indeed be that I am old—that waking seems but yesterday—or was it last night in my dreams?

Then came the delightful excitement of changing horses, dining off sandwiches, and flying from the trees as they circled past. I am quite sure no thought of sorrow dulled my gladness on that day; all was unmixed delight.

I fell asleep again and woke on being handed out of the coach and hearing confused talking, a light poked into my face completely roused me, and by the time I was wide awake and set on my feet the coach had driven off, and I was standing with my nurse and two men with lanterns by the side of a heap of luggage. This Roger and Harry, subsequently my great allies, shouldered, and we followed them a short distance to a door which opened into a small hall. After a short bustle and colloquy with a maid, my nurse took off my hat, pushed back my hair, and saying, "Now you are going to see your aunt," followed the servant into a sitting-room.

Little I knew for how many years that room would be dear to me—how sacred to my memory till I remember no more.

It was rather a lofty room, though small, the walls were panelled with crimson and gold, the borders of carved wood painted a light gray; the chairs matched the walls, light carved and gilt wood with oval backs and crimson seats; there were two armchairs and a cabinet, "sofas as yet were not" in rooms of this style. Before an embroidery frame, with candles on the table and a maze of gay silks by her side, sat a lady, young, tall, handsome,—the very image of my father. As we entered, the draught from the door disturbed the silks, and she looked up; she bowed slightly to the nurse, and, smiling kindly, held out her hand to me. I advanced with confidence, probably from her strong resemblance to my father, and put my hand in hers; she drew me to her and kissed me. I stood for some minutes silent and wondering, too young to feel embarrassed, too astonished to cry. Not a word broke the stillness; at last, with unaccustomed boldness, I lightly touched with my finger the flowers of her exquisite embroidery (that very white satin, now yellow; those very roses, now faded, are on my sofa cushion still; one bud especially has quite lost its bloom, but how dear to me its pale remains—its color evaporated in a tear shed by Phœbe).

She took my hand gently off, and, as if afraid of my being vexed, patted and kissed it; she put before me a book, and, opening it, pointed to the pictures, but I gazed at *her*.

What spell had fallen on us?

At last, scared by the silence, overpowered by her gentle, melancholy face, I broke from her and ran to hide against my nurse's gown. Nor was it till I found myself in a bedroom, where my supper was prepared, that I ventured to speak.

The reader has probably guessed, what I did not, that my Aunt Mabel was deaf and dumb.

It was striking eleven that night as I was put to bed, and though, no doubt, I asked a number of childish questions, I have no recollection of them or of the answers. I understood that I was to live with my aunt, and that I had a cousin, her niece, for she was herself unmarried, of whom also she had the charge. The next morning, when dressed, I was taken down to the same room I had been in the night before, and as I had been used to do, I walked up to my aunt and said, in my best manner, "Good-morning, Aunt Mabel."

She looked at me with a kind smile and a kiss, and nothing in the whole of my subsequent experience in the least resembles the sensation that then came over me. The utter uselessness of speaking, the weight of silence overpowered me. I felt perfectly helpless, and sat down to my bread and milk a melancholy child. This misery, however, was luckily soon to be relieved, for just as I had finished my breakfast and was doubting whether it might be right to get off my chair without asking leave, — which it was useless to do, and indeed the silence was so profound that I dared not have spoken,—the door opened and there entered Phœbe.

No words can tell the effect her appearance had on me; her young lovely face and form, her quick gestures, and, above all, her girlish voice, are before me now—a vision perfectly distinct from that which I can call up of her appearance at a later period. She came to me as the angel of resurrection from that tomblike abyss of silence and oppression. It was not till long after that I grew into a comprehension and appreciation of her beauty. I was then too young, and indeed she herself was but a girl of twelve, and her charms were only in their bud; it was the *life* of her that I felt; the gay laugh and the light grace with which she came into the room, a kitten scampering round her feet, and a spray of roses in her hand.

I was not a shy child, and when she knelt down by me and threw her arm round me, I willingly returned the caress, and said, though with a half terror of speaking, "May I get down?"

"To be sure," was the answer. And some telegraphic communication having passed between my aunt and cousin, I was carried off quite happy to romp in the garden.

My Aunt Mabel was my father's only sister; her other brother, who was the eldest of the three, had died some years before, leaving to her charge the orphan Phœbe, her mother being also dead, and now the occurrences I have related had added to her cares that of me.

She was in every way one of the most remarkable women I have ever met with; and a more judicious guardian could not have been found.

The only daughter of sensible parents, she had been instructed in every art that could enliven her solitary soul; and, her infirmity never having been made an excuse for ill-temper, her gentleness and affection made it appear an additional claim on the consideration of others.

My grandfather having left a good fortune, poverty never invaded her luxurious but unpretending retirement, and in Phœbe, who, having lived with my aunt from the age of two was far beyond her years, she had at once a companion and a friend. She was remarkably handsome, always dressed to perfection, and constantly occupied with some of the arts in which she excelled; she drew and embroidered exquisitely, knitted and netted with dexterity, and made the most delicate lace. Her library was well furnished, and her mind almost as well, for she read a great deal, and remembered all she read. Nay, besides teaching Phœbe all she knew, which included French and Italian grammar, I had no other teacher till I went to school, and did not find myself particularly backward in Latin, arithmetic, and the rudiments of Greek. Our lessons were all learned by heart, and then written out while she looked over us. She, of course, held the book, and we wrote in a sort of abbreviated language which would sadly have puzzled a stranger; more especially as, from the extraordinary quickness with which she discovered whether we were right, few of the sentences were ever completed.

By these means we did not learn quickly, perhaps, but we learned correctly, and many of her spare hours were devoted to writing out questions, to which we found the answers for her correction. An old French gentleman, a refugee, no doubt, came once a fortnight from the neighboring town, and after three hours spent in teaching Phœbe more or less well to play the piano, to dance, and to read and speak French, he put off the master, and, resuming the private gentleman, dined with us before returning home.

I recall with a sort of wonder the simple regularity of the household; how, day after day, and year after year, as if no note were taken of time, and no thought of change ever fell on that peaceful home, the same events recurred; and to me the same pleasures. One feeling I never did and never could get over; in the garden I could play, run, shout, and sing, but the house was to me a temple of silence—silence broken indeed often by the voices of Phœbe and myself, but never, I really believe, in all the years I lived there, by one hearty laugh on my part.

The first terror that my aunt's silence had occasioned me gave way to a feeling of tender reverence; there was something solemn to me in the grandeur of her handsome head and splendid expressive eyes that half revealed her mind, shrouded, as it were, in a fatal silence; so, though as I grew older my childish wonder wore off, my respect for that mysterious veil constantly increased, and I felt that if one day my aunt were to find the power of language, a spell, sacred to my heart and dear to my imagination, would be forever broken. When I, alone in the world to mourn for her, saw her eyes closed to this world's light, my first thought was "She is speaking now," and I felt a peculiar gladness that her first words should be in that heavenly tongue, which was doubtless as far beyond my comprehension as her deep-buried sorrows and unuttered joys had been.

Four years passed in happy monotony, and shortly before I was ten years old, I was sent to a public school. Of the effect that its discipline had upon my character I can hardly judge, for my heart clung always so closely to home, and the ambitions and strifes of school were so indifferent to me,—for I was neither robust nor clever,—that I believe my life and character were but little influenced by them. Phœbe constantly wrote to me, and the details of our home pets and village friends interested me far more than school escapades, or bedroom "chums." I always went home for the holidays; and, though Phœbe, as she grew older, paid occasional visits to distant friends, she always returned in time to welcome me, and remained during the whole of my vacation. I never missed her, and I never found her change, for with my growth she grew from a pretty girl to a lovely woman—ah! in my memory peerless! I became more and more capable of appreciating her, till at the age when boys are most susceptible, she was to me all in all. I followed her steps, I trod in her shadow: and, in short, was madly in love. Of this I am sure she was utterly unsuspicious; her simple heart was unconscious of itself, she never looked for admiration for she had never lacked it; that of her home circle was a matter of course; she was Queen of the Hearth, and she knew it, nor cared for more; but within a few months, doubtless, she found another life; for one day, just before the midsummer holidays, when I was sixteen, I received a letter dated from a friend's house, where she had been paying a long visit, to tell me she was going to be married.

An awful, blank, numb feeling came over me, relieved only by my indignant mortification as I felt that she had never even thought it possible that I, a child she had known almost from the cradle, could ever dream of loving her otherwise than as a brother; nay, perhaps if she had told the truth, Phœbe would have said as a slave; for she was somewhat imperious, but in her it was not a fault, only a beauty arising naturally from the unlimited sway she possessed over all who surrounded her.

I am blind? Well, yes, I *am* blind; she must have had faults, for she was mortal; but to this day they are to me but an additional charm. She was Phœbe, daughter of the sunbeams — a perfectly good-tempered waywardness, the arch petulance of a spoiled child, were only just a sufficient admixture of weakness to make her true womanly: and who could love an angel? We should soon tire of a being so perfect that it had no wants for us to gratify, or whims to humor.

It was not far from the midsummer holidays when I received this letter; and in her next she told me that Captain Howell was to pass part of them in our neighborhood; that she should be at home for the six weeks; married before my return to school, and then leave for India. In those days, going to India was a thing for life and death. Phœbe in India was Phœbe lost forever. My despair at this intelligence was not that of a boy. No fancy for drowning myself or devoting myself to celibacy entered my head, but I had lost all that I then lived for, and felt that I must begin a new chapter in existence. I took an opportunity of going to the neighboring town and spending all my ready money, of which I had generally plenty, in buying the handsomest ring I could find for Phœbe, and when the holidays came I mounted the coach with very mixed feelings.

As I got to the garden gate, and was on the point of getting down, I saw from my elevated position a white figure walking up the terrace,—it was Phœbe. The terrace was very near the road, but screened from it by a thick laurel hedge, and it was only by being so high up that I could see it. I took all in at a glance; Phœbe, in an evening dress of white—then very fashionable—the folds of the narrow skirt blown round her by the evening breeze, which also disturbed her thick curls; her face bright and eager, one hand holding her hat, the other through the arm of a gentleman—Captain Howell, her lover.

I vented my excitement in a tremendous leap to the ground. She must have just caught sight of me, for I heard her quick step as she ran to the gate calling for me, but I slipped round by a back path and flew into the house. I could not just then have faced Captain Howell. I put off the evil moment for an hour or so, but at last came tea-time, and the meeting was inevitable. Phœbe was just the same as ever,—lovely, affectionate, with her enchanting May-day manner and exacting caprice. Captain Howell I tried to ignore. I was, I believe, perfectly civil to him, and, to please Phœbe, gave him a full share of the obedience I yielded her; but of his position there and his rights I would not permit myself to think. He was a handsome, gentlemanly man, with a quiet, tender air, and a cool manner that contrasted strongly with Phœbe's light vivacity. He drove me half crazy by his forethought. Phœbe's wishes were fulfilled before they were formed. In vain I watched for opportunities of pleasing her. He forestalled every want, and left me without occupation. I followed her like a dog, doubtless to the great disgust of Captain Howell, till he one day laughingly said he believed I was jealous, and I had no choice but to laugh too—as Phœbe did. At last the weary time passed, weary, though I dreaded the end; and the evening came before the marriage—the last, the very last evening with Phœbe.

Captain Howell had been hanging about all the morning. Not that he saw much of Phœbe, for she was too busy packing; and to-day for the first time she showed frankly any regret at leaving her early home. A stray sigh, or some hint of sorrow, had now and then escaped her; but either out of compliment to her future husband, or because she was really happy, they were very rarely heard. But at breakfast on the last morning her eyes were unmistakably red, and for fully a quarter of an hour afterwards she sat on a stool at my aunt's feet, her head bent in that motherly lap, while Aunt Mabel's rare tears dropped on her shining hair. But there was business to be done, luckily for all. My aunt and Phœbe disappeared till dinner, and Captain Howell and I prowled about, too utterly désœuvrés to pretend to be company for each other. Shortly before dinner Phœbe came down; she went to the gate with Captain Howell, who took his last leave of her and rode off, she wandering back to the house, her eyes very full of her coming happiness.

Dinner was a melancholy meal; we could none of us eat, and yet we could not hurry it—it was the last. When it was over Phœbe went out into the garden, and I presently followed her, determined to offer my parting gift with as few words as possible, and so strangle my misery. We walked up and down for some time, talking by fits, but oftener silent, till at last she sat down on a bench. It was near evening, the sun threw ruddy flickering patches of light through the trees, but as yet no stars promised consolation for his departure—and to-morrow she was going—by next sunset would be gone.

"Phœbe," I said, cold and sick, "I have got you a wedding present, a ring; I hope you will like it—to keep—wear—remember."

My pulses choked me. I put it in her hand, and she looked at me, as I stood intending to fly as soon as I had given it; but tears were in her eyes, and I dropped on the seat by her side.

"Kiss me once—my love—love of my life. Phœbe *I* would have married you."

"Poor boy!" she said, gave me one deep kiss, and ran into the house. I sat like one frozen till I heard a bell ring, which startled me, and I went in. As I passed the drawing-room window I saw Phœbe, who had thrown herself on a settee, and with her face buried in a cushion—that cushion—was sobbing violently. By the time I went into the room my aunt had joined her, and they were engaged in a last silent conversation by signs.

I did not go to church next day, but I stood at the gate to see the last of Phœbe, as her husband carried her from the home of her youth, and an intense bitterness filled me as I rejoined my aunt, who had parted with her at the door.

That parting broke my Aunt Mabel's heart. No one who had not seen them together could imagine what Phœbe was to her. She had grown into such a comprehension of that entombed soul; there were so many impulses in my aunt, that finding no outlet in speech could only be known by one whose sympathies had been trained to read them, and that one a woman, that in losing Phœbe she lost as it were the complemental chord that made her life perfect, and she never was herself after. Ah, Phœbe! were you right to leave her so?

I went back to school at the end of the holidays, and when older I went to college, but my home was still with Aunt Mabel. Each time I came home I saw her more and more changed; as with a man in solitary confinement, solitude seemed closing on her: she would not engage a companion,—indeed, at this I do not wonder,—and in spite of reading, gardening, and charity, she altered visibly, and, without any apparent disease, sunk into a state of apathy which brought her to the grave. I was not all I might have been to her, perhaps,—all I *could* be I was; but Phœbe had absorbed me wholly, and I had no strength of mind to rise above the occasion.

• • • • •

Twelve years after this Phœbe returned; Captain Howell was dead, and she came home with one little girl—a second Phœbe, just fit to be a May queen. My Phœbe was altered in face, older, harder; in manner a shade harder too, perhaps, but with the same light vivacity as in her youth. Although we had at intervals corresponded,—but letters took four months in going to India then,—I think she had not realized that it was for the memory of my one first love that I had never loved again; perhaps she had never thought of it at all. Of course, I never said so to her, but a passion that had so influenced my whole life could not fail sometimes to betray itself, and Phœbe's friendship after her return grew warmer and deeper.

I do not know whether she would have married me—I never asked her—I would not insult her by supposing she loved me more than her dead husband. I would not have her loving me less; nor would I marry the mother of his child—Phœbe must be all or none of mine.

And now for more than twenty years she has been lying by my Aunt Mabel. Her daughter married before her death, and went to live in Scotland, and I am ending my life alone. My wedding coat never worn, and my Aunt Mabel's cushion, my mother's picture, and the ring I gave to Phœbe are my household gods; and a plot, unshorn by the mower, with a tombstone on either side, marks the spot where I shall rejoin the two women I have loved.

This, kind reader, is the whole of my old friend's manuscript, a record of a gentle, weak intellect, subjugated by feeling. I cannot, however, conclude without relating an incident that occurred at the time when I first met the Old Boy, and which was never fully explained to me till I read the foregoing story.

We made acquaintance at the dinner-table of a mutual friend, who had lived for many years in India, and whose wife, as I afterwards heard, had been the intimate friend of Captain Howell's lovely wife: it was some years after Phœbe's death, and I had never, of course, even heard her name. In the evening, Mrs. D—— happened to want something from another room, and, turning to her daughter, she said,—

"Will you fetch it, Phœbe?"

The Old Boy looked up.

"What, is there a Phœbe here, too?" said he.

"What else could I have called her?" was the answer.

Thenceforth the young lady had a devoted friend. He was always at her beck for a walk or a drive; her room was stocked with his little presents, and at his death none had more cause to mourn than the namesake of his only love.

Charlatan.—There can be no doubt as to the derivation of this word. It suggests itself at once to every one who, like myself, has but a moderate knowledge of Italian; and it may be found in any good English Dictionary from Johnson downwards.

Charlatan comes from the Ital. *ciarlatano*, and this from *ciarlare*, "to chatter," or rather "to talk much and in a light, frivolous, and boasting manner." From this verb also comes the subst. *ciarlata* "chattering." *Charlatan* thus exactly corresponds to our *quack*, for this comes from the verb "to quack," which Johnson defines "to chatter boastingly, to brag loudly, to talk ostentatiously," supporting his definition by the following quotations from Hudibras:—

> "Believe mechanick virtuosi
> Can raise them mountains in Potosi:
> Seek out for plants with signatures,
> To *quack* of universal cures."

Under *charlatan* he quotes the following from Browne's *Vulgar Errours*:—

> "Saltimbanchoes, quacksalvers, and *charlatans* deceive them in lower degree."

As for the derivation of *ciarlare* (pron. *char*lare, the *ch* as in *China*), it will be found, I think, in the Lat. *garrulus* (garrire, to prate, chatter). This may seem somewhat far fetched; but the Spanish equivalent for *ciarlare* is *charlar* (pron. the *ch* as in *China*), or *garlar*, which latter is evidently the same word as the Italian *garrulare*, a verb made from *garrulo*, or the Spanish *garrular*. That the hard Latin *g* is sometimes softened in Italian is shown by comparing *giallo* (pron. *j*allow, yellow) with the corresponding Lat. *gal*vus (gilvus, gilbus, galbanus), which Riddle says = χλωρός, light-green, or greenish-yellow. So *g*audium, *g*ioja (pron. *j*oya), *j*oy. It is no easy matter to find instances in which a hard Latin *g* has become *c* in Italian, still I find at any rate one; viz., Lat. *G*ades, Ital. *C*adice (Cadiz). The converse is more generally the case, as *c*astigare, Ital. *g*astigare; *c*atus (a tom-cat), Ital. *g*atto, etc.

The Lat. *ca* and *ga* generally remain hard in Ital., though they are very commonly softened in French. Cf. *c*ampus, *c*ampo, *ch*amp; *c*arus *c*aro, *ch*er; *c*astus, *c*asto *ch*aste; *g*amba (Lat. a hoof), Ital. *g*amba (a leg), Fr. *j*ambe; *c*astigare, *g*astigare, *ch*âtier; *c*atus, Ital. *g*atto, Fr. *ch*at.

I should not have entered into this perhaps wearisome detail, but that no one would, I think, be apt to believe in the derivation of *charlatan* from *garrulus* upon the mere assertion of any one, however good an etymologist. According to my views the steps of the process may be represented as follows: garrulus, garrulo, garrulare, *garlare* (Span. garlar, charlar), *carlare*, ciarlare (as in the Ital. *ciambra*, another form of *camera*, from the Lat. camera), ciarlata, ciarlatano, charlatan. All these words still exist with the exception of *garlare* and *carlare*, the steps I have supplied. As alike in sound, one might compare *C*arolus, Ital. *C*arlo, Fr. *Ch*arles.
—*Notes and Queries.*

From The Quarterly Review.

ON IRON MANUFACTURE.

THE returns of the iron manufacture for the past year have been completed; and they present a result to which we earnestly desire to draw public attention.

In the year 1840 the iron manufactured in the United Kingdom was estimated at a little more than 1,396,000 tons, and of this the "hot-blast" amounted to 625,000 tons, the cold to more than 771,000. In 1860 the total "make" had reached the enormous sum of 4,156,858 tons.* But the distinction between hot and cold blast *has ceased to be noticed in the returns*, and it is from other sources we have ascertained that of this total the portion of cold-blast cannot exceed the odd 156,858 tons. For many purposes, it is true, the cheapest iron is good enough. In earlier days the best materials were squandered on the commonest uses. But there was no such waste of power in 1840. If twenty years ago the supply of 771,000 tons of cold-blast was not more than sufficient, how far can one-fifth of that amount go towards satisfying the wants of the present time, when iron has been applied to so many uses? It is evident that inferior iron must be used for many purposes to which only the best should be applied.

We hear with satisfaction that a commission has been appointed by government to investigate the merits of the different qualities of iron. The commissioners, we understand, are men whose names justly claim our confidence, and we look forward to their report with much interest; but they have no easy task before them; for in a matter wherein the experience of different districts gives such various results, and the causes which bias the opinions of the witnesses are so numerous, the most conflicting evidence may be expected.

As an argument in favor of constructing iron vessels by private contract, Sir James Graham seems to rely (see *Times*, March 25th) on the great certainty which is attainable, in the case of iron as compared with wood, that proper materials have been used. We wish this were the case. As matters are now managed, we know of no security that the government possesses against the possible fraud or ignorance of a contractor for iron-work. When work is projected, the contractor is reduced by competition to the lowest possible estimate. He, to secure the contract, fixes a price which excludes the use of the best materials. He can buy pig-iron at prices varying * from 45*s.* to 105*s.*; and his first consideration is how much bad iron and how little good he can safely employ. In all probability the matter is further complicated by the intervention of middle-men, whose profits are virtually so much subtracted from the quality of the material. The contractor calculates that intermixture of the inferior qualities of iron will do much towards correcting their respective defects. But too much reliance must not be placed on this resource. *It is certain that by no combination of the inferior qualities can a superior quality be produced.* Manipulation, indeed, brings out the quality of all kinds of iron. But the limit is soon reached beyond which the inferior sorts cease to be improved by it; and they would be rendered absolutely worthless by the processes which are required to bring the superior to perfection. There is also a point beyond which the best iron deteriorates with further working. The horseshoe, made originally of the toughest merchant bar, is brought to the smithy again and again, till at last it breaks in two beneath the horse's foot.

It was for this reason, among many others, that we objected to the employment of scrap-iron for armor plates. But we have lately heard that the term "scrap-iron" has received a dangerous extension of meaning; that old rails have been included in the definition, and thus under a new name (such is the potency of words) a most unfit material has been introduced. No man who values his reputation would work up old rails (manufactured as they have been, for the most part, of *cinder-iron*) into merchant-bars; nor is there any process by which such a material can be fitted to resist the shock of an enemy's broadside.

The opinion which we ventured to express that "rolling" armor-plates was preferable to the more laborious and expensive method of hammering them, has been confirmed by further inquiry. The "pile" to form the rolled plate is heated by a single process, while the hammered plate is formed by the

* Blast Furnaces in Great Britain, January 1, 1861. Edwin Sparrow, Birmingham.

* See Edwin Sparrow's Iron Trade Price Current. Birmingham. Published monthly.

successive addition of slabs; and as at each addition the whole mass is replaced in the furnace, by these repeated heatings the quality of the earlier portion is damaged. Again, the rolled plate is subjected only to the equable and uniform pressure of the rolls; whereas, when the hammered plate is turned on its side and its edges are submitted to the action of the hammer, the force of the blows acting at a right angle to its previous direction has a tendency to disturb the welding, especially at the centre of the plate, which retains the heat longest. It is true that the greater solidity of the hammered plate is more likely to resist penetration; but by the repeated action of the fire and that of the hammer it is rendered more brittle. The question, however, can be settled only by experiment; and we are glad to hear that some important firms have received orders for rolled armor-plates. Whether the plates be rolled or hammered, true economy would be consulted by employing only the best iron, and we believe the efficiency of the plates would be increased by diminishing their size. If a long plate is struck by a ball, the reaction at the extremities is increased by its length, and moreover the increased size of the pile increases the difficulty of welding, whereas the smaller plate is not only more cheaply made, but more readily repaired. The method of grooving the plates, which is tedious and expensive, also adds much to the difficulty of repairing them, and should be abandoned.

The railway accidents of the last winter had no small effect in attracting public attention to the importance of "quality" in iron. But as far as regards the frequent breakage of the axles, it is by no means certain to what extent the iron was in fault. At the point where the axle of a railway carriage is immovably fixed in the wheel (for in railway carriages the axle revolves with the wheel, and not the wheel on the axle), the vibration of the axle suddenly ceases, and, where vibration ceases, crystallization and brittleness begin. This effect cannot be prevented by any quality of the iron; but it takes place much sooner when the quality is inferior. This is an obscure subject to which we beg earnestly to call the attention of scientific engineers, but thus much at least is certain: if it be desired to ascertain the original quality of the crystallized iron, the infallible test is to heat it red-hot and allow it to cool naturally. If after this process it does not regain its toughness, we may safely pronounce it to have been bad from the first.

The great drawback on the payment of railway dividends is the necessity which presses on most of the companies of prematurely relaying their lines. And the question is now, Shall the mistakes of their predecessors be repeated? or will the directors have the courage to propose and the shareholders the self-denial to sanction that which is required by the permanent interests of the company? It will no doubt be a great sacrifice to avoid reworking the old rails of cinder-iron; but cinder-iron is a material unfit for the construction of rails, whether the heads or wearing surface of the rails be of steel or not. Cold-blast iron, indeed, can be got only in quantities sufficient for a "doctor;" but good "hot-blast" made of "all mine" (that is to say, ironstone, without any admixture of cinder) may be obtained in abundance, and will make an excellent rail-bar.

We hope that the subject of *cast-iron* ordnance will receive the special attention of the Commission. We are persuaded that cast-iron may be produced of much greater strength than has hitherto been attained; and till its maximum power has been ascertained it is unwise to proceed in the expensive and tedious manufacture of wrought-iron ordnance. When some of the guns taken in the Crimea were examined in this country, and were found to be of extraordinary toughness, it was asked why we had no such ordnance, and the reply was, "that we had no such iron." This is not, or at least need not be, the case. Let the government resume the foundry operations at Woolwich which it prematurely abandoned, and take the place which it ought to hold as leader in all efforts for improving the national defences. Let it name the test it proposes, and invite the iron-masters to compete for the supply of the material. We are confident that a quality of iron will soon be attained which for ordnance purposes will equal the produce of Sweden or Russia. It is impossible to say to what extent our manufacturers—that portion of them, we mean, whose materials permit them to do so,—can yet retrace their steps and return to the cold-blast. But it is the public that must give the first impulsion to this improvement. The iron-masters can only act in obedience to the laws which regulate all commercial transactions. When the public are sufficiently enlightened to discover that the only cheap iron is that which will answer its purpose, the remedy is in their own hands. Supply will follow demand.

From Bentley's Miscellany.

OF STORM-BREWING AND SKYEY INFLUENCES.

(Continued from p. 203, No. 882.)

THERE is a branch of our stormy subject which, though already partially illustrated, may justify some further notice; namely, the sympathies ascribed, by poetical license or what not, to inanimate nature, in relation to struggling and suffering man, and *vice versâ*. No doubt that atmospheric changes materially affect the nervous system. Cuvier speaks of "cette malaise qui précède les orages dans les personnes nerveuses" *—a *malaise* of which few households are ignorant. Now in the last fiction quoted by us, Miss Bronte's "Villette," this *malaise* is copiously exemplified, with a curious degree of psychological and physiological interest, that indicates the personal experience of Charlotte herself. At one time Lucy Snowe is sitting at the fireside knitting: the wind has been wailing all day; but, as night deepens, it takes a new tone—an accent keen, piercing, almost articulate to the ear; a plaint, piteous and disconsolate to her nerves, trills in its every gust. "Oh, hush! hush!" she says in her disturbed mind, dropping her work, and making a vain effort to stop her ears against that subtle, searching cry. Three times in the course of her life events have taught her that these strange accents in the storm—this restless, hopeless cry—denote a coming state of the atmosphere unpropitious to life. Epidemic diseases, she believes, are often heralded by a gasping, sobbing, tormented, long-lamenting east wind.† At another time we see her in the empty *pension*, during the long vacation, the latter weeks of which have been tempestuous and wet. "I do not know why that change in the atmosphere made a cruel impression on me, why the raging storm and beating rain crushed me with a deadlier paralysis than I had experienced while the air remained serene; but so it was; and my nervous system could hardly support what it had for many days and nights to undergo in that huge empty house."‡ At another time we stand with Lucy, in the night-time, beside a newly sodded grave. "The air of the night was very still, but dim with a peculiar mist, which changed the moonlight into a luminous haze. In this air, or this mist, there was some quality—electrical, perhaps—which acted in strange sort upon me," * etc. And once more—to illustrate another aspect of these interacting sympathies and occult affinities—there is the apparition of the Nun, at whose going, "the wind rose sobbing; the rain poured wild and cold; the whole night seemed to feel her." †

* Cuvier, Progrès des Sciences, I. 265.
† Villette, ch. iv. ‡ Ibid., ch. xvi.

As a mere matter of history we all know how prompt men are to connect the phenomena of material nature with human incidents. That tremendous tempest which appalled the Spaniards at the siege of Mexico, is thus interpreted by the historian. The war of elements, says Prescott,‡ was in unison with the fortunes of the ruined city: it seemed as if the deities of Anahuac, sacred from their ancient abodes, were borne along shrieking and howling in the blast, as they abandoned the fallen capital to its fate. Men take earnest note, as Louis the Fifteenth (no longer *Bien Aimé*) lies a dying, while the whole court assists at the chapel, and priests are hoarse with chanting their Prayers of Forty Hours, and the heaving organ-bellows blow, that, "almost frightful!" the very heaven blackens; battering rain-torrents dash, with thunder; almost drowning the organ's voice; and electric fire-flashes make the very flambeaux on the altar pale.§ While Byron lay *in articulo mortis*, the poor Greeks of Missolonghi, who thronged the streets, inquiring into his state, regarded the thunder-storm which, at the moment he died, broke over the town, as a signal of his doom, and cried to each other, "The great man is gone!" ‖ Both Dryden and Butler make emphatic mention of the hurricane that signalized the day of Cromwell's decease.

Lamartine's animated description of the arrival of the Marseillais at Charenton, on the eve of their entry into Paris, expressly notes that, "by one of those strange coincidences which sometimes appear to associate great crises in nature with great crises in empires," a storm burst over the excited capital. A close and dense heat, he continues, had rendered respiration difficult during the day. Thick clouds, striped towards

* Villette, ch. xxvii. † Ibid., ch. xxxii.
‡ Hist. of Conquest of Mexico, bk. vi. ch. viii.
§ Carlyle, Hist. of French Revolution, v. i. ch. iv. ‖ Moore's Life of Byron, ch. lvi.

the evening with lowering lines, had, as it were, swallowed up the sun in a suspended ocean. "About ten o'clock the electrical matter disengaged itself in a thousand flashes, like luminous palpitations of the sky. The winds, imprisoned behind this curtain of clouds, disengaged themselves with a rush like a flood of water, bending the crops, breaking the branches of trees, carrying the tiles from the roofs. Rain and hail sounded on the earth, as if they had been violently pelted from on high. Houses were closed, streets emptied simultaneously." It is added, that the lightning, which glared incessantly for eight consecutive hours, killed a great number of the men and women who bring provisions to Paris during the night; that sentries were found killed, and their watch-boxes burned to a cinder; and that iron gates, bent by the wind or the lightning, were rent from the walls to which they were fastened by their hinges, and carried to incredible distances.* In the midst of this hurricane it was, that the conspirators of Charenton deliberated on the overthrow of the throne. At a lone house in the village were assembled blustering Santerre, and stammering, eager Camille Desmoulins, and burly, bull-headed Danton, and croaking, squalid Marat, and Fabre d'Eglantine, and Barbaroux, and others of less note or notoriety; while the dreadful pother o'er their heads resounded as proem or prelude to the greatest and bloodiest of revolutions. Well might the skies have their Marseillais Hymn, breathing fire and slaughter, as well as the Marseillais themselves. If

"A sudden gloom fills all the town
The wind comes sighing o'er the moors,
And wandering, moaning up and down,
Shakes with its trembling hand the doors,

when, in a modern ballad, "The Whisper in the Market-place,"

"When slowly through the Market-place
A stranger rode, but spoke to none," †

if this amount of skyey sympathy is poetically required for a single stranger and his mysterious advent, well might a storm of the first magnitude be brewed, and by poetizing historians be described in detail, to usher in the tramp, tramp of those Marseillais thousands.

* Histoire des Girondins, l. xix. § 15.
† Thornbury, Songs of the Cavaliers and Roundheads, 261.

We have seen how Shakspeare works up the storm on the eve of Cæsar's death. But we have not yet quoted a passage which specially recognizes the sympathy of the elements with the troublous time. "For now, this fearful night," says Cassius,—

"There is no stir, or walking in the streets;
And the complexion of the element
Is favor'd * like the work we have in hand,
Most bloody, fiery, and most terrible." †

Observe, too, the lowering, or rather the darkly, thickly veiled aspect of the heavens on the morning that King Richard arms him for Bosworth field. The doomed prince consults a calendar, to account for the sun's not rising. When, when will it be day?

"Give me a calendar.—
Who saw the sun to-day?
Ratcliff. Not I, my lord.
K. Richard. Then he disdains to shine; for, by the book,
He should have braved the east an hour ago:
A black day will it be to somebody.—
Ratcliff,—
Rat. My lord?
K. Rich. The sun will not be seen to-day;
The sky doth frown and lour upon our army.
I would these dewy tears were from the ground.
Not shine to-day!"

The night of Duncan's murder is unruly; lamentings are heard in the air, strange screams of death; a rough night, of which Lenox testifies that his young remembrance cannot parallel a fellow to it.‡ An elder remembrancer, who can count his threescore years and ten, and who has in his time experienced "hours dreadful, and things strange," declares "this sore night" to have "trifled former knowings." §. As closes, at sombre daybreak, the tragedy of Romeo and Juliet, in the tomb of the Capulets, "a glooming peace this morning with it brings," says Prince Escalus, as the mourners disperse, "The sun for sorrow will not show his head." ‖ So in Addison's tragedy: the dawn is overcast, the morning lowers, and heavily in clouds brings on the day, the great, the important day, big with the fate of Cato and of Rome.¶

* That is, *resembles.*
† Julius Cæsar, Act I. Sc. 3.
‡ Macbeth, Act I. Sc. 1. § Ibid., Sc 2
‖ Romeo and Juliet, Act V. Sc. 3.
¶ Cato, Act I. Sc. 1.

When Eve plucks the forbidden fruit, and eats, Milton tells us, "Earth felt the wound, —and Nature from her seat, Sighing through all her works, gave signs of woe That all was lost." Anon, Adam is enticed to share in the transgression. And then, too,—

"Earth trembled from her entrails, as again
In pangs; and Nature gave a second groan;
Sky lowered; and, muttering thunder, some sad drops
Wept at completing of the mortal sin. *

And again, after sentence has gone forth against the guilty pair, while Eve would fain still sojourn in Eden, there, though in fallen state, content, Nature gives the first unmistakable signs † that Paradise is indeed Lost.

Justly does Sir Walter Scott admire in Dryden's Theodore and Honoria (from Boccaccio) the preliminaries to the apparition —the deepening gloom, the falling wind, the commencement of an earthquake. "Nature was in alarm; some danger nigh Seem'd threaten'd, though unseen to mortal eye." ‡ Sir Walter himself was notably susceptible to, and observant of, impressions of this kind. Lockhart tells us how they stood together in the Canongate churchyard, while the turf was being smoothed over his old favorite, John Ballantyne's remains,—when, of a sudden, the heavens which had been dark and slaty, cleared up, and the midsummer sun shone forth in his strength. "Scott, ever awake to the 'skyey influences,' cast his eyes along the overhanging line of the Calton Hill, with its gleaming walls and towers, and then, turning to the grave again, 'I feel,' he whispered in my ear, 'I feel as if there would be less sunshine for me from this day forth.'" § Among the many examples the Waverley Novels afford of skyey sympathies, two occur to us, which may be taken to represent the class. One is where the Ellangowan retainers are searching for little Harry Bertram, after the gypsies and smugglers have made off with him, and away with the gauger. "The evening had begun to close when the parties entered the wood, and dispersed different ways in quest of the boy and his companion. The darkening of the atmosphere, and the hoarse sighs of the November wind through the naked trees, the rustling of the withered leaves which strewed the glades," etc., "gave a cast of dismal sublimity to the scene." * The other is where Sir George Staunton—the husband of Effie Deans—is crossing the Highland lake, in quest of that outcast son at whose unconscious hands his death is even now imminent. "Pull away, my lads," says Sir George to the rowers; "the clouds threaten us with a storm." And in fact, as we then read, "the dead and heavy closeness of the air, the huge piles of clouds which assembled in the western horizon, and glowed like a furnace under the influence of the setting sun—that awful stillness in which nature seems to expect the thunder-burst, as the condemned soldier waits for the platoon-fire which is to stretch him on the earth, all betokened a speedy storm. Large drops fell from time to time, . . . but the rain again ceased. . . . 'There is something solemn in this delay of the storm,' said Sir George; 'it seems as if it suspended its peal till it solemnized some important event in the world below.'" † Reuben Butler may object, with the query, What are we, that the laws of nature should correspond in their march with our ephemeral deeds or sufferings? but the objection goes for little either with Sir George Staunton or Sir Walter Scott.

Manzoni's description of the lazaretto, peopled with its sixteen thousand patients, during the plague at Milan, omits not to make atmospheric influences add to the horror of the scene. The disc of the sun, as if seen through a veil, sheds a feeble light in its own part of the sky, but darts down a heavy deathlike blast of heat, while a confused murmuring of distant thunder is overheard. Not a leaf stirs, not a bird is seen. Nature seems at war with human existence.‡ The fifth act of Talfourd's Castilian tragedy opens on the battlements of Toledo, with a stormy sunrise, portending what is to come. "Those ponderous clouds that drew an awful splendor from last evening's sun, Spread now on a black pavilion, where the storm Waits to make noontide terrible." So speaks Padilla, on the watch-tower. And when he and his boy are about to set forth to battle, the wife-mother's re-

* Paradise Lost, b. ix.
† Ibid., book x. line 180 *et sqq.*
‡ Translations from Boccace.
§ Life of Sir Walter Scott, ch. lii.

* Guy Mannering, ch. ix.
† The Heart of Mid-Lothian, penultimate chapter.
‡ I Promessi Sposi, cap. xxxiv.

monstrance is founded on these same skyey influences:—

"Oh, not to-day; all things in earth and sky
Are charged with terror; see the river's mists
Rise like huge shrouds to veil your battle-field,
And the air's fill'd with storm."*

Floribel, in the Bride's Tragedy, awaiting her beloved, and on the eve of her death by his hand, exclaims drearily, as she sits by the fire in Mordred's cottage, "How gloomy the clouds look, and the wind rattles among the brown leaves dolefully." In the next scene a mighty storm overhangs the huntsman in the wood—"the day is in its shroud while yet an infant"—and anon the "great tempest in his midnight car" comes forth, conquering and to conquer.

"And thro' the fiery fissures of the clouds
Glistens the warfare of armed elements,
Bellowing defiance in earth's stunned ear,
And setting midnight on the throne of day."†

Meet time for the cowering huntsman to find the murdered woman in the wood.

Meet and right too it is, on the same principle of electric affinities, or skyey sympathies, that when Violenzia parts with Ethel, she should have cause to exclaim, in her own despite, as she glances at the o'er-arching heavens, "But late so fair—and now, look, clouds arise, and the wind begins to blow. We shall have rain. I think you are not ominous. Well, good-night."‡ And that when the mischief at court begins to work, and tidings of it reaches Ethel in the camp, there should be a storm without to give tone to the opening lines of his soliloquy: "How the wind rushes and the gusty rain comes pattering in the pauses of the blast!"§ Campbell, in the feeblest of his longer poems, makes Theodric reach his dying Julia's abode amid a raging winter tempest—

"Without was Nature's elemental din—
And beauty died, and friendship wept,
within!"‖

Campbell's name, by the way, reminds us of what Bon Gaultier describes as having occurred at his funeral at Westminster Abbey. Milman, himself no mean poet, read the service, we are told; that service which may at no time be listened to without emotion; but in such a place, and in such circumstances, how solemn! As he read, the day which had been lowering, grew darker and darker, and when the requiem mourned along the echoing roof, and the coffin was lowered into the earth, a solemn shadow thickened over the spot, which was made more sad and solemn, by a wan and sickly beam that struggled in from a side window.

Then as the mimic thunder of the organ rolled away, by one of those strange coincidences which are often observed in nature, a low peal of thunder murmured along the heavens without, carrying the thought far, far away from this dim spot of earth to the great unfathomed world beyond."*

"Louder, louder, let the organ like a seraph anthem roll,
Hymning to its home of glory our departed brother's soul!
Louder yet, and yet more loudly let the organ's thunder rise!
Hark! a louder thunder answers, deepening inwards to the skies,—
Heaven's majestic diapason, pealing on from east to west,
Never grander music anthem'd poet to his home of rest!"

In connection with this particular we may notice what a graphic attendant at the funeral of Thomas Chalmers reports of skyey sympathies. The day he tells us, was one of those gloomy days, not unfrequent in early summer, which steep the landscape in a sombre neutral tint of gray—a sort of diluted gloom—and volumes of mist, unvariegated, blank, and diffuse of outline, flew low athwart the hills, or lay folded on the distant horizon. "A chill breeze from the east murmured drearily through the trees that line the cemetery on the south and west, and rustled against the low ornamental shrubs that vary and adorn its surface. We felt as if the garish sunshine would have associated ill with the occasion."† At how many common funerals how many common men have thought the like thoughts!

There are frequent examples of skyey influences in Galt's story of the Entail. Here is Charles Walkingshaw, just after he has learned his disinherited lot, and just before

* The Castilian, v. 1.
† T. Lovell Beddoes, The Bride's Tragedy, Act V. Sc. 2 and 3.
‡ W. Caldwell Roscoe, Violenzia, Act I. Sc. 1.
§ Ibid., Act III. Sc. 1.
‖ Theodric: A Domestic Tale.

* Bon Gaultier and his Friends. 1844.
† Hugh Miller.

his fatal illness—wandering distractedly down the Gallowgate. "The scene and the day were in unison with the tempest which shook his frame and shivered his mind. The sky was darkly overcast. The clouds were rolling in black and lowering masses. . . . The gusty wind howled like a death-dog among the firs [beside the Molendinar Burn] which waved their dark boughs like hearse plumes over him, and the voice of the raging waters encouraged his despair." *

Then again when James Walkinshaw is perplexed as to his future movements—where to go, and what to do—we read that the doubts, the fears, the fondness, which alternately swayed him, received "a secret and sympathetic energy from the appearance and state of external nature. The weather was cloudy but not lowering—a strong tempest seemed, however, to be raging at a distance; and several times he paused and looked back, at the enormous masses of dark and troubled vapor, which were drifting along the whole sweep of the northern horizon, from Ben Lomond to the Ochils, as if some awful burning were laying waste the world beyond them. . . . The uncertainty which wavered in the prospects of his future life, found a mystical reflex in the swift and stormy wrack of the carry, that some unfelt wind was silently urging along the distant horizon." † And, once more, when his widowed mother is on her dubious way, to take counsel with auld Leddy Grippy (Byron's favorite character in all modern fiction): "The twilight of the evening having now almost faded into night, she caught gloomy presentiments from the time, and sighed that there was no end to her sorrows. . . . The darkness of the road, the silence of the fields," etc., might awaken associations of anxiety and misgiving; "but the serene magnificence of the starry heavens inspired hope, and the all-encompassing sky seemed to her the universal wings of Providence, vigilant and protecting with innumerable millions of eyes." ‡

Even Miss Austen—homely, common-sensical, unromantic Jane Austen—employs in a quiet way the machinery under present review. But then it is in the congenial tale of "Northanger Abbey." Does not Henry Tilney fairly forewarn Catherine of what she may expect on becoming a guest at the abbey? The first night, after surmounting her "unconquerable" horror of the bed, she will retire to rest, he predicts, and get a few hours' unquiet slumber. But on the second, or at furthest the third night after her arrival, she will probably have a violent storm. Peals of thunder so loud as to seem to shake the edifice to its foundation will roll round the neighboring mountains; and during the frightful gusts of wind which accompany it, she will probably think she discerns one part of the hanging more violently agitated than the rest. And so on. That is all Mr. Tilney's fun. But sure enough the very night of her arrival was worthy of the abbey, and attuned the impressionable damsel's thoughts accordingly. "Catherine, as she crossed the hall, listened to the tempest with sensations of awe; and when she heard it rage round a corner of the ancient building, and close with sudden fury a distant door, felt for the first time that she was really in an abbey. Yes, these were characteristic sounds; they brought to her recollection a countless variety of dreadful situations and horrid scenes, which such buildings had witnessed, and such storms had ushered in." Gradually she is prepared for the worst. To her bedroom she goes, but not to bed—to bed—to bed! That were too dreadful. "The wind roared down the chimney, the rain beat in torrents against the windows, and every thing seemed to speak the awfulness of her situation." She is irresistibly tempted to examine that high, old-fashioned black cabinet—to unlock it—to make off with a mysterious manuscript. Then snuffs her candle—alas, *out*. Appalling position. "Darkness impenetrable and immovable filled the room. A violent gust of wind, rising with sudden fury, added fresh horror to the moment. Catherine trembled from hand to foot." In a cold sweat, she gropes her way to bed, though repose is impossible. "The storm, too, abroad so dreadful! She had not been used to feel alarm from wind, but now every blast seemed fraught with awful intelligence." *

Here again is another style of example to the main purpose, from one of Banim's Irish tales. Terence Delany is about to slay the proctor, Peery Clancy, beside an open grave,

* The Entail, ch. xxxvii. † Ibid., ch. lxvi. ‡ Ibid., ch. xcviii.

* Northanger Abbey, ch. xx. xxi.

but grants his victim a few minutes of grace to make his last prayer to Heaven. "He walked aside. By one of those singular coincidences which occur oftener than they are noticed, the face of night suddenly changed; the stars became extinguished, and the wind howled through the leafless branches."* All betokening a melodramatic crisis, ushered in accordingly. No sooner has Justice Rivers in Hood's novel, announced to Grace her engagement with the obnoxious Ringwood, than "a startling crash of thunder, as if dashing in the roof of the house, seemed to ratify the sentence just pronounced. The father sat still as unmoved and imperturbable as usual, though the flash which belonged to the shock had shivered a poplar in sight of the window; but it made the terrified girl start to her feet with a smothered scream, as she saw the green tree, upon which she had been gazing, instantaneously stripped and whitened by the rending off of the bark."†

Lest we should be overdoing the melodramatic section, take an illustration from that of a farce—in the case of Mr. Winkle on his way by sunset, to become a duellist, *malgré lui*. "The evening grew more dull every moment, and a melancholy wind sounded through the deserted fields, like a distant giant, whistling for his house-dog. The sadness of the scene imparted a sombre tinge to the feelings of Mr. Winkle."‡ Mr. Dickens is profuse in examples of our theme, melodramatic as well as burlesque. The night was dark, and a cold wind blew, driving the clouds fast and furiously, before it, when Ralph Nickleby went his way to keep his last appointment. Ere long, he hangs, a dead man, in a deserted lumber-room—his last look from the window having lighted on "the same black cloud that had seemed to follow him home, and which now appeared to hover directly above the house."§ Note the weather, too, and its associations, when Ada and Esther Summerson go to Cousin Richard's, neither of them in hopeful or lively mood. "It was a sombre day, and drops of chill rain fell at intervals. It was one of those colorless days when every thing looks heavy and harsh."‖ Even more profuse, perhaps, is Sir E. B. Lytton, in little sympathetic details of this sort. As Aram strides homewards to his solitary valley, one autumnal evening, Nature is described as seeming restless and instinct with change—there being those signs in the atmosphere which leave the most experienced in doubt whether the morning may rise in storm or sunshine—while in this particular period, the skyey influences seem to tincture the animal life with their own mysterious and wayward spirit of change. It is the night of Aram's interview with the Stranger.* So with the day on which the latter tempts Eugene to his crime. "It was a gloomy winter's day, the waters rolled on black and sullen, and the dry leaves rustled desolately beneath my feet. Who shall tell us that outward nature has no effect upon our mood? All around seemed to frown upon my lot."† Maltravers is talking with Florence, when, raising his eyes, he sees the form of Lumley Ferrers approaching them from the opposite end of the terrace: "at the same instant a dark cloud crept over the sky, the waters seemed overcast, and the breeze fell."‡ When Robin Hilyard warns the Earl of Warwick against Edward's false smile, and Clarence's fickle faith, and Richard's inscrutable craft, he takes his leave with these foreboding words: "'Mark, the sun sets!—and while we speak, yon dark cloud gathers over your plumed head.' He pointed to the heavens as he ceased, and a low roll of gathering thunder seemed to answer his ominous warning."§ Aspiring Glyndon, Zanoni's neophyte, retires to gaze on the stars: "But the solemn stars, that are mysteries in themselves, seemed, by a kindred sympathy, to agitate the wings of the spirit no longer contented with its cage. As he gazed, a star shot from its brethren, and vanished from the depths of space!"‖ Godolphin speeds to his interview with Constance—that crisis in his life. As the event is unhappy, naturally we read that "The day was sad and heavy. A low, drizzling rain, and laboring yet settled clouds, which denied all glimpse of the sky, and seemed cursed into stagnancy by the absence of all wind or even breeze, increased by those associations we endeavor

* Crohoore of the Billhook, ch. x.
† Tylney Hall, vol. iii. ch. ii.
‡ Pickwick Papers, ch. ii.
§ Nicholas Nickleby, ch. lxii.
‖ Bleak House, ch. li.

* Eugene Aram, book iii. ch. ii.
† Ibid., book v. ch. vii.
‡ Earnest Maltravers, book viii. ch. iii.
§ The Last of the Barons, book vii. ch. iv.
‖ Zanoni, book iii. ch. xii.

in vain to resist, the dark and oppressive sadness of his thoughts." * And, to give one more Lyttonian example, this little paragraph from the later history of Lucretia speaks for itself: "The following morning was indeed eventful to the family at Laughton; and as if conscious of what it brought forth, it rose dreary and sunless; one heavy mist covered all the landscape, and a raw drizzling rain fell pattering through the yellow leaves." † So commences significantly a chapter whose significant title is The Shades on the Dial.

Mark the opening paragraphs of "The Woman in White"—relative to Walter Hartright's expedition to Hampstead, on the memorable night of his roadside adventure with Anne Catherick. "The evening, I remember, was still and cloudy; the London air was at its heaviest; the distant hum of the street-traffic was at its faintest; the small pulse of the life within me and the great heart of the city around me seemed to be sinking in unison, languidly and more languidly with the sinking sun." ‡ Mr. Wilkie Collins is an artist—and artist-like is the striking of the keynote in passages of running accompaniment, such as these. So again on the night of Walter Hartright's visit to the Limmeridge churchyard, to keep watch for the white woman he erst encountered on the Finchley-road: "The clouds were wild in the western heaven, and the wind blew chill from the sea. Far as the shore was, the sound of the surf swept over the intervening moorland, and beat drearily in my ears, when I entered the churchyard. Not a living creature was in sight. The place looked lonelier than ever, as I chose my position, and waited and watched with my eyes on the white cross that rose over Mrs. Fairlie's grave." § Similarly, on the night of the lawyer's arrival at Limmeridge House, to arrange the marriage settlements: "The wind howled dismally all night, and strange cracking and groaning noises sounded here, there, and everywhere in the empty house." ‖ And, as stands to reason, it is on "a wild, unsettled morning" ¶ that the marriage ceremony comes off, between ill-starred Laura Fairlie and Sir Percival Glyde.

Nor can any attentive reader of Mr. Hawthorne's romances have missed the frequency of these and kindred phenomena, so closely interwoven with the progress and destiny of his characters. Here is conscience-stricken Arthur Dimmesdale speaking, as becomes his office, of judgment to come—at which little Pearl gives an elfish laugh; but "before he had done speaking, a light gleamed far and wide over all the muffled sky. . . . The great vault brightened, like the dome of an immense lamp. It showed the familiar scene of the street, with the distinctness of midday, but also with an awfulness that is always imparted to familiar objects by an unaccustomed light. . . . And there stood the minister with his hand over his heart; and Hester Prynne, with the embroidered [Scarlet] letter glimmering on her bosom; and little Pearl, herself a symbol, and the connecting link between these two. They stood in the noon of that strange and solemn splendor, as if it were the light that is to reveal all secrets, and the daybreak that shall unite all who belong to one another." * The stress laid on this meteoric appearance is thus far in keeping with the time and place of the story, that in those days the New Englanders interpreted all such phenomena (indeed, whatever occurred with less regularity than the rise and set of the sun and moon) as so many revelations from a supernatural source. The author doubts even whether any marked event, for good or evil, ever befell New England, from its settlement down to revolutionary times, of which the inhabitants had not been previously warned by some spectacle of this nature. *His* employment of them, we need not say, takes a wider range, and involves a subtler meaning.

Here again are Hester and little Pearl taking a forest walk—along a footpath that straggles onward into the mystery of the primeval forest—which hems it in so narrowly, and stands so black and dense on either side, and discloses such imperfect glimpses of the sky above, that, to Hester's mind, it images not amiss the moral wilderness in which she had so long been wandering. "The day was chill and sombre. Overhead was a gay expanse of cloud, slightly stirred, however, by a breeze; so that a gleam of flickering sunshine might now and then be seen at its solitary play along the path. This flitting cheerfulness was always at the

* Godolphin, ch. xviii.
† Lucretia, part ii. ch. xxiii.
‡ The Woman in White, vol. i. p. 3.
§ Ibid., p 144. ‖ Ibid., p. 258. ¶ Ibid., p. 315.

* The Scarlet Letter, ch. xii.

further extremity of some long vista through the forest. The sporting sunlight—feebly sportive, at best, in the predominant pensiveness of the day and scene—withdrew itself as they came nigh, and left the spots where it had danced the drearier, because they had hoped to find them bright."* Sunshine on her pathway, is not for such as Hester Prynne.

Or shall we glance at the pastor and his parishioner sitting down, side by side, and hand clasped in hand, on the mossy trunk of a fallen tree? "The forest was obscure around them, and creaked with a blast that was passing through it. The boughs were tossing heavily above their heads; while one solemn old tree groaned dolefully to another, as if telling the sad story of the pair that sat beneath, or constrained to forebode evil to come."†

One glimpse more of them, and it shall be a cheerier one. Hester has doffed, once and for all, the scarlet letter, as an outward and visible sign at least. And she finds exquisite relief, that stigma gone, and the pastor enters into her joy. The day has been gloomy; but now, as if the gloom of the earth and the sky had been but the effluence of these two mortal hearts, it vanishes with their sorrow. "All at once, as with a sudden smile of heaven, burst forth the sunshine, pouring a very flood into the obscure forest, gladdening each green leaf, transmuting the yellow fallen ones to gold, and gleaming adown the gray trunks of the solemn trees. The objects that had made a shadow hitherto, embodied the brightness now. The course of the little brook might be traced by its merry gleam afar into the wood's heart of mystery, which had become a mystery of joy.

"Such was the sympathy of Nature—that wild, heathen Nature of the forest, never subjugated by human law, nor illumined by higher truth—with the bliss of these two spirits."*

Is then the author of "Transformation" so objective a philosopher as to imply reality and self-existence in this flood of sunshine? Not at all. His doctrine it explicitly is, that love, whether newly born, or aroused from a deathlike slumber, must always create a sunshine, filling the heart so full of radiance, that it overflows upon the outward world. Had the forest still kept its gloom, it would, he says, have been bright in Hester's eyes, and bright in Arthur Dimmesdale's. Assuredly, in delicate symbolism of this peculiar kind, Mr. Hawthorne's tact is *sui generis*—so ingeniously fanciful is he, so quaintly suggestive, so profoundly humane.

* The Scarlet Letter, ch. xvi. † Ibid., ch. xvii.

* The Scarlet Letter, ch. xviii.

Bookbinding in Ancient and in Mediæval Times.—What are the best treatises relating to the art of bookbinding, and in what works, published either in this country or on the Continent, have good examples been figured? The old stamped bindings of the fifteenth and sixteenth centuries are often exceedingly interesting, and executed with great skill; the most tasteful productions of the *bibliopegic* art are those of the *renaissance* period, especially the choice relics of the Grolier or the Maioli collections, highly esteemed by lovers of old books in all countries. The Archæological Institute has announced a special exhibition of specimens of ancient bookbinding for their monthly meeting on April 5th, and numerous choice examples have been promised for the occasion. The collection will be open to the members and their friends during a few days, at 26 Suffolk Street, Pall Mall, and an opportunity thus afforded for some general investigation of the style and character of objects of this class, at various periods and in various countries. I should be much obliged to any of your readers who may be able to supply references to works upon the subject. Of course the notices scattered through Dr. Dibdin's publications are known to me; also the illustrated treatises by J. A. Arnett; that entitled *Ornamental Art applied to Ancient and Modern Bookbinding*, published by Cundall in 1848; the Specimens elaborately reproduced by Mr. Tuckett, a beautiful publication, of which, as I believe, two parts only have appeared; and a few other matters of minor note, published on the Continent. More ample information on the subject must doubtless have been given in other works. —*Notes and Queries.*

From The Saturday Review.

SELF-KNOWLEDGE.

We are sometimes told that a man cannot really know himself: and, from the days of the Seven Sages till now, we have had dictum upon dictum setting forth at once how desirable and how difficult a thing it is for him to obtain such knowledge. There are few subjects of which preachers and moralists are fonder; if the γνῶθι σεαυτόν originally came down from heaven, it has lived to take refuge in children's copy-books and in the margins of Treasuries of Knowledge. Like all apophthegms of the sort, it contains an element of truth; at the same time, like most apophthegms of the sort, it may easily be pressed and exaggerated in such a way as to contain much less truth than falsehood.

In one sense it is clear that every man of average understanding must know himself far better than he knows anybody else, or than anybody else knows him. He must know better than anybody else the history of his own actions, the circumstances under which they were done, the motives and objects which led him to do them. His knowledge of his own circumstances, motives, and objects may be far from perfect, but at any rate it is far more perfect than the knowledge which he can have of the circumstances, motives, and objects of anybody else. He is doubtless exposed to the various forms of what Butler calls self-delusion. He may refuse to look his own actions fairly in the face, and may invent excuses for himself which he would not invent for any one else. But self-delusion is, for the most part, voluntary—at all events, in its origin. It is not so much a lack of power as a perversion of the will. The self-deluded man does not want the mere power of self-knowledge, but he has lost the will—perhaps in the end he has lost the power—to judge himself fairly. Setting self-delusion aside, it is clear that a man must know himself much better than he can know anybody else. In the case of other men, he can at most see their outward actions—he cannot really look into their hearts. A certain combination of acuteness and experience may indeed enable a man to practise something very like discerning of spirits; he can, as the phrase is, see through everybody and every thing. But the very phrase of seeing through shows that there is something to be seen through; there are outward obstacles in the way of knowing other people which do not stand in the way of a man's knowledge of himself. To judge other people, he must argue, and compare, and follow the laws of evidence. To judge himself, he has nothing to do but to call his memory and his conscience into play. A man's worst and his best actions are probably known to himself alone. The right hand does many a good and many a bad deed which the left hand knoweth not. None but the actor can tell the circumstances which diminish the guilt of what is in itself a great crime, or the circumstances which diminish the merit of what is in itself a noble and virtuous action. The apparently criminal man may have a thousand excuses which can never be known to his prosecutor or his judge, and the apparently virtuous man may be conscious to himself of a thousand defects in his best actions, of imperfection or even corruption in his motives, which his admirers never dream of. Of a man's moral state as towards his own conscience, no one can know so much as himself.

And what is thus true of a man's knowledge of his own moral being is in some, though in a decidedly inferior, degree true of his knowledge of his own intellectual being. True it is that self-delusion comes in yet more strongly when a man tries to judge his own intellectual productions—his literary compositions, for instance—than when he tries to judge his own moral actions. Men are infinitely more vain and irritable under the criticism of the reviewer than they could be under that of the severest moral censor. Yet a man who can once look honestly at his own productions, knows a great deal about them which nobody else can know. He is alive to both beauties and faults to which nobody else is alive; and whatever we say of the beauties, the faults at least are commonly real faults. Every one who is much accustomed to speaking or writing, must know how often he is thoroughly disappointed with his own speech, book, or article, and is half angry, half pleased, to find that nobody else is disappointed. The truth is, that he set up for himself a very high standard and failed to reach it; and he is therefore himself disappointed because he knows of his failure.

But no one else knows any thing of his failure, because no one else knows any thing of the standard which he set up. Other people are satisfied if the result is positively good, because they do not know how much better the author meant it to be. Or, again, the reverse process takes place. Other people do not take in the real excellence of what a man produces. Readers, for instance, do not stop to appreciate the conscientious pains of a thoughtful and accurate writer. Most people who have much experience of such matters will testify that, whether a man can safely judge of his own writings or not, no other man can be safely trusted to improve them in detail.

How, then, is it that, while a man must, or at least can if he pleases, know himself both morally and intellectually better than anybody else can, yet the common voice of mankind refuses to accept a man's estimate of himself or to allow him to be a judge in his own cause? The common voice of mankind is perfectly right in so doing. A man's knowledge of himself, whether intellectual or moral, is a positive not a relative knowledge. He knows better than anybody else how he stands towards his own conscience; but he knows less than anybody else how he stands towards the rest of the world. And it is not a man's relation to his own conscience, but his relation to the rest of the world, which the rest of the world very properly takes as the groundwork of its estimate of him. Society, whether in the form of positive law or of mere social intercourse, does not so much regard the inherent virtuousness or viciousness of this or that course of action as it regards the effect which it may have upon society itself. A man who has, and rightly has, the full approbation of his own conscience, may often really do more mischief to others, and may very commonly be far more disagreeable to others, than one whose inspection of his own heart must discover things very much uglier in themselves. Let two men have a dispute; each vehemently maintains and conscientiously believes that he is alone in the right; yet one certainly, and both probably, will be set down by others as being in the wrong. It is not uncommon to say in such a case that the disputant does not know himself, that he does not know the weakness of his own arguments, and so forth. Now, in most instances, it would be truer to say that he knows himself and his own case thoroughly in themselves, but that he does not know his adversary and his adversary's case thoroughly, and that therefore he does not know himself and his own case in relation to his adversary. He knows his own circumstances, his own rights, wrongs, motives, provocations, etc., perfectly well; only he does not know equally well the rights, wrongs, motives, and provocations of his adversary. His arguments may be perfectly sound in themselves—perfectly convincing till they are weighed against other arguments which he has perhaps never heard of, and which, at all events, are not brought so forcibly home to him. Every man who knows any thing of courts of justice knows how convincing the arguments on one side seem, even to indifferent persons, till something equally or more convincing is brought forward on the other side. And a candid plaintiff or defendant will be perfectly astonished to find how much can be said against his own case which he never before thought of—enough commonly, if not to upset his own case, yet fully to justify the adverse party in disputing it. What a man therefore really wants, is not knowledge of himself, but knowledge of others, without which his very knowledge of himself may prove a snare. A third party looks on at two disputants. He does not know either so well as each knows himself, but his knowledge, though imperfect, is more equal. He may know one as well as he knows the other, which the disputants cannot do, and, with his imperfect but equal knowledge of both cases, he can weigh and compare the two in a way which is not possible to the more perfect but unequal knowledge of the two disputants. Society may very often, in one sense, condemn a man wrongfully—that is, it may not give him all the credit that is due to him for purity of motives; and at the same time, it may condemn him quite rightfully from its own point of view, which looks upon men, not as virtuous or vicious before their own consciences, but as useful or useless, agreeable or disagreeable, to mankind in general.

So with a man's intellectual position. A man may be conscious of real beauties and real faults in his works which others pass by; but others judge of his works in relation, not to himself, but to other men. They give him no credit for care the results of which are not clearly apparent, and they are not disposed to censure him for failures which nobody but himself knows to be failures. A man may have great powers and great knowledge, but if he will not use his powers or cannot use his knowledge, he must not complain if the world at large sets no store by either. A man of less powers and less knowledge, who makes the most of what powers and knowledge he has, is, as far as the rest of mankind are concerned, abler and more learned than one who has a really greater light, but who, perversely, or unluckily, hides it under a bushel. The general estimate of a man's intellect may be positively very unjust; he may know himself to be underrated or overrated; but, looked at, not positively but relatively and comparatively, it may not be far from the truth. Society regards not so much the amount of ability or the amount of knowledge as the way in which ability and knowledge are made available to the use of society. A man may know the positive amount of his own knowledge; but he cannot so well know the positive amount of the knowledge of his neighbor. For the most ignorant man will have some points on which he knows more than the best-informed. The world at large cannot tell, and does not care to know, the actual amount of a man's knowledge; it judges how much he knows relatively to itself—that is, how much he can make practically useful.

We all, then, know—or if we choose, may know—our own virtues and vices, our own knowledge and ignorance, better than anybody else can tell us—that is, we know them relatively to ourselves better than anybody else can tell us. But we shall find others far better monitors as to their value relatively to other people. The really difficult part of self-knowledge is for a man to be able to take his own measure, not only positively, but relatively—to know his place as regards others—not only to know whether an action is abstractedly right or wrong, but to know how it will affect others, and what others will think of it. It is an ugly doctrine that private vices are public benefits, but most certainly private virtues are often public evils. The self-knowledge which is so difficult to obtain is, in fact, knowledge of others and of our own position with regard to them. A man knows himself, in this sense, only by knowing his neighbor. He knows his own case by knowing his adversary's case. It is this calm, dispassionate power of going out of one's self and into another, of looking at one's self as one looks at another man, and looking at another man as at one's self, which is the real trial. Every man who does not play tricks with his conscience can take his own positive measure; but it requires a rather rare combination of gifts to take his own measure relatively to others. Yet, without such knowledge, a man does not really know himself, and so far the Seven Sages and the writing-masters preach a true morality.

Montrond is wonderful: apoplexy and gout do their worst, but cannot subdue his spirits and *esprit;* he killed us with laughing at his stories about M. de Talleyrand's death, which, though it deeply affected him, has still its ludicrous side: and his legacy of a standing-up desk to write at did not soften his natural inclination to be a little sarcastic. He said that when the signature to the retractation was signed, a priest declared that it was a miracle, on which he gravely said that he had already known of just such another miracle—that "when General Gouvins was killed, he, Montrond, with General Latour Maubourg, went to the spot where he lay, and that they asked the only person who had seen the catastrophe how it occurred; this was a hussar, who replied, "Le boulet l'a frappé, et il n'avoit que juste le temps de me dire, Prenez ma bourse et ma montre; et il est mort!'" This apologue, as you may suppose, was like a shell thrown into Dino's coterie.

Bob Bligh, when travelling with the Marquis of Ely through the Highlands, turned the marquis out of his own carriage, because he did not know who was the mother of Queen Elizabeth. In vain might he look for a travelling companion here. Do you recollect a story of Tom Stepney's about his countrymen, the Welsh? On the Restoration of Charles II. a form of prayer and thanksgiving was sent down into Wales, to be read in all churches and chapels. "This is all very well, perhaps, for Charles II.," said the Welsh; "but what is become of Charles I.?" Of Cromwell they had never heard a syllable.

A DARK HOUR.

"Leave me awhile! my heart is crushed, and some mysterious power
All the sad burden of my life has pressed into this hour.
Leave me awhile!—gay voices stir unfathomed depths of pain;—
Leave me to fight my fight alone, till I can smile again.
My spirit, like some angry wind that sweeps the wintry sky,
Gathers up all the darkest clouds, and whirls them swiftly by.
My weary eyes forget to gaze where spring's bright flowers abound;
Yet seek out all the faded leaves that die upon the ground.
With sunlight from the heart shut out, —no blue in all the skies,
I'm borne back to the olden time, and all its memories!
The absent ones—the changed—the dead—a long and sad array—
From the dim past stretch out their hands, and hold my heart to-day.
They come unsought, grave, sombre guests, those ghosts of loving hearts;
Each mocks me with some vanished joy, and then—too soon—departs.
So leave me now; for human words and human tears are vain;—
Leave me to fight my fight alone, till I can smile again."

There was no power on earth to soothe; we could but breathe a prayer,
That some good angel, passing by, would take her in his care;—
Would gently turn her tearful eyes from visions of the past,
And point to where her weary soul might find its rest at last.

—*Dublin University Magazine.*

A CHILD'S FIRST LETTER.

To write to papa, 'tis an enterprise bold
For the fairy-like maiden scarce seven years old:
And see! What excitement the purpose hath wrought
In eyes that when gravest seem playing at thought!

The light little figure surprised into rest,
The smiles that will come, so demurely repressed,
The long-pausing hand on the paper that lies,
The sweet puzzled look in the pretty blue eyes,—

'Tis a beautiful picture of childhood in calm,
One cheek swelling soft o'er the white dimpled palm
Sunk deep in its crimson, and just the clear tip
Of an ivory tooth on the full under lip.

How the smooth forehead knits; with her arm round his neck,
It were easier far than on paper to speak;
We must loop up those ringlets; their rich falling gold
Would blot out the story as fast as 'twas told.

And she meant to have made it in bed, but it seems
Sleep melted too soon all her thoughts into dreams;
But hush! by that sudden expansion of brow,
Some fairy familiar has whispered it now.

How she labors exactly each letter to sign,
Goes over the whole at the end of each line,
And lays down the pen to clasp hands with delight,
When she finds an idea especially bright.

At last the small fingers have crept to an end;
No statesman his letter 'twixt nations hath penned
With more sense of its serious importance, and few
In a spirit so loving, so earnest, and true.

She smiles at a feat so unwonted and grand,
Draws a very long breath, rubs the cramped little hand;
May we read it? Oh, yes; my sweet maiden, maybe
One day you will write what one only must see.

Is it surely a letter? So beautifully lies
Uncertainty yet in those beautiful eyes,
And the parted lip's coral is deepening in glow,
And the eager flush mounts to the forehead of snow.

'Tis informal and slightly discursive, we fear;
Not a line without love, but the love is sincere.
Unchanged papa said he would have it depart
Like a bright leaf dropped out of her innocent heart.

Great news of her garden, her lamb, and her bird,
Of mamma, and of baby's last wonderful word;
With an ardent assurance—they neither can play,
Nor learn, nor be happy, while he is away.

Will he like it? Ay, will he! what letter could seem,
Though an angel indited, so charming to him?
How the fortunate poem to honor would rise
That should never be read by more critical eyes!
Ah, would for poor rhymesters such favor could be
As waits, my fair child, on thy letter and thee!

—*Household Words.*

From All the Year Round.

THOMAS TURNER'S BACK PARLOR.

NOBLE and learned editors have given us innumerable volumes of the memoirs of statesmen, politicians, poets, and wits of the last century. Now here are two gentlemen, Mr. R. W. Blencowe and Mr. Mark Anthony Lower, who have had the reading of a manuscript diary in one hundred and sixteen stout memorandum-books, and instead of publishing it all have only sent a modest paper of extracts to the "Sussex Archæological Collections." The diarist is Mr. Thomas Turner, general shopkeeper at East Hothly, in Sussex. He sold grocery, drapery, haberdashery, hats, nails, cheese, brandy, paper, tobacco, and coffins; and in the parlor behind his shop he made entries not only as a tradesman of his dealings with his customers, but as husband, vestryman, neighbor, and a man of his home life, and his dealings with society at large. He was so much of a scholar that he had begun life as a village schoolmaster, taking threepence a week for educating the son of a country gentleman, and when he gave up school-keeping the odor of scholarship dwelt with him. He says, "Reading and study (might I be allowed the phrase) would in a manner be both drink and meat to me, was my circumstances but independent." His circumstances not being independent he had also a relish for calf's liver and hog's-heart pudding, and a weakness for strong beer, that he spills much ink in deploring.

When Mr. Turner was born, in the year seventeen twenty-eight, an admiralty survey of the British coasts had not a word for Newhaven, Worthing, or Brighton, and passed lightly over Hastings as a small town. In the days of Mr. Turner's father, judges in the spring circuits never ventured farther into the slough of Sussex than East Grinstead, or Horsham. Chancellor Cowper, when a barrister on circuit, wrote to his wife in sixteen ninety, that "the Sussex ways are bad and ruinous beyond imagination. I vow 'tis a melancholy consideration that mankind will inhabit such a heap of dirt for a poor livelihood. The country is a sink of about fourteen miles broad, which receives all the water that falls from two long ranges of hills on both sides of it; and not being furnished with convenient draining, is kept moist and soft by the water till the middle of a dry summer, which is only able to make it tolerable to ride for a short time. The same day I entered Surrey, a fine champagne country, dry and dusty as if the season of the year had shifted in a few hours from winter to midsummer." In such a district, with the wretched roads made passable by an occasional causeway of stones on one side, for the use of the farmers, who with their wives on pillions behind them jogged from village to town, lived Mr. T. Turner. In his young schoolmaster days, he desired to confine his over-easy temper within rules, and set down his determination to live a good, wholesome life, rising early, breakfasting between seven and eight, dining between twelve and one, not eating too much meat, and supping upon weak broth, water-gruel, or milk pottage, with now and then a fruit pie for a change, and to go to bed at ten o'clock. "If," he said, "I am at home or in company abroad, I will never drink more than four glasses of strong beer: one to toast the king's health, the second to the royal family, the third to all friends, and the fourth to the pleasure of the company. If there is either wine or punch, never upon any terms or persuasion to drink more than eight glasses, each glass to hold no more than half a quarter of a pint." Alas for these resolves on moderation!

Mr. Turner in his back parlor read books of all kinds. He desired to cultivate his mind in every corner, and set down the names of the books he read, with his opinions upon them. Within five or six weeks he digested Gay's Poems, Stewart on the Supreme Being, the Whole Duty of Man, the Universal Magazine, Paradise Lost and Regained, Othello, Thomson's Seasons, Tournefort's Voyage to the Levant, Young's Night Thoughts, and Peregrine Pickle. On one day he says, "In the evening I read part of the fourth volume of the Tatler; the oftener I read it the better I like it. I think I never found the vice of drinking so well exploded in my life, as in one of the numbers." The twentieth of June being his birthday, "I treated," he says, "my scholars with about five quarts of strong beer, and had an issue cut in my leg." "Sunday, I went down to Jones, where we drank one bowl of punch and two muggers of bamboo; and I came home again in liquor. Oh! with what horrors does it fill my heart, to think I should be guilty of doing so, and on a Sunday too! Let me once more endeavor, never, no never, to be guilty of the same again!" Mr. T. T. was a patriot, too. In seventeen fifty-six, a month or two after he had resigned his school to Francis Elless, he "heard of the loss of Fort St. Philip and the whole island of Minarco (Minorca). . . . Never did the English nation suffer a greater blot. O my country, my country!—O Albian, Albian! I doubt thou art tottering on the brink of ruin and desolation this day! The nation is all in a foment upon account of losing dear Minarco." On the whole, however, there were more occasions given by the war for rejoicing and bell-ringing than for despondency. East Hothly was in the neighborhood of Halland-house, an estate of the Duke of Newcastle's, where there were great doings when the duke came down, and where the duke's steward, Mr. Coates, set the example of loyalty by tapping the strong beer on all national occasions. Invited to one such gathering, Mr. Turner, before setting out, records in his diary that he is very miserable at the prospect of having to make a beast of himself before going to bed. "But what can I do? If I goe, I must drink just as they please, or otherwise I shall be called a poor singular fellow. If I stay at home, I shall be stigmatized with the name of being a poor, proud, ill-natured wretch, and perhaps disoblige Mr. Coates. Mr. Coates, representing the custom of Halland-house, no trifling matter to the general dealer in a village of some five hundred inhabitants, was not to be disobliged. Mr. T. Turner went, and drank health and success in a glass of strong beer apiece to: 1, His Majesty; 2, the Royal Family; 3, the King of Prussia; 4, Prince Ferdinand of Brunswick; 5, Lord Anson; 6, His Grace the Duke of Newcastle; 7, his Duchess; 8, Lord Abergavenny; 9, Admiral Boscawen; 10, Mr. Pelham of Stanmore; 11, the Earl of Anoram; 12, Lord Gage; 13, Marshal Keith, and several more loyal healths. "About ten I deserted, and came safe home; but to my shame do I mention it, very much in liquor. Before I came away, I think I may say there was not one sober person in company." This was a party of twenty, including the clergymen of that and the adjoining parish.

At the merry meetings of the tradesmen held among themselves, especially the rounds of supper parties given at Christmas, the wives got drunk with the husbands. "Their mirth being rather obstreperious than serious and agreeable. Oh! how silly is mankind to delight so much in vanity and transitory joys!" Thomas Turner was a prudent, thriving man, a churchwarden in his time, and arbitrator of the quarrels of the parish, who left a flourishing business to his son. His first wife, with whom he records all his quarrels, and of whom he records also his hearty liking and affection, was a prudent, thrifty woman, yet even she was sometimes brought home on a servant's back, after he had slipped away, as far gone as he dared to be, leaving her behind to make his excuses. When they played cards, it was brag or whist—usually brag—they played at, and we have record of pleasant sittings at cards between Mr. and Mrs. Turner and a couple of neighbors, which were continued as innocent entertainment all the night through. The stakes were small. The diarist records on one occasion special lamentation because he has lost at brag three shillings, which "might have been" given to the poor.

Mr. Thomas Turner, as became the tradesman of a hundred years ago, had a due reverence for rank. Here is one of his entries: "Sunday, July 10. The Right Hon. Geo. Cholmondely, Earl Cholmondely, Viscount Malpas, joint vice-treasurer of Ireland, Lord Lieutenant, cust. rot., and Vice-Admiral of Cheshire, Governor of Chester Castle, Lord Lieutenant of Anglesea, Caernarvon, Flint, Merioneth, and Montgomery, Steward of the Royal Manor of Sheen, in Surrey, and Knight of the Bath, being a visiting at Mr. Coates', was at church this morning." So Mr. Turner worshipped the lord on that Sunday at any rate.

On the 15th of October, 1756, having been just three years married, the diarist in the back parlor behind the shop, looks back on a series of matrimonial quarrels, and on afflictions "which we have justly deserved by the many anemosityes and desentions which have been continually fermented between us and our friends." But now, he adds, we "begin to live happy; and I am thoroughly persuaded, if I knew my own mind, that if I was single again, and at liberty to make another choice, I should do the same; I mean, make her my wife who is so now." The chief of the "fermenting parties" was —of course—his wife's mother, Mrs. Slater, a very Xantippe, he says, "having a great volubility of tongue for invective, and especially if I am the subject; though what the good woman wants with me I know not."

It was the refuge-slag of the extinct iron works that hardened the narrow slip of Sussex road that could be travelled over in the winter-time, when, a little more advanced in the world, Mr. Turner kept a horse, saddle, and pillion of his own; before he could do that, he hired or borrowed. Thus he writes one day, in the damp autumn weather: "My wife and I having fixed to go to Hartfield, my wife endeavored to borrow a horse of Jos. Fuller, Tho. Fuller, Will Piper, and Jos. Burgess, to no purpose, they having no reason for not doing it, but want of good-nature and a little gratitude; though I make no doubt but they will, some or other of them, be so good-natured as soon to come and say, 'Come, do write this land-tax or window-tax book for us;' then I always find good-nature enough to do it, and at the same time to find them in beer, gin, pipes, and tobacco; and then poor ignorant wretches, they sneak away, and omit to pay for their paper; but, God bless them, I'll think it proceeds more from ignorance than ill-nature. My wife having hired a horse of John Watford, about four o'clock we set out on our journey for Hartfield, and as we were riding along near to Hastingford, no more than a foot's pace, the horse stood still, and continued kicking up until we was both off, in a very dirty hole (but, thanks be to God, we received no hurt). My wife was obliged to go into Hastingford House, to clean herself. My wife and I spent the even at my father Slater's. We dined off some ratios of pork and green sallard."

When there was a race of any sort at Lewes, Mr. Turner went to see it, and came home in such a state as to call for the reproach on himself in his diary that he "behaved more like an ass than any human being—doubtless not like one that calls himself a Christian." On the whole, however, he was a good, church-going householder. This is a Sunday record, for example: "My whole family at church—myself, wife, maid, and the two boys. We dined off a piece of boiled beef and carrots, and current suet-pudding, and we had, I think, too extreme good sermons this day preached unto us. Tho. Davey at our house in the even, to whom I read five of Tillotson's sermons." This unfortunate Thomas Davey must have stood in very particular need of edification; for Tillotson's sermons are poured into him whenever he appears. Soon afterwards we read of another Sunday; "Tho. Davey came in the evening, to whom I read six of Tillotson's sermons." This was a stormy time in the back parlor. A little before we had read: "This day how are my most sanguine hopes of happiness frustrated! I mean the happiness between myself and wife, which hath now continued for some time; but, oh! this day it has become the contrari!" And a little afterwards we read: "Oh! how transient is all mundane bliss! I who, on Sunday last," (when Thomas Davey had the six sermons read to him), "was all calm and serenity in my breast, am now nought but storm and tempest. Well may the wise man say, 'It were better to dwell in a corner of the house-top, than with a contentious woman in a wide house.'" On the following Christmas-day, "the Widow Marchant, Hannah and James Marchant, dined with us on a buttock of beef, and a plum suet-pudding. Tho. Davey at our house in the even, to whom I read two nights of the Complaint." Thomas Davey had material for a complaint of his own, we think; but Doctor Young's Night Thoughts was a favorite work with Mr. Turner.

Mrs. Porter, the clergyman's wife was not always civil to her friends in their character as tradespeople, but when she was, it was a great pleasure to serve her. "I went down to Mrs. Porter's," writes the diarist one day, "and acquainted her I could not get her gown before Monday, who received me with all the affability, courtesy, and good-humor imaginable. Oh! what a pleasure it would be to serve them was they always in such a temper; it would even induce me, almost, to forget to take a just profit. In the even I read part of the New Whole Duty of Man." A few days afterwards, he says, "We supped at Mr. Fuller's, and spent the evening with a great deal of mirth till between one and two. Tho. Fuller brought my wife home upon his back. I cannot say I came home sober, though I was far from being bad company. I think we spent the evening with a great deal of pleasure." Sometimes there were drunken fights between neighbors as they met each other on their way home from their several merry meetings. T. T. records a great fight with Doctor Stone, the occasion of which he was much puzzled to remember the next morning. Another night there was a more considerable fight, from which T. T. escaped on the horse of a friend who was interposing in his favor.

Mr. Porter, the clergyman, who was a man of some substance, a Greek scholar and a pastor, long kindly remembered in the parish, joined with his wife in many of the festive riots that were in those days looked upon as celebrations of good fellowship, and from which he could not easily have withdrawn himself without being regarded as a churl. The wine-drinking among the polite, good society, with its three-bottle-men, was represented among village tradesmen chiefly by the drinking of strong beer and spirits. Here, for example, is the plan of a merry-meeting at Whyly: "We played at bragg the first part of the even. After ten we went to supper on four boiled chickens, four boiled ducks, minced veal, sausages, cold roast goose, chicken pastry, and ham. Our company, Mr. and Mrs. Porter, Mr. and Mrs. Coates, Mrs. Atkins, Mrs. Hicks, Mr. Piper and wife, Joseph Fuller and wife, Tho. Fuller and wife, Dame Durrant, myself and wife, Mr. French's family. After supper our behavior was far from that of serious, harmless mirth; it was downright obstreperious, mixed with a great deal of folly and stupidity. Our diversion was dancing or jumping about, without a violin or any music, singing foolish healths, and drinking all the time as fast as it could be well poured down; and the parson of the parish was one among the mixed multitude." Mr. Turner slipped away unobserved at three o'clock in the morning, leaving his wife to make his excuse. Though very far from sober, he came home safely without tumbling, and at ten minutes past five his wife was brought home by Mr. French's servant. She was hardly got into bed when some returning revellers, with the parson and his wife at their head, beat at the outer door. The parson's wife, Mrs. Porter, "pretended she wanted some cream of tartar; but as soon as my wife got out of bed, she vowed she should come down. She found Mr. Porter, Mr. Fuller and his wife, with a lighted candle and part of a bottle of wine and a glass. The next thing," says T. T., "was to have me down-stairs." As he would not come down, they went up to him, dragged him out of bed, made him put on his wife's petticoats, and dance without shoes and stockings, until they had emptied the bottle of wine, and also a bottle of their victim's beer. Doubtless they were punishing him for having left their company. It was not till about three o'clock in the afternoon that these people found their way to their respective homes. On the Sunday following, the diary says, "We had as good a sermon as ever I heard Mr. Porter preach, it being against swearing."

Of the prevalence of the habit of swearing the back parlor diary gives frequent illustration. The debates at the vestry meetings seems to have consisted chiefly in successive rounds of oaths. "In the even I went down to the vestry; there was no business of any moment to transact, but oaths and imprecations seemed to resound from all sides of the room; the sounds seemed to be harsh and grating, so that I came home soon after seven. I believe, if the penalty were paid assigned by the legislature, by every person that swears that constitute our vestry, there would be no need to levy any tax to maintain our poor." The poor might literally have been fed upon curses. Again, on another day, he wrote; "After dinner I went down to Jones to the vestry. We had several warm arguments at our vestry to-day, and several volleys of execrable oaths oftentime redouned, from almost all parts of the room. A most rude and shocking thing at public meetings."

Mrs. Turner had continual ill health; the diarist becomes melancholy and affectionate as her life draws to a close. His recreations have to be enjoyed without her. She can no longer go to see the mountebank at the next village, or the æsmorama, or the person at Jones' with an electrical machine. "My niece and I went to see it; and thoo I have seen it several years agoe, I think there is something in it agreeable and instructing, but at the same time very surprising. As to my own part, I am quite at a loss to form any idea of the phœinomina." The wife dies at last, and the diarist observes: "I may justly say with the incomparable Mr. Young, 'Let them whoever lost an angel, pity me.'"

Two or three years after the death of his "dear Peggy," Mr. Turner, who pined in his journal "for want of the company of the more softer sex," lost his friend Mr. French, "after a long and lingering illness, which it is to be doubted was first brought on by the to frequent use of spirituous liquors, and particularly gin. If it was possible to make any estimate of the quantity he drank for several years, I should think he could not drink less, on a moderate computation, than twenty gallons a year." This was looked upon as a degeneracy by the diarist. "Custom," he says, "has brought tea and spirituous liquors so much in fashion, that I dare be bold to say, they often, to often, prove our ruin. I think, since I have lived at Hothly, I never knew trade so dull, or money so scarce, the whole neighborhood being almost reduced to poverty."

We part from Mr. Turner with the approach of the event that brought his diary to an abrupt end. About four years after the death of his Peggy, he married Molly Hicks, a girl with expectations of property, and the daughter of a yeoman, though herself a servant to Luke Spence, Esq., of South Malling. The courtship was tremendously fatiguing. On one day, says the worthy little shopkeeper, who owns that neither he nor his Molly are good-looking, "in the afternoon, rode over to Chiddingly to pay my charmer, or intended wife, or sweetheart, or whatever other name may be more proper, a visit at her father's, where I drank tea, in company with their family and Miss Ann Thatcher. I supped there on some rasures of bacon. It being an excessive wet and windy night, I had the opportunity, sure I should say the pleasure, or perhaps some might say the unspeakable happiness, to sit up with Molly Hicks, or my charmer, all night. I came home at forty minutes past five in the morning—I must not say fatigued; no, no, that could not be; it could be only a little sleepy for want of rest." These night-watches of courtship, filled, he says, with serious discourse, were rather frequent, and at last the book in the back parlor contained the honest confession: "Very dull and sleepy; this courting does not agree with my constitution, and perhaps it may be only taking pains to create more pains."

Such a sketch of the life of a village shopkeeper a hundred years ago, reminds us of a change of manners as conspicuous among the people as among the clergy of the rural parishes. With all the defects peculiar to provincial life—as there are defects peculiar also to life in great cities—at the present day, we are surely wholesomer and happier than we could possibly have been, and we live longer lives than we could easily have lived, under the social conditions which afflicted Mr. Turner, grocer, draper, chandler, etc., of East Hothly, and which impoverished so many of his neighbors.

Dr. Eiselt, of Prague, has made a very important discovery connected with researches for the detection of contagious miasma in the air. In the foundling hospital at Repy, near Prague, there were, among two hundred and fifty children, between the ages of six and ten years, ninety-two cases of blennorrhea of the ocular conjunctiva. This epidemic ophthalmia fully convinced Dr. Eiselt that the contagion could be transmitted by other means than by contact. He instructed the nurses to carefully avoid touching the eyes of the patients; but, notwithstanding the greatest precautions, the doctor and his assistants were attacked by the same disorder. Then, by the aid of the Aeroscope of M. Pouchet, he examined the atmosphere of one of the sick wards, and in the first current of air through the apparatus he distinctly saw little pus cells, which had undoubtedly served as the vehicle of contagion. Several members of the Imperial Medical Society of Vienna, appreciating the high importance of this discovery, have united together to pursue researches in the matter.

Swift observes, that the accommodating your wants to your means is like cutting off your feet to avoid the expense of shoes.

From The Spectator, 27 April.

THE PROGRESS OF SPAIN IN THE WEST.

There is one country in the world, and only one, which benefits by the disruption of the American Union. To the world in general that event is an unmixed injury, the loss of a great example, the destruction, if we may so speak, of a political lighthouse. To England and to France, in a less degree, it involves besides, present annoyance and future danger to their commerce. Russia fears the loss of a valuable, though eccentric, ally; Germans sympathize in the humiliation of their second home; while the continent of America, from Florida to Paraguay, foresees in the reckless action of the South the coming triumph of the buccaneers. To Spain, and Spain alone, is the disruption an unmixed good. The rooted antipathy to Spain which the Americans inherit, with better prejudices, from the Puritan settlers, has been fostered by events and successive Governments into a political passion. The only European race the Americans have ever conquered are Spaniards and their descendants. The territories Americans most ardently covet are the rich islands of the Gulf, and the wide and half-populated states stretching down to Panama, which are all held by men of Spanish lineage and tongue. Spaniards have put Americans to death, justifiably, it is true, but still for enterprises with which the dominant class enthusiastically sympathized. In revenge an American President assembled a congress of envoys to consider publicly the easiest means of plundering Spain. Offers to buy Cuba were ostentatiously put forward in Presidents' speeches, and Spain, smarting at once under insult and invasion, felt herself compelled to keep up a war armament in the island, while still unable to commence the contest. The disruption at once terminates the pressure. The South alone is scarcely a fair match for Spain. Without the help of the North she could hardly defend her own coasts, certainly land no army of invasion in Cuba itself. The captain-general, whose duty has hitherto been divided between pocketing the profit of slave-smuggling and watching the intrigues of the fillibusters, draws a freer breath. Cuba is safe for the present, and its Government, by a not unnatural transition, employs the garrison relieved from watch for purposes of aggression. Still more naturally, a captain-general, once disposed to the aggressive, turns his eyes to the great and unprotected island which stretches into the Gulf, not a hundred miles from his own windows, and half of which is still, in the proud theory of Spaniards, a *de jure* colony of Spain.

For months past the Government of Cuba has been in communication with Santana, the most powerful man in the Mulatto Republic of Dominica. Whether he is an ordinary traitor, or a politician afraid of the blacks of Haiti, or, as is most probable, at once far-sighted and venal, matters little. By his connivance, small parties of Spaniards have been landed on the coast, part of the mulatto population have been induced to accede, the Spanish flag has been raised, and the Republic annexed by popular outcry to the Spanish crown. Special correspondents do not yet include Dominica in their travels, but, in the absence of further evidence, it is probable that the mulattoes really favor Spain, which may have granted them guarantees against the blacks. The captain-general of Cuba, delighted with his success, at once accepted the annexation, subject always to the veto of the crown, and despatched a powerful armament to maintain the new authority. The expedition comprises, it is said, five thousand men, and as that number is about the force the Cuban Government could spare, the statement is probably accurate. They have landed in safety, and the chances of local resistance are exceedingly small. The Spanish soldiers are among the best in the world, accustomed to the climate, and aided by the faction which has summoned them to its aid. Haiti, no longer under the rule of a single unscrupulous chief, is powerless to aid any who may resist, and, indeed, is reported willing to accept a Spanish protectorate. The negroes may fight, but they are no match for a regular army, and unless Europe interferes, Hispaniola—we use the name as including both sides of the island—may be considered once more Spanish. Europe, in this case, means simply England. The French Government is probably favorable, certainly not hostile to the expedition, and no other power of the Continent is even tempted to interfere. The responsibility rests on England alone, and her position becomes painful in the extreme.

On the one hand, the duty of incessant repression which seems to be imposed by circumstances on England is to the last degree invidious. This country has politically no animosity to Spain, whose recent progress in civilization, the improvement of her revenue, and the development of her military strength have been watched with unfeigned pleasure. A weak Spain is a temptation to France, of which it is well to be permanently rid. The Spanish character, as it exists in the mass, when not displayed in religious persecution, creates in England a decided feeling of respect. If Spain regained her hold of Mexico, England would certainly not regret the change. Her dominion on the

American continent was civilization compared with the rule of the wretched savages and half-breeds, whom a century of revolutions have thrown up to power, as the scum rises to the top of a perturbed cesspool. It is not against our interests that Spain, if honestly independent, should extend her influence, or even her direct authority. We are bound by no treaties to Haiti, and by no sympathies with the race of deteriorating savages who have destroyed the trade and the prosperity of the Queen of the Antilles. If the Spaniards would govern the island as the English govern Barbadoes or Ceylon, the annexation would be an unmixed benefit to the world as well as to the population.

But there is no chance whatever of Spain consenting to any arrangement of the kind. Not to mention the notorious faithlessness of her court, a faithlessness which has maintained the slave-trade in spite of a direct money payment for its abolition, the interests of Spain are opposed to any such stipulation. With Cuba tilled by a slave population, Hispaniola cannot be cultivated by freemen. The free blacks, in fact, will not work for pay. The country does not admit of European labor, and immigrants, whether imported from China or the African coast, are sure under Spaniards to become slaves. The existing population may be left in the mountains to avoid internecine war, but the slaves, who have over and over repeopled Cuba, will soon find labor for the plantations of Hispaniola. No power could prevent the Cuban planters, secure always of a fresh supply, from exporting their surplus to the neighboring island, and in a few years slave-breeding would become as important a trade in Cuba as in Virginia or Maryland. The result would be a direct extension of slavery, the one evil Great Britain stands pledged before Europe to prevent. To what other end have all our efforts against the slave-trade been directed? England has not expended millions to increase the horrors of the middle passage by the cramming the preventive squadron now entails. Her object has been to prevent the extension of the area of slavery by cutting off the sources of supply, and to this object she must adhere. Even if Spain would honestly adhere to the provisions of the treaties, and treat the importation of slaves as piracy, the situation would still be but little improved. The internal slave-trade would still be operative between Cuba and the new possessions, and slavery would be extended over another country at present free from the presence of the crime.

We have no sympathy with the fruitless anarchy to which one of the most beautiful islands in the world has been condemned. We can accept with cordial pleasure any evidence of the renewed vitality and even the revived ambition of the Peninsula. But there are moral considerations superior both to civilization and political friendship, and they call imperatively on Great Britain to forbid the extension of slavery over or among a new population inhabiting a country nearly as large as Ireland, and twice as rich in natural capabilities.

From The Spectator, 27 April.

CIVIL WAR IN AMERICA.

THE heavy thunder-cloud of war which has for some months lowered over the United States has now broken over South Carolina. The first success has been won by the Southern Confederacy. The Montgomery Government has proved that it can act as well as threaten. On the 13th of April, Fort Sumter surrendered to General Beauregard, and the stars and stripes no longer fly from any point in the harbor of Charleston. How has this been brought about?

The question lay between the recognition of the revolted States and the enforcement of the law; between the surrender of such Federal rights and properties as yet remained intact, and the retention of them, and for some weeks the course of the Lincoln Government was clouded with doubt. The President was too slow to please his impatient friends, and too menacingly reserved to please his enemies. The action of the Border States has been of a character to compel discretion and embarrass action. What they would do were war to arise was a question of great moment. Then the treasury at Washington was empty, the forts of the nation were unguarded and ungarrisoned, the munitions and weapons in store had been drained off to a large extent by the traitorous action of the Buchanan Government, and no provision has been made for supplying the President with the means of executing any steady and vigorous policy. Fort Sumter was beleaguered, and no government which valued its honor and its future could dream of sacrificing that garrison and its gallant commander. Fort Pickens was threatened by the forces of the Confederacy, and Key West and Tortugas lay at their mercy—if they only had a navy. All this time the President was said to be doing nothing but make appointments, but the jeers of his enemies were ill-founded. The treasury has been filled by the spontaneous offering of five times as much money at easy rates as was required. Forts have been secured, ships of war made ready, cannon, arms, and munitions have been quietly collected, troops have been concentrated, transports chartered. Why nothing was known of all this arose from the fact that by the exercise of threats of dismissal an amount of secrecy had been obtained unknown for many years. It is a mark of the decision and energy of the Government that it has been able to impose secrecy, and some mark of confidence that it can command money. It is a sign of a settled course of policy that Mr. Lincoln refused to receive in any way the commissioners from the Southern Confederacy, but what is that policy?

The *Times* correspondent, who has been in Washington, and evidently in close communication with the capitol, answers the question thus. "Be satisfied," he writes, and he repeats the same thing several times, "be satisfied of this—the United States Government will give up no power or possession which it has at present got. By its voluntary act it will surrender nothing whatever. No matter what reports may appear in the papers, or in letters, distrust them if they would lead you to believe that Mr. Lincoln is preparing either to abandon what he has now, or to recover that which he has not." If that be Mr. Lincoln's policy, and we have no better information, the next question is, how will he carry it out?

The first attempt has failed in a striking and flagrant manner. Early in April the Government of Washington had caused a considerable force of troops to assemble at New York; had chartered a small squadron of powerful steamers, and fitted up three men-of-war to act as convoy. It was said this armament was simply intended to make good existing deficiencies and next contingencies; that it would not go near Charleston, but steering further southward, reinforce Key West, and Tortugas, two posts of importance in the Gulf, and perhaps throw men and stores into Fort Pickens. When the bulk of the fleet had sailed on the 10th of April, the real object was disclosed—Fort Sumter was to be relieved, peaceably, if possible, but relieved. The Southern general had evidently got some inkling of this, for on the 7th he cut off the supplies of the fort. On the 10th he learned from Governor Pickens that President Lincoln had formally given notice that supplies would be sent to Major Anderson, peaceably, or by force. Thereupon General Beauregard, obtaining authority to do so from Montgomery, summoned Fort Sumter. Major Anderson refused to surrender; on the 12th the Southerns bombarded the fort, and on the 13th the garrison surrendered. At that very moment part of the relieving force was in the offing, and thus General Beauregard only anticipated the plans of the Northern army by a few hours. Here we have two central facts: the expedition to relieve the fort was planned at Washington, and executed by the orders of President Lincoln; the measures taken to seize Fort Sumter in anticipation were executed by the authority of President Jefferson Davis, and the two Confederacies are, therefore, officially at war. It would be quite legitimate to infer further that the *New York Tribune* was correct when it said, in speaking of the Fort Sumter expedition, "If rebellious cannon are now fired upon the flag of the United States (as in the case of the Star of the West), going out on an errand of peace, we may be sure that the United States will respond, and that effectively." The *New York Herald* was right for once when it began its "sensation" comments on the news from Charleston with the words, "Civil war has begun."

Thus, then, the prospect of the future is dark and lowering. The North has men, and what is more, money. In England sufficient account has never yet been taken of the vast strength which the North has in reserve—its free spirit, liable to be roused to fanaticism. Once thoroughly roused, the North will act with all the energy of the Anglo-Saxon race, and it is difficult to conceive the defeat of nineteen millions of free people by the comparatively small white population of the South. On the other hand, there is a fanaticism also in the South. There is plenty of material for armies in the "mean whites," and plenty of soldiership as well as statesmanship in the slave-owning, slavery-glorifying aristocracy. Money may be the weak point in the Southern armor, but they have even got money for present needs. The relative power of the two sections at the outset would be unequal, for the South has larger forces at its immediate disposal. As the Northern attempt to relieve Fort Sumter has roused the South, so we believe there are two acts which the South might do which would rouse Northern fanaticism. One is to close the Mississippi, or exercise sovereign rights thereon, impeding free transit; and the next is the reported scheme of marching on Washington. In any case "the Great Republic is gone." There can never more be one United States of America, and the chance is that out of the coming strife several Confederacies will arise. The tendency to split off from the centre has gone on without cessation since Washington's death; now, one whole group of States has broken utterly the Federal ties. Why should the process not go on?

From The Spectator, 4 May.

THE CIVIL WAR IN AMERICA.

We know at last the opinion of the silent North, and with the knowledge, the lingering hope of averting civil war has suddenly disappeared. The attack on Fort Sumter released the lawyer-like though firm mind at the head of the administration from its constitutional qualms. That attack, at all events, was overt rebellion, and Mr. Lincoln set himself, with the steady calmness he has throughout displayed, to bring the question to the issue of the sword. In a proclamation, which as a summons to civil war reads strangely formal, he called upon the States for an army of seventy-five thousand men, and in a few hours the reticent hesitation which has hitherto marked the North had disappeared. The Free States unanimously resolved to support the honor of their flag. Pennsylvania voted $3,000,000 and thirty thousand men, and rich individuals offered $50,000 apiece, in anticipation of the loan. In New York, the only great State in which Southern interests are strong, the merchants resolved unanimously to support the Government, while the Legislature voted three millions for war purposes, with only one dissentient. No vote of men is recorded, but the troops ready for immediate action in the city alone are estimated at twenty-five thousand men. In both States, moreover, the mob, always suspected of Southern sympathies, has shown itself hostile to the slaveholders, and compelled all doubtful newspapers to hang out the Union flag. The rush of volunteers in the city itself was so immense, that the police were called out to maintain order. In Rhode Island, always an independent little State, so eccentric that the South relied on its support, the governor offered a thousand men, with himself in command, for instant action. Massachusetts voted a regiment, which has arrived in Washington. The West may be relied on to a man, Ohio instantly raising twenty thousand men, Illinois offering thirty thousand, and Indiana double her contingent. The feeling in the country districts especially is most earnest, the quiet, half-Puritan freeholders looking evidently to issues even wider than the mere safety of the Union. The spirit of the people reacted upon the administration. The President has still the disposal of a naval force, though composed of somewhat heterogeneous elements. He has thirteen steamers, all above fifteen hundred tons, though not, we imagine, all completely equipped, off Charleston, and fourteen more vessels are ready for despatch in the navy-yard of New York. The Mediterranean squadron also will soon be at his disposal, and the sailors of the Union are Northern men. Mr. Lincoln has accordingly proclaimed all the ports of the South blockaded, and declared that all Southern privateers captured while assailing Northern vessels shall be condemned as pirates. If that threat be earnest, and not the mere expression of a legal fact, the Federal Government has thrown over the dream of a purely defensive policy, and is resolved not simply to resist, but to subdue, the South.

The Southern Confederacy is not behind its rival either in energy or speed. It has secured, at the very outset of the war, an advantage which may prove incalculable. The Border States, so long hesitating, have decided at last. On the receipt of the President's summons, Missouri and Kentucky blankly refused obedience, and announced their determination to aid the South. North Carolina seized the Federal forts. Virginia, whose territory almost surrounds Columbia, seceded, and menaced the navy-yard in Norfolk Harbor, a position which commands the entrance to the Chesapeake. The State troops attacked the great arsenal at Harper's Ferry, which was saved only by the resolution of the Federal guard, who burnt the buildings, destroyed the stores and arms, and retreated on Pennsylvania. Arkansas is admitted by the Northern press to be already gone, and though Maryland is doubtful, the action of the secret societies is energetically for the South. They have already prohibited the march of Pennsylvania troops, and enforced their prohibition by breaking down the bridges. The whole of the Slave States, Delaware excepted, may therefore be held to have joined the South, which thus commands a population of eight millions of whites. The Southern President has summoned an army of one hundred and fifty thousand men, his loan of £3,500,000 has all been taken up, and he has issued letters of marque for all Southern privateers. The North and the South are frankly ranged in open hostility, on an issue adequate to the frightful calamities to be risked, and with means we fear too equal for a hope to be entertained of a rapid or decisive termination.

It is in vain to predict the issue, but there are some considerations which may enable us to form an opinion more or less defined. The South has as yet the advantage in means, leaders, and position. With the help of the Border States Mr. Davis commands at least two millions of men capable of bearing arms, all thoroughly acclimatized, all accustomed to the rifle, and most of them inured to civil conflict on a smaller scale. He has obviously arms and ammunition in plenty, money enough for immediate needs, and the immense advantage derived from repudiating the pecuniary claims of the

North. His forces, moreover, are united by impulses which of themselves ensure discipline and obedience. Placed between the North and the slaves, accustomed to obey an hereditary aristocracy, without education, and almost without food, the mean whites range readily under discipline as stern as that of regular armies. Their leaders, moreover, are men accustomed to command, better educated than their rivals, and willing to acknowledge all ability at hand without regard to nationality. They must have from ten to twenty teachers, available men who have commanded, or at least fought, in European armies, some of them—such as Henningsen—of unquestionable ability. Their leader, Mr. Davis, himself commanded the volunteers in the Mexican campaign, while his personal energy extorts the admiration of those who detest his principles and his cause. He has, too, an incalculable superiority of position. His base of operations is beyond invasion. The Cotton States are, in fact, though not in geography, tropical deltas, provinces full of swamp, ravine, and forest, in which an invading army could not advance a mile a day. It might as well try to cross Bengal in presence of the British. While his base is thus secure, the actual contest will be carried on on friendly soil. The Border States, and more particularly Virginia, must be the ultimate if not the immediate battle-field. The first struggle, it is evident, will be for Washington. The North cannot surrender the historic capital, bad as its military position may be, without at the same time surrendering their claim to be a nation. Nor, however expedient the step, would Northern feeling tolerate a measure which deprived the people of their great link with the past, of the only historic spots belonging to the Republic, and of the centre to which all eyes habitually turn. Yet Washington is for the moment undoubtedly in serious danger. The secession of Virginia and the partial insurrection in Maryland cuts the capital off from its Northern supports, while it is exposed by the loss of the Border States to the full weight of Southern attack. The troops of the Confederacy may surround Washington without ever quitting a friendly soil, while the North must either cut a way through Maryland defended by a Southern army, or confine their efforts to reinforcements by sea. The latter, an indifferent expedient at best, is rendered none the more easy by the loss of Norfolk, which commands the Chesapeake, and by the fact that the Virginians can effectually close the Potomac. The only resource of the North will be to hold open a route through Maryland, as through any other enemy's country, and it is this effort which will throw the brunt of the war upon the territory round the District of Columbia.

On the other hand, the North, though less happily placed for the immediate struggle, exceeds its rival in all the sources of permanent military strength. Its population is more than double that of the Southern States, and unmenaced by the existence of a servile caste. This population bear to-day the relation to the Southerners which their Puritan forefathers bore to the Cavaliers who planted Maryland and Virginia. Slower, and perhaps less chivalrous, the spirit of the Puritan is the more earnest and persistent, and once aroused, rises to a pitch of enthusiasm which renders victory or destruction the only possible alternatives. The Puritan has always been victor in the end, from Marston Moor to the last struggle in Kansas, and his feeling seems now thoroughly aroused. The North possesses also ten times the wealth of the South, an inexhaustible commissariat, the command of the sea, and the sympathy of all European nations. She still lacks leaders, the trading politicians being wholly unequal to a great emergency, Mr. Lincoln himself rising only to the rank of honest respectabilities, and the most prominent of Northern partisans, Colonel Fremont, being still absent in London. Nineteen millions of Anglo-Saxons, however, engaged in a death struggle, and without formulas to restrain ability, must produce a great man, and with a leader their organization will be complete. Above all, their cause, apart from political issues, is palpably based upon the right. Politicians may chatter about State prerogatives and the declaration of independence, protective tariffs and the value of cotton, but the cause of the war is slavery. The South supports the institution, the North denounces it, and as the contest widens to the full breadth of that great issue, we cannot doubt on which side victory will remain. That it will so widen is a conclusion to which patient observers, however reluctant to admit an opinion so terrible in its immediate effects, will, we fear, gradually be forced. The imagination is baffled in the effort to imagine terms of peace not involving the submission of the South. The two countries are so inextricably linked by geographical position, that permanent separation seems all but impossible. Half the rivers which drain the West debouch at points in Southern possession. The frontiers touch each other across a continent, a distance of three thousand miles. The capital of the Free States, defended by Free troops, stands upon Slave soil. The South is dependent on the North for food, the North on the South for manufactures. Tariffs are impossible while half the national frontier is in the hands of foreign allies, with widely different interests, and economic faiths. The two bodies must be allied on *some* basis, and if the tendency of the world be towards freedom, that basis cannot be submission to the slave power.

To England the immediate effects of the contest can only be disastrous. The war, while it disturbs all trade with the North, interrupts the supply of our one essential staple. Cotton, it is true, may continue to be shipped, but a blockade, however unreal, always raises prices, and it is not only cotton, but cheap cotton, which Lancashire requires. So long as the slaves are uninterested, an additional supply from India, and the few smaller markets may keep the mills at work; but the probability of disturbances in the interior increases with the protraction of the struggle. The mere excitement of the contest must impede cultivation, and the next crop, if the war continues, must be unusually short. There is a danger, too, which Americans will not admit, but which is nevertheless not beyond the range of calculation. Men's ideas grow broader with strife, and the Northern population may yet ask themselves why they should fight for a purely political issue—why not declare war on slavery itself? Most Americans at present would start back with horror from a proposition they deem equivalent to a servile war; but vindictiveness is a plant of rapid growth, and the South, which has already summoned the Indians* to its aid, may teach the North to avail themselves of yet more terrible allies. The first stroke levelled at slavery will be the death-warrant of American cotton cultivation.

* And negroes!—*Living Age.*

From The Economist, 4 May.

THE EVIL AND THE GOOD IN THE AMERICAN CIVIL WAR.

THE war which has at length broken out in America, in spite of the truly legal caution and forbearance of the President, through the presumptuous aggression of the seceders, will no doubt be fierce and bloody. No one can think of it without dismay; no one can even venture to predict what may be its results and where it will end. The Southern leaders have unquestionably the whole responsibility of this fatal step. The blood which has at length begun to flow must be upon them and on their children. They originated the quarrel by their passionate desire to extend the shameful institution of which they are so proud. At every fresh turn of the dispute they have been the aggressors. They not only declined to submit to a constitutional defeat, but their statesmen had prepared by years of secret treason for the rebellion of last November. When they had consummated their purpose, and found the Northern States still long-suffering, still reluctant to precipitate the unhallowed strife, and yet intent on holding their ground in the Federal property still remaining to them, —they profited by the delay which the intercession of the Border States secured, only to mature their aggressive measures, and then did not hesitate to break the truce and plunge the country into civil war. Their plans are well conceived and ably executed. They are directed by a man of prompter mind and more vigorous decision than President Lincoln, and for a time they will probably be successful. The Border States, after causing a delay long enough to serve the purposes of Mr. Jefferson Davis, are now going off with rapid explosions to the enemy. Virginia has seceded, and on the attempt of her troops to seize the Federal arsenal at Harper's Ferry, it was blown up and abandoned by the officer in command. North Carolina has again seized the Federal forts. Even Maryland is fiercely divided. The war feeling is strong in Tennessee. Kentucky, alone, appears still to incline to the Northern side. A march on Washington was apprehended; and the Northern States, at length aroused to the true character of the position, were slowly sending in their succors to the President, while the Southern army was said to be completely organized. Blood has been already shed by the secessionists both at Baltimore and Harper's Ferry, and every hope of compromise was at an end.

Such news seems pure evil. And that it is the herald of frightful calamities, no thoughtful man can deny. Still it is not in our estimation evil quite unmixed and unfathomable. Black as the storm is, we believe there is promise of light through it. Let us take the worst feature first; and the worst feature about the war undoubtedly is that the eventual victory of the North can scarcely carry with it eventual success. We speak of the Northern victory as ultimately certain, because a wealthy and free population of twenty millions cannot but conquer in the long run in a contest with a poor free population of the same race, numbering at most seven millions even if we give the South the whole of the Border States. That the North may be beaten at first, we regard as exceedingly probable. But that a defeat will only animate the Northern States to greater and greater exertion, we consider absolutely certain. And in the long run no doubt wealth and numbers must decide this fatal strife. But suppose the war ended, and ended by the defeat of the Southern Confederation, will victory mean success? We think not. It may bring back one or two doubtful States within the Union. It may restore Western Virginia, Missouri, and Kentucky,—possibly even North Carolina to the United States; but in the Gulf States at least victory would be conquest, and conquest only. No one doubts that in these States the secessionist party has always had an enormous majority,* which is likely to be increased by civil war into a feeling of ferocious unanimity. Those States may be conquered, may be held in military possession, but they can scarcely again be expected to take a voluntary part in the political institutions of the United States. Unless the issue of civil war were a slave insurrection which should put an end to the institution of slavery altogether as the result of a train of events which it is utterly impossible to measure or foreshadow,—the Gulf States can never again be reasonably expected to act in political concert with the North. Whatever result, therefore, a Northern victory might have,—it could not be a political recovery of the Gulf States. It seems as certain as any human event can be, that by them at least the step taken can never be retraced. It follows, therefore, that the war, bloody and perhaps long as it may be, will be in this respect a fruitless war. The blood of Americans will be poured out by Americans, without any hope of achieving the end which is apparently the only legitimate end of such a war. After the conflict is over, the rival parties will be politically just where they were when it began,—except that mutual animosities will be deeper, both parties will be poorer, and both parties more vindictive than at the outset. The North will beat the South in the end, but when it has done so, we do not see what the Government can do, except leave the South to follow its own devices at the last as it might do at this moment. Surely, nothing can well be blacker than a prospect of a war at once vindictive, bloody, and fruitless.

This is the dark side of the prospect, and a very dark side indeed it seems. There is, however, not a little to be said on the other side. And the main consideration appears to us to be that the war will draw together the Northern States as they have never been drawn together yet,—will teach them the all-important character of the slavery issue,—will sweep the political horizon of those petty political controversies which have long frittered away the attention of statesmen and diverted them from the really great issues which were slowly maturing beneath the surface of society—and finally will impress them with the absolute necessity of a closer union, a stronger central power, a suppression of those repulsive forces which keep State and State jealous and apart,—in one word, with the duty of turning the Federal Government into a really supreme power.* Such, we think, may, and most probably will be, one result of the disastrous conflict in which the United States are now engaged.

As a secondary and casual advantage, the struggle will liberate from the authority of the Border States all those sections which are already prepared and anxious to extinguish slavery. This would be difficult to effect without war. While the State organization is still perfect, the stronger party will carry the State. For example, in Virginia the State has declared for the South, but Western Virginia is almost entirely in sympathy with the North. Again, in Kentucky there seems to be a very large Northern party, and the same is true of Tennessee. Nothing but war probably could dissolve those State-chains which bind the reluctant freeman to the corrupt and corrupting domestic institution in such cases as these. But war will enable these fragmentary States, chafing under their hateful connection with districts of quite different political tendencies, to achieve their liberty and seek protection of the Union. This would be in itself no small gain. But the one gain which alone can compensate the North for the horrors of civil war, is the growth of genuine Republican conviction to which it will probably give rise;—the learning of the great lesson that there can be no hearty political alliance between freedom and slavery, and no genuine freedom without a strong central government and the surrender of those atomic political privileges which minister to local jealousies and general anarchy.

For the South we see no possibility of a good issue for the war which its statesmen have provoked and commenced. The greater their temporary success, the greater must be their ultimate humiliation. Their policy seems to us able and masterly, but utterly short-sighted. To rouse by gratuitous insult the mettle of a nation three times as numerous and far more than three times as

* Excuse us, good Economist: most people in the loyal States, believe the majority will be found to be the other way. Of capitalists (including slaveowners) we fully believe a majority in every State (except, perhaps, South Carolina) to be in favor of Union and peace.—*Living Age.*

* "*Turning* it into a really supreme power"? It has always been so; and the nation means to show this to friends as well as to enemies.

powerful, to force them by aggressive steps into a struggle in which the sympathy of every free and civilized nation will be with the North, seems like the madness of men whose eyes are blinded and hearts hardened by the evil cause they defend. Had they been wise, they would have trusted all to delay and their own obstinate purpose. As it is, they rush on a war which, whether it end in their mere exhaustion or in the horrors of a servile insurrection, cannot but end in humiliating disasters, which will excite no pity, because they have been positively courted by the Southern leaders.

MILTON: WAS HE AN ANGLO-SAXON SCHOLAR?—The similarity between the Anglo-Saxon poem of Cædmon, paraphrased from Genesis, and some parts of Milton's *Paradise Lost*, is so striking as to have led many distinguished scholars to believe that Milton must have perused Cædmon in the original, and have borrowed his plot from the Anglo-Saxon poet. This appears extremely probable, and is so well stated by Mr. Westwood in his beautiful and most instructive work, *Palæographia Sacra Pictoria* (Lond. 1844), that I hope a corner may be found in "N. & Q." for Mr. Westwood's note.

"The plot of this paraphrastic history in fact so much resembles that of the *Paradise Lost*, that it 'has obtained for its author the name of the Saxon Milton.' (Wright, *Biogr. Brit. Liter*. p. 198.) When, however, the following circumstances are taken into consideration, I think we are, on the other hand, fully warranted in supposing that this striking resemblance was not altogether accidental, but resulted from Milton having borrowed his plot from the Anglo-Saxon poet. The MS. of Junius was published in 1655.* About this period Milton was engaged upon his *History of England* previous to the Norman Conquest, such a publication would therefore find its way to him. *Paradise Lost* was published in 1667, but its composition occupied a number of years. (See the *Life of Milton* by his nephew Edward Philips, Pickering's edit. of *Milton's Poet. Works*, 1826, vol. i. p. lxii.) And we learn from Philips that it was at first intended for a tragedy; 'and in the fourth book of the poem there are six verses, which, several years before the poem was begun, were shown to me and some others as designed for the very beginning of the said tragedy.' *These verses commence with what stands as the 32nd line of the 4th Book.* Now it will be at once remembered that the first three books are occupied with the history of the expulsion of the Devil and his angels from heaven, their discussions, etc., and it is precisely this portion of the Anglo-Saxon Paraphrase which is so strikingly similar to the *Paradise Lost*. Can it be supposed that Milton was ignorant of the publication of Junius? And is it not evident that the first three books of the *Paradise Lost* were an after-thought, entirely induced by the plot of the Paraphrase?" Vide *Palæographia Sacra Pictoria*: or *Select Illustrations of Ancient Illuminated Biblical and Theological Manuscripts*. By J. O. Westwood, F.L.S., etc.

* "Cædmonis Monachi Paraph. Poet. Genesois, etc. Anglo-Saxonice conscripta et nunc primum edita a Francisco Junio F. F. Amst. 1655."

Professor Andras, in his *Disquisitio de Carminibus Anglo-Saxonicis Cædmoni Adjudicatis* (Parisiis, 1859), points out by numerous quotations the passages in which Milton may have been indebted to Cædmon for his imagery and language.—*Notes and Queries.*

SATIRICAL ALLUSION TO JOHNSON.—The date of the satire is 1772, in which year Nugent's translation of Fray Gerundio was published under the direction of Baretti. Prudentio, after pointing out faults in Gerund's much-applauded sermon, says:—

"Instead of the acclamations which these simpletons gave thee upon finishing thy exhortation, thou shouldst have had that which was given to Father Friar Crispin, suiting thee as well as it did him, who without doubt must have been the Friar Gerund of his time:—

"All pretenders to style before Crispin must vanish,
Who speaks Spanish in Latin and Latin in Spanish,"
"Huzza!"*—Vol. i. p. 553.
History of Friar Gerund, London, 1772.
—*Notes and Queries.*

* The passage is badly translated. The original is,—

"No merecias, que al acabar la Platica, en lugar de los vitores con que te aclamáron los simples, te hubiesen aplicado este otro vitor, que te venia tan de molde como al Padre Fray Crispin, que sin duda debió de ser el Fray Gerundio de su tiempo:—

"Vitor el Padre Crispin,
De los cultos culto Sol
Que habló Español en Latin
Y Latin en Español."—Tom. iii. p. 139.
Historia de Fray Gerundio, Madrid, 1822.

I presume that "Huzza" is put after the couplet in English, as the equivalent of Vitor.

From The Spectator.

THE TURKISH BATH. *

If there be any one human contrivance of which it can with truth be said that it is absolutely perfect, that one is the bath of all baths, the Turkish, "the bath"—we quote Mr. Wilson—"that cleanses the inward as well as the outward man, that is applicable to every age, that is adapted to make health healthier, and alleviate disease whatever its stage or severity." It combines the various good qualities of all other kinds of bath, with none of their defects and inconveniences; whatever good is done partially and uncertainly by any one of them, that the same Turkish bath does thoroughly and without fail; and in the sense of enjoyment and exalted vigor of mind and body which it always imparts, it fairly beats them all put together. "None but a Frank," exclaims Mr. Urquhart, "would call a miserable trough of water a bath." The boxed-up vapor bath is just a degree better, and no more; and all the tedious and irksome processes of the water-cure establishments, ingenious as many of them are, and useful as they have been in their time, may now be classed with the efforts of a barbarous age to provide for urgent wants by means of rough-and-ready substitutes for arts not yet developed. A man may be content to appease his hunger in the Australian bush with damper and half-charred mutton, but he would not prefer them to such a dinner as he could have in a London club; and it is only under stress of circumstances that any one, who knows the transcendent merits of the Turkish bath, will ever condescend to return to the meaner expedients that satisfied him in his days of comparative ignorance.

It may serve as physic to our pride of progress to remember how long we have wilfully deprived ourselves of this inestimable invention, which was one of the earliest perfected by man. It was in use among the Phœnicians, from whom, probably, it was borrowed by the Greeks, along with the letters which Cadmus gave them. From the Greeks it passed to the Romans, who propagated it in Britain; but it became extinct there after the Saxon invasion, and the same fate befell it in every other part of the Roman world except the Byzantine empire, where it was at once adopted by the Turkish conquerors. "A people," says Mr. Urquhart, "who knew neither Latin nor Greek have preserved this great monument of antiquity on the soil of Europe, and present to us, who teach our children only Latin and Greek, this institution in all its Roman grandeur and its Grecian taste. The bath, when first seen by the Turks, was a practice of their enemies, religious and political; they were themselves the filthiest of mortals; yet, no sooner did they see the bath than they adopted it, made it a rule of their society, a necessary adjunct to every settlement, and princes and sultans endowed such institutions for the honor of their name." Perhaps we have great reason to rejoice that when the Turks first set foot in Europe they were not well supplied with soap, for had they been so, they might have fallen into the same error as ourselves, exaggerating the cleansing effects of simple ablutions with soap and water, and disregarding the incomparably more efficient means of purification afforded by the processes which the Greeks employed. Hear Miss Nightingale: "By simply washing or sponging with water you do not really clean your skin. Take a rough towel, dip one corner in very hot water—if a little spirit be added to it, it will be more effectual—and then rub as if you were rubbing the towel into your skin with your finger. The black flakes which will come off will convince you that you were not clean before, however much soap and water you have used. These flakes are what require removing. And you can really keep yourself cleaner with a tumbler of hot water and a rough towel, and rubbing, than with a whole apparatus of bath, and soap, and sponge, without rubbing." Perfect cleansing of the skin is not the only thing accomplished in the Turkish bath; quite other effects are produced by the various applications of hot and cold air and water; but the cleansing of the skin is thorough. All the superfluous thickness of the cuticle is converted into pulp, and is rubbed off in rolls that "fall right and left as if spilt from a dish of macaroni." The quantity of this dead matter which will accumulate in a week, obstructing the seven million pores of the skin,—Mr. Erasmus Wilson has counted them,—depressing its vascular and nervous energy,

* *The Eastern or Turkish Bath:* Its History, Revival in Britain, and Application to the Purposes of Health. By Erasmus Wilson, F.R.S. Churchill.

and impairing its elastic tone, forms, when dry, a ball of the size of the fist. When it is all rubbed and washed away, the bather laid on the couch of repose in the frigidarium, and the cooling completed, then, says Mr. Urquhart, "the body has come forth shining like alabaster, fragrant as the cistus, sleek as satin, and soft as velvet. The touch of the skin is electric."

The Turkish bath is much less complex in plan than those of Greece and Rome, and differs from the latter especially, and very advantageously, as Mr. Wilson thinks, in the much more moderate temperatures employed in it. Its essential apartments are three, a large airy hall, a middle chamber, and an inner chamber. The hall serves both as a vestiarium, or dressing-room, and a frigidarium, or cooling-room; the middle chamber is the tepidarium, or warm room, in which the bather courts a natural and gentle flow of perspiration, and prepares himself to encounter the higher temperature of the inner chamber, which corresponds to the calidarium or sudatorium of the Romans. Both these chambers are heated by furnaces beneath the floor, and the air in them may be either dry or mixed with watery vapor, as it always is in the baths of Constantinople, where its presence implies a low temperature, because watery vapor is scalding at 120 degs., though it is possible to remain for a short time without injury in dry air at double the temperature of boiling water. After a visit to the first Turkish bath erected in London, a private one, a gentleman wrote to an incredulous friend as follows: "I have been at Mr. Witt's bath; all that he told was true. I cooked a mutton chop on my knee, and in eating it afterwards the only inconvenience that I experienced was in the matter of the bread; it became toast before I could get it to my mouth." So curiously different is the action of heat on living and dead organic matter; and this is not a new fact revealed by the bath. Many years ago "Sir Charles Blagden remained for ten minutes in a room heated to 260 degs.; Sir Francis Chantrey's oven in which his moulds were dried, and which was constantly entered by the men, was heated to 350 degs.; the ovens in the slate-enamelling works of Mr. Magnus of Pimlico, also habitually entered by the workmen, have a temperature of 350 degs.; and the oven in which Chabert, the so-called fire-king, exhibited in London some years back, was heated to 400 and 500 degs." The Roman baths in republican times were moderately heated, but Seneca complains that in his day the heat was "like that of a furnace, proper only for the punishment of slaves convicted of the highest misdemeanors. We now seem," he says, "to make no distinction between being warm and burning." In some of the baths erected in England, the part of the calidarium immediately over the furnace, where the heat is greatest, is surrounded with curtains forming an enclosed chamber, which corresponds to the laconicum of the ancient thermæ. Mr. Erasmus Wilson has sat for at least ten minutes in the laconicum of Mr. Urquhart's bath at Riverside, and felt not the slightest inconvenience, though the temperature was 240 degs., that is to say 28 degs. above the boiling-point of water; but he deprecates the indiscriminate practice of such experiments. High temperature may be proper as curative means in special cases, but they should only be administered under medical guidance. These exceptional cases apart, "the purpose of the bath is to *warm*, to *relax*, to induce a *gentle*, *continuous*, and *prolonged perspiration*. It is obvious that a gentle temperature will effect this object more thoroughly and completely than a burning, parching temperature of 150 degs. and upwards. Our purpose is not to dry up the tissues, to rob the blood of its diluent fluid, but to soften the callous scarf-skin that it may be peeled off, and to take away the excess of fluids pervading the economy, and with this excess any irritant and morbid matters which they may hold in solution." Hence the best temperature, in Mr. Wilson's opinion, is one that ranges in medium limits, between 120 degs. and 140 degs. In the Turkish bath, as it at present exists in the East, inconvenience resulting from its temperature is scarcely possible, "whereas in the high temperature at present in use in London, 170 degs. and 180 degs. of dry air, disagreeable and even dangerous symptoms are extremely common."

The first indication of mischief, under these circumstances, is an increased rapidity of the heart's pulsations, generally accompanied with a feeling approaching to faintness. These symptoms sometimes occur to the beginner in the use of the bath, even when the heat is not excessive, and are a sign to him that he should instantly step out of the calidarium into the tepidarium, if there be one, or otherwise into the frigidarium. "The uneasy feeling soon passes away, and then he should return to the calidarium. He may do this as often as he likes, and with the most perfect safety; and with this hint it will be his own fault if he suffer any inconvenience whatever." Another caution which the neophyte should observe is to put on his clothing slowly and composedly when the bath is ended, and to avoid hasty movements, in which lies the only possible danger of catching cold after a well-conducted bath. It is impossible to take cold while perspiring freely in the calidarium; it is equally impossible whilst the pores remain firmly closed after the cooling has been duly effected; the only danger lies in the unseasonable renewal of the perspiration. It is to prevent this that when a Russian has heated himself in a vapor bath he immediately plunges into snow, and that the last operation in the English calidarium is to douse the bather with cold water, an act which is inexpressibly grateful to the sensations, and in which there is not the shadow of danger. You may take a cold with you into the calidarium, but it will be your own fault if you do not leave it behind you there when you come out; and your liability to a fresh attack will be diminished by every subsequent visit, for the bath will render you almost casehardened against the influence of cold. A friend of Mr. Wilson, regular in his habits, active and moderate in his diet, but so encumbered with fat that he could not walk the length of a street without panting, has become a new man under the regular use of the bath. "He looks fresh and well, and more shapely; he knows no fatigue in walking; during the late severe winter he has required no great-coat; in the midst of the bitterest frost he walked to the Serpentine in his shirt-sleeves, with his coat upon his arm, and his clothing is now his only incumbrance." A fine athletic child of five years old, brought up in Mr. Urquhart's bath, and who has never worn other clothes than a loose linen garment, was met one wintry day, when the snow was on the ground, walking in the garden, perfectly naked. "Do you feel cold?" he was asked. "'Cold!' said the boy, touching his skin doubtfully with his finger, 'yes, I think I do feel cold.' That is, he felt cold to his outward touch, but not to his inward sensations, and it required that he should pass his finger over the surface of his body, as he would have done over a marble statue, to be sure, not that he was cold, for that he was not, but to be convinced that his surface felt cold."

The ladies and gentlemen of Cuba wear pocket-handkerchiefs in full dress, but it is only for show; our northern use of such articles is to them unknown, for their beneficent climate exempts them from that ignoble necessity. The Greeks and Romans enjoyed the same happy immunity. The handkerchief which they used occasionally, but not habitually, was a *sudarium*, a cloth for wiping away perspiration, and not needed for other purposes. Now it was certainly not the climate of Rome or of Athens that preserved their inhabitants from catarrhs and the *madidi infantia nasi*; it was the bath; and why may we not hope that the bath will do as much for us?

Race-horses, prize-fighters, prize-rowers, and others, undergo an arduous course of training that they may be brought into the highest state of physical vigor, by the removal of all effete matter from their bodies, and the deposit of new and sound matter in its place. Precisely the same kind of physical improvement is effected in his own person by the frequenter of the Turkish bath, without effort and without exhaustion. The Romans kept their armies in health and strength by means of the bath; and by the same means we English may indefinitely increase our individual and collective capacity for action. "Let us suppose," says Mr. Wilson, "that we have the power, by an easy, pleasant process, of extracting the old, the bad, the useless, even the decayed and diseased stuff, from the blood and from the system by means of the bath; how simple the operation by which we could give back in its place wholesome and nutritious material. Where would be atrophy and scrofula if we had this power?—and this power is, I believe, fast approaching, fast coming within our reach, by means of the Eastern bath. We squeeze the sponge as we will; we replenish it as we will." Further on he adds:

"'One of the most important properties of the bath is its power of preserving that balance of the nutritive functions of the body which in its essence is health; in other words, preserving the *condition* of the body. The healthy condition implies an exact equipoise of the fluids and the solids, of the muscular and the fatty tissues, of the waste and the supply. This state of the body is normally preserved by a proportioned amount of air, exercise or labor, and food; but even the air, the exercise, the labor, and the food must be apportioned, in its kind and in its order, to the peculiar constitution of the individual. Those who have ever had occasion to reflect on this subject, must have felt the difficulties which surround it, and have been aware how extremely difficult it is to say what may be faulty in our mode of using these necessaries of our existence. If I were asked to select an example, as a standard of the just equipoise of these conditions, I should take the ploughman; intellect at the standard of day-to-day existence, moderate food, vigorous but not over-strained labor, plenty of air, and plentiful exposure. But who would care to accept existence on such terms as these? Give us brain, give us mind, however ungovernable, however preponderant its overweight to the physical powers, however destructive to the powers of the body. In a word, we select a morbid condition: our meals, our air, our exercise, our in-door and out-door habits are all unsound; we prefer that they should be unsound; the necessities of our life, of our position, require that they should be unsound. How grand, therefore, the boon that will correct these evils without the necessity for making any inconvenient alteration in our habits!

"That Boon is the Bath. The bath promotes those changes in the blood for which fresh air is otherwise needful. The bath gives us appetite, and strengthens digestion. The bath serves us in lieu of exercise. 'The people who use it,' writes Mr. Urquhart, 'do not require exercise for health, and can pass from the extreme of indolence to that of toil.' How glorious a panacea for those home-loving matrons whom no inducement can draw forth from their *Lares* and *Penates*, to enjoy a daily wholesome exercise, and who, as a consequence, become large, and full, and fat, and bilious, and wheezy; and who, in their breach of Heaven's law, lay the foundation of heart disease. 'A nation without the bath is deprived of a large portion of the health and inoffensive enjoyment within man's reach; it therefore increases the value of a people to itself, and its power as a nation over other people.'"

"Where is Shebbeare? Oh, let not foul reproach,
Travelling thither in a city-coach
The pillory dare to name; the whole intent
Of that parade was fame, not punishment,
And that old, staunch Whig, Beardmore, standing by,
Can, in full court, give that report the lie."
Churchill, *The Author*, 1, 301.

Shebbeare was sentenced to stand one hour in the pillory at Charing Cross. Beardmore, then under-sheriff took him there in one of the city coaches, and allowed him to stand *on* "the wood," his head and hands not being put through, with a servant in livery holding an umbrella over him. At the end of the hour Beardmore took him back. For this, on the motion of the attorney-general, the Court of King's Bench issued an attachment against Beardmore. The whole court were indignant at the sentence not being fully executed, and Mr. Justice Wilmot cited a case from the year-books in which large damages were recovered against a defendant for beating his adversary's attorney, and the reason assigned was, "*Quia* the defendant, *quantum in se fuit, non permisit regem regnare;*" and, added his lordship, "it may, with at least as much propriety, be said of this under-sheriff in the present instance, that, *quantum in se fuit, non permisit regem regnare.*" Beardmore was sentenced to two months' imprisonment in the Marshalsea, and fined fifty pounds. (*R.* v. *Beardmore*, 2 Burr. 792.)—*Notes and Queries.*

"We," observes our Paris contemporary, the *Cosmos*, "have the pleasure of announcing, as almost certain, the discovery made by M. Hermann Goldschmidt, of a ninth satellite to the planet Saturn, situated between Hyperion, the seventh satellite observed by M. Lassel, and Japhet. We could give the numbers which express the distance of the new satellite from Saturn, and its mean diurnal motion, but prefer waiting till the measures are verified. Since the 10th of this month, M. Goldschmidt has not lost sight of his brilliant conquest, and he will follow it step by step until it attains its greatest elongation. It will probably be named Chiron, the last son of Saturn.

GARIBALDI.

The fourth number of Rodenberg's *Deutsches Magazin* contains an article by Alexander Herzen, from which we borrow this interesting extract: "I became more intimately acquainted with Garibaldi at London in 1854, when he returned from South America as captain of a vessel then lying in the West India Docks. I went to visit him with one of his former comrades in the Italian war and with Orsini. In his thick light-colored overcoat, his colored handkerchief round his neck, and his cap, he seemed to me more a perfect seaman than the leader of a Roman army, whose statuette, fantastically attired, was at that day sold all over the globe. The good-humored simplicity of his behavior, the absence of all pretentiousness, and the unmistakable kindness of heart with which he received us, soon gained him my liking. His crew was composed chiefly of Italians. He was the head and commander, and a stern commander in the bargain,—of that I am convinced,—and yet he was beloved and venerated by all, for they were proud of their captain. He gave us breakfast in his cabin, consisting of some peculiarly prepared South-American oysters, dried fruits and port. All at once he sprang up, exclaiming, 'Stay; I must drink another wine with you,'—ran up the companion, and presently a sailor brought in a bottle. What might not be expected from a man who had just come from the other side of the ocean? It was, however, nothing more than Belette, a country wine of Nice, Garibaldi's home, which he had brought back from Monte Video. I felt, through our simple, social converse, that I was in the presence of an extraordinarily powerful nature. Without employing phrases or commonplaces, he displayed himself perfectly as the popular leader who had astounded even old soldiers by his bravery, and it was easy to recognize in this simple ship-captain, the wounded lion who, after the fall of Rome, retired only step by step, and when he had lost his comrades, called together soldiers, peasants, robbers, any one he could find in San Marino, Ravenna, Lombardy, Tessino, in order to deal a fresh blow at the enemy. And all this took place over the corpse of his wife, who had succumbed to the fatigues and terror of such a campaign! So early as 1854, his views varied from those of Mazzini, although they remained good friends. He told Mazzini in my presence, that it would not be well to offend the Piedmontese Government: the main object now was to shake off the Austrian yoke; and he doubted greatly whether Italy were so ripe for an United Republic as Mazzini thought. He was decidedly averse from any attempt at a revolution. When he sailed from London to Newcastle to take in coals from the Mediterranean ports, I told him that his seaman's life pleased me extraordinarily, and that he had chosen the better part among all the refugees. 'And who prevents others from doing the same?' he said, warmly; 'it was always my darling dream,—you may laugh at it or not,—and I still cherish it. The people in America know me. I could have had there three or four ships under my command, and taken on board the whole of the emigrants,—the sailors, the officers, the laborers would all have been refugees. I ask you, what is to be done now in Europe? A man must either be a slave, or let himself be ruined, or live peaceably in England. Settling in America is even worse: for in that case all is over: that is a land in which a man forgets his native country; he acquires a new home and different interests. Men who settle in America part eternally from our empire. What could be better than my plan? (And here his face glowed.) The whole emigration assembled round a few masts, and traversing the ocean, hardened by a rough sailor's life in a struggle with the elements and danger—that would be a floating emigration, unapproachable and independent, and ever ready to land on any shores.' At this moment he appeared to me like one of the classic heroes, a figure from the Æneid, who, had he lived in a different age, would have had his legend and his 'Arma virumque cano.'"

THE LIVING AGE.

No. 889.—15 June, 1861.

CONTENTS.

PUBLISHED EVERY SATURDAY BY

LITTELL, SON, & CO., BOSTON.

ARMY HYMN.

BY OLIVER WENDELL HOLMES.

"Old Hundred."

O LORD of Hosts! Almighty King!
Behold the sacrifice we bring!
To every arm thy strength impart,
Thy spirit shed through every heart!

Wake in our breasts the living fires,
The holy faith that warmed our sires;
Thy hand hath made our nation free;
To die for her is serving thee.

Be thou a pillared flame to show
The midnight snare, the silent foe;
And when the battle thunders loud,
Still guide us in its moving cloud.

God of all nations! Sovereign Lord!
In thy dread name we draw the sword,
We lift the starry flag on high
That fills with light our stormy sky.

From treason's rent, from murder's stain,
Guard thou its folds till peace shall reign,
Till fort and field, till shore and sea
Join our loud anthem, PRAISE TO THEE!

—*Atlantic Monthly.*

MY HOLIDAY.

THE town is blackening on the sky,
  Its muffled thunder rolls away,
To weary heart and languid eye
  There beams a holier light of day.
O sorrow-lined and throbbing brow,
  Long pressed against the bars of toil,
What ecstacy awaits thee now
  On yonder sunny stainless soil!

The opening landscape stretches wide,
  An endless swell of hill and plain,
With, through the golden haze descried,
  A distant glimmer of the main.
The woodland minstrels carol clear
  From out each green sequestered nook,
And 'neath their leafy haunts I hear
  The laughing answer of the brook.

And losing here all sense of wrong,
  I feel no more the clutch of care,
And dream a world of light and song
  Where all are happy, all is fair.
But o'er me steals the envious eve,
  And spreads a veil of sober gray,
When, as I take reluctant leave,
  A glory dies along the way.

The fading landscape fills with change,
  The flowers grow sadly pale and droop,
And writhing trees with shadows strange,
  Across my darkening pathway stoop.
Long branches thrust from bank and crag
  Seem, in the dim and dubious light,
Bare withered arms of some lone hag,
  Whose incantations thrill the night.

Again the engine thunders on—
  My car of triumph hours before—
The vision and the bliss are gone,
  Yet memory hoards her golden store.
And there, perchance, may burst a gleam
  In after hours of weary noise,
That may recall this passing dream
  Of happy sights and holy joys.

—*All the Year Round.*

THE VOLUNTEER TO HIS TOOTH-BRUSH.

I LAY no stress upon my dress,
  No dandy arts are mine:
A sponge and tub for morning scrub,
  A wash hands ere I dine:
Two hair-brushes together plied
  (I could make shift with one),
A rude skin-parting roughly made—
  And so my toilette's done.

And yet, all Spartan as I am,
  A pang my hand doth stay,
When stern Macmurdo order gives,
  "Your tooth-brush fling away!"
I little thought, when in the ranks
  A rifle first I bore,
That when gunpowder's day set in,
  Tooth-powder's day was o'er.

Defiance in the foeman's teeth
  I am prepared to fling;
But leaving my own teeth uncleaned
  Is quite another thing—
By turning Rifle Volunteer
  John Bull his teeth doth show,
And I should like my ivories
  To be a polished row.

What if the British Lion draws
  His weapons from their sheath,—
Out of their velvet shows his claws
  Out of their lips his teeth—
Will there be less of terror hid
  In that grim mouth or paws,
When nail-brush to his feet's forbid,
  And tooth-brush to his jaws?

We're ready when we're called on,
  To take the field—I know:
And though mere babes in arms, we'll try
  A brush with any foe.
But betwixt us and the foemen,
  As fierce the brush will be,
If we are first allowed a brush
  Betwixt our teeth to see.

That cleanliness to godliness
  Is next allied we're told:
And though I'm no Diogenes
  Still to my tub I hold.
But tubs and Turkish towelling
  Upon campaign, I know,
Are luxuries which Volunteers
  Must cheerfully forego.

With unblacked boot I'm game to shoot,
  To fight with unbrushed hair,
But thou, my tooth-brush—I had hoped
  That thee at last they'd spare.
In pack or pocket, fob or pouch,
  For thee there's surely room,
Whatever Spartan Napier preach,
  Or stern Macmurdo doom!

—*Punch.*

From The Quarterly Review.

1. *L'Esprit des Auteurs, recueilli et raconté,* par Edouard Fournier. Troisième Edition. Paris, 1857.
2. *L'Esprit dans l'Histoire. Recherches et Curiosités sur les Mots Historiques.* Par Edouard Fournier. Deuxième Edition. Paris, 1860.

MANY years before "aerated bread" was heard of, a company was formed at Pimlico for utilizing the moisture which evaporates in the process of baking, by distilling spirit from it instead of letting it go to waste. Adroitly availing himself of the popular suspicion that the company's loaves must be unduly deprived of alcohol, a ready-witted baker put up a placard inscribed "*Bread with the Gin in it,*" and customers rushed to him in crowds. We strongly suspect that any over-scrupulous writer who should present history without its pleasant illusions, would find himself in the condition of the projectors who foolishly expected an enlightened public to dispense (as they thought) with an intoxicating ingredient in their bread.

> "Pol, me occidistis, amici!
> Non servastis, ait, cui sic extorta voluptas
> Et demptus per vim mentis gratissimus error."

"A mixture of lie doth ever add pleasure. Doth any man doubt that if there were taken from men's minds vain opinions, flattering hopes, imaginations as one would, and the like, but it would leave the minds of a number of men poor shrunken things, full of melancholy and indisposition, and unpleasing to themselves?" So says Lord Bacon; and few aphorisms in prose or verse are more popular than Gray's "Where ignorance is bliss, 'tis folly to be wise." The poet may have been true to his vocation when he rhymed, rather than reasoned, in this fashion; but the philosopher would have been lamentably untrue to *his*, had he seriously propounded a doctrine which any looseness of interpretation could convert or pervert into an argument against truth, knowledge, or intelligence. Fortunately, the context shows that he was speaking of what is, not of what ought to be, and was no more prepared to contend that credulity and falsehood are legitimate or lasting sources of mental gratification, than that the largest amount of physical enjoyment may be ensured by drunkenness. After speculating a little on the prevalent fondness for delusion, he concludes: "Yet howsoever these things are in men's depraved judgments and affections, yet Truth, which only doth judge itself, teacheth that the inquiry of truth, which is the love-making or wooing of it, and the belief of truth, which is the enjoying of it, is the sovereign good of human nature."

This last emphatic sentence should be kept constantly in mind during the perusal of the books named at the head of this article. The object of the first, "L'Esprit des Auteurs," is the unsparing exposure of literary plagiarism in France. In the second, "L'Esprit dans l'Histoire," the learned and ingenious author gallantly undertakes to investigate the title of the leading characters in French history to the wisest and wittiest sayings, and some of the noblest doings, recorded of them. Kings, generals, and statesmen, are all thrown into the crucible, and in many instances we are unable to say of them (what Dryden said of Shakspeare) that, burn him down as you would, there would always be precious metal at the bottom of the melting-pot. Not a few subside into a mere *caput mortuum*, or emerge "poor shrunken things," with no future hold on posterity beyond what long-indulged error may maintain for them. On the other hand, the value of the genuine gem is ineffably enhanced by the detection of the counterfeit; and there is more room to walk about and admire the real heroes and heroines in the Pantheon or Walhalla when the pretenders are dismissed. At the same time, we cannot help wondering at the favor with which M. Fournier's disclosures have been received by his countrymen; and we might be disposed to admire rather than to emulate his courage, if analogous results were likely to ensue from an equally rigid examination of the recorded or traditional claims of Englishmen. But, in the first place, there is good reason to believe that he carries scepticism to an undue extent, and insists on an amount of proof which, by the nature of things is commonly unattainable. In the second place, our English habit of fully and freely canvassing assumed or asserted merit at its rise, and of immolating instead of pampering our national vanity, if (as in the case of the Crimean War) occasionally detrimental to our credit and influence abroad, carries at least one compensation with it. We have little cause to tremble lest our long-established idols should be thrown down.

We propose, therefore, besides profiting by M. Fournier's discoveries, to extend our researches to general history and biography, ancient and modern. Most especially let us see whether the Plantagenets, Tudors, and Stuarts, owe as much to borrowed plumes as the Capets and Bourbons; whether the stirring and pithy sentences of Wolfe and Nelson are as much a myth as those of Desaix and Cambronne; whether our English worthies, civil and military, have been portrayed with the same exclusive reference to artistic effect, and the same noble independence of strict accuracy, as the French.

Before setting to work in right earnest on his more limited task, M. Fournier throws out a strong intimation, that he could likewise shatter the foundations of many a fair structure of Greek and Roman heroism if he thought fit. Nor would it be altogether safe for the worshippers of classical antiquity to defy him to the proof.

"The intelligible forms of ancient poets,
The fair humanities of old religion,
The power, the beauty, and the majesty
That had their haunts in dale or piny mountain,
Or forest, by slow stream or pebbly spring,
Or chasms and watery depths,—all these have vanished;
They live no longer in the faith of reason."

Most of the associated traditions have necessarily vanished with them, or cut a sorry figure without their mythological costume. What are Romulus and Remus without their descent from Mars and their wet-nurse of a wolf? or what is Numa without Egeria? If one part of a story is palpably and confessedly fiction, can the rest be admitted without hesitation to be fact? Until nearly the middle of the eighteenth century, the earlier portions of Greek and Roman history were as implicitly believed as the later, and, from their exciting character, naturally sank deeper into the popular mind. In ignorance or forgetfulness of occasional hints thrown out by riper scholars, writers like Echard, Vertot, Rollin, and Hooke persevered in copying and amplifying the narratives of Herodotus, Livy, and Plutarch, as confidently as those of Thucydides, Cæsar, and Tacitus. The spell was not effectually broken till Niebuhr (improving on MM. De Pouilly and De Beaufort) undertook to show, principally from internal evidence, that nearly the whole of the received history of Rome for the first four or five hundred years was apocryphal. An able review of the ensuing controversy will be found in the introduction to "An Inquiry into the Credibility of the early Roman History," by Sir G. C. Lewis, who objects to Niebuhr's method, and insists with excessive rigor that external proof or testimony is the only trustworthy source or test.

"Historical evidence," he says, "like judicial evidence, is founded on the testimony of credible witnesses. Unless these witnesses had personal and immediate perception of the facts which they report, unless they saw and heard what they undertake to relate as having happened, their evidence is not entitled to credit. As all original witnesses must be contemporary with the events which they attest, it is a necessary condition for the credibility of a witness that he be a contemporary, though a contemporary is not necessarily a credible witness. Unless therefore, an historical account can be traced, by probable proof, to the testimony of contemporaries, the first condition of historical credibility fails."

No account of Rome or the Romans for more than four hundred years after the foundation of the city fulfils this condition; and the first book of Livy, containing the regal period, can lay claim (when thus tested) to no higher authority than Lord Macaulay's "Lays." Livy states that whatever records existed prior to the burning of Rome by the Gauls (three hundred sixth-five years after its foundation), were then burnt or lost. We are left, therefore, in the most embarrassing uncertainty whether Tarquin outraged Lucretia; or Brutus shammed idiotcy, and condemned his sons to death; or Mutius Scævola thrust his hand into the fire; or Curtius jumped into the gulf (if there was one); or Clœlia swam the Tiber; or Cocles defended a bridge against an army. Livy confesses his inability to fix the respective nationality of the Horatii and Curiatii; and Sir George Lewis presses with unanswerable force the absurdity of supposing that Coriolanus acted a twentieth part of the melodramatic scenes assigned to him; as, for example, that, with Tullus Aufidius at his side, he was permitted at his mother's intercession, to lead back the Volscians thirsting for revenge.

Herodotus has fared even worse than Livy at the hands of some modern critics (although, by the way, the tenor of recent discoveries has been much in his favor); and Mr. Gladstone's argument for converting Homer into a regular annalist on the strength of the minuteness and verisimilitude of his descriptions and details, would serve equally well to prove that Robinson Crusoe actually inhabited his island, or that Gulliver was really wrecked at Lilliput. We can fully sympathize with the amiable, eloquent, and accomplished Chancellor of the Exchequer in his eagerness to rehabilitate Helen, socially and morally, by showing in what high esteem she was held by Priam; but unless she was superior to all female weakness, there was a matter which occasioned her more anxiety than her character. Sir Robert Walpole used to say that he never despaired of restoring a woman's placability, unless she had been called old or ugly. Now the age of this respected matron has been discussed with more learning and critical skill than gallantry; and the prevalent opinion of erudite Germany seems to be that she was past sixty when Homer brings her upon the stage.

We could fill pages with the sceptical doubts of scholiasts, who would fain deprive Diogenes of his lantern and his tub, Æsop of his hump, Sappho of her leap, Rhodes of its Colossus, and Dionysius the First of his ear; nay, who pretend that Cadmus did not come from Phœnicia, that Belisarius was not blind, that Portia did not swallow burning coals, and that Dionysius the Second never kept a school at Corinth. Others, without incurring any suspicion of paradox, have exposed the monstrous exaggerations of the Greeks in their accounts of the invasions of Xerxes, whose host is computed by Lemprière (that unerring guide of the ingenuous youth of both sexes) at 5,283,220 souls. "This multitude, *which the fidelity of historians has not exaggerated*, was stopped at Thermopylæ by three hundred Spartans under King Leonidas."* The Persian commissariat must have been much better regulated than the French or English before Sebastopol, if half a million of fighting men were ever brought within fifty miles of Thermopylæ. Still there may have been enough to give occasion for the remark of the Spartans, that, if the Persian arrows flew so thick as to intercept the sun, they should fight in the shade—enough also to elicit the touching reflection of Xerxes as he gazed upon the assembled host; if, indeed, this should not be rejected as out of keeping with the mad pranks he played on the first occurrence of a check.

This is one of the instances in which, as Sir George Lewis would admit, internal evidence is superior to external. Herodotus was four years old when the Persian invasion commenced: he was only thirty-nine when he recited his History at the Olympic Games. He must have conversed with many who had been personally engaged in the war: he was truthful, if superstitious and credulous; and contemporary testimony might doubtless have been procured, that, to the best of the deponent's belief, the Persian army drank up rivers on their march. Internal probability or improbability must also be allowed considerable weight, when we have to deal with the records of a later age. Modern chemists have been unable to discover how Hannibal could have levelled rocks, or Cleopatra dissolved pearls, with vinegar. Napoleon at St. Helena occasionally read and commented on the alleged traits of ancient valor and virtue:—

"He strongly censured what he called historical sillinesses (*niaiseries*), ridiculously exalted by the translators and commentators. These betrayed from the beginning, he said, historians who judged ill of men and their position. It was wrong, for example, to make so much of the continence of Scipio, or to expatiate on the calm of Alexander, Cæsar, and others, for having slept on the eve of a battle. None but a monk excluded from women, whose face glows at their approach, could make it a great merit in Scipio not to have outraged one whom chance placed in his power. As to sleeping immediately before a battle, there are none of our soldiers, of our generals, who have not repeated this marvel twenty times; and nearly all their heroism lay in the foregoing fatigue."

Napoleon might have referred to Aulus

* Lemprière's "Classical Dictionary." Last edition. Title *Xerxes*. "To admit this overwhelming total, or any thing near to it, is obviously impossible."—*Grote*, vol. v. p. 46. Mr. Grote accepts the tradition of the three hundred Spartans, whom respectable authors have computed at seven thousand, and even at twelve thousand.

Gellius, who, after a mocking allusion to the continence of Scipio, and a similar instance of self-restraint practised by Alexander towards the wife and sister of Darius, adds :—

"It is said of this Scipio, I know not whether truly or otherwise, but it is related that when a young man he was not immaculate; and it is *nearly* certain (*propemodum* constitisse) that these verses were written by Cn. Nævius, the poet, against him :—

"'Etiam qui res magnas manu sæpe gessit gloriose;
Cujus facta viva nunc vigent; qui apud gentes solus
Præstat; eum suus pater cum pallio uno ab amica abduxit.'

I believe that these verses induced Valerius Antias to express himself concerning the morality of Scipio in contradiction to all other writers, and to say that this captive maid was not restored to her father." *

It is hard on Scipio to be deprived of his prescriptive reputation for continence on no better testimony than this. But "be thou as chaste as ice, as pure as snow, thou shalt not escape calumny." A German pedant has actually ventured to question the purity of Lucretia. By way of set-off, Messalina has been brought upon the French stage as the innocent victim of calumny. A Roman courtesan, so runs the plot, so closely resembled her as to impose upon the most charitable of her contemporaries, and make them believe that she was engaged in a succession of orgies, while she was spinning with her maids. She is killed just as the terrible truth dawns upon her, without being allowed time to clear herself. The combined part of the courtesan and the empress was one of Rachel's masterpieces.

It has been thought odd that so wise a king as Philip should have exclaimed, on witnessing Alexander's Rarey-like adroitness in taming Bucephalus, "Seek another kingdom, my son, for Macedon is too small for thee;" and Cæsar's exhortation to the pilot, *Cæsarem vehis*, has been discredited by Napoleon and others † on the ground that the incident is not mentioned in the "Commentaries." Neither is the voyage during which it is supposed to have happened, which was an ill-advised and unsuccessful attempt to reach Brundusium by sea. Although the pilot recovered his presence of mind sufficiently to mind the helm, the vessel was obliged to put back, and the entire adventure was one which Cæsar had little cause to remember with complacency. He is equally silent as to another rash expedition, in which he ran imminent risk of being taken prisoner by the Gauls. If his mere silence is decisive, we must also reject the story of his crossing the Rubicon, which is told with striking and minute details by both Plutarch and Suetonius, who report his words thus: *Eatur quo deorum ostenta et inimicorum iniquitas vocat. Jacta alea esto.*

The most remarkable incident of his death is one of the most puzzling instances of popular faith which we are acquainted with. How, and when, came the *Et tu, Brute*, to be substituted for the more touching reproach set down for him by the only writers of authority who pretend to give the precise words? According to Plutarch, Casca having struck the first blow, Cæsar turned upon him, and laid hold of his sword. "At the same time they both cried out—the one in Latin, 'Villain Casca, what dost thou mean?' and the other in Greek to his brother, 'Brother, help!' Some say he opposed the rest, and continued struggling and crying out, till he perceived the sword of Brutus; then he drew his robe over his face, and yielded to his fate." * Nicolas Damascenus mentions no one as speaking except Casca, who, he says, "calls to his brother in Greek, on account of the tumult." † The statement of Suetonius is, that Cæsar was pierced with twenty-three wounds, without uttering a sound beyond one groan at the first blow; "although some have handed down, that, to Marcus Brutus, rushing on, he said Καὶ σὺ, τέκνον." In some editions of Suetonius the words *καὶ σὺ εἶ* (or *εἷς*) *ἐκείνων* are added, which would make "And you, my son, and you are one of them." ‡ The "son" is supposed to imply

* "The Attic Nights of Aulus Gellius," B. vi. c. 8 (translated by Beloe), vol. ii. p. 23.

† "In reading, Napoleon leant to scepticism and paradox; as for instance, he ridiculed as improbable the story of Cæsar's escape in the boat, and his speech to the boatman, and was much inclined to disparage the talents, and more particularly the military skill, of that extraordinary man."—Lord Holland's *Foreign Reminiscences*, p. 296. The Duke of Wellington always professed the highest admiration of Cæsar's military talents.

* Plutarch's "Life of Cæsar." In the "Life of Brutus" nothing is said of the effect of Brutus' appearance.

† "Fragmenta Historicorum Græcorum," vol. iii. p. 445.

‡ The Rev. Charles Merivale, who, in the text of

something more than an ordinary term of affection, for in a preceding passage, after naming several Roman ladies with whom Cæsar had intrigued, Suetonius adds, "Sed ante alias dilexit M. Bruti matrem, Serviliam."

The history of modern Europe is susceptible of the same threefold division as that of Greece and Rome. It comprises the fabulous, the semi-fabulous, and the historic, period. We regret to say that Arthur and his Round Table belong to the first—so indisputably belong to it, that archæologists are still disputing whether the bevy of knights and dames, on whom poetic genius has recently shed fresh lustre, are the creation of French Britany or the veritable progeny of the ancient Britons, whose Welsh descendants claim them as the brightest ornament of their race.* Charlemagne belongs to the second period, and what we read of him and his court is a mixture of ill-ascertained truth and proved or proveable fable. His paladins are as mythical as Arthur's knights, and many of the traditions that do him most honor have been rudely shaken.

So prodigious an amount of learning and acuteness, German and English, has been brought to bear on Anglo-Saxon history, that no excuse is left for illusion, however pleasant. Dr. Reinhold Pauli has carefully examined the authorities for the popular stories of Alfred the Great, and reluctantly admits that they are far from satisfactory. We are not prepared to give up the story of the burned cakes because it is not to be found in the extant fragments of his Life by his friend Asser, but our faith is somewhat shaken in that of his venturing into the Danish camp in the disguise of a minstrel, when we learn that it is not told of him by any of the old Saxon writers, that it is told of another Saxon monarch, and that it breathes more of the Scandinavian-Norman than the Saxon spirit.*

The Chancellor Lord Eldon, who took his bachelor's degree in 1770, used to say "An examination for a degree at Oxford was a farce in my time. I was examined in Hebrew and in history: 'What is the Hebrew for the place of a skull?' I replied 'Golgotha.' 'Who founded University College?' I stated (though, by the way, the point is sometimes doubted) that King Alfred founded it. 'Very well, sir,' said the examiner, 'you are competent for your degree.'" If Alfred founded the oldest college, he, in one sense, founded the university; but the sole authority for the hypothesis is a passage in Asser, which is no longer to be found.†

We are gravely told, on historical authority, by Moore, in a note to one of his Irish "Melodies"—

"Rich and rare were the gems she wore;"

that during the reign of Brian, king of Munster, a young lady of great beauty, richly dressed, and adorned with jewels, undertook a journey from one end of the kingdom to another, with a wand in her hand, at the top of which was a ring of exceeding great value; and such was the perfection of the laws and the government that no attempt was made upon her honor, nor was she robbed of her clothes and jewels. Precisely the same story is told of Alfred, of Frothi, King of Denmark, and of Rollo, Duke of Normandy.

Another romantic anecdote fluctuating between two or more sets of actors, is an episode in the amours of Emma, the alleged daughter of Charlemagne, who, finding that the snow had fallen thickly during a nightly interview with her lover, Eginhard, took him upon her shoulders, and carried him to some distance from her bower, to prevent his footsteps from being traced. Unluckily, Charlemagne had no daughter named Emma or Imma; and a hundred years before the

his valuable work, "The Romans under the Empire," adopts the current story, says in a note, "Of course no reliance can be placed on such minute details. The whole statement of the effect of the sight of Brutus upon Cæsar may be a fiction suggested by the vulgar story of the relation between them."

* See Wright's edition of "La Mort d'Arthure," in three volumes. London, 1858. As to the worthlessness of the earliest histories of Arthur and Charlemagne, on which the latter are mainly based, see Mr. Buckle's *History*, 292, 297.

* "König Aelfred und seine Stelle in der Geschichte Englands, von Dr. Reinhold Pauli." Berlin, 1851; pp. 130-132.

† See Gough's edition of "Camden's Britannia," fol. 1799, p. 299, and "Thorpe's Translation of Lappenberg's *History*," Preface, p. 38. Mr. Hallam says, in his Introduction to the "Literature of Europe," vol. i. p. 16 (6th edit.), "In a former work I gave more credence to its foundation by Alfred than I am now inclined to do."

appearance (in 1600) of the *Chronicle* which records the adventure, it had been related in print of a German emperor and a damsel unknown. Let us hope, for the honor of the fair sex, that it is true of somebody. Fielding, after recording an instance in which Joseph Andrews' muscular powers enable him to ensure the safety of Fanny, exclaims, "Learn hence, my fair countrywomen, to consider your own weakness, and the many occasions on which the strength of a man may be useful to you;" and he exhorts them not to match themselves with spindle-shanked beaux and *petit-maitres*. Could we put faith in Emma's exploit, it might justify an exhortation to the male sex to give the preference to ladies strong enough to carry a husband or lover on an emergency; especially when we remember the story of the women of Weinberg, who, when that fortress was about to be stormed, obtained permission to come out, carrying with them whatever they deemed most valuable, and surprised the besiegers by issuing from the gate each carrying her husband on her back.

The story of Canute commanding the waves to roll back rests on the authority of Henry of Huntingdon, who wrote about a hundred years after the death of the Danish monarch. Hume treats the popular legend of fair Rosamond as fabulous. According to Lingard, instead of being poisoned by Queen Eleanor, she retired to the convent of Godstow, and dying in the odor of sanctity, was buried with such marks of veneration by the nuns as to provoke a rebuke from their diocesan, who reminded them that "religion makes no distinction between the mistress of a king and the mistress of any other man."

Blondel, harp in hand, discovering his master's place of confinement, is also a fancy-picture; for the seizure and imprisonment of Richard were matters of European notoriety. What is alleged to have befallen him on his way home has found its appropriate place in "Ivanhoe;" and the adventures of monarchs in disguise, from Haroun Alraschid to James the Fifth of Scotland, so frequently resemble each other that we are compelled to suspect a common origin for the majority.

The statement of a Welsh writer of the sixteenth century, that Edward the First gathered together all the Welsh bards and had them put to death, is implicity adopted by Hume, and made familiar by Gray:—

"Ruin seize thee, ruthless king;
Confusion on thy banners wait."

It is glaringly improbable, and rests on no valid testimony of any sort.

Miss Aikin was, we believe, the first to demolish the credibility of the celebrated story, that Cromwell, Hampden, and Arthur Hazelrig, despairing of the liberties of their country, had actually embarked for New England (in 1638), when they were stopped by an Order in Council. The incident is not mentioned by the best authorities, including Clarendon; and there is no direct proof that either of the three belonged to the expedition in question, which, after a brief delay, was permitted to proceed with its entire freight of Pilgrims.

"As for the greater number of the stories with which the *ana* are stuffed," says Voltaire, "including all those humorous replies attributed to Charles the Fifth, to Henry the Fourth, to a hundred modern princes, you find them in Athenæus and in our old authors. It is in this sense only that one may say '*nil sub sole novum*.'"* He does not stop to give examples, but there is no difficulty in finding them. Thus the current story is, or was, that Baudesson, mayor of Saint Dizier, was so like Henry the Fourth, that the royal guards saluted him as he passed. "Why, friend," said Henry, "your mother must have visited Bearn?" "No," replied the mayor, "it was my father, who occasionally resided there." This story, which is also told of Louis the Fourteenth, is related by Macrobius of Augustus.

Dionysius the tyrant, we are told by Diogenes of Laerte, treated his friends like vases full of good liquors, which he broke when he had emptied them. This is precisely what Cardinal Retz says of Madame de Chevreuse's treatment of her lovers.

The epigrammatic remark given by H. Say to Christina of Sweden, on the revocation of the Edict of Nantes by Louis the Fourteenth, "He has cut off his left arm with the right," belongs to Valentinian. That of the peasant to the same monarch, "It is useless to en-

* "A. M. du M . . ., Membre de Plusieurs Académies, sur Plusieurs Anecdotes." (1774.)—*Voltaire's Works*.

large your park at Versailles; you will always have neighbors," is copied from Apuleius, and has been placed in the mouth of a Norfolk laborer in reference to the lordly domain of Holkham. Henry the Fourth, when put on his guard against assassination, is reported to have said, "He who fears death will undertake nothing against me; he who despises his own life will always be master of mine." This recalls Seneca's "*Contemptor suæmet vitæ, dominius alienæ.*"

Fabricius, in conference with Pyrrhus, was tempted to revolt to him, Pyrrhus telling him that he should be partner of his fortunes, and second person to him. But Fabricius answered in scorn, to such a motion, "Ah! that would not be good for yourself, for if the Epirotes once knew me, they will rather desire to be governed by me than by you."* Charles the Second told his brother, afterwards James the Second, who was expressing fears for his safety, "Depend upon it, James, no one will kill me to make you king."

There is a story of Sully's meeting a young lady, veiled, and dressed in green, on the back stairs leading to Henry's apartment, and being asked by the king whether he had not been told that his majesty had a fever and could not receive that morning, "Yes, sire, but the fever is gone; I have just met it on the staircase dressed in green." This story is told of Demetrius and his father.

The Emperor Adrian meeting a personal enemy the day after his accession to the throne, exclaimed, "*Evasisti*" ("you have escaped"). Philip, Count of Bresse, becoming Duke of Savoy, said, "It would be shameful in the duke to revenge the injuries done to the count." Third in point of time is the better-known saying of Louis the Twelfth, "The king of France does not revenge the injuries of the Duke of Orleans." Instead of being uttered in this laconic form to the Duc de la Tremouille, it formed the conclusion of an address to the deputies of the city of Orleans, who were told "that it would not be decent or honorable in a king of France to revenge the quarrels of a Duke of Orleans."

The three last are amongst the examples adduced by M. Suard† in support of his theory, very different from Voltaire's, respecting the causes of the similarity between striking sayings and doings, which, he contends, is too frequently accepted as a proof of plagiarism in the later speaker or actor, or as affording a presumption of pure fiction from the first. We agree with M. Suard; and an apt analogy is supplied by the history of invention. The honor of almost every important discovery from printing to the electric telegraph, has been vehemently contested by rival claimants; and the obvious reason is that whenever the attention of the learned or scientific world has been long and earnestly fixed upon a subject, it is as if so many heaps of combustible materials had been accumulated, or so many trains laid, any two or three of which may be simultaneously exploded by a spark. The results resemble each other, because each projector is influenced by the same laws of progress; and as the human heart and mind retain their essential features, unaltered by time or space, there is nothing surprising in the fact of two or more persons similarly situated acting on similar impulses or hitting on similar relations of ideas.

This theory, which we believe to be true in the main, has one great recommendation. It is productive, not destructive. It doubles or trebles the accumulated stock of originality; and whenever we light upon a fresh coincidence in nobility of feeling, depth of reflection, readiness or terseness of expression, we may exclaim, "Behold a fresh instance of a quality that does honor to mankind." We have collected some striking specimens in addition to those already mentioned; and if many of them, individually taken, are familiar enough, their juxtaposition may prove new. Sydney Smith says of Mackintosh, "The great thoughts and fine sayings of the great men of all ages were intimately present to his recollection, and came out dazzling and delighting in his conversation." We may at least assist in purifying and utilizing, if we do not greatly augment, the store of these invaluable elements of entertainment and instruction.

The right wing of Hyder Ali's army, in

* Bacon's "Apophthegms."

† "Notes sur l'Esprit d'Imitation," published after his death, with additions by M. Le Clerc, in the "Revue Française," Nouvelle Série, tom. vi. On the subject of coincidences in fact and fiction, see also Keightley's "Tales and Popular Fictions," chap. i.; and the Preface to his "Fairy Mythology."

an action against the English under Colonel Baillie, was commanded by his son, and intelligence arrived that it was beginning to give way. "Let Tippoo Saib do his best," said Hyder; "he has his reputation to make." What is this but the reply of Edward the Third when exhorted to succor the Black Prince of Crecy?

Commodore Billings, in his account of his Expedition to the Northern Coasts of Russia, says that when he and Mr. Main were on the river Kobima, they were attended by a young man from Kanoga, an island between Kamschatka and North America. One day Mr. Main asked him, "What will the savages do to me if I fall into their power?" "Sir," said the youth, "you will never fall into their power if I remain with you. I always carry a sharp knife; and if I see you pursued and unable to escape, I will plunge my knife into your heart; then the savages can do nothing more to you." These recall the words of the French knight reported by Joinville: "Swear to me," said Queen Margaret, "that if the Saracens become masters of Damietta, you will cut off my head before they can take me." "Willingly," replied the knight; "I had already thought of doing so if the contingency arrived."

Florus, describing the battle in which Catiline fell, says, "*nemo hostium bello superfuit.*" The day after the battle of Rocroy a French officer asked a Spaniard what were the numbers of their veteran infantry before the battle. "You have only, replied he, "to count the dead and the prisoners." * A Russian officer being asked the number of the troops to which he had been opposed, pointed to the field of death and said, "You may count them; they are all there."

The *veni, vidi, vici*, of Cæsar has given rise to an infinity of imitators; one of whom has improved upon it. John Sobieski, after relieving Vienna in 1683, announced his victory over the Turks to the pope in these words: "*Je suis venu, j'ai vu, Dieu a vaincu*" —"I came; I saw; God conquered." Cardinal Richelieu acknowledged the receipt of a Latin work dedicated to him thus: "*Accepi, legi, probavi.*"

When Cæsar slipped and fell, on landing in Africa, he is reported to have exclaimed: "Land of Africa, I take possession of thee!" Thierry, in his "History of the Norman Conquest," says:—

"The duke (the Conqueror) landed the last of all: the moment his foot touched the sand, he made a false step, and fell on his face. A murmur arose, and voices cried, 'Heaven preserve us! a bad sign.' But William, rising, said directly, 'What is the matter? What are you wondering at? I have seized this ground with my hands, and by the brightness of God, so far as it extends, it is mine, it is yours.'"

Froissart relates that Edward the Third fell with such violence on the sea-shore at La Hogue that the blood gushed from his nose, and a cry of consternation was raised: but the king answered quickly, and said, "This is a good token for me, for the land desireth to have me;" "of the which answer his men were right joyful."

When Mirabeau exclaimed, "I know how near the Tarpeian Rock is to the Capitol," he may have been thinking of Pope Alexander the Sixth's words, "Vide, mi fili, quam leve discrimen patibulum inter et statuam." But no parallel has been found for Chancellor Oxenstiern's famous remark to his son, although the reflection is precisely what we should have expected to find in some ancient cynic or satirist.

The anecdote-mongers of antiquity relate of Pompey, that, when the danger of a meditated voyage (to bring provisions for Rome in a scarcity) was pressed upon him, he said: "This voyage is necessary, and my life is not." Maréchal Saxe, starting for the campaign of Fontenoy, at the risk of his life, said to Voltaire: "*Il ne s'agit pas de vivre, mais de partir.*" Voltaire put aside the remonstrances of his friends against his attending the rehearsal of "Irene" with the remark: "*Il n'est pas question de vivre, mais de faire jouer ma tragédie.*" Racine had anticipated both Voltaire and the Maréchal by a line in "Berenice:" "*Mais il ne s'agit de vivre, il faut régner.*"

Voltaire, speaking highly of Haller, was told that he was very generous in so doing, since Haller said just the contrary of him. "Perhaps," remarked Voltaire, after a short pause, "we are both of us mistaken." Libanius writes to Aristænetus: "You are always speaking ill of me. I speak nothing but good of you. Do you not fear that nei-

* "The Life of Condé." By Lord Mahon (Earl Stanhope), p. 22.

ther of us shall be believed?" "Themistocles in his lower fortune leaned to a gentleman who scorned him; when he grew to his greatness which was soon after, he sought to him. Themistocles said: 'We are both grown wise, but too late.'"* If all the good sayings attributed by Plutarch to Themistocles really belonged to him, they would suffice to place him amongst the wisest and wittiest men of antiquity. But Plutarch, like Voltaire, seldom resists the temptation of a good story; and even the celebrated "Strike, but hear!" is shaken by the fact that Herodotus, the earliest reporter now extant of the debate of the admirals, makes no mention of the speech, and represents Adeimantus, the Corinthian admiral, as the person with whom Themistocles had an altercation upon that occasion; while Plutarch puts the Lacedæmonian admiral, Eurybiades, in the place of Adeimantus; and adds the incident of the intended blow arrested by the words "Strike, but hear!"

The lesson of perseverance in adversity taught by the spider to Robert Bruce, is said to have been taught by the same insect to Tamerlane.

"When Columbus," says Voltaire, "promised a new hemisphere, people maintained that it could not exist; and when he had discovered it, that it had been known a long time." It was to confute such detractors that he resorted to the illustration of the egg, already employed by Brunelleschi when his merit in raising the cupola of the cathedral of Florence was contested.

The anecdote of Southampton reading "The Faery Queen," whilst Spenser was waiting in the ante-chamber, may pair off with one of Louis XIV. As this munificent monarch was going over the improvements of Versailles with Le Notre, the sight of each fresh beauty or capability tempts him to some fresh extravagance, till the architect cries out, that, if their promenade is continued in this fashion, it will end in the bankruptcy of the State. Southampton, after sending first twenty, and then fifty guineas, on coming to one fine passage after another, exclaims, "Turn the fellow out of the house, or I shall be ruined."

The following lines form part of the animated description of the Battle of Bannockburn in the "Lord of the Isles:"—

"'The rebels, Argentine, repent!
For pardon they have kneeled.'
'Ay, but they kneel to other powers,
And other pardon ask than ours.
See where yon barefoot abbot stands,
And blesses them with lifted hands!
Upon the spot where they have kneeled
These men will die, or win the field.'"

A note refers to Dalrymple's "Annals," which state that the abbot was Maurice, abbot of Inchaffray, and the knight to whom the king's remark was addressed, Ingleram de Umfraville. The same mistake is attributed to Charles the Bold before the battle of Granson, to the Duc de Joyeuse before the battle of Courtray, and to the Austrians at Frastenz.

In the scene of "Henry VI.," where Lord Say is dragged before Cade, we find:—

"*Dick.* Why dost thou quiver, man?
Say. The palsy, and not fear, provoketh me."

On the morning of his execution, Charles I. said to his groom of the chambers, "Let me have a shirt on more than ordinary, by reason the season is so sharp as probably may make me shake, which some observers will imagine proceeds from fear. I would have no such imputation; I fear not death."* As Bailly was waiting to be guillotined, one of the executioners accused him of trembling. "I am cold" ("*J'ai froid*"), was the reply.

Frederic the Great is reported to have said, in reference to a troublesome assailant: "This man wants me to make a martyr of him, but he shall not have that satisfaction." Vespasian told Demetrius the Cynic, "You do all you can to get me to put you to death, but I do not kill a dog for barking at me." This Demetrius was a man of real spirit and honesty. When Caligula tried to conciliate his good word by a large gift in money, he sent it back with the message: "If you wish to bribe me, you must send me your crown." George III. ironically asked an eminent divine, who was just returned from Rome, whether he had converted the pope. "No, sire, I had nothing better to offer him."

Lord Macaulay relates of Clive, that "twice, whilst residing in the Writers' Buildings at Madras, he attempted to destroy himself, and twice the pistol which he snapped at his own head failed to go off. This circum-

* Bacon's "Apophthegms."

* "Memoirs of the Two Last Years of the Reign of King Charles I." By Sir Thomas Herbert, Groom of the Chambers to his Majesty. London, 1813.

stance, it is said, affected him as a similar escape affected Wallenstein. After satisfying himself that the pistol was really well loaded, he burst out into an exclamation that "surely, he was reserved for something great." Wallenstein's character underwent a complete change from the accident of his falling from a great height without hurting himself.

Cardinal Ximenes, upon a muster which was taken against the Moors, was spoken to by a servant of his to stand a little out of the smoke of the harquebuss, but he said again that "that was his incense." * The first time Charles XII. of Sweden was under fire, he inquired what the hissing he heard about his ears was, and being told that it was caused by the musket-balls, "Good," he exclaimed, "this henceforth shall be my music."

Pope Julius II., like many a would-be connoisseur, was apt to exhibit his taste by fault-finding. On his objecting that one of Michel Angelo's statues might be improved by a few touches of the chisel, the artist, with the aid of a few pinches of marble dust, which he dropped adroitly, conveyed an impression that he had acted on the hint. When Halifax found fault with some passages in Pope's translation of Homer, the poet, by the advice of Garth, left them as they stood, but told the peer that they had been retouched, and had the satisfaction of finding him as easily satisfied as his holiness.

When Lycurgus was to reform and alter the state of Sparta, in the consultation one advised that it should be reduced to an absolute popular equality; but Lycurgus said to him, "Sir, begin it in your own house." Had Dr. Johnson forgotten this among Bacon's "Apophthegms" when he told Mrs. Macaulay, "Madam, I am now become a convert to your way of thinking. I am convinced that all mankind are upon an equal footing, and, to give you an unquestionable proof, Madam, that I am in earnest, here is a very sensible, civil, well-behaved fellow-citizen, your footman; I desire that he may be allowed to sit down and dine with us"?

In allusion to Napoleon's shaving, Talleyrand observed to Rogers, "A king by birth is shaved by another. He who makes himself *roi* shaves himself." A prince by birth, the great Condé, was shaved by another,

* Bacon's "Apophthegms."

and one day, when submitting to this operation, he remarked aloud to the operator, "You tremble." "And you do not," was the retort. M. Suard supplies a curious parallel to this anecdote by one of an old and infirm *Milord Anglais* who was going through the marriage-ceremony with a young and lovely girl, and held her hand in his, "You tremble." "Don't you?"

The French *Ana* assign to Maréchal Villars, taking leave of Louis XIV., the familiar aphorism (founded on a Spanish proverb), "Defend me from my friends; I can defend myself against my enemies." Canning's lines—

"But of all plagues, good Heav'n, thy wrath can send,
Save, save, oh! save me from the candid friend,"

are a versified adaptation of it. Lord Melbourne, on being pressed to do something for a journalist, on the ground that he always supported his lordship when in the right, retorted, "That's just when I don't want his help. Give me a fellow who will stick by me when I am in the wrong." Louis, by the way, complied with the Maréchal's request, for when told by a pretended friend of his that he was making a good thing of his command, "*Il y faisait bien ses affaires,*" the king replied, "*Je le crois, mais il fait encore mieux les miennes.*"

Louis XIV. is reported to have said to Boileau, on receiving his "Epistle" on the passage of the Rhine, "This is fine, and I should have praised you more had you praised me less." Unluckily, Queen Marguerite (la Reine Margot) had already paid the same compliment to Brantome; and the palm among courtly repartees must be given to Waller's on Charles II.'s asking him how it happened that his panegyric on Cromwell was better than his verses on the Restoration, "Poets, your majesty, succeed better in fiction than in truth."

It is unnecessary to repeat Wilkes' witty but profane remark on Lord Thurlow's exclaiming, "When I forget my king, may my God forget me." Lord John Russell states that Burke, on hearing this, remarked, "And the best thing He can do for him." One of Bacon's "Apophthegms" is, "Bion was sailing, and there fell out a great tempest, and the mariners, that were wicked and dissolute fellows, called upon the gods; but Bion said to them, "Peace! let them not know you are here."

Care must be taken to distinguish the cases in which, from failure of collateral proof, or internal evidence, or the characters of the relaters, the repetition or re-appearance of the story raises a reasonable suspicion of its authenticity; and it unluckily happens that quaint instances of ill-nature, absurdity, stupidity, or worse, are even more likely to be produced in duplicate or triplicate than heroic actions and generous impulses.

Mummius told the commissioners who were employed in carrying the plunder of Corinth, including many masterpieces of Grecian art, to Rome, that he should insist on their replacing any that were destroyed or injured. An Englishman, on hearing of Canova's death, asked his brother if he meant to carry on the business.

One of the petty tyrants of Italy, during the Middle Ages, was met on the middle of a bridge, by the bearer of a sentence of excommunication. He asked the messenger whether he would eat or drink, and cut short his astonishment by explaining that the alternative thereby proposed was whether he would eat up the Papal bull, seal and all, or be flung over the parapet into the river. Martin of Galway, "Humanity Dick," made nearly the same proposal to an Irish process-server, who was foolish enough to venture into a district where the royal writs never ran.

"In such partial views of early times," says Savigny, "we resemble the travellers who remark with great astonishment that in France the little children, nay, even the common people, speak French with perfect fluency."* There is not a country in Europe, and hardly a country in England, where they are not ready to name some individual traveller by whom the same astonishment was expressed. The echo which politely replies, "Very well, I thank you," to the ordinary inquiry after health, may be heard (*mutatis mutandis*) in Gascony as well as at Killarney. Who has not laughed at the story of the letter-writer who concludes: "I would say more but for an impudent Irishman who is looking over my shoulder, and reading every thing I write," with the self-betraying denial of the Irishman? The story may be read in Galland's *Paroles Remarquables des Orientaux*. It is not impossible that this comic incident or fiction gave Frederic the Great the hint for the terrible *coup de théâtre* in the tent of the officer who, when all lights had been forbidden under pain of death, was found finishing a letter to his wife by the light of a taper: "Add a postscript. Before this reaches you I shall be shot for disobedience of orders;" and shot he was. Mrs. Norton has based a beautiful song upon this event, which is only too well attested.

The same spirit of inquiry which may rob us of some cherished illusions may also relieve human nature from an unmerited stigma of barbarism or cruelty. Thus Heyne absolves Omar from the crime of burning the library of Alexandria; and serious doubts have assailed the authenticity of the order attributed to the legate at the sack of Beziers in 1209: "Kill them all. God will recognize his own." M. Fournier has devoted an entire section to the charge against Charles IX., of firing on the Huguenots with an arquebuss from the window of the Louvre during the Massacre of St. Bartholomew; and his verdict, after collating the authorities, is "Not proven." In the "Journal" of Barbier the scene is laid in the balcony of the palace of the *Petit Bourbon*, pulled down in 1758.

Shenstone defined good writing to consist in or of "spontaneous thought and labored expression." Many famous sayings comprise these two elements of excellence; the original writer or speaker furnishing the thought, and the chronicler the expression. When the omission, addition, or alteration of a word or two will give point and currency to a phrase, or even elevate a platitude into wit and poetry, the temptation to the historian or biographer seems irresistible.

Chateaubriand, in his *Analyse Raisonnée de l'Histoire de France*, relates that Philip the Sixth, flying from the field of Crecy, arrived late at night before the gates of the Castle of Broye, and on being challenged by the chatelain, cried out, "*Ouvrez; c'est la fortune de la France*" ("Open; it is the fortune of France")—"a finer phrase than that of Cæsar in the storm; magnanimous confidence, equally honorable to the subject and the monarch, and which paints the grand-

* "The Vocation of our Age for Legislation and Jurisprudence," chap. ii

eur of both in the monarchy of Saint Louis." The received authority for this phrase was Froissart, and it will be found faithfully reproduced in the old English translation of Lord Berners. The genuine text is now admitted to be, "*Ouvrez, ouvrez, c'est l'infortuné Roi de France*"—("Open, open; it is the unfortunate king of France"). Buchon, the learned editor of the French Chronicles, hastened to Chateaubriand with the discovery, and suggested the propriety of a correction in the next edition of his book, but found the author of the "Genius of Christianity" bent on remaining *splendide mendax* and insensible to the modest merit of truth.

Chateaubriand was no less zealous for the authenticity of Francis the First's famous note to his mother after the battle of Pavia: "*Tout est perdu fors l'honneur*," which, till recently, rested on tradition and popular belief. The real letter has been printed by M. Champollion, from a manuscript journal of the period, and begins thus:—

"Madame,—Pour vous advertir comment se porte le ressort de mon infortune, de toutes choses n' m'est demouré que l'honneur *et la vie qui est saulvé*, et pour ce que en nostre adversité cetta nouvelle votis fera quelque resconfort, j'ay prié qu'on me laissât pour escrire ces lettres, ce qu'on m'a agréablement accordé."

M. Fournier suggests that the current version may be traced to the Spanish historian, Antonio de Vera, who translates the alleged billet: "*Madama, toto se ha perdido sino es la honra.*"

In a note to the "Henriade," Voltaire says that Henry the Fourth wrote thus to Crillon:—

"Pends-toi, brave Crillon; nous avons combattu à Arques, et tu n'y étais pas. Adieu, brave Crillon; je vous aime à tort et à travers."

The real letter to Crillon was written from the camp before Amiens seven years after the affair of Arques, and is four times as long. It begins:—

"Brave Crillon, Pendes vous de n'avoir este près de moy, lundi dernier, à la plus belle occasion," etc., etc.

Henry seems to have been in the habit of telling his friends to hang themselves, for there is extant another billet of his, in the same style to one who had lost an eye:—

"Harambure, Pendes-votis de ne vous être trouvé près de moy en un combat que nous avons en contre les ennemys, où nous avons fait rage," etc. "Adieu, Borgne."

The naval history of England affords a striking example of the same sympathizing spirit of noble emulation. "See," cried Nelson (at Trafalgar), pointing to the Royal Sovereign as she steered right for the centre of the enemy's line, cut through it, and engaged a three-decker, "see how that noble fellow Collingwood carries his ship into action." Collingwood, delighted at being first in the heat of the fire, and knowing the feelings of his commander and old friend, turned to his captain, and exclaimed, "Rotherham, what would Nelson give to be here!" *

Strange to say, the French historians have once given credit for an honorable action, which was never performed, to Englishmen. The President Henault relates that an English governor had agreed with Du Guesclin to surrender a place on a given day if he was not relieved, and that, Du Guesclin's death occurring in the interval, the governor came out with his principal officers at the time fixed, and laid the keys on the coffin of the constable. Unluckily a contemporary chronicle has been produced, in which it is stated that the garrison tried to back out, and were brought to reason by a threat to put the hostages to death.

Froissart relates in touching detail the patriotic self-devotion of Eustache de Saint Pierre and his five companions, who (he says) delivered up the keys of Calais to Edward the Third, bareheaded, with halters round their necks, and would have been hanged forthwith but for the intervention of the queen. The story had been already doubted by Hume on the strength of another contemporary narrative, in which the king's generosity and humanity to the inhabitants are extolled; when (in 1835) it was named as the subject of a prize essay by an antiquarian society in the north of France, and the prize was decreed to M. Clovis Bolard, a Calais man, who took part against Saint Pierre. The controversy was revived in 1854 in the *Siècle*, by a writer who referred to documents in the Tower as establishing that Saint Pierre had been in connivance with the besiegers, and was actually rewarded with a pension by Edward.

* Southey's Nelson, ch. 9.

On the other hand, the account given by Froissart of the return of the French King John (the captive at Poitiers) to England, by no means bears out the chivalrous turn given to it in the *Biographie Universelle*. On hearing that his son, the Duke of Anjou, left as hostage, had broken faith, the king, says the writer, resolved at once to go back, and constitute himself prisoner at London, replying to all the objections of his council, that "if good faith were banished from the rest of the world, it should be found in the mouths of kings." Froissart attributes the journey to a wish to see the king and queen of England. "Some," remarks M. Michelet, "pretend that John only went to get rid of the *ennui* caused by the sufferings of France, or to see some fair mistress."

The adoption of the Garter for the name and symbol of the most distinguished order of knighthood now existing, is still involved in doubt. The incident to which it is popularly attributed was first mentioned by Polydore Virgil, who wrote nearly two hundred years after its alleged occurrence. The age of the Countess of Salisbury is objected by M. Fournier, but there is much more force to our minds in the established fact that her husband died in consequence of bruises received at the jousts preceding the foundation of the order; nor is it likely that such an incident would have been suppressed by Froissart, who makes no allusion to it, although he is the principal authority for her amour with the king. Polydore Virgil's history appeared in 1536. In 1527, at the investiture of Francis the First, John Taylor, Master of the Rolls, in his address to the new knight, stated that Richard Cœur de Lion had once, on the inspiration of Saint George, distinguished some chosen knights by causing them to tie a thong or garter round the leg. Camden and others suggest that Edward the Third, in remembrance of this event, gave the garter as the signal for a battle, probably Crecy, in which he proved victorious. But the very number and variety of these speculations show that the real origin of the symbol cannot be traced. The motto is equally unaccountable, although as fit for the purpose as any other maxim or apophthegm, whether connected with a tale of gallantry or not.*

As numerous questions of authenticity are made to turn on the want of contemporary testimony when it might reasonably be expected to be forthcoming, it may be as well to call attention to what Varnhagen von Ense notes in his "Diary:"—

"Humboldt confirms the opinions I have more than once expressed, that too much must not be inferred from the silence of authors. He adduces three important and perfectly undeniable matters of fact, as to which no evidence is to be found where it would be most anticipated: In the archives of Barcelona, no trace of the triumphal entry of Columbus into that city; in Marco Polo, no allusion to the Chinese Wall; in the archives of Portugal, nothing about the voyages of Amerigo Vespucci, in the service of that crown."*

In Grafton's Chronicles, comprising the reign of King John, there is no mention of Magna Charta. But it has been suggested that the period of publication (1562) and his office of printer to Queen Elizabeth may account for the omission.

Humboldt's remarks refer to a reading at Madame Recamier's, in which he had pointed out some inaccuracies in the received accounts of the discovery of America. Robertson states that "Columbus promised solemnly to his men that he would comply with their request (to turn back), provided they would accompany him and obey his command for three days longer, and if during that time land were not discovered, he would then abandon the enterprise, and direct his course towards Spain." A closer examination of the authorities has shown that no such promise was given or required.† Robertson accepts without questioning the traditional account of Charles the Fifth's celebrating his own obsequies in his lifetime, as well as that of his fondness for mechanical contrivances:

"He was particularly curious in the construction of clocks and watches; and having found, after repeated trials, that he could not

* See "Memorials of the Order of the Garter," etc. By G. F. Beltz, *Lancaster Herald*. London, 1841. The various suggestions and theories of Ashmole and others, with the evidence, are carefully reviewed in the preface. Recent and remarkable as was the adoption of the Tricolor, its origin is already involved in doubt.

* "Briefe von Alexander von Humboldt an Varnhagen von Ense," etc. 3rd edit., p. 57. "We have read books called Histories of England under the reign of George II., in which the rise of Methodism is not even mentioned."—(Macaulay.)

† See Humboldt's "Géographie du Nouveau Continent," vol. i.

bring any two of them to go exactly alike, he reflected, it is said, with a mixture of surprise as well as regret, on his own folly, in having bestowed so much timo and labor on the mere vain attempt of bringing mankind to a precise uniformity of sentiment concerning the profound and mysterious doctrines of religion." *

Mr. Stirling and M. Mignet are at issue as to the credibility of the alleged obsequies; and although they both state the predilection of the retired emperor for mechanics, it is very unlikely that the variations in his clocks led him to any reflection bordering on toleration or liberality; for almost with his dying breath he enjoined the persecution of heretics; and we learn from Mr. Stirling, that "In taking part in the early religious troubles of his reign, it was ever his regret that he did not put Luther to death when he had him in his power." At all events, the tradition may have suggested Pope's couplet, although he has given a different turn to the thought—

"'Tis with our judgments as our watches; none
Go just alike, yet each believes his own."

It is related of Raleigh, that, having vainly endeavored to ascertain the rights of a quarrel that fell out beneath his window, he exclaimed against his own folly in endeavoring to write the true history of the world. We have found no authority for this anecdote, and the famous one of his cloak first occurs in Fuller's "Worthies." When Sir Robert Walpole, on being asked what he would have read to him, replied: "Not history, for that I know to be false," he was probably thinking less of the difficulty that struck Raleigh, than of the presumption of some writers of his day, in pretending to be at home in the councils of princes, and to be perfectly acquainted with the hidden springs of his own measures or policy.

In France, writers of eminence have openly professed their indifference to strict accuracy. Besides the memorable *Mon siège est fait* of Vertot, we find Voltaire, on being asked where he had discovered a startling fact, replying, "Nowhere; it is a frolic (*espiègrie*) of my imagination." The frolic was, that, when the French became masters of Constantinople in 1204, they danced with the women in the sanctuary of the church of Sainte Sophia. Some modern French historians have not disdained to follow in his track.

"Like old Voltaire, who placed his greatest glory
In cooking up an entertaining story,
Who laughed at Truth whene'er his simple
tongue
Would snatch amusement from a tale or song."

We should like to know whether M. Lamartine had any warrant beyond his own rich imagination for these passages in his description of the battle of Waterloo:—

"He (Wellington) gallops towards two of his dragoon regiments drawn up on the edge of the ridge. He has the curbs of the bridles taken off, so that the animal, carried away by the descent and the mass, without the hand of the rider being able even involuntarily to check it, may throw itself with an irresistible rush and weight on the French cavalry—a desperate manœuvre, worthy of the Numidians against the Romans, and which the size and impetuosity of the British horse rendered more desperate still. He has brandy served out to the riders to intoxicate the man with fire, whilst the trumpet intoxicates the horse, and he himself hurls them, at full speed, on the slopes of Mont St. Jean." *

A little farther on, we find the duke on his eighth and wounded horse, although it is notorious that Copenhagen carried him freshly through the entire battle; and towards the end—

"He sends from rank to rank to his intrepid Scotch the order to let themselves be approached without firing, to pierce the breasts of the horses with the point of the bayonet, to slip even under the feet of the animals, and to rip them up (*éventrer*) with the short and broad sword of these children of the North. The Scotch obey, and themselves on foot charge our regiments of horse."

M. de Lamartine is a poet, and may have imported in his own despite a flight or two of original invention into his prose. But M. Thiers is a grave statesman as well as a brilliant and picturesque narrator. His information is derived principally, almost exclusively, from French sources. His point of view is essentially and invariably French, and his works afford an unimpeachable test of the kind of history most esteemed by his

* Robertson's "Charles the Fifth," book xii. Compare Stirling's "Cloister Life of the Emperor," and Mignet's "Charles Quint." Sir Condy's rehearsal of his own wake in "Castle Rackrent" is said to be founded upon fact.

* "Histoire de la Restauration," vol. iv. p 246.

countrymen. The scene is the channel before Boulogne, where, on the 26th August, 1804, a squadron of French gunboats were engaged against an English squadron of frigates and other vessels.

"The emperor, who was in his barge (*canot*) with Admiral Brieux, the Ministers of War and Marine, and several marshals, dashed into the middle of the gunboats engaged, and, to set them an example, had himself steered right upon the frigate, which was advancing at full sail. He knew that the soldiers and sailors, admirers of his audacity on land, sometimes asked one another whether he would be equally audacious at sea. He wished to edify them on this point, and to accustom them to brave recklessly the large vessels of the enemy. He had his barge taken far in advance of the French line, and *as near as possible to the frigate*. The frigate, seeing the imperial flag flying in the barge, and guessing perhaps its precious cargo, had reserved its fire. The Minister of Marine, trembling for the result to the emperor of such a bravado, tried to throw himself upon the bar of the rudder to change the direction; but an imperious gesture of Napoleon stopped the movement of the minister, and they continued their course towards the frigate. Napoleon was watching it, glass in hand, when all of a sudden it discharged its reserved broadside, and covered with its projectiles the boat which carried Cæsar and his fortune. *No one was wounded, and they were quit for the splashing of the shot.* All the French vessels, witnesses of this scene, had advanced as fast as they could to sustain the fire, and to cover, by passing, the barge of the emperor. The English division, assailed in its turn by a hail of balls and grape, began to retrograde little by little. It was pursued, but it returned anew, tacking towards the land. During this interval a second division of gunboats, commanded by Captain Pevrieu, had raised anchor and borne down upon the enemy. Very soon the frigate, much damaged and steering with difficulty, was obliged to gain the open sea. The corvettes followed this movement of retreat, several much shattered, and the cutter so riddled that it was seen to go down. Napoleon quitted Boulogne enchanted with the combat in which he had taken part, the rather that the secret intelligence coming from the coast of England gave him the most satisfactory details on the moral and material effect this combat had produced." *

According to the English version, the damage to our ships arose from their pursuing the French under the fire of the batteries. But the internal evidence of the narrative is enough. By way of *pendant* to Napoleon attacking an English frigate in his barge, M. Thiers should reproduce, as the representation of an historical fact, the picture, once in high favor for snuff-boxes, of a line of English soldiers recoiling from a wounded French grenadier, who waves his sword with one knee upon the ground. Beyle (Stendhal), who was with the French army during the whole of the Russian campaign of 1812, ridicules the notion of speeches on battle-fields, and declares that he once saw a French general lead a gallant charge with a piece of coarse ribaldry; adding, that it answered the purpose perfectly well. It is certain that most of those reported by historians were never made at all. The Duke of Wellington did not say "Up, guards, and at them," at Waterloo; he never took refuge in a square; and his "What will they say in England if we are beat?" was addressed to some officers of his staff, not to a shattered regiment. The best of his biographers, the chaplain-general, relates that, in the affair of the 11th December, 1813, the duke rode up to the 85th regiment, and said, in his (the subaltern's) hearing, "You must keep your ground, my lads, for there is nothing behind you."

"Follow my white plume," the traditional rallying cry of Henry IV., is quite consistent with Brantome's description of him at Coutras, "with long and great plumes, floating well, saying to his people, *Ostez-vous devant moy, ne m'offusquez pas, car je veux paroistre.*" The noble speech given to Henri de la Roche Jaquelcin is too finished and antithetical for the unpretending character of the man: *Si j'avance, suivez-moi: si je tombe, vengez-moi: si je recule, tuez-moi.* This young hero had no quality of a leader beyond chivalrous gallantry and courage, and looked to no higher reward for his services, if the Royalist cause had triumphed, than the command of a regiment of hussars. The real hero of the Vendean insurrection was the Marquis de Lescure. His widow married Henri's brother before the publica-

* "Histoire du Consulat et de l'Empire," vol. v. p. 229. Compare James' "Naval History," vol. iii. p. 333. This writer deduces from the affair that the gunboats could not face the cruisers, adding, "None knew this better than Napoleon. The affair of 25th August, of which he had *unintentionally* been an eye-witness, convinced him.

tion of her memoirs, and thus the name of La Roche Jaquelein has become imperishably associated with the most brilliant episode of the Revolution.

Voltaire makes Condé throw his baton of command over the enemies' palisades at Fribourg. Other accounts say "his marshal's baton." He was not a marshal; he did not carry a baton; and what he threw was his cane. A finer trait is told of Douglas, who, on his way to the Holy Land with Bruce's heart, took part with the Spaniards against the Moors, and lost his life in a skirmish:—

"When he found the enemy press thick round him, he took from his neck the Bruce's heart, and speaking to it as he would have done to the king had he been alive, he said, 'Pass first in fight as thou wert wont to do, and Douglas will follow thee or die.' He then threw the king's heart among the enemy, and rushing forward to the place where it fell, was slain. His body was found lying above the silver case." *

An attentive bystander reports a very sensible speech as made by Condé at Lens. "My friends, take courage; we cannot help fighting to-day; it will be useless to draw back; for I promise you, that, brave men or cowards, all shall fight, the former with good-will, the latter perforce." The authenticity of the brief dialogue between the spokesmen of the French and English Guards at Fontenoy is now generally allowed. Lord Charles Hay, hat in hand, steps forward, and says with a bow, "Gentlemen of the French Guards, fire." M. d'Auteroches advances to meet him, and saluting him with the sword, says, "Monsieur, we never fire first; do you fire." It is a question whether, with the musketry of 1745, the first fire was an advantage or the contrary.†

Lord Macaulay tells an anecdote of Michael Godfrey, the Deputy-Governor of the Bank of England, who was standing near King William and under fire at the siege of Namur. "Mr. Godfrey," said William, "you ought not to run these hazards; you are not a soldier; you can be of no use to us here." "Sir," answered Godfrey, "I run no more hazard than your majesty." "Not so," said William; "I am where it is my duty to be, and I may without presumption commit my life to God's keeping; but you—" While they were talking a cannon-ball from the ramparts laid Godfrey dead at the king's feet. *

When Charles XII. of Sweden was entering his barge to lead the attack on Copenhagen he found the French ambassador at his side. "Monsieur," he said, "you have no business with the Danes: you will go no further, if you please." "Sire," replied the Comte de Guiscard, "the king, my master, has ordered me to remain near your majesty. I flatter myself you will not banish me to-day from your court, which has never been so brilliant." So saying, he gave his hand to the king, who leaped into the barge, followed by Count Piper and the ambassador.

The dying words of Wolfe are well known, and well authenticated. On hearing an officer exclaim, "See how they run," he eagerly raised himself on his elbow, and asked, "Who run?" "The enemy," answered the officer; "they give way in all directions." "Then God be praised," said Wolfe, after a short pause; "I shall die happy." † His antagonist, the Marquis of Montcalm, received a mortal wound whilst endeavoring to rally his men, and expired the next day. When told that his end was approaching, he answered, "So much the better; I shall not live then to see the surrender of Quebec."

Napoleon stated at St. Helena that Desaix fell dead at Marengo without a word. Thiers makes him say to Boudet, his chief of division, "Hide my death, for it might dishearten the troops"—the dying order of the Constable Bourbon at the taking of Rome. The speech ordinarily given to Desaix, and

* "Tales of a Grandfather," vol. i. c. xi.

† The prowess of Dr. Adam Ferguson, the chaplain of the 42d Highlanders, or Black Watch, who charged with his men at the battle of Fontenoy, in flagrant defiance of the prohibition of his colonel, is related "Quart. Rev.," vol. xxxvi., p. 196. He was very young at the time, and the Celtic blood is hot; but it is possible that he acted upon the same principle as another chaplain of Highlanders (mentioned by Dr. Carlyle), who accompanied his regiment in America in a very dangerous charge, not from love of fighting, but because the soldiers were young and had never been in action before, and he thought that his presence (being the only officer well known to them) would give them confidence.

* Macaulay's "History," vol. iv. p. 589.

† "History of England, from the Peace of Utrecht." By Earl Stanhope (Lord Mahon), vol. iv. ch. xxxv. His lordship has rescued two other curious and now familiar anecdotes of Wolfe from oblivion or neglect.

inscribed on his monument, is confessedly a fiction. What passed between him and Napoleon, when they first met upon the field, has been differently related. One version is that Desaix exclaimed, "The battle is lost!" and that Napoleon replied, "No; it is won: advance directly." That of M. Thiers is, that a circle was hastily formed round the two generals, and a council of war held, in which the majority were for retreating. The First Consul was not of this opinion, and earnestly pressed Desaix for his, who then, looking at his watch, said, "Yes, the battle is lost; but it is only three o'clock; there is still time enough to gain one." Here again a kind of parallel is suggested. The Baron de Sirot, who commanded the French reserve at Recroy, was told that the battle was lost. "No, no!" he exclaimed, "it is not lost; for Sirot and his companions have not yet fought." * Desaix, it will be remembered, had turned back without waiting for orders on hearing the firing; and M. Thiers thinks that if Grouchy had done the same at Waterloo, the current of the world's history might have been reversed. He is welcome to think so; but the Hero of a Hundred Fights thought differently. A drawn battle and a short respite were the very utmost Grouchy's timely arrival could have gained for his imperial master.

All the flashes of instinctive heroism and prescient thirst of glory which are commonly ascribed to Nelson are indisputable. It has been vaguely rumored, indeed, that the signal originally proposed by him at Trafalgar was, "*Nelson* expects every man to do his duty," and that *England* was substituted at the suggestion of Hardy or Blackwood. According to the authentic narrative of Southey, Nelson asked Captain Blackwood if he did not think there was a signal wanting. "Blackwood made answer that he thought the whole fleet seemed very clearly to understand what they were about. The words were scarcely spoken before that signal was made which will be remembered as long as the language or even the memory of England shall endure." Nelson's last intelligible words were, "Thank God, I have done my duty."

Dying words and speeches present an ample field for the invective faculties of biographers and historians. It is reported that Louis XIV.'s to Madame de Maintenon were, "We shall soon meet again;" and that she murmured, "A pleasant rendezvous he is giving me; that man never loved any one but himself." Of Talleyrand M. Louis Blanc relates, "When the Abbé Dupanloup repeated to him the words of the Archbishop of Paris, "I would give my life for M. de Talleyrand," he replied, "He might make a better use of it," and expired.

Do such narratives command implicit faith? Did Goethe die calling for light? or Frederic Schlegel with *aber* (*but*) in his mouth? or Rabelais exclaiming, "Drop the curtain; the farce is played out"? or Chesterfield just after telling the servant, with characteristic politeness, "Give Dayrolles a chair"? or Locke remarking to Mrs. Masham, "Life is a poor vanity"? Did the expiring Addison call the young Earl of Warwick to his bedside that he might learn "how a Christian could die"? Was Pitt's heart broken by Austerlitz, and were the last words he uttered, "My country, O my country"? * George Rose, who had access to the best information, says they were; and says also that the news of the armistice after the battle of Austerlitz drove Pitt's gout from the extremities to the stomach. But the Duke of Wellington, who met Pitt at Stanmore Priory shortly after the arrival of the news, always maintained that Pitt's spirit was not by any means broken by the disappointment. On plausible grounds it has been alleged that Canning's last illness was aggravated by suppressed anger at one of Lord Grey's attacks; that he had serious thoughts of being called up to the House of Peers to answer it; and that his dying words were, "Give me time! give me time!" Lord Chatham made his son read to him, a day or two before he died, the passage of Pope's "Homer" describing the death of Hector, and when he had done, said, "Read it again."

The peculiar taste and tendencies of our neighbors across the Channel have produced a plentiful crop of melodramatic scenes, with words to match. Their revolutionary annals abound in them; many true, many apocryphal, and not a few exaggerated or

* "The Life of Condé." By Earl Stanhope (Lord Mahon), p. 30.

* We have reason to believe that the precise account of what passed at Pitt's death-bed, including his last words, will be given in Earl Stanhope's forthcoming work.

false. The crew of *Le Vengeur*, instead of going down with the cry of *Vive la République*, shrieked for help, and many were saved in English boats. The bombastic phrase, *La Garde meurt et ne se rend pas*, attributed to Cambronne, who was made prisoner at Waterloo, was vehemently denied by him; and when, notwithstanding his denial, the town of Nantes was authorized by royal ordinance to inscribe it on his statue, the sons of General Michel laid formal claim to it for their father. It was invented by Rougemont, a prolific author of *mots*, two days after the battle, in the *Indépendant*. *

M. Beugnot, provisional Minister of the Interior, was the author of the eminently successful hit in the Comte d'Artois' address at the Restoration: "Plus de divisions; la paix et la France! Je la revois, et rien n'y est changé, si ce n'est qu'il s'y trouve un Français de plus." His royal highness, who had extemporized a few confused sentences, was as much surprised as any one on reading a neat little speech comprising these words in the *Moniteur*. On his exclaiming, "But I never said it," he was told that there was an imperative necessity for his having said it; and it became history. †

M. Seguier denied, *La cour rend des arrêts et non pas des services*. M. de Salvandy claimed, *C'est und fête Napolitaine, Monseigneur; nous dansons sur un volcan*—addressed to the Duke of Orleans (Louis Philippe) at a ball given to the King of Naples on the eve of the Revolution of July.

It has been the fashion of late years in France to depreciate the capacity and the wit of Talleyrand, in forgetfulness that, if the good sayings of others had been frequently lent to him, *on ne prête qu'aux riches*. M. Fournier asserts, on the written authority of Talleyrand's brother, that the only breviary used by the ex-bishop was *L'improvisateur Français*, a compilation of anecdotes and *bon-mots*, in twenty-one duodecimo volumes. Whenever a good thing was wandering about in search of a parent, he adopted it,—amongst others, *C'est le commencement de la fin*. We have heard that the theory of royal shaving, already mentioned, was Napoleon's; and the remark on the emigrants, that they had neither learnt nor forgotten any thing, has been found almost verbatim in a letter from the Chevalier de Panat to Mallett du Pan from London in 1796. When Harel wished to put a joke or witticism into circulation, he was in the habit of connecting it with some celebrated name, on the chance of reclaiming it if it took—

> "He cast off his *jokes* as a huntsman his pack,
> For he knew when he pleased he could whistle them back."

Thus he assigned to Talleyrand in the "Nain Jaune" the phrase: "Speech was given to man to disguise his thoughts." In one of Voltaire's dialogues, the capon says of men: "They only use thought to sanction their injustice, and only employ words to disguise their thoughts." There is also a couplet by Young:—

> "When Nature's end of language is disguised,
> And men talk only to conceal their mind."

The germ of the conceit has been discovered in one of South's Sermon; and Mr. Forster puts in a claim for Goldsmith on the strength of Jack Spindle's remark in the "Citizen of the World," that the true use of speech is not so much to express our wants as to conceal them. He also claims for Goldsmith a well-known joke, attributed to Sheridan on his son's remarking that he would descend a coal-pit for the pleasure of saying that he had done so, and discovers the embryo of Lord Macaulay's New Zealander in a letter from Walpole to Sir Horace Mann: "At last some curious traveller from Lima will visit England, and give a description of the ruins of St. Paul, like the editions of Balbec and Palmyra." * The New Zealander first came upon the stage in 1840, in a review of Ranke's "History of the Popes;" but the same image in a less compact shape was employed by Lord Ma-

* When pressed by a pretty woman to repeat the phrase he really did use, he replied, "Ma foi, madame, je ne sais pas au juste ce que j'ai dit à l'officier Anglais qui me criait de me rendre; mais ce qui est certain est qu'il comprenait le Français, et qu'il m'a répondu *mange*."

† Sir Henry Bulwer adopts a somewhat different version in his "France, Social, Literary, and Political," vol. i. p. 181. His chapter on Wit is one of the best in a book which is of much deeper significance than its light and pleasant tone has led ordinary readers to perceive.

* Forster's "Life of Goldsmith." Second edition. Vol. i. p. 341. The remark on the true use of speech being to conceal our wants also occurs in "The Bee," No. 8.

caulay in 1824, in the concluding paragraph of a review of Mitford's "Greece."*

Talleyrand had frequently the adroitness or good luck to get credit for saying of others what was said against himself. Thus, *Qui ne l'adorerait? Il est si vicieux*—was said by Montrond of him, not by him of Montrond. Again, when he told a squinting politician, who asked how things were going on, *A travers, comme vous voyez*, he can hardly have forgotten "the frequent inkstand whizzing past his ear," with the accompaniment of *Vil émigré, tu n'as pas le sens plus droit que le pied.*† Both Rogers and Lord Brougham give him the interrogatory to the sick or dying man, who cried out that he was suffering the torments of the damned, "*Déjà?*" M. Louis Blanc says:—

"It is also related—and it is by priests that the fact, improbable as it is, has been silently propagated—that the king (Louis Philippe) having asked M. de Talleyrand if he suffered, and the latter having answered, 'Yes, like the damned,' Louis Philippe murmured this word, *Déjà?*—a word that the dying man heard, and which he revenged forthwith by giving to one of the persons about him secret and terrible indications."

The repartee will be found in one of Le Brun's Epigrams, and has been attributed to (amongst others) the confessor of the Abbé de Ternay and to the physician of De Retz. The French have a perfect frenzy for *mots*. No event is complete without one, bad, good, or indifferent. When Armand Carrel and Emile Girardin had taken their ground, and the seconds were loading the pistols, Carrel says to Girardin, "If the fates are against me, monsieur, and you write my biography, it will be honorable, wont it—that is to say, true?" "Yes, monsieur," replied Girardin. This is related by M. Louis Blanc ("Histoire des Dix Ans") with apparent unconsciousness of its extreme discourtesy or absurdity. "If you kill me, you wont write what is false of me?" "No."

On the fate of Louis Seize being put to the vote, Siéyes provoked by the urbanity of some of his colleagues, is reported to have exclaimed *La Mort—sans phrase*. He always denied the *sans phrase*, and Lord Brougham proves from the *Moniteur* that he was guiltless of it. M. Mignet relates of him, that, on being asked what he did during the Reign of Terror, he made answer, "*J'ai vécu*"—"I lived." This also he indignantly denied. Victor Hugo (in "Marion de Lorme") has versified another similar *mot* of the period:—

"*Le Roi à l'Angely.* Pourquoi vis-tu?
L'Angely. Je vis par curiosité."

During the same epoch Siéyes, in correcting the proof-sheets of a pamphlet in defence of his political conduct, read, "I have *abjured* the republic," printed by mistake for *adjured!* "Wretch!" he exclaimed to the printer, "do you wish to send me to the guillotine?"

As regards the famous invocation to Louis XVI. on the scaffold, *Fils de Saint Louis, montez au ciel*, the Abbé Edgeworth frankly avowed to Lord Holland, who questioned him on the subject, that he had no recollection of having said it. It was invented for him, on the evening of the execution, by the editor of a newspaper.* During more than forty years no one dreamed of questioning Mirabeau's apostrophe to M. de Dreux Brezé. "Go tell your master that we are here by the will of the people, and that we will not depart unless driven out by bayonets" ("*et que nous n'en sortirons que par la force des bayonnettes*"). On the 10th March, 1833, M. Villemain having pointedly referred to it in the Chamber of Peers, the Marquis de Dreux Brezé rose and said:—

"My father was sent to demand the dissolution of the National Assembly. He entered with his hat on, as was his duty, speaking in the king's name. This offended the assembly, already in an agitated state. My father, resorting to an expression which I do not wish to recall, replied that he should remain covered, since he spoke in the king's name. Mirabeau did not say, *Go, tell your master*. I appeal to all who were in the assembly, and who may happen to be present now. Such language would not have been tolerated. Mirabeau said to my father, 'We are assembled by the national will; we will

* "When travellers from some distant region shall in vain labor to decipher on some mouldering pedestal the name of our proudest chief, shall hear savage hymns chaunted over some misshapen idol over the ruined dome of our proudest temple."—*Miscellaneous Works*, vol. i. p. 188.

† Words addressed by Rewbell to Talleyrand at the Council Board, quoted in a note to Canning's "New Morality," in the "Antijacobin."

* Mr. Macknight quotes it with implicit faith in its authenticity.—*History of the Life and Times of Edmund Burke*, vol. iii. p. 505.

only go out by force (*nous n'en sortirons que par la force*).' I ask M. de Montlosier if that is correct (M. de Montlosier gave a sign of assent). My father replied to M. Bailly, 'I can recognize in M. Mirabeau only the deputy of the bailiwick of Aix, and not the organ of the National Assembly.' The tumult increased; one man against five hundred is always the weakest. My father withdrew. Such is the truth in all its exactness." *

Another of Mirabeau's grand oratorical effects (April 12, 1790) was based upon a plagiarism and a fable: "I see from this window, from which was fired the fatal arquebuss which gave the signal for the Massacre of St. Bartholomew." † He stole the allusion from Volney. Charles the Ninth did not fire from the window in question, if he fired on the Huguenots at all.

Horne Tooke is believed to have written the speech inscribed on the pedestal of Beckford's statue at Guildhall, purporting to be the reply extemporized by the spirited magistrate to George the Third. He himself had no distinct recollection of the precise words; and contemporary accounts differ whether his tone and manner were becoming or unbecoming the occasion.

It is well known that the great commoner's celebrated reply to Horace Walpole (the elder), beginning, "The atrocious crime of being a young man," is the composition of Dr. Johnson, who was not even present when the actual reply was spoken. Only four complete speeches of Lord Chatham's have been reported with any approach to fidelity —two by Francis and two by Boyd.

When the great Duke of Marlborough was asked his authority for an historical statement, he replied, "Shakspeare; the only History of England I ever read." Lord Campbell, whose reading is not so limited, remarks that Shakspeare, although careless about dates, is scrupulously accurate about facts, "insomuch that our notions of the Plantagenet reigns are drawn from him rather than from Hollinshed, Rapin, or Hume." Accordingly, he requires us to place implicit faith in the immortal bard's version of the affair between the chief justice and Prince Hal, even to the order or request put into the prince's mouth on his accession to the throne:—

> "Therefore still bear the balance and the sword."

"I shall prove to demonstration," says Lord Campbell, "that Sir William Gascoigne survived Henry IV. several years, and actually filled the office of chief justice of the king's bench under Henry the Fifth." "The two records to which reference has been already made," says Mr. Foss in his "Lives of the Chief Justices," "contain such conclusive proof that Sir William Gascoigne was not re-appointed to his place as chief justice, that it seems impossible that any one can maintain the contrary." In one of these, an issue roll of July, 1413 (four months after the accession of Henry V.), Gascoigne is described as "late chief justice of the bench of Lord Henry, father of the present king," and the date of his successor's appointment turns out to be March 29, 1413, just eight days after Henry the Fifth's accession; from which Mr. Foss infers his especial eagerness to supersede his father's old and faithful servant. Both Lord Campbell and Mr. Foss are convinced of the occurrence of the main incidents, the blow or insult and the committal. But the story did not appear in print till 1534. Hankford, Hody, and Matcham have been started as candidates for the honor of this judicial exploit by writers of respectability; and the late Mr. Henry Drummond proves from an ancient chronicle that identically the same story was told of Edward the Second (while Prince of Wales) and the chief justice of Edward the First.

Whether Richard the Second was slain by Sir Pierce of Exton, or starved to death in Pontefrac Castle, is still a question. Zealous antiquaries have doubted whether he died there at all. Halliwell, after alluding to the authorities, remarks: "Notwithstanding this exposure (of the body) the story afterwards prevailed, and is related by Hector Boece, that Richard escaped to Scotland, where he lived a religious life, and was buried at Stirling. The probability is that the real history of Richard's death will never be unravelled." *

Rabelais has co-operated with Shakspeare in extending the belief that Clarence was

* *Moniteur*, March 11, 1833. In Bailly's "Memoirs," published in 1804, there is a third version.

† The speech is somewhat differently reported by Thiers, "Révolution Française," vol. i. p. 148.

* Halliwell's "Shakspeare," vol. ix. p. 220.

drowned in a butt of Malmsey at his own special instance and request; and in a deservedly popular compilation, the precise manner of immersion is brought vividly before the mind's eye of the rising generation by a clever wood-cut.* Mr. Bayley, in his "History of the Tower," can suggest no better foundation for the story than the well-known fondness of Clarence for Malmsey. "Whoever," says Walpole, in his "Historic Doubts," "can believe that a butt of wine was the engine of his death, may believe that Richard (the Third) helped him into it, and kept him down till he was suffocated."

Well might Dryden say that "a falsehood once received from a famed writer becomes traditional to posterity." Learned antiquaries will labor in vain to clear the memory of Sir John Falstolfe, identified with Falstaff, from the imputation of cowardice, yet there is strong evidence to show that he was rather hastily substituted for Sir John Oldcastle, whose family remonstrated against the slur cast on their progenitor in "Henry the Fourth;" and that, instead of running away (as stated in the first part of "Henry the Fourth") at the battle of Patay, Falstolfe did his devoir bravely.†

Shakspeare's Joan of Arc is a mere embodiment of English prejudice; yet it is not much farther from the truth than Schiller's transcendental and exquisitely poetical character of the maid. The German dramatist has also idealized Don Carlos to an extent that renders recognition difficult; and he has flung a halo round William Tell which will cling to the name while Switzerland is a country or patriotism any better than a name. Yet just one hundred years ago (in 1760) the eldest son of Haller undertook to prove that the legend, in its main features, is the revival or imitation of a Danish one, to be found in Saxo Grammaticus. The canton of Uri, to which Tell belonged, ordered the book to be publicly burnt, and appealed to the other cantons to co-operate in its suppression—thereby giving additional interest and vitality to the question, which has been at length pretty well exhausted by German writers. The upshot is, that the episode of the apple is regulated to the domain of the fable; and that Tell himself is grudgingly allowed a commonplace share in the exploits of the early Swiss patriots. Strange to say, his name is not mentioned by any contemporary chronicler of the struggle for independence.*

In a former number we intimated an opinion that the story of Amy Robsart, as told in "Kenilworth," "is for the most part faithful." A pamphlet has since appeared in which its faithfulness is plausibly impugned;† and another opinion incidentally hazarded by us in favor of a romantic story has been perseveringly and ingeniously assailed by Mr. Charles Long; who has not yet succeeded in convincing us that "Wild Darell" was unjustly suspected, or that Chief Justice Popham came honestly by the old mansion and wide domains of Littlecote.

Popular faith is ample justification for either poet or painter in the selection of a subject; and for this very reason we must be on our guard against the prevalent habit of confounding the impressions made by artistic skill or creative genius with facts. We cannot believe that Mazarin continued to his last gasp surrounded by a gay bevy of ladies and gallants, flirting and gambling, as represented in a popular engraving; and a double *alibi* flings a cold shade of scepticism over "The last Moments of Leonardo da Vinci, expiring at Fontainebleau in the arms of Francis the First," as a striking picture in the Louvre was described in the catalogue. Sir A. Callcott's picture of *Milton and his Daughters*, one of whom holds a pen as if writing to his dictation, is in open defiance of Dr. Johnson's statement that the daughters were never taught to write.

Until three or four years ago a portrait at Holland House was prescriptively reverenced as a speaking likeness of Addison, and a bust was designed after it by a distinguished

* "Stories selected from the History of England, from the Conquest to the Revolution, for children." Fifteenth edition, illustrated with twenty four wood-cuts. (By the late Right Hon. J. W. Croker.) London, [illegible] "Tales of a Grandfather" was suggested by this book.

† "Journal of the British Archæological Association," vol. xiv. pp. 230–236. The paper was contributed by Mr. Pettigrew.

* "Die Sage von dem Schuss des Tell. Eine historisch-kritische Abhandlung, von Dr. Julius Ludwig Ideler." Berlin, 1836. "Die Sage vom Tell aufs neue kritisch untersucht, von Dr. Ludwig Häusser. Eine von der philosophischen Facultät der Universität Heidelberg gekronte Preisschrift." Heidelberg, 1840. Another learned German, Palacky, in his "History of Bohemia," has placed Zisca's skin in the same category with Tell's apple.

† An inquiry into the particulars connected with the death of Amy Robsart (Lady Dudley)," etc. By T. J. Pettigrew, F.R.S., etc. London, 1859.

sculptor. It turns out to be the copy of a portrait of Sir Andrew Fountayne, still in the possession of his descendant, who has miniatures placing the identity beyond a doubt.

Each branch of the Fine Arts has contributed its quota to the roll of unexpected successes and sudden bounds into celebrity. There is the story of Poussin impatiently dashing his sponge against his canvas, and producing the precise effect (the foam on a horse's mouth) which he had been long and vainly laboring for; and there is a similar one told of Haydn, the musical composer, when required to imitate a storm at sea. "He kept trying all sorts of passages, ran up and down the scale, and exhausted his ingenuity in heaping together chromatic intervals and strange discords. Still Curtz (the author of the *libretto*) was not satisfied. At last the musician, out of all patience, extended his hands to the two extremities of the keys, and, bringing them rapidly together, exclaimed, "The deuce take the tempest; I can make nothing of it." "That is the very thing," exclaimed Curtz, delighted with the *truth* of the representation." * Neither Haydn nor Curtz, adds the author from whom we quote, had ever seen the sea.

The touching incident of Chantrey working for Rogers as a journeyman cabinet-maker at five shillings a day was related by himself; and a mould for butter or jelly was the work which first attracted notice to the genius of Canova.

The romance of the Bar diminishes apace before the severe eye of criticism. Erskin went on telling everybody, till he probably believed what he was telling, that his fame and fortune were established by his speech for Captain Baillie, made a few days after he had assumed the gown. "That night," were his words to Rogers, "I went home and saluted my wife, with sixty-five retaining fees in my pocket." Retaining fees are paid to the clerk at chambers, and the alleged number is preposterous. At a subsequent period we find him hurrying to his friend Reynolds with two bank-notes for £500 each, his fee in the Keppel case, and exclaiming, "*Violà* the nonsuit of Cowbeef." Cowbeef must have been already nonsuited if the sixty-five retaining fees, or half of them, had been paid.

Equally untenable is the notion that Lord Mansfield dashed into practice by his speech

* Hogarth's "Musical History," vol. i. p. 293.

in *Cibber* v. *Sloper*, in reference to which he is reported to have said that he never knew the difference between no professional income and three thousand a year. From the printed reports of the trial it is clear that Serjeant Eyre, instead of being seized with a fit, and so giving Murray his opportunity, made a long speech, and that Murray was the fourth counsel in the cause. It was tried in Dec. 1738, the year after the publication of Pope's couplet—

"Blest as thou art with all the power of words,
So known, so honored in the House of Lords,"

rendered more memorable by Cibber's parody—

"Persuasion tips his tongue whene'er he talks;
And he has chambers in the King's Bench Walks."

In these and most other instances of the kind, it has been truly said, *the* speech was a stepping-stone, not the key-stone. Patient industry and honest self-devotion to the duties of a profession are the main elements of success.

There is no valid ground for disputing the "*Anche io sono pittore*" ("I, too, am a painter") of Correggio on seeing a picture by Raphael, although it has been given to others; nor the "*E pur se muove*" ("It moves notwithstanding") of Galileo, which he muttered as he rose from the kneeling posture in which he had been sentenced by the Inquisition to recant his theory of the earth's motion. Lord Brougham, M. Biot, and other admirers of this great man, however, thinking the story derogatory to him, have urged the want of direct evidence on the point. "I could prove by a very curious passage of Bulwer," says M. Fournier, "how Archimedes could not have said 'Give me a *point d'appui*, and with a lever I will move the world.' He was too great a mathematician for that." We are not informed where this very curious passage is to be found; and Archimedes asked for a place to stand on, not a fulcrum, nor did he specify the instrument to be employed. *

Sir David Brewster, in his excellent Life of Newton, says that neither Pemberton nor

* "Archimedes one day asserted to King Hiero, that with a given power he could move any given weight whatever; nay, it is said, from the confidence he had in his demonstrations, he ventured to affirm that if there were another earth besides this we inhabit, by going into that he would move this wherever he pleased."—Langhorne's *Plutarch*.

Whiston, who received from Newton himself the history of his first ideas of gravity, records the story of the falling apple. It was mentioned, however, to Voltaire by Catherine Barton, Newton's niece, and to Mr. Green by Mr. Martin Folkes, the president of the Royal Society. "*We saw the apple-tree in* 1814, *and brought away a portion of one of its roots.*" * The concluding remark reminds us of Washington Irving's hero, who boasted of having parried a musket bullet with a small sword, in proof of which he exhibited the sword a little bent in the hilt. The apple is supposed to have fallen in 1665.

Sometimes an invented pleasantry passes current for fact, like the asparagus and *point d'huile* of Fontenelle, invented by Voltaire as an illustration of how Fontenelle would have acted in such a contingency. One day, when Gibbon was paying his addresses to Mademoiselle Curchod (afterwards Madame Necker), she asked why he did not go down on his knees to her. "Because you would be obliged to ring for your footman to get me up again." This is the sole foundation for the story of his actually falling on his knees, and being unable to get up. There is another mode in which a mystification, or a joke, may create or perpetuate a serious error. Father Prout (Mahony) translated several of the "Irish Melodies" into Greek and Latin verse, and then jocularly insinuated a charge of plagiarism against the author. Moore was exceedingly annoyed, and remarked to a friend who made light of the trick: "This is all very well for you London critics; but, let me tell you, my reputation for originality has been gravely impeached in the provincial newspapers on the strength of these very imitations." Lauder's fraud imposed on Johnson, and greatly damaged Milton for a period. Diligent inquiry has brought home to a M. de Querlon the verses attributed to Mary Queen of Scots, beginning:—

> "Adieu, plaisant pays de France!
> Oh, ma patrie,
> La plus chérie,
> Qui as nourri ma jeune enfance," etc.

Cicero complained that funeral panegyrics had contributed to falsify the Roman annals, and *éloges* have done the same ill service to the French.

* "Life of Newton," vol. ii. p. 27, note.

Party malice has poisoned the streams of tradition, whilst carelessness, vanity, or the wanton love of mischief has troubled them. Sir Robert Walpole was accused of the worst cynicism of corruption on the strength of his alleged maxim: "All men have their price." What he really said was: "All *these* men have their price," alluding to the so-called "patriots" of the opposition. Many still believe Lord Plunket to have denounced history as an old almanac, although its real expressions notoriously were, that those who read history, like certain champions of intolerance, treat it as an old almanac. Torn from the context, Lord Lyndhurst's description of the Irish as "aliens in blood, language, and religion," sounds illiberal and impolitic. Taken with the context, it is merely a rhetorical admission and application of one of O'Connell's favorite topics for Repeal, when he wound up every speech by reminding his "hereditary bondsmen" that they had nothing in common with their Saxon and Protestant oppressors.

Hero worship pushed to extravagance, as it recently has been by one popular writer in particular, is quite as mischievous as the spirit of depreciation and incredulity. "The world knows nothing of its greatest men;" or, rather, the world is required to accept no proof of greatness but success. Voltaire illustrates the matter by three examples. "You carry Cæsar and his fortunes;" but if Cæsar had been drowned. "And so would I, were I Parmenio;" but if Alexander had been beaten. "Take these rags, and return them to me in the palace of St. James;" * but Charles Edward was beaten. Nelson's early boast, that some time or other he would have a gazette to himself, would be remembered (if remembered at all) as a mere display of youthful vanity, if he had been killed at the commencement of his career; and to all outward seeming, the ebullition of conceit is rarely distinguishable from the prompting of genius or the self-assertion of desert. In strange contrast to Nelson, Wel-

* "This is a fresh example of Voltaire's mode of dealing with facts. His shoes being very bad, Kingsburgh provided him with a new pair, and taking up the old ones said, 'I will faithfully keep them till you are safely settled at St. James'. I will then introduce myself by shaking them at you, to put you in mind of your night's entertainment and protection under my roof.' He smiled, and said, 'Be as good as your word.'"—*Account of the Escape of the Young Pretender*, first published in Boswell's "Johnson."

lington had so little of either quality, that, when a captain, he applied to the lord-lieutenant of Ireland (Lord Camden) for an Irish commissionership of customs, with the view of retiring from the army.

If the question is, how cherished and elevating impressions may be needlessly impaired, it should be observed that almost all heroes and men of genius suffer more or less whenever they are brought down from their pedestals and compelled to mingle with the crowd. "In the common occurrences of life," writes Wolfe, "I own I am not seen to advantage." Yet it is precisely in the common occurrences of life that Mr. Thackeray insists on exhibiting him; and the utmost skill of his accomplished painter of manners has been vainly exerted to obviate the depreciating effects. The impression conveyed in "The Virginians" of Washington, Franklin, Dr. Johnson, and Richardson, is equally unfavorable, and for the same reason. They are introduced doing what they did no better (if not worse) than ordinary mortals; and their images are brought home to us by peculiarities of dress and personal appearance, which were against all of them, except Washington. All accounts agree that Clive's person was ungraceful, that his harsh features were hardly redeemed from vulgar ugliness by their commanding expression, and that he was ridiculously fond of dress. In a letter to his friend Mr. Orme, he says: "Imprimis, what you can provide must be of the best and finest you can get for love or money: two hundred shirts—the wristbands worked; some of the ruffles worked with a border either in squares or points, and the rest plain; stocks, neckcloths, and handkerchiefs in proportion." Surely, the most consummate master of the prose epic, whose scenes, exclusively domestic, should be laid in England, could not meddle with the hero of Arcot and Plassey without degrading him. Or, supposing the novelist to deal only with the heroes of the tongue and pen, can he hope, by dint of versatility and comprehensiveness, to identify himself with all the leading spirits of one epoch after another so as to make each speak in character: to be Swift, Addison, Pope, Prior, Gay, Arbuthnot, and Bolingbroke, or Burke, Johnson, Franklin, Goldsmith, Fielding, and Richardson, by turns? If he cannot, however admirable his genius, he is doing unmixed harm, as well by lowering greatness in popular estimation, as by encouraging a school, which, it has been wittily said, bids fair to be to literature what Madame Tussaud is to art.*

Montaigne contends that, in treating of manners and motives, fabulous incidents, provided they be possible, serve the purpose as well as true. They may, if they are only wanted as illustrations; but to argue from them as from proofs, is to repudiate the inductive philosophy, and resort to the worst sort of *à priori* reasoning. Not long since an eminent naturalist surprised the public by a theory of canine instinct which placed it very nearly on a footing with the human understanding. This theory turned out to be based upon anecdotes of dogs, which some lads in one of the public offices had composed and forwarded to him, commonly as coming from country clergymen. Where is the difference in soundness between theories of animal nature based on such materials, and theories of human nature deduced from fictitious incidents, or, like some of Montesquieu's on government, from travellers' stories about Bantam or Japan? †

It may naturally be asked whether we have any new test of heroism or criterion of authenticity to propose? By what process is the gold to be separated from the dross? How are the genuine gems of history to be distinguished from the paste or glass imitations? Is there no spear of Ithuriel to compel counterfeits to resume their natural proportions by a touch? Or if Hotspur thought it an easy leap to "pluck bright honor from the pale-fac'd moon," can it be so very difficult to drag modest truth from the bottom of her well?

The archbishop of Dublin, on being asked to frame some canons for determining what evidence is to be received, declared it to be impossible, and added that "the full and complete accomplishment of such an object would confer on man the unattainable attribute of infallibility." ‡ His celebrated pam-

* Some thoughtful remarks bearing on this topic will be found in an Essay, by Sir E. Bulwer Lytton, on the Difference between Authors and their Works. It originally appeared in "The Student."

† "He said, 'The value of every story depends on its being true. A story is a picture of an individual, or of human nature in general: if it be false, it is a picture of nothing.'"—*Boswell's "Life of Johnson."*

‡ "Historic Doubts relative to Napoleon Bona-

phlet will afford little aid in the solution of the problem: for the existence of Napoleon Buonaparte was never denied in any quarter, and is affirmed by the complete concurrence of contemporary testimony. This cannot be predicated of any events or current of events with which it may be sought to establish a parallel; and it is little to the point to urge that many of the individual exploits attributed to Napoleon are as improbable as any contested period of history, sacred or profane. His grace must also admit that the invention of printing, with modern facilities of communication, have effected an entire change in the quality and amount of evidence which may be rationally accepted as the foundation of belief. A statement published to the whole civilized world, and remaining unchallenged, stands on a widely different footing from a statement set down by a monk in his chronicle, of which nothing was heard or known beyond the precincts of his convent until after the lapse of centuries. And what were his means of information when he wrote? Probably some vague rumor or floating gossip carried from place to place by pedlers and pilgrims. There is a game called Russian Scandal, which is played in this fashion: A. tells B. a brief narrative, which B. is to repeat to C., and C. to D., and so on. No one is to hear it told more than once, and each is to aim at scrupulous accuracy in the repetition. By the time the narrative has been transmitted from mouth to mouth six or seven times, it has commonly undergone a complete transformation. The ordinary result of the experiment will afford an apt illustration of the value of oral testimony in times when the marvellous had an especial attraction for all classes—

> "The flying rumors gather'd as they rolled;
> Scarce any tale was sooner heard than told,
> And all who told it added something new,
> And all who heard it made enlargements too;
> In every ear it spread, on every tongue it grew."

But we must be on our guard against assuming that events never took place at all, because there are material differences between the best accredited accounts of their occurrence. Lord Clarendon says that the royal standard was erected at Nottingham on the 25th of August, "about six of the clock of the evening of a very stormy and tempestuous day." Other contemporary writers name the 22nd as the date of this memorable event. An equal amount of discrepancy will appear on comparing the accounts given by Clarendon, Burnet, Woodrow, and Echard, of the condemnation and execution of Argyle in 1661. On what day, at what time of the day, and by whom, the intelligence of Napoleon's escape from Elba was first communicated to the members of the Vienna Congress, are doubtful questions to this hour. Yet that the standard was erected, that Argyle was executed, and that the news of Napoleon's escape did reach Vienna, will hardly be disputed by the most sceptical historians of posterity.

Again, the strangeness, or even absurdity, of an article of popular faith, is no ground for contemptuously rejecting it. "What need you study for new subjects?" says the citizen to the speaker of the prologue in Beaumont and Fletcher's "Knight of the Burning Pestle." "Why could you not be contented, as well as others, with the Legend of Whittington, or the Story of Queen Eleanor, with the rearing of London Bridge upon Woolsacks?" Why not indeed, when a learned antiquary, besides putting in a good word for Eleanor and the woolsacks, maintains, plausibly and pleasantly, the authenticity of the legend of Whittington, and most especially the part relating to the cat? *

Among the least defensible of Mr. Buckle's paradoxes is his argument, that historical evidence has been impaired by writing and printing, and that unaided tradition is the safest channel for truth. He deduces this startling conclusion from equally strange premises: 1, the degradation of the bards or minstrels, the professional guardians and repositories of legendary lore, when their occupation's gone; 2, the permanent form given to floating error when enbalmed in a book. But the second assumes that a story

parte." Ninth Edition. London, 1839. The various known modes of testing history are enumerated and discussed by Sir George C. Lewis, in "A Treatise on the Methods of Observation and Reasoning in Politics." In Two Volumes. 1842. Chap. 7.

* "The Model Merchant of the Middle Ages, exemplified in the Story of Whittington and his Cat: being an Attempt to rescue that interesting Story from the Region of Fable, and to place it in its proper Position in the legitimate History of the Country." By the Rev. Samuel Lysons, M.A., Rector of Rodmarton, Gloucestershire, etc., etc. London and Gloucester, 1860.

is cleared of falsehood by being handed down orally from age to age, as the purification of Thames water is promoted by length of pipe; and the first is like objecting to railroads that the old mail-coaches have been doomed to decay. It is rather against his theory that most of the disputed actions and phrases belong to the oral epoch; and fortunately no vital interest of any kind depends on their being recognized as facts.

One of Bubb Doddington's maxims was: "When you have made a good impression, go away." To all who dislike the illusion-destroying process, we should say: "When you have *got* a good impression, go away; but keep it for your own private delectation, and beware of generalizing on it till it has undergone the ordeal of inquiry." After all, the greatest sacrifice imposed upon us by inquirers like M. Fournier, is the occasional abandonment of an agreeable error, amply compensated by the habits of accuracy and impartiality which they enforce, without which there can be neither hope of improvement for the future nor confidence in the past. They have rather enhanced in value than depreciated the common stock of recorded or traditional wit, genius, virtue, and heroism; and if the course of treatment to which the reader is subjected sometimes resembles the sudden application of a shower-bath, his moral and intellectual system is equally braced and invigorated by the shock.

Queen Elizabeth's Verses, written while Prisoner at Woodstock.—A conjectural amendment of the verses cited by Hentzner in his *Itinerary*, is given by Walpole in his partial reprint, and is thence copied into Percy's *Reliques*. In comparing the latter verses with the original, I was much struck with the liberties which I think Walpole has taken, with what we may presume to have been a tolerably accurate transcript by Hentzner from the original writing in charcoal. To elucidate the matter, I subjoin three versions; the first, Walpole's *as quoted by Percy;* the second, Hentzner's (from the edition of 1617); the third, what I would suggest *may* have been the original:—

Walpole.

"Oh, fortune, how thy restlesse wavering state
Hath fraught with cares my troubled witt!
Witness this present prison, whither fate
Could beare me, and the joys I quit.
Thou causedest the guiltie to be losed
From bandes, wherein are innocents inclosed,
Causing the guiltles to be straik reserved,
And freeing those that death hath well deserved,
But by her envie can be nothing wroughte;
So God send to my foes all they have thoughte.
"Elizabethe, Prisonner."

Hentzner.

"Oh fortune, thy Wresting vvavring state
Hath fraught vvith Cares my troubled vvitt
Whose vvitnes this present prisonn late
Could beare where once vvas Ioy sloune quitt
Thou causedst the guiltie to be losed
From bandes vvhere innocents vvehre inclosed
And consed the guiltles to be reserued
And freed these that death had Vvell deserued
But allhereni, can be nothing Vvroughte
So God send to mÿ foës althey have tought.
"Elisabethe the Prisonner."

Probable Original.

"Oh Fortune! thy restless wavering state
Hath fraught with cares my troubled witt,
Whose witness, this present prisonn late
Could beare, where once was Joy slaine quite;
Thou causedest the guiltie to be losed
From bandes where innocents were inclosed,
And caused the guiltless to be reserved,
And freëd those that Death had well deserved;
But all-herein,—can be nothing wrought
So God send to my foes all they have thought."

I think that we must presume that Hentzner copied these verses as accurately as his small knowledge of the English language would allow; and we cannot conceive him writing the line, "*Could beare where once was Joy sloune quitt,*" if it had really stood "*Could beare me, and the joys I quitt;* the sense at the same time demanding that the words, "*whose witness,*" should be governed by the following, "could beare." Walpole has nipped in the bud the poetical and pathetic phrase, "where once was Joy slaine quite," for the sake of an apprehended improvement in the metre. I believe, however, that any of your readers who are versed in the English metres of this, and especially of an earlier period, will find but little fault with the flow of the amended verses. The words *fortune, witness,* and *guiltless,* must be read as trisyllables. It is hardly fair to attempt to cramp and alter verses of the middle of the sixteenth century, so to make them comfortable to our modern metre.

There seems to be an allusion in verses 3—8, to a *previous* occupation of the prison by some person who "Death had well deserved."

Query. Who was this released criminal?—*Notes and Queries.*

CHAPTER XII.

Mrs. Grant's father had been the youngest son of a Scotch peer, from whose ancient title the broad lands which gave it, had, in great part, fallen away. The pride of his family, however, had outlived its property; and it was sorely ruffled by his marriage, in early life, to the daughter of an Aberdeen merchant in the Baltic trade. When his noble kinsmen, judging him unworthy of his ancient pedigree, determined, in solemn conclave, to wash their hands of him and his Janet, Peter Muirhead, that stout Baltic trader, her father, offered to take into partnership his son-in-law, the Honorable Fergus M'Cauldie, upon the sole condition of his sinking the aristocratic prefix to his name. To this proposal Fergus acceded eagerly, and in the first heat of his anger against his relatives, threw the first syllable after the prefix. The invoice of the new firm were headed "Muirhead and Cauldie." Under that name it throve. He and his Janet knew no hard times, until the days of the Danish imbroglio and the bombardment of Copenhagen. That disaster did them irreparable damage; and the chief consolation they could find under its crushing was the fact that good Baillie Peter had not lived to see the firm in the list of sequestrations. Want of spirit was not among the qualities inherited by Fergus from his ancestry. He strove manfully against adverse fortune; but in vain. Then came a keener stroke. His Janet died. Then came other business misfortunes. Last of all, he himself sickened unto death, and found himself dying without having been able to make more than the very slenderest provision for his little Elsie. He had named her after a sister, his special friend and playmate in the old days at the Keep of M'Cauldie. He had seen no more of her, for years, than of his other kinsfolk; but the warming of his own heart towards her in his dire extremity seemed to promise that some tenderness for him might lurk in hers.

He wrote accordingly, in simple, touching terms, to crave her guardianship for the little girl, her namesake, and signed the letter with the full signature, so long disused, "Your dying brother, Fergus M'Cauldie." Well was it for his suit he did so. The Honorable Mrs. Gillespie, such was now Sister Elsie's name, had neither a very good heart nor a very bad; but she was well astride of the family hobby. The curtailment of his honored patronymic had been in her eyes all along an offence less pardonable in her once dear brother Fergus, than even the mésalliance with Miss Muirhead. She, therefore, noted the reinstated letter and apostrophe as signs of contrition and returning grace. A little lassie bearing name Elsie M'Cauldie must neither be left upon the wide world, nor even entrusted to the mercies of some stray Muirhead cousin. No letter came, however, and Fergus' sick heart grew sicker. But one day, waking from a feverish doze, he was aware of a tall female figure by his bedside, surmounted by a face whose features showed familiar through their strangeness. He turned more fully round in bed, stretched out a thin hand, and said:—

"Is that you, Sister Elsie?"

"Ay, just so, Brother Fergus."

"God bless you, then, you'll tak' the mitherless bairn when I'm gone, Elsie!"

"Bide a wee till I speer at her, Fergus."

Both brother and sister had gone back to words and accent in use in "auld lang syne" at the Keep.

"Elsie, dear! Elsie!" cried the father, louder than his voice had rung for many a day.

"Ah, weel, she's a true M'Cauldie, Fergus," said her aunt, as the little girl, running in at her father's call, stopped short half-way, at seeing the tall, strange lady.

"So said her mither, and was proud o' it; though I would leaver have had mair blink of the mither's eye in the lassie's."

"What, your wife, Janet Muirhead, proud to think her bairn a true M'Cauldie?"

He nodded an affirmative.

"Then there was some sense in your Janet after a', maybe."

"Some!" smiled the sick man, with ineffable expression of a love that would not sicken and die with him.

"I'll see to the bairn, Fergus," said his sister: "mair or less, that is," she added, with characteristic caution.

"The Lord reward you," he replied, "as you shall deal wi' her."

The Honorable Alexander Gillespie was almost as well descended as his wife. He was a man of middling ability and easy character, over whom she exercised a temperate but unquestioned sway. Their combined family connections, and her energetic use of their interest, had obtained for him a lucrative appointment on the outskirts of official grandeur. He was permanent in a department whose heads were fluctuating, and high enough up to come often into official contact with his chiefs. His social points of contact with them were not a few, hers with their wives and kinswomen more frequent, and more carefully cultivated still. So Mrs. Anderson said truly, that her friend, Elsie Grant, the paymaster's wife had been brought up among great folks.

But the Honorable Alexander had a paralytic stroke in course of time, so severe as to disqualify him for farther discharge of his official duties. The retiring pension was but small, and the narrowed income drove the Gillespies from the great metropolis to its northern sister.

The younger Elsie was the good angel of the house in Edinburgh, the kindest of nurses to her aunt's husband, and the most considerate of companions to herself, whose temper was not sweetened, nor her mind mellowed, by the change in her outward circumstances.

Though Mrs. Gillespie never ceased to regret London society, nor spared disparagement, upon occasion, of such substitute for it as Edinburgh could afford, she nevertheless availed herself to the utmost of the advantages which her Scotch parentage and noble extraction gave her, for access to the "superior circles" of Auld Reekie. Her niece must, of necessity, often accompany her to public or private entertainments; and at one of the former made acquaintance with an ensign of a Highland regiment quartered in the castle. Mr. Grant was not meanly gifted by nature in mind or body, and personally was not undeserving of any young lady's regard. What drew Elsie towards him, strongly and specially, from the very first, was the circumstance that he was from Aberdeen, and knew some of her mother's friends, one which, by some instinct, she never mentioned to her aunt. But that keen-witted lady did not need the additional reason which such knowledge might have afforded, for discouraging, as soon as she perceived it, the growing intimacy between Elsie and Mr. Grant. She ascertained that he had committed the rash act of entering the British army without any farther qualifications than high courage, fair talents, and an earnest admiration for a soldier's career. He had little more money than sufficed for the purchase of his first commission, and was entirely without family interest of any kind or degree. Now, the Honorable Mrs. Gillespie knew enough of the War Office, as of other offices, in those good old unreformed times, to perceive at once how high the young ensign was likely to reach in the military hierarchy; and she determined, neither unkindly, nor unwisely, to put him at once upon his honor with Elsie. Mr. Grant, therefore, waited on her, at her own request, to receive "an intimation upon an important matter."

"Would you make a baggage-wagon wife of the puir lassie, Mr. Grant? I'm tauld it's but a weary way of life," she said, reverting, as she always did, when moved, to the old pronunciation.

"Ah, but I hope, dear madam—"

"Weel, young gentleman, bide till your hopes are hatched a bit."

That was fair and forcible he could not deny. Poor lad. They were addled in one way before hatched in another.

No word had passed between him and Elsie, so he applied first for leave, then for exchange into a regiment on active service abroad. Years went by. He had gotten a wound and a medal; three varieties of fever; two of ague; much commendation as an active and efficient officer; frequent sciatica; and very grizzled hair. He was moreover, lieutenant, without purchase, in a company commanded by a puppy having less then one-third of his own time of service, when news came that Elsie M'Cauldie was an orphan again: for both her uncle and her aunt were dead. The regiment was, happily, no farther off than Ireland, otherwise his purse might not have allowed of the journey to Edinburgh.

The bloom was off her beauty certainly; but that assurance of loving-kindness which Ned Locksley could read on it some years later kept a wondrous loveliness on every feature. And the poor lieutenant read a special love-look through the loving-kindness which smiled on all. Elsie was glad to see him—almost delighted, spite of what she must have thought his long and fickle desertion of her.

"Your aunt said, Miss M'Cauldie, that a

baggage-wagon wife would have but a weary life of it, and with that word warned me off. For your sake I took the warning, hoping and striving through bitter years to win some other thing to offer you. I have no more now than I had then: less, for I was then young and hopeful. But you are lonely, and I have brought you back one thing increased—a luckless soldier's love."

Elsie thought it wealth, and took the treasure for better or worse. The few pounds her father had left her were but little increased by a legacy from her aunt. Lieutenant Grant applied for a paymastership by which to add a few pounds to his annual pay. He was actually appointed on the sole score of his character; and a brevet on a birthday made him captain. What can the vulgar outcry mean about deserving officers overlooked in our army.

Ned's new little acquaintance, Amy, was, as she had told him, her parents' only child, born and bred, as her dolls demonstrated, at a time when the station of her father's regiment had been shifting with more than usual rapidity. Having once visited the paymaster's quarters, and having done so, thanks to Miss Amy, in the character of a house-friend, Ned often found his way there again; most of his evenings being spent either with the Grants or with his first friends, the Andersons.

Personally, therefore, he was not much affected by the evening amusements of his comrades in barracks, nor disturbed by the "skylarking," of which he heard either in O'Brien's rollicking brogue, or in the major's wrathful murmuring against "unseemly practical jokes." Captain Rufford, indeed, by way of daring his dependant, Jones, had suggested to that officer—since Mansfield had been dipped in a solution of liquid blacking and water, and Garrett had an eyebrow shaved, his dress-boots filled with the contents of a mustard pot—that it was hardly fair to let the third "griff" off unscathed. But Jones fought shy of the suggestion, alleging Ned's intimacy with the major, "who'll make the confoundedest kick-up about conduct unbecoming a gentleman and an officer, if there's a scrimmage with his friend Lockaley."

In truth, Ned was known to share his senior's aversion to the noble sport of "badger-baiting," and looked him as if his teeth, albeit unofficial, might meet through where they bit, as well as the major's. He, therefore, enjoyed immunity from annoyance, until the arrival of a fourth youngster, who had been prevented by illness from joining on the same day as himself and the other two. This Milward was a lad of gentlemanly appearance; of well-proportioned, but very slender frame; of handsome, but very delicate features; with a mouth which might have been reckoned pretty in a girl, but betrayed in one of the ruder sex symptoms of weakness and irresolution. He showed the same distaste as Ned for stupid and noisy rioting; but with a shrinking very different from the masterful bearing of the self-possessed Etonian. The latter, who had left the mess early one evening, was at work some hours later over his Hindustani, when he heard a light, quick step run along the passage, and a hurried, hesitating knock against his door.

"Come in."

In came Milward, rather pale, but with a flush on his cheek-bones.

"Hulloa, Milward! Sit down in the big chair whilst I put the books away."

"Thank you. Hush! Is that them?"

"Is that who? What's up, old fellow?"

"To tell you the truth," said Milward, turning red all over now, "I took the liberty of running in here because there was a threat of 'spunging me with my clothes on.'"

"Whose threat—Rufford and that lot's?"

"Yes."

"Well, that romping is bad enough when O'Brien and his set are at it; but they do it for fun. As for that brute, Rufford, and that fool, Jones, they are unbearable. I'm glad you came in here. I'll give them a lesson if they follow you."

"It's very kind of you," said Milward. "I was ashamed of bolting in, because I know you hate this kind of thing."

"I do; but I wasn't eight years at Eton without being equal to this emergency, mind you, Master Milward. Aint they whitewashing the corridor up here?"

"Hardly *white*washing. It's a dirty yellow ochre in the pots outside."

"All the better. Just pick the stoutest sticks out of the fagot in my coal-bunk, will you, and look in the right-hand corner of the cupboard below for a coil of rope there is, I think. I'll be back in a second."

In he came again accordingly, with two big pots of the dismal ochre wash.

"What on earth are you at?" asked Milward.

"You'll see time enough. But be quick: I heard them banging open your door down-stairs as I went out."

Ned produced a hammer and a few stout nails out of the miscellaneous stores of his cupboard. Then mounting on a chair he nailed three or four stout sticks at right angles to the lintel. They made a sort of projecting platform, to the edge of which he fastened a length of rope nailed at one end to the woodwork of the door. Then he poised the pots upon the sticks so nicely that the door in opening must jerk the rope's end, and an avalanche fall.

"A very neat booby-trap," said he. "Let the stormers assault."

He put a bolt across the door, remarking as he did so:—

"Staple wont hold long. Hon. Company's barrack-master is not much of an ironmonger."

They heard two or three doors opened and shut with a bang along the passage. Then came a knock at his.

"Hulloa!"

"Seen Milward anywhere?" inquired the voice of Jones.

"Oh, dear, yes! He's in here. We're having tea and muffins," quoth Ned, in modulated tones.

Jones was at a nonplus. He had suggested that Milward might have taken refuge in some other officer's quarters; but had not reckoned upon finding him with Lockslcy.

There was a noisy deliberation outside, then another knock, and a more decided voice than the lieutenant's, cried, insolently,

"None of your nonsense, youngster, come out!"

"Who, I?" said Ned, blandly still.

"No! that milksop of a Milward, quick now!"

"Not till we've done the muffins," quoth Ned in reply.

The answer came in a savage kick, which made the color pots tremble; but could not dislodge them, so crafty was their adjustment.

Ned took no notice. A second kick followed, and a rush against the door.

"You had better not, gentlemen, for your own sake," cried Ned, with perfect good-humor; "I can't abear being disturbed at tea."

There was laughter outside, apparently at the baffled assailant, whose wrath, waxing hotter, vented itself in another kick, which almost upset the pots, and loosened the treacherous staple alarmingly.

"Pray don't, sir; you'll disturb your digestion by such strong exercise after meals."

Crash went the staple. In rushed Rufford. Smash went the pots upon his head; and his best uniform—they had dined in full-dress that evening—was dripping and done for.

"There! My best milk-jug broke!" said Ned. "Beg pardon, gentlemen, you may pick up the bits outside."

With one vigorous shove, he sent the captain reeling into the passage, followed by a volley of potsherds. He slammed, and double-locked the door.

Rufford was furious; but the laugh was loud against him, not only among the strangers, well soaked with claret, but even among his own admiring jackals. He put the best face upon the matter that he could, and beat a hasty retreat to change his drenched regimentals before seeking consolation in cards and broiled bones. Thenceforward he watched, with not unnatural eagerness, for some opportunity of turning the tables upon his antagonist: but came to the sullen, though sound, conclusion, that he was, in most things, more than a match for himself. He changed his tactics; took no notice of Ned; but instead of attempting to bully young Milward any more, treated him with studied politeness and cordiality, paying him many little attentions, which began insensibly to win the weak lad's confidence.

Jones, as usual, took his cue from the captain; and pasty-faced Mansfield, the "griff" with a turn for cards, took his from Jones. Milward soon began to fancy that he could do no better than conquer his first prejudices, rub off his home fastidiousness, and prove his manhood by conforming to the customs of such kind comrades. This somewhat nettled Ned; but, absorbed in his sorrows and his studies, he could not afford the matter more than a passing thought upon occasion.

These studies he cherished no less as a present solace than as a preparation for the future, and found in them escape from thoughts and feelings which the mechanical duties of the drill-ground left active still. Though not popular with comrades of his own age and standing, from whom he kept, in some respects, aloof, his good sense, his good-humor, and his proficiency in all manly exercises, fruit of his double training on Cransdale Moors and in the playing-fields at Eton, kept him from the invidiousness of actual unpopularity. His chiefs formed from the first the highest opinion of him, and the major had already caused his name to reach the superior authorities, as that of a young officer of extraordinary promise. For some chance reason, the stay of his batch at the Chatterham depôt was unusually prolonged; but the time at last came in view when they must proceed to their distant destination. Messrs. Rufford and Jones, who had early intimation of the fact, felt, that if profit was to be made out of any of them, it must be made without further delay. The design upon Garrett had been abandoned. He really was too stupid to learn play, too little spirited to play without learning. Milward gave better hopes; weak enough to be led, he was quick enough to learn, and conceited enough to be coaxed or carried beyond his depth. The worthy pair found Mansfield an admirable, though unconscious, assistant in their design. He had a very tolerable taste for gambling, with not much more acquired knowledge of play than Milward's superior wit soon enabled him to gain; and he being pitted against Mansfield, nothing loath, learned confidence in his own skill and judgment.

So they fooled him on; sometimes in fair duel, so to speak, sometimes in square games, where the presence of a confederate, as partner on either side, made the direction of matters both easy and unsuspicious. Rufford had poor luck at play, and was subject, though he handled his cards well upon the whole, to unaccountable inadvertencies, which would sweep off in a turn the previous gains of steady skill and equable fortune. Milward was sharp enough, as he thought, to take special note of this; and having had some unexpected minor successes to whet his appetite, determined on a regular set-to with the captain. To beat the man who had bullied him at first, and then had come round and acknowledged his social and manly qualities, would be greater glory than even gain. Jones made some apparent attempt to dissuade him from this rash purpose.

"Old Rufford knew a thing or two. When put upon his mettle, he was an ugly customer. In fact, he shouldn't himself half like a stand-up fight with him—if it wasn't that's to say, for those absent fits of his, which made such 'mulls' of his play now and then."

"Ah, but that's the very thing, you see, Jones. I own I am an inferior player, in some respects, to Rufford; but I have concentration," said the silly lad, drawing his lips tighter across his teeth, as if with instinctive consciousness of the feeble point of his handsome countenance.

"Yes, you command your attention better than Rufford, I think," answered the other; "which is strange enough, seeing what an old hand he is."

"I'll tell you what, Jones, it's all bosh about not getting old heads on young shoulders. Some youngsters are born with young heads on; but others with old ones all along; don't you see, eh?"

Jones did see, very plain.

At the bottom of the long mess-room at the company's barracks, Chatterham, were two little sitting-rooms, right and left. One was in general use as a smoking-room, the other comfortably furnished, was but seldom used, except as a kind of drawing-room when there were many seniors, or "distinguished visitors," at the depôt mess. Rufford and Jones had weighed very deliberately the arguments for or against making this room the scene of the gambling tournament.

"It was one of the scaliest points about young Archer's affair, Jones, that Plumer of 'the Dashers,' held the party in his own rooms. Floods of bosh were poured out upon it. We can't afford 'ugly circumstances' so soon after. Now, the little room to the left is public, though private to all intents and purposes, for there's not a fellow goes in there once in three months."

"No, that there isn't," said Jones; "and it's fusty enough in consequence."

"Never mind that, my boy; we can leave

the door open to air the atmosphere, which will look fair, and above board, you know, in case of impertinent inquiries. The odds are 'any thing to one' against any fellow lounging in, as we sha'n't play till very late, eh?"

"All right, then. It's a judicious idea enough."

Next morning, Ned, who by chance had got up unusually early, took it into his head to breakfast before, instead of after, parade. To the discomfiture of the messman, he ensconced himself in the uppermost corner of the long room, demanding coffee and poached eggs at an abnormal hour. Before these were ready, the old major looked in.

"Oh, there you are! You are early this morning. Here's the book I promised you. I keep up my old Indian habits, a canter before early parade; so I'm off round the Long Meadows. Look in to-night, will you? the Grants are coming."

The book was a relief, spite of the crabbed Oriental character. Ned kept on deciphering it to while away the time, with occasional interruptions, to shout at the dawdling messman.

Breakfast was so long in coming, that the second cup of coffee was but just poured out, when the bugle parade-call rang in the barrack-square. Up jumped Ned. Where should he put the major's book? The little sitting-room was a safe place; so he opened the door, went in, and placed it on a stand in the corner by the mantelpiece.

Parade was dismissed, when a young engineer officer cried out,—

"Locksley, didn't you say you should like to see the 'flying sap' to-day? There's a party going down to the lines with Dickson. They marched half an hour ago; but I have a trap outside, and I'll drive you down, if you've had your breakfast."

"Well, I've had half of it, or thereabouts. All right; I shall be glad of a lift."

And the young men drove off together.

The Sappers and Miners had a tent on the ground. And there was lunch, in due time, at some interval in action. Then, when the serious work was over, as men and officers were still full of "go," a couple of "scratch elevens" were got up, and Ned must needs play. "Too late for mess," was the word, when dinner-time was come; but as the lunch-commissariat had been liberal, a fair enough ration was fidgeted out all round. When they got back to barracks, he had only just time to dress and run down to the major's. It was past eleven o'clock before he left. The Andersons and he walked home with the Grants, as the night was very fine. Twelve struck by the town clock some time before he reached the barracks. As he passed the sentry, he bethought him of his book.

"I'm not on duty to-morrow morning, and shall have time for a grind."

So he went up to the mess-room in search of it. In the antechamber he asked a sleepy-looking waiter for a flat candlestick, saying that he was going into the left-hand sitting-room for a book, left there that morning.

"Then you wont want no light, sir," said the servant, "there's several officers as *is* in that little room to-night, sir."

Before he was half-way up the long room itself, his ear caught a burst of exultation from Milward's voice, noisier but seemingly somewhat thicker also than usual.

"By George! who'd a thought it? That's the fourth game I've beaten you, captain. I should think you were most sick of it by this time."

"Fortune of war!" said Rufford, in answer, quietly. "Turn and turn about, you know."

"Ha! ha! yes! but your turn seems longish a coming," cried Milward. "Jones, my boy, give us a glass of champagne to toast our luck, eh? No, confound it, none of those long-necked apologies for a wine-glass. Give it us in a tumbler, man; can't you? I'm thirsty. Here, Rufford, here's better luck to ye!"

"Don't drink now, Milward; don't, if you'll take my advice," answered Rufford. "I never do when at play. Keep your head cool, for I mean to cut out your work yet for you. I must have my revenge."

Ned, who by this time was in the room, noted the captain's look and tone at these last words, with misgiving. He had a half a mind to stay and see that Milward, with all his folly, got fair play. Second thoughts told him there would be little use in that, as he couldn't do much more than tell an ace from a knave on the cards himself. He went therefore to the corner to take his book. As he turned his back to do so, he thought, and yet he could not make sure of it, that he heard an ominous whisper.

"What brings the major's jackal poking his nose in here, eh?"

This turned him again. He determined to stay.

"Any objection to one's looking on a bit?" he asked of Jones.

"Oh, dear, no!" said Milward, before any one else could answer. "Sorry I can't let you cut in yourself, if you'd like to take a hand; but it's a regular stand-up between Rufford and me to-night. Have glass o' wine?"

"No, thanks!" He put his foot upon the hind rung of Milward's chair, crossed his arms, and looked on. No one could object to this, after what Milward had said; the circumstance would have been too suspicious.

The first game of Ned's looking on, Milward won again, to his own unbounded satisfaction. The second, Rufford called for double or quits on the whole score of the evening, and won it. Nothing could be more moderate than his conduct to all appearance.

"Tell you what, Milward, we'll leave off, if you like, now; not a scratch on either side."

"Hardly a revenge, is it?" said Jones.

"No, confound it, none at all," backed up Mansfield.

Two other officers, who had been half dozing on a sofa, started up, inquiring what the row might be; and on hearing the case concurred "it's monstrous good-natured of Ruff; but hardly fair upon him."

No such incentives indeed were needed to spur Milward on, for the greed of gambling was on him just then, as well as its mere recklessness. But if any one word had been wanting, the chance expressions of these lookers-on—who had neither knowledge of his intended victimization, nor interest in it—supplied its room.

"Good-natured of him! Ha, ha, ha! That's a good 'un. I have beaten him five games out of six; and he's to be so kind as to let me off, because he's had the luck to get the best of a double and quits. And that was a regular fluke," ran on the doomed simpleton. "I don't want to say any thing unpleasant, but the blundering way he played those clubs of his last hand, was almost enough to ruin any cards he held. What's your stake, Ruff? My deal."

"Well, then, if you 'mean business,' youngster," said the captain, with a new assumption of superiority in his tone galling enough, though by no means outrageous, "say twice what we did the last time."

Milward winced at the proposal. His antagonist, who faced him, could see what Ned, from behind his chair, could not—a tremulous motion of the weak upper lip.

"A leetle too much of a good thing, eh? How's that, with *your* judgment, to back your luck?"

"Done with you!" cried Milward. "Please cut; the deal is mine."

The cards were balanced evenly, yet in the end the captain won.

"We play on, of course," said the loser, nervously, and in a hurried, would-be hectoring tone. "Stakes as before. I may right myself yet."

"As you please," answered the captain.

Milward leant eagerly forward. All crowded round. Even Ned unfolded his arms and laid his elbows on the back of Milward's chair, bringing his chin down on his hands, that his eyes might be nearer the board.

Rufford's play was very deliberate. Milward's not quite so much so. Do what he would, they could all detect an occasional tremor in his hand. Again, however, the mere chances of the game seemed to be fairly divided between them. Up to the last trick it would have been unsafe to decide upon the winner.

At this crisis, Rufford leaned back in his chair, and looked, with sarcastic smile, into his adversary's eyes.

"I really beg your pardon; but it only strikes me now. If you should win this game, it will be but a drawn battle. Not worth one's while that, after all said and done."

"Well, what of it?"

"Why, let's double stakes as they stand now; and let these cards decide."

Milward hesitated, and his hand trembled evidently.

"Funky?" sneered the captain, with a look for which Ned, right opposite, would have liked to send his fist between his eyes. Rufford read his meaning right enough; and caught at the notion of a double revenge, like lightning.

"What! Show the white feather, Milward, with your original backer at your back, too? He'll be ready to do for you the same kind office he did for me, no doubt."

"As how?" said Milward.

"Whitewash you, should need be, to be sure."

There was a titter, in which Milward joined hysterically.

Ned's brow darkened. It was his old weak point to pick up a challenge at any cost.

"Come!" said the captain. "Can't you find the pluck between you both?"

"Shall I?" said Milward.

"I'll halve the damage," whispered Ned, beyond himself at the growing insolence on Rufford's face.

"Done with you, then, Rufford," cried the other. "Knave!"

"Queen!"

"King!"

"Ace!"

"Let's see, how does it stand?" said the captain, with affected unconcern. "Hundred and twenty-five, doubled once, two hundred and fifty. Doubled again, wasn't it? Just five hundred. I like round numbers. If a cheque wont be convenient, I'll take an I. O. U. There's an inkstand on the sideboard in the mess-room, I believe."

CHAPTER XIII.

That active and intelligent officer of the county force, Police Constable Hutchins, had need of the fullest exercise of his intelligence and activity.

The case was one of "howdacious buglary," as he himself said at Rookenham.

There could be no suspicion of connivance with any of the servants, for the doors of the passage inwards had not even been attempted; whereas forcible entrance had manifestly been made from without. There were plain enough traces on the fine gravel under the window, of the presence of the "parties concerned," who had taken, however, the precaution of scuffling, in such wise as to baffle any attempt to identify boot-marks.

Had they been "put up to the plant" by any of my lord's establishment, they would not have made the very serious mistake of breaking in on the left, instead of the right side of the great stone mullion. This mullion divided a two-light window of very doubtful "Gothic," the two lights being, in fact, two separate windows, lighting two separate little outer-rooms or passages, and the heavy clumsy mullion, itself a device for concealing the butt end, if one may say so, of the party-wall which divided them. Any one effecting entrance from without through the right-hand window, would have the door of the strong-room, in which the plate was kept, on his left hand, the party-wall on his right. Should he effect it, as the depredators did on this occasion, through the left-hand light, the party-wall would, of course, be on his left hand, the entrance to a sort of cabinet of curiosities on his right. The burglars having, as it would seem, a vague notion that valuable booty lay hereabouts, were wanting in the knowledge, accessible to any inmate of the house, of the relative positions of the plate and china stores.

It must have been a horrible disappointment to them after all their trouble, risk, and really hard work in forcing the well-fastened door, to find themselves in a museum rather than in a silversmith's. In a merely scientific point of view, the confusion of their topographical acumen must have been mortifying; and the financial failure of the speculation even more sad. One really could have found little heart to blame them had they vented their disappointment on the china generally, and enriched Lord Royston's collection by some additional specimens of "crackled" porcelain. Their abstinence from this obvious gratification of feeling gave P. C. Hutchins a respectful estimate of their prudence.

"Smashes o' crockery," remarked that officer, "hoften spile sport by givin' alarm to hinmates. Parties as can't keep their temper are hapt to put their foot in it at work o' this kind."

That they were practical philosophers, as well as men of self-control, and schooled in that wisdom which coined the proverb, "half a loaf, better than no bread," appeared from the further circumstance, noted by the keen inventorial eyes of Mrs. White, that they had taken with them, after all, such matter for consolation as the most valuable and portable of the non-earthenware articles of virtu could afford.

"Whatever will my lord say, to be sure? There's things and things is gone, as he'd sooner lost a dozen of silver forks and spoons as sich."

The hue and cry raised in the county was ineffectual. Futile was the activity of P. C. Hutchins, vain his intelligence and that of his local superiors. It was with mingled feelings of indignation and pride that he found himself brought at last into contact with detectives of vulpine reputation from the metropolis. Actual acquaintance with such ornaments of Scotland-yard could not but in itself be gratifying to a professional man; but the local constabulary feeling enjoyed—how should it not?—a profounder, if less ostentatious, gratification in the baffling of metropolitan acumen by the mystery which provincial acuteness had failed to penetrate.

"And you'll keep your eyes open, officer," said Inspector Ferritts to Hutchins, as a parting salutation before leaving for town.

"Catch a weasel asleep, inspector!" answered that officer.

Tommy Wilmot had caught several lately, not asleep indeed, but still had caught them, and presented their lithe little corpses to Mister Watson for the increase of his admonitory exhibition in the open air. Poacher against poacher! It was almost as unfair as the mutton bones, which the wolf reproaches the shepherds for grilling, in the old Greek fable.

But the fact was, that Tommy was as tender of the game, in his way, as Mr. Watson himself. He was not the man to rifle "nestisses," nor to pity the riflers on four feet or on two. He was as good as an underkeeper in matters of preservation, only he could not keep from sharing sport in due season. Father and mother were still obdurate, refusing their sanction to his regular enrolment under Watson, who by way of accustoming them to what he saw was, after all, inevitable, would ask of Tommy, in their presence, to do odd jobs in the keeperin' line for him, just now and then, on pretext that some press of work was leaving him no regular hand unemployed and available. Now, it befell, not long after the failure of the London detectives at Rookenham, that irregularities and offences had been rife upon the Cransdale trout-burns on the upper moors. Certain fishes had been found dead on the banks, at higher and drier elevations than any to which their own saltatory performances could have enabled them to reach. No "spoor" of otter was traceable, nor did the spotted silver of the luckless trout show marks of the incisors of their amphibious enemy.

"Can't say whether 'um's bin wired or netted, or what not," grumbled the old keeper.

"Tell 'ee what now, Tommy, set a thief to catch a— no, there; no need to take no offence, Tommy. I've a knowed you a'most as long as your own father, lad; and though I owes 'ee a grudge or two on fur and feather 'count, I don't believe there's a 'onester young feller not hereabouts, all *but* the poachin'. Howsomedever, what I meaned war this: my lord aint pertickler about the upland burns, so I don't want no 'rests made, nor nothin' like; but if you'd look into this here a bit, Tommy, and see what it is they does, and who does it, and let 'em know we can't quite stand it, not if things is to go on as they 'as; why, somethin' mought come on it, pertickler o' makin' things pleasant wi' your father and me about 'ee, Tommy!"

Never had Mr. Watson been known by Tommy to deliver himself of so lengthy a discourse. He was much moved by the circumstance, and by the evidence it disclosed of an interest in his own heart's wishes, and of a good-will, surviving in spite of frequent, aggravated, and old-standing provocations.

Nay, Mr. Watson went so far as to beg the loan of Tommy's services, by personal application from his father. It could not, under such condescension, be refused; so Tommy, strapping a fishing creel across his shoulders in token of his temporary rank on special service, betook himself to the moors to right the wrongs of the moorland trout.

It was three days after entering on this confidential enterprise that he determined—having completed a first cursory reconnaissance of the whole campaigning ground—to make detailed and minute examination of all and several the "likely places," where lines, nets, or wires might lurk unperceived. The hot noon found him at a notable spot, kneeling upon a ledge of stone which formed the brim of one of the deep basins, wherein the eddying waters stayed their speed below the Pixie's pillar, not far from the spot of Ned Locksley's adventure with poor Benjy.

He had tucked up his coat-sleeve at the wrist, and passed his hand cautiously along the under side of the ledge beneath the water, without encountering any suspicious substance. But such a superficial search proved little. He stood up, passed the strap of the fish-basket over his shoulder, and deposited that receptacle upon the grass, in which the cheery chirrup of a million grasshoppers made merry music.

He untied his neckcloth, loose as it was, and thrust it into the pocket of his velveteen coat. Then he divested himself of that garment utterly, and tossing it aside upon an ant-heap, caused a total eclipse over that region, which must have disconcerted the astronomical expectations of the ants—if they have any. As he wore no waistcoat, nothing farther was needed to set his upper limbs at liberty but to tie his braces round his waist and roll up his shirt-sleeves to the shoulders. This done, he laid himself flat, face foremost, upon the rim of the pool again, his head downwards, after a most apoplectic fashion, one hand grasping the outer stone ledge; the other, groping deep in the cool water.

He was thus all unknowing of the approach of a blue-coated figure coming up the bank at a cautious distance from the water, which, by reflecting, might have betrayed its advance. But when the "determination of blood to the head," necessitated by his posture, became temporarily unendurable, he looked up, and turning him round upon his seat, was aware of the presence and close contact of Police Constable Hutchins.

"At it again, eh?" said that functionary.

"At what again, pleaceman?" answered Tommy.

"Come none o' that ere," retorted the man in blue.

"None of what ere?"

"None o' your sorce, young man, when took in the hact o' sich ingratitude."

If the features of Police Constable Hutchins had ever caught from the countenance of the Chairman of Quarter Sessions any vestige of its force of magisterial rebuke against offenders, some reflection of that awfulness, he thought, must at this moment be causing Tommy Wilmot's heart to quail.

It is sad to state, however, that this hardened offender showed a contemptuous composure under the just wrath overhanging him. After a moment's hesitation, during which the thought of jerking the peace officer over his head into the pool caused his fingers to contract and clutch at nothing, he said, in a tone between provocation and playfulness,—

"I don't want no rows wi' nobody. Now git along, pleaceman, do!"

"I'm a goin' to git along, in discharge of my dooty, young man," answered Hutchins, unhesitatingly; "and do you git up and come along wi' me, without makin' no rows, and it'll be the better for you."

Tommy stood up, not to comply with this summons by any means. Still the sense of responsibility, and even of official dignity, was on himself as on his adversary; so he contented himself with saying,—

"Tell 'ee what now, pleaceman; this ere's some mistake o' yourn. I'm a doin o' my dooty, and you med go do yourn; I don't want no more words about it."

"Likely not," answered the other; "has for words, you may keep 'em for the justices, if so be you's rather. But if wirin' o' trout *his* your dooty, young man, happrehension of parties offending *his* mine, and *no* mistake."

"Oh, that's what you'm up to, be it?" cried Tommy, tickled by the policeman's blunder. "Ha'nt 'ee 'eared as Muster Watson's set I to look arter the lads that's bin a fishin' foul up 'ere now."

"I've a heard nothing of the sort," answered Hutchins, with evident incredulity.

"Then you've 'eared it now, and that's 'nuff, I s'pose," growled Tommy, interpreting and resenting the doubts upon the other's face.

"What!—set a thief to catch a thief, has Mr. Watson, eh?"

"Thief yoursen', you puddin'-faced peeler!" cried young Wilmot, enraged beyond measure at hearing from a foe's lips the same ugly phrase which had hurt him from a friend's.

There was a fulness of feature, combined with absence of color, about the worthy policeman's countenance, which accounted for, if it did not justify, the disparaging epithet long since fixed upon him by the less reverent portion of the village lads. His temper was gone, whither Tommy's had preceded it.

"Likely tale, *hin*deed; to take a Cransdale keeper hout o' Cransmere lock-up. A hofficer of my 'experience aint to be took in so easy, no, not by no means." And he looked round for any suspicious circumstance, on which to found a formal charge.

"What's in yon basket, eh? fair fishin' gear, or foul, I wonder. I shall *hinsist* upon yer shewing me, young man!"

"Wish 'ee may get it!" said Tommy, sulkily.

"Hindeed!" cried the policeman, making a quick snatch at it, as he spoke.

But Tommy likewise snatched at it, catching the leather belt only, which broke with the violence of the tug on either side, and, the lid opening as the basket fell, its contents rolled out upon the trampled grass.

Tommy Wilmot was thunderstruck.

"Wusser nor I thort!" cried the constable. He whipped out a pair of handcuffs, and had one of them on one of Wilmot's wrists before the young man recovered his senses, and darted a few yards aside.

Then the policeman pounced upon an object on the grass, caught it up, and thrust it into his left-hand breast pocket in a moment.

He rushed at Wilmot, who shook him off; but made no attempt at escape.

"So sure as Heaven's aboove—" began the young man.

"Shut up wi' that," cried Hutchins, and rushed at him again; but again his powerful opponent shook him off, and stood at bay, without attempting to escape.

"Tell 'ee what, pleaceman, you let I goo hands free; an' I goos wi'out no more ado, I does. But you and I med both be dead i' bottom o' yon pool afore 'ee takes I down to Cransmere han'cuffed!"

The policeman was no coward, and would have done his duty to the death, if need were. But he knew his man, and knew him by experience for more than his own match in any encounter. Moreover he saw him stand his ground, where a race for liberty was clear before him.

"Put on yer coat, then, and come along."

As Wilmot obeyed the order, the constable picked up the other scattered articles, and returned them to the basket, of which he took possession; then, side by side, in silence, he and his prisoner on parole went downwards from the moor.

"I really can see no course but to commit you for the present," said Squire Jekyll, when he had heard the policeman's story in his private justice-room, and had ascertained from Wilmot that, beyond a simple and absolute denial of any guilt or guilty knowledge on his own part, he had no account to give of the damning circumstance.

"There can be no doubt as to the identity or ownership of this article," continued the magistrate, taking from a drawer in his bureau a list of the missing articles advertised after the Rookenham robbery.

"Let me see," and once more he picked up from the table what Hutchins had seized upon the grass and pocketed. "It corresponds exactly;" and he read off from the paper, "'No. 56, oblong tortoise-shell box, lined with ivory, outer surface inlaid with gold ornaments in the "renaissance" style; centre, an oval medallion, with portrait of "Madame de Pompadour" in miniature, by Boucher; initials, F. B., under lady's left breast.' There can be no doubt that this is the box described, forming part of the valuables abstracted from the family mansion of Lord Royston. You must see yourself that, upon your total failure to account for your possession of this box, or, more exactly, of its presence in your fish-basket, it must be my plain duty to have you kept in custody till further investigation."

Tommy shook his head mournfully; he had no objection to offer. But whilst the magistrate was sealing up the stolen box, he asked of him whether he might communicate with Mr. Locksley at the Lodge in the Park.

"By all means," answered the squire; "will you write, or shall I send down and ask him to come over?"

"Ah, do 'ee, sir, and beg o' him, for any sake, to come over at once; on'y don't 'ee tell un, please, what I'm in trouble about, till I've seed 'un mysen'."

This the squire promised also.

The handcuffs still dangled upon Tommy's wrist. The policeman locked the second loop round one of his own with an apologetic look.

"I'm hanswerable to justices for 'ee, now, you see, young man."

"All right," said Tommy, in profound dejection.

"But, I say, pleaceman?"

"Well, what?"

"I'd tak' it kind o' 'ee to say nought o' what's brought me so, no sooner nor 'ee can help, ye know."

"Never fear, young man," answered the constable, with a pompousness, which not even his intended good-nature could suppress. "Discretion is the duty of a hofficer in my position."

Before dusk Mr. Locksley was ushered in. He was mounting for an evening ride over the estate when Squire Jekyll's messenger arrived; so he set off immediately.

"Policeman over zealous, I suppose," he said, cheerily, on entering. "I have seen Watson on my way over, Tommy; I understand it's all right about your roving commission as keeper of the trout-burns. But you've had so many difficulties about that sort of thing before, that you mustn't be hard on the constable for having his suspicions."

Tommy shook his head.

"Wish it wur that, sir. This is 'nother guess sort o' thing, this is."

"An unlucky blow, Tommy? You were always too ready with your fists."

Mr. Locksley's kind, apologetic tone was more than the lad could bear. He laid his arm upon the table, and his face upon his arm, and sobbed aloud.

"Tommy Wilmot! man! Look up like a man, and tell me what's amiss."

"They thinks it wur I as broke into my lord's at Rookenham, they does!"

"About as much as I did, Tommy!" said out, at once, the generous, open-hearted gentleman, under whose eye the boy had been born and bred.

"God bless 'ee for that, sir!" cried the prisoner, starting to his feet, and shaking off, as an evil spell spoilt, the despondency which had cowed him hitherto. He took a turn up and down the narrow crib; then begged his good friend to sit down upon the single chair, whilst he himself sat on the raised boards on which the rare inmates of Cransmere lock-up slept.

"What on earth can have put such a notion into their heads, Tommy?"

"I suppose them as put that box into my basket," answered he, with a forced laugh, which was a miserable failure.

"What box? You must remember I know nothing of what has happened, except that I find you here, where I am sure, as I said, that you have no right to be on any such score as that."

Thus encouraged, Tommy told him precisely what had passed, and of his own utter amazement at the unexpected appearance of the costly toy.

"It's most unaccountable," said Mr. Locksley, "and I should do you no service in hiding from you that, in the eyes of any one who didn't know you as I do, the thing would look very serious. But you shall have the benefit of lawyer's advice when the case comes on, and I'll see the squire myself and find out when it will."

"Thank'ee, sir," said Tommy, with a sincerity of tone which made up for the scanty allowance of grateful words.

"What shall I say at home, Tommy? Stories go about so, we sha'n't keep it long in some shape from father and mother, I fear."

"No! nor I wouldn't wish to't," he answered, "on'y I'd sooner have 'em 'ear it from a genelman like you, sir, as don't think I dun it, than be vrighted out o' their vour wits like by some lyin' gossip."

"All right, then, Tommy; I'll call in at once when I get over. I suppose there's nothing I can do for you to-night here? Shall you want any money?"

"No, thank'ee, sir! I've a bit i' my pocket if I shuld."

Mr. Locksley held out his hand to the poor lad, who wrung it with an eager grip, which told his appreciation of the friendly confidence put in him under such cloudy circumstances.

The elder Wilmot was a man of little judgment, and therewith pig-headed, as will not seldom befall. Mr. Locksley was surprised and shocked to find that Tommy's own father did not, as he had done, repudiate instinctively the supposition of the lad's guilt.

Disobedience to the just and reasonable commands of parents is, doubtless, offence enough in itself, and the fruitful parent of offences; but Tommy's disinclination for pursuits of horticulture could hardly be set down as regular rebellion, since he did continue to work among the lettuces and cabbages. But there was more of the despot than of the father in John Wilmot's estimate of his own authority. He seemed to think that hands which showed small aptitude for handling rakes and waterpots might naturally hanker after a burglar's crowbar. When he had heard Mr. Locksley's story and had recovered from the first emotion of surprise, he set himself to inveigh rather against his son's undutifulness than against the enormity of the suspicion of his guilt. The mother, too, true to her early prejudice against all poaching characters,—whom, indeed, she had but too good cause to think capable of the most outrageous crimes,—wept bitterly over Tommy's disgrace, and wrung her hands in despair, saying little else than this:—

"Guilty or not guilty, 'tis the poachin' as has brought it on us!"

An expression of opinion embodying, as Mr. Locksley felt, but too much of a truth likely to tell against her boy upon his trial.

The "big room" at the Cransmere town-hall was not very spacious, but such space as it contained beyond what was absolutely required for the magistrates' table was crammed to overflowing when Tommy was "had up." Three of P. C. Hutchins' blue-coated comrades were present from the county town itself, under the command of an inspector; and even their united imperiousness could scarcely keep the eager prying townsfolk from sweeping on to the tabooed parallelogram, to the confusion of magisterial order and the abrogation of all formal judicial action whatsoever.

There was a side-room at the upper end where the magistrates assembled, and whence in due time they issued in awful conclave to take their seats within the jeopardized "reserve." Squire Jekyll was there, and Mr. Locksley, Sir Henry Hebblethwaite, and Mr. Mapes, of Maperly; the magistrates' clerk, of course, an attorney on the part of Lord Royston's man of business, and another retained, according to Mr. Locksley's promise, "to watch the proceedings on behalf of the defendant." The lock-up had no means of communication with the "big room" save through the principal staircase, and P. C. Hutchins, with Tommy in charge, had no small difficulty in pushing his way through the crowd, even when assisted by a spirited diversion "ab intrà" upon the part of the inspector himself. Poor Tommy Wilmot! He was holding his head high, as becomes a lad of spirit, conscious, as it would seem, of innocence, when he first came in contact with the edge of the packed assembly. But his head hung on his breast before the policemen had elbowed and hustled themselves and him half through. The hot breath of his slanderers literally made his cheek to burn, for their lips almost touched his ear as he was pushed past them.

"Who'd a thowt it, o' Lodge-gairdner's son too? But, there, pride must have a fall. Them Wilmots was a stuck-up lot allays!"

"Pleaceman don't look so main bad nayther; thay sed, as Tommy had nigh throttled 'un too, thay did."

"How much wur it he'd spent o' what he gotten for the goods, eh? 'Twur old Levi, at Saint Ivo's, bought the main o' it vrom 'un, I 'eard saay—"

"You see what cooms o' poachin', Billy," said one hortatory matron to a loutish lad of fourteen or fifteen, in a tattered smock, beside her.

It cut Tommy to the heart, that his own mother said little else to him.

"Poachin' indeed, old gowk," objected a notorious setter of springes to the speaker. "There's as good as Tommy Wilmot has been up here along o' poachin', as 'ud be sheamed to steal the valley o' a toothpick, let aloan 'ousebreaking'."

This roused him again. To be cowed before such a creature as "Snivelling Sam," was a degradation to which he could not consent. He set his neck stiff, his teeth firm, and his eyes straight, and looked his gainsayers in the face once more.

"Lor'! 'ow 'ardened 'e do seem, look 'ee!" said several charitable females, in a breath.

The process was little likely to soften an offender, so far.

A first and unexpected consolation was in store for him, however, when he had reached the outmost row. Foremost amongst the strugglers against that living hedge of constables, so conspicuous for gaps, stood Benjy Cottle, the poor idiot boy. Who when he saw his kind friend Tommy captive and distressed, seemed with an apprehension quicker than his wont, to know that something was wrong, and forthwith began to vent his own alarm and grief in piteous howls.

"Don't 'ee hurt 'un, pleaceman, now, don't 'ee, ow, ow, ow!"

"Silence!" cried Sir Henry Hebblethwaite.

"Silence!" re-echoed the inspector.

But Benjy's lamentations rent the stifling air.

"Remove that noisy brat."

"Suttinly, Sir 'Enry," said the ever officious Hutchins. Sooner said than done. There was no thrusting Benjy summarily through the dense mass of townsfolk; and as for handing him out over their heads, as suggested by the inspector, his lively kicks and bites, and other practical remonstrances, made it a task of evident impossibility.

"Can't any one get him to hush up, at all events?" asked the less irascible squire.

"Perhaps his friend, the defendant," suggested, meekly, the magistrate's clerk.

This was an admirable idea, and, seconded by the defendant aforesaid, proved eminently successful. Upon being remonstrated with, and re-assured by, Tommy, and farther bribed by a promise of future peppermints, Benjy ceased his lamentations; but held his place in the front row still.

Justice thereupon entered undisturbed upon her august proceedings.

They were few and simple. The policeman was sworn, and gave his evidence, uncontradicted of course by Wilmot. The latter, when called upon to account for the presence of the box in his basket, could only suggest that some one, who had a spite against him, and was himself concerned in the robbery, must have placed it there.

"Some one who had a spite against you! Have you any reason to suppose that any person has one?" inquired Sir Henry.

"Not exactly," he answered.

"Not exactly? that's not exactly an answer, is it? Who is likely to have a spite of the sort against you?"

Tommy could have bitten his tongue out. The truth was, his acceptance of office under Watson had been counted an apostasy in certain sporting circles in the neighborhood. It had come to his ears that they had been aware of it, though the police had not; and that opinions derogatory to Tommy's sense of honor and goodfellowship had been expressed, in terms less choice than forcible, in the tap-room of the Blue Cow. Threats of "serving him out" had accompanied these candid expressions of opinion; and his exculpatory theory had certainly been, that some of the dregs of the "poaching lot" in Cransmere having tampered in the robbery, had fixed on this means of inculpating him, and diverting suspicion from themselves.

But the slanders he had just heard against himself, though they made him savage, had no power to make him mean.

Every man, woman, and child, but Benjy, had some harsh word against the poacher on their lips.

Now, he had been a poacher, with distinctions and reservations, of a sportsmanlike character, it was true; still a poacher, and for that belied. He was feeling with keen indignation, in that self-same hour, how cruel the injustice might be which made "poacher" and "thief" convertible terms. He shrunk, therefore, for the lad had a fine heart, from endorsing that injustice, even against possible enemies. Not another word, upon the subject of any spite against himself could the magistrate now get out of him.

"I suppose it would be right," said Sir Henry to his brethren, "that there should be some formal identification of the stolen article?"

"Just so," said the attorney present on Lord Royston's part. "Mrs. White, Sir Henry, the housekeeper at Rookenham, is here, prepared to give evidence."

Mrs. White, was at this juncture introduced.

"Where is the box in question?" asked Sir Henry. Hutchins produced it, sealed up, as it had been by Squire Jekyll, on the afternoon of Tommy Wilmot's arrest.

But when the seals were broken, and the paper wrapping thrown aside, and the box held out to Mrs. White for her inspection, there was a fresh outburst from Benjy,—

"Gi' it I! gi' it! Yon's my coffin, my pretty little coffin for the mousey!"

"Silence!" again cried Sir Henry.

"Silence!" again re-echoed the inspector.

"Hush up now, Benjy," said Wilmot, "like a good lad."

Far from it. Was this indeed a hall of justice, and his lawful property to be kept unjustly from him?

"Gi' it I, pleaceman! Oh, do, pray, please

gi' it I! My pretty coffin, for my poor dear mousey!"

"What's that the brawling brat says?" inquired the peppery baronet. "If the police force of this county were worth their salt, they would know their duty better than to let us be interrupted by idiots after this fashion."

But the quick ear and attention of the attorney for the defendant had noted the protestations of the boy. There was a possible clue, so he caught at the thread eagerly.

"With your leave, and that of the bench, Sir Henry, this seems to me to deserve considerable attention. Allow me, gentlemen; is that your box, my boy?"

"Nonsense!" cried Sir Henry. "How can the box be the boy's, when there's Mrs. White here to prove it part of Lord Royston's property. Besides which, how could a brat like that come by a box like this?"

"Ah, that indeed is quite a separate question. But excuse me, Sir Henry, I appear for the defendant, and prefer conducting my client's case my own way."

"As you please then, Mr. Attorney," growled the baronet.

The lawyer turned to Benjy.

"Is that your box, my boy?"

But Benjy's fitful intelligence failed to detect a friendly tone in the question, and he gaped upon the questioner with open mouth and lack-lustre eyes. This was embarrassing. The attorney was, however, a man of expedients. If Benjy's attention could be turned from himself again upon the toy, he knew that his chance of eliciting an answer would be tenfold. So he took it in hand, with "by your leave, Sir Henry," and passing it close under the idiot's face, repeated his question, "Is this your box, my boy?"

"'Ees it be!" cried Benjy, clutching at it.

"And where did you get it?" boldly asked the attorney, with a double inward apprehension, lest the child should obstinately refuse to answer; or lest he should blurt out something which might mar, instead of mending the case for Tommy.

"Nigh t' peat-pools," answered he without a second's hesitation.

The attorney could not resist a glance of satisfaction towards Sir Henry.

"Where are these peat-pools?" he asked of the policemen.

"Further edge of the moor, towards the quarries," said two, in a breath.

"Well, you're a good boy, and shall have some peppermints," continued his interrogator, who had noticed the soothing effect of that expectation upon him previously.

It occurred to Sir Henry, that there might lurk herein a savor of tampering with the witness; but the examination of Benjy being necessarily informal, he feared to risk its utter interruption by objecting.

"Didn't you say it was mousey's coffin, eh?"

"'Ees it be. Poor dear, wee mousey!"

"And what have you done with mousey, my boy?"

"Put 'un in yon basket," pointing to the fishing-creel upon the table.

"Ah yes! poor wee mousey!" said the sympathizing attorney. "So you put him in the basket, box and all, did you, till you could bury him?"

"'Ees, put 'un into pit hole like t'owld saxton," replied Benjy, with unusual lucidity before Sir Henry could object that the attorney must really not put such leading questions.

"How came this poor child to have access to your basket, Wilmot? Has he been in your company lately?"

"Why, yes, sir; I tak' my vittles at his mother's these day or two, since I wur set to mind the burns up at moor."

"Gentlemen!" said the attorney turning round to the bench, "here is evidence, most unexpected and most unexceptionable, of the fact that, as my client has all along asserted, this box was placed without his privity in the position where it was accidentally discovered by the policeman. The very circumstances under which that poor innocent's witness has been elicited remove, thank God, any suspicion of collusion. My duty is not concerned with suggesting how the child came into possession of the box, but is best discharged by claiming, as I now do, for my client an instantaneous and honorable acquittal."

There was a cheer from the audience at this little speech. Tommy had learnt, however, to hold their judgment cheap. He turned on them a look of such contempt as few could fail to understand.

"What!" said Sir Henry, in a confidential undertone to his brother magistrates, "are we to let off this poaching scamp, and lose the first clue that has been come across to the Rookenham affair, on the score of an idiot's cock-and-bull about a dead mouse?"

"By the way," interrupted Mr. Mapes, "the boy said he put the *mouse* into the basket; the *box* was rather a suggestion of the defendant's attorney, wasn't it?"

"Policeman Hutchins," he then asked, "the boy says he put a dead mouse into the basket: did you happen to see one when its contents fell out?"

"No, sir. Nor I don't think there could have been one neither, for I picked up what was on the grass after pocketing the box; and I didn't see no mouse, I'm positive."

Policemen are but human. The vanishing of all prospect of a share in the reward advertised for the fortunate man who should prosecute to conviction any party concerned in the great Rookenham burglary disposed him to attach less weight than Tommy's attorney did to the evidence in favor of the defendant.

"And what did you do with what you picked up, constable?" said Tommy's adviser.

"Shoved hall into the basket agen."

"Has the basket been opened since?"

"Not as I knows on, sir."

"May I suggest a search of its contents," he asked of the authorities.

"By all means," they assented.

One by one the articles contained were handed out and laid upon the table. A bit of chalk, a lump of bees'-wax, an old steel tailor's-thimble, a pocket songster, a hank of stout thread, a rude apology for a fly-book—with some admirably tied flies in it, however, as Mr. Mapes, an enthusiastic angler, at once observed; a clasp knife, a roll of gut, and, last of all, a very dirty, tattered pocket-handkerchief. Then the basket was held upside down and shaken. No mouse appeared.

A shade of disappointment clouded for a moment the attorney's face; Sir Henry brisked up again; but once more Benjy interposed to guide the investigation.

"'Ees, yon be my poor mousey, tied up in t' hanchefut."

"Tied up in what?"

"In t' lad's ankecheef," explained Tommy.

"Shake it out, policeman," said the squire, who shrunk from contact with the unsavory rag himself.

It might once have been, as its manufacturer intended, a rough white cotton article imprinted with the representation of a blind man and his dog, surrounded by the versicles of the beggar's petition. But if no other coloring had ever wrought confusion in its design, the strong, mordant purple of the juice of squashed blackberries had effectually obliterated all. The holes and tatters went impartially in both directions of warf and woop. No mouse fell out, but in one corner two knots appeared, and being with some toil unfastened — sure enough, the corpse of a poor little shrewmouse was discovered in an early stage of decomposition.

"I think after this corroboration, gentlemen," again interposed the attorney, "I need hardly renew my appeal. It is bare justice that my client should not only be discharged, but with the acknowledgment that there remains neither particle of evidence nor ground of suspicion against him."

Though it was evident the magistrates assented, there was no cheering this time; for Tommy, as if to forbid it, turned round once more and scowled angrily at the assembly. Then he put his hand up to his forehead, pulled his forelock towards Mr. Locksley, shook hands with his attorney, and began at once, with scant ceremony, to elbow his way out of the crowd, whose sympathies he scornfully rejected.

There was a further difficulty with Benjy, whom P. C. Hutchins took upon him to detain, and endeavored with no sort of success to cross-question about the finding of the enamelled box. "Nigh t' peat-pools" he repeated once or twice, and thenceforward devoted his whole flickering attention to the shrewmouse's unsavory carcass. Being allowed to wrap it up in his handkerchief again, he consented to accompany the policeman home, upon stipulation that opportunity should be afforded him of investing in peppermints the sixpence which, with praiseworthy faithfulness to his promise, the triumphant counsel for the defence had bestowed upon him. Hutchins was commissioned by the magistrates to make careful inquiries from Widow Rizpah, and empowered, if necessary, to search her cottage. It was not, however, till some weeks after that any thing appeared to corroborate or invalidate Benjy's assertions; and then one of the Cransdale underkeepers picked up, not five hundred yards from the peat-pools, an old-fashioned silver pencil-case, which Mrs. White identified as also forming part of Lord Royston's stolen goods. But a sullen indignation glowed like red-hot embers in the mind of Tommy Wilmot. It seemed to him upon regaining his liberty as if there was little more warmth in his parents' reception of him than there had been readiness in their conviction of his innocence: and the forwardness of the Cransmere gossips to believe the worst of him was an iron that had entered into his soul. The long-coveted underkeepership—should his father consent to his accepting it, as Mr. Locksley was most anxiously urging on him now to do—seemed to have lost its charm, it was already tainted with the reproach of being a turn-coat's bribe.

A wall of ice, upon which the glow of his own anger made no more thaw than an Esquimaux's camp-fire upon a "hummock" in the arctic seas, seemed to have interposed between his father and himself; and even his mother's tears seemed to freeze upon it into mere icicles, because he suspected that she, possibly, still suspected him. The warm breath of a genial confidence could alone melt the dense and cold obstruction, and from no quarter of the domestic heaven did such a soft south wind blow.

He took, without apparent increase of reluctance, the paternal rakes and watering-pots in hand, and went to work once more among the "cabbidge and lattices" which his soul spurned. He brooded and brooded, but hatched no egg of intent, cockatrice or wholesome barn-door chick; until one day, mowing on the lawn by the Lodge windows, without evil intent of eavesdropping, certain words smote his ear between the tinklings of the sharping-stone upon the scythe.

"So Ned sails this day three weeks. O Robert, I can hardly think all real now."

He didn't catch the answer.

"But we'll go down to Chatterham, dearest, wont we, to spend the last week at least with him."

Tommy moved off; but he had heard enough.

"Go for a sodger, eh? To the East Injies, along with Master Ned. I can't abide things as they is at home much longer, nor I wun't."

Two days after Mrs. Wilmot was crying her heart out in Lucy's little breakfast-room, reproaching herself, too late, with a woman's ready repentings.

"Oh, deary, deary, deary me, ma'am, to think we should a druv' un to 't. Our Tommy's tuk' an' started."

M. E. Lagout has presented a report to the Paris Academy of Sciences, on the employment of sea-weed, applied in layers against the thin walls of habitations, to prevent sudden variations in and excess of temperature. The marine algæ, such as sea-wrack, may be termed a *sea-wool*, which has this advantage over ordinary wool, that it does not harbor insects, and undergoes no change by dryness or humidity, provided it be not exposed to the solar rays; in that case it undergoes a complete transformation; from being brown and flexible, it becomes white and almost rigid. In the dark, on the contrary, it is unchangeable, unfermentable, imputresent, uninflammable, and unattackable by insects. At first it has the objection of being hygrometic, but a single washing in fresh water removes the salt, and then its properties become so beneficial, that a celebrated architect has styled it the "flannel of health for habitations." It has been applied successfully between the tiles and ceiling of a railway station also in a portable house intended for the use of officers at the Camp of Chalons: also double panels, the intermediate space being filled with seaweed, have been prepared for the construction of temporary barracks at the isle of Reunion. The consulting committee of Public Health, the Society of Civil Engineers, the council for Civic Structures, etc., have expressed their approval of the judicious employment of the marine algæ, and state that the popularization of this process will be of great service in dwellings, especially in those of the humbler class, as it renders them both more agreeable and salubrious. It can be obtained for about twenty shillings the ton, which quantity is sufficient for upwards of an hundred square yards of roofing.

From The North British Review.

Horæ Subsecivæ. By John Brown, M.D., F.R.S.E. First Series. Second Edition. Edinburgh, 1859.

Horæ Subsecivæ. Second Series. Edinburgh, 1861.

THIS book must be a great consolation to Mr. John Stuart Mill. That great writer and thinker has lately told us, in an essay full of gloomy forebodings, that every fresh originality of character is disappearing so rapidly from our society, that any deviation from one uniform type will soon become so rare as almost to be monstrous. This melancholy conviction gives rise to vaticinations still more dismal. And if it be true that the once rich and various life of Great Britain is now fused into one homogeneous social system, no wonder that thoughtful men should look to the future with more anxiety than hope. But to us the case does not appear so desperate as to Mr. Mill, for we do not think the world so monotonous. It is quite true that the remotest districts have now been brought so much nearer one another than they used to be, that the modes of thought of town and country have been assimilated in a remarkable manner. We are all interested and excited by the same things, and very much in the same way. In every corner of the three kingdoms people are engaged at the same moment in abusing Major Yelverton or in deifying Garibaldi. Every pulse of the great nation beats with its mighty heart; and though it is not impossible that Edinburgh should be in a ferment and London apathetic, London can hardly be moved very deeply without Edinburgh or without Kirkwall being almost equally agitated. It is true also, that this closer contact of remote districts has produced some bad effects, as well as effects that are unquestionably beneficial; and of these perhaps, it is not the least formidable that "the circumstances which surround different classes and individuals, and shape their characters, are daily becoming more and more assimilated." But though this may in some respects be an evil, we do not think it quite so serious an evil as Mr. Mill does, simply because we do not believe that the characters of individuals are shaped entirely by the circumstances which surround them. We do not believe, therefore, that by this assimilation of circumstances all variety will be blotted out from the picture of English life. The characteristic distinctions between the different classes of society are not so broad now as they were in the last generation, and every day they are growing finer and more evanescent. But this is no new phenomenon in the history of manners. It would not be very easy, perhaps, to find a characteristic squire now-a-days, like Sir Edward Bulwer Lytton's Hazeldean, or a characteristic parson like his Dale; but Squire Hazeldean and Parson Dale have only followed Squire Western and Parson Adams, as they themselves had long ago followed Sir Hugh Evans and Holofernes. Every element in these characters which is owing directly to the circumstances that surround them, has disappeared, or soon will disappear, from our modern manners. And if human life were a bad theatre, where the plumes and the tartan make all the difference between the Macbeth of to-night and the Hamlet of to-morrow, it would be reasonable enough, in the disappearance of such elements of difference as these, to see the approach of that dreaded uniformity which would surely be one of the greatest calamities for the national mind.

But though men may no longer differ greatly from one another, merely in virtue of their different conditions, it seems to us that the diversities of natural character will nevertheless remain as inexhaustible as ever. Even in these bad times, when the public voice is, no doubt, monotonous enough, when "the organs of public opinion" are all engaged in expressing the same sentiments, and inculcating the same doctrines, and the *Eatanswill Gazette* suspends its heroic struggle with the *Eatanswill Independent*, only in order to re-echo the proclamations of the *Jupiter*, there still remains, we are convinced, enough of individuality, enough of energy, and, what is quite as much to the purpose, enough of devotion also, among quiet, simple, sequestered people to save us from the Chinese stagnation which Mr. Mill so mournfully predicts. And if any of our readers is more inclined to agree with Mr. Mill than with ourselves on this subject, let him turn for consolation to Dr. John Brown. The Horæ Subsecivæ of this Edinburgh physician will reveal to him, if he will take the trouble to read it, not only the existence of "marked character" in one author, but of whole worlds of doctors, carriers, clergymen, shepherds, and, let us not forget to add, dogs,—all strongly marked characters, and all as different from other doctors, clergymen, and the rest, as Dominie Sampson differs from Dr. Proudie. And, in this point of view, Dr. Brown's originality is probably all the more important because of the manner in which it is expressed. For although we cannot attribute to the "influences hostile to individuality," so powerful or so unlimited an operation as Mr. Mill seems inclined to do, it is impossible for any thoughtful man not to see that such influences are truly at work; and perhaps, they are at work so extensively nowhere as in the world of letters.

We do not mean to say that the number of original and powerful writers now living, and publishing books, is either actually or comparatively small. The ten years—to go no further back—which elapsed between "Vanity Fair" and "Adam Bede," have given no contemptible amount of new and admirable writing to the world. We are not speaking of such great masters as Thackeray and George Eliot. And yet it might be curious to consider the extent to which the greatest writers of our day have allowed their thoughts to be directed and colored by that of the age in which they are living. Even the most illustrious of them all, the poet who of all modern poets is the most profoundly thoughtful and meditative—we mean Mr. Tennyson—seems far oftener to be moulding into some exquisitely beautiful shape the thoughts of an intellectual and highly cultivated age, than to be taking things new and old from the inexhaustible treasury of an individual mind, richer by the gift of nature than the accumulations of great libraries could make it. It need hardly be said that this is true of Mr. Tennyson only in a very limited sense. The commonest thoughts, when he utters them, are transfigured and glorified by the touch of a great imaginative poet; and the thoughts he is most fond of uttering are not common. It is in much humbler regions of literature than any that are haunted by his Muse, and yet in regions that are neither unimportant nor unadorned by talent of a very high order, that the absence of individuality is to be remarked.

What the cause of this effect defective may be, we do not stop to consider; but it is certain that, while we find writings every day in reviews and magazines and newspapers, which show great cleverness, learning, scholarship, every kind of ability, it is rarely indeed that we find any which show character. Now, Dr. Brown's Horæ Subsecivæ is only a collection of miscellaneous articles, some of them reprinted from magazines and newspapers, some published apparently for the first time in their present form; but we think it worth while to occupy some space with a notice of them, not because of any exceptional degree of talent which they evince, but because of that individuality which Mr. Mill finds nowhere, and which we have owned that we find very seldom in the "literature of the day." Dr. Brown is not without admirable talents as a writer; but the chief value of his book consists in the freshness and force of character which it describes very well and often in others, and displays as prominently in himself. The charm of these papers, in short, consists in the constant presence of the author. Dr. John Brown talks familiarly with his readers, instead of exerting himself to write for them; and there is so much of ease and richness of thought and feeling, so much love and goodness as well as genius and culture in his conversation, that these fugitive pieces have a value in our eyes a great deal higher than that of far more pretentious, laborious, and deeply considered books. The one defect, the appearance of which at least is inseparable from this kind of writing, is both the result and evidence of the originality which makes it valuable; we mean the exaggerated importance which the writer is sure to attribute to the things and persons which interest himself. We remember how Lord Cockburn was accused of thinking Edinburgh a bigger place than London. We should not be surprised if the same charge were brought against Dr. John Brown. In both cases it is a misapprehension. It is quite impossible for such men to

"Take the rustic murmur of their burn
For the great wave that echoes round the world."

But, however paradoxical it may seem, the most original mind is the most sensible to the form and pressure of the life that surrounds it. The freshest and richest nature is always the most alive to the things that are passing. And when such a writer as

Lord Cockburn, or as Dr. Brown, has received a lively impression of any kind, he is by no means disposed to conceal the traces of it out of deference to criticism. He is fearless of literary circles. He is never thinking of the Café Procope; and since he looks at the world for himself, and judges its life by no artificial standard whatever, his own genial enjoyment will seem to him sufficient warrant for attaching importance to the sayings and doings of men. People who have formed a fixed set of associations out of books and newspapers, may possibly think things trivial which he finds to be instructive and interesting. But that is because they are conventional and sophisticated. Their life is a kind of cut-and-dry criticism. Dr. Brown's very criticism is buoyant and vigorous life. There is a great deal of the schoolboy about our doctor's love of dogs and horses. There is something of the same quality in his hearty dislikes and exuberant admirations. Sometimes we think this leads him wrong, as when he talks of Mr. Harvey's pictures as if they were works of great genius. Generally it leads him right, as when he condemns that big impostor Festus. But, right or wrong, his severity and his praise alike are generally to be traced much more to the genial than to the intellectual nature of the critic. We do not mean that his judgments are capricious. He has a very fine critical faculty; and his natural taste has been chastened and educated by the constant and reverential contemplation of excellence. But the one thing he requires in writing or in painting is, that he himself should be moved by it; and if that is done, he is independent of external rules. His private judgment is not to be affected by the weight of authority. He is entitled, in short, to say with a more famous essayist: "J'ay une ame libre et toute sienne, accoustumée à se conduire à sa mode."

The preface to the first series of Horæ Subsecivæ contains a very unnecessary apology for what the author describes as "the tendency in him of the merely ludicrous to intrude, and to insist on being attended to and expressed." This is a very inadequate account of a rich and penetrating humor, not unworthy of so enthusiastic an admirer of Charles Lamb. He has not indeed—who ever had?—the wild yet tender imaginative wit of Elia, so subtle and wonderful, that even Scotchmen adore him, when he is "bleating libels against their native land." But he has the genuine humor which, in his own words, is "the very flavor of the spirit, its rich and fragrant *ozmazome*, having in its aroma something of every thing in the man, his expressed juice." Dr. Brown's humor illustrates admirably the definition of a thoughtful writer, whose own wit, by the way, was rather leathery,—Archdeacon Hare, who explains humor as "a sense of the ridiculous, softened and meliorated by human feeling." This is a true but hardly an adequate definition; for it fails to express how thoroughly the humor and the feeling interpenetrate each other. The two elements cannot be separated by the most searching analysis. Nor is the result, though always humanizing, so invariably gentle as one might suppose. Dean Swift, at least, is an illustrious example to show that some slight infusion of gall is by no means inconsistent with true humor; and it might not be impossible to name another instance almost as striking among our great living authors. But we have quoted Archdeacon Hare, chiefly to show how broad a distinction there is between such humor as Dr. Brown's, and the mere tendency to be always joking, with which he seems modestly afraid that it may be confounded. There is a great deal of fun in Dr. Brown: his gravely comic power is inimitable; but it is hardly ever, as it seems to us, the purely ludicrous which gives occasion for its exercise. The incongruity which moves him is that of ideas, and not of words. Sometimes his humor is merely quaint, as when he says of an eloquent talker, "He flowed like Cæsar's Arar, *incredibili lenitate*, like linseed out of a poke." Generally it is so deeply interfused with the human feeling of Mr. Hare's definition, that the smile with which we receive it is very nearly akin to a tear. It looks at the realities of life, and reveals at a touch the infinity and the limitations of our nature, as only the greatest masters of the human heart can reveal it in fiction. And for this very reason, perhaps, it is more felicitous nowhere than in cases where duller men would be puzzled to understand how human feeling should be imported into the matter at all. His descriptions, or rather characters of dogs, for example, are really like nothing so much, either in the result or in mode of treatment, as the Ellistons and Captain Jacksons of Elia. We do not put Toby on a par with Captain Jackson; but the peculiarities of his mental organization are made known to us in much the same way. The most impalpable niceties of the character are seized with the same firm and delicate touch, and brought out, one after another, with the same gradual art, till the picture is complete. And we know nothing anywhere, except in Charles Lamb, which in the least degree resembles the grave fun with which the whole dog is then presented to us. Nor in this process does the one artist ever degenerate into caricature any more than the other. We have not personally known his Tobys and John Pyms, and their fellows; but we feel there is no reason why we should not have met them. They are actual canine beings; and it is as impossible to mistake them for one another, as it is to forget the individuality of the characters of a great dramatist in their general resemblance and their common nature. Unfortunately, we cannot support this opinion by extracts, for we have no room for any complete picture; and we have not the heart to tear any into fragments. But there are two characteristic anecdotes, which we cannot resist. Our readers must understand that Dr. Brown, when a boy, had brought a shepherd's dog from Tweedside to Edinburgh :—

"She came, and was at once taken to all our hearts — even grandmother liked her; and though she was often pensive, as if thinking of her master and her work on the hills, she made herself at home, and behaved in all respects like a lady. When out with me, if she saw sheep in the streets or road, she got quite excited, and helped the work, and was curiously useful, the being so making her wonderfully happy. And so her little life went on, never doing wrong—always blithe, and kind, and beautiful. But, some months after she came, there was a mystery about her. Every Tuesday evening she disappeared. We tried to watch her, but in vain. She was always off by nine P.M., and was away all night, coming back next day wearied, and all over mud, as if she had travelled far. She slept all next day. This went on for some months, and we could make nothing of it. Poor, dear creature, she looked at us wistfully when she came in, as if she would have told us if she could, and was especially fond though tired. Well, one day, I was walking across the Grassmarket with Wylie at my heels, when two shepherds started, and, looking at her, one said, 'That's her; that's the wonderfu' wee bitch that naebody kens.' I asked him what he meant, and he told me that for months past she had made her appearance by the first daylight at the 'buchts,' or sheep-pens, in the cattle market, and worked incessantly, and to excellent purpose, in helping the shepherds to get their sheep and lambs in. The men said, with a sort of transport, 'She's a perfect meeracle—flees about like a speerit, and never gangs wrang wears, but never grups, and beats a' oor dowgs. She's a perfect meeracle, and as soople as a mawkin.' Then he related how they all knew her, and said, 'There's that wee fell yin; we'll get them in noo.' They tried to coax her to stop, and be caught, but no: she was gentle, but off; and for many a day that 'wee fell yin' was spoken of by these rough fellows. She continued this amateur work till she died, which she did in peace."

We think our readers will thank us for transferring what follows to our pages :—

"It is very touching the regard the south country shepherds have for their dogs. Professor Syme, one day, many years ago, when living in Forres Street, was looking out of his window, and he saw a young shepherd striding down North Charlotte Street, as if making for his house. It was midsummer. The man had his dog with him, and Mr. Syme noticed that he followed the dog, and not it him, though he continued to steer for the house. He came, and was ushered into his room. He wished advice about some ailment; and Mr. Syme saw that he had a bit of twine round the dog's neck, which he let drop out of his hand when he entered the room. He asked him the meaning of this, and he explained that the magistrates had issued a mad-dog proclamation, commanding all dogs to be muzzled or led on pain of death. 'And why do you go about as I saw you did before you came in to me?' 'Oh,' said he, looking awkward, 'I didna want Birkie to ken he was tied.' Where will you find truer courtesy and finer feeling? He didn't want to hurt Birkie's feelings."

We did not intend to quote more about dogs; but is there not something at once very absurd and very touching about this :—

"Puck had to the end of life a simplicity which was quite touching. One summer day, a dog-day, when all dogs found straying were hauled away to the police-office, and killed off in twenties with strychnine,

I met Puck trotting along Princes Street with a policeman, a rope round his neck, he looking up in the fatal, official, but kindly countenance in the most artless and cheerful manner, wagging his tail and trotting along. In ten minutes he would have been in the next world; for I am one of those who believe dogs *have* a next world, and why not? Puck ended his days as the best dog in Roxburghshire. *Placide, quiescas.*"

It is plain that, even in the dog-days, Dr. Brown would have no sympathy with the timid scholastic Gray, who said with some indignation, when he was asked if that was his dog, "Do you suppose that I would keep an animal by which I might possibly lose my life?"

The same faculty for seizing the subtlest distinctions of character, which enables Dr. Brown to describe his dogs so admirably, is displayed quite as effectually when he is dealing with men. We do not know that he gives evidence anywhere of that highest imaginative power which consists in the invention of a character; but in the exposition of an actual character, a man whom he himself has seen and known, it would not be very easy to mention many writers by whom he has been surpassed. And this is neither a small talent nor a very common one. It is a much slighter achievement, as it seems to us—and certainly it is a far less useful one—to collect a number of salient features, to solder them cleverly together, and call them a man or a woman, as some of our very popular novelists are much in the habit of doing, than to represent an actual human being as he lived, not by describing attributes merely, but by drawing his character. The power of conceiving an original character is, no doubt, among the rarest and highest of gifts. No description, however excellent, of real people will place a writer on the same level as the great dramatists or the great novelists. But you may count on your fingers the dramatists and the novelists who in this sense are entitled to be called great. As soon as the invention ceases to be human and true, the most dazzling effects of humor or of pathos will give the cleverest caricaturist no right or title to a place beside Sir Walter, or Fielding, or Jane Austen. And no inferior exhibition of imaginary persons is half so excellent a thing, in our view, as the most unpretending portraiture of people who have really existed. With all the amusement we have derived, and hope still to derive, from their productions, the talents of a second-rate novelist—and we should include some very distinguished names in that category—do not appear to us to be so admirable, nor their functions nearly so estimable, as those of the quiet and truthful painter of the things and persons his own eyes have witnessed. To invent a true and many-sided human being, ideal or real—a Hamlet or a Jonathan Oldbuck, a Portia or an Elizabeth Bennet—demands all the qualities which Dr. Brown evinces in describing his own friends, and an imaginative power in addition, which infinitely transcends them all. It is a very different matter to invent traits of character, however funny or however beautiful, or in however clever a combination, without that marvellous interfusion of individual traits with the characteristics common to humanity, which makes the resemblance between the people we see in the world and those we meet with in the great masters of imaginative literature. This may be done with very brilliant effect; but it shows the absence and not the possession of the excellences that are necessary for the exposition of true characters, whether actual or imaginative. We have no hesitation in saying that it required a far higher and more capacious mind, a finer insight, and, in every sense of the word, more genius, to delineate such a character as that of the late Dr. Brown in the way our author has done it, than to invent a score of the grotesque exaggerations which have moved the tears and the laughter of this most sensitive generation.

We mean no disparagement when we say that Dr. Brown generally approaches the people he is describing from the outside. If he remained there we could say nothing worse of him. But however he begins, he has almost always penetrated to the heart of a man before he has done with him. And if it be accompanied in any sufficient degree by feeling and humor, there is, after all, no finer instrument for the detection of character than a keen, rapid, and comprehensive eye for external peculiarities. Dr. Brown says he thinks that he could have been a painter; and it is certain that he possesses the prime requisite of being able to see the outward form of men and things. Nor would it be easy to present in words a more vivid image of a picture than he can when he pleases. Here, for example, is a sketch from the beginning of "Rab and his Friends:" "Does any curious and finely ignorant woman wish to know how Bob's eye at a glance announced a dog-fight to his brain? He did not, he could not, see the dogs fighting; it was the flash of an inference, a rapid induction. The crowd round a couple of dogs fighting is a crowd masculine mainly, with an occasional active compassionate woman fluttering wildly round the outside, and using her tongue and her hands freely upon the men as so many 'brutes;' it is a crowd annular, compact, and mobile; a crowd centripetal, having its eyes and its heads all bent downwards and inwards to one common focus." This clear perception of physical appearances is employed with great skill and success in Dr. Brown's biographical sketches. It is by penetrating observation of all the lovely organs of a life that he seems to arrive at the idea of the life, and he evolves the idea for the benefit of his readers in much the same fashion,—

> "As when a painter poring on a face
> Divinely through all hindrance finds the man
> Behind it, and so paints him that his face,
> The shape and color of a mind and life,
> Lives for his children, ever at his best
> And fullest."

There are two peculiar worlds of which, by sketches of some remarkable inhabitants of both, Dr. Brown gives us glimpses—the medical and the clerical. There are no professions of which the human element ought to be more interesting for laymen; and we cannot help thinking there are none for which, in this aspect, literature has hitherto done less. A good biography of any kind is rare; but rarest of all, is a good biography of a clergyman. One reason may be, that the dignity of their calling makes it so impossible for clergymen to regard it merely as a profession, that it hardly occurs to them or to their biographers to look at their relations with the rest of the world from the human point of view at all. And it is not impossible, that, while the great difficulty of all biography is to trace the intricate connection between the one man whose life is being written, and the qualities ascribed to him which are common to all men, that difficulty may be greatly increased when the subject of the life is a divine. For the qualities which make the life of such a man worth writing, are those of all others which the finest hand is required to individualize. Devotion, for example, and love of truth, identify no man. They are qualities of which we have the vaguest and least personal conception. But, unless the biographer of a man whose life was illustrated chiefly by devotion, or spiritual feeling, or love of truth, be a very able and discriminating person indeed, he is almost sure to think that he has done his work when he has pronounced a panegyric on such characteristics as these. To show how they *were* characteristic, not of good men, but of the one good man whose life he is writing, and no other, is the most subtle and delicate office a biographer can be called on to perform. Nothing short of dramatic genius can bring out clearly the fine evanescent lines by which such a man's personal peculiarities are interwoven with the sublimest feelings and emotions that elevate humanity. The best illustration of this rare and happy art that we could quote from Dr. Brown's book, would be his picture of his father; but we find that, if we were to begin to copy that, we should not be able to spare our readers a single sentence; and it is far too long to transfer entire to our pages. Another illustration may be found in a notice of Dr. Chalmers, in a paper contributed to this journal several years ago, from which, therefore, we do not need to quote.*

Perhaps we could find nowhere a more quiet and graceful picture, without any exaggeration or straining for effect, than the touching and beautiful character of "Uncle Ebenezer," the well-known pastor at Inverkeithing. It is little to say, that such things as this give a truer insight into the life and nature of a certain class of Scotch divines than any amount of lives and church histories:—

"Uncle Ebenezer flowed *per saltum*: he was always good and saintly, but he was great once a week; six days he brooded over his message, was silent, withdrawn, self-involved; on the sabbath, that downcast, almost timid man, who shunned men, the instant he was in the pulpit, stood up a son of thunder. Such a voice! such a piercing eye! such an inevitable forefinger, held out trembling with the terrors of the Lord! such a power of asking questions, and letting them fall deep into the hearts of his

* *North British Review*, vol. viii., No. xvi., page 462.

hearers, and then answering them himself with an 'Ah, sirs!' that thrilled and quivered from him to them! . . . Nothing was more beautiful than my father's admiration and emotion when listening to his uncle's rapt passages, or than his childlike faith in my father's exegetical prowess. He used to have a list of difficult passages ready for 'my nephew;' and the moment the oracle gave a decision, the old man asked him to repeat it, and then took a permanent note of it, and would assuredly preach it some day with his own proper unction and power. One story of him I must give. . . . Uncle Ebenezer, with all his mildness and complaisance, was, like most of the Brownes, *tenax propositi*, firm to obstinacy. He had established a week-day sermon at the North Ferry, about two miles from his own town, Inverkeithing. It was, I think, on the Tuesdays. It was winter, and a wild, drifting, and dangerous day; his daughters—his wife was dead—besought him not to go; he smiled vaguely, but continued getting into his big coat. Nothing would stay him, and away he and the pony stumbled through the dumb and blinding snow. He was half-way on his journey, and had got out the sermon he was going to preach, and was utterly insensible to the outward storm; his pony, getting its feet *balled*, staggered about, and at last upset his master and himself into the ditch at the roadside. The feeble, heedless, rapt old man, might have perished there, had not some carters, bringing up whiskey-casks from the Ferry, seen the catastrophe, and rushed up. Raising him, and *dichting* him with much commiseration and blunt speech: 'Puir auld man, what brocht ye here in sic a day?' There they were, a rough crew, surrounding the saintly man, some putting on his hat, sorting and cheering him, and others knocking the balls off the pony's feet, and stuffing them with grease. He was most polite and grateful; and one of these cordial ruffians having pierced a cask, brought him a horn of whiskey, and said, 'Tak that, it'll hearten ye.' He took the horn, and, bowing to them, said, 'Sirs, let us give thanks;' and there, by the roadside, in the drift and storm, with these wild fellows, he asked a blessing on it, and for his kind deliverers, and took a tasting of the horn. The men cried like children. They lifted him on his pony, one going with him; and when the rest arrived in Inverkeithing they repeated the story to everybody, and broke down in tears whenever they came to the blessing. 'And to think o' askin' a blessin' on a tass o' whiskey!' Next Presbytery day, after the ordinary business was over, he rose up—he seldom spoke—and said, 'Moderator, I have something personal to myself to-day. I have often said that real kindness belongs only to true Christians, but,'—and then he told the story of these men—'but more true kindness I never experienced than from these lads. They may have had the grace of God, I don't know; but I never mean again to be so *positive* in speaking of this matter.'"

We wish Dr. Brown had not omitted in his Second Series the two professional papers to which he alludes in the preface. The essays of that kind in his first volume are among the most interesting and valuable that he has written; and they are so because they deal far less with the mere details of his art, in which doctors only are likely to be interested, than with the far larger question of the way in which the art can be taught and learned, so as to afford the best chance of its being exercised for the benefit of men. The mere acquirements of the physician are only alluded to; but the way in which these acquirements can be turned to practical account is discussed in more than one excellent paper, which neither young doctors nor patients of any degree of age or experience can read too often or think over too thoroughly. The position of the medical profession has greatly changed within the last half-century. People no longer expect quite the same things from their doctor; and, fortunately or unfortunately, they are no longer inclined to feel the same unquestioning confidence that they will receive what they do not expect. The edge of the old sarcasm is blunted. A physician is not now an unfortunate gentleman who is expected to perform a miracle every day. Most of us have been made to understand that the issues of life are not in the pharmacopœia; and, in the natural progress of things, the very time when the mere accumulation of learning is beginning to afford less and less consolation to the mind of a much suffering universe, it is in itself growing vaster and more imposing. The science is crowded and overwhelmed with details in every direction. Nervous and hypochondriacal persons suffer frightfully from Mr. Churchill's advertisements of books. It is only too evident from that appalling evil, that every minute organ of the human frame is the centre of a whole system of diseases, all too probably in active, though hitherto unsuspected operation, at the very moment we are trying to spell out for the first time their cacophonous and mysterious titles. And when he turns from the diseases incident to humanity, to the almost equally numerous and distinct sciences, by the aid of which medicine proposes to combat those diseases, the reflecting layman begins to fear his well-armed champion almost as much as his natural enemy. He cannot bring himself to believe in the possibility of moving lightly under so elaborate and cumbrous a panoply. Such a layman will find some comfort in several of Dr. Brown's papers; for this is the aspect of his "noble and sacred" profession with which those papers are concerned. We believe with him that that profession requires more "intellect, energy, attention, patience, and courage, and that singular but imperial quality, at once a gift and an acquirement, presence of mind—*ἀγχίνοια*, or nearness of the *νοῦς*, as the subtle Greeks called it—than almost any other department of human thought and action, except perhaps that of ruling men." We make no doubt that these qualities are to be seen in operation every day, it is not for us to say where or how: but in writing, they are explained nowhere that we know of with more "sense and genius," than in the book before us.

We had marked for quotation some passages from his criticisms on art, but we have left no room to insert them. We have hinted already, that on this subject we do not always agree with him. The eye, it is said, sees no more than it brings with it the power of seeing; but some eyes bring with them the power of seeing a great deal more than the painter has had the power of showing; and in such eyes, it is not impossible for a daub to appear a masterpiece. But, after all, it is not often that we disagree with Dr. Brown; and where we are at one—to take his distinction—we know no abler exponent of the *soul* of painting than he. With the *body* he does not meddle. But in perception of the thought and feeling of a great picture, and in the faculty of teaching others to understand these things also, he is truly excellent; and this is the one essential element of good art-criticism. We know few things of this kind better than his description of Wilkie's "Distraining for Rent," or of Turner's "Rizpah," except some of Mr. Thackeray's criticisms, and of course, and above all, those of the most mistaken, most unmannerly, and best art-critic that ever wrote—Mr. Ruskin.

We are not going to criticise it, and we have no doubt that it is well known already to most of our readers; but we cannot part from this book without boldly asserting that "Rab and his Friends" is, all things considered, the most perfect prose narrative since Rosamond Gray. We can find in many books *a wider* combination of excellences, but so perfect a combination of those which do belong to it of humor and pathos, and genuine human feeling, in none.

We have been going back in this article to those half-forgotten days when Quarterly Reviewers, instead of writing elaborate essays, actually ventured to criticise and talk about nothing but the book before them. We have given a few extracts, after the fashion of those good old times, when Mr. Mudie and his colleagues did not put books into more hands than reviews. But we are not aware that the elder brethren we have been imitating ever indulged in wholesale panegyric. They let no author go without explaining, with something like paternal kindness, to him and the world, the nature of all the faults with which his excellence might happen to be alloyed. If we are like them in the rest, we will resemble them also in that; and before we bid farewell to an author who has been both amusing and instructing us, we mean to take the liberty of indicating some of his defects. It seems to us, for example, that there is a want of fusion in the longer and more important essays; and Dr. Brown interrupts his own sound thinking and good writing a great deal too often, to give us scraps of other people's. We do not object to his Latin and Greek in moderation; but the tender melancholy with which he sees "the tide setting in against the *literæ humaniores*," induces him to tag to his discourse rather too many patches from that quarter, and "quote quotation on quotation" a little too frequently. There is something a little irritating in the very appearance of pages so deformed with dashes, italics, and inverted commas; and still more so, in such awkward and even dangerous collisions between Greek definite and English indefinite articles, as even Dr. Brown's great skill and practice in driving half a dozen languages at once, have not enabled him to avoid. This is one fault of his otherwise admirable style.

Another is, the trick of running a simile to death. Dr. Chalmers, for example, is the sun for half a dozen pages, and then he is a river for half a dozen more. But we must own that, even when his figures of speech are long enough to be wearisome, they have always the merit of bringing out clearly and graphically the meaning they are meant to convey; and this is so rare a merit in new similes and short ones, that it almost induces us to forgive our old friends the sun and the river, even when they have grown to be unwieldy. The worst sin remains. Dr. Brown has studied many great philosophic writers, and knows how to reverence their greatness; and yet there seems to us something singularly free and easy, careless and disrespectful, in his dashing way of disposing of their merits occasionally in half a line. We limit this criticism to his *Excursus Ethicus*. Elsewhere his tone is different; but that disquisition reminds us of nothing so much as the great Madame de Stael's famous question to Schelling, "Monsieur voudriez-vous bien m' expliquer votre système en peu de mots?" She thought, "a petit quart d' heure" was quite enough for such a purpose; and Dr. Brown, in the Excursus, seems to think so too.

Our readers do not need to be told again, even after all this fault-finding, that good sense, sagacity, scholarship, humor, and genius, are not to be found in finer combination anywhere than in those two excellent books, in which Dr. Brown has given us the fruit of his leisure.

City and Suburb. By F. G. Trafford, author of "The Moors and the Fens," and "Too Much Alone." Three vols. London: Charles J. Skeet, 10, King William-street, Charing-cross.

This is a first-class novel. The author's name is not known to us, for it has not been our good fortune to have seen either of the works referred to in the title-page; but this we feel no hesitation in affirming that such a book as "City and Suburb" cannot fail to attract universal attention. It mainly devotes itself to giving in detail what reads as if it were an actual biography of a proud, highly gifted young man, unaided by friends, flinging himself into the midst of the great battle of life in London, and eventually, by integrity, energy, and talent, coming out of the strife—a conqueror! The hero and his family are all pictures drawn from life, and so distinctly portrayed that they must ever after remain impressed upon the memory as persons with whom one has been well acquainted. In the midst of the family group is one of those creatures,—the curse and the plague of many a homestead,—a beautiful, brainless girl, an unceasing cause of anxiety to all who bear her name, a creature of impulse, with no principles to guide her, and no strong feelings to hold her. In the following manner she is described upon her first appearance:—

"She was just one of those tiresome women who make the best of every thing till they weary of it; and if she had been shipwrecked on some distant island, she would first have shrieked till she had no voice left, and then have fascinated the chief of the tribe, and played at queen till she tired of her lord and her subjects, when she would have compassed heaven and earth to get off in the first vessel, the sail of which she saw against the horizon."

The power of the author does not consist merely in a clear analysis and a just description of character. Scattered profusely over the pages of the work will be found many wise, thoughtful, and just sentiments, the ripe results of practical wisdom and well-used experience. A single extract will prove this:—

"I would," says the author, "lift up my voice against an error of the day, against the idea that man can triumph over circumstances otherwise than by adapting himself to them. His will proves an engine of power in a sensible and an adaptable man, but it is an engine of destruction in the hands of an obstinate clever fool. The cant of the day is in favor of a man adhering to any determination once made, through misery and poverty to possible success. I believe I advise you better, my reader, when I say that the best laborer in the Lord's vineyard is he who, let him be working ever so hard in his own fields, is ready to leave those fields and seek work elsewhere, when the servants of God—circumstances—prove to him that his work in them will be but fruitless and his labor vain."

We recommend "The City and Suburb" as one of the most interesting and instructive novels we have ever read; a book calculated to afford pleasure to all classes of readers—the humble and the great—to women as to men.—*London Review.*

From The Spectator, 11 May.

CIVIL WAR IN AMERICA.

It is sometimes a misfortune to be too well informed, and it is one from which the British public suffers on American affairs. Intelligence reaches them in such masses, accompanied with such a profusion of detail, and explained by such an abundance of commentary, that the broad features of the position are scarcely to be released from the wrappings in which they are enveloped. Yet they are sufficiently simple when once the details are thrust aside. That lingering doubt which seems still to affect all English minds, and which springs from an unwillingness to credit events fraught with such unmixed evil, has no place in America itself. There the single order of the day, which all men consciously or unconsciously obey, is best defined in the old Marshal's habitual signal, "Forwards!" Two hostile nations are ranging themselves for battle, and their forces are rapidly crossing the intervening space. Every obstacle, physical and moral, which interfered with actual collision, is being rapidly removed. The leaders of the South, who retain the initiative they have always assumed, have determined to make Columbia their first battle-field, and their troops are pouring towards Washington in detachments. The nearest body has already arrived at Richmond, and it is calculated that by the 1st of May the Southern President will have twenty-five thousand men ready for the attack. They have no hostile territory to cross to reach their goal. The Convention of Virginia, assembled in secret session, has resolved to anticipate the people, and prevent the protest of the Western division by voting the State into the Confederacy of the South. The men of the Western counties, the Americans who own no slaves, and the Germans who hold slave-labor noxious or unprofitable, will doubtless organize a party of their own. But they are shut out from the body of the state by mountains, are essentially slower than their rivals, whose movements are quickened by fear, and will probably find it to their interest to restrict their energies to the supply of both the combatants with food. They have no control over the route to Washington, from the South, and President Davis is organizing his attack from the base of a powerful and friendly state, occupied by nearly a million of whites, and able for a time to supply all necessary commissariat. His road is clear whenever he thinks the hour for action has arrived.

On the other side, the obstacles which existed last week are disappearing with a speed which might suggest to many minds the notion that Providence *designed* the contest to be summarily fought out. Had Delaware seceded, the advance of the Northern troops by sea, always slow, might have been still further delayed, but Delaware has decided to support the Union. Maryland again, holds all the land routes between Washington and the North, and for weeks Maryland has been supposed heartily friendly to the South. In this event the President must either have conquered Maryland—a difficult and tedious enterprise — or carried on the contest in a besieged city accessible only from the sea. The action of the secret societies, however, seems rather to control the capital than the state. The mob of Baltimore, always the most bloodthirsty in the Union, who attacked the Massachusetts militia, and hunted for Mr. Sumner to hang him for his presumption in passing through their city, are not apparently supported by the majority of the state. The people are disinclined to secede; and as the Northern troops are competent, if necessary, to raze Baltimore, the Maryland routes must be considered no longer closed. Indeed, one line *viâ* Annapolis, is already held by regular forces, and as soon as the Western contingents now assembling at Harrisburg—the point in Pennsylvania at which the Western strikes the Southern system of railways—arrive, the power of the Baltimore rowdies will be at an end. Civilized men will not regret if a city which fosters associations like the "Blood-tubs" and Plug-uglies—associations compared with which a gang of coiners is a civilized community — should meet the fate it has so long deserved. Maryland once out of the path, the North and South stand face to face on their chosen battle-field. The South may be considered arrived, and the North is pushing rapidly to the front. Two regiments of the Massachusetts men had arrived, one in Washington and the other at Annapolis, while four New York regiments are reported in the capital. Six companies of flying artillery were in readiness at Washington, while from Maine to Annapolis the road was strewed with regiments all marching in the same direction. The news from the West is so fragmentary and uncertain, and all the facts indeed so obscured by clouds of enthusiasm and grandiloquence, that an accurate estimate of Northern numbers is not to be obtained. It would seem certain, however, that Pennsylvania, New Jersey, Rhode Island, and New York—the states nearest the scene of action—will have thirty thousand men in the field in good time, while this number will be doubled by the arrival of the Western contingents, and those of the New England States. Behind them a reserve is springing up which, if the war fever does not cool, will in three months amount to half a million—enthusiastic even if half trained. The character of these battalions it is more difficult to estimate, as the unlimited publicity of America makes every grumble seem important, but they are composed chiefly of two classes—the very flower of American youth, and the lawless, excitable scamps who, under the name of rowdies, are the terror of every Northern city except Boston. These men, if shot in sufficient numbers for disobedience, will make good soldiers, but if the discipline falls short in sternness, their irregular habits will detract greatly from their efficiency. As a whole the force is probably equal to that of the South in courage, superior in *morale*, and inferior only in capacity for discipline and obedience. For a permanent contest, too, they have probably the advantage in artillery. The North is full of cannon, of sorts, and as a navy-yard cannot well be ordered South, Mr. Floyd could not deprive the Federal Government of the stores intended for the ships. Such as they are, another week will report them in position for the defence of Washington, threatened by an equal army from the South.

In a contest like this, in which the people supply the resources their Governments do not possess, materiel is nothing in comparison with a cause. This is said in England to be lacking, but we think with only apparent justice. A nation which is defending its capital from attack cannot be said to lack a cause, even though the assailants should be seceders from herself. Even admitting, what we should strenuously deny, that the South had a claim to Washington, as standing on slave soil, the slaveowners could have no right to seize it while still in possession of their rivals, without negotiation. Still less can they pretend to close the right of way between the capital and the provinces, to annex Maryland without the consent of her population, or declare Wheeling, tilled by freemen, part of a confederacy based on the divine right of slavery. Least of all—for here the South comes in conflict with the facts of nature—can they expect to retain peacefully the mouths of rivers which drain the territory of their foes, to shut the West from the Mississippi, and Pennsylvania from the Potomac. The pretext for war is a dispute on boundaries: ample justification, even if the case is to be judged by the narrowest canons of international law. In truth, however, the present issue is far wider and deeper than this, while other controversies lie behind, so inevitable and yet so broad, that all but enthusiasts shrink from looking steadily at the prospect. It is absolutely essential, not to this or that settlement, but to any settlement whatever of the existing contest, that the two parties should comprehend their precise comparative strength, and all modes of trial have been rejected save the sword. The South abolished trial by the ballot-box when she revolted against the election of Mr. Lincoln. Trial by argument is impossible, for the adversaries have no *locus standi* common to them both. International diplomacy is equally fruitless, for each party thinks its strength enables it to dictate the terms. There is reason to believe that upon this point very wild delusions prevail upon both sides. The South has been taught, and believes that the Northerners are cowards, incapable of organization, demoralized by labor, and too divided by social strife to unite for resistance to an aggressive and kindred republic. It was the South, the planters allege, which beat England in the last war, which conquered Mexico, and which furnished generals, commodores, and statesmen to the entire Union. The North has been told, and believes, that the South is full of Union men, is frightened by the dearth of food, afraid of the mean whites, afraid of the four million of slaves, without money, and without cohesion. The one delusion is perhaps as baseless as the other, but each is in its own section absolute. The South has for years treated the North as a strong ally treats a weaker but still useful friend. The North, on its part, has given way to that sort of facility with which men often yield to the tyranny of the weak. Till these delusions are dispelled, and North and South understand their relative strength and weakness with some precision, negotiation can have no permanent effect.

We say this is the present issue, but behind it, ever drawing nearer, is the portentous issue on which American politics have for thirty years depended. The ultimate object of the South is the predominance of slavery; the ultimate object of the North is its subjugation. As yet the South has the advantage of its cynicism. It acknowledges its evil end, while the North, aghast at the results a war on slavery must entail, is vainly seeking some other terminus to the struggle. Already, however, as the strife extends, and the North becomes clear that the South is no enemy to be despised, men are habituating themselves to a design which, at first, seemed too terrible for discussion. Already it is said slaves are property, and if Northern property is to be attacked at sea, why not Southern property on land? As long as there remains any hope of negotiation, any conceivable *via media* short of a war of subjugation, the North will hesitate to risk the freedom of slaves. But the moment that day passes, and the North finds that the slaves are the prime source of an enemy's military strength, the idea of striking a final blow, of settling the conflict and its cause together, will gain ground in the national imagination. The idea of humanity is powerful in the nineteenth century, but care for the lives of their enemies will not long check a race naturally vindictive, whose blood is mounting rapidly to fever heat. It is not improbable that the great controversy may be precipitated by isolated movements conducted by single men. Already the surviving son of John Brown, "Osawatomie Brown," is collecting his friends to carry out his father's plans, and, if possible, avenge his father's execution. There are many John Browns among the abolitionists, and they are not of the class which forgets that all men lie always under sentence of death, or stop an idea because it may involve a life.

The war, we repeat, is already one for the boundaries of two great nations, and will become one to decide whether slavery shall extend or be finally extinguished.

From The Spectator, 11 May.

THE LAW OF THE AMERICAN SEAS.

The civil war in the States, besides the general injury to humanity, threatens to inflict a special mischief upon commerce by unsettling maritime law. Most of the principles hitherto observed are wholly or partially unsuited to so unexpected a condition of affairs, and every application of the law involves millions of property, perhaps even the future of states. Sir Richard Bethell, whose influence on politicians we last week denied, is this week arbiter of an important branch of politics. A blunder on his part may cost us more than one by the Foreign Secretary. Take, for instance, the question of the rights of belligerents. Lord John Russell states, acting on advice, that the principle in force is to admit any power as a belligerent possessed of a certain amount of force. The South possesses such a force, and must therefore be recognized as a belligerent. This amounts in practice to a recognition of the South for all maritime purposes, and will create extreme irritation in the Government with which, for moral reasons, Great Britain is bound to sympathize. England, of course, is bound to adhere to a principle if clearly defined, but this rapid decision seems to indicate a slight bias towards the South.

Then as to blockades. A blockade, it is announced, to be respected must be effective, a principle perfectly intelligible. But it is one America has not yet accepted, she indeed having lately raised the strange point that no state can blockade its own ports. The latter quibble, invented to compel the king of Naples to restore an American ship seized off Palermo, will, of course, be silently laid aside. But no one can doubt that the North will interpret "effective" blockades as loosely as it can, or that a violation of an ineffective blockade will produce intense irritation in the American mind. It is true the European powers, as matters stand, can enforce their own principle, but this country does not desire, in enforcing it, to drift into a position of hostility to men who are contending against an insurrection raised by slave power.

These points, however, are simple compared with those involved in the question of neutral goods. Northern goods, for example, may be taken in British vessels by Southern privateers. Are those goods liable to seizure or not? Clearly, if the Southern Confederacy were not entitled to the rights of belligerents, they could be punished as pirates. But they are declared entitled, and the law is still to be sought. By European law, settled at the Treaty of Paris, "the neutral flag covers enemies' goods, with the exception of contraband of war." But this law has never been formally recognized by America, which did not accede to the Convention of Paris. It is in accord with the right of neutrals so long upheld by America, but it is not the recognized law, and will be far less popular now that it will transfer the carrying trade at once to the British flag.

Then again as to privateers. The European world has agreed to abolish privateers. America has distinctly refused to accept that arrangement. Are privateers to be recognized or not? If they are not, they must be treated as pirates, and the Southern marine is at once swept off the seas. If they are, of what value is an arrangement to which one of the greatest of maritime states refuses to accede, and is allowed to continue to refuse? The complications are endless, and Lord Palmerston distinctly refused even to reply to questions on the law the Government intended to enforce. Every vessel, therefore, which sails for America, sails with a liability to attack, the extent of which its owners cannot appreciate.

Perhaps the simplest and, in the end, the fairest arrangement would be to notify that the European Governments intended to enforce their own law except as regards privateers. But this rule implies a wide exception in favor of the South, and we hold that the radical principle of British policy should be, granted a doubt, to explain that doubt in favor of the North. It is with them, and not with slaveowners, that our permanent sympathies must lie, and our interests are not very deeply endangered. We want nothing of the South except cotton, and, friendly or hostile, she must either sell her cotton or perish from inability to feed her slaves. To carry out the whole law of Europe is, however, impossible without coercing North as well as South, and the partial arrangement brings some large advantages. It would give to the British the whole of the carrying trade, both North and South, and preserve the communication of both parties with each other and the European world. It would enable the North and South to ship their wheat and cotton, and thus reduce the amount of suffering this iniquitous war must, in any case, produce, by exempting the North from the stoppage of her trade, and Lancashire from the interruption of her cotton supply.

From The Examiner, 11 May.

ASPECTS OF AMERICAN AFFAIRS.

THE struggle has at length fairly begun; and while we now talk of it in England, it is not improbable that the first sanguinary encounter may have taken place. The position of the capital has naturally been the first object of solicitude on both sides. Surrounded by the States of the Confederacy, the little territory of Washington has for weeks lain defenceless against surprise, yet no attempt whatever has been made; and the last advices state that the road from Annapolis, by which reinforcements from the North could most easily arrive, had not been stopped as there was reason to apprehend it would have been. The respite thus afforded has been used by General Scott to throw up outworks on several points in the vicinity of the city, and to organize every available species of defence in the suburbs. Several regiments have already made their way from Pennsylvania, New York, Delaware, and Massachusetts; and every day the route remains open, the number of the garrison is certain to be further increased. There is said to be no lack of warlike stores at Washington, and great confidence is felt in the judgment and decision of the veteran in command of the place. Why it has not been attacked during the period that it lay defenceless nobody seems exactly to understand. It is perhaps to be accounted for by the supposition generally credited in New England, that notwithstanding all their menace and bluster, the Confederates shrink from hazarding a decisive move before they are better prepared to meet the consequences of a reverse. The morrow of their first signal defeat will be for them one of unspeakable peril, not by reason of its strategic results, which may be immaterial or may be retrieved, but because the tidings of the overthrow of the Planter Army, spreading as they are sure to do like wildfire from one end of the Confederate States to the other, will whisper in the ear of many a bondsman in the tempting words of the old Jacobite song:

> "Now, or never,
> Now, and forever."

Few who know the instinctive and traditional spirit of those who have deliberately planned and executed the movement for secession, can doubt the earnestness or gallantry with which they will meet the onslaught of the men of the North. For years, almost for generations, they have been taught and they have been accustomed to consider themselves as an ascendant class, not only as regards their colored dependants, but as regards their more industrious and money-loving fellow-citizens of New England. In Congress and in the general Administration they have managed to possess themselves of a predominant power, resembling in many essential features that which has been so long enjoyed by the owners of real property amongst ourselves. New England presidents have been nearly as rare as plebeian premiers with us; and though the rigorous distribution of seats both in the Senate and in the House of Representatives according to territorial delimitation and electoral numbers, has rendered any preponderance of votes like that to which we are compelled to submit, impossible in America, the planter interest has long succeeded in exercising an overbearing influence both in the Legislature and the Executive Government. It would be strange if habits of irresponsible authority over their social inferiors, and of commanding superiority over their political equals, did not generate among the planters fixed belief in their own superior fitness and capacity to bear rule. We know how intense is a similar persuasion among our own nobility and gentry, though refinement of manners interdicts the unnecessary assertion of the claim in openly offensive phrase. The representative men of our great cities and manufacturing districts are indeed more effectually excluded from all participation in the profits and honor of power than the men of New England and of the Western States have ever been.

But there are many points of analogy between the relative positions of the men of industry and the men of leisure on the opposite sides of the Atlantic: and if we would estimate correctly the temper of haughty defiance with which the battalions of the South will be led into the field, we must bear in mind the elements that constitute their military *morale*. Amongst these ought not to be forgotten a greater familiarity with the discipline and habits of the camp. The Americans of our day have had indeed but little opportunity of acquiring a knowledge of the profession of arms, as that calling is understood in Europe; but of such opportunities as they have had, a far greater number of the young men of Virginia and Carolina have availed themselves, than of Massachusetts or Michigan: and upon the whole we may safely assume, that hand to hand, and man for man, the troops of the Confederacy would be more than a match for those of the Union. President Davis and his military advisers well know, however, that it is not upon these terms they will have to meet the fearful issue they have raised. The resources of the North in men and *materiel* are vastly greater than any at their disposal; and hence, no doubt, arose the impression that instead of giving time for levies, drill, equipment, and concentration, the Confederate chiefs would try to strike the first important blow by the capture of Washington. That they have not done so augurs better for their prudence and their foresight, than for the actual strength of their position. Masters of the capital, they might indeed have had the satisfaction of inditing instructions to their representatives at foreign courts from the official chambers occupied formerly by Jefferson and Monroe. But once there, it would have been difficult for them to have abandoned the metropolis, and perilous to have undertaken its defence when besieged, as besieged it would surely be. In point of fact the soldiers of the North could desire nothing better than that the seat and centre of war should be fixed beyond the limits of the residuary states, and that all the suffering and loss which the presence of war entails should be confined to one devoted region specially claimed by their antagonists as their own.

With the command of the sea, and industrial occupations uninterrupted within their borders, the still-United States need best calculate how long they would continue the contest, and how many men and dollars per month they would invest in ultimate victory as a grand speculation. The saucy secessionists, indeed, have not scrupled to avow their belief that the "money-worshippers of the North" would sooner tire of civil war than "the sons of Southern chivalry." But there is something more than merely growing tired to be considered in the matter. Beleagured in Washington and blockaded at Charleston and New Orleans, it is difficult to imagine a case more desperate than that of the Confederates must speedily become. The retention of the capital, no matter by what deeds of heroism and self-devotion, would do nothing to overawe mutiny and revolt among the negroes; and we shrewdly suspect that after a short time nothing will suffice to repress movements of that description but the presence everywhere of disciplined masses under military command. Whenever these are drawn away from any important district by the necessities of the campaign in the Border States, the danger of servile insurrection will be imminent.

This, then, we take to be the reading of the circumspection shown by President Davis and his ministers, as far as events are yet known to us. Meanwhile agents of both sides are known to be in this country engaged in the purchase of vessels capable of being fitted out as ships of war. Pending the decision of the British and French Governments with respect to the threatened resort to the practice of privateering, it is useless to enter into any discussion on the subject. But if ever there was an occasion there is one now on which it is justifiable for the rest of Christendom to take a peremptory tone in the interests of humanity, and to bring its whole concentrated pressure to bear upon combatants who threaten to resume semi-barbarous methods of warfare which the rest of the civilized world have agreed to repudiate.

From The Economist, 11 May.

THE LEGAL RELATION OF ENGLAND AND OF INDIVIDUAL ENGLISHMEN TO THE CIVIL STRUGGLE IN THE UNITED STATES.

NOTHING is more desirable than that we ourselves should have, and that the rest of the world should have, accurate notions of our precise position with respect to the civil conflict which is in progress between the now disunited States of America; and, at the same time, not many things are more difficult. The case is so new that it is difficult to realise its true features and to apprehend distinctly its proper relations either to recognized principles or to our own interests. Curiously, too, we in England have generally been the belligerent and America the neutral nation; and, now that the position is reversed, in some not unimportant points our former tenets are the more agreeable to them and their former tenets are more agreeable to us. In these circumstances our duty is a duty of caution. We should be wary in acting, and almost as wary in speaking: we should be very slow to do any act which would embroil us in a discord from which neither of the combatants can hope for any thing but disaster; and we should be slow, too, in committing ourselves to any international *formulæ* which might in the rapid course of events, from the unforeseen effect of some omitted consideration, commit us to the very course of conduct we wished to avoid, and immerse us in the dangers we had hoped to shun.

Some important conclusions, however, can be laid down very easily and very clearly. In the first place, we should on no account as yet recognize the Southern States as a new nation. Such an act would be wholly uncalled for, either by precedent, by reason, or by natural feeling. We cannot, with our ethical maxims, be over-ready to favor a federation of which slavery is not the accident but the principle: reason tells us that we should be slow to offend a government with which we are in amity by recognizing any seceders from it: the established precedents of international law tell us that we have our choice, and that there is no call upon us to recognize the Southern States of America unless we like it.

On the other hand, we are bound by all sound principle and by precedent to recognize the Southern States as belligerents. Common sense tells us that when two great sections of a nation are contending, whether the cause of strife be mastery on the one hand or independence on the other, or any other cause whatever, it would not only be absurd but wicked to treat either of the combatants as a herd of rioters or casual breakers of the peace. The two parties themselves are obliged to treat each other more or less according to the international law of belligerent relations, and lookers-on must do so also. We adopted this course in the case of Greece and Turkey; and though in no other respect are the Northern States of the Union at all like the empire of Turkey, they are like it in being the state from which the secession is in progress. Both are, to use a phrase familiar to all Scotchmen, the *residuary* states; and the entire difference of collateral circumstances must not withdraw our attention from the single material consideration. It is scarcely necessary to point out what would be our position if we did not recognize the South as having the usual rights of belligerents. We should then be constant and close spectators of a maritime conflict in which we gave one party all the rights of civilization, and the other party none of the rights; in which we recognized one party as regular combatants, and treated the other as tumultuous rebels; in which we, though constantly professing neutrality, should be in fact taking by distinct policy a definite side. It will be very difficult for England as it is to stand clear of all collision in the complicated naval war which seems to be close at hand. Though the force of privateers and other ships that the South can raise will be petty in comparison with European ideas, it is nevertheless considerable, and may come into collision with us at very many points, and therefore it is our clear interest as well as our great duty to steer clear of the conflict by maintaining an *absolute* neutrality.

This absolute neutrality would in one respect be very favorable to the North. It would compel us to deal with a blockade of the Southern ports as if it were an ordinary blockade between hostile nations. It has been questioned whether a nation could blockade its own ports, and it would be a serious question whether a Government would be justified in using such an extreme expedient to quell a mere local disturbance, or a riot in a town, or some series of acts by a municipality which it did not recognize. But when the ordinary rules of real war are by admission to regulate the conflict, the right of blockade must be accepted as one of the inseparable peculiarities of the adopted code.

It is possible that the American navy may at present be too dispersed to make such a blockade effective for the present, and it is also possible that now that the cotton crop of this year has been shipped, the Southern States will not much care for it for the present; but still it is one of the not improbable incidents of a not very distant future, and therefore it is important to observe that the admission of the South to the *status* of a belligerent will then be as advantageous to the North, as for the moment it is advantageous to the South itself.

These considerations are the most important of any at the present juncture as to the conduct of England as a State. It remains to consider the conduct of individual Englishmen, and on this point the English law is tolerably clear. The Foreign Enlistment Act, which is held to be only declaratory of the common law, is express on the one most essential point. It has been thought that letters of marque could be issued to Englishmen, and that British ships could be fitted out as privateers in London or in Canada, but such acts are as plainly illegal as any words can make them. The Act says: "That if any person, within any part of the United Kingdom, or in any part of his majesty's dominions beyond the seas, shall, without the leave and license of his majesty for that purpose first had and obtained as aforesaid, equip, furnish, fit out, or arm, or attempt or endeavor to *equip, furnish, fit out, or arm*, or procure to be equipped, furnished, fitted out, or armed, or shall knowingly aid, assist, or be concerned in the equipping, furnishing, fitting out, or arming of any ship or vessel, with intent or in order that such ship or vessel shall be employed in the service of any foreign prince, state, or potentate, or of any foreign colony, province, or part of any province or people, or of any person or persons exercising or assuming to exercise any powers of government in or over any foreign state, colony, province, or part of any province or people, as a transport or store ship, or with intent *to cruise or commit hostilities against any prince, state, or potentate*, or against the subjects or citizens of any prince, state, or potentate, or against the persons exercising or assuming to exercise the powers of government in any colony, province, or part of any provinces or country, or against the inhabitants of any foreign colony, province, or part of any province or country, with whom his majesty shall not then be at war;" shall be guilty of a misdemeanor, and be punishable personally by fine and imprisonment, while the ship so equipped is to be forfeited with its stores and ammunition.

It is happily, therefore, clear that we should not be tempted to embroil ourselves with either party in this disastrous conflict by permitting individuals to fit out privateers to aid and assist the other. It would have been very dangerous to England if our law had by any inadvertence allowed any unauthorized acts of individual intervention. We might then have been drawn into the conflict at any moment by some thoughtless act of some reckless individual, or the overbearing passion of either of two most passionate combatants.

This would have been aggravated if the North should persevere in their unwise declaration to treat the Southern privateers as simple pirates, and to visit them with the appropriate penalties. If, indeed, the United States had been wise enough to abolish privateering when requested to do so by the Congress of Paris, they would have had a clear right to act in the manner proposed. But now they have claimed the right of fitting out privateers for themselves, and are bound to afford to their *brethren* of the South the same advantage of those rules of warfare which they claim for themselves. They are bound in duty to carry on a civil war by the rules which *they* admit to be binding for all other war.

On the whole, therefore, it may be said that the duty of England and of Englishmen is for the moment plain and simple, though painful as in such terrible events any duty must be. It is to stand steadily apart from a course of events in which our participation would help no one who should be helped, and aid no cause which ought to be aided. As nations and as individuals, it is our evident interest and an incumbent obligation on us to take no part, by word or deed, with either party,—unaffected either by the Free-Trade enthusiasm on the one hand, or the Anti-Slavery enthusiasm on the other.

From Once a Week, 11 May.

AMERICA—ITALY—AUSTRIA.

American affairs were the grand interest of last week, as they are likely to be of many weeks to come. That Fort Sumter was overpowered could surprise nobody who knew the locality and circumstances; and that the President should issue a manifesto was a matter of course. What the reason is we hardly know; but there seems to be a disposition on both sides the water to disparage Mr. Lincoln. Not only is he blamed for inaction; but the quality of his action is found fault with in a way which appears to really impartial people, unjust. There is no use in judging him by the standard of anti-slavery; for he is not an anti-slavery man. He is opposed to the extension of slavery to new territory, against the will of the general community: and this is the ground on which he was elected. Beyond this his opinions cease to be a matter of practical interest; for he has not to deal with slavery in any of the States. He favors the more liberal section of his Cabinet; and, if forced to pronounce on the institution where it exists, it is probable that events would soon make an abolitionist of him. But with this the public has at present nothing to do. His proclamation is plain in its terms, and decided in its tone. As for the delay of five weeks in declaring war, if it had not been a necessity, it would have been a merit. But the President had no choice. When he took possession of the political edifice which looked from the outside so noble and venerable, he found it pillaged and half in ruins. The treachery of Mr. Buchanan's executive had disorganized and beggared the whole Federal Government, leaving to the new President the task of reconstituting all the departments, routing out remaining traitors, and finding better men to fill their places; replacing stolen stores, filling the empty treasury, in short, making his own tools, and fetching his materials before he could go to work. If overwhelmed by the Slave States which surround Washington before he was ready, he would have ruined the country. If he had driven the Border States to a premature decision, he would have been answerable for civil war. It will be a matter of wonder hereafter that five weeks sufficed him to get his government to work, so far as to enable him to issue his proclamation on the fall of Fort Sumter.

The importance of the responsibility of the first bloodshed is shown by the efforts made on each side to make the other begin. There has been more lawlessness in the Northern cities than has become known through the newspapers,—the good citizens being well aware that Southern money was in the pockets of the special mob in each place which harassed the prominent republicans and abolitionists. It has been hard work guarding one another and their houses and public halls, and exercising their rights of assembling and speaking under mob-intimidation; but it has been harder work to keep the young men passive where the object was to provoke a street fight, in order to say that the first blood was shed in the Free States. The aim was baffled. The first aggression was committed at Charleston; the first wounds were given in the attack on Fort Sumter; and the first deaths (except by accident) were inflicted at Baltimore, the capital of a Slave State, and the port which is, next to New York, the most deeply engaged in the illicit African slave-trade. The Southern section, after driving on a revolutionary policy for thirty years, made a groundless secession; and has now begun a causeless war. The North is so far responsible that a manly conduct and demeanor would have precluded the mischief, and that irresolution, bred of vanity, fear of loss, and idolatry of the Union, has encouraged both the delusions and the audacity of the South; but beyond this indirect responsibility, the North has no share in the disruption of the Union. Whatever its past faults may have been, its present course is clear; and it may enter on its task of self-defence with the stout heart and strong arm which properly belong to the defensive party in cases of pure aggression.

It may:—but will it?—That is the question anxiously pressed on every hand. In the first American revolution the constant and terrible difficulty was the uncertainty of civic and military support. Royalists were making secret mischief in all the towns; traitors were sowing discontent everywhere, as they are in Southern Italy now; the soldiers started off homewards at critical moments, or ignored opportunities of attacking the enemy, and shirked decisive action of any kind. These things were worse than the poverty of the towns, the defencelessness of the rural districts, and the want of shoes and weapons for the soldiers. Will it be so again? It was a civil war then; it is a civil war now: will the peculiar temptations of civil war operate now as before?

As far as we can judge, it will not be so. There must, it is true, be many Northern citizens whose hearts are half in the South, through the intermarriage of hundreds of families of the two sections; but in most of these cases, the Southern relatives are of the Union party, who are averse to secession and war. Their inability to act and speak under the pressure of the Secession leaders is an incitement to their friends in the Free States to put down the tyranny as quickly as possible. The fathers and brothers who live on free soil will fight stoutly to put down the rebel authorities who keep sons and daughters and sisters trembling and grieving on their plantations, expecting a rising of the negroes every hour, and seeing nothing but ruin and death in prospect for all who have, willingly or not, turned traitors to the republic.

The Southern trade, for which so much has been sacrificed, is at an end, after all; and the merchants are astonished to find how little they care about it. Except for family connections, Northern citizens are now free to encounter their enemy; and, as has been shown, these family connections are often the strongest incitement of all. Then there is a long accumulation of resentment of Southern insults, and disgust at Southern barbarism and braggartism. Above all, there is an intense sense of relief at throwing off the incubus of slave-institutions, and being restored to caste among the nations of the civilized world. All these things being considered, and the great population and wealth of the country allowed for, it is no wonder that the tramp of troops is heard with enthusiasm in town and village throughout the Free States; that farmers leave the plough, and clerks the desk, and students their colleges, and professional men their clients, to march to Washington. It is no wonder that money flows thither in a full stream, nor that women are as eager as men in offering such service as they can. Under the present awakening, there will be a quick weeding-out of traitors from all the services. From the highest ranks of the army and navy to the lowest of the customs or the post-office, there will be a watch kept upon all half-hearted, and an expulsion of all false-hearted officials; and there can hardly be many of either, now that all question of compromise or reconciliation is over.

The share that the great North-West is claiming in the struggle seems not to be attended to on our side the water; but it is highly important. The stout and prodigious population there have learned by the Kansas question how to appreciate the South,—or its aggressive forces at least. Their pride in their first President renders them intensely loyal. Their commerce is imperilled by the secession of the lower Mississippi

States; and it is certainly the opinion of good judges in the older parts of the Union, that when the Western men begin to swarm down the Mississippi, and attack the seceding States in rear, while a blockade is instituted at sea, they will leave little to be done elsewhere. When we heard last week of encampments at Washington, the collision at Baltimore, and the secession of Virginia, we perhaps did not think of looking further into the interior; but we may perhaps see the scale finally turned by the forces of the West.

It is a matter of congratulation that the Border States have seceded. They are torn by divisions; at least the three principal ones, Virginia, Kentucky, and Missouri; and half-hearted states are better on the enemy's side. Of all parties concerned, the Union men of those States are perhaps the most to be pitied. Impoverished and degraded by slavery, they have long struggled to rid themselves of it, and now they are to be carried over by their own legislatures to the desperate side, to fight and pay for slavery. They are one of the many elements of peril to the secessionists. Many of them will no doubt cross the frontier, leaving land and negroes to confiscation. Those who cannot so escape must suffer bitterly, whatever happens, before the issue is reached.

All that we hear from trustworthy sources confirms the belief that the secession cause is desperate from the beginning. There is certainly no mistake as to the dearth of money and food, the pressure of debt, the disaffection of the planting interest generally, and the enormity of the lies with which these truths are covered. The numbers of volunteers given in the newspapers could not be actually furnished if the plantations were left entirely unguarded, and the negroes wholly neglected. The impression is strengthened by the braggart tone of the administration and its organs. When it is announced that the Cabinet at Montgomery read Mr. Lincoln's proclamation "with shouts of laughter," people at a distance know what to think. It is the same with the protestations of the loyalty and zeal of the slaves. "Ignorance or worse" is the verdict of all impartial persons on such statements. The warfare is likely to be of a desultory, skirmish sort, judging by the extent of the frontier and the character of the people; and that kind of warfare is likely to convey to the negroes in a very short time a true notion of the real character of the struggle. When the cause is once understood by any single negro, the vanity of the race may be trusted to spread it from the Ohio to the Rio Grande.

Last week the commissioners from the Southern Confederacy arrived, and there was a good deal of curiosity about the precise object of their coming. It was rumored that one of their objects was to raise a loan; but few would credit it. There is no belief that adequate security exists; and if it did, it would be of no value when proffered by men who are implicated in acts of repudiation. Not only have some of the seceding states made themselves notorious by their repudiation of debts, but some of the new Administration, and especially its head, are under that disgrace in the eyes of the world. It was so desperate a notion that Mr. Jefferson Davis' Government could expect to obtain money from Europe, that it was extensively disbelieved.

The subordination of the selfish to the sympathetic spirit in our North American colonies has been admirable throughout the last five months. They have expressed regret, which no one doubts to be genuine, at their neighbors' strife. But sooner or later they must consider the effect on their own interests; and last week we perceived indications that the time had come. The colonists everywhere, from the Atlantic to the furthest frontier of Canada, anticipate a great immigration from Europe, as the tide will turn from the shores of the United States to theirs. Their ports and their shipping, and their canals and railways will all be wanted for the new commerce which must flow in when half the American ports are blockaded, and the commercial world of the Union has gone soldiering. The issue of letters of marque by the Montgomery Government, and President Lincoln's notice that privateering will be treated as piracy, must give over the carrying trade to the merchant navies of other countries, and especially of our own.

The Fourth-of-July celebrations will be something singular and memorable this year. Congress will meet, to sanction civil war. There will be a hush of boasting, which is on that day usually so resonant in the land. The true patriots, who have thus far saved the republic from a servile war, may give thanks and rejoice; but the rest of the nation must gaze down with horror into the impassable chasm which has opened in their national structure.

It was satisfactory to all England to hear Lord John Russell's reply to an inquiry as to our position in regard to this great event. "For God's sake, let us keep out of it!" said our Foreign Secretary, of this quarrel: and the words may be taken as, and will be, those of the country at large. Ministers are in consultation with the law officers of the crown, in order to attain the utmost discretion in guarding British rights without taking any part in American quarrels.

There is no week now which does not bring important news from the Continent. Last week we were supplied with the particulars of the reconciliation between Garibaldi and the minister and general of the king. The candor and nobleness of the man were just what might have been expected from him; but the whole affair leaves a painful impression of insecurity. Garibaldi has been so often misled now that his self-recoveries cease to inspire confidence. He cannot resist the influence of associates; and his associations are determined by the craft of others. For the present, however, he is induced to be quiet.

The schism in the clerical body in Italy became avowed last week in a distinct manner. It appears that the Italian clergy, who venerate the pope's spiritual power too highly to apprehend any danger to it from the loss of temporal possessions, are under apprehension for religion from opposite sides. They fear the worldliness and superstition of the Ultramontane clergy on the one hand, and the inroads of Protestantism (so called) on the other. Speaking accurately, it is not, for the most part, Protestantism which conflicts with Catholicism in Northern Italy; for the Waldenses never having been Catholics are not Protestants. They hold the ancient faith which has come down from a time prior to Romanism, being preserved in the seclusion of Alpine life, unchanged from century to century. They have come out into the world with their faith now,—have a fine cathedral at Turin, and many churches elsewhere,—and are persuaded that it is their mission to convert Italy from Romanism. What schismatics from the Romish Church could not effect, they believe to be their work, as holding an unchanged faith older than either; and their success is understood to have been considerable within the last fifteen years. To encounter at once this body and the pope's proud and rancorous and rapacious priests, the liberal clergy have formed associations in all the provinces, and issued declarations of their objects. They propose unions and congregations for the guardianship and promotion of civil, for the sake of religious, liberty; and that, when these centres of action are in work, they shall send deputies to a general assembly, which shall institute a complete organization. A journal is to be set up, to restrain the encroachments of Protestant doctrine: the assembly is to determine controversies by the canons of the Councils, to the exclusion of party authority: and the aim of the whole scheme is the reconciliation of religion with an advancing civilization, in avowed and steadfast opposition to the party in the Church which stakes its interests on a system of political rule, and social morals and manners, which is the disgrace of Christendom. Every member must be a friend to civil and religious liberty, and a loyal subject of King Victor Emmanuel. We have no news from Italy more significant than this.

The great continental event of the week was the opening of the Council of the Austrian Empire on May-day. The emperor spoke as if he really believed the existence of his empire to depend on the working of his new constitution. His call to the people of the various provinces to help the effective working can hardly seem to himself likely to avail, amidst the clash of interests and of claims, and the general distrust of his own stability. Whatever may happen, however, it is a memorable incident that an emperor of Austria has avowed to the whole world that the welfare of his crown and people depends on the success of any new representative system whatever.

Mr. Ravenstein's work on "The Russians on the Amur," which we lately announced, will be ready in a few weeks. It will consist of two parts, one historical, the other geographical, statistical, and commercial. The former will give the history of Russian adventure on the Amur in the seventeenth century to the treaty of Nerchinsk; the Amur, whilst in possession of China; the labors of the Roman Catholic missionaries in Manchuria; and lastly, the proceedings of Russia since the appointment of General Muravief-Amursky as governor-general of Eastern Siberia in 1848. Very few of these late events have become known to the public, and the author has been able to avail himself of information communicated to him by gentlemen who have themselves taken a part in the occupation of the country. Mr. Ravenstein charges Mr. Atkinson, who lately published a work on the same subject, with never having been on the Amur, the information which his "Travels on the Amur" contains, and the illustrations, having been taken from Mr. Maack's book.—*London Review.*

THE LIVING AGE.

No. 890.—22 June, 1861.

CONTENTS.

NOTE. — We have copied aforetime many articles from English papers, the writers of which seemed strangely ignorant of the merits of the great question, because it is important to us to know how it is regarded by that nation. We looked forward to the great awakening which should follow their knowledge of the uprising of the American people. The Manchester manufacturers, and the whole nation, have so great an interest in the peaceable production of cotton, that we expected a great difficulty in their seeing the truth; but their hardness of heart is greater than we anticipated, and seems to show that their *Government* desires the breaking up of the United States. It has been in haste to act in this direction. We do not believe that this is the desire of the people of Great Britain.

NEW BOOKS.

A MEMOIR OF JOHN FANNING WATSON, the Annalist of Philadelphia and New York. Prepared by request of the Historical Society of Pennsylvania, and read in their Hall, 11 Feb., 1861. By Benjamin Dorr, D.D. With an Appendix by Mr. Watson's daughter, Mrs. Lavinia F. Whitman.

[Man and boy we knew Mr. Watson for fifty years. He was gentle, kind, courteous; independent and firm in his opinions. We had the privilege of intimate knowledge at a time when a very sore calamity befell him, especially trying to him in many points, and are thankful for the example of the unswerving Christian graces of humility, submission, and fortitude which converted it into a blessing. We cherish his memory, and thank his daughter for this book.]

PUBLISHED EVERY SATURDAY BY

LITTELL, SON, & CO., BOSTON.

THE SPECTRE AT SUMTER.

I STOOD on the walls of Sumter
  As the solemn night came down
On the lone, beleaguered fortress,
  On the traitor camp and town;
While through the lurid heavens
  Sped the red-hot shot and shell,
As if by mad fiends driven
  From the open mouths of hell;
While the flag of a sovereign nation
  On the palpitating air,
Still waved from its lofty station
  Amid the fiery glare.

And I saw where fiercest, direst,
  Raged the terrible battle-storm—
Where the bursting shells fell hottest,
  There towered a spectral form:
I knew by its proud erectness,
  By its calm, determined mien,
By the strong arms sternly folded,
  By the deep, clear eye serene,
'Twas that old man, lion-hearted,
  Of the dark and terrible frown,
The genius of retribution—
  Old Osawatomie Brown.

"'Tis well!" he murmured, softly,
  "O traitorous, coward band!
Ply your engines fiercer, faster,
  'Gainst the flag of your native land!
Rain your deathful hail more hotly
  On the heads of that faithful few,
Stifled and faint and famished,
  With their flag of truce in view!

"Roar louder, ye murderous cannon!
  With every echoing boom
O'er the hills of the sturdy Northland
  Sweeps the story of Sumter's doom;
And I hear above your thunder
  The shout of a warrior band,
Waked suddenly from slumber,
  To strike for their native land.

"As the lion of the desert
  Leaps fiercely from his lair,
And gazes down the distance
  With fixed and fiery glare—
As the bolt along the storm-cloud
  Quivers in fierce unrest,
Ere it burst in triple vengeance
  On earth's rent and quivering breast—
E'en so the sons of Freedom
  For one dreadful moment stand,
Till your murderous hand uplifted
  Is struck at your native land.

"Strike fiercer, faster, murderers!
  Steeped to the core in sin,
See, the flag of your country drooping—
  Aim at it once again!
All Sumter's guns are voiceless,
  And the flames are hot within,
And faint are her brave defenders—
  Aim at her once again!
Ha! dastards, cravens, cowards,
  Ye are brave and knightly men!
Your foes disabled, silenced—
  Fire on them once again!

"Ah! mine is the unsealed vision,
  And mine is the prophet ear;
Ye may laugh in your mad derision,
  But the day of doom is near!
New-England's hills will echo
  With the warrior's battle-cry,
And New York's Excelsior banner
  'Mid shoutings kiss the sky:
From the free North's lakes and rivers,
  O'er the distant prairie's breast,
From true-souled Pennsylvania,
  And the bold, unfettered West—
Like the roar of the mountain torrent,
  Like the shriek of the tempest comes,
'God and our country ever!
  Our banner and our homes!'

"Oh! this is the day I prayed for,
  When against the wintry sky,
With the rope around my throttle
  Ye hung me up to die—
The day when my free-born brothers
  In their lofty faith will rise,
And wipe from their fair escutcheon
  The stain that on it lies—
When manhood, crushed and blighted,
  Trampled and bruised and torn;
And womanhood, lashed, polluted,
  The victim of lust and scorn,
From their fainting spirits lifted
  The burden and the blight,
May wake from their loathsome serfdom
  To revel in freedom's light.

"My country! O my country!
  I have called on you oft before,
Would God that my strong appealing
  Might enter your souls once more!
As you value the boon of freedom,
  So fearlessly won for you,
Strike home for your firesides bravely,
  And a whole free country too!
Let your proud flag kiss the heavens
  With never a blot or stain;
O'er bleeding human chattels
  Never to float again!"

—*Tribune.*

From Blackwood's Magazine.

THE EXECUTOR.

CHAPTER I.

"The woman was certainly mad," said John Brown.

It was the most extraordinary of speeches, considering the circumstances and place in which it was spoken. A parlor of very grim and homely aspect, furnished with dark mahogany and black haircloth, the blinds of the two windows solemnly drawn down, the shutters of one-half closed; two traditional decanters of wine standing reflected in the shining, uncovered table; half a dozen people all in mourning, in various attitudes of surprise, disappointment, and displeasure; and close by one of the windows Mr. Brown, the attorney, holding up to the light that extraordinary scrap of paper, which had fallen upon them all like a thunderbolt. Only half an hour ago he had attended her funeral with decorum and perfect indifference, as was natural, and had come into this parlor without the slightest idea of encountering any thing which could disturb him. Fate, however, had been lying in wait for the unsuspecting man at the moment he feared it least. He had not been employed to draw out this extraordinary document, nor had he known any thing about it. It was a thunderbolt enclosed in a simple envelope, very securely sealed up, and delivered to him with great solemnity by the next of kin, which carried him off his balance like a charge of artillery, and made everybody aghast around him. The sentiment and exclamation were alike natural: but the woman was not mad.

By the side of the table, very pale and profoundly discomposed, sat the next of kin; a woman, of appearance not unaccordant with that of the house, over fifty, dark-complexioned and full of wrinkles, with a certain cloud of habitual shabbiness, not to be cast aside, impairing the perfection of her new mourning. Her new mourning, poor soul! got on the strength of that letter containing the will, which had been placed in her safekeeping. She was evidently doing every thing she could to command herself, and conceal her agitation. But it was not a very easy matter. Cherished visions of years, and hopes that this morning had seemed on the point of settling into reality, were breaking up before her, each with its poignant circumstances of mortification and bitterness and dread disappointment. She looked at everybody in the room with a kind of agonized appeal—could it really be true, might not her ears have deceived her?—and strained her troubled gaze upon that paper, not without an instinctive thought that it was wrongly read, or misunderstood, or that some mysterious change had taken place on it in the transfer from her possession to that of Mr. Brown. His amazement and dismay did not convince the poor dismayed woman. She stretched out her hand eagerly to get the paper to read it for herself. He might have changed it in reading it; he might have missed something, or added something, that altered the meaning. Any thing might have happened, rather than the reality that her confidence had been deceived and her hopes were gone.

"Did you know of this, Mrs. Christian?" said the rector, who stood at the other end of the room with his hat in his hand.

Did she know! She could have gnashed her teeth at the foolish question, in her excitement and exasperation. She made a hysterical motion with her head to answer. Her daughter, who had come to the back of her chair, and who knew the rector must not be offended, supplied the words that failed to her mother: "No; we thought we were to have it," said the poor girl, innocently. There was a little movement of sympathy and compassion among the other persons present. But mingled with this came a sound of a different description; a cough, not an expression of physical weakness, but of moral sentiment; an irritating, critical, inarticulate remark upon that melancholy avowal. It came from the only other woman present, the servant of the house. When the disappointed relation heard it, she flushed into sudden rage, and made an immediate identification of her enemy. It was not dignified, but it was very natural. Perhaps, under the circumstances, it was the only relief which her feelings could have had.

"But I know whose doing it was!" said poor Mrs. Christian, trembling all over, her pale face reddening with passion. There was a little movement at the door as the servant-woman stepped farther into the room to take her part in the scene which interested her keenly. She was a tall woman, thin and dry, and about the same age as her accuser. There was even a certain degree of likeness between them. As Nancy's tall person and white apron became clearly visible from among the little group of gentlemen, Mrs. Christian rose, inspired with all the heat and passion of her disappointment, to face her foe.

"Did *you* know of this?" said the excellent rector, with his concerned malaprop face. Nancy did not look at him. The three women stood regarding each other across the table; the others were only spectators—they were the persons concerned. The girl who had already spoken, and who was a little fair creature, as different from the belligerents as possible, stood holding her mother's hand tightly. She had her eyes on them both, with an extraordinary air of control and unconscious authority. They were both full of rage and excitement, the climax of a long-smouldering quarrel; but the blue eyes that watched, kept them silent against their will. The crisis lasted only for a moment. Poor Mrs. Christian, yielding to the impulse of the small fingers that closed so tightly on her hand, fell back on her chair, and attempted to recover her shattered dignity. Nancy withdrew to the door; and Mr. Brown repeated the exclamation in which his dismay and trouble had at first expressed itself, "Certainly, the woman must have been mad!"

"Will you have the goodness to let me see it?" said Mrs. Christian, with a gasp. It is impossible to say what ideas of tearing it up, or throwing it into the smouldering fire, might have mingled with her desire; but, in the first place, she was eager to see if she could not make something different out of that paper than those astounding words she had heard read. Mr. Brown was an honest man, but he was an attorney; and Mrs. Christian was an honest woman, but she was next of kin. If she had known what was in that cruel paper, she might not, perhaps, have preserved it so carefully. She read it over, trembling, and not understanding the very words she muttered under her breath. Bessie read it also, over her shoulder. While they were so occupied, Mr. Brown relieved his perplexed mind with a vehemence not much less tragical than that of the disappointed heir.

"I have known many absurd things in the way of wills," said Mr. Brown, "but this is the crown of all. Who on earth ever heard of Phœbe Thomson? Who's Phœbe Thomson? Her daughter? Why, she never had any daughter in the memory of man. I should say it is somewhere like thirty years since she settled down in Carlingford—with no child, nor appearance of ever having had one—an old witch with three cats, and a heart like the nether millstone. Respect? don't speak to me! why should I respect her? Here she's gone, after living a life which nobody was the better for; certainly *I* was none the better for it; why, she did not even employ me to make this precious will; and saddled me—me of all men in the world—with a burden I wouldn't undertake for my own brother. I'll have nothing to do with it. Do you suppose I'm going to give up my own business, and all my comfort, to seek Phœbe Thomson? The idea's ridiculous! the woman was mad!"

"Hush! for we're in the house of our departed friend, and have just laid her down," said the inappropriate rector, "in the sure and certain hope—"

Mr. Brown made, and checked himself in making, an extraordinary grimace. "Do you suppose I'm bound to go hunting Phœbe Thomson till that day comes?" said the attorney. "Better to be a ghost at once, when one could have surer information. I'm very sorry, Mrs. Christian; I have no hand in it, I assure you. Who do you imagine this Phœbe Thomson is?"

"Sir," said Mrs. Christian, "I decline to give you any information. If my son was here, instead of being in India, as everybody knows, I might have some one to act for me. But you may be certain I shall take advice upon it. You will hear from my solicitor, Mr. Brown; I decline to give you any information on the subject."

Mr. Brown stared broadly at the speaker; his face reddened. He watched her get up and make her way out of the room with a perplexed look, half angry, half compassionate. She went out with a little of the passionate and resentful air which deprives such disappointments of the sympathy they deserve—wrathful, vindictive, consoling herself with dreams that it was all a plot, and she could still have her rights; but a sad figure, notwithstanding her flutter of bitter rage—a sad figure to those who knew what home she was going to, and how she had lived. Her very dress, so much better than it usually was, enhanced the melancholy aspect of the poor woman's withdrawal. Her daughter followed her closely, ashamed, and not venturing to lift her eyes. They were a pathetic couple to that little group that knew all about them. Nancy threw the room-door open for them, with a revengeful satisfaction. One of the funeral attendants who still lingered outside opened the outer one. They went out of the subdued light, into the day, their hearts tingling with a hundred wounds. At least the mother's heart was pierced, and palpitating in every nerve. There was an instinctive silence while they went out, and after they were gone. Even Mr. Brown's "humph!" was a very subdued protest against the injustice which Mrs. Christian had done him. Everybody stood respectful of the real calamity.

"And so, there they are just where they were!" cried the young surgeon, who was one of the party; "and pretty sweet Bessie must still carry her father on her shoulders, and drag her mother by her side wherever she goes; it's very hard — one can't help thinking it's a very hard burden for a girl of her years."

"But it is a burden of which she might be relieved," said Mr. Brown with a smile.

The young man colored high and drew back a little. "Few men have courage enough to take up such loads of their own will," he said, with a little heat; "I have burdens of my own."

A few words may imply a great deal in a little company, where all the interlocutors know all about each other. This, though it was simple enough, disturbed the composure of the young doctor. A minute after he muttered something about his further presence being unnecessary, and hastened away. There were now only left the rector, the churchwarden, and Mr. Brown.

"Of course you will accept her trust, Mr. Brown," said the rector.

The attorney made a great many grimaces, but said nothing. The whole matter was too startling and sudden to have left him time to think what he was to do.

"Anyhow the poor Christians are left in the lurch," said the churchwarden; "for, I suppose, Brown, if you don't undertake it, it'll go into chancery. Oh! I don't pretend to know; but it's natural to suppose, of course, that it would go into chancery, and stand empty with all the windows broken for twenty years. But couldn't they make you undertake it whether you pleased or no? I am only saying what occurs to me; of course I'm not a lawyer—I can't know."

"Well, never mind," said Mr. Brown; "I cannot undertake to say just at this identical moment what I shall do. I don't like the atmosphere of this place, and there's nothing more to be done just now that I know of. We had better go."

"But the house—and Nancy—some conclusion must be come to directly. What will you do about them?" said the rector.

"To be sure! I don't doubt there's plate and jewelry and such things about—they ought to be sealed and secured, and that sort of thing," said the still more energetic lay functionary. "For any thing we know, she might have money in old stockings all about the house. I shouldn't be surprised at any thing, after what we've heard to-day. Twenty thousand pounds! and a daughter! If any one had told me that old Mrs. Thomson had either the one or the other yesterday at this time, I should have said they were crazy. Certainly, Brown, the cupboards and desks and so forth should be examined and sealed up. It is your duty to Phœbe Thomson. You must do your duty to Phœbe Thomson, or she'll get damages of you. I suppose so—*you* ought to know."

"Confound Phœbe Thomson!" said the attorney, with great unction; "but notwithstanding, come along, let us get out of this. As for her jewelry and her old stockings, they must take their chance. I can't stand it any longer—pah! there's no air to breathe. How did the old witch ever manage to live to eighty here?"

"You must not call her by such improper epithets. I have no doubt she was a good woman," said the rector; "and recollect, really, you owe a little respect to a person who was only buried to-day."

"If she were to be buried to-morrow," cried the irreverent attorney, making his way first out of the narrow doorway, "I know one man who would have nothing to do with the obsequies. Why, look here! what right had that old humbug to saddle me with her duties, after neglecting them all her life; and, with that bribe implied, to lure me to undertake the job too. Ah, the old wretch! don't let us speak of her. As for respect, I don't owe her a particle—that is a consolation. I knew something of the kind of creature she was before to-day."

So saying, John Brown thrust his hands into his pockets, shrugged up his shoulders, and went off at a startling pace up the quiet street. It was a very quiet street in the outskirts of a very quiet little town. The back of the house which they had just left was on a line with the road—a blank wall, broken only by one long staircase-window. The front was to the garden, entering by a little side-gate, through which the indignant executor had just hurried, crunching the gravel under his rapid steps. A line of such houses, doleful and monotonous, with all the living part of them concealed in their gardens, formed one side of the street along which he passed so rapidly. The other side consisted of humbler habitations, meekly contented to look at their neighbors' back-windows. When John Brown had shot far ahead of his late companions, who followed together, greatly interested in this new subject of talk, his rapid course was interrupted for a moment. Bessie Christian came running across the street from one of the little houses. She had no bonnet on, and her black dress made her blonde complexion and light hair look clearer and fairer than ever; and when the lawyer drew up all at once to hear what she had to say, partly from compassion, partly from curiosity, it did not fail to strike him how like a child she was, approaching him thus simply with her message. "O Mr. Brown," cried Bessie, out of breath, "I want to speak to you. If you will ask Nancy, I am sure she can give you whatever information is to be had about—about aunt's friends. She has been with aunt all her life. I thought I would tell you in case you might think, after what mamma said—"

"I did not think any thing about it," said Mr. Brown.

"That we knew something, and would not tell you; but we don't know any thing," said Bessie. "I never heard of Phœbe Thomson before."

Mr. Brown shrugged up his shoulders higher than ever, and thrust his hands deeper into his pockets. "Thank you," he said, a little ungraciously. "I should have spoken to Nancy, of course, in any case; but I'm sure it's very kind of you to take the trouble—good-by."

Bessie went back blushing and disconcerted; and the rector and the churchwarden, coming gradually up on the other side of the road, seeing her eager approach and downcast withdrawal, naturally wondered to each other what she could want with Brown, and exchanged condolences on the fact that Brown's manners were wonderfully bearish—really too bad. Brown, in the mean time, without thinking any thing about his manners, hurried along to his office. He was extremely impatient of the whole concern; it vexed him unconsciously to see Bessie Christian; it even occurred to him that the sight of her and of her mother about would make his unwelcome office all the more galling to him. In addition to all the annoyance and trouble, here would be a constant suggestion that he had wronged these people. He rushed into his private sanctuary the most uncomfortable man in Carlingford. An honest, selfish, inoffensive citizen, injuring no one, if perhaps he did not help so many as he might have done—what grievous fault had he committed to bring upon him such a misfortune as this?

The will which had caused so much conversation was to this purport. It bequeathed all the property of which Mrs. Thomson of Grove Street died possessed, to John Brown, attorney in Carlingford, in trust for Phœbe Thomson, the only child of the testatrix, who had not seen or heard of her for thirty years; and in case of all lawful means to find the said Phœbe Thomson proving unsuccessful, at the end of three years the property in question was bequeathed to John Brown, his heirs and administrators, absolutely and in full possession. No wonder it raised a ferment in the uncommunicative bosom of the Carlingford attorney, and kept the town in talk for more than nine days. Mrs. Thomson had died possessed of twenty thousand pounds: such an event had not happened at Carlingford in the memory of man.

CHAPTER II.

THE divers emotions excited by this very unexpected occurrence may be better evidenced by the manner in which the evening of that day was spent in various houses in Carlingford than by any other means.

First, in the little house of the Christians. It was a cottage on the other side of Grove Street—a homely little box of two stories, with a morsel of garden in front, and some vegetables behind. There, on that spring afternoon, matters did not look cheerful. The little sitting-room was deserted—the fire had died out—the hearth was unswept—the room in a litter. Bessie's pupils had not come to-day. They had got holiday three days ago, in happy anticipation of being dismissed forever; and only their young teacher's prudential remonstrances had prevented poor Mrs. Christian from making a little speech to them, and telling them all that henceforward Miss Christian would have other occupations, but would always be fond of them, and glad to see her little friends in their new house. To make that speech would have delighted Mrs. Christian's heart. She had managed, however, to convey the meaning of it by many a fatal hint and allusion. In this work of self-destruction the poor woman had been only too successful; for already the mothers of the little girls had begun to inquire into the terms and capabilities of other teachers, and the foundations of Bessie's little empire were shaken and tottering, though fortunately they did not know of it to-day. Every thing was very cold, dismal, and deserted in that little parlor. Faint sounds overhead were the only sounds audible in the house; sometimes a foot moving over the creaky boards: now and then a groan. Up-stairs there were two rooms; one a close, curtained, fire-lighted, stifling, invalid's room. There was Bessie sitting listlessly by a table, upon which were the familiar tea-things, which conveyed no comfort to-night; and there was her paralytic father sitting helpless, sometimes shaking his head, sometimes grumbling out faint, half-articulate words, sighs, and exclamations. "Dear, dear! ah! well! that's what it has come to!" said the sick man, hushed by long habit into a sort of spectatorship, and feeling even so great a disappointment rather by way of sympathy than personal emotion. Bessie sat listless by, feeling a vague exasperation at this languid running accompaniment to her thoughts. The future had been blotted out suddenly, and at a blow, from Bessie's eyes. She could see nothing before her—nothing but this dark, monotonous, aching present moment, pervaded by the dropping sounds of that faint, half-articulate voice. Other scene was not to dawn upon her youth. It was hard for poor Bessie. She sat silent in the stifling room, with the bed and its hangings between her and the window, and the fire scorching her cheek. She could neither cry, nor scold, nor blame anybody. None of the resources of despair were possible to her. She knew it would have to go on again all the same, and that now things never would be any better. She could not run away from the prospect before her. It was not so much the continuance of poverty, of labor, of all the dreadful pinches of thrift; it was the end of possibility—the knowledge that now there was no longer any thing to expect.

On the other side of the passage Bessie's own sleeping-room was inhabited by a restless fever of disappointment and despair and hope. There was Mrs. Christian lying on her daughter's bed. The poor woman was half-crazed with the whirl of passion in her brain. That intolerable sense of having been duped and deceived, of actually having a hand in the overthrow of all her own hopes, aggravated her natural disappointment into frenzy. When she recollected her state of exultation that morning, her confident intentions—when they were to remove, what changes were to be in their manner of life, even what house they were to occupy—it is not wonderful if the veins swelled in her poor head, and all her pulses throbbed with the misery of the contrast. But with all this there mingled a vindictive personal feeling still more exciting. Nancy, whom she knew more of than any one else did—her close, secret, unwavering enemy; and even the innocent lawyer, whom, in her present condition of mind, she could not believe not to have known of this dreadful cheat practised upon her, or not to care for that prize which, now that it was lost, seemed to her worth every thing that was precious in life. The poor creature lay goading herself into madness with thoughts of how she would be revenged upon these enemies; how she would watch, and track out, and reveal their hidden plots against her; how she would triumph over and crush them. All these half-frenzied cogitations were secretly pervaded—a still more maddening exasperation

—by a consciousness of her own impotence. The evening came creeping in, growing dark around her—silence fell over the little house, where nobody moved or spoke, and where all the world, the heavens, and the earth, seemed changed since this morning; but the wonder was how that silence could contain her,—all palpitating with pangs and plans, a bleeding, infuriated, wounded creature—and show no sign of the frenzy it covered. She had lain down to rest, as the saying is. How many women are there who go thus to a voluntary crucifixion and torture by lying down to rest! Mrs. Christian lay with her dry eyes blazing through the darkness, no more able to sleep than she was to do all that her burning fancy described to her. She was a hot-blooded Celtic woman, of that primitive island which has preserved her name. If she could have sought sympathy, here was nobody to bestow it. Not the heart which that poor ghost of manhood in the next room had lost out of his chilled, bewildered bosom; not Bessie's steadfast, unexcited spirit. The poor soul saved herself from going wild by thinking of her boy; holding out her passionate arms to him thousands of miles away; setting him forth as the deliverer, with all the absolute folly of love and passion. He would come home and have justice done to his mother. Never fancy was more madly unreasonable; but it saved her from some of the effects of the agitation in her heart.

On the other side of the road, at the same hour, Nancy prepared her tea in the house of which she was temporary mistress. There could not be any doubt, to look at her now, that this tall, dry, withered figure, and face full of characteristic wrinkles, was like Mrs. Christian. The resemblance had been noticed by many. And as old Mrs. Thomson had not hesitated to avow that her faithful servant was connected with her by some distant bond of relationship, it was not difficult to imagine that these two were really related, though both denied it strenuously. Nancy had a friend with her to tea. They were in the cheerful kitchen, which had a window to the garden, and a window in the side wall of the house, by which a glimpse of the street might be obtained through the garden-gate. The firelight shone pleasantly through the cheerful apartment. All the peculiar ornaments of a kitchen — the covers, the crockery, the polished sparkles of shining pewter and brass—adorned the walls. Through it all went Nancy in her new black dress and ample snowy-white apron. She carried her head high, and moved with a certain rhythmical elation. It is surely an unphilosophical conclusion that there is no real enjoyment in wickedness. Nancy had no uneasiness in her triumph. The more she realized what her victory must have cost her opponent, the more entire grew her satisfaction. Remorse might have mixed with her exultation had she had any pity in her; but she had not; and, in consequence, it was with unalloyed pleasure that she contemplated the overthrow of her adversary. Perhaps the very satisfaction of a good man in a good action is inferior to the absolute satisfaction with which, by times, a bad man is permitted to contemplate the issue of his wickedness. Nancy marched about her kitchen, preparing her tea with an enjoyment which possibly would not have attended a benevolent exercise of her powers. Possibly she could almost have painted to herself, line by line, the dark tableau of that twilight room where Mrs. Christian lay, driving herself crazy with wild thoughts. She did the gloom of the picture full justice. If she could have peeped into the window and seen it with her own eyes, she would have enjoyed the sight.

"I'll make Mr. Brown keep me in the house," said Nancy, sitting down at a table piled with good things, and which looked an embodiment of kitchen luxury and comfort, "and get me a girl. It was what missis always meant to do. I'll show it to him out of the will that I was left in trust to be made commforable. And in course of nature her things all comes to me. It's a deal easier to deal with a single gentleman than if there was a lady poking her nose about into every thing. Thank my stars, upstarts such like as them Christians shall never lord it over me; and now I have more of my own way, I'll be glad to see you of an evening whenever you can commforable. Bring a bit of work, and we'll have a quiet chat. I consider myself settled for life."

The young surgeon's house was at the other end of the town; it was close to a region of half-built streets—for Carlingford was a prosperous town—where successive colonies were settling, where houses were damp and drainage incomplete, and a good practice to be had with pains. The house had a genteel front to the road, a lamp over the door, and a little surgery round the corner, where it gave forth the sheen of its red and blue bottles across a whole half-finished district. Mr. Rider had come home tired, unaccountably tired. He had kicked off one boot, and taken a cigar from his case, and forgotten to light it. He sat plunged in his easy-chair in a drear brown study—a brown study inaccessible to the solaces which generally make such states of mind endurable. His cigar went astray among the confused properties of his writing-table; the book he had been reading last night lay rejected in the farthest corner of the room. He was insensible to the charms of dressing-gown and slippers. On the whole, he was in a very melancholy, sullen, not to say savage mood. He sat and gazed fiercely into the fire, chewing the cud of fancies, in which very little of the sweet seemed to mingle with the bitter. He had been the medical attendant of Mrs. Thomson of Grove Street, and had assisted this afternoon at her funeral, and you might have supposed he had hastened the advent of that melancholy day, had you seen his face.

On the whole, it was a hard dilemma in which the poor young man found himself. He, too, like Nancy, kept realising the interior of that other little house in Grove Street. Both of them, by dint of that acquaintance with their neighbors which every body has in a small community, came to a moderately correct guess at what was going on there. Young Mr. Rider sat in heavy thought, sometimes bursting out into violent gestures which fortunately nobody witnessed; sometimes uttering sighs which all but blew out his lights—impatient, urgent sighs, not of melancholy, but of anger and resistance—the sighs of a young man who found circumstances intolerable, and yet was obliged to confess, with sore mortification and humbling, that he could not mend them, and behoved to endure. The visions that kept gliding across his eyes drove him half as wild as poor Mrs. Christian: one moment a pretty young wife, all the new house wanted to make it fully tenable; but he had scarcely brought her across the threshold when a ghastly figure in a chair was carried over it after her, up-stairs into the bridal apartments, and another woman, soured and drawn awry by pressure of poverty, constitutionally shabby, vehement, and high-tempered, pervaded the new habitation. No use saying pshaw! and pah!—no use swearing bigger oaths,—no use pitching unoffending books into the corners, or breathing out those short, deep breaths of desperation. This was in reality the state of affairs. Midnight did not change the aspect it had worn in the morning. Pondering all the night through would bring no light on the subject. Nothing could change those intolerable circumstances. The poor young surgeon threw his coat off in the heat and urgency of his thoughts, and pitched it from him like the books. There was no comfort or solace to be found in all that world of fancy. Only this morning sweeter dreams had filled this disordered apartment. In imagination, he had helped his Bessie to minister to the comfort of the poor old sick parents in Mrs. Thomson's house. Now he knitted his brows desperately over it, but could find no outlet. Unless some good fairy sent him a patient in the middle of the night, the chances were that the morning would find him pursuing that same interminable brown study of which nothing could come.

Mr. Brown's house was an old house in the middle of the town. The offices were in the lower floor, occupying one side of the building. On the other side of the wide, old-fashioned hall was his dining-room. There he sat all by himself upon this agitating night. It was a large, lofty, barely furnished room, with wainscoted walls, and curious stiff panelling, and a high mantle-shelf which he, though a tall man, could scarcely reach with his arm. It was dimly lighted, as well as barely furnished—altogether an inhuman, desert place—the poorest though the grandest of all we have yet looked into in Carlingford. Mr. Brown was not sensible of its inhospitable aspect; he was used to it, and that was enough. It occurred to him as little to criticise his house as to criticise his manners. Thus they *were*, and thus they would continue; at least he had always believed so till to-night.

He sat in his easy-chair with his feet on the fender, and a little table at his elbow with his wine. As long as their was any thing in his glass he sipped it by habit, without being aware of what he was doing; but when the glass was empty, though he had two or three times raised it empty to his lips, he was too much absorbed in his thoughts to replenish it. He was not by any means a handsome man; and he was five-and-forty or thereabouts, and had a habit of making portentous faces, when any way specially engaged in thought; so that, on the whole, it was not a highly attractive or interesting figure which reclined back in the crimson chair, and stretched its slippered feet to the fire, sole inmate of the dim, spacious, vacant room. He was thinking over his new position with profound disgust and perplexity. Nevertheless, it cannot be denied that the subject lured him on, and drew out into stretches of imagination far beyond his wont;—hunting all the world over after Phœbe Thomson! But, after all, that was only a preliminary step; he was required only to use reasonable means, and for three years. If she turned up, there was an end of it; if she did not turn up — here Mr. Brown sprang up hurriedly and assumed the favorite position of Englishmen in front of his fire. There, all glittering in the distance, rose up, solid and splendid, an appearance which few men could see without emotion—twenty thousand pounds! It was not life and death to him, as it was to poor Mrs. Christian. It did not make all the difference between sordid want and comfortable existence; but you may well believe it did not appear before the lawyer's eyes without moving him into a considerable degree of excitement. Such a fairy apparition had never appeared before in that cold, spacious, uninhabited room. Involuntarily to himself, Mr. Brown saw his house expand, his life open out, his condition change. Roseate lights dropped into the warming atmosphere which had received that vision; the fairy wand waved through the dim air before him in spite of all his sobriety. The wiles of the enchantress lured John Brown as effectually as if he had not been five-and-forty, an old bachelor, and an attorney; and, after half an hour of these slowly growing, half-conscious, half-resisted thoughts, any chance that had brought the name of the dead woman's lost daughter to his memory, would have called forth a very different "confound Phœbe Thomson!" from that which burst from his troubled lips in the house in Grove Street. Possibly it was some such feeling which roused him up a moment after, when the great cat came softly purring to his feet and rubbed against his slippers. Mr. Brown started violently, thrust puss away, flung himself back into his chair, grew very red, and murmured something about "an ass!" ashamed to detect himself in his own vain imaginations. But that sudden waking up did not last. After he had filled his glass and emptied it—after he had stirred his fire, and made a little noise, with some vague idea of dispelling the spell he was under—the fairy returned and retook possession under a less agreeable aspect. Suppose *he* were to be enriched, what was to become of the poor Christians? They were not very near relations, and the old woman had a right to leave her money where she liked. Still there was a human heart in John Brown's bosom. Somehow that little episode in the street returned to his recollection—Bessie running across, light and noiseless, with her message. How young the creature must be, after all, to have so much to do. Poor little Bessie! she had not only lost her chance of being a great fortune, and one of the genteel young ladies of Carlingford, but she had lost her chance of the doctor, and his new house and rising practice. Shabby fellow! to leave the pretty girl he was fond of, because she was a good girl, and was every thing to her old father and mother. "I wonder will they say that's my fault too?" said John Brown to himself; and stumbled up to his feet again on the stimulus of that thought, with a kind of sheepish not unpleasant embarrassment, and a foolish half-smile upon his face. Somehow at that moment, looking before him, as he had done so many hundred times standing on his own hearthrug, it occurred to him all at once what a bare room this was that he spent his evenings in—what an inhuman, chilly, penurious place! scarcely more homelike than that bit of open street, across which Bessie came tripping this afternoon, wanting to speak to him. Nobody wanted to speak to him here. No wonder he had a threatening of rheumatism last winter. What a cold, wretched barn of a room! He could not help wondering to himself whether the drawing-room were any better. In the new start his long-dormant imagination had taken, John Brown actually shivered in the moral coldness of his spacious, lonely apartment. In his mind he dare said that the Christians looked a great deal more comfortable in that little box of theirs, with that poor little girl working, and teaching, and keeping all straight. What a fool that young doctor was! what if he did work a little harder to make the old people an allowance? However, it was no business of his. With a sigh of general discontent Mr. Brown pulled his bell violently, and had the fire made up, and asked for his tea. His tea! he never touched it when it came, but sat pshawing and humphing at it, making himself indignant over that fool of a young doctor. And what if these poor people, sour and sore after their misfortune, should think that this too was *his* fault?

CHAPTER III.

Next morning Mr. Brown, with his hands in his pockets and his shoulders up to his ears as usual, went down at his ordinary rapid pace to old Mrs. Thomson's house. Nancy had locked the house-door, which, like an innocent almost rural door as it was, opened from without. She was up-stairs, very busy in a most congenial occupation—turning out the old lady's wardrobe, and investigating the old stores of lace and fur and jewelry. She knew them pretty well by heart before; but now that, according to her idea, they were her own, every thing naturally acquired a new value. She had laid them out in little heaps, each by itself, on the dressing-table; a faintly glittering row of old rings and brooches, most of them entirely valueless, though Nancy was not aware of that. On the bed—the bed where two days ago that poor old pallid figure still lay in solemn ownership of the "property" around it—Nancy had spread forth her mistress' ancient boas and vast muffs, half a century old; most of them were absolutely dropping to pieces; but as long as they held together with any sort of integrity, Nancy was not the woman to lessen the number of her possessions. The bits of lace were laid out upon the old sofa, each at full length. With these delightful accumulations all round her, Nancy was happy. She had entered, as she supposed, upon an easier and more important life. Mistress of the empty house and all its contents, she carried herself with an air of elation and independence which she had never ventured to display before. No doubt had ever crossed her mind on the subject. She had taken it for granted that the expulsion of the Christians meant only her own triumph. She had even taken credit, both to herself and other people, for greater guiltiness than she really had incurred. The will was not her doing, though Mrs. Christian said so and Nancy was willing to believe as much; but she was glad to be identified as the cause of it, and glad to feel that she was the person who would enjoy the benefit. She was in this holiday state of mind, enjoying herself among her supposed treasures, when she was interrupted by the repeated and imperative demands for entrance made by Mr. Brown at the locked door.

Nancy went down to open it, but not in too great a hurry. She was rather disposed to patronize the attorney. She put on her white apron, and went to the door spreading it down with a leisurely hand. To Nancy's surprise and amazement, Mr. Brown plunged in without taking any notice of her. He went into the parlor, looked all round, then went up-stairs, three steps at a time, into the best parlor, uncomfortably near the scene of Nancy's operations. There was the old cabinet for which he had been looking. When he saw it he called to her to look here. Nancy, who had followed him close, came forward immediately. He was shaking the door of the cabinet to see if it was locked. It was a proceeding of which Nancy did not approve.

"I suppose this is where she kept her papers," said Mr. Brown; "get me the keys. I want to see what's to be found among her papers touching this daughter of hers. You had better bring me *all* the keys. Make haste, for I have not any time to lose."

"Missis never kept any papers there," said Nancy, alarmed and a little anxious. "There's the best china tea-set and the silver service—that's all you'll find there."

"Bring me the keys, however," said Mr. Brown. "Where did she keep her papers, eh? You know all about her, I suppose. Do you know any thing about Phœbe Thomson, that I've got to hunt up? She was

Mrs. Thomson's daughter, I understand. What caused her to leave her mother? I suppose you know. What is she? How much can you tell me about her?"

"As much as anybody living," said Nancy, too well pleased to divert him from his inquiries after the keys. "I was but a girl when it happened; but I remember it like yesterday. She went off—missis never liked to have it mentioned," said Nancy, coming to a dead stop.

"Go on," cried Mr. Brown; "she can't hear you now, can she? Go on."

"She went off with a soldier—that's the truth. They were married after; but missis never thought that mattered. He was a common man, and as plain a looking fellow as you'd see anywhere. Missis cast her off, and would have nothing to say to her. She over-persuaded me, and I let her in one night; but missis wouldn't look at her. She never came back. She was hurt in her feelin's. We never heard of her more."

"Nor asked after her, I suppose?" said the lawyer, indignantly. "Do you mean the old wretch never made any inquiry about her own child?"

"Meaning missis?" said Nancy. "No—I don't know as she ever did. She said she'd disown her; and she was a woman as always kept her word."

"Old beast!" said John Brown between his teeth; "but, look here; if she's married, she is not Phœbe Thomson. What's her name?"

"I can't tell," said Nancy, looking a little frightened. "Sure, neither she is—to think of us never remarking that! But dear, dear! will that make any difference to the will?"

Mr. Brown smiled grimly, but made no answer. "Have you got any thing else to tell me about her? Did she ever write to her mother? Do you know what regiment it is, or where it was at that time?" said the attorney. "Think what you are about, and tell me clearly—what year was she married, and where were you at the time?"

Nancy grew nervous under this close questioning. She lost her self-possession and all her fancied importance. "We were in the Isle o' Man, where the Christians come from. I was born there myself. Missis' friends was mostly there. It was by her husband's side she belonged to Carlingford. It was about a two miles out of Douglas—a kind of a farmhouse. It was the year—the year—I was fifteen," said Nancy, faltering.

"And how old are you now?" said the inexorable questioner, who had taken out his memorandum-book.

Nancy dropped into a chair and began to sob. "It's hard on a person bringing things back," said Nancy,—"and to think if she should actually turn up again just as she was! As for living in the house with her, I couldn't think of such a thing. Sally Christian, or some poor-spirited person might do it, but not me as am used to be my own mistress," cried Nancy, with increasing agitation. "She had the temper of—oh! she was her mother's temper. Dear, dear! to think as she might be alive, and come back to put all wrong! It was in the year 'eight—that's the year it was."

"Then you didn't think she would come back," said Mr. Brown.

"It's a matter o' five-and-thirty years; and not knowing even her name, nor the number of the regiment, nor nothing—as I don't," said Nancy, cautiously; "and never hearing nothing about her, what was a person to think? And if it's just Phœbe Thomson you're inquiring after, and don't say nothing about the marriage nor the regiment, you may seek long enough before you find her," said Nancy, with a glance of what was intended to be private intelligence between herself and her questioner, "and all correct to the will."

Mr. Brown put up his memorandum-book sharply in his pocket. "Bring me the keys. Look here, bring me *all* the keys," he said. "What's in this other room, eh? It was her bedroom, I suppose. Hollo, what's all this?"

For all Nancy's precautions had not been able to ward off this catastrophe. He pushed into the room she had left to admit him, where all her treasures were exhibited. His quick eye glanced round in an instant, and understood it. Trembling as Nancy was with new alarms, she had still strength to make one struggle.

"Missis' things fall to me," said Nancy, half in assertion, half in entreaty; "that's how it always is; the servant gets the lady's wardrobe—the servant as has nursed her and done for her, when there's no daughter—that's always understood."

"Bring me the keys," said Mr. Brown.

The keys were in the open wardrobe, a heavy bunch. John Brown seized hold of the furs on the bed and began to toss them into the wardrobe. Some of them dropped in pieces in his hands and were tossed out again. He took no notice of the lace or the trinkets, but swiftly locked every keyhole he could find in the room—drawers, boxes, cupboards, every thing. Nancy looked on with fierce exclamations. She would have her rights—she was not to be put upon. She would have the law of him. She would let everybody know how he was taking upon himself as if he were the master of the house.

"And so I am, my good woman; when will you be ready to leave it?" said Mr. Brown. "You shall have due time to get ready, and I wont refuse you the trumpery you've set your heart upon. Judging from the specimen, it wont do Phœbe Thomson much good. But not in this sort of way, you know. I must put a stop to this. Now let me hear what's the earliest day you can leave the house."

"I'm not going to leave the house!" cried Nancy; "I've lived here thirty years, and here I'll die. Missis' meaning was to leave me in the house, and make me commforable for life. Many's the time she's said so. Do you think you're going to order *me* about just as you please? What do you suppose she left the property like that for but to spite the Christians, and to leave a good home to me?"

"When will you be ready to leave?" repeated Mr. Brown, without paying the least attention to her outcries and excitement.

"I tell you I'm not agoing to leave!" screamed Nancy. "To leave!—*me!*—no, not for all the upstarts in Carlingford, if they was doubled and tripled. My missis meant me to stay here commforable all my days. She meant me to have a girl and make myself commforable. Many and many's the time she's said so."

"But she did not say so in the will," said the inexorable executor; "and so out you must go, and that very shortly. Now don't say any thing. It is no use fighting with me. You'll be well treated if you leave directly and quietly; otherwise, you shan't have any thing. The other keys, please. Now mind what I say. You're quite able to make a noise and a disturbance, but you're not able to resist me. You shall have time to make your preparations and look out another home for yourself; but take care you don't compel me to use severe measures—that's enough."

"But I wont!—not if you drag me over the stones. I wont go. I'll speak to Mr. Curtis," cried the unfortunate Nancy.

"Pshaw!" said John Brown. Mr. Curtis was the other attorney in Carlingford, the one whom probably Mrs. Christian had in her mind when she threatened him with her solicitor. He laughed to himself angrily as he went down-stairs. If he was to undertake this troublesome business, at least he was not going to be hampered by a parcel of furious women. When he had locked up every thing and was leaving the house, Nancy threw open an upper window and threw a malediction after him. "You'll never find her! It'll go back to them as it belongs to," shouted Nancy. He smiled to himself again as he turned away. Was it possible that John Brown began to think it might be as well if he never did find her? The prophecy certainly was not unpleasant to him, though poor Nancy meant it otherwise. Mr. Brown hurried up the monotonous side of Grove Street, we are afraid not without a little private exhilaration in the thought that Phœbe Thomson was not unlike the proverbial needle in the bundle of hay. The chances were she was dead years ago; and though he would neither lose a minute in beginning, nor leave any means unused in pursuing the search for her, it was certain he would not be inconsolable if he never heard any more of Phœbe Thomson. Doubtless he would not have acknowledged as much in words, and did not even have any express confidences with himself on the subject, lest his own mind might have been shocked by the disclosure of its involuntary sentiment. Still he took an interest in Mrs. Thomson's bequest, greater than he took in the properties intrusted to him by his other clients. He could not help himself. He felt affectionately interested in that twenty thousand pounds.

But as he came up to it, John Brown remembered, with a little interest, that spot of the quiet street where Bessie, yesterday, ran across to speak to him. He could not help recalling her appearance as she approached him, though young girls were greatly out of his way. Poor Bessie! The baker's cart occupied at that moment the spot which Bessie had crossed; and one of the Carlingford ladies was leaving the door of the Christians' little house. Mr. Brown, though no man was less given to colloquies with his acquaintances in the street, crossed over to speak to her. He could not help being interested in every thing about that melancholy little house, nor feeling that the very sight of it was a reproach to his thoughts. Poor Bessie! there she stood yesterday in her black frock—the light-footed, soft-voiced creature—not much more than a child beside the middle-aged old bachelor who could find it in his heart to be harsh to her. Across that very spot he passed hastily with many compunctions in the mind which had been roused so much out of its usual ways of thinking by the events and cogitations of the last four-and-twenty hours. The lady to whom he paid such a marked token of respect was quite flattered and excited to meet him. He was the hero of the day at Carlingford. The last account of this extraordinary affair was doubtless to be had from himself.

"You've been at the Christians'. I suppose you were there for some purpose so early in the morning," said the abrupt Mr. Brown, after the necessary salutations were over.

"Yes—but I am a very early person," said the lady. "Oh, forgive me. I know quite well you don't care to hear what sort of a person I am; but really, Mr. Brown, now that you are quite the hero of the moment yourself, do let me congratulate you. They say there is not a chance of finding this Phœbe Thomson. Some people even say she is a myth and never existed; and that it was only a device of the old lady to give her an excuse for leaving you the money. Dear me! *did* you ask me a question? I forget. I am really so interested to see you."

"I like an answer when it's practicable," said the lawyer. "I said I supposed you were about some business at Miss Christian's house?"

"I must answer you this time, mustn't I, or you wont talk to me any longer?" said the playful interlocutor, whom John Brown could have addressed in terms other than complimentary. "Yes, poor thing, I've been at Miss Christian's, and on a disagreeable business too, in the present circumstances. We are going to send our Mary away to a finishing-school. So I had to tell poor Bessie we shouldn't want any more music-lessons after this quarter. I was very sorry, I am sure—and there was Mrs. Mayor taking her little girls away from the morning-class. When they expected to get Mrs. Thomson's money they had been a little careless, I suppose; and to give three days' holiday in the middle of the quarter, without any reason for it but an old person's death, you know—a death *out* of the house—is trying to people's feelings; and Mrs. Christian had given everybody to understand that *her* daughter would soon have no occasion for teaching. People don't like these sort of things; and Mrs. Mayor heard of somebody else a little nearer, who is said to be very good at bringing on little children. I said all I could to induce her to change her mind; but I believe they're to leave next quarter. Poor Bessie! I am very sorry for her, I am sure."

"And this is how you ladies comfort a good young woman when she meets with a great disappointment?" said John Brown.

"La!—a disappointment! You know that only means *one thing* to a girl," said the lady, "but you're always so severe. Bessie has had no *disappointment*, as people understand the word; yet there's young Dr. Rider, you know, very attentive, and I do hope he'll propose directly, and set it all right for her, poor thing, for she's a dear good girl. But to hear *you* speak so—of all people—Mr. Brown. Why, isn't it your fault? I declare I would hate you if I were Bessie Christian. If the doctor were to be off too, and she really had a disappointment, it would be dreadfully hard upon her, poor girl; but it's to be hoped things will turn out better than that. Good-morning! but you have not told me a word about your own story—all Carlingford is full of it. People say you are the luckiest man!"

These words overtook, rather than were addressed to, him as he hurried off indignant. John Brown was not supposed to be an observant person, but somehow he saw the genteel people of Carlingford about the streets that day in a surprisingly distinct manner—saw them eager to get a little occupation for themselves anyhow—saw them coming out for their walks, and their shopping, and their visits, persuading themselves by such means that they were busy people, virtuously employed, and making use of their life. What was Bessie doing? Mr. Brown thought he would like to see her, and that he would not like to see her. It was painful to think of being anyhow connected with an arrangement which condemned to that continued labor such a young soft creature—a creature so like, and yet so unlike, those other smiling young women who were enjoying their youth. And just because it was painful Mr. Brown could not take his thoughts off that subject. If Phœbe Thomson turned up he should certainly try to induce her to do something for the relations whom her mother had disappointed so cruelly. If Phœbe Thomson did not turn up—well, what then?—if she didn't? Mr. Brown could not tell: it would be his duty to do something. But, in the mean time, he did nothing except shake his fist at young Rider's drag as it whirled the doctor past to his patients, and repeat the "shabby fellow!" of last night with an air of disgust. John Brown had become very popular just at that moment; all his friends invited him to dinner, and dropped in to hear about this story which had electrified Carlingford. And all over the town the unknown entity called Phœbe Thomson was discussed in every possible kind of hypothesis, and assumed a different character in the hands of every knot of gossips. Nobody thought of Bessie Christian; but more and more as nobody thought of her, that light little figure running across the quiet street, and wanting to speak to him, impressed itself like a picture upon the retentive but not very fertile imagination of Mrs. Thomson's executor. It troubled, and vexed, and irritated, and unsettled him. One little pair of willing hands; one little active cheerful soul; and all the burden of labor, and patience, and dread monotony of life that God had allotted to that pretty creature; how it could be, and nobody step in to prevent it, was a standing marvel to John Brown.

CHAPTER IV.

Mr. Brown was well known everywhere as a famous business man—not perhaps in that sense so familiar to modern observers, which implies the wildest flights of speculation, and such skilful arts of bookmaking as ruin themselves by their very cleverness. Mr. Brown did not allow the grass to grow below his feet; his advertisements perpetually led off that list of advertisements in the *Times* which convey so many skeleton romances to a curious public. All over the country, people began to entertain guesses about that Phœbe Thomson who was to hear something so much to her own advantage; and Phœbe Thomsons answered to the call through all the breadth of the three kingdoms. Mr. Brown had a detective officer in his pay for the whole year. He made journeys himself, and sent this secret agent on innumerable journeys. He discovered the regiment, a detachment of which had been stationed at the Isle of Man during the year 1808; he went to the island; he left no means untried of finding out this hypothetical person. Nearer at home, Mr. Brown had made short work of Nancy, who, too deeply mortified by the failure of her hopes to remain in Carlingford, had returned to her native place with a moderate pension, her own savings, and her mistress' old clothes, not so badly satisfied on the whole, but still a defeated woman. While poor Mrs. Christian, compelled by sore dint of time and trouble to give up her forlorn hope of getting justice done her, and reclaiming the wealth that had been so nearly hers from the hands of Mr. Brown, was half reconciled to him by his summary dealings with her special enemy. A whole year had passed, and other things had happened at Carlingford. Everybody now did not talk of Mrs. Thomson's extraordinary will, and John Brown's wonderful chance of coming into twenty thousand pounds. People had even given over noting that the young doctor had thought better of that foolish fancy of his for Bessie Christian. All the persons in this little drama had relapsed into the shade. It was a very heavy shadow so far as Grove Street was concerned. The little pupils had fallen off, collected again, fallen off once more. If the cheerful glimmer of firelight had never failed in the sick-room—if the helpless old father, sitting in that calm of infirmity and age, making comments which would have irritated his careful attendants beyond bearing if they had not been used to them, never missed any thing of his usual comforts—nobody knew at what cost these comforts were bought. But there did come a crisis in which patience and courage, and the steadfast soul which had carried the young breadwinner through the drear monotony of that year, failed her at last. Her mother, who was of a different temper from Bessie, and had gone through a thousand despairs and revivals before the young creature at her side began to droop, saw that the time had come when every thing was at stake; and, more reluctantly and slowly, Bessie herself came to see it. She could not set her back against the wall of that little house of theirs and meet every assailant; she could not tide it out in heroic silence, and abstinence alike from comfort and complaint. That was her natural impulse; and the victory, if slow, would have been certain: so Bessie thought at least. But want was at the door, and they could not afford to wait; something else must be attempted. Bessie must go out into the market-place and seek new masters—there was no longer work for her here.

This was how the scene was shifted in the following conclusive act.

John Brown, travelling, and fuming and aggravating himself much over the loss of his time and the distraction of his thoughts, was in London that day—a May-day, when everybody was in London. He had seen his detective, and no further intelligence had been obtained. Phœbe Thomson was as far off as ever—farther off; for now that all these efforts had been made, it was clear that either she must be dead or in some quarter of the world impervious to newspaper advertisements and detective officers. Mr. Brown bore the disappointment with a very good grace. He felt contented now to slacken his efforts; he even felt as if he himself were already the possessor of old Mrs. Thomson's twenty thousand pounds. As he went leisurely through the streets, he paused before one of those "Scholastic Agency" offices which abound in the civilized end of London. It was in the ground-floor of a great, faded, sombre house, in a street near St. James' Park—a place of aching interest to some people in that palpitating world of human interests. It occurred to Mr. Brown to go in and see if there were any lists to be looked over. Phœbe Thomson might have a daughter who might be a governess. It was an absurd idea enough, and he knew it to be so; nevertheless he swung open the green baize door.

Inside, before the desk, stood a little figure which he knew well, still in that black dress which she had worn when she ran across Grove Street and wanted to speak to him; with a curl of the light hair, which looked so fair and full of color on her black shawl, escaped from under her bonnet, talking softly and eagerly to the clerk. Was there no other place he could send her to? She had come up from the country, and was so very reluctant to go down without hearing of something. The man shook his head, and read over to her several entries in his book. Bessie turned round speechless towards the door. Seeing some one standing there, she lifted her eyes full upon John Brown. Troubled and yet steady, full of tears yet clear and seeing clear, shining blue like the skies, *with a great patience*, these eyes encountered the unexpected familiar face. If she felt an additional pang in seeing him, or if any grudge against the supplanter of her family trembled in Bessie's heart, it made no sign upon her face. She said "good-morning" cheerfully as she went past him, and only quickened her pace a little to get out of sight. She did not take any notice of the rapid step after her; the step which could have made up to her in two paces, but did not, restrained by an irresolute will. Probably she knew whose step it was, and interpreted rightly, to some superficial degree, the feelings of John Brown. She thought he was a good-hearted man—she thought he was sorry to know or guess the straits which Bessie thanked Heaven nobody in this world did fully know—she thought, by and by, shy of intruding upon her, that step would drop off, and she would hear it no more. But it was not so to be.

"Miss Christian, I want to speak to you," said John Brown.

She turned towards him directly without

any pretence of surprise; and with a smile, the best she could muster, waited to hear what it was.

"We are both walking the same way," said Mr. Brown.

In spite of herself amazement woke upon Bessie's face. "That is true: but was that all that you had to say?" said Bessie, with the smiles kindling all her dimples. The dimples had only been hidden by fatigue, and hardship, and toil. They were all there.

"No, not quite. Were you looking for employment in that office? and why are you seeking employment here?" said the attorney, looking anxiously down upon her.

"Because there's a great many of us in Carlingford," said Bessie, steadily; "there are half as many governesses as there are children. I thought I might perhaps get on better here."

"In London! Do you think there are fewer governesses here?" said Mr. Brown, going on with his questions, and meanwhile studying very closely his little companion's face; not rudely. To be sure it was a very honest direct investigation, but there was not a thought of rudeness or disrespect either in the eyes that made it or the heart.

"I dare say it's as bad everywhere," said Bessie, with a little sigh; "but when one cannot get work in one place, one naturally turns to another. I had an appointment to-day to come up to see a lady; but I was not the proper person. Perhaps I shall have to stay at home after all."

"Have you any grudge at me?" said Mr. Brown.

Bessie looked up open-eyed and wondering. "Grudge? at *you*? How could I? I dare say," said Bessie, with a sigh and a smile, "mamma had, a year ago; but not me. The times I have spoken to you, Mr. Brown, you have always been kind to me."

"Have I?" said the lawyer. He gave her a strange look, and stopped short, as if his utterance was somehow impeded. Kind to her! He remembered that time in Grove Street, and could have scourged himself at the recollection. Bessie had taken him entirely aback by her simple expression. He could have sobbed under that sudden touch. To see her walking beside him, cheerful, steadfast, without a complaint—a creature separated from the world, from youth and pleasure, and more comfort even—enduring hardness, for all her soft childlike dimples and unaffected smiles—his composure was entirely overcome. He was going to do something very foolish. He gasped, and gave himself up.

"If you don't bear me a grudge, come over into the Park here, where we can hear ourselves speak. I want to speak to you," said Mr. Brown.

She turned into the Park with him quite simply, as she did every thing without any pretence of wonder or embarrassment. There he walked a long time by her side in silence, she waiting for what he had to say, he at the most overwhelming loss how to say it. The next thing he said was to ask her to sit down in a shady, quiet corner, where there was an unoccupied seat. She was very much fatigued. It was too bad of him to bring her out of her way.

"But it is so noisy in the street," said Mr. Brown. Then, with a pause after this unquestionable truism, "I've been thinking about you this very long time."

Bessie looked up quickly with great amazement; thinking of her! She was wiser when she cast her eyes down again. Mr. Brown had not the smallest conception that he had explained himself without saying a syllable, but he had, notwithstanding, leaving Bessie thunderstruck, yet with a moment's time to deliberate. While he went on with his embarrassed, slow expressions, fancying that he was gradually conveying to her mind what he meant, Bessie, in a dreadful silent flutter and agitation, was revolving the whole matter, and asking herself what she was to answer. She had ten full minutes for this before he came to the point, and before, according to his idea, the truth burst upon her. But it is doubtful whether that ten minutes' preparation was any advantage to Bessie. It destroyed the unconsciousness, which was her greatest charm; it made an end of her straightforwardness; worst of all, it left her silent. She gave a terrified glance up at him when it actually happened. There he stood full in the light, with all his awkwardnesses more clearly revealed than usual; six-and-forty, abrupt, almost eccentric; telling that story very plainly, without compliment or passion; would she have him? He was content that she should think it over—he was content to wait for her answer; but if it was to be no, let her say it out.

Strange to say, that word which she was exhorted to say out did not come to Bessie's lips. Perhaps because she trembled a great deal, and really lost her self-possession, and for the moment did not know what she was about. But even in her agitation she did not think of saying it. Mr. Brown, when he had his say out, marched up and down the path before her, and did not interrupt her deliberations. Another dreadful ten minutes passed over Bessie. The more she thought it over, the more bewildered she became as to what she was to say.

"Please would you walk with me to the railway," were the words that came from Bessie's lips at last. She rose up trembling and faint, and with a kind of instinct took Mr. Brown's arm. He, on his part, did not say any thing to her. His agitation melted away into a subdued silent tenderness which did not need any expression. He took her back into the streets, all along that tiresome way. He suffered the noise to surround and abstract her without any interruption which would make her conscious of his presence. It was a strange walk for both. To have called them lovers would have been absurd—to have supposed that here was a marriage of convenience about to be arranged would have been more ridiculous still. What was it? Bessie went along the street in a kind of cloud, aware of nothing very clearly; feeling somehow that she leant upon somebody, and that it was somebody upon whom she had a right to lean. They reached the railway thus, without any further explanation. Mr. Brown put the trembling girl into a carriage, and did not go with her. The Carlingford attorney had turned into a paladin. Was it possible that his outer man itself had smoothed out and expanded too?

"I am not going with you," he said, grasping her hand closely. "I wont embarrass or distress you, Bessie; but, recollect you have not said no; and when I come to Grove Street to-morrow, I'll hope to hear you say yes. I'll let you off," said John Brown, grasping the little soft hand so tight and hard that it hurt Bessie, "I'll let you off with liking, if you'll give me that; at my age I don't even venture to say for myself that I'm very much in love."

And with that, the eyes, which had betrayed him before, flashed in Bessie's face a contradiction of her elderly lover's words. Yes! it astounded himself almost as much as it did Bessie. He would still have flatly contradicted anybody who accused him of that folly; but he went away with an undeniable blush into the London streets, self-convicted. A year's observation and an hour's talk had resulted in a much less philosophical sentiment than Mr. Brown was prepared for. He went back to the streets, wondering what she would like in all those wonderful shop-windows. He traced back, step for step, the road they had come together. He was not six-and-forty—six-and-twenty was the true reading. That was a May-day of his youth that had come to him, sweet if untimely; a missed May-day, perhaps all the better that it had been kept for him these many tedious years.

And though Bessie cried all the way down to Carlingford, the no she had not said *did* not occur to her as any remedy for her tears; and, indeed, when she remembered how she had taken Mr. Brown's arm, and felt that she had committed herself by that act, the idea was rather a relief to Bessie. "It was as bad as saying yes at once," said she to herself, with many blushes. But thus, you perceive, it was done, and could not be altered. She must stand to the consequences of her weakness now.

It made a great noise in Carlingford, as might be supposed; it made a vast difference in the household of Mrs. Christian, which was removed to the house in which she had formerly hoped to establish herself as heir-at-law. But the greatest difference of all was made in that dim, spacious, wainscoted dining-room, which did not know itself in its novel circumstances. That was where the change was most remarkably apparent; and all these years Phœbe Thomson's shadow has thrown no cloud as yet over the path of John Brown.

From Chambers's Journal.

FRANCES BROWNE.

Few of our readers can be unacquainted with the story of Eurytus, the blind Spartan, who, when he heard that the Three Hundred were defending the pass of Thermopylæ against the Persian host, called for his arms, ordered his helot to lead him to the field, and, rushing on his country's foes, was pierced by the spears and arrows of the invaders. The Spartan's chivalry has been the theme of poet's song and historian's page, and after the lapse of more than two thousand years, still stirs the heart and dims the eye. But there are nobler deeds than his, wrought by weaker hands, tried by greater privations. To risk a life upon which the shadow of darkness has fallen, with the certainty of gaining after death an immortality of fame, is not the most exalted heroism. Many have sought the shadow of death as a refuge from the shadow of darkness, and with the knowledge that their name and memory would be buried with their bones. But to meet the decrees of fate with a calm and undaunted front; to fight the battle of life single-handed against poverty, blindness, and a host of relentless combatants, when you must first dig for the iron wherewith to forge the armor and fashion the sword; to contend day after day, and year after year, for no guerdon but bread, and no statue but the *statu quo:* this is a heroism greater than that of the Spartan, and deserving more honorable record than that at Thermopylæ: "Stranger, go tell the world that I strive on obedient to the gods' commands."

Yet this heroism has been displayed in our own day by her whose name stands at the head of this paper, and whose long and hard struggle for the means of life has hitherto left her little leisure for doing justice to her powers in a work of sustained effort; but who, by the munificence of the Marquis of Lansdowne, in presenting her with a gift of one hundred pounds, at a time when health and funds were much exhausted, has at length found an opportunity of giving to her country's literature a work of fiction worthy of her pen. The publication of these volumes * affords us an occasion for sketching the brief story of the life of their authoress.

* *My Share of the World.* By Frances Browne. London: Hurst and Blackett. 1861.

Frances Browne was born on the 16th of January, 1816, at Stranorlar, a mountain village in the county Donegal, Ireland. Her great-grandfather managed to run through a good estate, and his descendants were left with limited means. Her father was glad to fill the office of postmaster in the village. Frances was the seventh child in a family of twelve; and at the age of eighteen months, not having received the benefit of Jenner's discovery, she lost her sight by the small-pox. She had no teacher even in the elements of learning. Her knowledge of grammar and geography was acquired by listening to her brothers and sisters, as they read aloud their lessons for the village school; and we have heard her say, that the first geographical problem which puzzled her was, how Columbus could have hoped to reach the coasts of Asia by sailing west, till a neighbor solved the difficulty by explaining that the earth was a globe; "but to comprehend this fully," she observed, "cost me the study of a sleepless night." To understand the world's angles and asperities was a problem still in store for her, and soon to occasion her many sleepless nights.

Meanwhile the pursuit of learning was followed with an ardor which alone animates those who have to contend against the greatest obstacles. Step by step she advanced along the rugged road to the jealously guarded tree of knowledge. There were no guide-posts to direct the wayfarer, and many tolls were demanded of her. To gain time for her brothers and sisters to read to her, she did the household work assigned to them. To gain their inclination, she bribed them by telling them stories of her own invention, or which they had formerly read to her, but forgotten. She acquired a knowledge of French in exchange for lessons in English grammar, given to the daughter of the village teacher. She impressed on her memory the day's reading, by repeating it all over to herself in the silence of the night. Among the works that were thus mastered were Hume's *England*, and the twenty-one volumes of the *Ancient Universal History*. But it was a great event for the future novelist when the *Heart of Mid-Lothian* fell into her hands, her acquaintance with works of fiction being previously limited to such books as *Susan Gray*, the *Negro Servant*, and the

Adventures of Baron Munchausen; for in Frances Browne's youth there was no bookseller's shop within three counties of Stranorlar, and circulating libraries were things undreamt of.

About the end of her fifteenth year, having heard much of the *Iliad*, she obtained the loan of Pope's translation. "It was like the discovery of a new world," she writes to a friend, "and effected a total change in my ideas on the subject of poetry. There was at the time a considerable manuscript of my own productions in existence, which of course I regarded with some partiality; but Homer had awakened me, and in a fit of sovereign contempt, I committed the whole to the flames. After Homer's, the work that produced the greatest impression on my mind was Byron's *Childe Harold*. The one had induced me to burn my first manuscript, and the other made me resolve against verse-making in future." In this resolution she persevered for nearly ten years, till, in the summer of 1840, having heard a volume of Irish songs read, she could no longer keep silence, and a poem was composed, called *The Songs of our Land*, which was first printed in the *Irish Penny Journal*, and may still be found in Duffy's *Ballad Poetry of Ireland*. Then followed contributions to the *Athenæum*, *Hood's Magazine*, and Lady Blessington's *Keepsake*. Her verses were copied into the journals of the day; and she felt herself a poetess. At length the thought came to her in the long, sleepless nights, could she not, though sightless and friendless, make her own way in the world? Alas! the golden age had gone by, when, like Blind Harry, she could earn food and shelter by reciting the productions of her muse to chiefs and dames. Yet there were other walks in literature where bread might be got as well as fame. She would leave her native hills—but not Parnassus—and make the venture, though clouds and darkness rested on it. This purpose was carried into effect in the spring of 1847, when the terrible famine which made such devastation in her country began. Having no resources but a pension of twenty pounds, granted from the Royal Bounty Fund by Sir Robert Peel, and no companion but her sister, she crossed the channel for the land of Burns, and as she went, she sang:—

"I leave the spring-time by thy streams, with dreams that will not part,
And on thy hills what kindred names without one kindred heart!
They will not miss my steps at hcart, or shrine, or social band;
Oh, free the homeless heart goes forth—yet fare-thee-well, my land!"

Edinburgh was the city selected for her residence. There her genius, worth, and industry procured her the means of life, and made her many friends, among others Christopher North, and the proprietors of this Journal, to which the second piece of prose composition she ever attempted was contributed.* She wrote tales and sketches, essays and reviews, leaders and songs, for various newspapers and magazines; refusing no employment, however uncongenial, and acquitting herself as conscientiously in a story-book for children, as in writing for the entertainment of their elders. During her residence in the northern capital, she published a volume of *Lyrics and Miscellaneous Poems*, which she dedicated to the late Sir Robert Peel, in grateful recollection of his liberality and kindness; a series of *Legends of Ulster*, her native province; and *The Ericksons*, a tale for the young. She found her abilities for prose-writing gradually strengthen and improve, but her fortunes did not brighten in equal proportion. Sometimes ill-health, sometimes a dishonest publisher, was the drawback to her prosperity. Yet when things were at their best, there were two to be maintained; and ever mindful of the claims of kindred, Frances, out of her poverty, contributed to the support of her mother, as she has done for seventeen years past. No wonder if at times she felt the burden of life heavy, and mourned in the bitterness of her soul, "that the waters of her lot were often troubled, though not by angels."

In 1852, after a residence of five years in Edinburgh, she removed to London. Her sister married soon after, and returned to Scotland; and upon a friend condoling with Frances on her loneliness, she smilingly replied: "Oh, you know, in the absence of other relatives, an author may manage very well with the help of the relative pronouns." Since that period, she has had the assistance

* "The Lost New-year's Gift," March 8, 1845, No. 62, 2d Series.

of a secretary for a few hours every day, her lengthened service to literature not yet enabling her to have one entirely at her command. In those hours she has written songs which have pleased many who little guessed under what circumstances they were dictated.

Frances Browne's poems are, in truth, her best biography, for they show us her energy of mind, her resolution of character, her scorn of mean and soulless men, her love of the brave, the wise, and the good. Unlike the poems of Blacklock, which abound with complaints of the difficulties and distresses of his situation, his "rueful darkness" and "gloomy vigils," her lyrics contain little allusion to her outward life, and are altogether silent on the subject of her great calamity. With Voltaire, when some one was holding forth on De la Motte's blindness, she thinks that the public is concerned only with the powers of the author's mind, and not with the misfortunes of his body. But the circumstances of her life have given her a color to, if they have never formed the burden of, her song. Poverty having been her portion from the cradle, her sympathies are with the poor, "the wearers of the world's old clothes." Years of loneliness have made her look longingly forward to that better time when "none will lead a stranger's life," and to that happier shore, "where hearts will find their own." She deems this age but a material one, wherein the statesman's notion of the highest good is, that

"People and press no questions ask,
But joyfully pay taxes;"

while

"The sun of the priest's millennial views,
Is no dissent, and all the dues;"

and the trader's, that

"There will be no Gazette to fear,
But profits quite surprising;
With wages falling every year,
And the markets always rising."

In such an age, the poet is, she complains, out of place. 'Tis a cruel fate, which banishes him from his native heaven, and binds him to the clay—cruel as that which brings the wild swan from the purple heights of morn, to the dust and dulness of earth. This thought is beautifully expressed in the following touching poem, called

"THE WILD SWAN.

"An arrow sent from the hunter's string,
When the moorland sky was gray,
Had smote the strength of the wild swan's wing,
On his far and upward way;
Pinion and plume of vigor reft,
Drooped like boughs by the tempest cleft
On some green forest tree,
And never might that wild swan soar
To the purple heights of morning more;
Or westward o'er the hill-tops cleave
His course through the cloudy isles of eve,
And the sunset's golden sea.

"The light of the lovely lakes that lie
Among green woods was gone
From all his days, but the years went by,
And the lonely swan lived on,
A captive, bound to the dull earth then,
With wingless creatures, and weary men
Who could not quit the clay;
He grew like them, as a dweller must,
At home with the dulness and the dust,
Till faded from his memory's hold
The life and the liberty of old,
Like a far forgotten day.

"Yet ever as from wood and wave
The smile of the summer went,
And his kindred's march passed south, above
The spot where he was pent,
With their wavy lines, and their wings of snow,
And their trumpet's notes sent far below
To bid that lingerer rise,
The swan would gaze as the host swept by,
And a wild regret was in his cry,
As if for the nobler part and place
He lost, in the freedom of his race—
In the joy of streams and skies.

"Falls not that wild swan's fortune oft
On souls that scorn the ground,
Whose outspread wings the deadly shaft
Of an earthward fate hath found;
And narrowed down to some dusty scope
The tameless strength and the tireless hope
That for the skies were born;
Till in the lore of that lifeless lot
Their glorious birthright seems forgot,
As dimness deepens and grayness grows,
And year by year with its burden goes
To the night that knows no morn?

"Yet over the prison-house at times,
Great thoughts and voices go,
That wake with the mind-world's mighty chimes,
Their buried life below
And the bowed of bondage lift their view
To the heaven that lies so far and blue
In its boundless beauty yet,
But never can they that realm regain,
The wing is withered, the cry is vain—
So downward turn they, eye and heart,
And learn, but not with a ready heart,
Of that wild swan—'Forget!'"

But wherever our poet finds heroism, honesty, worth, there she reverently bows down; and never did preacher convey more beautiful a lesson on the brotherhood of all good men, however their lots may differ, than is contained in the poem of *Mark's Mother*.

"Mark, the miner, is full fourscore,
But blithe he sits at his cottage door,
Smoking the trusty pipe of clay,
Which hath been his comfort many a day,
In spite of work and weather;
It made his honest heart amends
For the loss of strength and the death of friends;
It cheered his spirit through the lives
And management of three good wives—
But now those trying times are done,
And there they sit in the setting sun,
Mark and his pipe together.

"From harvest-field and from pasture-ground,
The peasant people have gathered round:
The times are rusty, the news is scant,
And something like a tale they want
From Mark's unfailing store;
For he is the hamlet's chronicle,
And when so minded, wont to tell
Where their great-uncles used to play—
How their grandames looked on their wedding-day—
With all that happened of chance and change,
And all that had passed of great or strange,
For seventy years before.

"But on this evening, it is plain,
Mark's mind is not in the telling vein,
He sits in silence and in smoke,
With his thoughts about him like a cloak
Wrapped tight against the blast;
And his eye upon the old church spire,
Where falls the sunset's fading fire—
And all the friends his youth had known
Lie round beneath the turf and stone,
While a younger generation try
To touch the keys of his memory
With questions of the past.

"'Good Mark! how looked the Lady Rose
Whose bower so green in our forest grows,
Whom old men name with a blessing still
For the torrent's bridge, and the village mill,
And the traveller's wayside well?'
'Like my good mother, neighbors dear,
How long she lies in the churchyard here!'
'Well, Mark, that bishop of kindly rule,
Who burned the stocks, and built the school,
How looked his Grace when the church was new?'
'Neighbors, like my good mother, too,
As those who saw could tell.'

"'Then, Mark, the prince who checked his train,
When the stag passed through your father's grain?'
'Good neighbors, as I live, his look
The light of my blessed mother's took,
As he bade them spare the corn.'
Loud laugh the peasants with rustic shout:
'Now, Mark, thy wits are wearing out.
Thy mother was but a homely dame,
With a wrinkled face and a toil-worn frame;
No earthly semblance could she bear
To a bishop learned, and a lady fair,
And a prince to kingdoms born.'

"'Nay,' saith the pastor, passing by,
As the stars came out in the evening sky—
'That homely dame hath a place and part
Time cannot wear from the old man's heart,
Nor many winters wither;
And know ye, friends, that the wise and good
Are all of one gracious brotherhood;
Howe'er their fortunes on earth may stand,
They take the look of their promised land—
So bounteous lady, and bishop kind,
And prince with that royalty of mind,
Were like Mark's blessed mother.'"

With the above—which would be a sufficient answer to those critics who imagine that, like her own Ben Ezra, she only "sees of each soul the losing side"—we must conclude our notice of Frances Browne's poetry, and take a rapid glance at the prose work already referred to as her latest effort, *My Share of the World*.

This book is the autobiography of Frederick Favoursham of Liverpool, by turns artist, tutor, phrenologist, writer for the daily press, private secretary, holder of a government office, and finally of a large estate and many thousands. The scenes to which the author thus introduces us are various, showing considerable knowledge of men and things. The characters that play their part in the story are numerous—perhaps too numerous—but some of them are undoubtedly original. There is a young gentleman of fifteen, who despises *Jack the Giant-killer* and *Robinson Crusoe*, and considers the learning of his letters just a waste of time, but who dotes upon Foxe's *Martyrology* and *The Inquisition Displayed*, and will at any time lay down his knife and fork to hear about eternal punishment, or to meditate upon a tract he is composing on The Fall of Man. There is an old lady who is haunted at the full of the moon by the fear of the Jesuits, and goes shouting through the house: "Down with the pope!" There is a female phrenologist, who proves to be one of the women whom our hero's father had wheedled into a pretended marriage, who advises Frederick "to take care of his conscientiousness," and evinces her own by employing him as her assistant at the rate "of sixpence for every single, and a shilling for all double characters." There is a newspaper contributor who grumbles that his talents are not appreciated by editor or proprietor, and promises to revenge his wrongs by "pillorying the whole staff to all posterity in his great poem, The Guild of the Giftless;" solacing himself meantime by ascribing all the misfortunes of his life to his wedding-day, which "furnishes him with satisfactory reasons why he is not rich, wise, and celebrated—even the shortcomings of his previous life being laid at its door. 'Mr. Favoursham,' he would say, in moments of extraordinary confidence, 'how could I succeed, with that fate hanging over me? It cast a shadow on my prospects, though I did not know it: a man never does well who has something looming in the distance.'"

Nor are actors of a higher type and finer mould wanting in the drama. There is Frederick's mother, who is so lonely and heartbroken under her husband's desertion and profligacy, yet whose dying injunction to her son is, "Never forget he is your father, and do not let him want in his old days; and if you marry, be a good man to your wife, for women have a poor turn in this world; and if you don't, live like the holy virgins, that will come in white to the gates of heaven." There is Frederick's first and only love, a fine ideal nature, "with a born relationship to the arts and the muses," whom the fates join to a reckoner of sums and manufacturer of ginghams, surround by savers of candle-ends and makers of economical puddings, and consign at last to "the night-duty in this inglorious campaign of ours." There is her grandfather, a kindly old squire, with good word and hearty greeting for peasant and retainer, but who has never been himself since the murder of his only son, and who is quite bowed down by the suicide of his granddaughter, the sole comfort of his age. There is a brave and gifted Frenchman, whose love for the memory of the first Napoleon is greater than his love of friends or kindred, of fame or fortune; who has led a life almost as wandering and full of adventure as Candide's; who turns up in Frederick's painting-days, and befriends him in various emergencies, gets his father off a trial for bigamy, and our hero himself off a platform when he breaks down in a lecture, consoles him on the marriage of his first love with the remark: "You have missed Lucy somehow, but not the dream of your youth: you will never frown upon her because the joint is overdone, or the linen not mended;" who sings him the finest of songs, and gives him the wisest of counsel—except on the subject of astrology, and the partiality of Providence for red-haired people.

Then we have quaint pictures of the goings on of an "unco righteous" family, startling pictures of lives of blood and darkness, comic pictures of the whims and caprices, the failings and follies of men of the brush and men of the pen. We have glimpses of the homes of two brothers who had made their fortune in the slave-trade, one of whom turns to the deaconship of a chapel, the other to rum and limes, for consolation in his old days. We have sketches of mercenary love, hypocritical love, revengeful love, love to the wrong person. We have the portrait of a son unconsciously engaged in taking down his father's trial for bigamy. We have—but type and paper fail us to tell more than that we have the promise of another novel from the author, who, in the person of Frederick Favoursham, thus addresses the reader: "Having told my own tale, it would please me to tell some other people's whom I have mentioned in the course of it, thus taking a hint from the lady of the *Arabian Knights*, to prolong my literary life."

We think that that capricious calif, the Public, will be as pleased to listen to Frances Browne's stories as she will be to relate them; and as one of the ministers of his royal pleasure, we promise, when his majesty next yawns, to clap our hands, and usher in for his diversion the author of *My Share of the World*.

From Blackwood's Magazine.

SPONTANEOUS COMBUSTION.

In the year 1725 the Sieur Millet of Rheims rejoiced, or sorrowed, in a wife who was almost daily intoxicated. One evening, as he deposed, he retired to bed at eight o'clock, leaving her in the kitchen. About two in the morning he was awakened by a stench: he ran down to the kitchen, and there found the body of his wife, or rather the remains of her body, lying at a foot and a half's distance from the fire. A part of the head, a few of the vertebræ, and the lower extremities, were all that remained unconsumed. A foot and a half of the flooring was burned, but a kneading tub and trough, which were very near the body, were untouched. This was Millet's statement on his trial; for (owing to his having a very pretty servant-maid in the house, for whom he was thought to have an attachment) a suspicion had fallen on him of having murdered his wife, and burned the body to avert suspicion. The defence set up for him was, that the woman died of "spontaneous combustion;" and this was the verdict returned.

In the year 1847 the Countess of Görlitz was found burned in her private apartment, and two medical men reported, on evidence, that the cause of death was spontaneous combustion. Suspicion having fallen on one of the servants, Stauff, he was brought to trial; and in 1850 the long investigation ceased with the conviction of Stauff, who subsequently confessed his guilt, and was executed.

Between 1725 and 1850 the condition of scientific knowledge had been much changed; yet even in 1850 the laws of nature and the laws of evidence were so little understood by the mass of men, that Spontaneous Combustion continued to find believers, and continues to find them still. We propose, therefore, to lay before our readers a full account of the evidence, and the arguments adduced by those who believe in the phenomenon; and to examine these by the light of positive knowledge. There are few subjects that better illustrate the facility with which theories are formed and accepted, even by men whose scientific training ought to have taught them more circumspection and a truer appreciation of evidence. For the belief is not merely a vulgar error, it is an error countenanced by many scientific authorities; and although, when we come to examine the data on which it is founded, and the gross violation of chemical and physiological laws which it implies, the value of that authority will disappear, yet the fact that such authority can be cited for so preposterous a hypothesis is in itself instructive, and justifies our particular consideration of it. We give below a list of authorities. * It is unnecessary to cite authorities against the hypothesis: we shall have the far higher authority of positive laws to adduce, and will only mention, in passing, that no chemist of any eminence now sanctions the possibility of the phenomenon. Indeed, chemistry must relinquish her best-established truths before the hypothesis can be accepted. But as this kind of argument is more satisfactory to the scientific world than to the general public, we shall reserve it till the evidence of the alleged "cases" has been disposed of. In minds not long familiarized with the certainties of science, and the grounds upon which its conclusions are established, there is always a lurking distrust with regard to the conclusions of science, and a proportionate readiness to reject them in favor of the observations of some "eye-witness." There is in general but little appreciation of evidence, and none at all of the thousands of observations, scrutinized and verified with anxious care, upon which a scientific generalization, or law of nature, is founded. There is also a great readiness to believe in the marvellous. Our first object will therefore be to examine the evidence.

* Alberti: *Ob ein Mensch von selbst lebendig entzündet*, 1755; *Philosophical Transactions*, 1774. Lecat: *Relation de trois cas de combustion humaine* (Precis des Travaux de l'Acad. de Rouen, ii.). Dupont: *Diss. de corporis humani incendiis spontaneis*, 1768 Lair: *Essai sur les combustions humaines produites par un long abus des liqueurs spiritueuses*, 1800. Kopp: *Diss. de causis combustionis spontaneæ in corp. hum. factæ*, 1800. Koester: *Diss. de combustione corpor. hum. spont.*, 1804. Chirac: *Considerations sur la combust. humaine* (Thèses de Paris, An. xiii.). Charpentier: *Recherches physiol. pathol. et chimiques sur les phénomènes de la comb. humaine* (Bulletins de la Fac. de Med. de Paris, vii.). Fontenelle: *Recherches chimiques et med. sur les combust. humaines spontanées*, 1828. Fodéré: *Médicine Légale*, iii. Orfila et Devergie: *Comb. humaine* (Encyclopédie Moderne, vii.). Breschet: *Combustion humaine* (Nouveau Dict. de Médicine). Marc: *Comb. humaine* (Dict. des Sciences Médicales). Apjohn in *Cyclopædia of Practical Medicine*. Hooper's *Medical Dictionary*, by Grant, 1848. Beck: *Medical Jurisprudence*. Strubel: *Die Selbstverbrennung des Menschlichen Körpers*, 1848. Briand et Chaudé: *Manuel Complet de Médicine Légale*, 1858.

After noticing the incredulity excited by the narratives, M. Breschet says: "Les *nombreuses observations* que l'on possède de la combustion humaine, et les historiens qui nous le ont transmises, ne permettent pas de porter l'incrédulité jusqu'à nier l'existence de ce phénomène. Il nous suffira de nommer Lecat, Vicq d'Azir, Lair, Kopp, Dupuytren, et Marc, pour ne plus conserver de doute sur la réalité des combustions humaines." In Hooper's *Medical Dictionary* we find a similar statement: "The *number of cases on record* is so considerable as to leave no doubt of the reality of some process of igneous decomposition appearing during life under circumstances quite different from those of ordinary combustion from the application of fire." Now it is clear from these statements that the writers are very imperfectly acquainted with the laws of evidence. They speak of "observations" and "cases" when nothing is more certain, or indeed more generally admitted, than that no single *observation* has ever been made, no single *case* of spontaneous combustion has been established, otherwise all incredulity would vanish. The records referred to are not records of observations and cases, but are stories *purporting* to be cases—stories of events which are explained on the assumption of spontaneous combustion, because the ordinary explanations are at fault. After thus confounding the *guess* of a reporter with an *observation*, the writer continues: "*Little is distinctly known* concerning these mysterious cases; for it is a remarkable fact, that *in no instance has any witness been present* at the precise moment when the patient took fire." The stories of ghosts and spirit-rappings have a better claim to be regarded as evidence, since, absurd as the interpretations may be, the facts are vouched for by eye-witnesses. In the stories of spontaneous combustion there is no eye-witness, there is only a guess in the dark. When M. Breschet refers with emphasis to the historians who have transmitted the stories, and thinks that the reality of the phenomenon is established because respected names can be cited among the believers in it, he forgets that these authorities are only repeating the *reports* of ignorant and unscientific people narrating what they saw and inferred *after* the event. A list of names far more imposing might be drawn up as historians of witchcraft and apparitions. But the question is not, Who believes the phenomenon? it is, Who has any direct evidence to offer? Who saw the rise and progress of the combustion? And the answer is simple: The evidence is never of a *direct* and positive kind. No one has ever seen the phenomenon; no one pretends to have been present when the living body spontaneously burst into flame; no one even pretends to be fully acquainted with all the circumstances and conditions preceding the event. That the phenomenon ever did occur is, therefore, wholly hypothetical. It is an *inference* called upon to explain appearances which otherwise do not seem explicable. Not knowing how the body in question *was* burned—not understanding by what ordinary means it *could have been* burned under the circumstances—men assume an extraordinary process. The basis of their argument is flat ignorance. They know nothing, and infer all. On a similar basis many equally absurd explanations are daily erected unsuspiciously. The mind in its impatience cannot rest without an explanation of some kind. When men see huge boulders heaped somewhat in the shape of a rude pulpit, they invent an "explanation," and we have the legend of the Devil's Pulpit, because they are not content to sit down in quiet ignorance. When men see tables moving, and hear strange noises which they "cannot explain," they straightway begin explaining them as the work of spirits. When an epidemic breaks out, we hear on all sides confident explanations of it from gentlemen who have attended chemical lectures, and attribute it to "ozone" or to the "want of ozone." In these and a hundred similar examples, no attempt is made to prove the presence of the assumed cause, or to prove that the particular cause, *if* present, would necessarily produce this particular effect. But for a scientific hypothesis, one at least of these preliminaries is indispensable. If observation had detected any causal relation between ozone and the epidemic, there would be a scientific justification for the inference that ozone was now actually at work; we might, provisionally, assume the presence of ozone, because, if present, it would account for the epidemic. Or, on the other hand, if the presence of ozone in unusual abundance were proved, we might infer that this was one cause of the epidemic, and *then* proceed to test the inference. But to assume the presence of the agent, and also to assume its causal relations, and to make both these assumptions merely as an alleviation of our impatience, may be the practice of the vulgar—it is not the method of a philosopher.

Yet it is obvious that both these assumptions are made in the hypothesis of Spontaneous Combustion. In utter ignorance of *how* the death was caused, men assume that it was caused by spontaneous combustion; and they imagine they bring evidence in proof of this assumption when they show how little evidence there is for any other. They forget that there is *no evidence at all.* Granting that it is absolutely impossible to suggest any acceptable explanation of the cause of death, this impossibility is no evidence that the cause was spontaneous combustion: there is simply *absence* of evidence. We cannot account for the phenomenon. Nor is this difficulty removed by our inventing an explanation which has no guarantee of evidence. If in this ignorance we must guess at a cause, the guess should at least be one of probable or possible causes; and spontaneous combustion is *impossible.*

The matter stands thus: A body is found burned; the circumstances attending the burning are unknown; they have to be *inferred;* but, in the absence of the usual indications, we are unable to assign any of the ordinary causes: a hundred suppositions are possible, but there is no direct evidence for any one; each must, therefore, be tested by its inherent *probability.* If we said that the body was burned by the hot breath of a dragon, we should have as much evidence for the assertion as if we said the body spontaneously ignited—that is to say, we should have no evidence at all. Our opponents, in refuting the dragon hypothesis, would not trouble themselves about the evidence, but would point out the high degree of improbability in the assumption of a dragon, and the want of any warrant for supposing that the dragon's breath could burn a man. In like manner the philosopher troubles himself but little about the evidence of spontaneous combustion contained in the recorded stories, because he can prove that the phenomenon itself is impossible.

As we are addressing the general public, and not merely a public of scientific men, we shall consider the alleged evidence, since, if we can show that this evidence, upon which so much reliance is placed, is absolutely *worthless* because it is never direct, and never establishes the smallest presumption in favor of spontaneous combustion over any *other* imaginary cause, we shall gain a more willing hearing to the scientific arguments which prove the absurdity of the hypothesis.

Liebig, who has treated this question in a masterly manner, * remarks that the descriptions of cases which belong to the last century do not proceed from highly cultivated physicians, but from ignorant persons unpractised in observation, and the descriptions all bear the stamp of untrustworthiness. "In these accounts it is usually stated that the body entirely disappears down to a greasy stain on the floor and some remains of bones. Every one knows this to be impossible. The smallest bit of bone in the fire becomes white and loses somewhat of its bulk; but of its weight there remains from sixty to sixty-four per cent of earthly matter, commonly retaining the original form of bone." So little reliance can be placed on the reports of persons unaccustomed to scientific observation, that in the Görlitz trial the female attendants who had washed and clothed the dead body deposed that there were neither arms nor head; another witness saw one arm, and a head of the size of a man's fist; a third, a physician, saw both arms and head of the usual female size.

Let us now examine the chief cases more nearly.

Mary Clues, of Gosford Street, Coventry, aged fifty-two, and much given to drinking, was found burned to death one morning. The following is the description of the room and the appearance of the body, sent to the Royal Society by Mr. Wilmer, the surgeon: "Her bedroom was next the street on the ground-floor, the walls of which were plastered and the floor made of bricks. The chimney is small, and there was a grate in it, which from its size could contain but a very small quantity of fire. Her bedstead

* Liebig: *Zur Beurtheilung der Selbstverbrennungen des Menschlichen Korpers,* 1850; and in *Familiar Letters on Chemistry,* XXIV.

stood parallel to, and at the distance of three feet from, the chimney. The bed's head was close to the wall. On the other side of the bed was a window opening to the street. One curtain only belonged to the bed, which was hung on the side next the window. She was accustomed to lie upon her side, close to the edge of the bedstead next the fire; and on Sunday morning, March the 1st, tumbled on the floor, where her helpless state obliged her to lie some time, till a neighbor came accidentally to see her. With some difficulty she was got into bed. The same night, though she was advised to it, she refused to have any one sit up with her, and at half-past eleven one Brooks, who was an occasional attendant, left her as well as usual, locked the door, and went home. He had placed two bits of coal quite backward upon the fire in the grate, and put a small rushlight in a candlestick, which was set on a chair near the head of the bed, but not on the side where the curtain was. At half-past five the next morning a smoke was observed to come out of the window in the street, and upon breaking open the door some flames were perceived in the room, which, with five or six buckets of water, were easily extinguished. Betwixt the bed and the fireplace lay the remains of Mrs. Clues. The legs and one thigh were untouched. Except those parts, there was not the least remains of any skin, viscera, or muscles. The bones were completely calcined, and covered with a whitish efflorescence. The skull lay near the head of the bed, the legs towards the bottom, and the spine in a curved direction, so that she appeared to have been burnt on her right side with her back towards the grate. When the flames were extinguished, it appeared that very little damage had been done to the furniture of the room, and that the side of the bed next the fire had suffered most. The bedstead was superficially burnt; but the feather-bed, sheets, and blankets were not destroyed. The curtain on the other side of the bed was untouched, and a deal door near the bed not injured. I was in the room about two hours after the mischief was discovered. I observed that the walls and every thing in the room were colored black. There was a very disagreeable vapor; but I did not observe that any thing was much burnt except Mrs. Clues, whose remains I saw in the state just described. The only way I can account for it is by supposing that she again tumbled out of bed on Monday morning, and that her shift was set fire to either by the candle on the chair or a coal falling from the grate; that her solids and fluids were rendered inflammable by the immense quantities of spirituous liquors she drank, and that when she was set fire to, she was probably soon reduced to ashes, for the room suffered very little." * The only objection to this account is the hypothesis that the woman's body was rendered inflammable by the liquors she had drunk, a hypothesis we shall hereafter show to be utterly at variance with fact. Take that away, and the case is simply one of a woman burnt to death, and being at the time either too drunk or too helpless to make an alarm which would have brought assistance. We have cited the case because it is one constantly referred to by the advocates of spontaneous combustion; and, for the same reason, we will give another, also taken from the same source.

Grace Kett, the wife of a fishmonger, aged sixty, was in the habit of leaving her bedroom, half dressed, to smoke a pipe. This habit continued several years. On the 9th April, 1744 she quitted her bed as usual: her daughter who slept with her, did not perceive her absence till the morning. On going into the kitchen she found her mother stretched on her right side, with her head near the grate. The body was extended on the hearth, with the legs on the deal floor, and it had the appearance of a log of wood consumed by fire without apparent flame. On beholding the spectacle, the girl ran in great haste, and poured some water over the body to extinguish the fire. The fetid odor and smoke which exhaled from the body almost suffocated the neighbors who had hastened to the girl's assistance. The trunk was in some measure incinerated, and resembled a heap of coals covered with white ashes. The head, the arms, the legs, and the thighs had also participated in the burning. This woman, it is said, had drunk a large quantity of spirituous liquor, in consequence of being overjoyed to hear one of her daughters had returned from Gibraltar. There was no fire in the grate, and the *candle had burnt entirely out in the socket of the candlestick, which was close to her. Her*

* *Philos. Transactions*, 1774, p. 340.

dress consisted of a cotton gown. These final details are surely sufficient to lead to a conclusion. In a stupefied state of drunkenness she had probably fallen over the candle, which had ignited her cotton dress. But, even if this were not the cause, it is certain that the recorded evidence gives no hint of spontaneous combustion. The old woman is found burned—cause not apparent; so that the verdict might have been "died by the visitation of God," as in the following case, recorded in the *Methodist Magazine* for 1809: "Mr. O'Neil, keeper of the almshouse in Limerick, was awakened about two o'clock in the morning by a person knocking at his room door; upon which he arose, and having inquired who knocked, he opened the door; and going with the person who called him into his apartment, which lay under Mrs. Peacock's room, he found a dead body lying on the ground, burning with fire and red as copper, having dropped down from the loft, which was on fire. Examining the loft, he saw a large hole, the size of the dead body, burned through the boards and ceiling. Having, with assistance, quenched the fire about the hole, he examined by what means the body had taken fire, *but could find no cause.* There was no candle or candlestick near the place, no fire in the grate, but what was raked in the ashes, as in the manner of preserving fire by night. The room was examined, and nothing had taken fire but that part of the floor through which she had fallen. Even a small basket made of twigs, and a small trunk of dry wood which lay near the hole, had escaped. This phenomenon was the next day examined by the mayor, clergymen, and several gentlemen of the city. The *impossibility of ascertaining the cause of the fire*, the extraordinary circumstance (?) of no part of the room being burnt but the centre of it, through which she had fallen, added to the *well-authenticated circumstance of her recent diabolical imprecations and lies, obliged every observer* to resolve so awful an event into the visitation of God's judgment in the punishment of so daring and persevering a sinner." That the *Methodist Magazine* should record such a case is conceivable enough; but that Professor Apjohn should, in the pages of the *Cyclopædia of Practical Medicine*, reproduce it as evidence of spontaneous combustion, adding that he does not solely rely on the *Magazine*, but has received confirmation from "an intelligent lady residing in Limerick, who had personally inspected the floor through which the hole had been burned," is a curious example of what even professional men will at times accept as evidence in favor of preconceived ideas. It is true that Professor Apjohn is, or was, a chemist. But how little the laws of chemical action were impressed upon his mind, may be judged by the following preposterous story, which he also gives: A. B., a woman of about sixty years of age, retired one evening to bed, with her daughter, both being, as was their constant habit, in a state of intoxication. A little before day some members of the family were awakened by an extremely offensive smoke, which filled their apartment; and on going into the chamber where the old woman and her daughter slept, they found the smoke to proceed from the body of the former, "which appeared to be burning with an internal fire. It was as black as coal, and the smoke issued from every part of it. The combustion having been arrested, which was effected with difficulty, although there was no flame, life was found completely extinct." Up to this point there is nothing remarkable, but we must call attention to one important detail: no mention is made of the position of the body; we are not told whether it was on the floor, at some distance from the bed, or *in* the bed. Yet the absence of this statement vitiates what follows: "Her daughter, who slept in the same bed, sustained no injury; *nor did the combustion extend to the bed-clothes*, which exhibited no other traces of fire than the stains produced by the smoke." This preservation of the bed-clothes, which, Professor Apjohn is careful to inform us, was confirmed by the Rev. Mr. Ferguson of Dublin, is either the most irrelevant detail a scientific man could possibly adduce, or is a miracle which must have staggered a chemist: it is utterly irrelevant if the body were not *in* or *close* to, the bed, since in that case there could be no reason to expect the bed-clothes to be ignited; and he might as well have laid stress on the fact of some curl paper on the table having escaped. It is a miracle if the burning body were in the bed, and the bed-clothes escaped; for although Professor Apjohn, in common with some others, chooses to assert that the flame of spontaneous combustion is a *peculiar* flame, "not readily communicable to inflammable bodies placed in its vicinity"—an assertion founded on some misinterpreted facts, and in glaring contradiction with many other facts and with chemical laws—yet he must be perfectly aware that, in the recorded cases, while some objects escape combustion, there are always other objects which *have* been burned; and it will be difficult for him to show why the old woman's nightdress should ignite, and not the sheets in contact with that dress. We assert, that if the body were on the floor there is nothing remarkable in the escape of the bed-clothes; if the body were in the bed, the escape of the bed-clothes is—a fiction. "According to the testimony of one of the relations, who is represented as a woman of the strictest veracity, there was no fire whatever in the room." Perhaps so; but were there no matches? no lighted candle? no means of setting combustible bodies alight? On this point, silence. "The subject had been grossly intemperate for several days before her decease, having drunk much more ardent spirit at this period than usual." *That*, according to the professor, is the explanation of the case.

Yet it is "from the cases just related, and from several others which might be quoted," that a grave professor, in a medical treatise of authority, which would be looked up to by hundreds of practitioners, conceives it to be "fully proved that the human body is capable of being reduced to such a state as to undergo spontaneously, or upon the contact of flame, rapid changes analogous to those which may be effected by the agency of fire." More worthless evidence was never brought forward to support a more improbable hypothesis.

Let us turn to some of the cases adduced by other writers. The Countess Cornelia Bandi, of Cesena, in Italy, aged sixty-two, in excellent health, and *not* given to intoxication, was accustomed to bathe her body in camphorated spirits of wine. One evening, having felt very drowsy, she retired early to bed. Her maid remained with her till she fell asleep, and then quitted the room to return the next morning, and find the remains of her mistress in a horrible condition. At the distance of four feet from the bed was a heap of ashes, in which the legs and arms were alone untouched; between the legs lay the head. The brain, together with half the posterior part of the cranium, and the whole chin, had been consumed; three fingers were found in a state of coal, and the body was reduced to ashes, which, when touched, left on the fingers a fat and fetid moisture. A small lamp which stood on the floor was covered with ashes, and contained no oil. The tallow of two candles was melted on the table, but the wicks still remained, and the feet of the candlesticks were covered with moisture. The bed was not deranged; the bed-clothes and coverlid were raised up, as is the case when a person gets out of bed. We do not profess to explain the cause of death in this case. As in so many other cases, the details are too scanty for judgment. But there is *no one* detail which points to a spontaneous ignition of the body.

Dr. Beck quotes, with great confidence, the following case, for which he is indebted to the researches of W. Dunlop, Esq., of New York: Hannah Bradshaw, aged about thirty, was a *healthy*, hearty-looking woman, neat in her person and manner of living, but not remarkable for sobriety or chastity. On the evening of the 31st December, she desired a young woman, who worked for her, and was going home, to come again early the next morning; and about seven o'clock the same evening another acquaintance parted from her, at which time she seemed to have drunk a little too freely. She was neither heard nor seen till the next morning, when the young woman returned to her work. After knocking and calling, and having waited till half-past eleven, this person, by the aid of a man who lived below, got in through a back window, and opened the door. On looking within a screen, which went right across the room, and was fitted to the ceiling, she discovered Hannah, or rather her mutilated remains. The bones were lying near the middle of the floor, wherein a hole of about four feet in diameter was quite burnt away, and the bones were on the ground, about a foot beneath that part of the floor. The flesh was entirely burnt off the bones of the whole body, except a small part on the skull, a little on one of the shoulders, the lower part of the right leg and foot, which was burnt off at the small, almost as if cut off and left lying there. *The stocking was burnt off as far as the leg, and no farther. The bowels remained uncon-*

sumed. One of the sleepers which lay under the shoulders, was burnt almost through. Part of the head lay on the planks at the edge of the hole, and near it was a candlestick, with a part of a candle in it, thrown down, but it did not appear to have touched any part of the body, or to have set any thing on fire (?). The leg of the rush-bottomed chair, and about half the bottom, were burnt, so far as they were within compass of the hole in the floor, and no farther. Is it justifiable to see any evidence of spontaneous combustion in this story? How can any one assume that the candle did not set any thing on fire? No one was present from the commencement to the close; no one, therefore, could say what had been the course of events. A similar objection falls upon the next case:—

"By a letter from General William Shepherd, it appears that on the 16th March, 1802, in one of the towns of Massachusetts, the body of an elderly woman disappeared in the space of about one hour and a half. Part of the family had retired to bed, and the rest were gone out. The old woman remained awake to take care of the house. Soon after, one of the grandchildren came home, and discovered the floor near the hearth to be on fire. An alarm was given, a light brought, and means taken to extinguish it. While these things were doing, some singular appearances were observed on the hearth and contiguous floor. There was a sort of greasy soot and ashes, with the remains of a human body, and an unusual smell in the room. All the clothes were consumed. The fire had been small." *

Small? But is there any necessity for its having been large? One spark suffices to kindle a huge flame in a substance really combustible.

We will not repeat Liebig's analysis of the case reported by Battaglio, which he has completely exposed. Let us rather quote the very modern example reported in the *Edinburgh Journal of Medical Science*, December, 1852, the reporter being a medical man:—

"On the evening of the 29th of July last, the body of John Anderson, æt. fifty, about five feet four inches in height, and of a spare habit, a carter of wood from the forest of Darnaway to the pier of Nairn, and a notorious dram-drinker, was found dead by the road-side, seven miles from Nairn, and in a state of combustion, the process having proceeded so far as blackening and charring of the body and head, and complete disfiguration of the features—so much so, that the person was only recognized from his horses and carts being known. The case was taken up medico-legally by the Procurator-Fiscal of the county of Nairn, and I was requested to inspect the body, and report. On approaching the unfortunate man's dwelling, on the forenoon of 31st July, I found that the funeral had passed on to the churchyard of the parish of Dyke; and, after a little explanation to the attendants, I succeeded in getting a hurried autopsy within the church. On removing the grave-sheet, I found a black, incinerated, and stiffened body. The legs and arms were crossed, the latter raised from the chest. The position was one of ease; and the body had not been touched since first rolled up. The eyes, ears, and nose were burned away, teeth clenched, and from the mouth bubbled out some white froth and gas. The lining membrane on the inside of the lips and cheeks was quite burned; also the edges of the tongue, and the hair and skin of the head. The skin and cellular tissue of the body were much charred: the thighs not to the same extent; and the burning had ceased about midway between the knees and feet, where there was a reddish and slightly blistered line. The back was not so much destroyed. The pharynx, œsophagus, etc., exhibited no appearance of burning. The villous coat throughout was much congested, and that of the stomach presented those cherry-red appearances, with thickening, which are sometimes noticed in the stomachs of drunkards. It was almost empty, gave out no smell of alcohol, nor did the contents, on after examination. On opening the peritoneum, there was a great escape of fetid gas. The bowels were healthy, but dry from heat. The state of the heart, blood, and lungs, could not be examined.

"On inquiry, I found the wretched man's history to be the following: he has been a carter, as above stated, for several years; has drunk, at least of ardent spirits, *daily*, on an average, a common bottleful, besides porter, beer, etc.; left Nairn on the day of his death intoxicated; in passing an intermediate village, was seen coming on 'all fours' out of one of those many 'publics' which are the opprobria of our smaller towns and villages in the north of Scotland. He was, however, one of those 'soaking' individuals, who much sooner lose the locomotive balance than a knowledge of his situation and work; hence, when on his cart, he could talk and manage his horses tolerably well. He had a brother carter with him, a neigh-

* Beck, p. 577.

boring toll-keeper, who was sober; and they parted company at the toll-gate of Harmuir, within half a mile of the place where the body was found. Before this, however, Anderson wished his pipe to be lit and handed to him; but his friend, thinking that he had no need of a smoke, merely put a little fire on the old tobacco ash, when he drew, and immediately said, 'She is not in.' The conversation went on for ten minutes, when the poor man turned his horses' heads homewards. All this time the pipe was in his hand. The tollman, who was much on the road with him, declared that Anderson seldom lighted his own pipe, and never almost knew him to carry lucifers. The dress was a woollen shirt, canvas frock, corduroy trousers, and a 'wide-awake.' The weather was very warm and dry. When a little farther on his way homewards, smoke was seen rising up from the cart in which the man was, and which contained a good deal of hay, by a herd-boy on a neighboring rising ground, about one-fourth of a mile distant. The man was next seen to descend from the cart, to stand, then to stagger and fall. The horses stood still. In a few minutes smoke again appeared from the ground, when the boy ran down, and found the body lifeless, black, disfigured, and burning. He hurried to a cottage close by, and returned with a woman having a water-pail, with which they drew water several times from a rivulet almost at their feet, and thereby extinguished the burning body and garments. The position was on the back, inclining to one side; arms and legs as before mentioned. The time that elapsed between the boy seeing the man come down from his cart and the water being dashed on, is represented as not more than fifteen minutes. The body was wrapped into a sheet, and removed home. The pipe was found lying below the body with the cap on, apparently as it had been put into his hands. The clothes were all consumed, except the lower parts of the legs of the trousers, where the burning had ceased, and a small portion of the shirt, frock, and hat, immediately between the body and the ground. There was none of the hay burned.

"*Remarks.*—The case at first sight appeared to me to have arisen from the clothes having by some means caught fire, and the smoke therefrom producing death by asphyxia—the subject being much intoxicated; but second thoughts demonstrated a few points not reconcilable to my mind with this view, such as the position on the back, etc.—the event taking place in the open air—rigidity of the limbs—no trace of fire—and the rapidity and extent of the combustion, whilst this latter (compared with the accounts of martyrs, suttees, and others who have been consumed, and the great quantity of fuel and the time that have been required), and no apparent struggle or attempt having been made to cast off the burning garments, or to quench the flames in the brook running alongside, whilst the man was not at all in a state of insensibility from his potations, led me to the belief, that it was no ordinary combustion from the application of fire. I have, then, been induced to regard it as a case of progressive igneous decomposition, commencing during life without the application or approach of any hot or burning body, as believed in by several continental physiologists of eminence. Such a state of matters I know has been regarded by many as almost fabulous; but the numbers of general instances from good authorities, and from all parts of the world, of spontaneous combustion, or, as Beck more properly terms it, preternatural combustibility of the human body, and written on by Dr. Mason Good, and received into the Statistical Nosology from the General Register Office, now in the hands of most medical practitioners, under the appellation of *catacausis ebriosa*, show that the doctrine cannot be wholly set aside."

First remark the reliance placed on the numbers of "instances from good authorities"—instances which the reader has been able to appreciate—and then examine the evidence here offered. In the first place, the testimony is that of a toll-keeper and a herd boy, surely, not the most reliable sources to which one would look for accuracy in description. Then observe what were the appearances noted. The body was *charred*—that is, burned, as it always is superficially when the clothes take fire. The man's clothes were woollen shirt, canvas frock, and corduroy trousers, which, once ignited, would in the open air burn well enough. He was drunk. He had a lighted pipe, which was found *under* his body. The cart was full of hay. The clothes were consumed, except where the burning of the body had ceased—or, to state the case more accurately, the burning of the body ceased where the burning of the clothes ceased.

It is unnecessary to multiply examples. One more case, that of the Countess Görlitz, shall suffice. On the 13th June, 1847, between three and four in the afternoon, on her husband's going out to dinner, the countess, a healthy active woman of forty-six, retired to her apartment to arrange some household matters, as was her wont.

The servants, except Stauff, had permission to go out. The apartment consisted of an antechamber, and a chamber, into which opened a sort of closet, large enough to contain an ottoman, on which she commonly took her siesta. In one corner of the room was a Russian stove, and in another her *schreibpult*, a writing-desk, which those unacquainted with German furniture may form an idea of by imagining a large chest of drawers, with a folding-board to serve as writing-table. On his return in the evening, the count knocked at the door of the anteroom, but, receiving no answer, he went out again. This was about seven. He came back at nine. During his absence a bright light, which speedily disappeared, had been noticed at the closet window, and a thick smoke from the chimney which corresponded with the stove in the parlor. At nine o'clock the count ordered the servants, who had then returned, to go in search of their mistress: they not obtaining entrance, workmen were sent for to break open the doors, which were locked. The keys were afterwards not to be found. The smoke which issued from the rooms prevented their being entered till one of the windows was forced. On this being done, flames burst out simultaneously from the hangings, the writing-desk, and the floor underneath it. The dead body of the countess was found a foot from the writing-desk, with the feet towards the middle of the room and the head towards the window. There was no appearance of fire about it, or at the part of the inlaid floor on which it rested. On its removal a few buckets of water sufficed to extinguish the fire. On this being effected, a rush of smoke issued from the open door of the closet, which was found to proceed from the ottoman being on fire. No other object in this apartment was touched, and in front of the ottoman lay one of the countess' slippers uninjured. On the following morning, Dr. Graff was called in officially, and found the apartments in that state of disorder usual after a fire. The writing-desk had been mostly consumed, and the papers it had contained, partly burned, lay scattered about the room. The ottoman was displaced, and nearly in its centre was an almost oval hole caused by the combustion of the hair mattress and stuffing. On proceeding to view the body, Dr. Graff observed the remaining slipper on one of the feet, *and uninjured*. The dress on the upper part of the body was almost wholly consumed. The head exhibited the form of a nearly shapeless black mass, in which the mouth was imperfectly distinguished, with the charred tongue protruding from it. The body lay on its left side, the head and chest retracted, the neck everywhere blackened and charred, as were the skin and muscles on the fore and upper parts of the chest, the former being thus affected to within an inch of the pit of the stomach. The marks of the action of fire did not extend quite so far along the back part of the trunk. The joints of both upper extremities were flexed, and their surfaces charred, except at the hands. The left shoulder and the right elbow-joints were laid open. From the former of these the blackened humerus, and from the latter the heads of the radius and ulna, protruded. The skin in the vicinity of the left knee was slightly acted on. The body exhaled an empyreumatic odor. The further examination of it was objected to.

"Considering (1) that the deceased had been in full bodily vigor; (2) that she had been seen by her servants the evening before in good health; (3) that she had not gone to bed, but must have been occupied at her writing-desk; (4) that in case of the fire having been accidental, she might have escaped from it, or at least have called for assistance, of which there was no indication, though she was close to a window; and (5) that as the traces of the fire and the carbonization of the body were chiefly about the head, and that the open mouth and protruded tongue were indicative of suffocation and impending asphyxia, Dr. Graff reports it as highly probable that this had been one of the rare instances of what is termed *spontaneous combustion*; a supposition, in his opinion, which alone could explain the circumstances that the deceased had been unable to call for assistance or to save herself, as she must have done had the light on the writing-desk caught her hair or headdress."

This opinion Dr. Graff so far qualified next day, as to report further that his conclusion in regard to the high probability of death by spontaneous combustion, in this instance, was a hypothesis only admissible in the absence of *indications of violence on the body*, the abstract possibility of which he was not prepared to deny. Another report was furnished by Dr. Stegmayer in

December, 1847, in which he could not say whether there had or had not been any thing in the mode of life or constitution of the countess which supported the hypothesis of spontaneous combustion; but Dr. Siebold, on the 12th April, 1848, sent in a report decidedly to the effect that the countess had perished by spontaneous combustion; and in proof of the occasional occurrence of such a phenomenon, he referred to the cases collected by Devergie in his article in the *Dictionaire de Médicine*. He viewed the body on the night of the fire. The surface of the head and neck had a shining fatty appearance, as if covered with a coat of varnish. *There were no marks of fire on the clothes anywhere beyond the margins of the burns on the body.*

Although the death of the countess took place in June, it was not until the 26th November that the count intimated that an inquest would be held. Next day the cook detected a quantity of greenish matter (verdigris) in a sauce intended for the count. About the same time suspicion was awakened against the man-servant, Stauff, from the discovery of some jewels belonging to the countess in the possession of one of his relatives at a distance. Yet, in spite of the suspicions against Stauff, Dr. Siebold considered, from the facts of the case, that the burning of the countess could not have been the result of *design* nor of *accident*. The combustion of the desk and the portion of the floor could not have done it. The corpse was found out of the reach of these, and on a part of the floor to which the fire had not extended. The doors and windows were closed, so that the desk and floor were rather charred than burned. Besides, the *disproportion* between the extent of the burns on the body and the quantity of the combustibles consumed was too great to allow him to admit that they had been caused by the burning of the furniture. Dr. Siebold further contended, that spontaneous combustion alone could satisfactorily explain the circumstances of the case: such as the limitation of the burning to the upper part of the body and of the dress, while it had extended to the upper extremities; the greasy coating on the mirror and the oil-painting; and the appearance of the burned parts. Supposing that the combustion had begun at the head, and that the eyes had only been partially involved in it, the countess might at the moment have been in a state to run to the bell-pull, and in her agony to pull it till it gave way. The flame seen from a house opposite the closet window showed that she had been lying on the ottoman when the head had taken fire [not a bad example this of the way events are *shown!*], which accounted for the hole burned in the ottoman, as well as the finding the slipper in this room. He further conjectured that the countess was in the act of running to the window to call for assistance when she had fallen before the writing-desk and set it on fire.

This case is of great interest, as presenting many of those inexplicable details which in other cases have led to the inference of spontaneous combustion. Indeed, the account of the position of the body and the state of the objects in the room, is such as to baffle every attempt at explanation. Nevertheless, there was evidence against Stauff sufficient to convict him, and he confessed the crime. His confession makes us fully alive to the facility with which our guesses may shoot wide of the mark, though seeming probable. Read again Siebold's conjectures, and compare it with this confession of the murderer. Stauff declared that he had entered the room of the countess to announce that he was going out, when, finding no one in the room, he was tempted by some articles of value he saw there to commit a robbery. While doing so the countess came in: a struggle took place, and he seized her by the throat and strangled her. He afterwards placed the body on a chair, and, putting around it a quantity of combustible articles, set fire to them. We here see the value of Siebold's induction, that the body could not have been burned by accident, nor by design, because there was not a sufficient quantity of combustibles to account for so great an extent of burning. This induction is one constantly made; the fact being, as Liebig remarks, that the cause of death by burning has this peculiarity, that it consumes the fuel which supports it, so that the fuel does not remain unaltered, like the knife with which a man has been murdered. Had there not been the discovery of the jewels in Stauff's possession, and some other facts tending to criminate him, and had the cause of the countess' death remained a mystery, we should have seen this story quoted in cyclopædias and treatises as one of the striking "cases" of spontaneous combustion. And certainly, until the murderer confessed his guilt, the "evidence" was of such a character as to lend itself to the wildest suppositions. It is the same with the other cases. Had any one been present during any of the recorded cases, he would doubtless have been able to clear up all its seeming contradictions; but as nobody ever was present, we are left to the wide field of conjecture.

We do not mean to insinuate that in all the other cases a murder had been committed, and the dead body burned to conceal the fact. This may have been sometimes done; but it is perfectly consistent with experience to believe that drunken persons, or persons stupefied by the smoke, may have perished without raising any alarm. The following case, given in the *Journal of a Naturalist*, will show this: A travelling man, one winter's evening, laid himself down upon the platform of a lime-kiln, placing his feet, probably numbed with cold, upon the heap of stones newly put on to burn through the night. Sleep overcame him in this situation, the fire gradually rising and increasing, until it ignited the stones upon which his feet were placed. Lulled by the warmth, the man slept on; the fire increased, until it burned one foot (which was probably extended over a vent-hole), and part of the leg above the ankle, entirely off, consuming that part so effectually, that a cinder-like fragment was all that remained—and still the wretch slept on! and in this state was found by the kiln-man in the morning. Insensible to any pain, and ignorant of his misfortune, he attempted to rise, but, missing his shoe, requested to have it found; and when he was raised, putting his burnt limb to the ground to support his body, the extremity of his leg bone crumbled into fragments. Still he expressed no pain, and probably felt none. Had the fire extended further, this man would have been burnt to death slowly while sleeping, and would have never made an effort to escape.

We close here that part of our argument which relates to the evidence of cases. Reviewing this evidence, we find that, even on the very questionable assumption of the testimony having been both accurate and exhaustive, there has been nothing whatever to prove spontaneous combustion over and above the presumption which may arise in its favor on account of the difficulty of otherwise accounting for the deaths. The exclusion of ordinary causes may lead to the inference of *some* extraordinary cause, but it does not prove that this extraordinary cause is spontaneous combustion rather than any other. If I place a china vase upon the mantelpiece, and, on quitting the room, lock the door, having ascertained that no one is in the room, and find, on my return, the vase shattered on the floor, I shall certainly be puzzled "to account for it." No one has entered the room; no cat, dog, or bird was shut up in the room. The ordinary causes seem therefore excluded; but, shall I be justified in concluding that the vase spontaneously leaped from the mantelpiece? You would laugh at such a supposition, and would declare that it was, in the nature of things, an absolute impossibility that china vases should spontaneously leap. Now, although the impossibility of spontaneous combustion in a living organism is not so *obvious*, it is, to the well-informed physiologist, little less certain, than the impossibility of spontaneous movement in a china vase. Having shown, therefore, that the phenomenon is merely inferred in order to explain certain appearances, we will now show that the inference is one which is utterly unjustifiable, because it contradicts the well-established laws of nature.

Professor Apjohn, believing that his stories prove the reality of the phenomenon, asks, "Whence arises that extreme degree of *inflammability* of the human body, in virtue of which its combustion is so readily produced, and, occurring at any point, is *propagated with rapidity* to distant parts?" We answer that the human body *cannot* be rendered inflammable while living; and that a chemist should not only know this, but know that the rapid *propagation* of flame in the living body is as utterly impossible as the enclosure of space by two parallel lines. "The human body," he says, "is a combustible compound." True enough; and a diamond is combustible. But the human body is not a compound *easily* combustible, and cannot propagate its combustion like inflammable bodies. Its combustion is hindered by the *water* it contains. The living body consists of three-fourths of water, which, we need scarcely say, acts as a damper on the *propagation* of flame. This fact, however, does not damp the ardor of the advocates of spontaneous combustion. They admit that under ordinary circumstances the body is not easily combustible; but they assume that under extraordinary circumstances it may become so. Two hypotheses are advanced which are supposed to render this probable. The first is, that the bodies of habitual drunkards are so saturated with alcohol that they become preternaturally combustible. The second is, that "certain modifications" take place, "owing to diseased conditions," by which the body becomes preternaturally combustible.

When alcohol is taken into the stomach, it is absorbed into the blood-vessels, and is carried by the torrent of the circulation to the various tissues, especially to those of the liver and nervous centres, for which it seems to have a marked preference. But elementary knowledge of physiology ought long ago to have taught men that the idea of the living tissues being saturated with alcohol is absurd. The thing cannot be done. If life is to continue, only a very slight quantity indeed can be carried to any one tissue; and that slight quantity does not, and cannot, *remain* there. The blood which carried it there carries it away again. It is thrown out of the body, at each moment, by the breath, through the skin, and through the kidneys. If more alcohol be taken than can be rapidly got rid of in this way, death ensues from alcoholic poisoning. Few men could survive after drinking a bottle of brandy; and supposing this all to remain in the body, it would be far from "saturating the tissues" of a man whose body contains ninety pounds weight of water. Indeed, to suppose the tissues saturated with alcohol, is to overlook all physiological conditions—the incessant chemical changes upon which life depends would all be rendered impossible by alcoholic saturation. It is when we wish to preserve the tissues against chemical change that we place them in alcohol—and these are dead tissues.

So unfortunate is the hypothesis we are combating, that if even its premises be granted, its conclusions must be rejected. We might grant the possibility of the tissues being saturated with alcohol, without in the least relinquishing our position that the living body cannot be thereby rendered easily combustible. Make the body a mere living keg of brandy; let its ninety pounds of water be changed into brandy and water; nay, let the water be entirely removed; saturate the tissues with alcohol, soak them in it, and bring a lighted candle into direct contact with it—even then the body will not flame! the brandy will blaze away, but not the body. When all the brandy has burnt away, the body will be found black, dry, and charred, but not flaming nor destroyed. The truth of this is seen every Christmas, when our children shout around the snap-dragon. The raisins are steeped in brandy, the brandy is lighted, and blazes with blue and joyous fury; but the raisins are so little affected by all this flame, that the children pop them into their mouths as fast as they can. The reason is simple: it is a chemical law, admitting of no exception, that *a body which is in itself difficult of combustion cannot be rendered less so by the presence of a body easily combustible.* The raisins are not easily combustible, and are not rendered more so by the presence of brandy, which burns readily. In the brandy or out of it, the raisins are equally slow to burn.

The same is true of the living, or moist tissues. They are not made of asbestos; they will burn if a proper degree of heat be applied, which will first evaporate their liquids; but they are slow to burn, and are not inflammable like paper or straw, which, when once ignited, propagate the flame to distant parts, away from contact with the original cause of ignition. Light a piece of paper at one end, and the whole is quickly destroyed. Light a piece of flesh at one end, and it will only be the end in contact with the flame which will burn: remove the flame, and the flesh ceases to burn. To prove that alchohol will not make this flesh an iota more combustible, the following experiment will suffice. We placed three small strips of uncooked beef in brandy, and left them to soak there for several weeks, in a well-corked bottle. The first piece was removed, and held in the flame of a candle; it at once caught fire, and blazed: the alcohol was burned away; the flame then ceased, and the meat remained. The second piece was left in a vessel with the whole of the remaining alcohol. On applying the flame, there was a blaze, which lasted, as before, while the alcohol lasted; the meat would not burn. The third piece was then held in the flame, and as long as it was in direct contact with the flame it burned, but no sooner was it removed from this contact than the burning ceased. It is thus clear that, supposing the drunkard's tissues to be thoroughly soaked in alcohol (which they cannot be during life), and supposing a flame brought into direct contact with his body, that would only be a *local* burn, there could not be propagation of the flame from one part to another. To burn a body there must be the direct contact of combustible substances at a very high temperature—even fat cannot be kindled at less than 800° Fahrenheit. If, therefore, it is a *fact* that the body is difficult of combustion, and if it is a *law* that such bodies cannot be rendered less difficult of combustion by the mere presence of alcohol, or any other easily combustible substance, but only by the *removal* of that which makes the combustion difficult, then we are entitled to say that it is impossible to render living bodies preternaturally combustible.

We have used this word "impossible," several times, and may perhaps to many readers have seemed rash in using it. Who can pretend to assign the limits of possibility? Does it not seem presumptuous to decide beforehand on what is possible, what impossible? As a general rule, it is so; yet there are not a few cases in which the word impossible may in all modesty and with all firmness be pronounced. Whatever contradicts a law of nature will at once be admitted as coming under this category; and the only hesitation which can be felt in so classing it, is hesitation as to whether the law be really a law of nature, or only an empirical generalization. It is clearly impossible that two parallel lines should enclose space. It is impossible that the angle of reflection should be other than the angle of incidence. It is impossible that gravitation should act inversely as the mass. It is impossible that animals should continue to grow and exercise their vital activities without the agency of oxygen, or without exchanging carbonic acid for that oxygen It is impossible that a tissue in which nitrogen forms an integral element should continue to be nourished without a supply of nitrogen in its food. We might multiply examples indefinitely, but enough have been cited to indicate the nature of the warrant which may sometimes exist for the use of the word impossible; and we conceive that Mr. Mill has failed to seize the real logical conditions when he objects to all propositions that assert impossibility, except those of number and extension. "The non-existence of any given phenomenon," he says, "however uniformly experience may have testified to the fact, proves at most that no cause adequate to its production has yet manifested itself; but that no such causes exist in nature can only be inferred if we commit the absurdity of supposing that we know all the forces in nature."* To make good this position, we must assume that an *extension* of knowledge would not only be an *addition* of positive truth, but the *destruction* of positive truth—that when we learned something more of the properties of an object, it would necessarily force us to unlearn what we already knew. But this is not always the case. That water will dissolve salt, and that oxygen will combine with iron, are positive truths which will survive when our knowledge of the other properties of water and oxygen are multiplied a thousand-fold; and as positive facts they are unassailable. That water may be so saturated with salt as to be unable to dissolve fresh salt thrown into it, is not a fact destroying the absoluteness of the proposition, "water will dissolve salt;" nor is the proposition "oxygen combines with iron" affected by the fact that a coating of paint will protect the iron from oxidation. Mr. Mill seems to us to be confining himself only to a certain kind of propositions when he says, "That no variation in any effect or consequent will take place while the whole of the antecedents remain the same, may be affirmed with full assurance. But that the addition of some new antecedent might not entirely alter and subvert the accustomed consequent, or that antecedents competent to do this do not exist in nature, we are in no case empowered positively to conclude." Now it is surely impossible for a vertebrate animal to continue to live in an atmosphere of carbonic acid, or oxide of carbon. Igno-

* *Logic*, b. v. c. v. vol. ii. p. 407,

rant as we are of many causes and forces, we have positive knowledge of two facts: first, that a vertebrate animal cannot continue to live without breathing; and, secondly, that it cannot breathe in an atmosphere of carbonic acid. Some new antecedent may be introduced which will greatly alter some one of the accustomed effects — as damping the gunpowder will alter the effect of applying to it a lighted match. But although the process of respiration may be altered or prevented, it cannot be sustained, except by an exchange of carbonic acid and oxygen. A *new* animal existing under new conditions may be conceived as capable of living in an atmosphere of carbonic acid; but not the animal known to us as vertebrate. If we know any thing positively, we know that; and no extension of our knowledge of the forces in nature can overturn that.

In the case of Spontaneous Combustion, it may be asked whether some extension of our knowledge may not render it probable. It is certain that we have much to learn about the living organism and its possible changes; yet that any extension of knowledge should set aside what is positively known, we cannot admit. The *law*, that a body not easily combustible cannot be rendered more so by the presence of another body which is easily combustible, is a law expressive of the very nature of combustion; and the *fact* that living bodies are not easily combustible, is a fact which must remain as long as living bodies are what they are. To render the body easily combustible, we must remove the obstacle; but that obstacle is an integral constituent of the body: *without* water the tissues are not capable of forming part of a living organism, and *with* water they cannot be made easily combustible.

And this leads us to the second hypothesis by which certain modifications of the body, under diseased conditions, are supposed to render it preternaturally combustible. If these conditions removed the water, life would cease; if they did not remove the water, the body would not be inflammable. There is no escaping this dilemma. We need not pause to repeat Liebig's decisive refutation of the various suppositions respecting the gases said to be generated in the body and diffused throughout the tissues. Only gross physiological ignorance could in our day rely on such hypotheses. For if we suppose the gases abundant and conveniently distributed, as those hypotheses demand, the body is not thereby rendered more combustible. Distend the cellular tissues with the most inflammable of gases—phosphuretted hydrogen—and the gas will flame, but not the tissue.

Some writers avoid the danger of assigning a particular cause, and rely on general vague assertions. A clamorous appeal is made to Ignorance: "How little we know! how many phenomena baffle explanation! chemistry and pathology are as yet in their infancy!" There is nothing like the respect of ignorant men for ignorance. Credulity is always rampant when it can get on such a pedestal. Wholly unacquainted with the chemical and physiological processes of vital organisms, men have the most perfect reliance on any wild supposition they may invent or hear. "May there not be certain conditions produced by disease which would set at defiance all that chemistry teaches, or produce a state of preternatural combustibility?" In asking this question, men imagine they display philosophic caution. It is ignorance of philosophic method which they display. Their pretended caution is founded on the wildest fictions. Had the *fact* of spontaneous combustion been *proved*, there would be some warrant for supposing it due to morbid conditions. But is an outrage on logic to assume the *possibility* of a cause as a proof of its *existence?* A body is found burned, the cause of the burning is not apparent. Men choose to explain this by assuming that the body spontaneously ignited. When others deny that there is any evidence for such an assumption, a reference is made to historical testimony. On inspection, this testimony turns out to be *not* by any means testimony to the fact of spontaneous combustion, but only to the fact that bodies have been found burned under unexplained circumstances. Science, therefore, disregards this testimony, and asserts that the pretended explanation is inadmissible, because it involves contradiction to the most positive laws of nature. Whereupon the advocates wish to be cautious, and ask, *May* it not be possible, under peculiar conditions? and with similar caution, they conclude that because the result is *possible* we are to believe it *actual*.

To sum up in a sentence the result of the preceding paragraphs, we may say that Spontaneous Combustion in the living organism is a fiction adopted to explain circumstances which do not carry their explanation with them. As a fiction it is discredited by its open contradiction to all known truths. It is impossible; and if it could be shown to be possible, nay, eminently probable, there would still be no evidence which could make us believe that it had actually taken place. Between a possible or probable event, and an event which has passed from probability to fact, the gulf is wide. The supposition that Spontaneous Combustion *did* occur because it *might have* occurred, becomes all the more preposterous when we learn that the only reason for supposing that it might have occurred, is a desire to prove that it did occur. Neither Logic, on the one hand, testing the evidence, nor Science, on the other hand, testing the inferences, gives the slightest countenance to Spontaneous Combustion; and the continuance of its advocacy in dictionaries, cyclopædias, and works on medical jurisprudence, is a disgrace to the science of our day. *

* It is maintained, though with some qualification, in one of the latest works of medical jurisprudence which have fallen in our way; viz., the 6th edition of Briand and Chaudé's *Médicine Légale*, 1858. But in Taylor's *Medical Jurisprudence* it is decisively condemned.

Anecdotes from Luther's Table-Talk.—There was a miser, who when he sent his man to the cellar for wine, made him fill his mouth with water, which he was to spit out on his return, to show he had drunk no wine. But the servant kept a pitcher of water in the cellar, wherewith, after taking his fill of the better drink, he managed to deceive his master.

An idle priest, instead of reciting his breviary, used to run over the alphabet, and say: "O my God, take this alphabet, and put it together how you will!"

I am a great enemy to flies: *Quia sunt imagines diaboli et hæreticorum.* When I have a good book, they flock upon it and parade up and down upon it, and soil it. 'Tis just the same with the Devil; when our hearts are purest, he comes and soils them.

All wild beasts are beasts of the law, for they live in fear and quaking; they have all swarthy and black flesh, by reason of their fear, but tame beasts have white flesh, for they are beasts of grace; they live securely with mankind.

Not long since King Ferdinand came into a monastery where I was, and going over it was attracted by these letters, written in large characters, on the wall:—

"M.N.M.G.M.M.M.M."

After reflecting some time on their meaning, he turned to his secretary, and asked him what he thought they signified? the secretary replied: "Your majesty will not be angry at my interpretation?" "No, truly," said the king. "Well, then," returned the secretary, "I expound the letters thus: M.N. Mentitur Nausea (the archbishop of Vienna); M.G. Mentitur Gallus (the court preacher); M.M.M.M. Mentiunter Majores (the Franciscans); Minores, (the Carmelites); Minotaurii (monks of the Alps); all are liars." The king bit his lips, and passed on. 'Twas a very ingenious explanation of Mr. Secretary's.

A Rod in Pickle for Rogues.—A Bill now before Parliament declares the selling of any article with a false quantity affixed to it to constitute a misdemeanor, punishable as fraud by fine and imprisonment. This, if it passes, will be a piece of legislation apparently based upon severely classical principles, whereas the false quantity which will subject its perpetrators to punishment is no mere mistake in thieves' Latin, but the wilful and fraudulent substitution of short measure for that which ought to be longer. It is to be wished that all offenders of this kind should have an "imposition" set them consisting of exercitations upon that *Gradus* which they would not reach Parnassus by climbing, although they would perform a kind of labor resembling too much poetry in the peculiarity of being unproductive.—*Punch.*

In certain places on the sea-coast, where the usual means employed for fixing the shifting sands, or dunes, have failed, such as planting the maritime pine, certain kinds of grass, acacias, etc., it has been found that the *ailanthus* is perfectly successful, even in the most arid places. A landowner near Odessa has for the last sixteen years planted a considerable extent of surface with this fast-spreading tree, and an almost impenetrable forest exists where formerly was only a dreary, barren waste.

From The National Magazine.

THE CITY TURKISH BATH.

I HAVE just experienced a new sensation. I seem to have become young again; my eye is bright, my step is light, my heart beats high with hope. I just met a man who tried to do me an injury—I forgave him; I know that I have a bill coming due to-morrow, and very little at my banker's to meet it with —yet I smile. I rose this morning with an aching head and a heavy heart, life seemed to me a poor affair; this goodly frame, the earth, a sterile promontory; this excellent canopy, the air, this brave overhanging firmament, this majestical roof fretted with golden fire, no other thing than a foul and pestilent congregation of vapors; and now I am in Araby the blest, and I glow and brighten in the dawn of young desire, the purple light of love.

It came about in this way. I met Smithers, who said to me, "Old chap, you don't look quite the thing—come with me, and have a Turkish bath." I immediately declined. In the first place I had not the time, and, secondly, I was afraid the heat would make me feel faint. The first difficulty was got over, but as to the last I had serious doubts. A Turkish Bath might be a very capital thing for some people, but I was sure it would never do for me. However, Smithers talked me over, and away we went to the City Turkish Baths, South Street, Finsbury Square. A knock at the door brought to view a page who opened it, and immediately guessed my purpose. I had to take off my boots, and put on a pair of red slippers; then I was conducted to a little curtain box in which to strip, and then, arrayed in a sheet, I was walked down to a hot-air room, in which, as nude as possible, I was requested to take a seat on a wooden bench, in common with other gentlemen clad in an equally scanty manner. Very great city men were here, and very pleasantly did we chat, all of them equally in favor of the Turkish Bath. One assured me it was the jolliest thing in the world after you had been out to dinner, and taken too much wine; another said he had been such a martyr from rheumatism as to be unable to move a limb, and now he could walk with comfort; other gentlemen were suffering from that tendency to obesity which is the characteristic of the human animal when highly fed, and here he was getting reduced to gentility as speedily as possible. I was certainly surprised to find the shampooers—there are four of them, very civil and skilful men—in such good health. One of them had come there in very poor condition, and had gained considerably in muscle and strength; yet here they sit the live-long day, shampooing their fellow-creatures, and breathing an atmosphere where the heat is never less than one hundred and eighteen or one hundred and twenty degrees. In this room the bather sits till a gentle perspiration breaks out; he then goes into a hotter room, at a temperature of from one hundred and forty to a hundred and fifty, where he perspires in earnest, there is no mistake about it. The melted matter runs from every pore, and to a man who has never had much severe exercise—who has been hide-bound all his life, the relief is most grateful. After he has remained there about a quarter of an hour he is then taken back to the room which he first entered. Here he is shampooed, that is, kneaded from head to foot; every part of his body is operated on, and, if very fat, perhaps he rises from the operation a little sore. The man is done first on one side, and then the other, literally from the crown of his head to the sole of his foot, old joints are rubbed and made flexible. I did hear of one elderly gentleman who had a couple of his ribs broken while undergoing the process; but at such a place as the City Turkish Baths, under the superintendence of Mr. Dool, or the proprietor, you need fear no catastrophe of that kind. Further joys yet await the bather. After the shampooing process comes the relief of a warm and cold shower-bath. You are taken into another compartment, the atmosphere of which is not kept up by any mode of heating. Here the attendant bids you stand and receive a copious shower of warm water; next you are well wiped down, and then cold water is turned on, and for a moment you feel staggered, and involuntarily gasp for breath. Now comes the crowning luxury. You are wiped dry, wrapped in a sheet, a kind of turban is wrapped round your head, and you are taken up-stairs to lie down on a downy couch, to smoke it may be—and if you wish to enjoy yourself thoroughly you certainly will—a first-rate cigar, and a capital cup of coffee, and then you and your fellow-bathers recline, like the gods on hills together, careless of mankind. If it be evening you are further regaled by musical performances of no ordinary character. The half-hour thus occupied I believe you will find the happiest in your life. You cannot feel dejected or sorrowful; you have shaken off the accumulated crust of years; your skin is as supple as a youth's; you feel once more the elasticity of a youth. I have seen a man take his first bath the very picture of despondency; I could see, in addition, no small degree of timidity as to the result. He has sat down on the wooden bench in the first room in no enviable state, but as the skin began to glisten, one by one his humors fled away, and he leaves the place rejoicing as a strong man to run a race. There is no doubt about it—the Turkish Bath is a wonderful boon to this country. It is needed especially in this age of anxiety, and in this city of dust, and smoke, and dirt. I know I went from mine the other day to a turtle lunch given by energetic Mr. Train, at St. James' Hall, with an appetite which an epicure would have forfeited a thousand to possess—an appetite which would have made vinegar drink as the choicest Falernian, and turned the coarsest crust into a delicacy worthy of that crew of epicures headed by Mark Antony and Cleopatra, the company of the Inimitable Livers. I now understand why the latter, as she was about to die, after lamenting over the body of her Roman lover, and embracing his coffin, ordered a bath to be prepared for her. Plutarch tells us, "After bathing she lay down and enjoyed a splendid banquet." It was the bath that nerved her for her work, to apply to her bosom—on which an Imperator had reclined—an asp, and to fall down dead on her golden couch. I also understand how greatly the poet erred when he wrote,—

> "When the heart of man is oppressed with cares,
> Their weight is dispelled if a woman appears."

He should have said for "woman" "Turkish Bath," and he would have been right.

The philosophy of the Turkish or Roman Bath is not difficult to understand. Nature intends us to get rid of our waste through the skin, but we clog it up, and have, in consequence, more or less congestion of the liver, intestines, and kidneys. The number of diseases for which the Turkish Bath is recommended, even by medical men, is so large, that it would seem to be a general specific. There can be no doubt that its virtues are very great in all cases where there is a vitiated condition of the blood, arising from a languid condition of the skin and circulation, or any specific poison lurking within it. We have heard such miraculous tales told respecting its powers in curing rheumatism, that we cannot doubt its value. Mr. Erasmus Wilson also states that it is wonderfully efficacious in many skin diseases. It has been objected that in all cases of disease of the heart the Turkish Bath would prove injurious; but Mr. Wilson, in a lecture lately delivered upon the use of the bath, energetically denies this statement. "I believe," he says, "just the contrary—that many diseases of the heart may be cured by a judicious use of the Thermæ; and in the very worst cases it would prove to be the very best remedy that could be employed." In some cases, indeed, the heart's action is accelerated by the use of the bath, but a moment's sojourn in the Frigidarium, with its plentiful supply of pure oxygen, instantly calms any perturbation. Those who have not accustomed themselves to the bath, sometimes complain of feeling a fulness in the head, but this objection can be met by simply wrapping a towel round the head. That the Turkish Bath will before long be esteemed a necessary part of every gentleman's house is exceedingly probable.

"The bath," says Mr. Erasmus Wilson, "promotes those changes in the blood for which fresh air is otherwise needful. The bath gives us appetite, and strengthens digestion." The bath serves us in lieu of exercise. "The people who use it," writes Mr. Urquhart, "do not require exercise for health, and can pass from the extreme of indolence to that of toil." How glorious a panacea for those home-loving matrons whom no inducement can draw forth from their Lares and Penates to enjoy a daily wholesome exercise, and who, as a consequence, become large, and full, and fat, and bilious, and wheezy, and who, in their breach of Heaven's law, lay the foundation of heart disease. "A nation," says Mr. Urquhart, "without the bath is deprived of a large portion of the health, and inoffensive enjoyment, within a man's reach; it therefore increases the value of a people to itself, and its power as a nation over other people."

We must quote here Mr. Wilson's summary of the benefits resulting from the use of the bath. "It is a preservative of health by maintaining a vigorous condition of the body, a state the best suited for the happiness of the individual, as rendering him in the highest degree susceptible of the enjoyment of life, and a state the most advantageous to social interests, as insuring the highest working condition. The bath is preventive of disease, by hardening the individual against the effects of variations and vicissitudes of temperature, by giving him power to resist miasmatic and zymotic affections, and by strengthening his system against aberrations of nutrition and the fecund train of ills that follow disturbance of the nutritive functions; namely, scrofula, consumption, gout, rheumatism, diseases of the digestive organs, cutaneous system, muscular system—including the heart, nervous system—including the brain, and reproductive system. The bath is a cure for disease when the latter state is already established. and is a powerful and effective medicine." The bath must be this, and more than this, if, as Mr. Urquhart tells us—"the body has come forth shining like alabaster, fragrant as the cistus, sleek as satin, and soft as velvet."

Nor will it end here. I see Admiral Rous maintains its use in getting racehorses into proper condition.

The objects now sought by the use of the Turkish Bath are more numerous and diversified than is generally supposed. This will be seen from the following interesting analysis, furnished by the City Turkish Baths, in South Street, Finsbury Pavement. The analysis extends to two hundred and twenty-one baths, and shows—

Bathers.	Pleasure.	Colds.	Rheumatism and Gout.	Other Ailments.
Frequent,	54	3	8	4
Occasional,	53	4	14	9
1st Bath,	47	4	9	12
	154	11	31	25

Total, 221.

Among the "other ailments" not especially classified above may be enumerated Dyspepsia, Sore Throat, Weakness in the Legs, General Debility, Epilepsy, and affections of the Liver and Kidneys. For all these ailments the Turkish Bath has already been used under medical direction, and with manifest advantage. Its value in cases of Gout and Rheumatism has now for some time been generally acknowledged.

A PHYSICIAN, residing in the Philippine Islands, has written home to say that on a recent occasion, one of his attendants being bitten with a very venomous serpent, and having tried various remedies in vain, as a last resource he bethought himself of giving him a bottle of cocoa wine (a strong alcoholic drink). In a short time after the wine was swallowed, and the man became drunk, but seemed free from the agony which he was previously suffering. As he became sober, the pain re-appeared, so a second bottle was given to him, and after that a third with a like good effect. The swelling went down in his arm, and he was in a short time cured. There is a saying in some countries that drinking alcohol to intoxication is a specific against the venom of serpents, but we have never heard of so well-authenticated an instance as this. The instance is the more remarkable as a bite from a similar species of serpent which bit the physician's attendant has been known to be fatal in a few minutes.

WE announce with much regret the premature death of one whose early promise gave high hopes of future eminence. From his father, Henry Nelson Coleridge, and his mother, Sarah Coleridge, the daughter of the poet and philosopher, Herbert Coleridge seemed to have inherited all the genius of that gifted family. His career at Oxford was crowned with the highest attainable honors. He took a double first in the Easter term of 1852. On leaving the University he was called to the bar, but literature continued to occupy his leisure. He became secretary to the Philological Society, and was associated with the Dean of Westminster in a project for rescuing from oblivion and restoring to the English language words used by the best writers of the seventeenth century, but not acknowledged by Johnson and his successors. For the last five years, we believe, his life and energies have been gradually undermined by the fatal disease which so often accompanies genius and sensibility, and which has now brought him to an early grave.—*Guardian.*

From The Examiner.

Memoirs of Royal Ladies. By Emily Sarah Holt. In two volumes. Hurst & Blackett.

THIS book might have been shortened by omitting the first two of its ten biographies, which do not read well, and contain nothing at all interesting or instructive. The best that can be said of them is that Miss Holt has diligently connected some bare dates with a few monkish fables about two women who were not "royal ladies," and of whom one was a passable saint of the thirteenth century, and the other a confirmed sinner of the fourteenth. For Ela, Countess of Salisbury, place in the volume is claimed because her husband was son of Fair Rosamond, whom by the way Miss Holt would make a lawful queen of England, to the consequent bastardizing of Kings Richard and John. We are told that Ela was "one of those fair creatures who in the midst of gloom around them gleam forth as sparks of light in the dim expanse of the past," and that she was "an angel surrounded by demons." But all we learn about her is that she was the good wife of a brave soldier; that she was not willing to be run away with during her husband's lifetime by a wicked knight; that she is said to have had a wonderful dream which revealed her son's death to her; and that her last years of widowhood were spent in one of the abbeys which she gave her wealth to found. From her was descended Alicia, Countess of Lancaster. Miss Holt has been at pains to collect a few ugly illustrations of this woman's predilection for the poisoning of her own husbands, and other evil dealing with the husbands of others; not the sort of person of whose career one would expect to hear any thing from a lady who is at full liberty to please her taste in the selection of her subjects.

Of the rest of the book we can speak more favorably. The story of Joan, wife of the Black Prince, for instance, was worth telling, and is here well told. There is just so much of the public history of the time worked into the narrative as will suffice to make the private story clear. Joan's life was a remarkable one. In childhood she had been betrothed to the Earl of Salisbury. But he went abroad and seemed to have forgotten his intended bride; so in her twenty-fourth year there was made for her a fresh engagement; this time with Sir Thomas Holland. But before the completion of the marriage contract, the old suitor appeared with a fierce claim on his bride. Some time was spent in hot dispute, and the matter was settled only by reference to Pope Clement the Sixth, when he decided for the knight against the earl. After a few years, during which four children were born, Sir Thomas died; and, as a wealthy young widow, Joan did not lack suitors. One of them, an intimate follower of the Black Prince, asked his master to sue for him. Then followed a scene which Mr. Longfellow must have studied before writing his "Courtship of Miles Standish." Edward had a liking of his own for the lady, but

> "Friendship prevailed over love, and the prince went out on his errand."

Joan did not exactly say,

> "Why don't you speak for yourself, John?"

but she made answer to her visitor, "Lord Prince and fair cousin, I cannot cease to remember that I am of the blood royal of England, wherefore I have determined never to marry again, save unto a prince renowned for quality and virtue—like yourself." The chronicle tells of a kiss which followed this frank statement, and presently the Lady Joan became Princess of Wales.

She was well fitted for her station. At one time, when her husband was fighting in Spain, and she was left Regent of Aquitaine, she took wise measures to defend the territory from the attacks of the Spaniard, Enrique de Trastamare. After the prince's death she applied herself to the education of their little boy, King Richard. She was not a wise instructress. It is likely that the luckless king owed much of his haughtiness and waywardness, and not a few of his false notions of kingship, to her influence.

It was Joan who, together with John of Gaunt, gave encouragement to Wyclif. In 1378—not in 1382, the date given by Miss Holt—when the Reformer had been brought up for trial at Lambeth, she sent a messenger to the judges, and bade them desist from all further measures, if they loved the widow of the Black Prince and the mother of the king.

The last chapter in her life is a sad one. In 1385 her son, Sir John Holland, picked a quarrel with a nobleman and killed him. The king, when he heard of it, condemned his brother to death. The princess, after vainly suing for reversal of the sentence, went down to her Castle of Wallingford, and died within four days.

Next to her account of the Princess Joan, we like best Miss Holt's memoir of Jane of Valois, daughter of Lewis the Eleventh of France. Born in 1464, Jane had a hard life to live. Ugly and even deformed, her father hated her from her childhood, his hatred being increased by that strong devotional bias in her which Romish writers exaggerated into a miraculous piety. When she was five years old, it is recorded, the king sternly enjoined her to spend less time over her prayers. "The little princess gently, though firmly, refused to obey." As usually happened in such cases, but not till next year, the Virgin Mary appeared for her consolation.

For political purposes she was married, when thirteen years old, to Lewis of Orleans, and her husband followed the example of her father. When he was in prison she begged him to let her share and so relieve his misery, and when refused she pawned her jewels that he might have better food and shelter, till her perseverance had procured his freedom. Yet his treatment of his ugly wife was uniformly brutal. While duke he barely tolerated her; as soon as he became king he discarded her with papal sanction, so to make room for a younger and handsomer, although less pious, queen. At this change, indeed, she was not altogether sorry. She could have no pleasure in the life of a dissolute court, and it was a small loss to be parted from a husband who had ill-used her for a score of years. She devoted herself to religious offices and to the consummation of that saintly character for which she had at any rate been trained in sorrow. In company with four high-born ladies, like-minded with herself, she visited hospitals, tending the sick and feeding the poor. Her own food generally consisted of a few ill-dressed herbs. Good cookery might have produced sinful indulgence. Every day she beat her breast with flint stones, and through a wooden cross of her own making she drove five silver nails, which had formerly belonged to her favorite lute, and wore it next to her body, so that she might be continually pricked and scratched. She liked to be despised, and enjoyed insult as much as other women relish flattery. The happiest day of her life was one on which she heard that she was "an ugly, ill-shapen creature, and one of the most disagreeable women in the world." So at least says the pious author of "La Vie Merveilleuse de Jeane de Valois," who also recounts many edifying miracles attendant on her death and burial.

Of the six other memoirs here given we need not say much. One relates to Constance, the gentle wife of John of Gaunt, and contains some passages which may contribute to an understanding of her husband's public life. In writing of Jona, Queen of Spain, Miss Holt, without assigning any proper reason, falls foul of the current judgment concerning Ferdinand and Isabella. Indeed, she seems to have been unacquainted with the late Mr. Prescott's brilliant history of those sovereigns. But she is thoroughly at home in tracing the life of Margaret of Austria, a notable woman, who aptly indicated her career in the odd motto which she chose: "Fortune infortune fort une." Before she was full twenty-five she had been successively Queen of France, Princess of the Asturias, and Duchess of Savoy; once divorced and twice widowed; the other quarter century being occupied with the governing of Flanders, quibbling with her father and brother, and treating with a great number of suitors, chief of whom was our English Henry the Seventh.

M. Otto Struve, surprised at the important results obtained by the expedition to the Peak of Teneriffe, under the direction of Mr. Piazzi Smith, proposed to the Emperor of Russia to establish a permanent observatory on Mount Ararat, near Tiflis. This proposal was favorably received, and the sum of £5,000 appropriated for the necessary constructions, and half that sum for the purchase of instruments.

From The Saturday Review.

CROCHET-WORK AND NOVEL-WRITING.

SOME ten or fifteen years ago, when crochet came into fashion, no one would have been rash enough to predict that it was to exercise a material influence on literature. And yet it was written in the book of fate that such was to be the effect of this trifling though elegant accomplishment. Before the crochet period there was a vast field for industry open to female fingers and minds—Berlin wool. In many houses relics of that age, as the old ballad puts it:—

" Still for a monument doe lye,
And there exposed to lookers' viewe
As wondrous strange they may espye—"

and now and then you find yourself sitting on a cushion of roses so glowing red that they almost scorch your pantaloons, while for a support to your back you have the ruins of Pæstum or the Temple of Baalbec. But the manufacture is no longer carried on, except in remote districts; the discovery of crochet banished the art, and in so doing seriously affected the industrial resources of the fancy-working classes.

Berlin wool, considered as an occupation, had this special virtue, that it suited every possible variety of temperament, and was adaptable to minds of all calibres. For matter-of-fact Marthas, whose leanings were of the practical and utilitarian order, there were slippers, and kettleholders, and other articles belonging to the prosaic department of fancy-work; while for " burning Sappho " there were shepherds, and bandits, and tastefully tattered beggars, upon which she might expend her superfluous ideality. Crochet, on the other hand, is not a soul-satisfying pursuit. It appeals rather to the mechanical than to the imaginative faculties of the mind. There is, perhaps, a certain rhythmical charm about the language in which its principles are conveyed, and on some ears the cadences of " loop six, drop one, chain three," etc., may fall quite as soothingly as a good deal of the verse that is turned out every day by our minor minstrels. But there is also a " damnable iteration " about it, and it is obviously an employment wholly inadequate to meet the requirements of a being afflicted with what, in the language of the intense school, is called a Yearning after the Infinite, or even with the milder form of the disease known in psychical pathology as a Craving for the Ideal. It may be all very well for the mentally weaker sisters, who find that to weave the warp and weave the woof in strict accordance with the directions and patterns given in the *Ladies' Newspaper* is a sufficient demand upon their intellectuality; but with these higher natures such an occupation could only end in spiritual atrophy. Thus thrown out of employment, what could be more natural than that they should take to novel-writing? The craft was one which presented many analogies to the lost art of working in Berlin wool, and with a little dexterity might be conducted upon precisely the same principles. It was only necessary to go to the nearest library, instead of to an embroidery shop on Ludgate-hill, for a pattern and materials, to employ a good stout serviceable commonplace instead of coarse canvas for a basis, and then, having set up the frame and got every thing ready, to fill in boldly with words instead of with worsted. There was also this pleasant fiction common to both processes—that the work, although apparently taken up as a mere agreeable pastime, was in reality useful. The bandit or beggar was to form the seat of a chair; the novel was written " with a purpose." It is true that the chair when finished was not very generally sat upon, while the novel very frequently was—at least in the metaphorical or slang sense of the expression—but these untoward results have nothing to do with the original intention of the artist.

Arguments are scarcely necessary in such a case, but if any proof of all this be required, we simply refer to the facts that the discovery of crochet synchronises in a most remarkable manner with the gushing forth of that torrent of female novels which still pours steadily upon us, and that a large proportion of these productions will be found on examination to furnish ample internal evidence of the Berlin-wool mind. There are some who will wax indignant at this, and fling such works as *Jane Eyre* and *Adam Bede* in our teeth, but they need not hope to entrap us into platitudes about genius being of no sex. We are not going to be as weak as Hamlet and speak to them " by the card," because they happen to be as " absolute knaves " as the First Gravedigger. All we mean to say is that we believe there are a great many novels which would never have been written had working in Berlin-wool continued to be a fashionable employment, and which are, in effect, the cries of crocheted-out embroidresses, complaining that they have no fancy-work to do.

From The Dublin University Magazine.

MINA: A MODERN PATRIOT.

> "Such be the sons of Spain, and strange her fate!
> They fight for freedom, who were never free."
> —Lord Byron. *Childe Harold, Canto* 1.

Guerilla warfare, originating in a local term,* has passed into an acknowledged system, a branch of organized tactics, and is considered by many of our modern Folards, Guischardts, and Montecuculis, as not only an important but even a decisive element of national defence, peculiarly applicable to mountainous countries, where great lines of communication are few, and easily broken. It has also been recommended, amidst the host of theories born of the invasion panic, as well adapted to England, where the land is generally level, and a net-work of roads; because, say these advocates, every farm-house is a post, and every hedge-row a rampart. We are not going, at present, to dispute these premises, which seem to involve something of contradiction, or to show that our Rifle Volunteers (more power to them, as we say in Ireland) have not one jot of the guerilla in their composition, or are little likely to be rendered available in that capacity. They are intended for and are capable of much better service, as they will show should the opportunity occur. We only propose to cast a glance at recent history, in one or two instances, and to see what its pages teach us on the subject of guerillas.

Hofer, the "Tell of the Tyrol," as he has been called, and with more justice than flattery, though less fortunate than his prototype; and Espoz y Mina, the renowned Spanish partisan, have won enduring reputation by their exploits as guerilla leaders. Garibaldi once ranked in this list, but he has soared far above it, and is now entitled to be enrolled as conqueror and liberator on a grand scale. His renown rivals that of Scanderbeg, without even the blemish of early though almost unconscious apostasy. Hofer did wonders in the campaign of 1809, almost annihilated the division of Lefebvre, which thrust itself into the Caudine forks, at Innspruck, as Dupont did at Baylen, and retarded, though he could not prevent, the subjugation of his country. His trial and execution in 1810 was an act of petty revenge, which endeared his memory to millions, and exalted his fame, while it inflicted indelible disgrace on the conquerors.

When the Spanish regular armies were successively and easily swept from the field, during the Peninsular contest, by the legions of Napoleon, the military strength of the country resolved itself into independent bands, each under a favorite leader, hanging perpetually on the flanks, intercepting the supplies, and harassing, without effectually staying, the march of the invaders. Those who imagine that the tide was checked, not to say turned, by these hordes of banditti, under a patriotic name, for such they were in reality, would do well to consider what a great authority, and a personal observer, Sir William Napier, says on this particular point. Speaking of the exploits of Mina, he observed: "The communications of the French were troubled, and considerable losses inflicted upon their armies by this celebrated man, undoubtedly the most conspicuous person amongst the Partida chiefs. And here it may be observed, how weak and inefficient this guerilla system was to deliver the country, and that even as an auxiliary, its advantages were nearly balanced by the evils." The greatest of these evils lay in the mutual detestation engendered, and the reciprocal cruelties resorted to. A war of retaliation leads to barbarism in its direst shape, and the patriotic devotion of the Spanish guerillas was too often disgraced by savage acts, which might be emulated but scarcely surpassed by Caffres and New Zealand cannibals. They expected no quarter, and seldom extended any to their prisoners. *Væ victis*, war to extermination, was their motto and practice. Often they were not content with the infliction of death on their opponents, unaccompanied by protracted torture. The alcalde of Frasno, an old man, was burnt alive by the Spaniards, his own countrymen, because he happened to be taken amongst a party of French. The system thus adopted on both sides has no parallel in modern warfare, except in Calabria, where the proceedings of the French under Manhès, against the *Masse*, as they were called, or more properly the insurgent bands of robbers, and their corresponding resistance, were characterized by the same unmitigated ferocity, and at the same pe-

* From the Spanish *Guerra*, a small war, or skirmish, a body of partisans.

riod. If a Frenchman took a Calabrese, he stripped and hung him up by a hook in the ribs to a tree, there to perish by degrees. This spectacle was witnessed by officers of the writer's regiment, who were taken prisoners at Palmi, on their march to Naples, in 1809. If a Calabrese took a Frenchman, he also stripped him, rubbed him over with oil, and then roasted him by a slow fire. But, be it remembered, that both in Spain and Italy, the foreign invaders took the lead in all these indescribable horrors, and are assuredly answerable for the consequences.

Napier mentions a startling fact, that notwithstanding the violent measures resorted to by the Partida* leaders in Spain to fill their ranks, deserters from the French, and even from the British, formed one-third of their forces. It would be absurd to argue that patriotism could have had any thing to do with the feelings of this contingent. Release from discipline and the hope of pillage must have been their only incentives. One of the first exploits of Mina was to slay the commander of a neighboring band, because, under the mask of opposing the public enemy, he relaxed himself by plundering his own countrymen. The historian then goes on to say: "The guerilla system in Spain was the offspring of disorder, and disorder in war is weakness, accompanied by ills the least of which is sufficient to produce ruin. It is in such a warfare that habits of unbridled license, of unprincipled violence and disrespect for the rights of property are quickly contracted, and render men unfit for the duties of citizens; and yet it has been cited, with singular inconsistency, as the best and surest mode of resisting an enemy, by politicians who hold regular armies in abhorrence, although a high sense of honor, devotion to the cause of the country, temperance, regularity, and decent manners form the very essence of the latter's discipline." We quote this passage the more readily, as in the present day there are not wanting writers who maintain that England, the richest country in the world, traversed and intersected like a gridiron, by highways and railways, with a concentrated population of twenty millions, could be best defended by guerilla warfare.

The entire number of guerillas in Spain never much exceeded thirty thousand. Lord Wellington, at the desire of the British Government, sent presents to the principal leaders, acknowledging the importance of their services, which he thought of more value than they really proved, because at that time he only knew them by report. "When he afterwards advanced into Spain," says Napier, "and saw them closely, he was forced to acknowledge that, although active and willing, they were so little disciplined that they could do nothing against the French troops, unless the latter were very inferior in numbers. If the French took post in a house or church, of which they only barricaded the entrance, the guerillas were so ill-equipped as military bodies, that their enemy could remain in security until relieved. In like manner Napoleon, reprimanding his generals for suffering the Partidas to gain any head, observed, that when cut off from communication with the English ships, they were a nullity!"

The leaders of the guerillas were men from every class of society, including monks and doctors, peasants, artisans, cooks, and collegiate scholars. Some were named from a deformity, others from the fashion of their clothes; but each had his sobriquet, founded on a moral or physical characteristic. It has never been clearly decided whence or wherefore Juan Martin Diaz, *the Empecinado*, derived his strange agnomen. Some say he was so designated from his swarthy complexion; others, that finding his family murdered by the French, he made an oath of vengeance, and smeared his face with pitch, not to be washed off until the final expulsion of the invaders; as old General Thomas Dalziel would never suffer his beard to be shaved, under a vow, after the execution of Charles the First, until the House of Stuart was restored. This Empecinado was as bloodthirsty as he was active and enterprising; but in the former quality he was even exceeded by a female demon, named Martina, whose band infested Biscay. She murdered friends and foes with such balanced impartiality, that Mina was compelled at last to hunt her down, until the truculent Amazon and her whole gang were surprised and shot off at once upon the spot.

There were two Minas, nephew and uncle. Xavier, the first and youngest, called also the Student, had but a short career, being taken prisoner by Suchet in 1809, in the neighborhood of Pampeluna. While reconnoitring by moonlight, in the hopes of surprising a valuable convoy, he stumbled on a French patrol, when it was too late to retreat. He had been proscribed as a bandit, nevertheless his life was spared, but he was kept a close prisoner, and his services were lost to his country. Nothing could be more romantic and marvellous than his adventures, achievements, and escapes, until the night of his capture. Once near Estella, he was driven to an insulated rock, which could only be assailed on one side. That point he defended until darkness set in, and then lówering himself and followers by a rope, he slipped away without losing a man. When his unexpected loss occasioned many disputes as to who should succeed him, Espoz y Mina, who had hitherto served under his nephew, yielded with considerable reluctance to the general wish which nominated him as chief. He had been brought up as a tiller of the land, and was scarcely able to read or write; but on the call of the Junta, summoning all children of the soil to the defence of their country, he came forth from obscurity, and took up arms with the rest. Until accident made him a leader, his opportunities had been few; but no sooner did he assume command than his daring and decided character immediately exhibited itself. Echevarria had created a schism in opposition, and called off many partisans. The force became divided and enfeebled. Mina lost no time in bringing the question to issue. He surprised his rival, shot him, with three of his subordinate officers, and reunited the wavering band. No sooner was this competitor disposed of than Mina encountered a more subtle danger through the treachery of one of his own sergeants, who, from the evil expression of his countenance, had received the distinctive appellation of *Malcarado*, or foul faced. Disliking the new commander, he determined to betray him to the enemy, and with this object entered into arrangements in concert with the French general, Panettier, whose brigade was in the vicinity, to surprise the guerilla chieftain in his bed. The attempt very nearly succeeded; but Mina, obtaining a few minutes' notice to prepare, defended himself desperately with the bar of the door, until his chosen friend and comrade, Gustra, arrived to the rescue with a few followers, and enabled him to escape. Mina, with the rapidity of lightning, collected his band, repulsed the enemy, took Malcarado prisoner, and executed summary justice on him without delay. The village curé and three alcaldes, who were found to have abetted in the plot, were hung side by side upon the same tree, and their houses burned to the ground. No sharper practice had ever been exhibited in the old border warfare between feudal chieftains; but Mina's uncompromising severity, at the outset, terrified the discontented and the plotters, and secured for him, in all his future operations, the implicit obedience of his followers, and the ready co-operation of the country people and local authorities.

An account of Mina's guerilla exploits was written in 1811 by a Spanish colonel, Don Lorenzo Ximenes, who had served with, and describes him from close intimacy. From this narrative, which may be fully relied on, with memoirs of a later date, we collect the following particulars.

Mina was a well-made man, of a florid aspect, robust in form, and about five feet eight inches in height. When the Spaniards took up arms, in 1808, against the French, he was in the twenty-sixth year of his age, having been born at Ydocin, near Pampeluna, in 1782. He had a fixed idea that women interfered with public life, and were, above all other impediments, the heaviest clog on military operations. Under this conviction he avoided female society as resolutely as Charles the Twelfth did, and never suffered any officer or soldier of his band to be accompanied by such an incumbering addition to his light marching order. He was sparing of speech, but frank in manner, lived almost as abstemiously as a hermit, drank no wine, seldom slept more than two hours in the night, and then always with his loaded pistols in his girdle and the door of his room locked, if he chanced to enjoy the unusual luxury of a bed-chamber. This arose not from fear, but to be prepared, as much as possible, against the many chances of surprise or assassination. The great feature of his tactics was perpetual movement, so that his enemies should be misled by conflicting rumors as to his "whereabouts," unable to fix him in any assigned locality, or to calculate when and where his attack would strike them. With this leading object ever in view, he was habitually incommunicative and mysterious as a hieroglyphic. His most trusted lieutenants never knew the intended line of march nor the game in view until the prize was almost within their grasp. When the drum or bugle was heard, whether for ordinary parade or immediate and desperate service, neither officer nor soldier could tell, but all were required to appear fully equipped, the mounted officers in the saddle, and the mules, with their scanty baggage, loaded for the march. In fact, his entire success depended on profound secrecy and correct intelligence. When least expected, he appeared suddenly, placed himself at the head of his men, issued no complicated orders, but simply exclaimed, "Follow me!" In this manner he often marched thirty miles, with only an occasional halt of a few minutes; and on a particular expedition, where he succeeded in surprising and capturing, near Estella, a large convoy of French stores and provisions, he moved through by-paths in the mountains full forty miles without allowing refreshment either to horses or men for the whole day. At that particular period, he was utterly without provender, and his band must have dispersed for a time had he not, fortunately, replenished his commissariat at the expense of the enemy. When he had a superabundance he was most liberal, and gave freely to the peasants of an impoverished or plundered district, as well as to his own people, without requiring payment. His name became so popular that, if supplies were forthcoming at all, they poured into his cantonment or bivouac, when neither fear nor lucre could obtain a market for the regular troops.

Whenever a volunteer of infantry joined Mina he was only allowed to bring with him a pair of sandals, half stockings, breeches, and jacket. His own personal wardrobe was confined to the clothes on his back. He required no sumpter mules to carry articles of luxury nor even of necessary convenience. When his shirt was dirty, he went to the nearest farmhouse, asked for the owner, entered, and said, "I am Mina; the shirt I have on requires washing, give me a clean one." The countryman complied invariably, and if there was time, washed the exchanged shirt and then got back his own; if not, he kept Mina's, and Mina his. The arms of the band, in general, were outwardly rusty and ill-looking, but particularly well cleaned within, and the locks and flints in excellent condition. Not Gromwell himself was more emphatic in the order, "Keep your powder dry." If the bayonets were encrusted with blood it was seldom washed off. On one occasion he directed a detachment of thirty men to load each musket with three balls; "and I know that they obeyed me," said he, "for at the first discharge, they killed or wounded sixty people."

Mina's cavalry seldom reached two hundred. They were the best-equipped portion of his troops; dressed like hussars, with blue jackets and pantaloons, and caps similar to those of the regular army, with this exception, that they had a piece of red cloth about a yard long hanging down the back, in a point from the cap, and terminated by a gold tassel. All wore sandals and spurs. Mina himself never wore jack or half boots, but sandals, that he might escape the more readily by climbing up the side of a mountain, in case (as frequently happened) his horse should be shot or exhausted. Several times he saved himself in this way, almost miraculously.

If a juvenile recruit applied for enlistment in the cavalry, Mina began by minutely examining and questioning him in person; after which he called for the commanding officer of the infantry and said: "This boy wishes to serve in the cavalry; take him first with you, and let me know how he gets on." In the first action that took place a mounted captain kept him close to himself, and narrowly watched his behavior. At the fourth, if he stood fire resolutely, and showed an ardent spirit, the captain brought him to the chief and made his report: "The lad will do; he is worthy to die for his country." Mina then gave him a horse and arms, and kept his own eye upon him in the hour of battle. On this system his small troop of equestrians were composed of the most devoted and intrepid Spaniards in the peninsula. There was amongst them a boy, scarcely fourteen years of age. He was mounted on a pony, with arms in proportion to his size and youth—a small double-barrelled carbine, with pistols and sword. He was always in the advanced guard and first in a fight. Once, he found himself in the midst of five French troopers, and called on them to surrender. They, observing a strong party of Mina's cavalry closely following their young leader, turned about, and were in the act of galloping off, when "*el chico*" (the fine boy) charged one of them, knocked him off his horse, and, at the same time, seized the bridle of a second, until some of his companions came up and put them both to the sword. Mina saw the exploit, and exclaimed, "*El chico* is the bravest man in the division!"

The French designated Mina the King of Navarre. Whenever he entered a house, every thing he wanted was laid before him ere he could ask for it. The whole province thought it an honor to have him for a guest, and none of his officers were suffered to pay for their meals. There might have been policy as well as love in this, under the idea that they would take without ceremony if not ceremoniously treated. Mina adopted an ingenious plan of ridding himself entirely of French spies, without inflicting on them the extreme penalty, as by the articles of war of all nations "in such cases provided." When his outposts seized and brought one of this suspected fraternity before him, he caused the prisoner to be stripped naked, to see if he concealed scraps of paper, plans, or drawing. If any thing of the kind was found, he called one of his chosen guard and said, "Take this fellow, he is a spy; cut off his right ear." The soldier, who had been pretty well practised in this work, drew out his sword and performed the operation with the dexterity of a regular surgeon. That part of the ceremony concluded, "Viva Mina" was stamped on the forehead of the culprit with a red-hot iron. He was then kicked out, indelibly branded for the rest of his life. So ashamed were the sufferers under this disgrace that they shrank from showing themselves, and in more than one instance were found lying in the hills, starved to death.

Mina established a hospital for his sick and wounded, near a beautiful little village called Estella, on the brow of a mountain. It was attended by six female nurses and two excellent surgeons. The French discovered the exact spot, and made several attempts to surprise the hospital, but never with success. Mina was always made aware of their approach. The inhabitants of the village then, at his signal, turned out in a body, and carried away the invalids in biers, on their shoulders, at least six leagues into the mountains, where they remained, in inaccessible security, until the enemy retired. In this same mountain was a cave where he fabricated his own gunpowder, with which he was, in general, well supplied. His operations were principally confined to his native province of Navarre, every inch of which, mountain and plain, he was acquainted with from infancy, and could traverse by night without a guide.

Mina encouraged the Navarrese to traffic with the French, and gave them passports for the purpose, by which means he secured many articles essential to the comfort and advantage of his men that he could not otherwise obtain. If those who wished to trade were rich, he exacted permissory fees from them, which went towards the pay of his soldiers, and more particularly to the remuneration of the peasants and others who brought him information of the movements of the French. To these allies he was unbounded in liberality, and they, in return, supplied him with information worth more than its weight in gold. Not a man could stir in the enemy's quarters without his being immediately acquainted with it. If the alcaldes, or justices of the peace, of a village were ordered by the French general to make any requisition, and did not at once communicate the particulars to Mina, he paid them a domiciliary visit in the night, and shot them incontinently. Nine of these judicial episodes illustrated his career. If he obtained the necessary information, he took his steps accordingly, either to intercept the supply, cut off the escort, or delay their march. Every volunteer who joined his band had an ample supply of wine, meat, and bread. Every thing he took in action he was allowed to consider his own, but not until the battle was over. Marauders who left off fighting to plunder prematurely were fusiladed on the spot without even a drum-head court-martial.

Mina's field manœuvres were simple and concise. His "Dundas" would not have occupied half a page. "Form column!—line-of-battle!—charge!" This was all. He could not say, with old Sir Andrew Agnew, at Fontenoy, "Lads, dinna pull a trigger till ye spy the ruffles on their sarks," for the French in Spain wore no ruffles, and not always shirts: but his word was, "Never fire till you feel sure of hitting your mark." Gaming of all sorts was prohibited in his camp, and neither officer nor soldier possessed a pack of cards. When duty was neglected, punishment fell on all alike, without distinction of rank. He invariably rejected "regulars" when they offered themselves. "These automatons," said he, "are mere book-men and theorists, made to fail. They pretend to every thing, and do nothing." The book-men and theorists repaid the compliment in full, for from the Duke of Wellington downwards, they held the irregulars in sovereign contempt. "Clear the way, canaille!" was Murat's word when he rode in singly amidst a cloud of Cossacks. Both sides were wrong, as extremes are never right.

Gurichaga, Mina's second in command, was also a remarkable man, with many requisites for his post—the only person in whom the chief had implicit confidence, and sometimes consulted. He was about the same age, taller and thinner, with less self-command, of a most hasty and insolent temper, of moderate talents, but brave as a Paladin of old, fiery in action, and powerful with the sword. He was severe with the troops; but as he never spared himself either in toil, privation, or battle, they feared, respected, and obeyed him. He watched every one in action, and upon his report they were degraded or promoted. Every man knew the country and the mountain passes as well as their leader did; and when the pressure of circumstances required, Mina dispersed his band, naming a particular rendezvous, perhaps twenty leagues off, where they never failed to arrive, even though the intermediate country might be held by divisions of the enemy. A remarkable instance occurred in 1810, when he was surrounded by twenty thousand French, who had received orders to destroy him and his corps at all hazards. Mina knew the full extent of the danger that threatened him, but with his three thousand men, remained in the mountains for fifteen days, treating the beleaguering host with the utmost contempt. At length, about dusk on an autumnal evening, he saw himself fairly surrounded by four columns, bearing down upon his front, flanks, and rear, and taking up ground preparatory to attack on the following dawn. Mina was now fairly encompassed in a net, from which extrication seemed impossible. With the greatest coolness he called his officers round him. "Gentlemen," said he, "we are rather unpleasantly situated here. Let every captain look to his own company. The rendezvous will be at such a place (naming one), the rallying word—Mina: and now let every man disperse, and make the best of his way." The order was obeyed instantly, and without noise. The French deployed their columns at daybreak in the morning; but where they expected to catch the sleeping weazels, they found nothing but untenanted furze. In five days afterwards, there was Mina again upon their track, committing his usual audacious depredations, ten leagues from his circumvented lair, and without the loss of a single man.

Not long after this, on the 22nd of May, 1811, Mina achieved the greatest of all his exploits—a deed of partisan daring and success almost equal to that of Sarsfield in 1690, when he sailed from Limerick, took, and blew up King William's battering train, and effected the raising of the siege with the liberation of the beleagued city. A column of twelve hundred French infantry was escorting a convoy of eight hundred Spanish prisoners and a considerable amount of treasure to France. Mina attacked them at the Puerto de Arlaban, near Vittoria, with the most triumphant result. The prisoners were restored to freedom, and their joy at their unexpected deliverance exceeded all bounds; but it was checked by the death of many of these unarmed captives, indiscriminately confounded with their guards, and thus unfortunately killed in the melèe. The victory was also stained by the deliberate murder of six Spanish ladies, who for being attached to French officers, were in cold blood executed after the fight was over. Such instances were not solitary where the *lex talionis* seemed to be the recognized military code on the part of all the belligerents. Massena, whose baggage was captured, intended to travel homeward by this convoy, but disliking the order of the march, he remained in Vittoria until a better opportunity, and thus Mina lost the chance so nearly thrown in his way of adding to his trophies a French marshal of the empire of the highest reputation. Franceschi, a young French general of rising fame, was taken in this miserable way, at an earlier period, and died a prisoner.

Mina had struck a blow that resounded far and wide through the country. The enemy for the moment was paralyzed at his daring and good fortune; but he was surrounded by watchful opponents, and a sudden onset of cavalry, a single neglect by an outpost, might at any moment force him to abandon his prize. He had no time to waste either in delay or deliberation. His next object was to place the prisoners he had emancipated beyond the casualty of recapture. He marched through many villages, and across many mountains, sometimes in a narrow defile, at others across an open plain, and not unfrequently close to the French lines. He moved in the direction of Valencia for the purpose of opening communication with Duran and the Empecinado, to whom he despatched messengers, requesting them to coöperate with him by passing along the banks of the Ebro, to protect his own passage across. He waited with anxiety eighteen days for an answer from the Empecinado, but none arrived. That partisan had, unfortunately, been attacked at the precise juncture, and lost his artillery. Mina then resolved to execute his project alone. He ordered some boards to be placed on cars, with preparations to construct a bridge, and spread a report that he intended to cross the river at a certain point. The carts and wagons, loaded with these materials, he moved down in the day-time towards the water. The French drew nigh and waited anxiously, expecting Mina and his troops. In the mean while he started at dead of night, marched twelve miles below the point where it was given out that he intended to throw his bridge, and coming to the banks of the Ebro, jumped off his horse and said, "Here is the spot where I intend to carry you across." The whole column was halted without noise or confusion. Mina forced his own horse into the river to try the depth, and finding it practicable, ordered a hundred men to get up behind a hundred of the cavalry, and plunge into the stream. In this manner the eight hundred enfranchised prisoners were taken over, and safely landed on the other side before the French were aware that he was not on his way to the bridge. As soon as this manœuvre was successfully accomplished, Mina exclaimed, "Now, Spaniards, you are safe from all danger of recapture." He then divided two handkerchiefs full of dollars amongst them, saying they had as good a right to share in the plunder of the French as he and his own people had, and, wishing them farewell, galloped back into the river with his cavalry, leaving twenty dragoons and an officer to escort them on their route to Valencia.

This extraordinary leader might often have doubled or trebled the amount of his force, so popular had his successes made him; but he had no personal vanity, no desire to be the general of a host; his ambition was bounded to the reputation of first of the guerillas, and he was often heard to say, he could manage four or five thousand men, but that he should be lost at the head of a regular or numerous army.

In October, 1811, Mina descended from the mountains of Leon, and entered Navarre with an organized band of above five thousand in number. They were well armed, but in want of clothing and ammunition, with which, through the agency of Mr. Tupper, our consul at Valencia, they were soon abundantly supplied. A general plan of invasion was discussed, in conjunction with Duran and the Empecinado, but the three leaders were unable to agree, and each then acted upon his own resources. Two were speedily discomfited, but Mina contrived to cut off and either kill or make prisoners of a whole battalion of Italians, while crossing a plain in the neighborhood of Huesca. The French generals, Reille and Musnier, exasperated at this misfortune, spread around their columns to intercept him; but he contrived to evade them, and, between fighting and rapid marches, reached Motrico, on the coast of Biscay, with his captives. The Iris, an English frigate, took some off his hands, and the remainder were sent on to Corunna, through the Asturian mountains, but only thirty-six out of three hundred arrived. The rest were shot by the escort, under pretext that they made a noise near a French post! These, and similar acts, such as shooting prisoners in retaliation, in the ratio of ten or even twenty to one, as practised by the curate Merino, Napier says, "were recorded with complacency in the English newspapers, and met with no public disapprobation."

On the 7th of April, 1812, Mina attacked and defeated with great loss a Polish regiment, escorting an enormous convoy of treasure, prisoners, baggage, camp followers, and invalided officers returning to France. All the Spanish prisoners were released, and joined Mina's band; and it was said that at least one million of francs (£40,000), fell into his hands, besides the equipages, arms, stores, and a quantity of church plate. On the 28th of the same month, he captured another convoy; but he had now become so notoriously formidable, that General Abbé, recently appointed French governor of Navarre, directed every corps in his command to unite in combined movements to put him down. Abbé was an active, able officer, and Mina with much difficulty escaped from his clutches. He was often heard to say that no general ever gave him so much trouble, or proved so truly formidable to him. In 1813, after the battle of Vittoria, when Clauzel, with the wreck of the French army, was slackly pursued by the Duke of Wellington, Mina displayed tactical ability far beyond what might have been expected from a partisan general. He imposed upon Clauzel a belief that the whole allied army were close upon his track, took from him three hundred prisoners, and forced that skilful strategist to destroy some of his artillery and heavy baggage, and retire rapidly to Jacca. During the blockade of Pampeluna by O'Donnel and Carlos D'Espana, Mina and his guerillas again did good service as a covering corps. But when the Allies entered France, the Spaniards began to pay off old scores on their invaders by plundering and murdering to such an extent, that Lord Wellington was compelled to send the greater portion of them back to their own country. Some of Mina's battalions mutinied, and were foremost in these excesses, which materially impeded the English general's comprehensive plans, tarnishing at the same time their own reputation, and exposing themselves to defeats which somewhat diminished the credit of their renowned commander.

The subsequent career of Mina, although he lived to 1836, and reached the age of fifty-four, furnishes less satisfactory and less remarkable materials for biography than his short and meteoric course as a leader of guerillas. In that capacity alone we treat of him in this short notice. After the general peace of 1814, he soon discovered, in common with all Spaniards who really loved their country, that in fighting for the restoration of Ferdinand the Seventh, they had restored a monarch who was almost equally compounded between despotism, imbecility, and a systematic evasion of his solemn engagements. Mina endeavored to produce a reaction against the existing system, in his native province, but failed, and sought an asylum in France, where Louis the Eighteenth not only protected, but granted him a pension. In 1822 he returned to Spain, under an expectation that Ferdinand would, at last, be true to the constitution to which he had most reluctantly yielded under compulsion. Mina was then appointed Captain-General of the three armies of Navarre, Catalonia, and Arragon, but again, in 1823, found it prudent to leave Spain, and come to England. He was cordially welcomed as a hero and patriot of the first order, and great attempts were made to lionize him, from which he shrank with unaffected modesty. Sheridan Knowles inscribed "Virginius" to the guerilla chief, with this laconic flourish: "Illustrious man! to you I dedicate this play. Who will demand my reasons?" On the accession of Queen Christina, Mina returned to his own country, received an important command, and took an active part against Don Carlos. But he added little to his earlier fame in that sanguinary contest, his measures partaking fully of the savage animosity with which it was pursued.

From Chambers's Journal.

SCIENCE AND ARTS FOR APRIL.

The Society of Acclimation at Paris have recently received, as a present from the Duke of Hamilton, a fine ox, one of the aboriginal British breed, of which two small herds still survive on the estate of Earl Tankerville, in Northumberland, and at Hamilton Park. The Society having lost their flock of llamas and alpacas by epizoötic disease, are taking measures to replace them, and M. E. Roehn is to be sent out to South America to collect another pack, and to take charge of a breed of merinos, which is to be introduced at Buenos Ayres. The expedition thus offers a twofold advantage; but it will be, as we know from Mr. Ledger's experiences, both difficult and dangerous.—M. Roy has investigated the causes of the cholera and fever which prevail in Algeria, and traces it to the nature of the soil. In the region of volcanic and primitive rocks, the clay contains phosphorus; and this acted on by fogs and dews which contain ammonia, undergoes a concentration of whatever noxious quality it may possess, and being diffused in the atmosphere, enters the lungs with respiration, and occasions fever. M. Roy, by way of testing his theory, has created an atmosphere of this nature by artificial means, and by breathing therein has produced in himself all the symptoms of the African fever.—We may expect to hear, in the course of a few years, of arid wastes converted into fruitful fields in Algeria, seeing that the French government still continue their beficent work of artesian well-boring. There are now fifty wells in the province of Constantine, yielding, in all, nearly four thousand litres of water per minute; and this precious benefit has been obtained at a cost of less than three thousand francs for each well. If a party of well-borers were sent in advance of the expeditions to explore the interior of Australia, most of the risk which now attends endeavors to penetrate that unknown region would be removed.

M. Eugene Risler has published his researches on the part played by iron in the nutrition of plants, showing that in the roots, seeds, and white portions of the growth, the iron appears as protoxide, and as peroxide in the green portions and in the ruddy leaves of autumn. Expose vegetables to air and light, and the protoxide becomes peroxide, and with a rapidity proportionate to the intensity of the light. The chlorophyll is green because of combining the two oxides—blue and yellow; and the two form a voltaic pair which decompose water, and the carbonic acid held in solution, while the hydrogen and carbon enter into the organism. Nocturnal nutrition is oxidation; diurnal nutrition is deoxidation; and to quote M. Risler's description, "the vegetable tissue is formed somewhat like that of weavers': night being the warp; day the weft, with the iron of the chlorophyll to serve as shuttle."—A curious plant, the *Drosera*, has been talked about at a scientific gathering in London, which instantly kills all the flies that settle on it, and is so exceedingly sensitive, that the hairs with which it is furnished will converge on the application of one six-thousandth of a grain of nitrate of ammonia, while a single hair is affected by one sixty-four thousandth. Is this to be accepted as another illustration of the analogy between the animal and vegetable organization?—To pass from botany to zoölogy, we take pleasure in calling attention to the series of *Zoölogical Sketches* now in course of publication, comprising drawings, with notes, of animals in the Zoölogical Society's collection. The drawings are by Wolf, and Mr. P. L. Sclater is editor of the work; which to mention is equivalent to describing the publication as highly meritorious.—Now that Mr. Du Chaillu has lectured on the gorilla before the Geographical Society and the Royal Institution, and shown his specimens, and that the narrative of his adventures is to be published by Mr. Murray, we may expect that some enterprising traveller will ere long fetch over a few living gorillas for exhibition in the Zoölogical Gardens.

The Philosophical Institute at Melbourne has changed its name, and is now the Royal Society Victoria. Judging from the fourth volume of its *Transactions*, published last autumn, the cultivation of science is not likely to be neglected in our distant colony; we find a paper on lightning-conductors—on the turning-point of the wind, with a scheme for developing or discovering it by a system of antipodal observations: another by Mr. J. W. Osborne describes a method of photolithography, whereby the impression on the sensitive paper can be inked and transferred to stone. A map, as a specimen of the process, is published with the volume; and a wood-cut is also given as demonstration that a native wood, *Callistemon salignus*, is almost if not quite equal to European box for the purpose of the engraver. We find also a report by a committee on the animal, vegetable, and mineral resources of Victoria, with remarks on the climate. The lowest temperature of the air recorded in the colony during a series of years is forty-five degrees; the highest, seventy-two degrees. The mean at Melbourne is fifty-seven degrees, but during hot winds the temperature mounts to one hundred and eleven degrees. In 1858, the rain-fall at Melbourne was twenty-three and one-half inches, about the same as the annual average at London. Concerning mineral resources, the report sets forth that a considerable quantity of salt is made from the water of shallow lakes in different parts of the colony: it describes various kinds of available building-stone; and should any enterprising emigrant think of establishing pottery-works, he will feel interested in the fact, that coal and good china-clay may be had for the digging; clay suitable for drain-pipes and tiles is also abundant; and the tile-works are flourishing, for experience has demonstrated that tiles are far preferable for roofing purposes to slate or iron in the Victorian climate. In the time of the gold-fever, bricks were made and sold at from £12 to £20 a thousand, which have since actually melted away under the heavy rains; the quality is now first-rate and the price reasonable; and the Chinese immigrants, we are told, are making a good kind of blue brick.

The Epidemiological Society, finding publicity desirable, have printed the first part of their *Transactions*, containing papers read at their meetings on the special subject to which they devote themselves; so that readers who wish to know what steps have been taken in the science of epidemiology may now gratify their wish.—A member of the British Association is working at a question in natural history which ought to interest our naval authorities; namely, the history and habits of the teredo, the worm which does so much mischief to wharfs, piles, and ships, by burrowing in the timber. The cost of the havoc wrought by this apparently insignificant creature in the port of Plymouth alone, amounts to some hundreds of pounds every year. The ports which lie most directly upon the sea are the most infested, for fresh water is fatal to the teredo. Hence Hull is uninfested, while at Yarmouth and Lowestoft the piles and sheathing suffer from a worm which is of the same species as that which prevails on the coast of Holland. The species found at Plymouth and some places in Wales is Norwegian. The question is so important, that the Netherlands and the French government each appointed a commission some years ago to investigate it; but we hear that an application to the admiralty for leave to make a series of experiments at Plymouth, with a view to suggest a remedy, or discover means of prevention, received for answer, "it was not expedient." However, the problem will perhaps be worked out by the British Association; meanwhile, those who want information concerning the teredo will find it in a report published, with engravings, by the Royal Institute of Amsterdam. The subject is the more important, seeing that some of the little borers of the Mediterranean pierce holes in the gutta-percha coating of telegraph cables, and so interrupt the communication.

The President of the Royal Society's first soirée for the season was made the occasion for exhibiting important scientific experiments, and philosophical apparatus, besides works of art. Dr. Tyndall showed, reflected on a screen in a dark room, the spectra produced by various metals under combustion, and many a spectator became aware, for the first time, of the wonderfully beautiful colors evolved by silver, copper, and other metals when thus treated.—Mr. Wheatstone's telegraph sent messages from one end of Burlington House to the other, through a length of the same cable as is used for his metropolitan telegraph system; fifty separate wires enclosed within one small india-rubber rope.—Of that new and remarkable substance—ebenite, numerous specimens were to be seen, having all the appearance of jet ornaments, fashioned into rulers, paper-knives, and other useful appliances; but its chief claim to notice, appears to be its extraordinary electrical properties. The electrical machine exhibited by Mr. Varley had a disk of ebenite three feet in diameter; which, for experimental purposes, is pronounced by distinguished electricians to be superior to glass. Moreover, it has the further advantage of not being brittle, for the principal ingredients of ebenite are india-rubber and sulphur. Examples of Bunsen and Kirchoff's spectrum analysis were shown by Professor Roscoe with the colored lines peculiar to the various metallic and alkaline bases in perfection. Concerning this subject, we take the opportunity to remark that Bunsen's experiments would not have been so much talked of as a new discovery had chemists been acquainted with optical science; for the analytical powers of the spectrum have long been familiar to opticians. Brewster's *Edinburgh Journal* for 1826, contains a paper by Mr. Fox Talbot on Colored Flames, in which the author distinctly shows that, while no difference could be detected in the color of the flame of strontium and lithium in ordinary circumstances, a striking difference could always be discerned and demonstrated by means of the spectrum; and in another place, describing the soda-line, he says that the spectrum affords to chemical analysis a means of detecting quantities however minute, and however combined, which it would be impossible to discover by any other known analytical apparatus. It is but justice to Mr. Talbot to recall the facts which, more than thirty years ago, established his claim as a discoverer in highly important branches of optics and chemistry. In taking leave of this subject for the present, we may mention that Kirchoff is applying the spectrum to analysis of the sun's atmosphere, and with results, concerning which we hope ere long to have something unusually interesting to make known to our readers.

Rymer on Shakspeare and Milton.—In the neighing of a horse, or in the growling of a mastiff, there is a meaning, there is a lively expression, and, may I say, more humanity than many times in the tragical flights of Shakspeare.—When some trifling tale as that of Othello, or some mangled, absurd, undigested, interlarded history on our stage impiously assumes the sacred name of Tragedy, it is no wonder if the theatre grow corrupt and scandalous and poetry from its ancient reputation and dignity is sunk to the utmost contempt and derision. (*Rymer's Short View of Tragedy.*)—With the remaining Tragedies I shall also send you some reflections on that Paradise Lost of Milton's, which some are pleased to call a poem.—*Rymer's Tragedies of the Last Age Considered.*

Pope on Shakspeare and Milton.—Shakspeare generally used to stiffen his style with high words and metaphors for the speeches of his kings and great men: he mistook it for a mark of greatness. This is strongest in his early days; but in his very last, his Othello, what a forced language has he put into the mouth of the Duke of Venice!—This was the way of Chapman, Massinger, and all the tragic writers of those days.—[It was mighty simple in Rowe, to write a play now, professedly in Shakspeare's style, that is, professedly in the style of a bad age.] Milton's style, in his Paradise Lost, is not natural; 'tis an exotic style.—As his subject lies a good deal out of our world, it has a particular propriety in those parts of the poem; and, when he is on earth, wherever he is describing our parents in Paradise, you see he uses a more easy and natural way of writing.—Though his formal style may fit the higher parts of his own poem, it does very ill for others who write on natural and pastoral subjects. Philips, in his Cyder, has succeeded extremely well in his imitation of it, but was quite wrong in endeavoring to imitate it on such a subject . . . Chaucer and his contemporaries borrowed a good deal from the Provençal poets: the best account of whom, in our language, is in Rymer's piece on Tragedy. "Rymer a learned and strict critic?"—"Ay, that's exactly his character. He is generally right, though rather too severe in his opinion of the particular plays he speaks of; and is, on the whole, one of the best critics we ever had."—*Spence's Anecdotes.*

DR. WATTS TO JONATHAN.

A Spiritual Communication. Medium, Miss Punch.

Let Dons delight to shoot and smite
  Their fellers, no ways slow,
Let coons and wild cats scratch and fight,
  'Cos 'tis their natur' to;
But, Yankees, guess you shouldn't let
  Sitch 'tarnal dander rise:
Your hands warn't made to draw the bead
  On one another's eyes.

—*Punch.*

From The Saturday Review, 11 May.

AMERICA.

THROUGH the cloud of newspaper magniloquence which envelopes American transactions, a serious feeling of irritation and warlike excitement may be discovered in the North. Even the city of New York, which had always supported the pro-slavery party, has been moved by the danger of the Federal capital, and by the destruction of the United States' squadron at Norfolk. Volunteers are offering their services, several militia regiments have marched southwards, patriotic subscription-lists are rapidly filling up, and the newspapers are already discovering heroes to applaud. A Captain Jones, who destroyed some arms and stores at Harper's Ferry, instead of leaving them for the Virginians to use, is proclaimed by one journal the first hero of the war. The favorite of the moment, however, is the officer who surrendered Fort Sumter—prudently, perhaps, and certainly without the loss of a man. Major Anderson, according to the enthusiastic reporters, is no speaker; but it seems to be his practice to attend meeting after meeting, and "his presence itself is a speech." The loquacity and exaggeration which have long been applied to trivial affairs tend to vulgarize and distort the events of a great and unexpected crisis. There seems to be no doubt that the North has at last been aroused from its hesitation and timidity, and Americans, whatever may be their political faults, are not likely to prove cowards in the field. The Federal Government relies entirely on the contingents of the loyal States, for the small standing army is rapidly melting away through the disaffection of the Southern officers. Washington and the District of Columbia are enclosed in the territory of Virginia and Maryland, and a hostile force is stationed within two or three miles of the city on the opposite bank of the Potomac. The attack of the Baltimore mob on a Massachusetts regiment which was marching to the support of the President, has produced general and just indignation in New England, Pennsylvania, and New York. The right of passage through the State of Maryland will be maintained by force; and it is scarcely probable that a local opposition to the advance of reinforcements will be further attempted. It will not be difficult, in the course of a few days, to concentrate twenty thousand men at Washington; and a smaller force would effectually secure the city from attack. The arrangements for providing food and stores for the garrison will be troublesome and expensive, though not impracticable. If the capture of the town is understood to be impossible, the Southern troops may perhaps abstain from taking the offensive, and the probability of a collision might in that case be indefinitely postponed.

New York politicians assert that the secession of Virginia is so far advantageous that it presents an enemy within reach of attack. Plans for seizing Baltimore and occupying Richmond, as the basis of ulterior movements on Charleston and Montgomery, are for the moment thought plausible and likely to be effective. It is not perhaps impossible to collect an irresistible army which might force its way into South Carolina and Alabama, but an enterprise of such magnitude will not be undertaken merely to gratify a feeling of resentment, when it is obvious that it can produce no solid or lasting advantage. The insults and injuries which have been inflicted on the Union by the seceding States leave the original quarrel substantially unaffected. In calmer moments, it was universally admitted that the subjugation of the South was impossible, and the obstacles to reconquest are not diminished by the secession of Virginia and North Carolina. The conditions of peace and the mode of prosecuting war are ultimately determined rather by the position and interests of the belligerents than by sentiment or passion. The Northern States have nothing to gain by a prolonged campaign, and although their resources are great and their population pugnacious, they have no institutions adapted to a war of invasion. The lawyers and shopmen of New York are willing to risk their lives for the honor of their country, but they cannot permanently be spared from home. The rural districts, from the scarcity of hired labor, still more urgently require the presence of the farmers who cultivate the soil. The mythology of the original rebellion against England has so far superseded the history of the time that few Americans are aware of the difficulty with which Washington kept an army together during the War of Independence. By almost impossible miscarriages the English Government achieved a triumph of imbecility which has naturally been turned to account in the boastful narrations of the successful party. The seceding states, in defence of their own dominions, are not likely to emulate the military administration of Lord North. There is at present nothing to fight for but the possession of Washington; and it is absurd to suppose that the capital of the United States will finally be retained where the legislature must deliberate in the midst of a foreign territory. It is not improbable that the Congress, which is summoned to meet on the 4th of July, will be forced to transfer its sittings to a more convenient spot; but Mr. Lincoln will probably be able to retain possession of the city to the end of the war.

It was the interest of Mr. Jefferson Davis and his colleagues to precipitate a collision for the purpose of driving the Border States out of the Union; but since the object is accomplished, having attained practical independence, the Southern Government has nothing more to fight for. Retaliatory measures against Virginia will only destroy any remaining attachment to the extinct constitution, and the maritime operations which are threatened, although they may be annoying, can, from their nature, only be temporary. As both parties in the quarrel will find their account in bringing it to an end, their is no reason to anticipate a long and destructive war. The Free States ought to congratulate themselves on getting rid of their fractional responsibility for the slavery which was protected by the law and force of the Union. Peace and prosperity will, in a few years, replace the population which they have lost by the secession; and if their Federation can hold together, it will still form a great and powerful republic. It is not improbable that the Southern Union may modify its internal institutions by placing some check on the caprices of the multitude. The corruption and recklessness which are thought endurable at New York or Philadelphia might be dangerous in the midst of a slave population; and it seems that the revolution has hitherto been directed by the owners of property and the natural leaders of society. Nothing in the proceedings of the Government of Montgomery equals in meanness and stupidity the bargain by which, in the midst of the crisis, Pennsylvania and Massachusetts sold the interests of the country for a selfishly protective tariff. Statesman-like directness and sagacity have hitherto only been displayed on one side in the quarrel. The President of Montgomery was selected for his known ability by the leaders of the party. Mr. Lincoln's nomination was an election manœuvre, only rendered possible by his acknowledged obscurity.

The neutral attitude assumed by Kentucky creates an additional complication. A state which refuses obedience to the constitutional demands of the President may legally be considered as in open rebellion; but any attempt at coercion, even if it were practicable, would only change passive resistance into open hostility. In a civil war, neutrality involves repudiation of allegiance, and the Union is as much at an end for Kentucky as for Florida or South Carolina. The Border slaveowners are perhaps deterred from joining the cotton Confederation by their desire that a fugitive slave law should still be in force on the opposite shore of the Ohio. No underground railway to Canada would be necessary if the State of Ohio were a foreign country in its relation to Kentucky. The confusion of rights and duties which is natural to America may perhaps lead to the belief that the Federal Constitution may be repudiated for purposes of allegiance, and yet retained as a security for slave property. Thoughtful friends of the Union may well be alarmed at the discovery that secession is possible under various forms, and in more than one direction. The great chasm which has opened between North and South may possibly produce a transverse fissure of East and West. The states on the Upper Mississippi are agreed with the Atlantic provinces on the question of slavery, but their interests are wholly opposed to protective tariffs. The sanctity of the Federal bond is finally destroyed, and fresh causes of difference among the remote and dissimilar states will constantly arise. In the prosecution of the actual war, there will be many degrees of energy; and unequal losses, sufferings, and exertions will necessarily lead to dissatisfaction and complaint. The expediency of avoiding further internal disputes furnishes an additional reason for the adoption of a pacific policy by Mr. Lincoln's Government. If terms of accommodation can be devised, there is no fear that an arrangement will be impeded by the warlike ardor of commercial ports which are already trembling for their shipping and their trade.

From The Spectator, 18 May.

THE DUTY OF ENGLAND IN THE AMERICAN STRUGGLE.

A ROYAL proclamation published on Tuesday last defines with some care the official attitude of Great Britain in the American crisis. The Government is strictly neutral in the contest, and British subjects are ordered to be strictly neutral too. They are forbidden to enlist for land or sea service on either side, to supply munitions of war, to equip vessels for privateering purposes, to engage in any transport service, or do any other act calculated to afford direct assistance to either of the great parties to the struggle. British subjects infringing any of these rules will be liable to penalties for a misdemeanor, not a very formidable threat when the composition of British juries is considered, and to any punishment a successful enemy may deem it politic to inflict.

The proclamation seems, at the first glance, just enough, and perhaps an official declaration of neutrality was all but unavoidable. But it is nevertheless a misfortune that our first official act in connection with the struggle should be one which tends directly to the benefit of the South. Englishmen, as subjects of a power in alliance with the United States, had, till this declaration, a right to enter into its service, a right wholly unaffected by the fact of the service being against rebels instead of Indians or Mexicans. Nobody "proclaims" the Irishmen who rise in the Austrian army or the Englishmen who accept the summons of Garibaldi. By prohibiting enlistment the order deprives the United States of all the aid it might, without that order, have obtained. That aid is by no means nominal or limited to the moral force which is so serious an incentive in war. The Canadas, if let alone, might, in an anti-slavery struggle, have been ranked as Northern States, and one "British" regiment has already marched for Washington *viâ* Baltimore. British sailors, too, are sure to be engaged in thousands on the Northern side, and to deprive them of the protection their nationality might have afforded, is *pro tanto* to limit the resources of the North. It may be argued that the South is equally deprived of this advantage, but the remark is sound only in appearance. Nothing in the proclamation stops a shipowner of Liverpool or the Clyde from selling ships to the South, and it is in steamers, not in men to man them, that President Davis is deficient. The richer treasury, too, would always attract the men, even if sailors were devoid of prejudices, and indifferent to the cause for which they fought. That is not the case even with Englishmen, while the fishermen of Canada are as hostile to slavery as the sailors of Connecticut. That there is no intention on the part of government to favor the South may be readily believed, but the advantage incidentally gained by the slaveholders makes it all the more imperative to decide the position we intend permanently to occupy. The *policy* of England is neutrality, but its *bias* remains to be defined.

One party, more influential than numerous, and strangely powerful in the Press, would sway us slowly in the direction of the South, and many who sympathize heartily with freedom still believe that our interests link us strongly with the seceded states. It will not, we think, be difficult to show that their arguments are based upon a delusion, and that our direct pecuniary interests are bound up for the moment with the Government of Washington. The one thing, we admit, which really governs the pecuniary side of the question, is cotton. Northern wheat is acceptable, but we can purchase wheat over half the world. Northern customers are pleasant, but they do not purchase so much as the Australians, will soon be outbid by the Chinese, and have just imposed a tariff to check their own demand. The one necessity is cotton, and our supply of cotton depends on the friendliness of the North. It is with Mr. Lincoln, and not President Davis, that the power of stopping the supply now rests. If the South were at war with us to-morrow, she would still be powerless to withhold her supply. She must sell cotton, or lose her slave property, and, directly or indirectly, she must sell it to us. So keenly is this felt at Montgomery that President Davis has ordered all privateers to abstain from attacking ships engaged in the cotton trade, under whatever flag, and the order may be obeyed. An effective blockade will, it is true, close the sea route; but as long as the internal route is clear, we shall still get our supply. It is when the North resolves to stop the cotton in transit that the pressure will be most severe, and it is therefore on the carriers and not on the growers of the produce that our interests depend. The South must sell, but the North need not transmit, and it is therefore on Northern, not Southern, forbearance that we have to rely. It is true a military advance southward from Washington might imperil a whole crop, by leading to an enfranchisement of the slaves; but this movement we are in any case wholly powerless to prevent. We could not interrupt such an advance even if we would, while British feeling would, under any circumstances, prohibit the attempt. Active interference—such, for instance, as breaking the blockade of Charleston, and maintaining a fleet outside the bar to prohibit its renewal—would secure to cotton the cheapest of all routes. But active interference is not suggested, and short of that, our interests lie in maintaining our friendly alliance with the North.

We have confined the argument to our interests in the matter, because apart from cotton there is nothing to discuss. The war, whatever its nominal issues, whether Federal sovereignty or state rights, free-trade or the Morrill tariff, the Republican constitution or the birthplace of the President, is really a war for and against slavery. The seceding states secede because their property is in danger; the conservative states march against them because they will not place that property out of danger by submitting to terms dictated in the interest of slavery. *Punch* explains the position accurately when he makes the contending gladiators fight in the presence of a negro "Cæsar" Imperator. The victory of the South must enlarge the area over which the crimes involved in that word can be perpetrated with impunity; the victory of the North must tend to restrict it, even if slavery, as the cause of all disunion, should not be abolished altogether. In any result, except the submission of the North—even the improbable one of a speedy compromise—Maryland, Delaware, Western Virginia, and probably Kentucky, must cease to be slave soil, and the slavery question be decided *pro tanto* on the side of freedom. In such a contest Englishmen, however interested in cotton, can as a nation have but one bias and one duty to perform. Their function on earth, at all events, is not to enchain the slave. They may not be able to offer active support to the cause they have at heart. They may deem it right that in this as in so many other instances the evil acknowledged to exist should be extinguished from within, that slaveholding should be ranked among the offences beyond the reach of force; but accepting this neutral point, they bind themselves all the more stringently to beware lest any act, however legitimate, any profession, however plausible, should really tend to the advantage of the cause which they abhor. Among such unconsciously evil professions we must, we fear, place the formal declaration of neutrality.

From The Spectator, 18 May.

THE PROGRESS OF EVENTS IN AMERICA.

Mr. Lincoln can wait. By the law to which he appeals, he is bound to allow "illegal combinations" twenty days before he disperses them by force. The time of grace expires on the 5th of May, and until that date the President will continue his preparations without intermission and without bravado. Though without an army, and almost without a fleet, he is still the chief of a great military race, and the force which is rapidly assembling at his call would be formidable in a European war. In addition to the seventy-five thousand men already summoned, forty thousand more have been demanded, and are to be enlisted for three years, the most formidable announcement we have yet received. It looks as if the President, who at least is aware of his own will, were contemplating a war which will last for three campaigns. The regular army, shattered to pieces by defections, by the retirement of Southern officers, and by the treachery of individuals like Twiggs, is to be reinforced instantly to twenty-five thousand men, who, it must be remembered, will *not* have the Southern frontier to defend.

Rumors are afloat of a still more decisive increase to the regular army, while volunteers, enlisted for no definite period, continue to pour in. These calls are in no sense formal, for the number asked for is invariably supplied with a rapidity and ease which reminds European observers rather of an Austrian conscription than an enlistment of free soldiers. Surprise at the numbers, however, disappears, when it is remembered that the American people, though equal in number to those of England and Wales, have not yet raised an army exceeding our volunteers. It is the willingness of the people which is marvellous. The summons to the first Massachusetts regiment reached Boston in the evening, and was not in circulation till full midnight. At daybreak the *regiment had cleared the town* in its march on Washington, enthusiasm having remedied every want. Ten thousand men are now collected within the capital, ten thousand more are marching through Pennsylvania and Maryland, and not one Western man has yet arrived. The scarcity of arms, though not yet serious, is beginning to be felt, but orders of imperial magnitude have been forwarded to Europe, and the local factories are in a condition of fierce activity. Colonel Colt, in particular, whose loyalty had been questioned, has equipped an entire regiment with repeating rifles. Money is forthcoming in any amount. The *Herald* estimates the amount already given by individuals at five and a half millions of dollars, and this is independent of the State and Federal contributions. The marine department, though not quite so talkative,—for private enterprise cannot make a navy,—is equally earnest in preparation. The Federal squadrons have not arrived, but orders have been issued to enlist eighteen thousand sailors, to equip every thing in the shape of a steamer that will float, and to secure as many private vessels as their owners can be induced to lend. As yet it is impossible to form even an idea of the fleet at the President's disposal; but it seems certain that he has six or seven war vessels of some size, and an unlimited force of transports, but a great deficiency of small steamers capable of being armed. Already Charleston and the Virginian ports are effectually blockaded, and the mouth of the Potomac is said to be swarming with small vessels. No order seems to have been given about privateers, and it is possible that in the face of the European decision on this point the President prefers for the present to retain all available maritime force in his own hand.

Mr. Lincoln, as we have said, waits, and the constitutional delay has encouraged the belief, still popular in England, in the possibility of compromise. Despite the barometer, a lull is taken for the cessation of the storm. Reports of negotiations, overtures, armistice, are freely repeated, and the terms of agreement discussed as if a conference were at hand. Most of these prophecies are dictated by a secret sympathy with the South but all, whether honest or only intended to embarrass, are, we believe, equally without foundation. It is, we repeat, impossible for the two parties even to negotiate until their comparative strength has been defined. There is no *locus standi* for peaceable discussion. Nobody supposes, we presume, that the President intends to give up Washington, or discuss terms in which that proposal is included. But to retain Washington Maryland must be retained, and Maryland is not yet aware that her function in politics is for the present quiet obedience. Nor can the President, if so inclined, surrender Western Virginia, which is as free as New York, to the clutches of slaveholders eager to avenge her treason to the South. Yet her old spirit has departed strangely out of the Old Dominion if she submits to see her territory partitioned without a stroke in its defence. These States are as tenacious of their boundaries as any European kingdom, and the right of villages to secede, though a logical consequence of Calhoun's principles, is not yet admitted even by the South. Mr. Lincoln, moreover, has announced pretty openly his view of the first campaign. He intends to enforce the right of way through Baltimore in such style that the question shall not be again raised during the war. He will retake Harper's Ferry, Fort Monroe, and Norfolk in Virginia, and exact the restoration of the *matériel* plundered thence, and now stored up in Richmond. And then, with Maryland, Delaware, and Virginia finally detached from the South, he will announce the next object of the campaign. This programme is scarcely favorable to compromise, and the people, the only authority superior to the President, seem as little disposed to treat. Their real leaders, indeed, amazed at the unanimity which prevails, are lending their ears more and more readily to the counsel of those who would terminate not only the quarrel but its cause. The country folk of the North are fairly roused, and they add to the fixed will of the English people something of the vindictiveness which marked the race they have supplanted. They look on the quarrel, not as we are inclined to do, as a fit of irresistible ill-temper, but as the natural outburst of a sore festering for thirty years. This generation has grown up hearing only of slavery, seeing every consideration kept down by fear of emancipation, listening to stories of horrors done on the border land by slave-owners, brooding over a sullen resolve, if ever the outbreak should arrive, to end the peril once for all. The hour has now arrived, and the quiet men who in six hours had exchanged their beds for marching order, will not be daunted by the length of the conflict or the results it may involve. But we shall be told, if the North will not yield, the South may. Already, Mr. Davis, who was just now so loud about his visit to the capitol, pledges himself only to resist the subjugation of the South. As Virginia is included in the South, and the partition of Virginia is a certainty, that menace does not bear its English interpretation. It still means war, though it assumes that the cause of war is a just right of self-defence. That the planters are taken by surprise at the attitude of the North is probable, but their leaders always expected war, and cowardice is never the vice of an aristocracy of race. They could obtain no terms which would leave slavery any thing but a tolerated nuisance, and they will, unless their character and their means have been alike misjudged, submit as yet to none. When slave property is valueless, compromise, based on the surrender of guarantees for slavery will be possible, but scarcely before.

It is difficult, futile as speculation on such a point must be, not to speculate on the character of the virtual leaders in this war. Mr. Davis seems intelligible enough,—a man with the power which ability, unchecked by scruples or by fear, must always yield; But Mr. Lincoln is more difficult to read. Five-sixths of the speeches attributed to him are inventions as baseless as any Belgian canards. He is a silent man, too, lacking in a very remarkable degree the American faculty of effective declamation. Even his acts may be interpreted on two hypotheses, his decision being always hampered by more or less of formula. He levies an army as he would call out the posse commitatus, declares civil war by a notice against illegal combinations, and subjugates a state by a legal plea in favor of a right of way. But we see no act of his which indicates vacillation, and incline, under the evidence as yet produced, to believe him equal to the situation. He is, we suspect, a great man after the American type. An English statesman in his position would have been content to know that his own will was fixed, and gone straight forward, without a thought of the popular view of his resolve. American statesmen are drilled out of individuality, and Mr. Lincoln, with a will of iron and a heart to face all difficulties, still waited for the people. The silent masses have spoken at last, and Mr. Lincoln, confident of the one judgment which he fears, has in all subsequent acts shown himself as inflexible as a czar. A little letter has just been published from Mr. Seward, the "compromising" Secretary of State, which, to our thinking, lets a flood of light upon the character of the President. He was asked about some proposed armistice, and replied: "That sort of business ended on 4th March."

The Union is indivisible now as when the inaugural address was spoken, be the consequences of the doctrine what they may.

LIGHTS AHEAD! OR, THE PIONEER SHIP.

First and alone, o'er deeps unknown
Columbus steered his bark;
Fell Mutiny within its breast
Had reared her horrid serpent crest
To force him back;—when hark!
"Lights ahead! Our goal is won!"
And those who cursed at set of sun
Join in the shout "Our goal is won!"
The nations hear and follow.

First and alone, o'er deeps unknown,
Columbia steers her bark,
Say, can she ride that restless sea
The people's will, so strong, so free?
Fearless she floats; and hark!
"Lights ahead! The way is found!"
All Europe rises at the sound,
"The way to Liberty is found!"
The nations hear and follow.

First and alone, o'er deeps unknown,
Still moves the guiding bark;
Fell Mutiny within its breast
Again has raised her horrid crest
To force it back! But hark!
"Lights ahead! our quest is o'er!"
"*Our flag shall wave o'er all the shore!*"
"Columbia RULES for evermore!"
The nations hear and follow.

M. H. G.

Newark, N. J., May, 1861.

THE MASSACHUSETTS LINE.

BY THE AUTHOR OF "THE NEW PRIEST."

AIR: "*Yankee Doodle.*"

I.

Still first, as long and long ago,
Let Massachusetts muster;
Give her the post right next the foe;
Be sure that you may trust her.
She was the first to give her blood
For freedom and for honor;
She trod her soil to crimson mud:
God's blessing be upon her!

II.

She never faltered for the right,
Nor ever will hereafter;
Fling up her name with all your might,
Shake roof-tree and shake rafter.
But of old deeds she need not brag,
How she broke sword and fetter;
Fling out again the old striped flag!
She'll do yet more and better.

III.

In peace her sails fleck all the seas,
Her mills shake every river;
And where are scenes so fair as these
God and her true hands give her?
Her claim in war who seek to rob?
All others come in later—
Hers first it is to front the Mob,
The Tyrant and the Traitor.

IV.

God bless, God bless the glorious state!
Let her have way to battle!
She'll go where batteries crash with fate,
Or where thick rifles rattle.
Give her the Right, and let her try,
And then, who can, may press her;
She'll go straight on, or she will die;
God bless her! and God bless her!

—*N. Y. Evening Post.*

OUR COUNTRY.

Ye sailors on the mighty deep,
Ye soldiers on the land,
Your sacred oaths we bid ye keep,
We bid ye faithful stand.
This broad land, this whole land, this free land is yours,
It is the noble Union your constancy secures!

No narrow state in this dread hour
Shall dare to claim your birth,
Allegiance to the Federal power
Is more than home or hearth.
This broad land, this whole land, this free land is yours.
It is the noble Union your loyalty secures!

Keep ye the mighty river
Unbroken in its tide,
And the hills that stand forever
Let no mean hand divide.
This broad land, this whole land, this free land is yours,
It is the noble Union your fidelity secures!

The laws your fathers writ in blood
No impious thought shall break,
The flag they bore through fire and flood
Let no true heart forsake.
This broad land, this whole land, this free land is yours,
It is the noble Union your bravery secures.

—*Transcript.*

THE DARKENED PLEIADES.

"Like the lost Pleiad seen no more below."

They fall from heaven! the guilty seven!
Fall from our banner's starry heaven!
One Pleiad lost drags down the host,
And strives, like Lucifer of old,
To rob the skies of half their gold.

They have not failed. They are but veiled;—
Spots mar the disk. The light has paled;—
But treason's blot abideth not;—
And all those glorious orbs in heaven
Attract and hold the wandering seven.

M. H. G.

Newark, N. J., May, 1861.

INK, BLOOD, AND TEARS.

(THE TAKING OF FORT SUMTER.)

A FORTY-HOURS' bombardment! Great guns throwing
  Their iron hail: shells their mad mines exploding:
Furnaces lighted: shot at red heat glowing:
  Shore-batt'ries and fort-armament, firing, loading—
War's visible hell let loose for forty hours,
And all her devils free to use their powers—
And yet not one man hit, her flag when Sumter lowers.

"Oh, here's a theme!" quoth *Punch*, of brag abhorrent,
  "'Twixt promise and performance rare proportion!
This show-cloth of live lions, giving warrant,
  Masking some mangy, stunted, stuffed abortion:
These gorgeous covers hiding empty dishes,
These whalelike antics among little fishes—
Here is the very stuff to meet my dearest wishes.

"What ringing of each change on brag and bluster!
  These figures huge of speech, summed in a zero;
This war-march, ushering in *Bombastes'* muster:
  This entry of *Tom Thumb*, armed like a hero,
Of all great cries e'er raised o'er little wool,
Of all big bubbles by fools' breath filled full,
Sure here's the greatest yet, and emptiest, for John Bull.

"John always thought Jonathan, his young brother,
  A little of a bully; said he swaggered:
But in all change of chaff with one another,
  Nor John nor Jonathan was e'er called 'laggard.'
But now, if John mayn't Jonathan style 'coward,'
He *may* hint stripes and stars were better lowered
From that tall height to which, till now, their flag-staff towered."

Punch nibbed his pen, all jubilant, for galling—
  When suddenly a weight weighed down the feather,
And a red liquid, drop by drop slow falling,
  Came from the nib; and the drops rolled together,
And steamed and smoked and sung—"Not ink, but blood;
Drops now, but soon to swell into a flood,
Perchance e'er Summer's leaf has burst Spring's guarding bud.

"Blood by a brother's hand drawn from a brother—
  And they by whom 'tis ta'en, by whom 'tis given,
Are both the children of an English mother;
  Once with that mother, in her wrath, they've striven;
Was't not enough, that parricidal jar,
But they must now meet in fraternal war?
If such strife draw no blood shall England scoff therefore?

"If she will laugh, through thee, her chartered wit,
  Use thou no ink wherewith to pen thy scoff;
We'll find a liquor for thy pen more fit—
  We blood-drops—see how smartly thou'lt round off
Point, pun, and paragraph in this new way:
Till men shall read and laugh, and, laughing, say,
'Well thrust! *Punch* is in vein: 'tis his red-letter day.'"

The weight sat on my quill: I could not write:
  The red drops clustered to my pen—in vain;
I had my theme—"Brothers that meet in fight,
  Yet shed no blood!"—my jesting mood turned pain.
I thought of all that civil love endears,
That civil strife breaks up and rends and sears,
And lo! the blood-drops in my pen were changed to tears!

And for the hoarse tongues that those bloody gouts
  Had found, or seemed to find, upon my ears
Came up a gentle song in linkèd bouts,
  Of long-drawn sweetness—pity breathed through tears.

And thus they sang: "'Twas not by chance,
  Still less by fraud or fear,
That Sumter's battle came and closed,
  Nor cost the world a tear.
'Twas not that Northern hearts were weak,
  Or Southern courage cold,
That shell and shot fell harming not
  A man on shore or hold.

"It was that all their ghosts who lived
  To love the realm they made,
Came fleeting so athwart the fire,
  That shot and shell were staid.
Washington with his sad, still face,
  Franklin with silver hair,
Lincoln and Putnam, Allan, Gates,
  And gallant Wayne were there.

"With those who rose at Boston,
  At Philadelphia met;
Whose grave eyes saw the Union's seal
  To their first charter set.
Adams, and Jay, and Henry,
  Routledge and Randolph, too—
And many a name their country's fame
  Hath sealed brave, wise, and true.

"An awful host—above the coast,
  About the fort they hung;
Sad faces pale, too proud to wail,
  But with sore anguish rung.
And Faith and Truth, and Love and Ruth,
  Hovered the battle o'er,
Hind'ring the shot, that freight of death
  Between those brothers bore.

"And thus it happed, by God's good grace,
  And those good spirits' band,
That Death forebore the leaguered place,
  The battery-guarded strand.
Thanks unto Heaven on bended knee,
  Not scoff from mocking scorn,
Befits us, that to bloodless end
  A strife like this is borne!"

PRAYERS SET FORTH BY ALONZO POTTER, BISHOP OF PENNSYLVANIA.

PRAYER IN TIME OF PUBLIC CALAMITIES, DANGERS, OR DIFFICULTIES.

O MOST mighty God! King of kings and Lord of lords, without whose care the watchman waketh but in vain, we implore, in this our time of need, thy succor and blessing in behalf of our rulers and magistrates, and of all the people of this land. Remember not our many and great transgressions; turn from us the judgments which we feel, and the yet greater judgments which we fear; and give us wisdom to discern, and faithfulness to do, and patience to endure, whatsoever shall be well pleasing in thy sight; that so thy chastenings may yield the peaceable fruits of righteousness, and that at the last we may rejoice in thy salvation; through Jesus Christ our Lord. *Amen.*

PRAYER DURING OUR PRESENT NATIONAL TROUBLES.

O ALMIGHTY God, who art a strong tower of defence to those who put their trust in thee, whose power no creature is able to resist, we make our humble cry to thee in this hour of our country's need. Thy property is always to have mercy. Deal not with us according to our sins, neither reward us according to our iniquities; but stretch forth the right hand of thy Majesty, and be our defence for thy name's sake. Have pity upon our brethren who are in arms against the constituted authorities of the land, and show them the error of their way. Shed upon the counsels of our Rulers the spirit of wisdom and moderation and firmness, and unite the hearts of our people as the heart of one man in upholding the supremacy of Law, and the cause of justice and peace. Abate the violence of passion; banish pride and prejudice from every heart, and incline us all to trust in thy righteous Providence, and to be ready for every duty. And oh, that in thy great mercy, thou wouldst hasten the return of unity and concord to our borders, and so order all things that peace and happiness, truth and justice, religion and piety, may be established among us for all generations. These things and whatever else thou shalt see to be necessary and convenient for us, we humbly beg through the merits and mediation of Jesus Christ our Lord and Saviour. *Amen.*

PRAYER FOR THOSE EXPOSED TO DANGER.

ALMIGHTY God, the Saviour of all men, we humbly commend to thy tender care and sure protection, thy servants who have gone forth at the call of their country, to defend its government and to protect us in our property and homes. Let thy fatherly hand, we beseech thee, be over them; let thy Holy Spirit be with them; let thy good angels have charge of them; with thy loving kindness defend them as with a shield, and either bring them out of their peril in safety, with a heart to show forth thy praises forever, or else sustain them with that glorious hope, by which alone thy servants can have victory in suffering and death; through the sole merits of Jesus Christ our Lord. *Amen.*

IN THE TIME OF WAR AND TUMULTS.

O ALMIGHTY God, King of all kings, and Governor of all things, whose power no creature is able to resist, to whom it belongeth justly to punish sinners, and to be merciful to them that truly repent, save and deliver us, we humbly beseech thee, from the hands of our enemies; abate their pride, assuage their malice, and confound their devices; that we, being armed with thy defence, may be preserved evermore from all perils, to glorify thee, who art the only Giver of all victory; through the merits of thy only Son, Jesus Christ our Lord. *Amen.*

A COLLECT FOR PEACE.

O GOD from whom all holy desires, all good counsels, and all just works do proceed, give unto thy servants that peace which the world cannot give; that our hearts may be set to obey thy commandments, and also that by thee, we, being defended from the fear of our enemies, may pass our time in rest and quietness; through the merits of Jesus Christ our Saviour. *Amen.*

A PRAYER FOR THE PRESIDENT OF THE UNITED STATES AND ALL IN AUTHORITY.

O LORD, our heavenly Father, the high and mighty Ruler of the universe, who dost from thy throne behold all the dwellers upon earth, most heartily we beseech thee with thy favor to behold and bless thy servant, the President of the United States, and all others in authority; and so replenish them with the grace of thy Holy Spirit, that they may always incline to thy will, and walk in thy way. Endue them plenteously with thy heavenly gifts; grant them in health and prosperity long to live; and finally, after this life, to attain everlasting joy and felicity; through Jesus Christ our Lord. *Amen.*

From The New York Tribune, 28 May.

A PARALLEL.

A HUNDRED and fifty years ago, Scotland, then an independent kingdom, was, by an act of her own Parliament, annexed to England, and became a part of the British Empire. Scotland consented to the union on certain clearly expressed conditions in regard to her peculiar code of laws, her established Church, the number of her representatives in the House of Lords, and other like matters.

Now, suppose the Scotland of to-day, under the false pretext that the quuen or her Parliament had violated some of the conditions of the act of union, should summon her ancient Parliament, repeal her act consenting to the union with England, hunt up some seedy scion of the house of Stuart, place him on a throne in the dilapidated palace of Holyrood, and hail him "King of Scotland." Suppose the new king and Parliament should raise an army and fit out ships to maintain her rebellion, seizing Stirling Castle, Edinburgh Castle, and the other royal keeps and garrisons from John O'Groat's house to the Tweed; stealing all the arms in the arsenals and all the treasure in the coffers of her majesty, and proceeding to bombard and reduce the only two or three loyal fortresses north of that river.

Suppose nearly all the Scotchmen in the British army and navy should turn traitors to the crown, and surrender important posts on the land and valuable ships on the sea into the hands of the rebels—the rebel officers taking new commissions in the Scotch service. Suppose the Scots should pour troops in large masses down upon the English borders, commanded by officers who had just deserted the service of Queen Victoria, and furnished with cannon, rifles, powder, shell and shot, stolen from her garrisons; and from strategic points should threaten to sack Newcastle and Carlisle, to burn Liverpool and Bristol, and to speedily take possession of London, and organize their treasonable Parliament at Westminster, and lodge their fugitive king in Buckingham Palace.

Giving rein to the mob and license to ruffianism, suppose the Scotch should maltreat every English tourist found among their lakes and mountains, and every English merchant trading to their cities, scourging some, hanging others, and hunting all who tried to escape over the border like beasts of prey; and (perhaps worse than all in this venal age) utterly refuse to pay their indebtment to the merchants of London and Liverpool, and the manufacturers of Manchester and Birmingham, and return their protested notes accompanied with the most insulting letters.

Among other acts of the so-called Scotch Parliament, suppose they should pass a law authorizing letters of marque, whose every provision was redolent of rascality, offering a temptation to every corsair that infests the seas to take commissions and sweep the ocean of English commerce — stimulating their thirst for gold and blood by a reward of £20 sterling for every English mariner whom they would shoot, drown, or butcher.

In the face of these facts, and while England was putting forth all her might by land and sea to crush this rebellion, appealing to the loyalty of her own people and the sympathy of constitutional governments to sustain her, suppose Mr. Douglas or Mr. Fessenden should propose a resolution in the American Senate urging the government of the United States to recognize the independence of Scotland, while the American President should issue a grave proclamation recognizing the Scotch rebels as "belligerents" in the international sense of that term, and proposing to treat their letters of marque as legal documents, and all ships, goods, and men captured under them as prizes and prisoners, according to the law of nations. What would Lord John Russell, Lord Palmerston, the Earl of Derby, and Messrs. Richard Cobden and John Bright say of this conduct of their "American cousins"? Would they not ask, Does not the government of the United States remember that it has a solemn treaty of amity and commerce with the United Kingdom of Great Britain and Ireland; that Scotland is embraced within this geographical designation; that Victoria I. is the sovereign of this realm, and not Charles III.; that our gracious ruler dwells at Buckingham Palace, and not at Holyrood House; that the British Parliament sits at Westminster, and not at Edinburgh; that a scion of the illustrious house of Russell is our Foreign Secretary, and not some rebel Rob Roy of the Highlands; that our ambassador at Washington is Lord Lyons, and not a bevy of wandering fugitives from beyond the Tweed, styling themselves "Commissioners"?

And, more than all — suppose it should turn out that this Scotch rebellion was utterly causeless and wanton, and was set on foot not because of any violation of the act of Union, but, under false pretexts, was fomented for the purpose of establishing despotism at home, extending the curse of human slavery into all the colonies of Great Britain, and ultimately re-opening the African slave-trade to supply the victims of their cupidity. What, then, would the people of England, and of the whole civilized world, say of such conduct on the part of the American Government?

THE LIVING AGE.

No. 891.—29 June, 1861.

CONTENTS.

☞ Mr. Motley's Letter to *The Times* will be printed in full in the next number of *The Living Age.*

Poetry.—The Union Volunteers, 770. Back again, 770. Origin of Species, 782.

Short Articles.—Improvement in Iron Manufacture, 781. Influence of Air on Generation, 781. Queensland, Australia, 789. Chinese Mind, 803. Re-Issue of *Punch,* 808. Locality of the Eternal Inheritance, 814. New Brunswick, 814. Collieries and Colliers, 824. Oxide of Antimony in Borneo, 824.

NEW BOOKS.

The Partisan Leader. Part Second and Last. A Key to the Disunion Conspiracy. New York: Rudd and Carleton.

PUBLISHED EVERY SATURDAY BY

LITTELL, SON, & CO., BOSTON.

For Six Dollars a year, in advance, *remitted directly to the Publishers,* the Living Age will be punctually forwarded *free of postage.*

Complete sets of the First Series, in thirty-six volumes, and of the Second Series, in twenty volumes, handsomely bound, packed in neat boxes, and delivered in all the principal cities, free of expense of freight, are for sale at two dollars a volume.

Any volume may be had separately, at two dollars, bound, or a dollar and a half in numbers.

Any number may be had for 13 cents; and it is well worth while for subscribers or purchasers to complete any broken volumes they may have, and thus greatly enhance their value

THE UNION VOLUNTEERS.

BY GEORGE BOWERYEM.

WE arm by thousands strong,
To battle for the right,
And this shall be our song,
As we march into the fight;
With our country's banner o'er us,
And traitor-ranks before us,
Let Freedom be the chorus
Of the Union Volunteers!
Now hearken to the cheers
Of the Union Volunteers!
[Chorus of cheering.]

When the battle rages round,
And the rolling of the drum,
And the trembling of the ground,
Tell usurpers that *we come*,
Then the war's deep-mouthed thunder
Shall our lightnings cleave asunder,
And our enemies shall wonder
At the Union Volunteers!
Shall wonder at the cheers
Of the Union Volunteers!

True loyal sons are we
Of men who fought and died
To leave their children free,
Whom dastards now deride!
Tremble, traitors! at the beaming
Of our starry banner gleaming,
When like a torrent streaming,
Come the Union Volunteers!
Dealing death amid their cheers,
Come the Union Volunteers!

When Union men unite,
Heart to heart and hand to hand,
For Freedom's cause to fight,
Shall wrong the right withstand?
With our country's banner o'er us,
And rebels base before us,
And Liberty the chorus
Of the Union Volunteers!
How terrible the cheers
Of the Union Volunteers!

Where Freedom's banner waves,
Over land or over seas,
It shall not cover slaves!
They shall touch it and be free!
Tremble, tyrants! at the flashing
Of our arms, when onward dashing,
You shall hear their fetters crashing,
Broke by Union Volunteers!
And your slaves give back the cheers
Of the Union Volunteers!

God of Freedom! give thy might
To the spirits of thy sons!
To their bayonets in fight!
To the death within their guns!
Make their deeds in battle gory
Burn and brightly shine in glory
When the world shall read the story
Of the Union Volunteers!
And echo back the cheers
Of the Union Volunteers!

—*N. Y. Evening Post.*

BACK AGAIN.

BACK again
Comes the Swallow, twittering at our windows,
Skimming over meadow, over mere,
And the meadow speckles o'er with daisies,
And white lilies spring upon the mere,
As to woo him, as to deck with beauty,
Fitting pathway for his dipping breast.

Back again
Comes the Bee, with busy vernal humming,
Through the garden, round the scented lime;
And the flowers ope their painted petals,
And the rose sighs forth her perfumed breath,
To allure him, wearying with sweet languor,
Clasped and clinging to her crimson heart.

Back again
Comes the Heron to the windy beech-tree;
Comes the Song-Thrush to the knotty thorn;
Comes the Crake with harsh voice to the brook.
And the beech puts out her soft green leaflets,
And the maythorn clothes herself with whiteness,
And the thick grass rises by the brook.

Back again
Come into their old familiar places,
All the wanderers at sweet spring-time's call;
And all nature flushes out her welcome,
Throbbing in each vein with tremulous joy.
All—all—all of love—love—love is telling,
Answering life with life and love with love.

Back again
Thou, too, comest to our quiet village,
Brightest, fairest of the guests of spring-tide;
And again thy light foot haunts our pathways,
And again thy sweet voice thrills our pulses;
And our meadows, glades, and woods are dearer
As thy presence is among them all.

Back again
Come, responsive to thy gentle presence,
All the chafings, longing, and unquiet;
All the yearnings of the heart, when fancy,
Gazing keenly down the winding lanes,
Seems to see thy dress in distance waving,
Seems to hear the music of thy voice.

Back again
Comes the craving, fearing some chance meeting;
Comes the hoping, dreading some chance greeting;
Comes the weary journey o'er the moorland;
Comes the watching o'er the walls that hold thee;
Comes the sad, the heavy, turning homewards,
'Mid the shadows falling thickly round.

—*Fraser's Magazine.*

From Chambers's Journal.

THE ANTE-NUPTIAL LIE.

PART I.

On the morning of my twenty-third birthday, I awoke early, and with a profound sense of happiness and thankfulness. My five years of married life, without having been a realized dream or sentimental idyl, had enclosed the happiest and worthiest period of my existence. Tracing the details of it, I rejoiced to think my worst difficulties were overcome, and that strong affection and deep-rooted esteem had changed an anxious course of duty into blessedness and fruition.

My husband, Mr. Anstruther, had yielded to my earnest wish to celebrate our wedding anniversary in our country home, and had granted me just three days snatched from the toil of active parliamentary life, to taste my holiday; and I was tasting it slowly, but with intense enjoyment, as I stepped out that morning upon the dewy lawn, and devoured, with my aching London sight, one of the loveliest park-landscapes in England. I looked in the distance upon low ranges of hills, blue in the early misty light, and granting, here and there, peeps of the adjacent sea, sleeping quietly beneath the rosy amber of the eastern sky, and immediately at my feet upon flower-gardens planned and cultivated with all the exigence of modern taste, and glowing with a hundred dyes. My mind recurred involuntarily to the narrow court in which my father's house was situated, and to the dreary prospect of brick and mortar, of factory chimney and church steeple, which for eighteen years had bounded my horizon; and if the recollection brought with it the old inevitable association, I was able to thank God that now no pulse beat quicker, no traitorous thrill responded.

How strange it seems that fate should come upon us with such overwhelming suddenness, that we are not suffered to hear the approaching footstep or see the outstretched arm, but are struck down instantly by the blow which might perhaps have been withstood, had a moment's warning been granted! I went back to the house that morning with the most absolute sense of security and happiness; but on the threshold of the breakfast-room I met my husband, and the first glance at his face told me something was wrong. His face was always grave—it was now stern; his manner was always reserved—it was now severe.

I had approached him naturally with smiling face and outstretched hand, anticipating his congratulations; but I stood still at once, as efficiently arrested as if he had held a drawn sword at my breast.

"That is right," he said; "come no nearer!" Then, after a pause, he added, "You have been up some time; let us have breakfast at once;" and he opened the door of the room for me to enter. I took my place, and went through the accustomed forms without a word. I saw he wished me to eat and drink, and I did so, although the effort nearly choked me. Indeed, I was thankful for the few minutes' respite, and was striving to command my resources for the approaching conflict with all the strength of mind I possessed. I was not altogether ignorant of what had come upon me; there could be between us but that one point of disunion, that one cause of reproach; and surely, surely, neither God nor man could condemn me as without excuse upon that score!

While I ate he walked deliberately up and down the room, making no pretence to eat; and as soon as I had finished, he rang the bell to have the table cleared, and then sat down before it opposite to me. "We have friends asked to dinner to-day to celebrate the double anniversary of our marriage and your birthday—have we not?" he said, leaning his arms heavily on the table, and gazing steadily into my face. "I shall not meet them. I fear it will be impossible for me ever to recognize you as my wife again!"

I think he expected that the cruel abruptness of this announcement would strike me swooning, or at least convicted, at his feet; but it did not. My heart did for a moment seem to stand still, and every drop of blood faded from my cheeks, but I did not tremble or flinch under his hard scrutiny. I was even able to speak.

"Tell me at once," I said, "the meaning of this. You are under some delusion. What have I done?"

As I spoke, his face softened; I could see, in spite of the iron mould of his physiognomy, the instinctive hope, the passionate yearning produced by my manner; it was very evanescent, however, for almost before I had gathered courage from the look, it was gone, and all the hardness had returned.

"I am not the man," he said, "to bring a premature or rash accusation especially against the woman I have made my wife. I accuse you of having deceived me, and here is the proof."

He opened his pocket-book slowly, and took out a letter. I recognized it instantly, and my heart sank. I had sufficient self-command to repress the cry that rose instinctively to my lips, but no effort could keep back the burning glow which dyed face and hands like conscious guilt.

My husband looked at me steadily, and his lip curled. "I will read the letter," he said.

The letter began thus: "You have told me again and again that you loved me; were those words a lie? You shall not make good your Moloch offering, and sacrifice religion and virtue, body and soul, youth and happiness, to your insatiate craving after position and wealth. This man is too good to be cajoled. What if I showed him the pledges of your love? taught him the reliance that is to be placed on your faith? Why should you reckon upon my submission to your perjury?"

The letter ran on to great length, mingling vehement reproaches with appeals and protestations of such unbridled passion, that as my husband read them his voice took a tone of deeper scorn, and his brow a heavier contraction.

The letter was addressed to me, on the back of the same sheet on which it was written; it was not dated beyond "Tuesday evening," but the postmark unusually legible, showed May 19, 1850—just three days before we were married. My husband indicated these facts with the same deliberation that had marked his conduct throughout, and then he said, "I found this letter last night in your dressing-room after you had left it; perhaps I ought not to have read it, but it would now be worse than mockery to make any excuses for so doing. I have nothing more to say until I have listened to your explanation. You tell me I am under a delusion—it will therefore be necessary for you to prove that this letter is a forgery."

He leaned back in his chair as he spoke, and passed his hand over his forehead with a gesture of weariness; otherwise, he had sustained his part in the scene with a cold insensibility which seemed unnatural, and which filled me with the most dreadful foreboding of failure and misery. I did not misjudge him so far as to suppose for a moment that he was as insensible as he appeared, but I perceived that his tenacious and inflexible nature had been cut to the quick both in its intense pride and love, and that though the wound bled inwardly—bled mortally, perchance—he would never utter a cry, or even allow a pang.

Alas! alas! he would never forgive me. The concealment, the deception, as he would call it, which had appeared to me justifiable, would seem crime and outrage in his eyes. I lowered my head beneath his searching gaze, and remained silent.

"You have nothing to say?" he inquired, after a vain pause for me to speak. "You cannot deny that letter? God is my witness," he said, solemnly, "that I wish to be a merciful judge. I may hold extreme views of a girl's folly, a woman's weakness: you would only be vain and faithless, like your sex, if you had played with this young man's feelings, and deceived his hopes. Is this your explanation?"

It was a very snare of Satan offered for my fall—one easy lie, "I deceived him, but never you." And the way of forgiveness was open. I saw he was clinging to the hope with a concentrated eagerness it was impossible for him entirely to disguise. Oh! was it necessary for my punishment that the hard task should be made harder by that relenting glance?

I only hesitated for a moment; the discipline of the last five years had not left me so blind and weak as even in this supreme emergency to reject truth for expediency. However he might judge me, I must stand clear before God and my conscience.

"No, Malcolm," I said desperately; "the truth is rather as it first appeared to you. I have been guilty in this matter, but my fault is surely one that you will consent to pardon; for even were it greater, I think our five years of happy union might turn the scale in my favor."

"Yes," he said; "you have borne with the difficulties of my temper with angelic patience, until the passion which induced me to marry you, despite of many obstacles, was weakness in comparison with the love I had for you—yesterday. Only tell me I have not been your dupe throughout—only,—" He broke off abruptly. "I can bear no more fencing round the point," he said, harshly; "one word is enough—did you love this youth?"

"I did from childhood, with all my heart and soul."

"Up to the date of that letter?" he asked quietly, but the muscles worked round the clenched lips.

"Yes, and beyond it," I found courage to say; but hardly had the words been spoken, when I felt I had exceeded the limit of his endurance. An involuntary oath escaped his lips.

I saw there was no hope for me in deprecation and irresolution; I must speak to the point, and decisively. "I have a right to be heard before I am condemned," I said, "and I claim my right. I confess I loved the youth who wrote that letter, but it would have been a miracle had it been otherwise. You know from what a life you rescued me: a prisoner in the dull rooms above my father's bookstore, without a pleasure, a friend, a hope in life. You were astonished at my proficiency in unusual studies: if at that time an active brain had not driven me to intellectual labor, I should have gone mad in the midst of my austere and desperate loneliness. I was scarcely fifteen when Duncan Forsyth, a kinsman of my father, came to study medicine in our city university, and to live as boarder in our house. I say it was inevitable that such a connection should in due course ripen into love. He was young, gifted, and attractive, but it would have needed but half his endowments to win my heart then. I was nothing but a blind, passionate child, neglected utterly till he flattered, caressed, and wooed me. I think he loved me with all the faculty of love he had, and for a time we were very happy. To me it was a delicious dream—Have patience with me, Malcolm; I must tell all the truth. My dream, at least, was brief enough; I soon awoke to discover, it little matters how, that the lover I was canonizing in my imagination, as the type of heroic virtue, was unworthy. For awhile, I would not believe; when conviction became inevitable, I clung desperately to the forlorn hope of reform. It was in vain; his vices were too confirmed and tyrannous for even my influence—and it was great—to overcome. Then I gave him up. I thought the struggle would kill me, for my foolish soul clung to him desperately, but I could not mate with drunkenness and dishonor. My father, who had approved of our engagement, and who did not know or believe the facts concerning him, upbraided and coerced me; Duncan himself, relying on my weakness, tried all the skill he had to move me, till I was nearly frantic in my misery.

"It was just at this crisis that you first saw me, visited my father's bookstore, and desired to be made known to me. What followed, I need not tell. You told me you loved me well enough to marry me, despite of social inferiority, if I thought I could love you in return—if I had a young girl's free heart to give you. You insisted upon this, Malcolm—I dare not deny it—and I came to you with a lie in my right hand! Here lies my offence, and God knows, I do not wish to palliate it; but before you utterly condemn me, consider the temptation. My father forbade Duncan the house, and threatened me if I dared to tell you the truth concerning him; but I hardly think that would have moved me, had I not persuaded myself also that I was justified in deceiving you. Had I told you I loved Duncan Forsyth, you would have given me up, and shut against me all the vague but glorious hopes such an alliance offered; but more than all, I knew this unworthy love must soon die out, and that my deep recognition and reverence for your goodness and excellence would end in an affection stronger and deeper than the weak passion of a girl. Before God, I vowed to do my duty; from that hour, I have striven, with his help, to keep my vow; and save in that preliminary falsehood, Malcolm, I have never wronged you."

My husband had recovered his self-command while I was speaking, but the last phrase seemed to overthrow it again. "Wronged me!" he repeated, and the intonation quiet as it was, thrilled me like physical pain, it was so hard and unrelenting. "I wish to be calm, Ellinor," he continued, "and therefore I will speak briefly. You seem to think you have extenuated yourself by your confession. To my heart and mind, you are condemned past forgiveness. Nay, do not plead or protest," he said, with a haughty movement of restraint, as I was about to approach him; "it is a point for feeling, not casuistry, to decide. You understand fully the delusion under which I married you. I imagined I took to my arms a pure-hearted girl, fresh and innocent as her seclusion warranted me to believe her: instead of that, I find myself to have been cajoled by a disappointed woman, with a heart exhausted by precocious passion. You think it excuse sufficient that it was your *interest* to deceive me; to my mind, the fact adds only insult to the injury. Ellinor, you have ruined the happiness of my life. While I have been resting on the solace of your love, worshipping you for your sweet patience with a temper roughened by many causes unknown to your inexperience, it has all been the insensibility of pre-occupation, or at best a miserable calculation of duty. So gross is your sense of conjugal faith, that because your treachery has been only of the heart, you dare to say you have never wronged me, and to call upon God to approve your virtue because the lapse of time and better influences, I trust, have enabled you to school a disgraceful passion, and offer a measure of regard in return for the immeasurable devotion I have felt for you."

He paused in spite of himself, unable to proceed, and before he could prevent me, I had thrown myself at his feet. It was in vain to argue—to fight against his hard words; I could only implore.

"Malcolm," I cried, "you cannot believe what you say. Your affection has been the chief happiness of my happy life; you could not desire, you could not exact from a wife a deeper love, more entire and minute, than I feel for you. Forgive this one deception, Malcolm; believe me now."

I would fain have been eloquent, but sobs choked my voice. I was completely overcome; and when he forcibly extricated himself from my hold, I fell almost prostrate at his feet. He lifted me up coldly, but courteously, and placed me on the sofa.

"Pardon me," he said; "this excitement is too much for you, and can do no good. When you are calmer, we will conclude this matter."

There was the same cruel decision of tone and aspect in his manner which had marked it throughout the interview, and which convinced me he still adhered to his original purpose. I felt my situation was desperate, and that the time for prayers and tears was over. Were all my hopes of the future—his happiness, too, in which was involved my own—to be dashed to pieces against the rock of his unjust severity? Was it required of me to submit passively to disgrace and misery? In a moment, I, too, had taken my resolve, and conquered my agitation; I rose up nerved and calm, and spoke accordingly.

"One word before you leave me," I said. "However this ends between us, you do not, I suppose, desire to inflict upon me unnecessary shame and exposure? I request you, as a personal favor—it may be the last I shall ever ask—to postpone your decision till to-morrow, and help me to-day to entertain our friends as much as possible in the accustomed manner. Do you hesitate, Malcolm?"

His face flushed; some impulse seemed to incline him to refuse, but he checked it. "It shall be as you desire," he said, coldly; and left me alone—alone with the conviction of a blasted life!

For a few moments, with my hands clasped over my eyes, to shut out the redundant sunshine, I sat trying to realize my position. Granting that the threatened separation was effected with a so-called due regard to my honor and future relations with society, all that I valued and cared for in life would be irremediably destroyed. What honor remains to the wife repudiated by an honorable husband? What chance of happiness for her when at the same time he is the centre of her affection, of all her worldly ambition and hope? Doubtless, I was tolerant to my own transgression, but I alone knew the force of the temptation. I alone knew—what, alas! I felt my husband would never believe—how near extinction was the old love smouldering beneath its own contempt, and how strong the gratitude and esteem he had already excited. Oh, could I but convince him of my love for him! I rose up and paced the room. I felt he judged me harshly, was severe even to cruelty; but then I knew the innate inflexibility of his temper, and his rigorous sense of truth and duty. I knew how love, pride, and self-esteem had been all alike wounded, and [illegible] even in the extremity of my misery almost more than I pitied myself. Still, I would not accept my ruin at his relentless hands; I was a true wife, and would not submit to the position of a false one. I had avowed to love and honor him till death parted us, and nothing but compulsion should make me abandon my post.

I scarcely know how I got through that day; but the necessity for self-command was so stringent, that I could not but meet it. Fortunately, our guests were only a few country neighbors, for it was in the height of the London season, and I in some measure supported myself by the belief that their unsuspicious cordiality was not likely to make any discoveries. Mr. Anstruther's hospitality was always splendid, and his deportment as host peculiarly gracious and inviting, and if there was any difference on this occasion, it would be impalpable to all but a very keen observer. I perceived, indeed, a change in the aspect of the countenance I had long studied so closely, and beyond that, the intonation of his voice when addressing me fell hard and constrained upon my shrinking ear. It was over at last; and I saw our last guest depart smiling and congratulatory with the consolation at least left me that I had acted my part successfully.

The next day, the trial was renewed. Mr. Anstruther wrote me a few words, saying it was his intention to return to his parliamentary duties that day, and that he deemed it advisable I should remain in the country. His final determination and all accessory arrangements should be made known to me through the family lawyer, which would spare the pain of a second interview. "Cruel!" I said to myself, crushing the letter in my nervous hand, and for a moment a passionate feeling rose in my heart that I would suffer things to take their hard course, and leave duty and effort unattempted. It was but a brief paroxysm; for at the same instant I saw a tiny, white-robed figure flitting across the lawn towards my open window, and the sweet, shrill voice of our little daughter crying aloud, "Mamma, mamma, may I come in?" I stepped out and met her; stooped down and kissed the eager, upturned face; and with that quiet kiss I renewed my vow, and strengthened it with a prayer.

"My darling," I said, "go into papa's study, and tell him mamma is coming to speak to him, if he is not busy." She ran away on her errand, and I followed at once; I did not mean to be refused. It was well I did so, for he had already risen, as if to leave the room, and had taken the child in his arms, to carry her away with him. As I entered, his face flushed with a mixed expression of anger and pain; but he was soon calm again, sent away our little girl, and then placed me a chair. "There is no occasion for me to sit," I said, with a voice as steady as concentrated resolution could make it; "I shall not need to detain you long. I come to say, Malcolm, that I am quite willing to obey you so far as to remain here while you return to London, but that I must positively refuse to have any interview with your lawyer."

"You refuse!"

"I do refuse, and that finally," I pursued, "for it would answer no end. I could only tell him what I come now to tell you, that no power save physical coercion shall separate me from you. I know it is in vain to extenuate my fault in your eyes, but it is at least one on which no legal proceedings can be raised: you cannot divorce your wife because she told you an ante-nuptial lie. It remains to you to abandon or malign her, but I will be accessory to no mutual arrangement. My duty is by your side while life lasts, whether in weal or woe, and I will hold my post. That is, henceforth I will consider this our home, and will remain here, unless driven from it. I am now, as before, your true wife in heart and soul, as in word and deed; as anxious to fulfil my sweet duty to you, with no hope in life so strong as your forgiveness."

I had said my say, and was going, for I dared not trust myself longer, dared not even look into my husband's face to read the effect of my words, but he arrested me with a peremptory motion.

"Am I to understand, Ellinor, that you mean to defy my determined purpose; and in spite of alienation and contempt, to insist upon the shelter of my roof, or rather to exile me from a place which would be intolerable under such circumstances? Do not be afraid, if you will consent to a formal separation, that the terms of it shall fail in all possible delicacy and liberality, but I cannot live with the wife who has cheated me of her first kiss."

"I *am* resolved," I answered. "I am able to say no more. I think I see my duty plain, and I mean to strive to do it. You must follow your own will; it will be for me to endure."

He paced the room in strong excitement.

"I cannot bear it," he said; "it would eat my life out! You shall have our child, Ellinor, if she is the motive of this strange, unwomanly resolution: far be it from me to torture the heart of the mother! She shall be yours unreservedly, and her interests shall never suffer one whit. You know how I love that little creature; there was but one thing dearer: judge, then, by this of my intense desire to sever the connection between us."

"Cruel! unmerciful!" I exclaimed with an impulse of bitterness I could not resist, but I stopped as soon as the words had escaped me: to upbraid, was no part of my purpose.

"It is in vain," I said, "to think to move me by any words, however hard. I have nothing more to say. Let me go, Malcolm;" and I turned and fled from the room.

PART II.

Then began as hard a struggle as any woman could have been called upon to endure. My husband went up to town that same day, and Parliament sat late that year. During all that time, he never wrote to me, nor, save from a casual notice of him in the papers, did I know any thing of his movements. The intolerable suspense and misery of such a separation may be conceived. My love for him, indeed, was no mere dutiful regard, but of that profound yet passionate nature which men of his stern and reticent character seem calculated, by a strange contrariety, to excite. Add to this, that I knew myself to be exposed to the pitying wonder and suspicion of the world at large.

Mr. Anstruther's character stood above imputation, but I at the best was but a successful *parvenue*, and had at length no doubt stumbled into some atrocious fault beyond even his infatuation to overlook. The very servants of the household whispered and marvelled about me; it was inevitable that they should do so, but all this added bitterness to anguish.

Worst of all, there was a wistful look in Florry's childish eyes, and a pathos in her voice as she pressed against my side, to stroke my cheek, and say: "Poor mamma!" which almost broke my heart with mingled grief and shame. She, too, had learned in her nursery that her mother had become an object of compassion.

It was the deep sense of pain and humiliation which my child's pity excited, which aroused me to make some attempt to relieve my position. I sat down, and wrote to my husband. I wrote quietly and temperately, though there was almost the delirium of despair in my heart. I had proved that an appeal to his feelings would be in vain, and I therefore directed my arguments to his justice.

I represented to him briefly that his prolonged neglect and desertion would soon irretrievably place me in the eyes of the world in the position of a guilty wife, and that for my own sake, but still more for the sake of our daughter, I protested against such injustice. I told him he was blighting two lives, and entreated him, if forgiveness was still impossible, at least to keep up the semblance of respect. I proposed to join him in London immediately, or to remain where I was, on condition of his returning home as soon as Parliament was prorogued.

I waited with unspeakable impatience for a reply to this letter, and the next post brought it. How I blessed my husband's clemency for this relief! My trembling hands could scarcely break the seal; the consideration of the sad difference between the past and present seemed to overwhelm me—it was not thus I had been accustomed to open my husband's letters, feeling like a criminal condemned to read his own warrant of condemnation.

The letter was brief, and ran thus:—

"As the late events between us have been the subject of my intense and incessant deliberation since we parted, I am able, Ellinor, to reply to your letter at once. I consent to return and attempt the life of hollow deception you demand, under the expectation that you will soon become convinced of its impracticability, and will then, I conclude, be willing to consent to the formal separation which it is still my wish and purpose to effect."

"Never!" I said, crushing the hard letter between my hands, and then my passion, long suppressed, burst forth, and throwing myself on my knees by my bedside, I wept and groaned in agony of soul. Oh! I had hoped till then—hoped that time might have softened him, that the past might have pleaded with him for the absolution of that one transgression. Had my sin been indeed so great that the punishment was so intolerable? And then I thought it all over again, as I had done a thousand times before in that dreary interval, weighing my temptations against my offence, and trying to place myself in my husband's position. I did not wish to justify it: it was a gross deception, a deliberate falseness; but then I was willing to prostrate myself in the dust, both before God and my husband, and to beg forgiveness in the lowest terms of humiliation and penitence. But the pardon granted me by the Divine, was steadily refused by the human, judge—against his hard impenetrability I might dash my bleeding heart in vain. What should I do? What should I do? Which was the path of duty? And frail and passionate as I was, how could I hold on in such a rugged way? Had I not better succumb?—suffer myself to be put away, as he desired, and close the door of hope on what was left of life? My child—he said he would give me up my child. Then resolution arose renewed. For that child's sake, I would not yield. I could not endure the thought of separating her from such a father's love, care, and protection, and of chastening with sorrow and humiliation her opening girlhood. No; with God's help she should yet honor and revere her mother. However my husband judged me, that one fault had not cut me off from all moral effort hereafter. I would not be vanquished by it. I would, as I had said, keep my post as wife, insist, if need be, on external forms, and leave no means untried of patience, meekness, and womanly art, to melt down the iron barrier between us.

I should weary the reader if I detailed all the minute plans I formed, but at last I rose up from the prayers by which I strove to strengthen and sanctify my purpose with a firm heart and new-born hope of success. That evening, I sent for Florry to keep me company in the drawing-room; I told her her favorite stories, played her her favorite tunes, and joined with her in singing a simple evening hymn, which was her supreme delight. Then I took her up to the nursery myself, and bade her good-night with as much of the serene feeling of old as perhaps I could ever hope to know again.

I also, holding my husband's letter in my hand, told the assembled servants I expected their master home to-morrow, and gave the necessary orders in such a natural and collected manner as must have gone far to disarm their suspicions. Then the long night—then the expected day. I knew the hour when he must necessarily arrive, and, taking Florry with me, I went to a certain part of the grounds which commanded a view of the public road. I was externally calm; the morning's discipline had made me that, but the subdued excitement was intense. Florry ran and chattered by my side as children do, little guessing, poor innocents, the cruel strain they often make on their mothers' patience. It chanced, as sometimes happens, that the very intensity of our anxiety caused us to miss our object; the train was evidently behind time, and our attention, so long kept at full stretch, began to slacken, so that when Florry, who had wandered to some little distance from me, espied the carriage, it was so near the park-gates, that there was no chance of our reaching the house before it. I was vexed at my purpose being thus partially defeated, and, taking the child's hand, hurried back by the shortest route.

Mr. Anstruther was waiting us in the accustomed room. Still holding Florry's hand, I went in to face the dreaded meeting. The first glance at his face nearly overcame me, he looked so worn and harassed: true, that might have been from parliamentary hours and hard committee-work, but it is a plea a woman's heart can rarely withstand. Florry ran into his arms, talking eagerly of how glad we were to see him, and how dull poor mamma had been without him, and the momentary diversion gave me time to rally my failing calmness. "We are very glad you are come home, Malcolm," I said, at last, approaching him, and laying my hand on his. "Are you very tired? Do not trouble to dress before dinner to-day."

Perhaps my self-possession was overdone, so difficult is it in such cases to keep the golden mean; for I saw the unusual color mount even to his forehead, and he replied in a hurried voice, as he slightly returned the pressure of my hand: "I could scarcely sit down to table in this state—I shall not keep you waiting long;" and with Florry in his arms—I could see how he tightened his embrace of the child—he left the room.

I did not sit down and weep, although I was sick at heart. I had imagined it would be something like this, and had fortified myself to endure it. I sat there thinking, till I heard him come down-stairs, and then I went into the drawing-room. Immediately on my entrance dinner was announced, and he offered his arm to lead me to the room, just as he had always been accustomed to do when we were alone. There was no hesitation, no perceptible difference in his manner; I saw he had made up his mind to do it. During dinner, we talked but little, but even in days of old he had been wont to be absent and taciturn. Florry came in with the dessert, and her sweet prattle was felt to be a gracious relief by both. I soon rose and took her away with me, keeping her with me, and amusing her with talk and music until her bedtime. My husband joined me at the usual time, and though he did not voluntarily converse, he replied to any thing I said without apparent constraint. Before the servants, his manners were scrupulously as of old; indeed, so undemonstrative was his natural character, that it required no very great effort for him to appear the same. I indeed felt a radical difference, which cut me to the heart: the hard tone, the averted or chilly glance convinced me of the reality of our altered relations. Could I live such a life as this?—so near, yet so far off. I had a vague perception that every day we spent like this would make the separation more complete and fatal. Had I not better make one last attempt, before I was chilled into silence and fear of him? Perhaps he resented the dignified and all but peremptory tone I had assumed in my letter, and was still to be moved by entreaty and penitence. Acting on the vague hope, I put down the work on which I had tried to engage myself, and went up to the sofa on which he was lying.

"Malcolm," I said, leaning over the head of it, partly to sustain my trembling limbs, partly to secure a position of advantage, "is this the way we are to live together? I cannot resign myself to it without a word, without knowing better what are your feelings towards me. Am I to believe you will never forgive me? Do you hate me?"

He rose impatiently from his recumbent attitude, so as to be able to look into my face. "What do you mean by forgiveness, Ellinor?" was his answer—"the old love and esteem restored? Your own sense must convince you you ask an impossibility—a broken mirror can't be pieced again. Don't let us rake up the miserable ashes of our feud. I am here at your desire, willing to maintain your credit in the eyes of society. I have yielded so far out of regard for our little girl, of a solemn consideration of my own marriage-vows, and your exemplary performance of a wife's external duty. Do your duty now, Ellinor, and obey me when I charge you not to urge me on this topic again; it is unwise."

"This night shall be the last time," I said; "so suffer me to ask you one more question. Do you doubt my assurances of affection for yourself? Can you believe, in the face of the evidence of all our married life, that, however I deceived you in the beginning, I did not soon bring to a wife's duty a wife's entire and passionate devotion?"

"Ellinor," he exclaimed with sudden excitement, "you are mad to torment me thus! You compel me to say what had better remain unsaid. I repudiate your boasted love, which you parade as if it were the triumph of virtue. Had it been mine, as I believed and you swore it was before God, it should have been the crown and glory of my life; as it is, I care nothing for a sentiment provoked by habit, and cherished as a point of calculated duty. One word more: you think me cruelly intolerant, but I must follow the bent of my nature. Some lies I could forgive—or even, perhaps, some grosser sins—but yours cheated me into an irrevocable act, and defrauded me of the best and strongest feelings of my nature. Do I hate you? No, I cannot hate Florry's mother and my own intimate and cherished companion; but I hate myself for having been befooled so grossly, and almost loathe the wealth and its accessories for which you perjured your soul."

I was silent, but it was by a powerful effort. I could scarcely restrain myself, with all my power of self-control, from saying,

"Now that I understand you fully, let us part; I could not brook the mockery of intercourse." But the thought of Florry closed my struggling lips. "For her sake, for her sake," I repeated to myself. "The last hope, the last, the last chance of happiness is gone, but duty remains." I looked up at my husband, deadly pale, I knew, but calm. "Are you resolved," I asked, "to separate from me eventually? I claim it from your honor to answer me that question now."

"I care little," he said bitterly. "The sharpness of the sting must abate some day, and we shall become indifferent, like our neighbors; meanwhile, the effort may be salutary. No," he added haughtily, as he perceived I was not satisfied with the reply, "I am willing to pledge my word that I will never force you into a separation on this account. So long as you think proper to claim my protection, it is yours, only we must avoid such scenes as these;" and so the case stood between us.

From that time, my life became a hard monotony. To all appearance, there was no change in our relations; we went the same round in social life as of old, and, as I have said before, my husband's natural character gave little scope for self-betrayal. Occasionally, some outside comments reached us, but they were generally expressive of the belief that Mr. Anstruther's temper was becoming more morose than ever, and of pity for the poor wife who was allied to it. He certainly did become more irritable and exacting. I could see daily the bitter effects that his disappointment in my sincerity produced, how his fine nature was growing warped and soured. It was not so much towards myself that these effects were manifested—he kept too rigid a control over our relations; but it grieved me to notice it in his impatience with his inferiors, and even with our little tender Florry, and in his cynical and cruel judgment of the world at large. He had always been very much absorbed in political affairs, and ambitious for distinction, but now he seemed to throw heart and soul without reserve into the arena, and to struggle for the stakes with the eagerness of a gambler. There had ceased to be any communion between us. In past days, hopes and schemes had been discussed with me, and I was proud to believe my influence had often availed with him for good. I cannot describe the intensity of my misery at this time. Not to speak of alienation and mistrust in the midst of daily intercourse, which alone contains almost the bitterness of death, I saw myself the cause of deterioration in one dearer to me than life, and He who meted my punishment to my offence knows that no heavier cross could have been laid upon me. Once or twice, I again attempted expostulation, but I soon learned to desist; it was of no avail, but to provoke some hard reply, which would otherwise have remained unspoken. Then I turned to my daughter: it was for her sake I endured this life, this daily martyrdom, and I would not miss my reward. I devoted myself to her education, so far as my numerous avocations allowed, for I was scrupulous in the performance of all the duties of my station, and in any which my husband would suffer me still to perform for him. I strove with intense anxiety to make her attractive to her father, and to cultivate her affection and esteem for him. That he loved her passionately, I knew, but, as was his wont, he manifested the feeling but little; perhaps in this case he was checked by her inevitable preference for her mother, or by the difficulty of ever having her to himself. To me she was the one solace and spur of existence, and life began to brighten when, resigned to suffer myself, I dreamed and planned her future.

Thus, more than a year passed on monotonously; fruitlessly, so far as I could see, for my husband was as far off from me as ever. Sometimes, indeed, I hoped I had extorted some portion of respect from him by the sustained performance of my routine of duty, but his heart seemed turned to stone.

At last the gloomy depth was stirred. O God! I had prayed for the movement of the healing angel's wing, not for a stroke of judgment!

One evening during the session, I was sitting up awaiting his return from the House. I was not accustomed to do so, but on this occasion, I was deeply interested in the result of the night's debate, and added to that, I was uneasy about Florry, who had been slightly ailing all day, and seemed increasingly restless as the evening advanced. When he came in, he looked surprised to see me up, for it was already nearly three o'clock in the morning, and I could see that he seemed wearied and annoyed.

"You are anxious, I suppose," he said, "for the news I bring. Well, the ministers are thrown out."

I knew he, and, indeed, the country in general, had been quite unprepared for such a result, and that personally it was a severe mortification to him. As I involuntarily looked at him with an expression of earnest concern I hardly ventured to express, I saw his face soften. Perhaps in that moment of vexation, he yearned for the sympathy of old. Should I dare to risk another appeal?

"Malcolm," I said; but at the now unfamiliar name, his brow clouded again, and I finished my speech with some measured expressions of regret. I knew I should damage my cause if I were to attempt to press into my service a momentary weakness he was ashamed to feel. I could not, however, command my feelings sufficiently to speak of Florry, and after leaving him, I flew up-stairs to my child's room, and putting down my candle, sunk on my knees by her bedside. Oh, how my heart ached! I felt this life was killing me, and that one of my moments of abandonment was come. Before, however, I gave full vent to my tears, I paused midway, as it were, to look at Florry, and that look dried them up. I felt my cheek blanch, my eyes start; I felt —who has not felt it?—a premonitory horror chill my blood. I had left her pale and restless an hour before, now her face was tinged with a crimson heat, her lips dry and parted, and she was moaning heavily. I touched her burning hand, her burning brow, and the shadow of that awful calamity seemed to fall before me. I did not moan, I did not even appeal; despair straitened my heart.

Mr. Anstruther I knew was still up. I went down stairs with a strange quietness, and re-entered the room.

"I do not wish to alarm you," I said, and my own voice had a strange sound to me, "but Florry is not well. She has been ailing all day, but her appearance now frightens me. Will you send some one for a physician at once?"

I waited for no reply, but went back to the room. The fire in the grate was laid, but not lighted; I kindled it. I changed my evening dress for a morning-gown, doing all mechanically, as if under a spell I could not resist. Then I sat down by the bedside to watch my child and await the doctor. I seemed to hold all my faculties in suspense; no tear must blind my eye, no tremor unnerve my hand, until this agony had reached its crisis: then let life and hope go out together.

My husband and the doctor came in after what seemed to me an intolerable interval, but at first I only saw but one. Who knows not in such cases how the very soul seems hanging on the physician's first glance, drinking life or death from it? I drank death. The steady, professional gaze did not deceive me, but the stroke was beyond my taxed endurance, and I fell senseless on the floor.

Thank God, it was but a brief weakness. For the few days that that sweet life was left to me, I held my post unconscious of fatigue, enabled to comfort and sustain, and even smile upon my darling through her brief struggle with death. God bowed my stubborn heart, and strengthened me with the might of submission. I seemed, in the strong light of this fiery trial, to see the past more clearly, to acknowledge that I had not humbled myself sufficiently under the chastisement of my own sin.

It was midnight when she died. I was holding her in my arms, hushed and grief-stricken, when I saw that unspeakable change pass over the sweet face which tells the sinking heart the awful hour is come. Her laboring breath fluttered on my cheek, the look of love that still lingered in the glazing eyes fixed upon my face died out, and I was childless.

My husband was standing at the foot of the bed, watching the scene with an agony all the keener that he suffered no expression of it to escape, but as the last faint struggle ceased, and the baby-head fell prone upon my breast, I saw the strong frame quiver, and drops of perspiration start upon his forehead.

"God forgive me," he said in a stifled whisper, "for every harsh word spoken to that angel child!" Then as his eyes fell, as if involuntarily, upon me, the expression of stern anguish softened for a moment to one of pitying tenderness. "Poor Ellinor!—poor mother!" he added, "you think me a hard man, but God is my witness, I would have saved you that little life at the cost of my own."

"It would have been but a cruel compromise," I answered; "and yet—O my darling, how I have loved you!"

My husband had turned away a moment, as if to pace the room, but at the sound of my cry of irrepressible anguish, he came back hastily to the bedside, and bending over me, tried to separate me gently from the dead child in my arms.

As I felt the touch of his hand, his breath upon my cheek, caressing, warm as of old, it recalled, even in that moment of supreme bereavement, the passionate yearning of my heart, and yielding to the uncontrollable impulse, I threw my arms around his neck.

"Only give me back what is in your power," I cried—"give me back your love and trust—our old happiness, Malcolm, and even the death of our child will not seem too hard a sacrifice!"

There was a moment's breathless pause, then he raised me in his arms, and strained me to his heart in a close, vehement embrace.

"God forgive me," he said, "for what I have made you suffer! If your love has survived my long intolerance, I may well trust you, Ellinor. If I have the power left to comfort you, be to me again all, and more than all that I remember in the sweet past. A hundred times during the last few melancholy days have I been on the point of confessing my injustice, and entreating your forgiveness; only it seemed to me a mean thing to take advantage of the softness of sorrow. Life is not bearable without you, Ellinor: only satisfy me once more that I have not worn out your heart—that it is not magnanimity, but love."

I did satisfy him. We began henceforth a new life, chastened, indeed, by the shadow of a little grave, but a life, I trust, humbler and more blessed than the old past had been.

Any improvement in the manufacture of iron, whereby its quality may be enhanced or its price diminished, is now of more than ordinary value to this country. The most recent practical advance of this sort consists in the easy conversion of impure cast iron into good malleable wrought iron, by adding carbonate of soda to it in a fused state. The reason of the inferiority of crude pig to wrought iron consists chiefly in the impurities (silicum, sulphur, phosphorus, carbon, etc.) which the former contains. When the iron containing these is melted for some time with carbonate of soda, the latter dissolves nearly all the extraneous matter away, and leaves the metal in a state of comparative purity. A lump of common pig iron, very impure and nearly as brittle as glass, was treated in this manner. After removal from the crucible, and hammering at a red heat to remove the adhering slag, it was of such excellent quality that it could be drawn into rods and forged either hot or cold, whilst the granular fracture of the cast iron was replaced by a fibrous structure. The iron likewise resisted the action of acids better than the ordinary malleable metal, and in other respects acted as if it were of extreme purity. There are practical difficulties in the way of treating large bulks of cast iron in this way, owing to the length of time likely to be occupied in the conversion of a mass of any considerable thickness, and the infusible nature of the resulting metal; but for small castings the process is perfect, the action of the soda imparting to them great toughness in a very short time, and rendering them not liable to fracture. The amount of carbonate of soda used is stated to be inconsiderable.—*London Review.*

Experiments on the Influence of Air in promoting the so-called Spontaneous Generation.—Every one is acquainted with some curious experiments that were made some time ago by Loewel, showing that supersaturated solutions of different salts crystallise immediately the air is let in upon them; but not so if the air be previously filtered through asbestos, or be calcined before it comes in contact with the saline solution. M. Terreil has just made known to the Academy of Sciences at Paris the result of some experiments similar to those of Loewel; but instead of water supersaturated with some salt, he used some organic liquid, such as urine, which is extremely favorable to the production of those myriads of microscopic beings that are always found to be present in liquids containing organic matter undergoing decomposition. Now the author has shown that when the air that covers such a liquid has been filtered through cotton or asbestos, or has been calcined before it is allowed to lie upon the liquid, no microscopic animals or vegetables are developed, even when the experiment lasts for months together. On the contrary, if air in its natural state be allowed to come in contact with the liquid, the latter is very soon covered with mildew, or other inferior fungi.—*London Review.*

From Blackwood's Magazine.

THE ORIGIN OF SPECIES.*

A NEW SONG.

HAVE you heard of this question the doctors among,
Whether all living things from a Monad have sprung?
This has lately been said, and it now shall be sung,
Which nobody can deny.

Not one or two ages sufficed for the feat,
It required a few millions the change to complete;
But now the thing's done, and it looks rather neat,
Which nobody can deny.

The original Monad, our great-great-grandsire,
To little or nothing at first did aspire;
But at last to have offspring it took a desire,
Which nobody can deny.

This Monad becoming a father or mother,
By budding or bursting, produced such another;
And shortly there followed a sister or brother,
Which nobody can deny.

But Monad no longer designates them well—
They're a cluster of molecules now, or a cell;
But which of the two, doctors only can tell,
Which nobody can deny.

These beings, increasing, grew buoyant with life,
And each to itself was both husband and wife;
And at first, strange to say, the two lived without strife,
Which nobody can deny.

But such crowding together soon troublesome grew,
And they thought a division of labor would do;
So their sexual system was parted in two,
Which nobody can deny.

Thus Plato supposes that, severed by fate,
Human halves run about, each in search of its mate,
Never pleased till they gain their original state,
Which nobody can deny.

Excrescences fast were now trying to shoot;
Some put out a feeler, some put out a foot;
Some set up a mouth, and some struck down a root,
Which nobody can deny.

Some, wishing to walk, manufactured a limb;
Some rigged out a fin, with a purpose to swim;
Some opened an eye, some remained dark and dim,
Which nobody can deny.

See, hydras and sponges and star-fishes breed,
And flies, fleas, and lobsters in order succeed,
While ichthyosauruses follow the lead,
Which nobody can deny.

From reptiles and fishes to birds we ascend,
And quadrupeds next their dimensions extend,
Till we rise up to monkeys and men—where we end,
Which nobody can deny.

Some creatures are bulky, some creatures are small,
As nature sends food for the few or for all;
And the weakest, we know, ever go to the wall,
Which nobody can deny.

A deer with a neck that is longer by half
Than the rest of its family's (try not to laugh),
By stretching and stretching, becomes a Giraffe,
Which nobody can deny.

A very tall pig, with a very long nose,
Sends forth a proboscis quite down to his toes;
And he then by the name of an Elephant goes,
Which nobody can deny.

The four-footed beast that we now call a Whale,
Held his hind-legs so close that they grew to a tail,
Which he uses for threshing the sea like a flail,
Which nobody can deny.

Pouters, tumblers, and fantails are from the same source;
The racer and hack may be traced to one Horse:
So Men were developed from Monkeys, of course,
Which nobody can deny.

An Ape with a pliable thumb and big brain,
When the gift of the gab he had managed to gain,
As a Lord of Creation established his reign,
Which nobody can deny.

But I'm sadly afraid, if we do not take care,
A relapse to low life may our prospects impair;
So of beastly propensities let us beware,
Which nobody can deny.

Their lofty position our children may lose,
And, reduced to all-fours, must then narrow their views;
Which would wholly unfit them for filling our shoes,
Which nobody can deny.

Their vertebræ next might be taken away,
When they'd sink to a shell-fish, or spider, some day,
Or the pitiful part of a polypus play,
Which nobody can deny.

Thus losing humanity's nature and name,
And descending through varying stages of shame,
They'd return to the Monad, from which we all came,
Which nobody can deny.

[The foregoing lyric may be better understood by a few condensed extracts from the two works which have suggested it. We venture to think that the similarity of opinions exhibited in those

* *The Origin of Species, by means of Natural Selection.* By Charles Darwin, M.A. 1859.
The Temple of Nature; or, the Origin of Society. A Poem. By Erasmus Darwin, M.D. 1803.

works is not accidental, but is an example of the recurrence of a family type.

From the "Origin of Species."

"It has been asked by the opponents of such views as I hold, how, for instance, a land carnivorous animal could have been converted into one with aquatic habits? I think such difficulties have very little weight. Look at the family of squirrels. I can see no difficulty, more especially under changing conditions of life, in the continued preservation of individuals, with fuller and fuller flank-membranes, each modification being useful, each being propagated, until, by the accumulated effects of this process of natural selection, a perfect so-called flying squirrel was produced. It is conceivable that flying-fish, which now glide far through the air, slightly rising and turning by the aid of their fluttering fins, might have been modified into perfectly winged animals. In North America the black bear was seen by Hearne swimming for hours with widely open mouth, thus catching, like a whale, insects in the water. Even in so extreme a case as this, if the supply of insects were constant, and if better adapted competitors did not already exist in the country, I can see no difficulty in a race of bears being rendered, by natural selection, more and more aquatic in their structure and habits, with larger and larger mouths, till a creature was produced as monstrous as a whale."

"If we must compare the eye to an optical instrument, we ought, in imagination, to take a thick layer of transparent tissue, with a nerve sensitive to light beneath, and then suppose every part of this layer to be continually changing slowly in density, so as to separate into layers of different densities and thicknesses, placed at different distances from each other, and with the surfaces of each layer slowly changing in form. Let this process go on for millions on millions of years, and during each year on millions of individuals of many kinds, and may we not believe that a living optical instrument might thus be formed, as superior to one of glass as the works of the Creator are to those of man?"

"I believe that animals have descended from at most only four or five progenitors, and plants from an equal or lesser number. Analogy would lead me one step further. I should infer from analogy that probably all the organic beings which have ever lived on this earth have descended from some one primordial form, into which life was first breathed."

From the "Temple of Nature."

"Nursed by warm sunbeams in primeval caves,
Organic life began beneath the waves.
First Monas moves, an unconnected point,
Plays round the drop without a limb or joint;
Then Vibrio waves," etc.

"These, as successive generations bloom,
New powers acquire, and larger limbs assume,
Whence countless groups of vegetation spring,
And breathing realms of fin and feet and wing."

"Hence, ere vitality, as time revolves,
Leaves the cold organ, or the mass dissolves,
The reproduction of the living Ens,
From sires to sons, unknown to sex, commence.
Till as, ere long, successive buds decay,
And insect-shoals successive pass away,
Increasing wants the pregnant parents vex,
With the fond wish to form a softer sex."

NOTE. — "It would appear that vegetables and animals were at first propagated by solitary generation, and afterwards by hermaphrodite sexual generation; — but the larger and more perfect animals are now propagated by (separate) sexual reproduction only."

"The Mosaic history of Paradise and of Adam and Eve has been thought by some to be a sacred allegory,—and that this part of the history where Eve is said to have been made from a rib of Adam might have been a hieroglyphic design of the Egyptian philosophers, showing their opinion that mankind was originally of both sexes united, and was afterwards divided into males and females; an opinion in later times held by Plato, and, I believe, by Aristotle, and which must have arisen from profound inquiries into the original state of animal existence."

"It has been supposed by some that mankind were formerly quadrupeds as well as hermaphrodites; these philosophers, with Buffon and Helvetius, seem to imagine that mankind arose from one family of monkeys on the banks of the Mediterranean, who accidentally had learned to use the adductor pollicis, or that strong muscle which constitutes the ball of the thumb, and draws the point of it to meet the points of the fingers, which common monkeys do not; and that this muscle gradually increased in size, strength, and activity, in successive generations, and, by this improved use of the sense of touch, that monkeys acquired clear ideas, and gradually became men."

"It may appear too bold, in the present state of our knowledge on this subject, to suppose that all vegetables and animals now existing were originally derived from the smallest microscopic ones, formed by spontaneous vitality, and that they have, by innumerable reproductions during innumerable centuries of time, gradually acquired the size, strength, and excellence of form and faculties which they now possess."]

From All the Year Round.

THE FAMILY AT FENHOUSE.

I WAS to be a governess; but I could not obtain a situation. My poor mother had been insane for many years before her death; one of my brothers was deaf and dumb, another was deformed, while none of us showed either health or vigor. In a word, there was no escaping the fact that we had the seeds of some terrible disease sown thickly among us, and that, as a family, we were unhealthy and unsafe. I was the eldest and the strongest, both in mind and body, but that was not saying much. I was always what I am now, tall and gaunt, with the spasmodic affection which you see in my face, as nervous as I am now, and nearly as thin; short-sighted, which made my manners doubly awkward, and they would always have been awkward from my nervousness and ungainly figure; and with an unnaturally acute hearing, often followed by attacks of unconsciousness, which sometimes lasted many hours, and rendered me, for the time, dead to all outward life.

Unpromising as our family condition was, when my father died and left us destitute, it was absolutely necessary that those of us at all capable should get something to do, and that the rest should be cared for by charity. The last we found more easy to be accomplished than the first. Many kind hands were stretched forward to help the helpless of us, but few to strengthen the weak. However, after a time, they were all settled in some way or other, and were at last secured from starvation, while I, who had been considered the most hopeful, was still unprovided for, looking vainly for a situation either as governess or companion. Both were equally difficult to procure. On the one side my manners and appearance were against me, on the other, my family history. As I could not deny my inheritance of disease and insanity, mothers, naturally enough, would not trust me with their children, and I was not sufficiently attractive for a companion. People who can afford companions want something pliant, bright, animated, pleasant. No one would look at my unlovely face, or hear the harsh tones of my voice—I know how harsh they are—and pay me to be an ornament or pleasure to their lives. So, as I tell you, I was refused by every one, until I began to despair of success, and without blaming any, to understand that the world was too hard for me, and that I had no portion in it.

As my last venture, I answered an advertisement in the Times for a companion to a lady in delicate health, living in the country. My letter was replied to in a bold manly hand, and a meeting arranged. I was to go down that next day by train to a place about twenty miles from London, and find my way from a certain railway station named, two miles across the country—conveyances not to be had—to a village called Fenhouse-green. A mile farther would bring me to Fenhouse itself, "the seat of Mr. and Mrs. Brand." The note was couched in a curiously sharp, peremptory style, and pompously worded. I remember, too, that it was written on a broad sheet of coarse letter paper, and sealed with what looked at first sight to be a large coat of arms, but which, when examined, proved to be only a make-believe. With my habit of making up histories out of every incident that came before me, I decided that the writer was a military man, wealthy and high born; and that, about to leave on foreign service, he wished to place his young and beautiful wife in careful hands so as to ensure her pleasant companionship during his absence. I made quite a romance out of that peremptory letter with its broad margin and imposing seal.

"They will never take me when they have seen me!" I sighed, as I settled myself in the third-class carriage which I shared with three soldiers' wives and a couple of Irish laborers, and I wished that I could have exchanged my fate and person with the meanest among them. Though they were poor, they were not under a curse, as I was; though man had not uplifted them, Fortune had not crushed them as she had crushed me. I was weeping bitterly behind my veil, overpowered with my own sadness and despair, and almost decided on not going farther to meet only with fresh disappointment, when the train stopped at my station, and I let myself drift down the tide of circumstance, and once more dared my chance.

Asking my way to Fenhouse-green, much to the astonishment, apparently, of the solitary station-master, I struck into a rugged by-road, which he said would take me there. The two miles' walk seemed as if it would never end. The road was lonely, and the country desolate, ugly, and monotonous; nothing but a broad ragged waste, without a tree or an autumn flower to break the dead dreariness of the scene. I did not meet a living creature until I came to an unwholesome-looking collection of cottages, covered with foul eruptions of fungi and mildew starting out like a leprosy upon the walls. Where the village-green should have been, was a swamp, matted with confervæ. It was a place to remember in one's dreams, from the neglect and desolation, the hopeless poverty and feverish squalor of all about.

If this was the village of which the writer had spoken so pompously as his property, and of which I had imagined all that was charming and picturesque, it did not argue much for what had to come; and I began to feel that I had painted too brightly, and, perhaps, had ranked my chance too low. The place frightened me. I went through, glad to escape the stupid wonder of the pallid women and children who came crowding to the doors, as though a stranger were a rare and not too welcome sight among them. Indeed, some seemed to have a kind of warning terror in their looks when they pointed in the direction of the House, as they called it; and one old witch, lifting her stick, cried, "Surely, surely, not there belike!" in a tone which froze my blood. However, it was too late now to recede; so, full of an indescribable terror, I went on my way, until I arrived at Fenhouse, where my future was to lie.

It was a lonely house, standing back from the road, completely shut in, in front, by a tangled shrubbery, while at the rear stretched a close dark wood with a trailing undergrowth of briers and thorns. The gate hung broken, supported by one hinge only; the garden was a mass of weeds and rubbish; the flower-beds overgrown with grass and nettles; and what had once been rose-trees and flowering shrubs, left to wither and die, stifled by bindweed and coarser growths. The house was of moderate size, two-storied, and roomy, but so neglected and uncared for, that it looked more bleakly desolate than any thing I had ever seen before. My dream of the young and beautiful wife had vanished, and I felt as if about to be ushered into the presence of some fantastic horror or deadly crime. The wet leaves plashed beneath my feet, and sent up their clouds of autumn odor—the odor of death: unsightly insects and loathsome reptiles glided before me with a strange familiarity, which rendered them yet more loathly; not a bird twittered through the naked branches of the trees. The whole place had a wild, weird, haunted look; and, shivering with dread at I knew not what, I rang the rusty bell, hanging lonely out of the chipped and broken socket. The peal startled me, and brought out a small terrier, which came running round me, barking furiously and shrilly. The door was opened by a ragged, slip-shod servant-girl, and I was shown into a poorly furnished room, which seemed to be a kind of library; to judge at least by the open bookcase, thinly stocked with shabby books. The room was close and musty; the fire in the grate was heaped up carefully towards the middle, and the sides blocked in by bricks. It was a mean fire: a stingy, shabby fire.

After waiting for some time, a gentleman and lady came in. She was a pale, weak, hopeless-looking woman, very tall, fair, and slender, with a narrow forehead, lustreless light blue eyes with no eyelashes, scanty hair, straw-colored ill-defined eyebrows, and very thin pale lips. She was slightly deformed, and carried her arms thrust far back from the elbow, the hands left to dangle nervelessly from the wrists. She stooped, and was dressed in a limp, faded cotton gown, every way too scanty and too cold for the season. When she came in, her eyes were bent towards the soiled, gray carpet, and she never raised them, or made the least kind of salutation, but sat down on a chair near the window, and began to unravel a strip of muslin. The gentleman was short and thick-set, very active and determined looking, with dark hair turning now to gray, a thick but evenly cut moustache, joining his bushy whiskers, the large, square heavy chin left bare; overhanging eyebrows, with small, restless, passionate eyes beneath; in his whole face and bearing an expression of temper amounting to ferocity.

He spoke to me peremptorily and haughtily; asked me my name, age, family condition, previous history, as if he had been examining me on oath, scarcely waiting for my answers, and all the while fixing me with those small, angry eyes till I felt dazed and restless, as creatures under torture. Then he said, abruptly,—

"You have a strange look—a scared look, I may call it. How have you come by it?"

"I am of a nervous temperament, sir," I answered, pulling at the ends of my gloves.

"Nothing else? Nothing hereditary?"

"Yes, sir," said I, as steadily as I could; "there is hereditary misfortune among us."

"Father or mother?"

"Mother."

"Ah!" said the man, rubbing his moustache, and looking at me with eyes all aflame; "so much the nearer and more dangerous."

"I am not dangerous," I said, a little too humbly, perhaps; but that man was completely subduing me. "I am nervous, but I have no worse tendency."

He laughed.

"Perhaps not," he said, with a sneer that made my blood curdle; "no one ever has. Don't you know that all maniacs are philosophers, when they are not kings and queens? Shall I take you on trust, then, according to your own estimate of yourself, or discharge you at once, according to mine?"

"I think I may be trusted, sir," I answered, looking everywhere but into his face.

"What do you think, Mrs. Brand?" he said, turning to the pale woman unravelling her strip of muslin, and who had not, as I thought, looked at me once yet.

"She is ugly," said she, in a dull, monotonous voice; "I don't like ugly people."

Mr. Brand laughed again.

"Never mind that, Mrs. Brand; goodness don't go by looks, does it Miss—Miss what? Are you a name or a number?"

"Miss Erfurt."

"Oh, yes! I forgot—Jane Erfurt—I remember now, and a queer name it is, too. Does it, Miss Jane Erfurt?"

"Not always, sir," I said, moving restlessly.

"Well, Mrs. Brand, what do you say?"

"She is ugly, and George will not like her," said the lady, in the same half-alive manner.

"Who the deuce cares!" shouted Mr. Brand, flaming with passion on the instant. "Let him like it or not, who cares for a stupid fool, or for what he thinks? That, for his liking!" snapping his fingers insolently.

The lady's face grew a shade paler; but, beyond a furtive, terrified glance at her husband, she took no notice of his words. He then turned abruptly to me, and told me that I was to hold myself engaged to perform the duties of companion to Mrs. Brand, and that I was to enter on those duties early next week.

"But without the lady's consent?" said I, too weak to resist, and too nervous to accept.

She put away her muslin and rose. "Mr. Brand is master here," she said: "do what he tells you: it saves trouble."

The week after I went to Fenhouse, as the companion of Mrs. Brand.

The first day's dinner was a strange affair. After we had seated ourselves, to what was a very scanty supply, there lounged in a youth of about seventeen: a heavy, full-blooded, lumpish being, with a face devoid of intelligence, but more animal than imbecile; not specially good tempered, but not vicious, a mere idle, eating-and-drinking clown, scarcely raised above the level of a dog or a horse, and without even their instinctive emotions. What an unwholesome, unnatural circle we made! I longed for a little healthy life among us, and turned with a feeling of envy and relief to the commonplace servant-maid; who, if not intellectual, was at the least more in accord with pure ordinary life than we.

There was ill-blood between Mr. Brand and Master George, as the boy was called; and I soon understood why. His mother's only son by a former marriage, and heir of the neglected lands lying round Fenhouse, he stood in the way of his step-father, whose influence over his wife was supreme, and who, but for the boy, would have absolute possession of every thing. He had married for money, and had been balked of half his prize. I used often to wonder that the two were not afraid to trust themselves in the hands of one so passionate and unscrupulous; but, though Mrs. Brand was undisguisedly afraid of her husband, and the boy was not too stupid to understand that he was hated, and why, neither seemed to look forward to evil days. I do not think that they had mind enough to look to the future in hope or dread. Mother and son loved each other, with the mute instinctive love of dumb animals—a love in which both would be helpless to save if bad times came. They were not much together, and they seldom spoke when they met; but they sat close to each other, always in the same place and on the same chairs, and Mrs. Brand unravelled her eternal slips of muslin, while her son gathered up the threads and thrust them into a canvas bag.

I had been there a fortnight, and I never saw either of them employed in any thing else; and I never heard half a dozen words pass between them. It was a silent house at all times; and, more than this, it was a house full of hate. Save this dumb-animal kind of love between the two, not a ray of even kindly feeling existed among any of us. The servant was the mark for every one's ill-temper, while I stood out as a kind of pariah among them all, not even dignified by active dislike. I was shunned, and could not understand why I was there at all. The lady never spoke to me, not even to say good-morning; she gave me no duties, but she forbade me no employment. I was free to do what I liked, provided I did not make my existence too manifest to her, and did not speak to her husband or Master George. If by chance any thing like a conversation began—for Mr. Brand had his talkative moods in a violent, angry kind of way—she used to order me out of the room, in just the same tone as she used to speak to the dog. If I remonstrated, as I did once, her only answer was, "You can go if you like; *I* did not hire you."

One thing especially troubled me. It troubled me because, like all morbidly imaginative people, any thing of a mystery terrified me more than an open danger; and this, of which I am going to speak, was a mystery. The boy took no notice of me at the first. He never spoke to me when he came into the room; he passed me in the fields as if he did not see me; indeed he had always that manner to me—he did not see me—I did not exist for him. I was well content that this should be; but, after I had been there a short time, Mr. Brand began to make distinct mischief between us. From brutish indifference, Master George passed rapidly to brutish aggression. When he met me in the lanes and fields he made mouths at me, and once he flung stones and mud as I passed him; at table he would kick me silently, and whenever I caught his eye he made hideous grimaces, muttering in his broad, provincial accent, "Mad dog! mad dog! We hang mad dogs hereaway!" His insolence and brutality increased daily, and Mr. Brand encouraged him. This was the mystery. Why should he wish this lad to hate me?

There was a plot underneath it all which I tormented myself to discover. Day and night the thought haunted me, till I felt growing crazed with dread and terror. I could not conceal my abhorrence of the youth—I was too nervous for that—nor hide the fear with which that wicked man inspired me. I was as helpless as the poor pale woman there, and as thoroughly the victim of a stronger fate.

One night Master George had been more than usually intolerable to me. He had struck me openly before both father and mother, had insulted my misfortunes, and spoken with brutal disrespect of my family. It was a wild winter's night, and the howling wind shook the windows and dashed the trailing ivy-leaves sharply against the panes: a fearful night, making all visions of freedom and escape impossible; a night which necessitated one to be content with one's own fireside, and forbade the idea of wandering farther. Yet it was something worse than death to me to be shut up in that mean room, with its squalid furniture and scanty fire, with such companions, and to feel that I could not escape from them—that they might ill-treat me, mock me, persecute me as they would, and I was bound to bear all without protection or means of escape. The stormy night had excited me, and I felt less than ever able to bear all the insolence and brutality heaped upon me. When Master George struck me again, and called me "mad dog," something seemed to take possession of me. My timidity and nervousness vanished, and I felt as if swept away in a very tumult of passion. I do not know now what it was that I said or did, but I remember rising passionately from my place, and pouring out a torrent of bitterness and reproach. I was almost unconscious of what I was doing, for I was literally for the moment insane; but I remember the words, "You shall die! you shall die!" rising like a scream through the room. I have not the slightest recollection of how I left the parlor, nor how I got to my own chamber, but it was past midnight when I awoke from what must have been a kind of swoon, and found myself lying on the floor.

The wind was still raging, howling through the trees outside, tearing down branches, and scattering the dead leaves like flakes of frozen snow upon the ground. Every door and window shook thoughout the old house, and the wild moaning in the chimneys came, startling, like the cries of tortured beings. Confused and giddy, I rose up out of my trance, stiff with cold and scarcely conscious. But as my brain grew clearer it grew also feverish, and I knew there was no rest for me to-night. My hearing began to be distressingly acute, and every painful thought and circumstance of my life rose up before me with the force and vividness of living scenes actually present to my senses. I paced my room for some time in a state of despair, wringing my hands and sobbing violently, but without tears. By degrees a little calmness came to me, and I determined to go down-stairs for a book. I would get some quiet, calm, religious book, which would soothe me like a spiritual opiate, and take me out of the abyss of misery into which I had sunk. What friend, indeed, had I in the world, save the Great Father above us all?

As I opened the door I fancied I heard a stealthy step along the passage. I held my breath to listen, shading the candle with my hand. I was not deceived; there *was* a step passing furtively over the creaking boards in the direction of Master George's room. I shrank back into the doorway. Yet there was nothing to alarm me. A quiet footfall at midnight might be easily accounted for: why should it affect me with mistrust and dread? and why should I feel this overpowering impulse to go towards the sound? I scarcely knew what I expected to find; but something stronger than myself seemed to impel me to the discovery of something horrible; and placing the candle on the floor, I crept noiselessly along the passage, every nerve strung to its utmost tension.

Master George slept in a room at the end of the back-stairs gallery, which ran at right angles to the passage in which my room was situated. My door faced Mr. and Mrs. Brand's; Master George's faced the kitchen stairs, and was properly the servant's room, but she had been moved to a small closet near to me, Mr. Brand not approving of her holding so large a chamber for herself, neither willing to allow the boy any thing of a better class. When I stood by my door I could see Mr. and Mrs. Brand's room; but it was only by going the whole length of the back-stairs gallery that I could get to Master George's. I could see now, however, that his door was open, for a ray of light fell along the staircase wall, and I could hear his heavy snoring breath. And I heard another sound. I heard a man's step in the room; I heard the boards creak and the bed-clothes softly rustle; I heard an impatient kind of moan, as of some one disturbed in his sleep, and then a heavy blow, a stifled groan, a man's deep-drawn breath, and the quick, sharp drip of something spilt upon the floor. Dumb from terror, I stood in the doorway of the boy's room. Pale, heavy, motionless on the bed lay the youth, his large limbs carelessly flung abroad in the unconsciousness of sleep, and his face as calm and quiet as if still dreaming. The sheets were wet with blood—red—the light of the candle glistening upon a small red stream that flowed over the side of the bed, on the floor beneath. At a little distance stood Mr. Brand, wiping a knife on a handkerchief. He turned, and our eyes met. He came up to me with an oath, caught me by the throat, and drew the knife across my hands. I remember no more until I awoke in the broad daylight, and found myself in the midst of a crowd gathered round my bed.

Curious eyes stared at me; harsh voices mocked me; rough hands were laid upon me; and I heard myself branded with the burning name of Murderess. Red tracks made by a woman's naked feet—made by *my* feet—led from the boy's room to mine; each track plainly printed on the bare uncarpeted floor—tracks of a woman's feet, and of none other. There was no explaining away these marks and signs of guilt. Who would believe me, a half-mad lonely stranger with such a family history as mine, and, according to popular belief, at any moment liable to make a murderous attack against any one offending? Had not this unhappy youth notoriously offended, and had I not, only that very evening, openly defied and threatened him? Escape was impossible. To all the evidence heaped up against me with such art and cunning, I had but an unsupported assertion, which would be set down as maniacal raving, and only deepen the case against me.

All day I lay there; all that weary sobbing winter's day; and when the night came they fastened me with cords, and left me once more alone. I was so well secured—bound hand and foot, and triply bound—that it was not thought needful to watch me; and they were all too much excited and overwrought to wish to remain through the night with a lunatic murderer, as I was called. So they went, and Mr. Brand locked the door, saying, as he turned away, "We must have no more such dangerous fits of madness, Miss Erfurt!" with a sneer on the word.

I was too hopeless and desolate to think of any plan of escape, feasible or not. The reaction had set in, and I was content to lie there in quiet, and to feel that I had done with life forever. It had not offered me so many joys that I should grieve to leave it, and for the shame—who cares for shame in the grave? No; I was content to have done with all that had weighed upon me so long and heavily. I had no one to mourn for me, no one to love me, with a broken heart and a sorrowful faith: I was alone—alone—and might well die out at once, and sleep tranquilly in my murdered grave. And I was not unhappy, thinking all these things. Perhaps my brain was slightly paralyzed, so that I could not suffer. However it might be, it was a merciful moment of calm.

It was nearly three o'clock, when I heard a light hand upon the door. The key was turned softly in the lock, and, pale and terrible, like an avenging ghost, the poor bereaved mother glided into my room. She came up to my bed, and silently unfastened the cords. She said no comforting word, she gave me no kind look, no pitying human touch, but in a strange, weak, wan way, she unbound me limb by limb, until I was free.

"Go," she then said, below her breath, still not looking at me. "I do not love you, and *he* did not; but I know that you are innocent, and I do not want your blood on my head. My turn is to come next, but I do not mind, now he has gone. Go at once; that sleep will not last long. I made it come for you."

Without another word she turned from the room, leaving the door open. I got up as she bade me. Without energy, without hope, I quietly dressed myself, and left the house, going forth into the darkness and desolation, more because I had been bidden to do so, than to escape a greater peril. I wandered through the by-roads aimlessly, nervelessly; not shaping my course for any goal, but simply going forwards, to wherever chance might lead me. A poor woman gave me some milk, and I slept, I believe, once beneath a haystack. I remember lying down there, and finding myself again after many hours. In time—I cannot tell you how or when, nor how long I had been out in the fields, but it was evening, and the lamps were lighted—I was in London, reading a description of myself posted up against the walls. I saw myself described as a murderess and a maniac, and a reward offered for my apprehension; my dress, my manners, appearance, gait, voice, all were so minutely noted, as to render safety impossible. Seized with terror I fled: I fled like a wild being haunted and pursued, and I have never rested since.

A Handbook to the Colony of Queensland, Australia. By the Editor of the "Australian and New Zealand Gazette." London: F. Algar.

THIS pamphlet, which completes the series of handbooks to the Australian colonies, gives, within a narrow compass, full information respecting the climate, political institutions, etc., of Queensland, together with a statement of the advantages which are offered by that colony to intending emigrants.

From Fraser's Magazine.

CONCERNING THINGS SLOWLY LEARNT.

You will see in a little while what sort of things they are which I understand by *Things Slowly Learnt.* Some are facts, some are moral truths, some are practical lessons; but the great characteristic of all those which are to be thought of in this essay, is, that we have to learn them and act upon them in the face of a strong bias to think or act in an opposite way. It is not that they are so difficult in themselves; not that they are hard to be understood, or that they are supported by arguments whose force is not apparent to every mind. On the contrary, the things which I have especially in view are very simple, and for the most part quite unquestionable. But the difficulty of learning them lies in this: that, as regards them, the head seems to say one thing and the heart another. We see plainly enough what we ought to think or to do; but we feel an irresistible inclination to think or to do something else. It is about three or four of these things that we are going, my friend, to have a little quiet talk. We are going to confine our view to a single class, though possibly the most important class, in the innumerable multitude of Things Slowly Learnt.

The truth is, a great many things are slowly learnt. I have lately had occasion to observe that the alphabet is one of these. I remember, too, in my own sorrowful experience, how the multiplication-table was another. A good many years since, an eminent dancing-master undertook to teach a number of my schoolboy companions a graceful and easy deportment; but comparatively few of us can be said as yet to have thoroughly attained it. I know men who have been practising the art of extempore speaking for many years, but who have reached no perfection in it, and who, if one may judge from their confusion and hesitation when they attempt to speak, are not likely ever to reach even decent mediocrity in that wonderful accomplishment. Analogous statements might be made with truth, with regard to my friend Mr. Snarling's endeavors to produce magazine articles; likewise concerning his attempts to skate, and his efforts to ride on horseback unlike a tailor. Some folk learn with remarkable slowness that nature never intended them for wits. There have been men who have punned, ever more and more wretchedly, to the end of a long and highly respectable life. People submitted in silence to the infliction; no one liked to inform those reputable individuals that they had better cease to make fools of themselves. This, however, is part of a larger subject, which shall be treated hereafter. On the other hand, there are things which are very quickly learnt; which are learnt by a single lesson. One liberal tip or even a few kind words heartily said to a manly little schoolboy, will establish in his mind the rooted principle that the speaker of the words or the bestower of the tip is a jolly and noble specimen of humankind. Boys are great physiognomists: they read a man's nature at a glance. Well I remember how, when going to and from school, a long journey of four hundred miles, in days when such a journey implied travel by sea as well as by land, I used to know instantly the gentleman or the railway officials to whom I might apply for advice or information. I think that this intuitive perception of character is blunted in after years. A man is often mistaken in his first impression of man or woman; a boy hardly ever. And a boy not only knows at once whether a human being is amiable or the reverse; he knows also whether the human being is wise or foolish. In particular, he knows at once whether the human being always means what he says, or says a great deal more than he means. Inferior animals learn some lessons quickly. A dog once thrashed for some offence, knows quite well not to repeat it. A horse turns for the first time down the avenue to a house where he is well fed and cared for; next week, or next month, you pass that gate, and though the horse has been long taught to submit his will to yours, you can easily see that he knows the place again, and that he would like to go back to the stable with which, in his poor, dull, narrow mind, there are pleasant associations. I would give a good deal to know what a horse is thinking about. There is something very curious and very touching about the limited intelligence and the imperfect knowledge of that immaterial principle, in which the immaterial does not imply the immortal. And yet, if we are to rest the doctrine of a future life in any degree upon the necessity of compensation of the sufferings and injustice of a present, I think the sight of the cab horses of any large town might plead for the admission of some quiet world of green grass and shady trees, where there should be no cold, starvation, over-work, or flogging. Some one has said that the most exquisite material scenery would look very cold and dead in the entire absence of irrational life. Trees suggest singing-birds; flowers and sunshine make us think of the drowsy bees. And it is curious to think how the future worlds of various creeds are described as not without their lowly population of animals inferior to man. We know what the "poor Indian" expects shall bear him company in his humble heaven; and possibly various readers may know some dogs who in certain important respects are very superior to certain men. You remember how, when a war-chief of the Western woods was laid by his tribe in his grave, his horse was led to the spot in the funeral procession, and at the instant when the earth was cast upon the dead warrior's dust, an arrow reached the noble creature's heart, that in the land of souls the man should find his old friend again. And though it has something of the grotesque, I think it has more of the pathetic, the aged huntsman of Mr. Assheton Smith desiring to be buried by his master, with two horses and a few couples of dogs, that they might all be ready to start together when they met again far away.

This is a deviation; but *that* is of no consequence. It is of the essence of the present writer's essays to deviate from the track. Only we must not forget the thread of the discourse; and after our deviation we must go back to it. All this came of our remarking that some things are very quickly learnt; and that certain inferior classes of our fellow-creatures learn them quickly. But deeper and larger lessons are early learnt. Thoughtful children of a very few years old have their own theory of human nature. Before studying the metaphysicians, and indeed while still imperfectly acquainted with their letters, young children have glimpses of the inherent selfishness of humanity. I was recently present when a small boy of three years old, together with his sister, aged five, was brought down to the dining-room at the period of dessert. The small boy climbed upon his mother's knee, and began by various indications to display his affection for her. A stranger remarked what an affectionate child he was. "Oh," said the little girl, "he suspects [by which she meant *expects*] that he is going to get something to eat!" Not Hobbes himself had reached a clearer perception or a firmer belief of the selfish system in moral philosophy. "He is always very affectionate," the youthful philosopher proceeded, "when he suspects he is going to get something good to eat!"

By *Things Slowly Learnt*, I mean not merely things which are in their nature such that it takes a long time to learn them; such as the Greek language, or the law of vendors and purchasers. These things indeed take long time and much trouble to learn; but once you have learnt them, you know them. Once you have come to understand the force of the second aorist, you do not find your heart whispering to you as you are lying awake at night, that what the grammar says about the second aorist is all nonsense; you do not feel an inveterate disposition, gaining force day by day, to think concerning the second aorist just the opposite of what the grammar says. By *Things Slowly Learnt*, I understand things which it is very hard to learn at the first, because strong as the reasons which support them are, you find it so hard to make up your mind to them. I understand things which you can quite easily (when it is fairly put to you) see to be true; but which it seems as if it would change the very world you live in to accept. I understand things you discern to be true, but which you have all your life been accustomed to think false; and which you are extremely anxious to think false. And by *Things Slowly Learnt* I understand things which are not merely very hard to learn at the first; but which it is not enough to learn for once, ever so well. I understand things which when you have made the bitter effort, and admitted to be true and certain, you put into your mind to keep (so to speak); and hardly a day has passed when a soft quiet hand seems to begin to crumble them down and to wear them away to nothing. You write the principle which was so hard to receive, upon the tablet of your memory; and day by day a gentle hand comes over it with a bit of india rubber, till the inscription loses its clear sharpness, grows blurred and indistinct, and finally quite disappears. Nor is the gentle hand content even then; but it begins, very faintly at first, to trace letters which bear a very different meaning. Then it deepens and darkens them day by day, week by week, till at a month's or a year's end the tablet of memory bears, in great, sharp, legible letters, just the opposite thing to that which you had originally written down there. These are my *Things Slowly Learnt.* Things you learn at first in the face of a strong bias against them; things when once taught you gradually forget, till you come back again to your old way of thinking. Such things, of course, lie within the realm to which extends the influence of feeling and prejudice. They are things in the accepting of which both head and heart are concerned. Once convince a man that two and two make four, and he learns the truth without excitement, and he never doubts it again. But prove to a man that he is of much less importance than he has been accustomed to think; or prove to a woman that her children are very much like those of other folk; or prove to the inhabitant of a country parish that Britain has hundreds of parishes which in soil, and climate, and production, are just as good as his own; or prove to the great man of a little country town that there are scores of towns in this world where the walks are as pleasant, the streets as well paved, and the population as healthy and as well conducted; and in each such case you will find it very hard to convince the individual at the time, and you will find that in a very short space the individual has succeeded in entirely escaping from the disagreeable conviction. You may possibly find, if you endeavor to instil such belief into minds of but moderate cultivation, that your arguments will be met less by force of reason than by roaring of voice and excitement of manner; you may find that the person you address will endeavor to change the issue you are arguing, to other issues, wholly irrelevant, touching your own antecedents, character, or even personal appearance; and you may afterwards be informed by good-natured friends, that the upshot of your discussion had been to leave on the mind of your acquaintance the firm conviction that you yourself are intellectually a blockhead, and morally a villain. And even when dealing with human beings who have reached that crowning result of a fine training, that they shall have got beyond thinking a man their "enemy because he tells them the truth," you may find that you have rendered a service like that rendered by the surgeon's amputating knife—salutary, yet very painful—leaving forever a sad association with your thought and your name. For among the things we slowly learn, are truths and lessons which it goes terribly against the grain to learn at first; which must be driven into us time after time; and which perhaps are never learnt completely.

One thing very slowly learnt by most human beings, is, that they are of no earthly consequence beyond a very small circle indeed; and that really nobody is thinking or talking about them. Almost all commonplace men and women in this world have a vague but deeply rooted belief that they are quite different from anybody else, and of course quite superior to everybody else. It may be in only one respect they fancy they are this, but that one respect is quite sufficient. I believe that if a grocer or silk-mercer in a little town has a hundred customers, each separate customer lives on under the impression that the grocer or silk-mercer is prepared to give to him or her certain advantages in buying or selling which will not be accorded to the other ninety-nine customers. "Say it is for Mrs. Brown," is Mrs. Brown's direction to her servant when sending for some sugar; "say it is for Mrs. Brown, and he will give it a little better." The grocer, keenly alive to the weaknesses of his fellow-creatures, encourages this notion. "This tea," he says, "would be four-and-sixpence a pound *to any one else*, but *to you* it is only four-and-threepence." Judging from my own observation, I should say that retail dealers trade a good deal upon this singular fact in the constitution of the human mind, that it is inexpressibly bitter to most people to believe that they stand on the ordinary level of humanity; that, in the main, they are just like their neighbors. Mrs. Brown would be filled with unutterable wrath if it were represented to her that the grocer treats her precisely as he does Mrs. Smith, who lives on one side of her, and Mrs. Snooks, who lives on the other. She would be still more angry if you asked her what earthly reason there is why she should in any way be distinguished beyond Mrs. Snooks and Mrs. Smith. She takes for granted she is quite different from them: quite superior to them. Human beings do not like to be classed, at least with the class to which in fact they belong. To be classed at all is painful to an average mortal, who firmly believes that there never was such a being in this world. I remember one of the cleverest friends I have—one who assuredly cannot be classed intellectually, except in a very small and elevated class—telling me how mortified he was, when a very clever boy of sixteen, at being classed at all. He had told a literary lady that he admired Tennyson. "Yes," said the lady, "I am not surprised at that: there is a class of young men who like Tennyson at your age." It went like a dart to my friend's heart. *Class of young men*, indeed! Was it for *this* that I outstripped all competitors at school, that I have been fancying myself an unique phenomenon in nature, *different* at least from every other being that lives, that I should be spoken of as one of *a class of young men!* Now, in my friend's half-playful reminiscence, I see the exemplification of a great fact in human nature. Most human beings fancy themselves, and all their belongings, to be quite different from all other beings, and the belongings of all other beings. I heard an old lady, whose son is a rifleman, and just like all the other volunteers of his corps, lately declared that on the occasion of a certain grand review her Tom looked so entirely different from all the rest. No doubt he did to her, poor old lady, for he was her own. But the irritating thing was, that the old lady wished it to be admitted that Tom's superiority was an actual fact, equally patent to the eyes of all mankind. Yes, my friend: it is a thing very slowly learnt by most men, that they are very much like other people. You see the principle which underlies what you hear so often said by human beings, young and old, when urging you to do something which it is against your general rule to do. "Oh, but you might do it *for me!*" Why for you more than for any one else, would be the answer of severe logic. But a kindly man would not take that ground: for doubtless the *Me*, however little to every one else, is to each unit in humankind the centre of all the world.

Arising out of this mistaken notion of their own difference from all other men, is the fancy entertained by many, that they occupy a much greater space in the thoughts of others than they really do. Most folk think mainly about themselves and their own affairs. Even a matter which "everybody is talking about," is really talked about by each for a very small portion of the twenty-four hours. And a name which is "in everybody's mouth," is not in each separate mouth for more than a few minutes at a time. And during those few minutes, it is talked of with an interest very faint when compared with that you feel for yourself. You fancy it a terrible thing when you yourself have to do something which you would think nothing about if done by anybody else. A lady grows sick, and has to go out of church during the sermon. Well, you remark it; possibly indeed you don't; and you say, Mrs. Thomson went out of church to-day; she must be ill; and there the matter ends. But a day or two later you see Mrs. Thomson, and find her quite in a fever at the awful fact. It was a dreadful trial, walking out, and facing all the congregation: they must have thought it so strange; she would not run the risk of it again for any inducement. The fact is just this: Mrs. Thomson thinks a great deal of the thing, because it happened to herself. It did not happen to the other people, and so they hardly think of it at all. But nine in every ten of them, in Mrs. Thomson's place, would have Mrs. Thomson's feeling; for it is a thing which you, my reader, slowly learn, that people think very little about you.

Yes, it is a thing slowly learnt: by many not learnt at all. How many persons you meet walking along the street who evidently think that everybody is looking at them! How few persons can walk through an exhibition of pictures at which are assembled the grand people of the town and all their own grand acquaintances, in a fashion thoroughly free from self-consciousness! I mean without thinking of themselves at all, or of how look; but in an unaffected manner, observing the objects and beings around them. Men who have attained recently to a moderate eminence, are sometimes, if of small minds, much affected by this disagreeable frailty. Small literary men, and preachers with no great head or heart, have within my own observation suffered from it severely. I have witnessed a poet, whose writings I have never read, walking along a certain street. I call him a poet to avoid periphrasis. The whole get-up of the man, his dress, his hair, his hat, the style in which he walked, showed unmistakably that he fancied that everybody was looking at him, and that he was the admired of all admirers. In fact, nobody was looking at him at all. Some time since I beheld a portrait of a very, very small literary man. It was easy to discern from it that the small author lives in the belief that wherever he goes he is the object of universal observation. The intense self-consciousness and self-conceit apparent in that portrait were, in the words of Mr. Squeers, "more easier conceived than described." The face was a very commonplace and rather good-looking one; the author, notwithstanding his most strenuous exertions, evidently could make nothing of the features to distinguish him from other men. But the length of his hair was very great: and oh, what genius he plainly fancied glowed in those eyes! I never in my life witnessed such an extraordinary glare. I do not believe that any human being ever lived whose eyes habitually wore that expression: only by a violent effort could the expression be produced, and then for a very short time, without serious injury to the optic nerves. The eyes were made as large as possible; and the thing after which the poor fellow had been struggling was that peculiar look which may be conceived to penetrate through the beholder, and pierce his inmost thoughts. I never beheld the living original, but if I saw him I should like in a kind way to pat him on the head, and tell him that *that* sort of expression would produce a great effect on the gallery of a minor theatre.

The other day I was at a public meeting. A great crowd of people was assembled in a large hall: the platform at one end of it remained unoccupied till the moment when the business of the meeting was to begin. It was an interesting sight for any philosophic observer seated in the body of the hall to look at the men who by and by walked in procession on to the platform, and to observe the different ways in which they walked in. There were several very great and distinguished men: every one of these walked on to the platform and took his seat in the most simple and unaffected way, as if quite unconscious of the many eyes that were looking at them with interest and curiosity. There were many highly respectable and sensible men, whom nobody cared particularly to see, and who took their places in a perfectly natural manner, as though well aware of the fact. But there were one or two small men, struggling for notoriety; and I declare it was pitiful to behold their entrance. I remarked one in particular, who evidently thought that the eyes of the whole meeting were fixed upon himself; and that as he walked in everybody was turning to his neighbor, and saying with agitation, "See, that's Snooks!" His whole gait and deportment testified that he felt that two or three thousand eyes were burning him up: you saw it in the way he walked to his place, in the way he sat down, in the way he then looked about him. If any one had tried to get up three cheers for Snooks, Snooks would not have known that he was being made a fool of. He would have accepted the incense of fame as justly his due. There once was a man who entered the Edinburgh theatre at the same instant with Sir Walter Scott. The audience cheered lustily; and while Sir Walter modestly took his seat, as though unaware that those cheers were to welcome the Great Magician, the other man advanced with dignity to the front of the box, and bowed in acknowledgment of the popular applause. This of course was but a little outburst of the great tide of vain self-estimation which the man had cherished within his breast for years. Let it be said here, that an affected unconsciousness of the presence of a multitude of people is as offensive an exhibition of self-consciousness as any that is possible. Entire naturalness, and a just sense of a man's personal insignificance, will produce the right deportment. It is very irritating to see some clergymen walk into church to begin the service. They come in, with eyes affectedly cast down, and go to their place without ever looking up, and rise and begin without one glance at the congregation. To stare about them, as some clergymen do, in a free and easy manner, befits not the solemnity of the place and the worship; but the other is the worse thing. In a few cases it proceeds from modesty: in the majority from intolerable self-conceit. The man who keeps his eyes downcast in that affected manner fancies that everybody is looking at him. There is an insufferable self-consciousness about him; and he is much more keenly aware of the presence of other people than the man who does what is natural, and looks at the people to whom he is speaking. It is not natural nor rational to speak to one human being with your eyes fixed on the ground; and neither is it natural or rational to speak to a thousand. And I think that the preacher who feels in his heart that he is neither wiser nor better than his fellow-sinners to whom he is to preach, and that the advices he addresses to them are addressed quite as solemnly to himself, will assume no conceited airs of elevation above them, but will unconsciously wear the demeanor of any sincere worshipper, somewhat deepened in solemnity by the remembrance of his heavy personal responsibility in leading the congregation's worship; but assuredly and entirely free from the vulgar conceit which may be fostered in a vulgar mind by the reflection, "Now everybody is looking at me!" I have seen, I regret to say, various distinguished preachers whose pulpit demeanor was made to me inexpressibly offensive by this taint of self-consciousness. And I have seen some, with half the talent, who made upon me an impression a thousand-fold deeper than ever was made by the most brilliant eloquence; because the simple earnestness of their manner said to every heart, "Now, I am not thinking in the least about myself, or about what you may think of me: my sole desire is to impress on your hearts these truths I speak, which I believe will concern us all forever!" I have heard great preachers, after hearing whom you could walk home quite at your ease, praising warmly the eloquence and the logic of the sermon. I have heard others (infinitely greater in my poor judgment), after hearing whom you would have felt it profanation to criticise the literary merits of their sermon, high as those were: but you walked home thinking of the lesson and not the teacher: solemnly revolving the truths you had heard; and asking the best of all help to enable you to remember them and act upon them.

There are various ways in which self-consciousness disagreeably evinces its existence; and there is not one perhaps more disagreeable than the affected avoidance of what is generally regarded as egotism. Depend upon it, my reader, that the straightforward and natural writer who frankly uses the first person singular, and says, "I think thus and thus," "I have seen so and so," is thinking of himself and his own personality a mighty deal less than the man who is always employing awkward and roundabout forms of expression to avoid the use of the obnoxious *I*. Every such periphrasis testifies unmistakably that the man was thinking of himself; but the simple, natural writer, warm with his subject, eager to press his views upon his readers, uses the *I* without a thought of self, just because it is the shortest, most direct, and most natural way of expressing himself. The recollection of his own personality probably never once crossed his mind during the composition of the paragraph from which an ill-set critic might pick out a score of *I's*. To say "It is submitted" instead of "I think," "It has been observed" instead of "I have seen," "the present writer" instead of "I," is much the more really egotistical. Try to write an essay without using that vowel which some men think the very shibboleth of egotism, and the remembrance of yourself will be in the background of your mind all the time you are writing. It will be always intruding and pushing in its face, and you will be able to give only half your mind to your subject. But frankly and naturally use the "I," and the remembrance of yourself vanishes. You are grappling with the subject; you are thinking of it and of nothing else. You use the readiest and most unaffected mode of speech to set out your thoughts of it. You have written *I* a dozen times, but you have not thought of yourself once.

You may see the self-consciousness of some men strongly manifested in their handwriting. The handwriting of some men is essentially affected; more especially their signature. It seems to be a very searching test whether a man is a conceited person or an unaffected person, to be required to furnish his autograph to be printed underneath his published portrait. I have fancied I could form a theory of a man's whole character from reading, in such a situation, merely the words "Very faithfully yours, Eusebius Snooks." You could see that Mr. Snooks was acting when he wrote that signature. He was thinking of the impression it would produce on those who saw it. It was not the thing which a man would produce who simply wished to write his name legibly in as short a time and with as little needless trouble as possible. Let me say with sorrow that I have known even venerable bishops who were not superior to this irritating weakness. Some men aim at an aristocratic hand; some deal in vulgar flourishes. These are the men who have reached no further than that stage at which they are proud of the dexterity with which they handle their pen. Some strive after an affectedly simple and student-like hand; some at a dashing and military style. But there may be as much self-consciousness evinced by handwriting as by any thing else. Any clergyman who performs a good many marriages will be impressed by the fact that very few among the humbler classes can sign their name in an unaffected way. I am not thinking of the poor bride who shakily traces her name, or of the simple bumpkin who slowly writes his, making no secret of the difficulty with which he does it. These are natural and pleasing. You would like to help and encourage them. But it is irritating when some forward fellow, after evincing his marked contempt for the slow and cramped performances of his friends, jauntily takes up the pen and dashes off his signature at a tremendous rate and with the air of an exploit, evidently expecting the admiration of his rustic friends, and laying a foundation for remarking to them on his way home that the parson could not touch him at penmanship. I have observed with a little malicious satisfaction that such persons, arising in their pride from the place where they wrote, generally smear their signature with their coat-sleeve, and reduce it to a state of comparative illegibility. I like to see the smirking, impudent creature a little taken down.

But it is endless to try to reckon up the fashions in which people show that they have not learnt the lesson of their own unimportance. Did you ever stop in the street and talk for a few minutes to some old bachelor? If so, I dare say you have remarked a curious phenomenon. You have found that all of a sudden the mind of the old gentlemen, usually reasonable enough, appeared stricken into a state approaching idiocy, and that the sentence which he had begun in a rational and intelligible way was ending in a maze of wandering words, signifying nothing in particular. You had been looking in another direction, but in sudden alarm you look straight at the old gentleman to see what on earth is the matter; and you discern that his eyes are fixed on some passer-by, possibly a young lady, perhaps no more than a magistrate or the like, who is by this time a good many yards off, with the eyes still following, and slowly revolving on their axis so as to follow without the head being turned round. It is this spectacle which has drawn off your friend's attention; and you notice his whole figure twisted into an ungainly form, intended to be dignified or easy, and assumed because he fancied that the passer-by was looking at him. Oh, the pettiness of human nature! Then you will find people afraid that they have given offence by saying or doing things which the party they supposed offended had really never observed that they had said or done. There are people who fancy that in church everybody is looking at them, when in truth no mortal is taking the trouble to do so. It is an amusing though irritating sight to behold a weak-minded lady walking into church and taking her seat under this delusion. You remember the affected air, the downcast eyes, the demeanor intended to imply a modest shrinking from notice, but through which there shines the real desire, "Oh, for any sake, look at me!" There are people whose voice is utterly inaudible in church six feet off, who will tell you that a whole congregation of a thousand or fifteen hundred people was listening to their singing. Such folk will tell you that they went to a church where the singing was left too much to the choir, and began to sing as usual, on which the entire congregation looked round to see who it was that was singing, and ultimately proceeded to sing lustily too. I do not remember a more disgusting exhibition of vulgar self-conceit than I saw a few months ago at Westminster Abbey. It was a week-day afternoon service, and the congregation was small. Immediately before me there sat an insolent boor, who evidently did not belong to the Church of England. He had walked in when the prayers were half over, having with difficulty been made to take off his hat, and his manifest wish was to testify his contempt for the whole place and service. Accordingly, he persisted in sitting, in a lounging attitude, when the people stood, and in standing up and staring about with an air of curiosity while they knelt. He was very anxious to convey that he was not listening to the prayers; but rather inconsistently, he now and then uttered an audible grunt of disapproval. No one can enjoy the choral service more than I do, and the music that afternoon was very fine; but I could not enjoy it or join in it as I wished for the disgust I felt at the animal before me, and for my burning desire to see him turned out of the sacred place he was profaning. But the thing which chiefly struck me about the individual was not his vulgar and impudent profanity; it was his intolerable self-conceit. He plainly thought that every eye under the noble old roof was watching all his movements. I could see that he would go home and boast of what he had done, and tell his friends that all the clergy, choristers, and congregation had been awe-stricken by him, and that possibly word had by this time been conveyed to Lambeth or Fulham of the weakened influence and approaching downfall of the Church of England. I knew that the very thing he wished was that some one should rebuke his conduct, otherwise I should certainly have told him either to behave with decency or to be gone.

I have sometimes witnessed a curious manifestation of this vain sense of self-importance. Did you ever, my reader, chance upon such a spectacle as this: a very commonplace man, and even a very great blockhead, standing in a drawing-room where a large party of people is assembled, with a grin of self-complacent superiority upon his unmeaning face? I am sure you understand the thing I mean. I mean a look which conveyed that, in virtue of some hidden store of genius or power, he could survey with a calm, cynical loftiness the little conversation and interests of ordinary mortals. You know the kind of interest with which a human being would survey the distant approaches to reason of an intelligent dog, or a colony of ants. I have seen this expression on the face of one or two of the greatest blockheads I ever knew. I have seen such a one wear it while clever men were carrying on a conversation in which he could not have joined to have saved his life. Yet you could see that (who can tell how?) the poor creature had somehow persuaded himself that he occupied a position from which he could look down upon his fellow-men in general. Or was it rather that the poor creature knew he was a fool, and fancied that thus he could disguise the fact? I dare say there was a mixture of both feelings.

You may see many indications of vain self-importance in the fact that various persons, old ladies for the most part, are so ready to give opinions which are not wanted, on matters of which they are not competent to judge. Clever young curates suffer much annoyance from these people: they are always anxious to instruct the young curates how to preach. I remember well, ten years ago, when I was a curate (which in Scotland we call an *assistant*) myself, what advices I used to receive (quite unsought by me) from well-meaning but densely stupid old ladies. I did not think the advices worth much, even then; and now, by longer experience, I can discern that they were utterly idiotic. Yet they were given with entire confidence. No thought ever entered the head of these well-meaning but stupid individuals, that possibly they were not competent to give advice on such subjects. And it is vexatious to think that people so stupid may do serious harm to a young clergyman by head-shakings and sly inuendoes as to his orthodoxy or his gravity of deportment. In the long run they will do no harm, but at the first start they may do a good deal of mischief. Not long since, such a person complained to me that a talented young preacher had taught unsound doctrine. She cited his words. I I showed her that the words were taken *verbatim* from the *Confession of Faith*, which is our Scotch Thirty-nine Articles. I think it not unlikely that she would go on telling her tattling story just the same. I remember hearing a stupid old lady say, as though her opinion were quite decisive of the question, that no clergyman ought to have so much as a thousand a year; for if he had, he would be sure to neglect his duty. You remember what Dr. Johnson said to a woman who expressed some opinion or other upon a matter she did not understand. "Madam," said the moralist, "before expressing your opinion, you should consider what your opinion is worth." But this shaft would have glanced harmlessly from off the panoply of the stupid and self-complacent old lady of whom I am thinking. It was a fundamental axiom with her that her opinion was entirely infallible. Some people would feel as though the very world were crumbling away under their feet if they realized the fact that they could go wrong.

Let it here be said, that this vain belief of their own importance which most people cherish, is not at all a source of unmixed happiness. It will work either way. When my friend, Mr. Snarling, got his beautiful poem printed in the county newspaper, it no doubt pleased him to think, as he walked along the street, that every one was pointing him out as the eminent literary man who was the pride of the district; and that the whole town was ringing with that magnificent effusion. Mr. Tennyson, it is certain, felt that his crown was being reft away. But on the other hand, there is no commoner form of morbid misery than that of the poor nervous man or woman who fancies that he or she is the subject of universal unkindly remark. You will find people, still sane for practical purposes, who think that the whole neighborhood is conspiring against them, when in fact nobody is thinking of them.

All these pages have been spent in discussing a single thing slowly learnt: the remaining matters to be considered in this essay must be treated briefly.

Another thing slowly learnt is that we have no reason or right to be angry with people because they think poorly of us. This is a truth which most people find it very hard to accept, and at which, probably, very few arrive without pretty long thought and experience. Most people are angry when they are informed that some one has said that their ability is small, or that their proficiency in any art is limited. Mrs. Malaprop was very indignant when she found that some of her friends had spoken lightly of her parts of speech. Mr. Snarling was wroth when he learned that Mr. Jollikin thought him no great preacher. Miss Brown was so on hearing that Mr. Smith did not admire her singing; and Mr. Smith on learning that Miss Brown did not admire his horsemanship. Some authors feel angry on reading an unfavorable review of their book. The present writer has been treated very, very kindly by the critics; far more so than he ever deserved; yet he remembers showing a notice of him which was intended to extinguish him for all coming time, to a warm-hearted friend, who read it with gathering wrath, and vehemently starting up at its close, exclaimed (we knew who wrote the notice), "Now, I shall go straight and kick that fellow!" Now all this is very natural; but assuredly it is quite wrong. You understand, of course, that I am thinking of unfavorable opinions of you, honestly held, and expressed without malice. I do not mean to say that you would choose for your special friend or companion one who thought meanly of your ability or your sense; it would not be pleasant to have him always by you; and the very fact of his presence would tend to keep you from doing justice to yourself. For it is true, that when with people who think you very clever and wise, you really are a good deal cleverer and wiser than usual; while with people who think you stupid and silly, you find yourself under a malign influence which tends to make you actually so for the time. If you want a man to gain any good quality, the way is to give him credit for possessing it. If he has but little, give him credit for all he has, at least; and you will find him daily get more. You know how Arnold made boys truthful; it was by giving them credit for truth. Oh, that we all fitly understood that the same grand principle should be extended to all good qualities, intellectual and moral! Diligently instil into a boy that he is a stupid, idle, bad-hearted blockhead, and you are very likely to make him all *that*. And so you can see that it is not judicious to choose for a special friend and associate one who thinks poorly of one's sense or one's parts. Indeed, if such a one honestly thinks poorly of you, and has any moral earnestness, you could not get him for a special friend if you wished it. Let us choose for our companions (if such can be found) those who think well and kindly of us, even though we may know within ourselves that they think too kindly and too well. For that favorable estimation will bring out and foster all that is good in us. There is between this and the unfavorable judgment all the difference between the warm, genial sunshine, that draws forth the flowers and encourages them to open their leaves, and the nipping frost or the blighting east wind that represses and disheartens all vegetable life. But though thus you would not choose for your special companion one who thinks poorly of you, and though you might not even wish to see him very often, you have no reason to have any angry feeling towards him. He cannot help his opinion. His opinion is determined by his lights. His opinion, possibly, founds on those æsthetic considerations as to which people will never think alike, with which there is no reasoning, and for which there is no accounting. God has made him so that he dislikes your book, or at least cannot heartily appreciate it; and that is not his fault. And, holding his opinion, he is quite entitled to express it. It may not be polite to express it to yourself. By common consent it is understood that you are never, except in cases of absolute necessity, to say to any man that which is disagreeable to him. And if you go, and, without any call to do so, express to a man himself that you think poorly of him, he may justly complain, not of your unfavorable opinion of him, but of the malice which is implied in your needlessly informing him of it. But if any one expresses such an unfavorable opinion of you in your absence, and some one comes and repeats it to you, be angry with the person who repeats the opinion to you, not with the person who expressed it. For what you do not know will cause you no pain. And all sensible folk, aware how estimates of any mortal must differ, will, in the long run, attach nearly the just weight to any opinion, favorable or unfavorable.

Yes, my friend, utterly put down the natural tendency in your heart to be angry with the man who thinks poorly of you. For you have, in sober reason, no right to be angry with him. It is more pleasant, and indeed more profitable, to live among those who think highly of you. It makes you better. You actually grow into what you get credit for. Oh, how much better a clergyman preaches to his own congregation, who listen with kindly and sympathetic attention to all he says, and always think too well of him, than to a set of critical strangers, eager to find faults and to pick holes! And how heartily and pleasantly the essayist covers his pages, which are to go into a magazine whose readers have come to know him well, and to bear with all his ways! If every one thought him a dull and stupid person, he could not write at all. Indeed, he would bow to the general belief, and accept the truth that he is dull and stupid. But further, my reader, let us be reasonable when it is pleasant; and let us sometimes be irrational when *that* is pleasant too. It is natural to have a very kindly feeling to those who think well of us. Now, though, in severe truth, we have no more reason for wishing to shake hands with the man who thinks well of us, than for wishing to shake the man who thinks ill of us; yet let us yield heartily to the former pleasant impulse. It is not reasonable, but it is all right. You cannot help liking people who estimate you favorably, and say a good word of you. No doubt we might slowly learn not to like them more than anybody else; but we need not take the trouble to learn *that* lesson. Let us all, my readers, be glad if we can reach that cheerful position of mind at which my eloquent friend Shirley and I have long since arrived, that we are extremely gratified when we find ourselves favorably reviewed, and not in the least angry when we find ourselves reviewed unfavorably; that we have a very kindly feeling towards such as think well of us, and no unkind feeling whatever to those who think ill of us. Thus, at the beginning of the month, we look with equal minds at the newspaper notices of *Fraser;* we are soothed and exhilarated when we find ourselves describes as sages, and we are amused and interested when we find ourselves shown up as little better than geese.

Of course, it makes a difference in the feeling with which you ought to regard any unfavorable opinion of you, whether spoken or written, if the unfavorable opinion which is expressed be plainly not honestly held, and be maliciously expressed. You may occasionally hear a judgment expressed of a young girl's music or dancing, of a gentleman's horses, of a preacher's sermons, of an author's books, which is manifestly dictated by personal spite and jealousy, and which is expressed with the intention of doing mischief and giving pain to the person of whom the judgment is expressed. You will occasionally find such judgments supported by wilful misrepresentation, and even by pure invention. In such a case as this, the essential thing is not the unfavorable opinion; it is the malice which leads to its entertainment and expression. And the conduct of the offending party should be regarded with that feeling which, on calm thought, you discern to be the right feeling with which to regard malice, accompanied by falsehood. Then, is it well to be angry here? I think not. You may see that it is not safe to have any communication with a person who will abuse and misrepresent you; it is not safe, and it is not pleasant. But don't be angry. It is not worth while. That old lady, indeed, told all her friends that you said, in your book, something she knew quite well you did not say. Mr. Snarling did the like. But the offences of such people are not worth powder and shot; and besides this, my friend, if you saw the case from their point of view, you might see that they have something to say for themselves. You failed to call for the old lady so often as she wished you should. You did not ask Mr. Snarling to dinner. These are bad reasons for pitching into you; but still they are reasons and Mr. Snarling and the old lady, by long brooding over them, may have come to think that they are very just and weighty reasons. And did you never, my friend, speak rather unkindly of these two persons? Did you never give a ludicrous account of their goings-on, or even an ill-set account, which some kind friend was sure to repeat to them? Ah, my reader; don't be too hard on Snarling: possibly you have yourself done something very like what he is doing now. Forgive, as you need to be forgiven! And try to attain that quite attainable temper, in which you will read or listen to the most malignant attack upon you, with curiosity and amusement, and with no angry feeling at all. I suppose great people attain to this. I mean cabinet ministers and the like, who are daily flayed in print somewhere or other. They come to take it all quite easily. And if they were pure angels, somebody would attack them. Most people, even those who differ from him, know that if this world has a humble, conscientious, pious man in it, that man is the present Archbishop of Canterbury. Yet last night I read in a certain powerful journal, that the great characteristics of that good man, are cowardice, trickery, and simple rascality! Honest Mr. Bumpkin, kind-hearted Miss Goodbody, do you fancy that *you* can escape?

Then we ought to try to fix it in our mind, that in all matters into which taste enters at all, the most honest and the most able men may hopelessly, diametrically, differ. Original idiosyncrasy has so much to say here; and training has also so much. One cultivated and honest man has an enthusiastic and most real love and enjoyment of Gothic architecture, and an absolute hatred for that of the classic revival; another man equally cultivated and honest, has tastes which are the logical contradictory of these. No one can doubt the ability of Byron, or of Sheridan; yet each of them thought very little of Shakspeare. The question is, *what suits you?* You may have the strongest conviction that you ought to like an author; you may be ashamed to confess that you don't like him; and yet you may feel that you detest him. For myself, I confess with shame, and I know the reason is in myself, I cannot for my life see any thing to admire in the writings of Mr. Carlyle. His style, both of thought and language, is to me insufferably irritating. I tried to read the *Sartor Resartus*, and could not do it. So if all people who have learned to read English were like me, Mr. Carlyle would have no readers. Happily, the majority, in most cases, possesses the normal taste. At least there is no further appeal than to the deliberate judgment of the majority of educated men. I confess, further, that I would rather read Mr. Helps than Milton: I do not say that I think Mr. Helps the greater man, but that I feel he suits me better. I value the *Autocrat of the Breakfast-table* more highly than all the writings of Shelley put together. It is a curious thing to read various reviews of the same book; particularly if it be one of those books which, if you like at all, you will like very much, and which if you don't like you will absolutely hate. It is curious to find opinions flatly contradictory of one another set forth in those reviews by very able, cultivated, and unprejudiced men. There is no newspaper published in Britain which contains abler writing than the *Edinburgh Scotsman*. And of course no one need say any thing as to the literary merits of the *Times*. Well, one day within the last few months, the *Times* and the *Scotsman* each published a somewhat elaborate review of a certain book. The reviews were flatly opposed to one another; they had no common ground at all; one said the book was extremely good, and the other that it was extremely bad. You must just make up your mind that in matters of taste there can be no unvarying standard of truth. In æsthetic matters, truth is quite relative. What is bad to you, is good to me perhaps. And indeed, if one might adduce the saddest of all possible proofs, how even the loftiest and most splendid genius fails to commend itself to every cultivated mind, it may suffice to say, that *that* brilliant *Scotsman* has on several occasions found fault with *Fraser's Magazine*, and specially with A. K. H. B.!

If you, my reader, are a wise and kind-hearted person (as I have no doubt whatever but you are), I think you would like very much to meet and converse with any person who has formed a bad opinion of you. You would take great pleasure in overcoming such a one's prejudice against you; and if the person were an honest and worthy person, you would be almost certain to do so. Very few folk are able to retain any bitter feeling towards a man they have actually talked with, unless the bitter feeling be one which is just. And a very great proportion of all the unfavorable opinions which men entertain of their fellow-men found on some misconception. You take up somehow an impression that such a one is a conceited, stuck-up person: you come to know him, and you find he is the frankest and most unaffected of men. You had a belief that such another was a cynical, heartless being, till you met him one day coming down a long black stair, in a poor part of the town, from a bare chamber in which is a little sick child, with two large tears running down his face; and when you enter the poor apartment you learn certain facts as to his quiet benevolence which compel you suddenly to construct a new theory of that man's character. It is only people who are radically and essentially bad whom you can really dislike after you come to know them. And the human beings who are thus essentially bad are very few. Something of the original Image lingers yet in almost every human soul. And in many a homely, commonplace person, what with vestiges of the old, and a blessed planting-in of something new, there is a vast deal of it. And every human being, conscious of honest intention and of a kind heart, may well wish that the man who dislikes and abuses him could just know him.

But there are human beings whom, if you are wise, you would not wish to know you too well. I mean the human beings (if such there should be) who think very highly of you; who imagine you very clever and very amiable. Keep out of the way of such! Let them see as little of you as possible. For when they come to know you well, they are quite sure to be disenchanted. The enthusiastic ideal which young people form of any one they admire is smashed by the rude presence of facts. I have got somewhat beyond the stage of feeling enthusiastic admiration, yet there are two or three living men whom I should be sorry to see. I know I should never admire them so much any more. I never saw Mr. Dickens: I don't want to see him. Let us leave Yarrow unvisited: our sweet ideal is fairer than the fairest fact. No hero is a hero to his valet: and it may be questioned whether any clergyman is a saint to his beadle. Yet the hero may be a true hero, and the clergyman a very excellent man: but no human being can bear too close inspection. I remember hearing a clever and enthusiastic young lady complain of what she had suffered on meeting a certain great bishop at dinner. No doubt he was dignified, pleasant, clever; but the mysterious halo was no longer round his head. Here is a sad circumstance in the lot of a very great man: I mean such a man as Mr. Tennyson or Professor Longfellow. As an elephant walks through a field, crushing the crop at every step, so do these men advance through life, smashing, every time they dine out, the enthusiastic fancies of several romantic young people.

This was to have been a short essay. But you see it is already long; and I have treated only two of the four Things Slowly Learnt which I had noted down. After much consideration I discern several courses which are open to me:—

(1.) To ask the editor to allow me forty or fifty pages of the magazine for my essay.

(2.) To stop at once, and allow it to remain forever a secret what the two remaining things are.

(3.) To stop now, and continue my subject in a future number of the magazine.

(4.) To state briefly what the two things are, and get rid of the subject at once.

The fundamental notion of Course No. 1

is manifestly vain. The editor is doubtless well aware that about sixteen pages is the utmost length of essay which his readers can stand. Nos. 2 and 3, for reasons too numerous to state, cannot be adopted. And thus I am in a manner compelled to adopt Course No. 4.

The first of the two things is a practical lesson. It is this: to allow for human folly, laziness, carelessness, and the like, just as you allow for the properties of matter, such as weight, friction, and the like, without being surprised or angry at them. You know that if a man is lifting a piece of lead he does not think of getting into a rage because it is heavy; or if a man is dragging a tree along the ground he does not get into a rage because it ploughs deeply into the earth as it comes. He is not surprised at these things. They are nothing new. It is just what he counted on. But you will find that the same man, if his servants are lazy, careless, and forgetful; or if his friends are petted, wrong-headed, and impracticable, will not only get quite angry, but will get freshly angry at each new action which proves that his friends or servants possess these characteristics. Would it not be better to make up your mind that such things are characteristic of humanity, and so that you must look for them in dealing with human beings? And would it not be better, too, to regard each new proof of laziness, not as a new thing to be angry with, but merely as a piece of the one great fact that your servant is lazy, with which you get angry once for all, and have done with it? If your servant makes twenty blunders a day, do not regard them as twenty separate facts at which to get angry twenty several times. Regard them just as twenty proofs of the one fact, that your servant is a blunderer; and be angry just once, and no more. Or if some one you know gives twenty indications in a day that he or she (let us say she) is of a petted temper, regard these merely as twenty proofs of one lamentable fact, and not as twenty different facts to be separately lamented. You accept the fact that the person is petted and ill-tempered: you regret it and blame it once for all. And after this once you take as of course all new manifestations of pettedness and ill-temper. And you are no more surprised at them, or angry with them, than you are at lead for being heavy, or at down for being light. It is their nature, and you calculate on it, and allow for it.

Then the second of the two remaining things is this—that you have no right to complain if you are postponed to greater people, or if you are treated with less consideration than you would be if you were a greater person. Uneducated people are very slow to learn this most obvious lesson. I remember hearing of a proud old lady, who was proprietor of a small landed estate in Scotland. She had many relations, some greater, some less. The greater she much affected, the less she wholly ignored. But they did not ignore *her*; and one morning an individual arrived at her mansion-house, bearing a large box on his back. He was a travelling pedler; and he sent up word to the old lady that he was her cousin, and hoped she would buy something from him. The old lady indignantly refused to see him, and sent orders that he should forthwith quit the house. The pedler went; but on reaching the courtyard, he turned to the inhospitable dwelling, and in a loud voice exclaimed, in the ears of every mortal in the house, "Ay, if I had come in my carriage-and-four, ye wad have been proud to have ta'en me in!" The pedler fancied that he was hurling at his relative a scathing sarcasm: he did not see that he was simply stating a perfectly unquestionable fact. No doubt earthly, if he had come in a carriage-and-four, he would have got a hearty welcome, and he would have found his claim of kindred eagerly allowed. But he thought he was saying a bitter and cutting thing, and (strange to say) the old lady fancied she was listening to a bitter and cutting thing. He was merely expressing a certain and innocuous truth. But though all mortals know that in this world big people meet greater respect than small (and quite right too), mo[illegible] mo[illegible]tals seem to find the principle a very unpleasant one when it comes home to themselves. And we learn but slowly [illegible], a pl[illegible] in seeing ourselves plainly subo[illegible] about Por- other people. Poor Oliver Gold[illegible] ker's Lit- very angry when at the club one [illegible] he was stopped in the middle of a story by a Dutchman, who had noticed that the Great Bear was rolling about in preparation for speaking, and who exclaimed to Goldsmith,

"Stop, stop; 'Toctor Shonson is going to speak!" Once I arrived at a certain railway station. Two old ladies were waiting to go by the same train. I knew them well, and they expressed their delight that we were going the same way; "Let us go in the same carriage," said the younger, in earnest tones; "and will you be so very kind as to see about our luggage?" After a few minutes of the lively talk of the period and district, the train came up. I feel the tremor of the platform yet. I handed my friends into a carriage, and then saw their baggage placed in the van. It was a station at which trains stop for a few minutes for refreshments. So I went to the door of the carriage into which I had put them, and waited a little before taking my seat. I expected that my friends would proceed with the conversation which had been interrupted; but to my astonishment I found that I had become wholly invisible to them. They did not see me and speak to me at all. In the carriage with them was a living peer, of wide estates and great rank, whom they knew. And so thoroughly did he engross their eyes and thoughts and words, that they had become unaware of my presence, or even my existence. The stronger sensation rendered them unconscious of the weaker. Do you think I felt angry? No, I did not. I felt very much amused. I recognized a slight manifestation of a grand principle. It was a straw showing how a current sets, but for which Britain would not be the country it is. I took my seat in another carriage, and placidly read my *Times*. There was one lady in that carriage. I think she inferred, from the smiles which occasionally for the first few miles overspread my countenance without apparent cause, that my mind was slightly disordered.

These are the two things already mentioned. But you cannot understand, friendly reader, what an effort it has cost me to treat them so briefly. The experienced critic will discern at a glance that the author could easily have made sixteen pages out of the material you have here in one. The author takes his stand upon this—that there are few people who can beat out thought so thin, or say so little in such a great number of words. I remember how my dear friend, the late editor of this magazine (whom all who knew him well miss more and more as days and weeks go on, and never will cease to miss), used to remark this fact in those warm-hearted and playful letters of his, with wonder not unmingled with indignation. And I remember how a very great prelate (who could compress all I have said into a page and a half) once comforted me by telling me that for the consumption of many minds it was desirable that thought should be very greatly diluted; that quantity as well as quality is needful in the dietetics both of the body and the mind. With this soothing reflection I close the present essay.

A. K. H. B.

THE distinguishing characteristic of the Chi[illegible]se mind is this—that at all points of the circle [illegible]scribed by man's intelligence it seems occa[illegible]onally to have caught glimpses of a heaven far [illegible]yond the range of its ordinary ken and vision. [illegible] caught a glimpse of the path which leads to [illegible]litary supremacy when it invented gunpow[illegible] some [illegible]nturies before the discovery was [illegible]y [illegible] other nation. It caught a glimpse [illegible]he pa[illegible] which leads to maritime supremacy [illegible]en it made, at a period equally remote, the [illegible]covery of [illegible] mariner's compass. It caught [illegible]th which leads to literary su[illegible] the tenth century, it invented [illegible]ss; and, as my illustrious friend [illegible]Sir E. Landseer) has reminded me, it has caught from time to time glimpses of the beautiful in color and design. But in the hands of the Chinese themselves the invention of gunpowder has exploded in crackers and harmless fireworks. The mariner's compass has produced nothing better than the coasting junk. The art of printing has stagnated in stereotyped editions of Confucius, and the most cynical representations of the grotesque have been the principal products of Chinese conceptions of the sublime and beautiful. Nevertheless, I am disposed to believe that under this mass of abortions and rubbish there lie hidden some sparks of a Diviner fire, which the genius of my countrymen may gather and nurse into a flame.—*Lord Elgin's Speech at the Lord Mayor's Dinner.*

From The Examiner.

The Life of Richard Porson, M.A., Professor of Greek in the University of Cambridge from 1792 *to* 1808. By the Rev. John Selby Watson, M.A., M.R.S.L. Longman and Co.

THIS is a weak book on a strong man. Mr. Watson's opening "Remarks on Biography" discourage the reader at the outset, and are found in the end to have supplied only too true a measure of his literary skill and taste. He must be, we think, an extraordinarily wakeful man who does not go to sleep in the course of reading Mr. Watson's first three pages and a half, if he should incautiously attempt to read them without an interval of rest. They contain in a highly concentrated form the soporific principle diffused through sermons of weak preachers. Thus he begins:—

"The charms of fiction are much less forcible than those of truth. Histories of imaginary personages, however strikingly represented, are much less interesting than those of eminent characters that really existed. The man who read Robinson Crusoe as a true tale found much fewer attractions in it when he was told that it was an invention.

"The desire to know how our fellow-creatures, especially the most distinguished of them, have lived, is the cause that biography gains so much attention. Whoever relates the life, or any considerable portion of the life, of any remarkable person, has the satisfaction of expecting that his narrative, unless given in an absolutely repulsive style, will attract some share of regard."

So he goes on. Presently, after pointing out that no human character is perfect, and that the biographer must be sincere, he makes a quotation upon which the profound comment, if made from the pulpit, might be warranted to soothe into instant sleep the best half of a congregation.

"'Nature, apparently,' said Styan Thirlby, as we are told by Mr. Nichols, in his 'Literary Anecdotes,' 'intended a kind of parity among her sons; but sometimes she deviates a little from her general purpose, and sends into the world a man of powers superior to the rest, of quicker intuition and wider comprehension; this man has all other men for his enemies, and would not be suffered to live his natural time, but that his excellencies are balanced by his failings. He that by intellectual exaltation thus towers above his contemporaries, is drunken, or lazy, or capricious; or, by some defect or other, is hindered from exerting his sovereignty of mind; he is thus kept upon the level, and thus preserved from the destruction which would be the natural consequence of universal hatred.'

"Whether the mass of mankind would ever rise to destroy a fellow-creature possessed of unrivalled intellectual powers, may be doubted; for it might be expected that such a being would act so as to secure the approbation and esteem of at least a majority of those around him; but it is certain that men distinguished by eminent mental abilities are often drawn down, whether by the influence of others, or by their own imprudence and misconduct, to a condition far below that of many others who are too much their inferiors in mind to be able even to estimate their merits. It is not necessary to recur to the lives of Edmund Smith, or Samuel Boyse, or Edgar Poe, for examples of such degradation; for almost every man, whether high or low, whether of little education or of much, has seen something of the kind among his own connections or acquaintances. Those who contemplate the lives and fortunes of mankind, too often, as they increase their knowledge increase their sorrow. If they discover great merits in eminent characters, they find them, perhaps, the more they search, obscured by such defects as they could at one time have scarcely imagined. They find gold, but gold mingled with clay."

We dare not try the effect of continuing this extract through the entire page that follows, written in the same lethargy of amazing dulness, and ending with the novel comparison of the course of life to a river. The preamble closes with this summary of Porson's character:—

"The man whose life we propose to relate was eminently distinguished for tenacity of memory, quickness of perspicacity, and accuracy of judgment; and we shall see how much these qualities appear to have contributed to his comfort."

A few new letters of little interest; copious extracts from Porson's writing, good, but for want of shrewdness in selection, not so suggestive as they ought to be; a pleasant gathering of familiar stories about Porson from Beloe's Sexagenarian, Barker's Literary Anecdotes, and the Porsoniana in Roger's Table Talk; a great deal of not so much masterly as schoolmasterly discussion over Greek, and weak digression—now into a long history of Ireland's Shakspeare forgeries, that starts only from the fact of Porson's having refused to certify their genuineness, as he was "slow to subscribe to articles of faith;" now into a long history of the argument in the Church on 1 John 5 : 7,—these are the points representing the chief merits and faults of Mr. Watson's "Life of Porson." Nearly all the advantages of an admirable subject for a book that might be at once learned and popular have been missed by the biographer. There is no better presentiment of the character of Porson than the current anecdotes afford, no sounding the depths of his strange nature.

But even when badly told there must be much to interest us in the life of a man born about a hundred years ago, whose father was a poor Norfolk weaver and clerk in the village church, and whose mother had before marriage been a maid-servant, yet of whom it is to be shown how the wonderful powers for which he was conspicuous even in boyhood, by their own force and in spite of a rugged character, raised him to an acknowledged rank as the first Greek scholar in Europe. With poor village teaching and the help of his father's taste for arithmetic, young Porson entered heartily into mathematical studies, and at ten years old "was greatly attracted by logarithms." The parish clerk's wonderful son interested the parish clergyman, an excellent man, who educated five sons for the University (in which the four who survived all obtained fellowships), and got the value of a fortune from his scanty income of two hundred a year. He was a man to be found roasting a turnip for his supper, rocking a cradle and reading a book, all at one time. To this excellent clergyman's house the parish clerk's remarkable son trudged every Monday morning with a week's provision on his arm, to be gratuitously taught by him together with his sons. But the other boys could not keep pace with Porson, who had been gifted from birth with a supernatural grasp of memory that would hold any thing and every thing, and keep its hold for any length of time. The kind-hearted clergyman, Mr. Hewitt, represented the boy's powers to a wealthy and benevolent neighbor, Mr. Norris, founder of the Norrisian professorship of Divinity at Cambridge. Mr. Norris having sent him to Cambridge that his powers might be tested by examination, undertook to help him forward in his studies, and contributed largely to a fund—of which Sir George Baker, then President of the College of Physicians, became treasurer—for the education of the marvellous weaver's son at a firstrate school and at the University. He went to Eton, knowing by heart the Latin books he was required to study there, was put through the common routine, and clearly enough despised it. Once when he was to construe Horace in class he had not his book, and took an Ovid which another boy thrust into his hand, from which he appeared to read while he went accurately through all the business of the lesson. As Eton is now open to public question, let us cite Porson's opinion of the worth of the teaching he got there :—

"According to the 'Short Account of Porson,' he himself used to say that he added little to his acquirements at Eton except facility in Latin versification, as he had read with Mr. Hewitt, before he went thither, almost all that was required of him in the school, and had learned many portions of Horace, Virgil, Homer, Cicero, and Livy by heart. He was unwilling to own that he was, on the whole, greatly indebted to Eton, but he must, as the writer remarks, have been 'much obliged to the collision of a public school for the rapidity with which he increased his knowledge, and the correction of himself by the mistakes of others. *Magnos enim viros non schola, sed contubernium facit.*'

"Mr. Kidd says that Porson, when he entered Eton, was 'wholly ignorant of quality;' and that 'after he had toiled up the arduous path to literary eminence, he was often twitted by his quondam schoolfellows with those violations of quality which are common in first attempts at Latin verse.' 'Our Greek Professor,' he adds, 'always felt sore upon this point. One of his best friends and greatest admirers has preserved a copy of verses, which indeed evince the rapid progress of his mind, but would not do honor to his memory.'

"That he could repeat by heart almost all the books read at Eton, before he became an Etonian, he himself told Mr. Maltby, and said that almost the only thing he recollected with pleasure during his Eton course was the rat-hunting with which the boys amused themselves in the Long Hall."

There was no adaptation of the teaching to the powers of the boy, who simply despised the work set before him. He had a healthy contempt for the vanity of modern classical versification, and when the *Musæ Etonenses* afterwards appeared, his opinion was that such exercises were fit only to be thrown behind the fire. Porson at Eton, as everywhere else, was a satirist, with a rough sharp wit that generally came victorious out of encounters. A disputant with him in his later life wound up an argument by saying to Porson, "My opinion of you is most contemptible, sir." "I never knew an opinion of yours that was not contemptible," Porson replied. Of a boy at school with an ungainly figure who was one of his butts, he said that Murphitt never need be conquered by a cork; he had but to swallow a tenpenny nail and let it work down through the twist of his body to come out a corkscrew at the other end. Which is, in the Watsonian style: "The sinuosities of his frame as it passed through would twist it into an excellent shape for a cork extractor." Mr. Watson gives extracts from Porson's Eton play, "Out of the Frying Pan into the Fire," which is in the library of Trinity College, Cambridge, but as he has evidently no very good perception of what is worth quoting and what is not, his account loses some of the interest it might have had.

Although Eton did not take to itself the honor of sending Porson to Cambridge, he was maintained there by the friends who had established among themselves the fund for his education, got his Trinity fellowship, and after a course of theological study, having, as he said, "found that I should require about fifty years' reading to make myself thoroughly acquainted with divinity, — to satisfy my mind on all points,—I gave it up." Dr. Postlethwaite, master of Trinity, desiring to put a nephew of his own into the lay fellowship that Porson applied for, the scholar, already famous, found himself, as he has said, a gentleman in London, with, sixpence in his pocket, upon which Mr. Watson sagely remarks: "This after awhile must have become literally true, for he lived, he said, at this period of his life for six weeks on a guinea, which, at sixpence a day, would leave him with sixpence only on the last day."

He still visited Cambridge, walking the whole distance from London in a day, and while he vigorously met the pressure of his poverty, friends and scholars who thought him ill-used, admired his learning and honored his sturdiness of character, were secretly conspiring to raise money that enabled them to present him with an annuity of one hundred a year. The names of the subscribers were withheld from him, and he took the annuity only on condition that the capital should be returned to its donors at his death. Dr. Postlethwaite also, eager to make amends for his bit of nepotism, was prompt and cordial in pressing upon Porson the Greek Professorship when it soon afterwards became vacant. It might then be held by a layman, but was worth in money only forty pounds a year. A canonry is now connected with it to endow it and secure a churchman in the chair. There were no lectures to yield fees, though Porson talked of lecturing; but it was fit that the first among Greek scholars should bear style in his own country and before foreigners as Mr. Professor Porson.

Mr. Professor, meantime living in London, still gave occasional evidence of his great learning; while at the Cider Cellars he was honored as "Dick," who could drink all night and every night. He was fast friends with Perry, writing political squibs, with and without Greek, in the *Morning Chronicle*, and he proposed marriage to Perry's sister and housekeeper, Mrs. Lunan, the good-tempered widow of a Scotch bookbinder, who had two or three children of her own. But he proposed marriage on condition that her brother was not to be told. One night when smoking his pipe with George Gordon at the Cider Cellars, he said to him, "Friend George, do you not think the Widow Lunan an agreeable sort of person as times go?" George did think so. "In that case," said Porson, "you must meet me to-morrow morning at St. Martin's in the Fields, at eight o'clock." That was the whole announcement to his groomsman of his private marriage. After the event he was urged to make it known at "the Court of Lancaster," as he called Perry's office in Lancaster Court, Strand, but he went off to spend the evening with a learned friend to whom he did not tell a word of his marriage, and with whom he sat as long as he could, before he adjourned as usual to the Cider Cellars until eight o'clock next morning. Maltby had met him in Covent Garden on the wedding morning, and observed his pea-green coat. "He was carrying a copy of *Le Moyen de Parvenir*, which he had just purchased off a stall, and holding it up, he called out jokingly, 'These are the sort of books to buy.'" In spite of the odd way of wedding, Porson was as good a husband as he could contrive to make himself, and learnt something of times and seasons during the year and a half that his wife, who was consumptive, lived. He himself had been troubled from youth with asthma.

"Porson's personal appearance, at the time of his marriage, was, when he was well dressed, very commanding. 'His very look,' says Mr. John Symmons, 'impressed me with the idea of his being an extraordinary man; what is called, I believe, by artists, in the *Hercules*, "the repose of strength," appeared in his whole figure and face.' 'His head,' says Pryse Gordon, 'was remarkably fine; an expansive forehead, over which was smoothly combed (when in dress) his shining brown hair. His nose was Roman, with a keen and penetrating eye, shaded with long lashes. His mouth was full of expression; and altogether his countenance indicated deep thought. His stature was nearly six feet.' Mr. Maltby, who became acquainted with him when he was under thirty, spoke of him as having been then a handsome man. His ordinary dress, especially when alone, and engaged in study, was careless and slovenly, but on important occasions, when he put on his blue coat, white waistcoat, black satin breeches, silk stockings, and ruffled shirt, 'he looked,' says Mr. Gordon, 'quite the gentleman.'"

Porson, like Dr. Johnson, was wakeful and averse from bed. He drank only in company, and, as a hundred stories affirm, would drink any thing; ink rather than nothing. His social humor made him dead to the fact that his friends of a night had beds to go to. Some of them kept him to strict rule, but if he accepted the rule that he was to go away at twelve, he would not stir until the clock struck. When his father was ill and he went down to him in Norfolk, living at his sister's house, he abstained considerably from all his rough ways, drank only two glasses of wine a day, went to church with his sister, and even stayed to the sacrament. But in town he followed his own habits. The booksellers offered him £3,000 for an edition of Aristophanes that his knowledge would have enabled him to complete in a few months. But he was not to be tempted. Yet he laid money by, small as his income was, and when he died left, to the surprise of everybody, eight or nine hundred pounds in the funds. Probably in his own quiet, uncommunicative way he had been attempting to make some provision for his latter years.

Porson's nose was vexed by his love of brandy and port. But at breakfast he chose to drink porter.

"One Sunday morning, when he was at Eton, he met Dr. Goodall, the provost, going to church, and asked him where Mrs. Goodall was. 'At breakfast,' replied the doctor. 'Very well, then,' rejoined Porson, 'I'll go and breakfast with her.' He accordingly presented himself at Mrs. Goodall's table, and being asked what he chose to take, answered 'Porter.' Porter was in consequence sent for, pot after pot, and the sixth pot was just being carried into the house, when Dr. Goodall returned from church.

"Mr. Upcott used to say that he was often to be seen at breakfast with a pot of porter and bread and cheese; and in the latter part of his life, in the dirtiest attire, and with black patches on his nose."

Of the Professor's memory

"'Nothing,' says the writer of the 'Scraps from Porson's Rich Feast,' 'came amiss to his memory; he would set a child right in his twopenny fable-book, repeat the whole of the moral tale of the Dean of Badajos, or a page of Athenæus on cups, or Eustathius on Homer.'

"Dr. Dauney of Aberdeen told Mr. Maltby that, 'during a visit to London, he *heard Porson declare*, that he could repeat Smollett's "Roderick Random" from beginning to end;' and Mr. Richard Heber assured Maltby that 'soon after the appearance of the "Essay on Irish Bulls," Porson used, when somewhat tipsy, to recite *whole pages of it verbatim* with great delight.' He said that he would undertake to learn by heart a copy of the *Morning Chronicle*in a week.

"One day Porson called on a friend who happened to be reading Thucydides, and who asked leave to consult him on the meaning of a word. Porson on hearing the word, did not look at the book, but at once repeated the passage. His friend asked how he knew that it was that passage. 'Because,' replied Porson, 'the word occurs only twice in Thucydides, once on the right-hand page, in the edition which you are using, and once on the left. I observed on which side you looked, and accordingly knew to which passage you referred.'"

But after all, he said, "his memory was a source of misery to him, as he could never forget any thing, even what he wished not to remember."

Of Porson's pleasant vein of wit records abound. When Gilbert Wakefield's Diatribe on Porson's Hecuba was about to be published, Porson was at a Club where the president proposed that each member should toast a friend and illustrate the toast by quoting Shakspeare. Porson's toast was Gilbert Wakefield, What's Hecuba to him or he to Hecuba?"

"The extravagant phrases in which Hayley and Miss Seward complimented each other, frequently called forth satirical remarks from Porson. One day he wrote for them the following dialogue:—

"Miss SEWARD *loquitur*.

"Tuneful poet, Britain's glory,
Mr. Hayley, that is you."

"HAYLEY *respondet*.

"Ma'am you carry all before you,
Trust me, Lichfield Swan, you do."

"Miss SEWARD.

"Ode, didactic, epic, sonnet,
Mr. Hayley, you're divine."

"HAYLEY.

"Ma'am, I'll take my oath upon it,
You yourself are all the Nine."

Everybody knows his saying of Bishop Pearson "that he would have been a first-rate critic in Greek if he had not muddled his head with divinity."

In 1806 the London Institution was established in the Old Jewry, with Professor Porson as its principal librarian, negligent enough to be told by the committee within a couple of years that he was grudged his salary of two hundred a year. In September, 1808, Porson, seized with apoplexy in the Strand, was carried as a stranger to the workhouse, and found there by Mr. Savage, the under-librarian, who had recognized him in the workhouse advertisement for the friends of "a tall man apparently about forty-five years of age, dressed in a blue coat and black breeches, and having in his pocket a gold watch, a trifling quantity of silver, and a memorandum-book, the leaves of which were filled chiefly with Greek lines written in pencil and partly effaced; two or three lines of Latin, and an algebraical calculation; the Greek extracts being principally from ancient medical works."

This attack was a precursor of his death, which happened on the 25th of the same month, when he was forty-nine years old. He lies buried in the chapel of Trinity College at the foot of the statue of Newton, with RICHARD PORSON written on a plain slab for his only epitaph. The fund that had been raised for his annuity, and which the contributors refused to take back, was spent in establishing the Porson scholarship, and the prize that, for 1861, has this week been divided between two gentlemen of St. John's, for their translation of a passage in the second part of Shakspeare's *Henry IV* (act ii. sc. 3) into Greek verse.

Punch; or, the London Charivari. Vols. I.—III. Re-issue.

THIS re-issue of the only comic journal which has succeeded in permanently establishing itself in England, carries us back twenty years at once; and it is very pleasant to be thus enabled to renew our acquaintance with the old jokes which we used to laugh at when we were so much younger than we are now. In his infancy, *Punch* was far less exclusively political than he has since become, his satire being directed towards social far more frequently than towards political objects. The general impression produced by looking over these volumes is, that in those early days the letter-press was, on the whole, superior, and the illustrations decidedly inferior, to the present standard.

THE *Cologne Gazette* states that the Archduke Ferdinand Maximilian, husband of the Princess Charlotte of Belgium, has had about thirty copies printed, for private circulation, of a work that he has written on the Brazils. The work, which is said to possess much ability and humor, is dedicated "To Charlotte, the companion of my travels and my life."

From The Saturday Review.

IRVINGIANA.*

AMERICA does well to cherish the memory of Washington Irving. If not one of her most vigorous or original thinkers, he is one of her most graceful and humorous writers. But it is not Americans alone who revere his name and delight in his books. England also ranks him among her classics—a pupil in the school of her essayists and historians in the past, and the friend of many of her most distinguished writers in the present century.

Between the date of Irving's first publication, *Salmagundi*, in 1807, and that of his last, the *Life of Washington*, which was completed in 1859, America has produced a literature of her own, and England has renewed her literary youth. In Irving's boyhood, the daughter-country could not point to half a dozen writers of mark. In his old age, she could boast of such historians as Bancroft, Prescott, and Mottley; of such poets as Longfellow and Bryant; of Cooper in fiction; of Emerson, and many other names in ethical and periodical literature. Within the same period the mother country has been no less fruitful. The eighteenth century saw three great English historians—the nineteenth has already produced thrice that number, any one of whom, threescore years ago, would have been considered a star of the first magnitude. Byron is not the greatest poet of the nineteenth century, but he is superior to the greatest poet of the eighteenth—Alexander Pope. In science, and in social and political philosophy, there is no parity between these epochs. Science, indeed, in the hands of such writers as Sir John Herschel and Mrs. Somerville, has created a literature for itself.

To have won and to hold a good position among such competitors, especially in an age which forgets almost as readily as it applauds, is the lot of few, and marks Irving for a vigorous as well as a graceful writer—as one of whom the time had need and with whom we cannot dispense. In the half century during which his pen was at work, how many lights, once burning and shining brightly, have been dimmed, if not entirely extinguished! What poem was more famous in its hour than *Lalla Rookh*? Who reads it now? *Roderick the Goth* was once on every library table—it is now seldom taken down from the library shelves. Much of Byron's verse has fallen into desuetude—most of Bulwer's novels are superseded. The half of Scott's writings has become a dead letter. Many whom the Quarterly and Edinburgh Reviewers loved in their day have died young. It is not so with Washington Irving. We do not claim for him a place beside the greatest minds of his age. He would have thanked us little for such an assumption. Yet, like his favorite, Goldsmith, he survives, while many more powerfully built and richly laden vessels have gone down. His *Life of Columbus* is as vital as Robertson's *America*, and has long outlived Southey's *Brazil*. Time has abated little of the freshness of his *Sketch-Book*, his *Bracebridge Hall*, or his *Astoria*. His *History of New York* made grave judges laugh fifty years ago, and, fickle as is the fashion of humor, it cannot now be read with unmoved muscles.

But literary excellence is not the only merit of Irving's writings. Their moral and social influence has been great and always good. It is not merely that he never penned a line which, dying, he would have wished to blot—that he never sought applause by tricks of language or extravagance of thought—that he never imported, as some English writers have done, into either his lighter or his graver works, paradoxes or prejudices from Paris or Weimar. He has never been disloyal to the classical school of England. His first love was given to Chaucer and Spenser—his second to the wits and poets who illustrated the eighteenth century. His acquaintance with the modern literature of Europe was considerable, but it never led him astray from his allegiance to Shakspeare and Milton. And he did more than this, perhaps unconsciously, but, without doubt, effectively. No one in his generation labored more effectually than Irving to reconcile the mind of the old country with the mind of the new. At the date of his earlier writings, England and America were on such terms as divide and cause houses to fall. They were jealous of each other, angry with each other—the elder member of the family accounting the younger a graceless and impertinent upstart; the younger regarding the elder as a peevish beldame, proud of heart

* *Irvingiana; a Memorial of Washington Irving.* New York: Charles Richardson. 1860.

and vixenish in temper. The *Quarterly Review*, for nearly thirty years after its commencement, rarely afforded a civil word to America. It is to Southey's honor that, Tory as he was in most respects, he uniformly protested against this uncharitable dealing. America, said Gifford and his train-band, has no established church, no army which a true soldier could review without inextinguishable laughter, no Magna Charta, no gentlemen, no ladies, no single element of national unity or greatness. She is one vast shop, if not, indeed, one huge gambling house, in which every man is seeking to enrich himself and to beggar his neighbor. If a traveller told the world that all was not barren between the Transatlantic Dan and Beersheba, he was singled out for abuse—he was a demagogue, an atheist, a fool, a dupe, a Sir John Mandeville; but if any one returned from the United States with a book written in the temper of Dr. Smellfungus, sniffling at American manners, and snarling at American institutions, him the *Quarterly* guide and philosopher hailed with bravos, and bade sit at his right hand. We have become, since that time, better instructed and more tolerant. We listen as willingly to a candid and well-informed observer, like Sir Charles Lyell, as to Mr. Dickens' or Mrs. Trollope's hasty "Notes." We admit that, if an American should come to Britain in quest of vice or folly, he will find them both in town and country. We, too, have our "wind-bags" in the Senate, and our coxcombs in the pulpit—have those who hasten to be rich, and those who hurry to poverty among us. *Præbemus crura sagittis.* Irving was one of the first who helped England and America to reconciliation. His writings, from the outset, were void of gall and bitterness; they were palpably formed on our best models, and so gratified our vanity; they abounded in charming pictures of our life and manners, and therefore soothed our jealousy. Travellers had averred that out of America no gentleman could come; but here was a most presentable gentleman at whose approach every door was opened—moreover, a modest, quiet gentleman, who excited no rivalry by the brilliancy of his conversation, for he was a silent man, but who conciliated all who approached him by his demeanor and courtesy. His works confirmed the influence of his presence. Like good conversation, they made no undue demands on the attention, while they attracted readers by a variety of topics, touched upon but not exhausted, and by the always well-chosen and often highly picturesque words in which those topics were presented. America had sent us, in return for favors received, an Addison not requiring a bottle of Burgundy to loosen his tongue, a Goldsmith who neither talked like Poor Poll nor flaunted in peach-colored coats.

Seldom has the current of a life—a literary life especially—run more smoothly than Irving's. Seldom can the retrospect of duties fulfilled or of work done have been more satisfactory. He was born in the state to which the wise man aspired. His family had neither poverty nor riches. His home was a happy one; his school education the best the times afforded; his brothers, who were several years older than himself, occupied themselves with literature and fostered his natural taste for it. He had the good fortune early to fall in with a stock of the best English authors, who wrote under the "great Anna," or the greater Elizabeth. His schoolmaster seems to have judiciously left the young Washington very much to himself, guiding, but not driving, him along the road of learning. He was innocent of Greek, and had but little Latin, but the loss of them was made up to him abundantly, at first by his familiarity with English classics, and afterwards by his acquirements in different European languages. He was early "dipped in ink," his literary productions dating from his nineteenth year. They were a series of essays on the theatrical performances and manners of New York, and were written under the signature of "Jonathan Oldstyle," for a newspaper entitled the *Morning Chronicle*, then edited by his brother, Dr. Peter Irving. This was a proper prelude to the *Sketch-Book*. As yet, however, his vocation to literature was not decided. He was very near becoming a painter. In 1804 he visited the south of Europe, some pulmonary symptoms having made it advisable for him to shun the extremes of his native climate. At Rome he became the friend of Washington Allston, who, with the enthusiasm of an artist, prompted his young countryman to take up his abode with him, and wield the brush and palette instead of the pen and ink-horn

For a few days the vision of artist-life pleased him; "but fears and doubts," he says himself, gradually clouded the prospect, and after an absence of two years, he returned to New York and became an attorney-at-law. Law, however, neither helped nor harmed Irving, for he never drew or held a brief.

In his twenty-fourth year (1807), Irving entered into literary copartnership with his brother William and Mr. Paulding, and amused or admonished "the Town"—as the public used to be called—with *Salmagundi; or, the Whim-Whams and Opinions of Lancelot Langstaff, Esq.* Here was a second graft from the British essayists. The piquant gossip of the time has become amusing history now; and *Salmagundi* is still read with interest on the other side of the Atlantic. But the humor is too local for transplantation, and these papers could not strike root in England. His next work, however, although perhaps Americans alone can fully enter into its humor, was by no means unpalatable in Britain. Of *Knickerbocker's History of New York*, Sir Walter Scott wrote in the following terms, in 1813: "Accept my best thanks for the uncommon degree of entertainment which I have received from the most excellent jocose history of New York. I am sensible that as a stranger to American parties and politics, I must lose much of the concealed satire of the piece; but I must own that looking at the obvious meaning only, I have never read any thing so closely resembling the style of Dean Swift as the annals of Diedrich Knickerbocker." How Scott welcomed the author of the work he thus applauded, at Abbotsford, a few years later is chronicled in the *Crayon Miscellany*, and in Lockhart's *Biography*. These veracious annals took in for a time some persons even in America, and drew upon Irving most undeserved and very absurd censure from the Historical Society of New York. These sapient censors were, it seems, of opinion, with Martinus Scriblerus, that he who makes a jest of antiquity is no better than Ham, the father of Canaan. But it was in critical Germany, where men are so prone to discover that "Garths do not write their own dispensaries," that the unintended mystification was most complete. Goeller, the editor of Thucydides, cites from this authentic narrative a passage in illustration of the Greek historian, "Adde locum Washingtonis Irvingii *Hist. Novi Eboraci*, Lib. vii., cap. 5." The book merited the praise of Scott. The style is excellent; the descriptions of nature and manners are happy, whether serious or humorous; and even the satire is, much of it, of that general kind which admits of transplantation.

In 1816—a year memorable for its commercial revulsions—good, as it often happens, under the guise of ill, befell Irving. The mercantile house with which he was now connected failed, and he was thrown upon his own resources for a livelihood. He accepted his altered fortunes cheerfully. He repaired to London. He studied English life where its features are best seen—in places remote from the social uniformity of the capital—and in 1810 published the first *number* of the *Sketch-Book* at New York, and the two volumes, so familiar to our eyes, at London, in 1820. *Bracebridge Hall* was written rapidly, and appeared in the following year; and in 1823 was succeeded by *Tales of a Traveller*, which, though it contained some excellent papers, was less successful—and, indeed, less deserving of success—than its two predecessors. Both in London and Paris, Irving was now a "lion," though, it appears, a very somnolent one at feeding-time, for it was often, if not always, his custom of an afternoon to sleep when beards were wagging at table. We suspect that his slumbers, like those of Lord North, permitted of a good deal of both hearing and marking his "commensales."

The United States of the New World, like those of the Old, have some customs which the parent country might perhaps imitate with advantage. Holland in the seventeenth, like America in the nineteenth, century, selected for its residents and representatives at foreign courts persons eminent for their services to learning and literature. Neither of these great republics thought that men are fit for ambassadors merely because of the length of their sheep-skins or their purses. The Lucys are an "ancient house," but they are not meet for all employments. In 1829 Irving was appointed Secretary of Legation to the American Embassy at London, and in 1842, Minister to Spain, an office which he occupied for the next four years. The latter appointment was an acknowledgment of the credit reflected on his country and himself by his *History of Columbus*, which he published in 1828, adding thereby to the nascent literature of America volumes worthy to rank beside those of Robertson, Prescott, and Helps. He had passed from fiction to facts at the instigation, or at least through the intervention of Alexander H. Everett, then Minister to Spain. Navarrete, about that time, had been collecting and publishing a series of important documents relating to Columbus, and Irving was invited to Madrid for the purpose of translating them. For a translation he substituted an original work, to which the *Voyages and Discoveries of the Companions of Columbus* became in due time a supplement, and for which one of the fifty-guinea gold medals provided by George IV. for eminence in historical writing was awarded him. Irving's fellow "medalist" on this occasion was no less an historian than the late Henry Hallam. His residence in Spain yielded more fruit; viz., the *Chronicle of the Conquest of Granada*, the *Alhambra, or the New Sketch-Book*, and the *Legends of the Conquests of Spain*. The series of the Spanish and Moorish subjects treated by Irving was completed by his *Life of Mahomet and his Successors* (1849-50). The latter is perhaps the least happy of Irving's undertakings. He has not added materially to Gibbon's splendid sketch of the Arabian legislator, and seems not to have been sufficiently aware of the apocryphal character of many of his vouchers.

Astoria and the *Life of Washington* are the last productions of Irving's fertile pen which we need mention, although they by no means complete the list of his writings. The former exhibits much of the pictorial power of Defoe, but without any of Defoe's predilection for rendering fact ancillary to fiction. Irving was attracted to the subject by an early fondness for the stories of the trappers and *voyageurs* of the West, among whom he had been thrown in his youth, and by his friendship with the projector of the *Enterprise beyond the Rocky Mountains*—the second title of his book—the late Mr. John Jacob Astor. He has accurately described in the following words the scope of this interesting narrative:—

"The work I here present to the public is necessarily of a rambling and somewhat disjointed nature, comprising various expeditions and adventures by land and sea. The facts, however, will prove to be linked and banded together by one great scheme, derived and conducted by a master-spirit. One set of characters, also, continues throughout, appearing occasionally, though sometimes at long intervals, and the whole enterprise winds up with a regular catastrophe; so that the work, without any labored attempt at artificial construction, actually possesses much of that variety so much sought after in works of fiction, and considered so important to the interest of every history."

When Irving was but five years old, Washington had "laid his hand upon the child's head and blessed him"—"a blessing" which the receiver of it believed "had attended him through life." To write a *Life of Washington* was "an idea which entered early into his mind." He looked forward to it, though long postponed, as "the crowning effort of his literary career." He lived long enough to complete his project, although he was more than threescore and ten years old when the first of five volumes was published. If the narrative bear some tokens of senescence, it also exhibits many of the best gifts of years and "old experience." The style of it is simple; the sentiments are untinged by prejudice; and the hero of it appears in Irving's pages as he was in life, a soldier, a statesman, and patriot, second to none, and superior to most of the worthies "in ancient or in modern books enrolled."

The general felicity which had marked Irving's manhood attended him to the close of life. In a retreat which he had singled out nearly half a century before it became his own,—Sunnyside, on the banks of the Hudson,—tended by kindred, and surrounded by friends who loved and revered him, honored by the great nation whom he had honored by his writings, having fulfilled every duty, having gratified every wish, and exempt at the last from many of the sufferings incident to long life, Washington Irving drew his last breath on the 28th of November, 1859.

The Recreations of a Country Parson. Second series. Parker, Son, and Bourn.

THIS book contains a second collection of the essays which have appeared in *Fraser's Magazine*, under the signature of A.K.H.B. They are not so much remarkable for the display of a rare literary power, or for display of any sort, as for the refinement of a thoughtful and therefore cheerful gentleness with which the common truths of every-day life are presented in them. It is rest to the weary to take up a book like this, alive with quiet fellow-feeling for the smaller as for the greater joys and troubles of humanity, flashing its playful satires that scorch nobody and appear only as breaks of light; and winning men to pleasant wholesome meditation by the charm of a manner that is to some of the good satire of the day as summer evening to the glare of summer noon, but to much more, as the quiet evening light to the mere whiz and flash and never-ending bang of a display of fireworks. Although the Country Parson's Essays are well known, nobody will mind reading twice over any thing that he has written. We will illustrate, therefore, his kindliness with one of his pictures of a form of the life concerning which he is especially entitled to say what he thinks.

"I think of the case of a clergyman who at his first start was rather fortunate: who gets a nice parish at six and twenty: I mean a parish which is a nice one for a man of six and twenty: and who never gets any other preferment, but in that parish grows old. Don't we all know how pretty and elegant every thing was about him at first; how trim and weedless were his garden and shrubbery; how rosy his carpets, how airy his window-curtains, how neat though slight all his furniture; how graceful, merry, and nicely dressed the young girl who was his wife; how (besides hosts of parochial improvements) he devised numberless little changes about his dwelling: rustic bowers, moss-houses, green mounts, labyrinthine walks, fantastically trimmed yews, root-bridges over the little stream. But as his family increased, his income stood still. It was hard enough to make the ends meet even at first, though young hearts are hopeful; but with six or seven children, with boys who must be sent to college, with girls who must be educated as ladies, with the prices of all things ever increasing, with multiplying bills from the shoemaker, tailor, dressmaker, the poor pastor grows yearly poorer. The rosy face of the young wife has now deep lines of care; the weekly sermon is dull and spiritless; the parcel of books comes no more; the carpets grow threadbare, but are not replaced; the furniture becomes creaky and rickety; the garden walks are weedy; the bark peels off the rustic verandah; the moss-house falls much over to one side; the friends far away grow out of all acquaintance. The parson himself, once so precise in dress, is shabby and untidy now; his wife's neat figure is gone; the servants are of an inferior class, coarse and insolent; perhaps the burden of hopeless debt presses always with its dull dead weight upon the poor clergyman's heart. There is little spring in him to push off the invasion of fatigue and infection, and he is much exposed to both; and should he be taken away, who shall care for the widow and the fatherless, losing at once their head, their home, their means of living? Even you, non-clerical reader, know precisely what I describe; hundreds have seen it; and such will agree with me when I say that there is no sadder sight than that of a clergyman, with a wife and children, growing poor as he is growing old. Oh, that I had the fortune of John Jacob Astor, that I might found, once for all, a fund that should raise forever above penury and degradation the widows and the orphans of rectory, vicarage, parsonage, and manse!"

A page or two afterwards we have in a note pleasant evidence of the way in which A.K.H.B. carried the hearts of his readers along with him. It is a note to this passage:—

"What a little end is sometimes the grand object of a human being's strivings through many weeks and months! I sat down the other day in a poor chamber, damp with much linen drying upon crossing lines. There dwells a solitary woman, an aged and infirm woman, who supports herself by washing. For months past her earnings have averaged three shillings a week. Out of that sum she must provide food and raiment; she must keep in her poor fire; and she must pay a rent of nearly three pounds a year. 'It is hard work, sir,' she said; 'it costs me many a thought getting together the money to pay my rent.' And I could see well, that from the year's beginning to its end, the thing always uppermost in that poor old widow's waking thoughts was the raising of that great incubus of a sum of money. A small end, you would say, for the chief thoughts of an immortal being!

Don't you feel, gay young reader, for that fellow-creature, to whom a week has been a success, if at its close she can put by a few halfpence towards meeting the term-day? Would you not like to enrich her, to give her a light heart by sending her a half-sovereign? If you would, you may send it to me."

This charming little charity sermon had, as the note shows, its reward in a collection, for, says the Country Parson,

"I cannot deny myself the pleasure of recording that for many days after the above paragraph was published (in *Fraser's Magazine* for June, 1860), there arrived by each morning's post little sums sent by all kinds of people, in distant parts of Britain, which made the poor widow quite rich."

These "Recreations of a Country Parson" make a book that should be bought and added to home furniture rather than borrowed from a circulating library. It is full of the domestic spirit, of its ready sympathies and charities, its meditation, and its quiet mirth.

Physico-Prophetical Essays on the Locality of the Eternal Inheritance, its Nature and Character, the Resurrection Body, the Mutual Recognition of Glorified Saints. By the Rev. W. Lister, F.G.S. Longman and Co.

Inscribed in capital letters at the head of this book is Newton's famous phrase, "Hypotheses non fingo," a motto which could not, without most ludicrous unfitness, be prefixed to any of the apocalyptic romances of the Cummings, McCauslands, Stanley Fabers, and the rest of that school. Truly does Mr. Lister say of these fantastic interpreters, that they have played such tricks with the subject of prophecy as have "rendered even its very name distasteful to sober-minded men, who have, perhaps, only occasionally directed their attention to it, and who have therefore seen little more than the fanciful interpretations which have been given to many of the expressions of Scripture, and which have made them feel that the language of the Bible may, in this way, be made to mean almost any thing which a lively fancy can suggest, and that any thing like certainty with regard to its meaning is not to be expected." He himself adopts an entirely different method, and his work, he believes, may be said to be in some respects the first of its kind, having in it little or nothing that is imaginative or speculative, or merely hypothetical. Its topics have been drawn directly and solely from Scripture, and its conclusions have not been sought intentionally, otherwise than by the strict path of demonstration. Of the two recognized methods of prophetical interpretation—the Figurative and the Literal—Mr. Lister adopts the latter only in the present volume. Its use, he thinks, should be the rule, and that of the opposite method the exception, and he has specially chosen for discussion a range of subjects among which such exceptions do not present themselves. Having then determined the meaning of a given prophecy, he has next endeavored to view the things predicted, when of a physical nature, in the light of legitimate science, and to explain them by examples drawn from actual nature, either past or present. For instance, he draws largely on geology and physical astronomy for illustrations of the nature of the transformed earth, without a sea, where, and not in heaven, he fixes the eternal abode of all the redeemed. He averts to the increase of habitable space, which will be obtained by the absence of the sea which now covers more than three-fifths of the surface of the globe, and the much greater gain in this respect which would ensue should the density of the earth become equal to that of some other planets—to that of Saturn, for instance, which is about eight times less than that of the earth—which latter he gives reason for believing to have been far less at one time than it is now, and to have been increased by the cooling and contraction of the crust. His reasonings of this kind, whatever be their force and conclusiveness, are generally based upon sound scientific data, but not invariably so, for he talks of an animating or vital principle of animal bodies, a thing which all biologists know to be a mere figment and not an entity.—*Spectator.*

New Brunswick as a Home for Emigrants. First and Second Prize Essays. By J. V. Ellis and James Edgar. St. John, N. B.: Barnes and Co.

These are the two Essays which have obtained the prizes of fifteen and ten guineas, offered for public competition in December last by the President and Directors of the St. John's Mechanics' Institute. Both of the successful competitors are, as might be expected, warm panegyrists of the colony to which they belong. We see no reason to doubt the justice of the committee's decision that Mr. Ellis' production is the better of the two.

From The Spectator, 25 May.

THE CIVIL WAR IN AMERICA.

MR. SEWARD'S letter to the American Minister in Paris, though telegraphed all over the Union, adds little to our previous information. The policy enunciated by the Secretary of State on 4th May is precisely the policy defined by the President on the 4th March. On the day of his inauguration Mr. Lincoln took up a position from which he has never yet receded, and which is simply the one any European monarch would assume. Secession, said the President from the steps of the Capitol, is impossible. To that dogma he has steadfastly adhered, and that dogma implies all. The ruler of an undivided state can enter into no negotiation with rebels, accept no mediation between the nation and its provinces, listen to no terms not prefaced by the acknowledgment of his authority. And therefore Mr. Lincoln refused even to see the "Commissioners" from Montgomery, and treated with scorn Governor Hicks' request for the mediation of Lord Lyons. The last act was not acceptable in England, but a proposal from Smith O'Brien at the head of an armed force to refer Irish rights to the mediation of Count de Flahault would scarcely, we imagine, find much favor in our eyes. There may have been some momentary indecision as to the opinion of the North, for republican statesmen are trained in servility to the popular will; but the opinion of the President himself has never swerved. Even his reasoning for subjugating the South has a European sound. He does not go to punish—what ruler ever did?—but simply to release the friends of the Union from their bondage; to relieve, as an emperor of the French would say, that excellent people which is deceived and tyrannized over by an execrable faction. And now the Secretary of State repeats to M. Thouvenel that the thought of a dissolution of the Union, peaceably or by force, has never entered the mind of any candid statesman in America. If the Union cannot be broken, the Southerners are rebels, and as rebels the Federal Government intends, and has always intended, to subdue them. The question at issue is not the will but the power of the Executive to carry out its plans.

Our information on that point is steadily enlarged by the mails which successively reach Europe. Of the resources of the South, it is true, exceedingly little is still known, for the facts which reach us are distorted on their transit through the North. According to New Yorkers the South is bankrupt, but the South has repudiated her debts owing to the North, and the sum thus saved will of itself suffice to keep an army in the field. The slaves will starve, say the Western States, without our wheat; but we do not find that the rice crop is diminished, and rice, though an inferior food to wheat, will keep men alive and in good working trim. There is plenty of it, the last report showing a cultivation of three hundred millions of pounds all grown within the Southern States themselves. Add to this supply the wheat and Indian corn grown within the South itself, and the great harvest of the Border States, and there will be little further hope of starving the insurrection out. The reports of the armed strength of the South are contradictory to a degree, but Mr. Davis' official statement is now before the world. He estimates his soldiers, semi-regular troops fairly trained, and to all appearance well armed, at thirty-five thousand men. In addition to these, he calls for one hundred thousand more, and as the eight millions who obey him are military in tone, he may obtain them for a time.

In the North every detail pleasant and unpleasant is instantly given to the world. There may be some exaggeration as to numbers, but we suspect less than is usually supposed, the precise muster of the regiment being usually published as it departs. The forces, then, at the disposal of Mr. Lincoln seem to consist already of a very indefinite number of regular troops—not eight thousand at the outside—thirty thousand volunteers in and round Washington, thirty thousand more on or ready for the march, and a reserve of a quarter of a million armed, organized, and partly drilled recruits. We give that figure as the nearest approach we can find to truth amidst a mass of contradictions. Besides these, he can rely for the time upon a population of nineteen millions, singularly apt to military life, burning with excitement, and soon to be provided with the European arms. The force is ample in numbers, and the President has adopted the best means to make enthusiasm permanently available. A great standing army, one hundred thousand strong, is being enlisted for three and five years, and will be organized during the time which must elapse before the fall of the leaf renders the climate of the Southern States tolerable to Northern men. They will have ample occupation up to that time in reconquering Maryland and Virginia, and resisting the attack Mr. Davis on the 8th of May was preparing to make upon the capital. The Virginians are evidently prepared to fight, and a martial population of a million whites will not be defeated, even with the aid of the Western counties, in less than a campaign. If, then, the enthusiasm lasts, the President ought, by the beginning of

November, to find himself with an army of one hundred thousand men accustomed to service, his communications secured by the occupation of Maryland, and his front cleared by the defeat of the Virginians.

The delay will test the one point on which the friends of the North are still in anxious doubt. Will the enthusiasm of the Free States endure up to the point of providing means for a long war? The enthusiasm, while it lasts, is of course irresistible, but will it last? It is one thing to march to Washington for a month's bivouac, and quite another to invade the South on a three years' campaign. Men who will encounter any danger are often afraid of hardship, and English officers distinguished at the Alma shirked a diet of green coffee and raw pork. Already the "pet regiment" of New York—the 7th—talks of returning when its thirty days are up, and thousands who would face cannon quail at the ruin a protracted absence from business would entail. Nor have the Americans, as yet, quite counted the money cost of a long war. The papers talk of twenty-three million dollars, as if that sum, magnificent as a subscription, were adequate to a campaign. They will be fortunate if in an enemy's country it will keep their fleet and army for a month. As they themselves acknowledge, they must carry everything from shells to rations, with them on their march, and an army of one hundred thousand men raises prices on a scale of which their experience in Mexico gave but a faint idea. We question if they have yet realized the most ordinary difficulties of the commissariat, whether the mere cost of carriage has entered into their calculations.

Nevertheless, admitting all this, and much more which will be patent to military men, allowing for that sickening reaction sure to follow a period of excitement, and estimating at their full value the party strifes, and party opposition which will supersede the present unanimity, the North is still, we maintain, strong enough to carry out the policy so determinately announced. The President, as we have said, is providing for the reaction. Granted a certain looseness of discipline, there will always be volunteers enough to keep an army of a hundred thousand men on foot. The West swarms with men to whom campaigning is enjoyment, the North with men whom every check will bring rapidly to the front. With regular pay and slack discipline there are enough of the fighting class without calling, except in emergencies, on the bone and muscle of the nation. The enthusiasm may die away, but there is no chance of Northern determination growing cold. The colonists maintained the fight for twelve years with Great Britain, and though Washington's force faded away as the harvest came round, it was always renewed, always as hostile to compromise with the foe. This generation, too, has been trained in hatred of the South, and an insulted American forgives about as readily as the Indian he expelled. The war, too, has revealed the fact that the old Puritan spirit, dead in the newspapers, survives among the people. The Massachusetts men quote texts about slaying which are not pleasant in adversaries' ears, and company after company gravely announces two prayer-meetings a week during the campaign, and invites its officers to join. Zerubbabel Peabody, yeoman, deacon, and volunteer, is not the kind of man whose hand turns back readily from the plough, or hesitates because the Amalekite is strong. Add to these facts that the war itself will turn thousands into soldiers whose trade is war, that the men of the Border must fight or perish, and that every skirmish will open new and terrible sores—be, as it were, a new baptism of hatred—and the fear of want of men will be speedily given up. The want of money is still less to be anticipated. The Americans trust in a delusion as to the probable expense, but they are quite able to sustain the reality. A debt of a hundred millions sterling would still leave them less taxed than any European race, and the South must be impoverished before themselves. The hatred of taxation is very deep, but necessity modifies prejudices of that kind in a marvellously brief space, and the race which begins with subscriptions will soon resign itself to making those subscriptions regular and proportionate.

Indeed, willing or unwilling, the Americans may make up their minds that the cheapness of their administration is finally at an end. If they subdue the South, they must for years maintain an army to keep down the embers of the conflagration. If they make peace after war, they must watch their frontier like a European power. Democracy may survive the struggle, but economy will have finally disappeared.

From The Economist, 25 May.

CIVIL WAR: THE PRICE AND THE PROFIT.

THE Americans are just now standing in one of those critical positions and at one of those perilous moments of a nation's life which determine its fate and its character during many future years and, possibly, many unborn generations. The ground is very narrow, and even as we write is being washed from beneath our feet: the moment is very short, and perhaps has already passed away. On what may now be decided—nay, too probably on what has been already done—will depend vast good, or almost incalculable evil. The peaceful disruption of the Union we should welcome most hopefully, as an almost unalloyed advantage. A civil war we cannot but regard as an almost unmitigated mischief. A breach cannot be healed by internecine hostilities; but it may easily be widened into an impassable gulf. Even if a rejunction were possible, and as desirable as the Northern Federalists appear to deem it,—who can hope for it through the medium of war? The South can never again expect to dominate the North. The North cannot seriously expect to subjugate the South; nor, as we have often urged, would it be worth their while to do so. To *lure* the seceders back into the Union would be a grand, and might be a beneficent achievement: to *force* them back neither is feasible nor would be profitable.

Neither party, therefore, can subdue or re-embrace the other—probably by no means, certainly not by fighting. But each may inflict upon its antagonist such fearful injury and suffering as will leave a legacy of undying hatred to their children and their children's children. The material mischief wrought by civil strife between the two sections of the Union will be as nothing to the ferocious passions which it will engender. The havoc it will make in their prosperity will be trifling in comparison with the havoc it will make in their morality, and their civilization. For, observe, it will not be like a duel between two courteous foes, who exchange shots with unruffled tempers and no consequences. It will not even be like a pugilistic contest between two angry English yeomen, who shake hands before the mill and share a pot of porter after it. It will be deadly, it will be vindictive, it will be bitter. It will partake both of the barbarism and the relentlessness which have shocked us so much in the narratives of personal encounters among individual Americans. It is impossible to foresee what extremes belligerents may not permit themselves, when reciprocal inflictions are every day inflaming tempers which combine Anglo-Saxon stubbornness witn Indian ferocity. Let us look forward for a moment to the *possible* developments which such a conflict may assume—the frightful extremities to which, step by step in the progress of exasperation, it may ultimately lead. The navies of the North blockade the Southern ports; close, if they can, all their issues to European markets; shut in, and by so doing render worthless, because unsalable, all those teeming products of tropical plantations by which planters purchase their luxuries and comforts, and in the growth of which they employ their slaves. The Southerners may *live* undoubtedly under such a blockade, for they can grow their own sugar, cattle, tobacco, rice, and Indian corn. But conceive the state of mind of some millions of men, who have hitherto been dependent on foreign commerce for nearly all articles of consumption, when deprived of wine, of tea, of clothing, and with wheat driven up almost to a famine price;—and at the same time, in order to maintain the conflict, taxed to an extent that only the most prosperous condition of trade could make endurable. Conceive the feelings of thousands of the population, thrown out of all their usual avocations, and driven by idleness and privation into habits of marauding, plundering, and piracy.

Then turn to the other side of the blotted and disfigured picture,—the rich commerce of the North preyed upon by Southern privateers; the merchants of Boston and New York deranged in their transactions, struck at in their credit; their debtors and customers turned into enemies and repudiators; their wealth deeply eaten into in order to support a war of which they perceive more clearly day by day the hopelessness and the waste, while day by day their passions and their pride become more inveterately interested in bringing it to a triumphant issue—even though that triumph must be inevitably barren. They will not be able to bear its continuance; they will not be able to swallow the humiliation of confessing themselves discomfited and baffled: may they not at last, in their perplexity and exasperation, be tempted into the supreme desperation of endeavoring to excite a servile war, and, in their frenzied and overheated brains, elevate the crime of slave insurrection, as the Southerners have already elevated the crime of slavery, into a solemn duty and a sacred right? Which party would conquer in the strife, if it ever reached so horrible a development as this, we do not care even to speculate: but that such a development should be among its not impossible and perhaps not very remote contingencies, is enough of itself to make the most infuriated opponents pause before they strike the first blow. We will not enter, even for a passing moment, into any strategic estimate of probabilities. It would be rash, and almost irrelevant, to ask with which party lie the best chances of mastery. We content ourselves with the position—which even excited passion must, we think, admit to be irrefragable—that, to whichever side the balance may incline, the mutual mischief inflicted must be literally incalculable; and that the completest *victory* which it is possible for the North to achieve would bring no *success* worth achieving. As we have said over and over again, stripping the question at issue naked, it resolves itself into this: "Why should the Federal Government fight to prevent the Slave States doing that which they will do just as certainly after defeat or after victory, as before the battle?—nay, which is already done, and which not the most sanguine Abolitionist believes can be undone?" Mr. C. Clay, indeed—in that strange letter which he has addressed to the *Times*, and which is a very model of feeble reasoning and questionable taste—would fain persuade us that his constituents know clearly what they are about to fight for, and that they really propose to themselves to subjugate the seceding States, and believe they shall easily succeed in doing so. We can only say in reply that we have never met any sober countryman of his bold enough to avow the same project, or to entertain the same expectation.

But while we look with such grief and deprecation on the prospect of a sanguinary and unnatural conflict between brethren for an undefined purpose and a barren triumph, we are optimists enough to contemplate the prospect of a peaceful separation and an amicable partition of joint possessions with much hope and even with positive satisfaction. We do not see why both parties, why Europe, why humanity at large, may not then be gainers by the catastrophe. The two Republics will be free, each in its own sense and according to the dictates of its own experience, to amend that constitution which the one Republic had so long felt, and sometimes avowed, to be full of perils and defects. They may become friendly rivals and competitors in the art of democratic statesmanship. They may strive with each other as to which shall first bring to perfection a system of genuine self-government. They may profit by each other's errors, may grow rich by each other's prosperity, may grow strong by each other's progress. The North, when it has shaken off the fetter, the complication, and the disgrace of its former connection with slave institutions, may become single-minded, honest, humane, and just, in its internal as in its foreign policy. It need no longer have its best and truest feelings lacerated by the scandals of a Fugitive Slave Law, nor have its reputation as a lover of consistent freedom stained by the restrictions on liberty of speech and writing which deference to Southern interests and prejudices has hitherto compelled it to impose or to connive at. There will be nothing now to prevent it becoming as civilized in manners and as stainless in conscience as any European State. Its twenty millions of freemen, with their wonderful energy, their elastic genius, and their rapid multiplication, must always ensure to the Northern Federation a proud and powerful position among the great nations of the world; and if, as we hinted last week, they can—now or ultimately, by deliberate arrangement, by direct purchase, or by gradual absorption—draw the boundary line so as to include *free* Virginia, *free* Maryland, and *free* Kentucky and Missouri, they will be the possessors of a territory which, for extent and variety and richness of resources, will leave them without excuse for coveting any other lands.

How will it be with the South? The Slave States also will be left with a noble empire and an almost boundless field. What they will do with their grand opportunities and their heavy responsibilities we will neither affect to prophesy nor stop to conjecture. They may no doubt misuse them grievously, —or they may profit by past experience and by newly acquired security and independence, to face their own great domestic difficulty as wise and good men should. We are even much inclined to hope that the institution of slavery may be mitigated, and that the negro population may be better off than of late, both as to actual condition and remote prospects. Certainly, the change can scarcely be for the worse. Under the influence of irritation from the ceaseless reproaches of Northern Abolitionists—as to the sting of which there can be no question; and under the influence of fear as to unconstitutional interferences—for which we are bound to say we believe there was no ground, —the planters and slave-owners of the South have gradually goaded themselves into a state almost of frenzy on all matters relating to THE critical question, which has at once perverted all their natural good sense and poisoned all their natural good feeling. It is not unreasonable to hope that, when once they become a homogeneous republic—a congeries of states in all of which slavery is a recognized and *undisputed* system—*controversy* on the subject may cease and *consideration* of the subject may begin. When the minds of their more far-seeing and sagacious statesmen are no longer maddened and blinded by a position of daily self-defence, they will surely be compelled by the undisguised greatness and peril of the question, to turn all their powers to its study and its solution; and the ingenuity and hardihood which is now devoted to defending the indefensible and canonizing the atrocious, may then be concentrated on the more reputable and more profitable task of facing and conjuring without delay a danger and a puzzle which, sooner or later, *must* be met and overcome. The *continuance* of the old Union had done nothing either for the limitation or the mitigation of slavery: year by year, census after census, its area extended and its worst features became exasperated;—the *disruption* of the Union can scarcely be so utterly unprofitable. If the menaced war either was or pretended to be a war for the extinction of slavery, or for the limitation of its area with a view to its extinction, then it might be a righteous even if not a hopeful war;—*not* being waged for such an end, it is not a just one, and it cannot come to good.

From The Saturday Review, 25 May.

THE AMERICAN STRUGGLE.

AMERICAN proclamations and despatches, like all other state-papers, express rather the judgment which it is desired that others should form than the opinions of their authors. In some cases, the statements and arguments which they contain are purely and almost ostensibly conventional. Neither governments nor insurgents wish to avow their own initiative when they have thought it for their interest to commence a war. Even Napoleon was in the habit of throwing the responsibility of a rupture on Austria or on Prussia, as soon as he had massed his troops and accumulated his stores at the points most convenient for invasion. Mr. Jefferson Davis, when he affects to complain of the hostile policy of the Government at Washington, can scarcely wish to be literally understood either by friends or enemies. It is sufficient for his purpose to sketch a form of apology for Southern aggression which partisans may adopt and fill up if the quarrel should hereafter collapse into a verbal controversy. The capture of Fort Sumter was assuredly not a defensive measure; and, as a military operation, it was successful in the definite object of forcing Mr. Lincoln to declare war. The secession of Virginia, of Tennessee, of North Carolina, and of Arkansas, was the reward of judicious and seasonable daring. Many sophisms and fallacies may be excused in a statesman who knows his own mind, and who is ready to strike at the proper moment. The Cabinet of the United States, relying, in the absence of a definite policy, on procrastination and unlimited concession, apparently forgot that the system of peace at any price can only be carried out by the consent of both disputants. Even after the bombardment of Fort Sumter, official persons in Mr. Lincoln's confidence still persevered in the cant of conciliation. Mr. Clay boasted of the prudence of the President in withdrawing from Harper's Ferry to avoid bloodshed, and only entreated that Virginia would be neutral in preference to joining the secession. The sudden and unexpected excitement which arose at Boston and New York seems at last to have frightened the authorities out of their cowardly inaction. Mr. Seward, whose agents in Europe had not long since promised a peaceful solution of the difficulty, now informs the amused diplomatists of the Old World that the Union, maintained by force, will continue to be, as heretofore, "the object of human affection and of human wonder." If the North had proved as insensible as the Government to the human affection of resentment, Mr. Jefferson Davis would not have failed to heap affront upon affront, until even official patience was compulsorily exhausted. The capture of Washington may have been prevented almost as much by the declaration of war as by the rapid advance of the Northern militia to its defence. The great vigor and wisdom of the Southern Government may perhaps continue to counterbalance the vast superiority of the United States in wealth and in military resources.

The practical tendency of the American mind displays itself in the general recognition of the material considerations on which the success of the secession will ultimately depend. Pro-slavery pampleteers expatiate on the enormous value of the cotton of the Gulf States, and solace themselves with the belief that the monopoly of the raw material involves the command of the industry and commerce of the Continent. The South has long seen with dissatisfaction that New York buys and sells the slave produce which is worked up into fabrics in Europe and in New England. Even the well-founded grievance of the Federal Tariff has caused less general discontent than the inability of Charleston and New Orleans to maintain a direct trade with foreign ports. If the new Confederation establishes its independence, there will probably be many attempts to compete by the aid of protective regulations with the skill, the capital, and the natural advantages of the rival Republic. The writers of the opposite party are equally disposed to assume that the political controversy will ultimately be decided on commercial grounds. With sounder reason, and with ampler knowledge of economical relations, they assert that it is impossible to interfere with the natural flow and balance of trade. Innumerable attempts to establish manufactures in the South have failed, not from the influence of the Government, but because the conditions of capital, of labor, and of outlet were unfavorable. European commerce seeks New York, because the North has a comparatively dense and wealthy population of buyers, and it keeps aloof from Charleston, because the cargo of a single ship might glut the markets of South Carolina for a year. The Cotton States import provisions from the West, which they can only pay for by the bills which are drawn against their cotton at the port of shipment. Not receiving their returns in cash, they forget that the transaction is substantially lucrative, and they vainly hope to be relieved by a political revolution from the unavoidable incumbrance of middle-men and agents at New York. Every planter is probably aware that he gets the price of his cotton crop, and yet the community of planters entertains a vague suspicion that the whole district is sometimes defrauded by the acute and grasping Yankees. The advocates of the established system, like all apologists for natural results, have the best of the economical argument, but it is impossible to say how far passion and prejudice may prevail over sound calculations of mutual interest.

A clever writer against secession shows that through the heart of the Upper Slave States, a highland district, unfavorable to negro labor, and unsuited for the growth of cotton, extends in a south-westerly direction from Maryland to within two hundred miles of the Gulf of Mexico. Commencing with the Southern range of the Alleghanies, the temperate region includes the Western half of Virginia, parts of North Carolina and Georgia, a third of Kentucky, and the East of Tennessee. The population of a million and a half consists of slaves only in the proportion of an eighth, and it is forcibly argued that with the separation of the South from the North, the numbers of negroes on the Border will tend to diminish. Missouri, with a small negro population, is almost surrounded by free districts, and even if all the Slave States join the Southern Confederation, the former conflict of passions and interests will constantly tend to revive within its limits. It is not impossible that some of the Border States may even lose a portion of their territory and population. Notwithstanding their nominal sovereignty, which has up to the present time been acknowledged and exaggerated by the Democratic party, the breaking up of the Union will produce so much confusion of allegiance as to leave questions of political connection to the decision of local feeling and of interest. It is impossible for Englishmen to estimate the comparative force of relations and motives which apparently baffle the ingenuity of the ablest American politicians. The most instructive commentaries on the current revolution are certainly not those which are most positive and dogmatic. It is tolerably certain that the secession will not add to the wealth, to the power, or to the happiness of the South; and it is at least doubtful whether the Union will suffer any material loss by the disruption which is calling all the Northern States to arms. For the present, however, the conflict appears unavoidable and imminent, and thus far the Government of Montgomery has displayed a great superiority of political aptitude.

The North appears to be wholly without a leading statesman, although General Scott may probably be capable of directing military movements. The Atlantic States are still proceeding vigorously with their armaments and subscriptions; and in the remoter regions of the West the war has perhaps already begun. It is said that warlike stores destined for the South have been seized on the Mississippi; a collision was expected at the important post of Cairo at the confluence of the Ohio with the Great River; and a regiment of Missouri militia has surrendered to the Federal forces. It seems to have been already discovered that volunteer regiments of shopmen and clerks are not well calculated for a campaign of invasion; and, according to late accounts, the Government proposes to raise a standing army of one hundred thousand men to serve during the continuance of the war. A large number of armed vessels has already been despatched southward to form the blockade of the confederated ports; and by land it is supposed that General Scott will occupy positions in advance of the capital on the territory of Virginia. Baltimore is in possession of Northern troops, and the blockade of the Virginian waters is said to be complete. Mr. Davis, on his side, issues letters of marque, which, however, will soon be only available to vessels issuing from foreign ports. He has purchased a few ships, which he proposes to arm; he recommends the foundation of gun-factories and of arsenals; and he also puts on paper an army of one hundred thousand men. In material strength, the Southern Union is greatly overmatched; but if a campaign really commences, Mr. Davis will have the incalculable advantage of an intelligible cause and of definite and attainable objects. Henceforth he has only to repel an invading enemy, which he can always meet in equal force, or out-number, while he is carrying on the war at home. The army of the United States, when it has vindicated the outraged honor of its flag, will only be employed for purposes of conquest, which, long after the secession, were repudiated by all American statesmen. On the whole, war will tend to consolidate the new Confederation, which might possibly fall asunder in peace through the operation of economical causes.

PRAYERS FOR THE COUNTRY.

IOWA.—The bishop has issued the following pastoral and prayer for use during the Civil War:—

To the Clergy of the Protestant Episcopal Church in the Diocese of Iowa and Kansas: —DEAR BRETHREN,—Our beloved country is threatened with the dreadful evils and miseries of civil war. Sedition, conspiracy, and rebellion are already in full existence in our midst. Under these circumstances, it is our duty to betake ourselves to special and earnest prayer, and to stand by the civil authority in this time of need and danger. Without reference to any past political difference among the people, and without any useless crimination as to the causes of the present disturbances, it is for us and for all our fellow-citizens now to manifest true loyalty to the constitution of the United States, and to do all in our power to retain and transmit those rich civil and religious blessings with which we have hitherto been favored by benignant Providence.

During the continuance of the existing troubles, the following prayer may be used in the performance of Divine Service; unless the one set forth in the Prayer-Book for a "Time of War and Tumults" should be deemed more suitable; or unless the one set forth by me in December last should be continued in use at your own discretion.

Your affectionate friend and bishop.

HENRY W. LEE.

Davenport, April 25, 1861.

PRAYER.—O Almighty God, the Supreme Governor of all things, whose power no creature is able to resist, to whom it belongeth justly to punish sinners, and to be merciful to those who truly repent; save and deliver us, we humbly beseech thee, from the perils, calamities, and miseries of discord, sedition, and civil war; appease the tumults that have risen up amongst us; prosper every effort for the maintenance of the laws, and may the supreme authority be so established by thy blessing, that peace and happiness, truth and justice, religion and piety may be continued among us for all generations. May the rulers and people of these United States be under thy special care and protection. May they be armed with thy defence, and dwell securely under the shadow of thy wings. O Lord, in the midst of judgment, remember mercy. Spare thy people, good Lord, spare them, and let not thine heritage be brought to confusion. Hear us, we beseech thee, for thy mercy is great; and after the multitude of thy mercies look upon us and upon our country through the merits and mediation of thy blessed Son Jesus Christ our Lord. *Amen.*

OHIO.—The bishop has issued the following pastoral and prayer, touching the Civil War:—

To the Clergy and Laity of the Diocese of Ohio:—DEAR BRETHREN:—In the present time of most sad and painful conflict, to whom should we go first, and always but to the Lord? Thither let us go every day, in private and family prayer, and on all occasions of public worship confessing our sins, seeking blessings on our country, strength and wisdom to those who counsel and strive in its behalf, that an honorable peace may soon be granted to all parts and sections of our divine land.

The following prayer is hereby appointed to be used in this diocese on all occasions of public worship, immediately before the General Thanksgiving, while the present state of war shall last.

CHAS. P. MCILVAINE.

Cincinnati, April 23, 1861.

PRAYER.—Almighty God in whom is all our refuge and strength, we beseech thee to look with favor and blessing upon our country, on which have come the grevious calamities of war. In the cause of rightful order and authority, and for the maintenance of just and equal laws, do we stand before thee, desiring not to trust in our own wisdom or strength, but to be strong in the Lord, and in the power of his might. In the name of our God do we set up our banners. The Lord hear us in the day of trouble. The name of the God of Jacob defend us. In all our ways, may we humbly and obediently acknowledge thee: and do thou, O Lord, direct our ways. Make us courageous in doing, and patient in suffering, whatever may be required of us. Strengthen the union of the people in loving devotion to their country and its government, and in all brotherly kindness one toward another. Rule thou in the councils and wills of those to whom, under thee, the safety of the land is committed. Restrain all evil passion among the people. Bring to naught all evil designs. Make all things work together for our good. While we shrink not from the painful duty before us, make us earnest for such peace as will maintain the supremacy of law, the securities of righteous liberty, the honor and welfare of the nation. Comfort and save with an everlasting salvation all those who shall suffer, and those who shall die in this strife, and at last unite us together in the blessedness of the kingdom of our Lord Jesus Christ, in whose merits alone we pray, and to whom, with the Father, and the Holy Ghost, be all honor and glory, world without end. *Amen.*

MARYLAND.—*Prayer for the President of the U. S.*—Bishop Whittingham, hearing that in one or two instances prayer for the President had been omitted by the clergy of his diocese, addressed a circular to each clergyman enjoining the use of the church prayer without omission. In the circular he says:—

"Such omission in every case makes the clergyman liable to presentment for wilful violation of his ordination vow, by mutilation of the worship of the church; and I shall hold myself bound to act on any evidence of such offence laid before me after the issue of this circular." They are clearly enjoined, he says, "by the word of God, to make supplication and prayer for the Chief Magistrate of the Union, and for all that are in authority."

LETTER FROM BISHOP POTTER OF PENNSYLVANIA.

BISHOP POTTER of Pennsylvania, has written the following patriotic letter in reply to a correspondent in Alabama:—

Philadelphia, May 13, 1861.

"MY DEAR SIR,—You 'beg me to explain how it is possible that I could, under the circumstances, give so much sanction and encouragement to those engaged in this unholy, unprovoked, wanton attempt to destroy us, and all that is dear to us.'

"Your misconception is so radical that I almost despair of correcting it. What you regard as an 'attempt to destroy you and all that is dear to you,' is considered by us as simply an attempt to defend ourselves and the capital of our country from threatened invasion, our constitution from destruction, and even our Southern brethren from that which is the surest protection of themselves and their peculiar institutions. From the secession of South Carolina to the storming of Fort Sumter the general Government remained all but passive. It then became indispensable that we should know whether it was a government, whether it could retain its hold of Washington, and whether the whole system that Washington and his compeers inaugurated in 1789 was not a delusion and imposture. This, my dear sir, is the whole story. Your theory not only disregards your own obligations under the Constitution, but it leaves to us no government, except in name—opening the door for perpetual discord, and for secession without end.

"I do not believe that at the North one man in fifty desires an invasion of your soil or the destruction of your social system. They simply desire that you should not break up the Union by your method of leaving it, but refer all subjects of complaint to a convention of all the states, which will be competent either to redress all grievances, or to provide a way in which you can retire from the Union without dissolving the whole fabric of our general government.

"Under the present exasperated state of the sections it is impossible to say to what length this conflict may go. But I assure you that in the few lines above you have the whole *animus* of the loyal states and of the Union men everywhere. Only the smallest number of fanatics think or talk of slavery. The whole question is one of self-defence, and of government or no government.

"Yours, sincerely,

"ALONZO POTTER."

THE IRISH IN AMERICA AND THE WAR.

A LETTER FROM ARCHBISHOP HUGHES.

THE Dublin *Freeman* publishes a letter from New York, in which Archbishop Hughes indicates the policy which the American Irish will pursue in the present crisis. It is, he says, fifty years since he took the oath of allegiance to the American constitution, and no change has since come over his mind as to his duties as a citizen. The government was then, as it is now, symbolized by the "Stars and Stripes," which has been his flag, and shall be to the end. Although expressed in roundabout phraseology, Archbishop Hughes' words imply sympathy with the North, an adoption of its quarrel, and a belief that the Irish in America hold the same views as himself. The "Stars and Stripes," at the request of Archbishop Hughes, have been suspended from the Roman Catholic cathedral at New York.

A TALL spar, a whole tree in fact, one hundred and fifty-nine feet in height, has been erected in Kew Gardens as a flagstaff. It is made of the Douglas pine imported from Vancouver's Island, and presented to the Gardens by Mr. Stamp, a timber merchant. It has been rigged and set up by sailors and riggers from Woolwich.

From The Examiner.

An Account of the Manners and Customs of the Modern Egyptians, written in Egypt during the Years 1833, '34, *and* 35, *partly from Notes made during a former visit to that Country in the years* 1825, '26, '27, and '28. By Edward William Lane, Hon. M.R.S.L., etc., Translator of "The Thousand and One Nights." Fifth Edition, with numerous Additions and Improvements, from a Copy annotated by the Author. Edited by his Nephew, Edward Stanley Poole, M.R.A.S., etc. Murray.

A FIFTH edition of a book which has already taken place in the standard literature of the country hardly requires commendation. Yet there are some considerations suggested by this new issue of the *Modern Egyptians* for which we must find room. It is the most successful work of its kind, of which we know, and it is noteworthy that its success arises altogether from legitimate causes. All its merits are real and solid, and it may serve as a model for its class, whether we regard its style or its matter.

The greatest merit of the book is its completeness. In evidence of this we may quote a playful remark made by Canon Stanley, a critic whose praise upon any subject connected with Eastern life must have great weight. "The *Modern Egyptians*," he says, "is the most provoking book I ever read; whenever I thought I had discovered in Cairo something which must surely have been omitted, I invariably found my new facts already recorded." Nothing seems to have escaped Mr. Lane's observations, or to have been forgotten in his description. If he is speaking of the religious ablutions of the Moslems, he explains how they are performed in some mosques by help of a tank, in others with aid of a reservoir having spouts, and each article with its appurtenances is carefully sketched. He cannot praise the beautiful eye of the Egyptian lady without giving a complete account of the black pigment applied to the edge of the eyelids, telling of the various materials used for it, and of the several modes of preparing it. These are illustrations taken from pages opened at random. Almost every other page is as precise in its mention of the particular custom under description; and the whole presents a very living picture of Egyptian life, thoroughly amusing to the casual reader, and as complete as the most careful student can desire.

No one, however, can charge Mr. Lane's volume with containing a wearisome rehearsal of dry facts. He has a happy art of teaching without seeming to be a teacher. Often his most important information is worked into an anecdote which thoroughly amuses us, and we hardly know, unless we stop to think of it, that we are being instructed as well as amused. Then again the anecdotes themselves are well chosen and well told, neither exaggerated nor diluted with waste words.

There is humor, too, in Mr. Lane's writing. Carefully avoiding all the artificial ways by which it is often sought to make travellers' books amusing, he always writes with dignity; yet we can never forget that we are in company with a thoroughly genial man. All the strange parts of Eastern life are heartily appreciated, and the comic side of an incident or opinion is not lost sight of. But Mr. Lane only laughs where he should. He laughs at the standard of propriety according to which it is more necessary for a lady to hide the back of her head than her face, and a greater offence to expose the face than almost any lower part of the person; but he never speaks harshly of real, even though they may be mistaken, notions of duty. This is especially seen in the account of the Moslem theology and ritual. No one need be told of the errors of the former or of the follies of the latter, nor can any good result from throwing ridicule upon them. They claim respect because of the honesty with which they are held and observed by worshippers to whom they are sacred. For his kindly sympathy with all that is good and true in Egyptian thought and character, no less than for his quiet satire of all that lies fairly open to the satirist, we like Mr. Lane's book.

The accidents of modern commerce join to make it still more valuable. During the twenty-five years or so which have elapsed since it was written, a far greater change has passed over Egyptian manners than had occurred in many previous centuries. Before long, Europeans journeying by the overland route to India or China will have rubbed down some angles of the native character that now resist their influence. Mr. Lane studied the country before change was at all marked, and thus his tale of the land of Egypt even now describes institutions old as Isaiah and Herodotus, that are now in their decay.

Many readers will remember the book as it first came out in the tiny paper-bound volumes through which the Society for the Diffusion of Useful Knowledge imparted sound information a quarter of a century ago. They will rightly value it as it now appears, newly and ably edited, a gem of good printing, and a descriptive work enriched with every illustration that could add distinctness to the text.

LETTERS from abroad speak of the subtle and incessant labors of the secessionists in Europe to procure the countenance of England and France during the time when our government, at the close of the late administration, was tending swiftly towards anarchy, and at the beginning of the present administration, where it was silently recovering itself and gathering its energies for that grand and irresistible descent upon the enemy which is now in progress. It was during this dark period that the plotters against our liberties were most busy in England and France, getting the ear of leading officials, and seeking to procure the committal of these nations to their base cause before the true representatives of the government to foreign powers should take their place. It was a great privilege which then fell to the lot of such loyal Americans as chanced to be in Europe, to stand up for the honor of the country, and withstand these treasonable schemes And no man can tell how much the timely utterance of a patriotic soul in England or France may have done to serve the national cause.

Mr. Motley's letter, which is presented in an abstract elsewhere in our columns, is a noble vindication of the government. He has worthily improved a great opportunity for setting us right before the eyes of Europe. Nowhere has Mr. Motley been more highly appreciated than in England. His fame as an historian, learned, veracious, and full of the "authentic fire" of liberty, and the high honors which the English themselves have conferred upon him, will lend to his eloquent statements such weight and secure for them so ready a hearing that not all the suggestions of the adversary, as we may reasonably hope, can by any means countervail them. Well has Mr. Motley used the chance to serve his country. Such influence and so worthy a field for its exercise are the fitting and much-coveted rewards of the labors of the scholar. Heartily do we congratulate Mr. Motley upon this worthy vindication of the government, and most heartily do we congratulate ourselves that we had in England a scholar so competent and so patriotic as he, to uphold the national honor and good name.—*Daily Advertiser*, 8 *June.*

Collieries and Colliers: a Handbook of the Law and leading Cases relating thereto. By John Coke Fowler, Esq., Barrister-at-Law, etc. Longman and Co.

THIS work is intended chiefly for the guidance of non professional persons in the many important transactions connected with collieries, which are effected without professional aid. The author's experience as stipendiary magistrate for the district of Merthyr Tydfil and Aberdare must have enabled him to form a tolerably exact conception of the kind of legal information most needed by those for whom he has written; and besides this, he has taken the precaution to submit certain parts of his work, which deal with peculiarly ticklish questions, to gentlemen distinguished for their great practical knowledge of colliery operations, whose suggestions he has carefully considered.—*Spectator.*

NATIVE OXIDE OF ANTIMONY IN BORNEO.—At a recent meeting of the Paris Academy M. Flourens read a paper by Dr. Phipson on a native oxide of antimony from Borneo. This substance constitutes an important ore of antimony, capable of yielding far more metal than the ordinary sulphuret generally used, and at much less expense. This native oxide is as yet little known; from the analyses of Dr. Phipson it is evidently antimonious acid, or stibiconise. It is found to accompany the sulphuret in large quantities, and is often seen in beautiful prismatic crystals nearly an inch long. The author shows that this native oxide of antimony has been formed in nature at the expense of the sulphuret or stibine; its comparative rarity in Europe explains the slight notice that has hitherto been bestowed upon this important mineral.

A SUBSCRIPTION has been set on foot by the students of Paris for the purpose of giving a banquet, at the Hôtel du Louvre, to MM. Jules Favre, Picard, and the other members of the democratic opposition. The authorization of the government has been obtained, and six hundred subscribers have given in their names.

13 Cents a No. 880 Six

FROM FRASER'S MAGAZINE.

Lightning Source UK Ltd.
Milton Keynes UK
UKHW031353031218
333390UK00013B/819/P